WASTE of the WEST:
Public Lands RANCHING

Lynn
Jacobs

Second Printing

This second printing of
Waste of the West features new cover art and better
cover stock. Typos and other minor problems have been corrected.

As we go to press
again, new material on public lands
ranching keeps pouring in (wish I could have
used it in the book). Thanks to everyone. Already it seems I have
enough written, verbal, and visual input to fill another book (perish the thought!).

By far most of this
new material reinforces the
basic premise of this book: public lands ranching
should be ended, ASAP. The situation is *not* significantly
improving as claimed by the industry, and *cannot* really improve so
long as public lands ranching continues. This is becoming increasingly evident
to more and more people. The movement is growing. Ranching has become a major issue.

Waste has been praised
by the public and ignored by the public lands
ranching establishment. With a little luck, and help from supporters,
this book and the message it carries will spread far and wide. Keep on truckin' !

1st printing: November, 1991. 2,000 copies.
2nd printing: December, 1992. 5,000 copies.

Produced, published, and distributed by:
Lynn Jacobs
P.O. Box 5784
Tucson, Arizona 85703
(602)578-3173

$28 (postpaid)
ORDER COPIES OF THIS BOOK FROM ADDRESS ABOVE.
INQUIRE ABOUT BULK ORDERS.

Cover illustration by: **Charles Thomas Illustration, Tucson, AZ.**
Printed by: **Arizona Lithographers, Tucson, AZ.**

ISBN 0-9629386-0-2

*For the Earth,
its defenders and healers,
and the Natural way.*

Table of Contents
for
WASTE OF THE WEST: Public Lands RANCHING
by Lynn Jacobs

FOREWORD

Shortly before he died in the Spring of 1989,
naturalist author Edward Abbey offered to write a foreword for this book.
Like many of us who are close to the Western wild,
Cactus Ed had come to understand that ranching is not natural to the wild West
but is instead its most deadly enemy.
This space is dedicated to his vision of a West free from ranching.

PREFACE

Planet Earth suffers from many devastating human impacts. Why, then, a book about the impact of Western public lands ranching, an obscure and seemingly minor issue?

The answer is simple and probably surprising: **Ranching has wasted and is wasting the Western United States more than any other human endeavor.** Ranching is by far the West's most environmentally destructive land use, and one of the rural West's most economically, politically, and socially harmful influences as well.

Bold claims, admittedly. To most readers, probably outrageous claims. Keep reading, and then judge them.

This volume never pretends to be a 2-sided presentation of the public lands ranching issue. It needn't be. In our cowboy-crazed culture all of us are from the day we are born relentlessly indoctrinated with the pro-ranching side -- ideas, misinformation, images, illusions, and, perhaps most of all, romanticism (see Chapter XI). By the time we reach adolescence we are conditioned to automatically reject anything even remotely anti-ranching. Ya-hoo, buckaroos!

This book, therefore, takes a much-needed look at the other side -- the neglected, hidden, nonfictional world of Western ranching that few people know. It scrapes off the bullshit and burns off the romantic fog. What's left is Western ranching in stark reality.

Why focus on Western public land? First, because the West is my native home and the region of the globe I am most familiar with. Second, because most of the West is *public* land -- about 3/4 of this used for ranching -- and it is easier to change public land policy than private. In other words, from my perspective ending public lands ranching is the simplest way to do the most good.

This book covers the environmental, economic, political, and social ramifications of ranching -- livestock grazing and related activities -- on Western public land particularly. To put ranching into perspective and help the reader understand the huge web of issues and interrelationships connected with it, the book branches off into several important tangential issues such as Western range history, world livestock production, animal welfare, and human diet.

Likewise, to give the reader a basis for understanding how ranching affects the West, the book explores range ecology and, to a lesser extent, rural Western politics, economics, and culture. For this reason the reader will also learn about ranching fundamentals, management, and administration.

In short, **Waste of the West** comprises a thorough and detailed explanation of what public lands ranching is, why we must end it, and how we may do so.

Most of the contents, however, also apply to ranching on private Western land, on public and private land in the East, and on rangelands around the world. Indeed, ranching is conducted in nearly all regions of the globe, and everywhere it causes a strikingly similar set of problems. Ranching, in turn, is a major component of world livestock production, which is Earth's most environmentally harmful land use (see Chapter VI).

Though this book's foremost purpose is to end public lands ranching in the United States, this effort is only a part of a much broader movement. We are in the midst of a life-or-death struggle to halt the deterioration of this planet's 5-billion-year-old natural evolution. We strive to reverse our progressive separation from Nature, not only for personal contentment and to protect ourselves and the environment, but now even to survive as a species. We seek to end the social and political injustice that is both a cause and a result of this situation.

So, while this book is specifically about public lands ranching, it is generally about environmental decay, fiscal and natural resource waste, social and political injustice, culturalization, and the dominant paradigm and alienation from Nature underlying it all.

The main purpose of this book is to *inform* so people will *act*. Because so few understand ranching and its influence, there is much latent energy and potential involvement.

I therefore write to reach as many people as possible. Because public lands ranching has such far-reaching consequences, I address the issue from the perspective of many different special interests. Ending public lands ranching is one goal they may all agree on: from hunters to animal welfare advocates, social workers to tax reform proponents, conservationists to recreationists, back-to-the-landers to average citizens. Accordingly, there should be something here to interest (and offend) nearly everyone.

In a time when we are rapidly destroying the planet's basic life-support functions, anyone who becomes well-informed and remains coolly intellectual about it must be either numb or emotionally handicapped.
--Dale Turner, Assistant Editor, *Earth First! Journal*

Why, I am frequently asked, did I undertake this project? Why the personal involvement in this issue?

As often happens, it all started innocently enough during childhood: traveling with my family, camping in the Sierra Nevada, hiking the brushy Southern California canyons and hills, playing in the backyard weeds and dirt . . . a few feeble roots in Nature that took hold.

I took natural science courses in college and sought out Nature while interned in the Army. In 1974 my partner and I homesteaded in a rural ranching area of Northern California and, later, with 2 children, in New Mexico and Arizona, until my children and I moved to Tucson in 1987. Before, during, and since that period, I/we traveled extensively and spent much time on public land throughout the West. During my early 20s I began to notice that land damage of many kinds was occurring nearly everywhere I went, and in most places most of it was caused by . . . yes, *ranching*. This expanding awareness, in combination with my growing relationship with Nature, gradually led me to get involved.

Along the way I began collecting information on public lands ranching and in 1986 published a 48-page tabloid on the issue entitled *Free Our Public Lands!* The 100,000 copies distributed around the US garnered thousands of letters of support, query, advice, and contribution. Thus began a more or less full-time, many-faceted personal effort to end public lands ranching called, appropriately, Free Our Public Lands!

It soon became apparent that the immensity and complexity of the issue could easily cause the project to expand far beyond the capabilities of any one person, or even several people. Even before starting this book I felt like an overworked Ann Landers for ranching victims.

Then in mid-1987, in a response to a letter, I asked a California publisher if he might want to publish my tabloid as a book.

Why a book? At first, merely to lend the tabloid's contents "more legitimacy" and reach a wider audience, as some people had suggested. Later, other reasons arose: The tabloid only summarized public lands ranching; the media habitually ignored, trivialized, or misrepresented the issue; and it seemed that only a lengthy, heavily illustrated book could sufficiently convey how the West was being ravaged and what could be done to stop it.

When the publisher answered my letter with "Sure, let's publish," I had no idea that it was the start of a writing marathon that would dominate my life for the next 3 years.

A simple re-edit of the tabloid soon mutated into a vast rewrite and expansion. I found that to explain the issue in sufficient detail I had to greatly lengthen the text. Many people provided suggestions, information, literature, photos, artwork, and moral support. It seemed that most periodicals I read contained something pertinent to public lands ranching, and libraries yielded dozens of source materials. I returned from trips to the Western range laden with scribbled notes and exposed film.

To make a very long story short, for 3 years "The Book" became an insatiable monster, consuming my time, resources, energy, health, family -- my life. Many unforeseen problems added to the burden. But the importance of the issue compelled.

Eventually I came to accept that a book on public lands ranching could expand indefinitely just as surely as the Free Our Public Lands! project had. I began incorporating new material only when essential, cut and condensed text, wrapped up loose ends, and called it a book.

Some people suggested cutting the length much further or watering down the content -- to make the book more palatable to the general reader. As expressed recently by the editors of *Sierra* magazine, "Journalists who ruminate in print about rangelands risk losing their readers." The book remains thorough, however; public lands ranching is too complex and widely misunderstood for a superficial summary to suffice. Relative to the dimensions of the issue, even this book is small. And the content remains true-to-life because I consider reality more important than the negative flavor it sometimes imparts. As Oscar Wilde wrote, "Truth is never pure, and rarely simple."

A few suggestions on using this book:

• Cultural conditioning provides each of us an overwhelming, unwitting, pro-ranching bias. So while reading if you find yourself involuntarily denying the evidence or having a compulsive emotional reaction, just remember the sagacious words of Firesign Theatre: "Your brain may no longer be the boss."

• It is not necessary to absorb everything in this book. If you get bogged down, set the book aside and come back to it later. Or skip ahead. If you think range soil ecology, for example, is dull, skim to the next section, taking in only graphics and the most obviously important points along the way.

• Due to the nature of the issue, some points may seem insignificant or exaggerated. This is illusory, however. For example, dead cattle may not seem an important source of water pollution -- unless you realize that each year *many thousands* of cattle carcasses rot in lakes, streams, and rivers around the *41% of the West* that is public ranchland.

• To those who have tried, it is notoriously difficult to portray the environmental effects of ranching on film. Please bear in mind that what you see in the photos is usually subtle, partial, and/or relative.

• Originally, I had intended not to cite references in this book. I believed, perhaps naively, that readers would judge the content on its own merits, not on how many citations I could dig up to bolster my position.

  After finishing about half of the text, however, I was finally convinced by well-meaning friends that many people find it hard to take a nonfiction work seriously, regardless of the content, unless it is extensively documented. Belatedly, I began documenting.

  Due to size limitations and readability, it would have been impractical to document every piece of or even most information in the book. The bibliography reflects source materials that seem particularly relevant to public lands ranching but does not include hundreds of other references used. As is, the bibliography contains about 500 sources.

• A name and date in parentheses, such as (Oppenheimer 1987), indicate reference to a source listed in the bibliography. Authors are listed there in alphabetical order by last name, followed by the date of publication.

  If text information is not followed by a citation, it means: (1) the information, though taken from a reliable source, was deemed not worth citing; (2) the source, though reliable, was judged not worth listing in the bibliography; (3) the information was entered before I began documenting, and the source was subsequently unavailable; or (4) the information is based on personal knowledge.

• This book derives information from a wide variety of sources and recognizes traditional science as only one of many perspectives. As you read, try to accept the validity of these various perspectives.

  Much of the content -- perhaps 1/3 or more altogether -- is drawn from personal experience. Some of this information is neglected or "undocumented" by the scientific com-munity, but this makes it no less valid and numerous eyewitnesses support it. Those who require authoritative scientific documentation or official government seals of approval for everything they think may be reading the wrong book.

  Ranching is so widespread, dispersed, obscure, and *misunderstood* that many of its effects have not been or cannot be scientifically documented in the usual manner. Specifics may be studied if they are recognized, but many are overlooked, and generalities may be difficult or impossible to document.

• A last word on science and documentation:

  Science is not truth, but an *approach* to the truth -- a malleable cultural tool. Depending on how it is used, science may be a method of fact finding, distortion, or concealment. Accordingly, you can "prove" nearly anything with science, even the "need" for tens of thousands of nuclear weapons

  Thus, within the obscure, basically self-governing business of public lands ranching, scientific documentation has become largely a game of justification. Ranching establishment professionals are by far the most numerous and skillful players in the game. Over the decades, they have conducted thousands of studies and cranked out thousands of reports, which they then interpret to promote ranching (see Understanding Livestock Grazing in Chapter III).

  Yet most of their reports and conclusions contradict one another! In short, though scientific documentation can be a useful educational tool, the prudent reader will recognize its limitations.

• This book is more or less "timeless" in that by far most of the information it contains remains consistent, with relatively minor fluctuations from year to year; specifics may change periodically, generalities rarely. The ranching establishment has been firmly entrenched in the rural American West for more than a century. Changes there occur very slowly. (We're hoping to remedy that.)

And finally:

Muy muchas gracias to the many humans who helped this book happen.

I am obliged to the hundreds of caring individuals and groups who provided source literature, photos, graphics, money, information, suggestions, encouragement, and other assistance.

To the several dozen people who made promises that went unfulfilled: a reassessment of your priorities might be in order. And to all those who carry on as if what's natural doesn't matter: *come on people; Earth needs your help!*

Thanks to those scores of talented writers from whose works I so liberally quote.

My appreciation to Ann Carr for her generous computer assistance, and to computer wizard Ron Schilling, who more than once saved me from the evil, text-eating computer monster.

Steve Johnson and Denzel & Nancy Ferguson deserve much praise for sharing their abundant knowledge and for courageously leading the way. So does George Wuerthner, whose insight and dedication are a major part of the effort. As do those exceptional others who have the vision and concern to question and confront the ranching imperative.

Thank-yous to the various specialists who reviewed portions of the text, including Bob Stack. To Paul Hirt and Susan Eirich-Dehne for helpful suggestions. And particularly to Denis Jones and Mark MacAllister for their excellent copy editing.

Without the invaluable editing, advice, and friendship of John Davis, this book might not exist. John's wholehearted dedication to a natural Earth is an inspiration to myself and many others.

Considering the circumstances, my children, Sky and Dusty, have been remarkably understanding and supportive (as well they are personally involved in the issue). Overall, they were of more help than hindrance. Thanks for putting up with an often-grouchy, over-burdened, home-schooling single parent.

And thanks most of all to the Spirit of the Wild, which makes it all happen.

This book evolved into a mammoth undertaking. My apologies to those with whom I failed to maintain correspondence or whose friendships I neglected, and to myself for assuming a decreasingly natural lifestyle and compromising my health in order to complete the project. It has been a willing sacrifice, however, for every time I spend time on the Western range I re-learn the importance of the effort.

A grass roots movement to end public lands ranching is growing on many fronts, but needs your help. So please, USE THIS BOOK!

Who made you such an authority when so many of the facts are slanted to your advantage?
--A Montana public lands rancher, in response to the tabloid *Free Our Public Lands!*

INTRODUCTION

Public land in southwest Wyoming. *(Kelly Cranston)*

The world we are told was made for man. A presumption that is totally unsupported by facts. There is a very numerous class of men who are cast into painful fits of astonishment whenever they find anything, living or dead, in all God's universe, which they cannot eat or render in some way what they call useful to themselves . . . .
--John Muir

Y ou and I and all Americans are joint land owners. Together as "the public" we own almost half of the land in the 11 Western states (Washington, Oregon, California, Nevada, Arizona, Utah, Idaho, Montana, Wyoming, Colorado, and New Mexico), which hold 90% of all federal land in the United States outside Alaska. If state, county, and city-owned land is included, 56% of the West is public land.

This public land encompasses an incredible amount and variety of country -- some of the most diverse and beautiful in the world, including the Grand Canyon, Yellowstone, Death Valley, the slickrock country of southern Utah . . . Few other countries have so much land open to all people.

Each year by the millions they come from throughout the United States and around the world to visit these public lands, pursuing various experiences. Millions of hunters and fishers, hikers and backpackers, picnickers and sightseers enjoy the public lands. For scientists and researchers they are invaluable, huge, open-air laboratories. To naturalists, they are the largest remaining wild areas in this country -- strongholds of natural diversity. They contain many natural resources and provide for a great variety of personal and commercial uses. They expand our physical, emotional, and spiritual horizons and help maximize personal freedom. Public lands are many things to many people.

Public lands are much more than all this, however. They are . . . exactly what they are: soil, water, and air; plants and animals; climatic, geologic, hydrologic, and biologic processes; ecosystems; interrelationships; evolution; life -- *existence*. Western public land encompasses 418 *million* acres of Nature, of largely untransformed natural being. It is a continuing, progressive creation -- the current, cumulative result of the 5-billion-year evolvement of this planet.

All native entities of public land, from microscopic soil bacteria to grizzly bears, from desert globemallow to giant sequoias, from hot springs to lava flows, whether they occur individually or as communities, whether organic or inorganic, all share one thing: the right to exist. And though continued existence is not guaranteed to all on this Earth, the opportunity to pursue natural existence without undue human interference should be. The environment itself has

National Forest in Oregon. *(USFS)*

the right to exist in a healthy, natural state, for its own sake, regardless of any human considerations.

For many people, the intrinsic value of Nature is something intuitively sensed yet rarely discussed. Standing amidst a sea of waving grass or engulfed in the roar and mist of a waterfall can fill one with awe and humility, and inspire a feeling of protectiveness. Unfortunately, we tend to bury these sentiments as we go about our daily lives.

Although we humans have developed extraordinary powers to manipulate our surroundings for our purposes, we always will remain a part of Nature -- a creation of our natural environment, a component of the whole. As such, we need to protect the whole to protect ourselves. Ironically, by unnaturally exploiting the environment for short-term gain, in the long run we hurt ourselves, and our descendants.

Therefore, we should not only be "owners" of public land but defenders of this land. We have the responsibility to use it wisely, if indeed we use it at all. Because we have developed the power to control the land, we must also protect and in some cases restore it, for both our sake and the planet's.

As collective public land owners, we have relied largely on various government agencies to implement our wishes for wise use and protection of the land. But our governments have not done, are not doing, and even refuse to do their job. In fact, with our governments' help, a small sector of the business community has continuously manipulated and exploited public land for personal gain for more than 100 years. Ultimately, we are all responsible. We should have stopped it long ago.

Unfortunately, the most harmful land use in all history is also one of the most subtle and least recognized -- livestock production. The seemingly benign act of raising livestock has caused more environmental damage than any other land use, not only in the western US, but throughout the world (see Chapter VI).

On Western public land this commercial exploitation is the product of a well-organized, powerful, private ranching business allied with an entrenched government bureaucracy. Through the years, the public lands grazing industry has been quietly receiving billions of dollars in taxpayer subsidies, corrupting our political system, defiling the social fabric of the rural West, and, perhaps worst of all, devastating the Western environment -- all to produce a tiny fraction of US meat.

At this point, you may again suspect me of exaggeration or even fabrication. This is understandable. Few of us are exposed to ranching other than through the usual fictional renderings of the romantic "Old West," as on TV and in Western literature. And as a people we have always idolized the legendary, independent, honest, tough, hardworking, resourceful, and in all ways virtuous

Western rancher and endorsed the products of his* endeavors. Mom, apple pie, the cowboy and his cows. Americans love a good Western!

Nevertheless, this nostalgic, idealistic image we have all been reared with is a vast falsehood, a monumental myth preserved by baseless tradition, our own yearning for romanticism, and the ranching establishment's efforts to capitalize on our yearnings. Therefore, the *real* story of Western ranching may come as a shock.

* In this book I purposefully use the male rather than neuter form in reference to the stock raiser in recognition that ranching is so completely male-dominated.

So now we come to the business which created the West's most powerful illusion about itself and, though this is not immediately apparent, has done more damage to the West than any other. The stock business.
--Bernard DeVoto, **The Easy Chair** (DeVoto 1955)

Chapter I
HISTORY OF PUBLIC LANDS RANCHING

Not until the hairy men from the East came did the West for us become "wild."
--Chief Luther Standing Bear of the Oglala band of Sioux

Only a hundred and some odd years ago, what we now call "The American West" was predominantly *wild*. With the exception of several scattered European settlements, the entire western portion of North America was one vast wilderness, a result of 5 billion years of Nature's continuing creation on this planet. The grasslands, deserts, forests, brushlands, and wetlands here were functioning at or near peak productivity. Plant and animal life and soil and water systems were at optimum abundance, diversity, and stability. The West was, relative to today, a Garden of Eden.

Native Americans, or "Indians," then were an integral part of this wilderness. For thousands of years they lived in and interacted with this rich and beautiful country. Although these people exerted many influences on their environment, as a whole they had an incomparably less destructive impact than those who would follow. Perhaps this was largely because they had lesser means to exploit and destroy. Whatever the case, at that time they felt the wilderness to be home, not an obstacle or enemy to be conquered.

Only a hundred and some odd years ago, nearly all of these original human inhabitants either died from introduced disease, were killed, or were removed to small, restricted areas to make room for incoming United States settlers, military and business interests. On many reservations, natives continued to die from starvation, exposure, or suicide even as their home, the wilderness, was ravaged.

The old Western myth was that these people were the salt of the earth, that they were people of astounding virtue. But these same people often were filled with greed and violence and corruption and racism.... No people went through an environment faster, and more destructively and wastefully than Americans have gone through North America.
--Historian Donald Worster, **Rivers of Empire**

The intruders came west for many reasons, some quite noble. Nonetheless, most of these early settlers, businessmen, and soldiers were not as portrayed in American history books. Few were the courageous, heroic, God-fearing people of tale and legend -- brave patriots who set out into the wilderness to face great peril with a burning desire to build a better America. No, most came west for more common purposes: to make more money, get free land, or escape various problems in the East. These newcomers originally were, or soon became, farmers, trappers, traders, miners, laborers, and merchants.

And then there were the stockmen -- the cattlemen colonists. The fiercely competitive, violent, and environmentally brutal nature of the early livestock grazing business attracted a somewhat different breed of people. Most of the participants fit into 3 distinct classes:

Hired manual laborers called *cow-boys* did the bulk of the chores for most ranching operations. These men typically were solitary drifters who took work here and there as the occasion arose. Of course nearly all originally had come from the Eastern US, where many had experienced unemployment or other personal difficulties. Many had lost their jobs in mills and factories. Many others were troubled, rootless veterans of the Civil War. Some were former insubordinate soldiers banished to the West to "protect the frontier," and some were desperate farmers who left the ravaged South after the Civil War. Some were luckless, would-be miners who began raising stock when for them the West's gold and silver rushes didn't pan out. Early cow-boys also included various Western riffraff -- the misfits, unfortunates, crooks and swindlers, outcasts and outlaws, loners and losers. There were many exceptions, but the sad fact is that early Western cow-boys by and large were an accumulation of what today would be termed "the dregs of society."

For them, "cow-boying" was an easy way to make a little money and escape from whatever problems drove them away from society and out onto the range.

Another class of stockmen could be termed *managing ranchers*. These included ranch foremen, managers, and working owners -- the professionals who kept ranches operating on a long-term basis. Some were former cowboys, but many had roots in other professions in the East. Many of these men were well-known for intolerance, ruthlessness, and violence, especially towards ranching competitors, rustlers, Native Americans, insubordinate cow-boys, and the land.

Ranch owners who made it big became *cattle barons*, the self-proclaimed aristocrats of the range, and joined a third class. This class was also composed of wealthy financiers -- the influential investors who put up capital to finance the huge grazing fiefdoms that soon dominated most of the West. These acquisitive, opportunistic entrepreneurs were already rich and powerful bankers, lawyers, politicians, publishing magnates, mining tycoons, timber barons, railroad kings, industrialists, and so forth. They were mostly absentee owners who lived in Western cities, back East, or in Europe and occasionally visited or vacationed on the ranches they owned or financed. They relished their role as ranching nobility, and Westerners came to treat them as such, and even today many Americans envy and aspire to be wealthy ranching moguls.

As a rule, the men who came West and entered the ranching business displayed greed, ignorance, and bigotry. They had little respect for themselves or others, much less for the land itself, other than for what it might provide them. Denying to ourselves the true nature of these early colonists in order to preserve our nostalgic, heroic image of the Old West can only prevent us from understanding the real history of the West.

Although greatly outnumbered by other settlers, these stockmen seized the vast bulk of Western land and turned it to cattle grazing. At that time in history most of the West was of little use to most settlers, and the prevailing attitude toward the land was "If nothing else, you can always graze it."

Men of every rank were eager to get into the cow business. In a short time every acre of grass was stocked beyond its fullest capacity. Thousands of cattle and sheep were crowded on the ranges when half the number were too many. The grasses were entirely consumed; their very roots were trampled into dust and destroyed. In their eagerness to get something for nothing, speculators did not hesitate at the permanent injury, if not the total ruin, of the finest grazing country in America.
--H.L. Bentley in 1898

Vikings carried livestock on their ships when they sailed to North America up to 500 years before Christopher Columbus (actual name Cristobal Colon), but the first livestock settled permanently in the "New World" were probably those brought by Columbus to the Caribbean island of Hispaniola on his second voyage, in 1493. Writer Kirkpatrick Sale relates in "The Columbian Legacy":

Within a year Columbus and a massive contingent of Spanish settlers had begun to change all that [the veritable "Garden of Eden" Columbus encountered on his first voyage] as the trees were cut down to make rancheros *for imported cattle and sheep and soon plantations for sugar and coffee. Pigs, goats, and horses were allowed to roam freely, and as a result destroyed forage, trampled native farmlands, and made savannahs bare.*

The first livestock introduced to the North American mainland are believed to have been cattle brought to Florida by Ponce de Leon in 1519. Cattle were imported into Mexico and the Eastern British colonies soon thereafter.

Grazers owned little or no land and their movements were known to few and questioned by none. The plentiful forage is evidenced now by words of early adventurers, as Fremont's ". . . tremendous areas of luxurious grass -- an inexhaustible supply;" Lewis and Clark's "These Western ranges have a luxuriant grass cover and will supply enough feed for all the cows in the world;" and Bradley's ". . . good, fine grasses grow evenly all over the country -- I believe that all the flocks and herds in the world could find ample pasturage (here)." Herdsmen rested secure knowing that over the next ridge was more free feed to the first comer.
--Laurence A. Stoddart, "Range Land of America and Some Research on Its Management" (Stoddart 1955)

Livestock grazing in the West began slowly. Hardy Spanish longhorn cattle, introduced from Mexico as early as the 1500s, were spread to California, Texas, and the Southwest. Shorthorn cattle from the Eastern colonies were gradually moved West over the years. By the 1800s both kinds, though in comparatively small numbers, had been moved into many parts of the West. Sheep, spread mainly from Mexico and California, generally followed not far behind. In 1850 there were less than a million cattle and perhaps a few million sheep (mostly in California) in the 17 Western states. With regional variations, numbers gradually increased during the 1850s and 1860s, with livestock relentlessly displacing native grazing animals and the peoples who depended on them.

Then in the 1870s and 1880s, with most Native Americans subdued and buffalo (bison) no longer in competition,

stocked and overgrazed that drastic environmental changes began to occur (see Chapter III).

Edible vegetation was so depleted that livestock starved to death during periods of drought or heavy snow, and in some places even during benign weather. In January 1887, for example, starving cattle ate the wool off dead sheep and then fell dead themselves. Massive die-offs occurred periodically during the latter decades of the 1800s, and to a lesser degree during the early 1900s (as they still do occasionally). Some die-offs were so bad that most livestock were lost over huge areas, even entire states. Emaciated cattle ate wood from trees. Rotting carcasses were sometimes so thick a person could throw rocks from one to the next.

Stockmen blamed these disasters on drought or storm, though such periodic atmospheric fluctuations are natural occurrences. Likewise, many contemporary ranching advocates make claims such as this one by grazing industry spokesman Thadis W. Box: "The period from the [sic] 1880 to 1905 was one of the driest in the past 1500 years" (Box 1987). Scientific studies and precipitation records prove these claims unfounded (see Air section in Chapter III).

In truth, the range was simply so devastated by livestock grazing that biological population controls began to kill off the cattle and sheep (which, unlike today, were rarely given supplemental feed to mitigate starvation). In retrospect the massive die-offs were a blessing -- Nature's method of self-protection -- for without them much of the West might have been transformed permanently into Sahara-like wasteland. Nature reduced 1884's estimated 35-40 million cattle to an estimated 27 million in 1890 (Holechek 1989). And despite it all the frenzied, profit-crazed cattlemen were eager to

transportation (including new railroads) and communications modernized, and livestock established and ready to multiply throughout the West, the true subjugation of the West began. Livestock grazing became an immense, booming business, and numbers of cattle and sheep increased by leaps and bounds. Stockmen and investors (mainly from the East and Europe) began to realize the huge profits to be made by running livestock across the Western range. Many of the West's most successful and powerful miners and other businessmen turned to stock raising. Word spread like wildfire, spurred on by fantastic claims of potential ranching profits in popular publications and promotional literature.

Livestock grazing suddenly became a mad rush to get rich quick. From ocean to prairie, livestock were propagated and crammed onto every conceivable piece of forage land (about 2/3 of the West altogether) in an all-out attempt to maximize profits. The 1870 estimated cattle population of 4-5 million in the 17 western states (Ferguson 1983) peaked at an estimated 35-40 million around 1884 (Holechek 1989). Ranchers showed little or no concern for the land itself as "forage fever" (similar to "gold fever") swept the West.

The range itself got little relief from heavy use, and there may not even today be a truly widespread recognition of the lasting impact of the damage to forage and soil started during that boom era.
--William Voigt, Jr., former Executive Director, Izaak Walton League, **Public Grazing Lands** (Voigt 1976)

The land suffered. Livestock stripped vast areas of ground cover as clean as a billiard table. By the early 1880s the Western range was so over-

Roundup following a hard winter in the late 1800s. *(Unknown)*

raise cattle numbers once again! Meanwhile, because sheep can survive in areas where cattle cannot and sheepmen had not yet fully expanded their efforts, the sheep population of the 17 Western states continued to climb and reached about 53 million that same year (Ferguson 1983).

The invention of barbed wire by J.F. Glidden in 1874 became the final nail in the coffin for Western range. With it our public land -- indeed, about 2/3 of the West -- came under the symbolic and actual stranglehold of the livestock grazing industry. With barbed wire, the most powerful stockmen divided the West among themselves and brought it under their control, where it has remained ever since.

For the last five years over most of the mountain states you have been definitely overstocking your ranges, and you glory in your shame. You have been eating off the good pasture grass, and you have eaten it so close in many regions that the water has washed away the soil over large areas, and the wind has blown a lot of it away, until some of the land is almost permanently ruined. It is all right to go ahead if you want to, under your rugged individualism, and overstock your ranges and eat off the good pasture; it is all right for you to hurt yourselves if you want to; but it is a shame to hurt the land the way you have been doing.

--Early Western government official (Willard 1990)

Those initial decades of grazing insanity depleted, degraded, or destroyed **over 700 million** acres of grassland -- nearly all grassland west of the Mississippi River (Ferguson 1983). To this day most of it has not recovered (*or been allowed to recover*) to anywhere near a natural condition, and much of it has been altered beyond recognition from a natural state. There is no longer any US grassland larger than a few thousand acres in a pristine state. We will never know what was lost.

Compounding the impact from their animals was that wrought by stockmen themselves. Ranchers, as much or more than any of the newcomers, engaged in many activities

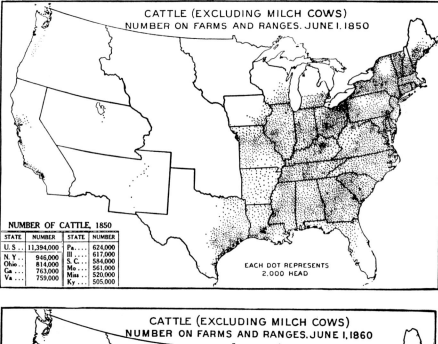

CATTLE (EXCLUDING MILCH COWS)
NUMBER ON FARMS AND RANGES. JUNE 1. 1850

EACH DOT REPRESENTS
2,000 HEAD

NUMBER OF CATTLE, 1850

STATE	NUMBER	STATE	NUMBER
U.S .	11,394,000	Pa....	624,000
N.Y..	946,000	Ill	617,000
Ohio.	814,000	S.C..	584,000
Ga ...	763,000	Mo...	561,000
Va ...	759,000	Miss	520,000
		Ky ...	505,000

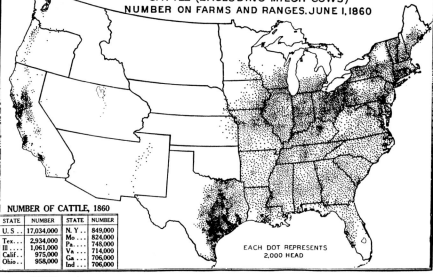

CATTLE (EXCLUDING MILCH COWS)
NUMBER ON FARMS AND RANGES. JUNE 1, 1860

EACH DOT REPRESENTS
2,000 HEAD

NUMBER OF CATTLE, 1860

STATE	NUMBER	STATE	NUMBER
U.S ..	17,034,000	N.Y..	849,000
Tex...	2,934,000	Mo ...	824,000
Ill	1,061,000	Pa...	748,000
Calif..	975,000	Va ...	714,000
Ohio..	958,000	Ga ...	706,000
		Ind ...	706,000

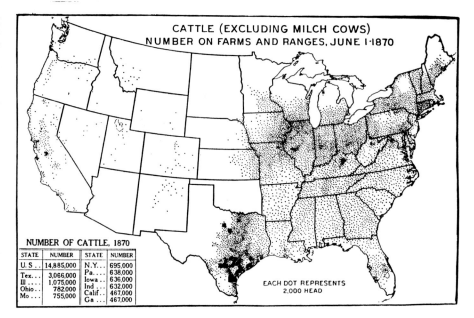

CATTLE (EXCLUDING MILCH COWS)
NUMBER ON FARMS AND RANGES, JUNE 1·1870

EACH DOT REPRESENTS
2,000 HEAD

NUMBER OF CATTLE, 1870

STATE	NUMBER	STATE	NUMBER
U.S ..	14,885,000	N.Y..	695,000
Tex...	3,066,000	Pa...	638,000
Ill	1,075,000	Iowa..	636,000
Ohio..	782,000	Ind ...	632,000
Mo ...	755,000	Calif..	467,000
		Ga ...	467,000

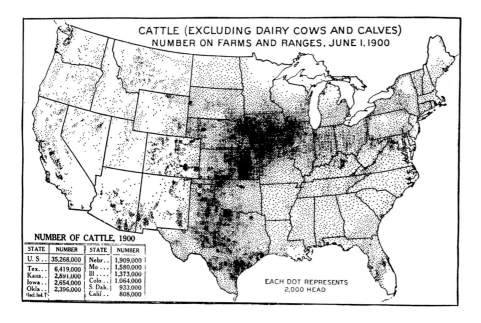

CATTLE (EXCLUDING DAIRY COWS AND CALVES)
NUMBER ON FARMS AND RANGES, JUNE 1, 1900

EACH DOT REPRESENTS 2,000 HEAD

NUMBER OF CATTLE, 1900

STATE	NUMBER	STATE	NUMBER
U. S ..	35,268,000	Nebr..	1,909,000
Tex...	6,419,000	Mo ...	1,580,000
Kans..	2,891,000	Ill	1,373,000
Iowa..	2,654,000	Colo ..	1.064,000
Okla..	2,396,000	S. Dak.	933,000
(incl. Ind. T.)		Calif ..	808,000

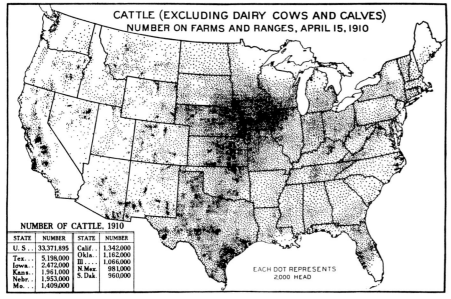

CATTLE (EXCLUDING DAIRY COWS AND CALVES)
NUMBER ON FARMS AND RANGES, APRIL 15, 1910

EACH DOT REPRESENTS 2,000 HEAD

NUMBER OF CATTLE, 1910

STATE	NUMBER	STATE	NUMBER
U. S ..	33,371,895	Calif..	1,342,000
Tex...	5,198,000	Okla..	1,162,000
Iowa..	2,472,000	Ill	1,066,000
Kans..	1,961,000	N.Mex.	981,000
Nebr..	1,953,000	S. Dak.	960,000
Mo ...	1,409,000		

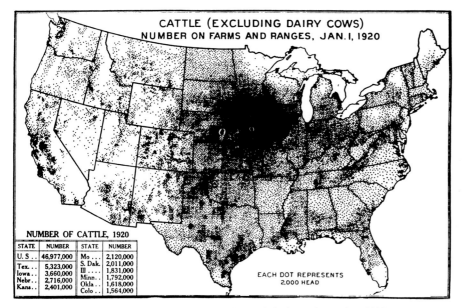

CATTLE (EXCLUDING DAIRY COWS)
NUMBER ON FARMS AND RANGES, JAN. 1, 1920

EACH DOT REPRESENTS 2,000 HEAD

NUMBER OF CATTLE, 1920

STATE	NUMBER	STATE	NUMBER
U. S ..	46,977,000	Mo ...	2,120,000
Tex...	5,323,000	S. Dak.	2,011,000
Iowa..	3,660,000	Ill	1,831,000
Nebr..	2,716,000	Minn..	1,792,000
Kans..	2,401,000	Okla..	1,618,000
		Colo ..	1,564,000

Note: Cattle distribution and numbers have remained relatively consistant since 1920.
US Government maps.

that spoiled the aboriginal Western landscape. Aside from stringing fences, they overfished, overhunted, and overtrapped wildlife; felled trees; built various harmful range developments; introduced exotic game animals that outcompeted indigenous species; spread non-native pasture plants; and generally manifested a heavy presence.

Within twenty years after the cowboy moved onto the last unsettled portion of the United States, a continuous line of inhabitants stretched from the Atlantic to the Pacific, for the cowboy had shown that this West had riches to plumb, fabulous wealth to yield to the hardy and adventurous, the sort of "risk-with-profit" that has always appealed to Americans.
--Joe B. Frantz and Julian Ernest Choate, Jr., **The American Cowboy**

Stockmen also seized the rural West politically and economically. With power based on great numbers of livestock and control of huge amounts of land and crucial sources of precious water -- and with a willingness to use violence to get what they wanted -- they banded together to form what is known today as the livestock grazing industry.

Local, area, state, and regional stockmen's associations were formed to protect ranchers' interests, and gunmen were hired to enforce their agreements. These associations came to exert tremendous power, legally and illegally restricting grazing access to certain lands, imposing self-serving regulations, running small-timers out of business in various ways, having dissenters murdered, and so on. Usually they were closely associated with state or territorial governments; their rules and regulations were often translated into actual law, or at least made the basis of legislation. Many laws throughout the West were made by and for the livestock industry during this period, and many of these laws stand today.

Largely through these associations and laws, wealthy ranchers came to rule the West with an iron fist. Nearly all Westerners paid deference to the "cattle barons" and "cattle empires." The sheriff always wore a cowboy hat (perhaps most still do). And as Joseph Nimmo, Jr., chief of the US Bureau of Statistics, related in *Harper's*, November 1886:

> The cattle-men and the cow-boys themselves supplied judges, jurymen, witnesses, attorneys, constables, and executioners. Sometimes a level-headed cow-boy was placed upon the judicial bench. . . . When the verdict of guilty was pronounced, a short shrift, and a stout rope, and a grave without a coffin or a winding-sheet, ended the proceedings. (Savage 1975)

Politicians, judges, lawyers, law enforcement officials, and others were *expected* to cater to livestock interests. Indeed, they were often influential ranchers themselves.

Stockmen's social powers became no less formidable. In **The Range Cattle Industry**, Edward Everett Dale writes:

> In addition to the rules of more or less local live stock associations, there gradually grew up in the range cattle area a body of precedents, customs, and principles, the whole forming a kind of unwritten law of the range known as "cow custom" which was in force and respected throughout the entire region. (Dale 1960)

The overwhelming influence of this "unwritten law" found its way not only into personal lives and customs throughout the rural West, but into actual law as well, especially at state and local levels.

In "The West Against Herself," Bernard DeVoto describes the aggressive cattlemen common in the formative years of the grazing industry:

> The cattlemen came from Elsewhere into the empty West. They were always arrogant and always deluded. . . . They thought of themselves as Westerners and they did live in the West, but they were enemies of everyone else who lived there. They kept sheepmen, their natural and eventual allies, out of the West wherever and as long as they could, slaughtering herds and frequently herdsmen. They did their utmost to keep the nester -- the farmer, the actual settler, the man who could create local and permanent wealth -- out of the West and to terrorize or bankrupt him where he could not be kept out. And the big cattlemen squeezed out the little ones wherever possible, grabbing the water rights, foreclosing small holdings, frequently hiring gunmen to murder them. (DeVoto 1955)

Conflicts between stockmen and other settlers were numerous. Those questioning stockmen's claims to power were dealt with swiftly and efficiently. Many were threatened, harassed, beaten up, and murdered. New settlers who clashed with established ranchers were driven off or killed. Farmers' crops were destroyed, many times intentionally, by marauding livestock. More Western homesteaders' hopes and hard work were crushed by ranchers and their cattle than by any other influence.

The movie Red River *begins with rancher John Wayne driving his cattle onto the vast range of a Mexican landowner. The Mexican's foreman rides into Wayne's camp and tells him that he and his stock must leave the next day. Wayne refuses, kills the foreman, and sends a messenger to the Mexican landowner informing him that Wayne now owns the land and will do whatever necessary to keep it.* Red River *is a cult film on how cattlemen won the West.*

A funny thing. Next morning the man that had been stampeding the herds was hanging from one of them trees -- considerably off to one side so's not to scare any cattle. He hung hisse'f so he wouldn't stampede no more cattle. That's what they said.
--From **The Longhorns** by J. Frank Dobie

Bloody battles or "range wars" were common even between stockmen themselves as they fought and killed each other trying to monopolize the dwindling, depleted forage land. When sheep began to spread through the West and compete with cattle, the war between cattlemen and sheepmen became especially gory. Initially sheepmen got the worst of it. Cattlemen attacked and looted sheep camps, burned camp wagons and provisions, and stole or killed horses and sheep dogs. Sheepmen often were beaten or murdered. For example, more than 30 men died in just a 3-year period in the Tonto Basin of central Arizona (Shanks 1984). Throughout the West, irate cattle ranchers killed hundreds of thousands of sheep by poisoning, clubbing, dynamiting them in close flocks, burning them in intentionally caused fires, driving flocks over precipices or into quicksand, and denying access to water and food (Roberts 1963).

However, sheep raising was highly profitable and increased steadily, eventually outdistancing cattle in value in many areas. In time, even many cattlemen decided to switch to the sheep business.

Sheep and cattle rustling was extremely common. The stolen animals were sold or added to existing herds. Suspected rustlers and sometimes competing herdsmen only accused of rustling were hanged for all to see. Rustlers even hanged less powerful rustlers as a warning to other rustlers to stay away from their turf.

(Unknown)

The more powerful stockmen forced out the less powerful, who had previously forced out the less powerful, and so on, as all jostled for position in this rangeland version of "king of the hill." The competition for grass had become the

the new gold rush, and any tactic was employed to get a bigger slice of the pie. The winners became rich and powerful; the losers left to seek greener pastures or died. By the time the undeclared range wars subsided, thousands of people lay dead. And stockmen's power in the rural West approached omnipotence.

Until the Sioux Indians were subdued, Wyoming was not safe for ranching; but with the conclusion of the Indian wars, the cattlemen immediately took possession of the old hunting grounds of the Sioux Indians. Cattle replaced the buffalo and antelope on the plains and foothills of the Rockies. Some of the early ranchers employed as many riders to protect their interests from the Indians as they used for running livestock.
--A.F. Vass, *Range and Ranch Studies in Wyoming* (Vass 1926)

Indian ricegrass, a staple of aboriginal Americans in much of the West, was mostly eliminated by livestock. *(Helen Wilson)*

In their conquest stockmen also murdered thousands of Native Americans, or hired mercenaries or pressured the US Army to do it for them. More than any non-military group, Western ranchers contributed to the Native's downfall and subjugation.

As soon as the federal government removed Native Americans from their homelands and onto reservations, cattlemen surged onto the newly vacant landscape. By the 1880s stockmen regularly grazed livestock in trespass on the "vast," "wasted" (ungrazed) Indian reservations as well. They began demanding that Western Congressmen reduce sizes of reservations. Congress often complied. For example, in the early 1890s the Blackfeet lost millions of acres when chronically trespassing ranchers convinced Congress to draft new treaties. Under pressure from stockmen, 4 reservations in Oregon comprising 3,567,360 acres in 1880 were reduced to 1,788,800 acres by 1890. Similar reductions took place in most Western states; *most* Indian reservations were reduced in size to accommodate US settlers, mostly ranchers. (Ferguson 1983, Shanks 1984)

Not satisfied, cattle ranchers continued to trespass the already reduced acreages. Indeed, throughout the West cattlemen not only ran thousands of cattle on Indian reservations but actually built homes there and claimed the land as their own. The government rarely tried to stop them. When it did, ranchers resorted to other tricks, such as driving cattle very slowly across reservations under pretense of moving them to other ranges, taking Native American wives to establish legal basis for grazing reservation lands, and consigning cattle to willing Native Americans (often bribed or supplied liquor) already living on reservations. Many trespassers simply claimed that they did not know where reservation boundaries were; when Congress finally appropriated money for surveys, stockmen pulled up stakes, destroyed boundary markers, and even murdered surveyors (Ferguson 1983). Pressure from Anglo ranchers was a major factor in the starvation, disease, and other hardship common on reservations.

Another change occurred in the second half of the nineteenth century. . . . A number of other wild resources that the Papago and Pima relied upon became so scarce [from livestock grazing] that to survive, they had to increase sales of whatever products they could muster in order to buy sufficient food.
--Gary Nabhan, **Gathering the Desert** (Nabhan 1986)

Even before their murder and banishment to the reservations Native Americans were harmed by the grazing industry in other ways usually ignored by historians. As livestock increased in numbers throughout the West, they depleted or extirpated hundreds of plants these peoples had for centuries depended on for shelter, clothing, bedding, basketry, tools, religion, magic, and medicine. They ravaged many of the food plants that produced the edible roots, bulbs, fruits, seeds, stalks, flowers, and leafy greens that composed *most* of the aboriginal diet. Along with the depletion in useful vegetation came a corresponding reduction in wild animals and pollution and depletion of critical water sources. By the time native peoples had been forced onto reservations, much of the West could no longer sustain them. (When plants, animals, water sources, and bottomland began disappearing from Navajoland in the 1880s, many believed the region had been bewitched.) Cattle and sheep also ate and trampled Native American crops, including those they planted after settling onto reservations. Thus, Native Americans became dependent upon domestic beef, their homelands and reservations became desolate, and their physical subjugation was complete.

Along with Indian reservations, stockmen grazed livestock in nearly every other possible grazing area ostensibly off-limits, or legally open, to their bovines. Grazing others' private property was common (as it still is); wire cutters allowed ranchers to expand their operations to almost any ungrazed land. Illegal grazing in National Parks was standard. For instance, in 1896 the US Cavalry drove 1000 cattle, 300 horses, and 189,500 sheep out of Yosemite National Park (Ferguson 1983). For years after Yellowstone National Park was established in 1872, stockmen trespassed thousands of sheep and cattle. Some ranchers even built cabins and mowed hay there (McNamee 1985). Government reports state that as late as the 1920s grazing in Grand Canyon National Park was so intensive that park rangers were complaining of spending too much time disposing of cattle carcasses.

Probably most private range land in the western states was originally obtained by various degrees of fraud in connection with the Homestead Act.
--Wesley Calef, **Private Grazing and Public Lands** (Calef 1960)

With the conquest of Native Americans, victorious military engagements with European powers, Mexico, and Russia, and massive land purchases, treaties, and other means of acquisition, the United States between 1803 and 1853 acquired the entire region that was to become "the West." Originally, nearly all of this land in the region to become the 11 Western states was under federal public ownership, excepting the old Spanish land grants in the Southwest and California and several million acres of other private holdings. By the early 1900s powerful stockmen would own about 1/3 of the West outright and control most of the other 2/3.

Ranchers gained ownership of federal land through various legal and illegal means, including outright theft, cheap sales that amounted to virtual giveaways of government land, and bribery or intimidation of government employees. Federal and, later, state governments gave away millions of acres as grants to encourage construction of railroads and roads; stockmen acquired much of this land for little or nothing, often through dubious means. Most of all, Congress enacted a series of laws designed to encourage settlement of the Western frontier, e.g., the Pre-emption Act of 1841, Homestead Act of 1862, Timber Culture Act of 1873, Desert Land Act of 1877 (of which one author estimated over 90% of land disposition was fraudulent), and Timber and Stone Act of 1878. Ranchers employed sundry schemes to gain title to more land than permitted under these acts. Often they would file claims under the names of employees, relatives, or people in other states, or invent fictitious names. Using a dozen aliases apiece, they would file claims to huge areas and through various methods later have the land transferred to their ownership. To qualify as homesteaders they would profess to have seen water where

there was none; throw together a few boards and claim it a dwelling; pretend to be homesteading property while only spending a day or two per year there; run a few furrows and say they were farming; splash a little water on the ground and claim to be irrigating; and so on. Altogether, the federal government transferred more than a billion acres west of the Mississippi to private ownership, 2/3 of it being given away in the form of grants and homesteads. Dominant ranchers even stole private land from less powerful settlers with help from their government yes-men. (Foss 1960, Ferguson 1983, Shanks 1984)

Some ranching empires became enormous. One Mormon cattle enterprise amassed a dominion of 2 million acres, or more than 3000 square miles of open range. The largest was a Texas spread of over 5 million acres, roughly the size of New Jersey! Operations controlling hundreds of thousands of acres were common. Some of these cattle kingdoms have been handed down or sold basically intact over the years and still exist today.

Dominant ranchers also gained control of large blocks of federal and state land through various means: controlling checkerboarded, multi-ownership land by buying up alternate sections (square miles); monopolizing water sources; purchasing strategic private land; agreeing among themselves to respect illegal boundaries; and pushing through bogus state laws which purported to give rights to federal lands (Foss 1960).

To defend "their" rangelands from others, stockmen erected thousands of miles of illegal fences on public land. Department of the Interior records show that from 1880 to 1920 many thousands of ranchers illegally fenced tens of millions of public acres, with as much as 8.6 million acres behind illegal fences in one year (1887). These records reflect only *reported* illegal fencing; actual acreage illegally fenced certainly was much higher. (Foss 1960, Culhane 1981)

By the end of the 19th century, stockmen had gained ownership of most of the more productive rangeland and water sources in the West. Most of the rest remained under public ownership, where it is today. One publication described these public lands as "the least desirable leftovers," land which "throughout almost 200 years of fraud, theft, chicanery, and unparalleled generosity in land disposition, nobody bothered to steal or dedicate to a specific purpose." Thus -- defined through default -- were born what are now "our public lands."

All he [the early Western stockman] *wanted from Washington was free use of public lands, high tariff on any meat coming from Australia and Argentina, the building and maintenance of public roads, the control of predators, the provision of free education, a good mail service with free delivery to the ranch gate, and a strong sheriff's department to arrest anyone who might think of intruding on the land. "I want no interference from the government," the rancher proclaimed, and he meant it.*
--from **Centennial** by James Michener

Despite the devastation caused by the livestock invasion of the 1870s and 1880s, extreme overgrazing continued into the 20th century. However, many Westerners were becoming increasingly alarmed at declining range productivity -- the depletion of water supplies, soil, game animals, and useful vegetation. Many more were calling for a halt to ranchers' reign of terror over the West. Even some stockmen began to recognize a need for regulation and stability in the grazing industry, especially for protection of forage and browse. But perhaps most importantly, powerful, established cattle ranchers desperately wanted to eliminate competition from their long-time rivals -- nomadic herders, mostly sheepmen. Gradually, over the years a number of measures were adopted to attempt to mitigate these problems.

In 1891 one of the first steps was taken when Congress passed a law setting aside federal forest reserves, eventually leading to the establishment of the United States Forest Service (USFS or FS) in 1905. The new federal agency enacted grazing regulations, created allotments, issued permits, and charged a nominal fee of 5 cents per month for each cow or 5 sheep grazed to help pay administrative costs. This effectively eliminated nomadic sheep and cattle herders on FS land. Grazing boards composed of local ranchers were set up and quickly became influential policy makers.

Ungrazed portion of Ruby Lake National Wildlife Refuge, NV, on left; BLM on right.

Powerful graziers were instrumental in creating the Forest Service and placing it under the jurisdiction of the US Department of Agriculture (USDA), rather than Interior, where by all logic it should have been located. A great many ranchers became district, forest, regional, and national Forest Service range and administrative officials, and many still are today. For example, Albert F. Potter, an influential Arizona Wool Growers Association official, became the agency's first Chief of Grazing. Indeed, the Forest Service during its early years was much more tied to the grazing industry than to the timber industry. This history helps explain why today's Forest Service is so dedicated to ranching. (Voigt 1976, Foss 1960, etc.)

Old aristocrats of the western rangelands were given preference rights without competitive bidding. Public-land leases essentially became property rights, bought and sold by ranchers as part of a ranch. No Forest Service administrator would dare substantially reduce or transfer a grazing lease from a large and influential cattle rancher, no matter how abused the public's land might be.

--Bernard Shanks, **This Land Is Your Land** (Shanks 1984)

The most productive public land was now under Forest Service administration. Stockmen and farmers owned most of the productive private land, and there were millions of acres of other private and state land. But there remained more than half a billion acres of "leftover" federal public domain, roughly half of the 17 western states. Many graziers did not even bother trying to patent this land because they thought they could control it through their possession of adjacent water and land, through brute force, and by other means. Few seemed to care what happened to this "waste" land, and unrestrained grazing continued there for decades. Again, abuse was so severe on the unadministered public domain that even many ranchers began to realize that something had to be done.

Cattlemen here were concerned about the land's lowered productivity, but, as with the large ranchers who spawned the Forest Service, they were more concerned about another problem -- continued competition from nomadic livestockmen, mostly sheepmen. In 1934 that problem was ended. With the support of the most influential cattlemen in the West -- many who were enticed by the promise of increased federal aid -- Representative Edward Taylor, a rancher from Colorado and sworn enemy of conservationists, pushed a bill through Congress. The Taylor Grazing Act of 1934 was adopted with the expressed intent of eliminating nomadic herding, as well as stopping indiscriminate settlement and grazing, stabilizing the grazing industry, restoring damaged lands, and fulfilling other lofty goals (USDI, BLM 1976).

The Taylor Grazing Act also created the Division of Grazing under the Department of the Interior, with Colorado stockman Farrington Carpenter as its first Director. As with the Forest Service, Congress enacted regulations, created grazing allotments, and charged a nominal 5 cent grazing fee. Leases were issued to the privileged few, generally the most wealthy and powerful cattlemen, especially those who helped create the Taylor Grazing Act, often those who had illegally fenced off public land. To help secure their control and abolish nomadic herders, only those with "base properties" -- well-established, substantial private ranch holdings near the public land to be grazed -- were eligible for leases.

Regulations were extremely loose, as they did not even

restrict numbers of livestock or season of use. Yet, as with the new Forest Service permittees, these changes did not sit well with many in a group who had for decades done whatever they damn well pleased on public land. Irate ranchers threatened to run Department of Interior representatives out of town. Some issued belligerent statements that they would shoot anyone trespassing on "their" range and declaring that they would tolerate no government interference with ranching operations on private or public land. They collaborated to overwhelm the Division of Grazing with threats, complaints, and demands. Despite it all, with support from the most powerful Western stockmen, the Taylor Grazing Act and Division of Grazing survived, albeit with little real power over public ranching practices other than nomadic herding (Calef 1960). In **This Land Is Your Land**, Bernard Shanks writes: "In a classic example of western control of federal land, the Taylor Grazing Act retained the elite stock raisers' dominance using a permit system, a small grazing fee, and a weak agency to manage the program." (Shanks 1984).

In its first year of operation, 1935, the Division of Grazing was assigned 60 Civilian Conservation Corps (CCC) camps with about 12,000 men to build fences, stock tanks, ranching roads, erosion control structures, and other livestock-related developments on public domain. The number of camps peaked at nearly 100 before the CCC disbanded in 1943. These years of CCC involvement were instrumental in subjugating the range for powerful livestock interests.

Through liberal interpretation of several phrases in the Taylor Grazing Act, Division of Grazing stockman/director Carpenter formulated administrative directives which established local "grazing advisory boards." Elected by local stockmen, the boards ostensibly would cooperate with agency district managers in planning for responsible management. State and federal boards were created as well. "Advisory" boards were likewise established by and for Forest Service permittees in 1950.

All these "advisory" boards were composed mostly of the same large-scale, aggressive, politically savvy ranchers who helped create the Forest Service and Taylor Grazing Act and awarded themselves federal grazing permits (or else stockmen who followed in their place). Most members were also livestock association officials, and many were bankers, real estate dealers, lawyers, timber barons, merchants, and mining tycoons. They realized, however, that it would be politically unwise if it appeared that big ranchers in livestock associations controlled the federal grazing administration apparatus. Consequently, to appease Congress and the public, a few token small-time ranchers were allowed onto the boards and placed into high-profile positions. The tactic remains common today.

Nonetheless, the grazing "advisory" boards assured powerful stockmen continued dominance. They quickly assumed nearly absolute power over grazing management decision-making; not even agency district managers dared challenge their authority. In **Private Grazing and Public Lands**, Wesley Calef affirms that, "the advisory board members were the effective governing and administrative body of each grazing district" (Calef 1960). Indeed, Division of Grazing Director Carpenter in his yearly report for 1935 referred to the boards as "the local governing agency as to all matters of a range regulatory nature" (Foss 1960). The

federal government even paid advisory board members $5 per day "expense salary," an appreciable salary in the 1930s.

In 1939, under close supervision of the grazing industry, the Division of Grazing was reorganized into the Grazing Service. This was no improvement. Congressional Representative Jed Johnson of Oklahoma later complained emotionally on the floor of the House:

> *But what did the Grazing Service do? They went out and practically turned it over to the big cowmen and the big sheepmen of the West. Why they even put them on the payroll. . . . It is common knowledge that they have been practically running the Grazing Service.* (Culhane 1981)

Seven years later, in 1946, again under the influence of powerful stockmen, the Grazing Service and General Land Office were combined to form the Bureau of Land Management (BLM). Due to industry pressure and lack of funds, administration and enforcement of grazing regulations had been practically non-existent. Now, with the formation of the BLM, many stockmen hoped that even the regulations that were enforced would be lost in the shuffle of reorganization.

They were not disappointed. Despite some of the founders' original intentions in creating the Forest Service

and BLM, both agencies promptly acquiesced to stockmen's expectations. This is not to say they did not in many ways represent an improvement over the prior *laissez faire* system, but that grazing and ranching abuses and political, economic, and social injustice continued largely unchecked.

Due to excessive grazing industry influence in agency formations, regulations were weak to begin with. But ranchers generally followed them only when they wanted to anyway. In fact, for years many ranchers refused to obtain permits, pay grazing fees, or follow any regulations whatsoever. When agency personnel attempted enforcement, traditional grazing industry power neutralized the challenge by applying political, social, and economic pressures where needed. In short, the Forest Service and BLM (and states, etc.) functioned more as grazing industry tools than true regulatory agencies.

The Forest Service, being older, better organized, and with more of a public mandate to safeguard natural resources, generally has had more capacity to curb abuses and more success at it. Yet livestock grazing and other abuses remain prevalent on National Forests. BLM, staffed mostly with ranchers and ranching advocates and administering primarily stockmen-dominated rangeland, has had little inclination to curtail ranching abuses.

Over the years the ranching story has taken many twists. An expanding Western population suppressed most outright social violence long ago, though it still does occur. Sheep populations exploded soon after cattle, peaking around 1910 and according to some estimates rivaling cattle in overall value. Sheep raising declined drastically in the 1930s and continued to decline, with a slight upsurge since 1978. Goat grazing also became popular -- and destructive -- until a lack of herders caused it to fall off in mid-century, again, with a recent slight upsurge. Stockmen used World Wars I and II as excuses to overstock public ranges even further (our brave fighting boys need more meat), compounding the massive environmental degradation. Livestock grazing joined unwise farming to cause the 5-state, 50 million acre Dust Bowl disaster of the 1930s.

Agency corruption and pro-ranching biases have remained prevalent all along, though things have begun to change somewhat in recent years. The fee for grazing livestock on public land has always been and remains extremely low. Various range management policies come and go, none significantly improving range conditions. Annual government expenditures on ranching have risen manyfold, allowing technologically based management programs under the guise of range "improvement" to exploit and damage the environment more and in more different ways than ever before. The livestock industry, promoting various state land-grab schemes (most notably the so-called "Sagebrush Rebellion" of 1979), has tried to take our public land away and ultimately transfer ownership to stockmen, thus far with little success. The government and public, and even the agencies themselves in several recent cases, have battled the grazing industry on reform issues. The industry has prevailed in almost every case, if not legally, then in practice on the ground. The "ecology movement" of the 1960s and 1970s resulted in a number of important environmental protection laws being passed, but thus far they are poorly enforced, particularly with regard to ranching. Vehemently opposed to each of these laws every step of the way was the ranching industry. (See Chapter IX for details.)

The regional landed aristocracy that emerged, with its attitude of aristocratic lawlessness, dominates public rangeland management to this day.
--Bernard Shanks, **This Land Is Your Land** (Shanks 1984)

The *real* history of the Western livestock industry is a century-long, continuing progression of corruption, trickery, thievery, harassment, persecution, brute force, and incredible insensitivity toward and destruction of the land -- a country mile from our idealistic cowboy fantasy. Ranching continues to be one of the most dishonorable episodes in American history, and denial will only allow this outrage to continue.
[Note: For more detailed studies of public lands ranching history, consult DeVoto 1955, Calef 1960, Foss 1960, Voigt 1976, Ferguson 1983, or Shanks 1984.]

At this point it is necessary to differentiate between what is being done and the people doing it. First, it serves no good purpose denying that in some ways the attitudes and tendencies of their predecessors have followed stockmen down through the years. As a group, even today's ranchers often display the intolerance, machismo, self-importance, environmental insensitivity, avarice, and drive-for-power that characterized early stockmen. As in any group, however, many modern stockmen are fine people who possess any number of good qualities. But this does not mean one must approve of their ranching. Historically, many individually fine people have been caught up in occupations, undertakings, or even lifestyles that have had disastrous impacts on the world and the people around them.

... as long as the rivers shall run and the grass shall grow ... till the cows come home ...

Chapter II
PUBLIC LANDS RANCHING TODAY

*Public land does not belong to the government,
nor to ranchers,
nor to any other special interest group*

More than a century has passed since that first wave of grazing exploitation left the Western environment in shambles. Looking back on those reckless times, most of us believe things are much different now. The great trail drives and bloody range wars ended long ago. We rarely hear of cattle rustlers being shot, much less hanged. The clearest picture most of us have of living livestock these days is the sight of them grazing along rural roadsides.

Many things are indeed much different now.

On the other hand, the situation overall has actually changed very little, despite claims to the contrary by the ranching establishment. Though less blatant, stockmen's power remains similarly overwhelming. They use subtler and more palatable methods to achieve their goals, but retain political and social hegemony over most of the rural West. As the following analysis will show, the range itself is in many respects even more degraded than 100 years ago, as our natural resources continue to be plundered year after year. And, sorry to say, the public is now being swindled more than ever. (The many reasons for our collective misunderstanding of modern ranching are explored throughout this book.)

The West is literally covered with livestock, from the highest elevation tundra to the driest sagebrush basins. . . . Livestock graze seven out of every ten acres in the West. . . .
--Florence Williams, "Who's at Home on the Range?" (Williams 1990a)

As it has been for a century, about **70%** of the 11 Western states is "open range" managed for livestock ranching (Fer-

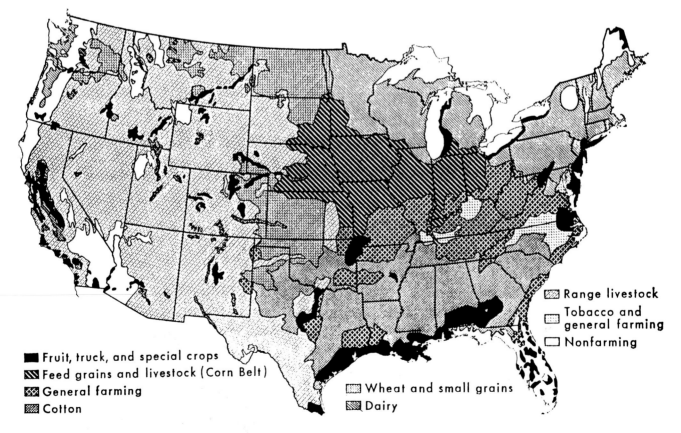

Range livestock
Tobacco and general farming
Nonfarming
Fruit, truck, and special crops
Feed grains and livestock (Corn Belt)
General farming
Cotton
Wheat and small grains
Dairy

Major agricultural land uses in US. Note the overwhelming predominance of "range livestock" throughout the West; the major use of some of the "nonfarming" areas is also ranching. *(USDA map)*

guson 1983). Basically, that's 7 of every 10 acres behind barbed wire fences with cattle, sheep, and/or other livestock grazing on them on some regular basis. That's roughly 525 million acres, representing more than 2 acres for every person in the United States.

Further, included in the ungrazed 30% of the West are inaccessible areas, dense forests and brushlands, the driest deserts, sand dunes, dry lake beds and salt flats, lava flows and cinder cones, extremely rocky areas, cliffs and mountaintops, cities and towns, roads and parking areas, airports, golf courses, your backyard, and every other place that cannot be used for livestock. In other words, in the American West almost every place that *can* be grazed *is* grazed. More than 2/3 of Montana, Wyoming, Colorado, New Mexico, Arizona, Nevada, Utah, and Idaho is grazed, and if not for farmland and dense forest more than 2/3 of the West Coast states would be grazed too. Livestock graze in most grasslands, forests, brushlands, wetlands, and

Cattle and sheep are found nearly everywhere in the West.

Cattle strip vegetation from between irrigated date palms in Death Valley, CA -- the place with the overall highest summer temperatures and one of the lowest precipitations on Earth.

deserts in the West, on almost any land with enough forage or browse to keep a cow or sheep alive. (Navajo herders even carry small sheep up steep rock walls on their backs, one by one, to reach the grassy tops of mesas.)

Of the grazed 70% of the West, 58% is publicly owned land used for commercial livestock. In other words, 41% of the West, or 306 million acres, is public land used for private ranching. An additional 5%, or 35 million acres, is grazed Indian reservation land.

Furthermore, the 11 Western states are home to about 98% of all public lands ranching in this country. The remaining 2% is mostly in the Midwest -- where about 325,000 BLM acres in 5 states and several million Forest Service acres (including National Grasslands) are grazed -- and in the South, where roughly 1.7 million FS acres are open to ranching. An additional 100,000 or so acres of National Forest in the East and some other non-Western federal, state, and county lands are commercially grazed, as are about 8 million BLM acres by 17,400 reindeer in Alaska. (USDA, FS 1988; USDI, BLM 1988; and other federal publications)

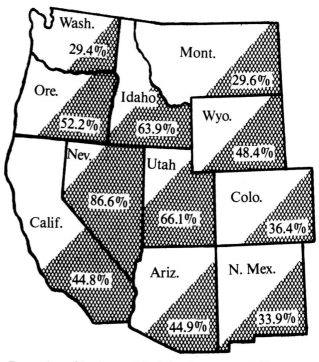

Proportion of land owned by federal government (does not include state, county, and city land). Roughly 80% of this federal land and 70% of all land in the West is used for livestock.

Two government agencies administer 85% of Western public ranchland -- about 260 million acres, or an area the size of the 14 Eastern seaboard states plus Missouri. Of this 85%, the Bureau of Land Management administers 63% (163 million acres) and the Forest Service administers 37% (97 million acres). Roughly 90% of Western BLM and 70% of Western FS land is managed for ranching. There are 140 BLM resource areas (local divisions) in the West. Each is grazed by privately owned livestock. Likewise, commercial livestock are allowed and encouraged on all of the West's 102 National Forests. National Forests in 24 Eastern states also allow ranching. BLM land accounts for 61% and

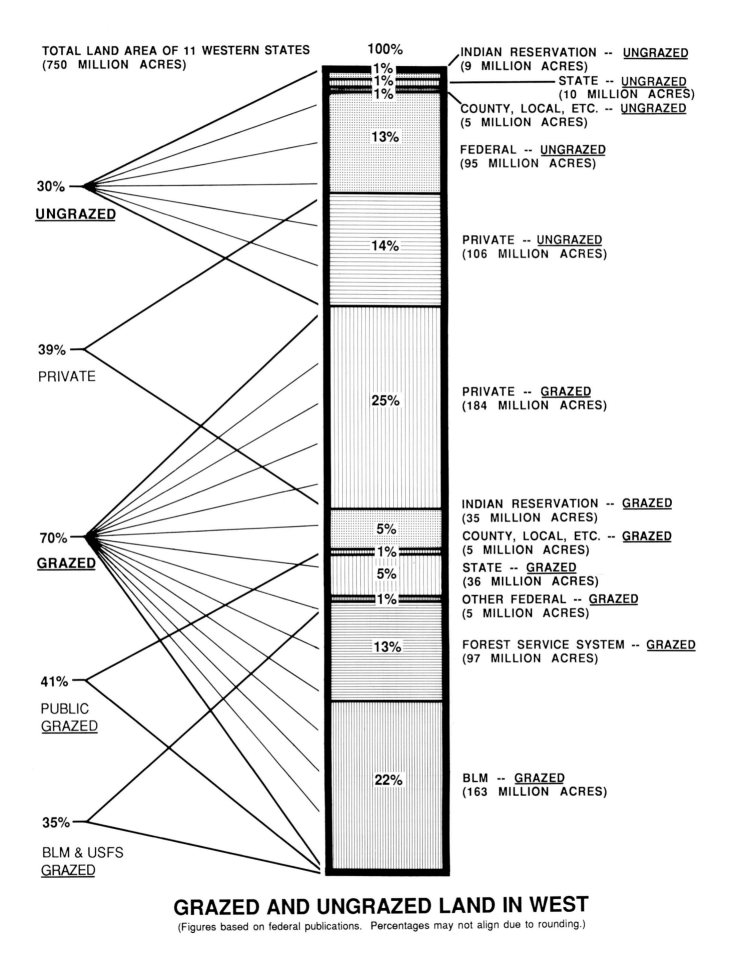

TOTAL LAND AREA OF 11 WESTERN STATES
(750 MILLION ACRES)

100%

INDIAN RESERVATION -- <u>UNGRAZED</u>
(9 MILLION ACRES)

1%
1%
1%

STATE -- <u>UNGRAZED</u>
(10 MILLION ACRES)

COUNTY, LOCAL, ETC. -- <u>UNGRAZED</u>
(5 MILLION ACRES)

13%

FEDERAL -- <u>UNGRAZED</u>
(95 MILLION ACRES)

30%

<u>UNGRAZED</u>

14%

PRIVATE -- <u>UNGRAZED</u>
(106 MILLION ACRES)

39%

PRIVATE

25%

PRIVATE -- <u>GRAZED</u>
(184 MILLION ACRES)

70%

<u>GRAZED</u>

5%

INDIAN RESERVATION -- <u>GRAZED</u>
(35 MILLION ACRES)

COUNTY, LOCAL, ETC. -- <u>GRAZED</u>
(5 MILLION ACRES)

1%
5%

STATE -- <u>GRAZED</u>
(36 MILLION ACRES)

1%

OTHER FEDERAL -- <u>GRAZED</u>
(5 MILLION ACRES)

13%

FOREST SERVICE SYSTEM -- <u>GRAZED</u>
(97 MILLION ACRES)

41%

PUBLIC
<u>GRAZED</u>

22%

BLM -- <u>GRAZED</u>
(163 MILLION ACRES)

35%

BLM & USFS
<u>GRAZED</u>

GRAZED AND UNGRAZED LAND IN WEST
(Figures based on federal publications. Percentages may not align due to rounding.)

Forest Service land 39% of their combined livestock production. (1987 USDA and USDI publications).

BLM land, being the "land nobody wanted" (or, more properly, the land that was wanted *least*), generally is the least economically valuable land in the West. Most is hot, dry, barren, rocky, and/or steeply sloped. Nonetheless, BLM administers many riparian areas, grasslands, and even forests. The lands administered by the Forest Service are of course mostly forested, but National Forests also include millions of acres of brushlands, shrublands, meadows, grasslands, and even deserts. Thirty percent of National Forest System land in the US is "open" rangeland (USDA, USDI 1979), and a forested area must be extremely thick with "dark timber" to be excluded from livestock grazing.

Publicly owned ranchlands also include many millions of acres of state, county, and even city lands; National Wildlife Refuges (administered by the US Fish & Wildlife Service); National Grasslands (FS); military reservations; and even some National Parks, Monuments, Recreation Areas, etc. (National Park Service); along with several million acres administered by several other federal agencies. Roughly half of designated Wilderness Areas (various federal agencies) are likewise grazed by livestock. Administration and management of these lands vary widely (see Chapter IX).

... the public rangelands exhibit examples of literally all of the recognized land forms ... [they] support all of the natural vegetation types known to the West....
--Fair Market Rental Value of Grazing on Public Lands, FS and BLM (Tittman 1984)

Is this public land impractical for livestock? Of course, but because edible vegetation grows here, it is used for ranching.

The vast bulk of Western BLM and FS land is divided into individual grazing allotments ranging in size from less than 40 acres to well over a million (Com. on Govt. Oper. 1986). Average state allotment sizes vary from 68,583 acres in arid Nevada to 2217 acres in comparatively well-grassed Montana (USDA, FS 1986; USDI, BLM 1986). Allotment boundaries are usually based on traditional and often obsolete ownership, fence, and grazing patterns; allotment configurations rarely make sense topographically or environmentally.

Livestock operators are issued permits or, on some BLM lands, leases, allowing them to graze cattle, sheep, goats, horses and other equines on certain allotments (USDA, FS 1986; USDI, BLM 1986). Much more than permission to merely graze livestock on an allotment, the grazing permit is essentially a *ranching* permit, allowing each permittee to manage and develop (that is, to *ranch*) that allotment for livestock. Indeed, ranchmen themselves have had perhaps as much impact on the land as their livestock (see Chapter IV). Thus, public lands grazing is a great misnomer, and we refer to the industry as public lands *ranching*.

Average size of BLM and Forest

Our BLM lands of the West. Approximately 90% of their area is used for ranching, yet all this land produces only about 1.1% of US cattle and sheep. *(USDA map)*

Our National Forests of the West. Although nearly 70% of their total area is used for livestock ranching, only about 0.7% of US cattle and sheep are produced there. *(USDA map)*

the remaining 1/4 run yearling cattle operations -- generally, they buy calves in spring, fatten them through the summer, and sell them in the fall -- or sheep operations. (Williams 1990)

Sheep, which are herbivores (eaters of various types of plants), are in the US West raised mostly in relatively cool, well-watered regions; on public land this usually means in higher elevations during summer. However, sheep are drought-resistant compared to cattle and prefer somewhat different vegetation, so they are found in many locales. Goats are primarily browsers (shrub and tree eaters), but are famous for their ability to eat almost anything organic. Although not nearly as numerous as sheep (there are only 1.6 million goats in the US, mostly in Texas), goats recently have gained popularity as "tools" for eradicating unwanted brush to increase rangeland productivity for cattle and sheep. Semi-domesticated buffalo and buffalo cross-breeds are grazed similarly to cattle in scattered locations, but are relatively few in number. Lastly, equines -- domestic horses, burros, donkeys, and mules -- which are all mainly grazers, are much less common than cattle and sheep; but many ranchers graze them in smaller numbers on public land for commercial as well as domestic purposes.

Service System allotments is about 8500 acres (USGAO 1988). Due to overlapping use, the average size of BLM and FS land allotted per Western grazing permittee is 11,818 acres (various 1987 federal publications). Including state and other government lands simultaneously grazed by permittees, the figure probably is closer to 15,000 (various 1987 federal publications). When a public lands rancher talks about "his" ranch he usually means his private property *and* "his" multi-thousand acre public lands grazing allotment. The public lands portion is usually many times larger than the private; in Arizona, for example, the average ratio is 7 public acres to 1 private acre.

Cattle and sheep have always comprised the vast majority of livestock on public land, with cattle currently accounting for about 8 times more total grazing pressure on Western federal rangeland than sheep (USDA, FS 1987; USDI, BLM 1988). (Nationally, cattle consume about 96% of the estimated total grazed forage [Joyce 1989].) Cattle, primarily grazers (grass and forb eaters), are nearly omnipresent in range and distribution. About 3/4 of public ranchers run cow/calf operations in which the basic "resource" is a herd of brood cows and the principal livestock income is derived from sale of "feeder cattle" (yearling heifers and steers) to commercial feedlots for fattening before slaughter. Most of

Goats can be particularly destructive to the Western range because they will eat almost any vegetative material, including many types of plants that cattle and sheep would not. *(Steve Johnson)*

The so-called "right" to graze livestock on federal public land is not a right at all, but a revocable *privilege* (Tittman 1984). Ranchers cannot legally own or have exclusive right to any federal land, claim resources thereon (except permitted use of forage and, unfortunately, water rights on some BLM lands), exclude any person from public land, or dictate any visitor's behavior. Stockmen granted the privilege to graze their livestock on the public's land are ostensibly required to pay their fees on time, adhere to all grazing and environmental regulations, mitigate environmental damage, and minimize conflict with other land users (see Chapter IX).

Grazing use is measured in units called Animal Unit Months, or AUMs. An AUM is defined by the federal government as the amount of forage and/or browse required to feed a cow and her calf, a horse, or 5 sheep or goats for a month. The AUM concept is somewhat arbitrary and malleable, so in practice AUMs vary from 600 to 1200 pounds of herbage (leafy plant material of any kind). Most fall between 800 and 1000 pounds, so an AUM averages roughly 900 pounds (USGAO 1988).

About 30,000 grazing permits and leases are issued on BLM and FS rangeland in the 11 Western states, with permittees paying an annual fee based on the number of AUMs (permitted and alleged to be) used. Some of these permittees graze more than 1 allotment, and 15% graze both BLM and FS lands, so the actual number of permittees grazing BLM and FS land in the 16 Western states is about 23,000. (Com. on Govt. Oper. 1986) Thus, in the 11 Western states only about **22,000** permittees graze BLM and Forest Service lands. That is 0.0088% of the US population, or 1 of 11,364 persons in the US, or less than the population of Barstow, California.

Furthermore, according to the Committee on Government Operations of the US Congress, the 23,000 public lands permittees in the 16 Western states (including North and South Dakota, Nebraska, Kansas, and Oklahoma) represent *less than 2%* of the 1.6 million livestock producers in the United States (Com. on Govt. Oper. 1986). Extrapolation shows the figure for the 11 Western states to be *1.375%, or closer to 1%*.

Many federal permittees graze livestock not only on BLM and/or FS lands but on other federal, state, and/or local government lands as well. Some hold a half dozen or more leases to various government and private lands. Thus, including *all* public lands there are approximately 30,000 public lands ranchers in the West, comprising *less than 2%* of US cattle and sheep producers. (Various government sources)

Less than 15% of original permits issued by BLM and FS remain with the family to which they were issued (Com. on Govt. Oper. 1986). The notion that most public lands ranching is done by descendants of the original settlers is another of the numerous powerful myths associated with the grazing industry.

Grazing permits generally are issued for a period of 10 years, and permit holders have first priority for renewal. In practice renewal is virtually automatic. Because of this livestock operators enjoy essentially permanent tenure on allotments and consider permits almost as private property (see Chapter VII).

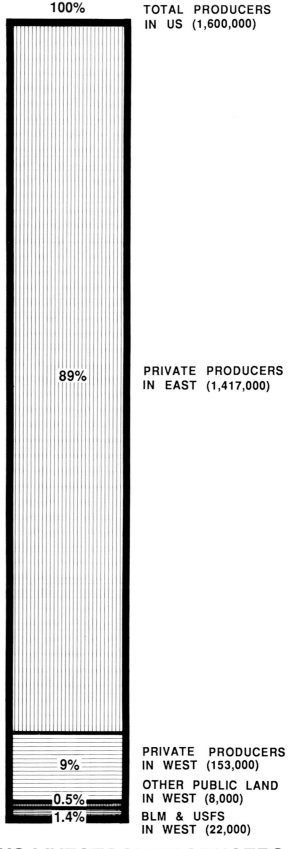

100% TOTAL PRODUCERS IN US (1,600,000)

89% PRIVATE PRODUCERS IN EAST (1,417,000)

9% PRIVATE PRODUCERS IN WEST (153,000)

0.5% OTHER PUBLIC LAND IN WEST (8,000)

1.4% BLM & USFS IN WEST (22,000)

US LIVESTOCK PRODUCERS
(US Government figures)

The Forest Service requires each permittee to own an adjacent or nearby "base property" -- deeded land of a certain minimum acreage (usually 40, 60, or 80 acres) which is used as a base for livestock operations on the grazing allotment (though, as mentioned, the original intent of requiring base properties was chiefly to exclude nomadic herders from the public range). Base property requirements for BLM permittees are somewhat different and vary from area to area; generally, the minimum size required is larger than what FS requires. When a permit is "sold" with a base property, it is returned to the government and nearly always reissued to the new property owner. (Most other land managing agencies require base properties, though the US Fish & Wildlife Service does not.)

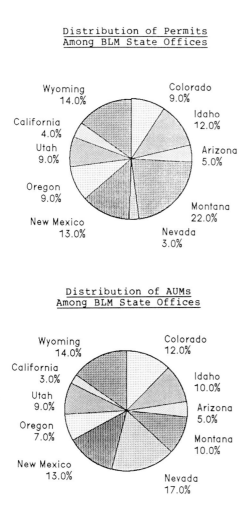

In some cases stockmen are granted grazing permits based on ownership of water rights on private or public land. In fact, grazing privileges on BLM land can now be granted to a stockman based solely on ownership of water rights to a single spring.

The number of permits varies little mostly because almost all grazable land is already being grazed. If agencies acquire new rangeland, it is apportioned among existing adjacent permittees. If for some reason a permittee decides to abandon a permit (almost unheard of), the agency involved reassigns the permit to an established adjacent or nearby

rancher. The Taylor Grazing Act, Forest Service mandates established at the agency's formation, and subsequent legislation have ensured that the federal permit system maintains the status quo.

Ostensibly, permittees are required to manage livestock operations in accordance with allotment management plans developed by the agencies in consultation with permittees. This results in each permit containing conditions specific to the allotment being grazed, such as maximum and minimum number of livestock, AUMs allotted, period and area of use, entry and exit routes, and so forth. Most public land is grazed during growing seasons, typically spring and/or summer but sometimes fall or even winter, but there are many areas in the warmer regions where it is permitted year-round (see Livestock Management in Chapter IV). The agencies have authority to adjust permit conditions or terminate permits at any time to allow for any number of variables, but they rarely do. Each agency has independent basic guidelines and regulations, but local agency administrators have wide discretion in adjusting permit terms. In practice, ranchers and rancher-staffed "advisory" boards often have more influence over permit conditions than do the agencies (see Chapter IX). (For a good discussion of the intricacies of BLM and FS grazing administration, see Chapters 3 and 4 in Wesley Calef's **Private Grazing and Public Lands**.)

. . . the little cattlemen have always fought the big one's battles, have adopted and supported their policies to their own disadvantage and to the great hurt of the West.
--Bernard DeVoto (DeVoto 1955)

There are small public lands ranchers, but corporate ranchers and large individual operators predominate; 40% of federal grazing is controlled by only 3% of permittees (Ferguson 1983). On BLM land, just 5% of cattlemen, those with herd size over 500, control 58% of all herbage allotted to livestock, and 32% goes to medium-sized operations -- 100-499 animals. Only 10% goes to the small rancher who owns less than 100 cattle (Atwood 1990). Forest Service stockmen with herd size over 500 constitute 12% of permittees and use 41% of AUMs (Com. on Govt. Oper. 1986). And merely 6% of Western sheepmen own 63% of all sheep (Ferguson 1983). Nonetheless, despite myths and misinformation, most of the 22,000 Western BLM and FS permittees, even most of the so-called "small-timers," are quite well-off financially (see Chapter XI). (On the national scale, nearly 80% of all beef processing is controlled by only 3 agricultural conglomerates: ConAgra Red Meat Company, IBP, Inc., and Excel; many cattle that graze public lands wind up in their feedlots [Zaslowsky 1989]).

[A 1982 US agricultural census] found that Arizona had 3346 farms and ranches that sold cattle. Of these, 97 farms and ranches accounted for $413 million of the $502 million in sales . . .
--1-17-86 *Phoenix Gazette*

At this point, one might reasonably ask what all these facts and figures amount to, food-wise. There are roughly 260 million acres of BLM and Forest Service System "grazing land" in the 11 Western states -- 35% of the land area of the West -- but how much of this country's livestock is produced there?

Two percent by weight, value, or livestock feed (food of any kind) (Com. on Govt. Oper. 1986). This will surprise most people, for we have always been led to believe otherwise. Ranching on federal land is insignificant to US food supply -- only 1 out of 50 pounds of combined beef and mutton. Alabama alone produces nearly this amount, mostly on pasturage!' Iowa produces more than 2 1/2 times as much, mostly with grain feed. (USDA 1987) The US imports more than 4 times as much (US Dept. of Com. 1986).

Even if all public lands in the West are considered together, their yield is insignificant. *All* Western public lands -- federal, state, and local together, roughly 306 million acres, or 41% of the West -- produce *less than 3%* of America's combined cattle and sheep feed. Nearly 6 times this amount is raised on the private ranchland that encompasses about 25% of the West. (Government publications)

Only 3% of US cattle feed is supplied by all Western public land. As for sheep, the Western grazing establishment has used deception and fabrication to persuade the American public that Western federal rangeland accounts for 40% or more of US sheep production. For example, USDA's *Livestock Grazing Successes on Public Range* claims, "Fully 50 percent of the Nation's marketable lambs and 20 percent of the calves going to feedlots are raised in the western public land states" (USDA 1989). "In the

western public lands states" is a sneaky way of making it seem that Western livestock production is public, when in fact it is overwhelmingly private. The truth is that all US public lands combined supply only about 15% of US sheep feed, or less than 1/3 of the West's sheep feed. By value and weight US cattle outrank sheep nearly 50 to 1, so sheep are insignificant to US livestock production anyway. (USDA 1987, various government publications) Another misconception is that most US sheep are raised for wool; 78% are raised for their meat (Joyce 1989).

Furthermore, merely 21% of US cattle and sheep feed comes from all the West, public *and* private (USDA, FS 1986; USDI, BLM 1986). Arkansas raises more cattle than Arizona; Wisconsin supports almost 3 times as many cows as Wyoming; and Nebraska's cattle production value is 16.6 times that of Nevada's! (USDA 1987) Private land (including Indian reservations) produces 18% of the West's 21%. Private land includes feedlots, irrigated pasture, and farmland for livestock, which together account for much of this 18%. In addition, a relatively large proportion of the West's livestock is produced on the Great Plains of Montana, Wyoming, Colorado, and New Mexico east of the Rockies. In short, *private* land is the true livestock producer in the West and the *East* is the true livestock producer in the US.

Public stockmen counter that while they supply comparatively few livestock, their contribution is vital because their

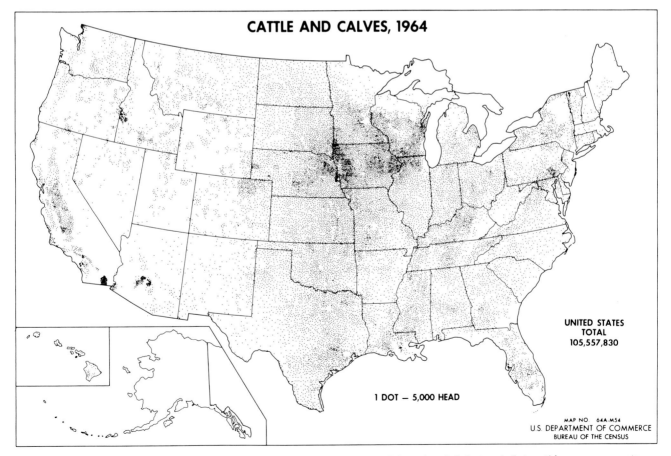

CATTLE AND CALVES, 1964

UNITED STATES
TOTAL
105,557,830

1 DOT — 5,000 HEAD

MAP NO. 64A·M54
U.S. DEPARTMENT OF COMMERCE
BUREAU OF THE CENSUS

Note: When comparing this map to the similar historic maps in Chapter I, keep in mind that each dot on this map represents 5000 -- not 2000 -- cattle. In the West, clusters and high densities of dots (and even many single dots) indicate areas of feedlots and irrigated pastures; only a minor portion of Western cattle are produced by open range grazing. Change in cattle distribution and numbers from 1964 to present has been insignificant.

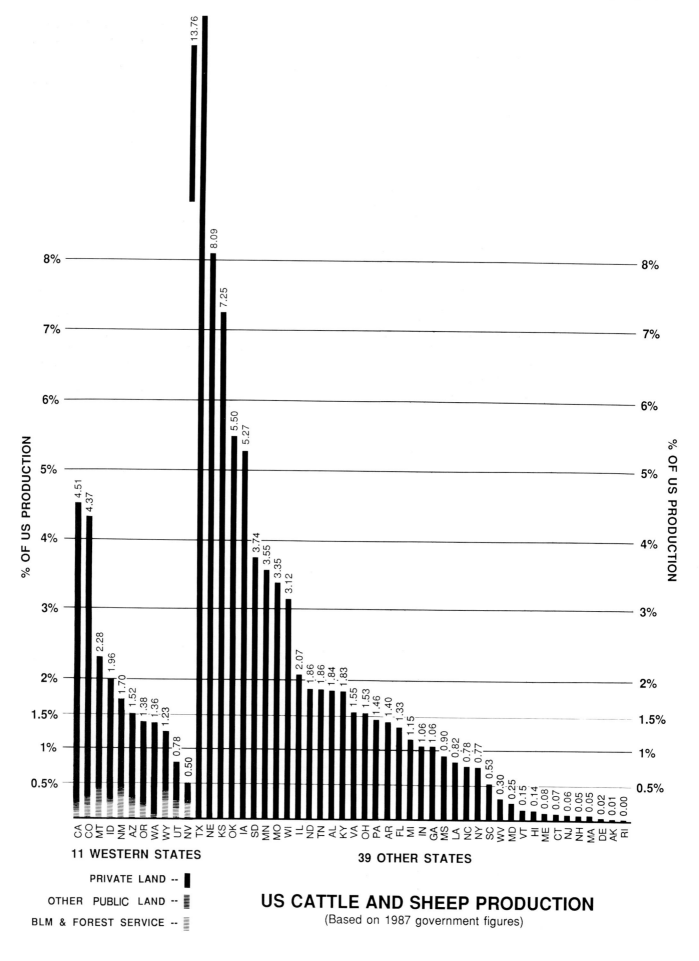

11 WESTERN STATES

39 OTHER STATES

PRIVATE LAND --

OTHER PUBLIC LAND --

BLM & FOREST SERVICE --

US CATTLE AND SHEEP PRODUCTION
(Based on 1987 government figures)

livestock are the "solar factories" that harvest this country's "forage resource" that would otherwise be "wasted." The Department of the Interior itself discredits their claim in its "Information Bulletin No.89- 93," stating that only 7% of US forage consumed by cattle and sheep comes from federal land (Atwood 1990).

The loss of the valuable renewable forage resource from public lands is, in effect, a loss to the entire nation. It is a loss our nation need not, indeed cannot, afford . . .
--From a joint statement by the Western states Farm Bureaus, Cattlemen Associations, and Wool Growers Associations

If the object is to grow more feed for cattle, study after study shows the same investment (in range development money) in the Piedmont states -- or just about anywhere else it rains -- would have a much higher payoff than spending it in the arid West. . . .
A Mississippi black in overalls isn't as photogenic as a cowboy with his pony, but he's sure a hell of a lot more efficient at raising beef.
--William Broly, "The Sagebrush Rebels"

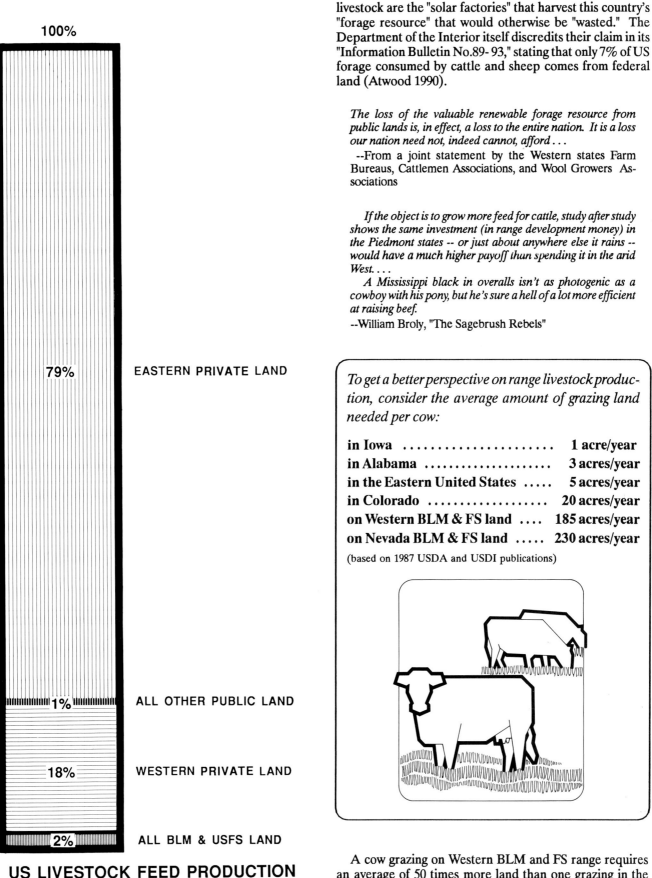

100%

79%   EASTERN PRIVATE LAND

1%   ALL OTHER PUBLIC LAND

18%   WESTERN PRIVATE LAND

2%   ALL BLM & USFS LAND

US LIVESTOCK FEED PRODUCTION
(Figures based on federal publications)

To get a better perspective on range livestock production, consider the average amount of grazing land needed per cow:

in Iowa	**1 acre/year**
in Alabama	**3 acres/year**
in the Eastern United States	**5 acres/year**
in Colorado	**20 acres/year**
on Western BLM & FS land	**185 acres/year**
on Nevada BLM & FS land	**230 acres/year**

(based on 1987 USDA and USDI publications)

A cow grazing on Western BLM and FS range requires an average of 50 times more land than one grazing in the East, while generally causing much more ecological damage and public expense. According to BLM itself, an average of 165 Western BLM acres are needed to feed a cow for a year, varying from 73 acres in Montana to 262 acres in Nevada (USGAO 1988). Therefore, even on the more live-stock-productive BLM land it takes about 20 times more land to support a cow than in the East.

While supplying only 2% of US livestock feed, Western federal land supplies only 9% of total AUMs of rangeland livestock grazing nationwide (Com. on Govt. Oper. 1986). Thus, the notion that public lands are the backbone of American open range grazing is another myth.

Despite being much larger overall than private land, BLM and FS land supplies only 11% of total Western livestock feed, ranging from 1.5% in New Mexico to 0.1% in Washington. These federal lands supply an average of 17% of each Western state's overall livestock feed, varying from 2% in Washington (the 26th ranking livestock state in the US) to 53% in Nevada (the 38th ranking livestock state). (Federal publications)

All Western federal, state, county, and city lands com-bined supply only about 18% of Western livestock feed requirements. This is primarily because public land is less productive than private and generally too arid, rugged, inaccessible, etc. for practical livestock grazing. The remaining 82% of Western livestock feed comes from the more productive private rangeland, pasture, and farmland used for livestock crops. (Government publications)

A cow can graze for about 3 1/2 months on the amount of forage produced in a month on an average grazing acre in Alabama, compared to only little more than a day on a month's production of forage on the average acre in Nevada, generally with much less environmental damage and public expense.

Because they are less livestock-productive than private lands, most public lands supply only a fraction of the total livestock food used by their permittees. The average BLM grazing season is only 4 1/2 months per year (USDA, FS 1986; USDI, BLM 1986), while according to the Forest Service, "In the West, NFS ranges supply an average of 25 percent of the permittee's annual requirements for livestock feed." (Figures for most other public ranchland are similar.) Accounting for the relative difference in BLM and FS live-stock production, this means that federal land supplies about *1/3* of public lands ranchers' annual livestock feed requirements, that an average permittee's livestock are on federal land only about *4 months* per year. Further, while some of these permittees hold permits to graze other government lands as well, many do not graze all or even most of their livestock on public land, so the discrepancy is

probably even greater. In short, public lands are little more than a *supplementary food source* for most "public lands" ranchers.

Public lands ranchers counter that public lands are vital as this supplementary food source and for calving grounds. What this actually means is that these ranchers have become habituated to using public land for these purposes. If they readjusted management, probably most of their ranching operations could survive without public lands. Obviously, reductions in overall livestock numbers would also have to be made, which is their main, underlying concern.

Why supplemental feed could not be obtained from private sources, livestock calved on private pasture and rangeland, or livestock numbers reduced remains un-answered. After all, a hungry stock animal eats whatever is available and cares not whether it is on public or private land. A cow can drop its calf anywhere, and the two can survive as well on private land as on public land (usually better). Depending on who you believe, only between 3% and 7% of all US calves are born on public land anyway. By public lands ranchers' logic, we could say that 100% of beef cattle are supported by this nation's highway system, since all of them spend at least some time there.

Without public lands grazing... 47% of all the beef cattle and sheep stock that graze the 11 Western states would be eliminated.

--Jeffrey C. Mosley, et. al. Seven Popular MYTHS About Livestock Grazing on Public Lands (Mosley 1990)

Though some public grazing proponents warn that the Western livestock industry would collapse without use of public lands, an un-tainted assessment proves this not only unfounded but ridiculous (see Chapter XI). The Committee on Government Operations of the US Congress states that public lands permittees "account for only 7% of the 386,000 producers in the 16 western states" (Com. on Govt. Oper. 1986). Only *16%* of the live-stock producers in the 11 Western states use public land, and, as explained above and else-where, of those who do relatively few are wholly or even primarily dependent upon it (USDA, FS 1986; USDI, BLM 1986). Even the highest figures provided by prominent spokespersons for the public lands grazing establishment itself claim that no more than 10% of US cattle ever touch public land (again, this for an average of only about 4 months each year) (Mosley 1990). Extrapolation from government figures suggests that the figure is closer to 7%.

The Bureau of Land Management, Forest Service, Soil Conservation Service, and Arizona State Land Department all have range specialists who are deeply involved in working with ranchers on improving and monitoring the condition of the lands, including much of the deeded range land. These bureaus will confirm that by and large the ranges are in very good condition.
--Southern Arizona public lands rancher G.E. Monzingo, in a Benson, AZ newspaper

In spite of more than forty years of federal administration, the condition of the public domain has remained virtually unchanged, judging from figures published under the auspices of the [BLM] itself. In 1936, 84% of the western rangelands were producing less than half of their potential forage; in 1954, 69% of the federal range was in fair condition or worse, and by 1974 this percentage had increased to 83%.
--Thomas R. Vale, "The Sagebrush Landscape" (Vale 1980)

Westerners are accustomed to the ubiquitous sight of barbed wire fences lining the roads in rural areas. Have we become so complacent about these fenced scenes that we fail to consider the land behind those fences?

In 1975 the BLM admitted that its own extensive survey data showed only 17% of its rangeland in good or excellent condition, 50% in fair, and 33% in poor or very poor condition (presented in *Range Condition Report* to the Senate Appropriations Committee, still the most current large-scale survey data available). Altogether, *83%* was in unsatisfactory condition -- essentially producing at *less than 50%* of its potential. The report concluded that although range conditions had improved in some respects since the early years of grazing, "public rangelands will continue to deteriorate. Projections indicate that in 25 years productive capacity could decrease as much as 25%." In other words, the overall condition of BLM rangeland was still deteriorating; the main "improvement" was that the rate of deterioration had been slowed (see Chapter XI). After this report came out, both BLM officials and the General Accounting Office criticized the data for *understating* the poor and deteriorating state of public range. (Ferguson 1983)

Eighty-two percent of beef production in the Western United States is attributable to *private* land, mostly irrigated pastures (12 million acres) and feedlots, with a smaller amount produced by the 184 million acres of private range that emcompass 25% of the West. The West's 306 million ranched public acres account for only 18% of the region's livestock. Hundreds of thousands of acres of public land would be needed to feed the cattle in the feedlot scene above.

Forest Service range condition figures at the time were nearly as bad: 24% "good," 44% "fair," 26% "poor," and 6% in "very poor" condition (USDA, USDI 1979). And though comprehensive state land range condition studies are rare, it is widely acknowledged that conditions on state rangelands are generally worse.

Despite misleading claims by the ranching establishment, the situation clearly has not changed much since the surveys of the 1970s. For example, a 1985 report prepared by the National Wildlife Federation (NWF) and the Natural Resources Defense Council (NRDC) titled *Our Ailing Rangelands: Condition Report -- 1985* concludes that recent data from environmental impact statements *prepared by BLM* under court order show that of Western BLM land *for which data was available* (about 80%), more than 71% (84 million acres) is in "unsatisfactory" condition -- meaning it is producing (producing basically *for livestock*) at **less than 40%** of its present (as opposed to pre-livestock) biological potential. (NWF 1985) A follow-up 1989 report prepared by NWF and NRDC entitled *Our Ailing Public Lands: Still Ailing* states that, "the data that are available do not reveal any significant improvement in range health since [1985]," and that "conditions are unlikely to improve" (NWF 1989). In the late 1980s, BLM itself stated that in areas of 5"-20" of precipitation (the vast bulk of BLM land) it may take 300 years, even under optimum ranching management, for livestock-damaged range to approximate original environmental health, summarizing that range managers "must be patient."

On a national scale, even John Block, Secretary of Agriculture during the Reagan administration, stated that at least 60% of all US rangeland is "overgrazed" (Akers 1983). Coming from people within the ranching establishment, few estimates are unbiased, nor do they take into account important and often obscure environmental factors; in truth, nearly all Western rangeland is being significantly damaged by livestock and/or their owners. Thus, "grazing" and "overgrazing" may be used almost synonymously in reference to Western livestock ranching.

This chapter summarizes the logistics of contemporary public lands ranching. But it doesn't explain what is happening to the land. The next 2 chapters attempt that. Ranching's environmental impacts can be separated into 2 groups -- those caused by the livestock themselves and those caused by range development by livestock owners and their government and private assistants. First, the livestock . . . .

> *I have a small herd of cows, but I had to buy my land.*
> *I feel that the public lands should be for nature and wildlife.*
> *If I plan to keep any of my land in a natural state,*
> *I have to keep the cows out.*
> --Bob Bertin, Houston, Texas,
> personal correspondence

Chapter III
LIVESTOCK GRAZING: ENVIRONMENTAL EFFECTS

Domestic livestock grazing has been the greatest environmental calamity ever to befall the Western United States.
--George Wuerthner, author and ecologist (Wuerthner 1989)

The effects of ranching on the Western landscape are pervasive, shaping the look of the West and causing more environmental damage than any other single agent.
--Dave Foreman, **Confessions of an Eco-warrior** (Foreman 1991)

No force in modern civilization has changed the Western lands as much as livestock grazing.
--Steve Johnson, Southwestern Representative, Defenders of Wildlife (Johnson 1985a)

Why no hue and cry to aid the range? The persistent myth of the cowboy retains its power, of course, so that to catalog his sins is to risk seeming un-American. But it's also true that the threats rangelands face seem soporifically benign at first glance. Old Bossy's dewy-eyed stare fails to stir the same measure of fear and anger as a chainsaw, a bulldozer, or John Sununu. Moved to confusion (or boredom) by a litany of rangeland ills, the general reader turns the page; the activist turns her or his energies to saving something more "majestic."
--The editors of *Sierra* magazine (Sierra 1990)

So, just how do "harmless" cattle and sheep harm the land? This simple question has no simple answer. Ask someone to explain Nature itself -- the virtually infinite number of complex interactions between myriad components of biologic, geologic, hydrologic, and climatic systems in ecosystems throughout the West.

Maybe a better question is: what in Nature does livestock grazing *not* adversely affect? Its influence is all-pervasive, as limitless as the environmental interrelationships it disrupts. As will be seen, no other land use is so destructive in so many ways.

Unfortunately, livestock's destructive influences are mostly unrecognized and thus uncorrected. Their geographic remoteness and subtle, dispersed, and insidious nature combine with our society's blind love affair with cowboys and cows to make livestock grazing the most misunderstood and neglected major environmental problem facing the rural West.

For simplicity's sake I have assembled livestock grazing effects under 6 basic headings: *Plants, Soil, Water, Animals, Fire,* and *Air*. Please keep in mind that these headings are necessarily general and impose artificial boundaries. They merely serve as organizational aids to facilitate understanding. In the natural world there are no such delineations.

Seemeth it a small thing unto you to have eaten up the good pasture, but ye must tread down with your feet the residue of your pastures? and to have drunk of the deep waters, but ye must foul the residue with your feet?
--Ezekiel: 34:18

Plants

They are taking the skin off the land.
--from the movie *The Emerald Forest*

The college textbook on zoology I am reading describes plankton as "both animals and plants which are collectively called 'oceanic meadows,' for they are the basis of food chains upon which larger organisms, such as fish, and even humans are dependent." It states that most of this planet's oxygen supply and an entire pyramid of life, including many terrestrial plants and animals, is dependent upon marine plankton. Similarly, the ocean ecologist Jacques Cousteau and other oceanographers conclude that plankton are vital to the health of the oceans and dependent terrestrial life. They warn of the dire consequences of overharvesting, poisoning, or otherwise harming these countless trillions of tiny floating organisms.

Grass and small herbaceous plants, along with co-dependent micro-organisms and insects, are the "plankton of the land." These countless trillions of small plants and animals are the base of an extensive, complex food web -- an almost infinite interdependency of life. As with ocean plankton, they are vital to the health of most terrestrial ecosystems. Like plankton, they provide oxygen to the atmosphere and, ultimately, nourishment to larger animals and necessities to humans. Additionally, they maintain soil, water, fire, and atmospheric dynamics.

Livestock grazing has destroyed the plankton of the land in the Western United States -- and around the globe -- more extensively than has any other human pursuit.

Consider that on the Western range today cattle and sheep outweigh all large native herbivores combined roughly 10 times over. It takes more than 20 pounds of herbage to produce a pound of beef (Zaslowsky 1989). A cow eats for about 8 hours a day to keep its 4 stomachs full, and an average cow consumes 700-800 pounds of vegetation per month. (Again, mature cattle average 800-1000 pounds -- 1 AUM -- monthly.) An average range steer eats 12,000 pounds of range plant material and 2850 pounds of feedlot food by slaughter time (Ferguson 1983). Sheep eat roughly 1/5 as much as cattle, and goats eat roughly 3/4 as much as sheep. Generally, a stock animal will eat approximately its weight in herbage per month.

(Greg Pentkowski)

Thus, on most Western rangeland domestic livestock eat *most* of the forage (grass, herbs, and other non-woody plants) and much of the browse (leaves and twigs on shrubs and trees). Indeed, they eat not only preferred grasses, but willow shoots, wild celery, young agave stalks, rosehips, lupine, honeysuckle, miner's lettuce, cottonwood saplings, wild tobacco, desert marigolds, clover, watercress, saltbush, mesquite pods, wild oats, mountain mahogany leaves, morning glories, reeds, wild strawberries, monkey flowers, vetch, mulberry leaves, bracken ferns, sunflowers, small aspens, dandelions, marijuana, apple leaves, cacti, acorns, peppermint, maple stems, *ad infinitum*. Government grazing management plans specifically call for heavy "utilization" of many of these and scores of other species.

If preferred vegetation is not available, as is often the case in the overgrazed West, cattle, sheep, and goats resort to eating decreasingly palatable species, such as sagebrush, scrub oak, bear grass, manzanita, yucca, tumbleweed, and cheatgrass, eventually eating nearly anything organic, including tree bark and, according to one eyewitness, old newspapers. This plasticity of diet allows ranchers to "mine" the public's range vegetation with their livestock year after year, eventually right down to the bare dirt, and is a key to range degradation.

Cattle-eaten yucca.

Cattle eating mesquite.

Cattle even eat cattails.

This stripping of the vegetation cover is livestock's most obvious impact. Many plants are simply ripped out of the ground roots and all and swallowed; sheep are especially destructive in this respect. However, most plants are damaged by being heavily cropped or browsed. ("Cropped" refers to the refers to the leaves and stems of non-woody vegetation being eaten off; "browsed" refers to the leaves and twigs of woody plants being eaten off.) When too much of a plant is removed or taken at the wrong time of year, its future growth is retarded. In fact, livestock usually remove more than half of the above-ground portions of most non-woody plants in their grazing areas and often graze during the weeks most critical to plant growth and development. When a plant is cropped or browsed too often in a single season or too heavily year after year, it dies. With the extreme grazing prevalent throughout the West, livestock stunt or kill *most* rangeland plants in these ways.

Cropping and browsing also destroy vegetation by preventing plants from seeding properly. Many plants are eaten before they are able to flower or produce seedheads or seed pods. As reserves in roots are depleted, other plants are so stunted in growth that they produce infertile or reduced numbers of seeds. The seeds that are produced may be eaten by livestock and rendered useless for reproduction (although seeds of several species pass through unharmed and may be spread through livestock feces). Due to reduced ground cover and other factors, many of the seeds that do fall to the ground are rendered sterile or caused to sprout at the wrong time of year by increased cold, heat, light or unfavorable moisture levels. On some soils, seeds of certain species may even be physically damaged by livestock hooves.

Indeed, perhaps even more destructive to vegetation than the actual grazing and browsing is the trampling that accompanies them. Most Western native plants -- those of the arid to semi-arid regions (most of the West) especially -- are ill-equipped to survive frequent, intense pounding from the cloven hooves of unnaturally managed, heavy, non-native ungulates. Small plants and seedlings are easily killed, and larger plants suffer physical disruption, injuries to root systems, exposure, and other damages. Vegetation has regularly been broken, beaten down, cut off, and crushed for over 100 years on hundreds of millions of Western acres.

Thus, livestock have transformed much of the West's relatively lush natural vegetation to wasteland. This biotic change is manifested in 4 basic ways:

● 1. *Decreasers:*

Most vegetation communities are a combination of many different plant species living together in competitive, yet mutually supportive, generally stable relationships. Though livestock are for the most part less selective than native herbivores, they nonetheless generally feed upon their favorite plants first -- the most palatable, succulent, and nutritious species, sometimes called "ice cream" species. On Western rangeland these include many of the important native grass and herbaceous perennials, and even several woody species such as whitesage, budsage, and bitterbrush. Livestock graze the tender tops first, then the coarser leaves, and finally the stems. Often these preferred plants are eaten to the ground before others are utilized. If they continue to be eaten year after year, these species are significantly reduced in number and range, and are thus termed "decreasers."

Because livestock spend more time in areas where these decreaser species occur, trampling and other detrimental effects are concentrated there, compounding damage from

This bull seems to prefer barrel cacti to grass and mesquite.

Stockmen "mine" vegetation with livestock, often right down to bare dirt. *(Richard Ginser)*

the grazing itself. As these desirable plants dwindle, they are sought more and more fervently by hungry livestock, creating a vicious circle of species extirpation.

As a result, the plants we see least on the range today are generally those livestock (and native animals) prefer most. The result of more than 100 years of livestock grazing has been virtual eradication of many of the most biotically productive native plant communities in the West.

● 2. *Increasers:*

Conversely, livestock graze less on the less nutritious, more fibrous, thorny, poisonous, and otherwise unpalatable plant species. Some species are protected from livestock by virtue of long taproots or extremely bitter taste, or because they hug the ground, possess stolons (runners) or rhizomes (underground stems), or are otherwise equipped to resist heavy grazing. These qualities, along with reduced competition for space, sunlight, water, and nutrients from decreasers, often allow these "undesirable" plant species to expand their numbers and territories. In other words, these "increaser" species fill the void left by the decreasers.

A livestock favorite, the distinctive sideoats grama was once a common resident of the West but, as a livestock decreaser, now survives as only a small fraction of its aboriginal population. *(Helen Wilson)*

An apparent increaser is not necessarily an increaser, however. Many areas are so denuded by livestock that certain plant species only *seem* to be increasers by simple virtue of being the only ones to survive in significant numbers. They have actually decreased in number and area, and only appear to be increasers in comparison to the ravaged decreaser species around them.

Nonetheless, many true increasers have indeed become dominant over large areas. Though these species were integral parts of original climax communities, they usually represented much smaller percentages of the total vegetation. Big sagebrush is a prime example. It originally composed 1/4 or less of the vegetation cover in bunchgrass communities throughout much of the Intermountain West. Today, on tens of millions of these same acres, big sagebrush forms essentially pure stands, interspersed not with grasses and forbs but with bare dirt. Depending on circumstances, prickly pear cactus may also be an increaser, and in some grazed areas prickly pear now grow so closely together that they are nearly impenetrable. Skunk cabbage and even wild iris can be increasers in heavily grazed wet meadows. Other prominent increasers include yarrow, tarbush, snakeweed, shadscale, rabbitbrush, mesquite, catclaw, and creosote.

Lakeview Cemetery in Montana's Red Rock Lakes Wildlife Refuge has not been grazed by livestock for 100 years. As a result of a century of livestock use, the thick native grasses and herbaceous plants on the left were replaced by the scraggly sage and other increasers on the right. *(George Wuerthner)*

● 3. *Invaders*:

Increasers do not encroach from without, but merely fill the empty niches within their own ranges left by ravaged decreaser species. If heavy grazing continues, even increasers are eventually killed out and their places taken by the true grazing "invaders" -- exotic herbaceous or woody plants, or opportunists native to that region but not to that site. These invader species may appear at the first sign of ecological stress, but do not become dominant until overgrazing is so severe that increasers decline.

Among the many notable invader plants are cheatgrass, tumbleweed, knapweed (all exotic to the US), halogeton, leafy spurge (native), a few species of mustards, filaree, thistles, and some shallow-rooted annuals and forbs (many of which are exotics). Most invader species are very hardy and resistant to drought, grazing, trampling, and other disturbances. Most are also unpalatable to livestock, provide less soil holding and building ability, are highly inflammable, and are of lesser value to wildlife. Many are thorny or poisonous to livestock. Annuals are prominent among invaders largely because they grow an entirely new generation

of plants from seeds each year and are therefore less susceptible to cumulative damage from trampling and other
impacts. Some invader infestations create conditions which
cause populations of "pest" animals to explode, further
favoring invaders over natural vegetation (discussed later).

> *The exotic plants saved the newly bared topsoil from water and
> wind erosion and from baking in the sun. And the weeds often
> became essential feed for exotic livestock, as these in turn were
> for their masters. The colonizing Europeans who cursed their
> colonizing plants were wretched ingrates.*
> --Alfred W. Crosby, **Ecological Imperialism** (Crosby 1988)

Ironically, invaders and increasers may play an important
role in the restoration of overgrazed land. Without them
there would often be little or no vegetation to hold soil,
provide cover for wildlife, and so forth. Though not as
valuable as native species, invaders and increasers are much
preferable to bare dirt. They are all that keeps much of the
Western range from becoming absolute wasteland. Invaders may pave the way for future restoration; if the land
is protected from further overgrazing, most invaders and
increasers will gradually be replaced by native vegetation.
(Feral animals sometimes play a similar role.)

On the other hand, depending on the unique circumstances of each area, some exotic invaders may colonize overgrazed areas and remain dominant long after livestock are
removed. In some areas these species show little obvious
sign of yielding to the natives even after decades of non-
grazing. Because of the long timeframes involved it may
thus seem that these vegetation changes are permanent.
However, close inspection of these livestock-excluded areas
reveals that on most a very gradual, steady recovery of native
vegetation is indeed taking place. While some invaders --
Bermuda grass and tamarisk, for example -- may be there
to stay, most have begun to yield to the natives in areas given
an extended reprieve from livestock.

Mostly because of livestock grazing, scores of increasers
and invaders have become dominant on more than 150
million acres of Western range, or more than 1/5 of the West.
Specific examples are plentiful. Indeed, most of the increaser and invader species listed above have replaced
native flora on millions of overgrazed acres apiece.

Yellow star thistle.

Yellow star thistle, for example, is a spiny, 3' tall plant that
produces numerous needle-sharp seedheads and which
may be toxic to cows and horses if eaten in quantity. It is
thought to have first arrived on this continent in California
in the mid 1800s in shipments of contaminated alfalfa from
southern Europe. The livestock explosion soon thereafter
opened the way for star thistle to spread throughout the
West. A recent *San Francisco Examiner* article explains:

> *Cattle ranchers, major victims of the thistle, have contributed
> significantly to its spread. Without cattle and sheep, whose
> hoofs break down the delicate fungal mat that once covered
> most western soils, the star thistle's seeds probably wouldn't
> have outcompeted the West's native perennial grasses.*

Overgrazing has helped spread yellow star thistle across
tens of millions of acres throughout the West, 8 million in
California alone. (Bashin 1990)

Cheatgrass, *Bromus tectorum*, is a prime example of a grazing
invader. Originally from the Eurasian steppes, it spread quickly
across the West with livestock in the late 1800s and early 1900s.
Many stockmen initially welcomed the spread of cheatgrass (as
they did tumbleweed), but soon discovered that as a forage
plant it was much inferior to the natives it replaced, that the
awned (barb-like) seeds lodged in the mouths and eyes of
livestock and caused injury, and that it was explosively flammable. Today, cheatgrass covers tens of millions of arid to
semi-arid acres throughout the West, often in single-species
stands such as the one above.

● 4. *Bare dirt*:

Bare dirt is desirable only where it occurs naturally.
Except for drier regions, this generally includes only small
percentages of the ground area. *Overgrazing has probably
resulted in more actual ground area in the West being converted to bare dirt, sand, and gravel than to a vegetation cover
of increasers or invaders.* Yet, range literature invariably
focuses on *changes* in species rather than overall *reductions*
in plant cover. This obscures the severity of the problem.

> *Cows and sheep are everywhere on public lands, wandering
> into most every available nook and cranny with something
> edible on it.*
> --Letter to the editor, *High Country News*

In describing these changes in Western vegetation, we
speak of what scientists call "biotic succession," or the

tendency of plant and animal communities to succeed or replace one another over a period of time in response to environmental or human influences. Biotic succession is influenced in two ways.

One influence is related to sudden changes in existing conditions. For example, extremely high winds in an area of dense coniferous forest may cause a "blowdown" of nearly all the trees. Soon thereafter a new community of plants begins to occupy the area, usually hardier "weeds" and forbs. These plants are gradually replaced by grasses and flowering perennials. Over the years this community is overgrown by a mixture of shrubs and bushes, which in turn is overgrown by a grove of aspens. Finally, the original conifers begin poking through and overshadowing the aspens, and eventually reclaim the area as a conifer forest vegetative community.

Quick changes in the environment, such as those induced by windstorm, fire, flood, drought, landslide, or insect outbreaks, are periodic natural occurrences to which biotic communities have been subject for millennia. Each "disaster" may cause dramatic changes. But because these disturbances occur infrequently and affect only limited areas, biotic communities reestablish and maintain their essential character. In the conifer forest, abrupt changes occur infrequently enough that most of the trees have time to reach maturity before the next disturbance hits. Although there are always some portions of the forest at earlier stages of succession, the forest as a whole maintains its coniferous character.

A second type of change in biotic communities occurs very slowly, usually in response to long-term climatic or geologic changes. For example, a long-term change in the storm track could cause a drying trend in climate and gradually move a conifer forest back through succession, finally resulting in some type of plant community adapted to a drier climate -- perhaps, again, the grasses and flowering perennials. Or, colliding crustal plates may create a new mountain range, with a "rain shadow" effect on the range's interior side and eventually producing a biotic community more adapted to aridity. These kinds of changes usually occur so slowly as to be imperceptible to humans.

Succession is a sliding scale, but to humans appears to occur in steps. Each change in the essential character of a a biome [particular biotic area] is termed a "stage of succession." All biotic communities are constantly changing, moving from one stage to another on the scale of succession, in response to both short- and long-term fluctuations in the environment. Changes may occur very quickly, as with the forest blowdown, or extremely slowly, over thousands or even millions of years, as with the drying climate. We humans see the sudden changes as "disasters" and rarely recognize the slow changes.

This is not to say that succession proceeds as a smooth, predictable pattern. It is more like a general trend with numerous variables. The natural environment provides succession many diverse influences, once again complementing biodiversity.

Generally, the more complex a biosystem, the more stages of succession it is subject to. The conifer forest discussed above went through at least 5 stages. Most grasslands have several stages. The simplest and least productive biosystems may have only 2 or 3. For example,

removing the vegetation from a creosote flat in the Mojave Desert usually results in a slight, temporary increase in a few native and/or exotic desert annuals and, eventually, the regrowth of most of the original creosote or a continuance of bare dirt.

A "climax community" is the final stage of succession -- a relatively stable biotic community natural to each unique physical environment, able to replace and regenerate itself and maintain its essential character over long periods of time. Every place on Earth with plant or animal life has a climax community. Each is determined by the area's unique set of long-term environmental influences, including climate, soil, and landform. Though the overall biotic character of each climax community is relatively stable, integral to each is a complex mosaic of areas in different stages of succession. This diversity strengthens systems dynamics and the climax community as a whole.

There are no "bad" climax communities; each is the one best suited to given conditions, and as such the most beneficial to the environment as a whole. Scraggly, scattered creosote with its few small companion plants is "good" on hot, dry desert flats because it is the most biologically productive stable community possible under such conditions. Nor are the earlier stages of succession "bad," for each has an important role in augmenting biodiversity and reestablishing the climax community after it has been disturbed. Even the most hated "weed" has an important place in succession.

The radical disturbances caused by overgrazing would have only minimally affected the essential character of the Western range if it had occurred as infrequently as natural disturbances -- say 15 or 20 years apart, and for only a few days at a time. But heavy grazing usually occurs every year, for weeks, months, or even year-round. Chronically overgrazed land cannot progress along the stages of succession back to its natural state. Hence, natural systems progressively deteriorate, and plants and animals populations simply never recover.

On the other hand, when long-term changes constitute a permanent change in the environment, succession gradually provides an area with a new climax community. This type of change usually requires centuries, and isn't the type of change we've seen in the West. Before European intervention, grama-buffalo grass, tule marsh, scrub oak, sage-bunchgrass, and scores of other major Western vegetative climax communities had existed relatively unchanged, aside from usual natural, periodic, localized disturbances, for many thousands of years.

What should be remembered is that Nature has already advanced each area's climax community as far toward the biologically productive side of the succession scale as possible for the given physical environment. Humans can temporarily increase the productivity of a given ecosystem only by artificially releasing energy stored in the ecosystem's biomass and soil, or by importing energy from other ecosystems. As a rule, drastic disturbances move succession toward the biologically less-productive side of the scale. The greater the disturbance, generally the less diverse and abundant the resulting biotic community. Continued livestock grazing leads to the replacement of climax vegetation with less and less productive plant communities and, finally, bare dirt, sand, and gravel. Recovery of the original climax community is hampered because the foundation of the ecosystem is damaged. The resulting degraded biotic community does not represent merely a step down in succession or change in the climax community but a breakdown of the whole process.

> *More US plant species are wiped out or endangered by livestock grazing than by any other single factor. Of the five plant species placed on the national endangered species list in August and September of 1989, for instance, three were victims of grazing.*
> --George Wuerthner, "The Price Is Wrong" (Wuerthner 1990b)

As a result of livestock grazing, numerous plant species throughout the West have been locally extirpated. In fact, hundreds of species likely were completely eliminated from many areas at the onset of heavy grazing in the late 1800s, even before knowledge of their existence could be documented. We will never know what has been lost. Because damage from overgrazing is often such a slow, insidious process, the gradual decline of many other species has not been properly linked to livestock.

For example, mushrooms and other fungi of scores of species grow in ranching areas of the West. But a century of overgrazing has so reduced the soil moisture, humus, host plants, and shading vegetation they depend on that many mushrooms are now rare in these areas. While some note that mushrooms grow prolifically on cowpies, these represent only a very small number of species, and some of these formerly grew on the dung of wild animals as well.

Livestock so drastically reduced many Western plant species in range and number that those species are now listed as Rare, Threatened, or Endangered. The following are a few examples:

The autumn buttercup is a species endemic to the upper Sevier River Valley in Garfield County, Utah. The *Endangered Species Technical Bulletin* reports:

> *Approximately 11 individuals survive on less than 0.01 acre of privately owned land that is highly vulnerable to continued grazing and habitat modification. Believing the species in imminent danger of extinction, the [government] has proposed to list it as Endangered.*

Even so, the *Bulletin* reports that the rancher landowner wants to increase grazing in the area by building a new stock watering pond, although he "may be willing to allow construction of a protective fence."

Grama grass cactus is a little-known cactus that often grows within the fairy rings formed by grama grass or ring muhly grass. It grows long, papery spines which look remarkably like the curled, pale blades of old grama and muhly grass. "Hiding" in the dead layers of these grasses helps grama grass cactus escape predation by rodents and other herbivores. Overgrazing of its only habitat in parts of New Mexico and Arizona has drastically reduced the cover formerly provided by these grasses, while trampling livestock have killed many. Consequently, the grama grass cactus is listed as "rare."

Golden buckwheat (*Eriogonum chrysops*) is a distant relative of cultivated buckwheat. According to the Center for Plant Conservation, though thought extinct and last seen in 1901, it was rediscovered in 1988 in Malheur County,

Oregon, on 3 barren, volcanic hilltops -- among the few places in its habitat not accessible to livestock.

The Tiburon Mariposa lily (*Calochortus tiburonensis*) grows only on the rocky upper slopes of Ring Mountain on the Marin Peninsula, north of San Francisco. Here, a remnant population finds shelter from the livestock grazing that has ravaged the remainder of its habitat for more than two centuries.

The Arizona agave was federally listed as Endangered in 1984. A report by Rick DeLamater and Wendy Hodgson of the Desert Botanical Garden in Phoenix states that "agave stalks provide an irresistible food for cattle" and that the agave's habitat, "including what we thought to be the most inaccessible areas, shows severe degradation by overgrazing." Studies show that less than 1/3 of the stalks of 3 types of agaves in the area reached maturity undamaged. The report concludes:

> *Cattle, overgrazing on lands administered by the U.S. Forest Service, are cited as the major threat to* [the Arizona agave's] *survival as well as to the population dynamics of* [other agaves in the area]. (DeLamater 1986)

Golden draba is a small member of the mustard family that grows in the spruce and alpine belts of California's high Sierra Nevada, where it has been relentlessly diminished by sheep and cattle grazing for more than 100 years. Golden draba is now listed as Rare in the state.

Clay phacelia is one of Utah's 190 globally Endangered species, many of which fell to livestock grazing. The world's only known population of this purple wild flower clings tenuously to a steep, shale-strewn hillside in central Utah. For years botanists have watched clay phacelia decline under the hooves of domestic sheep and have finally secured an agreement to erect a fence around the plants . . . rather than remove the sheep.

Colorado butterfly plant, Gila groundsel, Knowlton's cactus, Cusick's camas, Bitterroot milk vetch, solano grass . . . the list of livestock plant victims goes on and on. The Nature Conservancy reports that in California alone (which has nearly as many endemic plant species -- 1517 -- as all other states, except Hawaii, combined), more than 600 species are threatened with extinction. If nothing is done the state could lose 12% of its native plant species. Further, livestock grazing has been identified as a major factor in this threat. In Hawaii, livestock grazing, land clearing for pasture, development, and introductions of exotic species have caused a tenth of the estimated 1250 species of flowering plants that were present 200 years ago to become extinct. Probably half of the remainder has become Threatened or Endangered. The Center for Plant Conservation, in its *Endangerment Survey Summary* of December 9, 1988, offered a grim assessment:

> *3,000 of the approximately 25,000* [about 14,000 are in the 11 Western states] *species, subspecies, or varieties of plants native to the United States are at risk of extinction in the wild. For an estimated 200 species, we are too late; they are already extinct!*

The Center estimates that 680 of the species at risk will be extinct in the US by the year 2000. While many Endangered plants are indigenous to comparatively small areas and have succumbed mostly to intensive development, livestock grazing has forced more Western species to become Rare, Threatened, or Endangered than any other factor.

However, grazing's greatest impact on native vegetation has been -- far more than any other human influence -- **the depletion and extirpation of species over large areas.** Though they may not have been reduced to the point of imminent extinction, hundreds of native plant species have been reduced to only fractions of original populations over vast expanses, and have been eliminated entirely from many areas. Livestock grazing continues to be by far the most prevalent, insidious, and destructive force affecting native Western vegetation.

Soil Conservation Service range agronomists have for years conducted research with native plants and grasses, the object being to nurture them and eventually to reintroduce them into areas of degraded rangeland. The difficulty is that few native plants exist -- they have been trampled or eaten by livestock, and displaced by non-native species.
--David L. McWilliams, Rock Springs, CO, letter to the editor, 3-2-88 *Casper Star-Tribune*

Under many Western state laws it is illegal for a person to collect, kill, or otherwise harm certain rare plant species. You may even be cited for picking a wild flower. Yet, cattle and sheep are allowed to eat and trample these same plants by the thousands.

While grazing and trampling have wiped out much Western vegetation directly, livestock have also damaged native biotic systems in countless subtle and complex ways. For example, livestock negatively affect the *composition, range, distribution, density, size, health, diversity,* and *vertical stratification* of Western vegetation:

* *Composition* refers to the arrangement or mixture of the different plant species within a vegetative community. Vegetation composition determines relationships and inter-actions, and is crucial to animal, soil, water, fire, and air dynamics. For example, livestock grazing in a small Western canyon causes grasses and forbs to be replaced by rabbit brush and tumbleweeds. This new plant composition is less efficient at holding soil, so subsequent floods yield more soil erosion than before the replacement. The degraded soil, in turn, is even less able to support the original grasses and forbs, and the cycle repeats.

* *Range* refers to the general geographic area occupied by a plant species, while *distribution* refers to the placement of the species within its range. Although the two are often used interchangeably, they are not precisely synonymous. Range and distribution of plant species determine animal populations and also affect soil, water, fire, and air dynamics. For example, by shrinking the range and distribution of Indian ricegrass in portions of the West, livestock have likewise shrunk the range and distribution of some dependent seed-eating birds. (Range is also a generic term for open country; this second meaning is the more common usage in this book and can be determined by context.)

* *Density* refers to the number of individual plants of a given species within a given area, or how closely spaced individuals of a plant species are. The term also refers to the spacing of vegetation in general. Density usually indicates the importance or dominance of a particular species in a plant community; but, since density values indicate nothing about size, health, or how widespread a species is, this is not always so. Generally, livestock grazing has decreased the density of beneficial natives and increased the density of harmful exotics, with a significant decrease in overall combined plant density on most Western range (an increase in bare dirt). When livestock reduce or increase plant density, they once again negatively impact ecosystem dynamics. For example, overgrazing on bunchgrass/sagebrush rangeland in much of the Great Basin has so reduced the density of bunchgrasses that individual grass plants are no longer spaced closely enough to carry wildfires. The resultant loss of wildfire has given sagebrush a further advantage over grass because natural fire generally restricts the spread of sagebrush while actually stimulating the growth of many grasses.

* When assessing range conditions, range professionals generally survey the composition, range, and density of vegetation, but give little consideration to the *size* and *health* of individual plants. While composition, range, and density are important, individual plants must also be full-sized and healthy for ecosystems to function properly. For example, a full-sized, healthy buckthorn bush in a natural, non-live-stock area may produce 2 or 3 times more leaves, flowers, seeds, stems, and other organic materials than one in an overgrazed area. This superior bush will provide much more food, nesting, and shelter for wildlife. It will also supply more organic litter, better wind resistance, more shade producing branches, more soil holding roots, and so on.

Through the many influences described elsewhere in this chapter, livestock have caused most rangeland plants to be stunted and less vigorous today than in pre-livestock times. Wild sunflower plants in overgrazed areas are often only half the size of those in adjacent ungrazed areas. Sagebrush plants in grazed areas are typically short and misshapen, sparsely leafed, with many broken branches and little underlying organic litter. Cacti in livestock areas are often stunted, broken, and diseased.

Additionally, because range plants are heavily grazed or browsed, size relative to plants in ungrazed areas is reduced even further. For example, on most Western range grass plant density, health, and size has been decreased, but since livestock also keep most individual grass plants cropped to less than half their normal height, their *size* has been decreased relatively even more.

* Plant *diversity* refers to the number of different species as well as to the variety of plant types in a given area. Natural diversity is essential to ecological health and stability. In affecting all of the above negative changes in Western vegetation, livestock have greatly lowered plant diversity in most of the West. Heavily grazed areas commonly support less than half as many species and much less diversity of plant types. In Idaho an ungrazed stand of big sagebrush supported 31 species of plants, while a comparable grazed stand supported only 9 species (Ferguson 1983). Overgraz-

ing nearly always simplifies ecosystems, further increasing their susceptibility to disturbances, including continued overgrazing.

- Livestock likewise damage what is known as *vertical stratification*. Most natural plant communities are stratified, having a vertical arrangement of plants in several layers instead of an even distribution throughout all heights from the ground to the tops of the tallest plants. In the forest vertical stratification may be obvious as a surface layer of mosses and lichens, a low herb layer, a grass and tall herb layer, a shrub layer, a subcanopy tree layer, and a canopy tree layer. In grasslands, shrublands, and deserts, vertical stratification may not be as well-defined, but is nearly always present nonetheless. All grasslands have at least 3 stratification levels, and some have 4 or even 5.

Each layer provides food, shelter, nesting, and other necessities critical to certain animals at certain times, and certain combinations of layers are likewise necessary to the survival of many animals. Each layer also contributes its unique benefits to soil, water, fire, and air systems and other interrelationships. Livestock grazing depletes or fragments ground surface and lower vegetation layers, and may over time also significantly impact upper woody vegetation layers.

Natural diversity is a key to ecosystem health and stability. Ungrazed in the Sonoran Desert.

One little-appreciated factor in rangeland dynamics is the role of dead plant material. As old leaves, stalks, stems, flowers, and other plant parts wither and die they are acted upon in various ways and their nutrients are recycled throughout the biotic system. This dead organic material is essential to vegetation, soil, water, animal, and fire dynamics. In most ecosystems, 1/5 to 1/2 of all biomass (overall amount of organic matter) consists of dead plant material.

Accumulation of plant litter on the soil's surface is an ongoing process, and litter on the dry Western range depleted may require decades to replenish. Livestock inhibit or destroy the old growth vegetation needed as source material for organic litter. Particularly, they eat much of it and trample plants, damage soil, reduce available water, and cause other changes that ultimately deplete the amount of dead plant material. They break apart and scatter remaining organic litter. Additionally, much of the biomass that would otherwise eventually become dead plant material is removed from the ecosystem entirely when the domestic animal is moved off the range for eventual slaughter. Reduction of the organic litter layer has been extreme on most grazed land. On Nebraska's Sandhills Prairie, for example, removal of cattle for 4 years yielded a 300 + % increase in litter cover (Potvin 1984). Even in many forests, livestock are the main cause of organic litter depletion.

Inaccessible to cattle, this luxuriant mixture of vegetation assures high environmental quality.

The importance of organic litter to plant growth is graphically demonstrated here. I threw 2 small piles of a neighbor's cut brush down in a bare spot. Several months later plants growing in the area covered by the litter had twice the height and several times more biomass per unit of area than the plants in the surrounding area.

Livestock grazing damages vegetation in many other ways that are little understood or appreciated. For example, the leaves and branches of many plants in arid to semi-arid climates possess patterns or structures that gather rainfall and run it in toward the center of the plant, thus increasing the amount of water available to its roots. When livestock remove leaves or break branches, or otherwise alter plant patterns and structures, they reduce water-trapping capabilities. Conversely, water-stressed plants become more brittle and susceptible to physical damage from livestock.

Another example concerns plant reproduction. When livestock strip off the vegetation cover and deplete and displace the organic litter layer, they expose seeds on or immediately under the ground surface. Pecking and scratching birds and other foraging animals may then consume the seeds, leading to sparse regeneration. If you have ever had the bare ground of your garden de-seeded by foraging animals, you will appreciate this factor.

Moreover, many plants depend on lateral growth or rooting of broken segments for their spread. Others send runners out across the ground's surface that put down roots at certain intervals, creating new plants. Some have branches that sag as they mature, make contact with the ground, and send down roots at those points. Others, such as most cacti, possess segmented branches that break off easily, fall to the ground, and send down roots from points of contact.

Success for plants that spread in such ways depends primarily on (1) the health of the parent plant and spreading portion, (2) the condition of the soil and amount of ground moisture, and (3) how well and how long the spreading portion of the plant makes contact with the ground. Con-

sequently, livestock prevent the establishment of new plants by (1) damaging or killing the parent plant and spreading portion, (2) damaging the soil and causing it to dry out, (3) trampling and shuffling, thereby preventing the spreading portion from "seating" properly onto the ground and making prolonged, close contact. Further, trampling livestock often pull out or break off the small roots that have established themselves. Even where livestock aid in the spread of plant reproductive segments, such as cholla cactus, their other harmful effects usually result in reduced net reproduction. I have seen this in some deserts, where in ungrazed areas cholla sections fall off and reproduce successfully around their parent plants, while in nearby grazed areas where cattle have scattered cholla "balls" randomly across the landscape (to the great discomfort of my ankles), so few of the segments have rooted that their overall reproduction rate is far lower.

In most natural biotic communities, plants shade and protect each other. A closely spaced arrangement of undamaged plants provides "nursery protection" for seedlings and ground-level plants, shading them from the sun and helping protect them from foraging animals, wind, hail, frost, etc. To a lesser degree, it does the same for mature plants. It also conserves essential soil moisture by protecting the ground from the drying effects of sun and wind. In the soil, close spacing creates an interlocking network of roots which helps stabilize both the plants and the soil that anchors them. Tall, closely spaced, fully vegetated plants are even less susceptible to damage from trampling because, together, they form a thick mat which disperses hoof impact on each individual, including its roots.

An obscure indirect effect of livestock: According to the photographer, a botanist for the National Park Service, on overgrazed ranges hungry rodents may eat patches from saguaros and other cacti. (*Charles Conner*)

A grazed hillslope in a BLM Wilderness Study Area offers mostly cactus, snakeweed, rocks, and bare dirt. *(Dale Turner)*

A comparable ungrazed hillslope in the same area is covered with a lush diversity of grasses, flowering plants, shrubs, soil surface microflora, etc., as well as cactus and snakeweed. *(Dale Turner)*

Grassland

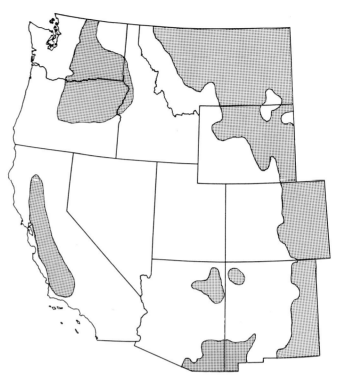

Rough Approximation of Major Grasslands
(Source: Vankat 1979)

Livestock have obliterated almost all of the West's original grasslands.
--Florence Williams, "The West's Time Capsules" (Williams 1990)

In sum, to the great harm of the environment, livestock have converted huge areas of the West to unpalatable, poisonous, thorny, unnatural, and comparatively unproductive vegetation or bare ground.

> *But, of all man's activities, grazing by livestock has been the most widespread and prolonged use and has had the most profound effect upon the Nation's ranges.*
> --US Forest Service, "An Assessment of the Forest and Range Land Situation in the United States" (USDA, FS 1980)

The Forest Service defines *range* as "land that provides or is capable of providing forage for grazing or browsing animals [read: 'livestock']." By this definition more than 80% of the West qualifies as range, including a complex array of more than 40 major ecosystem types, **all** of which have been significantly degraded by ranching. We may divide these into 4 basic categories:

Grass is a relatively recent botanic lifeform, having first appeared "only" about 60 million years ago. Prairie grassland developed around 15 million years ago, large herds of herbivores evolving along with it.

When settlers migrated west they found more than 1/3 of what was to become the 11 Western states covered primarily with grass. The extensive interior basins, valleys, plains, plateaus, hills, and even mountains supported a great assortment of climax grassland and grassland/shrubland combinations. But this new grassland was quite different from the more familiar lush, soggy pastures of the eastern US and northern Europe.

Prairie grasses are chiefly *sod-forming*, meaning they form a dense mat of stems and roots. Most have rhizomes, while a few have stolons. These structures produce a series of new shoots as they spread away from the parent plant. Sod grasses and most other prairie plants are *perennials*, coming up year after year from the same underground root system. Once established, they depend much less upon seeds than new buds for their spread. They rely on summer rainfall, and their growing season extends well into summer. Therefore, in the West sod grasses generally are limited to the Great Plains and portions of adjacent inter-Rocky Mountain plains, riparian areas, moist valley bottoms, the wet Pacific Northwest, and some high elevations.

Precipitation over most of the West is low during the summer months (and low overall), most of it ending by June. The grasslands there are dominated by *bunchgrass*, plants that grow in groups of upright stems, each tuft appearing as if held in a bunch. Single plants may form a hundred or more shoots, but these do not spread laterally as mats; they instead form dense clumps of aerial stems. Bunchgrasses generally rely on lingering winter moisture and spring precipitation. They mature and set seeds by mid-July, and become dormant in the dry summer. The plants may put on a new burst of growth during wet periods in the fall, especially in warmer climes.

A third category of Western grasses is the *annuals*, which live through the growing season, produce seeds, and then die. Each year a completely new generation is produced from seeds. Annual grasses normally inhabit mainly the dryer portions of the West, where precipitation is infrequent and erratic. Because their growing period is limited, most are smaller and less nutritious than bunch and sod grasses. Western annual grasses include wild oat, many of the bromes (foxtails, cheatgrasses), and some of the fescues and lovegrasses. Many are exotics.

Native annuals have been greatly depleted and even extirpated from many areas by overgrazing. Over even greater areas, however, ranching's "desertifying" effects have eliminated perennial ground cover and created conditions favorable to annuals. In most of these areas, exotic annuals have outcompeted the native annuals and perennials, replacing them on tens of millions of Western public acres. Due primarily to livestock grazing *most* of the West's annual grass cover is now composed of increasers and invaders, including many exotics.

Some Western grasses may vary in their growth-form, developing as sod, bunch, annual, or some composite form

of these, depending on conditions. Thus, livestock grazing tends to transform sod grasses into bunchgrasses and bunchgrasses into annuals.

Hundreds of different grasses are native to the West. Originally, much of the Midwest and intermountain prairie was carpeted with the rhizomatous grasses big and little bluestem, needle and thread grass, blue and hairy grama, and western wheatgrass; the stoloniferous buffalo grass; and the usually bunching wire grass. Large portions of Idaho and eastern Washington and Oregon were covered with Sandberg bluegrass, Idaho fescue, and the chiefly bunching, though sometimes rhizomatous, bluebunch wheatgrass. Scattered across many parts of the Great Basin were bunchgrasses such as bluebunch and western wheatgrass, bottlebrush squirreltail, sheep fescue, and Indian ricegrass. At least 23 million acres of California's valleys and hills (about 1/4 of the state) were spread with a great diversity of short and tall perennial bunchgrasses, including purple and nodding needlegrasses, with some sod grasses in moister areas. Finally, much of the mid-elevation portions of the Southwest supported lush stands of black and sideoats grama, Arizona cottontop, tobosa, wire, and other bunchgrasses.

The individual species vary greatly in their ability to withstand grazing pressure, but as a group the sod grasses generally fare much better. They have co-evolved over millions of years with herds of large, hooved herbivores -- mainly buffalo, but also elk, deer, pronghorn, and bighorns -- and, before the Pleistocene extinctions, with others -- camels, horses, mammoths, mastodons, ground sloths, etc. These grasses are adapted to occasional heavy grazing, and if not grazed too often will usually rejuvenate, even after being cropped to the ground. They have a high percentage of vegetative to flowering stems, so grazing has less impact on reproduction. Their new stems emerge horizontally, and their growth points are low to the ground, helping protect them from grazing damage. As mentioned, once estab-

Generalized depiction of the 3 major grass forms: annual (left), rhyzomatous (center), and bunch (right). *(Helen Wilson)*

lished, sod-forming grasses depend much less on seeds than on new buds for their spread. Their root systems are rugged and extensive, able to withstand tremendous trampling. A dislodged piece of root sod, thrown on bare ground nearby, may even reroot!

Semi-wild buffalo on a healthy prairie range in Badlands National Park, western South Dakota.

Depleted prairie grassland in Montana. *(USFS)*

All this is not to suggest that livestock have not been very destructive to the sod grasslands of the West, for they surely have. Where not under the plow, these grasslands have been seriously degraded by domestic grazing animals. Sod grasses are much more resistant to heavy foraging by large herbivores. However, they have been *far more heavily grazed* by livestock than have bunchgrass communities. To the untrained eye, the moist, uniform green of a sod grassland may look to be in much better condition than the scruffy tan, grey, and green of a bunchgrass community, but relative environmental damage may be similar.

Even the most pro-ranching of sources acknowledge the serious damage that livestock grazing has done to the prairie grasses of the West. For example, in the contemporary textbook **Range Management**, the authors have listed the results of 20 range studies done on short- and mixed-grass prairies in 7 Western plains states. Their table compares herbage production measured on moderately grazed sites to that measured on comparable sites ungrazed for 5 to 60 years. Of the 20 studies, 19 showed greater herbage produc-

tion on the nongrazed sites, with an average of 68% more on the nongrazed sites. (Holechek 1989)

Jared Smith in 1895 described the aboriginal great Western grasslands:

The prairies in their wild state were covered with the richest possible grass flora. There was no similar region that had so many useful species and so few poisonous or injurious ones. Almost any square mile of the whole extent of territory could furnish in one season 50 kinds of grasses and native forage plants, grasses that would make from one and a half to two tons of hay per acre as rich as that from an Old World meadow. (Smith 1895)

In 1899 Smith reported:

It is the common testimony of the older stockmen that in the early eighties the grass was often as high as a cow's back, not only along the river bottoms, but also on the uplands far from the creeks and rivers. . . . The grazing capacity of large bodies of land has been reduced within a period of twenty years from one head to 2 to 5 acres, to one head to 20 to 25 acres. (Smith 1899)

In 1940 grazing professional Kling L. Anderson reported in "Deferred Grazing of Bluestem Pastures":

Old grazing records show that prior to 1900 most of the bluestem pastures could be stocked at the rate of two acres for one mature cow or steer for a grazing season of six months beginning May 1. . . . At the present time the average grazing capacity is about seven acres per animal.

Similar references abound. Today, these once-lush prairie grasslands have recovered little, and in many ways continue to deteriorate. Many experts estimate that they have lost 50% or more of their productive potential to a century of livestock grazing.

Further east, ranching and, later, farming combined to devastate the comparatively well-watered tallgrass prairie. Tallgrass prairie is the world's most damaged ecosystem, in terms of percentage of land corrupted. According to The Nature Conservancy: "Once blanketing 142 million acres, tallgrass is considered extinct as a fully functioning natural ecosystem."

A study of historical accounts and the ecological research indicates that the vegetation of the sagebrush/grassland communities of the Intermountain West is distinct from the grassland vegetation of the Great Plains. Based solely on morphological characteristics, it is apparent that the vegetation of those two geographic areas evolved in response to different environmental factors. The vegetation of the Intermountain West did not coevolve with, and is therefore not adapted to, large grazing mammals.
--Katey Palmer, biologist (Palmer 1988)

Unlike sod grasses in the prairies of the central region of the US, Western bunchgrasses generally did not co-evolve with great herds of buffalo and other large, hooved herbivores. This different evolutionary history, combined with less precipitation, less dependable precipitation, and other factors, leave them ill-adapted to intensive grazing or trampling. To varying degrees, most bunchgrasses are severely damaged by livestock. Bunchgrasses generally show less ability than sod-forming grasses to adequately restore leaf area lost to grazing. Their ratio of flowering to vegetative stems is high, so their ability to reproduce after being grazed is low. Their new stems emerge vertically, with growing points elevated and exposed to grazers. Regrowth from trampled stems is unlikely, and tufts of even partially uprooted bunchgrass often die, even under moist conditions.

A cover of grass does not necessarily mean all is well. This slope in the Jackass Mountains of eastern Oregon is covered with cheatgrass, a livestock-spread exotic that replaced the much more beneficial native bunchgrasses and other plants. *(George Wuerthner)*

Pronghorn, bighorns, elk, mule and white-tailed deer were often present in the bunchgrass communities, but their smaller numbers and herd sizes, different behavior, and, importantly, their lower body weight prevented them from having as great an impact as did buffalo. Buffalo did occur west of the Great Plains, but in much smaller numbers and limited distribution. As evidence of this, scientists report that in the Intermountain West there are no native species of *Onthophagus*, a genus of dung beetle which occurs in association with dense herds of large mammals. In contrast, there are 34 species of the genus native to the Great Plains.

Native Western bunchgrasses have probably suffered as much at the hands of the grazing industry as any other plant group. For example, bluebunch wheatgrass is native to semi-arid land throughout Idaho, western Montana, eastern Oregon, and eastern Washington. It grows in 2-foot-high clumps, primarily at lower elevations. Individual plants can live 50-100 years. A cool-season grass, most of its growth occurs in spring; in the typical hot, dry summers it goes dormant. During wet periods in autumn it may break dormancy and grow until early winter.

Light grazing of bluebunch wheatgrass during summer dormancy, when most carbohydrate reserves are stored in roots, usually causes minimal damage to the plant. In fact, before the advent of fire suppression, wildfires burned these grasslands frequently with no long-term ill effect. But truly light livestock grazing is almost unheard of. As traditionally

Sign amidst lush grass in Badlands National Park, SD. Livestock have been banned from about half of the roughly 100,000-acre Park, making the ungrazed portion one of the largest ungrazed -- and healthiest -- grasslands in the West.

practiced, livestock grazing depleted the bunchgrasses repeatedly during one season, every year. In contrast, fires burned them at irregular but periodic intervals of perhaps 5 to 20 years. Cattle ate the grasses, converted them to energy, heat, body weight, and manure, then left the range completely, whereas fires left many more nutrients on the range in the form of ashes. And livestock trampled heavily. Over many thousands of years, the grasses adapted to influences of native animals and fire, but they have not adapted to the intensive grazing, trampling, and other impacts of exotic livestock.

Bluebunch wheatgrass at one time grew tall and abundantly throughout much of

A healthy bunchgrass community, ungrazed by livestock, is a biotic Shangri-la.

its range. Today, after a century of overgrazing, most of it has been replaced by cheatgrass, other exotics, and bare dirt.

As early as 1910, excessive grazing, as well as accidental and grazing industry-caused arson fires, reduced perennial bunchgrass on Idaho rangeland by 85%, diminishing the land's grazing capacity by 40%-75% (Ferguson 1983). Today, cheatgrass accounts for 75%-95% of southern Idaho's herbage production (Palmer 1988). Studying overgrazed Utah National Forests in 1918, range professional A.W. Sampson reported that "these and similar eroded lands would originally support a cow or the equivalent in sheep on from one-third to one-fifth the acreage required at the present time (Sampson 1918)." Conditions in Utah haven't changed much since.

In the hills and valleys of California, the native bunchgrasses and rhizomatous grasses were so incessantly grazed that today about 95% of the herbaceous cover in uncultivated areas is composed of non-native species, mostly cheatgrass and other weedy annuals from Europe (Holechek 1989). Exclusion of livestock for 16 years from a Southwestern semi-grassland site resulted in 45% more grass cover, a comparatively heterogeneous plant community, and 4 times more shrubs than adjacent grazed areas (Bock *et. al.* 1984). Concerning the Great Basin, Gleason & Cronquist state in **The Natural Geography of Plants**, "Heavy grazing has caused considerable diminution of the grasses over much of the area, until in some places there is no native grass left (Gleason 1964)." The story is similar all around the Western United States. One magazine article on livestock grazing concludes:

> *Unfortunately, the grasses were exhaustible. One can find them surviving in cracks between rocks, beneath clumps of sagebrush, clinging to the sides of cliffs; any place a cow can't reach.*

Overgrazing became a greater problem [than farming] *with increasing numbers of cattle* [on the prairie]. . . . *In the Desert Grassland . . . many factors may have been involved* [in historic vegetation changes], *but cattle grazing is thought to have been the most important. . . . Livestock grazing is also considered the primary cause of vegetation changes in the Palouse Prairie* [northwest US] *and California Grassland associations.*
--John L. Vankat, **The Natural Vegetation of North America** (Vankat 1979)

An intact, natural grassland is a wonderland of life and beauty. A healthy bunchgrass community may hold anywhere from a few to over 20 species of bunchgrass, a great variety of herbaceous, flowering plants, many brush and cactus species, trees along drainages and perhaps scattered around the landscape, yuccas, a carpet of soil lichen and mosses between the larger plants, even mushrooms -- in all, hundreds of species all growing together, along with an amazing variety of animals, as a complex yet harmonic intermingling of lifeforms.

Prairie-type grassland generally is not so rich in diversity of plant types, but usually contains an average of 125-150 plant species and numerous animal species. Here one finds many different grasses and flowering plants. Perennial forbs are widespread, especially members of the sunflower and legume families. Annuals typically comprise less than 5% of plant species. Thick stands of bushes and trees commonly line drainages, and woody plants, cacti and other "desert" vegetation may occur where the influences of soil, landform, fire, animal impact, and other factors create suitable habitat. While generally less biotically diverse than the bunchgrass community, prairie grassland usually has many more individuals and a much greater biomass per unit of area.

Grass
is
beautiful.

Correspondingly, there are few champions of grassland in this country. Defenders of the West's mighty forests, mountain ranges, rivers, lakes, canyons, and other such spectacular areas can be counted in the millions. Though grassland and semi-grassland probably cover more of the West than all of these areas combined, the vast majority of those interested in grass and grassland are connected with the ranching industry. With this in mind, it is no wonder that Western grassland continues to be abused.

Deterioration of forage is not always easy to detect. It can be a slow, insidious process.
--William Voigt, Jr., **Public Grazing Lands** (Voigt 1976)

When a plow rips into the earth, exposing the soil and uprooting native vegetation, even the most unobservant can see a big change. When a logging outfit cuts a forest, the results are painfully obvious. When a copper company scalps a hillside, leaving tailings in piles at the bottom, the destruction is immediate and evident.

Not so with livestock. Grazing damage usually occurs in slow increments. Like the hour hand of a clock, changes are imperceptible, yet relentless. Of all the major land uses, livestock grazing is not only the most destructive but the most insidious.

Unfortunately, grassland is not widely appreciated in this country. Indeed, probably most US Americans have a bias against grassland and other untimbered landscapes, assuming that trees are the natural and proper vegetation cover for the land. Charles A. White of the Iowa Geological Survey rightly challenged this assumption in 1870, saying, "There seems to be no good reason why we should regard the forest as any more a natural or normal condition of the surface than the prairies are (Malin 1956)." Indeed, grassland generally has the deepest, most fertile and productive soil, highest erosion resistance and water retention, and greatest biomass of animals of all the major bioregions.

Nevertheless, probably most people when traveling through a landscape of grass consider it with indifference. To them, grassland is monotonous and one-dimensional. Although literally thousands of kinds of plants and animals are found in the grass country, there is little conspicuous enough to excite their interest. No doubt much of the public's attitude toward grassland stems from the fact that most of the West's originally lush, productive ranges have been turned into scenes of desolation by a century of overgrazing. Exposed often to cross-fenced landscapes of closely cropped grass, bare dirt, and scattered cows, people simply don't have any idea what a healthy grassland would be like.

Squirreltail.
(Helen Wilson)

(Steve Johnson)

USDA reports that 718 million acres of unforested grassland and semi-grassland in the US are grazed by livestock (Akers 1983). Unfortunately, healthy, intact native Western grassland has been almost totally eliminated by cow and plow, and, to a much lesser extent, development. On public land, its destruction has been caused almost exclusively by livestock grazing and ranching activities.

Though we usually think of rangeland as being grassland, this is just one of several major Western vegetation types grazed by livestock. All other major Western vegetation divisions have been severely affected as well.

Knee- and thigh-high grasses of several varieties and river grass 8' tall (top right) blanket this ungrazed bottomland along a remote stretch of the Green River in northeast Utah.

On an area of Arizona grassland fenced from livestock for 40 years, we picked the 24 seedheads of different grass species above the line. On an adjacent comparable area outside the exclosure, we found only the 6 species below the line.

Forest

At the beginning the mountains and heavily timbered areas were used but little [for livestock], but as the situation grew more acute in the more accessible regions, the use of these areas became general and in course of time conditions within them were even more grave than elsewhere, for experience had demonstrated that they were in strong demand. The mountains were denuded of their vegetation cover, forest reproduction was damaged or destroyed, the slopes were seamed with deep erosion gullies, and the water-conserving power of the drainage basins became seriously impaired.
--Albert F. Potter, sheepman, principal founder of the US Forest Service and its first Chief of Grazing, in "The National Forests and the Livestock Industry," 1912

When Europeans arrived in the West they found much of it -- 25% according to *Forestry Almanac* -- timbered, especially along the Pacific Coast and at higher elevations in the interior. There was a wondrous variety of forested areas, from immense stands of the world's largest trees in the Pacific Northwest to tiny forests of pigmy pinyon-juniper on rocky slopes in the Great Basin to impressive cottonwood and mesquite bosques in riparian areas of Southwest.

Over the years more than 90% of the West's commercially exploitable old-growth forest has been logged, and though most of this has regrown with trees, little of it attains aboriginal forest health and integrity. (In the US as a whole, less than 5% of pre-European old-growth remains intact.) Since the Western deforestation of the 1800s and early 1900s, many areas have been cut again, some 2 or 3 or more times, with tremendous environmental impact. Today this plunder continues at an accelerating pace.

Though few people realize it, Western forests are also heavily grazed, generally with higher livestock densities than on open landscapes. For a century, nearly every forest in the West, even in the soggy Northwest, has been degraded by livestock. (On a recent stay in Mountain Home State Forest in California, we found cattle damage even in a densely vegetated sequoia grove amid the world's largest trees.) Indeed, as mentioned, in the early years of exploitation ranching was of much greater consequence than was logging in National Forests, and the US Forest Service was largely an outgrowth of the grazing industry (Foss 1960, Roberts 1963, Voigt 1976).

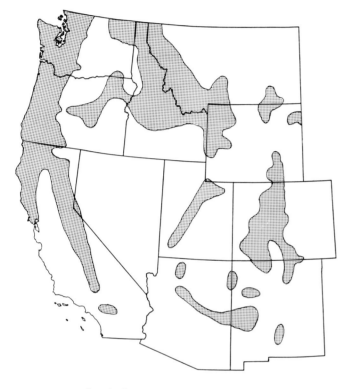

Rough Approximation of Major Forests
(Source: Vankat 1979)

About 70% of the total area of Western National Forests, or roughly 100 million acres, is currently managed for ranching -- essentially all that "feasibly" can be -- with by far most of this land grazed by livestock on some regular basis (USFS 1988). BLM reports about 25 million acres of forested land in the West, the vast bulk of it grazed (USDI, BLM 1987). And there are millions of acres of grazed state, other public, and private forest. The US Department of Agriculture reports that 246 million acres, or 63% of US forest, is "used for pasture" for livestock (Akers 1983).

Aside from logging, livestock grazing has caused and is causing far more damage to Western forests than any other forest use. This fact may not be readily apparent, for a number of reasons. But before discussing these it would help to understand just what a forest is.

A forest is more than just trees. According to ecologist George Wuerthner, a forest includes "the interrelationships between trees, soils, water, insects, fungi, fire, wildlife and a host of other influences most of us don't even know exist, much less understand." As with grasslands, healthy forests are a rich mixture of species, natural processes, and complex interrelationships. Through the millennia the right balance has been achieved for each unique geographic area. Though trees are the dominant plant type in a forest, there usually is an understory of brush and a ground cover of mixed grasses, forbs, and flowering plants, many able to subsist on scant sunlight. These plants serve many purposes to the trees and the forest as a whole, including holding and building soil, retaining water, moderating temperature, providing beneficial insect habitat, and so forth.

The natural forest is usually a jigsaw puzzle of different vegetation communities at different stages of growth. This mosaic provides diversity for overall health and biologic regeneration in case of fire or other disturbance. Likewise, the trees in healthy forests are of varying ages and sizes, from tiny seedlings to centuries-old giants, dispersed fairly randomly to assure maximum regeneration and distribution. Natural disturbance and fallen dead trees allow sunlight to reach lower levels, and through natural processes the larger forest trees usually are spaced far enough apart so that lower branches and some young trees receive adequate sunlight. This also allows smaller plant species to prosper between the larger trees, in turn helping sustain the forest as a whole. Directly underneath each tree, within its "fall line," is found a thick duff of fallen needles or leaves, twigs, bark, catkins or cones, and other tree parts. In this way each tree provides itself a rich compost that supplies nutrients, conserves moisture, builds topsoil, moderates soil temperature, and benefits the tree in many other ways.

Cattle in BLM forest. *(BLM)*

To most of us, as long as there are trees everything seems "park-like" and fine. When livestock strip off the grass and small plant cover of a forest, the large trees ("the forest") remain. Though the ecosystem may be greatly damaged, we cannot see the *whole* forest for the trees, so to speak.

But when a forest's smaller plant cover is denuded, the large trees themselves and the forest as a whole are eventually affected. Soil erosion intensifies; soil moisture decreases; air and soil temperatures reach greater extremes; localized, low-level air movement increases;

humidity decreases; beneficial animal habitat is destroyed; seed beds are damaged. Thus, in the long run large trees may become stunted, experience reproductive failures, be damaged by disease or insects, and so on. New trees cannot replace those that die since seedlings cannot establish in the overgrazed dry, hard ground.

Trees are likewise harmed when their underlying compost layer is disturbed. Normally, this organic litter layer is loosely matted together, cool, moist, aerated, and full of nutrients and beneficial microorganisms. Cattle in particular drag their feet as they walk, and all livestock tear apart and scatter this fertile overlayer, exposing it to light, cold, and heat, while at the same time compacting the underlying duff and soil, preventing aeration and, indirectly, killing microorganisms. As a result, trees suffer from a lack of moisture and nutrients that causes them to shed leaves, grow meager foliage, produce fewer and less fertile seeds, and be more vulnerable to insects and disease.

Dead trees and branches fall to the forest floor, where they may take longer to decompose than they did to grow. On the ground they are gradually reduced to humus by bacteria, fungi, and small insects. Like huge time-release vitamin capsules, they slowly release their nutrients into the soil and to plant roots.

These logs and branches may be periodically burned off by fires, without which they might accumulate to levels where they provide excessive fuel that results in highly destructive conflagrations. Where overgrazing depletes too much combustible organic ground cover, it prevents the spread of fire, or fire hot enough, to ignite these large branches and logs. In some sparsely forested areas where accumulation of duff alone isn't sufficient to carry fire, depletion of ground cover by livestock has reduced or eliminated forest fires altogether, to the forests' overall detriment (see Fire section of this chapter).

(Gila Trout)

Many people have a hard time believing that cows and sheep eat trees. Nevertheless, trees are a significant part of the diet of both in many areas. Trees preferred by livestock include oak, ash, walnut, willow, birch, aspen, alder, and

Ponderosa pine, eaten, stunted, and distorted by cattle -- one of the few survivors in a tree plantation in Prescott NF, AZ. (Rod Mondt)

This juniper, eaten and broken, stunted by general environmental degradation caused by livestock, probably will not survive.

This ash is likewise damaged and stunted.

cottonwood, though if need be they will eat almost any tree. Many times I have seen cattle eating pine, even pinyon pine!

Livestock eat the leaves and twigs from branches as far up the tree as they can reach (about 5 feet with cows), leading to the familiar "browse line" common in pictures of the African savanna. Livestock also eat tree saplings, and in winter leafless saplings; in some areas these compose a significant portion of their diet. According to the Forest Service, "Proper utilization of ash, walnut, etc. is 40% to 60% of available twigs." Many public land grazing allotment management plans expressly call for 30%-70% or so annual "utilization" of tree seedlings, and often more is taken. Thus, again, as large trees die from old age or the effects of overgrazing and small trees are eaten by livestock, the forest declines. Very sparse or even-aged stands of trees often indicate a history of heavy livestock use.

Trees are dying on this deteriorating BLM range. They are stunted; lower branches are gone; soil beneath is barren and damaged; saplings are eaten. This bottomland may have been covered with trees 150 years ago.

While cattle browse trees and damage forest ecosystems, they may also physically injure trees more directly, often by crashing through them and snapping off lower branches or breaking off small trees completely. Cattle also scratch against trees, breaking branches and rubbing off bark. They gouge trunks with their horns, opening the trees to disease and parasites. And they gnaw on bark to the point of girdling and killing trees. Wild animals such as elk and bears also injure trees, but they usually do so in more heavily forested areas where the damage usually adds to forest diversity and stability. Conversely, damage done by cattle is worst in the least forested areas.

In the drier parts of the West, mainly the Great Basin and Southwest where most forests are small and sparsely treed to begin with, livestock have been particularly destructive.

Cattle-grazed oak grove. Note lack of lower branches, ground cover, small trees. When old trees die, none will take their place. Santa Barbara Co., CA.

Lone pinyon pine shade tree begets cattle "sacrifice area."

In fact, most forests in these areas show more overall damage from ranching than from logging or any other activity. Due to aridity, ecosystems here are especially vulnerable to most of the livestock influences discussed.

In the summer, cattle often congregate under the largest, shadiest trees in these forests to spend the hottest part of the day. Here, they rut about, chew their cud (which they do about 8 hours a day), digest their food, and generally rest from eating (another 8 hours a day). The cattle shade tree is a common sight throughout the drier West: lower branches eaten or broken away; bark stripped from the trunk; bare, pounded dirt for many yards around; and piles of dusty manure scattered everywhere.

Many streams throughout the West are littered with the remains of what were once vigorous aspen groves. Aspen reproduce by sending up shoots from roots. If these young plants are constantly grazed off, eventually the parent trees will die of old age and aspen will disappear from the site.
--Livestock Grazing on Western Riparian Areas (Chaney 1990)

Though livestock affect all Western forest types in many ways, generally broadleaf woodlands experience more harm than do coniferous, largely because the former's saplings are more succulent and palatable. Among the most heavily damaged, for example, have been the West's shimmering aspen groves. Most are ravaged by livestock that eat and trample aspen sprouts and seedlings and other low-level vegetation, damage soil and bare it to the elements, and in many cases allow brush to take over.

The grassy oak woodland of Mediterranean California has for more than 2 centuries been experiencing a steady decline in oak trees, mostly due to cattle and sheep eating saplings. Five years after the University of California fenced 40 acres of its 4550-acre San Joaquin Experimental Range from livestock, the fenced plot supported 345 oak saplings per acre -- many times more than adjacent grazed land. According to The Nature Conservancy, an estimated 94% of California's interior broadleaf woodland has been sig-

Ungrazed by livestock, a mountain meadow in summer vibrates with life.

This meadow in a Wyoming National Forest is a pretty scene, but the grazing sheep do extensive damage. *(George Robbins Photo, Jackson, WY)*

nificantly damaged or destroyed, largely by the livestock that use the vast bulk of it.

Forest meadows are among of the most forage-productive areas in the West, so ranchers historically have made a concerted effort to concentrate their animals there. Large numbers of cattle are still driven into meadows to graze through the summer, and vast flocks of sheep are herded slowly through them, leaving devastation in their wake. The beautiful mountain meadows of the West have thus been especially hard-hit by overgrazing. Because they usually remain moist and green even when overgrazed, few people understand the magnitude of the damage.

Additionally, *most* of the overgrazed "meadows" found today on flats and valley bottoms in Western forests are actually artificial pastures. They were created by (or for) early stockmen who cut down trees to maximize forage for their livestock. Because of their prime growing locations, these "meadows" once contained some of the largest trees and most productive portions of the forest. Even where timber harvesting was the original reason for cutting, ranchers have prevented the forest from growing back by continuing to cut young trees and allowing their livestock to damage the land and eat and trample saplings.

California's beautiful oak woodlands are disappearing. Trees die or are cut, and few young ones take their place. The only small oak in this scene survives behind the protective barbs of the roadside fence.

A "meadow" (cleared livestock pasture) in a central California forest. Note stumps, lush vegetation on fenced roadside.

On a seven-day backpack trip in the rugged Blue Range Primitive Area in eastern Arizona, I came upon a fence crossing the Blue River. Upstream, where cattle grazed, there were no tree seedlings at all on the gravel bars, mudflats and terraces along the river. Downstream, where cattle had been removed for several years, young cottonwoods, willows, and sycamores were lush.

--Dave Foreman, **Confessions of an Eco-warrior** (Foreman 1991)

The West's riparian groves have suffered more overall from livestock than have any other timbered lands. Situated on bottomlands along perennially flowing or moist drainages, these luxuriant stands of huge trees included various combinations of cottonwood, sycamore, alder, elder, boxelder, maple, willow, walnut, hackberry,

mesquite, and others. Most covered hundreds or even thousands of acres and harbored an amazing variety and abundance of plants and animals. Riparian areas were the center of life in the West.

On public land *most* riparian groves have been virtually eliminated by overgrazing and grazing-induced flooding, and to a lesser extent by flooding caused by logging and unnatural fires, woodcutting, dams, and development (much of all this also a result of ranching). Overgrazing in watersheds caused drastic flooding that swept away the very bottomland these magnificent groves used to inhabit. Where large trees do remain, they may give the impression of riparian health; however, often all that survive are "historic" trees -- large individuals that were established before intensive livestock use began, or that established at some point in history when livestock grazing slacked off for a period. When these historic trees die they aren't replaced as long as heavy livestock use continues because saplings are eaten before they grow large enough to withstand intensive browsing. This appears to be the case along the Wild and Scenic Missouri River in Montana, where University of Montana researchers have discovered that livestock grazing is a major factor in the decline of the plains cottonwood; the deterioration has

Cottonwood

been masked to most observers because the remaining large historic trees give a false impression of riparian health (Wuerthner 1991).

Hardest hit have been the verdant cottonwood and mesquite bosques of the Southwest; by far most of them have been destroyed. The Fremont cottonwood/Gooding willow community, for example, is the rarest of the 104 major plant communities in North America. Although it never covered more than 1%-2% of the Southwest, livestock grazing led the way in reducing its area to (according to The Nature Conservancy) less than 1/1000 of 1% of Arizona and less than 1/100 of 1% of New Mexico. The most sensitive riparian areas succumbed first to the initial grazing frenzy of the late 1800s, but modern ranching prevents

Remaining live oak awaits its fate while shading its destroyers. When it dies there will be none. According to D.A. Duncan and W.J. Clawson in a presentation titled *Livestock Utilization of California's Oak Woodlands*, a study at the Hopland Station in the northern California foothills showed that after 5 years of protection from livestock an ungrazed study plot had 554 oak saplings per acre, compared to 0 saplings per acre on a plot grazed by sheep.

recovery and continues to cause new damage to riparian areas throughout the West (see Riparian Areas in this chapter).

natural fire, has eliminated most natural fire from *most* Western rangeland. Subsequent lack of fire, more than overgrazing directly, appears responsible for the spread of pinyon-juniper.

Generally, livestock grazing diminishes tree cover. However, under certain conditions overgrazing may increase the range and density of several kinds of trees.

Whatever the cause, the new P-J "forests" are comparatively dry, eroded, and devoid of plant and animal life -- as overgrazed as the grassland and semi-grassland they replaced. They are a human creation, like golf courses, and wherever they have been artificially produced by livestock the livestock, rather than the trees, should be removed.

Piñon Pine

Pinyon pine and juniper are the primary examples. These trees, often in mixed stands termed "P-J," currently cover about 75 million acres, about 1/10 of the semi-arid West. To justify destroying them to increase livestock forage, ranching advocates have greatly exaggerated the extent of their spread, but there is little doubt that pinyon and juniper have expanded their territory since the 1800s, "taking over" perhaps 20 million acres previously dominated by grass and grass/shrub combinations.

The exact reasons for this have not been determined, but it is no coincidence that overgrazing and P-J spread have occurred almost simultaneously. Overgrazing in P-J and potential P-J areas is very common, and the thin soils normally associated with this vegetation type make it highly sensitive to livestock influences. We know that livestock disperse juniper seeds through feces and their trampling tends to favor P-J seedlings over competing vegetation. And obviously livestock would rather eat grasses and most other herbaceous plants than pinyon and juniper. By stripping off this organic understory, however, livestock have precluded the natural fires that used to kill tree seedlings and revitalize forbs and grasses. This, in combination with the ranching industry's intentional war against

As young trees are eaten or succumb to other ranching impacts and old trees die, remaining trees (often used as shade) become foci for environmental damage, intensifying their extirpation.

A fenceline ungrazed on both sides. Note small oaks on both sides.

Most Western forest is grazed by livestock.

Brushland

Rough Approximation of Major Brushlands and Woodlands
(Source: Vankat 1979)

Because Western forests became fully stocked somewhat later than open rangelands, their greatest overall rate of livestock degradation probably occurred in the early 1900s (particularly during World War I). Forest conditions at that time have been described with terms like "devastation" and "holocaust"; indeed, many areas resembled barren deserts scattered with trees.

Thus, the forests were divested of their natural productivity, and those forests we think we know today are operating at much less productive levels. Livestock grazing may now seem less intense, especially compared to the historic past or to the more obvious damage of current open range grazing. Be that as it may, most Western forests are still stocked many times beyond their true carrying capacity, and this pressure perpetuates the dynamic state of degradation begun a century ago. Destructive modern range development (next chapter) has augmented this state, and in some ways cumulative damage continues to mount.

Primarily because woody plants block sunlight and occupy space that could be used by forage grasses, brushland/shrubland is the most maligned major biotic community in the West. The ranching establishment considers it a hindrance to profits and has waged unrelenting war against woody plants (see Plant Enemies in next chapter).

Unfortunately, few people of any persuasion have much good to say about brush. Perhaps this is because brush is not conveniently open to human access; you cannot walk over it as with grass or under it as with trees. Maybe it is because brush provides few apparent benefits to humans; it is not easily conquered and molded to our will. Or maybe it is because a thick stand of brush is hidden, mysterious, and even a little scary. Certainly it has much to do with the grazing industry's vilification of it for over 100 years.

Decades of differences in livestock grazing have apparently resulted in more juniper and less mesquite on the far side of the fence, vice versa on the near side. Gila NF, NM.

Brush (bushes) and *shrubs* are woody plants, with brush generally being larger and more tree-like, while shrubs are low to the ground. Scrub oak, greasewood, laurel, locust, sumac, winterfat, rabbitbrush, saltbush, tarbush, cliffrose, mountain mahogany, hawthorn, snakeweed, manzanita, acacia, chokecherry, ceanothus, creosote, serviceberry, Mormon tea, jojoba, soapberry, bur sage, burro brush, bitterbrush, blackbrush, buckbrush, buckthorn -- hundreds of varieties of brush and shrubs inhabit the West. Brushland and shrubland are areas where these woody plants are the predominant vegetation.

Though occasionally growing as dense, single-species stands, woody plants usually grow in mutually beneficial combinations of species. As with forests and grasslands, the natural brushland association is most often composed of a rich array of plant types and species.

Healthy, ungrazed sagebrush range also supports abundant grasses, flowering plants, cryptogams (see Deserts in this chapter), and animal life. Commonly, less than 10% of the ground is bare. This brushland in Craters of the Moon National Monument, ID gets only 10" annual precipitation.

Brushland performs all the essential functions of any other plant community. It builds and maintains soil, absorbs and retains water, blocks the elements, and all the rest. Even where brush forms tight, closed stands, it performs these jobs admirably. The ground beneath these stands is blanketed with a rich cover of organic litter dropped by the brush above. Pull back this thick layer and you'll find the soil beneath moist and dark, as it is well protected from sunlight, heat, cold, rain, wind. And, despite misconceptions, brush and shrubs provide habitat for the many and varied animals adapted to them.

While it is true that in some respects brushland has a lower capacity to perform these functions than does grassland or forest, as with any natural plant cover brushland is the most productive, stable biotic community for the given environment. The key here is *health*. Neither grassland nor brushland nor any other vegetation type perform natural functions well if abused by livestock.

Forget ranching industry "information"! Bushes and shrubs are not merely "transitional" plants or "disturbance species" occupying space until some other kind of vegetation takes their place, though they sometimes do play that role. Rather, they are part of the climax community throughout large areas of the West. This is well-documented

by the journals of early explorers and by scientific study.

Indeed, when Europeans arrived in the West they found much of it cloaked with brush and shrubs. Nearly every Western ecosystem supported woody vegetation, and even the grasses of the prairie were often interspersed with shrubs, such as buckbrush. There was a great diversity of woody plant communities, from widely spaced, low-growing, mixed desert shrubs in the lower Sonoran Desert, to vast sagebrush/grass-covered plains in western Wyoming, to huge stands of dense chaparral in California's hills and mountains, to tiny thickets of mixed shrubs in rocky outcroppings in eastern new Mexico to . . . The US Geological Survey identifies 15 major shrubland and grass-shrubland divisions in the West, with scores of subdivisions.

Today, most original brushland survives, though most has been damaged and much has been altered beyond recognition. Public lands ranching has played the major role in its deterioration. According to USDA, in the US (mostly in the West) shrubland range is in even worse condition than grassland range, with 55% and 53%, respectively, producing at less than 40% biotic potential and 85% of both producing at less than 60% potential (USDA, USFS 1980).

Brushland is affected by overgrazing in most of the same ways as grassland and forest. Brush and shrub seedlings are eaten and trampled. Mature plants are overbrowsed, giving them an excessively "hedged" appearance; many brush species, mountain mahogany for example, are highly desired as browse. Branches are broken and trampled. Plants eventually lose vigor, roots and branches die back, centers die out, and reproduction fails. Livestock strip off the ground cover of grasses and other small, herbaceous plants. They trample, displace, and destroy the organic litter layer and soil cryptogamic layer common to many brushlands (see Deserts in this chapter). Rain runs off instead of in, soil erodes . . . The whole familiar series of harmful effects proceeds.

Here, grazing cattle have converted dense shrubs interspersed with grass to scattered shrubs, woody debris, and no grass. Northern Nevada BLM.

As with pinyon-juniper, some brush and shrub species -- particularly catclaw, sage, snakeweed, and mesquite -- are resistant to grazing. As with P-J, they have in some areas become increasers or invaders at the expense of grass; thus, the grazing industry's "brush invasion." Overgrazing can indeed increase the range and density of brush, *but only some species under certain conditions*.

According to many range professionals, grazing's indirect effects, more than grazing *per se*, are responsible for the spread of these woody plants. For example, in his study of vegetational changes on Southwestern grassland and semi-grassland, **The Desert Grassland**, Robert R. Humphrey concludes:

> *The principal environmental factors that may have been modified are [1] climate, [2] grazing by domestic livestock, [3] plant composition, [4] rodents and rabbits, and [5] fire. Each of these appears to have aided in the spread of shrubs. The effect of some, as for example, climate, appears slight; that of others, such as grazing and fire, is of considerable importance.* (Humphrey 1967)

These 5 factors are most commonly cited as leading to the spread of brush throughout the West. Though Humphrey and most other range pros seem reluctant to state the obvious connection between livestock grazing and these other factors, I will do so here:

● (1)*Climate*, Humphrey agrees, has been a minor factor; in fact, there has been insignificant change in climate (see Air section of this chapter).

● (2) *Grazing by livestock* is listed as 1 of the 2 major factors, along with lack of fire, for the spread of woody plants. There are many influences involved, including: spread of seeds through fecal droppings (probably important to the spread of mesquite, for example); selective grazing (livestock eating the most palatable species and leaving the woody plants); trampling of smaller plants; reduced competition (removal of plant species that formerly served to limit other plant species' growth); damage to soil and water systems, which may favor woody plants over grasses; and removal of combustible plant matter which previously served to carry range fires.

● (3) *Plant composition* changes, including the increase in woody vegetation around the West, as previously explained, has been caused largely by overgrazing.

● (4) *Rodent and rabbit* population increases have also contributed to the increase in woody plants in some areas. These animals have accomplished this primarily by eating the more palatable species, spreading seeds in their droppings, and storing seeds underground, where they later germinate.

Increases in rabbits and other rodents are caused by the livestock industry in 2 basic ways: First, predator slaughter

Cattle on this New Mexico state range have decreased nearly all plant life, including brush by perhaps 50%. Roadside at right. Foreground was bladed.

The heavy cattle grazing to the left of the fence at center has caused a definite reduction of shrub and brush cover on this steep, rocky, semi-arid BLM range in central Arizona. Probably unbeknownst to the viewer, however, the lighter grazing to the right of the fence has caused a significant vegetation decline as well.

has allowed rodent populations to fluctuate wildly in many areas, causing them to periodically overuse smaller vegetation, favoring brush. Second, livestock grazing and certain ranching management techniques (next chapter) favor the spread of weedy species on which some rodents may thrive.

• (5) *Lack of fire* is, according to Humphrey, the major cause of the invasion of woody vegetation into Southwestern grassland and semi-grassland. Unfortunately, Humphrey failed to make the connection between the grazing industry and the lack of natural fire during the past 100 + years. Perhaps this is because range professional circles frown upon directly blaming ranching for anything more than the most obviously deleterious.

At any rate, by eating and trampling and causing other changes that radically decrease the amount of combustible material, livestock have eliminated natural fire from much of the range. Without periodic fire to rejuvenate grasses, destroy bush seedlings, and burn back small bushes, woody plants often have the advantage. This and the grazing industry's fire suppression campaign have been the 2 main elements snuffing out natural range fire in the West (see Fire in this chapter and Fire Management in Chapter IV).

Humphrey has changed his thinking somewhat. His recent book, **90 Years and 535 Miles**, compares photographs made in 1892-1893 in 205 locations along 535 miles of the US-Mexican border between El Paso and Yuma with recent photographs of the same locations. Conclusions on these comparisons were difficult because the 1892-1893 photos were made *after* many years of devastating overgrazing, and directly following a period of severe drought in which thousands of cattle in the area died of thirst and starvation. Even so, the photos and Humphrey's on-the-ground comments document a nearly universal reduction in grass and perennial herb cover, often accompanied by an increase in brush and annual forbs. A great many of his comparisons identify the impact from livestock as the probable main cause of change. Humphrey now concludes that climate "may be in part responsible for this change," that grazing is "in large part responsible for the change," and that "in many areas close grazing reduced the potential fuel; in others, fires would have been extinguished because they were seen as consuming valuable forage." (Humphrey 1987)

As a rule, increases in woody species from overgrazing are most pronounced in semi-arid regions. Livestock grazing in deserts usually decreases *all* vegetation, while grazing in moist regions generally causes native herbaceous perennials to be replaced by herbaceous increasers and invaders rather than woody vegetation. Large increases in bare dirt are common with livestock grazing everywhere.

While it is generally accepted that overgrazing has resulted in major changes to Western brushland vegetation, the nature and extent of these changes typically have been misinterpreted by those with vested interests in eliminating any and all brush. True to style, the grazing industry has blown "the brush invasion" totally out of proportion. For example, an article, "Man vs. Mesquite," in *Life* magazine, August 18, 1952, claims:

> A century and a half ago, there was hardly any in this country ... Mesquite march during the last 100 years has taken it from small riverside areas in which it grew in 1850 to the 75 million acres it now covers [in the US].

This claim, provided to the article's author by ranching advocates and still alive today, is grossly inaccurate. Many early explorers, including Stephen Long, Lieutenant Abert, and R.B. Marcy, noted what surely totaled millions of acres of mesquite on the plains and valleys of the Southwest more than 150 years ago. In fact, evidence indicates that (1) mesquite has expanded its general geographic range only slightly, (2) mesquite has occupied most of its current territory for centuries, (3) mesquite formerly grew across plains and valleys, not only along drainages, and (4) the biggest change in the nature of the average mesquite landscape has been that formerly open, grassy savanna scattered with large mesquite trees has become scrubland of densely packed, scraggly mesquite (Malin 1956). (As livestock grazing tends to transform sod grasses into bunchgrasses into annual grasses, so it tends to convert trees into bushes into shrubs.)

Numerous accounts by early Western explorers confirm that brush and shrubs have not increased nearly as much as claimed by the ranching establishment (Thwaites 1959, for example). Moreover, most of the brush and shrubs alleged to have "invaded" have actually been increasers, if even that. As natural components of mixed plant communities, they simply increased in density when livestock damaged their ecosystems. Or, in some cases, they only *seemed* to increase because they were the only plants left.

Whatever the case, most of today's brushlands and shrublands are generally incomplete, unhealthy, and unproductive as compared to those in pre-livestock times. Many have been turned into veritable biological wastelands. Frequently existing as stands of  only 1 or 2 species, their stunted, broken plants are interspersed with little more than bare, trampled dirt. In such condition, who would have much good to say about them?

Deteriorated sage/grass range in northern Nevada. Note healthy vegetation on ungrazed side of fence.

Desert

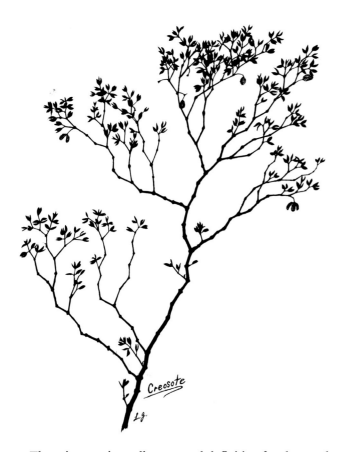

Creosote

l.j.

There is no universally accepted definition for the word "desert," but it is often considered to be a biotic region that receives 10" or less of precipitation per year. Under this interpretation, about 1/4 the area of the 11 Western states could be termed desert, including some portions of each of these states, even Montana.

The amount of vegetation cover should perhaps be as important a defining factor as the amount of rainfall. Many variables besides annual rainfall influence an area's amount of vegetation: type and season of precipitation; temperature; elevation; latitude; angle and lay of land; amount, speed, and direction of wind; soil color, texture, structure, and chemical composition; and so forth. There are areas receiving more than 10" annual rainfall that seem to be desert and areas receiving less than 10" that wouldn't be considered desert. When it comes down to it, each area is judged individually.

A true desert is not merely an area of sparse vegetation, but an area only capable of supporting sparse vegetation. There is an immense difference. Actual *desert* is not wasteland but simply another of the Earth's natural biotic regions. This helps explain why the Earth's human/livestock-created deserts, many of those in the "Old World" particularly, support a paucity of desert species compared to more natural deserts like those in North America.

Contrary to popular opinion, the "struggle for survival" in deserts is not necessarily harder than in other bioregions, just different. A healthy desert, like any natural bioregion, is a smoothly functioning group of ecosystems. Though deserts are capable of supporting only comparatively sparse vegetation, they produce the maximum abundance and diversity of plant and animal life possible *for existing climatic, geologic, and geographic conditions*. Having spent millions of years perfecting the art of using water to maximum benefit, deserts are the unsurpassed experts in conservation and effective use of water. Humans can only force deserts to produce more than what they would naturally on a transitory basis, and then only at the expense of the overall environment.

There are 4 main desert regions in the United States. The *Great Basin Desert* encompasses most of the high "sagebrush desert" that includes much of the area between the Rocky Mountains and the Sierra Nevada and southern Cascades. The *Mojave Desert* is the low-elevation, dry-summer desert covering most of southeastern California, southern Nevada, and northwestern Arizona. The *Sonoran Desert* of south and central Arizona is a warm, comparatively verdant desert with both winter and summer rainfall. And the *Chihuahuan Desert*, with a similar rainfall pattern to the Sonoran, is a somewhat higher and cooler desert covering much of southern New Mexico and western Texas. These 4 regions encompass the bulk of genuine desert in the West.

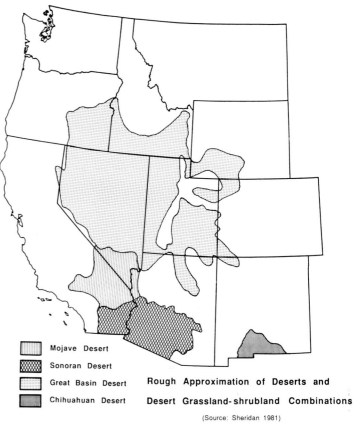

▦ Mojave Desert
▧ Sonoran Desert
☐ Great Basin Desert
▥ Chihuahuan Desert

Rough Approximation of Deserts and Desert Grassland-shrubland Combinations

(Source: Sheridan 1981)

The morning sun lights an impoverished land: greasewood wide-spaced, dirt and sand between, a little grass, a low, prickly, gray-green matted cover only at river's edge -- woefully overgrazed land. . . . Somehow a true desert is less bleak than this vista; a desert seems at equilibrium within itself, while this is but the tattered remnant of something better.

--Ann Zwinger, **Run, River, Run**

Much of today's West only superficially *appears* to be desert and would be more accurately described as "wasteland." Extensive overgrazing has caused what botanists term *desertification* (making desert-like -- something of a misnomer) throughout much of the West, including huge areas previously well-vegetated and still well-watered. Marginally arid areas generally are the first to succumb to desertification from overgrazing, but any place can be "wasted" or "cowburnt" and take on the outward appearance of desert. This is nicely demonstrated by former-grassland-now-wasteland areas in every Western state. While about 1/5 of the West could be termed true, natural desert, perhaps another 1/5 has been so thoroughly and incessantly grazed by livestock that it has taken on the superficial appearance of desert. The point is that this overgrazed land is *not* true desert and, further, that it does not function in the healthy, productive manner inherent in a natural desert.

Of course all this is not to say that the West's genuine desert has not been wasted as well. Indeed, it is the most vulnerable of all biotic regions to livestock damage. This is understandable when one considers that the last large native herbivore to occupy the arid West was the giant ground sloth, a browser extinct for more than 10,000 years. Additionally, desert experiences the greatest precipitation and temperature fluctuations of all biomes (biologic regions), which further augments its vulnerability. Already limited to a minimum of biomass, it is easily harmed by any kind or amount of livestock grazing. Once damaged, it usually does not recover for decades or even centuries.

For example, the Sonoran and Chihuahuan Deserts of the American Southwest are probably a million years old as deserts, and yet they have become perceptibly more barren during the past 100 years. . . . In short, these deserts have undergone desertification.

--Desertification in the United States by David Sheridan (Sheridan 1981)

Desert plants' relatively small stature, brittle nature, and slow growth rate make them highly susceptible to damage. And most desert vegetation is so scarce to begin with that it doesn't take much pressure from livestock to wipe it out completely. The few palatable plants that exist are quickly eaten. The combination of grazing, trampling, low rainfall, searing wind, and hot, glaring sun on exposed ground makes for conditions unfavorable to the establishment of seedlings.

This arid region near the Paria River in southeastern Utah naturally supports only sparse vegetation, but a century of livestock has in many areas left it little or (in this case) no vegetation. *(George Wuerthner)*

This former grassland may now seem a desert, but it is more correctly a wasteland. BLM, Northern Nevada. *(BLM)*

Bare spaces left where vegetation was removed are likely to remain bare for long periods. Additionally, the combination of overgrazing and infrequent, torrential desert rains results in disastrous flooding and soil damage and erosion. These influences make it difficult even for desert annuals to survive and reproduce.

Stock tanks, corral, pens, and ramp at foot of Kelso Sand Dunes, Mojave Desert, CA, an area of 4" annual rainfall. Cattle wander the scorching sand, devouring the scant greenery; hoof prints and piles of mummified cow turds defile the graceful, otherwise beatiful dunes.

The great majority of desert plants are easily harmed by livestock. For example, studies show that cattle stepping on and eating young saguaros and some other cacti are a major cause of their decline in Western deserts (Vankat 1979). Indeed, cattle frequently trample and eat cacti of many types -- even some species of cholla -- spines and all. Depending on hunger, they may also eat yucca, agave plants, ocotillo, and other unique desert vegetation.

As barren as the desert may at times appear, it is rarely truly so. Open desert areas or spaces between scattered desert shrubs are usually sprinkled with various cacti, succulents, short grasses, and other small herbaceous plants. They all contribute to the soil's meager organic content, soil stability, moisture conservation, and so on -- unless livestock get to them.

The desert's famous flowering annuals spring up in beautiful abundance following wet periods. A few months later, they

may be dead and shriveled, but their dry tops and slowly decomposing roots help anchor and fertilize the soil. Over much of the desert West livestock eat *most* live annuals, thus precluding seeding, pulverizing dead tops and roots, and preventing the establishment of seedlings.

In the desert, moisture is usually inadequate to support woody increasers or invaders; when woody plants die back, a few annuals and bare ground take their place. Studies by Cook and Child show that desert plants even moderately devegetated in one season were significantly lower in vigor than those left intact, even after 7 years (Cook 1971).

Though deserts support few and small trees (mostly along drainages), these trees are vitally important. They provide wildlife with shade, shelter, food, and nesting sites that often are wholly lacking on the open desert. Underneath, their shade, wind protection, and dropped organic material create a relatively moist, cool micro-climate where many small plants and animals thrive. These, and the dense lower branches, afford "nursery" protection for small trees, immature saguaros, cacti, perennial herbs, leafy grasses, and other plants vulnerable to full desert exposure. Unfortunately, shade-seeking cattle often congregate under desert trees, killing and driving off wildlife, breaking lower branches, trampling underlying vegetation, depleting organic litter, and drying out and damaging the soil below. Because overgrazed deserts are devoid of preferred forage and browse, cattle and sheep also eat from these trees, even thorn-covered palo verde, hackberry, smoke tree, and ironwood.

Researchers studied the effects of traditional sheep grazing on 4 BLM sites in the western Mojave Desert in 1978. They found a 60%-90% reduction in the cover of annuals and a 16%-29% decrease in perennials. The sheep also caused significant soil compaction, which hampers plant growth (see Soil section of this chapter). The study concluded that "These changes indicate that the range quality of the Mojave Desert is deteriorating under sheep grazing pressures."

Studies by the US Geological Survey at the Desert Laboratory west of Tucson show that the 869-acre section of desert on and around Tumamoc Hill, fenced in 1907 to exclude cattle, has transformed from mostly creosote and a few other shrubs to a comparatively lush vegetative mosaic that includes bursage, ratney, palo verde, burro weed, prickly pear, cholla, ocotillo, grasses, saguaros, and "over 400 other species." *Even mesquite increased dramatically.* While saguaros in grazed areas of Arizona continue to decline, the 55 counted on a 100 acre study area on a flat below Tumamoc Hill in 1907 increased to 205 in 1989. Runoff and soil erosion have decreased, wild animals are provided more favorable habitat, and students at nearby Pima College are provided more beautiful scenery, though few of them realize why.

Cryptogams protect soil in an ungrazed portion of Behind the Rocks, a Wilderness Study Area near Moab, UT. *(George Wuerthner)*

... the Columbia Basin's unspoiled steppe has a thin layer of mosses and lichens that completely clothes the earth between the shrubs, grasses, and forbs. These minute, fragile plants dry during the summer heat and become extremely brittle. They are unable to survive trampling by sharp-hooved sheep, cattle, and horses.

--Andrew Kratz and James Kagen in "Grasslands Amid the Forests" (Kratz 1986)

Desert plants differ from those of other biotic regions in several significant ways, but perhaps the most noticeable difference is that they are spaced widely apart.. However, while the open space between plants might seem to be only bare dirt, this is rarely the case. In fact, the surprisingly fertile soil common to most arid lands is rarely directly exposed anywhere, being well-protected in several basic ways.

An important ground cover found primarily in drier regions are soil microphytic or cryptogamic crusts, better known as "soil lichen layers." These variously colored crusts are dominated by cyanobacteria (formerly known as blue-green algae), the oldest form of life known, and also may include lichens, mosses, green algae, liverworts, microfungi, and bacteria. These mutually supportive, numberless tiny plants form a "living skin" over much of the soil surface and are in essence the topsoil of much of the West. Any soil that contains a high concentration of cryptogams may be termed

cryptogamic soil, but in some deserts cryptogamic crusts are extraordinarily well-developed and may represent 70%-80% of the living ground cover (Belnap 1990).

Cyanobacteria usually occur in the soil as filaments that compose an intricate webbing of minute fibers up to several inches deep which, along with other microflora, bind soil particles together and help prevent erosion. Cryptogamic carpets also infiltrate water, reduce evaporation, moderate soil temperature, trap wind-borne particles, physically and chemically create soil, bind important nutrients and keep them in upper soil horizons, fix nitrogen, contribute organic matter, provide a seed bed, and promote a wide variety of ground-dwelling animals.

Cryptogamic crusts are highly vulnerable to trampling and disappear rapidly whenever even moderate livestock grazing occurs. Thus, in most of the West, cryptogams and other small plants are found chiefly under the protective cover of larger plants and rocks, where livestock are unable to tread. Indeed, livestock grazing has destroyed more of the West's cryptogamic cover than all other human impacts combined! Where grazing is discontinued, cryptogams usually creep slowly out from their "hiding places" and recolonize exposed soil (Anderson 1982).

A loose pebblestone layer in the Sonoran Desert. Note seedlings and rabbit pellets.

In the more barren desert areas, soil is often protected by a tight surface layer of cobblestones, pebbles, or even coarse sand -- what is sometimes called "desert pavement." These inorganic protective layers are formed when smaller soil particles are blown or washed away from the desert surface over a period of time, leaving the heavier particles and/or stones as an overlayer. They serve to protect underlying soil and conserve water. With few large native animals to disturb them, these protective layers are a semi-permanent feature of many arid lands (and of some areas stripped of vegetation by livestock). Thousand-pound, trampling cattle quickly destroy them.

Even where desert soil is naturally open and exposed, Nature provides a protective covering. In these areas the soil surface itself hardens, forming a protective crust that shields it from the elements and keeps it from being displaced by wind, blowing objects, small animals, and so forth. When it rains, the crust immediately softens to allow water infiltration. This delicate soil crust is shattered by a half-ton, hooved beef as if it were pie crust.

Desert soil crust has been pulverized on left by tires and shoes, leaving a fine dust that is susceptible to the elements.

In the barren spaces between desert shrubs, the shrubs have created a spreading network of shallow roots to maximize their absorption of scant, infrequent rainfall. In many areas this web of roots just below the soil's surface is the desert's primary builder and stabilizer of soil. It is, of course, extremely vulnerable to the deeply cutting hooves of livestock.

Runoff flow is from right to left. Note smaller-grained sediments trapped behind the organic dike.

Sometimes open spaces of bare soil in the desert are sprinkled with a light covering of organic matter dropped from nearby plants. On the flat, gentle slopes common to many deserts, rainfall from intense cloudbursts runs in sheets, pushing this organic matter ahead of it, piling it into low, long, parallel "dikes." These dikes slow water runoff, enabling more water to infiltrate into the ground and minimizing sheet erosion. Later, the dikes may be gradually disassembled by gravity, wind, animals, etc. and redispersed over the soil's surface, ready to fulfill the same function once again. The larger and more sturdy of them remain to conserve water, build soil, and provide seed beds for the establishment of desert vegetation. Livestock deplete source materials and trample these dikes.

The above is just one example of the numerous unfamiliar but essential natural processes that keep desert ecosystems healthy. They go largely unnoticed, even by scientists, as do the ways in which livestock disrupt them.

In a nutshell, deserts are an absurd place to raise livestock. For example, on California's Mojave Desert, 108 ranchers graze livestock on 4,660,000 BLM acres of mid- to upper-elevation desert. This land -- about 5% of California -- produced 103,191 livestock AUMs in 1987, the equivalent of yearlong grazing for only 8599 cattle, or about *one cow per square mile*, about 1/600 of California's annual livestock production (while livestock production represents only 1/6000 of

(Bob Dixon)

the state's economy). Permittees pay little more than a penny per acre per year; their livestock cause extensive damage; and taxpayers shell out more money for or because of ranching than the value of their cattle (see Chapter VII for economic details).

It takes *hundreds* of acres of desert to keep a cow alive for a year. Nonetheless, Western deserts are grazed almost anywhere there is enough forage or browse to keep a cow or sheep alive. About the only place they are not is where livestock grazing is virtually impossible -- the hottest, driest, most desolate parts of southeastern California and southwestern Arizona, and some barren dry lake beds and salt flats in the Great Basin.

Where there before existed beautiful, living desert, there now exists true *wasteland*. Grazing desertifies even the deserts.

The most widespread and cataclysmic change in the desert [of the United States] in modern times has resulted from unrestricted grazing. . . . The desert in many places is one-tenth as productive for livestock as it was when white men first came on the scene.
--David F. Costello, **The Desert World**

(Paul Hirt)

Conclusions: Plants

The principal cause of desertification in the U.S., as in the rest of the world, is overgrazing by livestock.
--R. Neil Sampson, **Farmland or Wasteland** (Sampson 1981)

There is not an overgrazing problem, but a lack of rain problem.
--Northern Wyoming rancher

Livestock grazing has helped desertify more than 1/3 of the Earth's land surface. In the US West, it has helped desertify several hundred million acres -- *most* of the West -- converting well over 100 million acres of grassland and semi-grassland, brushland, and even forest to wasteland. Let's take a quick tour of the on-going destruction:

Only 130 years ago a great sea of grass stretched across western Texas, southern New Mexico, and southeastern Arizona. Today most of the area is basically "desert" in biological terms, often barren, and scrubby mesquite and catclaw have increased in density at the expense of other lifeforms on perhaps 20-30 million acres. The grassland and mixed grassland/shrubland of much of the Great Basin, once averaging about 80% bunchgrass and forbs to 20% shrubs and brush, has been converted into a wasteland of scraggly, broken sage, shadscale, snakeweed, cheatgrass, and tumbleweed, with a reversed ratio averaging about 20% grass (mostly exotic) and forbs to 80% woody vegetation (not including a much larger percentage of bare dirt, sand, and gravel). Most of California's once lush, grass- and flower-carpeted hills and valleys are now covered with sparse, overgrazed exotic grasses and "weeds" and bare dirt, transformed beyond recognition from their original state. The well-watered Pacific Northwest is still green, but much less so. In many areas its thick herbaceous cover has been cropped annually to near ground level, often replaced by exotics. The steppe-like grassy plains in portions of Idaho and eastern Oregon and Washington are now commonly barren and eroded. The Rockies, Sierra Nevada, and nearly all Western mountain ranges have been degraded by millions of sheep (the "hooved locusts" of which John Muir wrote) and cattle. Livestock have denuded and trampled the fragile deserts, canyons, and mountains of the fantastic Colorado Plateau of southern Utah and northern Arizona. Much of the marginally grazable true desert of the Southwest has been converted to wasteland. Likewise, the hot, barren, truly ungrazable low desert of southeastern California and southwestern Arizona is actually expanding its geographic boundaries as voracious cattle eat away at its fringes and higher elevations. And finally, the Great Plains of Montana, Wyoming, Colorado, and New Mexico today bears little resemblance to its former state in the times when great herds of buffalo, elk, and pronghorn roamed its vast, luxuriant spaces.

The grazing industry typically blames these changes on a drying climate (or sometimes plant evolution or development or road building or farmers using too much ground water or early beaver trappers eliminating beaver dams and lowering water tables or earthquakes [yes, earthquakes] or nearly anything but ranching). Climatic statistics, on the other hand, show no overall drying trend (see graphs in Air

Huge herds of sheep have desertified millions of Western acres. *(Paul Hirt)*

section of this chapter), and these other scapegoats are in truth relatively minor influences on overall Western vegetation.

Rain at the right time will make anyone look like a good rancher.
--Bill Brockman, Sawtooth NF, ID grazing permittee

As detailed elsewhere, experts in and out of the industry estimate that the Western range today is half or less as botanically productive as before the livestock invasion of the 1800s (some call it "the loss of the herbaceous component"!). For example, according to a 1990 report prepared for the US Environmental Protection Agency, "In 1980 the United States Department of Agriculture estimated that vegetation on more than half of all western rangelands was deteriorated to less than 40% of potential productivity, and to less than 60% of potential on more than 85% of rangeland" (Chaney 1990). This addresses *productivity* but does not take into account that most range plants are severely cropped down or browsed off and rarely allowed to attain full size. So the *actual* biomass of vegetation existing at any given time on today's Western range is undoubtedly far less than half that of 150 years ago.

To provide some veneer of justification and semblance of rationality for grazing public land, the ranching establishment alleges that livestock benefit Western plant communities by performing ecological functions similar to the native herbivores they replaced. This may sound good, but the influence of domestic livestock is vastly dissimilar to that of native grazers.

In natural situations wildlife are nomadic, bound by no fences or management schemes. Herds of grazing, trampling, wallowing, free-roaming buffalo and other ungulates create a complex mosaic of vegetation in varying states of recovery (though the bulk of the range remains old-growth). Periodic natural fires sweep through these plant communities, augmenting biodiversity and thus ecosystem

Plains lovegrass, a much diminshed native. *(Helen Wilson)*

Livestock desertification in northern Arizona. Adding insult to injury, the last juniper within miles has lost most of its branches for fence posts.

health and stability (see Fire section of this chapter). In contrast, managed livestock uniformly denude vegetation over vast areas, creating biotic monotones that are impoverished and prone to disease and pests. The resulting heavily grazed, homogeneous plant cover supports expansive, homogeneous fires, or more likely no fire at all.

Ranchers declare that livestock are needed to trample seeds into the ground, as did native ungulates. In practice, plants frequently never make it to seeding time in the first place or are eaten before they can drop seeds if they do. Often the environment is so degraded that seeds won't sprout, and what seedlings do come up are eaten or trampled to death. Moreover, for millennia throughout most of the West trampling by large

Surrounded by unscalable cliffs, this lushly vegetated grassy area has not been grazed by large herbivores for at least centuries, indicating that grassland does not require animal impact to maintain health or essential character (trees also grow in the nearby lowlands). Badlands National Park, SD.

Bluebunch wheatgrass and scattered sagebrush on an isolated, cliff-sided plateau at the junction of the Deschutes and Crooked Rivers in central Oregon. Much of the northern part of the Great Basin probably looked a lot like this 150 years ago, before the competitive balance was shifted by livestock. *(USFS)*

ungulates was a relatively minor influence on plant regeneration.

It is true, as the industry claims, that light grazing or browsing of certain plant species at just the right time of year can sometimes cause plants to produce more overall biomass (what ranchers call *productivity*) during a growing season than if left uneaten. For example, under certain conditions gentle pruning of the older leaves of some grasses allows more sunlight to reach plants' basal growth cells, increasing photosynthesis and their overall growth. However, this relatively insignificant result is rarely achieved within contemporary livestock grazing. Rather than increasing overall plant growth, the grazing and browsing common to most of the Western range stunts or kills most plants. And the alleged increase in total production of plant fiber does not reflect higher environmental quality; indeed, livestock eat and trample many, many times more than this additional amount.

The left plant wasn't clipped, the middle plant was clipped to three inches weekly, the right plant was clipped to an inch-and-a-half height weekly for each of six weeks.

(SCS, USDA)

The industry similarly argues that without livestock to strip off a grass plant's old, dead leaves the green portion of the plant will fail to receive adequate sunlight and eventually die. While this sounds almost plausible, few plant species require the removal of old plant material to receive enough sunlight. Those that do significantly benefit from physical removal are adapted to having this procedure performed by *fire* more frequently and effectively than by native grazing animals. They are certainly not adapted to annual multiple denudations by domestic livestock.

In natural situations most wild herbivores move continuously and eat selectively, with each species specializing on a uniquely different set of plants. In comparison, domestic livestock -- bred to eat a lot and gain weight -- are lazy creatures that wander only far enough to eat and drink (or find shade or salt). Eating less selectively, they crop the plants nearest them (some say even past satisfying their own nutritional needs) beyond the plants' ability to replenish themselves. Livestock, cattle especially, concentrate in certain areas for long periods, denuding the same vegetation repeatedly in a single season. They "ambush" each new blade of grass, seedling, or leaf as it emerges or re-emerges. Eventually so little stored nutrients remain that plants cannot reach maturity, set seeds properly, or survive dormancy. The damaged plants suffer drought much more frequently because their shallow, weak roots are unable to extract sufficient moisture from the soil or compete with "weedy" species. Roots shrink to compensate for lost above-ground biomass and cause the plant to become stunted and unable to carry out essential processes; it finally dies.

Consider for example that on most grazing allotments livestock remove 40%-90% of the above-ground biomass of most herbaceous plants at least once each year. After this drastic depletion of biomass, most native range plants require at least several years to

Ungrazed roadside at right is lush with vegetation and organic litter; heavily grazed plot at center supports roughly 10% as much biomass; and very heavily grazed pasture at left is nearly barren. NM BLM.

recover full size and health. Yet livestock defoliate them relentlessly.

For livestock to simulate the beneficial influence of wildlife, they would have to roam freely and unmanaged on an unfenced open range -- an inherent impossibility. Livestock are not American "common property" like wildlife; an unnaturally large percentage of livestock are culled each year; and most cattle and sheep would die quickly on the open range without extensive human intervention.

Cattle and sheep are ecological misfits. What worked well with isolated, drifting herds and small groups of buffalo, pronghorn, bighorns, deer, and elk on the Great Plains and other Western rangelands has not worked at all with cattle and sheep, either on the Great Plains, other grasslands, or anywhere else. The West was properly stocked with the appropriate animals 200 years ago.

(Steve Johnson)

Roughly 10% of all the land in the West has reached a state of severe desertification, meaning it has virtually lost its ability to support life. . . .
Florence Williams, "The West's Time Capsules" (Williams 1990)

Though we are led to believe otherwise, desertification continues to expand rapidly throughout most of the Western United States. In a 1981 report, the Council on Environmental Quality concluded:

Improvident grazing, or overgrazing, as it has come to be known, has been the most potent desertification force, in terms of total acreage affected, within the United States.

According to the report, about 225 million acres, mainly in the West (an area the size of the 13 original colonies) was undergoing severe or very severe desertification, while a similar sized area was threatened by desertification. An accompanying map by Professor Harold Dregne of Texas Tech University showed that overgrazing has helped increase desert-like conditions on 80% of the West, and that 36.8% of North America's dry land has suffered "severe" desertification. The report further stated that these figures probably *underestimate* the severity of loss and deterioration of soils. (Sheridan 1981, CEQ 1981) When the Reagan administration took power, distribution of the report was

LIVESTOCK GRAZING STUDY

In this century thousands of scientific (and pseudo-scientific) studies have been conducted to determine the effects of livestock grazing on Western vegetation (see bibliography). I could not begin to detail even a small percentage of these, but suffice it to say that -- even though most were conducted by ranching-oriented range professionals -- the great majority show grazing detrimental to most native plant species under most conditions, usually in direct proportion to the overall intensity of grazing. I offer the study report outlined below, "Effects of Grazing on the Vegetation of the Blackbrush Association" by Douglas L. Jeffries and Jeffrey M. Klopatek, as generally representative of many others, and more relevant than most for it includes as one of its comparison study sites an area *never* grazed by livestock:

Four communities or sites dominated by blackbrush were studied in the Kaiparowits Basin of southern Utah and northern Arizona. One site had been heavily grazed yearlong for about 100 years; the second had had 10 years of recovery from 100 years of heavy cattle grazing; the third had been lightly to moderately grazed in winter for 3 years (a new stock tank had opened it to livestock, whereas it was lightly grazed previously); and the fourth was a relict, ungrazed ecosystem -- an inaccessible mesa top (therefore, due to dryer soil and other conditions, probably inherently a less biotically productive site). Using traditional scientific methods the researchers measured the cover of different types of vegetation. Here are the results, the numbers indicating relative herbage cover:

	Heavy grazing	Recovering	Light grazing	Ungrazed Relict
Shrub cover	1405	1372	2874	3645
Herbaceous cover	102	127	256	1047
Cryptogamic cover	70	50	1196	2129
Total cover	1576	1549	4326	6821

Jeffries and Klopatek summarized their findings: The data indicate that even light grazing may reduce the cryptogamic cover in this system, and heavy grazing almost completely eliminates it [30 times more in relict than heavily grazed]. This agrees with the findings of [many other researchers]. . . . Herbaceous vegetation cover was greatly reduced on the grazed sites as compared to the relict site [10 times less on heavily grazed than relict]. . . . The shrub cover is reduced by heavy grazing [over 2 1/2 times less on heavily grazed than relict]. . . . The relict site had significantly more total cover than all other sites [more than 4 times as much as heavily grazed], and the lightly grazed site had significantly more than the heavily grazed and recovery sites. (Jeffries 1987)

"stopped cold"; since 1982 the word "desertification" has not officially been used by the federal government in reference to US rangelands (Zaslowsky 1989).

Daniel Stiles of the United Nations Environment Programme writes, "The surest -- and perhaps only -- way to halt desertification is to stabilize human population and reduce livestock herd sizes."

Grazing and especially overgrazing [are] still so widespread on the public lands that many say it looks as if the cows are being trained to eat rocks. . . .
--Candace Crane, "In the Shadow of Livestock" (Crane 1989)

(Courtesy of Farm Animal Reform Movement)

All-too-typical desertified range. Vale District, BLM, OR. *(George Wuerthner)*

(Courtesy of Farm Animal Reform Movement.)

The Status of Desertification in the United States

Overgrazing has helped put about 10 percent of the land in the United States, all in the West, in a state of severe or very severe desertification, according to Harold Dregne, head of the International Center for Arid and Semi-Arid Land Studies at Texas Tech University. While the most severely desertified areas are in the Southwest, millions of acres of land to the north are also losing their productivity. Of all the activities that cause desertification, overgrazing is the most potent in this country, according to a 1981 report by the U.S. Council on Environmental Quality. Source: Harold Dregne, "Desertification of Arid Lands," Economic Geography 53(4):325 (1977)

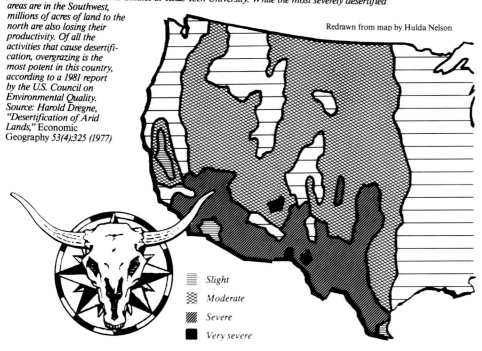

Redrawn from map by Hulda Nelson

Slight
Moderate
Severe
Very severe

Several decades after ranching was banned, 70,000-acre Fort Huachuca in southern Arizona can only be described as a plant wonderland -- one of the most botanically luxuriant and diverse areas in the Southwest. A short walk reveals scores of species and types of vegetation, many seldomly or never seen in nearby grazed areas.

Soil

. . . this nation and civilization is founded upon nine inches of topsoil and when that is gone there will no longer be any nation or any civilization.
--Dr. Hugh Bennett, US Soil Conservation Service

Soil is a collection of various-sized rock fragments, decaying organic matter, living organisms, atmospheric gases, and water solutions. Topsoil is the uppermost and generally most fertile soil horizon, and on the Western range is usually several inches thick.

Soil has been called "the soul of life itself." Without adequate and fertile soil, most terrestrial plant and animal life ceases. For over 100 years livestock grazing has been the major cause of both increased soil erosion and decreased soil fertility on Western public land. Most soil loss and damage is a result of livestock stripping off and trampling vegetation, though much loss and damage occurs even where vegetation remains intact.

As livestock injure and kill plants, fewer roots remain to hold soil particles together and masses of soil in place (some roots even excrete a substance that helps bind soil particles together). Consequently, surviving plants often are perched on little islands of self-protected soil/sod called *pedestals* (perhaps augmented by accumulated blowing particles captured by the plants). The scattered taproots of increasers and exotics and small, shallow roots of annual invaders do not hold the soil against the elements like the dense root masses of the natives they replace.

The soil's "living umbrella" of leaves and other plant matter is also depleted, and soil is bared to the elements -- raindrops, hail, wind, sunlight and other radiation, freeze and thaw, animal impact. Mechanically or chemically acted upon by these forces, broken apart by livestock hooves, loose soil particles succumb to gravity, or blow or wash away. (According to the US Soil Conservation Service, roughly 4/5 of US soil erosion is due to water and 1/5 to wind.)

Removal of protective vegetation and ground cover allows rain drops to hit the bare soil with great kinetic force, causing a physical displacement of soil particles termed "splash erosion." Damaged soil absorbs and retains less precipitation, leading to increases in both sheet erosion (displacement

Wind and water erosion on overgrazed slopes in the Tehachapi Mtns., CA. *(USGS)*

of a fairly uniform layer of soil by water runoff) and gully erosion (dislocation of soil due to trenching). For example, studies by Weltz and Wood showed suspended sediment production (representing eroded soil) 30%- 950% higher on pastures under several common grazing systems than on comparable pastures where livestock were excluded (Weltz 1986).

Livestock grazing or other vegetation destruction on steep slopes can even result in "massive downslope soil displacement," as demonstrated by this short story: Several years ago my 2 young children and I lived in a rural area of central Arizona. Our little homestead was nestled at the bottom of a river valley, accessed from

Eroding hills on BLM cattle range in Campbell County, northeast Wyoming.

On the far side of the fence, within the exclosure ungrazed for 40 years, this drainage is a low, wide swale with no banks, filled with grass and other small plants. Exactly at the fenceline, where it emerges into grazed range, it becomes a barren, eroded gully.

The topmost layer of soil is eroding as a broken crust from this grazed Arizona BLM range.

This expanding rim is actually the top soil layer eroding due to cattle trampling and removing protective vegetation.

above by a long dirt driveway. Not having been grazed by livestock for many years, the steep slope down which the driveway ran was well vegetated with bunchgrasses, flowering perennials, various shrubs, cacti, and many other plants.

One day the boys decided to play "slide down the hill on your butt." After an hour of this, a 5' x 10' strip had been denuded. When I found out about this, I told them that it "looked like a herd of cattle had stomped around there" and lectured them on the possible consequences. As if to prove

the point, after a rainy period a couple of weeks later that section of the hill slipped right off the underlying bedrock, leaving part of our driveway under a ton of mud and rocks. Massive downslope soil displacement is caused by livestock in many areas; it is common, for example, in the overgrazed central California hills.

Trails form as cattle walk along easy and well-traveled routes, alongside fences, around obstacles, and to and from

This 1977 windstorm removed 25 million tons -- as much as 12" -- of soil from 373 square miles of overgrazed range in south-central California. (Howard Wilshire)

Erosion of cattle trail along fence at right has removed up to 2' of soil.

Cattle trails on degraded NM BLM range.

food, water, salt, and shade. Depending on terrain, cattle trails can be anywhere from 1 to 5 or more feet wide. On slopes they often become gullies. Cattle may then create parallel new trails, which may join together with the old to form larger gullies, and so on. Probably several hundred thousand miles of cattle trails criss-cross Western public land and comprise a barren area of well over 100,000 acres. As well as causing environmental damage directly, cattle trails provide humans and vehicles (with their harmful influences) easier access to many areas by providing avenues of travel through thick vegetation.

Old cattle trails at center eroded a large chasm; new trails are rerouted to the left and right.

With their enormous weight and cloven hooves, standing cattle exert an average pressure of 24 pounds per square inch upon the soil's surface, and this pressure increases greatly when other feet are lifted and the animal is in motion (Ferguson 1983). This, their inbred awkwardness and decreased intelligence, and their unnatural impacts make cattle (and to a lesser extent sheep and goats) ideal soil destroyers, especially on the fragile soils and steep slopes common to the West. Their many areas of congregation exhibit especially degraded soil conditions. In contrast, wild animals travel carefully and lightly over the land (in part so as not to attract predators), avoid trampling individual plants, and rarely concentrate in one place for long.

Livestock cause extensive damage to the fragile soils of the Western range. *(Steve Johnson)*

Livestock physically alter the soil itself, setting into motion destructive ecological chain reactions. They upend and scatter small rocks that would otherwise stabilize soil, conserve water, promote plant growth, and provide habitat for small animals. They overturn large rocks and send them crashing down hillsides. They churn up the topmost soil while simultaneously compacting the under layer to create a "hardpan." Soil structure -- the arrangement of soil particles -- helps determine soil productivity, susceptibility to erosion, and other characteristics. Intensive grazing, of wet soils especially, can be particularly destructive because it compacts and destroys delicate soil structures that have usually taken decades to form. This reduces water infiltration, depletes groundwater supplies, and increases flooding and other detriments (see Water section in this chapter). Numerous studies show that livestock grazing under most conditions significantly compacts soil underlayers, decreases infiltration, and increases runoff (see Laycock 1967a, Orr 1975, Dadkhah 1980, Abdel-Magid 1987, and Stephenson 1987).

Compacted soils increase water loss through capillary action. Spaces between soil particles are reduced, and capillary action pulls more water more rapidly to the surface. The increased surface evaporation from soil water solutions may leave mineral crusts on soil surfaces that harm plant life. Organic wastes from livestock also add salts to the soil and exacerbate this mineralization problem.

Intensive or protracted livestock use breaks apart and scatters the protective inorganic, cryptogamic, and organic litter layers and exposes underlying soil. Churned up and scattered organic matter, no longer matted together or interlinked with the soil below, washes or blows away, further decreasing soil fertility. Remaining organic material then decomposes faster than it is replaced, with a net loss to the soil.

Through these and other influences, and through consumption and damage of a large percentage of the rangeland vegetation that would otherwise contribute to the organic litter layer, livestock reduce soil humus. *Humus*, partially decomposed organic matter incorporated into soil, is vitally important for maintaining proper soil pH, binding soil particles together, providing nutrients to plant roots and soil microorganisms, aerating soil, increasing soil moisture-holding capacity, and limiting the topmost soil's susceptibility to heat and frost.

Soil stripped of organic matter and ground cover, trampled, compacted, and bared to the sun and wind, dries out and cannot support original plant life. The resultant transition toward sparser, more desert-like vegetation is caused not only by an overall reduction in soil moisture but by greater *fluctuations* in soil moisture.

All these changes together kill off soil microorganisms -- bacteria, fungi, protozoa, algae, nematodes, etc. -- that would otherwise break down and recycle the chemical constituents of organic matter. Certain of these tiny organisms would also provide food for other small life, fix atmospheric nitrogen (alone or in conjunction with plant roots), form nitrates essential for plant growth, and even produce growth-stimulating substances necessary for vigorous plant growth. On healthy ranges microorganisms may occur by the billions in every cubic yard of soil; about 95% of them by weight live in the litter layer and top few inches of soil. No less important are the myriad other small soil creatures -- earthworms, mites, grubs, termites and other insects, etc. -- that would help infiltrate water; enrich, mix, and aerate soil; promote root penetration; and so on. As life-giving organic litter is depleted and topsoil is damaged and eroded, all these organisms decline.

The amount of organic material in the soil and the amount of organic litter also help determine the *color* of the soil and exposed ground surface. Livestock grazing's depletion of organic matter (sometimes in conjunction with increased mineralization, etc.) tends to cause the ground surface to lighten, intensifying reflected heat and glare (albedo), increasing aridity, killing soil microorganisms, and so forth. While darker ground may absorb more heat than lighter ground, the albedo effect, reduction of shade and protective organic cover, etc. of lighter colored grazed ground are together a much more potent aridifying influence.

Further, as livestock deplete low-level vegetation and the organic litter layer, they destroy the soil's protective, "shock absorbing" surface mat. Normally this mat functions to absorb and disperse the pressure from hooves as they thrust toward the soil and to physically shield the soil's surface from their abrasive action. When the mat is removed, pounding hooves hit the soil's surface with full force and compact subsurface layers, while their scuffling, scraping action tears apart and scatters the topmost soil.

By compacting the underlying soil, trampling also directly reduces soil aeration, slowing the flow of necessary oxygen to roots and soil organisms and of carbon dioxide back out to the soil surface. These exchange processes are imperative to a healthy biosystem, as is illustrated by the death of plants and soil organisms in waterlogged soil. Rainwater may accumulate on the surface of damaged soils,

compounding these problems and causing others, including again increased surface mineralization.

Between storms, plant roots tend to deplete moisture in the topmost layers of soil, thereby increasing the soil's capacity to absorb and infiltrate storm water that would otherwise run off. Some ranching proponents maintain that heavy grazing thus reduces drying of the topsoil by reducing root biomass. In truth, overgrazing's other environmental detriments are far greater soil-drying influences.

Continued livestock grazing causes a steady decline in the number and size of plants on the range, and a relatively even greater decline in the biomass of *dead* plants. Decomposing roots supply much soil humus, and humus to deeper soil that would otherwise lack organic matter. They feed termites and other soil-enhancing fauna and flora, provide channels for water infiltration, aerate the soil, give the seeds that settled into their empty holes favorable places to germinate, and create subterranean habitat for small creatures.

Most soil surfaces naturally contain many small pores that permit soil aeration and water infiltration. Vegetation provides a protective canopy that breaks the impact of rain on the ground, thereby retarding splash erosion and the clogging of these soil surface pores. By destroying this protective canopy, livestock allow the soil's surface to be "sealed," thus increasing runoff flooding and preventing aeration. When dry, this sealed soil surface becomes a hard crust which prevents seedlings from breaking though the soil's surface or their roots from penetrating to the soil below, which in turn further reduces vegetation cover.

Intact lower branches help trap organic matter that otherwise would wash or blow away, creating rows or piles of debris that serve important ecological functions. Livestock commonly break off and trample to pieces lower branches of trees and bushes.

Leaves, twigs, other fallen plant parts, and living plants themselves slow the velocity of low-level air flow and rainwater running over the soil's surface. This reduces wind erosion and allows water more time to infiltrate the soil and augment groundwater reservoirs. When livestock deplete vegetation and organic ground cover, few obstacles remain to slow wind and overland flow of water.

Similarly, as rainwater runs across the surface of the land it carries loose organic matter along with it. This debris accumulates against plants and other obstacles, forming low piles that act as small check dams to further slow runoff.

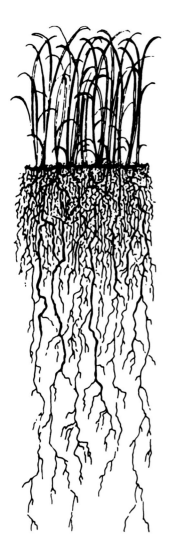

Later, they help build soil, conserve moisture, provide insect and small animal habitat, and so on. The loss of ground-level vegetation due to livestock grazing results in less organic debris, as well as more debris loss through flooding and erosion, leaving a greater percentage of exposed soil.

The above factors and others together may alter the soil's chemical and mineral composition, further decreasing fertility and once again affecting other interrelationships. Overgrazing-induced soil changes may also cause essential soil nutrients to be lost to the atmosphere as gaseous emissions. And in some areas increased runoff carries away nutrients important to plant growth (Schlesinger 1990).

According to ranching promoters, the manure left by livestock is an essential source of organic matter and soil fertility. What they invariably fail to mention is that *much more organic matter and nutrients are lost than returned*. The organic material left by livestock contributes many times less in organic weight and most soil nutrients than if it were left in herbaceous form. For example, less than 1/4 of the nitrogen consumed by range cattle is returned to the soil with manure (Hur 1985).

As livestock deplete vegetation and organic matter, they also retard soil formation. Less plant roots exist to break apart rock fragments. Decreased soil moisture impairs chemical and biological soil-forming processes. Reduced soil microorganisms mean slower breakdown of soil particles and less soil organic material.

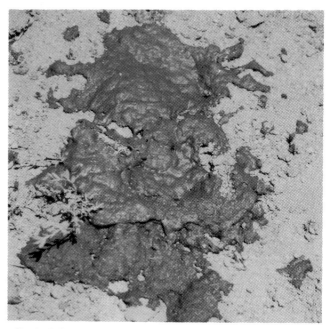

Cattle defecate about 12 times and 50 pounds per day. Their offerings vary greatly; due to disease, parasites, and other problems, many are liquid in form.

The luxuriant diversity of grasses and flowering plants in the livestock-ungrazed portion of Badlands National Park, SD, produces dark, moist, relatively fertile soil.

Cow flops, in contrast to nearly all other Western herbivore droppings, are produced moist (they are 85% water) and quickly lose ammonia (a gas containing nitrogen) to the atmosphere. In the arid to semi-arid conditions common to the overgrazed West, cowpies dry rapidly in the sun and heat up, killing the bacteria and fungi that would normally speed decomposition; they often remain intact for years. The large, flat, dry cowpie also kills the grass beneath it, whereas the fecal pellets of other dryland ungulates are smaller and roughly spherical. According to Paul Ehrlich's **The Machinery of Nature**, "Rather than tending to create a 'fecal pavement' as cattle droppings do, the pellets are readily broken down by decomposers, returning the nutients to the soil" (Ehrlich 1986).

As with all mammals, much of the biomass eaten by livestock is lost because it is converted to heat (a cow produces about 3500 Btu/hr) and motion by the animals' bodies. However, most livestock bodies themselves are taken from the range after a year or two, rather than being left there to die, decompose, and be recycled. Nutrients such as nitrates and phosphates are often already scarce in rangeland soils but, according to B.K. Watt and A.L. Merrill in "Composition of Foods," for each kilogram of choice grade beef from a whole carcass with bone (raw), 7.9 grams of nitrogen, 1.1 grams of phosphorus, and 0.55 grams of potassium (among other nutrients) are lost to grassland ecosystems.

Flat, wet cowpies tend to smother vegetation.

Wildlife pellets are easily scattered and provide more available nutrients.

In most natural situations the surface of soil is *uneven*, that is, there are numerous protrusions and concavities (they differ from soil pores discussed above). These irregularities come in many forms and sizes. Many result from plants pushing up and building small mounds of soil around their bases and thereby in effect creating depressions in the spaces between. Other irregularities are animal burrows, worm and insect holes, and footprints, scratchings, diggings, wallows, dirt baths, mineral and salt licks, and other effects of animal activity. Live roots often push up the soil's surface and dead ones cause it to subside. Cracks appear in drying soil. Cobblestone, pebblestone, organic litter, and soil lichen layers provide irregularity. Running water, hail, lightning, chemical action, falling tree branches, rolling

rocks -- many things can cause uneven soil surface. In addition, plants, rocks, branches, bones, and other objects are themselves a form of surface irregularity.

These irregularities serve important ecological functions. They slow water runoff and aid infiltration, help break ground-level wind, improve habitat for small animals, provide openings for seeds to enter the ground, and promote eco-diversity. In especially barren areas small depressions collect water, topsoil, and organic matter that would otherwise blow away, creating seedbeds for the seeds that also settle into them. These small mounds and ruts also function as "intakes" and "outlets" for water and air as part of the soil-air interface. During heavy rain, as water runs into depressions and sinks into the ground, displaced air within the soil moves to the tops of mounds and escapes into the atmosphere. Without protruding surface irregularities to release soil gases and equalize pressure, incoming water forms a uniform toplayer over these soil gases, decreasing infiltration while increasing runoff and soil erosion.

Though trampling by livestock may initially create an uneven soil surface, in the long run it has just the opposite effect. Soil structure collapses. Once the earth is stripped of vegetation and natural irregularities are reduced by trampling, then gravity, wind, and rain level the trampled dirt, usually within weeks or months. With fewer plants, animals, and healthy soil protective layers to form more *permanent* irregularities, soil simply flattens out over time, leaving the all-too-familiar "cowburnt" landscape. Extreme cases of overgrazing on clay soils have resulted in billiard table-flat and bare landscapes.

Some stockmen advocate intensive and frequent grazing, thinking that by maintaining a constantly disturbed soil surface they can offset the detrimental effects of heavy grazing. Scientific studies and actual grazing practice demonstrate that this simply does not work. Instead, the surface protrusions and concavities created by frequent livestock trampling are constantly destroyed and reformed, nullifying most of their potential benefits, while intensive grazing depletes vegetation, increases soil erosion, and all the rest.

When overgrazed soil loses its ability to support vegetation, vicious circles ensue; one aspect involves accelerated soil erosion. Unprotected from the elements, topsoil experiences higher and lower temperatures than before, and its surface is loosened by daily expansion and nightly contraction, especially during hard freezes. This loosened soil is much more susceptible to wind and water erosion, and on steep gradients this topsoil seems to "melt off" in a rain. Beneath the soil surface, less organic matter and roots exist to form small air pockets and buffer underlying soil from temperature extremes, causing soil organisms to die and soil structure to decline. When root systems shrink or die, they provide fewer pathways for water infiltration, increasing runoff and erosion, baring more dirt. Hotter topsoil increases evaporation, which increases upward water movement via capillary action, which then increases evaporation.

More radical temperature fluctuations adversely affect surviving plants and animals. For example, denuded, sunbaked soil may become hot enough to "scorch" or stunt seedlings, vines, and other sensitive ground-level vegetattion. More extreme soil temperatures kill or drive off moles, earthworms, termites, insect larvae, and other soil creatures that would have served to mix and aerate soil, aid water infiltration, and break down organic matter for use by plants. Roots in the upper soil are likewise more susceptible to injury from temperature extremes. In most plants, roughly half of the "action" occurs below ground, and in many as much as half their overall weight is roots.

Topsoil humus helps to physically retain water, so less organic matter means less soil moisture. Less humus in the soil also means less space between soil particles, leading again to increased upward water capillary action, more evaporation, and drier soil. Dry soil is affected by the various forces of chemical decomposition at different rates than previously, causing detrimental changes in soil nutrient content and availability and negatively affecting dependent plants and animals. The resulting decrease in numbers of, say, burrowing animals leads to reduced water infiltration and organic matter to lower soil levels, causing plant roots to concentrate nearer the surface. Plant life, now stunted and more susceptible to drought, dies back, and soil erosion further intensifies.

This leads inexorably to other effects, which in turn lead to still others . . . *ad infinitum*. Government statistics and grazing industry disseminations obscure the seriousness of the problem.

Severe grazing and erosion in central California hills. *(Howard Wilshire)*

On July 21, 1915, when both areas [study areas in Utah's Manti National Forest] *had been protected from grazing since August, 1914, a heavy rainstorm occurred in which area B received approximately twice as much precipitation as area A; but only about one-twelfth as much run-off and one-ninth as much erosion was recorded from area B as from area A. On August 5, 1916, area B was grazed closely by sheep, area A being at that time ungrazed. Late in the day of August 5, a rainstorm occurred in which both of the selected areas received an average of 0.25 of an inch of rain. Practically the same amount of run-off was recorded from the two areas, and the erosion from area B was one- half that from area A. . . .*

Since grazing was the only factor changed as compared with all previous records, it appears safe to conclude that the change in the ratios of run-off and erosion showing a marked increase in erosion on area B was due to grazing.

--A.W. Sampson, "Range Preservation and Its Relation to Erosion Control on Western Grazing Lands" (Sampson 1918)

The overall rate of topsoil erosion on public land may have, as claimed, decreased over most of the West since the initial grazing mania of yesteryear. This is largely because the most susceptible topsoil eroded first. But topsoil erosion is still extreme, even by the government's own reckoning, and especially so considering that the US Soil Conservation Service (SCS) estimates that *less than half the West's original rangeland topsoil remains*. In other words, there is now less than half as much topsoil to erode *from*. It's like the difference between losing $1 when you have $6 compared to losing $0.75 when you have only $3.

A similar critical factor often overlooked is that erosion removes the most productive soil first. Generally, the closer to the ground's surface soil is, the more available nutrients, organic material, and living things it contains. The top few inches of soil contain the vast bulk of organic matter and much more available nutrients and living things than do layers below. Losing the topmost few inches of soil to erosion is like losing many inches of soil below it. After the best soil is depleted, soil erosion may continue at a high rate even without continued livestock grazing. Since the most fertile soil generally occurs in conjunction with and is produced by thick grass and herbaceous plants -- and these are the very plants most sought out and consumed by livestock -- the best soil has been the most abused, eroded, and prevented from regenerating. Livestock are like roving topsoil terminators!

Also, though the rate of soil erosion by weight per acre is generally higher in the East than West, and higher on farmland than on rangeland, there are several reasons why soil erosion is even more of a problem in the West than in the East. First, the East -- especially Eastern farmland, where soil erosion rates are the highest in the US (largely due to higher rainfall) -- has far more soil to lose. Even if it lost many times more soil than it already has, it would still be in generally better shape soil-wise than the West. For example, according to SCS, "Unlike cropland, which can bear an annual soil loss of up to 5 tons per acre, the more fragile rangeland soils can tolerate an erosion rate of no more than 2 tons per acre" (USDA, SCS 1981). The West, its public land in particular, is so thinly covered with soil that much of it is already down to sand, gravel, or bedrock. Additionally, since in most plants roughly half the "action" occurs below ground, the reduction in the actual *volume* of soil leaves less room for roots, thus limiting the size, species, and type of plants.

Second, because of all this, soil erosion on Western public land has a relatively greater impact on native wildlife*, community watersheds, recreational values, and the like. Third, soil is generally *created* much faster in the East than West -- perhaps an average of 2 or 3 times faster. Fourth, there is more than twice as much non-arable grazing land as there is cropland in the United States. In the West, 525 million acres are grazed, compared to only 66 million acres farmed (mostly for livestock feed) -- 8 times more rangeland than cropland (US Dept. of Com. 1986). And fifth, grazing land produces scores of times less food value per acre than does cropland, so grazing's "justification factor" is vastly lower. (All of this is in no way intended to belittle the serious soil erosion problem in the East.)

* "Wildlife" in this book may refer to native animals *and* plants.

Non-arable grazing land suffers even more acutely from soil erosion and degradation than cropland does. . . . Over 2/3 of the nation's non-arable grazing land is sparsely vegetated Western rangeland. Little of the remaining 1/3 has an extensive vegetational cover. Rangeland receives almost no fertilizer or irrigation water to enhance its vegetational cover. So, when cattle denude it of over 50% of its vegetation -- and many cattlemen allow their animals to consume 80%-90% -- the land becomes virtually defenseless against erosion.
--Robin Hur, "Six Inches from Starvation" (Hur 1985)

In the US, Nature creates topsoil at an average rate of roughly 1 inch per 100 years, or 1 1/2 tons/acre/year. Under ideal conditions (in warm, humid grassland for example), the rate may be as high as 1 inch per 30 years (5 tons/acre/year), while under poor conditions (most Western rangeland for example), it may take several hundred years or more to produce an inch of topsoil (less than 1/2 ton/acre/year). (Pimentel 1976)

On healthy forest and range, soil erosion is minimal -- usually less than 1 ton/acre/year -- and for millions of years soil creation and erosion generally kept an equilibrium. But now SCS reports an average US topsoil erosion rate of 4.2 tons/acre/year for grazed forest and 3.1 tons/acre/year for grazed rangeland. (USDA, SCS 1981) Considering that Western grazing land is generally the least productive top-soil producer in the US and is already heavily damaged, it is safe to assume that most of the Western range is producing topsoil at far less than 1 ton/acre/year. In other words, Western rangeland is losing topsoil, mostly due to ranching, at least 4 to 5 times faster than it's being replaced. This is a conservative estimate; reports by food production expert David Pimental suggest that range soil is actually eroding roughly 20 times faster than it is being replaced.

Additionally, the subsoil in some parts of the West is prehistoric; that is, it developed in large quantities thousands of years ago during long periods of humid climate and abundant vegetation. Likewise, the deep aboriginal soil in many Western valleys is the result of thousands of years of silt deposition by natural floodwaters. These deep ancient soils are vitally important to many ecosystems. When this "reservoir" of soil is depleted, it cannot be replaced until the climate changes again.

1. The soil levels indicated by alluvium remnants in thousands of canyons in southeastern Utah represent what the canyons looked like barely a century ago. All the cutting and soil removal has taken place since the relatively recent pioneer occupation of the region. 2. One century of domestic livestock grazing in southeastern Utah has largely destroyed 4,000 years of natural soil-building alluviation in the region.
--F.A. Barnes, naturalist and author, *High Country News* (2-29-88)

Gully erosion on cattle range.

Sediment loosened by livestock is carried steadily downward away from its origin.

A fenceline demonstrates how potent livestock grazing is as a cause of soil erosion. The right side of the fence has been very heavily grazed by cattle for many years, the left side "only" heavily grazed (it too has lost much topsoil). Note lush vegetation on fenced roadside in foreground. BLM/state land, Grant Co., NM.

In a fine example of livestock industry misinformation, an article in *American Cattle Grower* stated that increased soil displacement caused by cattle actually *benefits* the West by leveling out uneven terrain and depositing eroded sediments in lowland areas, thereby creating more usable flatland! (Ferguson 1983) As if things aren't bad enough, how many stockmen are out there actually *trying* to increase soil erosion!?

Experts estimate that in the past 200 years human activities have depleted **75%** of US topsoil, about **85%** of this to the feet of grazing livestock or to the production of livestock feed. This loss represents a steady decline in environmental potential with each passing year. In the US only farming, which *intentionally* manipulates soil, outranks grazing as a cause of soil erosion and damage. Ever since Europeans arrived, in most of the West livestock grazing has been the major cause of soil displacement, loss, and damage. Even the BLM states that 40% of its land is seriously eroded (likely an ultraconservative estimate). (Ferguson 1983) More than 5 billion tons of US topsoil erode each year, and half a billion tons blow and flow off public land, mostly due to ranching (Akers 1983; USDA, SCS 1981). In sacrificing 41% of the West thusly, the public receives an insignificant 3% of national cattle and sheep production.

What this all adds up to is bad news for public land. There is less soil now than for millennia past, and this loss is compounded by soil degradation. Some desert areas are now only *1/10* as productive for livestock as they were when stockmen arrived in the West (Sheridan 1981). Even the most well-watered Western rangelands have lost large percentages of topsoil and soil fertility to livestock grazing.

The damage that began in the 1800s, and which continues to this day, has so changed the land that it should not be called grazing, but mining. Over vast areas of the West, the soil is gone. Viewed in the human scale by which we measure civilizations, such soil has become a non-renewable resource. It has been mined.

--Steve Johnson, SW Rep., Defenders of Wildlife (Johnson 1985a)

(Ginny Rosenberg)

Ranchers dump junk into gullies to help stem erosion.

Ranching's geologic impact goes beyond soil, however. Soil is mostly decomposed rock. In the long run rock is not static and dead, but an inextricable part of life on Earth. Substantial evidence suggests that though rock life seems motionless on the human scale (avalanches, earthquakes, and volcanos excepted), over the millennia rocks exhibit many of life's properties, even a certain consciousness. If geologic processes were sped up millions of times, we could see rocks being created, changing, interacting with their environment, "dying," and reforming, all with a pattern and sense of purpose similar to biologic lifeforms.

Though modern humans may not understand, many of their activities are altering these geologic processes, to the short- and long-term harm of other environmental components. For example, by decreasing soil formation and increasing erosive flooding, livestock grazing has reduced or removed much of the fine-particled alluvial soil (bottomland) from most Western floodplains. Some of this soil would have eventually been deeply buried and over eons turned into fine-grained sedimentary rock. But where it has been replaced by sand, gravel, and rocks, sandstone and sedimentary conglomerates will form instead. Because these two classes of rock possess differing properties, when they finally reappear at the Earth's surface they will have differing effects on the biosphere and character of the land. Finer-grained sedimentary rock usually provides a more fertile parent material for new soil, for example.

These possible scenarios are of course speculative, but it is certain that the great changes wrought by livestock grazing on Western soil formation, erosion, deposition, composition, mineral content, and so forth over time represent a substantial influence on the inorganic Earth, and thus the organic Earth. Our actions today will affect the condition of the planet far into the future.

The soil of the Western range is being treated like dirt. Cattle exclosure on far side of fence.

Water

Along with vegetation and soil, livestock grazing has severely affected what many people call the West's most essential element -- water. Water quality has suffered greatly, but more serious harm has been done to the *amount* of water absorbed, retained, and released slowly as surface flow.

This vast reduction in "the water supply" has been brought about mainly in 2 ways -- (1) degradation of watersheds and (2) damage to waterways and associated riparian areas. Most important from a strictly quantitative standpoint are the watersheds.

Watersheds

Livestock grazing operations have severely damaged or destroyed more pristine watersheds in the West than all other uses of the land combined.
--Edwin G. Dimick, **Livestock Pillage of Our Western Public Lands**

This here crick used to run, but it don't no more.
--Rangeland old-timer

To understand how watersheds affect surface water quantity, it is first necessary to understand the basic underground water system, which contains more than 99% of all unfrozen fresh water and is the source of most surface water. As water percolates down through soil layers, it enters permeable water-bearing strata of rock, gravel, or sand called *aquifers*. Some aquifers retain water in one place for long periods. But most aquifer water flows slowly diagonally downward roughly parallel to the slope of the land, eventually to appear as base flow for springs, streams, ponds, or lakes. Other aquifer water joins the large underground reservoirs of lowlands, where it may give rise to meadows or marshes, water deep-rooted plants, keep subsoil moist during dry seasons, and so on.

The *water table* of any area is the depth below which the ground is saturated with water. Water table levels depend on the amount of water absorbed into the soil and the amount of water allowed to escape back out through surface flow and/or evaporation. Nearly every place on Earth has ground water at some level below the surface.

A *watershed* is a particular area that drains into a creek, river, lake, other waterway or dry channel -- in other words, a drainage area. On a topographical map a typical watershed resembles the twigs, branches, and trunk of a tree, the trunk being the main drainage.

The three-dimensional watershed can be imagined as a funnel made from very thick, absorbent material. As sprinkled water hits the funnel's surface, most of it is absorbed quickly into the porous material and carried slowly downslope toward the neck of the funnel and gradually down the spout. Little water actually flows along the surface

unless the sprinkle turns into a lengthy downpour. After the sprinkling stops, by far most of the water is retained within the absorbent material itself; gravity works it slowly toward the spout, while capillary action brings a lesser amount to the surface to evaporate. In watersheds, water that does flow

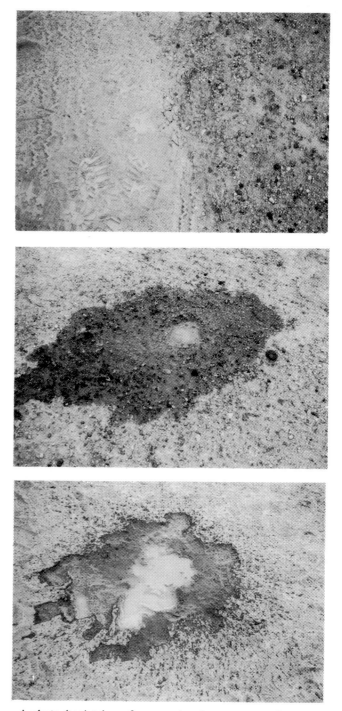

A photo (top) taken after a weekend camp-out on the range shows trampled dirt on left and undisturbed dirt on right. A quart of water poured onto the undisturbed ground had infiltrated into the soil several seconds later when the middle photo was taken. A quart poured onto the trampled ground was still largely puddled several seconds later when the bottom photo was taken; on sloping terrain, this water would have run off. Note soil displacement from splash erosion in bottom photo; on sloping terrain, much of this soil would join runoff.

along the surface and in waterways is slowed and infiltrated by organic litter, accumulated debris, fallen trees and branches, and living plants. Additional moisture is stored within all organic matter itself, and the soil's cover of dead plant material minimizes evaporation from the surface.

Livestock grazing is like throwing a sheet of plastic over a watershed. Organic matter that formerly slowed surface flow, stored moisture, and checked evaporation is eliminated. Studies show that depleted, damaged vegetation is less able to reduce runoff, shelter moist soil and snow from sun and wind, trap blowing snow, and in general preserve moisture. By damaging vegetation, drainages, soil protective layers, and the soil itself, livestock have destroyed the "sponge" that before soaked up and stored most of the West's precipitation.

Livestock damage watersheds, causing more runoff and flash floods. *(Bob Dixon)*

Thus, water that previously infiltrated into groundwater supplies to be released slowly as surface water throughout the year now runs quickly off watersheds, into and through waterways, and eventually into the oceans. As a result, the West's water storage capability has been tremendously reduced. Most watersheds have been rendered less productive, thousands of them greatly so.

We know that 150 years ago the area's [southeastern Arizona's] *streams were all perennial, and the only thing that has caused the change is the destruction of the watershed by grazing.*
--Grassland ecologist Carl Bock (Crane 1989)

When stockmen seized the West and livestock numbers skyrocketed in the late 1800s, water tables immediately began dropping in most grazed areas. Steadily since then *many thousands* of surface waters have vanished -- a greater relative percentage of them, of course, in drier areas where they were most needed. Thousands more now flow only intermittently, and so has every Western river been reduced in flow. All this is at the expense of environmental quality and agricultural, industrial, municipal, hydroelectric, recreational, and other human use.

Again, there has been **no** overall drying trend in Western climate during the past century to bring about these changes (see Air section of this chapter). While other factors -- notably groundwater pumping for agriculture (mostly for livestock production) and urban growth, irresponsible logging and mining activity -- have depleted Western water, by far the major force exhausting Western water sources has been and remains livestock grazing.

In 1600 B.C., Emperor Yu of China said, "To protect your rivers, protect your mountains." In the Western US, nearly all of the major waterways and 3/4 of the water supply for humans originates in National Forests -- generally the highest elevation lands in the West. But the grazing industry has not appreciated the importance of protecting these watersheds. To the contrary, ranchers manage most of these areas as livestock pastures, and some misguided or crafty stockmen actually promote heavy grazing in mountains, alleging that stripping off the ground cover will increase

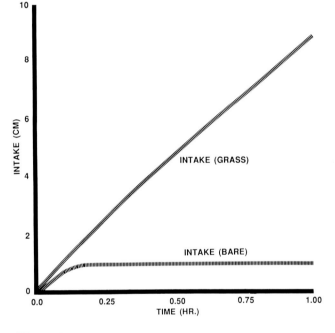

Water infiltration at Santa Rita Experimental Range, Arizona, 1975. According to soil scientist Bob Dixon, "Grazing down to bare ground reduces infiltration to just 1/10 of what it was with a grass cover."
(Source: Dixon 1978)

runoff to lower elevations, thereby increasing water available for human use.

In the 1930s, Trout Creek on the eastern slope of the Colorado Rockies disappeared. When I first saw it in 1937, a widening network of gullies fed into a dry streambed. On a return trip to the watershed in 1974, I noticed a striking difference: vegetation was filling the gullies, beaver dams stretched across a beautiful clear stream. What had happened? In the main, the Forest Service had removed several bands of domestic sheep that grazed the watershed.
--Noel Rosetta, "Herds, Herds on the Range" (Rosetta 1985)

Surface Waters

This awkward attempt to compare the value of healthy flowing streams alive with native trout and all their food chain, the welcome shade of the over-bending willow, and the smile of the buttercup; the scarlet gilia yielding under the soft foot of a furtive mule deer -- with the bawl of an auction-bound steer, shows what stratagems a land manager must adopt to justify restoring our native heritage.

--Janet O'Crowley, Chair, Board of Directors, Committee for Idaho's High Desert

A spring on BLM land in the mountains of White Pine County, north-central Nevada. How would you like a drink of the water?

As mentioned, livestock congregate around water, generally in greater concentrations, more frequently, and for longer periods than did native herbivores. Their excessive grazing and incessant trampling turn many riversides, creeks, springs, lakesides, marshes, wet meadows, sinkholes, bogs, bottoms, and otherwise moist areas into veritable quagmires. Ponds and small lakes are particularly susceptible, in large part because they usually have little flow to replenish them and dilute water-borne sediments, urine and manure.

Recently I visited Indian Spring southwest of Mono Lake. The willows had been trampled nearly to oblivion, and the spring itself was a muddy morass of hoof prints.

--The late David Gaines, Mono Lake Committee, Lee Vining, CA

Throughout the West livestock hooves annually churn springs, seeps, and other wet areas into mush, over time causing subsurface changes that physically block outflows. In many cases, trampling spreads water thinly into multitudes of hoof holes, dissipating flow and allowing water to become stagnant, reducing its availability and presenting health hazards to native animals.

Livestock's destruction of plant life around springs reduces or halts springflow. In a natural situation, plants help shelter springs, clean the water, and enrich, stabilize, and mechanically build up finely particled soil; through capillary action the plants draw underground water higher in relation to the levels of surrounding areas and increase outflows. Roots provide channels for water to rise to the surface. Unfortunately, vegetation around springs is typically eaten to nubs by livestock, beaten down and largely destroyed. Roots are mashed or scraped from the ground. Soil is often damaged and badly eroded, reducing plant biomass and lowering water retention capacities. Most livestock-impacted wet areas are trampled, barren mud, baked by the sun, and often highly mineralized.

Thus, in these ways, and especially through lowered water tables, over the years tens of thousands of Western springs have been depleted or eliminated. Although in most cases it is nearly impossible to conclusively document decades of livestock grazing as the cause, circumstantial evidence is overwhelming; indeed, livestock grazing has been the only significant human influence where most of these changes have occurred.

Cattle-ravaged warm spring in Nevada.

Unlike any other large native ungulates in the West, cattle stay around water indefinitely, or until the depletion of herbage forces them elsewhere. *(Bottom photo courtesy of Farm Animal Reform Movement)*

Tonto Creek was timbered with the local creek bottom type of timber from bluff to bluff, the water seeped rather than flowed down through a series of sloughs and fish over a foot in length could be caught with little trouble. Today this same creek bottom is little more than a gravel bar from bluff to bluff. The old trees are gone. Some were cut for fuel, many others were cut for cattle during droughts and for winter feed, and many were washed away during the floods that rushed down the stream nearly every year since the range started to deplete. The same condition applies to practically every stream in the Tonto.
--Fred Croxen, Senior Forest Ranger, Tonto National Forest, AZ, 1926 (Chaney 1990)

Livestock grazing's impact on Western creeks and streams is similarly overwhelming. As cattle walk along streamsides they cave in and disintegrate banks and kill the plants that formerly stabilized them (the banks, not the cattle!). Cattle also commonly lie on cool, moist banks and mash them down, killing vegetation. As they plod about in water, eating, drinking, and keeping cool, they kill aquatic vegetation that anchors streambeds. These and the other livestock impacts discussed below make streams wider and shallower. Grazed streams, where they still exist, are commonly 2 or 3 times as wide and 1/2 to 1/3 as deep as comparable ungrazed streams. For example, a study on Montana's Rock Creek found channel erosion 2 1/2 times greater on grazed portions than on an ungrazed portion

Small creek on BLM land near Cannonville, UT.

(Marcuson 1977). The resulting larger water surface area exposed to the sun and shallower water cause stream temperatures to rise.

As water warms, its oxygen and carbon dioxide-carrying capacities diminish, adversely affecting aquatic animals. An increase in water temperature of only 5 or 10 degrees can eliminate some species, fish particularly. Summer temperatures of many Western streams have been raised 10 degrees or more by livestock grazing, and now instead of 60s they often exceed 80 degrees F. Cold water fish such as trout are gradually replaced by "rough fish" such as carp (an exotic), suckers, dace, chubs, and squawfish that can tolerate higher water temperatures and lower oxygen levels (though this is not to say that livestock grazing has not also ravaged warm water fish).

LaBarge Creek, Bridger-Teton NF, WY, is stripped of vegetation, trampled, depleted, wide, shallow, warm, sediment-laden, and polluted -- all due to cattle grazing. *(George Wuerthner)*

Relatively few springs in the rangeland West are fenced from livestock; these are, but the fences are obtrusive, hard to maintain, cost the taxpayer, harm wildlife, and drive cattle out onto the more fragile surrounding range. *(George Wuerthner)*

This former lushly vegetated bog is now a cattle quagmire. BLM, NV.

Higher water temperatures, along with copious livestock manure and urine, sometimes cause severe algal blooms, which give water that "pea soup" appearance common to Western creeks these days. The oversupply of nutrients in warm water causes algal populations to peak; the algae die and their decomposition uses up virtually all dissolved oxygen. This sometimes causes tremendous die-offs of fish and other aquatic animals. In addition, higher water temperatures cause changes in the type and amount of aquatic vegetation, likewise harming ecosystem dynamics.

Rising water temperatures and widened channels also increase water loss through evaporation. As livestock have doubled or tripled the width of streams, so have they doubled or tripled water surface exposed to air. Similarly, because vegetation on the surface of the water and overhanging streams has been depleted, more water surface is exposed to sunlight and wind, further increasing evaporation. In turn, depleted water volume caused by this and other livestock influences means increased salinity, turbidity, and concentrations of pollutants.

When cattle stomp around in wet areas, their hooves often sink deeply into the mud, sometimes a foot or more. This displaces or kills numerous mud-dwelling creatures, many in hibernation, as well as insects in pupal and larval stages. This subsurface zoological community is generally more diverse and complex than either the watery or terrestrial communities above it, yet its demise goes unnoticed. Aquatic plants, trampled and left to rot in waterways or along banks, slowly decay and release their nutrients into the water, augmenting eutrophication and aggravating algal bloom. Water-filled hoof ruts at waterside become stagnant and putrid, increasing the possibility of disease.

As cattle stomp and shuffle through the water, they also displace rocks on stream and lake bottoms. These rocks, until displaced, offer shelter to many different small animals, places to birth and rear young, feeding spots, and hibernation sites. Without them many small invertebrates -- various worms, insect larvae, fresh water clams, snails, etc. -- do not survive. Silt and organic matter also settle around rock bases, securing them to stream or lake beds and promoting plant growth. This vegetation, in turn, stabilizes these sediments and filters out other water-borne sediments. The plants and animals killed also add to water pollution.

By displacing rocks and stirring up stream bottoms, livestock release large amounts of sediment into the water, further increasing turbidity. This reduces light penetration, in turn reducing aquatic plant photosynthesis, which further reduces dissolved oxygen levels. Additionally, these water-borne sediments harm or kill aquatic animals and plants.

Most natural streams are an alternating succession of riffles and pools. The rapids are vital to water aeration, which is necessary for water purification and to provide oxygen to aquatic fauna. A high rate of aeration is a function of both high turbulence and rapid water speed, both factors in effect increasing surface area exposed to the air. The cascading of rapids helps cool water, further increasing water's oxygen-absorbing ability. Rapids also fulfill the habitat needs of many animals, including limpets, caddis fly larvae, various rock suckers, darters, and trout. And functioning as check-dams, the high points under rapids slow floodwaters.

Oak Creek, Arizona. A deep pool teeming with aquatic life (and some terrestrial life) (left) and cascading rapid just downstream (right) indicate a healthy, little-grazed watershed and waterway.

Pools are likewise vital to healthy waterways, in large part because they contain such great *volumes* of water in relation to their surface areas. Pools embrace a different set and greater abundance of animal inhabitants, including sunfish, catfish, minnows, crayfish, fresh water shrimp, many insects and insect larvae, frogs, turtles, muskrats, beaver, and many more. In the still water of pools, fine-particled sediments, instead of being washed away, sink to the bottoms, as does decomposing organic debris, where they combine to create extremely productive subsurface habitats -- so productive, in fact, that some bottom muds contain more organic than inorganic material! Pools, as "speed dips," also team up with rapids ("speed bumps") to decrease the erosive power of floods. Additionally, being deep and slow-flowing, pools release a constant flow of cooling water slowly into streams.

In livestock-trodden streams, large-particled sediments, sand, and gravel from crumbling banks and sediments washed down from degraded watersheds settle into holes where the currents are less forceful. The reduction of deep holes diminishes volume and quality of habitat. Without deep holes, floodwaters flow even faster and level out rapids. This in turn causes floodwater speeds to increase further, causing more cut-and-fill, tearing out aquatic and streamside vegetation, killing wildlife, and so on. Doubling the velocity of streamflow quadruples its erosive power and gives it 64 times more bed-load and sediment carrying power (Chaney 1990). The end result to thousands of Western waterways has been wide, flat, barren, sun-baked, wind-blown, gravel-filled, scoured, flood-ravaged channels.

Increased quantities of water-borne sediments may also augment the amounts of dissolved minerals and change water pH. Changes in either of these factors can have deleterious effects on aquatic life.

Heavy sediment loads bury spawning gravels, fish eggs and embryos, and the essential foods of many fish. These effects (along with the aforementioned) have reduced or extirpated native trout, salmon, and other native fish around the West.

Water-borne sediments (along with livestock manure and urine) flow down degraded tributaries and enter ponds, lakes, and reservoirs, impairing their ecological health and limiting their lifetimes. They are likewise dumped into oceans, where they interfere with marine processes, harm sealife, and even dirty the sand on beaches. In winter sediment deposits loosed by livestock sometimes restrict stream and river channels, resulting in ice buildups and related problems.

In 1885 Terlingua Creek in southwest Texas was, according to the first homesteader in the area, ". .. a bold running stream, studded with cottonwood and alive with beaver." Today, it is wide, braided, and barely runs most of the year. There are few cottonwoods and no beaver. A century of livestock grazing was the only major variable in the watershed and drainage. *(George Wuerthner)*

Heavy sheep grazing in the Boise Mountains caused the flood damage and excessive sediment load seen here. Boise NF, ID. *(George Wuerthner)*

The role of aqueous and streamside vegetation in maintaining healthy waterways is too seldom acknowledged. Nevertheless, such vegetation is essential for many reasons.

Under natural conditions most lowland streams are deep and meander slowly in serpentine curves through dense stands of aquatic plants such as watercress, grasses, sedges, reeds, and cattail. This vegetation helps spread water out over bottoms of drainages, creating small pools and marshy areas. It maintains high water levels, shades and cools water, and provides important aquatic habitat, including large underwater areas hidden from predators. Livestock destroy this vegetation.

Aquatic plants filter out water-borne sediments, and also capture and break down nutrients and pollutants. Studies show that healthy aquatic plant systems filter out even extremely tiny particles -- a process important to water quality and natural functions. (Blum 1986).

Sediments trapped by plants on stream bottoms, for example, stabilize the bottoms and provide nutrients for growth. As these sediments build up slowly in the base of the vegetative mat, the plants grow taller at approximately the same rate. Even when buried suddenly under a thick layer of sediment, they have an amazing capacity to regrow quickly to their normal stature, ready to repeat the process. In this way, stream channels gradually rise and in turn raise water tables.

When livestock eat and trample aquatic plants, this process is reversed. Sediments are released into water, streambed stability declines, unprotected stream channels are cut by increased flooding, water tables drop, and so on. Water plants and streamside vegetation also serve the important function of slowing water. They minimize hydraulic action, especially at the water line, protecting streambanks from erosion and affording healthy habitat for plants and animals. Generally, sedges and grasses provide the best streambank protection; unfortunately, these are the plants most avidly consumed by cattle.

Aquatic plants produce oxygen and release it into the water, augmenting that taken through surface absorption, largely from rapids. As livestock kill this vegetation, the water's oxygen content is reduced accordingly, affecting water purity, aquatic animals, and even aquatic plants. Because small lakes and ponds, having very slow water movement and no rapids, are comparatively deficient in oxygen, aquatic plant life here is especially important as a source of oxygen.

When trees, branches, and other vegetative debris fall or wash into waterways, they provide many benefits to aquatic systems. This organic matter serves as food for midges, mayflies, snails, and crayfish, which then serve as food for fish, raccoons, birds, and so on. Much of the vegetative debris sinks to the bottom, where it enriches bottom muds and feeds aquatic organisms therein. Logs, branches, and accumulated organic matter in water provide cover and homes for numerous aquatic animals. A 1978 Oregon study by Swanson *et al.* found that large fallen trees provided 50% of fish habitat in small to medium-sized streams (Wuerthner 1989). Floating and above-water portions of logs and branches provide basking, perching, and foraging sites for turtles, various mammals, amphibians, birds, and insects.

Boulders, log jams, single logs, and/or accumulated debris often function as check dams to slow floodwaters. These obstructions block flowing water, causing eddies and backwaters -- important resting and nesting places for fish and other animals. Water cascading over these check dams digs pools into streambeds. These pools become

Denuded, trampled stream channels harm surface waters. BLM land in Utah. *(BLM)*

especially important to fish and other aqueous life during periods of low water. The cascading water is aerated and purified. Water above the dams is raised, increasing stream volume, creating more aquatic habitat, trapping sediments, lowering water temperature, and so on.

When washed into a river, old dead snags like this play a crucial role in stream ecology. Yet, in many areas of the West, such large trees are becoming a rarity due to livestock, which prevent regeneration and cause destruction by flooding. *(George Wuerthner)*

Look out! -- here come the cows again. By destroying riparian trees and other vegetation, they reduce the amount of vegetation that ends up in water. Sloshing through streams, they break apart and scatter logs, branches, and debris and destroy check dams. And by damaging watersheds, riparian zones, and waterways -- thereby increasing erosive flooding -- they cause waterways to be scoured of vegetation and check dams.

Streamside trees, willows, vines, berry bushes, cane, cattail, rushes, sedges, mints, grasses, and other moisture-loving plants provide habitat critical to a huge number and variety of animals. Many of the smaller animals -- beetles, ants, spiders, worms, flies, butterflies, moths, mosquitos, and so forth -- eventually fall into the water from overhanging vegetation, along with plant parts, to become food for fish and other aquatic animals (and to provide nutrients for plants). Researchers estimate that up to 99% of instream nutrients that produce the aquatic food web come from adjacent streamside plants (Blum 1986). Studies by William

Platts and Rodger Nelson on Big Creek in northeastern Utah showed streamside vegetation overhang averaged 10 times greater in the protected portion than in the grazed portion of the stream, with 2 of the grazed study sites having no overhang at all (Platts 1989a).

Vegetation overhanging bodies of water not only provides food and shade to wildlife, but also moderates air temperature. Cooler summer and warmer winter temperatures benefit the entire ecosystem. Overhanging vegetation and plants on the water's surface insulate the water below from ice-forming cold, and thus protect it from damage due to expanding ice and melting, scouring ice. When livestock reduce streamside vegetation, stream banks are likewise more susceptible to frost. Repeated freezing and thawing of the soil composing stream banks causes it to be loosened, pushed outward, and dropped into streams, which widens channels and increases sediment pollution (Bohn 1989). Waterside vegetation also slows winds that blow across the water's surface, thus limiting evaporation.

Streambanks stripped of protective vegetation experience increased freeze and thaw; soil loosens, pushes outward, and crumbles into channels.

The extensive overhanging and submerged root tangles of natural streamside vegetation generally protect banks from erosion better than does wire and rock "riprap." These root tangles and the undercuts created by them provide shelter and nesting for birds, fish, beaver, muskrats, water snakes, frogs, turtles, and many other animals. Long-term livestock use usually results in destruction of this vegetation and the undercuts. When floods caused by overgrazed watersheds tear away at unprotected banks, the banks can melt and wash away as readily as cake in the rain.

Many of the aquatic animals that benefit by waterside vegetation play critical roles in maintaining the integrity of wet ecosystems. Beaver, for example, build check dams that slow streamflow, reduce flooding, raise water tables, promote riparian growth, create

(Steve Johnson)

deep pools of excellent animal and plant habitat (and swimming for humans), trap nutrients and water-borne particles, decrease water pollution, and maintain lower water temperatures. Old beaver ponds eventually fill with rich sediments, become lush meadows with meandering streams, and later provide a fertile base for large trees.

Cattle, sheep, and goats consume seedlings and small trees -- cottonwood, willow, and aspen are prominent ex-examples -- needed by beaver for food, lodging, and dam construction. Livestock grazing in watersheds causes violent flooding that destroys beaver dams. Trampling livestock also damage beaver dams, as well as the banks and protective root structures needed for homes by bank beaver; cattle impacts reduce streamflow, and spread giardia and other beaver diseases. Irrigation for ranching destroys habitat, and stockmen slaughter beaver as pests.

Beaver dam in Bannock Mountains, ID. Livestock grazing and stockmen have reduced or eliminated beaver from much of the West. *(George Wuerthner)*

The estimated 400 million beaver in North America before European settlement have been reduced to fewer than 9 million today -- about 2% their original population (Kay 1988). Once found in incredible numbers in waterways throughout the West, beaver have been decimated not only by trapping but in many areas by livestock. By hurting beaver, or any other native aquatic plant or animal, livestock hurt aquatic ecosystems.

Recall that streamside vegetation, acting something like a sponge, functions to regulate local streamflow. During periods of high water, vegetated, porous banks absorb water, recharging adjacent aquifers and expressing water as pools and seeps along floodplains. During dry seasons, these stored waters continue to be released into waterways, augmenting flows from water tables fed by watersheds. This continuing dry season flow can mean the difference between life and death to numerous plants and animals. Where livestock grazing persists, streamside vegetation is destroyed and the land's ability to store water is greatly diminished.

> *Locations that as little as 18 months ago were essentially devoid of vegetation with badly eroded streambanks and often only intermittent flow had been transformed* [by fencing out livestock and other restoration techniques] *into productive areas characterized by dense vegetation, stable streambanks, and deep perennial streams often providing excellent fish habitat.*
> --*Public Rangelands* (USGAO 1988)

Numerous scientific studies (see bibliography) demonstrate that simply fencing livestock out of waterways can restore damaged streams from ephemeral/intermittent to perennial flow -- *even without reducing grazing in watersheds.* Most of these studies show dramatic increases in surface water quantities, and none that I am aware of have shown decreases. Some are nothing short of amazing.

Left photo shows the fenced boundary of Seedskadee National Wildlife Refuge in southwest Wyoming. The photographer took the center photo while standing at the fenceline looking at an ungrazed portion of the Refuge; the right photo was taken from the same spot looking at grazed land outside the Refuge. *(Kelly Cranston)*

One such study was done on Camp Creek in central Oregon (Winegar 1977). In 1875 the Oregon Surveyor General described the Camp Creek valley floor as an "ungullied meadow," with several marshes along its course and an abundance of bunchgrass on the uplands. After 28 years of heavy livestock grazing, the US Geological Survey described Camp Creek and its tributaries as they are today -- arroyos 15'-25' deep and 25'-100' wide, dominated by sagebrush and rabbitbrush. The previously perennial creek is now dry in late summer, and the once grass-covered uplands are mostly bare dirt with scattered juniper.

With a denuded watershed and without riparian vegetation to stabilize soil, Camp Creek became a conduit for enormous amounts of sediments. A downstream 531-acre-foot reservoir built in 1953 filled with about 1 million tons of eroded soil by 1970. Between 1965 and 1974, in an attempt to improve wildlife habitat and decrease turbidity, the Oregon Department of Fish and Wildlife and BLM fenced a 4-mile portion of the Camp Creek channel.

Before fencing, only 17 plant species, mostly "undesirables," were present within the area to be exclosed. In 1977, 45 species were identified, including willow and many rushes, sedges, and grasses. A wildlife inventory was conducted in July 1976. In 2.5 miles of unfenced creek channel only 75 members of 9 animal species were observed; 22 of these were sage grouse, which of course generally prefer sagebrush to riparian vegetation. In 2.5 miles within the exclosure 153 members of 27 species were observed. Today, beaver have re-established themselves and constructed many dams. Waterfowl and at least 12 mammals now use the protected area.

Camp Creek's sediment load was measured 3 times during run-off periods in 1972 and 1973. Water samples were taken from flows entering and leaving the fenced channel. Results of the 3 samplings showed that the non-grazed portion of the stream reduced sediment loads by 79%, 48%, and 69%. Turbid water taken from above the exclosure and left in a still bottle remained cloudy for several days. Samples taken from the outflow cleared and appeared to contain no suspended material within 3 hours.

Perhaps most impressive was the effect on Camp Creek's streamflow. Since the 1800s the creek has experienced only intermittent flow. A simple fence has restored perennial flow. Further, at times during dry periods water begins flowing 225 yards inside the upstream fence, flows at half a cubic foot per second through the fenced portion, and then disappears 30 yards outside the downstream fence.

In addition, due mainly to the protection of vegetation and the lack of streambed trampling, the level of the streambed within the exclosure is steadily rising. A measurement at one point in 1975 revealed 36" of soil deposition between the stream bottom's vegetative mat and the stony bed of 1966. Local water levels have risen accordingly. Lush vegetation covers the area; summer water temperatures have decreased; wildlife has re-established itself. In short, a simple fence has restored this 4-mile section of Camp Creek to its best condition in over 100 years.

Camp Creek is not unique. Most grazed Western streams could be fenced and show similar results -- as sections of many have. For example, a large portion of Big Creek in Rich County, northeast Utah, was fenced in the late 1970s. Studies there by Platts and Nelson showed that, compared to the fenced portion, the grazed portion of the creek had an average of less than 1/3 the bank stability (reflecting mostly vegetative cover), 64% steeper bank angle, 2 1/2 times less beneficial undercut, less than half the stream-shore depth, 18 times less overhanging vegetation, far less sedge cover, less fine sediment deposition, far more streambank erosion, a wider channel, and a lower water table. (Platts 1989a)

Indeed, today dozens of riparian and stream restoration projects are being undertaken using livestock exclosures, often in combination with check dams, plantings and seedings, and/or the removal of competing non-riparian vegetation. Other waterways are being restored by default as they are fenced off by land owners and governments for various reasons.

These protected segments represent only a tiny fraction of waterways on the Western range; but they offer overwhelming evidence of the advantages of excluding livestock. Though few of these areas yet approach pre-livestock productivity, most evince remarkable improvement.

My experience in the Gila National Forest of southwest New Mexico helped open my eyes. The setting is an intermountain valley at 6000' elevation, a moderately wooded area of about 20" annual precipitation. A half mile section of Sapillo Creek and its valley has been fenced for many years, excluding the otherwise prevalent cattle.

Looking down from a hilltop near our home, the valley to the left of the fence is comparatively barren and lifeless. Here, the shallow, algae-infested creek runs quickly through a 100' wide, gravelly drainage devoid of plant life except for several small, broken willows. Steep banks enclose most of the stream channel, inexorably eating away at the bottomland along its margins, expanding the gravelly wash. The bottomland is nearly as lifeless as the scoured wash. Here, small semi-arid weeds and scattered, stunted brush provide 30% ground cover at best. Only a score or so tattered, dying "remnant" cottonwoods survive. In 3 years of living beside this wasteland, we've see little more than occasional birds and rodents.

The valley to the right of the fence is a different world, however. The stream soon disappears behind lush foliage. From walking the area, we know that here the stream slows considerably and contains many small holes and riffles. Its channel narrows to 20'-30' and is enclosed by dense vegetation rather than cutbanks. Silt and sand, rather than rocks and gravel, cover the stream bottom. Watercress and other aquatic plants grow in slower pools and in small marshy areas. The valley floor is 70% covered with abundant and diverse vegetation -- cottonwoods, walnuts, ash, alders, willows, many kinds of bushes, grass, and flowering plants. Here we see animals often -- except of course cattle.

In summer much of its [Willow Creek's, in Central Oregon] streambed is dry. . . . Between the years 1975 and 1980 fences were constructed to exclude livestock, permitting recovery in approximately 7 miles of its channel through Crooked River National Grassland. By 1978 flow had become continuous within this 7 miles except for about 100' within a cattle watering access point . . . almost the entire streambed, approximately 5 miles above and below the exclosure were dry and exposed to the summer sun.
--Harold H. Winegar, "Streamflow Augmentation through Riparian Recovery" (Winegar 1982)

Livestock exclosures have increased streamflow everywhere they have been built. In fact, as with Camp Creek and Willow Creek, many of these streams often flow only within, and not outside, exclosure fences (Winegar 1982).

According to riparian specialist Harold Winegar, usable water could be increased by about 190,000 acre feet on Oregon's Ochoco National Forest simply by removing cattle for 10 years. Similar increases could be expected for most Western National Forests and BLM lands. Winegar further states that with only 5 years of no grazing on the Ochoco, fishery production could be expected to increase 150%. Yet the proposed management plan for this National Forest -- like many recent FS and BLM management plans -- actually proposes *increasing* livestock grazing levels, from 76,000 to 83,000 AUMs. Even with overwhelming evidence of grazing's destructiveness to waterways, our land managing agencies continue servicing ranchers at the expense of the environment.

A recent study in Wyoming found that of 262 miles of streams, only 2% function now as they did in 1850. Eighty-three percent of the streams were lost or destroyed by overgrazing and accelerated erosion. The remaining 15% were in fair to good condition.
--Charles Kay, wildlife ecologist (Kay 1988)

On a much smaller scale -- but important nonetheless -- is the loss of water simply from livestock *drinking* it. Cattle consume about 10 gallons of water daily; on hot, dry days intake may exceed 15 gallons. Relatively speaking, this is more than any wild large herbivore; elk, for example, though weighing about half as much, consume only 2-3 gallons daily (USDA, SCS 1976). Just one steer drinking from a small spring, seep, pond, or waterpocket can quickly deplete available water. In drier areas this water is often crucial to plants and animals, and sometimes humans.

Wherever livestock have access to surface water, such as at this point on an Oregon stream, they destroy vegetation, destabilize banks, and foul water. *(BLM)*

Biologists know that an acre of streamside habitat is as valuable as an acre of redwoods.
--The editors of *Sierra* magazine (*Sierra* 1990)

This stream in the soggy Wind River Mountains, Wyoming, may seem pleasant enough, but it has been heavily degraded by livestock. *(Paul Hirt)*

Almost any water in the dry West seems nice, at least nicer than no water. Most visitors to public land seem happy with whatever surface water they encounter. I have heard the most terribly denuded, trampled, polluted, flood ravaged, cutbank-enclosed waterways described as "such a pretty little creek," "a nice camping spot," "a great place to enjoy the outdoors," and so forth. This pleasant attitude in the face of overwhelming degeneration may simply indicate a high degree of tolerance in some people. Most, however, simply seem unaware of what they are looking at.

While our Western waterways may *seem* nice, we should realize that most are depleted and degraded, often extremely so. As expressed by Stephanie Wood, a range technician for the Beaverhead National Forest in Montana: "This kind of damage is so widespread that most people, including most range managers, have never seen a healthy stream channel (Wuerthner 1991)." Moreover, we need to understand that throughout most of the West a large percentage of waterways no longer exist. Amazing what a few harmless cows and sheep can do.

[Note: For further documentation of this section see Winegar 1977; Blum 1986; USDI, BLM 1989; and other sources listed in the bibliography.]

(George Wuerthner)

According to hydrologists Wayne Elmore and Robert L. Beschta, "Many people have never seen a healthy rangeland riparian area, since degradation was widespread before many of us were born."

The photo at right is of Pole Creek in the Sawtooth National Recreation Area, central Idaho. The photographer, naturalist George Wuerthner, writes that "The creek looks lovely to the untrained eye. However, it is severely degraded. The channel is wide and shallow. There is little overhanging vegetation and few undercut banks. No willows or shrubs."

In this photo, Pole Creek flows under a fence onto the grounds of a Forest Service ranger station, where there has been no livestock grazing for nearly 100 years. Note that it narrows and becomes deeper.

This photo was taken within the ungrazed ranger station compound. Now the creek is barely visible. Rather than being several feet wide and 1' deep, as in the grazed area, it is a foot or two wide and *3' deep*! Vegetation is taller; overhanging vegetation is everywhere; and undercut banks are common. Willows and shrubs line the creek. Water flows more slowly; is cleaner, cooler, and better protected from the elements; and provides a more natural, superior habitat for wildlife.

Yes, the grazed portion of Pole Creek in the top photo is pleasant to look at. Indeed, it is probably in fairly good condition compared to most rangeland streams. Nonetheless, it *is*, as the photographer notes, **severely degraded**.

(Photos by George Wuerthner)

Riparian Areas

A riparian area in northeast Utah, ungrazed by livestock.
(Kelly Cranston)

Even though wildlife riparian surveys are far from complete, the Arizona Game & Fish Department now identifies at least 137 species of fish, amphibians, reptiles, birds, and mammals that may face extinction if current habitat trends continue. About 80% of the above species (which does not include plants) are strongly affected by the destruction of riparian habitats. Since livestock grazing is by far the most common form of land use in Arizona and the other 11 Western states, it is not surprising that grazing abuse is a leading cause of riparian decline. Studies in every Western state have shown similar declines due to livestock grazing.
--Steve Johnson, Southwestern Representative, Defenders of Wildlife (Johnson 1987)

Scientifically, *riparian ecosystems* are defined as wetland ecosystems that have a high water table because of proximity to an aquatic system or to subsurface water. In other words, they are land surfaces that are close to water, but not under water. They derive a high amount of moisture from nearby surface and/or subsurface water, but aren't normally covered with surface water themselves.

When talking about riparian systems, one usually thinks of springs, streams, rivers, lakes, and other surface waters. But these aquatic environments are not, strictly speaking, physically part of riparian areas; it may help to discuss them as separate but closely related entities.

Some riparian systems are supplied moisture from ground waters that never appear as surface water in the immediate area. In other words, riparian ecosystems can exist even where there is no regular surface water nearby.

The *riparian zone* is defined as the strip of land bordering surface waters whose vegetation depends on a high water table. These zones, particularly those along streams and rivers, constitute most riparian acreage in the West. The term *riparian area* is commonly used to describe any area with riparian qualities.

In the US, riparian areas encompass less than 5% of the land (Chaney 1990). Riparian areas and associated waterways together cover only about 3 million acres and represent less than 1% of the area of Western public lands (USGAO 1988). Yet riparian areas are the most biologically productive of all Western ecosystems. Their deep, rich soils, flat expanses of bottomland, and abundant moisture support the greatest abundance and diversity of vegetation in the West. Accordingly, they are, acre for acre, among the most significant animal habitats anywhere. In many parts of the arid and semi-arid West, the large trees and dense vegetation common to riparian areas provide the only cool, shady places and thick cover for miles around. Lush riparian vegetation moderates air temperatures and protects wildlife from weather extremes. Riparian areas provide avenues and cover for animal movements and migrations, assuring wide distribution, minimum species inbreeding, and refuge from humans and their developments. On Western ranges, which are often characterized by relative uniformity over vast spaces, riparian areas provide habitat diversity, thus abundance and stability. Riparian systems are transition zones between aquatic and terrestrial ecosystems -- land-water interfaces -- containing organisms from both overlapping ecosystems, as well as organisms endemic to riparian systems.

Throughout most of the West, most animal species rely at some time in their lives on riparian areas. For example, 75% of wildlife species in eastern Oregon utilize riparian zones (Ferguson 1983). In the Elko, Nevada, BLM Resource Area, 80% of approximately 300 terrestrial wildlife species "are directly dependent on riparian habitat, or use it more than any other habitat" (Luoma 1986). In

A healthy, ungrazed riparian area is alive with abundance and diversity.

Arizona and New Mexico, 80% of all vertebrates depend on riparian areas for at least half of their life cycle; more than half of these are totally dependent on riparian areas. Riparian areas provide habitat for more species of birds than all other Western rangeland types combined, and in the Southwest more than half of bird species are completely dependent on them (Chaney 1990). Overall, 75% of all vertebrate species in the West in some way rely on riparian areas and associated waters (Williams 1990).

The extensive deterioration of western riparian areas began with severe overgrazing in the late nineteenth and early twentieth centuries.... Extensive field observations in the late 1980s suggest that riparian areas throughout the West were (are now) in the worst condition in history.
--*Livestock Grazing on Western Riparian Areas*, produced for the Environmental Protection Agency (Chaney 1990)

Unfortunately, cattle also find riparian zones immensely attractive. With lush, succulent vegetation, plentiful water, smooth, level ground, shade and shelter, riparian areas attract cattle like a magnet. Regardless of range conditions, riparian areas are their first target. Even a handful of cattle on a vast range will concentrate in riparian areas (Chaney 1990). Cattle are relatively lethargic, and once settled into this pleasant environment they stay indefinitely unless strongly induced to move. The BLM found that in the Great Basin all riparian land covers less than 2% of the area, yet receives 50% of the livestock pressure. Riparian meadows occupy only 1%-2% of the interior Northwest, but account for 81% of the forage removed by livestock. (Green 1989)

Therefore, riparian areas are exceedingly susceptible to damage from cattle grazing; generally, the narrower they are the more readily they are damaged. Until recent decades (and improved public relations) many range manuals referred to riparian areas as grazing "sacrifice areas."

Thus, riparian destruction is among the most environmentally disastrous aspects of public lands ranching, and many experts cite livestock grazing as the most harmful riparian influence on public lands. For example, a special report prepared for the US Environmental Protection Agency identifies livestock grazing as having "the most geographically extensive effects" on riparian areas Westwide, public and private land included (Chaney 1990). *Indeed, in the 70% of the West managed for ranching the vast majority of riparian areas have been and are being significantly damaged by livestock.* Of dubious consolation is that concentrating livestock on riparian areas in effect reduces pressure on neighboring countrysides .

"Cowed out" riparian zone on BLM land in Jordan Valley, Oregon. *(George Wuerthner)*

A riparian community impoverished by livestock is like a rainbow without color.

This is the same creek shown in the adjacent photo, as it flows onto a fenced, ungrazed roadside.

... the partial information that is available shows that there are tens of thousands of miles of riparian areas in the West, with only a small portion of them in good condition.... Poorly managed livestock grazing is the major cause of degraded riparian habitat on federal rangelands.

--US General Accounting Office, *Public Rangelands* (USGAO 1988)

Since riparian areas are such fruitful ecosystems, their functions are complex and varied, and so too are the impacts from livestock. Let's look at some of the basic functions of natural riparian systems and what effect livestock grazing has on them.

Most riparian areas in the West are situated alongside perennial watercourses or seasonal drainages. At higher elevations, riparian vegetation generally grows in narrow strips along fast flowing streams, around the perimeters of lakes, and in moist, boggy areas of seeps and springs. Cattle and sheep are usually brought into these places in late spring and remain until autumn, where they gobble down the luxuriant grasses and flowering plants and plod about in their self-made mire. In many areas, their destructive impacts can be easily seen right up to mountain headwaters, often above 10,000' elevation and occasionally as high as 12,000'. Harsh climatic conditions, thin soils, and low stream sediment levels make these high-elevation riparian areas quite susceptible to long-term damage from livestock.

When heavy rains or snowmelt send water rushing down from higher elevations, the water picks up particles of clay, silt, and fine sand along the way and carries them into streams. Upon reaching lower elevations, these flood-swollen waters spread out across the bottoms of canyons and valleys -- the *floodplains*. This dispersion causes the waters to lose speed and deposit their suspended sediments in a fairly even manner across canyon and valley floors. Each new flood drops another layer of these fine-particled sediments, over the years building up the wide strips of fertile floodplain soil called *bottomland*. This important process creates most riparian land in the West.

The combination of flat, deep, fertile soil with a constant supply of ground moisture provides riparian plant life an ideal medium. Most healthy riparian bottomlands support veritable jungles of vegetation usually consisting of at least 200 species of large and small trees, bushes, vines, grasses, flowering perennials, and other moisture-loving plants.

While these riparian plants owe their existence to the fertile soil and groundwater of the riparian system, conversely the soil and water owe their continued existence to these plants. Riparian vegetation and soil maintain a mutually beneficial equilibrium. As riparian plant life grows more profuse, it becomes better able to slow floodwaters and trap sediments, thereby adding to its base of rich topsoil. In turn, as more layers of topsoil are laid down, vegetation grows more profusely, enabling it to trap more soil, and so on. Additionally, the thicker the vegetation, the more able it is to filter out the finest waterborne particles -- generally the most fertile sediments.

When cattle deplete and destroy riparian vegetation, this cycle is reversed. Less plant cover means less soil trapped and deposited, reduced plant growth, even less topsoil. . . . With cattle depleting remaining vegetation at a quicker and quicker rate as it becomes scarcer, a downward spiral of botanic extermination ensues. Not only this, faster floodwater speeds due to depleted plant cover mean increased topsoil *erosion*, as well as decreased topsoil deposition -- a double whammy.

Under natural conditions, the topsoil composing most bottomlands is remarkably rich and fertile, due in large part to its high percentage of organic matter.

This riparian area was once lushly vegetated and filled with wildlife. A century of livestock grazing has left it as you see it now. *(Steve Johnson)*

Most riparian zones at lower elevations occur within the valleys and canyons of rivers and streams. Riparian dynamics here are somewhat different and more complex. As streams descend from the highlands, they spread out and slow down as their drainages gradually become more shallow, wider, and more level. Eventually, streams join together to form rivers that flow slowly through wide, flat valleys toward the oceans.

Lush riparian growth, animal droppings and remains, and organic material washed down in floods and trapped among riparian plants are the main constituents of this organic matter. Without the physical obstructions created by riparian plants and debris, rising floodwaters simply wash these vital materials away, eventually to be caught under bridges or in logjams, buried under coarse sediments, or dumped into reservoirs and oceans.

Livestock destruction of riparian vegetation is accomplished in much the same way as in any other ecosystem. These moisture-loving plants, being more leafy, succulent, and palatable, are more eagerly sought out and consumed by greater numbers of cattle. Being generally more leafy and succulent, many are also more fragile. Thus, because cattle congregate and spend so much time in riparian zones, damage is, overall, acre for acre, comparatively even greater than in dry areas.

Loss of riparian vegetation exposes moist soils to the sun and wind, leading to increased groundwater loss through evaporation. In some areas, increased capillary action from the water table close below has brought inordinate amounts of dissolved salts and minerals to the soil's surface, forming a sterile crust, changing plant composition and killing vegetation.

Healthy riparian vegetation even acts as a filter for adjacent surface waters. It screens out pollutants, sediments, and harmful debris that would otherwise enter surface waters from surrounding rangeland. (Green 1989) The fine-particled sediments, organic matter, and beneficial chemicals also trapped by this vegetative filter make riparian areas nutrient repositories for surrounding watersheds. Livestock open passages through riparian vegetation, deplete it, or destroy it altogether.

Plants draw water up through roots and transpire it through leaves into the air. Because of this, some argue that riparian vegetation wastes water. In fact, riparian plants conserve more than they transpire. Their organic litter layer helps soil absorb rainwater and percolate it into underground storage. Likewise, the organic litter helps absorb and store the occasional shallow floodwaters that spread across bottomlands. Riparian vegetation blocks sun and wind, limiting evaporation. Of the water that is "lost" into the air through transpiration by leaves, much eventually forms clouds and returns to the earth as precipitation anyway (as opposed to water that mostly *runs off* denuded

Russian olive thicket along the Rio Grande River in central New Mexico. When the leafless cottonwood and willow saplings in foreground leaf out, cattle will eat and trample them, allowing the thorny exotic to dominate, as it does in the background.

and degraded lands). We have already detailed many other ways in which vegetation, streamside vegetation in particular, conserves water.

As on rangeland, livestock in riparian areas reduce the amount and the diversity of vegetation. For example, tamarisk is a prolific riparian invader native to north Africa and southern Asia. The shaggy tree has replaced native species on tens of thousands of riparian acres in the West, much to the detriment of native animals. Livestock help spread tamarisk because they eat and trample cottonwoods, willows, walnut, sycamore, alder, etc. and thus give the unpalatable tamarisk the competitive advantage.

Similarly, damage and depletion of natural riparian vegetation reduces the diversity of animal habitat. Most Western wildlife depends on riparian vegetation for all or part of its needs, and much requires a combination of riparian and other biotic types to survive.

An important yet little-studied riparian process is the biogeochemical cycle that influences riparian and aquatic systems. Riparian areas are unique in that they contain large areas of water-saturated soil in conjunction with permanent, dense vegetation. The influence of both and the interaction between them helps keep riparian and aquatic systems in proper chemical balance. Livestock may upset this balance, with far-reaching but little understood consequences. (Green 1989)

Streams and rivers have a special relationship with the floodplains through which they flow. Over long periods, stream and river channels tend to meander from side to side

Thick -- ungrazed by livestock -- riparian vegetation traps flood debris. This debris is ecologically very important in many ways.

within the confines of their drainages -- a phenomenon called "sinuousity" -- from sweeping curves in narrow canyons at high elevations to great serpentine loops in wide lowland river valleys. If it were possible to look at a time lapse video of the movement of a stream or river channel within its canyon or valley, it might appear as a giant snake writhing back and forth from one side of the drainage to the other, now and then removing small portions of canyon and valley walls. In this way streams and rivers broaden their canyons and valleys over time, creating wide "overflow areas" -- floodplains -- that carry surplus floodwaters, dissipate destructive hydraulic action, and create fertile bottomland.

The increased speed and erosive power of livestock-caused floodwaters, in combination with other livestock impacts, has caused them to eat through stream and river meanders and eventually to widen and straighten water courses. Straighter courses, in turn, allow for even greater floodwater speed and erosive power. Streams are reduced in actual length, reducing overall water quantity as well as streamside and aquatic wildlife habitat.

Straighter courses also mean steeper stream slopes that further increase water speed and allow streams to carry coarser and larger amounts of sediments, which further erode channels and kill vegetation. These more erosive floods physically harm aquatic animals and displace channel bottoms, sweeping away and killing small aquatic animals that live in sand and gravel and under rocks, which in turn reduces the amount of food available for larger animals. Increased channel erosion, in conjunction with abnormally powerful and frequent floods eliminates sandbars that are essential for the establishment of some types of vegetation and that are important for animal habitat. Faster floodwaters racing through wider, straighter channels means the channels are able to contain much greater quantities of floodwater and that floodwaters are less likely to be spread out evenly over remaining bottomlands and deposit fine sediments.

As discussed, bottomland riparian vegetation extracts sediments, replenishes soil, provides organic litter, slows floodwaters, and thus replenishes groundwater supplies. Floodplains and their riparian vegetation, in turn, help maintain maximum water flows for the streams and rivers that helped create them.

Under natural conditions, streams and rivers meander very gradually. Sturdy masses of interwoven roots on channel banks allow only extremely slow bank erosion and lateral channel movement. Healthy watersheds rarely produce the violent, erosive floods necessary to tear apart these banks.

When cattle overpopulate a riparian ecosystem, bottomland vegetation is usually destroyed first, being generally less resistant to livestock use than the more luxuriant, well-watered, densely rooted, resilient streamside plant life. As a consequence, when streamside vegetation finally does succumb to livestock pressure and floodwaters break through its declining root masses, the denuded bottomlands behind them are suddenly laid open to massive erosion. Crumbling banks recede quickly, eating up precious bottomland as they go, often right up to canyon or valley walls. What is left is canyon and valley floors covered with sand and gravel, boulders, and massive corpses of uprooted trees -- now common scenes around the West.

Cattle-bombed riparian zone. Note erosion, absence of protective lower branches on trees, streamside depletion, and utter lack of ground cover, in contrast to fenced roadside in foreground.

Livestock overgrazing is the most pervasive cause of the deterioration of riparian ecosystems on public lands.
--Beverly I. Strassmann, "Cattle Grazing and Haying on Wildlife Refuges" (Strassmann 1983a)

The changes [from livestock grazing] *are usually small from year to year and often go unnoticed. They are, however, cumulative, and eventually represent major alterations. Ironically, local residents will often declare that a stream hasn't changed since their grandparent's time; they may be correct because many of the major impacts occurred before the turn of the century. The consequences of riparian degradation for fish and wildlife are the same whether it occurs as a sudden catastrophic event, such as a washout from a tailing pond, or a long series of small, cumulative events.*
--William S. Platts, "Fish, Wildlife and Livestock" (Platts 1990)

Consider these before-livestock descriptions of Southwestern riparian areas. From J.J. Thornber, an early botanist at the University of Arizona:

In moist valleys, cienegas [marshy areas along drainages]*, and occasionally canyons, tall sacaton grasses were the predominant plants. These valleys, examples of which are the Santa Cruz, San Pedro, San Simon, and Little Colorado, were veritable cienegas or flood plains over which the excess storm water spread from time to time in broad sheets, retarded by the accumulated vegetation of past years, and occasionally by groups of beavers' dams. . . .*

In **Desertification in the United States**, David Sheridan describes the Santa Cruz and San Pedro Rivers:

Water flowed through an unchanneled river that wound sluggishly across a flat, marshy area. Trout were abundant. Beavers built dams. There were giant cottonwood, mesquite, willow, sycamore, and paloverde, and grass -- grass tall enough to "brush a horse's belly," to shelter wild turkeys. Meandering, ungullied tributary creeks fed the river. (Sheridan 1981)

These river valleys represent 4 of Arizona's major drainages. All 4 are now bone dry along most of their courses, as are their former tributaries. Their broad, sandy and rocky beds are enclosed in many places by cutbanks, some of which reach 50' in height and run for miles. These washes are scoured periodically by violent floodwawaters that run off overgrazed rangeland. Most of the original bottomland and large trees were washed away long ago. There is very little grass of any kind, no beavers or trout, and little "accumulated vegetation." Few parts of them have any resemblance whatsoever to "cienegas." (Chapman 1948, Blum 1986, Hastings 1965)

Consider this excerpt from *Livestock Grazing on Western Riparian Areas*:

> *In 1976 the grazing permit for the allotment was relinquished by the permittee. The BLM used the opportunity to fence most of the creek and much of the watershed to exclude livestock.*
>
> *Riparian vegetation responded to rest from grazing and installation of a few instream structures to improve trout habitat by raising water levels and reducing erosion. Native perennial grasses increased throughout the fenced area. Previously decadent aspen groves expanded. Curlleaf mahogany began reproducing within the fenced area while outside the fence almost no seedlings survived grazing.*
>
> *Streambanks stabilized and erosion was reduced. The stream channel narrowed and deepened. Summer streamflow increased 400%, and depth of water increased 50%. Water temperatures and sediment load decreased.* (Chaney 1990)

As evidence of the diversity of problems caused by riparian livestock grazing, here are samples from a report by the General Accounting Office:

> *"The creek's riparian areas were in poor condition -- they had unstable banks and a declining trout population, which local BLM officials said stemmed from unrestricted grazing"; ". . . 118 streams* [in Nevada] *and found that over 80% of the 1,036 miles inventoried were in poor or fair condition"; ". . . the creek's riparian areas were overgrazed, causing the creek to dry up in the summer"; "The Audubon Society said overgrazing prohibited the regeneration of cottonwood trees critically needed as nesting sites for endangered bald eagles"; "The inventory showed that, primarily as a result of major floods and livestock overgrazing, the Burro Creek area had been devastated and stripped of vegetation"; "Degraded conditions were evidenced by eroded streambanks, shallow stream channel, and the elimination of a trout population"; "BLM said the area was eroding badly and producing excessive sediment"; ". . . the 2,000-acre allotment of the watershed has been reduced to bare ground, primarily through overgrazing by sheep and cattle."*

Little remains of this riparian area in the Challis National Forest, Idaho, except a stunted willow and an eroded gully. Note depleted range. *(George Wuerthner)*

Throughout the grazed 70% of the Western US, livestock grazing has been and continues to be the most widespread and potent force destroying riparian areas. For example, the Arizona Game & Fish Department reports that 97% of the state's original riparian habitat has been lost, with ranching the major factor (Wuerthner 1989a). According to the Arizona State Parks department, 90% of the original riparian ecosystems in New Mexico are gone. Assessments by BLM itself found that 80% of the 12,000 miles of streams and associated riparian zones on BLM land in Idaho are being damaged by poor management and 90% of 5300 miles surveyed in Colorado were rated in poor or fair condition due to livestock. (Wuerthner 1990b) California has lost an estimated 89% of its riparian woodland since 1848, largely to ranching, as well as farming, dams, placer mining, development, and other impacts. The Wyoming Game & Fish Department estimates a loss of 45% of the state's riparian area, again largely from ranching. In arid Nevada, a *BLM* report states, "Stream riparian habitat where livestock grazing is occurring [most of the state] has been grazed out of existence or is in a severely deteriorated condition" (Ferguson 1983); the Nature Conservancy reports that Nevada has lost more than 80% of its wetlands since the 1800s. In rangeland areas of every Western state, *most* riparian habitat has been seriously damaged or eliminated by livestock. (In the US overall, livestock grazing and other human influence has caused the loss of 70% of the original area of riparian vegetation [Joyce 1989].)

Under increasing public pressure to improve riparian areas, the Chair of the House Committee on Interior and Insular Affairs and the Chair of its Subcommittee on National Parks and Public Lands in 1986 asked the US General Accounting Office (GAO) to identify examples of successful riparian restoration efforts on public rangelands, to determine why they were successful and if those methods could be used on a widespread basis. In response, the GAO in 1988 released *Public Rangelands, Some Riparian Areas Restored but Widespread Improvement Will Be Slow*, which reviewed successful restoration efforts by the BLM and FS on selected riparian areas in 10 Western States. (USGAO 1988)

The report showcases these agencies' most successful restoration attempts. Failures were not included. According to the report, "We first requested lists of successful riparian management projects from the BLM and FS headquarters." In order to set the stage for continued heavy livestock grazing, these agencies seem to have made a special effort to provide the GAO with the most impressive examples of livestock *grazing* (as well as removal or reductions) being used as a restoration technique. The GAO selected 15 out of 35 example projects provided by the agencies, and later added 7 more, for a total of 22. Continued the GAO, "We selected projects . . . to illustrate several different techniques of riparian management."

In other words, due to both of the above factors, the report is subtly structured to promote the false impression that changing grazing systems has been much more successful in riparian restoration than it actually has been. In truth, as shown even in this report, by far the most numerous and successful restorations of riparian areas have been accomplished by *removal or drastic reductions* of livestock, not changes in grazing techniques. Regardless, the report dramatically displays the ability of riparian areas to make significant recovery if given a chance.

Of the 22 examples in the GAO report, half involved fencing and complete removal of livestock. Without exception, each of these ungrazed study areas soon displayed impressive improvement of riparian health, *except where cattle had broken through exclosure fences*. Though in some

cases developments such as rip-rap, in-stream structures, and vegetation planting were implemented in conjunction with livestock removal, in most tremendous riparian recovery occurred without these aids.

In the other 11 study areas discussed in the GAO report, riparian grazing was continued in some form, usually as an intensified "rest-rotation" system of grazing (basically, moving large groups of livestock about more quickly between smaller pastures). In most of these cases, livestock numbers were significantly reduced. Generally, riparian recovery increased in direct proportion to the degree that livestock populations decreased. Areas where efforts were made to keep livestock away from riparian zones and waterways experienced noticeably greater improvement than where grazing continued unabated. All but 1 of these studies involved concurrent riparian and/or range developments, *to a greater degree than on the ungrazed study areas*. This included fencing; rip-rapping; tree and shrub planting, grass seeding; in-stream structures of various kinds; bank protection; stabilizing eroded terraces and gullies in watersheds; water developments in uplands; transporting water to livestock away from riparian areas; and brush eradication, prescribed burning, and seeding in watersheds. In the single grazed study area where no developments were implemented, recovery was perhaps the least impressive of all 22 case studies. Some permittees indicated they didn't believe much more restoration could be accomplished in their grazed riparian areas without additional improvements, which was not the case with the ungrazed areas.

When The Nature Conservancy purchased a 5-mile stretch of west-central Arizona's Hassayampa River in 1986, the riparian area was as stripped and beaten by cattle as most other Western wetlands. Several years of no cattle later, preserve managers report "phenomenal recovery." Clear, cool water meanders slowly through a jungle of grasses, sedges, reeds, and rushes. Small, quiet, vegetation-filled ponds and bogs shelter wildlife. Dense thickets of bush willows and small trees line the wet zone, and the floor of the surrounding riparian forest is covered with organic matter and vibrant with living things.

The GAO reported numerous difficulties in completing the studies, particularly with respect to cooperation from grazing permittees. While visiting a number of the study sites, GAO staff found trespassing cattle or evidence of trespassing. The report stated, "As we saw, failure to keep livestock out of recovery areas long enough for vegetation to establish itself can ruin the progress made by months of effort and effectively doom projects to failure." Trespassing on one riparian project was so bad that the report stated:

We observed the project with BLM officials in October 1987. . . . They considered the project essentially a "showcase" demonstration area for visitor tours, the most recent of which was given about 2 weeks prior to our visit. However, when we arrived at the site we found that a large number of cattle had broken the exclosure fence and grazed the previously protected area to a desert-like condition. Essentially all of the regenerated grass in the area was eaten or trampled and most of the area was reduced to dust. The BLM officials expressed their surprise and dismay with the trespass. They stated, however, that such trespass was not uncommon and they would try to work more closely with the permittee to gain assurance the incident would not be repeated.

Many of the permittees involved in the study projects initially objected and provided little cooperation. According to the GAO report, "On most BLM projects, staff worked long and hard to convince the ranchers that healthy riparian zones would benefit their ranching operations and thereby obtain their voluntary cooperation." Most of those whose livestock numbers were not significantly reduced eventually began to support the projects, especially when they found the many taxpayer-sponsored developments starting to enhance their profit-making potential.

But most of those whose livestock numbers were reduced were not at all happy. Some exerted pressure on agency officials, forcing them to "modify" project plans to be more conducive to their ranching goals. Some demanded, and received, livestock developments in upland areas in compensation for reduced riparian grazing. In protest, some took to trespassing livestock in fenced study areas. Some cut fences and damaged non-grazing-related developments. Apparently one permittee, objecting to a riparian fence being built on "his" allotment without his approval, stole half the fence materials after the project was completed. The BLM "could not determine who was responsible for the theft."

The GAO report cited not only the permittees but the agencies themselves as obstacles to riparian restoration. Reportedly, many agency efforts to restore riparian areas are hampered by pro-grazing staff at both upper and lower levels. BLM employees trying to make management decisions protecting riparian areas apparently were pressured to back off. The report stated, "If the BLM is serious about more widespread riparian restoration, it will have to demonstrate its seriousness with concrete actions such as cutting AUMs or citing known trespass or other permit violations, when such actions are necessary."

In sum, these 22 projects (22 of the most successful projects on public land, remember) improved the condition of a total of less than 150 linear miles of Western waterways and adjacent riparian zones. The reported cost of 14 of these projects was (as of 1988) over $400,000 in government funds. Including the other 7 projects, as well as additional and indirect costs, total costs would undoubtedly run well over $1 million in taxes. The report concludes:

The successes of the projects to date need to be measured against the backdrop of work that remains to be done. . . . The available information is too incomplete for an estimate of how many miles of streams on BLM and Forest Service land are in less than satisfactory condition. It seems likely, however, from the partial estimates above, that the number of miles easily runs into tens *of thousands. In addition, many other types of riparian areas, such as springs and meadows, may also need work.* (emphasis added)

But even if these hundreds of millions of dollars are spent, improvement is never permanent as long as ranching continues. Tragically, as soon as riparian areas begin to recover the land management agencies are pressured to increase livestock grazing once again -- in direct proportion to the extent of recovery. The lush green (read: *greenbacks*) and water of a healthy riparian area are almost unbearably desirable to the rancher. He does his utmost to make sure the government doesn't "waste" this livestock potential. Few riparian areas, therefore, are allowed to make full and lasting recovery.

A riparian area on Sheldon National Wildlife Refuge, northwest Nevada, was fenced from cattle. Soon thereafter, dense vegetation covered the bare ground, aquatic plants stabilized the stream bottom, and the water level rose significantly, soaking the roots of the sagebrush in the foreground and killing the dryland plants. *(George Wuerthner)*

A number of reports similar to GAO's have been published in recent years (see bibliography). Prominent is a 1990 report produced for EPA titled *Livestock Grazing on Western Riparian Areas* (Chaney 1990). It essentially parallels GAO's report with before-and-after descriptions of grazed riparian areas and recovery efforts. As with the GAO report, only successful recovery efforts were showcased, this time in a dozen case studies in 8 Western states. Again, in general, the greater the degree of livestock reduction, the more dramatic the riparian recovery. And again, despite the admission of grazing devastation, a concerted effort was made to protect the grazing imperative:

Decreasing the number of livestock is commonly offered as the simple solution to degraded riparian conditions. But even under light stocking rates livestock tend to concentrate on riparian vegetation during various seasons of the year. Unless the reduction was extreme, it might not achieve the desired improvement in riparian conditions.

So why not simply make the reduction extreme? Answer: The grazing imperative (a fusion of tradition, politics, bureaucracy, cowboy idolatry, etc.) mandates that ranching continue indefinitely. Thus, again we are instead advised to advocate and finance more ranching developments and administration to mitigate riparian impact, rather than use "the simple solution."

During the most severe drought in decades, thirsty cattle badly damaged riparian zones on public rangelands in southern Idaho [BLM says it made a "mistake" in management.]. . . . An Idaho sports group, however, blamed the damage on pressure put on the BLM by ranchers and Idaho Sen. James McClure. R. Al Berry, a member of the Ada County Fish and Game League, told AP that cattlemen and McClure run the state, and if BLM officials tried to reduce grazing they'd lose their jobs.

--High Country News (12-7-87)

Millions of acres of Western riparian bottomland have been devegetated and converted to livestock pasture and crops.

Luxuriant riparian vegetation turns to trampled, barren mud at fence. The cattle responsible for the contrast lie in the shade of a large oak at right. Note corral at left.

Though riparian areas on public land have suffered extensively from livestock, those on private land have fared even worse. In the 1800s ranchers took control of *most* of the fertile riparian flats in the rangeland West, along with associated surface waters. So the most productive riparian lands throughout most of the West have been in the hands of ranchers hands for over 100 years. To increase livestock production, they have cut down most riparian trees and brush on their lands and turned these bottomlands into cow, sheep, and horse pastures. **Thus have ranchers destroyed the most productive wildlife habitat in the rangeland West.**

Sadly typical to the contemporary Western scene is the once productive river valley, now stripped of nearly all native vegetation, fenced into small rectangles dotted with grazing cattle and sheep, barren of wildlife. The once free-flowing river trickles over gravel and rocks down the middle of the valley, narrowly restrained by parallel, rip-rapped rock dikes. A few large trees survive along the waterway and in places along the many irrigation ditches that dump most of the river's water onto the alfalfa fields and closely cropped livestock pastures that cover the valley.

Domestic livestock have been and continue to be the principal destroyer of healthy riparian zones [on federal land].
--National Wildlife Federation, in 1990 letter to New Mexico State Game Commission

[Note: Studies on livestock's riparian and aquatic impacts are relatively numerous; see bibliography for many.]

A National Forest riparian zone is now pummeled dirt. *(USFS)*

Flooding

"I don't get it. . . . What do cows have to do with floods?" asked Rick.

"It's simple," answered his cousin. *"When the cattle strip the land bare, the rain runs off it as if it were concrete. Instead of soaking into the ground, it rushes into the nearest stream and down through the canyons. Places that once were fairly safe can be hit by worse floods than ever before."*

"Like here!" added Zelda knowingly.

"That's right," continued Roberto. *"But's that's not all of it. The floods carry tons of soil with them. They cause some of the worst soil erosion. And when the soil is gone, you can kiss this country good-bye."*

--Gerry Bishop, "Adventures of Ranger Rick," *Ranger Rick* (March 1985) (Bishop 1985)

Floods can be defined as periodic dramatic rises in water flow within drainages, sometimes causing overflows onto land that is normally dry. Flooding is a natural and in many ways beneficial occurrence, serving many important functions. Floods periodically flush out and keep open waterways that might otherwise become choked with vegetation or blocked by detritus washed in from tributary drainages. As mentioned, flood overflow is essential to the building of fertile bottomland. Natural floods help spread seeds and root stocks; germinate seeds; transport aquatic animals to habitat not normally accessible; grind rocks into gravel into sand into silt into clay; build productive deltas; establish sandbars; maintain proper dissolved mineral levels in oceans; and much more. In many arid to semi-arid areas, flash floods spread out evenly over alluvial fans and plains, dispersing needed moisture and fertile sediments. Aboriginal peoples depended on these fairly predictable high waters and deposited sediments to support agriculture.

In the past, the greatest natural floods did, of course, have significant influences on local environments and occasionally may even have seemed disastrous from a human perspective. However, because massive water runoff was relatively infrequent, affected lands had plenty of time to reestablish. Indeed, in the long run, these natural highest waters were essential to the health and character of many ecosystems. Because the aboriginal environment was in near peak condition, resistance to the potentially destructive powers of floods was very high.

A heavy summer storm struck in the hills and gulches above town and what marched down Mt. Pleasant's [Utah] main street was . . . a river of thick mud like concrete that, in a town of twenty-five hundred people, did half a million dollars' worth of damage in ten minutes. The range above town had been overgrazed and the storm waters which would have been retained by healthy land could not be retained by the sick, exhausted land.

--Bernard DeVoto, **The Easy Chair** (DeVoto 1955)

Buenos Aires National Wildlife Refuge, ungrazed by livestock, is on the far side of the fence. *(Steve Johnson)*

Watersheds degraded by livestock beget rampaging floods. *(Dave Foreman)*

Things changed with the introduction of livestock grazing in the 1800s. Violent flooding became commonplace throughout most of the West. Rather than mild flooding occasionally flushing out waterways, huge floods now ravaged stream and river channels. Rather than swollen streams and rivers gently overflowing their banks and moving slowly across bottomlands, massive floods turned whole canyon and valley floors into raging torrents, carrying away their topsoil and burying them under coarse sediments. Rather than moderate flash floods distributing moisture and sediments to alluvial outwashes, rampaging floodwaters cut deeply into the land and buried anything in the way downhill under tons of rock, sand, and gravel.

Intensified flooding due to livestock grazing triggered this massive landslide.

During the past 130 or so years, flood damage to the Western environment has been inestimably extreme. Billions of tons of topsoil, hundreds of thousands of acres of fertile bottomland and lush riparian land, billions of plants and animals, and millions of large trees have been swept away. Flooding, once a fairly reliable benefit to both environment and people, has become an uncertain and hated enemy.

Stockmen do not accept responsibility. And although ranching proponents offer 101 scapegoats, it is noteworthy that the peak in livestock numbers and commencement of greatly increased destructive flooding in each region occurred virtually simultaneously. For example, the period of 1875-1895 marked the beginning of this period in most of Arizona -- the same years livestock grazing reached its highest level. In most of California, where cattle numbers

peaked at an estimated 1.4 million in 1860, destructive floods and drought in the 1860s caused extensive damage that brought cattle numbers down to around 670,000 by 1870 (Cleland 1941). In the vast Rio Puerco Basin of northwest New Mexico, serious flooding and arroyo cutting increased in direct proportion to the increase in livestock numbers in the 1880s to early 1900s. In most of Wyoming serious flooding and cutbank formation suddenly began at the same time huge numbers of livestock arrived from Texas and the far West in the 1870s and 1880s. Coincidence?

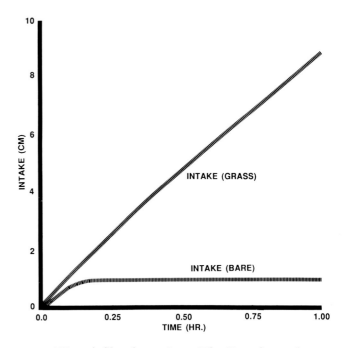

Water infiltration at Santa Rita Experimental Range, Arizona, 1975. Water not infiltrated = runoff; runoff = flood water quantity. (Source: Dixon 1978)

Livestock have caused this extreme increase in violent flooding mainly in 2 ways: (1) watershed degradation, and (2) damage to waterways and riparian areas themselves. The destructiveness of a particular flood depends on the amount of water it contains and the condition of the drainage through which it flows. In other words, because denuded and degraded watershed soils absorb much less water than previously, runoff is far greater and, thus, floods contain vastly greater volumes of water. These larger floods flow through degraded channels and riparian zones that are much more susceptible to flood damage.

Dense vegetation has an amazing capacity to hold water and percolate it into the soil and into aquifers, thereby limiting runoff and flooding. However, since livestock have for a century cut vegetative ground cover productivity by at least half on over half the West (livestock additionally eat and trample about half of surviving low-level vegetation annually), it is not surprising that rain and snowmelt runoff, and therefore major flooding, has increased dramatically during that period. Since plants eliminated by livestock were generally those most suited to conserving water, the increased runoff influence has been amplified.

As detailed, livestock have reduced the soil's water infiltration rate in many ways. However, the ground's ability to absorb and percolate water into aquifers also depends upon soil *quantity*. Soil holds water and releases it slowly into groundwater tables or surface flows. Where there is little or no soil, water runs quickly through underlying sand and gravel, hits bedrock, and flows off quickly into waterways. Topsoil likewise does a better job of holding and slowly releasing water than do underlying soil horizons. Since more than half of Western topsoil has been lost during the past 130 years, it is again not surprising that violent flooding has increased tremendously.

In "Land Erosion -- Normal and Accelerated -- in the Semiarid West," R.W. Bailey states that observations, measurements, and history "... amply justify the conclusions that many watersheds in the semi-arid West may develop a sufficiently complete plant-and-soil mantle to allow an infiltration rate equal to the greatest magnitude and intensity of storms." In other words, if undamaged, the plant and soil mantle of many watersheds in the semi-arid West will prevent serious flooding. As most of the rangeland West is in the semi-arid category, this means that before being grazed by livestock much of the West rarely experienced destructive floods.

This plant-and-soil mantle to storm equilibrium is verified by botanic, geologic, and hydrologic evidence from recent and prehistoric times. In their undamaged state watersheds have a far greater ability to absorb water and prevent flooding than is generally acknowledged. Unfortunately, undamaged watersheds are now extremely rare.

Both watersheds [along the Wasatch Front in Utah] *received equally heavy rain, yet the watershed of Parrish Canyon produced severe floods, whereas the adjacent Centerville Canyon produced little or no flooding. Investigation showed that the Parrish Canyon watershed was heavily overgrazed; whereas the Centerville Canyon watershed was protected from excessive grazing.*
--from **Environmental Conservation** by Raymond F. Dasmann (Dasmann 1972)

If the West had a regional landscape, as states have state birds, it would be the gully and wash. Over the last century, millions of them have been cut into the vast landscape, carrying off cubic miles of dirt, causing water tables to drop, and helping to turn intact arid land into sterile desert.
--Ed Marston, "Rocks and Hard Places" (Marston 1991)

Most of us view the common eroded gulch as one of the West's scenic natural attractions. However, it is rarely natural, and scenic only because we have come to accept it as such. In fact, just 130 years ago it was unusual to encounter an arroyo (eroded drainage with flat floors and vertical banks) or cutbank, or even a scoured wash, in most of the Western US. In the Southwest, for example, the only stream for which significant pre-1850 arroyo trenching is well-documented is the Rio Puerco in New Mexico (where currently exist vastly larger arroyos than at that time).

Then in the late 1800s something radical happened. According to Ernst Antevs' study "Arroyo-Cutting and Filling," "The native grazing ranges were denuded in one to a few decades after the introduction of livestock in large numbers, and a general arroyo-cutting followed promptly." J.J. Thornber, an early botanist studying Arizona rangelands, agreed that "This overstocking [in the late 1800s] soon resulted in destructive overgrazing and trampling out of large areas of forage producing plants, often beyond recovery." As a consequence, rainwater rushed down watersheds and, "Once in the cienegas and rivers, these accumulated waters developed into the most destructive floods, cutting in the rich alluvial soils of these formerly well-watered valleys, within the space of a remarkably few years, permanent channels 5 to 30 feet deep and 50 to 300 feet wide."

Arroyos, though best represented in the Southwest, are now common to landscapes throughout the rangeland West. They come in all sizes, from small, eroded gullies to gigantic chasms up to 100' deep, hundreds of feet wide, and over 100 miles long. Arroyos are incised in unconsolidated materials consisting of clay, silt, sand, and gravel. These channels were formed primarily when accelerated water runoff from livestock-grazed watersheds caused violent floods that cut into the alluvium of the (usually) overgrazed bottoms of canyons and valleys.

Arroyos and cutbanks usually begin in the main drainages where floodwaters are most concentrated. After forming, they work their way back up main channels and tributary drainages, undercutting falls and eating away at cutbanks -- something like an army of Pac Men -- creating heavily eroded, miniature Grand Canyons. Because floodwater concentrates in these eroded channels rather than spreading out evenly over floodplains, downcutting, side cutting, and undercutting are exacerbated and deposition of bottomland is minimized.

An arroyo on grazed range. *(Bob Dixon)*

Though arroyo formation was greatest during ranching's early years, it is still prevalent across most of the West. Moreover, the main reason that the rate of arroyo and cutbank formation has lessened during the latter part of this century is because the most arroyo-prone drainages have already been cut, not because grazing pressure and resultant flooding have significantly diminished.

Hanging roots indicate gully was recently cut; subsequent fencing from cattle has allowed new vegetation to begin recovery.

One of the simplest and cheapest ways to control small and medium gullies having small drainage areas is to fence them and exclude livestock . . .
--USDA, *Farmers' Bulletin #2171*

When a flood cuts into the drainage on the floor of a draw, canyon, or valley, long chains of destructive forces are unleashed. As channels cut lower into drainages, groundwater is drawn in laterally from adjacent bottoms and riparian zones and down to these lower levels. As a result, these bottoms and riparian zones dry out, stunting or killing vegetation and changing plant composition. Grasses, sedges, rushes, and other herbaceous perennials are replaced by annual forbs, cheatgrass, rabbitbrush, sagebrush, and bare dirt. Water levels drop below the roots of riparian trees, which then die.

For instance, the mesquite trees along the Santa Cruz River in southern Arizona originally grew to over 60' tall in huge riparian groves along much of this 100 mile long river valley. With the onset of heavy livestock grazing in the late 1800s, floods began cutting into the river bed and water tables began to drop. Mesquite roots, which can grow 300' or longer (the longest known roots of any plant) finally could no longer reach dependable moisture. Later, woodcutting and groundwater pumping augmented ranching's influence. Today, the river is gone and only a few stunted reminders of these once magnificent mesquite riparian forests survive.

Being barren and sun-baked, the walls of arroyos dry out quickly and effectively suck water from adjacent bottoms. In turn, when vegetation along drainages is depleted, violent floods are better able to rip into banks and expand cutbanks, causing further drying of adjacent land. In a similar manner, groundwater from surrounding uplands gravitates down and inward toward these incised channels, drying out the uplands as well.

One might imagine that surrounding groundwater draining down and in toward arroyo bottoms would increase streamflow there, but curiously just the opposite usually occurs. Arroyo beds, barren and composed of coarse sediments, are much less able to bring water to the surface than the well-vegetated, fine-soiled, fertile bottoms they replaced. Dried out, adjacent grazed land that once conserved water and released it gradually into drainages no longer does so.

Very active arroyo cutting on BLM land in the overgrazed Rio Puerco River drainage, NM. *(BLM)*

Large cutbanks on state land, Yavapai County, Arizona.

Across the West, cattle graze unchecked in stream bottoms, destroying riparian zones and causing serious erosion that in turn causes the deep-cut-bank streams that even old-timers think are natural conditions.
--Charles F. Wilkinson, professor, University of Colorado Law School

Ranchers commonly blame "the damnable weather" for all this. Many say that violent flooding, arroyos, and cutbanks have always been around. Of course, it does take a lot of rain or snowmelt to cause flooding anyplace, overgrazed or not. But blaming the weather for the flooding destruction of the past 130 years is like blaming the air or your lungs for your lung cancer after smoking 3 packs a day for 30 years.

Other ranching apologists promote the drying climate theory as the cause of the massive depletion of vegetation, water, and soil over the past century. Curiously, many of these same people concurrently push the violent weather theory to excuse the massive flooding and arroyo cutting of this same period. One well-known ranching proponent claims that "sudden violent showers" and "irregular occurrences of heavy storms" are what really caused the sudden appearance of arroyos, cutbanks, and tremendously destructive flooding in the West. Livestock were supposedly a minor influence, or at most merely a "trigger" that helped set off this deterioration.

If this were indeed true, wouldn't geologists and archaeologists have found much evidence of past periodic channel cutting and violent flooding in what is now the Western US? They haven't. Based on historical accounts and photographs, both K. Bryan and J.T. Duce, in separate studies, concluded that arroyo formation in the semi-arid West occurred at the time of livestock introduction and was not related to geomorphological processes (Palmer 1988). If livestock grazing is just a harmless "trigger," then what is the weapon, and why was it never detonated before?

Today, many other human activities contribute to increased flooding, including logging, mining, ORV (off-road vehicle) use, road building, and development (much of all this by the ranching industry). Many stockmen lay the blame on one or more of these factors. But consider this: Throughout most of the West accelerated and violent flooding began long before any of these other activities had a substantial influence. Further, in many watersheds that have experienced increased and ruinous flooding, livestock grazing was and still is the only significant human use.

In 1933 a portion of Wickiup Creek in central Oregon -- at the time, a wide, barren, trampled, arroyo -- was fenced from cattle. Fifty years later, a 94% decrease in incised channel area had occurred, and the clear, flowing creek was "almost completely obscured by grasses and sedges, and willow thickets . . ." (Clifton 1989)

[Note: Consult Packer 1953, Lusby 1970, Busby 1981, Debano 1989, and other references in the bibliography for more information on watershed runoff and flooding.]

The greatest damage from erosion on range lands occurs where the areas have been overgrazed and the ground cover destroyed or seriously impaired. Before the ranges had been overstocked and the ground cover impaired, erratic run-off and erosion were practically unknown. After the breaking up of the vegetative cover in the early nineties, however, many streams originally of steady year-long flow and teeming with trout became treacherous channels with intermittent flow through which the water from rainstorms was plunged, or rose and fell according to the size and frequency of the storms and carried so much sediment in the water that fish and similar life could not exist.
--Range professional A.W. Sampson (Sampson 1918)

Water Quality

I can imagine the splendor of a not-so-distant past when Westerners could drink from streams without fear of giardia and other water-borne illnesses. But now, whether it be drinking from an alpine lake, a Rocky Mountain waterfall or a canyon creek, that opportunity has been lost due to indiscriminate cattle grazing. . . .
--Ken A. Rait, Tucson, AZ, *High Country News* (9-12-90)

Even as livestock grazing has depleted or eliminated most Western water sources, so has it lowered the *quality* of remaining water. Experts estimate that 90% of the surface water on public land is significantly polluted. In the West, sediments loosed by livestock, pollutants washed off the overgrazed land, manure, urine, and dead cattle are the main sources of water pollution in most ranching areas (which, again, compose 70% of the West), as well as many downstream waterways. The Arizona Department of Environmental Quality reports that 95% of the state's surface waters are polluted, with livestock being the leading cause. In Utah, more than half of the high-priority nonpoint source watersheds identified by the Utah Department of Health suffer from excess salts, organic and chemical wastes, and sediment due to grazing. The *New York Times* reports that cattle "represent the West's largest source of 'nonpoint' water pollution" (Royte 1990). Nearly all surface waters in the West are fouled with livestock-related contaminants (Suk 1986).

These plains rivers are depressing and rather sinister to look at, and they always have been helping carry the mountains to the sea. But one reads with amazement descriptions of them before the Civil War. They were comparatively clear streams, streams whose gradual, geological erosion of the land had not been accelerated -- as it was when the cattle business came to Wyoming and Montana.
--Bernard DeVoto, **The Easy Chair** (DeVoto 1955)

As water runs off the denuded, degraded, depleted soil of watersheds, it picks up sediments and carries them into surface waters. Other sediments are contributed by degraded riparian areas, crumbling banks, and trampled, stirred up stream and lake beds. Much of the finer-particled sediment remains in suspension for days, or indefinitely if water remains in motion, as in flowing water or where livestock stir it up. The sediment is harmful to fish and other aquatic life. Field studies reveal 37%-59% decreases in biological productivity as a result of increases in water-borne fine sediments.

In the West, rangeland contributes 28% of the total sediment load (as with soil erosion, most sediment is from farmland) (Ferguson 1983). In the US, over half of the suspended matter in water supplies consists of particles washed off grazing land and cropland used to grow livestock feed (Hur 1985a).

In 1929 the US Geological Survey estimated that the San Juan and Little Colorado River watersheds, which drain the Navajo Indian Reservation, where overgrazing was then at a peak, contributed 14% of the Colorado River's water but more than half of its sediment. It called the Navajo Reservation "public enemy number 1 in causing the Colorado silt problem." Subsequent stock reductions brought corresponding reductions in siltation, though overgrazing remains the Navajos' most serious environmental problem (see Chapter IX).

Airborne pollutants from vehicular exhaust, industrial emissions, radioactive discharges, and so forth are spread by winds through the atmosphere, a portion settling gradually onto downwind rangeland around the West. Various solid and liquid toxic wastes are dumped there, along with other banishments from civilization and ranching operations, such as old equipment, vehicles, appliances, trash, etc. Mining wastes make a heavy contribution. As rainwater and snowmelt run quickly off damaged watersheds, harmful particles from all these sources, rather than being filtered through soil or held on land until rendered less harmful, are picked up and carried into streams, lakes, and oceans. Once in water supplies, they may be consumed by animals and people, causing or contributing to a variety of health problems. Thus, ranching's overall contribution to water pollution is much greater than indicated by figures for its direct contribution.

Similarly, as mentioned, aquatic vegetation filters out and breaks down sediments and pollutants. On public land, livestock grazing has removed and destroyed far more aquatic vegetation than has any other influence.

Livestock also cause chemical water pollution directly. Cattle produce about 50 pounds of manure each day, which contains large amounts of ammonia, nitrates, sodium, phosphates, potassium, and other elements that -- in the amounts commonly found in livestock-impacted streams -- harm plants and animals; nitrates in drinking water, especially, have been shown to be hazardous to humans. Cattle urine, of which each cow donates about 20 pounds per day, contains much ammonia, which in heavy concentrations is toxic to fish and other aquatic animals. Excessive sediment and foreign substances washed off rangeland and dissolved into or chemically transformed in surface waters also add to chemical pollution, as do ranching activities such as herbicide and insecticide spraying.

Livestock grazing sometimes lowers water quality by lowering water tables. Much of groundwater is saline or highly mineralized, especially at lower levels. When good quality groundwater is depleted, adjacent lower-quality water may flow in and mix with what remains. This fouled water may then appear as surface flow or be pumped for human use.

Similarly, livestock have lowered water quality by reducing surface flows. Less flow means less aeration and filtering through inorganic sediments and aquatic vegetation, as well as less *volume* of water to dilute pollution. The stock tanks that partially replaced depleted surface waters exhibit essentially no flow and little cleansing action.

Compared to nearly all wildlife, cattle are filthy , disease-ridden animals. If not for modern medicine, many would not survive.

Ranching operations are the main cause of water pollution on Western public lands.

Almost always, government agencies advise against drinking from natural water sources. The traditional explanation has been, "There might be a dead animal just upstream from where you are drinking." Except in the case of dead cows, this is basically a fable, nurtured by the ranching establishment for a hundred years and generally accepted by the American public. Indigenous Americans drank solely from natural waters for millennia and rarely fell ill as a result. Many thousands of mod-

Livestock grazing is the main reason we may no longer safely drink from natural water sources in the West (and, again, the main reason so many natural water sources no longer exist). Note cowpie at edge of creek. *(Bill Lewinson)*

ern Americans have become sick and some have died from doing so. When hard pressed, government officials will usually confess that livestock are actually the main culprits. Most Western communities utilizing surface flow for domestic water seem to agree; they fence off their watersheds and water sources, from livestock more than from people. In the East's Appalachian Mountains, where there are no livestock but many humans, hikers are provided dippers at stream crossings and most are unafraid to drink the water.

Regardless, many ranchers contend that *people* -- backpackers especially -- are the real transgressors behind biological water pollution on Western public land. Undoubtedly people *are* mostly to blame in a few small, heavily used areas. But how many humans defecate directly into a stream or lake? Cattle do, perhaps a million of them each day, on *most* public land. If 1 million cows each release 1 quart (2 of 50 pounds) a day into water (a conservative estimate), this means that at least 1000 tons of bovine excrement are discharged into our public waters every day. Though human excrement generally is more dangerous from a disease standpoint (at least to humans), people produce an average of only 0.33 pounds per day, an infinitesimal percentage of which is released into public waters. Thus, the daily direct human contribution is *tens of thousands* of times less.

Many diseases and disorders are spread via water-borne livestock pollution to wild animals and humans. Most are bacterial or protozoan in nature.

Various *salmonella* bacteria, spread by livestock through surface waters, cause disease to humans and wildlife. *Dysentery* may be spread through feces or water. *Anthrax* bacteria live in the stagnant pools and hoof ruts created by trampling cattle or sheep and infest mice, rabbits, and other wild and domestic animals, usually killing them quickly. A

similar bacteria-caused disease is *black leg*, which has killed many large herbivores over the years, though humans are immune. *Hoof rot* is also spread to ungulates through infected waters.

One disease of great concern is *giardiasis*, which is caused by giardia, a water-borne protozoan that parasitizes the intestinal tracts of humans and at least 40 wild and domestic animals, including cattle. More than 16 million Americans are currently thought to be infected with it, mostly from contaminated community water supplies in the East. Giardiasis can debilitate the body on a semi-permanent basis and cause acute abdominal pain, bloating, vomiting, and diarrhea, sometimes leading victims to seek hospitalization.

Countless thousands of people and wild animals have contacted giardia by drinking contaminated water from public land. Grazing industry apologists are currently busy trying to pin the blame for this giardia on beavers and humans. However, they ignore important facts. A main one is that giardia bacteria are often contracted from springs, streams, ponds, and lakes not inhabited by beaver and where human use is extremely light.

Consider, for example, that 20% of stock tanks tested in Arizona contained giardia. I have never seen any sign of beaver in a stock tank, and no other giardia-carrying mammals or humans use many of them either, so cattle are the only possible source. Many scientific questions about giardia remain, but overwhelming circumstantial evidence indicates that cattle are a major, and probably *the* major, purveyor of giardia to public waters.

This bloated carcass is actually *floating* downriver in at least 6' of water.

A dead cow is stranded on a gravel bar, unnoticed until downwind. The corpse lies like a beached hull, misted with flies. And more dead cows -- whether from infection, accident, or stupidity we can only guess. The aroma downriver of various states of decomposition ranges from unpleasant to pungent to nauseating.
--Ann Zwinger, **Run, River, Run**

Dead cattle are another source of biological water pollution. Seeing their bloated corpses floating down rivers, as I have many times, is not at all uncommon, especially during flooding. Other times, you will find them lying stiff-legged, half eaten by maggots, at the edge of a pond or stream, exuding foul fluids into the water. As you can imagine, a putrid, rotting, thousand-pound cow carcass can contribute to water pollution.

Also spread by livestock via surface waters are internal parasites. *Tapeworms*, various *roundworms*, and *pinworms* can be transmitted to wild animals and humans when affected cattle and sheep defecate into water.

Livestock's overall contribution to all the above-mentioned types of water pollution is vastly greater than that of all wildlife combined. Not only is there a far greater biomass of livestock, but livestock concentrate and spend much more time in and near surface waters. Being large, clumsy foot-shufflers, cattle keep sediments and waste products stirred up and in suspension. (Fecal *coliform* bacteria counts in these sediments may be 100 to 1000 times greater than in surface water itself.) And certainly, few other large animals evacuate their bowels and bladders directly into their own water sources.

Springs, creeks, ponds, and stock tanks are especially susceptible. Many are turned into virtual cesspools, heavily laden with manure, urine, rotting vegetation, and muck. Under these conditions, summertime fecal *streptococci* bacteria counts soar. On the other hand, *coliform* bacteria peak during spring runoff when large amounts of excrement are washed in from rangelands. Numerous studies show that prevailing livestock use increases stream bacteria levels as much as 1000%, and that levels may remain high for months after livestock are removed (Gary 1983, Blumm 1986, Tiedemann 1987, etc.).

Relative to all of the above, consider the State of Oregon's official definition of water pollution (similar to most states):

. . . such alteration of the physical and chemical or biological properties of any water of the state, including change in temperature, taste, color, turbidity, silt or odor of the waters, or such discharge of any liquid, gaseous, solid, radioactive, or other substance into the waters of the state, which will or tends to, either by itself or in connection with any other substance, create a public nuisance or which will or tends to render such waters harmful, detrimental or injurious to public health, safety or welfare, or to domestic, commercial, industrial, agricultural, recreational or other legitimate beneficial uses or to livestock, wildlife, fish or other aquatic life or the habitat thereof.

Obviously, under Oregon law (as under all other Western state water pollution laws) livestock are water polluters of the highest magnitude.

As the vast bulk of Western water is located on, flows through, or flows from public land, most surface waters in the West are affected by public lands livestock grazing. As mentioned, 75% of Western water for human use comes from National Forest land, most of it grazed by livestock.

(Ginny Rosenberg)

"THAT AIN'T THE KIND OF RENEWING THIS RESOURCE NEEDS !!!"

The drastic reduction in the amount of surface water in the West over the past century or so is a major adverse result of public lands ranching. If compressed into a single year, it would be declared a national disaster. The widespread pollution of what water remains adds insult to injury. The public and public land have a fundamental right to naturally occurring, clean water.

. . . grazing helps improve grass and crop production, control erosion, recharge aquifers, enhance riparian conditions, and provide water for recreational, agricultural, and other needs.
--*Livestock Grazing Successes on Public Range*, USFS, BLM, and Public Lands Council (USDA 1989)

They lie.
--Mike Roselle, progressive activist

Oman handed me a two-year-old photo that showed three cows wading in a mudhole embraced by bare, compacted dirt. I lifted my gaze from the photo to the pond, now rimmed with greenery and full of ducks and grassy nesting islands. We climbed over the fence and walked into the twenty-seven-acre oasis. Everywhere flax and aster were in blue and purple bloom, and thousands of willows, some waist high, were sprouting around the pond's perimeter. We pushed on toward the dike through Great Basin wild rye -- the native bunch grass that lapped the stirrups of the pioneers. A year ago the dike had been naked. Now it was filling in with western yarrow and small burnet, a good wildlife staple. Killdeer screamed, a marsh hawk wheeled and dipped, and redwings rustled through the cattails.
--Ted Williams, "He's Going to Have an Accident" (Williams 1991)

Animals

The grazing of domestic livestock on Western rangelands has probably had a greater adverse impact on wildlife populations than any other single factor.
--Steve Gallizioli, Research Chief, Arizona State Game and Fish Department (Ferguson 1983)

Do you realize that the small piece of plastic dropped along the way or left in camp is a thousand times more dangerous to wildlife (and livestock) than any cow?
--Jim Ellison, public lands rancher, Bond, Colorado, in a letter to the editor of *Colorado Outdoors* (Nov/Dec 1986)

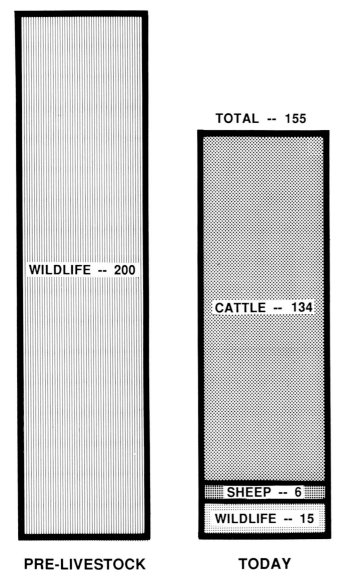

PRE-LIVESTOCK   **TODAY**

RANGE AUMS CONSUMED:
11 WESTERN STATES
(In millions of AUMs annually. Livestock and large wild herbivores. Rough conjecture based on various sources.)

Practically speaking, *there are no empty niches in a healthy ecosystem.* Aside from any additional deleterious effects livestock may have, every cow, sheep, goat, or other domestic animal on the open land is *replacing* naturally occurring animals -- taking up their "living space," so to speak. No matter the number of livestock or grazing method used, there is no way around this actuality.

When livestock deplete natural resources and occupy space, wild animals have less available for food, cover, shelter, perching, mating, nesting, hibernating, and so forth. Additionally, the mere physical presence of domestic stock interferes with territorial boundaries and behavior, and forces wildlife to seek larger domains and infringe upon and deplete their neighbors' habitat. In short, wildlife has less of what it needs to survive. As a general rule, when livestock are placed in an area, they eliminate at least roughly their weight in elk, raccoons, spiders, pronghorn, worms, badgers, moles, mice, microbes, salamanders, robins, and other wild animals that inhabit the area.

However, livestock's negative impact on wildlife is far greater than this simple rule indicates. Mark Dimmitt, curator of plants at the Arizona-Sonora Desert Museum in Tucson, states that, "Anytime you damage a plant, you affect the health of an animal." Indeed, botanists estimate that the loss of 1 plant species affects the life processes of, on average, at least 15 animal species. On the Western range livestock grazing has depleted or extirpated more native plant species and biomass than any other factor. For each domestic animal added to an ecosystem there is a much greater corresponding decrease in total wildlife biomass, affecting a great number of species.

To repeat, Western rangeland today is probably less than half as productive biotically as before the livestock occupation. Disregarding other factors, it stands to reason that rangeland now supports less than half the biomass of wild animals that it once did. Further, on most rangeland today livestock have stripped off at least half of the forage and much of the browse; most public lands grazing plans call for 30% to 70% herbage "utilization," while actual removal (and destruction by trampling, etc.) is often even higher. With all this in mind, it is easy to understand why many native animals have been devastated.

Bighorns forage on heavily grazed BLM cattle range near Cody, Wyoming, but if snow piles too high they may starve -- while the cattle responsible for the lack of forage are fed hay. *(George Robbins Photo, Jackson, WY)*

Large Native Ungulates

We have let cattle displace at least 90% of native ungulates in the West. If loggers wanted to replace 90% of the trees in the West with even-aged European pines, would we let that happen too?

--George Wuerthner, naturalist/author

Cattle alone now eat a greater relative percentage of Western vegetation than did all native large ungulates combined when they roamed in great herds and scattered bands 150 years ago. According to reasonable estimates, at that time buffalo, elk, deer, pronghorn, bighorns, and free-roaming horses consumed roughly 150-250 million AUMs from the range in the region that would become the 11 Western states. Today, based on government wildlife estimates (which may be inflated), these species combined consume approximately 15 million AUMs from the Western range. Domestic sheep currently eat roughly half this amount, whereas cattle eat perhaps 7-10 times this amount, or between 100 and 150 million AUMs. (Variations in estimates are due largely to differences in what constitutes rangeland." For instance, some types of pasture may be considered rangeland and some may not. Ultimately, however, nearly all Western land now used to produce livestock was originally rangeland.)

Therefore, the total amount of herbage eaten by all large herbivores, wild and domestic, on Western rangeland today is perhaps 130-170 million AUMs, compared to the 150-250 million eaten by wildlife 150 years ago. Of course, geographic use patterns are somewhat different now, so relative grazing pressures vary. For example, due to livestock water developments, some areas grazed by livestock now were never grazed by wild ungulates. Farmland now ungrazed was at one time prime wildlife range. And public and private range has experienced variations in management over the years. However, most of the West grazed by wildlife then supports relatively similar, corresponding -- *though lower* -- livestock levels now.

In a nutshell, this reaffirms that (1) today's rangland is far less productive, and far more degraded, than in pre-livestock times, and (2) livestock, unlike native herbivores, are destructive, and primarily caused this condition.

GRAZING AUMS CONSUMED BY WILDLIFE AND LIVESTOCK IN 11 WESTERN STATES
(conjecture based on various sources)

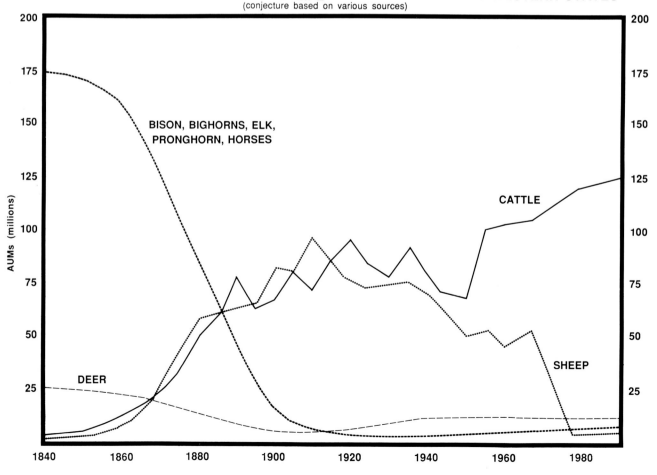

In other words . . .

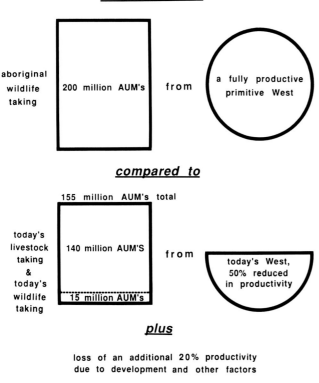

aboriginal wildlife taking

200 million AUM's   from   a fully productive primitive West

compared to

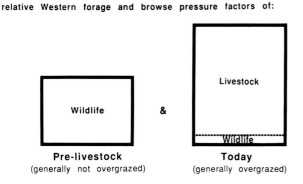

155 million AUM's total

today's livestock taking & today's wildlife taking

140 million AUM'S   from   today's West, 50% reduced in productivity

15 million AUM's

plus

loss of an additional 20% productivity due to development and other factors

equals

relative Western forage and browse pressure factors of:

Wildlife   &   Livestock

Wildlife

Pre-livestock
(generally not overgrazed)

Today
(generally overgrazed)

Further, there is an even greater relative loss to wildlife than the numbers of AUMs would indicate because livestock generally deplete and destroy the vegetation most beneficial to wild animals, largely because ranchers move their animals about to maximize consumption of preferred forage and browse in the most productive locations. Likewise, because so much of the West's preferred grasses, forbs, and browse are depleted, livestock frequently eat other types of vegetation, which accordingly leaves wildlife even less desirable vegetation in even less favorable habitat. There is therefore that much more competition between livestock and wildlife than commonly acknowledged by the grazing industry. For example, on many Great Basin sagebrush ranges, palatable browse, grasses, and forbs are so depleted by livestock that deer are forced to eat sagebrush, which they may survive on but not thrive on.

Additionally, since heavy grazing has depleted native forage and browse and degraded the range, poisonous increasers and exotics have become much more numerous and widespread. The great reduction in available food plants has forced wildlife to eat this toxic vegetation, causing a significant increase in the percentage of wild animals harmed or killed by this influence.

Finally, wild ungulates generally are more selective in their diet than are livestock, so they are more adversely affected by these radical vegetation changes. Much evidence indicates that livestock are better able than most wild herbivores to adjust their dietary needs to changing range conditions. Domestic cattle and sheep, spread over most of the globe, have adapted to and have been bred to eat whatever is available. Wild herbivores, on the other hand, have evolved slowly along with and so are adapted to certain plant species in certain habitats. In other words, though they may be selective within their forage area, livestock can survive on a greater variety of plants within a wider variety of conditions than most wild plant eaters (although within their own particular habitats most wildlife species would outcompete livestock without human intervention). In **Wildlife and America**, Frederic H. Wagner explains it somewhat differently:

> *Livestock, through centuries of selective breeding, appear more capable of shifting diets without so much detrimental effect on their nutrition. Consequently, as vegetation composition is altered through grazing, wild species may be affected detrimentally by slight or subtle changes while the range may still be in quite favorable condition for domestic animals.* (Wagner 1978)

All this doesn't take into account other negative factors such as introduced disease, loss of predators that normally keep wildlife populations healthy, hunting and trapping by ranchers, the effects of fences, human encroachment from ranching roads, and so on. No wonder populations of large herbivores -- and most wild animals -- plummeted when livestock grazing became intensive.

The decline of large herbivores on the Navajo Reservation in the late 1800s demonstrates ranching's impact. Navajoland visitors reported abundant game, including pronghorn, deer, and elk, in the early 1870s. Livestock numbers exploded soon thereafter and, as a result of overgrazing combined with hunting to eliminate livestock competition, by 1884 the Navajo Indian agent reported no game left. (White 1983)

(Paul Hirt)

Contrary to the claims of some ranching advocates, compared to today large wild herbivores were numerous throughout the aboriginal West. Historical records and scientific study indicate that only the driest deserts and other waterless, barren, or inaccessible areas lacked some type of large herbivore. The mid- and short-grass prairies, in fact, supported megafauna numbers second only to that of Africa's Serengeti.

Aside from heavy use in the vicinity of strategic watering places and salt licks, however, native animals did not cause long-term depletion of native vegetation. Normal seasonal migrations permitted recovery of the range. The animals moved slowly across the land, herds of different species often side by side, grazing and browsing as they went, usually not returning to the same area until several years later -- perhaps even 10 or more years later. Moreover, for millions of years they and the vegetation they ate evolved together, to each other's overall benefit. There existed a symbiotic, dynamic equilibrium, a natural balance between plants and animals.

When livestock were introduced into the West, this co-evolution mostly came to an end. As huge and wildly fluctuating numbers of domesticates were added to those of wildlife, the natural balance was quickly upset. Many species had to change habits and habitat to survive; in most areas populations significantly decreased or species disappeared altogether.

Native animals most noticeably affected by livestock have been the large, herding ungulates -- buffalo, elk, whitetail

(George Wuerthner)

and mule deer, bighorns, pronghorn, and free-roaming horses (see Competitors in Chapter IV). Somewhat resembling cattle, sheep, and goats in size, herding tendency, and food requirements, these were the animals most perceptibly vulnerable to degradation of their habitats, to introduced disease, and to being replaced, displaced, and destroyed by livestock.

Just 150 years ago, incredibly huge herds of buffalo roamed the Great Plains and, in lesser numbers, the grassy portions of the Intermountain West, even in the mountains themselves. However, even then buffalo numbers had been reduced by Native Americans, chiefly because introduction of the free-ranging horse in the 1500s allowed for much more efficient buffalo hunting and eventual overkill. Estimates place the buffalo population in North America at that time at 40-75 million, and in the area to become the 11 Western states at 7-12 million, with the greatest concentrations on the plains of Montana, Wyoming, and Colorado. Single herds sometimes numbered in the millions and stretched 100 miles or more in length. It is thought that these herds were the greatest animal concentrations in terms of biomass that ever existed.

There were 2 subspecies of buffalo: the *plains*, which in 1900 dropped to a low of only about 500 individuals, and the *woods*, which is said to be genetically extinct as a species.

Directly or indirectly, buffalo provided necessities to a great number and variety of creatures, including wolves, coyotes, foxes, grizzly and black bears, eagles, wolverines, buffalo birds (now ironically known as *cow*birds), magpies, prairie dogs, dung beetles, and many others. For instance, the numerous buffalo bones once scattered across the plains were an important source of calcium to small gnawing mammals. These animals, in turn, dug extensive tunnels into the prairie soil, benefitting soil and water systems, and so on.

Effects of the loss of the buffalo reverberated throughout the environment. The thousands of large buffalo wallows that once pock-marked Western grassland became ponds to be used by numerous plants and animals. The wallows provided dust, dirt, and mud some animals used for various purposes; they also furnished an environment favorable to certain plant species with few other places to grow on the open prairie; and they provided for a diversity of habitat, not only for species that specialized in buffalo wallow habitat, but for those that depended on a combination of wallow and other types of habitat. Abandoned buffalo wallows, which contained copious manure and captured runoff, rich sediments, and organic material, eventually provided fertile, moist seedbeds for lush vegetation and habitat for many wild animals. Some of the depressions left by these wallows, and traces of their unique biologic community, can still be seen on the prairie today.

That the buffalo's demise was due mainly to the US campaign (led largely by stockmen) to subjugate the "Indians" by destroying their livelihood and to a relentless quest for meat, hides, and sport, is well-documented. But livestock, too, had a heavy hand in the buffalo's annihilation. Especially in the later years, cattle competed with buffalo, persistently overgrazing their forage plants, introducing disease and crowding them out. As buffalo declined, livestock occupied nearly all of their former range, effectively eliminating opportunities for re-establishment.

Recovery efforts by concerned groups and individuals in the early 1900s gradually increased buffalo numbers and saved them from extinction. The US government established token buffalo herds in some Western states; their low numbers are now carefully controlled, often with sport hunting. In recent years, as a growing appetite for buffalo meat has led to "buffalo ranching" (see Chapter XII), the total number of buffalo in North America has risen to approximately 90,000 -- still only roughly 1/600th their aboriginal number. Most are *raised* on small, carefully fenced lands that better resemble cattle ranches than open buffalo territory. There are no longer any truly wild, truly natural buffalo.

A time would come when those plains would be a grazing country, the buffalo give place to tame cattle, farmhouses be scattered along the water courses, and wolves, bears, and Indians be numbered among the things that were.
--Francis Parkman, in the preface to the 1872 edition of **The Oregon Trail**

We've been under Forest Service management since the 1930's, and we don't believe there's overgrazing by cattle. If there's any overgrazing, it's by elk. The cattle have been undergrazing...
--Jim Webb, President, Arizona Cattle Growers Association, in 1988

(Steve Johnson)

Before European settlement, elk lived in a wide diversity of habitats across North America: from coast to coast, from northern Canada to Mexico. Historically, 6 subspecies have been described, all of which lived somewhere within the 11 Western states. Two are now extinct due to human impact.

Herds of hundreds and even thousands of elk roamed the Great Plains, inter-Rocky Mountain valleys, semi-arid grasslands and adjacent mountains of the Great Basin, hills and valleys of California, forests of the Northwest, and mountains and mesas of the Southwest. Estimates put the number of elk in the West at that time variously at 2 to 5 million, with the higher figure probably more accurate.

Over the years, elk were overhunted and pushed out of their former range by ranching, farming, and development. The survivors were those able to subsist in rugged, remote, heavily forested areas; now elk occupy less than 15% of their former range. Since reaching a low point of about 70,000 in 1920, elk recovery and reintroduction efforts (mainly for hunting purposes) have brought the number in the West up to about half a million -- perhaps 10% of their original number. In contrast, there are about 20 million cattle and 5 million sheep in the 11 Western states, representing roughly 100 times elks' biomass (USDA 1987).

In the West today, elk are found mostly in National Forests, in dense mountain timber and adjacent open spaces where they can forage and browse. Primarily grazers, elk and cattle eat many of the same plants. Competition between the two is intense in much of the remaining elk habitat, not only for food, but for salt, minerals, and sometimes even water. For example, thousands of elk in Yellowstone National Park and elsewhere in the Northern Rockies starved to death in the winter of 1988-89, in large part because elk are no longer able to migrate to lower-elevation forage lands or, when they do, they are unable to find enough to eat. Disease spread by livestock also hurt elk.

Perhaps as harmful has been cattle's social and psychological influence on elk. Studies by Nelson and Burnell in 1976 conclude that elk left an area where cattle were introduced, and that elk would not use a study management unit except for those areas ungrazed by cattle. Studies by Jeffrey in 1963 and Mackie in 1970 showed similar results (Wagner 1978). A study by Jon Skovlin in 1968 also found that elk use was significantly lower on ranges cohabited by cattle than in those where cattle use was restricted (Skovlin 1968). Many people contend that, in addition to related factors, the mere *presence* of cattle is repellent psychologically to elk and many other wildlife species.

Livestock grazing continues to be a major threat to elk survival. Although elk do survive, most do so only with human help (e.g., winter feeding and vaccination against disease) and by assuming unnatural habits and living under unnatural conditions. As with the buffalo, the elk is no longer a truly wild animal able to adapt and evolve in a natural manner.

Before fencing this area was prime wintering ground for elk. Since sheep have grazed here almost no natural grasses grow between the sage, and without them, the wind worries the soil, producing it into the air in streaming funnels.
--Ann Zwinger, **Run, River, Run**

(Steve Johnson)

The 2 species of deer native to the West are the whitetail and mule, the latter recognized by its larger ears and black-tipped tail. A mule deer subspecies, the blacktail, lives in the damp, dense forests of the Pacific Northwest.

Ernest Seton, an early 1900s wildlife expert, estimated that a deer population of around 13 million existed in the West in pre-Columbian times (Seton 1929). Most current authorities place that number then at 1/3 to 1/2 that amount, but it should be noted that most of today's "authorities" are somehow professionally involved in deer management programs and may, consciously or otherwise, foster misinterpretation. Although no one knows for sure, extrapolation and numerous descriptions by Native Americans and early explorers suggest that the pre-European deer population was at least 5 million and perhaps as high as Seton's estimate.

Today's 3.6 million deer (according to state fish and wildlife agencies estimates) comprise 2/3 of all "big game" animals in the 11 Western states. This helps explain why professional wildlife managers consider deer their "big game success story."

For several reasons deer numbers remained high while those of all other large herbivores plummeted. First, deer, like elk, have semi-successfully abandoned their former habits and territory. Until the mid-1800s deer, often in large groups or herds numbering in the hundreds, roamed not only forest and brushland, but open rangeland as well. Unlike today, deer felt as much at home on the open landscape as in brush and trees. In his journal, Meriweather Lewis of the Lewis and Clark expedition notes, "when [mule deer] are met with in the woodlands or river bottoms and are pursued they invariably run to the hills or open country as the elk do" (Thwaites 1959). When ranching and hunting pressures increased, those deer that lived in or moved to wooded areas and lived singly or in small groups were better able to survive.

Second, deer eat forbs, grasses, and even mushrooms but, more than the other large herbivores, they can thrive on browse. For them, cattle and sheep competition has always been less severe. (Also, though cattle and especially sheep eat much browse, deer can reach higher into branches, and can even stand on their hind legs to do so.) Originally, huge herds of deer roamed Western grasslands, often eating grasses and forbs more than browse. However, after they abandoned most of the open range -- and when much of their new and former habitat was overgrazed by foraging cattle and sheep -- they were able to switch to a heavily browse diet. While overgrazing livestock may under certain conditions increase the amount of woody vegetation, this "benefit" is more than offset by their detriments -- depletion of woody vegetation and browse on most land, overgrazing of other vegetation, depletion of water sources, introduced disease, physical presence, and so on.

During the late 19th and early 20th centuries, as habitat was severely grazed and hunters and ranchers took an increasing toll, deer numbers reached a low point of perhaps 2 million. But then a curious thing happened. As the years passed, and as humans acquired a greater technological ability to exploit the forests of the West, extensive logging, woodcutting, and explosive, destructive fires (caused ironically by fire suppression) resulted in brush, forb, and grass increases in many previously heavily forested areas.

Additionally, as the West's human population increased, so did the demand for "big game." Consequently, in recent years governments have managed much of the land heavily for deer and deer hunting.

Mainly due to these factors, the overall area of prime habitat has not decreased nearly as much for deer as it has for other large herbivores. However, most deer habitat is currently grazed by livestock, so available *food per acre* averages far less than in pre-Columbian times. In many areas, deer are undernourished due to livestock pressures.

Studies show that livestock grazing exerts other detrimental influences on Western deer populations. As with elk, deer do not mix well with cattle or sheep; they are rarely found together. Livestock spread disease and reduce or eliminate cover that deer, especially young fawns, need for protection from predators. They also cause deer to abandon feeding grounds, feed more heavily in riparian areas, increase the size of their home range, and spend more time traveling and feeding, rather than resting or interacting socially. (Loft 1987)

[Bighorns] *could not support the competition of the domestic sheep imported into their terrains, and suffered seriously from scab and other diseases contacted from these stupid, stunted cousins.*

--from **Wildlife in America** by Peter Matthiessen (Matthiessen 1959)

At perhaps 1% of their aboriginal population due mostly to ranching, bighorns are still harmed by livestock grazing and persecuted as competitors by Western stockmen. *(Steve Johnson)*

Bighorn sheep have been extirpated from well over 90% of their former range. Once roaming in herds across plains, plateaus, mesas, and valleys as well as mountains throughout the West, the bighorn is now restricted chiefly to steep, rugged mountainsides and rocky escarpments -- about the only places inaccessible to cattle and sheep. Knowledgeable and open-minded estimates of the West's pre-European bighorn population range from 2 to 3 million or more. They were more common than deer in many areas. Lewis and Clark, who traversed the northern West from 1804-1806, frequently reported seeing "great numbers of the bighorned animals" (Thwaites 1959). Native American pictographs and petroglyphs commonly featured bighorns. Today, Western bighorns number 20 to 30 thousand -- perhaps 1% of their former population.

Representations of bighorns are common in aboriginal pictographs and petroglyphs throughout the West.

Bighorns fare very poorly if forced to associate with livestock, and often abandon an area when livestock are introduced. Wildlife workers had this to say about bighorns in Utah's Canyonlands National Park:

> Prior to heavy livestock grazing pressure, bighorn sheep occupied much of the Park. Today [they are] restricted to canyons which were isolated from livestock grazing or to canyons where the physiography prohibited livestock from grazing the entire canyon.

Overhunting and habitat encroachment (both often attributable to stockmen) were important factors in bighorn population declines, but problems caused by ranching have been more harmful. They include inability of bighorns to share space with livestock, depletion of forage and browse, loss of water sources, harmful range developments, and introduced disease. There are at least 4 bighorn subspecies, each with different food preferences, that eat similar percentages of forage and browse. Normal bighorn diet consists mostly of grass, and thus food competition with livestock is considerable in many areas where bighorns survive. Corresponding increases in brush caused by overgrazing augment this competition in some areas. Wildlife expert Frederic H. Wagner reports

> There is a widespread view among wildlife specialists in the West that these kinds of changes were significant in exterminating bighorns from much of their former range and placing them in endangered status in the remnant areas still occupied. (Wagner 1978)

Scores of scientific studies (see the bibliography for some) show that livestock are deadly to bighorns in all these ways and more.

In short, the bighorn's plight is due mostly to ranching; further, livestock now monopolize most of the bighorn's former habitat, effectively preventing its recovery. If not for its ability to survive in impossibly rugged terrain, and governments' expensive efforts to save the species, the bighorn might have vanished long ago.

(Steve Johnson)

An exclusively North American animal, the pronghorn "antelope" (not a true antelope) includes 5 subspecies -- 4 in the West, one of which, according to wildlife experts, is "gravely endangered," and 1 in Baja California, near extinction. When pronghorn wandered most of the West 150 years ago, probably at least 10-15 million individuals inhabited the area that later became the 11 Western states. On the grassy plains, plateaus, and valleys, their huge herds, often numbering in the thousands, rivaled the buffalo's in size, and the two often moved across the landscape together.

As with the species described above, pronghorn suffered a drastic reduction in numbers during the 1800s. But, unlike elk, deer, and bighorns, pronghorn stayed in open country; because they generally prefer forbs, browse, and wildflowers to grass, competition from cattle for food was less intense. Nevertheless, continual overgrazing, overhunting (largely by ranchers), farming, and habitat intrusion (largely by ranchers and their livestock) eventually took their toll, reducing pronghorn to an estimated low of about 26,600 individuals in 1924.

Because cattle are more closely related to buffalo than to any other native Western animal, and because pronghorn are well-adapted to living near buffalo, pronghorn experienced less harm from cattle. In some areas, extensive overgrazing by cattle also caused an increase in forbs or sagebrush, which pronghorn do enjoy. Overall, however, cattle have been highly detrimental to pronghorn. For instance, cattle overgrazing has nearly eliminated the tall grass in which pronghorn, deer, and other large ungulates hide newborns and fawns from predators. On large portions of the semi-arid intermountain West, cattle have so denuded the range that pronghorn cannot survive; many studies document cattle/pronghorn food competition (Wagner 1978). In many areas, livestock grazing has caused brush to become so thick that pronghorn, which prefer open grassland/shrubland, have moved elsewhere or died.

Domestic sheep, with a diet much like pronghorn, were especially harmful when their numbers peaked in the early 1900s. For example, research biologist Don Ness states bluntly that, "all of northern Arizona was marvelous antelope range. Then it was sheeped to hell." When sheep herding finally succumbed to cattle ranching in the early 1930s, domestic sheep numbers took a dramatic fall -- while pronghorn numbers made a closely corresponding rise.

Due greatly to this decline in sheep numbers -- and to government recovery efforts, largely for hunting purposes -- state fish and wildlife agencies today estimate that about 700,000 pronghorn inhabit the 11 Western states, half of them in Wyoming (this figure may be inflated for political purposes). Unfortunately, some experts think the pronghorn population may currently be at or near its maximum, considering continued ranching pressures and other factors (Yates 1988). Unbelievably, today's pronghorn, at perhaps 5% of its original number, extirpated from the vast bulk of its range, and roaming in small bands in scattered locations, is proclaimed "a spectacular success" by ranchers and government range managers.

Malnourished pronghorn on depleted New Mexico BLM cattle range.

Now, because of the excellent range conditions, we have an overabundance of big game in [Utah] . . .
--Gary Rose, President, Utah Cattlemen's Association, 5-15-89 *Salt Lake City Tribune* (Government statistics show that all Utah "big game" combined consumes roughly 0.7 million AUMs, while Utah cattle and sheep consume more than 10 million AUMs.)

(Steve Johnson)

The 3 other large ungulates native to the West are the moose, mountain goat, and woodland caribou. In the West, moose live in the northern Rocky Mountains, in forested areas with lakes, swamps, or streams. Because of their limited range and watery habitat, effects from livestock might seem negligible, but this is not the case. Although overhunting has been the main cause of moose decline, introduced disease, range developments, general degradation of habitat, and competition for food with livestock, especially sheep, have also been factors. A study shows that, except in winter, moose diet in Montana and Wyoming consists of 20% browse, 10% grass, and 70% forbs -- a diet similar to that preferred by the domestic sheep that graze much of their habitat. Other studies have shown that moose have a low tolerance for the physical presence of livestock. The current Western moose population of several thousand is a fraction of what it once was.

The mountain goat, living at or above timberline in the high mountains of the Northwest and northern Rockies, has been less affected by ranching. Nevertheless, large herds of domestic sheep invade portions of its summer range; mountain goats moving in winter to lower mountain elevations often find forage and browse depleted by cattle and sheep. Introduced disease and range developments have taken a toll, though overhunting has been the mountain goat's greatest enemy. It has been eliminated from much of its former range in the contiguous US (though in some areas it has been introduced as a "game animal").

The large native Western ungulate probably least affected by livestock is the woodland caribou. Larger than a deer, smaller than an elk, this chiefly browsing animal inhabits boreal coniferous forests, glacial bogs, and wet meadows. Records show that the woodland caribou once roamed the forests of Washington, Idaho, Montana, and east to Maine. It currently survives in the lower 48 only in small resident populations in the mountains of northern Idaho and northeast Washington, with small numbers occasionally wandering from Canada into northwest Montana and extreme northeast Minnesota. Caribou are harmed by logging, road-building, mining, hunting, and many of the same livestock impacts that harm moose and mountain goats. Ecologist Jasper Carlton identifies the woodland caribou as probably the rarest and most endangered indigenous mammal surviving in the wild in the lower 48 states.

Big game populations on public lands are increasing in the presence of regulated livestock grazing.
--Mosley, *et al.,* Seven Popular *MYTHS About Livestock Grazing on Public Lands*

The grazing establishment counters that (1) "big game" numbers have increased since early this century and (2) ranching has continued during that period; therefore, (3) improved ranching management has caused or contributed to this increase (or, at least this proves that modern ranching is not harmful to these animals). In other words (or numbers), 1 + 1 = 3. As detailed elsewhere, decades of "big game" protection legislation and intensive reintroduction and restoration efforts (which ranchers have almost universally fought *against*) are actually responsible for these modest population increases. Regardless of increases or decreases, ranching was and is the most destructive influence on large Western herbivores. Indeed, "big game" numbers generally have increased most where livestock grazing has been "regulated" -- that is, *reduced.*

Although livestock grazing has been disastrous to wildlife, public lands managers do little to correct the situation. In 1976 the BLM employed an average of 1 full-time wildlife biologist for each 3.36 million acres -- an area the size of Connecticut. That year, the Forest Service employed 1 biologist for each 1.9 million acres (Ferguson 1983). In contrast, the agencies employ several times as many ranching-related professionals. BLM and FS generally manage for less than 1% as many deer, elk, pronghorn, or bighorns as cattle and sheep on the public's land. In most Western states, livestock grazing accounts for 80%-95% of total forage allocations on BLM and FS land, while the percentage for state-owned land is even worse. And these figures don't take into account livestock trespass, which is common.

One example: According to a report by the Committee for Idaho's High Desert, all 6 BLM resource areas in southern Idaho, representing 13% of all land in the state, have released proposed management plans since 1982. Livestock are scheduled to receive 90.6% of the total allotted forage, while all wildlife gets the remaining 9.4%; this, again, does not take into consideration livestock trespass and other factors described below. Adding insult to injury, all 6 plans schedule increases in projected forage allocations to livestock, ranging from 13% to 66%, with lesser increases to wildlife. These BLM plans are unfortunately typical.

On top of all this, what little herbage is allotted to wildlife is usually located in areas undesirable to ranchers anyway -- dry, inaccessible, rugged, steep, brushy, otherwise unprofitable, and generally the least ungulate-productive habitat. Most wild ungulates would not inhabit these areas if given a choice, but under the grazing establishment's influence prime habitat is monopolized for livestock.

For example, bighorn sheep in New Mexico's Gila National Forest *may* get 1% of total forage allocations, according to the forest management plan. But bighorns in the Gila rarely leave their rugged cliff and rocky hillside homes, while cattle enjoy the comfortable, level, well-watered valley bottoms, grassy flats, and gentle slopes. That 1% forage and browse *may* be there, but in order to utilize it, the bighorns must expend much time and energy moving over rugged terrain. Just to drink, they may have to climb down 1000' of steep, rocky escarpment. Ironically, bighorns may not want to leave their rocky homes except to drink, for, being relatively unvisited by cattle, these rugged hide-outs often support more available forage per acre than the more gentle and potentially productive, yet overgrazed, cattle terrain below.

Further, at least 1 and usually more "big game" species have been reduced or extirpated from almost every public grazing allotment in the West. Yet, even though many allotments could still support these species, very few management plans seriously consider recovery or reintroduction.

The buffalo is an excellent example. More than half the area of the West used to support some buffalo, and perhaps half of the public grazing allotments in the West could still. Yet only a handful out of tens of thousands do. Why? Because the ranching industry simply will not allow it; buffalo aggressively compete for forage and break through ordinary livestock fences. Therefore, the agencies rarely even consider reintroducing them.

Thanks to their owners and our government, cattle and sheep have other unfair advantages over their wild competitors. Livestock often receive veterinary treatment and supplemental food, water, salt, and minerals, whereas wild animals usually do not (and when they do, it is to compensate for habitat degradation and fragmentation.) If they severely overgraze, livestock can be moved to greener pastures or be given supplemental feed. Domestic stock are usually moved off the public range altogether during seasons when grazing is less profitable, while wild animals must struggle through the lean seasons on what remains.

For example, during summer livestock heavily graze elk winter foraging areas. As winter approaches, livestock are moved to lower elevations where they subsist on pasturage and stored feed. As elk migrate from the highlands down to their traditional winter foraging areas, they find little to eat. Occasionally they starve, but even if they do not, insufficient food often leads to reduced body weight, lowered resistance to cold and disease, less energy to escape and fight predators, reproductive failures, and impairment of bodily functions. Some elk may eventually die as a result, and herds may experience genetic setbacks, or fail to produce offspring sufficient to maintain viable populations.

A bighorn in Gila NF. The river canyon bottom is overgrazed and occupied by cattle (note muddy river water), so bighorns here climb down from their steep, rocky uplands only to drink.

After several days of grazing in this heretofore little grazed area, the herbage cover will be reduced by more than 80%, leaving little for wildlife through fall, winter, and early spring. *(USFS)*

Bighorns overcome their fear of humans -- potentially fatal in and of itself -- while searching for winter forage on overgrazed range. *(George Robbins Photo, Jackson, WY)*

Large native herbivores lived in habitats to which they were naturally suited -- not where people put them. Over millions of years, each plant and animal in these habitats evolved to co-exist with these grazing and browsing animals. In an amazingly complex web of interrelationships benefiting all involved, each plant and animal was adapted to all other plants and animals. Cattle and sheep were not participants for these millions of years, and are thus not adapted to these countless unique interrelationships in these ecosystems.

Recently I received a letter from a woman in New Mexico who echoed ranchers' arguments in asking if perhaps cattle and sheep are now semi-native to the West because they have been here for so long. I answered that perhaps they would be if left completely unmanaged and genetically unaltered for several thousand years -- an inherent impossibility with any domestic animal, but especially with commercial livestock.

America's domestic cattle and sheep are native to lush, well-watered, level-to-rolling grassland and grassy woodland of the Old World (which also are mostly overgrazed by livestock) -- environments completely unlike most public land in the West. (Even if these environments were quite similar geographically and climatically, however, livestock

Further complicating matters for wildlife, ranching pressures are continually changing, often drastically from day to day, season to season, or year to year. Because range management varies according to perceived livestock needs, market trends, opinions, fickle whims, and greed, wild animals must constantly adjust to simply survive. For millions of years wildlife evolved to endure periodic *natural* hardships, such as storms, floods, fires, and to adapt to gradual, *natural* changes in the environment occurring over centuries or millennia. But expecting wildlife to adapt to the unnatural changes caused by ranching is like asking a leopard to change its spots to stripes quickly and frequently.

To demonstrate: Some livestock management plans call for grazing of allotments on alternating years, purportedly to allow the range to recover in between. During off years, livestock are moved elsewhere. Thus, one year wild animals have relatively abundant grass, forbs, and browse; the next -- stubbles, sticks, and stems. On, off, on, off. Wild animals generally cannot adapt to these conditions, and usually they have no good habitat left to retreat to. And, given human inconsistency and the transitory nature of human goals, any adaptations they do make cannot possibly benefit species evolution in the long run.

On extremely overgrazed BLM cattle range in northern Wyoming, winter may prove fatal to some of these mule deer. *(George Robbins Photo, Jackson, WY)*

would not be suited to the West's vastly different biosystem.) As such, livestock are invaders from a foreign land. Today's cow is a relatively dimwitted, ponderous, slow, gluttonous beast, unlike any native American animal except for a superficial similarity to the buffalo. Domestic sheep are similarly unlike native bighorns, much as domestic goats are unlike mountain goats.

Although large native herbivores exerted some outwardly similar influences on the land, because they were *natural* components of the Western range their overall impact was not harmful. The impact from intensively managed, domesticated livestock was, however. And, the most cattle-like native American animal -- the buffalo -- outside of the Great Plains, occurred only in relatively small numbers. Moreover, especially on the prairies, native herbivores grazed and trampled heavily, but only for short periods. After denuding the vegetation in an area -- commonly a matter of hours or days, not weeks or months -- they moved on to greener pastures, usually not to return until well after plants had rejuvenated. If wildlife had grazed like cattle -- unnaturally, intensively, for long periods every year, and for millennia -- there would be no prairie, or non-wasteland, anywhere in the West.

I cannot believe that grazing on public land endangers wildlife.
--Peter Decker, rancher, former director of the Colorado Agricultural Department

Disease and Parasites

Just like all other natural, living beings, disease organisms and parasitic creatures by right of evolution have a place and purpose in Earth's 5-billion-year old scheme of things. Human misunderstanding notwithstanding, disease and parasites are a natural and beneficial part of any ecosystem.

In much the same way as predators do, disease strikes and kills the very old, ill, deformed, crippled, wounded, and otherwise impaired much more frequently than it does the healthy; weak individuals are naturally culled. Other species members are thus spared the task of expending valuable food, time, and energy caring for disabled members, thus strengthening the species.

When overcrowding threatens to cause food or water shortages, detrimental social behavior, fertility problems, and harmful inter- and intra-species relations, disease reduces the population to a healthier level. Though death by disease is an unpleasant thought, it is usually far better than slow starvation, and it is better for other species than having an ecosystem gradually devastated and subjecting myriads to suffering. Additionally, those individuals that become sick from disease but don't die often temporarily experience much lower reproduction rates, further limiting population. Under *natural* conditions, however, disease rarely makes deadly rampages through populations.

In many ways, parasites are larger versions of disease organisms. (Some protozoans straddle the fine line between the two.) They play a similar role, and indeed often carry and transmit disease. Nevertheless, under natural conditions, parasites rarely infest hosts so seriously as to impair normal functioning.

All the foregoing applies to humans, as demonstrated by severe and frequent disease epidemics and die-offs in overpopulated areas of the "Old World," or in areas where humans lived under grossly unnatural conditions. Before the development of "modern man," the vast bulk of human history shows disease to be a relatively benign influence. When "Old World" humans first domesticated livestock and began farming in roughly 9000-5000 B.C., they became overpopulated and concentrated, and created conditions favorable to the development and spread of virulent diseases. Viral and bacterial oscillation/interplay between livestock and humans produced variants of old diseases and many new and deadly diseases hitherto unknown to either, yet deadly to one, the other, or both. (Crosby 1988)

When Europeans arrived in North America, they brought with them these new diseases, and their old ones as well, most of which they had over time developed at least partial immunities to. The indigenous peoples of this continent had not, however. Some of these diseases spread through native tribes like the Black Plague had through 14th century Europe. It is now widely accepted that more Native Americans were killed by introduced disease than by bullets, starvation, and exposure combined. The US Army's use of smallpox-contaminated blankets as gifts to subdue Native Americans is also well-known.

A contaminated blanket was given to the native wildlife of this hemisphere, in the form of domestic livestock. American animals were ill-prepared for the diseases and parasites common to the Europeans and their cattle, sheep, goats, and horses. Not having evolved with many of these viral and bacterial diseases or parasites, native species were highly susceptible to and greatly harmed by them. Though some resistance has been built up during the past century or two, Western wildlife is still more vulnerable to many of these disorders than are livestock, all things being equal.

But all things are not equal. Cattle and sheep pervade the West in large numbers in heavy, usually stationary concentrations -- exactly the conditions most conducive to spreading disease and parasites. Management activities exacerbate this situation. Immunizations, antibiotics, insecticides, and such generally keep problems in check. But when a disorder does spread through a livestock herd, it may be transmitted to wild animals not normally exposed to it. There are also a number of diseases and parasites that domestic stock can transmit to wild animals, but to which they are resistant.

Additionally, the unnatural situations forced upon wildlife by livestock grazing and related ranching activities often stress native animals, making them overly susceptible to disease and parasites. For example, the lack of herbage due to overgrazing causes nutritional stress in wildlife that results in greater susceptibility to disease. Experts believe that this is currently a significant influence on the desert tortoise, whose population has recently been diminished by an incurable respiratory disease.

When wildlife concentrates in small areas where food and water remain, stress and susceptibility to disease are further increased. For example, Wyoming Game and Fish Department officials think widespread ranching that forces elk to concentrate in localized areas is a main reason the number of elk calves born in the state has declined in recent years; the disease brucellosis is the major factor.

In short, domestic stock serve as a vector to spread disease and parasites, both native and exotic, to wild animals throughout the West. Bighorn sheep are a prominent example. Many experts think that livestock-spread disorders are the main cause of declines in bighorn sheep numbers in much of the West.

In California, for example, the bighorn is threatened by livestock competition, habitat loss, and human intrusion and poaching; but, in many areas the greatest hazard to its survival is *pasteurella*, an always lethal, highly contagious bacteria. The bacteria's transmission process is not fully understood, but nose to nose contact between livestock and wildlife is one suspected mode, and recent tests show that the viral agent can live 24 hours outside the host and be transmitted through grass. Entire herds can be decimated in weeks.

From the 1940s through the 1960s, California experienced many declines and local extinctions of bighorns due to livestock-spread afflictions. Since then, the California Department of Fish and Game has taken many measures to reintroduce and protect bighorns. Yet, both native and reintroduced herds continue to suffer from livestock competition and introduced disease.

In the Sierra Nevada, the Sierra race of bighorn is currently threatened by both habitat intrusion and a *pasteurella* parasite, carried and spread by domestic sheep which are themselves resistant to its effects. Reintroduced herds of 43 bighorns in Lava Beds National Monument and 50 in Modoc National Forest recently experienced 100% mortality from *pasteurella*. Both herds were adjacent to domestic sheep grazing allotments. Although many bighorn herds could be protected from introduced disease by a 5-mile buffer zone between sheep allotments and bighorns, few public lands managers are willing to confront powerful local ranchers and insist on the necessary changes in land management plans.

In the Challis National Forest in Idaho, a recent *pasteurella* outbreak has resulted in 7 known bighorn deaths so far -- immediately after a herd of 200 domestic sheep grazed the area for the first time in years. Bill Foreyt, an associate professor of veterinary medicine, microbiology, and pathology for Washington State University, said of the outbreak, "The results show the [strain of] *pasteurella hemolytica* is definitely of domestic sheep origin." A similar virus killed between 125 and 200 bighorns in Hells Canyon in 1983, and 75% of a 100 animal herd in northeast Oregon in 1985, including the largest recorded ram in the US.

In a report entitled "Effects of Domestic Sheep Grazing on Bighorn Sheep Populations," N.J. Goodson states that "Co-use of ranges by domestic and bighorn sheep has been consistently linked with declines, die offs, and extinctions of bighorn populations from historical to recent times" (Goodson 1982). (See Jessup 1985 in the bibliography for numerous other examples.)

Disease and parasites are spread to wild animals through infected water, vegetation, manure and soil, flies and other insect carriers, physical contact with livestock, feed, and salt licks. Most large mammals and many other animals are susceptible to these disorders. (Incidentally, there are 50 diseases that cattle can and sometimes do transmit to people -- more than are transmitted by any other animal except the lovable family dog.) Following is a general list of afflictions spread by range livestock:

Anthrax bacteria can be transmitted through stagnant water, soil, and dead animals. A relatively common and sometimes deadly disease, all warm-blooded animals are susceptible, including humans, but cattle are most vulnerable. Flesh eaters such as coyotes, ravens, and vultures may contact anthrax from eating infected dead cattle or sheep, and may also spread it to other wildlife.

Brucellosis is another bacterial disease, various strains of which affect many warm-blooded animals, especially cattle. It causes cattle fetuses to abort in late pregnancy; in humans it causes flu-like symptoms that may persist from 3 days to 3 months. Bovine brucellosis may be spread through livestock food, water, and salt licks, as well as through physical contact with live or dead stock, aborted fetuses and, for humans, through the handling of dead bodies in slaughterhouses. Brucellosis was once the most serious human/animal disease in the US, but in 1935 the US launched an intensive eradication program and brucellosis infection is now reported in only 0.17% of US cattle, while many states are certified brucellosis-free (Wuerthner 1990).

Circling disease is a widespread infectious bacterial disease affecting livestock, humans, and wildlife. Affected animal stagger, circle, and make strange, awkward movements.

Encephalitis, an infectious disease affecting cattle, sheep, and goats, can be spread to wild animals and humans. The mortality rate in untreated individuals is high.

The infamous and deadly *foot and mouth disease* has not been reported in the United States since 1929. Large sums of money were spent eradicating it, and much is still spent by the government keeping it away from US borders. At one time foot and mouth disease spread by livestock killed many thousands of deer in the West. Between 1925-1927 in the Stanislaus National Forest, California, 22,000 deer were slaughtered to eradicate the disease after it had been introduced by cattle.

According to the *Sacramento Bee*, cattle may even be linked to *leptospirosis*, a liver-kidney disease that has killed hundreds of *sea lions* along the West Coast. Spread mainly through urine, humans and other animals incur the disease by swimming in or drinking infected waters. Humans and predatory and scavenging animals can also contact it by consuming the meat of infected livestock. Surveys indicate widespread leptospirosis in the US cattle population.

Cattle are susceptible to all 3 forms of *tuberculosis* and can spread the disease to certain animals, including bighorns, elk, deer, and mountain goats.

Pneumonia caused by livestock-spread bacteria has been implicated in the deaths of many wild animals. One type of *pneumophilic* bacteria exacerbates existing disorders, thus producing fatal pneumonia, while another causes the progressively fatal disease independently.

Livestock help spread a viral disease called *bluetongue* to deer, elk, pronghorn, bighorns, and other large mammals, sometimes with fatal results. A certain kind of gnat is also necessary for transmission; low elevation areas with stock tanks and high livestock densities are good gnat habitat.

The familiar bacterial disease *pinkeye* may strike humans as humorous, but it can be deadly to many wild animals because it causes blindness. Pinkeye is not a natural disease process in some wild animals. Spread by livestock, it is especially common to range and feedlot cattle, and affects 3% of all beef cattle.

Soremouth, a pox virus common to domestic sheep, can be transmitted to bighorns and others through direct contact or through the infected animals' shed scabs, on which the virus can remain viable in soil for 10 years. The infection causes painful sores and scabs on the face and can either be lethal to an animal or retard its growth.

Scabies is a highly contagious and often deadly skin disease spread by a tiny mite carried by cattle, sheep, wildlife, and humans. Livestock frequently transmit this disease to wildlife, especially to bighorn sheep. According to a report by the California Department of Fish and Game, "The introduction of domestic livestock onto bighorn sheep ranges in the late 1800s and early 1900s was followed by severe and widespread die offs of bighorn sheep attributed to scabies." Domestic sheep were the main culprit; when their numbers declined, so did bighorn mortality rates.

And yes, cattle and sheep do get *rabies*, though less than 10 cases a year are reported. Infected livestock may be dangerous during the middle stages of the disease. In Canada and much of the US more humans are bitten by rabid cows than by rabid bats!

A number of *protozoan-based diseases* are also transmitted from livestock to wildlife, and sometimes to humans. Other diseases are too numerous to include here.

More than 100 species of external and internal parasites affect cattle and sheep, of which a score or so significantly affect Western wildlife. *Anaplasmosis* is a disorder caused by one of the tinier of these parasites. Transmitted by mosquitos, ticks, horseflies, and other biting insects, it spreads quickly and can kill wild animals.

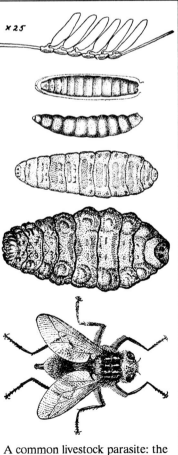

A common livestock parasite: the warble fly, from egg to adult

Several species of flies produce *parasitic larvae* that live within the bodies of cattle, sheep, and other domestic and wild animals. Many can make life miserable and some can be fatal. Among these are bot flies, blowflies, horn flies, warble flies, and screwworm flies. At one time, the screwworm fly, which arrived in this country with and was propagated by cattle, killed 60%-80% of all fawns throughout much of the southern United States, as well as many human babies. Their maggots consume living flesh inside wounds, increasing wound size sometimes until the victim is literally eaten to death. Blowflies are widespread on the range. Their maggots eat away at the skin surface of livestock and wildlife.

Livestock can also indirectly transmit disease to wild animals by spreading flies that carry disease. For example, there is strong evidence that a nose bot fly common to domestic sheep is a major cause of bighorn death from a disease syndrome called *chronic frontal sinusitis*.

Parasitic worms, spread to native animals and humans by livestock via shared ranges or water include stomach worms, bladder worms, tapeworms, lungworms, hookworms, pin worms, and various roundworms. (Some of these worms are also spread to people through inadequately cooked meat.) Victims die or suffer from malnutrition or internal hemorrhaging. *Liver flukes* kill livestock and wildlife in some areas of the West. Their life cycle takes them from animal feces, through certain species of snails, onto vegetation or into water, and back into large animals. Livestock help spread them. Cattle and sheep are also host to many different *ticks*, *lice*, and *mites*, a few of which can be transmitted to wild animals and humans.

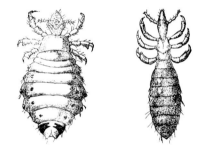

Two lice of cattle.

Ringworm, a contagious disease of the outer layers of skin caused by certain molds or fungi, creates round, scaly patches of skin almost devoid of hair. Able to live on most large animals and humans, it is sometimes spread by livestock.

Even *warts* can be spread from livestock to wildlife. Unbelievably, on cattle some of these ugly tumors become pendulous growths several pounds in size.

Various and numerous immunizations, antibiotics, medications and veterinary techniques have been employed over the years to protect livestock from the spread of disease and parasites -- some with success, most with tax money. In some cases, government efforts have stemmed outbreaks in wildlife. Usually, though, wild animals don't have the benefit of modern medicine when they become sick or infested.

As long as livestock remain nearly omnipresent in the West, we can expect disease and parasites to be spread to wild animals. Western wildlife is in a quandary, for the greater its concentrations, the more susceptible it becomes to livestock-spread disease and parasites. But it would be impractical to immunize and treat large numbers of wildlife without semi-domesticating them, thus destroying the essence of *wild* life.

Other Native Animals

(Greg Pentkowski)

Large native herbivores, though well below cattle and sheep on the rangeland totem pole, receive far more managerial benefit than other wildlife. Great government effort is expended to maintain sufficient numbers of "game" animals for hunters and fishers. But relatively little goes toward the tens of thousands of other species that inhabit (or formerly inhabited) public land. The Council on Environmental Quality observes that "$97 of every $100 spent by federal and state governments on wildlife management goes to less than three percent of the species; the ones used specifically for hunting, trapping or fishing." Much of what little the government spends on non-game species goes towards those already classified as Rare, Threatened, or Endangered.

The same influences that hurt pronghorn and elk hurt scaled quail, earthworms, garter snakes, and dragonflies. It would be impossible to list all the less-celebrated wild animals harmed by livestock grazing (or the many different ways they suffer), but here are a few: ant lions, armadillos, and alligator lizards; bass, bumblebees, and butterflies; cockroaches, coral snakes, and coatimundis; ducks, dip-

pers, and daddy longlegs; earwigs, egrets, and earthworms; ferrets, finches, and freshwater crabs . . . . Indeed, of the thousands of species of mammals, birds, reptiles, fish, amphibians, and tens of thousands of species of smaller animals native to the rangeland West, **most** have been harmed by livestock grazing. Even the BLM's Division of Wildlife calls livestock grazing the primary cause of the "unsatisfactory" condition of major portions of wildlife habitat on public land (Natural Resources Defense Council 1973).

Consider a few examples: The tiger salamander is the world's largest land-dwelling salamander. Being a moisture-loving creature native to most of the Intermountain West, livestock grazing has seriously affected its habitat and reduced its numbers. Yet the tiger salamander remains one of the anonymous thousands not considered in land management plans.

The great plains toad is a large, grey to olive-brown, blotched amphibian native to grassland and shrubby/grassy areas of the Great Plains from Montana to southern New Mexico, southern Arizona, and the Colorado River Basin of the Southwest. Livestock grazing has eliminated much of the native vegetation in its habitat; correspondingly, its food supply of insects, cutworms, and other small animals has been depleted. The great plains toad depends on moist, loose soil for burrowing, but trampling and destruction of native plants have caused soils to dry and harden. It needs ponds and other slow, shallow waters in which to lay eggs, but livestock have depleted and polluted suitable waters. If eggs are laid, they may be stepped on or buried by drinking livestock. Adult toads may be trampled when on the ground's surface or burrowed into wet soil.

More than 2000 species of bee inhabit the West. Over the last 100 million or so years, they have become morphologically, physiologically, and behaviorally attuned to native flowers. Though many species can utilize non-native flowers, the natives are most beneficial and some bee species have become so specialized that they are wholly dependent on only one or a few flower species. Bees depend on the nectar and pollen of certain wild flowers being available through the growing season(s). Though overgrazing has increased the number of flowers in a some areas, in general it has diminished the number and variety of herbaceous flowering plants in the West and depleted or extirpated required native flowers over vast areas. In addition, because livestock grazing tends to decrease diversity, the variety of plants blooming at any given time has been reduced and some portions of blooming seasons may be devoid of flowers. Livestock have thus destroyed many of the bees and other flying and crawling creatures that helped pollinate flowering plants as they consumed or gathered pollen and nectar -- creatures that were a food base for much other wildlife.

The spotted bat is another unacknowledged victim of the grazing industry. This rare large-eared bat lives in arid to semi-arid areas in every Western state except Washington. But how could livestock hurt bats?? Much of their food source of small, flying insects has been wiped out through the effects of overgrazing. Livestock have a definite, destructive influence on these bats, but not many scientists or range professionals make the connection. In the Southwest, the red bat, which is found primarily along riparian corridors, is listed as Threatened by the Arizona Game & Fish Department, due largely to livestock. Why? In Arizona the red bat roosts in the cavities of large riparian trees, primarily cottonwoods, most of which have been lost to the impact from livestock grazing.

Spotted bat.

Cottontail rabbits usually fare poorly on the common grazed range. Livestock remove cover needed for shelter, nesting, protection, and food. (Turkowski 1975)

Nor has the javelina escaped harm. The wild pig of the southern portions of Arizona, New Mexico, and Texas forages for grasses, cacti, beans, nuts, berries, fruits, grubs, and insects. Because grasses in these regions have been largely eliminated, cattle there draw heavily on other vegetation, especially the most palatable javelina food plants, thereby also reducing javelina grubs and insects that rely on these plants. For example, a 1942 University of California report titled "Mammals of the Big Bend Area of Texas" mentions the very small number of javelinas counted in a wildlife survey, and concludes that "heavy grazing by domestic stock has greatly reduced forage and shelter and probably has been an important factor in reducing the range and number of javelina."

Even such an unlikely creature as the northern bog lemming is violated by livestock grazing. This small vole-like mammal spends its life in cool, moderate- to high-elevation cirque bog basins and meadows in the mountains of extreme northern Washington, the Idaho panhandle, and northwestern Montana -- places you might not expect to find cattle. But as you may have guessed, the Forest Service does allow cattle grazing there, in the high wet meadows of all 5 National Forests in the area. Livestock, along with ORVs, snowmobiles, improper capturing techniques by biologists, and logging, have reduced the northern bog lemming's range and numbers so much that it is considered a "sensitive" species or "species of special concern" by various state and federal agencies.

Northern bog lemmings. *(Roger Candee)*

With the depletion of native grasses -- especially mature grasses with seedheads -- many seed-eating birds, rodents, and insects were devastated. With the removal of ground cover, a large percentage of small, moisture-loving, soil-dwelling creatures were killed off. With the loss of succulent low-level vegetation, many insects and their larvae, such as moths and butterflies and their caterpillars, bugs, and beetles (and the animals dependent upon them), were eliminated. These losses have had far-reaching, though largely unrecognized, impacts on Western ecosystems.

For example, a large percentage of insects that depend on low-level vegetation burrow into the top 1'-3' of soil for the winter, channelling and aerating the soil as they go. If they die there, their remains enrich the soil, but most emerge the following spring, further channelling and aerating the soil. Their loss has thus also lowered soil quality.

Similarly, a great many animals large and small live in the soil either permanently or at some stage of their lives, far more than we surface-dwellers realize. Thousands of species of microscopic creatures inhabit rangeland -- by the trillions, providing many essential, yet little-known, benefits to ecosystems. By far most of these animals utilize the topsoil. As mentioned, the SCS estimates that since the 1800s at least half of the West's original rangeland topsoil has been lost, mostly to ranching. In other words, these soil-dwellers have already lost half of their topsoil habitat.

The abundant, loose, moist, organic soil of ungrazed areas supports many more soil-dwelling creatures than does the soil of grazed areas. In this ungrazed scene, a colony of pocket gophers has pushed up numerous mounds of dirt, further promoting soil fertility.

By drastically depleting ground cover, trampling nests, and terrifying wildlife, livestock have reduced numbers of ground-nesting animals throughout much of the West and eliminated them from huge chunks of land. For example, a study by Thomas Overmire in 1964 showed that grazing reduced by 50% the breeding populations of Bell's vireos, birds which nest on or near ground level (Overmire 1964). When livestock numbers were increased dramatically at Oregon's Malheur Wildlife Refuge between 1940 and the 1970s, populations of ground-nesters such as mallards, Canada geese, and sandhill cranes plummeted correspondingly, largely because grazing livestock stripped off ground cover, leaving nests poorly concealed or in plain view for predators (Ferguson 1983). In southeastern Arizona, establishment of the San Pedro National Riparian Conservation Area and elimination of cattle grazing there several years ago has, according to preliminary results of a BLM study, increased the number of ground nesting song sparrows, yellow-breasted chats, and common yellowthroats by 100%-400%. Other animals that may be harmed by reduction of ground cover and associated impacts include ground doves, poorwills, horned larks, bobolinks, white-tailed ptarmigans, meadowlarks, some sparrows, many water birds, woodrats, some rabbits, a variety of shrews and mice, many reptiles and amphibians, and a huge number of invertebrates.

(Helen Wilson)

The wild turkey is another unrecognized livestock victim. Native mainly to open forest and brushy woodland, it was decimated in the West last century, not only by hunting but by gradual habitat deterioration from livestock grazing. Needing thick vegetation for cover and nesting sites, wild turkeys suffered greatly when livestock depleted tall grasses, flowering plants, and dense brush thickets in their range. Overgrazing also decreased their food supply of seeds, nuts, acorns, grass, forbs, tubers, and insects by depleting source plants, eliminating vegetation upon which their food insects relied, and drying up water sources. A comparison of young wild turkeys on heavily grazed and ungrazed lands revealed 580 young per 100 hens on ungrazed plots, compared to only 150 young per 100 hens on grazed plots (Gallizioli 1976).

Together with overhunting and habitat destruction (both largely by ranchers), commercial grazing helped reduce a pre-European US wild turkey population of roughly 10 million to about 20,000 by the 1930s. Intensive reintroduction and recovery efforts, mainly for hunting, have brought the wild turkey back to some areas in recent years, though

Wild turkey.

generally in greatly diminished numbers. The "incredible restoration" of the wild turkey touted by vested interests has increased its numbers to an estimated (again, perhaps overestimated) 1-2 million today, or about 10%-20% of its original population.

Other upland "game" birds such as ruffed grouse, blue grouse, chukars (exotic), and lesser and greater prairie chickens have also suffered, as have gambel's quail (Gorsuch 1934), Mearn's quail (Bishop 1965), and scaled quail (Goodwin 1977). Livestock have destroyed their food sources, cover, and essential understory vegetation. Sharp-tailed grouse, which depend on seed-bearing perennial grasses, have been extirpated from several states and now occupy about 10% of their original habitat.

Even the sage grouse has been decimated. One might imagine that the increase in sagebrush caused by livestock grazing would have boosted the numbers of this bird. Yet the sage grouse population today is only a tiny fraction of what it was before the livestock invasion (Wagner 1978). The main detriment is reportedly destruction of riparian areas, which contain vegetation and invertebrate foods essential for proper development of young sage grouse. Sage grouse also consume large amounts of forbs, perennial grasses, and nutritious shrubs on open sagebrush ranges -- foods that have been mostly eliminated by livestock. The Wyoming sage grouse population increased temporarily when stocking levels were reduced from those levels around the turn of the century (Patterson 1952); however, continuing progressive habitat deterioration during this century augments long-term Wyoming sage grouse decline. The Wyoming Game and Fish Department estimates that 50% of the state's original sage grouse habitat has been destroyed, mostly by ranching. Hunting seasons on the bird in Oregon and Washington were eliminated in 1985, and if present trends continue, the sage grouse may be extirpated there by the end of the century.

(George Wuerthner)

Livestock harm many species of waterfowl by eating their food plants, depleting surface water through overgrazing watersheds, damaging riparian areas, and polluting water, reducing nesting success and the likelihood of nesting attempts through the removal and trampling of residual cover, killing chicks in their nests by trampling, and disturbing birds' normal activities. Some ranching advocates maintain that livestock "help out" waterfowl by "opening up" dense wetland vegetation and providing nesting sites. In "Waterfowl Production in Relation to Grazing," L.M. Kirsch concludes "In reviewing the literature I was unable to find a single example of where grazing or other cover removal activities increased waterfowl production" (Kirsch 1969). In 1978, the Conservation Committee for the Wilson Ornithological Society reported that of 56 scientific papers dealing with effects of grazing on waterfowl, all but 1 reported decreased production or other detrimental effects (Strassmann 1983a).

Studies at Oregon's Malheur National Wildlife Refuge showed passerine (perching bird and songbird) counts 5-7 times higher on an ungrazed area of the Refuge (Taylor 1986). Indeed, populations of nearly all bird species almost invariably decline under conventional livestock grazing. R.F. Buttery and P.W. Shields reviewed a number of papers reporting the results of studies in many parts of the country and found this to be so; they also determined that a lessening of grazing pressure resulted in an increase of more than 100% in the small bird population (Buttery 1975).

(Steve Johnson)

The overwhelming impact of livestock grazing on wildlife, birdlife especially, was impressively demonstrated to my family and me a few years ago. On this hot, humid summer afternoon we were driving slowly south through the Sand Hills country of western Nebraska. The asphalt of the old, narrow, unfenced road was full of potholes, much as the countryside was pockmarked with circular lakes.

As we drove, at intervals of a mile or so we'd bounce over cattleguards set perpendicularly through fences, bringing alternations of ungrazed and grazed areas. Each ungrazed mile was thick with medium-high prairie grasses, flowering plants, and widely scattered brush of various kinds. Butterflies and other insects were in the air everywhere, and small mammals were occasionally visible through the lush vegetation.

A bounce back into a grazed section brought much sparser grass cropped to a few inches, few native flowers, and patches of invader plants such as thistles and mustards. Flying insects were scarce, and a few rabbits were the only non-bovine mammals to be seen -- noticeable because the meager vegetation afforded so little cover.

But most amazing were the birds. In the grazed sections, we saw them only occasionally, representing only a few species. Upon entering an ungrazed section, we actually had to reduce our already slow speed to avoid hitting the numerous birds fluttering up out of the grass and over the road. There were large numbers of at least a dozen different species, including meadowlarks, buntings, goldfinches, sparrows, warblers, and hawks. Though grazing damage is considerable throughout the West, rarely is the power of livestock to alter the landscape so clearly demonstrated.

To repeat, in most of the West more than half of all animal species rely on riparian zones and associated waters --

precisely the areas hardest hit by livestock. Because most waterways have been depleted or eliminated by overgrazing, wildlife that depended on them has died off; because water volume is much reduced, remaining animals are more easily taken by predators. For example, in Arizona and New Mexico more than 100 riparian species are Threatened or Endangered, more due to livestock grazing than to any other influence (Wuerthner 1989a).

The river otter is a good example. Once found in rivers throughout the West, it is now extinct in most of its former range. Due to overgrazing (and water withdrawal for livestock purposes), many streams and small rivers no longer have adequate flow to support river otters. Because of damage to waterways and riparian systems, in many areas the river otter's food supply of fish, frogs, crayfish, and other aquatic animals has been diminished, while prime denning sites have been reduced. Also, because many riparian trees (and beaver dams and ponds) have been eliminated by livestock, prime river otter habitat has been reduced.

River otter.

The yellow-billed cuckoo is another victim. In the West, this bird is largely dependent upon riparian zones. Once numerous, it is now rare in much of its range. According to Robert Ohmart of Arizona State University, in the last decade alone 5000 acres of cuckoo habitat along the Colorado River valley on the California-Arizona border have been reduced to only 200 acres, chiefly by ranching and tamarisk invasion.

Other examples are bluebirds, flickers, woodpeckers, and other birds that depend on cavities in large riparian trees for nest sites. By eating tree saplings and young trees, damaging soil, causing increased flooding and lowered water tables, etc., livestock have eliminated many of the trees these birds formerly utilized. The story is the same for hawks, owls, flycatchers, orioles, warblers, egrets, herons, bald eagles, tree swallows, raccoons, skunks, squirrels, lizards, and other animals that nest, roost, den, or find shelter in riparian trees and snags. For example, the National Audubon Society put pressure on Arizona's Tonto National Forest to curtail grazing there because "improper grazing prevented regeneration of trees essential to nesting bald eagles (Chaney 1990)." The ferruginous pigmy owl, one of the world's smallest owls, is listed as Threatened in Arizona due largely to ranching's destruction of riparian zones with their snags, degradation of upland habitat, and withdrawal of groundwater for pasture irrigation.

A public stream somewhere in southwest Wyoming is testimony to the impact of a century of livestock grazing. Thousands of Western waterways are in such condition and can no longer support the abundant aquatic life they once did. *(Kelly Cranston)*

A study on the Little Deschutes River in Oregon found trout populations 350% higher on ungrazed than grazed portions of the river (Lorz 1974). An ungrazed segment of Montana's Rock Creek produced 268% more trout (336% by weight) than a grazed segment (Ferguson 1983). Studies by A.S. Leopold show deterioration of streams and loss of trout in California (Leopold 1951). A recent overview of 5 separate studies determined that trout populations averaged 184% higher in ungrazed than grazed segments of the same streams (Wuerthner 1990a).

Indeed, where streams still exist, trout populations are commonly 2-5 times higher on ungrazed than grazed streams. Livestock grazing is often cited as North America's foremost cause of the drastic decline in native trout populations and a leading cause of salmon decline since the 1800s -- not only in the West but in the central and eastern regions as well (White 1989). A recent study report released by the Forest Service documents how livestock have hastened the decline of salmon (Durbin 1991). The American Families Fisheries Society states that fishing opportunities have been reduced by 60% to 90% because of livestock overgrazing on 68,000 miles of streamside cover in National Forests. According to trout authority Robert Behnke, overgrazing is the single greatest menace to trout streams today (Rosetta 1985).

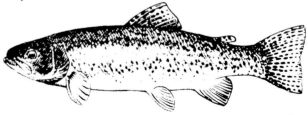

For example, in the Owyhee region of southwest Idaho, southeast Oregon, and northern Nevada, overgrazing has helped decimate the red-banded trout, a unique rainbow trout subspecies specially adapted to warmer water. Most red-banded trout that remain survive in small streams where grazing is restricted by rugged terrain. In the nearby Trout Creek Mountains of southeastern Oregon, the whitehorse trout, a subspecies of cutthroat, is a candidate for federal listing as Endangered due basically to the same influences (Wuerthner 1990a). And in northern Nevada, livestock helped put the Lahontan cutthroat on the Threatened Species list.

The Gila trout is a colorful fish once abundant throughout the Gila River drainage and perhaps others in the Southwest. It began suffering from extensive habitat degradation due to livestock grazing about 100 years ago (Behnke 1976, Platts 1978). Along with competition from exotics, logging, fire suppression, and mining, overgrazing almost exterminated the species by the early 1900s. The Gila trout was placed on the Endangered Species list in 1966. Reintroduction efforts in recent years have been unusually successful, but the fish's future remains uncertain.

Similarly in the Southwest, loss of aquatic habitat, destruction of streamside vegetation, siltation and other water pollution, dams and water diversions for livestock production, and other ranching factors helped put the Arizona trout and Little Colorado spinedace on the Endangered list, and hampered recovery efforts (Behnke 1976, Gallizioli 1976, Meehan 1978, Platts 1978, Nowakowski 1982) In fact, of 32 fish species native to Arizona, 5 are extinct and 21 of the remaining 27 are officially listed as Threatened or Endangered or are being considered for listing -- all due largely to ranching (Wuerthner 1989a).

Though livestock grazing has raised summer temperatures of thousands of Western streams, thus giving warm water fish an advantage over cold water fish, grazing's depletion and pollution of surface waters, reduction of fish food, and many other impacts have caused declines of warm water fish as well. For example, the Zuni bluehead sucker, native to several waterways in western New Mexico, is currently under review for listing as Threatened or Endangered due mostly to habitat destruction by livestock and dams and water withdrawal to support livestock production.

It is reported that some undescribed species of fish were wiped out long ago from streams that are now nonexistent (Ferguson 1983). Though dams and overfishing commonly are blamed for the declines in Western fish populations, most dams were built (primarily for livestock production) and most intensive fishing began decades *after* fish populations plummeted in the late 1800s and early 1900s. Overgrazing was and probably still is the main force ravaging the finny multitudes that once swam freely Western waterways.

Researchers found twice as many lizards (3.7 times by weight) on ungrazed study plots than on grazed study plots (Ferguson 1983). Livestock may be implicated in declines of many frog species over much of the West, including the relict leopard, Rio Grande leopard, and Tarahumara frogs, canyon and mountain treefrogs, and the Las Vegas leopard frog, which is probably extinct (the city of Las Vegas has covered most of its habitat in recent years). Most snakes, toads, and salamanders likewise fare poorly under livestock grazing pressure.

Livestock grazing harms most snakes -- garter snakes, for example -- which utilize surface waters, abundant protective vegetation, and insects and other small prey.

Although countless creatures have been harmed, the destruction of species and their habitat by livestock is rarely a dramatic event. Rather, it is a slow, insidious *process* continually taking place throughout the West. As with moderate levels of toxics or radiation, it may take many years or even decades, but the damage is nonetheless severe. Steve Johnson of Defenders of Wildlife writes that "Grazing is a subtle agent of change, making inroads on wildlife and its habitat that are slow and cumulative."

The badger, for example, was once common throughout the rangeland West. It survives in small numbers, and is locally extinct in many areas. Its preferred habitat -- open grassland and semi-arid grassland abundant in small mammals and various animal and plant foods -- has been extensively and intensively grazed for over 100 years.

When livestock damage an area it is seldom immediately obvious the ways in which wild animals suffer. For example, many species require different foods or vegetation types at different times of the year. Black bears are omnivorous. At times during spring and summer they become grazers and over half their diet may consist of *grass*. Thus, in some areas livestock become direct competitors with bears for forage.

Likewise, because most allotments are not grazed year-long, lingering, harmful grazing effects may go unnoticed while livestock are elsewhere. As another random example, the hard-packed soil caused by trampling cattle may months later prevent burrowing animals from digging tunnels and dens.

The effects on wildlife are sometimes very obscure: Surveys at the San Pedro National Riparian Conservation Area (mentioned above) show a large increase in the number of yellow warblers since cattle were removed several years ago. Yellow warblers feed primarily on insects in the upper riparian tree canopy. BLM staff report that the amount of understory vegetation and number of saplings has increased tremendously since cattle were removed from the Conservation Area several years ago. But, how could this so immediately benefit a bird that depends on the upper canopy for survival? BLM says it may be because most of the upper canopy insects spend their larval, pupal, and/or younger stages in lower vegetation or topsoil, where they are vulnerable to cattle.

Typically livestock so eat and trample vegetation that little remains above winter snowpack for wildlife. *(George Robbins Photo, Jackson, WY)*

Where ground cover vegetation grows high and dense, it is much more available to foraging animals above the winter snowpack. In contrast, forage plants on the typical grazed range are so closely cropped by livestock that for months at a time little or no edible plant matter is above the snow's surface. As a result, most winter foraging animals have been harmed, especially those less able to dig deeply into the snow for forage.

Also, where vegetation grows high and dense, much more snow is trapped and protected from melting than on grazed ranges. This snow cover provides insulation, providing for higher below-snow and in-snow rodent populations, which in turn provide a greater prey base for predators like weasels, red foxes, coyotes, hawks, and owls.

By closely cropping vegetation, livestock harm wild animals in many other subtle ways. For example, without full-sized vegetation many invertebrates lack protection from sun, wind, and rain. Many crawling organisms likewise lack refuge from ground-level predators. Web-spinning spiders lack attachment points to build webs high enough and large enough to catch most flying insects (livestock also regularly destroy their webs). And without tall plants,

whatever edible seeds, fruits, and greens do escape the jaws of cattle and sheep are trampled down (if not destroyed), to be eaten mostly by ground-level creatures -- to the deprivation of the herbaceous canopy-dwellers.

Fallen dead plants and loose organic litter combine to provide a cover of insulating material under which small plants escape frost or heat and keep moist; some species use this microclimate as a "greenhouse" to start seedlings. Many animals rely on this greenery during certain portions of the year. Livestock smash this canopy and deplete its source materials.

And, depletion of vegetation cover has unnaturally exposed numerous animals to the cross-hairs of human hunters, and to harassment, capture, and physical mistreatment.

This complex riparian interminglement of downed branches, litter, flood debris, and living plants is prime habitat for many animals. Ungrazed.

Logs, downed branches, and other plant parts such as yucca stalks, cactus skeletons, wild fruit and melon hulls, and pine cones, as well as leaf and organic litter, provide important cover, dwelling, hibernating, feeding, mating, and observation sites for thousands of species of small- to medium-sized animals. To many mammals, reptiles, amphibians, birds, arachnids, insects, and others, these ground-level organic objects are home. They give plants protective cover, provide a seed-bed, conserve water, enrich the soil, and so forth. Additionally, they give diversity and character to the land. Undisturbed rocks and stones serve similar purposes. (Turn over almost any fair-sized rock or other object and usually you'll find a surprising assortment of tiny creatures underneath.)

The bad news is, of course, that livestock spoil all this. They break apart and/or scatter logs, tree branches, rocks, and everything else on or near the ground, denying these objects fixed positions and prolonged contact with the ground, thereby impairing their usefulness to wild animals. Commonly, nothing remains but chaotic wasteyards. By desertifying the land, they make sure little new plant material grows and eventually falls to the ground to replace lost organic material.

Livestock keep these objects broken into small pieces, scattered, dried out, and constantly moving, thereby preventing wildlife from using them for many purposes. Consider bumble bees; some species cut small, round holes

in old yucca stalks and hive in the hollow interiors. Overgrazing has reduced yuccas in many areas, but as important to bumble bees, cattle often knock over and trample apart yucca stalks. Consider lizards; most species find shelter in, under, and between ground-level objects and organic litter, so they are particularly harmed by its loss and rearrangement.

Ponder the lowly sowbug or "pillbug." Most of us recognize these as the miniature trilobite look-alikes that roll up into tiny, gray balls when disturbed. Sowbugs find refuge in perpetually humid surroundings, in the mat of litter beneath vegetation, below fallen logs, under rocks -- in conditions similar to those experienced by their ancestors hundreds of millions of years ago. Here, in sowbug comfort, they spend most of their time, avoiding deleterious weather, safe from most predators, producing young. Usually at night, they crawl out to feed, mostly upon decomposing plant material. In turn, they feed many other animals, including various birds, toads, lizards, and large insects.

Look at cows and sheep from the sowbug's point of view. They invade your habitat like a tornado. Thousands of gigantic shuffling and trampling hooves break apart and scatter logs, branches, rocks, and the organic litter layer, exposing you and your comrades to the blazing sun, to wind and cold, to predators, leaving you homeless. Many sowbugs are smashed. The ground is also exposed, causing a chain reaction of damaging effects; especially harmful from your viewpoint is the drying of the soil. As the livestock deplete vegetation and prevent new growth, sowbug habitat inexorably declines. Less plant life inevitably means less decaying vegetation for you to eat. You soon die.

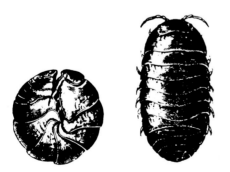

Some livestock effects may seem unimportant, but their cumulate impact may be significant. For example, as mentioned, overgrazing has caused a dramatic increase in the number of thorny and stickery plants on the Western range. This type of vegetation physically injures many wild animals, causing them to develop infections or lose the use of limbs or eyes. Some die from infection, and maimed animals are less able to fend for themselves and more susceptible to predation. Similarly, livestock have spread cheatgrass and foxtails across tens of millions of acres. As many dog owners will attest, the awned seeds of these plants often lodge in animals' eyes, ears, gums, or foot pads, from which they sometimes work their way into the animals' bodies, inflaming and infecting, sometimes causing blindness, hearing loss, or death.

On range ungrazed by livestock, healthy vegetation enhances the natural camouflage of these mule deer. *(George Robbins Photo, Jackson, WY)*

Again, many livestock effects are indirect and subtle, often poorly understood even by scientists. The link between livestock grazing and species decline is not recognized in many cases, purposefully ignored in others. For instance, many animals depend on specialized coloration and cryptic form to escape predation. When livestock change the character of the land, the effectiveness of these animals' camouflage -- developed over millennia -- is reduced. Suppose that over  several decades overgrazing sheep cause changes in the composition, texture, and color of the soil's surface. As a result, horned lizards, which evolved irregular, colored blotches to resemble specific soil surfaces, are more visible to hawks and other predators.

Reptiles, being ectothermic ("cold-blooded") creatures, need adequate plant cover, rocks, or other objects to provide shade from the summer sun. Without shade, they must go underground or die. (In some grazed areas, the compacted, hardened soil may prevent them from burrowing.) Where livestock have eaten and beaten vegetation, shade is often inadequate and reptiles are limited in daytime movement and less able to carry out normal activities.

Many small animals suffer the effects of livestock in a more direct and immediate manner -- *they are stomped on*. Domestic cattle are huge, obese (if not undernourished), and awkward animals. Their large, cloven hooves crash down billions of times every day around the West. Large herds of domestic sheep or goats aren't much better. Many animals, including insects, spiders, snakes, lizards, tortoises, toads, and various amphibians, rodents, and small mammals are maimed or killed. Ground-dwelling creatures are killed and injured as hooves crash into their burrows. Many animals cannot dig the burrows they use, and must rely instead on those dug by other animals. Thus, trampling livestock may leave them at the mercy of the elements. Baby animals are crushed in or thrown from their nests. In Old Spain, El Torro Ferdinando sat on a bee. In Idaho, a cow sat on and killed two baby Endangered whooping cranes.

(Greg Pentkowski)

If we get rid of the cattle that now infest our public lands in the American West we will then be making room for a much greater population of elk, pronghorn antelope, bighorn sheep, mule deer, black bear, grizzly bear, buffalo, mountain lion, javelina, jaguar, desert tortoise, moose . . .
--Late naturalist writer Edward Abbey

As habitats are degraded, the more livestock-sensitive species are reduced in numbers or extirpated from certain areas, a phenomenon called "localized extinction." The masked bobwhite is a good example. With the introduction of cattle in the late 1800s, the bobwhite's lush grassland habitat in New Mexico and southern Arizona was devoured and the bird declined rapidly (Brown 1977, Goodwin 1977). The last known bird in the US was killed in 1912, and within a few years it was also believed extinct in Mexico, its last stronghold. Unexpectedly, many years later a few masked bobwhites were found in a cage in Mexico. They were brought to the US and reared in captivity. Subsequent reintroduction efforts were unsuccessful until 1985, when the federal government bought a 112,500-acre ranch near

Sasabe, Arizona, on the Mexican border, established it as the Buenos Aires National Wildlife Refuge, removed the cattle, and reintroduced the masked bobwhite. With tall grass and a comparatively healthy environment, the masked bobwhite is making a comeback on the Refuge and may already have reached a viable breeding population. There are still no other known wild populations of masked bobwhite in the United States and only a small number in a small area in the overgrazed Mexican state of Sonora.

Northern bobwhite, of which the Endangered masked bobwhite is a subspecies. *(USFWS)*

Ungrazed Buenos Aires National Wildlife Refuge. *(Paul Hirt)*

Wildlife in ecologically limited or simplified habitats may be particularly sensitive to livestock grazing. For example, the island night lizard is a large, darkly mottled, nocturnal, omnivorous reptile native only to the San Clemente, San Nicolas, and Santa Barbara Islands off the Southern California coast. Even its restricted habitat -- a few widely scattered islands 60 miles out in the Pacific Ocean -- has been ravaged by introduced livestock! Consequently, with no refuge the island night lizard is Endangered.

Similarly, species with naturally small ranges may be devastated by livestock. The black toad, for example, is native only to the area around Deep Springs Valley in east-central California. Decades of intensive ranching there led to the toad being placed on the California Endangered list. The Oregon silver spot butterfly, which lives in the lush meadows of coastal Oregon, probably never did have a large range or great numbers, but grazing sheep have so reduced its range and numbers that the insect is now a candidate for listing as Endangered.

When a species' population is reduced beyond a certain level, inbreeding and genetic drift gradually weaken the species. The gene pool dwindles and social structure collapses. The species eventually reaches the point where it cannot maintain a viable population and goes extinct locally or throughout its range. Such has been the case for numerous Western species.

(Eric Twachtman)

Dunes tiger beetle, Uncompahgre fritillary butterfly, Hualapai vole . . . As with plants, the list of animal victims forced onto the Threatened and Endangered list by livestock goes on and on. One example that has gained some media and scientific attention is the desert tortoise, a resident of the arid West for more than 3 million years, one that individually may live to 100 years of age. At home in the sparsely vegetated low-elevation deserts of California, Arizona, Nevada, and Utah, its diet consists mainly of grasses, forbs, and low shrubs. An average cow (or 5 sheep) eat as much of this vegetation in 1 day as a desert tortoise does in a year. Actually, the desert tortoise hibernates 9 or 10 months of the year and eats only about 23 pounds of vegetation during the other 2 or 3 months. So, strictly food-wise 1 cow equals about 500 tortoises. By far most tortoise habitat has been occupied by cattle and sheep for over 100 years. Ninety percent, mostly BLM land, is grazed now. Most native tortoise food plants have been wiped out, so it isn't hard to see why habitat once supporting 2000 desert tortoises per square mile now supports at most 200-400 per square mile, why the reptile has been extirpated completely from much of its former range, and why it is now listed as Threatened in California, Nevada, and Utah, and probably soon will be in Arizona.

(Steve Johnson)

A 1983 study on BLM land in the Paiute Valley of southern Nevada showed that 109 desert tortoises had starved to death on a 1 mile square plot. Similar mass starvations of desert tortoises over large areas due chiefly to livestock competition are common during dry years. Tortoises may increase in numbers during wetter years, but the overall trend is downward.

An extensive study of desert tortoise mortality on BLM land in the Beaver Dam Slope area of Arizona and Utah (part of the longest-ever continuous study of a vertebrate) showed clearly that tortoises there were starving due to cattle grazing. (A friend writes that in a recent visit to this area she observed starving cattle "eating mesquite branches 3/4" in diameter.") Additionally, depletion of vegetation left tortoises without adequate shade from hot sun. Tortoises were also suffering a variety of malnutrition-related maladies and reproduction failures and being stepped on, overturned (which can kill them), and buried alive in burrows. Other ranching-related problems include compaction of soil needed for burrowing, harmful fires due to highly flammable exotic annuals, trampling of nest sites, and impacts from ranching activities. Nevertheless, BLM is considering *increasing* the number of cattle on the Beaver Dam Slope. (Jarchow 1987)

A 1990 FWS biological opinion documents numerous detrimental effects of ranching on the desert tortoise (USDI, FWS 1990). Even the Forest Service maintains, in *Run Wild: Wildlife/Habitat Relationships*, that, "Livestock have deleterious effects on tortoise populations and their habitat through trampling young, soft-shelled tortoises; damaging burrows and shrubs used by tortoises for shelter; and removing critically needed forage (Nowakowski 1982). Dr. Kristen H. Berry, the world's foremost authority on the desert tortoise, states that the animal could reach the brink of extinction by the end of the century:

We're seeing extirpation of whole populations. Many of the island populations have already fallen below viable levels.

Disease has recently taken a toll, probably due largely to increased susceptibility from stress caused by livestock pressures. Collectors have taken and killed millions, and development, mining, toxic dumping, and ORV use also harm tortoise habitat. But Berry cites livestock production as both the main historic cause of desert tortoise decline and the main threat to its future survival. (Berry 1978)

Desert tortoise hatchlings are easily killed by trampling livestock. *(Steve Johnson)*

The livestock users have always contended that there is no conflict between sheep and the desert tortoise.
--Frank Munoz, executive officer, Kern County [CA] Wool Growers Association (Hartshorn 1988)

The desert tortoise shows that the decline of one animal often leads to subsequent declines of others. The desert tortoise digs burrows up to 30' long and 15' deep. By a recent count, 362 species of commensal invertebrates and vertebrates utilize the tortoise's burrows, and many of them can live nowhere else or even dig burrows themselves (Carlton 1990). The drastic reduction in the tortoise population cannot help but lead to declines of dependent species.

Likewise, the general decline in wildlife caused by livestock means general decreases in prey and carrion and corresponding declines in populations of dependent predators and scavengers, such as hawks and turkey vultures.

As overgrazing progressively degrades an area, even livestock-tolerant species decline. For example, the Merriam's kangaroo rat generally maintains a fairly high population level on moderately grazed grassland (though not moderately grazed desert -- its chief habitat). But when grazing reaches the point where the grass is gone and little of the rat's food source of seeds and leafy ground cover remains, its numbers decline.

The Arizona Game and Fish Department reports that livestock grazing and associated activities are partially or fully responsible for the decline of 13 of 18 mammal species and 11 of 22 bird species now listed by the state as Threatened or Endangered (this not including impacts such as from ranching roads, etc.) (Wuerthner 1989a). Even BLM acknowledges a serious livestock/wildlife problem. In 1974 a BLM report stated that "uncontrolled, unregulated or unplanned livestock use is occurring in approximately 85% of the state [Nevada], and damage to wildlife habitat can only be expressed as extreme destruction." The next year a BLM study noted that 33 species officially designated as Endangered inhabited BLM land and that "public land management at existing levels may not insure the survival of

these endangered species" (CEQ 1975). In its Fall 1986 issue, *Advocate* magazine reported:

> There are currently 109 endangered species on BLM lands, but there are recovery plans for only 57. Of those 57, only 44 of the plans are being implemented. In fact, BLM has been trying to cut back on wildlife programs for 6 years, and this year requested a $2.16 million cut from their wildlife species program. . . . The government touts a "multiple use" philosophy for public lands, but clearly, livestock are favored.

Since the above was published, BLM has stated that it administers "habitat for over 3,000 wildlife species, including 127 Federally listed threatened or endangered plant and animal species and more than 800 species that are candidates for Federal listing" (USDI, BLM 1987). Similarly, the Forest Service reports that:

> National Forests and Grasslands are home to 140 plant and animal species listed as threatened or endangered. The Fish & Wildlife Service has approved [not implemented] recovery plans for 80 of these species. . . . An additional 761 species are considered sensitive . . . . (USDA, USFS 1987)

If habitat is severely affected throughout an animal's entire range, eventual extinction is possible. The Wyoming subspecies of the Canadian toad is one example. General degradation of its southeastern Wyoming habitat by extensive livestock grazing and range management was a major factor in its recent extinction.

According to The Nature Conservancy, in California alone 220 animal species are threatened with extinction. Thus, 1/5 or more of California's native animals could become extinct in the near future. In 1988 Defenders of Wildlife identified 498 US animal and plant species listed under the Endangered Species Act, 940 species qualified for listing but not yet listed, 3010 species needing further study, and possibly 200-300 species already extinct. Ranching has been a major factor in the decline of many of these.

Jared Diamond, a physiologist at UCLA, thinks that nearly all of the world's modern animal extinctions were caused by human influence. He identifies 5 major causes of these extinctions (and drift toward extinction). Livestock ranching is the *only* human activity on Western public land (and much of the Earth) to include all 5 of these influences to a significant degree. They are: 1. *Overkill.* For more than a century, the grazing industry has killed great numbers of predators, competitors, and pests. 2. *Habitat destruction.* Overgrazing and range development have caused more damage to the ecosystems of Western public land than any other single agent. 3. *Impact of introduced species.* Livestock themselves are the most destructive introduced species on Earth; however, the Western grazing industry has also introduced feral horses, dogs, and cats; many insects and parasites; and numerous plant species over millions of acres. 4. *Pollutants.* The grazing industry has polluted Western public land and water more than any other user, with herbicides, insecticides, pesticides, predacides, petroleum products, various chemicals, sediments, urine, manure, and dead livestock. 5. *Secondary effects -- decline or extinction of one species leads to decline or extinction of another.* The decline of numerous Western species at the hands of the ranching industry -- elk, prairie dogs, and slugs, for instance -- has lead to the decline of numerous dependent species -- in this case, grizzlies, burrowing owls, and skunks.

The International Union for the Conservation of Nature and Natural Resources concludes that habitat destruction is the Earth's major cause of extinctions, accounting for twice as many extinctions as overexploitation, which in turn accounts for twice as many extinctions as introduction of exotic species (CEQ 1981). However you slice it, livestock production (including ranching) is Western public land's and the planet's greatest cause of drift toward extinction (see Chapter VI for global impacts of livestock production).

Further, both natural and anthropogenic reintroductions of many extirpated species are made more difficult by livestock. For example, by outcompeting large herbivores, overgrazing, predator-protected livestock have reduced the wild prey base needed by wolves wandering into the Western US from Canada and Mexico and potentially for wolves reintroduced by humans.

> *Respected scientists and learned others already are warning that natural vertebrate evolution on this planet is coming to a close as a result of unnatural influence. Invertebrate and plant evolution may not be far behind. Ranching is the major cause in the rural Western United States.*

Because each species has different habitat requirements, livestock of course have varying effects on them. For example, where grazing has caused an increase in the  brush-to-ground -level vegetation ratio, the ground cricket, which needs thick organic cover at ground level, may be harmed more than the bush cricket, which spends most of its time in bushes.

Because there is such a huge variety of animals with such a wide diversity of requirements, livestock grazing is bound to (temporarily) benefit some species in some areas in some ways. Carp, an exotic, can tolerate water temperatures in the 70s and 80s F., so in streams where grazing has caused higher summer water temperatures, carp have replaced native cold water fish. However, grazing has also reduced streamflow, eliminated protective shelter, ruined spawning beds, polluted water, and decreased available fish food, so undoubtedly even carp are much less abundant overall than they would have been without the livestock influence.

Some species gain numbers in some areas and lose in others. For instance, the blacktail jackrabbit prefers forbs as a food source to grasses. In areas where grazing of grasses has favored "weedy" vegetation, blacktail jackrabbit numbers may rise. However, where grazing is so heavy that even most weeds cannot survive and no cover from predators remains, jackrabbit numbers decline.

Similarly, certain kinds of grazing in certain places at certain times of the year may have certain beneficial influen-

ces on certain species, certainly. Killdeer prefer to nest in short grass, so moderate grazing of tall grass just prior to nesting season might be of benefit at that time, if not outweighed by other detrimental livestock factors. Yes, in theory, some livestock effects could occasionally benefit certain wild animals. But in practice this rarely occurs. The detrimental effects almost invariably outweigh the beneficial, especially if range management is considered with the other effects. Shorter grass at nesting time isn't much good to killdeer if the creek they depend upon is dried up and their food supply of water-oriented insects and crustaceans is destroyed.

Cowbirds (formerly buffalo birds) *seem* to do well on cattle ranges (but much more so on irrigated livestock pastures), where they sometimes feed on insects stirred up by grazing cattle. However, the 40-75 million buffalo and millions of other large grazers cattle replaced were of much greater benefit, and huge flocks of buffalo birds followed the great herds, eating the much greater numbers of insects that were flushed up from healthy ranges. The vast native herds supported more buffalo birds then than erratically managed, sporadically grazed groups of cattle do now.

Because native herds were nomadic, buffalo birds could not afford to be tied to nests, and they evolved *brood parasitism* -- that is, they laid their eggs in the nests of other birds at the expense of their hosts' eggs and offspring. However, all involved survived and thrived over the millennia in Nature's balance.

With the introduction of livestock grazing and farming, buffalo birds necessarily became cowbirds and spread into many areas not evolved to accommodate them. There, through their brood parasitism, they have caused the near-extinction of 3 songbirds and decline of many others. However, the main reason cowbird populations in these areas are so high is because millions of acres of cropland, particularly grain fields, provide them abundant food, not because cattle provide much benefit.

A few animal species even seem to thrive because of livestock grazing. The zebra-tailed lizard, for example, runs through sandy washes and open areas with hard-packed soil and scant vegetation cover. Because grazing has increased flooding, creating more sandy washes, and decreased vegetative cover, uncovering and compacting bare dirt over large areas, the overall area of zebra-tail habitat may have increased. Despite negative livestock influences on the zebra-tail (trampling of the lizards and/in their shelters, depletion of food species, reduction of hiding places, etc.), grazing may have caused an overall increase in zebra-tail numbers.

However, while some species appear to benefit from livestock grazing, we must bear in mind that the Western landscape we see today is little like it was before Euro-Americans and their livestock arrived. The environment is now functioning on a much less productive level. On a human-created landscape where much of the wildlife has been eliminated, those animals that survive stand out starkly. Though their numbers may actually be smaller than in pre-livestock times, we may imagine them higher.

For instance, here is a common experience: You are driving along a rural highway early one summer morning. Looking out over the sparse, overgrazed landscape, you see here and there a foraging cottontail rabbit. Since the cottontails are the largest and most prominent objects, and you can see many of them scattered across hundreds of barren acres, they might seem abundant. On a comparable ungrazed landscape, you may be able to see only a few cottontails here and there in the thicker, taller vegetation. Though there are actually many more cottontails and other animals on the ungrazed land, you simply cannot see them.

And some species *appear* to be doing well simply because they are doing better than the more severely harmed species. For example, when you take a week-long camping trip to the lava country of northeastern California and the only large animals you see are 8 deer, 3 coyotes, 2 skunks, a beaver, a few bighorns, and 287 cows, it might seem that deer are doing well there. How are you to know that on that same trip 150 years ago, you would have seen a dozen deer, plus 6 coyotes, 4 beaver, a couple of foxes, 2 herds of pronghorn, 3 black bears, 2 badgers, 3 herds of elk, a porcupine, a bobcat, a group of raccoons, a weasel, 3 mink, a pack of wolves, a ringtail, and no cows? How can we conceptualize accurate comparisons when we have only experienced one half of that to be compared?

> *Livestock grazing has been proven to be essential to proper management of wildlife and other natural resources.*
> --From statement adopted by Western state Farm Bureaus, Cattlemens Associations, and Wool Growers Associations

> *The old slogan that "good livestock management is good wildlife management" should be laid to rest by range managers as it has been by wildlife professionals.*
> --Maitland Sharpe, Director, Environmental Affairs, Izaak Walton League of America

Because of this illusory abundance of some wild animals on some grazed lands, some ranchers claim their hooved invaders benefit wildlife. As Denzel and Nancy Ferguson noted in **Sacred Cows**:

> *Today, we hear that ducks cannot take their newly hatched ducklings to water unless cows first trample a path through the dense vegetation. Big game animals would certainly starve if cows failed to eat old growth vegetation and expose the new. Grasses would become extinct if cattle weren't around to trample the seeds into the soil. And if it weren't for the magic stimulating agent in the saliva of cows, plants would probably cease growing altogether. Yes, indeed, American wildlife is certainly blessed to have enjoyed the fabulous benefits of cows as a wildlife management tool.* (Ferguson 1983)

Many if not most ranchers practically take personal credit for any wildlife that survives on "their" public land allotment, promulgating any living creature larger than a rabbit. As the Fergusons point out, however, wildlife is also seen on highways, but that doesn't mean highways are a favored or useful habitat. In an absurd twisting of the truth, it is as if these stockmen somehow manufactured these animals themselves through the wondrous effects of livestock grazing, that there would be some kind of void otherwise. I am reminded of an eloquent and succinct statement by Mike Roselle, a socio-enviro activist: "They lie."

Although they may talk like it, stockmen did not *create* the land or the animals on it, and what few large wild animals remain do so in spite of -- not because of -- ranching.

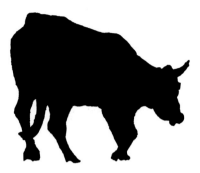

When a species increases to large enough numbers that it reduces livestock production, the grazing industry alleges it a "pest" -- the animal equivalent of a plant "invader." In damaging ecosystems and setting up conditions favorable for population explosions of certain species, overgrazing and range management (next chapter) are the principal causes of pest infestations in the rangeland West. Animals prone to becoming pests in this manner include grasshoppers, jackrabbits, various rodents, harvester ants, aphids, beetles, and crickets.

The grasshopper is perhaps the most renowned grazing industry pest. USDA calls it the most potent Western forage competitor. Grasshoppers rarely occur in large numbers on ungrazed range, plagues of them are signs of overgrazing. In fact, grazed land sometimes produces 50,000 or more grasshoppers per acre. Livestock grazing uncovers bare dirt in which hoppers lay their eggs, hastens egg development by permitting more sunlight to reach and warm the soil, eliminates vegetation needed by birds and other hopper predators, and causes other changes favorable to population explosions. Accordingly, many experts recommend a uniform grassy cover to reduce grasshoppers, and some suggest a barbed wire fence as the most effective method.

A curious personal experience exemplifies the livestock/ grasshopper connection: On the plains of southeastern Montana, a fence separates grazed from ungrazed grassland. The grazed side, where "hooved locusts" have eaten most grass and uncovered much bare dirt, is crawling with hoppers. The ungrazed side, with a thick, tall grass, supports perhaps 1/4 as many. Most surprising is that (until no food remains) the hungry hordes stay on the wasted side of the fence -- not the side with the vastly greater amount of food!

Natural population cycles evolved as part of ecosystem dynamics. Unnatural pest infestations are generally very sporadic, fluctuate to much greater extremes, and do not fit into ecosystem dynamics. They reduce species' habitat, genetic viability, resistance to disease and parasites, and so on.

Pest infestations usually intensify the effects of overgrazing. When a large number of grasshoppers graze an already overgrazed range, an ecosystem can be devastated. At this point, either a massive grasshopper die-off occurs, leading to extremely low numbers of grasshoppers the following year(s), or the grasshoppers transform into winged "locusts" and fly off to greener pastures, where they may wreak havoc.

Sometimes so-called "pests" only seem to be pests or are misleadingly portrayed as such. For example, in some areas of California and the Southwest, kangaroo rats of several species are poisoned as pests when their numbers reach "unacceptable" levels. Their numbers may actually be no higher than normal for their habitat -- the high points of natural population cycles. Yet, they are considered pests merely because they reach higher numbers than other wild plant-eating animals in their range. Their comparative success guarantees them a deadly fate.

Similarly, wild animals often become "pests" by default. Pocket gophers, for example, are sometimes considered pests because at certain times they do more damage to livestock operations than any other wild animal. Though the decrease in profits may be slight, stockmen strike out at whatever animal reduces production most. In this way, the ranching industry always maintains at least 1 pest animal enemy, thus garnering subsidy and sympathy.

When grazing is extreme, and perhaps compounded by pests, the land may become so thoroughly degraded that even pests cannot survive. These areas become biological voids, barren wastelands. Millions of acres in every Western state fit this description.

I am reminded of one area in particular. Though no worse than many, at the time it struck me that walking across this stark BLM flatland south of Grants, New Mexico, must be a lot like walking across one of the Moon's desolate "seas."

The Moon. *(NASA)*

This BLM moonscape south of Grants, New Mexico, is virtually worthless as animal habitat. Ungrazed highway right-of-way on left.

Nothing broke the monotony of the vast expanse of dry, hard dirt. Tiny stubbles of brown, amounting to no more than 5% ground cover, provided little protection to the exposed soil. Perhaps a few ants or beetles crawled across the ground, but I don't recall any animal. Exactly at the fenceline of the nearby ungrazed highway right-of-way the emptiness was magically transformed into a thick covering of foot-high grasses, forbs, and flowering plants, with flying insects buzzing about.

An ungrazed portion of Bosque del Apache National Wildlife Refuge, New Mexico, supports relatively abundant wildlife.

A recurrent premise in this book is that *Nature knows best how to "manage" itself*. Teddy Roosevelt, selective Nature advocate, once said of the Grand Canyon, "Leave it as it is. The ages have been at work, and man can only mar it." Well, the ages have been at work on *all* natural entities and processes.

Here we come to a key juncture in our quest to understand what ranching has done to the West. Before Euro-American conquest, western wildlife existed in relative stability. Populations did fluctuate, but as part of natural cycles following irregular but relatively dependable patterns beneficial to species and ecosystems alike. For millions of years in most cases, individual species have evolved to thrive as parts of these cycles.

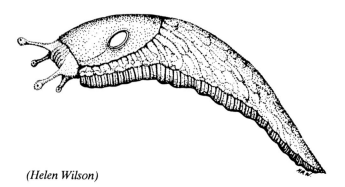

(Helen Wilson)

For example, during a series of wet years slugs naturally increase in number as more food becomes available and conditions remain moist. When dry years come, slug numbers drop. Slug species have experienced these irregularly

alternating wet and dry periods for millions of generations. Each succeeding generation is given the most-fit genes of the preceding to adapt to environmental changes. In this way, slugs evolve to both survive under a wide range of environmental conditions and thrive under specialized conditions.

All animal and plant species exhibit this duality. On one hand, long-term adaptations to various changes in environments have caused them to evolve to survive as wide a diversity of situations as possible. Thus, within certain limits slugs can live in a multiformity of habitats, under a variety of changing conditions.

On the other hand, to varying degrees all species are also specialists. Each has evolved to take advantage of certain aspects of its environment more fully than other species. In this way, each species maintains some competitive advantage. Thus, slugs are favored in certain habitat in areas of prolonged frost-free periods and high moisture with succulent herbaceous plants for food.

But specialization has its price. Many species have over millennia become so highly specialized that they are harmed by only slight unnatural changes in their environment. Though adapted to survive natural long- and short-term changes, they often cannot tolerate the radically different artificial changes caused by livestock.

Natural cycles are the pulsebeat of all life. All living things have evolved to survive between cyclic extremes. These extremes define the parameters of species evolution. Without them, species become simplistic and limited in their ability to survive environmental changes. Like muscles that go unused, species atrophy without the stimulation provided by natural cycles, evolution stalemates, and species decline.

Nature's cycles are usually relatively gentle, occurring gradually enough so species have time to adjust. For example, as an extended period of dryness progresses, instinct -- the cumulative result of thousands of generations of natural experience -- tells slugs to leave open areas and concentrate along waterways and in low, moist areas. Here they stay until moister conditions return, whereupon they recolonize uplands.

Natural extremes rarely reach far beyond established limits. The periods of dryness that drive slugs and other animals to waterways and low spots almost never last long enough to extirpate populations completely. If a dry period lasts so long as to constitute a change in climate, it does so slowly enough that slugs and other animals and plants can move to moister climes or evolve accordingly.

However, when unnatural changes, such as those caused by livestock, hit an ecosystem, wildlife is caught unprepared and may suffer extirpation. When a herd of cattle moves onto slug habitat, it quickly strips off most low-level vegetation, destroys shelter, damages and dries the soil, smashes slugs, and so on. Slugs do not know what to do; they have not adapted to these changes over the millennia and, unless such a cattle herd invaded extremely infrequently, they could never evolve to survive such radical, unnatural changes. For example, many slugs are too far from waterways to make it there on such short notice. Those close enough to do so find the riparian zones have been similarly damaged. A massive die-off of slugs occurs, perhaps affecting slug predators and others as well.

When livestock alter the necessities of any species, that species suffers. Because almost every natural component has become a necessity to some species, the drastic unnatural influence wrought by livestock has hurt *most* rangeland species.

"Natural disasters," such as tornados, landslides, avalanches, and volcanic eruptions, are also radical influences on wildlife, but they occur relatively infrequently, and usually in small areas. Rejuvenation begins soon thereafter and continues until the previous circumstances re-occur. In areas where radical natural changes, such as those caused by floods and fire, are periodic occurrences, wildlife has evolved to withstand them with minimum hardship and no long-term decline.

The impact of livestock pushes environmental changes and cyclic extremes far beyond natural limits. When the lushly vegetated area that supported slugs for millennia is suddenly stripped of most vegetation, and soil is exposed to the drying rays of the sun on an annual basis for periods of time far exceeding those caused by native grazing animals, fire, or other natural disturbances, slugs and many other animals and plants cannot survive.

Even if they don't die immediately, long-term survival is doubtful. Genetic changes made gradually and under natural conditions do not apply to radically different or fluctuating human-manipulated surroundings. Those genetic changes wildlife does make in response to these human influences will not apply to future environments where conditions will either continue to be radically different and fluctuating or (if humans end livestock grazing or fail to survive), revert back to (whatever is left of) Nature.

In other words, *livestock grazing throws evolution out the window.*

To the wild animal, the rancher means life . . . .
--Wyoming state Representative and rancher Jim Hageman

Livestock grazing is the single most important factor limiting wildlife production in the West.
--Philip Fradkin, "The Eating of the West" (Fradkin 1979)

(Lone Wolf Circles)

(George Wuerthner)

Fire

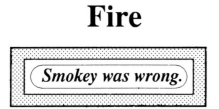

Smokey was wrong.

Fire is as natural to this planet as trees, brush, and grass. Indeed, most Western forests, brushlands, and grasslands *need* natural fire to maintain peak health. Their plant and animal species are well-adapted to periodic natural burns, and many actually thrive *because of* fire. Until recently, they had been doing so for thousands or millions of years.

Natural fire provides many important benefits to most Western ecosystems. It creates seedbeds; assists some species' seed germination; initiates sprouting of tender, nutritious new growth preferred by some animals; helps prevent insect and disease epidemics; neutralizes environmental toxins; recycles nutrients not otherwise recycled; diversifies habitat; and prevents excessive accumulation of combustible organic matter which could lead to explosive, destructive fires. For many plants, fire also functions something like an animal predator, "weeding out" the old, sick, deformed, and otherwise weak of the species, allowing stronger individuals to survive and pass on their more favorable characteristics to future generations.

But just as the plants, soil, water, and animals of the West have been denigrated by livestock grazing, so have fire regimes. Livestock alter: the amount, type, and location of combustible material; fuel moisture; humidity and wind speed at fire level; waterways and other natural firebreaks; and other factors which affect fire dynamics. This has changed the location, incidence, interval, burn time, size, and other characteristics of fire on most Western rangeland.

Fires now are generally much more sporadic and less frequent than 150 years ago. They are usually smaller, burn shorter and at different times of the day and year, leave dissimilar amounts and kinds of ash, and so forth. In many areas where livestock prevent fuel buildup, wildfire is now virtually non-existent. Where livestock are removed, usually natural fire quickly reestablishes itself, if given the chance.

In the Southwest, scattered mesquite trees were a component of many original bunchgrass communities. Lightning-caused fires periodically swept through such communities, burning any given area at intervals of roughly 5 to 20 years. The hotter of these fires burned off the tops of bunchgrasses (and forbs, flowering perennials, and other non-woody plants) and small mesquites alike, but roots of both almost always survived. (Widely scattered large mesquite trees usually were not burned.) Because bunchgrass regrows more quickly than mesquite, it gets a head start over mesquite for the first few years after a fire. But eventually mesquite begins to overshadow and dominate bunchgrass. Mesquite remains prominent until another fire comes through and once again gives bunchgrass the advantage. Fire dynamics maintained cyclic equilibrium and ecosystem health, diversity, and stability.

When livestock change an ecosystem they "play with fire," so to speak. As cattle overgrazed these Southwestern bunchgrass communities in the late 1800s, they stripped off so much ground cover that fire no longer made periodic sweeps. Mesquite was given the advantage and as a result outcompeted bunchgrass in many areas. The combination of overgrazing, harmful range management, and lack of natural fire continues to wipe out not only the native bunchgrasses but many other plants and animals, and even the mesquite in some areas.

This mostly natural fire in a mesquite grassland creates biologic mosaics and promotes healthy ecosystem dynamics. *(Geoff Babb)*

Natural fires can be started by volcanic activity, sparks from landslides or falling rocks, meteorites, or even spontaneous combustion of certain naturally occurring substances. However, the vast majority are started by lightning. This is significant, for lightning is usually accompanied by a storm's cool temperatures, high humidity or rain, and wind. The strong winds associated with thunderstorms often help ignite and spread fires, but the wind and the fires usually don't last long. More than 90% of lightning-caused fires in the West burn out or are rained out before reaching an acre in size.

Human-ignited fires, on the other hand, whether prescribed, accidental (ranching activities are one of the main causes of accidental fires in the West), or arson, rarely occur when or where Nature would have them. Most are started during the wrong weather at the wrong time of day and in the wrong part of the season. They occur too frequently or infrequently and too regularly or irregularly. Accordingly, anthropogenic fires are too big or small, long or short, hot or cool, smoky or clear, etc., to be of maximum benefit to ecosystems that evolved with certain fire patterns. Depending on a host of variables, human-caused fire may benefit or harm an ecosystem, but natural fire is usually much preferable in both the long and short term.

Additionally, a widespread policy of fire suppression by governments under pressure from timber and ranching interests has resulted in great increases in combustible material in many brushland and forest areas since around the turn of the century. Most fires in these areas, both accidental and purposeful in origin, occur when the weather is hot and dry with long-lasting winds -- conditions unlike those associated with thunderstorms. Thus, these fires spread explosively through tinder-dry fuel, often killing nearly everything in their path. They can be so intensely hot that they "scorch" the surface of the ground, change its chemical composition, kill soil microorganisms, and render uppermost soil sterile. (Conversely, livestock depletion of ground cover can result in fires too cool for ecosystems adapted to naturally hotter fires.)

Some natural fires started by lightning at the end of the dry season and onset of the thunderstorm season may also "burn hot" (though subsequent thunderstorms extinguish many). Most natural fires, however, occur as the thunderstorm season progresses. They burn relatively moist fuel and/or during wetter, cooler weather. Usually, they burn comparatively slowly and coolly. Even when strong winds whip them quickly through the grass, brush, or trees, fire temperatures stay comparatively low.

In timberland, most natural fires creep across the forest floor, consuming accumulated duff, dry grass and herbs, occasionally burning logs, small or dead trees, and patches of thick understory. Erratic storm winds may cause fire to leap-frog through the ground cover or up and down through the different foliage levels. In brushland, wildfires move steadily along beneath the brush canopy, consuming dead lower branches and the litter layer of leaves, twigs, and dry grass. Or where sufficient fuel has accumulated, flare-ups burn off brush completely. In grassland, fires sweep or creep across the landscape irregularly, burning off the old, dry vegetation and fertilizing the soil with nutritious ash.

Contrary to what we have been taught from infancy by Smoky the Bear, Bambi, and BLM's Johnny Horizon, natural fire is not an evil monster annihilating everything in its path. As mentioned, relatively few wildfires spread far. Most are extinguished by rain or diminishing thunderstorm winds, or quickly exhaust their fuel supplies. Many are blocked by streams, washes, rocky outcroppings, cliffs, animal trails, moist vegetation, and so on. Some do burn for days or weeks or even months, occasionally becoming gigantic in size, but even these benefit the ecosystems adapted to them.

Wildfire usually leaves a complex mosaic of burned and unburned areas, as well as individual trees and plants that survive the flames. Organic matter that is not yet ready to burn doesn't, and cliffs, rocky areas, waterways, irregularities in growth patterns, differences in fuel moisture, and weather changes during the fire all contribute to a mosaic effect and, eventually, to a complex of vegetation types in various stages of succession which promote ecosystem health, diversity, and stability. The unburned portions of mosaics allow many animals that cannot go underground, run, or fly away to escape the flames. They additionally provide source areas for revegetation of burned-over areas by less fire-tolerant plants and re-colonization by small animals. Ranching influences, particularly overgrazing, can cause either excessive or inadequate fire, and unnatural fire, all of which preclude this biodiversity-enhancing mosaic effect.

> In some places, the fire had reached the canopy, "crowned out," and incineration was complete. Where the fire had burned fitfully or not at all, there were brown or green islands of surviving vegetation. In many places, it was difficult for us to determine why the flames had skipped over a patch of ground. Already a mosaic of new vegetation was intermixed with the old.
> --Ed Grumbine, ecologist

Natural systems experience cyclic variations in their components. Each component is interlinked with all others in an incredibly complex network of interrelationships no person can fully understand. Because of this complexity, and because the time frames for these cyclic pulses are often longer than those familiar to us, we have a distorted view of many natural events, including fire, as catastrophes when in fact they are essential to maintaining ecosystems.

For example, the Yellowstone area wildfires of summer 1988 burned 1.6 million acres. Not since 1910, when 3 million acres burned, had the Northern Rockies seen fire on such a scale. Because the Yellowstone fires charred such a huge area for the first time in so long, they were widely perceived as "catastrophic." While it is true that historic fire suppression was a contributing factor to the size and intensity of the Yellowstone fires, there is also much evidence that fires of this magnitude naturally occur at intervals of roughly 100-300 years in the region's high country. Thus, the area's natural systems are adapted to, even dependent upon, this size and frequency of burns. (In 1991, the fires' benefits to the Yellowstone ecosystem are evident; the complex mosaic of fires has rejuvenated many biomes and enhanced biodiversity.)

Fire dynamics are influenced by many factors. The unique interrelationships between all components of each ecosystem dictate the timing, amount, and type of fire inherent to that ecosystem. In turn, each individual component of an ecosystem is best adapted to the fire dynamics unique to that ecosystem. In other words, fire is an integral part of ecosystem dynamics and species evolution.

Periods between natural fires generally are long enough so that climax vegetation reproduces and regrows to maturity, ground water is recharged, animals reestablish themselves, organic litter builds up enough to rejuvenate soil, and so forth. On the other hand, fires are generally frequent enough to assist with the reproduction of dependent species, maintain proper balance between animal species, recharge soil with ashes to maintain proper pH and nutrient levels, suppress plant diseases, and so on. When livestock grazing alters the natural timing of fire, these important interrelationships are impaired. For example, without frequent-enough grassland fires, some grass fungi may spread unchecked and eventually kill grass over large areas.

Fire recovery: A year after a lightning-ignited burn, this ungrazed mountainside is covered with luxuriant vegetation; leafy, fire-promoted species spring forth, and most burned-over perennials, brush, and trees sprout from rootstocks and bases. Dead trees and bushes provide important animal habitat.

Fire frequency ranges from 5-10 years (California chaparral) to 5-20 (short grass prairie) to 50-100 years (some mid-elevation Rocky Mountain forests) to essentially never (Olympic Peninsula rainforest and portions of the Mojave Desert). Intervals between fires depend on the unique characteristics of each ecosystem, so Nature best provides proper timing. Natural fire occurs on an irregular yet periodic basis. Like rainfall, fire is dependable yet variable. You know it will happen and when and where it might, but never exactly. In this way, fire provides maximum diversity of influence, thus diversity in the environment -- a basis of ecosystem health and stability.

Some plants are specifically adapted to fire and cannot survive without it. Giant sequoia trees are one example. Tom Swetnam, a researcher at the University of Arizona, has studied the tree rings of 1000-year-old sequoias. He says that fire scars among the rings indicate forest fires burned them at fairly regular intervals of 10-30 years, and similar burning probably occurred throughout many Western forests. These natural fires helped sequoia cones open and their seeds germinate, and thinned out competitive shade-tolerant trees and gave sun-loving sequoia seedlings more room. Experts are concerned that fire suppression may be a major factor working against the survival of these 1000-2000 year old trees, the largest living beings on Earth.

Having evolved with frequent fire, prairie plants keep most of their biomass and reproductive structures below ground. After a burn removes their above-ground portions, they regrow quickly from the protected portions in the soil. Some Western grasses and perennial flowering plants have life-spans of 100 years or longer and may sprout from the same burned-over base many times, though too-frequent fire can damage or kill them. Most grasslands burn during dormant seasons, after grasses have matured and cured on the stalk. Dormant grass buds are less susceptible than active buds to damage by fire, so artificial burning during the growing season is detrimental.

Chaparral and many other brush communities are highly dependent upon natural fire. Most of their woody species have numerous, thin stems and resinous, flammable leaves. They form many dead branches after reaching maturity, and their dropped litter is likewise highly susceptible to fire. The seeds of some brush species, some ceanothus and manzanitas for example, require fire scarification to germinate.

Livestock grazing often activates changes in fire dynamics that spell trouble for certain fire-dependent species. Quaking aspen, for example, depends on natural fire to create openings in thick conifer forests. Where fire has burned off all the trees in an area, aspen roots put forth shoots that quickly overshadow new conifer seedlings and form almost pure aspen stands. In some parts of the Rockies

A year before, a wildfire burned the right side of this hill -- ungrazed National Park Service land -- up to the fence at center but not beyond. Left of the fence is grazed National Forest land that could not carry the fire. Via fire, livestock unnaturally alter the character of the land.

heavy grazing has removed so much ground cover that fires cannot spread through the forest. This, combined with fire suppression and with cattle and sheep eating many aspen saplings, has resulted in depletions and local extirpations of aspens.

Manzanita is a red-barked shrub native to brushy areas over much of the West. As mentioned, the seeds of some manzanita species need fire to germinate. But livestock grazing and fire suppression for ranching have so reduced natural fire that in some areas manzanita has been outcompeted by less fire-dependent shrubs and trees, such as shrub oak, silktassel, oaks, and junipers; in many cases it has been replaced by bare dirt).

For thousands of years, people on different parts of the globe periodically burned off grass and sometimes brush and trees for various reasons. Largely because of this, it is argued that humans were the controlling force in these ecosystems -- that these ecosystems, grasslands especially, depended on human-caused fire to maintain their essential character. Usually the message underlying this supposition is that humans must manage these ecosystems, either with fire or (according to ranching advocates) with *livestock* because "fire is no longer a viable management alternative in our modern world."

The theory is contradicted by the facts. First, paleontological evidence shows that, even during humankind's multi-thousand year history of setting fires, anthropogenic fires were still much less widespread and influential than natural fires. In what is now the Western US, aboriginals had probably been setting fires for less than 5000 years, and evidence indicates that most of their mid- and tall-grass prairie burning took place in the past few centuries to improve horse pasture (White 1990). Second, scientific evidence also indicates that these same fire-impacted ecosystems *antedate the origin of fire-setting humans by 25 million years*. Third, numerous other studies show that, naturally, fire has a far greater (and much different) influence than large herbivores in defining the character of vegetation communities, grasslands especially.

Another misconception is that periodic fire will keep any land free from brush. In many cases the opposite is true. Most chaparral, brush, and shrub communities in the West have been subject to periodic fire for millennia. The most successful species of these communities survive fire, even if burned to the ground. After fires they send up new sprouts from near the ground line, and within several years the woody plants have regained their former height. The chaparral-covered foothills of California, some of which naturally burn at cycles averaging less than 10 years, are a prime example.

Due largely to the logging and ranching industry-inspired war against fire, and the attendant propaganda during the past century (see next chapter), natural fire has been neither understood nor appreciated in this country. Compounding common misconception, there are few natural fires for comparison anymore. These days many fires, in those areas where they still ignite, burn out quickly due to lack of fuel caused by overgrazing and other poor land management. We rarely hear about these fires. In other areas they explode into raging infernos due to bad timing and because relentless fire suppression allowed excessive build-up of coarse fuels. We hear about these often; they are the basis for misconceptions about fire in general. Further, due to our society's general lack of interest in grassland, forest and brush fire garners far more attention and research than grass fire.

> *Livestock grazing* [on public land] *helps prevent dangerous forest and prairie fires by preventing the buildup of excess combustible brush and forage.*
> --Patty McDonald, Executive Director, Public Lands Council

One often hears ranchers and range managers say that livestock are necessary on our rangelands -- grasslands, brushlands, forests, and even deserts -- to eat off vegetation and prevent the buildup of combustible plant materials, and thus destructive fires. When other arguments to justify livestock grazing fail, this one usually does the trick. After all, who wants to be accused of condoning destructive fires? But let's examine this argument.

In the first place, if it is indeed necessary to have herbivorous animals reducing the vegetation cover, then why shouldn't we let the native animals that supposedly did this for millions of years do it? Indigenous grazers, the plants they foraged, and fire had kept a remarkable balance. Livestock grazing is subject to the vagaries of politics, market fluctuations, and management irregularities, as well as the laws of Nature. Isn't this another argument to bring back the bison, to reestablish elk, bighorns, pronghorn, and prairie dogs on our public land?

Second, large areas of the West, in deserts especially, were not naturally frequented by fire, or large herds of herbivores. So fire prevention cannot reasonably be used to justify livestock grazing in these areas now, though it often is.

Third, it is much more beneficial to ecosystems to let organic matter build up and burn than to have livestock eat it and carry it off to feedlots and slaughterhouses, leaving a net loss of nutrients on the range.

Fourth, natural fire performs many important functions that any type of grazing cannot. For example, the rapid heating and cooling from fires helps break down rock and soil particles, assisting soil formation. Livestock may scatter rocks and displace soil, but they cannot break apart rocks or individual soil particles. Natural fire helps neutralize plant diseases, whereas livestock may help spread them. In many areas, the ashes left by fire are necessary to reduce soil acidity, whereas livestock cannot adequately reduce soil acidity. Wildfire may destroy or promote the seeds of various plant species according to Nature's way; livestock tend to harm natives. And (unless starving) livestock consume only palatable vegetation, whereas fire can recycle coarse grass, inedible forbs and brush, fallen tree leaves, down branches, logs, and other combustible organic matter. There is no adequate substitute for natural fire, especially not livestock.

Fifth, and perhaps most important, though livestock and fire share some similar influences, fire has always been a *much more potent* force than grazing animals in botanic/fire dynamics.

Yes, of course it is true that livestock have reduced the amount of combustible material on rangeland. It is true to the extreme! Most natural range fire ended suddenly when ground cover was stripped off by livestock in the late 1800s.

For example, the 112,500 acres of grazed grassland that is now the Buenos Aires National Wildlife Refuge experienced its first large natural fire since the 1800s -- a highly beneficial 12,500 acre blaze -- only a couple of years after the Refuge was established and livestock were removed in 1985.

Bare dirt does not burn, nor do mere stubbles of grass. Livestock have so widely and uniformly denuded and trampled the West that vast areas can no longer support fire. Many of these areas have deteriorated to the point that they could not support fire for a long time even if livestock were removed. (In contrast, native herds generally depleted the range much less severely, uniformly, and frequently, thus creating mosaics of fuel that were important to natural diversity.) Furthermore, the many cattle trails, ranching roads, cleared fencelines, stock trails and driveways, and other "improvements" act as firebreaks and, along with constructed firebreaks and grazing industry-inspired fire suppression, prevent fire from spreading and have virtually eliminated natural fire from many areas.

Fires on ungrazed roadsides in the West often burn only up to the fenceline because the denuded range on the other side cannot carry fire.

On the other hand, livestock have so overgrazed the West that much of it has been invaded by unpalatable and extremely flammable species, most notably cheatgrass from Russia. On millions of Western acres, cheatgrass is now the dominant grass species, often the *only* grass species. Much more likely to burn than any native grass, cheatgrass "burns hot" and can carry fire into and burn vegetation that would not normally burn, in many cases causing changes that further the spread of exotics. Thus have cheatgrass fires seriously damaged many Western ecosystems. (Ferguson 1983) Exotic vegetation supports inferior, unnatural fires.

Native bunchgrasses in much of the West were not contiguous in distribution, and carried fire poorly. Some arid to semi-arid areas, much of the Mojave and Great Basin Deserts in particular, historically did not produce the type and spacing of vegetation necessary to keep fire burning for more than short distances. Livestock-initiated invasions of annuals provided a flashy fuel source that resulted in intense, frequent fires that harmed wildlife not adapted to them. Many native desert shrubs, for instance, have declined as a result. (USDI, FWS 1990)

Additionally, livestock have so depleted ground cover that in some types of forest and brushland it no longer supports the relatively frequent fires that used to periodically burn off excess woody fuel. When these large-sized fuels finally do accumulate to the point where they may carry fire regardless of ground cover, they explode into destructive conflagrations. Thus, according to one study, "continued livestock grazing without fuel management will cause reductions in the frequency of low intensity fires, but will promote conditions that favor the occurrence of infrequent, high intensity fires" (Zimmerman 1984).

Another "stock" argument used often by grazing interests is that cattle and sheep, rather than fire, are needed to recycle range nutrients. This is false. When wild animals die, their bodies return to the earth to be reborn throughout the environment again and again. Livestock are shipped off to feedlots and slaughterhouses. In fact, this represents the loss of roughly 1/3 of all large animal biomass from the Western range annually. As we all know, livestock do leave manure upon the land. But compared to their detriments this isn't much of a contribution, and natural fire is a much more efficient rangeland recycler.

In sum, Western ranching has caused (1) a great decrease in the number and quality of natural fires and (2) a great increase in the number of destructive anthropogenic fires. The main factors have been livestock grazing, fire suppression, prescribed burning, range arson, ranching-caused accidental fires, and the primary and secondary effects of ranching roads and other range developments.

Few of us have ever witnessed a truly natural fire. As with the present condition of Western biologic, soil, and water systems, there is a strong tendency to accept the way things are as the way things were and never realize the difference.

> *The burned landscape is marvelous, mystical, alive with regeneration and fulfillment of natural processes.*
> --Greg King, environmental activist

A wildfire burns through a portion of ungrazed Fort Huachuca, Arizona, bestowing its many environmental benefits. *(Tony C. Caprio)*

Air

The atmosphere is commonly considered an unalterable, or even a nonentity. How could livestock grazing affect it?

Consider the usual overgrazed landscape. The air is dry, there being little vegetation to transpire moisture, or soil moisture to evaporate, or riparian vegetation or surface water to contribute to humidity. Without healthy, dense vegetation, air moves unhindered across the land, sucking moisture from remaining vegetation and soil. Lower humidity causes temperatures to reach greater extremes. Without dense vegetation to block and scatter the sun's rays, the naked earth becomes a reflector oven, further raising summer temperatures and drying out the air. Likewise, without the subdued colors of vegetation and organic ground cover to absorb and scatter sunlight, a harsh glare is reflected directly off the light-colored dirt, rocks, and sparse, dehydrated plant material. In the winter, the lack of thick, insulting vegetation and of the moderating effects of humidity and surface water cause lower temperatures.

Now, step across a fenceline, or back 150 years into the same landscape never grazed by livestock. Here, the air is moister. The flourishing vegetation, damp, deeper soil, and flowing water all contribute to higher humidity. Thick, healthy, full-sized brush, trees, and plant cover at ground level block air movement which would otherwise suck this moisture away and dry out the plant-soil mantle. Higher humidity moderates air temperatures and thick vegetation blocks and scatters the sun's rays, making it noticeably cooler in summer and warmer in winter. Leaves also absorb and scatter harsh sunlight, and that which is reflected from the ground gives off the subdued colors of herbaceous vegetation, cryptogams, and organic litter. Because dense vegetation and humidity scatter and dissipate sound waves, even sound is gentler here.

The following is from the 6-22-89 *Arizona Republic*:

Overgrazing by cattle in [this area of] *Sonora has made temperatures on the Mexican side of the border an average of 4 degrees hotter than on the Arizona side, according to Arizona State University climatologists. Moving even a few yards from Arizona into Sonora is "like stepping from a playground onto pavement," ASU's Robert Balling said Tuesday. The ASU group's findings are consistent with other studies . . . . A state agricultural agency in Sonora has calculated that for the past century, 300 times more cattle have roamed Sonoran ranges than the land could support, Balling said.* (Note: The range on the American side also is grazed, just not as badly -- perhaps with only 100 times as many cattle as the land can benignly support!)

Infrared and microwave observations of the 50,000-square-mile study area, taken by satellites, show that the Mexican side has lost more vegetation, loses soil moisture more quickly, and reflects more solar heat than the Arizona side.

So, air near the ground -- for its volume the most concentrated and environmentally significant air in the atmosphere -- is definitely affected by livestock grazing. But the air within, say, 200' of the ground still represents only a tiny fraction of the air volume above it. And when air is in motion local effects from the terrestrial landscape may be quickly dissipated into surrounding areas or the upper atmosphere. So livestock grazing's effect on climate is another matter.

Climate is commonly described as the average weather conditions over a long period of time, usually at least several decades. Most climatic changes are measured fairly easily. Yet determining the causes of those changes is difficult to impossible. Modern scientists can't say for sure if rain will fall tomorrow, much less prove, say, that sheep grazing increased the average amount of summer fog on the Falkland Islands from 3.7 hrs./day to 4.2 hrs./day from 1916 to 1957.

Even a small understanding of ecology tells us that any significant alteration in the environment will have repercussions in the surrounding environment. Obviously, climate affects surroundings. Conversely, though not so obvious, surroundings affect climate. Since ranching-caused alteration of Western ecosystems has been extreme, it is reasonable to assume that climate has been affected in some way. But ascribing general climatic changes to any human influence is still largely conjecture. And for every measured change in climate traced to an influence, any number of unrecognized, unrelated influences may be working to make the change more or less so.

Determining cause-and-effect on microclimates is a much easier proposition. As mentioned above, livestock grazing may cause obvious changes in humidity, temperature, air movement, light, and sound. It is reasonable, then, to conclude that when changes in many microclimates are taken as a whole the influence on regional climate may be appreciable. For example, overgrazed ranges commonly have an albedo 2 or more times higher than that of healthy ranges. Studies show that livestock-induced desertification in Africa's Sahel is increasing regional albedo as much as 4% and is probably affecting the climate (Schlesinger 1990).

We know that land masses heat up and cool off faster and to greater extremes than equivalent areas of water. This creates the comparatively low summer and high winter atmospheric pressure regimes found over continents. The resulting differences in seasonal atmospheric pressure between continents and oceans influence global storm patterns. Generally, low pressure pulls; high pressure pushes. Now, theoretically, since livestock have depleted vegetation in localized areas throughout the southwestern quarter of North America, average summer and winter temperatures may rise and fall accordingly, leading to lower summer and higher winter atmospheric pressures. This, in turn, could lead to changes in continental storm patterns, and some kind of change in North American climate. Or, if nothing else, the many localized warmer summer and cooler winter temperatures themselves would, at least in the lower level of air, amount to a cumulative, de facto change in regional climate. Thus, with respect to ground level temperature, humidity, wind, and albedo, much of the West has experienced a de facto change in climate.

Livestock grazing also affects air quality. Plants transpire oxygen into the atmosphere, which is currently 21% oxygen, having dropped slightly in the past few centuries. Livestock's depletion of vegetation in the West (and around the world) has undoubtedly decreased the atmospheric oxygen level by some small, as-yet undetermined degree.

Studies show that plant leaves also extract air-borne pollutants. Biotic degeneration caused by livestock has undoubtedly increased atmospheric pollution levels, again by some small, undetermined degree.

Increased dust can be linked much more easily to livestock. Bared and displaced soil is vulnerable to wind erosion. Heavier particles blow horizontally through the air. They pollute waterways, hamper and injure wildlife, damage vegetation, and bury small plants and animals, topsoil, and seeds. They pit windows and windshields, damage a wide range of developments, and degrade outdoor activities.

Fine grains may be carried high into the atmosphere as widespread particulate pollution. They block sun rays and reduce the amount that reaches the Earth's surface; trap solar radiation reflected from the Earth's surface; settle into streams, lakes, and oceans, and augment pollution and cause chemical and mineral changes. Settling dust dirties homes and businesses and affects many human developments and activities.

In some areas dust storms are natural occurrences. But their distribution, frequency, intensity, and destructiveness have been much exacerbated by livestock grazing. Worsening dust storms have been linked to livestock in many parts of the globe, including north Africa, the Middle East, China, Australia, and the Western US (Schlesinger 1990).

Dust storms sweep off Western ranchlands. Often called "natural" or blamed on drought, etc. by vested interests, dust storms in the American West usually are caused mostly by livestock grazing and ranching activities.

According to scientists, the Indus River region of eastern Pakistan and northwestern India was covered with dense vegetation 2000 ago. Since then, livestock grazing and farming have caused a Texas-sized area to evolve into barren waste -- the Great Thar Desert -- and precipitation to drop to below 10" per year. And yet the air over this region was and is *moist*, containing 80% as much water vapor as the air over tropical rainforests. In **Climates of Hunger**, Reid Bryson and Thomas Murray explain that the region's atmospheric dust, among the thickest and most persistent of any region on Earth, in several ways hinders the formation of monsoonal rain clouds.

Cattle are *ruminants*, named for a rumen compartment in their stomachs where cellulose is broken down by bacteria into cud and gas. A Colorado University study found that a cow belches or farts every minute and a half (much

more than most wildlife, or even Al Bundy or Sam Kinnison), emitting up to 400 quarts of methane gas daily. Scientists say methane is the second largest contributor (at 15%, behind only carbon dioxide) to the Earth's "greenhouse effect." (They think that global livestock production activities have also significantly increased the atmospheric CO_2 level, now 25% higher than preindustrial levels, which also accelerates the greenhouse effect.) Researchers further state that, after rice paddies, the main source of nonnatural methane in the Earth's atmosphere is the eructations (emitting digestive gasses via the throat), flatulence, and manure of cattle. Another significant contributor is the vastly increased numbers of termites found where forests and brushlands have been leveled for livestock; termites produce methane while digesting wood.

Excess methane gas accumulates in the upper atmosphere, where it acts as a blanket to trap energy from the sun reradiated from the Earth's surface, preventing it from passing into outer space as it would normally, thereby warming the Earth's atmosphere. According to most experts, in the 21st century the effects from this warming may well prove disastrous (Stone 1989). US and British study teams report that 1990 was the world's warmest year since records have been kept.

Today, scientists say there is twice as much methane in the air as there was 200 years ago (Worldwatch Institute 1990). Global atmospheric levels of methane grew by *1.5%* annually during the last decade. The Earth's cattle population grew by an even greater percentage, and is now growing faster than its human population. Could the world's 1.3 billion cattle with their yearly contribution of about 150 *trillion* quarts of methane be significantly warming the Earth's atmosphere? Many scientists think so. (Pearce 1989) In fact, in 1990 the US Congress authorized spending $19 million to study the livestock/methane problem, and the Washington-based Foundation on Economic Trends has filed a lawsuit accusing the Agricultural, Interior, and Energy Departments of failing to measure how much methane US livestock are contributing to the atmosphere.

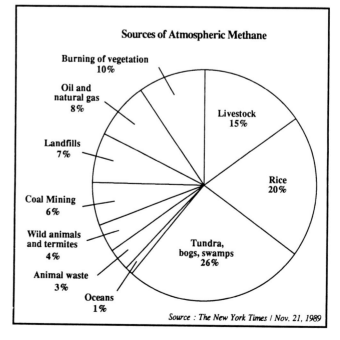

Sources of Atmospheric Methane

Burning of vegetation 10%
Oil and natural gas 8%
Landfills 7%
Coal Mining 6%
Wild animals and termites 4%
Animal waste 3%
Oceans 1%
Livestock 15%
Rice 20%
Tundra, bogs, swamps 26%

Source : The New York Times / Nov. 21, 1989

What we need is rain. And that is the universal cry of stockmen.
--Texas rancher

Drought does not cause desertification.
--Professor Harold Dregne, Texas Tech University

Vegetation transpires water into the atmosphere, augmenting precipitation. For example, studies show that warm, moist air rising from densely vegetated tropical areas promotes build-up of local thunderstorms so that these areas receive as much as 40% more rain than neighboring devegetated areas. Areas overgrazed and/or denuded of trees and brush for livestock production contribute significantly less moisture to the air. Additionally, dry air currents rising from hot ground weaken incoming storm fronts.

Many overgrazed regions of the Earth have been desertified with little apparent effect on climate. However, much evidence indicates that historic overgrazing in some regions has caused or contributed to a drying in climate, greater temperature fluctuations, etc., for example, in north Africa, northwest India, and portions of the Middle East and interior Asia. These areas all supported abundant life 10,000 years ago, just before the rise of pastoralism. However, overgrazing in these regions has continued for *centuries or millennia*, not merely a century or so as in North America.

Still, some people contend that livestock grazing has similarly desertified the climate of the Western US, and that consequently precipitation has decreased significantly since the 1800s. Conversely and conveniently, ranchers claim a drying climate -- not their livestock -- is responsible for the decline in range conditions since the 1800s. This is disproved by statistics (see graphs on following pages). In fact, the National Oceanic and Atmospheric Administration recently stated that in the past 93 years in the US there has been: "1. No great change in temperature.* 2. No great change in precipitation."

* Some experts cite a slight warming trend during the past decade or so.

Regardless, livestock's *influence* on Western climate may be significant. It may well be that the depletion of vegetation caused by livestock and the resulting change in the continental atmospheric pressure is initiating changes in storm dynamics that will result in *more* storms being drawn across the West, ironically counterbalancing the desertifying effects of overgrazing. Or it may be that other unrelated human-caused changes during the past century have had a similar influence. Or perhaps grazing's influence has been offset by a naturally occurring climatic fluctuation. And then, it could be that Western ranching has simply not had a strong enough influence to significantly affect climate, though this seems

doubtful. In any case, there are simply too many variables and unknowns to prove a definite cause- and-effect relationship.

One climatic change that does seem likely in recent decades, however, is the weather becoming more and more *erratic*, not only in the West but throughout the world. No doubt part of this is illusory; each year there are simply more humans and human developments to be adversely affected by weather extremes and, therefore, more "natural disasters." And with advanced communications we are more likely to hear about these events. Nevertheless, extremes in temperature, rain and snowfall, wind, violent storms, and other weather phenomena do seem increasingly frequent as the years pass.

Whenever the natural balance is upset, detrimental environmental changes, often radical, are the result. Climate is no exception. Though we may not understand how, it seems certain that human influence is significantly altering microclimates, regional climates, and world climate. Ranching -- as the rural West's most environmental destructive entity -- is playing some mostly unknown part in that change.

Trampling and overgrazing finish off the ground cover. Wind blows dust into the atmosphere, a devegetated land reflects the sun's rays back into the sky, heating the dust. There is little moisture to evaporate into the air from such a land, and when humid air moves into this dry region from elsewhere it is very difficult for rain clouds to form. Precipitation decreases over time, lakes and streams dry up, and a desert is created. . . . The notion that land is merely a passive factor in climatic change, reacting helplessly to the vagaries of rain and temperature, can no longer be accepted. . . . Conditions of land surface are inter-active with variables determining climate, and changes in the land can cause micro-climatic changes, with as yet unknown effects at the macro level.
--Daniel Stiles, United Nations Environment Program

As is traditional around the ranchland West, California ranchers recently blamed drought for barren ranges such as that on left. But look at the fenced roadside!

HISTORIC AVERAGE ANNUAL PRECIPITATION

(inches)

Graphs on the following 4 pages are based on averaged annual precipitation statistics from all official weather stations in each of the 11 Western states. Additionally, records from 13 stations in 10 Western states indicate relatively normal precipitation for the West as a whole for the period 1850-1890. Records for 1987-1990 show precipitation below normal for California and the Northwest and approximately normal elsewhere, except New Mexico and Colorado above normal. Records also show insignificant changes in seasonal precipitation patterns. *Claims of deteriorating range condition due to drying climate are unfounded.* (Source: **World Weather Records, Smithsonian Institution**)

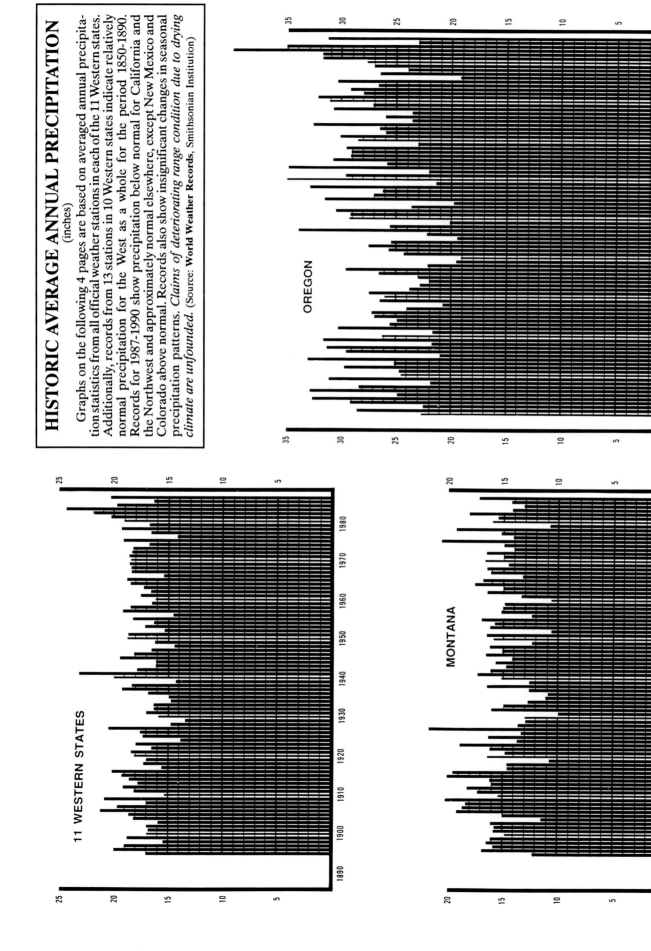

OREGON

11 WESTERN STATES

MONTANA

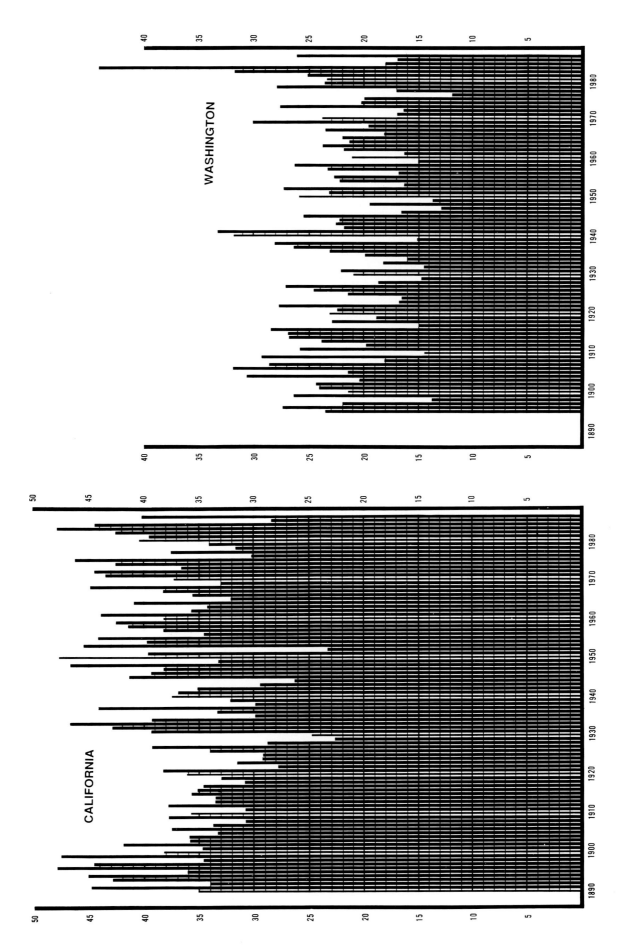

WASHINGTON

CALIFORNIA

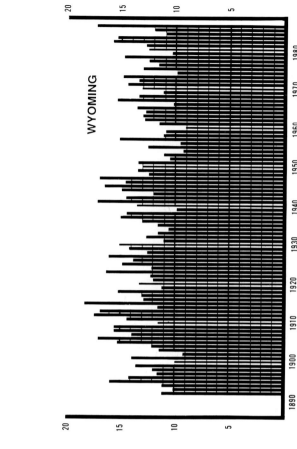

WYOMING

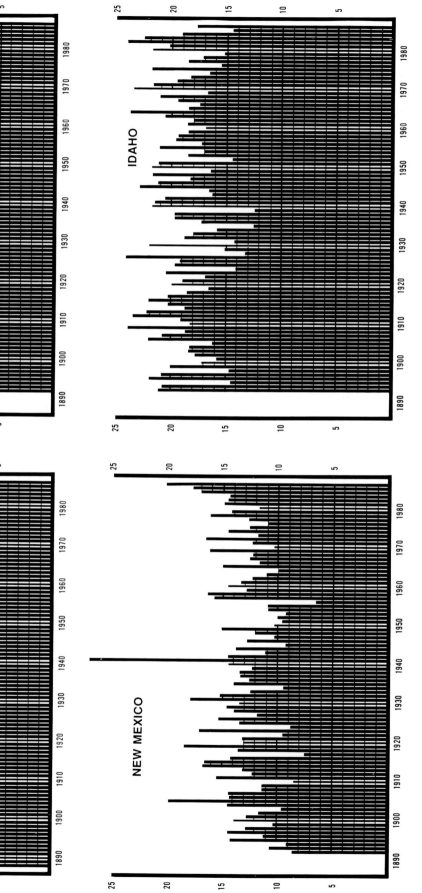

IDAHO

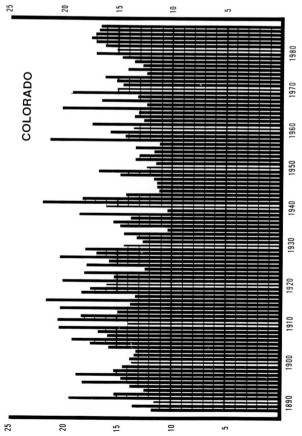

COLORADO

NEW MEXICO

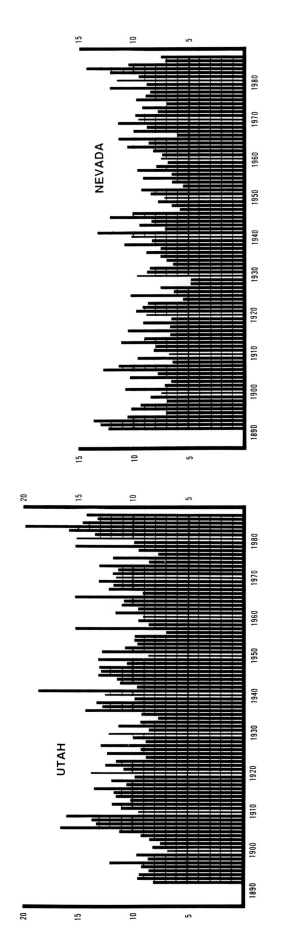

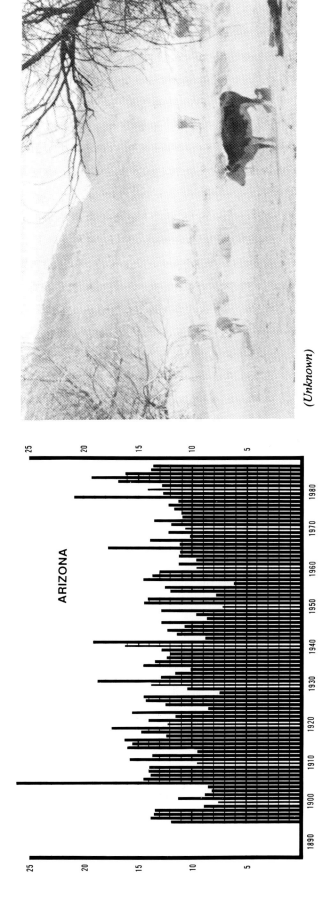

(Unknown)

Understanding Livestock Grazing

Seldom in history have so many been so thoroughly brainwashed by so few. The truth of the matter is: No industry or human activity on earth has destroyed or altered more of nature than the livestock industry. The slow-talking cowboy and his docile cows . . . are the center of a monstrous myth, a part of Americana that rests on concocted imagery and fabrication -- an enormous falsehood based on profound ignorance.

--from **Sacred Cows at the Public Trough** by Denzel and Nancy Ferguson (Ferguson 1983)

By now it should be apparent that domestic livestock do not belong on the Western range -- particularly public lands -- never did and never will. But I know many readers are still skeptical. Most of the West doesn't *look* devastated. Perhaps I exaggerate? Surely some kind of livestock grazing would be acceptable. If the situation is so bad, wouldn't we have heard a lot more about it? Wouldn't the public be outraged? Wouldn't the government have stopped it? Why should we care anyway? Aren't there more important issues?

Thoughts similar to these run through people's minds when confronted with the issue. All are reasonable reactions considering our culture's long-standing myths, social and political realities, and the nature of livestock grazing.

Americans mythologized the cowboy/rancher while steadfastly ignoring the ecological devastation wrought by his cattle and sheep.

--Charles Lee Atwood, *Restoring the Ravaged Range* (Atwood 1990)

The Western rancher is America's most enduring legend, our mythological national hero, and we all know that heroes do only good. To suggest that our shining paragon is causing massive environmental destruction amounts to sacrilege.

So there is great reluctance in our society to question what ranchers do on public land, or assign them or their animals responsibility for anything deleterious. This makes the problem difficult to address, for whenever it is approached it seems to melt away in a plather of cowboy sentiment. In fact, we usually end up changing the rules, or the public's reality, or the land itself, rather than offending or burdening public lands ranchers by asking them to stop what they are doing. (Ranchers' social and political clout is discussed in Chapters VIII and IX, respectively.)

The practice of grazing livestock on the western lands, 60% of which are publicly owned, is the least understood activity. . . . The public is misled by the Bureau of Land Management, which touts the land's importance for "red meat production." Confusion is added by the Marlboro Man image of the western stockraiser. The stockraiser who sincerely believes he is a conservationist raids and degrades the rangeland. . . . More than any other group rangemanagers are tethered by their chauvinistic devotion to ranching.

--Bernard Shanks, **This Land Is Your Land** (Shanks 1984)

Livestock grazing is also extremely low profile. It happens out on the range, out of sight and out of mind of the great majority of Americans. Stockmen like it that way; they figure the less the public knows, the less it will interfere. Since they have historically done pretty much what they want, why rock the boat? Government agencies and many politicians, as components of the ranching establishment, also have ample reason to keep the issue under wraps. Their general attitude: "Leave it to us; we're the experts; we're taking good care of your land; there's no reason for the public to get involved."

Years ago I learned a shocking fact. If you drop a frog into a pot of boiling water, naturally it will jump out. But if you place that frog in water of comfortable temperature and slowly heat it to boiling, the frog will sit there calmly as it boils to death, never noticing the heat coming on slowly and steadily, deadly.

--Nina Mohit, Prescott, AZ, *Prescott Peace News*

From 1960 to 1975 about 50,000 Americans died in the Vietnam War; it was the major news story of those years. During that same period a comparable number of Americans died in motor vehicle accidents *each year*.

Following a stream up the floor of a canyon, Joe [Feller, a law professor at Arizona State University] was struck with the horror of what he saw. Puzzled, he tried to imagine what natural disaster might have caused such devastation. A tornado? A fire? A flood? Finally he noticed the abundance of cow pies. "My God -- it's grazing! . . . with cowpies instead of shrapnel left behind."

--Ray Wheeler, "He Doesn't Give Up" (Wheeler 1990)

When a war or hurricane devastates the landscape, it makes headlines. When cattle do the same over a period of years, 1 mouthful and 4 hoof steps at a time, it's not even news. Livestock grazing is rarely a dramatic event. With most kinds of environmental exploitation, some outside force comes into an area and does something dramatically destructive. The place seems under attack. Maybe a development corporation builds a ski resort in a pristine mountain valley, or fur sellers club to death thousands of baby seals on the Arctic ice, or a mining company dumps toxic wastes near a residential area, or a timber sale allows a logging company to clearcut an old-growth forest. Usually though, when the attack is over, it's over, and restoration proceeds.

Cattle and sheep, on the other hand, have occupied most of the West for more than 100 years, quietly, insidiously, relentlessly degrading the land. They *stay* there forever, unless grazing is halted, so restoration *never* proceeds (as it does after a clearcut or tailings washout, for example). Instead, unrecognized progressive deterioration continues indefinitely.

But who wants to see, read, or hear about a bunch of munching cows? These other issues would seem more interesting, more exciting, even if the damage from livestock is a thousand times greater -- which it usually is. Other threats are perceived as more "imminent," more "immediate," even though livestock actually create a more imminent and immediate situation overall than any other entity. To a society jaded by dramatic events, ranching impact simply isn't very "mediagenic" or "sexy."

For example, the bones of more than 500 free-roaming horses, shot by public lands ranchers to reduce competition with their cattle, were found recently on BLM land in central Nevada. This gruesome discovery probably created for a few weeks more public furor against public lands ranching than all the industry's other effects combined -- effects which during that time period undoubtedly caused an overall environmental impact hundreds of times greater than the horse killings.

(Daniel Dancer)

The logging clearcutting in the photo at top right is a tragedy. The livestock clearcutting above is no less a tragedy. It occurs every year -- so recovery never proceeds -- and to a total area of the West many times larger than that affected by logging. *(Elliott Bernshaw)*

While we may find it aesthetically pleasing to see green rolling hills covered in sheep, and cattle roaming on the wide open range, we should not be tricked into thinking that these pastoral scenes are natural. They are industrialized landscapes that should be returned to nature.
--Dr. Michael W. Fox, **Agricide** (Fox 1986)

Imagine a typical Western landscape -- miles of rustic terrain. Over the years livestock grazing has eliminated half of the original vegetation and reduced species diversity by 50%. Most of the former creeks now flow only sporadically. Those that remain are enclosed by cutbanks, their streambanks trampled and water fouled. Half of the original topsoil has eroded away, and most of the wildlife is gone. Fifty cattle graze placidly on a creek bottom.

An "average American family" arrives on the scene. They see a pair of jeep tracks cutting up a hillside. "Why can't people stay on the roads?" Mother complains. They notice the freshly cut stump of a large creek-side tree. "Damn!" exclaims Father, "Doesn't seem right cutting a fine tree like that." On a creek bank, they stumble over some Coke cans, pieces of rotting watermelon, and a greasy rag. "How disgusting!!" the kids cry in unison. Father gazes nostalgically at the foraging cows and wonders how people can be so disrespectful of Nature.

My first backpacking trip, in a grazed county-owned wilderness, brought disappointment so subtle I didn't acknowledge it to myself, for like many Westerners, I accepted cows as part of the natural landscape.
--Candace Crane, "In the Shadow of Livestock" (Crane 1989)

Livestock grazing also differs greatly from other issues in being so widely and evenly dispersed. Says Bill Marlett of the Oregon Natural Desert Association, "I challenge anyone to go anywhere in the Western United States and travel for more than a day and not see extreme ecological damage caused by grazing." No commercial land use in the West comes close to utilizing as much area. In "A Public Beef," Dyan Zaslowsky goes so far as to state that, "Scientists have said for years that grazing by domestic livestock, particularly cattle, has diminished or destroyed more Western land than all other human activities combined" (Zaslowsky 1989). Grazing occurs in all of the West's 412 counties, excepting perhaps San Francisco County, which is completely occupied by the city. Because almost all grazable range (especially the more productive portions) either is or has at some time been grazed, very few places remain where a person can realistically compare grazed and ungrazed or never-grazed land.

Compounding the problem, like a child spreading unwanted peas out evenly across a dinner plate, livestock impacts are spread out relatively evenly across the land (about 70% of the West), making the damage seem far less significant than it actually is. Strip mining, oil drilling, commercial development, logging, and so on may do more damage to localized areas, but in the West nothing comes close to causing as much overall damage as livestock grazing, or provides less for humans relative to the amount of damage done. In short, ranching is nickel-and-diming the West to death.

Well then, if livestock are really so harmful, why hasn't research been done to document the damage? It has. Over the years literally *thousands* of studies have been conducted, in diverse terrain and conditions all over the West, to determine various environmental effects of livestock grazing (or, more accurately, the effects of the environment and manipulation of the environment on livestock production). Though I could not begin to describe or even list all these studies, many are detailed herein and/or listed in the bibliography.

Most of the data collected show that livestock grazing in any form significantly diminishes environmental quality. In fact, numerous studies show that traditional grazing reduces water infiltration; increases runoff, sediment loads, and erosion; lowers water quality; damages watersheds and riparian areas; degrades vegetation cover; harms wildlife; and much more.

The only environmentally harmless cattle are those painted on walls or otherwise intangibly rendered.

But just because studies show that cigarette smoking is harmful doesn't mean people will stop smoking, or that tobacco companies will stop selling cigarettes. The ranching establishment controlling public land *demands* that the land be grazed. So study results are commonly misunderstood, misused, distorted, refuted, or ignored.

Bernard Shanks writes in **This Land Is Your Land:**

In western legislatures, line-item budget appropriations provided land-grant colleges of agriculture and livestock with the means to conduct "studies," a popular academic industry during the 1960s and 1970s [and still]. Many of the studies were at best pseudo-scientific and designed with obvious biases, often to establish a need for predator control, lower grazing fees, vegetation manipulation, or simply the importance of livestock to the state's economy. (Shanks 1984)

Most grazing studies are instigated and/or funded by government land managing agencies, agricultural extensions, and/or range colleges at land grant agricultural universities. Most of the range scientists at these institutions are, in the words of Ed Marston, editor of *High Country News*, "handmaidens of the industry rather than independent researchers." A friend calls them "cow-centric." Job security for these professionals comes from serving their rancher clientele. To range scientists, continued grazing is universally preordained, and few question this overwhelming mandate, even if they realize its destructiveness. For example, several range researchers at the University of Arizona recently confided that they thought grazing public lands was a bad idea, but that if they didn't produce grazing-promoting studies, they would lose their jobs. Indeed, most range studies are implemented, in whole or large part, specifically to explore possibilities for expanded and more profitable grazing. Others look for ways to mitigate existing grazing problems without reducing livestock operations.

Range professionals have over the years explored nearly every conceivable method of increasing livestock profits. To get a better idea of what I mean, consider a sampling of titles of study reports: "Effects of Season and Stage of Rotation Cycle on Hydrologic Condition of Rangeland Under Intensive Rotation Grazing"; "Salt and Meal-salt Help Distribute Cattle Use on Semidesert Range"; "An Economic Analysis of Two Systems and Three Levels of Grazing on Ponderosa Pine-Bunchgrass Range"; "Vitamin A Reserves of Sheep Maintained on Mulga (*Acacia aneura*)"; "Changes in Perennial Grass Cover Following Conversion from Yearlong to Summer-Deferred Grazing in West Central New Mexico"; and "Accuracy of Roughage Intake Estimates as Determined by a Chromic Oxide in-Vitro Digestibility Technique." *Ad infinitum.*

Both the results and interpretations of the results of these kinds of studies are at best questionable. Often an individual or study team, if not already under a pro-grazing bias, is under subtle pressure to produce the desired results. The study plan itself is often faulty or contains built-in bias. Implementation and monitoring are improperly conducted. Important variables aren't taken into consideration. Questionable evaluation techniques and parameters lead to incorrect or slanted conclusions. Many reports, in trying to promote ranching, are filled with vague qualifiers, such as "appears to," "seemed to," "suggested that," "indicated that," "might," "may have," "can be," "could be," "has potential," "sometimes," and so on (see Holechek 1989 in bibliography for numerous examples). In this way, they mislead the reader without openly falsifying.

According to a NOVA video documentary, over 1 million scientific papers are produced every year in the US. Described was one scientific study which showed 70% of all scientific studies are in some manner invalid or fraudulent! The highly specialized, secretive, and influenced nature of the ranching establishment calls into question an even greater percentage of range studies.

Moreover, the studies themselves are nearly always environmentally destructive. Our public land is a guinea pig for range research. Each experiment requires the manipulation and damage of some aspect of the natural environment to produce the desired comparative effects. For example, a typical study will have a grazing range divided into several test areas of many acres each. The pastures are grazed under various management methods, and the results compared. Some pastures are heavily damaged, some moderately, and some lightly, but usually all exhibit more damage than if unmanipulated, and usually more damage than if grazed traditionally. Thus do hundreds of studies damage thousands of acres.

"Scientific" range study is a game, and the most skillful and the vast majority of the players are part of and funded by the ranching establishment. Those who follow the industry's established unwritten rules and produce "useful" (grazing-promoting) reports are the winners -- not only in terms of acceptance and credibility, but future government funding and private employment. Knowledgeable range professionals can pick out and cite whichever reports they need to "document" nearly anything they want to prove. Indeed, range studies so usually contradict each other that, even after nearly a century of research and thousands of experiments, range professionals frequently disagree on ranching methods and techniques. Thus, it would be pointless to use half this book to cite, compare, and discuss livestock grazing studies.

Interestingly, however, even most professional range studies strongly indicate that livestock harm overall environmental health. Even more curiously, few evaluation reports recommend significant reduction, much less removal, of livestock. Instead, they opt for practically any management scheme that protects grazing interests, usually some type of taxpayer-sponsored range development (or the ever-popular "no action" alternative). The study results are then used to justify and implement the new management plan.

Grazing studies are cranked out on a steady basis -- scores of them every year. Range research is itself an industry. (The Society for Range Management even sells a 336 page textbook on how to conduct range research.) Scientists, range professionals, agency personnel, and ranchers ponder the results and argue the merits and demerits of various grazing plans derived from pondering the results. The public generally stands by, hands in pockets, and leaves it all up to "the experts." Consistently and completely avoided is the most important question of all: *Is livestock grazing inherently a wise use of public land?*

Overgrazing is much too weak a term. Most of the public lands in the West, and especially in the Southwest, are what you might call "cowburnt." Almost anywhere and everywhere you go in the American West you find hordes of these ugly, clumsy, stupid, bawling, stinking, fly-covered, shit-smeared, disease-spreading brutes. They are a pest and a plague. They pollute our streams and rivers. They infest our canyons, valleys, meadows, and forests.
--Edward Abbey (Abbey 1986)

(Jim Stiles)

So, are public lands really under siege? On one hand, we say that public land is "overrun" with livestock that are causing more environmental damage than any other agent. On the other, we say that all public grazing lands combined -- 41% of the West -- produce only a tiny fraction -- 3% -- of this country's livestock. Isn't this a gross contradiction? To the contrary, that so few cattle and sheep can do so much damage is the perfect testament to public land's inherent unsuitability for livestock grazing.

Indeed, as proved every year, much of the West is impractical for livestock grazing merely in terms of available livestock herbage. Many cattle and sheep turned out onto the public range at the beginning of the grazing season barely maintain normal growth, lose weight, or eventually starve to death without supplementary feed. In other words, because the range is so sparsely vegetated (often due largely to past livestock grazing) livestock use as many or more calories searching for and consuming range herbage than is contained in the herbage. In **Livestock Pillage of Our Western Public Lands**, Edwin G. Dimick concludes that 75% of public grazing land "does not produce sufficient forage to qualify as rangeland." Including factors other than herbage, such as predators, disease, environmental damage, range developments, and so forth, perhaps none of Western public land is truly suitable for livestock.

Grazing of the grass cover by livestock is necessary to maintain the ecological balance.
--George D. Lea in **Grasslands of the United States**

Now, the livestock grazing industry would have us believe that it is merely replacing native grazing animals with domestic grazing animals. Consider the calculated words of recent BLM Director, public land rancher Robert Burford:

With regard to livestock grazing, the American rangelands have continuously been grazed for millions of years. The vegetation there evolved under the influences of grazing and fire. While the prehistoric grazers are now extinct, they were replaced with the buffalo, deer, elk, wild sheep, and antelope found by early European explorers nearly 500 years ago. Grazing is a natural process on rangelands . . . .

Cattle and sheep, the vested interests also insist, are merely harmless, roving lawn mowers and hedge trimmers, neatly clipping off and ingesting forage and browse otherwise "wasted," thus "stimulating new growth." Under their reality, how could their livestock be guilty of any more environmental damage than done by native grazers or your lawn mower?

What appears to be a rocky outcropping on the bottom of this valley is actually hundreds of sheep. Wind River Mountains, Wyoming. *(Paul Hirt)*

This contains a grain of truth, and may seem convincing to the uninformed. In reality, it is extreme exaggeration. Among the many things Burford and the others fail to mention is that there were many different kinds of native grazing animals. Each species had different types of influences on Western ecosystems than those of other species. Each had evolved for millennia to mesh into the web of interrelationships that composed the environment. Each had developed the qualities needed to fulfill important environmental functions. What we have today is an incredible overpopulation of just 2 exotic species -- cattle and sheep -- that do not and inherently cannot begin to fulfill these functions. The industry's simplistic, self-serving interpretation of the Western environment is overwhelmingly fictitious.

Further, as we have seen, every cow or sheep added to an ecosystem causes not only a corresponding, but much greater overall decrease in native lifeforms, as well as increased damage to soil, water, etc. And their impact is even greater than this because livestock are removed from the land and shipped off to feedlots (where, according to the *New York Times*, 82% of all American cattle eventually end up) and slaughterhouses. Even beyond all this, why would forage and browse plants be wasted if eaten by wild animals instead of livestock or, as would naturally be the case with most plants, just left to live out their plant lives unimpeded?

You must have proper grazing of some kind to maintain a healthy, viable grass resource. It's very similar to what would happen to your personal lawn if not mowed for some time.
--Pete Talbott, Chairman, Oregon Cattlemen's Association Public Lands Committee

BOVIS VAMPIRUS PROFITUS

Lawn grasses are characteristically short-leaved, and cutting them to the height of a lawn does not remove critical amounts of photosynthetic food and manufacturing material. These grasses are artificially seeded, watered, fertilized, and protected from invading weeds and hungry insects. Regardless of how shallow the roots become from leaf removal, water and nutrients are constantly available for regrowth.
--Edwin G. Dimick, **Livestock Pillage of Our Western Public Lands**

When the roving lawn mower image doesn't take hold as intended, many ranching advocates pull another from their bag of tricks. This one imagines that livestock grazing is not so bad because although some native plant and animal species decline, others prosper. Maybe somehow things just kind of even out? Perhaps cheatgrass takes over for native forbs, sagebrush replaces bunchgrass, thrashers substitute for meadowlarks, and cattle pinch-hit for bighorns. Things are reordered, but all in all nothing is lost -- a nice consolation prize, at worst. And as always, whatever the case, it is undoubtedly a small price to pay for maximum beef production and to keep cowboys happy.

As we have seen, however, this is a far cry from rangeland reality. From a human standpoint, certain plant species (increasers and invaders) may seem to benefit from livestock grazing. But if they actually do, they do so in numbers only, and usually on a temporary basis. Individual plants are usually broken and stunted, while their local survival is short-lived. Pest animal species may explode in numbers, only to suffer overcrowding, starvation, disease, parasites, or other detriments to their quality of life. Their unnatural, widely fluctuating populations exist under dire circumstances and are always in imminent danger of being wiped out.

When livestock graze an area, the destructive effects reverberate throughout the ecosystem, creating the familiar "ecological chain reactions" discussed in high school science. Follow one of these series of events to see how cattle help kill kingfishers: Trampling cattle compact and dry out the soil of a valley bottom, killing worms and insects, reducing food for moles and eventually lessening mole numbers, which in turn reduces the number of mole tunnels that formerly helped water infiltrate into the valley water table, lowering the water table and reducing flow in the nearby creek, causing the eventual death of a some cottonwood trees in marginally wet areas, which in turn reduces the number of tent caterpillars that rely on the cottonwoods, leading to a decrease in the number of moths falling into the creek, less food for fish, fewer fish, less food for kingfishers, thus, finally, fewer kingfishers.

The game can be played with any aspect of any ecosystem. It begins when the ecosystem is perverted by a significant, unnatural force and ends when you get tired of linking things together. The point is, naturally the chain reactions of an ecosystem function more or less smoothly, predictably, to the overall benefit of each of the individual parts and the ecosystem as a whole. When livestock introduce radical, unnatural changes to which no component of an ecosystem is (or possibly could be for millennia) fully adapted, detrimental effects are bound to occur and be passed along these chains of interactions indefinitely. An influence at any stage may have a greater or lesser impact than the one before or after, because each influence is unique. The chains usually snowball in number, but countering this usually is a general, progressive dissipation in relative impact as the interactions continue to spread (like ripples from a rock thrown in a pond). Individual effects at any point along the way may or may not seem significant, but the *cumulative* impact is usually considerable.

This northeast Arizona range has been severely degraded by a century of livestock grazing, but how many of us would know this to look at it today?

A ranching road winds through a rustic Western scene -- actually a heavily damaged ecosystem.

I have been a geologist in the "wild" West for 30 years now and I have driven to the end of a thousand dirt roads and hiked up a thousand canyons in our living desert. Please believe me, things are a lot worse than you think or **Sacred Cows** *says they are.*
--Bill Davis, "Our Living Desert Is Becoming a New Sahara" (Davis 1990)

When we look at the Western landscape, we may see plants being eaten and soil trampled by cattle and sheep. But we generally understand little of subsequent ecological chain reactions whose overall impact is much greater. Unfortunately, as soon as an influence becomes once-removed from plain view, its origin becomes irrelevant to 99% of people. Because secondary cause-and-effects are inherently vague, it is difficult to make the connection, even when we try. Even professional range ecologists exhibit little understanding of the myriad subtle, often nearly incomprehensible, effects of livestock grazing.

It really disturbs me to look at the Utah Travel Council Calendar. Every photo shows signs of overgrazing....
--Pamela M. Poulson, Chair of the Board, Utah Native Plant Society

Most people, however, don't even see the *obvious* effects of livestock grazing. They look out over the Western countryside and see a familiar land, as they imagine it has always looked. To them, it doesn't look so bad -- a little scruffy and barren, maybe, but then that's how the West is supposed to look, isn't it?

Most of us derive our "first-hand" knowledge of livestock grazing from viewing landscapes as we drive or walk alongside fences. But this can be deceptive (see photos at right). Looking down at a roadside, bare spaces between plants are easily seen. When gazing out over a roadside fence at a grazed vista, plants are viewed at a greater distance, horizontally, and appear much more closely spaced, perhaps as a solid mass of vegetation. It may be assumed that the spacing, condition, and composition of the plants marching off to the horizon are superior to those along the ungrazed roadside, when in fact nearly always the opposite is true. As they say, the grass looks greener on the other side. (Indeed, to convince the public of what good shape the range is in, the government land managing agencies sometimes leave wide strips of ungrazed range adjacent to highways, as the Forest Service commonly leaves strips of uncut forest along highways to hide clearcuts from the public [Dimick 1990].)

In Arizona, for example, about 97% of the land either has been or is being grazed at some time during the year. To find areas for study of ungrazed plants, botanists must search diligently, and often must resort to corners of old fenced cemeteries, or lofty buttes and mountain tops too steep even for a starving cow.
--Steve Johnson, Southwestern Representative, Defenders of Wildlife

Aside from our collective infatuation with cowboys and cows, probably our main obstacle to understanding is that most of the West is so different now than in centuries "B.C." (Before Cattle). Our environment was severely damaged beginning about 130 years ago and has been kept in a **dynamic state of degradation** ever since. Because little obvious new destruction takes place, one thinks that little damage is occurring, when in fact heavy damage is continually occurring. Thus, for example, it is understandable that pre-Columbian wildlife numbers are usually underestimated, even by experts.

Because many of the changes occurred long ago, land managers and environmentalists tend to accept the present condition as the starting point in any discussion. Thus, while many conservationists argue that livestock should be reduced or better managed on public lands, few challenge the basic assumption that the livestock industry is entitled to priority rights on public rangelands.
--George Wuerthner, "Counting the Real Costs of Public Lands Grazing" (Wuerthner 1989)

We tend to accept current conditions as the norm. We have nothing to compare them to because, of course, none of us was around 150 years ago to see the West in its natural condition. All we have are limited and often questionable descriptions by early explorers, trappers, and settlers (along with bits and pieces of scientific evidence). Nearly all of these people came from the comparatively lushly vegetated East or Europe. Many of them described any place without trees as "wasteland" or "desert," even the most verdant of Western grasslands. Landscapes covered with sagebrush, bunchgrass, and forbs were frequently termed "lifeless," "worthless," or "destitute." Consider, for example, an 1849 account by an explorer named Simpson: "the country is one extended naked, barren waste, sparsely covered with cedar and pine of a scrub growth, and thickly sprinkled with the wild sage, or artemisia" (Simpson doesn't even bother to include the unimpressive bunchgrasses and herbaceous plants that undoubtedly grew between and underneath the sage.) To almost all US Americans 150 years ago everything west of the Mississippi River was "The Great American Desert," as in this account from a popular journal of the time: "water-less, windswept land of sand and stone, this howling, hopeless, worthless cactus-bearing waste inhabited by savages of extreme fierceness and cruelty, and haunted by prowling beasts of unexampled ferocity."

Viewed from the fenced roadside (above), the grass on both sides of the fence looks uniform. Actually, the grass in the ungrazed right-of-way (middle) is nearly twice as thick as that on the grazed range (bottom).

Most early US Americans had little understanding or appreciation of the West, and this is surely reflected in their writings and actions. They were chiefly concerned with 2 aspects of their environment: (1) "game" animals and (2) forage for livestock. They therefore documented little else. Additionally, except for the earliest travelers, most of their descriptions of the early West were made along established routes, where heavy livestock grazing and other human impacts had already altered the landscape. (White 1990) And, of course, impressions varied according to the recent weather, season of year, particular year, and the traveler's character, intelligence, awareness, bias, and imagination.

Furthermore, because photography wasn't introduced to the West until just after the Civil War and did not come into general use until the 1880s, even the earliest photographs are too recent to show conditions before heavy use by livestock. (The famous early photographer William Henry Jackson, as part of the US government's Hayden Survey, did make a number of Western rangeland photos in the early 1870s, most of which show comparatively lush vegetation.) Thus, according to David L. McWilliams in the 3-2-88 *Casper Star-Tribune*, "Trotting out century-old pictures and comparing them with modern photos only verifies that the range is in as poor condition now as it was 100 years ago, and merely serves to obfuscate the issue of public lands degradation."

Even so, if we dig deep enough and read between the lines, we can get a good idea. Numerous historical accounts do confirm drastic, detrimental changes in plant and animal life, soil, water, and fire conditions throughout most of the West. These reports progressively establish livestock grazing as the biggest single perpetrator of these changes, particularly considering that it was the only significant land use over most of the West.

One of the most useful and informative descriptions of the early West was that of Meriweather Lewis and William Clark on their famous expedition across the northern Midwest, Rockies, and Pacific Northwest from 1804 to 1806 (Thwaites 1959). Their descriptions of the unconquered West are of a world we can scarcely imagine: landscapes filled with wildlife; great diversities of lush vegetation; highly productive, free-flowing rivers, creeks, and springs; abundant, dark, fertile soil; unaltered, unimpeded fire and other natural processes. Of the Montana plains, one excerpt from Clark reads, "we observe in every direction Buffalow, Elk Antelopes & Mule Deer inumerable and so jintle that we could approach them near with great ease." Another states,

We saw a great number of buffaloe, Elk, common and Black tailed deer, goats [pronghorn] beaver and wolves. Capt. C. [Clark] killed a beaver and a wolf, the party killed 3 beaver and a deer. We can send out any time and obtain whatever species of meat the country affords in as large quantity as we wish.

In the West today only ungrazed Yellowstone National Park supports nearly this variety and density of large wild animals. The Lewis and Clark journals tell of killing buffalo, elk, pronghorn, bighorns, deer, bear, and beaver almost every day for months at time. Clark's complaint of a *poor* wildlife day: "Saw but five Buffalow a number of Elk & Deer & 5 bear & 2 antelopes to day." In the 1990s, who would not be thrilled to see these animals in a single day? And most early explorers rarely bothered recounting sightings of smaller animals.

Lewis and Clark's and other historic journals attest that buffalo, elk, deer, bighorns, pronghorn, mountain goats, moose, horses, grizzly and black bears, wolves, foxes, cougars, bobcats, beaver, muskrats, river otters, fish, porcupines, wild turkeys and other "game" birds, waterfowl, snakes, prairie dogs and other rodents, most insects, and the vast majority of wild animals were all many times more abundant then than now. So too were native plants; the journals describe a great abundance and diversity of grasses and herbaceous vegetation, willows and deciduous trees, cattails, rushes, sedges, wild grapes, chokecherries, currants, wild cherries and plums, gooseberries, "red" and "yellow" berries, service berries, flax, dock, wild garlic and onions, sunflowers, wild roses, tansy, honeysuckle, mints, and more, a large number being edible. Most of these plants have been depleted through the many effects of livestock grazing for 100 years and are today comparatively scarce.

Of northwest Arizona (the remote "Arizona Strip" northwest of the Grand Canyon), the National Park Service states:

The vast flatlands and broad desert valleys, which are now wastelands of sagebrush, tumbleweed, and cheatgrass, were once rich with perennial grasses and flowering plants that the early explorers described as brushing up against their horses' bellies.

Ernst Antevs writes in "Arroyo-Cutting and Filling":

In Utah "grass was originally an important and conspicuous element of the foothill vegetation." In some places it formed pure grasslands, in others it was associated with shrubs. At present these vast uplands are dominated by sagebrush, rabbitbrush, and shadscale.

Jon R. Luoma relates in "Discouraging Words":

Here in the Great Basin, a typical scene was expanses of bluebunch wheatgrass, interspersed with sagebrush, and dozens of other species of grasses, shrubs, and wildflowers. Rodents -- ground squirrels, pocket gophers, mice -- abounded, as did their raptor predators, including ferruginous hawks, golden eagles, and kestrels. Sage grouse were abundant. The grasslands provided forage for tens of thousands of pronghorns, mule deer, and elk. (Luoma 1986)

Of the Sonoran "Desert," Padre Ignaz Pfeffercorn wrote in the 1760s:

On the hills, as well as on the plains, there are the most excellent pastures, where grow a superabundance of the choicest grass and all kinds of healthful herbs. Because of this Sonora has the most desirable conditions and conveniences for a considerable livestock industry . . . .

In 1926, Senior Forest Ranger Fred W. Croxen of the Tonto National Forest in central Arizona, wrote this account of the reflections of Florance A. Packard, "the oldest living man to settle in the Tonto Basin":

He told of blackfoot and crowfoot grama grass that touched one's stirrups when riding through it, where no grama grass grows at present. The pine bunch grass grew all over the Sierra Anchas in the pine type and lower down than the pine timber on the north slopes. There were perennial grasses on the mesas along Tonto Creek where only brush grows at the present time. Mr. Packard says that Tonto Creek was timbered with the local creek bottom type of timber from bluff to bluff, the water seeped rather than flowed down through a series of sloughs and fish over a foot in length could be caught with little trouble. Today, this same creek bottom is little more than a gravel bar from bluff to bluff. Most of the old trees are gone, some have been

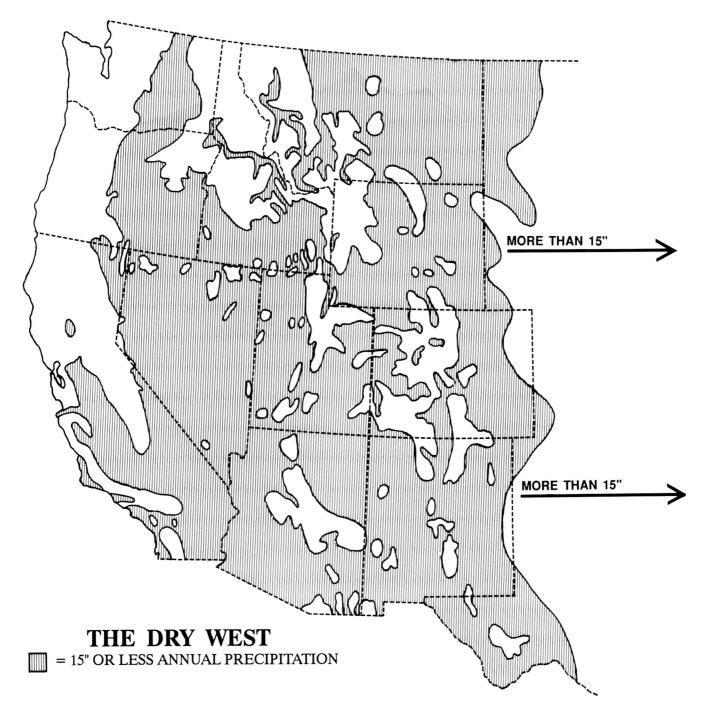

THE DRY WEST
▥ = 15" OR LESS ANNUAL PRECIPITATION

cut out for fuel, many others cut down for the cattle during drouths and the winters when the feed was scarce on the range, and many have been washed away during the floods that have rushed down this stream nearly every year since the range started to deplete. The same condition applies to practically every stream of any size in the Tonto.

Numerous similar descriptions abound. It is clear that enormous changes in the Western landscape have occurred since European settlement.

In 1930, an Indian returned to her former home in southern Utah for the first time in 40 years and observed the effects of white occupation. She noticed that, "This country is no good anymore; everything is dry; the creeks are cut deep; the plant foods are all gone."
--Charles Kay, wildlife biologist

Other misunderstanding stems from the fact that the most verdant and productive vegetation in the West is now gone. Originally, ranchers claimed the best forage plants on the most well-watered land throughout the West. After each rancher staked out his territory, his livestock relentlessly sought out and consumed the best of the best in each area. Every subsequent year for more than a century, ranchers and their livestock have searched out the best of the remaining best. Consequently, we have come to accept vegetation that is less and less productive as the norm, failing to realize what has been lost. Thus have the most biologically significant portions of Western public land also been the most heavily abused by livestock.

The best lands were privatized long ago, and what remains as public grazing lands is the ugliest, meanest, driest, least desirable country found west of the 100th meridian.
--George Wuerthner, writer/naturalist

The common public image of Western rangeland is "the rugged West," although what is actually "rugged" or "hardy" is not so much the land itself but our conception of living on that land -- a conception fostered largely by the ranching industry itself, ironically. Compared to the East (east of the 100th meridian, roughly), most of the West is dry. Approximately 80% of Western water falls on only 20% of the land, and 95% of all BLM land receives less than 15" of precipitation annually. The West generally is also much more precipitous, with a shallow, often alkaline, stony soil layer, or even no soil, and sparse ground cover. Accordingly, the West, rangeland especially, is much more "fragile" than the East, and ecosystems here are termed "unstable." The eastern US, mostly flat to gently rolling, well watered -- averaging more than 40" precipitation annually -- and fertile

The grassy green of a grazed range in a moist climate may seem in good condition, but most of this conception is relative.

This Black Hills, Wyoming, range is grassy and moist, yet severely overgrazed.

with deep soil, is much better suited for raising livestock. That 79% of all US livestock are raised there despite a higher human population density amply demonstrates this.

Grass, on the other hand, is to most people simply a green carpet. The kinds of plants, their abundance, and their vitality are matters which escape the casual. So long as all is green, all is well.
--Paul B. Sears, **Deserts on the March** (Sears 1967)

Understandably, most people think livestock grazing in wetter Western climes is relatively benign, that, in direct proportion, the drier the clime, the more damage from livestock. As suggested above, there is a measure of truth in this, but it isn't a great one. The wetter West contains more "stable" ecosystems but is also much more heavily stocked -- much of it literally *hundreds of times* more heavily stocked! And though the moister West is somewhat better suited to livestock than is the drier, it is still far behind the East, considering that generally the wettest parts of the Western range are steep terrain with comparatively sparse vegetation and shallow soil. (Even the East, however, is not really suited to domestic livestock and has thus been seriously damaged.)

In the moister West, most grazed range stays green through the growing season, and to most people if it is green it must be doing fine. But green isn't much good if plants are kept cropped short most of the year, year after year, and other livestock impacts are serious. Green is much less useful if composed of non-native plants. So, damage to these moister areas is often similar, relatively speaking, to grazed arid land. In fact, many parts of the comparatively moist plains of Montana, Wyoming, Colorado and New Mexico, the Pacific Northwest, and the high-elevation Western mountains are in terrible condition, even according to federal reports.Perhaps more importantly, why should even the wetter Western range be dedicated to livestock rather than wildlife?

I worked in the resource management division at Sequoia-Kings Canyon National Park for several years, and though we no longer had much cattle grazing there, I spent a considerable amount of time correcting meadow erosion which was caused by overgrazing during the 1930's.
--Steve Sorenson, Leucadia, CA, personal correspondence

Another important factor in our failure to understand the impact of livestock grazing is that **more than half** of the grazing potential of Western range was lost during the initial rush of grazing madness, the late 1800s and early 1900s. The 1934 Taylor Grazing Act grew partly out of reports to Congress that over 36% of public lands suffered "extreme depletion" and another 47% "severe depletion," in the language of the Grazing Service itself (Williams 1990).

A general land survey made by the US Department of Agriculture during the 1930s documented for the first time the extent of the damage. A resulting report stated, "A range once capable of supporting 22.5 million AUM's can now carry only 10.8 million" (US Senate 1936). Thus, any comparisons made after 1936 using this report are based on rangelands whose **productivity is estimated to have deteriorated by more than 50% from original conditions.**

Since 1936 the overall biomass of ground cover on most of the Western range has increased somewhat because plants in most areas have not been eaten as closely to the ground. While this may seem an improvement, the condition of the Western range has in many ways declined since the 1930s due mostly to continuing livestock grazing (see Chapter XI). And many areas, including those previously inaccessible to livestock, have experienced decreases in groundcover.

The 1936 report concluded that it would take at least 100 years to restore public rangeland to its original productivity. This was, of course, assuming that a sensible course of restoration would be pursued during the following 100 years; 50 years later, we have never come close. Restoration to anywhere near "original productivity" within another 50 years is impossible, especially given that most topsoil has been and continues to be lost and could not be replaced within this time frame even under optimum circumstances. Heavy ranching abuse has continued essentially unabated since 1936, and despite considerable artificial restoration effort the range we see today undoubtedly operates at less than half aboriginal capacity and is probably still declining in overall productivity.

Further, an additional, ever-increasing strain is placed on Western grazing land each year as more and more of it is converted to government installations, mining developments, reservoirs, fenced parks and recreation areas, roads, resorts, airports, and other developments, while ranchers and government try to maintain or increase numbers of livestock (this aside from grazing land expansions).

Also of note is that contemporary comparative studies of past and present livestock grazing usually consider today's full-grown range cattle (typically weighing about 1000 pounds) as representative of yesterday's cattle, when in fact the Texas longhorns common during grazing's early years averaged only about 650 pounds, and the typical cow at the turn of the century weighed around 800 pounds. Today's half-ton beeves probably eat about 25% more than their 800-pound predecessors (Wagner 1978), and perhaps 40% more

than the 650-pound longhorns. Additionally, in sheer numbers, in ranching's early days there were many times more sheep than cattle. So, then-and-now comparisons of livestock *numbers* are misleading and don't necessarily reflect relative grazing pressures on the land. For example, 1000 cattle in 1990 would eat roughly the same amount of vegetation as 1000 cattle *and* 1000 sheep in 1900.

All these factors, along with other intentional deceptions by the ranching establishment, have given us a very misleading picture of livestock grazing. Denzel and Nancy Ferguson, in **Sacred Cows at the Public Trough**, report that in the West as a whole there are now *more and bigger* cattle than ever before (Ferguson 1983). They and some other experts think that overall grazing pressure on public land may now be near an all-time high.

One question has always stuck in my mind: Why would anyone want to graze cattle in this type of environment [public land]. I still don't understand it. What a waste of land and water. Cattle can be grown on lots anywhere.

--Tom Thompson, Vail, CO, personal correspondence

The livestock grazing practiced on the comparatively sensitive ecosystems of the West amounts to an annual clearcutting of herbage. The peaceful-looking, pastoral scenes we see as we speed down the highway are in reality disasters to the natural systems of our public lands. Ranching is a subtle, silent, slow death to Nature.

Several years ago a range expert in New Mexico flew over the Trinity Site, where the first atomic bomb was tested. The area hasn't been grazed by livestock since the explosion, more than 40 years ago. He stated that range conditions 20 yards from the center of the blast were better than over 90% of New Mexico. (Foreman 1986) Food for thought.

Earl D. Sandvig, formerly a US Forest Service range specialist and employee for 36 years, now retired, said it plainly: "No use of our federal lands has caused so widespread and serious damage as livestock grazing" (Ferguson 1983).

What has four legs and doesn't belong here? What turns singing high-country streams into silent mud bogs? What reduces green hillsides to brown earth and dust? What wipes out entire species if they get in its way? Hint: It goes moo....

The single best thing that could be done for our Western lands, far and away, would be to get cattle off.

--Donald M. Peters, 5-30-90 *The Arizona Republic* (Peters 1990)

Home on the Range

Oh, give me a home
Where the buffalo roam
Where the deer and the antelope play
Where seldom is heard a discouraging word
And the skies are not cloudy all day

Home, home on the range
Where the deer and the antelope play
Where seldom is heard a discouraging word
And the skies are not cloudy all day

--Traditional

Home on the Range #2

Oh, give me a home
Where the buffalo roam
And the deer and the antelope play;

Where seldom is seen
The hamburger machine
And the flies are not swarming all day

--Edward Abbey

(Photo by SCS, USDA)

Things Aren't Always As They Seem
(A Short Story)

"Great spot!" I thought to myself as we sprawled onto some rocks near a small waterfall. It was a warm, clear spring day, and my kids and I were hiking up along a mountain stream and decided to take a rest. We had seen few obvious signs of cattle along the way -- a welcome change from the cowburnt wastelands we'd visited recently.

I got out the camera, but looking through the viewfinder something seemed wrong. Yes, the rocks in the creek seemed oddly strewn about. Looking closer, I saw that most of the small plants around them were dead. Cattle! Apparently, the plants had grown in favorable locations only to have their host rocks upended and scattered by trampling cattle. No doubt many small animals that dwelled or sheltered under these rocks were also killed.

Now I'm writing my observations.

I stoop down for a closer look at the creek bottom. The silt and organic matter that would normally settle around the rocks, secure their bases to the stream bed, and promote plant growth are churned up and washed away. At creekside, I notice small tree stumps -- the results of cutting for fence posts? (Later, we climb a ridge and find the omnipresent barbed wire barrier.) Cattle have eaten and trampled those small trees that haven't been cut.

Looking through the viewfinder again, I see rocks piled up along the bank on the far side of the creek. They have been rolled down the adjacent, steep hillside by cattle, precluding streamside vegetation. I cross the creek to study this rock levee. Like channelization, it prevents the stream channel from meandering. The tumbling rocks have bent or broken all of the surviving small trees at creekside. Dirt, sand, and gravel likewise have slid and washed down the slope into the creek. Cattle trails, hoof prints, and cow flops are obvious on the slope, and hillside vegetation is eaten and trampled.

I jump back across the creek once more and finally take a picture -- the one on the right.

Now, scanning up and down canyon, I notice that most lower leaves have been eaten off the larger cottonwoods, velvet ash, and Arizona walnut. Entire lower branches are broken off, and a haphazard jumble of broken branches, twigs, and overturned stones litters the ground.

In and along the creek grow moisture-loving plants such as algae, watercress, sedges, grasses, mullein, and monkey flowers, but it is clear that much has been eaten, trampled, and uprooted. What remains grows in broken clumps, matted together this way and that, sometimes covered with organic debris from uprooted plants and splattered with mud, sand, and gravel. I am guessing that riparian plant cover is only about half what it would be without cattle.

Further detracting from the experience are the many flies that make it unpleasant to stay in one place long. On the hike up here, I spotted a few cow pies rotting in the creek. So now I am wondering if we should have brought that canteen after all. So much cool mountain stream water, but should I risk getting sick, maybe for weeks or months with giardia? I drink it anyway.

We stretch out on bedrock, streamside. Looking into and around the creek, I see . . . muddy hoof ruts. Clumps of mud and roots lie dissolving and rotting in the slower water along the bank. Likewise, dead, rotting vegetation is exuding an oily scum into nearby stagnant, water-filled hoof holes. In some places, plants and their root masses have been "peeled" clean off the underlying bedrock by cutting and sliding hooves. The rock I am lying on is spattered and smeared with mud and bovine excrement.

Despite it all, this place is nice. But it lacks the abundance, vitality, integrity, and beauty of a natural ecosystem. Most of the Western landscape may seem pleasant enough, especially to those of us accustomed to concrete, metal, and plastic. But appearances can be deceptive. Most often, the pastoral Western panoramas we gaze upon are in reality settings for extensive ecological disasters.

Let's appreciate what remains of the wild West. But let's also keep asking what would, what should, this place be like?

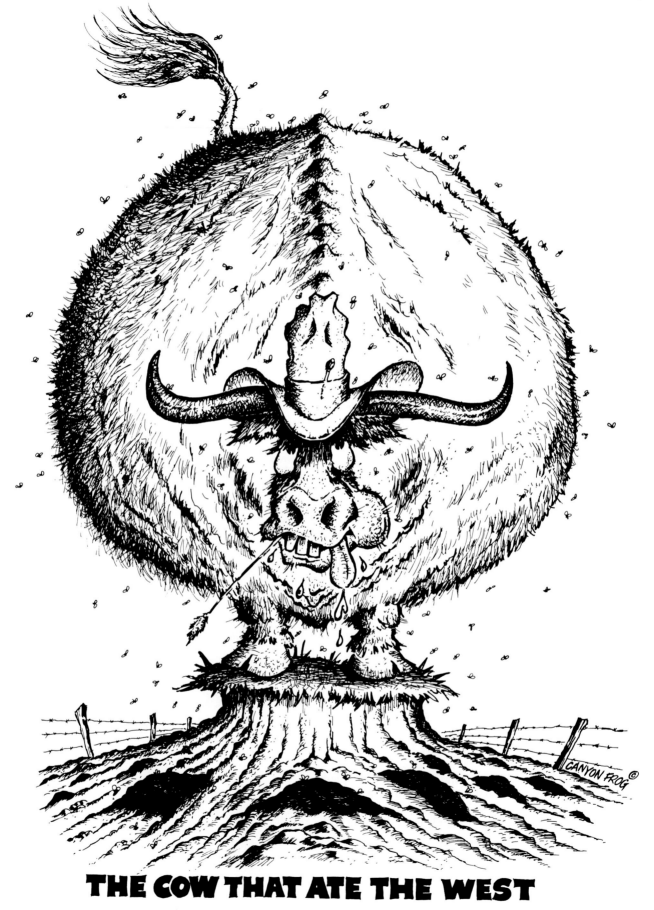

THE COW THAT ATE THE WEST

(Roger Candee)

(USDA)

Exclosures and Fenceline Contrasts

It's amazing how pervasive grazing has been. There aren't many pristine areas left.
--Nick Van Pelt, head of Natural Heritage Program for Utah Nature Conservancy (Williams 1990)

From the onset of the livestock invasion until the early 1900s stockmen grazed their cattle and sheep indiscriminately nearly every place with a blade of forage or leaf of browse. Even so, some of the West was inaccessible to livestock due to availability of water or rugged topography. As the years passed, water and access developments opened these areas to ranching, and soon few places remained that had not been significantly and (on the human timescale) irreversibly altered from original conditions.

Long before enactment of the Taylor Grazing Act in 1934, it became apparent that the productivity of the Western range was being seriously reduced. Even ranchers were calling for restoration of the West's public "forage resources." How this restoration would be accomplished was debatable, but one thing was certain: **stockmen would not remove their livestock**. The government would have to explore other possibilities.

Whatever the future held, scientific studies would have to be conducted to identify and measure ranching's effects on the range. But without ungrazed lands for comparison, how could this be accomplished? A series of fenced, ungrazed study plots would have to be established. To encompass the great diversity of grazing situations, plots would need to be located at representative sites, in varied terrain, and in disparate vegetative and climatic regimes throughout the rangeland West. To maximize their representative value, they would have to be numerous.

Consequently, in the early 1900s various government agencies established hundreds of "exclosures" to evaluate livestock impacts (or the lack thereof) and to serve as standards for assessing range condition. Hundreds more were built in the 1930s and 1940s, when thousands of men from the Civilian Conservation Corps (CCC) were placed at the disposal of the Division of Grazing (later the Grazing Service) and Forest Service. Since the 1940s, lesser numbers have been constructed sporadically for various reasons by government and private entities.

Most of Arizona rangeland probably has been grazed by livestock for more than a century. Changes in vegetation on some of these rangelands are so marked and so extensive that current concepts of natural vegetation are based on landscapes that are quite unlike those present before human obtrusion.
--Raymond M. Turner, et al., *Arizona Range Reference Areas*

Looking into a 75-acre livestock exclosure near Globe in central Arizona. Fenced in the 1950s, the protected land is slowly recovering and currently supports roughly twice the plant and animal biomass per unit of area as the grazed land around it. As is apparent in this photo, native grasses are reestablishing, whereas cheatgrass composes virtually 100% of the grass cover outside.

Today the West has a few thousand scattered livestock exclosures. Yet, all of them combined encompass only a minuscule fraction of the area of public land; they are tiny specks in a vast sea of overgrazing. The great majority enclose several acres or less, most less than an acre. Stockmen rarely tolerated anything larger, even though land retired from grazing was not included in grazing fees and minimally interfered with grazing operations.

These areas are now fenced from livestock, but are they truly representative of lands ungrazed by livestock? Do studies conducted thereon reflect land in a natural state? Not at all! Merely building a fence around an overgrazed acre does not magically transform it into a natural area. Livestock exclosures are unnaturally affected in the following ways:

- Most of these areas were heavily grazed by livestock for decades before being fenced, so residual effects linger.
- The physical disturbance of exclosure sites during construction and subsequent concentration of human impact in the areas influence their condition.
- Few exclosures are large enough to provide for proper ecosystem dynamics, e.g., seed dissemination, plant and animal migration, biologic succession, and genetic viability.
- Overgrazing, range developments, and other human obtrusion in surrounding areas affect the interiors of most exclosures and hamper restoration. Perimeter effects include excessive water runoff and soil erosion; sediment deposition; increased low-level wind speeds and drying of soil; decreased shade; reduction or elimination of natural fire; absence of native species needed for repopulation; diminishment of native animals; and net loss of organic matter, as it is blown and washed from comparatively verdant exclosures to surrounding depleted areas but not reciprocally replenished. Enclosed stream segments are affected by upstream ranching.
- Wild animals from surrounding grazed areas are attracted to ungrazed exclosure interiors, where they find a greater abundance of plant and animal food, shelter, nesting materials, moisture, etc. They therefore unnaturally affect and deplete exclosures.
- To "destroy the evidence" that livestock are damaging the land, express their displeasure with government interference, and allow their livestock to "utilize" what they consider "wasted" herbage, many ranchers covertly tamper with exclosures. They destroy exclosure vegetation, spread seeds of "undesirable" plants, damage soil with minerals or chemicals, "accidentally" leave gates open (though most exclosures don't have gates), break fence posts or push them over, and cut exclosure fences, all of which reduces or destroys exclosure validity.

- Perhaps most significantly, *most* exclosures have since their construction been grazed (often for long periods) by livestock that knock down or push through fences, thereby invalidating their value for comparative study.

Exclosures are often useful for limited comparisons, but they cannot be considered fully adequate for comparisons of grazed and ungrazed sites. The interiors of even the largest, oldest, most secure exclosures are corrupted relative to entire ecosystems never influenced by ranching.

One thing at least has been conclusively proved in this experiment, i.e., that the perennials which once flourished here and which have been decidedly injured by stock will again regain their ascendency over the weedy annuals when given a measure of protection. . . . the increased growth of an even partially protected area is phenomenal.
--Range professional D. Griffiths in 1910

A 200-foot-wide stretch of land containing 300 feet of stream was fenced, and recovery there he said, "shows that riparian areas can come back something fierce." Prunty [Jim Prunty, a former rancher and 20-year Forest Service employee] *said the exclosure is especially impressive because of the dramatic difference between the protected stretch and the heavily grazed sections upstream and downstream from it.*
--Ed Marston, "Ranchers' Hold on Agency Revealed" (Marston 1990)

One friend reports having a flash of understanding when he stood by a fence that separated grazed and ungrazed portions of the same creekbed. One side was lush and verdant. The other side looked like the face of the moon. Moo.
--Donald M. Peters, "Give Me a Range Where Never Is Heard a Discouraging Herd" (Peters 1990)

Fenceline of a 1-acre livestock exclosure at 9000' elevation in central Utah.

In 1932 a one-square mile livestock exclosure was constructed to study the effects of livestock grazing on the natural vegetation of the Jornada del Muerto, thirty miles north of Las Cruces, New Mexico. In 1935 vegetation was measured along permanent transects, and these measurements were repeated in the 1950s and again in 1980. In 1935 the vegetation both inside and outside the exclosure was dominated by black grama grass with almost no mesquite. By 1955, however, mesquite was clearly on the increase outside the exclosure, and black grama was declining. In 1980 the exclosure was a small island of grass, surrounded by country in which black grama was almost completely absent and mesquite was dominant. In addition, on what had been a more or less level plain, sand hummocks or coppice dunes like those along the route from Fort Bowie to Las Cruces had formed around the mesquite.

A similar pattern of change is reported for extensive areas of southeastern Arizona and southwestern New Mexico.

--Gary Nabhan in **Arizona: The Land and the People**

Despite their limitations, the great majority of livestock exclosures exhibit dramatic environmental recovery. For example, after SCS established several large exclosures on the Navajo Reservation in the 1930s, "The Service reported both dramatic recovery of the range and improved conditions of the [stock] animals in virtually all these areas and continued to report progress in succeeding years" (White 1983). Though not always visibly obvious, exclosure interiors commonly have at least *twice* the organic ground cover, overall biomass, numbers of individuals and species, topsoil, and soil moisture. I have visited scores of livestock exclosures, in every Western state, and **all** of them exhibited as good or better environmental condition (even herbage production) than the livestock-grazed land around them. For most, the comparison was not only impressive but remarkable. Curiously, on the other hand, nobody -- not even ranchers -- raves about the comparative range condition *outside* exclosures. Why do cattle so frequently risk bodily harm to break *into* exclosures?

Exclosures are among the few places left in the West where we can witness land and water that has not been directly affected by livestock for decades. Thus, these sites are irreplaceable, vitally important, and should be protected. Unhappily, they are not. Though most were originally well-constructed, they have over the years deteriorated to the point where probably most are broken into by livestock occasionally, many routinely. They are poorly maintained, if at all. For example, when I asked a Utah BLM range specialist why the few hundred yards of exclosure fences in his district could not be properly maintained, he replied that funding simply wasn't available (though it was for *hundreds of miles* of ranching fences).

A livestock exclosure at 8000' elevation in the Dixie National Forest, Utah. The interior supports several times the plant and (non-livestock) animal biomass, many more species, and moister, more fertile soil. Without this exclosure for comparison and under continued livestock grazing, how would we have any idea what this particular landscape should be like?

One by one, these last tiny representatives of a more natural environment are falling to ranching. Funding for new exclosures is scant to nonexistent, but new ones are much less useful than the old ones anyway.

If they won't end ranching, our land managing agencies at least should immediately begin protecting all existing livestock exclosures by maintaining fences, erecting new fences where necessary, and actively resisting trespassing and tampering ranchers. Also they should establish many large, new exclosures in representative areas of the rangeland West, enclose them with sturdy fences, and fully maintain and defend them. These ungrazed areas should not be mere acres, but *thousands or millions* of acres so we may eventually study whole, and largely unaltered, ecosystems and make valid comparisons. Allotments of habitual permit violators could be retired and established as units of this system of ranching-free zones; all the necessary boundary fencing would already be in place!

A fenced highway right-of-way in central Arizona.

Instead of having 3,778 acres [on the Box Allotment, Pawnee National Grasslands, CO] "*suitable and open to grazing*" *and only a mere 16 acres for exclosures, why not have it the other way around?*
--Cindy Bishop, Co-coordinator, Prairie Dog Rescue, Inc.

By far the most common livestock exclosure in the West is de facto -- the narrow, fenced strips along roadways. They provide a great diversity of grazed/ungrazed contrasts for almost every portion of the West. Even so, fenced roadsides are not fully adequate for comparative purposes, for most of the reasons listed above.

The grassland, roughly 300 acres, sticks out like a green postage stamp on the vast, dry range. Surrounded by high sandstone cliffs, its pastures have never felt the mandibles of a cow, sheep, or horse. The tall bunchgrasses here are native. There is no Russian thistle, no tumbleweed, no cheatgrass; there is not even sage.

The land is an almost intact gift from the past, and because of the meadow's pristine condition, scientists treat it as a rare clue to how the West might have looked before the arrival of Europeans.

The meadow's most striking feature is not grass; it is cryptogam from which the grass springs. Elsewhere in Canyonlands National Park, the cryptogam is pink and knubbly, just beginning to recover from years of intensive cattle grazing. But on these few hundred relict acres, it is a thick, dark, ancient matrix of lichen and moss.
--Florence Williams, "The West's Time Capsules" (Williams 1990) (Ranching guru Allan Savory insists that a large herd of cattle should be moved onto this secret meadow a.s.a.p.; he thinks the meadow is deteriorating due to lack of animal impact. See Savory's Salvation in Chapter XII.)

ROADSIDE

Between pavement and barbwire
Between cows and cars
Narrow strip
No cattle graze
tall grasses
short grasses
sage, yucca
other plants whose names
I do not know
Roots deep
tenacious
Tough survivors
I kneel and give thanks

--Michael Adams, Eldorado Springs, Colorado

In many areas of the West, *vacant lots in cities and towns* display the best range conditions -- by simple virtue of not having been used by livestock for so long.

With few exceptions and relatively speaking, the best environmental conditions in rangeland portions of each Western state are found where livestock have never grazed or have been excluded for long periods. Some of the best range conditions in southern Nevada, for example, are found on the vast, unranched Nevada Test Site. In Arizona, marginal desert grassland in the ungrazed Petrified Forest National Park averages more herbaceous cover than the overgrazed naturally grassy lowlands around it. Similarly, the buffalo-grazed "badlands" of Badlands National Park in South Dakota is luxuriant with tall grasses and flowering plants -- in contrast to short-cropped, depleted surrounding livestock-grazed prairie. Ungrazed portions of Vandenberg Air Force Base on California's central coast support a lush diversity of plants and animals compared to adjacent grazed land. Areas of the Colorado Plateau where one can experience a relict (never-grazed) environment include No Man's Mesa in the upper Paria Creek drainage, Powell Plateau in Grand Canyon National Park, and Romona Mesa, 10 miles northeast of Glen Canyon Dam on the Utah-Arizona border. Romona Mesa is a steep-sided, inaccessible table that has never been grazed by *any* large ungulate. Despite its rocky, windy, dry location, it supports a much more abundant and diverse biologic community than the vast grazed lowlands surrounding it.

For the past seven years, cattle have not been allowed to graze at the U.S. Army Pinyon Canyon maneuver site near Trinidad in southeastern Colorado. According to Tom Dougherty of the National Wildlife Federation, "The real paradox is that even with the maneuvers, which most people would believe tear up the soil, we're noticing that the vegetation and wildlife communities seem to be infinitely better off."
--from news release for the film *The New Range Wars* (National Audubon Society 1991)

This inaccessible, volcanic hilltop on Hart Mountain National Wildlife Refuge in Oregon is inaccessible to livestock and so supports a lush covering of bluebunch wheatgrass and other native plants -- in stark contrast to the sparse covering of mostly exotics on the grazed land below. *(George Wuerthner)*

One of the few large livestock exclosures of any kind on the Great Plains is the Rocky Mountain Arsenal near Denver, Colorado. The US Army fenced the 27-square-mile area during World War II and built chemical plants at its center, using the rolling open grassland around them as a natural buffer zone. After 47 years of complete protection from ranching, the area is so thick with wildlife that Wendy Shattil, a world-traveling wildlife photographer, describes it thus: "For public viewing and diversity and quantity of wildlife, I don't think there is anything that compares to this, outside of Yellowstone National Park." In a 3-12-89 *New York Times* article entitled "Nature Sows Life Where Man Brewed Death," William E. Schmidt reports:

This ungrazed roadside offers not only several times more ground cover and vegetative biomass per unit of area than the miles of livestock range around it, but more species and diversity of grass, flowering herbaceous plants, and cryptogams, plus all the wild animals that go along with them.

"The diversity and numbers of wildlife are so extraordinary that this winter the Army agreed to escort bus tours of bird watchers and other wildlife enthusiasts through the once-secret installation." The exclosure's lush, tall vegetation supports remarkable numbers of hawks, owls, golden and bald eagles, coyotes, prairie dogs, mule and white-tailed deer, badgers, and much more. The land outside the installation's fences seems desolate in contrast. The main difference is ranching. (Schmidt 1989)

Financing for study and maintenance of exclosures and relict areas is scarce, due largely to pressure from livestock interests. According to Canyonlands National Park biologist Tim Graham, "Funding has been abysmal. It's probably my cynical view, but if we knew what the landscape was like 200 years ago, we'd have a model we'd have to be working toward." Graham notes that this might "require a big change in behavior" on the part of stockmen, that some ranchers may want to keep a lid on such studies, and that the grazing industry carries a lot of weight to suppress such studies. (Williams 1990)

Inside the split-rail fence the growth was green and luxuriant. Outside there was no growth, just desert. The ranchers hate such exclosures because they teach the public that cattle are the scourge of the earth.
--Ted Williams, "He's Going to Have an Accident" (Williams 1991)

I have never known a person who, once being shown a dramatic fence line, does not become an advocate for range improvement.
--Johanna Wald, attorney for public lands issues, Natural Resources Defense Council (Zaslowsky 1989)

Following is a pictorial account of some representative livestock exclosures:

This fallow field on the Fort Apache Indian Reservation in east-central Arizona, fenced to prevent cattle from destroying crops, is a de facto exclosure, lush with vegetation compared to the thousands of grazed Reservation acres around it.

A small exclosure in the Hawksie-Walksie Wilderness Study Area, Oregon, with cattle and a beaten range beyond the fence in the middle distance. *(Nancy Peterson)*

On the left is a small BLM cattle exclosure near Deadhorse State Park in southern Utah. The contrast between grazed and ungrazed land seen here is typical for exclosures in the region. *(George Wuerthner)*

Boundary of a mile-square exclosure in southern Arizona, fenced in the 1940s..

A small cemetery (left) in pine-oak woodland near Palace Station in the Prescott National Forest, central Arizona. The burial ground has been fenced from livestock for nearly a century and supports perhaps 3 times as much ground cover as the surrounding woodland.

Near the cemetary, a portion of a forest meadow (right) has been protected from livestock for several decades. The exclosure is almost completely covered with many species of tall, thick grass; wild iris; herbaceous perennials; shrubs; and bushes; with many insects buzzing and crawling about. Outside the exclosure is trampled, mostly bare ground; stubbles of grass of only a few species; wild iris only half the size; mostly annuals rather than herbaceous perennials; fewer, smaller shrubs; eaten, stunted bushes stripped of their lower branches; and vastly fewer insects.

Lone Mountain Exclosure, established in 1935, is situated at 5500' elevation in the Coronado National Forest near the Mexico-US border in southeast Arizona. The protected 5 acres has made a fair recovery thus far, and supports about twice the amount and density of ground cover as the unprotected land around it. Parts of the exclosure harbor cryptogams; almost none of the grazed range has cryptogams. Quail, doves, songbirds, small mammals, and insects are more common inside the exclosure.

Two photos taken from the same spot on an exclosure fence, one facing the interior of the exclosure (left), and one viewing the cattle-grazed range outside (right). BLM, southeast Utah.

Roundup Flat Exclosure is located in a wide saddle at more than 9000' elevation on the Aquarius Plateau in south-central Utah. The Plateau rises to more than 11,000' and is the largest expanse of high country in southern Utah, but destructive cattle and sheep grazing is common throughout, even in the aspen groves and pine-fir forests.

When the acre plot was fenced in 1957, the protected land immediately began the restoration process, the current results of which can be glimpsed in these photos. The vast improvement in the vegetation is evident, but what is not so obvious is the concurrent improvement in soil, water, animals, and so on. Look closely, for example, at the difference in the amount of exposed ground in the photo at top right.

Imagine the incredible restoration if the entire Aquarius Plateau was a livestock exclosure!

Norrell Range Study Plot, created in 1937, is located at 2250' elevation about 50 miles east of Phoenix, Arizona. At 175 acres, it is among the largest livestock exclosures in the West.

Norrell provides a prime example of how deceptive the influence of livestock grazing can be. I first discovered the exclosure by chance. My family and I were driving through the sub-tropical Sonoran Desert on a small dirt road. Suddenly, I noticed a small Forest Service sign off to the left. We had been driving alongside a fence but until now I had seen nothing that would have indicated that it was the boundary of a livestock exclosure.

Even as I stood there reading that this place had not been grazed since 1937, I discerned little difference between it and the grazed expanse to my back. Only after I climbed the fence and began exploring did things finally click.

Outside of the exclosure, the ground cover was virtually 100% cheatgrass. Inside, cheatgrass still composed probably 90% of ground-level vegetation, but here and there stands of various native grasses were coming back. These grasses grew only to the fence-line, not beyond.

I was surprised to suddenly realize that the inside of the exclosure contained about twice the biomass of shrubs, bushes, and trees per unit of area as the ranchland that we'd been driving through. As you can see in the photos at right, the woody plants on the grazed range (bottom) are sparser, smaller, more scraggly, and have been divested of most of their lower branches.

I walked back and forth between the exclosure and the grazed range. Inside, with thicker vegetation and organic litter, I found more birds, small mammals, lizards, and insects; and more nests, burrows, and tracks.

I strolled up a small, sandy wash. Its banks were covered with grass and dried-out herbaceous plants. The dense bushes and trees overhanging the drainage had trapped piles of flood debris and dropped much litter of their own. Lizards scurried into this organic material at my approach. Further along, a covey of quail exploded from a brush thicket and a large owl winged silently from a palo verde.

I encountered and negotiated barbed wire and continued up the wash. Immediately the drainage widened. Its banks were bare and trampled. Little overhanging vegetation or organic litter. Few piles of debris for lizards. No dense thickets for quail. No clean, unmarked sand. Cow pies, hoof prints, and environmental travesty everywhere.

I headed back to the exclosure.

The exclosure featured on these 2 pages can be found along a small dirt road 30 miles northeast of Moab in east-central Utah. It covers a couple of acres of semi-arid (former) grassland at 5000' elevation.

Both photos above were taken from the same spot on the exclosure fence. The top right photo looks out toward livestock-grazed land typical to the region. Note that the cow pie -- much-touted by ranchers as an essential range fertilizer -- is like a drop in the ocean compared to the massive denegration wrought by their contributing animals.

The top left photo of the exclosure's interior reveals what much of the region might look like if similarly protected from livestock. Though mostly grass, the unranched land also supports many shrubs, bushes, trees, flowering plants, and cryptogams in and amongst the grasses.

The bottom photo displays a typical fenceline contrast.

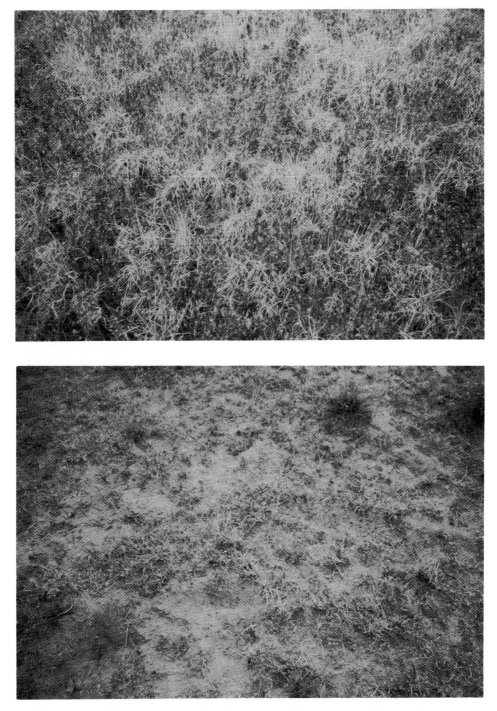

The ground within the exclosure (top photo) is so thickly covered with grasses, herbaceous plants, cryptogams, and organic litter that less than 5% of the actual ground surface is bare. Soil here is rich with humus, dark, moist, and wonderful to smell.

In contrast, bare ground on the grazed range averages about 50%. Soil here is exposed to the elements, eroded, light-colored, dry, and smells more like a dusty road.

Page Experimental Ranch was established in the 1940s by the University of Arizona as a place to research various agricultural techniques. To prevent roving cattle from disturbing the study projects, a square-mile section of Sonoran Desert (former) grassland was enclosed with barbed wire. Over the years, many experiments have been conducted thereon, but much of the exclosure remains basically natural, and most of it has seen few livestock for decades.

To visit Page you cross miles of typical state and private cattle-land -- rather barren, eroded country with sparse exotic grasses and scraggly, scattered shrubs, cacti, and mesquite. You might imagine that the area is naturally like this.

When you climb over the fence into the Page exclosure, however, you enter another world. Suddenly, as if by magic, you are immersed in a rich mosaic of life and healthy natural processes. Tall native grasses everywhere. Wild flowers of a dozen bright colors. Insects and birds fill the air. Small mammals and lizards scurry through thick grass and dense shrubbery. Large, healthy cacti. Small vines and strange-looking plants you have never seen. A glimpse of a kingsnake as it slithers into an ancient packrat nest. Curious and colorful bugs and beetles crawl across the thick organic compost -- a mat so thick that much of it feels spongy to your step. Fragrant and earthy smells hang in the moist air. You drift gently into another world . . . and for just an instant you feel an overwhelming primeval oneness with these wild and wonderful surroundings. . . .

And then a slap in the face!: you snap back into "reality" -- a university experimental area on the vast Arizona livestock range.

The livestock-grazed range adjacent to the exclosure (top) is typical of a large percentage of central and southern Arizona -- an impoverished land of mostly bare dirt. In comparison, the exclosure is a wonderland of Nature.

Health, integrity, abundance, and diversity are the rules inside Page; in contrast the land outside is ill, fragmented, deficient, and simplified.

Pull back the grass, scrape off the litter, and grab a handful of moist, dark, loose, humus-filled, microbe-enriched soil. Smells great!

The University of Arizona recently decided to sell Page and no longer maintains the protective fence. Already, cattle have broken into the exclosure and damaged some of the beautiful vegetation, and evidence strongly suggests that the local state-land rancher has several times twisted wire strands of the fence together to let his cattle in.

The ground just inside the exclosure fence.

The ground in the same location just outside the fence.

An unusual couple of yuccas in the Page exclosure. It is doubtful that these yuccas could have reached this size and perfection of shape under the abusive influence of cattle.

A scene outside. The lack of grass may make it seem that shrubs are doing well here; most shrubs inside the exclosure are hidden behind tall grass. Note these shrubs' poor condition.

This 2-acre BLM exclosure in Spring Valley near Majors, White Pine County, Nevada, hints at what ranching has done to much of the Great Basin. After 60 or 70 years of devastating livestock use, cattle and sheep were fenced off of this land in 1937. The subsequent 50 years of recovery is seen in these photos. The recovery is remarkable, but try to envision the aboriginal landscape.

View from the Majors exclosure fenceline looking at grazed range. Nevada, 87% of which is federal land, is the overall driest and naturally most barren state in the continental US. Still, for more than a century more than 80% of it has been used by livestock. As a result, a large percentage of Nevada now looks something like this.

Much of Nevada would look more like this if similarly protected from livestock for 50 years. Clearly, the exclosure has at least twice the plant biomass per unit of area and much healthier plants than the grazed range. If all federal land in Nevada was protected from livestock, the state could support many times more wildlife. Nevada might not be considered a wasteland.

Following is a pictoral account of some representative fenceline contrasts:

Fenceline during recent drought, west-central California.

Roadside on BLM range in central New Mexico.

View of roadside from grazed range, central New Mexico

Northeast Nevada.

Roadside in the Santa Fe National Forest, New Mexico.

Standing on a fence, looking at the ground through a wide-angle lens, at 8000' elevation in the Bighorn National Forest in north-central Wyoming. The right side of the fence looked like the left side only several days before -- when sheep were brought in. Hundreds of acres in the immediate area were similarly devegetated.

Cibola National Forest in west-central New Mexico.

Navajo Reservation, Arizona.

BLM land, somewhere in Nevada. *(BLM)*

National Forest *(USFS)*

Ungrazed roadside at left. West-central New Mexico.

BLM highway right-of-way in northwest New Mexico. Note the obsolete fence.

This side of the fence is grazed by cattle. Kern County, California.

Socorro County, New Mexico.

Central Nevada.

Freeway right-of-way in central Arizona.

Roadside on central New Mexico BLM range. Hundreds of square miles of grazed land similar to that on the right surround this lonely highway.

Healthy bunchgrass and brush end at the roaside fence.

Most livestock grazing in the West amounts to an annual clearcutting of ground-level vegetation. Freeway right-of-way, Yavapai County, Arizona.

BLM land, Valencia County, New Mexico.

The fenced roadside on the right is a veritable jungle of Johnson grass and other vegetation. Tumbleweeds have piled up against the fence on the barren left side. BLM land, Grant County, New Mexico.

Highway fenceline, Pawnee National Grassland, northeast Colorado.

Utah highway right-of-way. Note where cattle have reached through the fence for forage.

The narrow strip between the 2 fences has become a de facto exclosure. The wooden fence stretches for miles through similarly degraded terrain. The cattle are clustered around blocks of salt, an essential mineral.

Livestock Grazing Photos

Cattle and sheep grazing causes serious damage to much of the Bighorn National Forest in north-central Wyoming.

Livestock-grazed range in Big Bend National Park, Texas. Note the lack of ground cover, pedestaled plants, and severe erosion. Surviving plants are creosote. *(George Wuerthner)*

Cattle-caused arroyo-cutting near Tombstone in southeast Arizona. *(BLM)*

The right side of this fence was for decades more heavily grazed by cattle than the left side. As a result, creosote has mostly outcompeted the grass, shrubs, and other plants that survive on the left. In this case, creosote is an increaser. Such has been the case on millions of acres in the Southwest and California. Note the cattle trail on right.

A beaten riparian area along the Rio Grande River in central New Mexico. Note the stunted willows, paucity of riparian vegetation, hoof ruts, cattle trail, and, of course, cattle.

On steep, open slopes with plenty of forage, cattle tend to walk along contours as they graze, creating "terraces" such as these in central California.

A trampled-down bank and a cattle trail across a wash on BLM land in central New Mexico. Cattle prints mar the sand for miles up and down the wash.

Cattle-ravaged riparian area. Note the poor condition of the trees. Banches have been broken off, trampled to pieces, and scattered. *(USFS)*

Cattle grazing near Saratoga, Wyoming. Note the lushly vegetated roadside. *(Harvey Duncan)*

Cattle grazing on left; fenced roadside on right. New Mexico BLM.

Close-up of a boggy area in northern Nevada -- devegetated, trampled, and polluted by cattle.

Cutbanks and denuded, trampled drainages succumb to floodwaters from depleted watersheds.

More than 1000 sheep degrade this fragile sub-alpine meadow. *(BLM)*

Gully erosion of old cattle trails has formed gulches. Central California.

Deforested range in Coconino National Forest, northern Arizona, beaten by cattle.

Livestock have converted tens of millions of acres in the West into virtual biological wasteland.

Cattle turned this once-beautiful warm spring into trampled mire. Nevada BLM.

Ash Springs, Chiricahua Mountains, Coronado National Forest, southeastern Arizona. *(Paul Hirt)*

Gully erosion in coarse sediment on cattle-beaten range.

Cattle-beaten range in northern Wyoming mountains.

Gully erosion on barren California range.

Kern County, California.

Cattle and domestic horses degrade this BLM scene in the Owyhee Mountains, Idaho: an impoverished range; unstable and eroding streambanks; ravaged riparian vegetation, mostly liquidated long ago; turbid, polluted, depleted water; an obstructing fence; and utter lack of wildlife. Without livestock, this would be a verdant, dynamic ecosystem. *(George Wuerthner)*

Shade trees on open ranges become centers of activity -- thus destructive influence -- for cattle. The trees are damaged, stunted, and, finally, killed, and the nearby range is trashed..

Cattle harm the unique and impressive salt lakes on the plains in the geographic center of New Mexico. Long lines of hoof prints mar their smooth, white surfaces, and (as here) fences jut out into their salty expanses.

Kaibab National Forest, northern Arizona.

A roadside view in Southern California.

A dying riparian area in California. With continued livestock grazing, in several decades nothing will remain but a bare field. Note the cattle congregation area at upper right, fences, road, and denuded range.

Dying cottonwood on a dying range. Fallen branches are reduced to chaotic debris; organic litter is depleted; soil and roots are damaged. Note terracing on hill.

The top photo shows a mountain stream in Wyoming, trampled by cattle. The water is murky and algae-infested. Nearby, a cow splat covers a rock at stream's edge.

Top photo is of a cattle-trampled sub-alpine bog above 12,000' elevation in the White Mountains, Inyo National Forest, California. Bottom photo shows a nearby spring, fenced to protect the water from cattle for domestic use.

From sea to shining sea....

Los Padres National Forest. This cool, foggy, moist central California coast would, if not for livestock, be a paradise of green and gold.

A livestock-devastated landscape in central Utah.

Gully erosion caused by livestock. BLM land, Mariposa County, California. *(USGS)*

In many areas throughout the West, livestock reduce not only grass, but shrubs, herbaceous plants, and other vegetation types as well.

This cattle trail skirts a bluff and winds down to the Green River. BLM, northeast Utah.

Mounds and ruts created by cattle in a hot springs bog in Nevada. Some of the ruts are more than a foot deep.

Cattle-caused erosion in the Coronado National Forest, southeast Arizona. *(George Wuerthner)*

Our public land in Wyoming; sheep.

Sheep on ragged creosote range in Texas. *(SCS, USDA)*

Cattle create eroded trails as they move between areas of food, water, salt, and shade. Note that there is a cattle trail even through the thick brush in the left half of the photo (the large trees there are used for shade).

No single activity or combination of activities
has contributed more
to the deterioration of plant and animal life
than the nibbling mouths and pounding hooves of livestock.

--Richard and Jacob Rabkin, **Nature in the West** (1981)

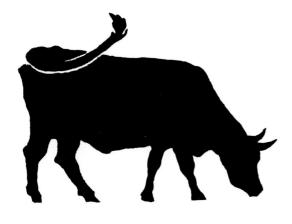

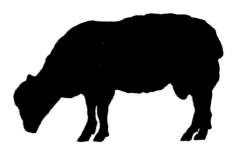

Chapter IV
RANGE DEVELOPMENT: ENVIRONMENTAL EFFECTS

Rancher Wayne brings in 200 head from March through July to feed on the lush spring growth on this typical 12,000-acre BLM allotment. The cattle spend their time on the fertile, grassy flats and along watercourses and moist drainages. They eat selectively, consuming the most nutritious bunchgrasses, herbaceous perennials, riparian growth, and choicest browse.

The first year his cattle grow fat, and Wayne is happy. The second year, he is still pleased, but at the end of the grazing season his cattle haven't gained as much weight. At the end of the third season, the year's herd is thinner still, and Wayne is beginning to worry.

The years pass. Soon after each of the intermittent wetter periods, Wayne's hopes rise with the new green growth, but this never lasts long; overall trend is downward. The allotment is progressively more ragged and cowburnt. Wayne's cattle become less selective, eat decreasingly palatable vegetation, and roam farther to find enough to eat. They are undernourished and disease-prone. Reproduction is low, mortality high.

Like most public lands ranchers, Wayne derives a minor portion of his total income from ranching public land. However, he is unwilling to admit the obvious -- that Wayne Allotment, like all public allotments, is an inherently lousy place to raise livestock. Rather, like his peers he blames failure on bad luck, bad weather, predators, high production costs, low beef prices, vandals, government rules and regulations, and so on. Wayne is committed -- socially, politically, habitually, and emotionally as much as financially -- to being a celebrated Cowboy with 12,000 acres and a 200-head herd. He is not about to cut his herd, and he knows the BLM won't force him to, to any significant degree.

Wayne is in a quandary, being adamantly opposed to reducing herd size, but realizing the need to increase the allotment's suitability for livestock to maintain herd size. Like most ranching advocates he inevitably sees only one solution: begin the government-sponsored range development process to artificially improve the range for livestock. Not only will this maintain Wayne's livestock production at government expense, but it will place the burden of responsibility for keeping the allotment productive squarely and permanently on government (taxpayers') shoulders. Once the range development program stabilizes a certain production level, government will be *expected* to maintain that level indefinitely. Though Wayne is happier, the story doesn't have a happy ending.

The West is systematically looted.
--Bernard DeVoto

A range improvement program may include wells, reservoirs, detention dams, ditches, water spreaders, storage tanks, pipe lines, spring developments, watering troughs, fences, corrals, loading chutes, dipping vats, cattle guards, weighing scales, riders' cabins, bridges, truck trails, stock trails, stock driveways, water-hauling roads, firebreaks, contour furrowing, check dams, diversion dams, subsoil sagebrush eradication, plowing and range reseeding, noxious and poisonous weed control, rodent control, insect control, predatory animal control, reseeding of logging roads and skid trails, brush burning and reseeding, and eradication of brush stands by chemical spraying.
--Phillip O. Foss, **Politics and Grass** (Foss 1960)

Livestock have wasted the West more than any other single agent, but they are helpless pawns in a complex game of maximum profit and power. Stockmen, government range managers, university and business professionals, politicians, and other components of the ranching establishment are in charge. And while the impact of livestock grazing is more than enough reason to end public lands ranching, *it is only half of the environmental story.*

For more than a century, in its attempt to maximize livestock production, this grazing establishment has in effect waged war against the Western environment.* The industry fights its war with what it calls "range improvements" and "range management," 2 basic weapons systems which together may be termed "range development." Its enemy in this never-ending battle is anything that inhibits or is perceived to inhibit maximum livestock production. As will be evident, this includes an incredible number and variety of living things and inanimate objects.

* Additionally and significantly, many ranchers habitually manipulate the land due to long-standing tradition, because it gives them a feeling of doing something worthwhile, or simply out of sheer boredom.

Famous Euphemisms: "Range Improvement."

Jim Stiles
© 1990

Range "Improvements"

Fixed developments on the open land that facilitate live-stock production may be termed "range improvements." As with "newspeak" in George Orwell's classic, **1984**, the wording is intended to rearrange the reality of whoever sees, hears, or uses it. By consistently calling anything they do to the land an "improvement," ranchers and their aides lead people to believe that these developments actually do *improve* the range, and should therefore be supported. Taking reality-bending terminology one step further, BLM recently has begun calling range developments "accomplishments." By constantly defining and redefining range terminology in relation to the land, the ranching establishment creates a widely accepted, malleable, self-serving reality.

Purposefully obscured is that these developments are designed to improve the land *for livestock grazing*. And though they may temporarily benefit livestock production, they usually degrade the environment and public use.

Millions of fences, stock tanks, and other range "improvements" have been constructed on our public land, the vast majority with our taxes (see Chapter VII). They and the land

they occupy are treated more or less as private property by stockmen. BLM does in fact consider some permanent structural developments made by ranchers on federal land to be private property, effectively privatizing the land they occupy.

Fences

Barbed wire is shaped like a certain attitude toward the world; it lends a taut-strung control over a large area. It works because it derives maximum cruelty from a minimum of material. Like many other elements of our culture, it is hated almost as widely as it is used.
--C.L. Rawlings, Western poet

The most conspicuous so-called range "improvement" is the ever-present barbed wire fence. Fences stretch for hundreds of thousands of miles across Western public land, almost all of which serve solely or primarily for livestock grazing management.

As mentioned, each Western public lands grazing allotment encompasses an average of more than 10,000 acres, or about 16 square miles -- representing a territory about 4 miles by 4 miles (though they are rarely square). Each of these 30,000 allotments is enclosed by boundary fences around its perimeter. Even if all allotments shared all boundaries and were perfectly square, this would still amount to 245,000 miles of fence. Allowing for boundaries shared with private lands and non-grazed public lands and the common irregular allotment shapes, the figure is certainly at least 300,000. However, most allotments are also cross-fenced, many heavily so, and other non-boundary fences on allotments run along roads, utility corridors, recreation area boundaries, and so on, altogether probably traversing at least as many miles as allotment boundary fences. Thus, we may reasonably estimate at least **600,000 miles** of livestock fences on Western public land -- more than enough to stretch to the moon and back, or around the Earth 24 times! Including private lands, which generally are more heavily fenced than public, the figure for the West is surely well over 1 million miles.

This corral is posted "NO HUNTING OR TRESPASSING" -- essentially privatizing the BLM land it occupies as well.

There are 2 basic types of fences. *Division fences* enclose the boundaries of a range grazing unit. They are used to divvy up our public land into manageable grazing allotments for use by private livestock interests. Division fences also divide these allotments into smaller parcels for conducting various grazing systems, segregating livestock into different age and sex groups, and keeping different owners' livestock within their respective grazing areas on joint allotments.

Drift fences are not intended as enclosures, per se, but as barriers to keep livestock in certain areas and prevent them from drifting to areas where they are not wanted. Many drift fences retain livestock in certain preferred grazing areas, often tying in to natural barriers such as steep ridges, ravines, and cliffs. Others keep livestock away from poisonous plants, extreme rockiness or brushiness, dangerous cliffs, or predators. Some drift fences are used to help funnel and then contain cattle during roundup. Still others keep cattle and sheep off roadways and out of campgrounds, recreation areas, or grass seeding areas. Drift fences may even be intended to keep competing wild herbivores away, or to exclude people from certain livestock areas.

Of course fences can also be used to protect the environment from livestock, as is often the case with National Parks, nature preserves, and such. Nonetheless, if there were no livestock on adjacent public land these fences would not be needed. For example, after livestock grazing was terminated in both Organ Pipe Cactus National Monument and Cabeza Prieta National Wildlife Refuge in southwestern Arizona, the long barbed wire fence separating the two no longer served any purpose and was removed.

Many well-meaning groups and individuals have proposed fencing livestock out of selected ecologically sensitive areas -- especially heavily "cattlized" riparian zones. Though their intent is commendable, this is a poor substitute for removing livestock from these areas. For instance, throwing cattle out of riparian zones and onto surrounding rangeland would result (and has resulted, where it has occurred) in more damage to these less heavily grazed and often more fragile areas. Riparian ecosystem consultant Harold Winegar concludes

Watersheds are all connected. If you move cattle out of the stream bottoms and into the uplands you will still be pounding to death the springs, seeps, and creeks, not to mention contributing to soil compaction over the entire uplands. More fences also entail more wells drilled, roads and stock tanks built, water sources developed, and other harmful ranching development.

Forest Service installing a fence on Montana range. *(USFS)*

Fences serve many other purposes, not the least of which is giving public land the appearance of private ownership. Stockmen benefit in several ways:

Probably most Americans, when confronting a barbed wire fence or gate, assume the land behind is privately owned or, if publicly owned, is off-limits. Many others are unable to cross over. This group of people -- sightseers, photographers, picnickers, hikers, campers, fishers, hunters, birders, rockhounds, Nature lovers, and so on -- represents the general public. In keeping this large segment of the population away from most public rangeland, fences help prevent the public from becoming aware of ranching abuses.

Others who visit public land for purposes of resource exploitation are generally well aware of land ownership, and so are not deterred by fences and gates. Indeed, most of these people are glad to have fences to filter out the general populace -- what they consider a nuisance and potential opposition. Consequently, in effect, what fences do is allow through those people who tend to exploit public land and bar those who would tend to defend it.

Additionally, by keeping the public off public land, ranchers minimize competition and hindrance from "nonconsumptive" land users. These people scare cattle and leave gates open. They complain about overgrazing, livestock-polluted water, lack of wildlife, and cow pies, flies, and cows in their camps. Some cut fences, punch holes in stock water tanks, take salt blocks, remove traps and poisons, damage corrals, vandalize ranching equipment, and shoot cattle.

Importantly, fences tend to foster in stockmen a sense of possession of public land. Barbed wire is a worldwide symbol of conquest and domination. Fences define boundaries of influence. Any land, enclosed and cross-fenced with barbed wire, seems under the  control or influence of the man for whom the fences were built. Stockmen cannot help but feel this sense of power; indeed, many relish it. The psychological motivation it gives helps provide the impetus they need to treat public land as their own.

If a permittee can demonstrate a need (or an apparent need) for a new fence on "his" allotment, construction is usually forthcoming. The BLM, FS, or other land managing agency almost invariably supplies planning and materials while, depending on circumstances, either the permittee or agency supplies labor. Quite often government plans construction and provides both. Additionally, the taxpayer usually assumes responsibility for fence building and maintenance between allotments, along roadways and utility corridors, surrounding federal installations, and around other government and private lands requiring exclusion of livestock.

Livestock fences on public land are of many different kinds, but by far most common is 3, 4, or 5 strands of barbed wire set on wooden, metal, or (very infrequently) reinforced concrete posts. First, sturdy, well-anchored corner and support posts are installed. Then strands of barbed wire are stretched tightly and nailed or wired to the "line" posts between. Or, barbed wire strands are simply stretched from tree to tree, or sometimes between rock faces. Posts are commonly spaced 20' to 30' apart, with 2 to 4 equally spaced wooden or special spiral metal "stays" holding barbed wire strands the proper distance apart so cattle can't push their way

through. Gates may be spaced miles apart or as closely as 4 or 5 per mile, depending on the wants and needs of the local rancher and the priorities of the local public lands managers.

Wire mesh fences are used on many allotments where sheep are grazed. Where tourism is important and scenic quality high priority, log or split rail fences are sometimes employed. In portions of the high country West, especially where moose wander right through ordinary fences and abundant lodgepole pine or other small, straight trees provide free fence materials, "buck-and-pole" fences are the way to go. Even rock walls are seen occasionally in some extremely rocky areas, usually where volcanic activity has provided numerous medium-sized rocks. And electric fences are increasingly popular on public land. Some of the more modern of these are set up in various grid patterns and connected to a central switchboard.

Electric cattle fence. *(Paul Hirt)*

In some grazed areas with significant pedestrian traffic, people cross fences on specially designed stairs or through U- or V-shaped chutes which allow through people but block cattle.

Where fences traverse exposed rock, holes are drilled and posts anchored into concrete. BLM land near Moab in southeast Utah.

Construction and maintenance of livestock fences is not the hokey, harmless activity pictured in cowboy movies and TV commercials. It often entails bulldozing vegetation, chainsawing trees and brush, girdling trees with wire (which often kills them), dislodging large rocks (from the ground, outcroppings, or cliff faces), excavating topsoil, sometimes even dynamiting. Fence building consumes endless rolls of barbed wire, millions of metal posts, tons of nails, staples, and wire stays -- from natural resources that could be left in the ground.

Where fences span drainages and low spots, boulders, logs, or other heavy objects are displaced and wired to strands for stabilization.

Lower branches of this tree were cut for fence posts, killing it.

For posts, stays, gates, corrals, etc., ranchers and government employees have cut branches from, or cut down, millions of trees and bushes. Stockmen often are given permission to cut wood for ranching materials in areas where cutting for all other purposes is disallowed. Not bothering with even the formalities, many ranchers simply cut whatever they want, whenever and wherever they want. Thus, in some areas of the West the sparse brush and tree cover has been depleted, disrupting environmental processes and other human use.

Some girdled trees grow around the wire, but many eventually die because the wire chokes off their vital cambium layer. Millions of trees in the West have been girdled for fences.

This oak bears old scars from barbed wire, which may have introduced the disease that killed it. Coronado National Forest in southeast Arizona.

Fences tend to be located where easiest to build and maintain, most convenient for ranching activities, and most profitable -- and often not where they are authorized. They run beside roads, lengthwise through canyon and valley bottoms, alongside waterways and drainages, along ridge tops, and across passes and saddles. Many bisect creeks and streams to provide water access to livestock in the numerous pastures that radiate out from water sources into the surrounding countryside. Thus, fences generally are concentrated where they most effectively interfere with natural processes, wildlife, and human visitors.

Wire fences on public land kill and maim many wild and domestic animals. Ranchers often complain about escaping calves and sheep, as well as adult cattle pushing through fences, so fences usually are built strong and tight, with close-spaced wires, the bottom wire close to the ground. Larger animals such as deer, elk, moose, pronghorn, and horses, in trying to cross fences, become entangled. Failing to clear the top strand, they may wedge a hind leg between the 2 uppermost strands and hang there to die from exposure or thirst, or to be eaten by predators. Or, in attempting to go under or through fences, animals may become entangled or pinch a leg in a tight spot. One study of the causes of accidental deaths of bighorns, for example, found 12% attributable to fences and other wire. Other bighorns were thought to have torn themselves free and escaped with serious injuries. (Ferguson 1983) Animals malnourished, diseased, or otherwise impaired due to ranching impacts are less able to negotiate fences.

Wide swaths are cut through woody vegetation to facilitate construction and maintenance of fences.

Wherever possible, the government and ranchers build roads to help in the construction and maintenance of fences. In gentle terrain, the rancher may simply drive cross-country in to and alongside fencelines, thereby creating new roads. A common rangeland sight is the miles-long, arrow-straight fenceline leading into the horizon with a paralleling dirt road at its flank, or on *both* sides.

After fences are completed or repaired, waste materials commonly are discarded onto the nearby countryside or left where they lay. Old or obsolete fences usually are left to rot or rust where they stand, leaving spaghetti-like strands of rusty barbed wire strewn across the landscape laying in wait for passing animals, humans, and vehicles.

(George Robbins Photo, Jackson, WY.)

Where fences or other obstacles block movement, livestock often travel alongside in a parallel manner, one animal following another, creating trails. Other trails are formed where livestock move along common routes to and from water sources, salt blocks, shade trees, and forage areas. Thus have been created tens of thousands of miles of wide trails across the West -- representing hundreds of square miles of trampled, bare dirt. Note the fenceline contrast. *(SCS, USDA)*

Dogs, coyotes, foxes, bobcats, raccoons, and other large to mid-sized mammals likewise die lingering deaths. Even smaller animals may entangle their fur in single barbs, or collide with fences and wound themselves, opening their bodies to infection, disease, and parasites. Fence wire in water is especially injurious to beavers, muskrats, river otters, fish, and diving waterfowl. Fences straddling waterways and drainages may also catch large amounts of flood debris, causing jam-ups and consequent flash flooding.

Birds crash into barbed fence strands, often when the strands are concealed by vegetation. Especially vulnerable are large birds of prey, waterfowl, and large night-flying birds such as owls and nightjars. Sandhill cranes and even Endangered whooping cranes have been killed on fences on National Wildlife Refuges in Oregon, Idaho, and Colorado.

Another problem with fences is that they impede migration and restrict free movement of many large animals, thus shrinking their territories and limiting access to key areas of food, water, minerals, mating, hibernating, etc. In fact, some ranchers build fences for the calculated purpose of keeping wildlife competitors off both their private property and "their" public lands allotments.

Pronghorn and bighorns are especially susceptible to being "trapped" by fences. When encountering a fence, they are prone to walk along rather than cross over. Thus, failing to reach necessary destinations, they sometimes die from thirst, starvation, or exposure. (In the early ranching years, market hunters purposefully drove herds of pronghorn and other large herbivores up against fences and slaughtered them in large numbers.)

From _The Coyote: Defiant Songdog of the West,_ Revised & Updated by Francois Leydet. Copyright (C) 1977, 1988 by Francois Leydet. Used by permission of the University of Oklahoma Press.

A cattle fence on the San Pedro River, Arizona. The washed-out portion in the background lurks underwater.

The public became aware of this problem only in winter 1983, when in southern Wyoming 700 pronghorn fleeing a series of blizzards stacked up against a barbed wire fence, where they starved and froze. The fence, enclosing more than 20,000 acres of private, state, and federal land, prevented the pronghorn from reaching their natural feeding grounds. Not wanting to remove the fence or modify its lower strand to accommodate wildlife and responding to a lawsuit by environmentalists, the rancher took his case to the Supreme Court. (A recent court decision ordered him to modify the fence's lower strand, but it remains to be seen if he will do so.) In recent years the government has in some areas provided "antelope guards" -- specially-designed grills similar to cattle guards emplaced along fences to restrict livestock but allow pronghorn passage.

Deer and elk jump most fences fairly easily, but like most large animals -- including bears, moose, mountain lions, and mountain goats -- they prefer walking along rather than going over, under, or through fences. Buffalo usually don't jump fences (though they are capable of it), but will push right through them, sometimes getting entangled.

(Brush Wolf)

To help confine sheep and reduce predation, sheep ranchers and government agencies have since the 1800s erected thousands of miles of net-wire fences across public land. This type of fence has been especially restrictive to some wildlife species, particularly pronghorn, which have consequently declined in many areas. For example, the *llano estacado* in southeastern New Mexico once supported one of North America's greatest pronghorn populations, but it crashed when a network of tightly woven sheep fences was erected on public lands in the area (Foreman 1991). Taxpayers have recently replaced some sheep fences with barbed wire, but thousands of miles remain.

Little recognized is that livestock grazing and roadside fences team up to cause millions of animal deaths each year. Most Western roadways are fenced to keep livestock off. The grazed countryside usually is barren compared to the luxuriantly vegetated, fenced, ungrazed roadsides -- hence the startling fenceline contrasts that confuse many a traveler in the West. Pavement runoff from rain accounts for much of this difference on downhill slopes, but the dramatic contrast usually begins exactly at the fenceline. Even on uphill roadsides, where runoff cannot reach, the contrast is usually striking. This difference is due to livestock grazing and is the cause of many wildlife deaths, for these lushly vegetated roadsides not only support a much greater number and variety of animals, but attract many of the surviving

animals from surrounding, overgrazed areas. Mammals, birds, reptiles, amphibians, rodents, and insects concentrate there. As they run, crawl, or fly across roads, after being scared or simply moving from one place to another, they are hit by oncoming vehicles. Vultures, crows, ravens, coyotes, raccoons, and other scavengers seek out these roadkills and often become roadkills themselves.

A pronghorn finds lush early spring grass along a highway right-of-way, its overgrazed range in the background. *(George Robbins Photo, Jackson, WY)*

The photographer claims that this mule deer was hit by a vehicle while seeking the comparatively abundant roadside vegetation. *(George Robbins Photo, Jackson, WY)*

Fences may contribute to environmental decline in other, seldom understood ways. For example, studies show that in some grasslands and deserts lacking natural high observation points, fence posts may allow predators "too good" a view of nearby prey, thus leading to overkill and eventual decline of predators as well. Once again, ecosystem components are simply not adapted to artificial developments.

Though fences are already nearly omnipresent, the Forest Service, BLM, and others have launched a campaign to build an even more complex network, to eventually include *hundreds of thousands of miles of new fences*. Ostensibly to "facilitate resource management," the effort is actually a desperate attempt to maintain livestock production levels by creating ever-smaller grazing areas of ever-more intensive management.

Expansion of rotation systems as planned will require extensive fencing of western ranges in the years ahead. Each grazing area would be fenced into subunits to be rotated according to plan by the stockmen whose livestock graze it. In effect, the West would be extensively subdivided into pastures if these plans are carried out.

--Frederic H. Wagner, *Livestock Grazing and the Livestock Industry* (Wagner 1978)

Water Developments

Every effort should be made to provide the water needed by livestock to fully develop the grazing potential of an allotment. This would include development of springs and seeps with known supply of season-long water, ponding of runoff, construction of ponds in areas of seasonably high water tables, or use of drilled wells or windmills. Some of these structures may supply only a few head of livestock with water for only a short time, but they will frequently encourage grazing in areas formerly unused.

--from "Managing Public Rangelands," a booklet by the US Forest Service

Stockmen discovered early that to control the range they had to control the water. Thus, through the Homestead Act and other legal, quasi-legal, and illegal means, most surface waters in the dry West became private property long ago, and remain so today. Ranches were established along almost every appreciable stream and in nearly every river valley in the rangeland West.

But cattle normally will travel only a few miles from water (sheep, somewhat further), and much of the Western range is farther from water than this, especially since so many natural water sources have been eliminated by overgrazing. Generally, livestock cannot survive more than a few days without water. Thus, without supplemental water it would be impossible to graze large areas of the West. Additionally, plentiful water allows livestock to consume coarser, less palatable, and more toxic vegetation (whose existence is also largely a result of overgrazing). So in dry and degraded areas water developments are spaced out evenly across the land to allow livestock more uniform and intensive use of forage and browse.

These artificial stock water sources, termed "tanks," dot the land like pepper on a map throughout all but the wettest regions of the West. (Look closely at a good Forest Service map and you will see, though many are not shown. Probably twice as many per unit of land pepper BLM land, though tanks usually are not shown on BLM maps.) Stock tanks commonly occur at an average of perhaps 1 per square mile, up to 4 or 5 per square mile in many areas. The vast majority of allotments have at least several tanks, and most have a dozen or more; thus, we may reasonably estimate **several hundred thousand** stock tanks on Western federal land. State and county lands are pocked with perhaps a couple hundred thousand more.

Most stock tanks are dirt. Ranging anywhere from bathroom-sized to acres in area, they are scraped into the living earth with bulldozers, back-hoes, and graders. This often involves bringing heavy equipment across land never even driven on before. The dam site and area to be covered by water, and the ground 10' to 20' all around the site, are cleared of trees, stumps, brush, rocks, and other large objects, destroying animals and their habitat in the process. The topsoil may then be removed and saved to line the dam and spillway. Dirt, sand, and rocks (and remaining plants and animals) are gouged out to form basins and shaped into dams across draws, gullies, arroyos, canyons, and other drainages. Additionally, trenches and/or levees may be scraped into the uphill countryside to divert more water into the prospective ponds. In flatter areas without well-defined drainages, stock ponds are scraped deeply into the terrain, blocked with long, low dams on the downhill side, and fed with long swales, trenches, or levees that capture water runoff from large areas upslope. Some are lined with plastic, clay, cement, oil, and other sealants. But most are "puddled naturally" by the trampling hooves of livestock, and by manure, urine, washed-in silt, and a build-up of salts and minerals left by evaporating water. Infrequently, tanks are fenced to exclude livestock in order to reduce physical damage to the dam and to reduce water pollution (which may cause livestock to become ill or infested with parasites), and water is delivered to stock through a pipe or access point.

The dirt tank fills with water during a good rain, if the dam doesn't wash away or the basin fill with sediment. If it holds water (perhaps 10%-15% of those I have witnessed don't), thereafter it becomes a livestock mud-wallow.

These tanks function partly and temporarily as check dams, as natural sediments and those loosed by overgrazing settle onto the bottoms of waters backed up behind the dams. However, the elevation difference caused by the dams (or *any* dam) also *increases* the water speed and scouring action of floodwaters in channels *below* the dams. This, in combination with the impact from overgrazing and tank building in drainages and surrounding areas -- plus the fact that livestock use and damage is extremely concentrated in tank areas -- usually leave drainages with significant net losses in vegetation, soil, and wildlife. Moreover, most tanks eventually (often suddenly) wash away, causing flooding and erosion to drainages far worse overall than if no tank were built in the first place. Thus, ranchers' claims of slowing channel erosion and providing for wildlife with stock tanks, though often palatable to the public, are usually the inverse of reality.

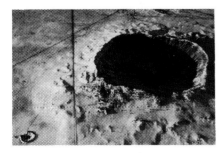

Mile-wide Meteor Crater near Winslow, Arizona on upper right; stock tank, lower left. *(Unknown)*

A washed-out large stock tank dam.

Constructing a large BLM dirt stock tank. *(BLM)*

Other common stock water tanks are metal, usually round and made from galvanized iron. These storage tanks, ranging in size from roughly a hundred to a hundred thousand gallons, commonly are fed via wells and windmills (invented in 1854), gas, diesel, propane, or electric pumps,

A Forest Service holding tank for cattle.

or springs or creeks via gravity flow through pipes. Small open metal tanks may double as water troughs. Troughs may be built onto the bottom of large tanks, or located nearby and fed through pipes. Water levels in tanks and troughs are regulated by float valves. Like some other structural range "improvements," these metal tanks are sometimes flown into remote areas with government helicopters, allowing ranchers to graze otherwise unexploitable land.

Other stock tanks are constructed from concrete, concrete blocks, rocks, sheet metal, logs, or whatever material is available, then caulked and coated with asphalt or some other sealant. Some are situated in natural slickrock catchments or blasted into bedrock. Some are designed to capture rainfall directly and channel it into storage. These are termed "trick tanks."

One trick tank I encountered on Forest Service land was constructed thus: A gently rolling area of about 1 acre of juniper woods was stripped of all vegetation, bladed flat with a gradual slope to one side, and covered with a thick sheet of plastic and layer of gravel. Rainwater ran off into a funnel-shaped galvanized gutter and then over the side of a hill into a large metal holding tank supported by a platform of timbers. From this tank ran underground pipes, with valves, to a large metal holding tank with a trough, and from there to a concrete stock tank with a trough. The side of the

holding tank was stenciled "PROPERTY OF U.S. FOREST SERVICE." A few cows were milling around in the surrounding acre of trampled, bare dirt. Who knows how much this project cost the public -- merely to help water 20 or 30 cows for a few months each year. Ranching contrivances such as this are common on public land.

Some stock tanks are even designed to capture windblown snow. This may include structural developments, bulldozing, and/or vegetation manipulation.

Where profitable, seasonal drainages are bulldozed to form dams, or dammed with concrete, sheet metal, lumber, rocks, logs, or whatever is available, and lined with plastic. Perennial streams are dammed (damned) similarly, with pipes or ditches sometimes running to stock tanks and troughs in more convenient locations. Springs are dug or blasted out, curbed, or capped off and the water piped to stock tanks or troughs.

A spring development; water is piped to a cattle tank some distance away. Note the roadside fenceline contrast, barren hillside, and cattle trail at top.

This rock and concrete cattle tank ties into the canyon walls. Note that the basin behind the dam has filled with rocks and gravel.

Where water is near but still inaccessible to livestock, they may be supplied the water with noisy and polluting water pumps. Or, wide trails may be cut through thick vegetation, rocky areas, or even down steep mountainsides so livestock can reach the water. Pumping plants are installed to lift water from deep canyons. Commonly water is piped for miles onto the dry range. If all else fails, water may be *trucked* to the thirsty animals. *Any* water is fair game to stockmen, and little gets away unaltered, undepleted, or unpolluted in most of the West.

(On BLM land a permittee who pays to develop a water source may become sole owner of associated water rights, even to the exclusion of all others, including wildlife. This rule applies only to BLM ranchers. On BLM and most other government lands, "use-it-or-lose-it" policies encourage ranchers to develop and degrade natural water sources.)

And this cattle tank is filled via a pipe at the center from a water truck that makes its rounds once or twice a week.

A spring (indicated by the dark area at left) has been rerouted to a metal stock tank (right center), leaving the spring's channel dry. Sheldon National Wildlife Refuge, Nevada. *(George Wuerthner)*

Well drilling in BLM's central Idaho lava country. *(BLM)*

These metal cattle watering tanks are filled regularly during the grazing season with trucked water. *(BLM)*

A BLM spring has been capped and piped to this cattle trough. *(BLM)*

This open metal stock tank is fed by a pipeline. *(BLM)*

According to the Forest Service, "Hauling water on dry ranges makes available herbage for grazing that otherwise could not be used."

Stock water pipeline being installed by the BLM. *(BLM)*

Stock tanks and other ranching developments are sometimes helicoptered in to remote or less accessible areas. *(Jim Brown)*

On a larger scale, the various government agencies allow the development of many streams and rivers on public land for ranchers' use. Diversion dams, reservoirs, channels, dikes, irrigation canals, and holding ponds are all constructed on public land so ranchers can water livestock on public land and raise livestock feed on private land. These "improvements" frequently deplete most of a waterway's water and sometimes drain streams entirely, lowering water tables, further drying up springs and creeks, and so on.

For example, due to livestock production the Yellowstone River between Yellowstone National Park and Livingston, Montana (a 60-mile stretch), has only 2 instead of many tributaries whose flow still reaches the river through the summer; most water is diverted by ranchers, and the land's

water retention capacity has been diminished by overgrazing (Wuerthner 1989). In Idaho's Sawtooth National Recreation Area (established by Congress in 1972 largely to protect anadromous fish habitat) water diversions for cattle pastures by the Busterback Ranch in late summer and early fall drain the entire upper reaches of the East Fork of the Salmon River. This stretch of river is described as once teeming with some of the world's farthest-ranging chinook, sockeye, and steelhead, but now these fish are rare. The Forest Service itself calls this "the single most important resolvable problem in restoring historic anadromous fish habitat in the state of Idaho." (Bagwell 1990) A Nevada rancher was recently served a cease-and-desist order to prevent him from continuing to take all water from a stream on public land and thereby eliminating miles of riparian waterway during hay growing season each year. And in southwestern Idaho, the Bruneau Hot Springs snail is being considered for the Endangered Species list chiefly because groundwater pumping by ranching operations in its range has lowered or dried up its springs (Wuerthner 1991).

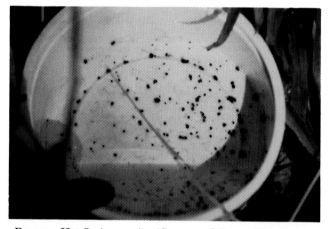

Bruneau Hot Springs snails. *(Courtesy of George Wuerthner)*

Water developments disrupt waterway dynamics, create the danger of dam-breaks and flash floods, release large amounts of sediments into waters, pollute waters with petroleum products, change water temperatures, block fish and other aquatic animal migration and movement, kill plants and animals, and more. For example, Rene J. Dubois of the Natural Resources Defense Council writes:

Channelization is a process which transforms streams into lifeless drainage canals. Bulldozers and chain saws denude the stream banks, while giant draglines cut new channels through the stream's natural bends, leaving behind piles of mud and debris. In most cases, adjacent wetlands are drained as well -- although they act as natural "sponges" absorbing floodwaters. Fish populations are virtually wiped out, waterfowl habitats are destroyed, and the recreational value of the streams is ruined.

In drought years, water diverted for livestock production sometimes reduces streamflow so drastically that fish and other aquatic animals are killed *en masse*. Such is currently the situation in Montana, where stock raisers are pushing the state to dam more streams, reimburse ranchers for leaving water in streams during dry years rather than use it for irrigation, and transfer water rights to stockmen outright. Already some Western state laws require that during drought ranching be given priority for available water, in some cases over all other uses.

A scene common to the rural West: the surface flow from this drainage is diverted for livestock pasture, livestock, and the ranch, leaving little or none for Nature and the public. *(Julia Fonseca)*

On an even larger scale, most major water development projects in the Western US were at least partially promoted by and now benefit the livestock industry, mostly to grow food for cattle. The massive environmental destruction and taxpayer waste caused by these water development boondoggles is the subject of other books, such as **Killing the Hidden Waters, Rivers of Empire**, and **Cadillac Desert**. In **A River No More**, Philip L. Fradkin relates: "Never in history has so much money been spent, so many waterworks constructed, so many political battles fought, so many lawsuits filed to succor a rather sluggish four-legged beast."

In the Northwest, livestock production accounts for over half of the water consumed in the entire region. Half of Arizona's water use is for livestock. According to a 1982 *Living Wilderness* article, 90% of the water taken from streams in the Colorado River basin is used for irrigation to grow hay and other crops for livestock (Wuerthner 1990b). Most of California's share of Colorado River water doesn't go to Los Angeles swimming pools but to irrigated pastures and cropland for cattle; overall, stockmen account for well over half of the state's water use. A recent federal hearings report on subsidized irrigation stated that 97.5% of Montana's water use was for some form of livestock production (Wuerthner 1991). Dr. Denzel Ferguson, co-author of **Sacred Cows**, reports that "Of the 100 billion gallons of water used daily in the U.S., 84% is used in 17 Western states, primarily to produce food for cows (Ferguson 1983)."

Livestock production accounts for *more than 70%* of water consumed in the 11 Western states (Hur 1985a). Moreover, in nearly half of the West (generally the most arid portions), in an average year *70% or more* of all surface water is taken, again mostly for livestock production (USDA, SCS 1981). In other words, considering these 2 factors and the loss of water flow caused by a century of livestock grazing, it becomes clear that without livestock production the volume of surface water flowing through about half of the West would be at least 2 and perhaps 3 or more times greater!

While ranchers have taken water for livestock production in most areas, they have intentionally decreased natural surface waters for livestock production in others. To utilize Western wetlands for grazing and haying, they have drained hundreds of thousands of acres of marshes, swamps, ponds, and wet bottoms -- formerly some of the most important wildlife habitat in the West. Most of this activity has occurred on private land, but its indirect effects have helped dry up public wetlands in many areas.

According to the photographer, this deep cut into a drainage in the Big Horn Mountains near Story, Wyoming, was caused by ranchers' misuse of irrigation water. *(George Robbins Photo, Jackson, WY)*

Meanwhile, back at the ranch:

Cattle visit stock tanks often. Here they congregate and spend much time, especially during the hot part of the day, lounging about, scratching, chewing cud. Thus, the area immediately surrounding tanks (springs, creeks, etc.) is severely trampled, devoid of ground cover, splattered with urine and littered with excrement. These places are commonly and rightly termed *sacrifice areas*.

The boundaries of sacrifice areas are usually well-defined as the extent of bare dirt around tanks -- commonly a radius of a few dozen yards. As the distance from tanks increases, livestock damage generally decreases, but definite impacts, associated cattle trails especially, are often discernable a mile or more away. A study at the Jornada Experimental Range in New Mexico showed that on unfenced range where stock tanks were spaced 7 to 11 miles apart, *most* vegetation was killed within 1 mile of tanks, about half was killed within 2 miles, and the impact was significant more than 4 miles away in all directions. In other words, almost the entire range was significantly affected.

A stock pond and the cattle drawn to it transform this draw's verdant landscape into a sacrifice area.. *(BLM)*

Ranchers are caretakers. In developing water sources we benefit the land, and we benefit the wildlife.
--Phelps White, past president, New Mexico Woolgrowers Association

Sure, they can say they are bringing in a permanent water supply where it was only intermittent before [often because of overgrazing] and that it helps wildlife. But they are putting it in so they can concentrate cows where cows wouldn't go before. Cattle stick pretty close to water, and they'll get all the grass and beat up the range. That's no benefit to wildlife.
--Bill Meiners, retired BLM range specialist (Luoma 1986)

According to many ranchers and range managers, their water developments are "vital" to wildlife. Many stock tanks are even called "wildlife watering tanks" by those who think the public gullible. In reality, the vast majority of tanks are built primarily to help spread livestock into lightly grazed areas, where water is scarce and cattle and sheep seldom wander. These areas are, of course, exactly where many remnant wildlife populations survive -- a convenient coincidence to justify the new "wildlife" watering projects.

Wildlife tends to shun these stock tanks, which are usually little more than nearly sterile, viscous mudholes frequented by hordes of bellowing cattle. Many large wild animals actively avoid cattle and/or sheep (and their smell), and thus tanks. Most small animals have been killed off or forced away from sacrifice areas, and many of those in surrounding areas may refuse to cross the wide "zones of nothing" around tanks, especially with livestock present. The sides of most troughs are too high for small animals to reach, anyway. Lucky for them; troughs and open metal tanks often become death traps to those birds and other small animals that do try to drink from them, fall in, can't get out, and drown. Few ranchers bother to provide "escape ramps," or even a simple stick from water line to trough or tank rim, which would save many of their lives. Needless to say, these dead animals do not enhance water quality.

less water, and can travel faster to and further from water than cattle or sheep, and many small animals drink dew or extract or metabolize most or even all the water they need from the food they eat. On the other hand, livestock's depletion of the West's most succulent vegetation has caused some wild species to depend more heavily on drinking water to maintain hydration.

Whatever the case, many stock watering developments would not have been constructed if ranching had not depleted natural vegetation and water sources in the first place. In many areas, tanks partially replace water lost to overgrazing. But livestock monopolize and degrade this replacement water and surrounding areas. According to retired BLM grazing management specialist Hugh Harper, "We are treating the symptom instead of the problem." Building artificial water sources ensures that the real problem -- livestock grazing -- will be ignored, if not worsened.

In other areas, tanks have been built where there was no surface water originally. Thus have land managers been able to "produce" certain animals, usually small numbers of elk, deer, or pronghorn, in places where they would not normally live. As shown in countless areas where non-native animals have been introduced (e.g. mountain goats in Olympic National Park, pigs in Hawaii, burros in the Southwest, cattle and sheep almost everywhere . . .), it is not a good idea to bring either wild or domestic animals into areas where they and the ecosystems

To those few wild animals that can reach them and choose to use them, open metal tanks such as this may become death traps and purveyors of disease and parasites.

Indeed, stock tanks and the livestock frequenting them are ideal purveyors of disease and parasites to what wildlife does come around. The water of dirt tanks, in which cattle trample, defecate, and urinate, usually has incredibly high bacteria and protozoa counts, and the mucky, heavily trammeled area surrounding tanks often is rife with disease and parasites.

Many stock ponds contain heavy concentrations of harmful dissolved and suspended substances, causing health problems to livestock and whatever wildlife may use them. Manure, urine, minerals, salts, settled air-borne pollutants, toxic wastes, and sediments from surrounding sacrifice areas and degraded ranges are carried down by runoff and deposited in these artificial depressions. Because these stock ponds are devoid of plantlife and open to full sun and wind, evaporation rates are astronomical, and these harmful substances build up in ever-greater concentrations, while frequent livestock trampling keeps them dissolved or in suspension.

In the context given, ranching advocates' claim that wildlife needs these foul, unnatural water sources is patently false. Most large wild animals drink less frequently, require

are not mutually adapted. This applies, for example, to winter grazing allotments where herds of sheep subsisting on snow seriously damage land normally lacking water for large numbers of ungulates.

From the standpoint of wildlife, stock watering developments differ from natural water sources in another important, but seldom considered, way: They are inherently *temporary and undependable* water supplies. Natural water sources

This obsolete BLM water development no longer produces water.

Most stock tanks are of little use to wildlife.

occur as long-established perennial surface flows, ponds, and lakes, or as intermittent -- yet relatively predictable -- springs, creeks, and ponds. Indigenous plants and animals have adapted to and depended upon these water sources for millennia. When changes in water availability did occur, they usually did so gradually enough that biota could adjust or migrate to more favorable areas.

Artificial water sources, in contrast, are nonpermanent and undependable. Take the common earth-fill dam type of tank, for instance: on the bottom of a small canyon in the hills of Southern California, a rancher uses heavy machinery to scrape out a basin and push the excavated material into a long dam across the drainage below. The basin soon fills and remains at least partly full from that point on. Assume that what wildlife survives in the grazed area comes to rely on the pond, natural water sources having been exhausted by cattle. Now, one spring day years later a snowmelt flood breeches the dam, and suddenly the tank no longer holds water. Soon thereafter, the cattle are moved to their summer pasture. The rancher doesn't repair the dam until December. In the meantime, the wild animals either die, or move out to suddenly overpopulate other areas.

Because most dirt stock tanks are built in overgrazed, flood-prone drainages, they trap large quantities of silt and other sediments. Animals, wild and domestic, sometimes get stuck and eventually die in the thick muck. Tanks often fill completely with these deposits within a few decades. At

(or before) this point, the dams themselves usually begin to crumble and wash away under the erosive influence of livestock, gravity, the elements, and floods. Because tanks are degraded by livestock and support little or no vegetation, few roots exist to hold the sediments or dams in place, as in a natural situation. When a dam finally goes, the thick, loose sediment layers filling the basin wash away quickly. What is left is a sacrifice area worse than that created by the bulldozer and livestock in the first place. Such situations are in fact very common.

Dirt tanks must be rebuilt or repaired periodically. The same holds true for all other artificial water developments; they break down or are damaged. Water may not again be available for weeks, months, or years, depending on knowledge of the occurrence, management priorities, availability of money and equipment, amount of precipitation, etc. Less efficient tanks are abandoned.

Many structural tanks are kept full only during grazing seasons, which on public land averages 4 months per year. Many other tanks are located inside corrals that are closed during periods of non-grazing. Most of the windmills and other water pumps that supply many water developments are turned off when livestock are elsewhere. In colder regions in winter, tanks that still contain water freeze over much more readily than natural water sources. To be of much use to wildlife, water sources must be clean, accessible, and dependable.

A washed-out stock tank dam on BLM land in central New Mexico. Note the size of the humans at top left.

Finally, stock tanks require an extensive network of roads for construction and maintenance, and fences to facilitate livestock utilization of the water.

In sum, stock watering developments are ugly sores upon the land. They harm ecosystems by bringing ranching degradations to areas that had little or no ranching previously. I have visited hundreds of stock tanks around the West and most have been barren, sterile, stinking, and polluted. Rarely does one see more than a few birds and insects using them. If government was really concerned with providing water to wildlife, it would stop building stock tanks and end livestock grazing.

After denudation and trampling by cattle concentrations near this BLM water development, floods from an overgrazed watershed ravaged the drainage. *(BLM)*

Close-up of the bank of a typical dirt stock tank.

On the few months per year when this trough contains water, cattle drive off what few animals would use it; when the cattle are gone, so is the water.

Roads

Cowboys weren't meant to walk ..."
--Joe B. Frantz and Julian Ernest Choate, Jr., **The American Cowboy**

Ever wonder why so many gravel and dirt roads criss-cross the Western range? So many of them seem to have no real purpose or destination.

Well, wonder no more; most are ranching roads. More roads have been blazed, bladed, and blasted through our public land to benefit the grazing industry than for any other reason. This incredibly huge and complex road network is perhaps the least recognized but most destructive of the major range developments.

Over the years, each stockman -- with help from government -- has developed roads to access nearly every portion of "his" allotment. These roads are used for building and maintaining range "improvements," implementing ranching management programs, procuring natural materials used for ranching projects, hauling supplies and water, managing and moving livestock; roads also are used as ranching firebreaks, for access to ranches themselves, and simply as a means for ranchers to oversee their vast grazing domains. In brief, they make public land accessible to and usable by the grazing industry.

The Forest Service reports more than 375,000 miles of officially acknowledged dirt roads on our National Forests, not including county, state, and federal rights-of-way; most are for logging (Foreman 1989). Many more miles traverse BLM, state, and other publicly owned lands. Additionally, hundreds of thousands of miles of unofficial, unrecognized, or de facto roads cover public land.

Typical local ranching road.

Nearly all of the West's 30,000 or so public lands grazing allotments are criss-crossed with dirt, gravel, and (occasionally) paved roads, whose main and often only purpose is for ranching. Again, each allotment averages roughly 10,000 acres, or an area about 4 miles by 4 miles if square. We may reasonably estimate that maintained ranching roads traverse each allotment at least twice, accounting for 8 miles per allotment, for a total of at least 240,000 miles.

The innumerable smaller dirt roads certainly cover at least this many miles, perhaps even an average of 1 linear mile per square mile, or twice this many miles. Thus, we may conservatively estimate that **0.5 million miles** of ranching roads exist on Western public land. This is more mileage even than for the Western public lands timber industry, whose roads are confined to comparatively small areas. Further, many timber roads are retired after logging has ceased, while ranching roads are almost always used indefinitely for ranching and other purposes. (This is not to minimize logging roads' overwhelming impact.)

Ranching roads wander along almost every valley and canyon floor, ridgetop, mountainside, plain, and plateau imaginable. In the grazed regions of the West, this vast, extensive road network provides access to almost every place grazed by livestock, leaving most of the West no more than a few miles from a road.

Many ranching roads on public land have existed for decades; some may now be used for other purposes, but generally their chief or only significant use remains ranching. Many other roads have been constructed in recent years by or with the permission of the government, usually in response to some perceived ranching need. When permission to build a road is not forthcoming, it can still be established under pretense of some other activity. For example, a rancher may obtain permission to clear a stock trail, path for a fenceline, or access to a fence post cutting area, whereafter the cleared corridor becomes the road originally wanted. New roads that access "public woodcutting areas" often become ranching roads.

Many other roads are developed illegally. Some ranchers simply blade new roads wherever they want. Why bother getting permission from government agencies that often don't care anyway? Why worry about getting caught when this remote activity is rarely viewed or understood by anyone who would inform the authorities? In the rare cases where illegal road builders have been prosecuted, they usually suffer only a slap on the wrist.

Many more -- perhaps most -- ranching roads are created as ranchers drive cross-country along convenient routes, then continue using these same tire tracks until new routes are formed. Other motorists may follow their lead. Once established, these routes are treated more or less as sanctioned roads by government. When they wash out or are somehow obstructed, ranchers simply begin driving new routes instead.

Many muddy tracks parallel the ranching road on right.

Stockmen in 4-wheel drive pickups, jeeps, all-terrain vehicles, and on dirt bikes keep these roads in a general state of disrepair because they patrol the countryside frequently, and in all kinds of weather. Wet roads become rutted, eroded mud bogs, and dry roads throw up thick plumes of lung-choking, vegetation-smothering, air- and water-polluting dust. Being familiar with these roads (and of the macho persuasion), many ranchers normally drive them at high speed, throwing up gravel and rocks that pit and crack oncoming motorists' windshields and endanger lives. Their speeding heavy-duty vehicles create "washboards" -- numerous parallel small bumps on road surfaces that make driving difficult and cause vibration damage to vehicles.

Ranching roads combined with fences beget hundreds of thousands of tax-sponsored cattle guards.

Probably most stockmen drive their vehicles *off-road* habitually, in all kinds of weather. Suppose, for instance, Rancher Clyde wants to mend a hole in a fence (or check on cattle, shoot coyotes, cut fence posts . . .) a mile from the nearest road. No problem. Clyde jumps in his pickup, drives on a road as near as possible, puts the truck in 4-wheel drive, and drives cross-country to the fence. The mile-long set of muddy ruts he left concerns him not. But now he sees an easier route back to the road, so takes that way instead. Thenceforth, he uses this latter route to access the area.

Though environmental damage from fences and stock water developments is enormous, that from ranching roads is more so. In fact, without the huge network of ranching roads, contemporary range development and livestock grazing itself would be nearly impossible.

Besides making it possible for extensive overgrazing and range development to occur, these roads have opened up huge areas -- *perhaps as much as half of public land altogether* -- to human access and abuse by a wide variety of interests. Consequently, woodcutting, hunting, plant and animal collecting, development, and off-road vehicle (ORV) use are occurring in many areas damaged by such activity. Littering, dumping of toxic wastes, theft of natural resources, artifact hunting, arson, and mindless vandalism are common along ranching roads. For example, according to ecologist Jasper Carlton, over half of human-caused "wild"fires begin along roads. Geologically fragile and botanically and zoologically sensitive areas have been opened up with reckless abandon, often with ruinous results.

More than any single human development, ranching industry roads have aided the exploitation, development, and desecration of our public lands and the rural West.

This eroded ranching road has been rerouted on the left. Coconino National Forest, Yavapai County, Arizona.

The mileage and distribution of ranching roads is mind-boggling; these roads have opened up nearly every livestock-grazed area in the West (*most* of the West) to vehicular access and its destructive impact.

Roads are themselves a substantial detriment to natural systems. First, every road is a sacrifice area. Each square foot of roadway is a square foot of biological void. Even a lone set of tire tracks across the landscape represents the denudation of about 1/8th of an acre per linear mile. Each linear mile of dirt road ruins an average of approximately 4 acres of ecosystem. Accordingly, Western public land's minimum of 500,000 miles of official and de facto ranching roads represents a bare area of about 2 million acres -- about the size of Delaware and Rhode Island combined.

A cattle guard awaiting emplacement in a highway through BLM land.

Many tons of topsoil have been excavated illegally from this site along a BLM ranching road.

Ranching roads promote all manner of environmental abuse, including illegal trash dumping.

To clear a ranching road through a riparian area, live and downed trees were bulldozed into this pile. Coronado National Forest, Arizona.

However, the overall physical impact is far greater than represented by these 2 million acres. Road construction activities kill plants and animals directly, and physically damage road sites and surrounding areas in many ways. Cut-and-fills are especially destructive as they displace and damage soil to a great depth, sever roots, destroy animals and their burrows, alter drainage patterns, and so forth. The steep slopes formed by cut-and-fills provide poor sites for vegetation reestablishment, and usually cause greatly increased water runoff and soil erosion, sometimes even landslides. Unless down to bedrock, the cut-out portion of a hill will expand until gravity and erosion finally level the slope beyond the angle of repose.

The eroded gash in this hillside is caused by runoff concentrated through a culvert under the ranching road at top.

Water infiltration through bare ground commonly is less than 1/3 that of comparable vegetated areas, so runoff from dirt roads is high. Soil damage is similar to that of extreme overgrazing. These factors combine to make dirt roadways prone to severe erosion. Many ranching roads are in fact highly eroded and washed away regularly. On steep, easily eroded slopes, they become gullies and arroyos. Roads are rerouted alongside these new drainages; eventually they too wash away and join together to form larger gulches. Runoff water and sediment from dirt roads adds to that of surrounding grazed areas, increasing sediment deposition.

Roads block waterways and drainages. Water often is rerouted through culverts or bridges, hindering or halting passage of fish and other aquatic animals. Flood dynamics are altered and drainage patterns upset. Because roads concentrate surface water flows, soil erosion downslope from roadways is accelerated, causing cutbanks. Upslope, drainages commonly are bladed and channelized with heavy equipment to funnel water through culverts.

Culverts impede the movement of aquatic life, pervert drainage patterns, cause increased downslope erosion -- and allow destructive roads to exist where they otherwise could not. *(Steve Johnson)*

Roads hamper interrelationships, fragment habitat, and create edge effects. They act as barriers to the normal movement and activity of native animals. Some very small creatures will not or cannot venture across these barren zones at all. Many small mammals, amphibians, and reptiles avoid roads, partly because they may be more easily espied and picked off by predators when on barren roadways. Some large animals, including turkey, elk, deer, mountain lions, and bears, for psychological reasons -- mainly, they associate roads with danger -- avoid crossing roads whenever possible, and are thus hampered in movement. They exhibit decreasing densities toward roads; for example, studies show that road densities of 6 miles or more per square mile can cut habitat use by elk and deer by up to 100% (Carlton 1990). Burrowing animals and soil dwellers, including worms, insects, and soil microorganisms, are blocked or killed by frozen, sun-baked, and otherwise hard-packed roadways. In summer, road surfaces may become too hot for certain reptiles, amphibians, and others to cross. For some populations and species, all these effects may lead to genetic drift and inbreeding, and thus reduced genetic viability.

Roads serve as pathways for humans and corridors for the spread of their opportunistic plants and associated pests and pathogens, thus harming wildlife and natural systems. As well, roads may effectively hamper normal migration patterns of many plant species, depending on their methods of propagation. Roads act as dams and diversions to alter runoff patterns, thereby restricting water to downhill vegetation. The overall effect on plant life can be seen along some roads, where vegetation on one side is sparser and/or composed of different species than that on the other.

Vehicular traffic scares animals and upsets their normal activities. Moving vehicles act as barriers to animal movement. Exhaust from vehicles contains heavy metals, carbon dioxide, and carbon monoxide, all of which may have a significant cumulative effect on wildlife.

Wildlife and animal rights groups estimate that 1 million vertebrate animals are killed on roadways in the United States *each day*. Ranching roads on public land cause many thousands of these deaths, not to mention killing millions of invertebrates each non-winter day.

A zebra-tailed lizard joins the mass of victims killed by Western ranching roads.

A large percentage of ranching roads must be wide and well-maintained to accommodate large stock transport vehicles. Ranchers require all-weather roads for well-drilling rigs, the transport of supplies and heavy machinery, and year-round access for ranching management and to ranch headquarters. Powerful ranching interests make sure their needs are given high priority in government road building and maintenance plans.

Indeed, as public lands ranching management becomes more intensive and range "improvements" more numerous, new ranching roads are being developed at an accelerated pace. Already, ranching roads are the single most destructive development on public land. If public lands ranching was ended and all associated roads decommissioned, what would soon follow would be one of the world's greatest environmental restorations.

Salt

Salt is a necessity to many wild and domestic animals, including livestock. A cow consumes 2 to 3 pounds of salt per month and will travel long distances to obtain the mineral. Ranchers are acutely aware of this and often use salt to coax cattle into less heavily grazed areas, in a manner similar to their use of stock ponds. In this way salt is used to distribute livestock more evenly over an allotment and thus to more fully exploit the range. In some cases this may, as claimed, lessen overgrazing in certain areas. More often, greater herbage utilization through salting simply means that a rancher spreads his livestock (sometimes *more* livestock) over more of the allotment, thereby further spreading livestock impacts.

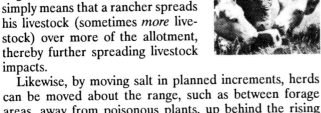

Likewise, by moving salt in planned increments, herds can be moved about the range, such as between forage areas, away from poisonous plants, up behind the rising snowline in spring and down from the lowering snowline in fall, or toward corrals at roundup. Thus, salt is a tool of livestock manipulation and range exploitation. Under both BLM and FS regulations, decisions on salting are solely the permittee's, with essentially no restrictions.

A black angus licks a mineral-salt mixture. Note the numbered ear tags.

Salt for range cattle commonly comes as 50 pound blocks. White blocks are pure sodium chloride; other colors indicate the addition of various other essential minerals. Usually salt blocks are simply thrown on the ground in the desired location. They may also be set on flat rocks or tree stumps, or placed in specially constructed salt block holders or covered feed troughs to keep them from dissolving in the rain or moist soil. This also minimizes competition from wild animals.

For convenience, ranchers most often locate salt blocks near established ranching roads, but they will punch in new roads if they feel the need. *Many thousands* of dirt roads in the West lead to nothing more than a few salt blocks. Many ranchers drive off-road across the landscape, dumping salt blocks from the back of their pickups wherever they think it

would benefit their operations, thus creating the beginnings of new roads as they go.

Salt blocks dumped only days ago are already becoming the center of a sacrifice area and surrounding range damage. BLM, southeast Oregon. *(Nancy Peterson)*

As with stock tanks, the areas around salt blocks quickly become sacrifice areas. Often covering acres, with numerous cattle trails radiating outward, many of these wastelands resemble wagon wheels when viewed from aircraft. Because trampling is so intense, and because salt tends to sterilize soil, damage may last for decades after an area is no longer used for salting livestock. *Hundreds of thousands* of salt blocks litter our public land, and each becomes the center of a sacrifice area.

Note: Bear in mind, however, that sacrifice areas are merely concentrated -- thus more obvious -- manifestations of livestock impacts. Even if livestock were distributed uniformly over the range, depending on circumstances, their overall impact may or may not be smaller.

Again, as with stock tanks, ranchers claim their salt blocks benefit wild animals and that without this salt much wildlife would perish. However, wild animals have been obtaining needed salt and minerals from food, natural licks, etc. since life began; there is clearly no need for ranchers to provide salt for wildlife.

They lie.
--Mike Roselle, activist

A wooden trough provides salt and supplemental feed to cattle, whose impacts are thus concentrated in this area. Note that the juniper, used by the cattle for shade, has lost all of its lower branches and is beginning to die. Gila National Forest, NM.

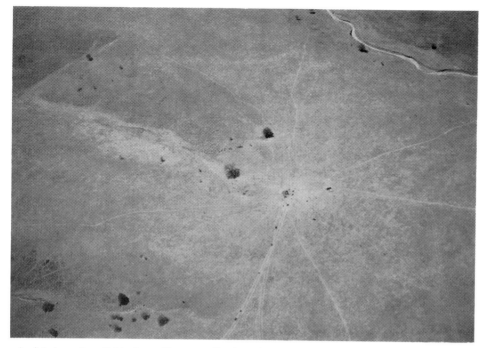

Aerial view of a salt block sacrifice area. Cattle trails radiate. Note the access roads at bottom center and the cattle (black dots). A wash stands out at upper right. *(Joanne Cockerill)*

in metal, plastic, or wooden feed troughs or thrown on the ground. All these areas, too, quickly become sacrifice areas -- localized wastelands. During hard winters or droughts, emergency supplemental feed is sometimes trucked in or dropped, at taxpayers' expense, from government planes or helicopters. BLM has been allowing long-term supplemental feeding on many desert allotments, thus allowing stocking levels in these areas to remain extremely high.

Water spreading is a technique of diverting flood waters from usually dry drainages onto the surrounding landscape with a system of dikes, dams, and/or ditches. Most water spreaders are long, low dikes bulldozed across wide, shallow drainages. Runoff is trapped and spread shallowly over a wide area behind the dike, with the intention of promoting forage growth, though it may or may not occur. Thousands of water spreaders have been built with tax monies on public land, many of them stretching across the range for a mile or more. Each one kills animals, scars the land with heavy equipment, displaces large amounts of topsoil, and robs runoff from downhill areas. Furthermore, their cost is not nearly compensated for by the increased amount of forage. Studies by the US Soil Conservation Service and the Bureau of Indian Affairs show only a slight increase in forage production, and that the costs to construct and maintain water spreaders are at least several times higher than the maximum benefits attained (Calef 1960).

Other Range Developments

Supplemental feeding creates sacrifice areas and exacerbates overgrazing.

On a properly and lightly stocked range, livestock would theoretically obtain all necessary calories and nutrients from native plants. But because public ranges are vastly overstocked and livestock are grazed when, where, and how they shouldn't be, supplemental feeding is a common practice -- even on BLM land, where supplemental feeding is officially not allowed except for "protein blocks" and other highly concentrated supplements. (These concentrated supplements allow an animal's digestive system to utilize less palatable vegetation, thus intensifying overgrazing.) When range livestock become chronically hungry or deficient in certain nutrients, they must be provided with imported food, or they will suffer and die. Various feeds -- hay, alfalfa pellets, block, cube, and meal mixtures, sometimes mixed with salt and/or minerals -- are supplied to livestock

Other range "improvements" on public land include *tens of thousands* of corrals, pens, and associated equipment. Corrals are used for sorting and handling livestock, especially at roundup. Pens are used for separating breeding animals from steers and heifers; dehorning, castrating, and branding; shearing sheep; dealing with sick or injured animals; holding work horses; and so on.

Within the corral area are chutes and loading ramps, and perhaps a scale for weighing. There may be a cattle "squeeze" for restraining animals; special compartments or chutes for spraying cattle and sheep with insecticides, fungicides, and fumigants; or a dipping vat for treating livestock for external parasites. Also within the corral area may be fences to funnel livestock into the corral; feed and water troughs; salt blocks; sun shades; and storage for fence posts, wire, oil, fuel, and other supplies.

The land in and around a corral becomes a super sacrifice area -- especially degraded by trampling, concentrations of manure and urine, spilled oil, fuel, chemicals, etc. With their large truck parking areas and tight networks of roads and cattle trails, most of these corral sacrifice areas represent the environmental obliteration of at least an acre, and, in many cases 5 or more acres of public land.

A corral in the (former) grassland of central California. Note the cattle trails leading toward the hills.

This corral under cottonwoods along the Rio Grande River, New Mexico, may seem pretty, but like all other corrals it is a sacrifice area. Ranching roads lead everywhere, there are no small cottonwoods, lower tree branches are gone, the ground is mostly bare, and cattle desecrate the nearby river. Stockmen often establish corrals in or near riparian areas for the purposes of easily locating water-oriented cattle, providing them herbage and shade, and procuring fence and corral building materials.

A corral made from cut trees and associated sacrifice area in dense forest, Kaibab National Forest, Arizona.

Where rivers, spring runoff, or deep gorges prevent sheep from crossing, government and/or ranchers build sheep bridges, some of which are quite extravagant. Similarly, where natural obstacles block rancher access, various kinds of cable crossings may be installed, again usually at government expense, often ostensibly for non-ranching purposes such as "public access," "fire fighting access," and the nebulous and baseless "to facilitate land management."

Tax-sponsored monuments glorify stock driveways on public land.

Stock driveways are wide, cleared zones allowing "trailing" of whole herds from place to place, usually from one grazing area to another or between ranch bases. *Stock trails* are simply trails used for the same purposes, though generally for smaller numbers of livestock. These "improvements" may be constructed anywhere a rancher deems it necessary to clear a path for more efficient movement of livestock, often through areas of rockiness, timber, or brush. There are tens of thousands of miles of stock driveways and stock trails on Western public land, which are in effect tens of thousands of acres of sacrifice area. Their environmental impact is similar to roads.

Ranchers cut or blast stock pathways into steep slopes and notches through obstructing steep-sided ridges, cliffs, saddles, rims, etc. to allow livestock passage. They cut openings through streamside vegetation and cut stream banks down to allow livestock access to water. They slash their way through thick forests and dense undergrowth. They even build "walkways" of firm ground into marshes, wet bottoms, and areas of overflow so cattle have access to as much forage as possible. Stockmen also cut and remove vegetation and displace rocks and soil to make trails for themselves and pack trails for their horses, so they may more easily move about allotments.

Shacks sometimes are built on public land to house cowmen or sheepmen attending to business in remote parts of the range. Range riders develop temporary and permanent campsites, often removing vegetation in the process, cutting and filling soil, constructing crude log or rock shelters, building fire rings, depleting local firewood, and scattering trash about -- thus creating human sacrifice areas. Their horses further deplete vegetation and trample soil.

A firebreak along a roadside fence. Ironically, the grass on grazed side is generally too sparse to carry fire!

Range fixtures also include tens of thousands of stone, metal, and concrete monuments that mark the boundaries of grazing allotments, as well as metal and wooden signs. Most are built or installed with tax dollars.

Tens of thousands of miles of firebreaks scar Western rangeland. Whether bladed, herbicided, or disced, the environmental impact is similar to that of dirt roads. And, as discussed, the ranching industry's great reduction of natural fire has been one of its most destructive influences.

Range "improvements" also include developments designed to restore livestock productivity to land degraded by livestock. This would include, for example, contour furrowing of overgrazed hillsides to reduce soil erosion and help reestablish forage. Other restoration developments include contour trenching; terracing and terrace stabilization; check dams and instream structures; rip-rap on banks; grass seedings and plantings of shrubs, bushes, and trees; and range fertilizations. Though all of these developments and more are necessitated by and constructed to improve livestock grazing, they are rarely directly linked to livestock grazing in government land management plans.

Additionally, phone, electric, water, and gas lines run long distances over public land to service public lands ranches, necessitating utility corridors and concomitant environmental damage. Considering that there are 30,000 base properties (not to mention auxiliary operations, electric pumps, etc.

A semi-permanent sheep camp on BLM range near Lovell, Wyoming, becomes a sacrifice area and helps spread overgrazing to the surrounding area. Hired cowboys live at these camps for weeks at a time. The agencies tell us that to prevent damage from long-term use, no one may spend more than 2 weeks in any one location on BLM or Forest Service land -- no one but stockmen, that is. *(George Robbins Photo, Jackson, WY)*

out on the range) spread more or less evenly across the rural West, necessitating *tens of thousands* of miles of utility lines and service roads, environmental damage from just the utility services for public lands ranching is clearly enormous.

The grazing industry is responsible for a bewildering array of other developments, contrivances, and environmental alterations which degrade our public land -- too many to detail here. For example, snow fences may be constructed on public land to protect developments such as corrals, pumphouses, and ranching roads. Wood, metal, or rock shelters protect livestock from winter storms. Even wind-blocks for livestock may be built; researchers are currently testing designs such as V-shaped and semi-circular high, solid fences.

Some "improvements" are so lacking in realistic justification that they may be considered little more than environmental vandalism. Actual examples include cutting down an entire pinyon tree to get a good fence post from the top, bulldozing a stand of brush so cattle may be more easily *seen* on the other side, and taking a chainsaw to a large, dead tree because the stump made a good place to set a salt block.

Range Management

Fences, tanks, roads, salt, corrals, and other "fixed" developments are one form of what the ranching establishment commonly terms "range improvements." Another involves general manipulation of the environment, and is perhaps more properly called "range management." This includes eradicating unwanted vegetation, seeding rangeland, killing predators, and so forth.

In their century-long effort to force the environment to conform, stockmen have offered a remarkable range of suggestions for range management. For example, some ranchers think the government should destroy entire forests to enhance their livestock operations. Some would seed whole allotments to exotic forage grasses. Many propose killing every large predator in their state.

What has actually occurred would shock most people. Most Western public land is subject to range management, and already a large percentage has been developed for ranching, the vast bulk utilizing our tax dollars. This ranges from national soil conservation programs, to state-assisted brush eradication projects, to county aid in poisoning gophers on a 5-acre piece of land. All have one thing in common: they pervert Nature to benefit ranching.

Plant Enemies

With the zeal of missionaries bringing The Word to heathens, range "scientists" are busy justifying the annihilation of certain ecosystems. This holy war is being fought with chainsaws, bulldozers, chains, torches, poison, and, like all wars, lots of propaganda. An entire vocabulary of pejoratives surrounds these efforts at biocide . . . . This rangespeak bears as much relation to science as the rantings of the new right evangelists bear to philosophy and logic.
--"Le Chat Noir," an environmentalist

As we now know, during the past century and a half livestock grazing has severely reduced or eliminated most native forage plants. Be that as it may, before Euro-American settlers arrived much of the West was covered by livestock-unpalatable vegetation. Forage plants were certainly important components of most vegetation regimes, but often other species were significant or dominant. Nonetheless, ranchers and range managers proceed blindly, assuming forage grasses are the ultimate goal for any landscape. (Of course, livestock consume a great variety of plants, but grass is the most profitable.)

We also have the dubious distinction as well regarding the number of species of undesirable vegetation. Let me list some of them: 1. Pinyon and juniper 2. Creosote bush 3. Mesquite 4. Cholla (pronounced CHOY-YA) 5. Oak shinnery 6. Sagebrush 7. Prickly pear.
--David W. King, President, New Mexico Association of Natural Resource Conservation Districts (USDA, USDI, CEQ 1979)

Consider the terminology used by vested interests to describe plants they don't like: "worthless," "unwanted," "unacceptable," "undesirable," "inferior," "rank," "overgrown," "overmature," "noxious," "poisonous," "decadent," "weedy." "Undesirable" to what? "Inferior" for what, and to whom? Why are plants "rank" when allowed to grow up closely together as they normally do instead of being eaten by livestock? Is a plant, any more than an animal, "overgrown" when reaching full size? When it gets old, is it "overmature," not deserving of life? (Is Grandpa "overmature"? Should he be put to death?) Why are plants termed "noxious" or "poisonous" when many animals other than cattle and sheep eat them? Can plants be "decadent"? What, really, are "weeds"?

Most of these terms would be laughable if not so widely accepted. We have been indoctrinated to believe that non-forage plants on rangeland are inherently "bad," that they have no justification for existence.

They [native "increasers"] are stable because millennia of co-evolution provided a full complement of native pathogens and debilitating creatures to limit these plants.

Nevertheless, because they are economically undesirable -- because we wish they weren't there -- much propaganda still portrays them as rogue organisms that have broken out and will destroy range, wildlife and the Western Way of Life if not beaten back by technology.
--Sam Bingham, "Barbarians Within Agriculture's Gates" (Bingham 1990)

So strong is our society's ranching orientation that we have been convinced that non-forage plants are not only bad, but even unnatural. To hear many ranchers talk, one would think these plants were practically nonexistent when livestock arrived in the West. Forbs, flowering annuals and perennials, and other non-woody, non-forage plants, they say, were "transitional" in nature, occurring only rarely where some major disturbance had temporarily cleared off the otherwise omnipresent grass cover. Supposedly, brush, shrubs, cacti, yucca, ocotillo, and other woody plants occurred naturally only in small stands in rugged terrain. Junipers and pinyons, they tell us, used to grow only in tiny stands on steep hillsides and rocky ridges. According to many of these people, even the West's coniferous forests have expanded greatly in size. These assertions correctly or partially apply to some areas, but as blanket statements they are ridiculous.

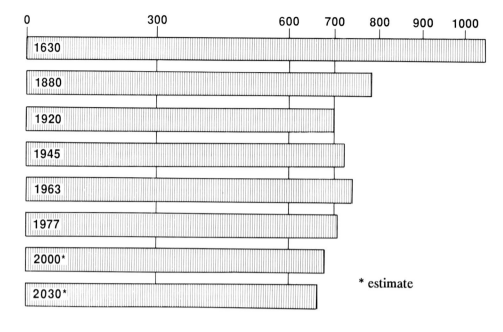

US LAND AREA IN FOREST (millions of acres)
(Source: US Forest Service) Note: This graph merely reflects acreage in trees, not forest *quality*.

Ranching promoters have painted themselves into a corner. On one hand, they insist that non-forage vegetation is native to only tiny portions of the West, that because of this most of the West should be managed for forage vegetation almost exclusively -- that is, for livestock forage. On the other, they don't quite know how to refute the overwhelming evidence that livestock grazing is what eliminated most forage in the first place. To escape this quandary, the industry has over the years developed a number of scapegoats: climatic changes; invasion of woody and weedy vegetation (it's the plants' fault); fire suppression; human causes; natural causes. The falsity of these claims is demonstrated elsewhere in this book.

Then again, many ranching advocates don't even bother with explanations or justifications. They see the West as a giant board upon which they play "Vegetation Manipulation for Maximum Profit." These people see the world as merely a collection of resources, and with themselves as managers of those resources for whatever goals they choose. What is natural doesn't matter. There need be no rationalization for manipulating ecosystems, for it is their manifest destiny to direct all natural processes towards their goals. This reality is unfortunately common to our modern world, from former Interior Secretary James Watt, who said that we may as well use up the world's resources now because Armageddon is coming, to range consultant Allan Savory, who insists that livestock can be used to mold the Earth into virtually anything we choose it to be, to the typical BLM range manager, who embraces some degree of both.

In many areas of the Forest, livestock graze in and adjacent to timber sale areas. Timber harvest removes woody vegetation allowing shrubs and grasses to increase for a period of time before trees become dominant again. The extra forage produced during this period can be used to increase cattle . . .
--US Forest Service

The grazing industry's plant enemies fall into 3 main groups -- trees, "weeds," and brush. That trees are natural to much of the Western landscape stockmen cannot deny, nor would the public tolerate the denuding of whole forests simply to create more livestock pasture, as they do with brushlands and "weed" areas. Besides, most Western forests provide a tolerable amount of livestock herbage anyway; widely-spaced trees allow plenty of sunlight to reach the forest floor, usually providing for a good covering of forage and browse plants. On open rangeland, a few trees per acre is even considered desirable as summer shade for livestock. Nonetheless, ranchers prefer to maximize profits by minimizing sun-blocking trees. Toward this end, they have for decades cut, ripped, burned, poisoned, and generally killed trees. In "Forest Land Grazing," Kingery and Graham relate that, "In the past, carrying capacity for livestock in forested areas was routinely increased by removing tree cover." The federal government reports that more than 260 million acres of US forests have been cleared *specifically for livestock* -- an area nearly the size of Texas and California combined.

This ranching deforestation continues today. John Robbins explains in **Diet for a New America**:

Since 1967 the rate of deforestation in this country has been one acre every five seconds. Many think our forests are being cleared to make room for urban development. But in fact, for each acre of American forest that is cleared to make room for parking lots, roads, houses, shopping centers, etc. seven acres of forest are converted into land for grazing livestock and/or growing livestock feed. (Robbins 1987)

More than 2/3 of the 70 million acres of US forest cleared between 1967 and 1975 was converted to grazing land, and most forest clearing still is for livestock production (Akers 1983). While much of this has been in the East, forests there generally regrow and heal more quickly than in the West. And while Eastern deforestation is generally more openly geared toward livestock production, Western stockmen needn't be so directly involved; as mentioned, most Western forests are naturally more open and sunny, and, moreover, the government and other land users do most deforestation for them.

On public land, the various governments conduct forest thinning, herbiciding, and prescribed burning -- usually ostensibly to benefit forest health or timber programs, sometimes openly to promote livestock grazing. Whatever the expressed or actual purpose, these programs benefit the ranching industry. Most forest areas with commercial quality timber have been logged at least once, many areas twice or thrice. Livestock grazing potential is a strong consideration behind many government timber plans, though this is rarely acknowledged, and, by the agencies' admission, logging is a main component of government long-range plans to expand grazing. The agencies often allow increased grazing in logged-over areas, especially clearcuts. Once logging opens up a forest area to allow a certain level of grazing, ranching interests do their utmost to keep the area as sparsely-treed in the future. At times this has resulted in conflicts between ranchers and loggers, but the level of grazing possible and allowed on most logged public forests is sufficient to keep ranchers satisfied.

Thus, other than the timber establishment, the grazing establishment is the strongest influence behind denudation of public forests. According to the USDA's *An Assessment of the Forest and Land Situation in the United States*:

Two half-square-miles deforested primarily for cattle grazing. BLM, Beaver County, western Utah.

> *Significant opportunities to increase range grazing occur on portions of the 488 million acres of commercial forest land. Commercial harvesting of mature tree stands will often result in temporary (5 to 10 years) production of grasses, shrubs, and forbs that are palatable to livestock. Intensive timber management practices such as thinning, pruning, and site preparation can be modified in scope, timing, and intensity to increase the amount, and to extend the period of forage production . . . (USDA, FS 1980)*

The National Cattlemen's Association and other public ranching organizations recently co-signed a National Forest Products Association letter to Forest Service Chief F. Dale Robertson demanding that the Allowable Sale Quantity in forest plans be *mandated*.

Thinning slash piled and ready to burn -- in preparation for increased livestock grazing. Black Hills National Forest, eastern Wyoming.

Forest thinning allows increased use by livestock. Apache-Sitgreaves National Forest, east-central Arizona.

Many "wildlife enhancement" projects on public forests entail tree thinning or clearing, usually, it is said, to benefit elk or deer. Roads, water developments, and fences are installed, and, curiously, livestock numbers are raised. Though an area may then be thrashed by cattle, the presence of a few more elk or deer will prompt range managers and ranchers to trumpet the "success" of the "wildlife" project.

Equally deceptive are many of the "firewood cutting" programs on public lands. Often, when stockmen want a grazing area thinned or cleared of trees not of sufficient size or quality for commercial logging, they pressure the agencies to open it -- often with new roads -- to commercial or personal-use firewood cutting. As expressed in a federal brush management manual, "The potential for harvesting cordwood should not be overlooked as an added incentive in the management of mesquite, juniper, oaks, and other appropriate species." Having woodcutters saw trees down and haul them away is profoundly easy for the ranching establishment. The cutters get the wood, the government the credit, the ranchers the profit, and the land and the public the shaft. The new roads become ranching roads; fencing, grass seeding, and stock water projects are begun; and small trees are killed from that point on. Presto! -- overgrazed woodland becomes overgrazed ranchland.

Another scam cooked up by Western ranchers in collaboration with self-serving water resource departments and their powerful constituents involves pushing government agencies to eradicate trees and brush to "improve watersheds." Watersheds stripped of their trees and brush, they say, shed water like a tin roof, shooting the increased runoff quickly down through drainages to fill reservoirs, where it may then be used by cities and agriculture. After the land is denuded, it is seeded with livestock grasses, and from that point on cut, burned, or sprayed to keep it free of woody vegetation. The vested interests may then claim that the increased grass cover infiltrates and releases more water into waterways than the original vegetation -- disregarding, of course, the impact of increased overgrazing.

Studies show that these projects generally don't produce much, if any, more water for reservoirs because devegetation, attendant soil damage, and overgrazing deplete prolonged surface flow. They also show that the money, materials, and effort expended, coupled with the environmental damage, don't begin to justify the extra water, and that woody vegetation must be re-eradicated indefinitely.

However, they usually do produce more livestock forage, and often this is a main reason our taxes keep being squandered.

For example, in Arizona thousands of acres of upland forest and brush have been cut, herbicided, and burned in an attempt to increase forage for livestock and water to the Phoenix metropolitan area. The Tonto National Forest's effort to keep Pinal Mountain grassy spawned one of the biggest conservation battles in Arizona history, as well as a book entitled **Sue the Bastards**. In another Arizona fiasco, the government spent millions of dollars on the Beaver Creek Project in Coconino National Forest to cut ponderosa pines, junipers, oaks, and brush from hundreds of acres to produce, according to a newspaper editorial, "about enough water to wet a dishcloth," and some additional forage. Yet, an association of government agencies is currently studying the prospects for vastly expanded devegetation in central Arizona forest and chaparral.

Another form of this ripoff involves eradicating trees and brush along waterways because they "drink up and transpire huge quantities of water." This has led to all sorts of crazy schemes, like a recent proposal by Arizona state officials to kill all cottonwoods along several rivers. This was done in the early 1970s by the New Mexico Soil and Conservation Service along a portion of the Mimbres River in southwest New Mexico. As related by Sharman Apt Russel in **Songs of the Fluteplayer**,

> They believed eliminating these great trees, some more than a hundred years old, would mean more forage for cattle. . . . Without the cottonwoods to hold the soil with their roots and break the impact of water, subsequent small floods swept over the denuded ground like an efficient mowing machine. When the channel was dry again, the eroded result could only charitably be called a river.

While it is a known fact that plants transpire water, any high school ecology student also knows that riparian vegetation also conserves water, as well as physically protecting waterways and providing many other benefits. However, less trees and brush means more forage, which means more livestock grazing.

Logging, forest health management, wildlife enhancement, wood cutting, or watershed or waterway improvement -- whatever the intentions -- stockmen are the long-term beneficiaries. Though they aid and abet whenever possible and are even in many cases the main motivating influence, they keep a low profile. Why incur public resentment for destroying trees when the government and other land users are doing it for them?

In quantity, leaves of some tree species can be poisonous to livestock, and they may be removed for that reason. Pine needles are blamed for Western livestock losses totaling millions of dollars. A recent article in the *Lassen County* [CA] *Times* is entitled "Pine Needles Threat to Pregnant Cows"; much of Lassen County and the West is covered with pines. While some ranchers are calling for action on this "problem," most are thus far reluctant to call for widespread "pine eradication" programs for this reason.

A killer [ungrazable plant] *is invading Montana! Like a cancer it is spreading at runaway speed, getting out of control, and destroying its victims* [ranchers].

--from an article in **The Stockmen's Journal**

Weeds, according to Emerson, are "plants whose virtues have not yet been discovered." But according to M.E. Ensminger in **The Stockman's Handbook,** "A weed may be defined as a plant (1) growing where it is not wanted and interfering with desired land use, or (2) with a negative economic value within the framework of current land use." According to ranching reality, then, a weed is any leafy, non-woody plant that detracts from livestock operations. Plants now called weeds were components of almost every pristine vegetation com-

"Larkspur -- a rangeland weed," according to the Forest Service. *(USFS)*

munity in the West. Even on the "pure" grassland of the prairies, many non-grass species flourished among the grasses, in separate stands, and where fire, animal activity, rocks, drainages, etc. interrupted the grass cover.

Forest Service employee poisoning larkspur via backpack sprayer. *(USFS)*

Approximately 455 acres of wet meadows will be sprayed in the Apache National Forest [Arizona] in June to control the wild iris . . . . The control project is part of the range improvement program on the Burro Creek Range Allotment.
--Arizona Daily Star, Tucson, AZ

Stockmen disdain "weeds" for many reasons. A great many, such as tumbleweed, mustard, thistle, cheatgrass, and yarrow, are of low palatability; as increasers or invaders, they have replaced forage plants over large areas. Some -- coneflower, ragweed, and paintbrush, for example -- are marginally grazable. Soil cryptogams are considered weeds because they allegedly prevent the establishment of forage. Locoweed, Johnson grass, milkweed, tansy mustard, goldenrod, threadleaf groundsel, larkspur, lupine, wild parsnip, and many other plants can be poisonous to cattle and sheep. (The government occasionally fences off poisonous plants from livestock, rather than eradicating

them.) Others, such as cheatgrass, foxtail, and various sticker-producing plants, may physically harm livestock. Some plants are destroyed because they are highly flammable. Some "drink up too much water." Some benefit insects and other wild animals not acceptable to the grazing industry. They damage or block stock watering developments. They hamper ranching activities. They're rank, coarse, unruly, stickery, stinky, strange: almost any excuse will do when an increase in preferred forage is the ultimate goal.

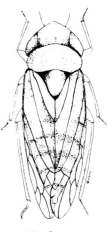

A leafhopper.

Interestingly, most of these plants are natives and, if not for stockmen, would not now be considered "weeds." Those that have increased their numbers and range have done so under the influence of livestock grazing. As related by range professional D. Griffiths in 1910, "The perennials, or more valuable species, have, it is true, disappeared; but they were not driven out by annuals, but on the contrary, by the rancher's cattle" (Griffiths 1910). Many other weeds are exotics that overgrazing has spread over huge areas.

Brush is the mortal enemy of the range manager . . . .
--Boysie E. Day, Professor of Plant Physiology, University of California, Berkeley (USDA, USDI, CEQ 1979)

Ranching roads and brush clearing open up formerly inaccessible, unexploitable, and unspoiled areas to livestock grazing and other harmful developments.

Healthy stands of brush provide for many and various animals, ecodiversity, productive watersheds, recreational use, and aesthetic enjoyment. Be that as it may, brush is the plant type most persecuted by the ranching establishment. Not only does brush reduce forage more than any other vegetation type, but it is the hardest to eradicate. Brush may "hide predatory animals," obscure views of livestock, or physically injure livestock with long spines or sharp, broken branches. Some species have poisonous leaves. Brush hinders the movement of livestock and cowboys.

Chaparral near Sequoia National Park, California, has been stripped from these ridges to increase cattle forage.

Ranching advocates similarly argue that brush never occurred as climax communities, that bushes and shrubs are merely "disturbance species" that occupy disturbed lands until grass once again covers the land. This may be true for some species in some areas, but much evidence suggests that *most* Western brushlands and shrublands have been around in one form or another for millennia (see Malin 1956, Thwaites 1959, etc.).

For example, though today big sagebrush covers fully 100 million acres -- more than 1/8 of the American West -- research indicates that it has increased its range only slightly, and that the significant change has been the increase in sagebrush *density* at the expense of other vegetation (Vale 1980). Regardless, more than 12% of sagebrush territory has been cleared of sage for livestock (though usually it eventually regrows under continued livestock grazing and lack of fire) (Ferguson 1983).

Some brush species provide livestock browse, but ranchers much prefer the potentially greater amount of herbage provided by grass. They see brushland as potential grassland. To them, every bush eliminated is that much grass gained. To this end they even kill individual brush plants. With brush eradication projects, some involving hundreds or thousands of acres, they have destroyed millions of acres of aboriginal brush.

Indeed, many brush eradication projects occur in places that never were primarily grass. Often it is assumed that any place with the apparent potential to grow grass originally was grassland, or, if not, at least *should* be grassland. And, with a few magic words from some industry "range expert," a brush eradication project is under way.

Through subsidization, brush clearance has grown to become an agricultural industry. It is a significant source of income for various seed, chemical, and machinery interests.
--Ian McMillan, **Man and the California Condor** (McMillan 1968)

The large acreage involved in shrub eradication projects is a telling commentary on the economic power and political influence of the range livestock industry in the intermountain West.
--Thomas R. Vale, "The Sagebrush Landscape" (Vale 1980)

Over vast areas, livestock have *reduced* the cover of shrubs and brush along with herbaceous ground cover. Ungrazed roadside on right.

Again, stockmen claim that brush has "invaded" and ruined their once-productive, grass-covered ranges. Again, partly true. However, in many areas overgrazing has actually killed off the original woody cover. This is especially true of arid regions, sensitive transition zone brushlands, low-elevation broadleaf woodlands, and riparian areas.

According to the ranching reality-makers, half or more of the area of former Western grassland has been "invaded" by shrubs, brush, trees, and weeds. According to USDA, "noxious" plants have "taken over" tens of millions of overgrazed acres and cost ranchers roughly $107 million annually in livestock deaths, birth defects, abortions, or emaciation. But calling it an "invasion" is a tremendous distortion. By growing a covering of woody plants or other vegetation unpalatable to livestock, in a sense the land protects itself from further overgrazing.

Stockmen's answer is to kill the offending plants, instigate range developments, and *increase* livestock numbers, leading to more unwanted vegetation, more eradication, more developments; in short, endlessly staving off livestock impacts and maintaining livestock numbers with more and more range management. Stockmen do not tolerate livestock reductions. Instead, the land itself must be changed, or grazing systems, or agency management, or even people's perception of the problem.

To maximize livestock production, ranchers and range managers seek to maximize vegetation that benefits livestock by minimizing that which doesn't. This is euphemistically called "type conversion" -- changing the vegetation from one type to another. In truth, stockmen find reason to kill nearly every kind of plant but preferred grass. Since so little preferred grass remains, vegetation manipulations are usually designed to erase *all* vegetation in a given area, in hopes that new growth will contain more grass. In so doing, the industry gives itself a "clean slate" on which to create a livestock-oriented landscape.

Since the early 1900s most biotic manipulation on public grazing allotments has been done by the various governments, bolstered in 1974 by the Federal Noxious Weed Act. Today, under a variety of rationales and pretenses, nearly every public land management unit in the West conducts vegetation eradication. Many means have been developed over the years. They are used singly or in various combinations now under the buzz phrase "integrated pest management." Described below are the 6 basic methods.

Mechanical Methods

Numerous and sundry mechanical means are employed to physically destroy plant enemies. Prominent among these is "chaining," in which a heavy chain (or a heavy cable) is dragged between 2 crawler-type tractors to rip out all woody plants. The heavy equipment and huge anchor chain kill wild animals, destroy nests and burrows, kill many non-woody plants, damage the soil, drag and dislocate large rocks, and generally trash the land. In **This Land Is Your Land**, Bernard Shanks reports that chaining has likewise effaced hundreds of federally "protected" Native American ruins and archaeological sites (Shanks 1984). After chaining, the woody debris is burned or left to rot.

In an average year hundreds of square miles of Western public land are chained, hundreds or even thousands of acres at a time. Utah State University research scientist Ronald Lanner a decade ago found that more than 3 million acres (the size of Connecticut) of public pinyon/juniper land had been chained for cow pasture (Shanks 1984). Lanner recently stated that the weight of published research does not support any of the reasons used to condone chaining. Yet,

common to the remote West is the chained landscape -- thousands of broken juniper, pinyon, greasewood, or sage skeletons scattered about the ravaged land, a few cows seeking forage among them.

A harrow is an agricultural implement consisting of a row or rows of metal teeth, spikes, or upright discs protruding downward from a supporting frame. Harrows are dragged across public land behind tractors to kill shrubs, brush, and other "unacceptable" vegetation. Similarly, railroad rails, channel irons, "H"-beams, and other heavy implements are pulled across the ground to break off and kill brittle shrubs in what is generally termed "railing." Environmental damage is similar to chaining.

Public land is even plowed and disced as if it was private farmland. With these techniques, soil is penetrated and displaced to the depth of a foot or more to kill offending vegetation -- sagebrush, creosote, and "weedy" plants in particular. These methods not only destroy *all* plants but damage topsoil, increase soil erosion, and destroy animals, soil dwellers especially, and their habitat.

Towed units chop as well as crush for better brush and slash treatment. On steeper slopes these units should be towed up and down the slopes to prevent erosion and avoid sideslip. Rolling choppers should move at high speeds for maximum effect. Production rates vary from two to nine acres per hour.
--From *Range Seeding and Brush Management* by Gilbert L. Jordan

Other machines and implements are driven or pulled across public land, raking, mowing, cutting, crushing, chopping, beating, shredding, and otherwise destroying "undesirable" vegetation. Sometimes vegetation is simply scraped off the land with bladed bulldozers. "Root plowing"

Chaining trees and brush in an attempt to increase cattle forage. *(SCS,USDA)*

by large tractors destroys brush roots to a depth of a foot or more. Some machines "grub" individual bushes or trees, cutting, ripping, and yanking roots, pushing or pulling plants out of the ground. Grubbing and "weed" killing are also accomplished by hand, with axes, mattocks, spades, and hoes.

The 72-ton machine ("tree crusher") uproots, crushes, and splinters juniper trees in one operation. Because most trees are pushed out of the ground before being crushed, the percent kill is high (about 80%). On fairly level terrain, this machine can crush about 4 ha [10 acres] per hour.
--from **Range Management** (Holechek 1989)

A BLM rotor-beater brush removal in Elmore County, Idaho. *(BLM)*

A BLM sage disking operation. *(BLM)*

Discing the range in the central California hills.

BLM land in Hamlin Valley, Beaver County, Utah.

A crawler tractor piling brush. *(SCS, USDA)*

Chainsaws are a favorite tool for increasing livestock production. BLM, McKinley County, New Mexico.

Large stands of trees and brush often are felled with chainsaws. Smaller stands may be cut with hand saws, axes, machetes, and brush hooks. Another method of "control" is "girdling" -- cutting off a strip of bark around the circumference of the trunk of a tree or large bush, which will kill it. Trees, brush, and weeds alike -- ranchers and range managers eradicate the unwelcome plants by just plain hacking away with axes, mattocks, hoes, spades, bushwhackers, weed whackers, hatchets, pruners, pocket knives, and potato peelers.

After vegetation is uprooted, cut, or by whatever manner taken to pieces, it may be pushed or raked into rows (windrowed) or piles and burned to prepare the land for intensified livestock grazing. Roads, fences, tanks, and other "improvements" may then be installed and management further intensified.

In Texas, where the golden-cheeked warbler depends upon mature Ashe juniper for nesting, removal of junipers as a range-improvement measure caused such a serious reduction in numbers that it was declared a threatened species by the U.S. Fish and Wildlife Service.
--Denzel and Nancy Ferguson, **Sacred Cows** (Ferguson 1983)

Chemical Methods

Without chemicals, life itself would be impossible.
--A motto of Monsanto chemical company

Aerial application of herbicides affords the possibility of chemically treating half of the United States acreage at one time or another.
--Maureen K. Hinkle, Environmental Defense Fund (USDA, USDI, CEQ 1979)

Herbicide application is a comparatively easy way for ranchers to destroy large areas of less-profitable vegetation (especially since the government usually does the work and the taxpayer foots the bill). Unlike mechanical methods, herbicides can quickly denude thousands of acres at a time.

This explains the strong push by the ranching establishment to increase herbicide use on public lands. With almost religious fervor, many recommend its application for virtually every vegetation eradication proposal. Behind it all are the huge national and multi-national chemical companies with their multi-million dollar promotion campaigns. With convincing presentations, they offer a variety of herbicides as the answer to a host of range problems created

"Spike got the brush. I got the grass."

An ad for range herbicide. Look closely. *(Julia Fonseca)*

or perceived by the grazing industry.

Major herbicides used on public ranges today include 2,4-D, Picloram, Dicamba, Atrazine, Dalapon, Tebuthiuron, Glyphosate, and Hexazinone. Of these, 2,4-D accounts for a large percentage of acreage "treated." Range managers sometimes test combinations of these.

The commonly used rangeland herbicides 2,4,5-T (a defoliant used in the Vietnam War) and Silvex were finally banned by the Environmental Protection Agency (EPA) in the early 1980s when they were found to be carcinogenic. They contain dioxin, a deadly poison shown to have adverse effects on wild and experimental animals. Dr. Diane Courtney, head of the Toxic Effects Branch of EPA's National Environmental Research Center, states that dioxin is "by far the most toxic chemical known to mankind," while Dow Chemical states that "2,4,5-T is about as toxic as aspirin." Near where 2,4,5-T was sprayed in Oregon National Forests, pregnant women experienced increased miscarriages, and birth defects, prompting rural rebellions with angry locals shooting at spray helicopters. Silvex and 2,4,5-T were outlawed under public pressure, and despite years of irrational defense by the chemical, timber, and ranching industries.

A Forest Service helicopter spraying herbicide on vegetation noxious to livestock. Beaverhead National Forest, MT. *(USFS)*

By far most range herbicide is applied in spray solution from small aircraft and helicopters equipped with sprayers. It may also be applied with boom-type broadcast sprayers mounted on trucks or pulled behind tractors, or with hand sprayers. The poison lands on foliage, enters through the leaf surface, and is translocated to the root system, where it kills the plant. Some herbicide comes in dry "bullets" or pellets, which may be applied aerially or by hand from vehicles, horseback, or on foot. These "soil applied" herbicides enter the soil in solution with precipitation and directly kill plants when absorbed by the roots. Trees and bushes may be killed individually with subsoil and trunk herbicide injectors.

There are 70 million acres of mesquite, 76 million acres of juniper, 96 million acres of sagebrush, over 40 million acres in scrub oaks, and 78 million acres of cacti which are significant contributors to unproductive rangeland. The benefits of herbicides are virtually self-regulating.... Our ecosystem is under dynamic change, whether managed by man or nature. It is important that we manage it in the proper direction.
--C.S. Williams, Business Manager, Dow Chemical Company, at a rangeland symposium (USDA, USDI, CEQ 1979)

Herbicide is used to kill sagebrush, snakeweed, mesquite, acacia, shadscale, greasewood, creosote, scrub oak, manzanita, rabbitbrush, other brush and shrubs, juniper, pinyon, tamarisk, cacti, yucca, and a great variety of "weedy" plants and livestock-unpalatable grasses. Herbicide also is used to kill regrowth following use of other methods of vegetation eradication.

The wide-spectrum herbicides commonly used on the Western range poison most or all plants in a given area. Eliminating vegetation has, of course, serious environmental consequences, too numerous to detail here. Animals that rely on these plants, especially smaller or sedentary animals unable to move to unpoisoned areas, suffer and die. Those that can relocate infringe upon existing residents. If vegetation is not soon replaced, soil erosion increases greatly. Cryptogamic plant communities are simultaneously destroyed, along with the stability and protection cryptogamic crusts provide the soil's surface and soil below. Consequently, water infiltration and retention may be reduced. After natural vegetation is removed, usually a more uniform cover of only a few plant species (often exotics) grows back or is seeded or planted, setting up conditions conducive to explosions of pest animals. Because of this, herbicide use is one of the main reasons for the dramatic rise in pesticide use in recent years.

A National Forest mountainside (background) divested of trees and brush by herbicide provides increased cattle forage.

Cattle seek herbage amongst herbicided juniper skeletons on west-central New Mexico BLM range.

One cannot help but question the wisdom of registering, selling and spraying an herbicide [picloram] known to persist in the environment, volatilize, leach into groundwater, damage non-target plants, contain carcinogenic contaminants, lack any acceptable chronic effects testing, affect humans adversely and display synergism and carcinogenicity.
--Mary O'Brien, National Coalition for Alternatives to Pesticides

Notwithstanding downplay by chemical companies and other vested interests, herbicides *are* dangerous poisons. Workers handling these chemicals have experienced numerous ailments. Though advertised as being non-toxic, or as losing their toxic qualities within hours or days after use, many herbicides have been shown to retain toxic qualities for weeks or months, or in some cases years. Research has proved that some accumulate in the tissues of plants and animals and in mothers' milk. Other studies show that these chemicals break down under natural conditions to form compounds sometimes more toxic than the herbicides themselves. Picloram is assumed to be carcinogenic even by the BLM, as is glyphosate by the EPA; nearly all the others are considered possible or probable carcinogens, even by the agencies. And, EPA regards some herbicides to have high leaching potential, making them hazardous to groundwater supplies.

Herbicide may enter animals' bodies by absorption through skin, lungs or breathing tubes, or in food and water. Small contaminated animals are eaten by larger ones, which are eaten by larger ones, and so on; depending on a host of variables, this chain of events may or may not increase concentrations of harmful chemicals faster than they break down into less harmful substances. Such an increase is called bioaccumulation. Although a waiting period of 2-3 months is recommended before grazing livestock, this is often not followed. Livestock themselves occasionally are sprayed, accidentally or because the rancher did not expend the effort to move them.

There are so many variables in the foliar application of herbicide that it is virtually impossible to guarantee environmental protection -- to predict for sure where the chemical will go or what it will do. These variables include wind speed; temperature; humidity; sunlight; precipitation; skill and attitude of the operator; marking of target area; type and condition of equipment; preparation of herbicide and condition of materials used; nozzle size, pressure, and orientation; spray pattern; flight height; obstacles such as powerlines, buildings, and high rocks; topography; condition, stage of growth, and height of both target and non-target plants; plant disease and insect damage; the species and behavior of animals; soil type and amount of soil moisture; amount and nature of any water which may be present; and management before and after "treatment." Many things can and often do go wrong. If the spray height is too high or nozzle holes too small, some of the herbicide mixture may volatilize and drift somewhere else. If the wind picks up, herbicide may end up on cattle or in other vegetation, streams, or someone's garden. If heavy rain falls soon after spraying, herbicide may be carried into waterways.

Soil-applied herbicides are likewise risky. In addition to many of the problems above, herbicide pellets or granules may be accidentally mixed with human food stores or water supplies, swallowed by wild or domestic animals, or dropped in non-target areas. Additionally, herbicide in pellet or granular form generally persists in a toxic state much longer than it does in spray form.

Another chemical method of killing unwanted plants involves pouring oil, diesel fuel, kerosene, and other poisons around the bases of offending plants. Ranchers also sometimes dump these substances on the stumps of bushes and trees after being cut. Much of this activity occurs without agency knowledge or consent.

Since the early 1980s, rangeland herbicide use has declined. As mentioned, EPA outlawed the formerly popular, more effective 2,4,5-T and Silvex, and public concern over the effects of herbicide use has risen dramatically. Even costs have become somewhat prohibitive, especially in drier, less productive, and degraded areas where there is so little potential forage that the cost-benefit ratio is glaringly disparate.

Despite the recent downturn, however, there is reason to fear herbicide will regain prevalence as public upheaval subsides. For example, BLM's recent Draft Vegetation Treatment EIS proposes to increase herbicide spraying in the West from the current average of 37,475 acres per year to 141,515 acres per year; 90% of this would be on rangeland. Ranching pressure remains strong, and the current Congress and Bush administration, like all others, contain many ranching advocates.

It is so popular in these days of environmental awareness to be opposed to herbicides and other pesticides as pollutants, that it takes courage to advocate their use, particularly on forests, ranges, and watersheds where livestock, wildlife, and streams are exposed....
--Boysie E. Day, Professor of Plant Physiology, University of California, Berkeley (USDA, USDI, CEQ 1979)

The ranching establishment has "treated" *many thousands of square miles* of public land with herbicide to kill both native and ranching-attributable "unwanted" vegetation. Environmental damage has been extensive, the results transitory, and the cost enormous. Once again, the treatment obscures the illness, or becomes part of the illness.

Treatment of the land and air and water with phenoxy herbicides is not the answer. They are part of the short-sighted cosmetic solutions supplied by the chemical industry and the government such as have long plagued the management of our public lands.
--Donna M. Waters & John C. Stauber, Coordinators, Citizens National Forest Coalition, Inc.

Junipers killed by herbicide.

In conclusion, herbicide use *may* increase forage production. But this increase can only be temporary so long as livestock use remains heavy; and, it occurs at the expense of the natural environment. Continued ranching inevitably leads to the same recurrent problems, and to more use of herbicide as a "quick fix." For example, one study of herbiciding on sagebrush rangeland showed increased livestock profits of 24% after preliminary application, but that re-application was expected to be necessary on an average of every 12 years (Holechek 1989). Indeed, it is commonly acknowledged that under continued livestock pressure the effective "treatment" life of herbicide is only 10-20 years, at which time herbicide must be reapplied. In this way, rangeland herbicide use is like narcotics addiction.

This central Arizona state range was once a land rich with life. Now, decades after being herbicided for cattle production, there are miles of overgrazed, barren waste.

Biological Methods

Infrequently, biological "controls" utilizing fauna and flora are used to manipulate vegetation on public ranges. Most notable has been the use of insects to eliminate "noxious" plants.

Plants introduced without their natural parasites often show dramatic initial reductions when these parasites are introduced. For example, early in this century the livestock-poisonous Klamath weed "invaded" overgrazed ranges in the Pacific Coast states and monopolized more than 250,000 acres near the Klamath River. "Control" efforts long seemed futile. Finally, a leaf-eating beetle (previously introduced into Australia from France) that feeds only on Klamath weed was introduced into these areas. The beetle proved effective -- *except*, curiously, along fenced, ungrazed roadways, where Klamath weed survived as part of a much more diverse and flourishing plant community. Here it waits today, ready to reinvade adjacent overgrazed ranges when the opportunity arises.

In New Mexico overgrazing has caused broom snakeweed (a native opportunist) to partially replace grass and other more "desirable" plants on an estimated 40 million public and private acres, including 60% of state-owned range. On 4 million acres it has choked out most other vegetation. Snakeweed in quantity is poisonous to livestock, causing sickness and aborted fetuses. It competes with forage plants, compounding depletion from overgrazing. Needless to say -- though they are most responsible for spreading the plant -- stockmen hate snakeweed. Therefore, the government hates snakeweed, and the public is supposed to hate snakeweed. Government and ranchers spend about $2 million annually just to fight snakeweed with chemicals.

According to New Mexico State University researcher David Richman, broom snakeweed in New Mexico has gone "out of control." He and others, along with USDA, are experimenting with biological methods of destroying snakeweed. They have imported an Argentine weevil that during its larval stage bores into the roots of snakeweed, then eats the plants. If proven feasible, the snakeweed-killing weevil may eventually be released on rangelands around the West.

But there always are complications when trying to manipulate the environment. Will the weevil itself get "out of control" and kill too much snakeweed? Snakeweed was an original and essential component of many Western vegetative communities, making up an average of about 10% of vegetation in its range. Shouldn't it be allowed its rightful place in the environment? Will the weevil kill non-target plants or cause some other unforeseen harm to the environment? Moreover, if livestock are the cause of the snakeweed "invasion," why aren't livestock removed from public lands instead of snakeweed?

Research on biological "control" is mostly a matter of experimenting to determine which organism most effectively kills an unwanted plant, what method of utilizing that organism is most efficient, and what complications might arise. These projects often prove prodigious and expensive -- especially when there really is no practical biological

"control" to be discovered! They likewise may be environmentally hazardous. For example, some insects introduced to kill "noxious" range plants kill other plants as well, upset natural processes, and pose threats to agricultural crops and ornamental vegetation. Close relatives of some plants targeted for biological extermination are on the Threatened or Endangered Species list and could be further reduced or extirpated. Research on imported parasitic plant fungi poses such a threat to the biosphere that it is carried out only in a custom-built, escape-proof greenhouse at an old Army biological warfare center at Fort Detrick, Maryland.

"Successes" in biological eradication of unwanted range vegetation are few and far between, but grants for research are numerous. In Montana, a fungus, a fly, and a few other insects are being considered to combat knapweed, which covers 4.5 million overgrazed acres of the 90-million-acre state. The situation is similar in Utah regarding the "invaders" squarrose knapweed and Russian knapweed; Utah State University researchers are also testing a naturally occurring parasitic rust on dyers woad, a kind of mustard that has spread across more than 150,000 overgrazed acres. In California, government researchers are testing, thus far with little success, weevils, flies, and fungi on yellow star thistle, a wickedly spiny exotic that has colonized more than 8 million acres in the overgrazed Golden State alone. In some states various insects have been suggested for killing leafy spurge. Worldwide, according to the Forest Service, only "57 attempts to partially or completely control plants biologically have been successful . . ."

Generally, the ranching community finds biological means too abstract and ineffective. Activity in this field is centered at agricultural colleges and agency research centers, where funding provides the impetus for research. And, though much hoopla is made over the fantastic potential for the biologic breakthroughs that will magically erase rangeland degradation, there is little reason to believe that this is much more than public relations hype.

Livestock Methods

A range ecologist for Rocky Mountain Forest and Range Experiment Station [FS], Duane Knipe was looking for an alternative to prescribed burning, herbicide treatment, or mechanical means such as root plowing or chain-dragging for shrub control. Goats seemed to fit the formula: browsers that were cheap and environmentally acceptable [emphasis added].
--Jan Barstad, "A New Look," *Arizona Highways* (March 1987)

Incongruous as it may seem, livestock themselves are sometimes used to help rid the range of "unwanted" vegetation. By manipulating the timing, frequency, intensity, and kind of livestock use, ranchers manipulate vegetation characteristics. Further, studies are underway to determine the effect of chemical and mineral supplements on forage and browse preference so livestock may be "induced" to eat selected plants. Ranching zealot Thadis W. Box reports that other studies are in progress to see if young livestock may be psychologically "conditioned to eat the plants we want them to eat (Box 1987)."

In a broad sense, *all* livestock grazing is a form of vegetation manipulation -- of favoring some plant species over others. Yet historically this was rarely a conscious attempt. With the recent downturn in herbicide use and mounting public opposition to traditional methods of destroying vegetation, livestock are increasingly used as an "environmentally acceptable" "management tool" ("tools that moo" is a current catch-phrase) specifically to eradicate certain species or types of plants. Flowery industry rhetoric portrays this as a great advance in "progressive, scientific range management." In practice, what it amounts to is that livestock are heavily concentrated on a target area for a certain period in hopes that they will eat and/or trample the unwanted plants into oblivion. This is commonly called "intensive herding."

For example, the "undesirable" plant leafy spurge has "invaded" roughly 3 million acres since it was first sighted in the US in 1827. In Montana, where longstanding cattle grazing has caused leafy spurge to spread over about 500,000 acres of public range, some ranchers are using dense herds of cattle to help eliminate it. Leafy spurge is sensitive to physical injury from intensive trampling; stems are broken and seedlings killed. In theory, when a tightly packed herd of cattle is placed in an "infested" area, the concentrated cows perforce step on and kill most of the spurge plants. In some areas intensive herding has had this intended effect; in others it has not. In either case, it may create or worsen other problems. Sheep and goats like to eat leafy spurge, so herds of these animals are being used to reduce the plant in some areas.

On some National Forests, goats are used to destroy brush to increase cattle forage. Concentrated herds of hundreds of goats are driven into brushy areas where essentially they eat every plant in sight, including all leaves and twigs from bushes. Often in combination with other methods of vegetation manipulation and grass seeding, depending on a host of uncontrollable variables, the goats may or may not have the intended effect of killing off the brush and allowing replacement by forage plants. Where they have, "success" has been highly publicized by ranching advocates. Where they haven't, the land often ends up even more degraded than before, and the ranchers and rangers keep it quietly under their cowboy hats.

In Colorado, ranchers have publicized great "success" using goats to destroy Gambel oak sprouts, increasing livestock forage in the process. On northeastern Arizona's Tonto National Forest in 1980, Dr. Duane Knipe of the Rocky Mountain Forest and Range Experiment Station launched a goat study. A herd of 240 angora goats was brought in to eradicate brush. "They ate everything, even the grass we planted after we burned the hill," said Knipe. (According to Dan Dagget, head of the mountain lion protection group Lions Unlimited, "Our source tells us that as many as 15 lions have been killed in the vicinity of that goat cell." This aspect of the study was never publicized.) After 2 seasons the goats were removed and the study was terminated due to extreme overgrazing. The goats were then moved to a ranch near Kingman in northwest Arizona, where 3 years later the rancher publicized his "success" decreasing brush and increasing grass with goats. He added reluctantly, "Our progress has been slower than I'd like because we haven't had much rain -- it all depends on rainfall." In checking official climatic records, however, one finds that rainfall in the area during the period was actually *higher* than normal.

They lie.
--Mike Roselle, progressive activist

To eradicate unwelcome plants, some ranchers experiment with intensive sheep herding. Others try combinations of livestock animals. For example, a mixture of cattle, sheep, and goats can be used to eliminate plant cover as thoroughly as herbicide. Intensive herding may also be used to augment other "control" methods or help prepare the soil for grass seeding, as was done recently with pig herds in Arkansas. In southern New Mexico, camels are being tested on "worthless" vegetation because, according to the experimenter, "they can eat things you wouldn't even want to pick up in your hand." Llamas have also been suggested. And rhinoceroses "because what they didn't eat, they'd bulldoze." Apparently all is fair in love, war, and public lands ranching.

Results, success or failure, are largely in the eye of the beholder. Suppose a huge herd of cattle is concentrated on a range covered with diverse native vegetation. The cattle trample and eat heavily until the area resembles a golf course, with mostly a single species of hardy, low-profile grass withstanding the onslaught. The cattle's owner is happy; to him that green stubble monoculture is much preferable to the less livestock-palatable native vegetation. Or, suppose he moves his herd slowly through a field of livestock-inedible wild flowers. The trampling destroys most of the flowering plants and gives the grasses underneath an advantage. Grass prevails for several years, and he feels successful. In our ranching-oriented society, ranchers, range college pros, and government range personnel define environmental quality to conform to ranching goals.

The "successes" are widely publicized, the failures rarely. Even when intensive herding results in forage *decreases*, ranchers are prone to feign success, for theirs is not merely an effort to increase forage but to maintain control of public ranching empires. They use alleged "successes" in using livestock to "improve" the range as an argument to justify their operations or even greater numbers and more intensive management of livestock. More than situational occurrences, this is a widespread, calculated attempt by ranching advocates to convince the public and government that "properly managed" livestock actually promote environmental health, that ranchers should therefore be given even more power over public land.

But it is hard to hide the fact that using livestock to correct livestock-caused problems is an inherently self-defeating proposition. Changes in the kind of livestock and method of management may alleviate some problems, but they invariably create others. Livestock management, particularly intensive herding, entails so many uncontrollable variables that effects on livestock or the environment cannot be predicted with any certainty, especially over years or decades. No amount of scientific knowledge or technological skill can change this.

Admittedly, intensive herding may more than other grazing strategies simulate the herding effect of wild herbivores. Depending on many often ungovernable and variable factors, it may or may not be less environmentally harmful. But again, livestock cannot go far toward imitating Nature.

Despite its increasing popularity, intensive herding will probably never gain widespread acceptance because it has many practical limitations. Endlessly moving herds about to keep them in the most profitable locations while simultaneously protecting the land under constantly changing environmental conditions is essentially impossible. Because herds must be watched closely, packed tightly, and moved often, intensive herding is labor intensive. Most ranchers are unwilling to work that hard or hire extra help. Intensive herding is ineffective against many unwanted species, including plants resistant to heavy cropping or trampling, as well as large bushes or trees. Obviously, it also is useless in areas where toxic or otherwise harmful plants may be encountered. And, except with goats and sometimes sheep, it doesn't work well in rugged country, which makes up a large percentage of the West. Even comments from the most "successful" intensive herders are rife with "Progress has been slower than expected . . .," "If the Forest Service had only let us . . .," "The weather hasn't been cooperating . . .," "If we'd only . . .," "Next year . . .," and so on. Results are rarely impressive. At worst, they are an environmental tragedy.

As with all artificial methods of destroying unwanted vegetation, intensive livestock herding is an extreme shock to any ecosystem. The resulting radical fluctuations in the amount of plant material may prove disastrous to many dependent animals or give rise to pest infestations. A livestock herd's grazing and trampling can lead to extreme soil erosion if a violent storm strikes before vegetation recovers. However, if adequate precipitation doesn't follow, vegetation may not recover at all. The heavy concentration of domestic animals in an area can spread afflictions to wildlife. Or it may raise sediment levels in waterways so high that aquatic animals and plants die. Recurring denudation

of vegetation may eventually eliminate certain native plants. Intensive herding, or any other type of livestock grazing, is simply not worth the risk -- especially when the ultimate goal is more livestock on the range.

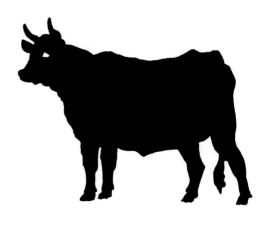

Fire Management

Fire has always been a part of the natural environment. However, BLM sees fire from two different aspects [sic]: wildfires that cause negative impacts and must be suppressed and prescribed fires that can be used toward achieving positive resource management objectives.
--BLM, *Managing the Nations* [sic] *Public Lands* (USDI, BLM 1987)

Fire management is the manipulation of fire to achieve defined goals. As you can probably guess, the main goal on public rangeland is promoting livestock production. This manipulation comes mostly in the forms of "prescribed burning" and "fire suppression" by various government agencies.

Smoke from a prescribed burn on winter range, Kaibab National Forest, northern Arizona.

Prescribed burning is intentional burning under formulated conditions. It is used to achieve many stated objectives, but, stated or not, foremost among these on public rangeland is eliminating competing vegetation to favor livestock forage.

Most grazing allotments contain areas covered with "unproductive" shrubs, brush, trees, "weeds," rough grasses, etc. When ranchers, grazing advisory boards, or agency range staff perceive fire as an effective means of removing this vegetation, they may include these areas as targets for prescribed burning in allotment or land management plans. BLM reports purposefully burning 101,756 acres in 1987, mostly for livestock, while the Forest Service confusingly reports what seems to be at least 420,000 acres of prescribed burning that year, perhaps 100,000 acres primarily to benefit ranching (USDI, BLM 1988, USDA, FS 1988).

To increase forage in forests and brushlands, government employees cut brush, small trees, and lower branches from trees, throw them in piles, and burn them when the weather allows. Another method of prescribed burning is torching individual plants. This is effective in killing certain species of trees and brush. Even flamethrowers are sanctioned weapons, as Theodore Knipe reports in *Javelina in Arizona*:

> *In some localized areas, during the dry periods, ranchers burn the spines off cacti so that cattle may readily feed on them. In this practice the ranchers burn* [with flamethrowers known as "prickly pear burners"] *all the cactus in the treated area and the cattle consume the entire plant.*

According to the ranching text **Range Management**, "Based on recent figures from south Texas, it costs about $0.35 per animal unit per day to maintain animals on prickly pear compared to $0.78 if relief corn is used or $1.09 for alfalfa."

A Forest Service employee igniting a prescribed burn. *(USFS)*

Torching individual plants in the Wenatchee National Forest, Washington. *(USFS)*

Overall, prescribed burning has 2 basic motivations: (1) to correct past (including fire) mismanagement and (2) to alter ecosystems to benefit certain commodity users, most notably loggers, stockmen, and hunters. BLM states, "Prescribed burning is used to enhance wildlife habitat, improve range forage mixtures, improve watersheds, improve the visual backdrop, and remove forest harvest residue." These are among the reasons most frequently given for prescribed burning. Others include: reduce the amount of combustible fuel, help prepare a site for grass seeding, and "open up" the land to access and use. On the Western range, they may all be translated as "improve habitat for livestock" or "mitigate ranching impacts." For example, the Sierra National Forest in central California plans extensive controlled burns over the next 10 years to "improve deer habitat." Coincidentally, it also plans vastly increased livestock grazing in the burned areas.

Prescribed burns vary in size from the area around a bush to many thousands of acres. The largest are usually subdivided and burned as blocks of less than a thousand acres on a continuing, daily basis. Burning may continue for weeks or months, spreading particulates that comprise the persistent, scenery-obscuring haze common to much of the West during "burn seasons."

In prescribing a burn, many factors must be considered, including fuel moisture, type, and distribution; soil moisture; size and shape of the fire area; topography; human developments; prevailing wind direction; and weather. When a burn plan is formulated, the public may be notified, the burn area ribboned or staked out, and fuel-breaks and firebreaks constructed (these too are environmentally destructive). Artificial fire designs vary considerably. For example, a firebreak may be cleared around the entire prospective burn area. When circumstances are deemed right, agency employees with drip torches initiate a long line of fire along the downwind firebreak's upwind side, and the backfire is allowed to burn upwind to the intended destination. Other employees with fire-fighting equipment wait at strategic locations around the perimeter to make sure the fire burns as planned.

Regardless, the fire may not behave as planned. "Controlled" fires commonly do get out of control and damage non-target areas. Many Western conflagrations began as "controlled" burns. Likewise, because prescribed fires are influenced by many uncontrollable variables, environmental protection cannot be assured. For instance, if a hot, dry wind arises suddenly, a controlled forest burn set to kill brush may be quickly whipped into a fierce blaze that kills large trees as well.

Anthropogenic fires do not provide the full benefits of natural fires, and are comparatively destructive in many respects. For example, because of precautions taken to minimize danger to personnel and prevent fires from spreading beyond planned perimeters, many prescribed fires do not burn hot enough to mimic the burn effect of natural fires.

Negative effects of prescribed burning may be briefly summarized as follows:

- reduction or elimination of natural fires causing reduction or elimination of native fire-dependent species;
- destruction of brushlands and dependent wildlife;

- in forests, a reduction of foliage height diversity, creating a 2-layered instead of multi-layered forest, with attendant reduction in wildlife diversity;
- in grass/shrublands, diminishment of native species along with target shrubs;
- because organic litter doesn't have time to rebuild and *all* of each target area is burned, there is more frequent and more complete loss of energy stored in ground litter than with natural fires;
- more frequent and more complete elimination of wildlife cover at ground level than with natural fires;
- recurrent, short-term elimination of ground level food supplies needed by wild animals;
- because prescribed fire is managed to burn *all* of a target area *evenly*, thereby creating a relative biotic monoscape, there is increased danger of pest and disease outbreaks;
- and, because prescribed burns provide much less diversity of impact than natural fires, there is a reduction in biome diversity.

Walking around this area a year after the fire, I was impressed with the irregularity of the burn. The fire spread through the crowns of the pine trees, killing many of them, but as much as a third of the ground cover was not burned at all. Low spots, fire shadows behind fallen logs, wet places, etc. were passed over by the rapidly advancing flames. These refugia probably insured the survival of all plant species, and within a year seedlings of the original plant species had already begun to reestablish on the burned areas. Unlike prescribed burns, which creep slowly over the ground into the wind, natural fires whip and swirl rapidly with the wind, leaping from ground to shrubs to trees and back again, while leaving irregular burned patches in numerous fire shadows.
--Steven P. Christman, Ph.D., "Timber Management Is Not Wildlife Management"

Compared to natural fires, prescribed fires generally are too big or small, hot or cool, frequent or infrequent, and so on to be of maximum benefit to ecosystems. For example, burning too frequently can reduce grassland nutrients by locking them up as less useable compounds and converting excessive amounts into heat. Burning too infrequently can result in a grassland being gradually succeeded by flowering plants and shrubs. Prescribed fires are often started during the wrong weather, at the wrong time of day, in the wrong part of the season, etc. For example, most natural fires burn near the end of or following growing seasons, after most animal inhabitants have finished breeding. Prescribed burning often is done preceding or early in growing seasons, when it may hamper breeding, destroy nests, and kill small animals.

Like other range vegetation eradication methods, fire is commonly misjudged or misused. For instance, young junipers and certain brush species cannot survive frequent burnings. Knowing this, range personnel may artificially burn overgrazed ranges (when overgrazing permits) at unnaturally frequent intervals in an attempt to eliminate these plants. "Weeds," too, frequently are burned off overgrazed ranges to favor forage grasses -- ironically, often favoring cheatgrass, tumbleweed, and other invaders more unwanted than the original "weeds."

The aftermath of a prescribed burn of a juniper forest: increased use by cattle assures environmental decline.

Of course, prescribed fire may be better than no fire at all. Lack of fire in an ecosystem adapted to fire leads to many problems, the most serious being an excessive buildup of combustible materials and the consequent potential for highly destructive fires. In many forest and brushland areas where fire has been suppressed for decades it may be necessary to carefully introduce prescribed fire until the excess accumulation of fuel has been gradually reduced to a level where balance is restored and natural fire can once more assume its rightful place.

However, it is a big mistake to think that because an area contains enough flammable material to burn that it is necessarily wise to burn it. Depending on circumstances, prescribed fire may or may not benefit ecosystem health more than lack of fire. But Nature, through millennia of influence, provides the *most* beneficial conditions, placement, and timing for fire. Likewise, fires respond to the influence of environmental variables too numerous, complex, and uncontrollable to be addressed in fire management plans. In the long run, natural fires result in much greater ecosystem diversity and health than could ever be produced by fire management personnel.

For example, most natural grassland fires are caused by lightning in late summer and the fall, after grasses have matured and dried. The darkened soil surface caused by natural grassland fires subsequently prompts earlier and greater warming of the soil in spring, favoring quick regrowth of certain early-season plants beneficial to wildlife and increasing the activity of nitrogen-fixing bacteria important to restoring the burned areas. Prescribed grassland burns, on the other hand, are often done during other seasons, when blackening of the soil is counterproductive, undoubtedly in many subtle ways not understood. Humanized, rather than natural, fire prolongs environmental deterioration and obscures the real problems behind our need to use prescribed burning in the first place -- overgrazing and fire suppression for the timber and ranching industries.

> *FIRE is a four letter word.*

Fire suppression is the effort to minimize natural fire. It comes in the form of (1) minimizing ignition sources, (2) manipulating the land to reduce the likelihood of fire, and (3) fighting wildfires themselves.

Fire suppression in the West began in earnest long ago, when early ranchers and loggers perceived that they could increase profits by "protecting" grass and trees from fire. Not understanding that fire actually helps maintain healthy grasslands and forests, they pressured the government to begin a fire suppression campaign in the early 1900s. Initially, the campaign accomplished what it was designed to do. Fire was reduced greatly in many areas, and ranchers and loggers were largely unimpeded by fire.

But soon their anti-fire effort began to backfire (so to speak). As the years passed, huge amounts of woody fuel accumulated in brushlands and forests. When fires did start, they often turned into raging conflagrations that destroyed all vegetation, including marketable trees. With fire suppression and overgrazing, shrubs, brush, and "weeds" encroached upon many grassy areas, eliminating forage plants.

Nevertheless, ranchers, timber interests, and government waged war against their perceived enemy with ever-more effective technology. The resulting greater accumulations of woody fuel led to increasingly destructive forest and brushland wildfires, which led to more intensive efforts to suppress them, which led to even more explosive fires, and so on. Dwindling amounts of grass were "protected from fire" with ever-greater fervor, which led to even greater encroachment of unwanted vegetation.

Decades of misunderstanding and bad-mouthing by vested interests cast fire into the role of hated villain. With massive ad campaigns featuring the immensely popular Smokey the Bear, the government convinced the public that fire is an inherently destructive enemy and should be fought with everything we can throw at it. Millions of children grew up knowing that "Wildfires are bad!", just as house fires are bad. Behind the cowboy and the policeman, the fireman became perhaps the most revered figure in Americana. Ultimately, fire suppression became its own best reason for being.

Yet, natural processes could not be circumvented indefinitely, and the destructive fire suppression policy probably stemmed as much from misunderstanding as from greed. In recent decades, many land managers have at least come to see the need for removal of excess combustible material to prevent explosive wildfires. Some have come to realize that ultimately more grass is created by fire than by lack of fire. Thus has prescribed burning become a main method of fire suppression and, to a lesser extent, of grassland maintenance. "Controlled" fire is also increasingly used as a land management tool for various other goals, such as eliminating commercially unprofitable trees from timber harvest areas.

There remains, however, a pervasive, overwhelming bias against natural fire. Few people understand the profound difference between anthropogenic and natural fire. Aside from some more enlightened people at a handful of National Parks and Forests, few public land managers seriously consider allowing natural fires to burn (and those who do are constantly badgered by the public and commodity users). Most prefer fire management because with it they maintain the *illusion of control* over the results. Their job is *managing* the land, and that is what they intend to do! The situation is perhaps worst on public grasslands, where agency staff generally are most reactionary and permittees are not willing to defer grazing for the year or two necessary for grasses to regrow after being burned. Compounding these problems is the fact that fire suppression has grown into a self-perpetuating, multi-billion dollar industry/bureaucracy.

Under pressure from ranching and timber interests, BLM, FS, and states still strongly oppose natural fire. They have a policy of stamping out all wildfires immediately, regardless of the circumstances. BLM boasts that "most wildfires are now brought under control sooner and the acreage burned is less than in the past." A popular Forest Service bumper sticker reads "PREVENT RANGE FIRES."

Of course, as detailed, due to extensive overgrazing much of the West no longer supports fire as it did 150 years ago. This is one of the main reasons the agencies support ranching. Supposedly, with it they neither have to fight so many fires nor use so much prescribed burning to reduce fire danger. Indeed, they commonly promote livestock grazing as "the only viable method of reducing the fire danger." This argument recalls the "we had to destroy the village to save it" mentality of the Vietnam War. When grazing is heavy enough to eliminate fire, it *is* extremely destructive environmentally. Often, however, heavy grazing gradually increases the amount of cheatgrass or weedy vegetation, necessitating the prescribed burning it supposedly obviates.

Further, by extinguishing natural fires, managers have in many areas favored larger and more intense fires in the future by maintaining larger blocks of landscape in about the same stage of fire recovery, with few natural fire breaks from previously burned-over areas. A natural mosaic of vegetation is less conducive to major conflagrations than is a uniform vegetation cover.

Additionally, many natural fires are extinguished to protect houses, barns, sheds, corrals, etc. on the thousands of ranching base properties scattered within and around public land; wooden fences, corrals, water developments, seedings, and livestock on public land are also protected. These developments are used to justify destructive fire suppression on hundreds of millions of acres of public land.

Fire fighting activities themselves are also environmentally destructive. A fire fight usually resembles a war zone, and is in fact executed much like a military assault on an enemy position. Scores, hundreds, or even thousands of personnel pour into a natural area, set up a base camp, and send out platoons to skirmish with the enemy. Dozens of heavy vehicles drive where no vehicle has driven before. The base camp quickly becomes a sacrifice area. Fire fighters with chainsaws, pulaskis, and shovels cut miles of fire lines across the land, and bulldozers scrape wide firebreaks through undisturbed country. All brush, logs, and snags with the slightest possibility of containing live coals are cut to pieces. Smoldering duff is ripped off the ground, and smoldering roots are hacked from the earth. Local water sources are degraded and depleted as millions of gallons are diverted to the fire. Aerial bombers drop thousands of gallons of fire-retardant chemical solution as helicopters shuttle personnel, supplies, and equipment.

A personal story provides an example: Years ago at our backcountry homestead in northern California my partner accidentally started a grass fire one dry, windy day. The fire spread quickly through the grass, small plant, and organic litter layer, consuming a bush here and there, blackening the trunks of a few pine trees. We put out about half of the fire ourselves (mostly to keep it off a neighbor's property), but a few dozen Forest Service fire fighters arrived when the fire reached about 7 acres in size. With fire trucks, hoses, chainsaws, axes, pulaskis, shovels, and boots, they did far more lasting damage to the land than the fire ever could have.

Slash burning with helitorch ignition. Removal of woody debris not only prepares the land for timber management, but increases forage and allows cattle and ranchers to more easily move about allotments. *(USFS)*

Many livestock grazing areas are targeted for fire extermination. Ironically, they are often so heavily grazed that fires cannot develop anyway.

Finally, fire research shows that fire suppression frequently has little to do with putting out fires, anyway. *Most large fires aren't stopped by fire fighting activities but by changes in weather, natural obstacles, or lack of fuel.* A good example is provided by the huge Yellowstone fires of summer 1988. They were fought for months at a cost of $120 million, but were finally extinguished primarily by cool, wet weather. As Montana naturalist George Wuerthner observed, "In essence, we often throw money away at fires just so we have the appearance of doing something."

Yet, the above notwithstanding, some Western ecosystems have not evolved with fire. For example, fire has been absent for thousands or perhaps millions of years in some wetlands, the wettest rainforests, the more sparsely vegetated deserts, and in high mountain areas. Ecosystems with infrequent lightning or little fuel build-up may not be prepared for frequent fire. In areas where fire is not a normal occurrence, lifeforms can be seriously harmed by it.

Normally, mere mention of the word "wildfire" is enough to throw stockmen into panic. But, strangely enough, range arson by ranchers is prevalent throughout the West. A stockman knows that if part of "his" allotment is too brushy or otherwise unproductive for livestock, all he needs to do is drop a match in the right place (maybe that chaparral-covered hillside he never liked much) at the right time (say, early afternoon on a hot, dry, windy day), and his problem will be solved.

Several years ago, my family and I were driving along a remote, rocky ranching road on BLM land in west-central Utah, near the Nevada border. We rambled on for some 30 miles through hills, over a small mountain range, and down into a large valley. All along the way, someone had set fires wherever the terrain turned brushy. The blackened areas, numbering 40 or 50, ranged from small patches that didn't have enough fuel to spread far to over an acre. Beyond the thick brush, the land was generally too overgrazed to support fire. Of course I suspected range arson and the next day called the local BLM office to see what their reaction might be. Well, they really didn't know, they said, but, yes, that kind of arson by ranchers was pretty common. No, they never caught them. From their tone, I doubted they ever tried.

To give you a better feeling for the ranching establishment's attitude toward fire on public range, here is another short story: Years ago, before I understood the full value of natural fire or destructiveness of unnatural fire, I took a seasonal job as a fire fighter with the Forest Service in Oregon. I spent most of my time helping cut and burn brush, small trees, and logging slash to make the forest more profitable for timber companies and ranchers, but 6 times that season we were called out to fight fires. Most of these fires were started by lightning, but one in particular seemed to have another derivation.

Said to be the second largest fire in Arizona history, it was a 50,000-acre blaze in the rugged, brushy hills and canyons of the Tonto National Forest north of Phoenix. Local and state fire fighters battled the blaze for a week, then called in reinforcements from other Western states. At its peak, more than 5000 men and women joined the campaign.

After being out on the lines for a few days, it became apparent that our illustrious Forest Service leaders were not actually trying to extinguish the fire, but to contain it within prescribed limits, while keeping it away from human developments. Some of this could be explained as the usual ploy to collect more hazard and overtime pay or reduce future fire danger, but somehow it seemed to go further than that.

One day while our fire crew was resting, the local public lands rancher arrived, and I overhead part of his conversation with one of the fire bosses. The smiling rancher seemed quite pleased with the development of the fire. Said he had no use for all that brush, anyway, as it "choked" the land, and that it was good to get it cleared out so they could get more grass going. Asking around, I discovered that the rancher had been here often, checking on the fire's progress.

Planting livestock forage grasses is usual government procedure after fires of any origin. Thus, when planned with foresight, range arson often results in not only elimination of "undesirable" vegetation, but government-financed grass seedings, complete with associated range "improvements." Every year thousands of "wildfires" of mysterious origin pop up on grazed land all over the West. The agencies are well aware of this practice, though they rarely openly admit it.

We must abandon our dictatorial approach to fire. Range arson should be stopped cold. Natural fire should be allowed to gradually re-establish itself as prescribed burning is reduced proportionally and eventually used chiefly as a protective measure around the perimeters of developed areas. Smaller developments in areas not easily defended from natural fire should be removed or considered expendable. Natural fire should be allowed to reassume its rightful place in the ecosystem.

Seeding

When cows are hungry, ranchers antsy and grumbling, and the public a willing patsy, you get on with the seeding.
--Denzel & Nancy Ferguson, **Sacred Cows**

Seeding is the dissemination of seeds for the establishment of desired vegetation -- thus, the elimination of unwanted vegetation. Seeding species include forbs and shrubs. For example, salt-tolerant shrubs such as fourwing saltbush are considered as having forage potential in arid regions and areas with excessive salinity. However, by far most seedings on public land employ livestock forage grasses.

Motivations for seeding include the usual "promote desirable vegetation," "enhance wildlife habitat," "improve watersheds," "improve aesthetics," and (following fire or other disturbance) "soil erosion control." But, once again, don't be fooled! Whatever the stated goal, forage for livestock is usually the underlying priority on grazed public land.

Seed may be broadcast onto any ground, but chances for success are much greater where a "seedbed" has been prepared. The most common way of preparing a seedbed is eliminating vegetation that would compete with the seeded plants. This can be accomplished through any of the methods of vegetation eradication discussed in this chapter.

Those used most often are prescribed burning, herbiciding, and certain mechanical methods. Most seedings on public land range from a few hundred to a few thousand acres in size.

As on a farm, a seedbed may be further prepared by mechanically breaking apart the soil to loosen it and allow seeds and water to enter more readily. With some mechanical methods, such as plowing, discing, and "ripping," vegetation may be killed and soil prepared simultaneously. The seeding site may also be prepared by mulching and/or fertilization, but due to exorbitant costs these are uncommon on open ranges.

IMPRINTING

A generally superior method of preparing soil for seeds is called "land imprinting." The "rolling rangeland imprinter" evolved during the 1970s in the mind of Bob Dixon, then a researcher for USDA's Agricultural Research Service (ARS). Dixon eventually was fired essentially because his invention threatened the entrenched petrochemical establishment. His imprinter is a heavy, rolling implement, usually towed behind a tractor. It leaves angular depressions in the soil in which rainwater, topsoil, litter, and seeds (natural or broadcast) accumulate. In cases of severe overgrazing in arid to semi-arid climes, depending on circumstances, this may promote establishment of new growth.

In each area, imprinting's potential benefits must be weighed against its known and potential detriments, such as impact on existing vegetation, small animals, burrows and nests, and archaeological sites; subsoil compaction; noise disturbance; use of fuel; work time; cost; etc. As with all methods of range manipulation, land imprinting should be considered a last resort for those areas where terminating grazing does not heal the land fast enough in relation to other factors. Though much preferrable to herbicides and usually to other methods of seedbed preparation, the imprinter has yet to become a widely accepted alternative.

(Bob Dixon)

Aerial seeding. *(USFS)*

As with herbicides, seeds may be broadcast across the land with aerial or ground equipment, or by hand. Dispersal by aircraft is the usual method following fire. If soil has been prepared beforehand, it may be loose and open enough so that seed eventually is covered by sloughing and settling soil. If not, an area may later be chained over, disced, or otherwise disturbed in order to cover the seed. Or, seed may be "drilled" into the soil with farm-style seed drilling equipment. Drilling is the preferred and most successful method if equipment availability, time limitations, soil type, and topography allow.

A drill seeding machine. *(Unknown)*

Grass species used in seedings vary according to climate, soil type, terrain, competing vegetation, and the kind of livestock to be fed. Generally, native grasses are more nutritious, live longer, grow taller, have deeper roots, and are much better adapted to wildlife. However, introduced species may be more readily established, drought tolerant, livestock-resistant, and, perhaps most important to ranchers, cost-efficient, quick-profit forage producers. So, public range management is geared overwhelmingly toward exotics. Because seed companies sell mostly exotics, native grass seed usually is expensive or unavailable; few in the ranching establishment request natives. Researchers at the Forage and Range Research Laboratory of Utah State University in Logan recently returned from the Soviet Union with more than 1000 species of forage grasses and seed samples which they will evaluate for introduction to the Western range.

Commonly used seeding species include the native fescue and grama grass and exotic Russian wildrye, sweet clover, orchardgrass, African lovegrasses, and others, but crested wheatgrass is easily the most popular. A cool season perennial, readily established, hardy, drought-resistant, fairly nutritious to livestock, resistant to grazing, and cheap, its admirers call crested wheatgrass "the golden grass" for both its color and the profits it often brings. A native of Turkestan in western Russia, crested wheatgrass was introduced to the West in 1898. Its use spread steadily, and in the latter decades of the 20th century CW has become the focus of a veritable rangeland mania, with public lands ranchers constantly prodding the government to plant more. As of 1990, more than 15 million acres of crested wheatgrass and many millions of acres of other exotic grasses have been seeded on Western federal land, alone, with more on the way.

"Grass seeding" has a pleasant ring to it, and planting grass seems like a positive thing to do. A stand of crested wheatgrass that has taken well may even look impressive -- somewhat like a sparse wheat field.

But, as with fire suppression and so much else, we have unwittingly been conditioned to accept rangeland grass seeding as environmentally beneficial when in fact the opposite is usually true. The heavy machinery commonly used in seeding damages topsoil and organic surface layers, compacts subsoil, and may increase soil erosion. It damages remaining plant roots and crushes small animals. It destroys animal nests, burrows, and habitat. It creates noise pollution, uses fuel, and all the rest.

Seedings take a year or more of protection from livestock to establish, so sometimes wild grazing animals, rodents, seed-eating birds, insects, and other "pests" must be "controlled" -- that is, *killed* -- until that time. (Ironically, some of these "pests" are caused by seedings in the first pace.) Some seedings require follow-up elimination of competing vegetation. Many require the construction of roads, fences, and firebreaks. And a few require fertilization or even mulching to establish well. Rangeland fertilization is geared toward supplying nutrients to seeding vegetation or preferred forage, and these increased nutrient levels sometimes harm native species. Fertilizers may also contaminate waterways and groundwater.

Seedings help spread exotic grasses, often far beyond seeding boundaries. Over the years, with the help of overgrazing, these exotics outcompete and preclude native plants, and thus their dependent animals. Western grasses have evolved with their companion plants and animals for an estimated 26-28 million years; additionally, they are generally more nutritious. Nonetheless, many range managers are only too happy to help the spread of exotics. Some ranchers are known to cavalierly spread exotic grass seed around allotments.

The agencies have been known to mistakenly use the wrong seed. For example, in fall 1988, the Forest Service accidentally seeded 6000 acres of the livestock-grazed Hells Canyon National Recreation Area with a grass seed mixture containing yellow star thistle, an exotic that in quantity can kill wildlife and livestock.

As with other methods of vegetation manipulation, seeding results depend on many unpredictable and uncontrollable variables. Many factors influence seeding establishment: suitability of soil and terrain; precipitation; flood, hail, freeze; seed viability; seed dissemination; seed soil coverage; soil erosion; competition from existing plants; disease or depredation by insects or rodents; and post-seeding management. The result may be a lot of bare dirt and/or a crop of less-welcome plants than those eradicated in the first place. For example, Idaho BLM's Burley District recently proposed herbiciding 1500 acres of a crested wheatgrass seeding "infested with broom snakeweed." Pests often become rampant in simplified plant communities and may eat everything within reach; biotic pathogens likewise more easily infest seeding monocultures. Many seedings receive inadequate precipitation and fail to germinate, or simply shrivel up and die.

But possibly the worst thing that can happen is for a seeding to *succeed*. If it does, hundreds or thousands of acres of diverse plant and animal life are transformed into a sterile monoculture, good for little more than grazing livestock. Because most seedings utilize exotic grasses, they eliminate whatever native plants have survived overgrazing. In fact, seedings commonly support only a few plant species, while adjacent areas (if not too overgrazed) usually support dozens of species of many types.

Native animals are likewise reduced or extirpated. Monocultures of seeded grass, whether native or exotic, support only small numbers of animal species compared to natural vegetation (even if overgrazed). Necessities provided by original vegetation -- food; shade; shelter; cover; nesting materials; mating, resting, and nesting sites; observation perches; territorial markers; and more -- are

This drilled BLM crested wheatgrass seeding has taken poorly, leaving mostly bare ground. *(BLM)*

diminished or eliminated. For example, studies show that range seedings reduce numbers of small mammals, and thus the prey base for raptors (Howard and Wolfe 1976). It has been said, only half in jest, that a field of Lehman's lovegrass (a popular exotic) is about as productive as a Safeway parking lot. Even the ranching text **Range Management** by Jerry L. Holechek *et al.* describes "extensive seedings of crested wheatgrass" as "nearly devoid of wildlife." Grass does not an ecosystem make.

Furthermore, the usual life-span of seedings is only 15-25 years, though some may last 30 years or longer (Ferguson 1983). These high-yield exotic grasses tend to deplete soil nutrients. Moreover, although extremely heavy grazing is often recommended to keep other plants from invading, with time seedings invariably deteriorate from overgrazing, competition from other vegetation, and/or inadequacy of sites to sustain them. Then they must be replanted or allowed to return to a more natural state. Range pros usually choose the former. Even if they choose not to replant, depleted sites may take decades to rejuvenate. With continued heavy grazing, they end up in far worse condition than if never seeded in the first place. Thus does seeding beget more seeding indefinitely.

The results of probable range arson: the lighter patches (except snow on mountaintops) are crested wheatgrass seedings. BLM land in central Nevada.

And then, after cattle stamp around the area for a time, soil erosion accelerates. Then the rancher may get a government reseeding project going . . . and perhaps a stock watering project financed . . . and some fencing along the seeding boundaries . . . . And so it goes on our public land.

Range seedings largely are an attempt to farm non-farm land, to compensate for overgrazing while ignoring and in fact furthering overgrazing. Generally, they are expensive, unreliable, and environmentally destructive.

Similar to seedings are "plantings," in which live trees, shrubs, or even cacti are set into the ground. Most rangeland plantings are attempts to revegetate areas denuded by livestock; often riparian areas are re-planted. However, species used are often specifically geared toward providing food for livestock, and grazing is rarely permanently terminated in revegetated areas. Though necessitated by overgrazing private livestock, these plantings nearly always are sponsored by government,

Devegetated and seeded previously, this portion of the Dixie National Forest, Utah, was reseeded with wheatgrass in 1953. Today, under the continued influence of livestock, the range is once again covered with scraggly brush. It will probably be reseeded again and again; judging from the sign, the Forest Service actually seems proud of it. *(George Wuerthner)*

As mentioned, though increased livestock forage isn't always stated as the major objective of grass seeding, close inspection reveals that on rangeland it usually is. For example, under pretense of "soil erosion control," burn areas often are seeded by the government with crested wheatgrass. Crested wheat is a better forage plant than it is an erosion control plant, and natural revegetation will cover a burn as well or better in many cases. Often, cattle are heavily grazed on wheatgrass-seeded burn areas only a year or two after fires, devouring the very grass that the government claims was planted to prevent soil erosion.

often the SCS. Experiments currently are underway with plantings of salicornia and other salt-tolerant plants which might be used as livestock feed in saline desert areas or near the ocean.

To summarize, though it has done more to destroy livestock forage grasses than any other entity, the ranching establishment is out to abolish nearly all vegetation but livestock forage grasses. Vegetation eradication has degraded tens of millions of public acres, and the industry envisions ever-expanded manipulation. BLM's recent Draft Vegetation Treatment EIS, for example, proposes to increase "treatment" to about 375,000 acres annually through chainings and rollerchoppings, chemical application, burning, and intensive livestock grazing -- in order to "modify desired plant communities" and "to remove undesirable plant communities." Including programs by the Forest Service, SCS, ASCS, FWS, NPS, states, counties, agricultural colleges, ranchers, and other entities, vegetation on probably *more than a million public acres annually* is manipulated for ranching purposes.

It is the frustration and challenge, but indeed also the beauty and reward of range management to conserve and enhance resources not by massive action but by skilled redirection of natural forces. . . . We need to seek better range management technology with unflagging determination. This should be the cornerstone of national range management policy. . . . Surely we should expect to see on every hand a veritable whirlwind of activity in range improvement . . . .

--Boysie E. Day, Professor of Plant Physiology, University of California, Berkeley (USDA, USDI, CEQ 1979)

This livestock grazing, together with the projects undertaken to replace existing vegetation with that favored by livestock, have altered the entire physical aspect of vast expanses of the Public Lands from the native, perennial vegetative complexes to monocultures or essentially bare-ground areas of accelerating erosional activity.

--from a 1973 lawsuit by the Natural Resources Defense Council

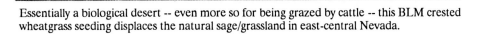

Essentially a biological desert -- even more so for being grazed by cattle -- this BLM crested wheatgrass seeding displaces the natural sage/grassland in east-central Nevada.

Animal Enemies

In the eyes of graziers, basically there are 3 requirements for an acceptable environment -- grass, water, and livestock to eat and drink them. All else is questionable, if not expendable, a possible hindrance to profit and power.

The ranching establishment's assault on the environment, therefore, includes campaigns against a huge number and wide variety of animals. Most of the score or so native large mammal species in the West have been decimated by ranching, both intentionally through slaughtering efforts *and* indirectly through the harmful effects of livestock grazing and ranching developments. Indeed, most larger and a great many smaller animal species are in some way assailed as enemies. The mass carnage carried out for the sake of privately owned livestock continues today throughout the grazed 70% of the West, including public lands, and even in adjacent ungrazed areas.

Though definitions given by ranching advocates vary, most animal enemies fall into 4 main subdivisions: Carnivores and omnivores are (1) *predators* if able to kill a sheep, calf, or goat. Herbivores are (2) *competitors* if they eat enough forage or browse to decrease the amount available to livestock. Many smaller animal species are (3) *pests* if they occur in large enough numbers to affect production in some manner. And a huge number of animals are considered (4) *no-goods*, inherently "no good" because they are perceived as possessing some offensive characteristic.

Predators

Nature does not care whether the hunter slay the beast or the beast the hunter. She will make good compost of them both, and her ends are prospered whichever succeeds.
--John Burroughs

A *predator* is an animal that survives by killing and eating other animals. We usually think of large mammals with sharp teeth, but predators include many birds, reptiles, amphibians, fish, insects, arachnids -- a high percentage of species in the animal kingdom. The West supports thousands of predator species, but those that concern us here are the score or so species of large mammals and birds capable of or accused of killing livestock.

Predators and their prey are mutually adapted and highly beneficial to each other. How could such huge numbers and varieties of both have survived together for millions of years otherwise?

Indeed, predators are an essential part of any healthy ecosystem. By culling "inferior" animals, they keep wildlife populations physically and genetically healthy. They help check populations of many animal -- and thus, plant -- species that might otherwise increase in numbers, burden ecosystems, and subject numerous other animals to suffering and death. (For example, predator eradication is a major factor allowing *livestock* overpopulation and overgrazing!) Likewise, predators prevent certain species from outcompeting or overconsuming others, thereby protecting species diversity, which is a key to ecosystem health. They kill animals that fall into situations from which they cannot extricate themselves and that would otherwise die slowly of thirst, starvation, injury, or exposure. Predators remove carrion that would become health hazards. Additionally, they provide aesthetic and recreational enjoyment, and scientific and symbolic meaning to humans. Perhaps most important, predators are natural beings with the will to exist.

The Kaibab mule deer herd offers a famous example of what can happen when predators are removed from an ecosystem. The setting was the beautiful, forested, high plateau on the north rim of the Grand Canyon, where some 20,000 sheep and cattle had been introduced in the late 1800s. Before 1906 an estimated 4000 Rocky Mountain mule deer shared the plateau with the livestock and many predators.

In the early 1900s tourists, including some of America's most powerful people, enjoyed watching the mule deer in the meadows. With their support and under recommendation from government authorities, President Teddy Roosevelt -- rancher, big game hunter, and selective wildlife advocate -- in 1906 declared the area a national game preserve. Subsequently managed to maximize the deer population, soon even the cattle and sheep were removed to make room for more deer. Federal trappers were sent in. They exterminated the area's grey wolf population and killed more than 700 mountain lions, 5000 coyotes, 500 bobcats, uncounted eagles, and non-target species.

Without competition from livestock, under protection from hunting, and with few remaining predators, the deer population exploded, increasing at an estimated 20% per year. In 1924 the number on the Kaibab Plateau was estimated at 100,000. Apparently the plan to increase deer numbers had worked . . .

. . . far too well. For as the deer increased in numbers they intensely overgrazed the plateau, stripping shrubs bare, eating leaves and twigs from trees as high as they could reach, devastating grass and herbaceous ground cover. In many areas, an estimated 80%-90% of the forage was gone.

Now, 80%-90% denudation of forage is common on livestock allotments, and people rarely take notice. But when it is caused by wildlife on a popular national wildlife preserve overlooking the Grand Canyon, overgrazing becomes a major crisis. For years, controversy raged over what should be done.

In the meantime, Nature took care of the problem. Between 1924 and 1930, an estimated 80,000 deer starved to death. Another 10,000 died between 1930 and 1939. Today, predators are still too few, and it is said that the Kaibab deer herd of perhaps 10,000 is still damaging the plateau environment. Yet, livestock also currently graze most of the plateau, and to anyone who knows the area their destructive impact is obviously far greater than that of the deer. The grazing establishment still kills predators on the plateau.

Undoubtedly, the major sources of prejudices against predators are the stories told by those who kill them: the ranchers, hunters, trappers, and even some biologists working for the government with monetary interests in predator elimination.
--Bob Jessup, wildlife biologist, author

Despite expanded ecological research and modern information dissemination, predators remain maligned and misunderstood. Much of our society still vilifies them as immoral, bloodthirsty killers to be scorned, feared, and hated.

The fact is a predator kills to eat -- whatever acceptable prey is available and within its capability, generally as quickly and efficiently as possible. It is guided by hunger and instinct, not driven by bloodlust and cruelty. It feels no hate, no guilt, no remorse doing what comes naturally. And, in the West, aside from grizzly bears, predator attacks on humans are almost unknown.

A man who kills more game than he'll ever need calls himself a sportsman. But if the same fellow finds a coyote that has killed more than it needs, he will call the animal ruthless and greedy.
--Jed Hill, Southern California old-timer

Most hunters condemn predators because of their depredations on game species. They see predators as competitors. Yet, in the biological web, the number of prey more determines the number of predators, not the reverse. As humans overpopulate and degrade the Earth, they are the cause of most competitive conflict; predators have always been regulators of the natural balance that prevents conflict.

Some animal advocates, hoping to save "cute" animals from "cruel death" at the jaws of predators, would like to see predators eliminated from some areas. They don't understand Nature.

And stockmen, more consistently and vehemently than any, damn predators for more evils than even humans are capable of. They say that predators kill out of viciousness, cruelty, and even "for fun" (as evidence, they frequently exhibit gruesome photographs of predator victims). Allegedly, predators are cold-blooded murderers that wantonly attack and "steal" their innocent livestock. Without predator "control," they say, Western ranching surely would be wiped out by these homicidal maniacs. They insist that predators and livestock cannot co-exist. They are perhaps right only on this last count.

We have laid out an incredible feast of livestock on our public lands. In a very real sense, we are the intruders.
--Marty Stauffer, from the TV series *Wild America*

Ranching, not predators, is the real problem. As livestock grazing and range development exterminated most of their wild prey, predators were forced to eat livestock. A degraded biosystem makes for poor hunting, unstable prey populations, and hungry predators. Overgrazing also eliminated the tall grass needed by livestock mothers to hide their newborns and young from predators. Thus, in traveling about the West, one generally finds the greatest incidence of livestock predation on the most overgrazed ranges.

Then, too, domestic animals, having lost most of their ability to evade predators, make easy prey. Studies show that through evolution each kind of predator has an ingrained sense -- composed of shape, smell, movement, etc. -- of what constitutes its natural prey. Scientists call this its "prey image." Though this instinct guides them in hunting, when their natural prey is gone, predators often must necessarily turn to livestock to survive. Discovering what an easy meal sheep or cattle make in the midst of a ravaged habitat, many understandably develop a dependency on livestock.

Even so, when predators do prey on livestock, generally they take the weakest animals. (On overgrazed ranges all livestock may be weak, and this is much more true of cattle than sheep.) In this way, predators cull animals that perhaps should not survive to suffer, spread disease, propagate inferior genes, or ultimately be sold to unsuspecting consumers. Needless to say, few ranchers appreciate this free service.

Though livestock may die from any number of causes, if the cause is unknown stockmen usually blame predators.

Predators often are wrongly blamed for killing stock. Very few predator kills are actually seen by people. Yet, when a rancher discovers a coyote, bear, or eagle feeding on a sheep carcass, he commonly *assumes* it was killed by the predator, though there is a good chance the sheep died from disease, infection, exposure, poisonous plants, or a gunshot wound from a disgruntled hunter. In one study, professional autopsies showed that only 10% of the dead livestock studied were actually killed by predators.

When a rancher finds a predator-killed sheep or cow carcass but no predator, he often goes after *all* predators in the area, sometimes those not even capable of killing the dead animal. Wildlife biologist Bob Jessup puts it this way: "Instead of tracking down the one animal responsible for livestock losses, ranchers usually find it preferable to begin a regime of unselective poisoning and trapping -- on their land or open [public] range -- killing hundreds of individuals, and possibly missing the one actually responsible for livestock attacks."

I remember once telling Jewel Smith [an old rancher] *about a friend seeing a young Black Bear treed by Coyotes in the Gila Wilderness. "Why didn't he shoot that li'l bear," she asked, "and the coyotes, too?" It was inconceivable to her that anyone would see a varmint of any sort and not kill it.*

--Dave Foreman, **Confessions of an Eco-Warrior** (Foreman 1991)

Many predators are killed not because livestock have been killed, but simply *because they are predators*. For generations stockmen have habitually killed all the predators they can, as casually as most of us swat flies. Killing predators also gives many stockmen a psychological boost -- a feeling of doing *something* to improve ranching conditions; some ranchers are essentially *addicted* to killing.

No quarter was given to the predators. They were regarded as bad animals -- evil creatures that attacked human beings and livestock alike; therefore, they were proscribed and pursued whenever and wherever they appeared.

--**Wild Enemies** by J.J. McCoy, naturalist and former rancher (McCoy 1974)

Probably no aspect of public lands ranching stirs such emotions or has induced such a plethora of publicity as its brutal predator "control" effort. Though surely not the most environmentally harmful of the industry's general activities, it is considered by many to be the most disgusting. Perhaps

no issue reveals so well the true nature of the power exerted by Western stockmen. Even with growing public opposition, the ruthless butchery that began when ranchers took control of the rangeland West more than a century ago continues unabated. The various ways the ranching establishment kills predators are described below.

● Guns

12-gauge pump shotgun loaded with BB shot is good for hunting pups that have left the dens but are still together. They may be found lying under sagebrush or among rocks and are more easily hit with a shotgun than with a rifle when they start to scatter.

--from **The Clever Coyote** by Stanley Young and Hartley Jackson (Young 1978)

More than anything, Western cowboys are famous for their guns -- their "most faithful companions." In the grazing industry's formative years, predators were shot whenever they were seen. Even today most ranchers carry rifles in their pickup trucks and many shoot at every predator and stray dog they see (if they aren't able to run over them first). Many hunt predators with trained dogs or hire others to do so. The animal is tracked down, cornered or treed, and shot. Some lure and shoot predators using special calls that sound like prey in distress or like animals seeking others of their species. Some use scent lures. Little of this slaughter has much to do with livestock protection, but is done "on principle," "for sport," or because, as Champ Clark writes in **The Badlands**, "killing varmints helps ease frustrations."

Under various state and federal wildlife protection and game laws, much of this shooting is technically illegal. But nearly all of it occurs in remote areas where getting caught is unlikely. Getting charged and punished is even more improbable. Most Western state stock killer laws are so loosely worded and weakly enforced that ranchers may shoot predators essentially at will.

Government predator "control" agents have gunned down millions of large predators since the early 1900s, including many thousands of stray dogs. With the ban of many predator poisons in 1972, they have stepped up the shooting spree, often using helicopters or fixed-wing aircraft. Typically, aerial predator "control" agent-"sportsmen" chase coyotes until they drop from exhaustion or roll over and expose their vul-

From The Coyote: Defiant Songdog of the West, Revised & Updated by Francois Leydet. Copyright (C) 1977, 1988 by Francois Leydet. Used by permission of the University of Oklahoma Press.

" PREDATOR CONTROL"

(John Zaelit)

nerable underparts in a canine plea for mercy. Or coyotes are lured into the open with helicopter or truck placements of "bait draws." Then they are shot with 12-gauge shotguns or high-powered rifles. These aerial killers are especially deadly in winter, when snow is deep and predators have few places to hide. Francois Leydet describes the organization of one of these aerial hunts in his excellent book, **The Coyote**:

> *The operation, directed by ADC [Animal Damage Control] district supervisor Wes Bonsell, was organized like a military campaign. There were the ground forces -- ADC field district assistants Arnold Bayne and John Foard, and ranch manager B.W. Cox, in the pickups. And there was the aviation -- the B.A.F., as I came to all it, Bonsell's Air Force: the Supercub spotter plane, with Wes riding as spotter, and the gunship helicopter.* (Leydet 1977)

Many wealthy public ranchers think it great sport to spend the weekend shooting coyotes from their own private aircraft. One in Wyoming patrols "his" public lands sheep allotment in his noisy ultra-light, shotgun in hand.

At least 1/3 of animals shot do not die immediately. Many live out their days in agony, dying slowly from infection or starvation. Others are crippled for life. Commonly seen on the Western range are coyotes and other predators with legs, jaws, and other body parts shot off.

● Traps

> *Few men could endure to watch for five minutes an animal struggling in a trap with a crushed and torn limb ... Some who reflect upon this subject for the first time will wonder how such cruelty can have been permitted to continue in these days of civilization.*
> --Charles Darwin, 1863

The first traps set by Western ranchers to kill predators were snares. Snares usually involve a noose that constricts around a trapped animal's neck, choking it to death under its own weight or holding it until the rancher comes by and slays the animal. Large animals trapped in snares often struggle for hours or days before finally dying. Leg snares

are also used. Wire leg snares often strip the skin and flesh of a struggling animal's leg right off the bone. Most non-target species caught in snares must be tranquilized to be removed alive. Few trappers carry tranquilizer; thus, most non-target snare victims are killed. Ranchers and government agents still commonly use snares to kill predators.

In the past, another method of "trapping" involved staking a tame wolf, one raised in captivity, where it would attract a wild one. A man hiding downwind behind a tree or rock would then shoot the wild animal.

Another method still used to kill large predators is digging a large pit and lining the bottom with sharp, upright "pungi sticks" (such as were made famous by the Vietnam War). The pit is carefully covered and camouflaged, and the large animal (possibly human) that falls into it is impaled and usually killed.

The leghold trap was invented in medieval Europe by wealthy land barons to catch *human* trespassers and poachers. The metal, spring-loaded leghold trap was introduced into the US in 1840 and has remained virtually unchanged ever since. Its use spread quickly throughout the continent, revolutionizing the trapping industry and increasing stockmen's ability to kill predators. Today, ranchers and government predator "control" agents use leghold traps extensively. Stockmen also discretely encourage, assist, and/or hire private trappers to kill predators on private and public lands. Their motto: "The essence of trapping is secrecy."

Public domain in northern Arizona.

A predator trap is placed in a location where the intended victim is likely to come across it. A meat or scent bait is placed in or about the trap as a lure and the trap is set. When the victim steps into the trap, powerful jaws snap shut and the animal's leg is held firmly, as in a vise. The trapper then comes by, dispatches the animal with a rock, club, or gunshot, and resets the trap. This is the best-case scenario, anyway.

The reality is usually even more unpleasant. When the steel jaws snap shut, the trapped animal suffers immediate pain said to be similar to that of a car door slamming on a human hand. Often leg bones are broken. A study by the Louisiana School of Veterinary Medicine showed that more than 90% of coyotes caught in leg-hold traps suffered broken bones (Grandy 1989).

Oddly, a broken bone may be the desperate animal's best hope, for the break may allow it to yank or chew off the trapped limb segment completely -- what trappers term "wringing off." Most of these animals later die from starvation, predation, or infection. But some survive, and consequently many 3-legged coyotes, bobcats, deer, and other animals hobble about in the wild.

itself, the steel jaws slowly work into its flesh, often to the bone. Muscles, tendons, and ligaments are torn, cut, and crushed, while often blood flow is cut off. Bones may be broken or dislocated as the animal thrashes about to free itself. Some animals go into shock and die. Some suffer gangrene. Some are eaten by predators. Babies starve to death in their dens and nests while their imprisoned parents await their fate. Mates stand by helplessly as their partners suffer in jaws of steel.

Western state laws require trappers to check their traps at regular intervals, often every day. But most trappers leave their traps unattended for days. According to several government trappers, leghold traps are checked an average of twice a week, or "at the trappers' convenience," often only on weekends. Thus, trapped animals suffer and frequently die from exposure, thirst, starvation, or attacks from predators.

When the trapper finally does come by, the animal may suffer more severe pain. Wild animals usually don't die easily, and many are stoned to death or succumb to multiple wounds from a gun, shovel, or club.

This non-target trapping victim -- a lactating female coyote -- was later released with an amputated foot, and survived. *(Paul Tebbel)*

(Dick Randall)

Large animals may be trapped on the leg, foot, nose, or head. On small animals the trap may snap shut on almost any part of the body. As a trapped animal struggles to free

(John Zaelit)

A Denver Wildlife Research Center study, aimed at coyotes, reported that of 1119 animals trapped, injured or killed [by USDA's Animal Damage Control], only 138 were the targeted coyotes. The remaining victims consisted of 21 non-target species, including hawks, golden eagles, song birds, rabbits, and deer, as well as 63 domestic animals.

--Tanja Keogh, U.S. Predator Control -- a Legacy of Destruction (Keogh 1988)

In livestock areas, traps are most commonly set for coyotes, mountain lions, bobcats, and bears. But traps are indiscriminate. Any animal attracted to the bait or happening by may fall victim. In fact, most reliable studies and expert testimony have shown that between 2/3 and 3/4 of animals trapped are "non-target" species (Keogh 1988). Casualties include many deer, wolverines, martins, badgers, beaver, opossums, porcupines, raccoons, skunks, rabbits, ringtails, javelina, armadillos, groundhogs, humans, eagles, hawks, owls, vultures, crows, ravens, magpies, wild turkeys, quail, songbirds, kingfishers, tortoises, domestic dogs (frequently) and cats, domestic livestock (!), and many others. For example, ADC reported "inadvertently" killing 555 badgers, 1117 raccoons, and 764 javelina in 1988 (Satchell 1990) (numbers of unreported victims are undoubtedly much higher). Says Dick Randall, a federal predator "control" agent for 10 years, now working to protect wildlife, "my trap victims included bald and golden eagles, a variety of hawks and other birds, rabbits, sage grouse, pet dogs, deer and antelope, badgers, porcupines, sheep and cows" (Malachowski 1988). This, from a skillful and conscientious trapper. Most ranchers are little bothered by killing these non-target animals; indeed, as detailed later in this chapter, many would just as soon eliminate most of these "troublesome" animals.

Trappers keep or sell many of these non-target animals for their fur, meat, feathers, etc. Though many of those animals they don't keep are found dead or must be killed, some are well enough to be released, often after having their foot cut off. Of these, many are permanently disabled or so seriously injured they eventually die. One study showed that 25% of released animals appearing to have no injuries were subsequently found to have died from gangrene as a result of prolonged constriction of blood flow in the leg.

Another trap less commonly used is the so-called "killer" or body-gripping trap, also termed a "conibear." This spring-loaded device snaps shut with great force on whatever portion of the victim's body enters the open square and activates the tripping mechanism. The animal is crushed or suffocated. Unfortunately, of conibear trapping incidents studied by the US Humane Society, "Nearly 50% of the animal victims did not die, but suffered serious injuries, sometimes for days (Grandy 1989)." Ranching interests usually set conibears at the burrow entrances of suspected predators and competitors.

I mentally totalled up our "score" [for the day]: *a raccoon, a fox, a hog-nosed skunk, shot and killed; a fox, a ringtail, a raccoon, released with the loss of a foot; a fox, a raccoon, and an ewe released unharmed. Forty-three traps re-set and re-baited, now all ready to spring. And all for what? Because of an unsubstantiated report that a coyote's track had been seen in the area!*
--Francois Leydet, **The Coyote** (Leydet 1977)

Trapping on public land, though prevalent, is an obscure, secretive, nearly unregulated activity -- and trappers prefer it that way. Much of it is illegal, and nearly all of it is cruel and environmentally destructive. A common misconception, one that stems largely from our romantic image of the Old West "mountain men," is that trappers are rugged, outdoors-loving sportsmen who trap on foot or horseback. In truth, most are professional predator and/or fur trappers who run scores of traps from 4-wheel drive pickups and jeeps, often off-road, to the further detriment of the land. They may take hundreds of animals, and some make tens of thousands of dollars annually. Many "hobby" trappers also use public land, but even they rarely walk more than half a mile from their vehicles to and from their traps. The inherent nature of trapping seems, generally, to attract the unintelligent, inept, and irresponsible. Indeed, a long-term computer operator at NCIC (National Crime Investigation Center) remarked once that he had never run the name of a trapper through the system that didn't have a yellow sheet. (Marten 1991). An amazingly large percentage of trappers are felons. It is clear to me that many trappers are simply sick individuals who feel the need to kill or hurt, and trapping offers them one of the few culturally and legally sanctioned means of doing so.

There is a growing movement in this country to outlaw the steel leghold trap, as it has been in at least 65 other countries. (All leghold traps I find end up in thick brush or deep water.) But, as usual in the West, the ranching industry still pulls the strings, and the trapping continues.

For more than 50 years, the American Humane Association in Denver has had a standing offer of $10,000 for the invention of a humane trap. To qualify, the trap must be efficient and economical, practical for widespread use. No one has collected the $10,000. Could it be there is no "humane" way to take wild animals from their homes?

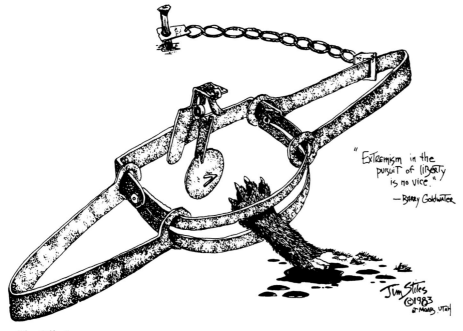

"Extremism in the pursuit of liberty is no vice."
-- Barry Goldwater

(Jim Stiles)

Three out of four animals caught in traps are non-target or "trash" animals, including pets and endangered species. Fewer than 1% of all trappers rely on trapping to make their living. Trapping targets healthy animals that would otherwise survive. Health officials now say trapping does not control diseases, and may even promote their spread.

--*The Compendium Newsletter* (May-June 1989)

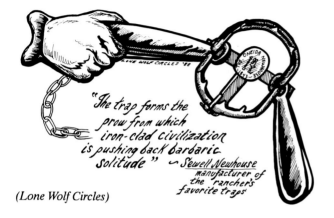

"The trap forms the prow from which iron-clad civilization is pushing back barbaric solitude" ~ *Sewell Newhouse manufacturer of the rancher's favorite traps*

(Lone Wolf Circles)

●Poisons

A 1979 U.S. Department of Interior Fish and Wildlife study by Dr. Stephen Kellert of Yale University deals with public attitudes toward critical wildlife and natural habitat issues. This included public opinion toward the use of poisons to minimize agricultural loss due to wildlife. . . . Sheep producers and cattlemen strongly approved of poisons and constituted just about the only group in the entire study to favor this control strategy.

--From the report, *1080* (Defenders of Wildlife 1982)

(Dick Randall)

Poisons are the cheapest way to kill large numbers of predators. During the early years of Western ranching, the predator "control" arsenal acquired various deadly poisons -- arsenic, strychnine, sodium cyanide, and others. These were inserted into bait, usually meat or carcasses of cattle, sheep, deer and other foods favored by predators.

The 1940s ushered in a whole new era of predator eradication with the introduction of the extremely lethal toxicants thallium sulfate and sodium monofluoroacetate (Compound 1080, or "1080") -- developed in Germany during World War II. They replaced many of the older poisons and soon became widely popular.

Also introduced in the 1940s was a revolutionary, deadly new predator weapon. The "coyote getter" is a pistol-cartridge-powered cyanide gun that fired a puff of deadly sodium cyanide dust into the mouth of any carnivore, omnivore, or carrion-eater that tugs on its scented wick. On contact with the moisture in the animal's mouth (or eyes, or wherever it hits) gas is released and the animal is gassed to death (or blinded). A highly effective killer, the coyote getter quickly gained widespread use. Eventually it was usurped by a newer model, the spring loaded "M-44" (sounds like a war, appropriately) coyote getter, which is still in use today. Over the years coyote getters have killed countless thousands of predators, non-target animals, and even a few humans.

(John Zaelit)

During the heyday of the predator poisons, the public didn't have any idea that Western rangelands, mostly public land, were laced with every kind of poison known to humans.
--Dick Randall (Pacelle 1988)

During the 1950s and 1960s, poisons became the rangeland rage. Contaminated livestock carcasses were routinely left on grazed land across the West. Meat baits tainted with 1080 were placed at 6 mile intervals in huge grid patterns over vast areas. From trucks, horses, trail bikes, and airplanes, millions of strychnine-laced tallow pellets were scattered over the Western landscape, even where no livestock grazed. In 1970, the Division of Wildlife Services alone set out 10,800 Compound 1080 baits, 805,000 strychnine baits, and 32,933 coyote getters. According to government-calculated toxic kill patterns, just these 1080 baits alone were estimated to be sufficient to poison 248,832,000 acres for coyote "control" -- an area 2 1/2 times the size of California. Other federal agencies, states, counties, and ranchers waged their own, even more secretive poison wars.

These deadly poisons took their toll on much more than predators. Wildlife experts estimate that more than 2/3 of poison kills are non-target animals. Of course, to a large degree results depend on the skill of the handler, and some poisons are more specific than others. But relatively speaking most predator poisons are indiscriminate. And most were over-applied irresponsibly and often illegally.

Millions of non-target animals have been killed, including scavengers such as crows, ravens, jays, magpies, eagles, hawks, badgers, weasels, mink, raccoons, ground squirrels, bears, dogs (including sheep dogs) and cats, and any other animal attracted to dead meat. For example, poisons, traps, and degradation of habitat by livestock were chiefly responsible for extirpating the wolverine from more than 2/3 of its native range. According to ex-predator "control" agents, they were encouraged by their superiors to ignore and not report non-target deaths.

These rodents were trapped, are now being inserted with poison, and will be left out on the range to kill predators. *(Dick Randall)*

Opposition to range poisons grew during the 1960s and early 1970s, chiefly as part of the growing environmental movement. Thallium sulfate, nonspecific and slow to kill, was finally banned in 1967. Predator exterminators turned to 1080. But 1080 is little better. According to one source, "The symptoms of 1080 poisoning appear in from 30 minutes to 2 hours and are characterized by severe convulsions. Death ensues in two to three hours and there is no known antidote." Former EPA Administrator William Ruckelshaus called 1080 "one of the most dangerous toxics know to man." Less than 1/500 of an ounce will kill a grown human. It decomposes only when burned or immersed in large quantities of water, is white, tasteless, odorless, water soluble, easily absorbed through stomach, lungs, or breaks in the skin, and has been evaluated and listed as desirable for use as a chemical warfare agent by the military. So potent is 1080 that, like DDT, it can kill as many as 5 animals in a bioaccumulative chain reaction. According to the EPA, "1080 is highly toxic to all species," and according to authorities, prior to 1963 there were at least 13 fatal cases, 5 suspected deaths, and 6 non-fatal cases of 1080 poisoning in humans. Between 1974 and 1982, the Rocky Mountain Poison Center in Denver, alone, was consulted on treatment of about 100 cases of poisoning by 1080 and 1081 (a very similar toxin used chiefly as a rodenticide) (Defenders of Wildlife 1982).

The photo at top shows federal agents injecting sheep carcasses with 1080. Above, a badger is dead after eating from a poisoned sheep carcass. *(Dick Randall)*

Finally in 1972, after the highly publicized 1080 deaths of many eagles in Wyoming, President Nixon signed an executive order halting the use of all poisons to kill predators on federal land. Unfortunately, rancher Ronald Reagan eagerly rescinded the order in 1982, reinstating the use of sodium cyanide and 1080 in sheep collars -- a "trial balloon" for 1080. The grazing industry is the main force behind the effort to bring 1080 back into general use, and under a sympathetic George Bush this may soon be the case.

Today some Western sheep ranchers fit their animals with collars (cost: about $20 apiece) containing pouches of concentrated solutions of Compound 1080 -- "enough to kill 300 25 pound dogs" or "26 children weighing 35 pounds each." When a sheep dies or is killed, the animal that consumes it ingests the poison, then dies and transfers the poison to various scavenging larvae, worms, beetles, birds, and mammals, which in turn pass it on to others. Even sheep themselves sometimes die from eating vegetation contaminated by 1080 collars punctured by thorns or barbed wire. Tests show that for many reasons the collars do not work as intended. (Defenders of Wildlife 1982)

(George Wuerthner)

One recipe for death calls for a number of live coyotes to be tied up and their mouths wired shut. While they are being tormented in this way, adrenaline pours into the terrified animals' systems, creating strongly scented bladders and anal glands, which, when cut out of the still-living animals, provide "passion" bait for poison stations.

--Hope Ryden, **God's Dog**

Most poisons are still legally unavailable for use on range predators, but according to Dick Randall, "there has always been a black market for strychnine, 1080, and others." Many toxicants are smuggled in from Mexico, where they are legal. And other over-the-counter pesticides, such as the dewormer Warbex, are readily available. Randall adds, "the 'grapevine' has told ranchers that if they want to kill something they don't need strychnine or 1080 -- they can go out and buy these pesticides which will do even better because they [broad spectrum pesticides] kill everything" (Pacelle 1988). Some stockmen even use toxic Prestone antifreeze. Ranchers are currently lobbying heavily for the legal return of 1080, as well as strychnine and other deadly poisons.

Poison advocates argue that toxins are a humane alternative for killing predators. Yet often predators and, especially, non-target victims don't eat enough poison to die "quickly" and instead suffer for hours, days, or weeks. They may wander the landscape in torment or writhe on the ground, wracked by pain, dying gradually or eventually recovering. Even under the best of circumstances, most poisons cause agonizing pain before death.

. . . a frenzy of howls and shrieks of pain, vomiting and retching as froth collects on his tightly drawn lips . . . A scant six to eight hours after eating his meal, Mr. Coyote is breathing his last, racked [sic] by painful convulsions, [dying from] the most inhumane poison ever conceived by man . . . .

--Montana rancher, State Senator Arnold Rieder, describing the effects of 1080 poisoning in a newspaper article (Strychnine is said to be even more painful, though quicker.)

● Denning

Another method of killing predators is "denning." The object of denning is to kill predator young, usually coyote pups, sometimes foxes, wolves, mountain lions, bobcats, or others, in their dens. There are dozens of forms of denning, all of them gruesome. If possible, the denner simply digs back into the den and

Coyote pups. (Dick Randall)

strangles the young barehanded, shoots them, or kills them with any implement at his disposal. In another form, a piece of barbed wire is shoved into the back of the den and rotated until it catches on a pup or kitten's fur. Or a hook may be used. The youngster is then fished out and shot or its head is bashed in. In another form of denning, the inside of the den is turned into a blazing inferno with a flamethrower, or filled with poison gas. One form involves smoking the

Digging out a coyote den. (Dick Randall)

animals out with a smoke bomb or fire and dispatching the choking, blinded pups or kittens with a club or shovel. In still another, dry brush is packed into the den hole and set on fire, and the entrance is covered with a rock. In theory, the animals suffocate from the smoke, but, as Dick Randall relates:

(Dick Randall)

... they'd often end up scrambling for the cracks of light at the entrance in desperation. You could hear them yowling when they hit the flames. They burned alive." (Malachowski 1988)

(Dick Randall)

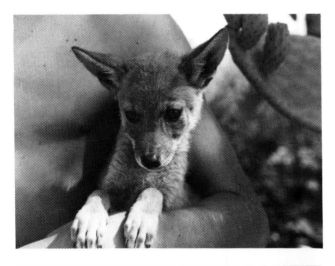

(Dick Randall)

● Dogs

Trained dogs -- usually hounds -- are used to pursue and tear apart their wild predator cousins, to lure coyotes into the open for shooting, and to locate dens. Government predator "control" agents sometimes use these methods, but many more ranchers own such specially trained dogs. Commonly they train their dogs to chase and kill *any* wild animal encountered.

● Non-lethal methods

There are non-lethal means of discouraging predators, but most are expensive and/or ineffective, and most stockmen harbor deep antipathy toward predators and prefer to kill them. Hog wire or wire mesh sheep fences are used in some sheep grazing areas. They are expensive and rarely keep predators away completely, so they are usually considered supplementary protection. Electric fencing has shown to be likewise. Guard dogs have been effective in keeping predators away in some cases, though they necessitate additional human supervision and monetary expense. According to an article in *Arizona Highways*, public lands rancher Bill Conway "welcomes [his guard dogs] barking all night because it deters coyotes and mountain lions." Wildlife and visitors to public land might not appreciate the all-night barking as Bill does. Some ranchers herald guard donkeys as the solution, while others say llamas, ostriches, or emus. Intensive livestock herding has also been promoted as a predator preventative. Supposedly, the natural instincts of a large herd cause it to fight off predator attacks more effectively. There is some truth in this, but a large, densely packed herd requires extensive fencing or humanpower (money) to keep it together, and livestock have lost much of their herding instinct through domestication. Other predation-reducers include shed-lambing, providing winter shelters, removing carrion from lambing and calving pastures, and simply more vigilant human supervision.

The battery-powered sheep collar features flashing lights and sirens, all electronically triggered by the sheep's sudden movement when attacked by a coyote.... After 10 seconds, the alarm automatically shuts off for 10 minutes, allowing the excited sheep to calm down, then resets itself. An electric eye activates the collar only at night, when most coyote attacks occur.
--High Country News (8-1-88)

Non-lethal methods also include bells, warning sirens, taped recordings of scary sounds, other sound-repelling devices, bright lights, wild colors, electric shockers, and other generally ineffective and often daffy deterrents. Hundreds of non-lethal methods of thwarting predators have been tested by the government in recent decades, including repellent and aversive scents, attractive scents (to draw predators elsewhere), and antifertility agents, none of which have gained much acceptance. Consider this one by the University of Wisconsin and the US Fish & Wildlife Service's Denver Research Center: "this approach involves an attempt to make coyotes 'allergic' to ovine antigens so that a depredating coyote would react in the form of a fatal anaphylactic shock or a sufficiently painful response to constitute an aversive stimulus."

All the above non-lethal methods are environmentally obtrusive and/or harmful. While differing factions debate the merits and demerits of various predator "control" methods, completely ignored as always is the most important question of all -- what are livestock doing on public lands in the first place?

We run most of the coyotes on our ranch with pickups. We must have had three our four chases a week in 1973. Everything stops when you do this. You pile into the pickups, and go racing across the country after him at top speed, whatever the terrain . . . [then kill him].
--Ellis Whitney, public lands rancher, 4-term New Mexico state legislator

Some ranchers torture captured predators. They purposefully leave them in traps to gradually die from thirst, starvation, or exposure. They may slowly torment trapped animals by beating, stoning, burning, shooting, or slashing them. Or they may saw off their lower jaws, wire their jaws shut, blind them, cut off their legs or tails, or otherwise mutilate them and then release the unfortunate animals. Some public relations-minded stockmen insist that this kind of activity ended long ago, but their claims simply are not true.

I know a sheep rancher out here -- you wouldn't believe that guy! He's boasted about the coyotes he's trapped, how he takes a burlap bag, cuts out a hole for the head and two holes for the front legs, pulls the bags on the animals, pours kerosene on, sets them on fire and turns them loose. And he laughs when he tells that, as if it were the greatest thing!
--Dick Randall (Pacelle 1988)

In the early years, grazing industry and government were largely synonymous. Community, county, and state governments passed stock killer laws, supplied bounties, and generally helped kill predators whenever they could. Federal involvement began in 1890, leading to creation of USDA's Biological Survey. In 1907 private and government interests killed at least 1800 gray wolves and 18,000 coyotes. Federal, state, and county governments paid bounties for various varmints. Yet, in these early years, government activity was sporadic, minimally organized, and mostly undocumented.

Then in 1914 the Predatory Animal and Rodent Control become an autonomous part of the Biological Survey. In 1915, ostensibly compelled to maximize livestock production for World War I, organized federal involvement in predator "control" began in earnest when Congress appropriated $125,000 to be used by the Biological Survey for killing predators in Texas. Stockmen argued that since they were paying fees (10 cents/AUM in 1915) to graze federal land, the federal government ought to be responsible for protecting their livestock from predators (say what?). Soon the Western ranges were divided into supervised districts and federal, state, county, and private monies were used to coordinate the attack against the predator enemy.

For the benefit of the new men on the force I wish to state that we grade their catches in the following manner: One fox is worth 1/2 point, 1 coyote or 1 bobcat is 1 point, 1 bear is 10 points, 1 lion 15 points, 1 wolf is 15 points . . . . It is necessary to have 15 points or 1/2 point per day for the time you work in order to get on the honor roll . . . REMEMBER OUR SLOGAN, BRING THEM IN REGARDLESS OF HOW.
--M.E. Musgrave, Predatory Animal Inspector, 1923

In 1931 Congress enacted the Animal Damage Control Act, which authorized the Secretary of Agriculture to eradicate a host of "destructive" animals, including wolves (which by then had already been nearly eliminated from Western ranges), coyotes, bobcats, prairie dogs, gophers, ground squirrels, jackrabbits, and others. In 1939 this program was placed under the jurisdiction of the Department of the Interior. In 1986, under pressure from powerful ranchers, the federal government moved the Department of Animal Damage Control back to USDA, an agency more sympathetic to the ranching industry's desires.

ADC kills everything from blueberry-eating geese to domestic cats "making noise in buildings," but according to ADC its principal mission is the protection of livestock. According to critics, ADC's principal mission is perpetuating its own bureaucracy by protecting livestock. This year, many of its 700 agents will trap, snare, den, poison, or shoot tens of thousands of predators, including coyotes, bobcats, foxes, black bears, and lions. The 1971 "Cain Report" sponsored by the Department of the Interior and Council on Environmental Quality stated that problems with the federal predator program stemmed in part from the fact that,

. . . . several hundred control agents today are the same persons for whom for many years the job requirements and measurement of an agent's success have been the killing of large numbers of predators and of personal, uncritical response to the complaints of stockmen. Agents are frequently long-time acquaintances, friends, and neighbors of the individuals demanding service.

ADC's 1990 Draft Environmental Impact Statement for long-term management of its Animal Damage Control Program is, according to Humane Society Vice President for

Wildlife John Grandy, "just awful in every respect": "All this document does is glorify the status quo. It's more of slaughter the West." Indeed, the EIS is so full of inaccuracies and distortions to promote ranching and its own interests that it is widely considered a bad joke. The Sierra Club's Atlantic Chapter concludes its blistering 39 page commentary with "this draft EIS is without redeeming value."

To minimize public scrutiny and opposition, ADC is extremely secretive. For example, throughout the United States ADC distributed only 1000 copies of the draft EIS mentioned above. ADC field agents do their killing quietly; its officials issue no public messages or information handouts; and its offices are purposefully located where they will receive little attention. Arizona's state ADC office, for example, is situated in an unmarked building in an obscure Phoenix small-business district; workers at a neighboring business didn't even know who occupied the office until years after ADC moved in. Understandably, few Americans have ever heard of ADC.

ADC logo on the cover of its 1989 report. Turn this book upside down, and the cow becomes a cowboy.

This mindless killing of coyotes, cougars, bears, and everything else that doesn't produce wool or beef on the public lands by the ADC is a sickening example of a government agency out of control. While this slaughter is presumably undertaken to protect the heavily subsidized stock industry, I suspect an equally compelling motive is the preservation of the jobs of the government's hired guns, the federal trappers.
--Jack T. Spence, Condon, MT, in a letter to the editor of *High Country News* (3-11-91)

Other federal agencies are, to a lesser degree, involved in murdering predators. Many states and counties also fund predator "control" programs. Western state game departments are especially sensitive to pressure from ranchers to fund predator kills. Some states still finance predator bounties, and counties are allowed to contract for the killing of wildlife to benefit stockmen. Some ranchers pay bounties or hire professional hunters and trappers to kill predators on private and public lands. And, because of the overwhelming influence of ranchers on early and subsequent Western state legislation, many hunting laws today are geared toward unrestrained slaughter of livestock predators, competitors, and pests. Predator bag limits in most states are set to keep predators at very low densities. (New Mexican laws still on the books, though not enforced, require hunters of certain game species to kill a wolf or mountain lion for each game animal they take!)

The verified government body counts are staggering but account for only a small fraction of the total kill. Moreover, according to a special report on the 4-11-90 *CBS Evening*

News, ADC agents are routinely pressured to underestimate kills and to disregard non-target kills. And many government kills, especially poison kills, cannot be verified.

Stockmen have for decades waged their own extensive, intensive extermination programs; indeed, common knowledge on the Western range is that *stockmen and their hired hands kill far more predators than does the government* (documentation of this is, of course, essentially impossible). And by ranchers' own declaration, if ADC and other government predator programs were discontinued, ranchers would simply kill that many more predators themselves. Several wildlife experts have even suggested that many ostensible "predator kills" by ranchers are made instead more for personal possession or sale of pelts, stuffed heads, claws, teeth, bear fat, and such.

Sheepmen! I'm sick to death of them. They're a bunch of whining crybabies. Calling me up at all hours of the night, whining and crying for more traps, more poison, more attention. "Where's your husband? Why isn't he out here? Send him out here right away!"
--Wife of former federal predator "control" agent Dick Randall

Officially, sheep protection is the main justification for most predator "control" in much of the West. Yet, in many areas where predator "control" occurs, cattle are the animals being grazed. The foxes, bobcats, lynx, eagles, and others being killed are not even able to kill cattle, or usually even their calves.

Stockmen and their government agencies greatly exaggerate (often astronomically) the number of livestock killed by predators. Western public lands ranchers typically report yearly sheep and calf losses of 2%-5%, up to 10% and even higher (Ferguson 1983). Two House of Representatives reports in the 1960s and 1970s found these claims to be unfounded. Other studies show actual predator kills of usually under 1%. Sheepmen -- relatively speaking predators' worst enemy -- claim predator losses of $20-$25 million or more annually, while non-ranching sources consistently cite $4-$10 million (Ferguson 1983). According to Defenders of Wildlife, "Less than 550 of the 20,000 commercial sheep producers in the West -- less than 3% -- suffered about one third of the West's total lamb losses to coyotes (Defenders of Wildlife 1982)." Predictably, public lands sheep ranchers report far higher losses than private.

While most graziers habitually inflate predator losses, many ranchers, to cover up poor ranching practices or to make a bid for more subsidies, regularly blame *all* livestock losses on predators. The ranching community by mutual understanding quietly agrees that these "little white lies" are necessary to the continuation of government predator "control" programs and public sympathy and support. Conveniently, the owner of livestock lost to predation may also deduct the value of the loss from his federal income tax!

And I killed so many coyotes I got ashamed of myself. I think I got 700 and some coyotes in three months. Of course next spring, I didn't notice any difference in the amount of telephone calls I got. It was the same old whine, "The coyotes are putting us out of business, the coyotes are eating us up."
--Dick Randall

Furthermore, minimal correlation exists between predator "control" activities and reported losses to predators. Heavy losses have been reported consistently for a century, regardless of the intensity of predator programs. A recent National Audubon Society report states: "The Fish & Wildlife Service [under whose jurisdiction ADC was at the time] did not have the data which would justify the existence of its control programs, since it could not show the total amount of losses to coyote predation, the number of coyotes causing damage, or the relation of control methods to predator damage reduction."

Of course many ranchers, those of the Old West mode especially, don't bother with explanations or legalities. Here is a shocking but too-typical case in point, from the 8-11-88 *Tucson Citizen*: The article reports that southeastern Arizona public lands rancher Eddie Lackner *admitted* to killing 9 black bears *in one year* on the 2 National Forest allotments totalling 14,000 acres where he enjoys grazing privileges. According to an Arizona Game & Fish officer,

"He didn't just shoot the bears, he let them die slowly in traps." The official said they probably died from thirst and exposure, their legs shredded by the jaws of the huge leg-hold devices. Lackner also admitted to killing 27 mountain lions since 1976, and word has it that he has also killed many other bears and mountain lions, bobcats, and any other predators or competitors he could trap or pump lead into.

According to the article, although Lackner could have been charged on 4 different counts, fined, and jailed, he instead was sentenced to 2 years probation by the Graham County prosecutor -- a distant relative who has hunted on "Lackner's" ranch. Even if convicted on all counts, Lackner's crimes would have been relatively minor infractions under existing laws. Arizona Fish & Game claimed it was unable to press charges. The Forest Service smacked Lackner's hand smartly by revoking 1 of his 2 grazing permits for 2 years -- the first time a grazing permit in Arizona has been suspended for such reasons. Many of the cattle from this allotment were moved to adjoining state grazing land. Also, at Lackner's request the Forest Service road leading onto the allotment where the offenses occurred was closed with a fence, meaning other public lands users must obtain Lackner's permission to enter the Forest through Lackner's private land. On top of all this, even Forest Service documents show that Lackner's allotments were overgrazed. Forest range chief Larry Allen concedes that FS might have been "a little too accommodating toward the livestock interests." But that's not all. Since the Lackner case was filed, Game and Fish documents reveal that 2 more bears and at least 25 more (and still counting) mountain lions have been killed by Lackner and federal predator agents on "his" allotments .

The huge, 16" jaw, 2" teeth, steel leg-hold traps Lackner used to kill the animals would have been illegal if used by anyone but a rancher. Only in stock killing cases is such a large trap legal. Arizona Fish & Game officer Dave West stated, "If a person got caught in it they would never have been able to get out."

Non-ranchers are required by law to check their traps daily. Ranchers face no such requirements. According to an agent of the Arizona Game & Fish Department, "Ranchers who use this technique drop by their traps about once a month and kick aside the desiccated remains of whatever bear or mountain lion [or non-target animal] that has died there. Then they reset their trap and go about their business."

As a stockman, Lackner has legal rights far beyond those of mere mortals. As with other Western states, Arizona has special statutes allowing ranchers to kill actual, suspected, or even *possible* predators in many different ways legal only to them. No proof of actual or intended predation is required. Ranchers can kill as many predators as they like, anywhere, at any time of the year. They don't have to pay a fee, use legally established hunting methods, or report their kills for most species, as all other people are required to do. (Under Arizona and some other state laws,

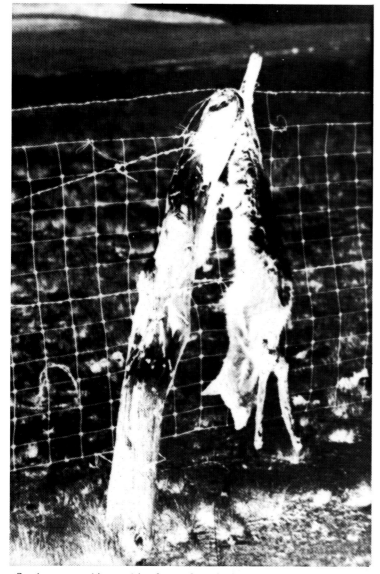

Stockmen use this repulsive form of voodooism to take out frustrations and to induce surviving predators to leave the area or meet the same fate. Where they are to go is a mystery when nearly every suitable habitat is occupied by livestock (or other predators). *(Unknown)*

ranchers are required to report all bear and lion kills, but it is well-known that few do.) Only a rancher can kill as many mountain lions as he wants. Only a rancher can legally kill any animal on public land he dislikes.

Of the few wildlife protection laws that do apply to ranchers, few government officials are inclined to interpret these laws so as to incriminate stockmen. However, even if laws were passed to strictly forbid ranchers to kill any predator, it is widely acknowledged -- boastfully by stockmen themselves -- that most predator slaughter would continue unabated.

Idaho's [and any Western state's] agrarian history has left us with an institutionalized kneejerk reaction when it comes to predators: In any encounter with domestic livestock, the predator must lose. It is a reaction that deserves some reassessment.
--Pam Morris, managing editor of *Idaho Mountain Express*, in *High Country News* (10-15-87)

Ranchers with chronic problems from predators on public lands must change their grazing practices. Cow-calf operations should be discontinued in brushy, rugged areas of public land that are in prime lion and bear habitat. Such allotments should either be restricted to steers, which are less prone to attack by lions and bears, or be retired in favor of wildlife.
--David Brown, wildlife biologist, author, and former chief of game for Arizona Game & Fish Department (Brown 1985)

A rancher beheaded and skinned this bobcat. *(Steve Johnson)*

"Predator control" has in reality been a ruthless campaign of genocide against many animal species. As a result, *most* large predators have been extirpated from much or most of their former ranges, and some are on the Endangered Species list. Following are species-by-species descriptions of the ranching establishment's continuing offensive against its major "varmint" enemies.

• Grizzly bear

Excepting the polar and Kodiak bears, the world's largest and strongest terrestrial predator is the grizzly bear, *Ursus horribilis*, a magnificent and much misunderstood animal. Like Kodiaks, grizzlies generally are recognized as a subspecies of brown bear, *Ursus arctos*. There is much disagreement on classification of varieties.

Grizzlies resemble their black bear cousins, but are larger, with a prominent hump in the shoulder and longer, straighter claws. Fur commonly is brown with silver-tipped hairs, but grizzlies vary greatly in coloration and other features. Adult grizzlies in the continental US typically weigh 300 to 600 pounds, occasionally 800 pounds or more. Most stand 3'-5' high at the shoulder and about 6'-7' end to end. Males generally are much larger than females.

The Great Bear can run more than 40 miles per hour, live to 30 years of age in the wild, and is so powerful it can crush a hereford's skull like an eggshell. Grizzlies are very broadly territorial and range widely, as individuals, or in families or small groups of families. They require large areas with a variety of terrain and food sources.

Grizzlies are gatherer-hunters and will in fact eat practically anything that lives or once did. They kill and eat many kinds of animals, but studies show that *70%-80%* of their diet in the Lower 48 consists of *plant* foods, often grass and sedges. (However, their diet probably has become more plant-centered since the most predatory bears were killed off over the years.) Their most significant nutritional component is plant protein. Grizzlies generally dislike human flesh and usually keep their distance from people. Nonetheless, more than any Western carnivore they do kill and sometimes eat humans, though so rarely that there is a greater risk of being killed by a falling tree. Their few attacks on people almost invariably occur when the bears are cornered, provoked, wounded, or when protecting young (especially), bedding sites, or food. Humans are the grizzly's only enemy.

A grizzly bear eating berries. *(George Wuerthner)*

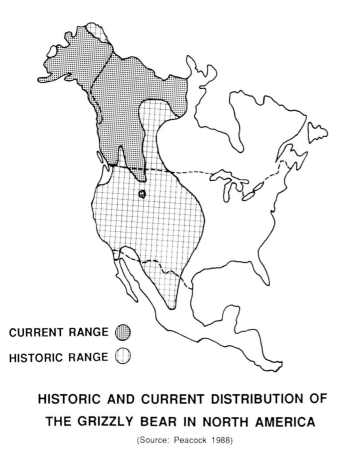

CURRENT RANGE ◉

HISTORIC RANGE ◐

HISTORIC AND CURRENT DISTRIBUTION OF
THE GRIZZLY BEAR IN NORTH AMERICA

(Source: Peacock 1988)

Because the grizzly needs a large, pristine, and diverse habitat, his continued existence guarantees survival of many forms of life. He is a measure of the health of the whole system.
--Annick Smith, from *Great Bear*

When Europeans arrived on this continent, a conservatively estimated 100,000 grizzly bears roamed plains, plateaus, valleys, mesas, hills, and mountains of the West. The explorers Lewis and Clark in their 1804-1806 journey reported sighting grizzly and black bears most days and killing at least a few of them almost every week (Thwaites 1959). Seventeenth century Spaniards in California occasionally reported seeing 50 or 60 grizzlies in one day, many of them feeding in actual herds (McNamee 1985). Grizzly range encompassed the entire western half of what is now the United States, excepting arid regions and the wettest portion of the Pacific Northwest. Unlike today, pre-European grizzlies lived an open and sunny existence, roaming freely across the landscape -- grasslands, low-elevation woods, and riparian zones (even within deserts) included.

There was no attempt to isolate the livestock killers; all grizzlies were sheep and cattle killers to the stockman and therefore they were executed whenever and wherever they were encountered.
--J.J. McCoy, **Wild Enemies** (McCoy 1974)

The griz fell victim to the standard livestock scenario: as ranchers took over most of the West in the mid-1800s, they killed as many grizzlies as they could. Their livestock so overgrazed the grizzly's habitat that its food source of grass,

forbs, leaves, berries, fruits, nuts, roots, tubers, insects, and grubs was seriously depleted. Range management and overgrazing's secondary effects drastically reduced the number and variety of prey animals, and riparian and waterway damage lowered fish populations. In a twist of irony, surviving grizzlies sometimes of necessity took to eating the livestock that had ravaged their habitat. David Brown relates in **The Grizzly in the Southwest**, "Like the wolf, the opportunistic grizzly was not about to forego a new and readily available food source -- not when this new-found prey had depleted the grizzly's natural food supplies (Brown 1985)."

Nevertheless, the grizzly never was the rabid livestock killer portrayed. Grizzly expert Doug Peacock writes:

Protecting livestock was ostensibly the principal reason for killing grizzlies. Yet few bears actually preyed on domestic animals. Bears were shot due to ignorance, irrational hatred, and the illusions of what constituted duty or sport. (Peacock 1988)

Early explorers, trappers, and settlers across the West shot all grizzlies they encountered as a service to stockmen and to general human advancement. Some used dynamite. In California, many early ranchers made sport and money by staging grizzly/bull fights. The bears usually won, but ranchers provided them a never-ending supply of bulls. (McNamee 1985) By the end of the 1800s, grizzlies were extirpated from much of the West.

With grizzlies on the run in the early 1900s, livestock interests stepped up the slaughter. The plains grizzly, a variety that once preyed on bison and pronghorn but was forced to prey on livestock, was driven to extinction. The federal government trapped, shot, and poisoned remaining grizzlies without restraint. Stockmen shot them on sight or paid bounties. According to Lance Olsen, Director of the Great Bear Foundation in Missoula, Montana, "By the 1920s, grizzlies survived only in remote and rugged mountains where the livestock industry had not yet penetrated." As with so many Western species, the grizzly was forced to change its habits and confine itself to inhospitable areas rarely visited by humans or their livestock. In Mexico, griz held out in small numbers in the northern Sierra Madre until the 1960s when ranchers launched a final assault with guns, traps, and poisons.

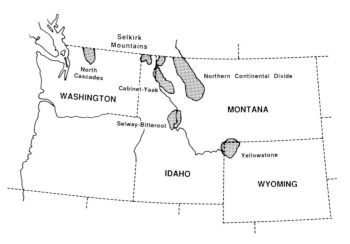

OCCUPIED GRIZZLY BEAR ECOSYSTEMS IN THE LOWER 48 STATES

(Source: Peacock 1988)

In the US West today 99% -- *including the best* -- of the grizzly's former habitat is no longer home to these awesome omnivores. In California, whose state flag features the grizzly, a grizzly population of about 20,000 -- possibly the second highest brown bear concentration in the world -- was reduced to zero. In the 48 contiguous states probably less than 800 grizzlies survive in 6 relatively small enclaves at high elevations in the northern Rocky Mountains, mostly in Wilderness Areas and National Parks. Only 2 of these enclaves harbor enough grizzlies to be considered sufficient for genetically viable, self-sustaining populations -- the Northern Continental Divide and the Greater Yellowstone Ecosystems (including Glacier and Yellowstone National Parks). Nearly all surviving grizzlies live on public land. (Brown 1985, McNamee 1985, Peacock 1988)

Unfortunately, livestock, sheep especially, are grazed in or near most of these rugged, remote areas. And grizzlies occasionally do eat a dozen sheep or a few cows. As one grizzly expert put it, "These docile, defenseless flocks of sheep must to a grizzly seem like some benevolent soul has set the table." Nonetheless, depredation has been exaggerated by ranchers, who aim to make sure grizzlies are not allowed to make a comeback.

Systematic extermination of grizzlies continued into the 1970s. Since then, many "problem" grizzlies have been killed by government officials, while poachers, slob hunters, and general development in their range have taken a heavy toll. But conflict and slaughter in or near these high elevation sheep allotments probably continues as the major single factor working against their survival.

Records show that in the second largest grizzly population in the Lower 48, the Greater Yellowstone Ecosystem, 20 grizzlies were killed on sheep allotments between 1970 and 1975. Curiously, since 1975, when grizzlies were officially classified as a Threatened species, there have been no grizzly killings reported on Yellowstone-area sheep ranges. Why? Because grizzly killers are now subject to fines and official investigations. Now the rule, even more than before, is "shoot, shovel, and shut up."

For example: In 1978 in the Targee National Forest portion of the Greater Yellowstone Ecosystem there were 2 known grizzly killings by sheepherders. In a 1980 report to the Wyoming Department of Game & Fish, biologist Larry Roop stated,

One of these was discovered only because it was a radio-collared bear. The other was discovered by a researcher in a sheepherder's camp. Because of the discovery the researcher was threatened and was unable to collect the skull for study. . . . There were four more Grizzly Bear mortalities strongly suspected, but not confirmed, in the Targee National Forest during 1979. All of these losses were associated with sheep grazing.

A 1979 report by the Yellowstone Interagency Grizzly Bear Study Team stated that "Information gathered by undercover agents and volunteered by sheepherders indicated that at least three other grizzlies and possibly as many as *fourteen* have been killed in the last two years . . . ."

A 1988 report prepared by the Greater Yellowstone Coalition states that since 1975, 20% of all known and probable grizzly mortalities resulted from conflicts between bears and livestock. The report also noted that livestock may eliminate or reduce the plants grizzlies need for food, leading indirectly to increased mortality, either through starvation or by forcing the bears to forage more widely, bringing them into contact with people. Forty-four percent of the Greater Yellowstone Ecosystem is open to livestock grazing.

The situation is even worse in the largest grizzly enclave, the Northern Continental Divide Ecosystem in Montana, where 31 of 35 reported "grizzly bear control actions" between 1967 and 1983 were related to sheep depredations. Further, biologists agree that there is *at least* 1 unknown death for every known kill. (Dogmeat 1986)

The [cattle-eating grizzly] *was captured, tranquilized, fitted with a radio-transmitting collar, and transported far from Choteau* [Montana] *to the western side of the Continental Divide. Within days the bear was back, killing cattle again, and this time was killed in a state-sanctioned hunt. Ranchers tend to think that predatory animals caught in the act of killing livestock should receive no second chances.*
--Henry Schacht, Farm Reporter, 10-23-87 *San Francisco Chronicle*

Not only does the ranching industry bear (so to speak) more responsibility than anyone else for grizzly extermination, but also for subsequent failure to reintroduce the bruin. There are biologically excellent reintroduction sites for the grizzly in every Western state, except perhaps Nevada. Yet, even with the promise of guaranteed compensation for livestock losses, the industry refuses to reconsider its opposition. Thus, despite legal mandates, no Western state plans to reintroduce the animal. The grizzly's needs, the public's desire, environmental integrity -- all take a back seat with the Imperial Graziers at the wheel.

(Brush Wolf)

The heedless [grizzly] bear that roamed the open and fed by day is gone. His place is taken by bears that feed secretly, silently, by night, in cover -- always secretly. ... He has retreated to secluded fastnesses, to wild and inaccessible regions of thicket and mountainside. He is changed in temper as in life, and the faintest whiff of man scent is now enough to drive him miles away.
--Naturalist Ernest Thomas Seton

●Black bear

The black bear is the most numerous and widely distributed bear in North America and has been a resident of the continent for about 500,000 years. Though similar in appearance to the grizzly, this bear is generally smaller and darker, with shorter, more curved claws, a straighter nose, larger ears, a small white patch on the chest, and no shoulder hump. As with grizzlies and humans, appearance and behavior between individuals vary greatly.

Adult black bears generally weigh from 150 to 450 pounds, measure 2'-3' at the shoulder and about 5' long. Females usually are smaller than males. Their fur is black or dark brown, occasionally cinnamon, or even blonde. Like grizzlies, black bears have poor eyesight, good hearing, a keen sense of smell, great intelligence, and are easily irritated. They are fine runners, swimmers, and, unlike the straighter-clawed grizzlies, adept tree climbers. Black bears are more territorial than grizzlies, but loosely so, also wandering great distances in search of food, singly or mother and cubs together.

Like the grizzly, the black bear has flat molars and sharp front teeth; its herbivorous/omnivorous diet includes berries, acorns, grasses, leaves, cactus fruits, bulbs, bark, roots, honey, bird eggs, grasshoppers, ants, termites, grubs, fish, small mammals, an occasional larger animal, and carrion. In some areas frequented by tourists, black bears eat tourist treats and garbage. Though even less dangerous to people than grizzlies, they are much more numerous and likely to make contact with humans.

Like most Western predators, black bears are opportunistic scavengers. Most bears readily eat from cattle and sheep carcasses. Though probably most eat livestock as carrion only, they are from circumstantial evidence, or simply on principle, declared stock killers and relentlessly hunted and killed. Others, by eating livestock carrion, acquire a taste and begin killing livestock for food, whereafter they are pursued unto death. Those few black bears that kill livestock regularly do so because they are driven to by an overgrazed habitat or presented an almost irresistible offering of unprotected mutton or beef for their dining pleasure. Most never set teeth on livestock, but they too are often pursued and killed, simply because they are bears. And, many are killed by traps and poisons as non-target species.

Early Western settlers often could not tell if they were killing black or grizzly bears, but to them it did not matter. With help from government predator "control" in the early 1900s, black bears were killed so indiscriminately that in 1919 even a chief federal predator "control" agent, J. Stokley

Ligon, reported, "Few of the black and brown bears are really destructive to livestock, most ranchmen are so unfair as to condemn all the animals for the crimes of a few." By the late 1920s both black and grizzly bears had been so reduced in numbers and range that Ligon reported, "Poverty stricken ranges, as a result of excessive range utilization, and drought often render their usual food so scanty that out of need bears become killers; hence, as respects losses from bears, forage conservation would result in increased savings of cattle and sheep." (Brown 1985)

Until the 1920s black bear decline in the West generally paralleled that of the grizzly, but after, the grizzly gradually slid toward oblivion, while the black bear partially recovered. One reason is that predator "controllers" began focusing more attention on the grizzly. More importantly, loss of the grizzly's open habitat to ranching and settlement made it impossible for the animal's low reproductive rate to recoup relentless attrition from stockmen and their bear-hunting allies. The black bear, on the other hand, needing a smaller home range and naturally more a creature of the forest, was more resilient.

Since the early 1920s black bears have expanded their populations and territories, though not nearly to their original numbers or range. Although they live in mountainous and forested areas in every Western state, black bears have been extirpated completely from numerous mountain ranges, and where they do survive they do so in much smaller numbers. Increasing evidence indicates that in recent years their numbers are once again declining. In the West, their most deadly enemy is still ranching. In 1988 ADC alone *reported* killing 289 black bears, while perhaps thousands were killed through other government predator programs and, mostly, by stockmen themselves. Each year, thousands more are precluded from existence due to a degraded range and ranching developments.

Like the grizzly, the black bear has necessarily changed its habits and habitat since Europeans and their livestock arrived in the West. As opposed to pristine times when it roamed freely between vegetation zones in diverse terrain, the black bear now stays almost exclusively in or near the protective cover of thickly forested areas; it is secretive, primarily nocturnal, and seldom seen, except as a camp robber or garbage eater.

●Wolf

The wolf was this continent's premier, most ubiquitous predator, inhabiting nearly every terrestrial ecosystem before the arrival of Europeans. Two species are native to North America. The red wolf, *Canus niger*, is a small wolf somewhat resembling a coyote. Once found throughout the "Civil War South," it was extirpated from its range entirely and survives today only in captivity and as several small reintroduced populations at the Alligator National Wildlife Refuge in coastal North Carolina and Cape Romain National Wildlife Refuge in coastal South Carolina. Another reintroduction proposal for Tennessee-Kentucky was scrapped when both state wildlife agencies withdrew their support because of objections from livestock interests, while the current reintroductions are saddled with many restrictions due to stockmen. No red wolf reintroduction site is large enough to maintain genetically healthy populations, but they are a beginning.

Many varieties of gray wolf, *Canus lupus*, once inhabited all but the driest portions of the West and, curiously (at least according to most experts), most of California. Many subspecies are now extinct. The gray wolf looks something like a large German shepherd, weighs usually from 50 to 120 pounds, and measures 2'-3' tall and about 4' long in head and body. Depending mostly on environment, gray wolves may vary in color, from pure black or white to the usual gray to brown, gold, or tan.

Wolves are highly social animals, and their social structure is complex. Their packs usually consist of a couple and their young, along with some close relatives, numbering up to 15 or so. Packs larger than this are less efficient, so wolves regulate pack size carefully. The Mexican variety of wolf (*C.l. baileyi* -- named, ironically, after an early wolf eradicator), the most distinct North American subspecies, lives in smaller groups of up to 6. The famous "lone wolves," of which there are comparatively few, are mostly younger wolves that were driven away from oversized packs. They live alone without social territories until accepted into another pack or until they join other lone wolves. In natural situations, wolves usually mate for life; if one of a couple dies, the other usually never mates again. Their average yearly litter is 6 pups. They are prolific reproducers, if not disturbed by humans and if food is adequate.

Wolves are very playful and affectionate, and genuinely enjoy and appreciate each other. They are highly intelligent, much more so than domestic dogs. Their only real enemies are humans, and rarely bears.

Gray wolves travel widely in search of food, and may cover 30-125 miles in a day. A pack's well-defined but dynamic territory may be anywhere from 50 to 5000 or more square miles, depending on numerous environmental variables. Hunting is done in packs in a very organized, cooperative fashion, usually not by outrunning but by circling and wearing down their prey. Much more carnivorous than coyotes, wolves feed only rarely on wild berries, fruits, grass, or other plant foods. Gray wolves favor deer, elk, pronghorn, buffalo, moose, and other large mammals, but will eat small mammals and rodents, reptiles, amphibians, birds, fish, and even insects and earthworms. They much prefer to kill their own food, but will eat carrion if they must. A wolf can eat 20 pounds of meat at one feeding.

Wolves have been around the West in one form or another for an estimated 15 million years. (Before the Pleistocene extinctions, dire wolves also roamed the continent.) Before Europeans and their livestock arrived, gray wolves ranged over prairie, mesa, valley, and mountain alike. The Lewis and Clark expedition of 1804-1806 reported numerous wolves along most of its route across the northern West. Like grizzlies, wolves are top-level predators and their influence on Western ecosystems was profound.

The Indians understood it all along. They would watch attentively as early settlers sought to render wolfless the surrounding countryside by pumping dead cows full of poison and setting them out in their fields. Such behavior amazed Native Americans. Their explanation for it was that, among palefaces, it was a manifestation of insanity.
--Ted Williams, "Beast of Lore" (Williams 1988)

For more than 1000 years, the wolf has been the most misunderstood of all predators. While Native Americans knew and did not fear the wolf, the "great" cultures of Europe turned it into a symbol of the Devil -- largely because of centuries of predation on European livestock. Thus, the Europeans who arrived on this continent in the 1500s brought with them an intense fear of wolves, cultivated by centuries of horror stories by superstitious, religious peoples who had lost connection with the natural world. These early settlers were terrified by wolves howling around them at night -- wolves that killed and ate their livestock and left bloody bones for them to find! Rumors of wolves attacking people ran rampant, and the settlers' fear bordered on hysteria. The wolf was considered an especially evil enemy, to be unquestioningly destroyed. (In Virginia, settlers began converting the natives by offering them one cow for every wolf destroyed.) Descendents of these American colonists brought this unreasonable fear of the wolf with them when they "settled" the West in the 1800s. Passed down through the generations, it persists even today.

There never was any real basis for this paranoia. In all of North America there has never been a documented case of a healthy, wild pure wolf killing a human. Jim Johnson of the Endangered Species branch of FWS says that "people hiking in the woods are more likely to be eaten by a cow than a wolf." Fact is, wolves immediately flee at the slightest sign of humans. Even when people threaten their home or young, they keep their distance. Indeed, researchers have carried off their pups while the parents followed for miles, whining all the while. Except toward prey, wolves are extremely shy and gentle animals.

The livestock industry has been united to have the wolf forever removed from its domain. Powerful political forces were mustered to enlist the aid of the U.S. government in the total removal of the premier livestock predator from Western rangelands and to insure that no reservoir of breeding wolves remained for reinfestation. No refuge for wolves was to be permitted.
--David E. Brown, **The Wolf in the Southwest** (Brown 1984)

Wolves can easily kill a sheep or calf, and are quite capable of bringing down an adult cow; however, they prefer full-grown sheep and yearling cattle. In the late 1800s, with their natural prey severely reduced by overgrazing and overhunting (largely by ranchers), wolves came to rely on livestock for food. In fact, the intensity of wolf predation on livestock coincided perfectly with the overgrazing of their habitat -- not so much because livestock numbers were high as because wild prey was scarce. The omnipresent herds of docile, practically defenseless animals (the tough Texas longorn partially excepted) afforded wolves an endless supply of easy prey on an otherwise nearly empty hunting ground.

By taking livestock from grossly overstocked ranges, wolves were in a sense merely culling surplus animals. And, though wolves generally prey on weak and inferior animals, to them *all* livestock must have seemed weak and inferior. As naturalist Ted Williams writes, "As wolves view the universe, the torpid, dull-witted creatures we call 'livestock' qualify eminently as 'infirm'" (Williams 1988).

Wolves surely did kill a large number of stock, but ranchers grossly overestimated losses. Wolves found scavenging livestock remains were routinely blamed for those deaths, though the animals often had died from other causes. Wolf prints around a sheep carcass were more than enough reason to kill every wolf in an area. And as always, stockmen greatly exaggerated predations to elicit sympathy and support from the public and government. Eventually *all* wolves were condemned as stock killers.

And so stockmen's fear turned to hate. The slaughter intensified, with guns, snares, traps, and animal carcasses poisoned or laced with broken glass (which causes one of the most excruciatingly painful deaths imaginable). By the 1880s ranchers and government were paying wolf bounties. For example, in 1883 Montana's first state-sponsored wolf bounty brought in 5450 dead wolves for the $1 bounty. By 1905 the Montana state legislature had increased the bounty to $10 and ordered the state veterinarian to inoculate all trapped wolves with scarcoptic mange and release them into the wild. Between 1883 and 1918, 80,730 wolves were bountied in Montana, while many thousands more were killed without bounty. The story was similar in every Western state, and within a few decades the Western wolf population was cut in half.

However, wolves are wary and intelligent animals with high reproductive potential. They were not to be so easily eradicated from the West. Early wolves were vulnerable due to their pack structure, territorialism, and repeated use of wolf pathways, and they accepted a wide variety of baits and blundered into the most obvious traps. But they learned quickly, and the last wolves in this country died hard. Some became experts at uncovering traps and taking bait; some learned to avoid poisoned bait; the survivors changed their habits and avoided humans unequivocally.

WOLF DISTRIBUTION

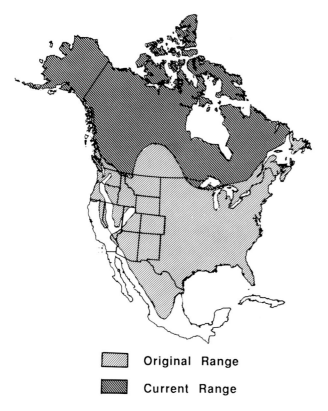

▨ Original Range

▨ Current Range

Eventually, the Great Provider -- Uncle Sam -- was called into the genocide campaign. "Sportsman" President Teddy Roosevelt damned the wolf as "the beast of waste and desolation," and in 1915 the federal government passed a law requiring extermination of all wolves on federal lands, including National Parks. Soon, skilled, well-equipped federal predator "control" agents spread across the land. By the 1940s wolves survived only as scattered individuals and a few small groups; in the 1950s and 1960s only a few rugged scragglers remained; and from the 1970s on wolves were reported only as occasional wanderers from Canada and Mexico.

Thus did the ranching establishment almost single-handedly exterminate the gray wolf from the American West. As an idea of the size of this war, in all more than $100 million (perhaps $0.5 billion in today's dollar) in wolf bounties has been paid in the US and Canada since the early years. Bounties are still paid in a few areas. As a sadly humorous example, in 1986 the Brazos County, Texas, treasurer paid out $225 for 30 sets of "wolf" ears under the county's ancient predator laws. The ears were probably those of dogs or coyotes. The treasurer was informed that there haven't been wolves in the area for decades, and county officials subsequently voted to stop paying the $7.50 bounties. Today, stockmen in Alberta and British Columbia, along with the hunting establishment, continue to kill Canadian wolves, sometimes with bounties, while in Mexico ranchers and population pressures have nearly driven the gray wolf to extinction.

We're going to fight this to the bitter end. We're just not going to have wolves.
--Joe Helle, National Wool Growers Association, sheep rancher

In the past few decades, the occasional wolves crossing the borders from Canada and Mexico into the US have excited the fears of stockmen and the imaginations of wolf advocates. Thus far, the public's growing demand for wolf reintroduction has been consistently overpowered by ranchers' vehement insistence that wolves shall never again roam the West. Wolf recovery efforts have been thwarted on 3 main fronts: the Southwest, northern Rockies, and Yellowstone National Park. (Additionally, a reintroduction proposal for Olympic National Park -- a prime site -- was recently defeated by area stockmen.)

Keep them [all Mexican wolves in the US] in the zoos. They're not smart enough to survive . . . that's why they didn't survive before.
--Gerald Maestas, New Mexico State Game Commission chairman, 1-29-88 *Albuquerque Journal*

The last few wolves in New Mexico were killed for ranchers by a federal agent in the late 1960s. In Arizona, the famous Aravaipa Wolf was taken "quietly" (so as not to arouse public displeasure) in 1970 by a private trapper for a reputed bounty of $500 put up by local stockmen. Ironically, even before this time, with growing support from the public, the US Fish & Wildlife Service -- the same agency largely responsible for exterminating the wolf, now entrusted with its recovery -- had been considering wolf reintroduction plans for the Southwest.

Under the federal Endangered Species Act of 1973, the Mexican subspecies of gray wolf was in 1976 determined to be in extreme danger of extinction and listed as Endangered, mandating the federal government to take whatever steps necessary to save it. The Mexican Wolf Recovery Team was established in 1979. In 1982 the team wrote a reintroduction plan that was approved by the US and Mexican governments and drawn up by the Recovery Team. Under the plan, only a token number of wolves would be reintroduced in 1 or a few locales. Each locale would be, according to project director Norma Ames, at minimum "a 200 square mile piece of public land with as little impact by livestock or humans as possible." Each wolf would be fitted with a radio collar for tracking purposes, and each collar would contain a radio-activated tranquilizer dart so wolves could be immediately subdued if they wandered onto land used by livestock. Reintroduction was tentatively scheduled for the late 1980s or early 1990s.

Originally, New Mexico, Arizona, and Texas were considered for reintroduction. But in 1986, with complete disregard for the Endangered Species Act, ranchers forced a bill through the Texas legislature which made re-introduction of wolves in that state illegal. In 1987 FWS asked New Mexico and Arizona to consider possible reintroduction sites in those states.

New Mexico proposed the wild, remote Animas Mountains in the extreme southwestern part of the state (excellent wolf habitat) and the Air Force's White Sands Missile Range (not great wolf habitat, but also not grazed by livestock, therefore having the least potential opposition). The New Mexico Cattle Growers Association (NMCGA) reacted by threatening to have all state game personnel supportive of the plan fired. Shortly thereafter, the Animas Mountains were dropped from consideration, and the commander of the White Sands Missile Base alleged that the Air Force could not support the plan because it did not want wolf biologists on the Missile Range because they might get hurt. (Interestingly, on this same range have been a 10 year mountain lion study, a public sport hunting season on introduced oryx and ibex, researchers studying a protected herd of bighorn sheep, and other human activities.) Meanwhile, New Mexico's best reintroduction site, the huge Gila/Blue Range Wilderness complex in the southwest, was not seriously considered due to ranchers' clout in that area.

With pro-ranching politics-as-usual, wolf reintroduction in New Mexico is unlikely. Indeed, in 1986 Governor Gary Carruthers (a close friend of James Watt and long-time public lands ranching supporter) appointed a past president of the NMCGA to head the New Mexico Game Commission. Of the reintroduction effort, current NMCGA president Denny Gentry stated "We've put [federal and state officials] on notice that we will take whatever legal action and political action is necessary to stop it." Gentry further promised that ranchers would "shoot the damn things as fast as they're released."

The fact that efforts to reintroduce the gray wolf into Arizona wilderness are being squashed by the Arizona Game & Fish Director is an indication of the choke-hold welfare ranchers have on our public lands.
--John Patterson, teacher and environmentalist, in letter to the Arizona Game & Fish Department

Over in Arizona, things were little different. The state Game and Fish Director agreed to evaluate no less than 15 potential reintroduction sites. However, though many of the sites were physically adequate for wolves, a new Game and Fish director soon thereafter bowed to industry pressure, saying he had to "put the plan on the back burner" for alleged "lack of public education" on the wolf. In a telephone interview, a Game and Fish official described the department's 3-point reintroduction plan as (1) breeding, (2) identifying reintroduction sites, and (3) educating the public. Consequently, it may be 10 years or more before wolves are "on the ground" in Arizona, if ever. Yes, he said (covertly), stockmen are chiefly responsible, but we "must accept reality."

In October 1987, with Texas, New Mexico, and Arizona all refusing to cooperate, the FWS Region 2 Director in Albuquerque announced: "We have no sites. The [Mexican] wolf reintroduction program is now terminated." Many people feel FWS never was serious about reintroducing the Mexican wolf into the Southwest and was just going through the motions to appease the public and to superficially acknowledge the Endangered Species Act. Whatever the case, Southwestern stockmen have crushed the program, as they promised they would.

Presently, there are only 38 Mexican wolves in captivity, 30 of which are in the US. Few have been bred because there aren't more pens to hold their progeny. With each passing year they lose more of the wildness they need to survive as a natural species. They live in cages and eat dog food.

The Southwest has changed drastically since wolves were a functioning part of the ecosystems of the region. If those changes are too drastic, then the restoration of the Mexican wolf in the wild is no longer a reasonable possibility in this region.
--Bill Montoya, Director, New Mexico Department of Game & Fish

Opposition to recovery for the gray wolf also has been vehement in the Rockies. Strongly influenced by the ranching industry, most state officials there have expressed outright hostility to any reintroduction effort. The Colorado Game and Fish Commission approved a resolution opposing "every person or entity" that would even suggest returning the wolf to the state, (Brown 1988) as did the Idaho Game & Fish recently.

Even so, the northern gray wolf has a much better chance of reinhabiting lost habitat than does the Mexican wolf of the Southwest. Wolves naturally were much more numerous in well-watered regions, where their prey base of large ungulates was more abundant. (Between 1880 and 1920, the grazing industry killed more than 100,000 wolves in the northern Rockies alone.) There remain vast, comparatively wild spaces of suitable habitat in the northern Rockies, especially in central Idaho, which contains the largest block of Wilderness in the lower 48. And the Canadian wolf population is still large enough to spin off occasional individuals and packs into the remote mountains of Montana, Idaho, and Washington (where 2 wolf dens were discovered recently).

Public support for the wolf in the northern Rockies has grown strong in recent years, and tentative recovery plans were gradually developed. In August 1987, compelled by the Endangered Species Act, FWS Regional Deputy Director John Spinks signed a wolf recovery plan that called for establishing 10 wolf packs each in northwest Montana and north-central Idaho, and reintroduction to Yellowstone National Park. Just a month later, under pressure from stockmen, FWS Director Frank Dunkle (former chairman of the Montana Republican party), announced he was shelving the plan as "foolhardy." Said Joe Helle of the National Sheep Growers Association, "We got it stopped. We still have the political clout . . . ."

Nonetheless, Yellowstone National Park, from which wolves were extirpated in 1926, remains prime for wolf reintroduction. According to wolf researcher David Mech, "Yellowstone is a place that literally begs to have wolves." Already home to the grizzly, it is a large and relatively wild area with abundant large prey. With the wolf's return, the alleged "overgrazing" by "overpopulations" of elk, buffalo, and moose in Yellowstone would be alleviated. There is even strong evidence that grizzlies (a Threatened species) would benefit from wolf reintroduction because they often displace wolves from carcasses.

The wolf recovery plan for Yellowstone proposed reintroducing a minimum of 10 wolf pairs in the Greater Yellowstone Ecosystem as an "experimental population." There are 50 livestock operators in the recovery area, with only 5000 cattle and 6000 sheep, all outside the National Park. Under the plan, any wolves wandering into livestock areas on public or private lands could have been killed. The federal government also guaranteed reimbursement for the full cash value of any livestock verified as lost to wolves. A coalition of conservation groups, the National Park Service, and the US Fish & Wildlife Service promoted the plan. In 1985, William Penn Mott, Director of the National Park Service, also announced his support for wolf reintroduction in Yellowstone National Park.

Despite all this, with their heavily pro-ranching Wyoming Congressional delegation firing the big guns, the Royal Ranchers stopped the plan dead in 1987. Park Service Director Mott quickly changed his tune, saying he would not support the plan unless Wyoming's Congressional delegation did. Joe Helle provided the eulogy, saying that [after 15 million years] "the wolf's place is gone," and that sheep growers, on the other hand, had been ranching for generations, and would be for years to come.

Much to the dismay of stock-men, wolves are reintroducing themselves in the northern Rockies. In the mid-1980s, 12 gray wolves wandered down from the Canadian wilderness into Glacier National Park -- the first known resident pack in the American West since wolves were all but eradicated there half a century ago. They bred, while another new pack was reported to the east on the Rocky Mountain Front. One pack moved back into Canada, however, and in 1986

(Lone Wolf Circles)

the other was massacred by government predator "control" agents after eating livestock. Today, the roughly 10 to 20 wolves remaining in the Northern Continental Divide Ecosystem (greater Glacier National Park ecosystem) constitute a very fragile population. (ADC recently shot from a helicopter another wolf accused of preying on a rancher's livestock near Marion, Montana.)

A national wildlife organization, Defenders of Wildlife, has independently raised more than $30,000 and offered to compensate northern Rockies ranchers for all verified livestock kills by wolves; it has thus far compensated 2 ranchers for livestock kills; in one incident there was strong evidence that coyotes had made the kills. Most area ranchers rejected this profit guarantee as a "public relations ploy" and continued to demand death for all stock-eating wolves. Meanwhile, one conservationist complained, "National conservation groups like 'Defenders' defend cows, ranchers, FWS and their fat budgets with money they should be using to sue FWS for violating the Endangered Species Act."

Recovery plans included radio collars for all reintroduced wolves, recapture of stock killers, laws to permit ranchers to kill stock-killing wolves, and guaranteed government compensation for lost livestock. Montana and Idaho ranchers nonetheless vowed to fight all wolf recovery efforts.

Some of the arguments given by ranching advocates for opposition to wolf recovery are ridiculous, if not humorous. Idaho Senator Steve Symms, in response to letters requesting his support for reintroduction in the northern Rockies, stated that wolves "pose a real danger to humans." Wyoming Senator Alan Simpson maintained that wolves *eat* humans. Not to be outdone in bias or ignorance, Wyoming Senator Malcolm Wallop told the Wyoming Stock Growers Association in June 1985 that proposed wolf reintroductions "threaten the state's tourists as well as ranching industries," and that "there's [sic] 50,000 wolves in Minnesota and that should be enough to keep them off the endangered species list."

Politicians and Western ranchers would do well to consider those nationally *Threatened 1200 or so wolves of a different subspecies* in northern Minnesota (along with perhaps 50 in northern Wisconsin and Michigan). Generally, they coexist amid 9800 farms that raise 91,000 sheep and 234,000 cows. There, an average of less than 5 cows and 13 sheep per 10,000 animals grazed are lost to wolves annually, and ranchers are reimbursed by the government for all losses (though some ranchers there do kill wolves illegally). Wolves there do not significantly deplete wildlife or pose problems to human use of the land (other than the abovementioned livestock kills), much less to humans themselves. In Minnesota, wolves have been accepted by most farmers as a natural part of the environment. (Wuerthner 1987)

We killed off the goddamn things once. Now they want to bring 'em back.
--Montana public lands rancher Butch Krause, *People* (9-24-90)

Despite all this, the future for the wolf in the West is not hopeless. An increasingly informed public, already favoring wolf reintroduction, can only become more pro-wolf. By a margin of 6 to 1, visitors to Yellowstone National Park said the presence of wolves would enrich their Park experience. A study by Alister Bath of the University of Wyoming revealed that 48.5% of Wyoming's citizens support wolf reintroduction, while 34.5% are opposed. Wildlife biologist David Brown reports:

When a preliminary telephone survey aimed at determining the public's attitude toward wolves showed that 61% of the 726 Arizona households queried favored bringing the wolf back to the state, the Arizona Game and Fish Commission discontinued the survey rather than offend influential livestock raisers. (Brown 1988)

A questionnaire by Arizona Game & Fish also showed 2/3 of state residents supporting wolves, even in rural areas. New Mexico surveys show 76% support for the wolf. Other surveys in Montana show good public support for wolf reintroduction. According to Hank Fischer of Defenders of Wildlife,

Throughout the US as a whole there is overwhelming support for wolf recovery and reintroductions. Even opinion polls conducted closer to areas where wolves might actually dwell show a majority of people favoring wolf recovery.

And while survival of the Mexican wolf is in doubt, Canada's wolf population, though under attack, still survives in numbers large enough to help repopulate the US.

[FWS biologist] *Bangs took a poll of the meeting room packed with wool growers to see how many favored reintroduction of wolves. Not one hand went up.*
--*High Country News* (2-12-90)

Since the 1800s gray wolves have changed greatly in habit and habitat. Today they are chiefly nocturnal, having learned to minimize exposure to humans. Likewise, they have necessarily become wasteful of food, having learned not to feed in the daylight or remain near their kills for long. As has their habitat, so has their social order been fragmented, further threatening their survival. No longer do wolves roam the grassy plains or open mesas. Rather, they slink through the remote, cold forests of the North, as far from people as they can get. Territory size is also necessarily much larger now, as their remaining habitat is much less productive and they must range farther to find food. A larger territory also brings them more deadly contact with humans.

Correspondingly, areas for reintroduction must be quite large, perhaps roughly 50 miles in diameter. And though there are many sites of sufficient size that would fit wolves' needs, *all* would result in conflict with stockmen. According to some "reasonable" ranching apologists, we should reintroduce wolves only where there are no livestock and wolves will not travel into livestock areas. Great, but *where is that place*?? Since livestock are grazed within 20 or 30 miles of every potential wolf reintroduction site in the West, and wolves may travel beyond permissible boundaries, that leaves nowhere for wolves.

We reached the old wolf in time to watch a fierce green fire dying in her eyes. I realized then, and have known ever since, that there was something new to me in those eyes -- something known only to her and to the mountain.
--Aldo Leopold

The wolf belongs in the West.

Its howl is an inspiration to all who know and love the Earth.

Bring back the wolf!

(George Wuerthner)

(George Wuerthner)

●Coyote

The coyote, *Canis latrans*, also known as "prairie wolf," "brush wolf," or "little wolf," resembles a medium-sized dog with a pointed nose and bushy tail. It is in fact more closely related to domestic dogs than wolves. There are many subspecies described. Usually weighing from 15 to 45 pounds, the animal measures slightly less than 2' high at the shoulder and about 3' in body length. Its color ranges generally from gray to reddish gray. The coyote is said to vary more in individual characteristics than any other North American mammal.

(Steve Johnson)

If they aren't killed by people, coyotes usually live 10 to 15 or more years. They average bearing 5 to 10 pups a year, sometimes 15 or more. Unlike wolves, coyotes may be either polygamous or monogamous, and are only loosely social. They travel and hunt alone, in pairs, or in packs. The coyote's greatest enemy, aside from humans, is the domestic dog. Coyotes can run 40 mph, swim fast, and sing well.

For perhaps 1 1/2 million years, coyotes have roamed the Western landscape. (The canine family itself probably originated in North America and migrated to the Old World, not vice versa.) For thousands of years, indigenous Americans have in many ways venerated the coyote. Perhaps more than any other animal, the coyote represents the spirit of the West.

No such sentimental feelings as the foregoing, however, are to be found in the hearts of the stockmen. Summed up in toto, this feeling on the part of the majority of the livestock interests is: "To you, Mr. Coyote, unending vengeance, and warfare to extermination!"
--from **The Clever Coyote** by Stanley Young and Hartley Jackson, federal predator "control" agents and advocates (Young 1978)

Possessing great intelligence and adaptability, the coyote is by far the most successful large predator in the West. Despite relentless persecution by the grazing industry and others, it has not only survived but expanded its range, though in considerably reduced numbers. Today, the coyote is said to have the largest range of any North American mammal, inhabiting almost the entire continent except northeast Canada.

Though technically carnivorous (in the order *Carnivora*), coyotes are highly omnivorous scavengers. Of hundreds of their scats I have seen around the West, most contained plant material, often more than half. The coyote diet consists mostly of small rodents and rabbits, reptiles, wild fruits and berries, grasshoppers, grass, seeds, birds, deer . . . and sometimes livestock.

From _The Coyote: Defiant Songdog of the West_. Revised & Updated by Francois Leydet. Copyright (C) 1977, 1988 by Francois Leydet. Used by permission of the University of Oklahoma Press.

A coyote is the most destructive thing God ever put on this Earth.
--rancher Harold Anderson, Lavina, Montana

The coyote's story is similar to that of so many others. Before the advent of ranching, it was incredibly abundant as compared to today, and was much more a pack animal with vastly different habits. According to Francois Leydet in **The Coyote: Defiant Songdog of the West**, "Early reports tell of a hundred or more coyotes being sighted in a single day, of packs of 20 or 30 chasing deer or antelope or straggling buffalo, of bands of coyotes ringing the campfire at night" (Leydet 1977). Today, though ranchers claim coyotes are "everywhere," it is rare to see more than a dozen or so in a day, including those in packs.

Early settlers shot coyotes on sight to protect livestock and promote general human advancement. The 1800s livestock invasion devastated coyote habitat, depleting their animal and plant foods. By necessity, coyotes increasingly turned to killing livestock, and ranchers increasingly turned to killing coyotes.

In fact, after wolves were exterminated, coyotes killed more stock than any other predator. As Native Americans, wolves, and bears faded from the West, the stockmen-conquerors' new rallying cry became, "The only good coyote is a dead coyote!" In the 1800s, ranchers, bounty hunters, and professional hunters and trappers killed millions. When the federal government joined in the slaughter early this century, the ranching industry became optimistic that perhaps coyotes could be eliminated completely from the West. Exciting the stockmen's imagination, the 1934 Department of Agriculture Year-book announced the government's ultimate goal as "total extirmination of the coyote in the United States."

Since 1915 federal agents alone have reported killing approximately 5 million coyotes. Ranchers and others have taken many millions more than this (though, again, little of this widespread, secretive slaughter is documentable). The killing continues essentially unabated in recent decades. According to Donald Balser, chief of Predator Damage Research at the FWS's Denver Wildlife Research Center, "The ADC took 74,000 coyotes in 1974. We know of 224,000 that were taken by others besides our trappers. Probably a half million or more coyotes are killed every year by man." The 1987 ADC *reported* coyote kill was 84,000. (Malachowski 1988)

This coyote was indiscriminately and intentionally killed by a ranchman in a pickup.

Coyotes are poisoned, trapped, snared, shot, denned, chased by fierce dogs, and run over with vehicles. No other predator has been so ruthlessly and gratuitously pursued. Because there are so few other predators left, the coyote has felt the brunt of ranchers' wrath. Hundreds of university grant research studies on coyotes and how to kill them or prevent them from eating livestock have been conducted in recent decades. Since 1972 even a government periodical has been dedicated to the death and deterrence of coyotes -- *The Coyote Research Newsletter*. Roughly 60% of federal predator "control" efforts are directed at coyotes.

Indeed, perhaps 60% of remaining livestock predators are coyotes. For several reasons they were not so easily quashed as bears, wolves, and others. First, overgrazing, along with elimination of wolves and other predators, helped periodically increase coyotes' food supply of rodents and grasshoppers ("pests") in some areas, partially compensating for degradation of their habitat. Sparse ground cover also allowed coyotes to spot and capture remaining prey more easily. With their unique adaptability, coyotes were better able to take advantage of these changes than are other predators.

Second, coyotes learned to be efficient stock hunters while evading their pursuers. Through years of persecution, many learned to immediately run from human scent or sound, hide from horses and vehicles, walk away from poison baits and traps, hide their dens better and refrain from barking or yipping near them, and kill livestock only where they could get away with it. Those that survived were those most skilled at stealth and hiding, and poisoned carcasses taught them to take only live stock. Also, like many Western species, coyotes adopted a chiefly nocturnal lifestyle. With their great resiliency, coyotes were better able than most predators to make this transition to nocturnal prey.

Third, coyotes and some other species increase their reproduction rates in response to attrition. For example, if half the coyotes in a certain area are killed, remaining coyotes produce larger litters, breed at a younger age, and procreate more frequently and take more prey, including more livestock. Studies show reproduction rates increase as much as 30% in response to population reductions (Pacelle 1988). The degree of increase generally corresponds to the degree of reduction, and populations grow exponentially from one generation to the next. One study shows that more than 50% of coyotes in a given area must be killed each year to significantly reduce their long-term population. And, when coyotes are severely reduced or extirpated from an area, coyotes from surrounding areas can move in to balance populations. Consequently, with the coyote, eradication efforts constitute an especially senseless slaughter and futile waste of taxpayers' money.

Tell you the truth, coyotes don't do anywhere near the damage a lot of ranchers and hunters claim they do. A sheep could die from disease, being lost, dogs -- anything. God knows its suicidally dumb. And if a coyote walks by the carcass, it gets the blame.
--Bill Austin, federal predator "control" agent

Coyotes are not the mass murderers of livestock portrayed by the grazing establishment. But since they kill far more livestock than any other Western predator, many ranchers have an almost paranoid delusion about coyotes. The average annual 5%-10% loss of sheep and 1%-3% loss of cattle to coyotes reported by stockmen has repeatedly been shown to be at least twice as high as actual losses. In 1984 the US Fish & Wildlife Service (which had jurisdiction over ADC at the time) estimated that more than $51 million in livestock were lost to coyotes alone that year. This figure was calculated using numbers supplied by its rancher constituents, and is widely known to be far higher than actual losses. According to J.J. McCoy in **Wild Enemies**, reasons given by wildlife conservationists for inflated figures include, "extreme bias and prejudice against coyotes by the sheepmen, failure to distinguish between coyotes that killed sheep and those that scavenged lambs and ewes that died from other causes, exaggerating sheep losses for tax purposes, and an attempt to increase federal subsidies" (McCoy 1974). Additionally, many supposed coyote kills are done instead by individuals or packs of domestic and feral dogs and dog-coyote hybrids; in some areas these types of animals make most predator kills on livestock. Wildlife biologist Dr. Franz Camenzind testified in 1982 that, "Although the number of coyotes killed by all methods in the last 12 years has more than doubled, the industry continues to claim increasing livestock losses" (Defenders of Wildlife 1982). Nevertheless, Merritt Clifton reports in "The Myth of the Good Shepherd" that in the US today ranchers accuse coyotes of killing over 900,000 sheep annually -- 9% of the nation's total! -- for a loss of $83 million (Clifton 1990).

This skinned coyote carcass was left on the roadside near the entrance to Canyonlands National Park, Utah. *(Bonnie Hood)*

According to sheepmen with whom we have talked, it is doubtful if any sheep has died a natural death in the past century; extermination of all coyotes, whatever the environmental costs, is their battle cry.
--Congressman John D. Dingell of Michigan (Ferguson 1983)

According to Edward Abbey, "It's true that coyotes eat sheep. But do they eat enough sheep?" Yes, coyotes do sometimes kill sheep, infrequently calves and, rarely, grown cows. But relatively few do so on a regular basis. Of those that do, many have been injured or crippled by gunshot wounds, traps, and vehicles, so are less able to procure their normal wild prey. Most coyotes never lay teeth on livestock, except occasionally as carrion. Studies show that coyotes actually prefer livestock as carrion (favoring *old* carrion!) to killing it themselves. Ironically, most of a coyote's meat diet consists of rabbits, other rodents, and grasshoppers that compete with livestock for forage.

Similarly, claims that coyotes kill for fun or willfully torture their prey are little more than horror stories spread by ranchers and uninformed hunters to drum up hatred for their perceived competition. A coyote kills to eat, usually going for the throat and subduing its prey as efficiently as it can. A wriggling animal is difficult to eat, and coyotes do whatever necessary to still their prey. If at times while hunting they bite off a calf's tail or fail to kill an animal completely before they begin to dine, thus offending our human cultural sensibilities, it is incidental to their purpose.

Traditionally, ranchers throw slaughtered coyotes in piles so they may appreciate the cumulative results of their efforts and engage in a little bravado and good-natured competition with other area stockmen. Such piles are in fact quite common; I have encountered them several times while visiting ranches around the West. Usually they are hidden from view behind a back shed, under the overhang of a barn, or perhaps under a tree. *(Dick Randall)*

Rather than beef or mutton, this coyote's stomach was filled with rodents. Millions of coyotes are wrongly blamed for livestock predation, and indiscriminately killed. *(Dick Randall)*

For refusing to succumb to relentless oppression, coyotes have been vilified with "sly," "crafty," "cunning," "tricky," "wily," "shifty," "devious," and other evil-sounding adjectives. Stockmen see coyotes as "cowardly thieves" of livestock that don't have the courage to stand up in the light of day in front of their cross-hairs to be punished for their sinful deeds. Perhaps, to men so used to getting their way, the idea of anything on the range -- especially a "smart-assed coyote" -- not being under their control is intolerable. They also blame coyotes for spreading rabies and other disease, to cattle especially. However, coyotes and their prey animals coexisted and thrived together for over a million years, and cattle have been shown to spread more disease than coyotes.

Some coyotes are killed by rural residents to protect poultry, chicken eggs, dogs, and cats. Many are trapped for their pelts, which may bring $15 or $20. Others are killed for what is termed "sport" by hunters and varmint callers. Still others are killed out of a warped sense of what constitutes "fun" or "duty to humanity" by emotionally sick individuals. A quote from **The Clever Coyote** by Young and Jackson typifies the mentality of many:

A dead coyote family. *(Dick Randall)*

"The trapping of coyotes is a popular and often profitable form of recreation for many farm [ranch] boys, private professional trappers, or those seeking a short respite in the out-of-doors" (Young 1978). Far more coyotes are killed by or for ranchers than by or for any other group.

Despite it all, many stockmen advertise their "respect" for "Mr. Coyote," usually in the form of a reluctant admiration for the skill and tenacity of their "worthy adversary." By thus humanizing the coyote, they suggest that its demise is less a ruthless slaughter than a noble contest between equals (as if a coyote is equally equipped or seeks to engage in battle). While openly espousing their supposed respect for the coyote, these same stockmen destroy the unfortunate animal with reckless abandon for the slightest perceived offense.

Nevertheless, there have always been a few ranchers who recognized value in coyotes and other predators. They find it more profitable to allow coyotes to prey on the small rodents, rabbits, and grasshoppers that compete with livestock for herbage than to wage war against these predators which kill so few of their stock anyway. In recent decades, more ranchers have come to understand the economics of predator "control," though they still represent only a small minority of Western ranchers. These ranchers have limited their slaughter of coyotes to known stock killers or, in rare cases, have stopped killing predators altogether.

Prominant among these is Dayton O. Hyde, owner of a 6000-acre private ranch in Oregon and author of a dozen books. In his latest book, **Don Coyote**, Hyde pushes ranching tolerance to new limits, befriending a coyote and praising coyotes for their contributions to a healthy environment and successful ranching. Near the end of his book, however, Hyde clarifies his priorities, speaking to coyotes in general, telling them, ". . . as long as you make me more money than you cost me, I intend to keep you around." (Hyde 1986)

Texas House Speaker Gib Lewis was recently invited by ranchers on an aircraft mission to shoot Coyotes, who had allegedly been eating the Texas ranchers' calves, because, he said, "they know I like to kill." Proving adept at aerial gunning, Lewis murdered 90 Coyotes.
--Editor John Davis, *Earth First! Journal* (June 1988)

Elimination of the coyote is like a carrot in front of the ranching industry's nose. Many graziers have convinced themselves and each other that, "If we just could get rid of coyotes this'd be damned good stock country!" Others perceive the delusion, but continue the slaughter anyway to quell their anger or because killing coyotes is "traditional." In a word, coyotes have become a universal scapegoat for the industry. You may not be able to solve ranching problems, but you can always blow a hole in a coyote.

(Paul Hirt)

(Dick Randall)

It is a mistake to attempt to analyze cattlemen's attitudes about coyotes from the standpoint of logic. . . . Cattlemen are willing to pay from their own pockets more than $120 an hour to have coyotes gunned from helicopters. . . . All this has little to do with ranching or economics, but is, instead, a stubborn vestige of macho frontiersmanship, identifying the ranchers as practicing Westerners out of the old mold. The calves saved would not even pay for the ammunition and gasoline, not to mention time.

--Denzel & Nancy Ferguson, **Sacred Cows** (Ferguson 1983)

Today, though relentless persecution and habitat destruction has greatly reduced their numbers and extirpated them completely from a few areas, coyotes continue to range throughout the rural West. The coyote may put its tail between its legs and slink away at the slightest sign of a human, but thus far it survives the onslaught.

●Foxes

Four species of fox inhabit the West -- the red, gray, swift, and kit. The **red fox**, *Vulpes vulpes*, is the most common and familiar of the 4. It is also the largest, averaging about 2' long in head and body and 10-15 pounds. This species is usually reddish-yellow with a white underside, but it may be black (the famous "silver fox") or one of many variations. Regardless of color phase, a red fox may always be recognized by its white-   tipped tail.

Red fox. *(Peg Millet)*

The red fox is found throughout most of the West, except along the coast and most of the Plains and Southwest. It ranges a territory usually 1 to a few square miles, depending mostly on food availability. Red foxes may be active at any time, but are most so at night, dawn, and dusk. They are superb swimmers and do not hesitate to go into water after prey. All foxes are inveterate trotters, and can fox trot at a steady 5 miles per hour seemingly forever.

More like the coyote than are the other foxes, the red fox is the Western fox most adapted to human activities, and has, therefore, replaced the gray fox over much of its range. To some degree, it has learned to evade guns, traps, and poisons. The red fox has survived the human onslaught, but in reduced numbers and not nearly so well as the coyote.

The **gray fox**, *Vulpes cinereoargenteus*, resembles the red fox, but is a little smaller and more weasel-like, with a longer, more slender body and longer tail, which has a black median strip down its length and is tipped with black. The salt-and-pepper coat is reddish underneath. This is the only American fox that can climb trees.

The gray fox inhabits mostly the southern half of the West, northern California, and western Oregon. It prefers wilder regions than the red, which helps explain why it has not fared so well. Unfortunately, it is also more susceptible to traps and poisons. The gray fox has disappeared completely from many areas, and survives elsewhere only in small numbers.

Vulpes velox is known as the "**swift fox**" because of its quickness trotting or running across the open Great Plains where it resides. This fox is much smaller than the red and gray, being generally 15" to 20" in head and body and weighing 4 to 6 pounds. Its coat is buffy-yellow, and more uniformly colored than the red and gray, with a black-tipped tail.

The swift fox is less wary than the red and gray, and is more easily trapped, poisoned, and shot. Because it inhabits open plains and intermountain valleys of the inland West, it has suffered more from farming, livestock grazing, and, especially, the "control" programs directed at larger predators. Indeed, as an unintended victim of the grazing industry's omnipresent predator extermination campaign, the swift fox has been decimated.

The **kit fox**, *Vulpes macrotis*, is sometimes considered a subspecies of swift fox. Generally even smaller than the swift, it has exceptionally large, sensitive ears, a pale gray body washed with rust, a whitish belly, and a black-tipped tail. It is a very shy, gentle fox. If this animal isn't cute, nothing is.

The kit fox is primarily nocturnal, remaining in its burrow during most of the day. It prefers the open, dry country, grassy plains, scrubland, and sparse juniper woodlands of the Great Basin and the Southwest, including Southern California. Like the swift fox, it has been devastated by traps and poisons set to catch larger predators, as well as development, farming, and grazing. It is the rarest American fox.

All foxes are opportunistic, omnivorous feeders. Their intelligence and acute hearing and sense of smell make them superb hunter-gatherers. Their prey normally consists mostly of rodents and insects (again, ironically, animals that compete with livestock for herbage), reptiles, birds, and eggs. When prey is plentiful, foxes may stash the surplus and return to feed on it from time to time. Their plant foods include wild fruits and berries, nuts, acorns, and occasionally greens.

A kit fox. *(George Wuerthner)*

Rarely, a fox may take a fawn, lamb, or (extremely rarely) a small calf, especially if the habitat is degraded. Though the value of livestock taken by foxes in the West is minuscule, to the ever profit-minded stockman it is excessive. Thus, many foxes (even swift and kit foxes, which would be hard-pressed to kill the smallest lamb) are shot, trapped, poisoned, and, as they are great den diggers, denned. Probably even more foxes have been killed unintentionally as a result of indiscriminate predator eradication.

Many of the 30,000 or so public lands ranchers on base properties spread across the rural West keep poultry and domestic pets. Because foxes sometimes feed on eggs, chickens, turkeys, and other small domestic animals, ranchers are all the more vehement in their persecution of foxes. Under their pressure and that of farmers, fox bounties are still paid in some states and counties. In the past, many foxes were trapped for their pelts, but with the rise of fox farming in recent decades wild fox fur is no longer in great demand, so ranchers and farmers stand alone as the fox's greatest adversaries.

●Mountain lion

(Dick Randall)

Called mountain lion, cougar, lion, panther, painter, puma, and a dozen other names, *Felis concolor* is a magnificent feline. Its 27 described subspecies range from British Columbia to Tierra del Fuego, making it the most widely distributed American cat, and before the Europeans' arrival the most widespread "New World" predator. Though most popularly called mountain lion, the animal is at home in a great variety of terrain, from sweltering, jagged desert escarpments to icy high mountain forests. The mountain lion that once inhabited the entire area that became the contiguous United States now survives only in much reduced numbers in the most rugged, wildest West, and as a population of 30-50 of the Florida panther sub-

species in the swamps of southern Florida. Otherwise, predator "control" has eliminated cougars east of Texas and the Rocky Mountains (and throughout much of the Americas).

The mountain lion is a *large* cat, measuring 4'-5' in head and body and 2'-2 1/2' at the shoulder and weighing 80-200 pounds, occasionally more (the largest are over 300 pounds). Coat color generally is tawny to grayish, with a lighter underside and dark brown tip to its long tail, but it may vary greatly according to geographic area. A pure black mountain lion has been spotted a few times recently at Point Reyes National Seashore north of San Francisco.

Mountain lions have no definite mating season, so their spotted cubs, numbering usually 2 or 3, may be born at any time of the year. Normally they live 10 to 15, occasionally 20 or more, years. They have few enemies besides humans, and are considered remarkably free of disease and parasites.

Pumas are chiefly nocturnal, now even more so as a defense against human assault. Their wail at night excites the fears of some people, who perceive it as a fiendish, unearthly shriek. However, the cougar is the most timid of all the world's large cats. Solitary, secretive, wary, and elusive, it is so seldom seen by humans that a glimpse even of its footprints is a special treat.

Reports of mountain lions attacking and eating humans are almost invariably spread by the ignorant, gullible, overly excitable, or paranoid, and by ranchers and hunters seeking to give the animals a bad name. Of the 52 documented lion attacks on humans in the past 100 years in the US and Canada, only 10 were fatal. Most attacks are thought to be the result of lions incapacitated by old age, injury, or disease, mistaking humans for prey, or of aggressive people provoking the attack.

The mountain lion is the most agile and skillful hunter in the West. A cougar can leap 40', and one was seen jumping 18' *straight up* into a tree. Like most cats, it can run very fast for short spurts, but tires quickly. So in hunting it stalks, or sometimes ambushes, its prey, then makes a quick dash and powerful leap upon the victim, killing it quickly by breaking or biting its neck. In the pre-European West, mountain lions used to eat their fill, then later return to the carcass, but due to persecution they rarely do this anymore.

Because the cougar is such an effective hunter, it can afford to be a selective consumer. When habitat permits, therefore, most of its prey will be deer -- overwhelmingly its favorite food -- and a cat may take 50 deer annually. That Western deer numbers have remained relatively much higher than those of other large mammals since last century is a major factor in the mountain lion surviving even as well as it has. On the other hand, because it kills deer, many hunters have teamed up with ranchers to eradicate the big cat, conveniently unaware that much greater numbers of both cougars and deer coexisted for millennia. The West's low "game" populations are caused by ranching, introduced disease, overhunting, and habitat development and fragmentation, not by predation.

Cougars establish distinct territories of 100 to 300 or more square miles and roam within these borders, but will wander 100 miles away if need be. When deer are scarce, they may eat porcupine (a favorite in some areas), elk, pronghorn, bighorns, javelina, beaver, rabbits, mice, coyotes, raccoons, skunks, wild turkeys, rabbits, fish, slugs, grasshoppers, and a great variety of other animals. Like all cats, they are almost exclusively carnivorous. But unlike many, the cougar will not scavenge or eat carrion unless it has no choice.

The big cats also kill and eat livestock. Though studies show they rarely attack cattle weighing over 500 pounds, a mature mountain lion has little problem bringing down a medium-sized heifer or steer, and a calf or sheep makes a tasty treat. What hungry person would refuse a plate of food set at her or his feet? Yet, lions that eat cattle or sheep in their home range are branded "bad" and relentlessly pursued.

Mountain lion food.

There have been many accounts of one puma killing 30, 40, or even up to 192 sheep in one night. Such mass slaughter, usually put down as performed in an excess of "blood lust," results from the fact that the cat's urge to pounce upon a victim is constantly being reactivated by the penned-in animals helplessly milling about it. The situation it finds itself in is quite abnormal, and so, too, is the puma's reaction.
--C.A.W. Guggisberg, **Wild Cats of the World**

Still, few mountain lions kill livestock regularly or in large numbers. Again, losses claimed by ranchers usually have little to do with reality. As with all large predators, the grazing industry branded cougars as varmints and has for more than a century persecuted them with genocidal fervor.

Being powerful and exceptionally elusive animals, however, they were not easy to kill. Because pumas disdain old meat, poisoning was not effective. Stockmen got a lucky shot off here and there, but the real killing was done with dogs and traps, often by professionals. Bounty hunters sometimes followed stock-killing lions for months. With experienced dogs, they were often able to tree or corner the cats and shoot them. Though cougars are wary of traps, trapping became much more effective when it was discovered that they were attracted to catnip and other scents.

Stockmen commonly and discreetly pressure state game and fish departments to increase allowed predator kills under the guise of protecting "big game" species, primarily deer, from predation. However, for decades the big cat has been hunted for "sport," often by or with assistance from ranchers. In recent years the puma's popularity as a "game" animal has grown rapidly. Many public lands ranchers have set up guide services for hunting the animals with dogs

(many often already owned packs of hounds for hunting predators). Wealthy "sportsmen" (many of them ranchers themselves) are taken out on horseback to a public grazing allotment. A pack of dogs finds a cougar's scent and pursues the terrified animal until it becomes so exhausted or scared that it climbs a tree. With the dogs barking and the mountain lion cowering in fear, The Great Hunter rides up, dismounts, aligns the cross-hairs of his $1000 high-powered rifle, and blasts the cat out of the tree. For his service the stockman receives $100-$200 a day and the satisfaction of knowing one less lion lives. In winter, when tracks can be followed indefinitely, cougars are pursued by "sportsmen" on snowmobiles.

Southern Arizona public lands rancher Doug Cumming is one such professional hunting guide. On his ranch he keeps 5 well-trained hounds for pursuing predators. Customers from around the US pay hundreds of dollars apiece to visit "his" ranch, jeep out onto the range, and "bag" a mountain lion. Cumming, now 82, remembers when "there were lots of wolves around." He has been a lion and coyote hunter all his life. A rural newspaper submits that, "Cumming is a defender of mountain lions and coyotes, but hunts the cats to save his herd of cattle."

A surprisingly large percentage of ranchers own hounds trained to pursue mountain lions and other predators, and to kill "pests."

Just 20 years ago, every Western state and Canadian province paid bounties on mountain lions. Texas and Wyoming, where the mountain lion has been practically exterminated, still classify the animal as a "varmint" species. But, in recent years, as cougar populations plummeted and environmental awareness grew, most Western states removed the mountain lion from their varmint lists and assigned it "big game" status, meaning ranchers may still kill them whenever they claim predation, though other people must obey hunting regulations to kill the animal. Regardless of current legalities, stockmen continue their own covert slaughter of cougars, often hiring professional hunters.

In the Southwest, ADC currently is lobbying county governments for local funds to match federal funds to mount "pre-emptive" campaigns against lions that *may* kill cattle. In Arizona, hunting is allowed year-round. Estimates from Arizona Game & Fish biologists and experienced hunters range from 100 to 600 lions killed by ranchers each year, in addition to annual "sport" hunting kills (often by ranchers) of about 200 out of the state's estimated 2500 resident adults (Dagget 1990). The situation in most Western states is similar. The Yuma puma, which ranges the hot, arid flats, mountains, and tangled bosques of the lower Colorado River valley, recently was the first Western mountain lion subspecies designated as Threatened. It may be one of the most endangered animals on Earth; yet year-round hunting of the cat is still allowed, as is its slaughter as a stock predator.

I would like to say I can feel for these people who want to protect the mountain lion. These people, however, are obviously city dwellers. The lion is one of the most deadly killers in the world. My ancestors fought him well over 100 years ago.
--public lands rancher Lewis Oliver, Grant County, New Mexico

In 1983 the New Mexico Department of Game and Fish released a report concluding that the state's mountain lion population had dropped sharply and that livestock depredation was infrequent and economically insignificant. Livestock losses to lions in New Mexico that year were estimated at $30,000, yet government agents spent $90,000 in tax dollars to kill mountain lions. New Mexico ranchers continue to pressure state legislators to return the lion to its former "varmint" status, to be killed by anyone, any time, any place. Some ranchers promote serious proposals to eliminate the lion from New Mexico completely, as they did the wolf, grizzly, and jaguar; so too do many ranchers in every Western state.

New Mexico's Game and Fish Commission is in hot water following what many say was an illegal picnic. Four of the five commissioners took an unpublicized horseback trip to the Guadalupe Mountains, where they met for a barbecue with ranchers who want the state to kill more mountain lions. . . . Soon after the horseback ride and picnic the commissioners approved new rules allowing "preventative" killings of mountain lions without requiring proof that a particular cat killed livestock. (Note: A judge in Santa Fe subsequently upheld the legality of the killing, even while acknowledging that the meeting violated the Open Meetings Act.)
--High Country News (6-22-87)

Hughes is a leader among ranchers urging lion trapping. She estimates that her family's ranch lost nearly $50,000 in livestock to verified lion kills over the last five years. "We expect a certain percentage of losses, but not years in which we are suffering the loss of 70 to 80 percent of our income just from lion losses alone," she says. The [New Mexico] game department pays Hugh's father $35,000 a year under a contract to trap lions in the Guadalupes.
--High Country News (7-6-87)

The mountain lion population of aboriginal California is estimated to have been roughly 20,000. Historically, ranchers have been the state's biggest killers of mountain lions. Along with hunting, fire suppression, overgrazing, and habitat destruction, ranchers' predator elimination programs nearly extirpated the cat from most of the state by 1973, when a moratorium was imposed on lion hunting. Though ranchers continue to kill them secretly, the lion population has subsequently risen, with estimates varying from 2000 to 5000. In 1986 the moratorium was ended, and

the California Fish & Game Commission has twice since tried to institute trophy hunting of lions. Fortunately, the Mountain Lion Preservation Fund has blocked these efforts in the courts.

With comparatively strong mountain lion protection and much rugged, inaccessible habitat, California probably has the largest population of any Western state. Counting such an elusive animal is difficult guesswork at best, and few mountain lion censuses have even been attempted. In fact, most state Game & Fish Departments have no idea how many lions live in their states, though they continue to legally allow ranchers to kill them. For example, estimates of the number of big cats in Colorado range only from 1500 to 3000, yet stockmen may kill them as stock predators. In Nevada, where the lion population is probably even lower, ADC alone killed 41 mountain lions in 1988.

The mountain lion is extirpated from most of its natural range, and remaining populations are very sparse. Current ostensibly "high" populations are at most 1/5 original numbers, probably far less. Most Westerners have never seen a lion print, much less the animal itself. In sum, ranching is by far the biggest single factor in the decline of the West's mountain lions. Lion skin never did have much commercial value, and today its chief value is as a trophy or rug to decorate the floor or wall of a hunter's or rancher's den.

So a mountain lion kills a few sheep. What do we expect? Should we extirpate the lions to make the world safe for livestock? I think not.
--The late David Gaines, ecologist, Mono Lake Committee, letter to editor of 7-24-86 *Mono Herald*, Lee Vining, CA

●Lynx

The lynx, *Felis lynx*, is a medium-sized, powerfully built cat with long, sturdy legs, a black-tipped, stubby tail, and triangular ears tipped with tufts of black hairs. A close relative of the bobcat, it lives in far northern and high mountain country and has adapted to the cold by growing a warm coat of fur and large paws, which in winter are so thickly furred that they serve as snowshoes. The lynx is much more a forest animal than the bobcat, inhabiting rough, mountainous terrain, sometimes swamps, only occasionally venturing into broken or open country.

Lynx mark their typical 8-12 square mile territories with tree scratches, droppings, and urine. In hunting, the lynx usually stalks its prey as closely as possible, then pounces on it in 1 or 2 bounds. Its diet consists mainly of snowshoe hares, supplemented with rodents, birds, and fish, occasionally a young deer or fox -- or a sheep or very rarely a young calf.

Its remote habitat and primarily solitary, nocturnal behavior help protect it, but a predator in the West has little chance of escaping the ranching industry, or humans in general. Bounties were paid. Shooting, poisoning and trapping (often as a non-target animal) by sheep and cattle interests and their government agents, fur trapping, overhunting, and habitat intrusion, have greatly lowered the lynx's numbers and extirpated the cat from much of its southern range. Whereas the lynx originally ranged well south into the Rocky Mountain West and Oregon mountains, it is now rare in the lower 48.

(Helen Wilson)

● Bobcat

The bobcat, *Lynx rufus*, is slightly smaller than the lynx, measuring about 2' to 2 1/2' in head and body, 14" at the shoulder, and weighing from 15 to 30 pounds. Its legs are more slender and feet smaller. The ears are less conspicuously tufted, if tufted at all. The shorter coat is of varying shades of buff or brown, with many indistinct dark spots. The "bob" tail, from which the bobcat derives its name, is tipped black on the upper side only. Like all cats, the bobcat's long whiskers are equipped with sensitive nerves to determine the width of tight places. Its surreal yowling is a sound not soon forgotten.

Bobcat *(Steve Johnson)*

Though the lynx is closely related, the bobcat is a distinct species and seems to have been present in North America long before the lynx crossed over the Bering Strait from Asia. The bobcat is much more widespread than the lynx, inhabiting sagebrush country, semi-desert regions, forests, brushlands, wetlands, rimrock areas, and a wide variety of habitat throughout the West, as well as the East. Like the lynx, it marks its roughly 8-12 square mile territory with scratchings, droppings, and urine. And, like the lynx, the bobcat is a chiefly solitary and nocturnal animal -- much more so since human intrusion.

Bobcats prey mostly on small mammals and birds, and they are good fishers. They eat larger prey, such as deer, pronghorn, sheep, and calves, only when smaller game is scarce (such as on overgrazed ranges) or as fresh carrion (or, in the Northern Rockies, when deep snow makes deer comparatively easy prey). A bobcat sometimes will leap on the back of a larger victim, such as a deer, then bite the neck just below the back of the skull to kill the animal. The desperate prey may run for a long distance with the bobcat riding on its back, biting and scratching to bring it down.

Bobcats generally cause little livestock loss, only occasionally killing a sheep or small calf, though they some-

times become costly to sheep ranchers during lambing season. In a study by Charles C. Sperry of the US Bureau of Sport Fisheries and Wildlife, in which the stomachs of 3538 bobcats were examined for their contents, investigators found that rodents constituted 46% and livestock only 2% of the animals' diet. Significantly, 70% of these study bobcats came from the 15 Western states and most of them had been exterminated as stock killers by federal agents at the request of ranchers. In another study, this one on the rocky Snake River Plain in southeastern Idaho, Theodore N. Bailey found no remains of sheep in 300 bobcats' stomachs and feces.

Bobcats eat mostly small mammals -- here, a jackrabbit -- and birds. *(Steve Johnson)*

Bobcats, though shy and secretive, are unfortunately one of the easiest animals to trap, and prime pelts fetch as much as $200. Yet the ranching industry has been the most overall potent factor in the bobcat's decline in the West; the cat survives at a small fraction of its aboriginal population. Since 1915 the federal government alone has reported killing roughly a million bobcats and lynx, primarily for stockmen. Ranchers and their attendants have trapped, shot, poisoned, and denned bobcats for more than a century, and, as always, livestock and range development have . . . .

Early bobcat killers labeled the animal "wildcat" because it fought so fiercely for its life when cornered or trapped. May the wild cat outlast cattle and sheep and continue to roam the wild West!

A bobcat in a steel leghold trap. *(Paul Tebbel)*

●Jaguar

POSSIBLE FORMER JAGUAR RANGE

America's other big cat, the jaguar, has been all but forgotten by wildlife and land management agencies. . . . What right have Americans to expect other countries to protect el tigre, *it might be asked, if we do not demonstrate an effort of our own?*
--Wilderness (Winter 1988) (Brown 1988)

Few Americans realize that before European intervention jaguars roamed what is now the Southwestern United States for tens of thousands of years. The world's third largest cat was a widespread resident of parts of Southern California, much of Arizona and New Mexico, and most of Texas. It ranged as far east as Louisiana and north as far as northern Texas, the Sangre de Cristo range in New Mexico, the Grand Canyon in Arizona, and the southern Sierra Nevada Mountains in California. Early explorers reported numerous jaguars in the swampy jungles of the Colorado River delta.

Panthera onca is one of the most beautiful animals on Earth. It is the largest and most powerful wild cat in the Americas, and around the globe only tigers and African lions are bigger. Jaguars average around 150-225 pounds, but occasionally weigh up to 350 pounds. They measure 4'-5' in head and body and 2'-2 1/2' at the shoulder.

The jaguar's tawny coat is uniformly spotted with black. The spots on sides and back form rosettes with small black dots in the centers, and the white belly, legs, face, and tail are covered with black spots.

Like mountain lions, jaguars are basically territorial animals. In northern Mexico they are known to roam areas of roughly 200-1000 square miles. They favor open forests, scrublands, savannas, swamps, and riparian areas.

The jaguar's extremely strong jaws, with heavy bones and massive teeth, allow it to kill its prey by crushing the skull or biting between vertebrae and neatly severing the spinal cord. In the northern part of its range, its favored food is javelina, and to a lesser extent deer, but a variety of other mammals, fish, ground-dwelling birds, and reptiles are also important foods. Many people are terrified of jaguars, though attacks by jaguars on humans are almost as rare as attacks by mountain lions.

Also like mountain lions, jaguars occasionally eat livestock. Nevertheless, jaguars that hunt livestock are likely to be diseased, crippled, old, have blunted teeth, or be otherwise incapacitated. As a rule, they take inferior livestock from depleted ranges.

To put it simply, the Jaguar was incompatible with the livestock industry. . . . Several of the Jaguars reported taken . . . were poisoned by US predator control agents . . . Most of the rest were taken by ranchers and their employees.
--David Brown, **The Wolf in the Southwest** (Brown 1984)

To the stockmen who invaded the West, **no** amount of livestock depredation was acceptable. The jaguar would go the way of the wolf, grizzly, and others. Hundreds were slaughtered in the late 1800s. The last jaguar in California reportedly was killed in 1860. In Arizona, where the cat held out longest, the reported jaguar kill was 23 in the first decade of the 1900s and 15 in the second; *actual* kills undoubtedly were far higher. In the 1920s, the reported kill dropped to 8; in the '30s, 5; in the '40s, 6; and in the '50s, only a few. (Over the same half-century, 6 jaguars were reported killed in New Mexico, where the last known was killed in 1925, and about a dozen in Texas, where the last was reported destroyed in 1946.) In Arizona in the '60s, 3 jaguars died, and the '70s and '80s had 1 recorded death each. Thus did the industry's guns, dogs, and traps effectively extirpate the jaguar from the United States.

The jaguar still survives in Mexico, where it is known as *el tigre*, and in Central and South America. Individual jaguars occasionally wander over the border from Mexico into southern Texas, New Mexico, and Arizona, but while trying to recolonize their northern habitat invariably they are killed, usually by stockmen.

The most recent killing occurred in southeast Arizona's rugged Chiracahua Mountains, where 2 birders reported seeing a jaguar in 1986. The most frequently related version of the story goes like this: In 1988, a public lands rancher/hunting guide from nearby Willcox, after tracking the jaguar with his hounds for 3 days, finally bayed the animal and shot it. To show off his success, the killer took the carcass to town, where people came to see the dead beast and some took pictures. It is said a celebration of sorts took place in the small, rancher-dominated community.

Killing a jaguar or possession of jaguar parts is a Class II misdemeanor in Arizona, with a possible fine of around $750. According to local newspapers, although the Arizona Game & Fish Department is fully aware of the murder, it is unable to press charges. It found no *corpus delicti*, and locals are afraid or unwilling to finger the murderer, who is part of a locally powerful ranching family with "a reputation for vengeance." "They're real wild west," a Game & Fish Commissioner said "The fear is genuine." The local livestock community is protecting him, and it has not disavowed the jaguar killing.

Ironically, jaguar killers in the US cannot be prosecuted under the federal Endangered Species Act. Though the jaguar was federally listed as Endangered in 1972, it is now considered "extinct" -- not Endangered -- in the US, so it has no protection under the Act. This loophole apparently was arranged at the insistence of the livestock industry.

Endangered status for the [jaguar], [political experts] *say, could entail restrictions on habitat destruction or even pressure for reintroduction, measures that would prove extremely unpopular with the politically powerful cattlemen who worked so hard to exterminate the animal. Pressure from ranchers has blocked any protection possible from either state or federal government.*
--Dan Dagget, environmental journalist

Possible reintroduction sites exist in the mountains of southeast Arizona, southern New Mexico and Texas, but jaguars do not transplant well. They wander so widely that even the largest transplant areas may not contain them; individuals have been known to travel more than 500 miles. Some say no transplant areas of adequate size remain. Actually, this tendency to wander long distances could also be considered a major factor favoring reintroduction. Perhaps the best hope for the jaguar's recovery in the Southwest US is to protect its few remaining ranges in northern Mexico and wait for individuals to wander north across the border. However, the number of reported jaguar sightings in the US has dropped sharply in recent years, indicating that the cat is in trouble in Mexico. (The last sighting in the US was made in 1988 by a couple of javelina hunters about 15 miles north of the Mexican border.) Unfortunately, hope for the jaguar's recovery seems slim in light of Mexico's extreme human overpopulation and economic crisis, and its continued slaughter by Mexican stockmen.

Realistically, the long-term prognosis for the jaguar's survival in northern Mexico is almost as poor as its chances are for recovery in the US. If the jaguar is to return to its rightful place on the Western landscape, something radical must happen soon.

●Ocelot

The ocelot, *Felis pardalis*, is another little-known predator victimized by ranching. This beautiful cat resembles a small jaguar, with similar coloration and lines of elongated spots, more nearly stripes than spots, that serve as excellent camouflage. Most ocelots measure 2 1/2'- 3' in head and body and weigh 20-40 pounds.

Ocelots live in tropical and subtropical forests, riparian zones, thorn scrub, and rocky areas, and spend much of their time in trees. Basically nocturnal, they often pass the day asleep on the branch of a tree or in thick brush. They are also good swimmers. The ocelot diet consists mostly of small mammals and birds. They will eat small livestock or raid hen houses if circumstances dictate, but generally they shun humanity and rarely show themselves in the open.

Before the livestock invasion, the ocelot inhabited a range that included southern portions of Arizona, New Mexico, and Texas. Apparently, they were not uncommon

in the low mountains and riparian zones in and near the Tucson basin and Salt River Valley near what is now called Phoenix.

Ocelots were killed to protect livestock or as non-target species in predator "control" efforts, and for their valuable, attractive skins. Habitat destruction, especially of riparian areas, by ranching has been a major detriment. Today, ocelots are effectively extirpated from the Southwest, though a few hang on in southern Texas, especially along the lower Rio Grande Valley.

An ocelot.

●Jaguarundi

Yet another native cat extirpated from the Southwest is the jaguarundi, *Felis yagouaroundi*. This intriguing animal is smaller than the ocelot, usually weighing 15-18 pounds, or about twice the size of the average house cat. Jaguarundis come in 2 color phases, red and gray -- sometimes in the same litter. The coat is uniform in color, ranging from fox-red to chestnut or blackish to brownish-gray.

With its small, flattened head, short legs, elongated body, and very long tail, the jaguarundi looks almost as much like a weasel or otter as a cat. It slinks along the ground through the lowland thickets and river bottoms it inhabits, and even enjoys swimming.

Jaguarundis are much more terrestrial than ocelots, living and hunting mainly on the ground. They are also less nocturnal than most cats, and frequently patrol their thickly vegetated haunts in broad daylight. Food is mostly ground-dwelling birds and small mammals, but they can take young deer, and even an occasional sheep or small calf if they must.

The jaguarundi's demise was accomplished like the ocelot's -- with the ranching industry's dogs, guns, poisons, traps, and overgrazing. Like the ocelot, it also suffered greatly as a non-target species, though it wasn't killed so much for its skin. And like the ocelot, the jaguarundi that once inhabited southern portions of Arizona, New Mexico, and Texas now survives only in small numbers in southernmost Texas.

It is time to see the border cats -- Jaguar, Ocelot, and Jaguarundi -- not as tropical exotics who infrequently visit north of the Rio Grande or Gadsden Purchase line, but as integral and proper resident members of the natural community of Arizona, New Mexico, Texas, and even California.
--Dave Foreman, environmental activist

●Golden eagle

Aguila chrysaetos, the golden eagle, is a noble raptor, a symbol of courage, strength, and freedom, and Mexico's national symbol. It is also foremost among the ranching industry's predatory bird enemies. Eagles have no natural enemies.

The golden eagle is a large, powerful bird, with a hooked bill and strong talons. It measures 6' to 7 1/2' in wingspan and 30" to 40" in total length. As with most eagles, females are significantly larger than males. Its color is uniformly brown, with a golden wash over the back of the head and neck and a faintly banded tail.

The golden eagle may be found in almost any terrain, being a year-round resident throughout nearly the entire rural West. It glides and soars on air currents, circling, scanning the earth with sharp eyes, dipping and rising, occasionally beating its great wings, frequently changing direction, until it spies a prey animal.

Unfortunately, the golden eagle has often been pictured as cruel and savage, always ready to dive-bomb some innocent victim. Even today some people believe old tales of golden eagles carrying off young children and devouring them in secret caves. As usual, stockmen are foremost among the detractors. They accuse the birds of, among other things, killing (and even carrying off) large numbers of lambs and calves. In truth, golden eagles may occasionally take a small deer or other immature large mammal, a lamb, or even a very small calf, if nothing else is available (as is often the case on livestock ranges). Normally, they feed on rabbits, squirrels and other rodents (animals that compete with livestock for forage), snakes, birds, and carrion. As for "carrying off" young livestock, a golden eagle is incapable of carrying more than 5 or so pounds, so the most that one could fly away with would be the smallest newborn lamb or an aborted fetus. At least 5 major studies on eagles and their predation on livestock, including one by the Advisory Committee on Predator Control, show that livestock losses to eagles are frequently exaggerated.

Be that as it may, stockmen have shot, trapped, and poisoned golden eagles for more than a century. Eagles feeding on livestock carrion often were wrongly blamed for the deaths. Ranchers and many other early Westerners compulsively shot at any large bird in the sky.

Golden eagles were finally given federal legal protection in the 1960s only after conservationists pointed out that the bird was in serious difficulty due to indiscriminate slaughter by ranchers and "sportsmen." The Golden Eagle Protection Act was passed in 1962, due in large part to research that showed the bird's main food consists of rodents that compete with livestock for forage. But, as usual with wildlife protection laws, ranchers were exempted; by obtaining a special permit they were allowed to kill any golden eagles they accused of killing stock.

Furthermore, as we have seen time and again, legalities have little do with what actually occurs out on the range. Thousands and thousands of golden eagles have been killed illegally since their protection law was passed in 1962. Illegal bounties are still paid. Many ranchers, sheepmen especially, shoot at, trap, or poison golden eagles or any large predatory bird.

For example, in 1971 the remains of 48 golden and bald eagles were discovered in Wyoming. Tests showed that they died from thallium sulfate poisoning. A rancher arrested for the crime admitted to 29 counts of violating state game laws for shooting antelope, inserting thallium sulfate into their carcasses, and leaving them as bait. Ostensibly, since the prosecution could not prove the rancher (as usual a politically powerful individual) intended to kill eagles rather than coyotes, he was given the minimum penalty under law -- a $675 fine.

A golden eagle poisoned by ADC. *(Dick Randall)*

peoples, though, ironically, by collecting condors for ceremonial use they contributed to the bird's demise. (Smith 1978)

In contrast, early European settlers regarded the vulture as dirty, destructive, dangerous, an ill-omen, and a carrier of disease. According to Dick Smith in **Condor Journal**, "Many early settlers were convinced that condors attacked living cattle and sheep, carried off calves and lambs, even infants and small children." Early Spanish ranchers killed them often, as did the American stockmen and others who followed, sometimes "just for target practice." (Smith 1978)

As the abundant wildlife of the Pacific West was gradually replaced by livestock, and as habitat was impinged upon by ranches and farms, the California condor slid toward extinction. Yes, cows and sheep mostly replaced wildlife as a food source (95% of its diet during the last century was cattle, sheep, ground squirrels, deer, and horses, in that order), but the condor was used to finding plentiful carrion at all times of the year, not just when ranching allowed for it. Variations in ranching practices caused irregular annual and seasonal fluctuations in available carcasses, as did the long-term effect of massive livestock and wildlife die-offs caused by overgrazing and drought.

The condor was in trouble as early as the mid-1800s. In the 1880s, California even passed a bill outlawing the killing of condors. Few were aware of the law, however, and fewer still were inclined to obey it. In fact, though thousands of condors have been killed illegally, in all history there is only 1 record of someone being successfully prosecuted for killing a condor. That man was fined $50 in 1908. (McMillan 1968)

With the onset of the Gold Rush in 1849, a great number of condors were killed for their quills, which were in vogue for carrying gold dust. Many people shot them indiscriminately. Egg collectors took a heavy toll. By the turn of the century, most California condors were gone, and by mid-century most experts had given up the species as lost. In the mid-1900s, pesticides began to contaminate the bodies of the few remaining, while "progress" reared its ugly head and invaded the condor's habitat.

In recent decades, as modern ranching reduced livestock deaths, dead stock were removed from the range, and various dangerous substances were introduced into livestock, the already dubious substitute condor food source -- dead cows and sheep -- became increasingly inadequate. Olive Kingston Smith explains in **Condor Journal** that in the 1970s,

> Do the [condor] *flocks that forage the ranges of modern cattle ranches where herd animals are scientifically bred and fed reproduce? No one really knows, but many are beginning to question as Dick* [Smith, a condor expert] *did, whether this vaccinated, supplementally fed, and hormone injected food supply disrupts delicate mechanisms of the condor's breeding cycle.* (Smith 1978)

> *A sheep rancher, who killed two golden eagles in San Luis Obispo County about 1946, said he would shoot any condors which he saw near his sheep. He refused to be convinced that condors were not predatory.*
> --Carl Koford, **The California Condor**, in 1953

Ranching is the most pernicious, persistent factor in the California condor's decline. Stockmen, sheepmen especially, shot many, thinking them golden eagles, or because, as one writer put it, "they made almost irresistible targets." Some were killed in the massive rodent poisonings of the late 1800s and early 1900s. According to Oliver J. Austin, Jr. in **Birds of the World**, "Many were poisoned by strychnine which ranchers inserted into cattle to kill wolves and coyotes." In June 1941 a condor was found dead in a metal stock tank, presumably drowned. In the 1940s, when the condor population was estimated at about 100, there were several documented incidences of stockmen killing condors. In later years, ranchers using Compound 1080 against predators murdered others. Additionally, 10 condors -- about 1/4 the population at the time -- were found dead during 1080 squirrel poisoning in the 1960s. Six more were examined and discovered uninjured. How many flew away to die in solitude is unknown. In fact, there is considerable evidence showing that a large percentage of ranching-related condor deaths went undiscovered or unreported and, what's more, for decades government officials collaborated with ranchers to hide incriminating condor deaths. (Koford 1953, McMillan 1968, Smith 1978)

> *I doubt that any other region in the world has seen poison used so extensively, so effectively, or with as much ingenuity as in the range of the California Condor. . . . In my view, poison not only is a probable cause of condor decline but has undoubtedly caused serious and inexcusable losses.*
> --Ian McMillan, **Man and the California Condor** (McMillan 1968)

By 1967 the total number of known California condors was about 50; by the end of 1982 it was only 19. An M-44 coyote getter claimed one of these just before the last wild condors were taken into captivity. Of the last 3 wild condors, 1 died in a leghold trap.

As the big bird declined in recent years, various steps were taken to try to save it from extinction. Road kills and stillborn calves were left near where condors were known to live. The government enforced protection laws. Small portions of condor range were closed to public access, development, and mining -- though rarely to ranching. In the latter 1980s, in a desperate attempt to thwart extinction, the US Fish & Wildlife Service took all condor eggs from their nests and captured all wild condors. Several chicks have been reared in captivity, and all 40 of the Earth's largest flying birds now spend their days in cages at the San Diego and Los Angeles Zoos.

Little of the California condor's homeland is being protected from "progress" or ranching. Chances for the species' successful reintroduction and recovery in the wild seem slim.

●Raven

What? Ravens kill livestock!? Ranchers traditionally have shot ravens as vermin. Now, believe it or not, ravens have been added to their predator list. Maybe stockmen are simply running out of eligible predator enemies? Perhaps some drunken cowboys took Alfred Hitchcock's classic horror film *The Birds* too seriously?

(Roger Candee)

funding will increase by about 40%.
--naturalist/author Byrd Baylor in 3-20-88 *Arizona Republic*

According to a handful of ranchers, ravens have killed hundreds of their livestock in recent years. Probably the most vocal of these raven-haters is a wealthy former president of the Arizona Cattle Growers Association, public lands rancher Jack Metzger, promoted as one of the most environmentally enlightened ranchers in the state. (A day with him on his ranch showed me that this isn't much of a claim.) Under pressure from Metzger and other stockmen, ADC in Arizona and other Western states has begun to shoot ravens and poison them with starlacide-tainted beef and chicken eggs. For example, in 1988 in Nevada, government hunters shot 109 ravens blamed for taking "20 lambs, 2 calves, 50 hen eggs, and 25 golf balls (valued at $2 each)" (Satchell 1990). However, ranchers across the West discreetly dispatch thousands of ravens each year.

The common raven is one of the most familiar Western birds, and to those who know it well it is a wonderful animal. It is distinguished from crows by its voice, habit of soaring, and larger size, thicker bill, and wedge-shaped tail. Ravens are found throughout the West in an incredible variety of habitats, from the baking, 130 degree floor of Death Valley to the frosty shorelines of northern Cascade alpine lakes. Spirited birds, they ride the wind currents, skim along sheer cliff faces, speed across cliff tops out into the void above vast canyons, dive, climb, float, even play tag with one another as they soar about -- apparently for the sheer joy of it. Ravens are brilliant, omnivorous opportunist-scavengers, which largely explains why they have fared so well in the face of ranching and other human encroachment. Like vultures, they may feed on cattle and sheep carcasses.

At the request of ranchers, poison bait traps were set out [by ADC], in an effort to stop ravens from striking young cattle. The ravens reportedly kill calves by poking their eyes out and harassing young animals until they bleed to death. Juve [Director of Arizona ADC] said the Flying M Ranch near Flagstaff reported that 16 calves were killed by ravens last winter.
--Associated Press, June, 1989

. . . the ADC has been poisoning ravens on two Arizona cattle ranches for the past two years, and now pending is an application to poison ravens anywhere in the state "as needed." They have already sent forms out to cattlemen, polling them on the need to control these crazed killers. If this succeeds, their

The graziers allege that flocks of these black devils (and magpies, in some areas) attack helpless calves and sheep, poke their eyes out, and ravage every external orifice until the animals bleed to death. Then the bloodthirsty demons descend upon the lifeless victims en masse and pick the bones clean. Non-ranchers have yet to witness the gruesome spectacle.

According to many experts, the stockmen's claims are false. In fact, rarely do ravens kill an animal larger than an insect. And a study by Dr. Bernd Heinrich of the University of Vermont shows that ravens are incapable of penetrating the hide of a calf or cow, much less of killing a cow or calf. According to a report on the study:

In order to observe raven activity, Heinrich set out calf carcasses to attract them. Until the carcasses were ripped open (either by Heinrich or coyotes), the ravens were unable to feast on the meat. They have neither the power nor the beak formation to pierce the hides.

In California, Arizona, and other Western states, it is illegal to kill a raven or to keep one as a pet, even an injured raven that would otherwise die in the wild. Penalties are stiff. Yet ranchers and government agents may massacre flocks of them.

A recent TV news show ran a story of a young local boy who found a crippled raven, nursed it to health, and kept it for years as a pet. The boy grew close to the bird and came to love it as a brother. When Arizona Game & Fish officials found out, they invoked the law declaring raven possession illegal and confiscated the bird. The boy was heartbroken. But Game & Fish wasn't through; they then killed the bird because, they said, it couldn't be rehabilitated and released into the wild.

> *A controlled program to control predators is the best way I can imagine to have our natural environment adjusted by man to enhance his livelihood. The controls should not be just for predators, but for any effective means to enhance our subsistence . . . .*
>
> --John McRae, public lands rancher, Miles City, Montana

Besides all the foregoing, Western stockmen kill other animals as predators or suspected predators, or to protect livestock from injury. For example, many ranchers shoot ospreys, vultures, large hawks, and even owls, believing them eagles or other livestock predators. Some shoot or trap badgers, fishers, and wolverines because these animals may seem large enough and ferocious enough to kill or injure a calf or sheep.

The theory behind predator killing is still there: If you kill lots of predators, especially coyotes, foxes, mountain lions, bears, then cows and sheep can sleep in peace. It's time we recognize that this philosophy has never worked, and never will.
--Dick Randall (Pacelle 1988)

On January 15, 1980, one of the livestock industry's foremost representatives declared, "I would like to say as a sheep producer, I cannot accept any level of predation" (Malachowski 1988). In other words, he will not accept anything less than the government preventing *all* predation on his livestock.

"Reasonable" people say we need a "balanced" predator control program that "controls" predators enough to minimize stock losses but not so much that it harms the environment. This is not reasonable. It's like saying a reasonable approach to burglary is to allow the theft of only 3/4 of a person's belongings. Moreover, it has been shown that to maintain minimal predation levels, predator populations must also be kept to minimal levels -- small fractions of original densities -- so low, in fact, that often they are not able to maintain genetic health in the long run.

Janice Grauberger, a spokesperson for the National Woolgrowers' Association, stated in 1987 that "All that stockmen have ever asked for is that people take a common sense look at the reintroduction of wolves or the purposeful reintroduction of any predator where livestock are being raised." Well, I challenge anyone to find an area in the West large enough that wolves or any other large predator would have no contact with livestock, and large enough for that species to maintain a viable population. This country needs such places, but they do not exist. Even most Wilderness Areas are infested with cattle or sheep. Grauberger's words

are simply empty rhetoric designed to make her business appear reasonable and placate opposition to predator slaughter.

Even if ranching did have an appropriate place in the West, which it does not, predation is a natural occurrence and anyone in the ranching business should be prepared to suffer livestock losses to predators, as herders historically have for thousands of years. If losses on an allotment are so great that a rancher simply cannot stay in business, then he should not be in business. This is something ranchers, government, and the public all must sooner or later realize.

By far the most vocal, vehement, and deadly enemy of Western predators has been and remains the public lands rancher. Yet, the total amount of meat from sheep and cattle killed by predators on public land each year would, if distributed evenly, provide each American only *1/12* ounce (about the weight of a peanut) of mutton and beef (US government publications). Ranchers counter that without predator "control" keeping the predator population low the amount would be vastly higher. If this was true, then historical fluctuations in predator slaughter should reflect corresponding rises and falls in livestock predation. They don't.

The massive slaughter of predators in western states continues in an effort to protect the private interests of a few thousand cattle and sheep ranchers, with total disregard for both its cost to the nation's taxpayers and its impact on the nation's wildlife and public lands.
--Sava Malachowski, "Bloody Shame" (Malachowski 1988)

I'm sick of hearing about the slaughter of mountain lions, bears and wolves, and having to listen to John Wayne wannabes mewling about their property rights. . . . Ranchers are just going to have to accept the fact that certain natural hazards go along with driving cows on public land. Among those are gopher holes, lightning strikes, rattlesnakes, flash floods and, yes, predators. . . . I object to the wholesale slaughter of the public's wildlife so that a few dozen ranchers can sustain an uneconomical "lifestyle" that became an anachronism 50 years ago.
--Richard Lessner, "Dancing With Wolves: Ranchers Should Lose This War" (Lessner 1991)

Competitors

"Competitor" is a term not often used by stockmen or their government bureaucracies, but it accurately describes the industry's attitude and activities relative to many wild animals. A *competitor* may be defined as any wild or feral animal that normally eats significant amounts of what livestock might eat. This definition would include a great number of species the ranching establishment usually calls "pests," and there is often a fine line between the two. This section, however, will focus on those animals more conventionally regarded as competitors -- mainly the large herbivores. (See next section for "pests.")

Since bison, deer, elk, and antelope competed with domestic cattle and sheep for the grazing lands, it was axiomatic that these wild grazers had to be eliminated or at least reduced in numbers to the point where they no longer posed a major threat to livestock. Accordingly, ranchers, aided by Indians and contract hunters, launched a concerted campaign on the grazing mammals, and by the end of the nineteenth century, deer, antelope, elk, and bison were nearly exterminated, with only small herds scattered over what was once a very large range.

--J.J. McCoy, **Wild Enemies** (McCoy 1974)

A century ago ranching, and later other human exploitation, hit Western wildlife like a nuclear bomb. Millions of large herbivores were slaughtered and replaced by livestock. Overgrazing depleted the food supply and ravaged the habitats of those that remained. Many fell to introduced disease and parasites. Within a few decades, many species survived only as tattered remnants of their former populations.

Overall, the 1920s were a low point. After that, abandonment of thousands of small homesteads, efforts to mitigate ranching impacts, increased concern for wildlife, tighter "game" restrictions, restoration programs, and the creation of National Parks and National Wildlife Refuges all began to reverse the trend. Since then, populations of most large herbivores have rebounded somewhat, though they are still only small fractions of their original numbers. Populations of others, including many predators and small animals, continue to decline.

Today, livestock grazing and related activities remain the major factors preventing wildlife recovery on Western public land. In this way, without having to fire a shot, the ranching establishment eliminates most competitors from most areas or pushes them into areas not well suited to livestock (or most wildlife either, unfortunately). Yet, even

(Photo courtesy of Steve Johnson)

today's relatively tiny wild large herbivore populations are unacceptable to stockmen striving to **minimize** competition. Stockmen continue to intentionally kill wild competitors, and their government agencies continue to give livestock overwhelming priority in management plans. Thanks more to ranching than any other factor, it is possible to walk for days across public land and never see a large native herbivore other than an occasional deer.

They call them "mammal control agents." . . . And I could tell you how the sheepmen shoot game animals, deer and antelope by the hundreds and treat them with poison of their own. I know where there are 14 deer baits right now . . . . It would make your hair stand on end, all the things I really have seen.
--Dr. Stanley A. Cain, Assistant Secretary of the Interior for Fish and Wildlife, in a statement to a Congressional subcommittee in 1966

● Deer

Because deer are (now) primarily browsers, stockmen are less prone to think of them as competitors. This is another reason deer numbers remained comparatively high while other "big game" species plummeted. Nonetheless, overgrazed ranges may have a 35% to 60% dietary overlap between cattle and deer, and even greater competition between sheep and deer. Heavy goat grazing (which is gaining popularity) can virtually ruin a

A mule deer on healthy range not used by livestock. *(George Robbins Photo, Jackson, WY)*

range for deer. Thus, many ranchers shoot deer regularly, allegedly for sport or venison, but often as much or more to reduce competition. Because deer hunting is one of this country's favorite outdoor activities, few people question ranchers' motives.

● Pronghorn

On lightly grazed ranges, competition between cattle and pronghorn usually is no more than 15% of their diets, but on heavily grazed ranges competition can be significant. Sheep and pronghorn normally have a 40% dietary overlap; and, as mentioned, overgrazing on sheep ranges can create serious competition. Damage claims for lost herbage awarded ranchers by the state of Colorado are figured on the basis of 13 pronghorn equalling 1 cow.

To the partial credit of some of the more enlightened private lands ranchers, pronghorn have been tolerated, or even encouraged (nearly always as a "big game" species) in recent years and have increased in numbers on some private

Pronghorn on cattle-grazed Wyoming range. *(George Robbins Photo, Jackson, WY.)*

rangelands, especially in Wyoming. Public lands ranchers, however, have not been so generous; their opposition keeps pronghorn numbers relatively low. They shoot pronghorn discreetly as competitors or ostensibly for sport, on private or public land. With government help, they organize special "damage control" hunts to bring pronghorn numbers down to "acceptable" tiny levels. They compel Western state game and fish departments to trap and relocate "problem" pronghorn. More than any other group, they pressure states and federal agencies to maintain population ceilings which keep pronghorn at only small fractions of aboriginal numbers. On Montana's Charles M. Russell National Wildlife Refuge, it took a federal court ruling against livestock operators to uphold the right of the Refuge to allot more herbage to pronghorn and other wildlife than to the permittees' cattle. Nearly all pronghorn range in the West is used for livestock ranching.

● Bighorn

Bighorns eat many of the same foods as cattle and sheep, but because they have been reduced to tiny populations that survive only in remote, rugged, livestock-unproductive locations, they pose little competitive threat. Yet stockmen continue to shoot bighorns (legally or otherwise) as competitors and to

oppose recovery and reintroduction efforts. In recent years, they have even gone to court to block bighorn reintroductions. In one case, livestock interests pressured a court to forbid BLM to transplant 18 bighorns onto BLM land in Big Jacks Creek Canyon in Owyhee County, Idaho (where they had been extirpated by ranching long before) unless the Idaho Department of Fish & Game first administered vaccines to the animals and checked them for disease and parasites that might affect livestock. All parties complied. Stockmen in some Western states are pressuring state game and fish departments to require veterinarians to inspect, treat, and certify as disease-free all transplanted wildlife -- an economic impracticality that would effectively end many recovery efforts. The public might reasonably ask why an area's cattle and sheep are not required to be checked and vaccinated at stockmen's expense to protect transplanted wild animals.

●Buffalo

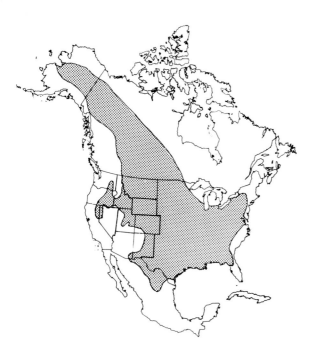

APPROXIMATE PRE-EUROPEAN PRIMARY BUFFALO RANGE

Buffalo on average are half again as big as cattle, are much stronger, more agile and intelligent. They can push over or through most livestock fences. They are (were) the cow's premier forage competitor. Thus, the Western stockman fears the free-roaming buffalo as much as the wild wolf. A large percentage of the variously estimated 40-75 million buffalo massacred (hundreds of millions, altogether, including progeny) a century ago were slaughtered to make room for cattle. Competing, disease-carrying livestock destroyed many. And ranchers have continued to slaughter buffalo ever since.

Though early ranchers helped push the unfortunate animal nearly to extinction, contemporary stockmen have not relented; most of them vehemently resist buffalo recovery or reintroduction proposals. For example, south-central Wyoming's Red Desert, last home of free-ranging buffalo in this country and even today one of the largest unfenced tracts of land in the lower 48 states, is considered a prime reintroduction site. Local ranchers oppose a proposal to transplant "surplus" buffalo from northwest Wyoming's National Elk Refuge to the Red Desert, ostensibly because buffalo will spread brucellosis to their cattle, and, according to Leonard Hay, a member of the Rock Springs Grazing Association's board of directors, because "Bison will compete with livestock for forage, particularly winter range forage." Local BLM officials say there is enough forage for both the cattle and a token number of buffalo. A past president of the Wyoming Wildlife Federation, Ron Smith, points out that buffalo can simply be inoculated against brucellosis before being transplanted (inoculation is considered 70%-90% effective). But the transplant is unlikely. Again, why shouldn't the cattle be removed from Red Desert BLM land and replaced with buffalo?

Yellowstone National Park harbors one of the world's largest "free-roaming" buffalo populations -- currently about 2200 animals altogether. The Park's northern herd of approximately 1000 had in recent years been expanding northward into historic wintering habitat in the Yellowstone River Valley in Montana. As usual, most of the valley is owned and/or grazed by stockmen.

These men [buffalo hunters] *have done in the last two years, and will do in the next year, more to settle the vexed Indian question than the entire regular army has done in the last 30 years. They are destroying the Indian's commissary; and it is a well known fact that an army losing its base of supplies is placed at a great disadvantage. Send them powder and lead, if you will; but, for the sake of lasting peace, let them kill, skin, and sell until the buffalos are exterminated. Then your prairies can be covered with speckled cattle and the festive cowboy, who follows the hunter as a second forerunner of an advanced civilization.*

--US Army General Sheridan, 1870s

Ranchers shot some of the Yellowstone buffalo as they ventured beyond the Park's northern boundary into the Land of Bovine. The Park Service attempted to drive them back into the Park with trucks, helicopters, rubber bullets, cattle grates, and loud noise. On April 19, 1985, the Governor of Montana signed HB 763, which allows the hunting of any buffalo that wanders out of Yellowstone National Park. The Park Service considered other alternatives and finally decided to build a 6-mile-long, 6-foot-high, heavy-duty woven wire fence to block the buffalo's movement out of the Park. The fence cost half a million dollars, blocked elk migration, and created an eyesore in the National Park. It was only partially effective. Over half of Yellowstone's northern herd -- at least 569 animals -- were shot in the winter-spring of 1988-89. Reportedly, only 4 were killed during the 1989-90 season, but government officials predict hundreds will be killed in coming years.

In 1990, eighty miles south in Wyoming, ranchers have pressured the state to allow for the first time hunters to kill 20 bison straying from Grand Teton National Park and the National Elk Refuge (see Wuerthner 1990). In southeast Utah's Henry Mountains, drought and overgrazing -- by far mostly by cattle -- recently induced the state Division of Wildlife Resources to issue 115 special buffalo hunting permits -- in addition to the usual 65 -- to minimize competition with livestock.

Ranchers next to or near some buffalo reserves are pushing for the slaughter of these few remaining behemoths under the premise that they spread brucellosis to cattle -- this, despite evidence that, "no cases have surfaced in which cows have been infected [with brucellosis] from bison" (*E* magazine, May/June 1990). Experts say that *cattle* spread this disease -- to each other and to wild animals. At Yellowstone, where the brucellosis argument is being used, almost all cattle have been inoculated against the disease.

The Parker Land and Cattle Co. of Dubois in northwest Wyoming recently filed a damage claim for over $1.1 million (the state's largest ever) against Wyoming Game & Fish, Grand Teton National Park, BLM, FS, and FWS. The company contends that the agencies are to blame for the ranch's cattle herd contacting brucellosis from either buffalo or elk, leading to the quarantine and mandatory slaughter, sterilization, or castration of its entire 622 head cow/calf herd -- this, despite a statement by the Wyoming state veterinarian that there is no proof the cattle contacted the disease from wildlife. The Parker Company, like many other ranches, is demanding stepped-up wildlife vaccination against brucellosis and the immediate slaughter of any wild animals even remotely suspected of carrying the disease. (Rancher-oriented Western Congressmen currently are backing legislation introduced by Sen. Conrad Burns of Montana that would force the federal government to pay ranchers for testing cattle that were "exposed" to brucellosis by wildlife in the area.)

> *Imagine not that the bison are invading the ranches, but that the ranchers' cattle are occupying the bison's ancient turf.*
> --Mike Bader, Alliance for the Wild Rockies

●Elk

Concerning Elk. They are very destructive animals.
--Hubert Lauzon, public lands rancher

Elk average almost as much as cattle in weight and eat many of the same plants (though 1/3 to 1/2 as much); thus, they are formidable competitors. Dietary overlap may be 50% or higher, and on badly overgrazed winter ranges elk may starve while cattle usually munch hay. Elk may also damage fences and in winter abandon livestock-overgrazed ranges in favor of private pastures and feed supplies. Modern elk generally keep to high elevations and stay near the cover of forests, but few elk ranges are not also used by livestock. Elk and livestock do not mix well, and since livestock arrived in the West elk have been getting the worst of it. Ranchers long ago fenced elk out of most of their natural ranges and relegated them to a marginal existence on less favorable lands -- what now mostly comprise public lands. But because elk travel much farther from water than do cattle, the construction of many new stock tanks has allowed cattle to invade much of this formerly inaccessible elk habitat.

An elk in an autumn meadow during rut.*(George Wuerthner)*

Probably no other wild competitor stirs such violent opposition in ranchers as elk. Since the 1800s many stockmen have routinely shot elk to give their cattle more to eat, often under the protective banner of "hunting." Elk hunters are a powerful special interest in the West; but, ironically, their traditional "hunter/cowboy camaraderie" has been a major factor in keeping elk numbers low. In recent years, some of the more enlightened elk hunters have challenged stockmen's efforts to prevent elk recovery, though with only limited success. Detailed below are a few of the livestock/elk conflicts raging around the West.

In Arizona (and New Mexico), the largest of all elk, the now-extinct Merriam's elk, has been replaced with other subspecies, which now number perhaps 20,000 and survive only in the east-central to north-central forests of the state. In the 1950s, ranchers' complaints led the state Game & Fish Department to "shoot the heck out of the elk herd," but in recent years elk hunters have fought back, and a major confrontation is brewing. Ranchers claim that elk overgraze winter ranges, damage fences, and eat their hay and salt blocks. In fact, an Arizona Cattle Growers questionnaire returned from 40 of 147 area permittees shows: (1) an average of 473 elk per ranch/allotment, which, if representative of the other 107 permittees, would total 70,000 elk -- 10 times more elk than exist in that area!, (2) an elk salt use of *6 tons* per ranch, (3) the presence of elk is (suddenly) the worst of their ranching problems, followed by dense tree growth, hunters, vandalism, and predators, (4) an average hay damage of $1100 per ranch, and (5) elk depletion of 69% of the grass and 31% of the browse on their allotments! Steve Gallizioli, Vice President of the Arizona Wildlife Federation, took a cattlemen-sponsored tour to witness the elk devastation. He reports:

It was billed as a tour to show everyone the magnitude of the "elk problem" on the Apache-Sitgreaves National Forest. . . . We saw nothing to substantiate what he [local rancher] said about numbers of elk and their predations. Ironically the only evidence we actually saw which indicated there had been too many animals on the area was a forest allotment overgrazed by cattle. A swarm of locusts couldn't have done a better job on the area.

Hunters claim that cattle, which account for at least 12 times as many AUMs in the area, are doing the overgrazing and should be reduced on public land. It is a common conflict, this struggle over "natural resources" -- the ranchers historically in control, the hunters demanding their slice of Nature's pie. According to an article in an area newspaper, "When it came to actually making formal suggestions on what big game policies and regulations ought to be changed this coming year, the proposals from the ranchers present all had one aim -- drastically reducing elk herds." A recent statement by a spokesman for Arizona stockmen demanded that the state's elk population be immediately reduced by 61%. He also wanted Arizona Game & Fish to be held liable for any elk impacts on ranchers' private or public land ranching operations, and demanded that ranchers be given a portion of the state's revenues from sales of big game hunting permits and tags. Hunting and bag limits were to be set in accord with ranchers' desires, and the Arizona Game & Fish Commission was to be appointed to include at least half livestock interests. Both ranchers and hunters agree there should be more range "improvements."

In Arizona's Prescott National Forest, Mike Oden, a public lands ranching permittee, recently pled guilty to illegally killing 6 elk. Investigators believe 11 and as many as

20 may have been shot -- 1/3 of the area's elk herd. Some of the animals were probably "gut shot" -- that is, purposefully shot in the stomach or intestines and allowed to wander far away from the scene of the crime to die slowly from infection or other complications. According to the Arizona Game & Fish Department in their Nov. 15, 1989, *Wildlife Newsletter*, "Oden reportedly shot or ordered his employees to shoot as many elk as possible because he believed they were competing with his cattle and feared their presence might cause the U.S. Forest Service to reduce his grazing permits . . . ."

In Utah in the early 1900s, pressure from stockmen prompted the state to establish the Board of Elk Control, which, along with attrition from ranchers and others, nearly extirpated the animal from the state. In southeast Utah in 1988, a handful of public lands ranchers hired a powerful range consultant firm to block an attempt by the Forest Service to reintroduce elk onto their historic range in the Manti-LaSal National Forest. After subjecting government agencies and numerous groups and individuals to a lengthy battle, their appeal was recently denied. FS reintroduction plans (along with various appeasements to local stockmen) are scheduled to proceed, though it remains to be seen if these elk will survive covert "lead poisoning" promised by ranchers.

In northeast Nevada, another proposal to reintroduce elk -- into Nevada's largest and best elk habitat -- was dropped in 1985 after 13 years of planning. Under pressure from a handful of stockmen (including a past president of the National Cattlemen's Association) and the ever-pro-ranching Nevada legislators, the Nevada Department of Fish & Wildlife abandoned its reintroduction plans. According to a local newspaper, "Nevada legislators were rumored to have threatened the Nevada Department of Fish & Wildlife with reprisals if the reintroduction occurred."

Elk once were abundant in northeast Nevada and southwest Idaho, but livestock grazing and extermination by local ranchers 20 to 30 years ago have destroyed the area's elk, except for a herd of 30 in a remote area of Owyhee County, Idaho. Nevada DF&W studies show that at least 400 elk could live in the area without significantly affecting ranching, that these elk would equal or exceed the economic value of area livestock while consuming less forage, and that rancher use of BLM lands (most of the area is BLM land) contributed only 0.26% to the total income of 3 area "cow counties."

As with so many other animals, the most persistent, deadly influence on elk is ranching.

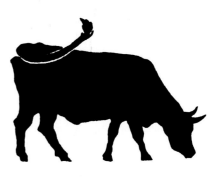

●Horse

Are the West's free-roaming horses and burros wild or feral? Do they have a place on public land? If so, where and how many? Should they be allowed to occupy their entire range or be limited to certain areas? These are sticky questions, and people have many varying and often emotional answers. Each person must make up his or her own mind based on consideration of environmental and other impacts, knowledge of the animals, and intuition.

Technically, they probably are feral animals, having descended from escaped domestic stock. However, fossil evidence indicates that some species of horse evolved on the North American continent perhaps 60 million years ago and disappeared only about 7000 years ago -- probably due largely to attrition by humans. Some evidence suggests that vestigial populations may have survived up until 3000 or even 1000 years ago. Equines are therefore much better adapted to North American ecosystems than are cattle or domestic sheep. This is a main reason horses took so readily to the West when the Spanish reintroduced(?) them to the continent in the 16th century.

Strays from Spanish missions and settlements formed wild bands and spread quickly across the West. Native Americans captured and tamed many of these. History books notwithstanding, other than introduced disease the use of horses was probably the greatest contributor to the downfall of indigenous Americans in the West in the 17th, 18th, and early 19th centuries. With the horse, they could travel great distances much more quickly and carry (therefore own) many more possessions, thus radically altering the ways of life that had served them well for millennia. They were able to slaughter many more large game animals than they could eat or use. Horses in domesticated, sedentary herds ate crops and overgrazed surrounding areas, destroying plants and small animals used for food and other necessities. With the horse, Native Americans were able to invade each others' homelands and wage war as never before. Thus, the warring, nomadic Native Americans that Euro-Americans met when they came West in the mid-1800s were already vastly changed from a century or two before. (Malin 1956; White 1983) (Historically, livestock domestication fostered the rise of many aggressive civilizations; for example, domestication of the alpaca and llama was a major factor in the rise of the conquering Incas in South America.)

By the end of the 18th century, horses, also called mustangs, roamed about half of the continent and numbered an estimated 2 to 10 million individuals. This population level continued until the livestock invasion of the mid-19th century. Evidence indicates that during this period the horses of North America filled "their" habitat and reached a relatively stable population. Overgrazing was a minimal problem until the introduction of huge numbers of cattle and, later, sheep.

To clear the way for cattle and help destroy "the Indian menace," white invaders slaughtered not only the buffalo and "redskins" themselves, but the horses they had come to depend on. During the late 1800s, millions of horses were shot, poisoned at water holes, and driven over cliffs. In California, for example, to increase cattle forage, early Spanish ranchers drove thousands of horses over cliffs or into the sea (McNamee 1985). Thousands more were shot for target practice or sport. As the incoming hordes of cattle were given the advantage and began seriously overgrazing the range, horses found it more difficult to survive and reproduce, further reducing their numbers. Introduced disease took a toll.

Early Western newspapers contain many accounts of mass slaughters of hundreds or thousands of horses to keep them from competing with cattle, such as this from a Nevada newspaper: "Nine wild horses are all that remain now of a band of nearly 2,000 of the fleet-footed animals that romped over the hills and valleys of the Toiyabe National Forest three years ago and these nine are due to be exterminated if federal hunters and livestock owners can get within rifle shot of them . . ." (Young 1985)

Augmenting the overgrazing, introduced disease, and relentless attrition by the ranching industry, commercial "mustanging" became a booming business in the early 1900s. Mustangers, working independently, paid private and government bounties, or hired by stockmen, rounded up millions of horses and sold them as work or saddle animals or to slaughter houses where they were processed for pet food, chicken feed, fertilizer, and glue. Methods of capture included: roping; roping a tire to horses' necks to eventually wear them down; "creasing," whereby a rifleman would attempt to graze the spinal nerve on top of the neck to incapacitate the animals; "walk down," where 2 or more riders working in relays would follow a band for days until the horses became too tired, footsore, or indifferent to resist the riders (sometimes "running them down until their legs became bloody stumps"); and "corralling," in which men on horseback, in vehicles, or (later) in aircraft drove a band up against fences or canvas walls and funnelled them into a corral, or trapped them in a narrow, steep-walled canyon. (Young 1985)

Additionally, many thousands of horses on public land were captured by ranchers and used as saddle stock and draft animals. Compensating for this somewhat, horses abandoned by or escaping from ranchers joined or formed wild bands; thus, ironically, stockmen are partly responsible for their own "horse problem." Because of this, and subsequent hybridization, few free-roaming horses still have much original Spanish blood.

strong sentiment developed to get rid of them.
--Paul H. Roberts, former Forest Service official, **Hoof Prints on Forest Ranges** (Roberts 1963)

It's really a matter of greed. The cattlemen pay ridiculously low grazing fees, and now they're afraid that the horses are going to spoil their little game.
--Hope Ryden, author, widely considered the foremost authority on free-roaming horses

The Taylor Grazing Act of 1934 gave the ranching industry added organization to and the government the means to destroy free-roaming horses. By the 1940s the horse population was so low that people began to worry (or *hope*, in the case of most stockmen) that free-ranging horses would be extirpated completely from the West. Some demanded federal protection. Foremost among these was Velma Johnston, who later came to be known as "Wild Horse Annie." In 1950 Annie began an energetic campaign for legislative protection, which in 1959 resulted in passage of Public Law 86-234, known as the "Wild Horse Annie Act." This act outlawed the use of motor vehicles and aircraft and the poisoning of water holes for capturing or killing horses. It helped slow the slaughter, but was difficult to enforce. By 1970 the US free-roaming horse population had dropped to a low of about 17,000.

I am especially angry at the BLM and Forest Service because I have been a member of the International Society for the Protection of Mustangs and Burros since its inception. My friend, "Wild Horse Annie" Johnston was the president. The ranchers in Reno, Nevada, burned her in effigy because of her efforts on behalf of these animals.
--Rosemary Henry, Pinyon Hills, California, personal correspondence

The continuing lobbying efforts and letter writing campaigns of concerned groups (and thousands of school children) during the 1960s finally culminated with the passage of the Wild Free-roaming Horse and Burro Act of 1971, which outlawed killing, capturing, or harming the animals without government authority. This Congressional act stated that horses and burros were "fast disappearing from the American scene" and called for "protection, management, and control" of animals described as "living symbols of the historic and pioneer spirit of the West" (ironically, about the same words sometimes used in Congress to describe public lands ranchers -- those people who have killed more horses than any other). With the added protection of the 1971 act, the "wild" horse and burro population rose quickly and reached roughly 50,000 in 1976, and perhaps as high as 70,000 in the early 1980s. *But...*

As soon as the horse population began to rise, stockmen once again put the screws to the BLM. Under authority of the 1971 act, BLM in 1973 began identifying free-roaming horse and burro "herd management areas" and setting limits on how many mustangs or burros each area would be allowed "*based on availability of resources.*" With the sneaky rhetoric, these limits were based overwhelmingly on projected competition with cattle and sheep. In 1988, BLM stated that "the appropriate management level Bureauwide

is expected to be approximately 31,000 wild horses and burros" (USDI, BLM 1988). Also that year, the Forest Service estimated that "1,225 wild horses and 350 wild burros are the appropriate management levels" for FS land (USDA, FS 1988). In other words, the federal government claims that Western lands once supporting millions of horses (an estimated 1 million in Nevada alone) and burros can now support only about 32,600.

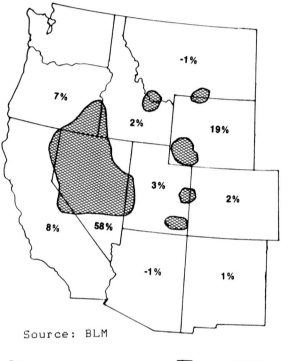

Source: BLM

% - Percentage of Total Population   ▨ - Major Wild Horse Areas

The intent of Congress is to preserve some symbols, not expand the herds.
--John Boyles, chief of BLM's Wild Horse Bureau (Satchell 1987)

BLM determines the status of each management area's free-roaming horses and burros yearly. Old, sick, and lame animals (or those claimed to be) may be killed. Thousands of "surplus" horses and burros are captured, usually with helicopters, and trucked to corrals. There they are processed and offered for adoption (generally, a 4-per-year limit) to anyone who pays the adoption fee and maintains the animals for 1 year. All adopted animals are supposed to go to good homes, but many wind up being abused, butchered and fed to pets, or sold for slaughter, to rodeos, etc.

A federal court of appeals in San Francisco recently stated BLM's "adopt-a-horse" program was a "farce" because it failed to screen out commercial interests. The court ruled that BLM is prohibited from transferring title to federal free-roaming horses or burros to anyone known to use the animals for commercial exploitation. BLM itself admitted that several thousand horses taken under large-scale adoptions have been sold for slaughter, and that thousands of others have been sold or abused. A 1990 GAO report affirms that at least 4000 were sold for slaughter from 1985 through 1988 by horse traders who took advantage of the program, and that the same fate probably met most of the 16,000 other horses given away through one part of the program. The report indicated that thousands more were illegally sold and cruelly mistreated, that BLM knowingly gave horses to commercial interests, that there is little evidence of horses overgrazing federal lands, and that ranchers have been allowed to increase cattle numbers on some allotments after horses have been removed, concluding, according to Knight-Ridder Newspapers, that the adoption "program has been run largely to satisfy ranchers who graze cattle on the land."

Since 1973, about 100,000 horses and burros have been taken from the range and "adopted." But, the adoption market is now saturated, and more than 10,000 animals are being held in federal corrals (some for 4 years), where, according to many sources, food, treatment, and conditions in general are poor. Each year thousands more are born on the open range and thousands more are captured and added to the already overflowing corrals. (BLM claims a natural "wild" horse population increase of 25% per year, though a 1982 study by the National Academy of Sciences concluded that the rate is 10% or less.) BLM, rather than reducing cattle numbers, has proposed that these "unadoptable" thousands be killed or auctioned off *en masse*. A growing number of people say BLM is purposefully rounding up far more horses and burros than it can accommodate so as to make slaughter or auction to large-scale commercial interests seem like the only alternatives.

Leaving no stone unturned, BLM has for years been funding research for fertility control and genetic manipulation to reduce horse numbers. Some horses already have been implanted with contraceptive drugs. Naturalists and others express concerns over how this interference may affect the animals' behavior, physical health, and gene pool.

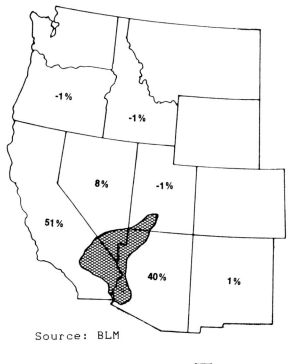

Source: BLM

% - Percentage of Total Population   [icon] **Major Burro Area**

●Burro

Burros were used as pack animals by early prospectors and shepherds because they could travel long distances and subsist on desert vegetation. Some were later abandoned in favor of newer forms of transportation. Others escaped to the open range. They survived and prospered in the low deserts of southeastern California, western Arizona, extreme southern Nevada, and extreme southwestern Utah.

Burro range is generally unproductive for cattle, though most is grazed by cattle nonetheless; parts of it are too barren and dry for even stockmen to utilize. Thus, as competitors burros are somewhat less persecuted by the grazing industry than are horses. They are killed in some areas, however; for example, the carcasses of at least 51 burros were recently found on cattle range in Mojave County, Arizona, probably killed by local ranchers.

Free-ranging burros have damaged some parts of their fragile, hot desert range, especially near water, though damage generally has been less than that from cattle. To protect the environment, burros have been removed from the Grand Canyon, most of Death Valley, and some other areas. To protect livestock interests, they have been removed from many other areas.

Today, thousands of burros also await adoption in BLM corrals. The free-roaming burro population has declined greatly in recent years and now stands at less than 5000. The government plans further reductions.

Feral burros in lower elevation Mojave Desert, California.

[Stockmen] *are very disturbed that the BLM cannot seem to do what Congress told it to do, which is manage the numbers of wild horses. When there's not enough forage to go around, it's always the livestock that gets cut.*
--Deloyd Satterthwaite, Nevada Cattlemen's Association president, 10-21-89 *Arizona Republic*

Stockmen generally support BLM's program to clear the range of horses and burros. But many of them think BLM isn't doing enough. In other words, horses are still getting some of "their" forage. Since the 1971 act stockmen, their legal representatives, and the state of Nevada have filed a number of lawsuits against BLM to force it to further reduce horse numbers; Nevada, for instance, wants a 10,000 head ceiling in the state (USDI, BLM and USDA, FS 1980). For example, Nevada rancher Joe Fallini recently won a court decision forcing the federal government to remove 1100 (all but 150) horses from the allotment he grazes cattle on. Of "his" *700,000-acre* "ranch" -- *98% of which is public land* -- Joe says, "I call it split-estate land. The public owns certain rights, and we have a certain possessory interest through use." In some Western states, the courts have even ordered BLM to remove free-ranging horses from *private* ranchland, essentially at the owners' request.

Pro-horse groups have filed a similar number of lawsuits to force BLM to halt various roundups, treat captured animals humanely, and screen potential adopters. In all, more than 20 lawsuits have been filed since the inception of the 1971 Wild Free-roaming Horse and Burro Act, with the ranching industry prevailing in most cases.

Also since the 1971 act, BLM has investigated *hundreds* of cases involving harassment, illegal capture, or killing of free-roaming horses and burros on public land. The agency acknowledges that detection and prevention of these activities is "difficult." In other words, the ranchers' war against the horse continues unabated.

Perhaps the most prominent example is the recent discovery of scattered remains of hundreds of horses on remote BLM land in central Nevada. In August 1988, a charter helicopter pilot spotted the sprawled bodies of many horses on the slopes and in the washes near a spring. He notified BLM, whose investigators found 41 dead horses. Subsequent searches of the general area turned up groups of horse remains in various locations, which 2 months later totaled 451 bodies over 160 square miles of rangeland. All had been shot. Continued searching has so far revealed the bodies and bones of a total of 524. Some estimates place the number at around 1000. Many, perhaps most, will never be found. Undoubtedly, BLM could expand the search indefinitely and discover slaughtered horses throughout its 75,000 square miles of horse range in the West. (Even more recently, an Arizona newspaper reported that as many as 400 horses and *200 deer* were killed near the new Great Basin National Park in east-central Nevada, "allegedly by the employees of ranchers seeking to protect *their* grazing land . . ." [*Tucson Citizen*, 6-9-89 (emphasis added)]. Said undersheriff Harry Collins, "They shot them in the stomach, so these animals would wander" and take hours to die and spread the carcasses widely.)

The appalling discovery in central Nevada touched off a rare but brief public outcry, nationally broadcast TV programs, magazine articles, and a widespread demand for action. BLM launched an extensive investigation. In a *People* magazine article (Brower 1988), Nevada BLM chief investigator Len Sims stated, "People know who did it, but they are reluctant to talk to me. They say they don't want to get killed." A local former mustanger, Jimmy Williams, seemed to confirm this when he confided, "I don't want my bones bleaching out there." Sims also "watches his backside" these days.

Of the killings, BLM spokesperson Bob Stewart said, "The carnage that occurred out there was terrible, almost unbelievable." But Art Bergonzoni, son of a local public lands rancher, begs to differ. In an Austin, Nevada, saloon, he thundered at the *People* reporter, "They should shoot every damned one of them! They eat all the grass! The

taxpayers is paying for them suckers and what good is they?" Outside the saloon, another public lands rancher snapped, "Whoever is killing those horses should get a medal."

Denying industry involvement, Nevada Cattlemen's Association president Deloyd Satterthwaite said he "cannot believe" that ranchers committed such atrocities, while NCA spokesperson Vickie Turner declared, "There are too many horses out there, but ranchers aren't killing them." Soon thereafter, a federal grand jury indicted 5 area cowboys for killing some of the horses (though as usual none were convicted).

This particular horse slaughter is unusual only in the large number of horses killed at one time and in having been discovered and revealed to a large segment of the public. According to Jimmy Williams, "The ranchers used to shoot just a few at a time and nobody paid much attention. The only difference now is they got a lot more ambitious." Many rural folks are well-aware that ranchers have always discreetly dispatched horses they think compete with their livestock. BLM itself reports recent cases of horses being intentionally tortured and maimed, as is the case with predators (USDI, BLM, USDA, FS 1980). And it is widely known that stockmen often shoot a horse or two to draw predators away from their livestock, or for carcasses to poison and leave for predators. For example, a northeast California rancher, Bobby Gene Bunyard, recently was charged by state and federal wildlife officials with gunning down a horse and then injecting its body with strychnine, which later killed a "protected" golden eagle. Again not surprisingly, the court system found the defendant not guilty by reason of insufficient evidence.

If all illegal horse killers were arrested and convicted, *hundreds* of Western ranchers would go to jail.

Even on northern Wyoming's Prior Mountain Wild Horse Range, free-roaming horses must compete with cattle. *(George Robbins Photo, Jackson, WY)*

Wild horses and burros which are protected by law are proliferating to such as extent that they are not only driving out all wildlife and livestock in many areas but also ruining range resources for generations to come.

--Ronald A. Michieli, as Executive Director of the Public Lands Council, which "represents the ranchers who graze livestock on Federal lands in Western states"

BLM estimates in 1989 show about 30,000 horses and 5000 feral burros roaming 47.5 million acres of its public land in 10 Western states, and that there are approximately 42,000 free-roaming horses and burros on all public land (understandably, very few survive on private rangeland). American Humane Association studies and other estimates place the figures at about 2/3 these numbers. Regardless, even BLM figures (which are for many reasons distorted to favor ranching) show that horses receive less than 5% as many AUMs in their range as do cattle and sheep.

Nonetheless, with great mock-concern, the agencies and ranchers claim that horses and burros are overgrazing the land and trampling water sources. Of horse grazing, public lands rancher Demar Dahl complains, "There was no vegetation left, and they ruined the springs -- did incredible damage!" (Satchell 1987). While it is true that in some areas horses have had an obvious impact, usually the main reason their influence seems significant is because they aggrevate an already severe livestock overgrazing situation. Head for head, cattle are more destructive to Western ecosystems than are horses. And while BLM estimates place the Nevada free-roaming horse population at about 20,000 (probably high; still Nevada has over half of the US BLM total), USDA figures place the number of cattle in the state at 620,000 -- 31 times the number of horses. In other horse areas, the disparity is even greater.

Regardless, some ex-public lands ranchers actually claim they were "driven out of business by wild horses." Their claims basically are cover-ups for poorly run operations, livestock overgrazing, and the fact that public land is simply an impractical place to raise commercial stock.

Wild horses trampling water holes? What do you think bovines do? Drink through a straw, maybe? Ranchers destroy more grazing land by overgrazing it, driving over it with their pickup trucks, and mismanaging it than any wild animals ever did.
--Reno Gazette-Journal letter to the editor

In conclusion, tens of millions of "wild" horses and tens of thousands of feral burros have been killed over the years by public lands ranchers and their government and private assistants. The 30,000 or so that remain represent probably less than 1% of their 19th century population. Compared to cattle and sheep, the damage they do is minuscule.

Yet, nearly all public lands ranchers want their numbers cut much further, and many want free-roaming horses and burros eliminated altogether. Conservationists contend that any AUMs gained by removal of horses and burros will just be used to further increase cattle and sheep numbers; this does indeed seem to be the trend.

At least a dozen organizations are dedicated to protecting free-roaming horses and burros. Some of them and some other groups and individuals think horses and burros should be given free reign throughout Western public land. Others think they should be restricted to certain areas. Some ecologists and others think that neither domestic stock nor "feral" equines belong in the ecosystems of public land. Whatever you believe, isn't it reasonable that as long as millions of domestic livestock are allowed on public land, so should a significant number of free-roaming horses and burros?

The free-roaming horses in Nevada are not true wild horses in the biological sense, for they all derive from fully domesticated ancestors and have not lost the genetic traits peculiar to domestic horses, but there are historically significant aspects of their origin which makes them a unique biological phenomenon.
--The Wild Horse in Nevada by Cheryl A. Young (Young 1985)

●Prairie dog

Prairie dogs are the worst thing to happen to rangeland.
--A rancher at the Nucla, Colorado, World Prairie Dog Shoot

Perhaps as important as any large herbivore to pre-livestock Western grassland and semi-grassland was the prairie dog. Belittled as a destructive "pest" by ranchmen, in reality it is (was) one of the industry's foremost competitors.

The prairie dog is a yellowish, plump rodent resembling a squirrel, about a foot long and weighing 1-3 pounds. It has short legs, small ears, and keen, high-set eyes. A uniquely North American mammal, its ancestors evolved on this continent about 35 million years ago, and the subsequent genus *Cynomys* has been found nowhere else on Earth. Five subspecies comprise 2 species: the blacktail, which lived throughout the Western plains from southern Canada to northern Mexico, and the whitetail of the inter-Rocky Mountain West. Combined, their ranges covered the entire eastern half of the 11 Western states. Both species live in open, relatively flat, treeless areas abundant in short to medium grass.

(Helen Wilson)

> *The clans mainly live in peace, with much sunbathing and grooming, often standing or sitting side by side with their forelegs around one another. Clan members are identified by touching noses and sometimes "kissing." Tribal in nature, the clan offers complete community cooperation. The members share burrows in time of danger, defend one another from strangers, share sentry duties, and generally live a tranquil life of respect for one another.*
>
> *--from* **Little Dogs of the Prairie,** Jack Scott and Ozzie Sweet

Prairie dogs are very social, playful, and affectionate animals that live together in clans within larger colonies called "towns." They carefully craft complex, interconnecting burrows with small mounds at each entrance, and may create more than 50 burrows per acre. Prairie dogs occasionally eat forbs, seeds, and insects (of which grasshoppers are a favorite), but by far their preferred food is grass. This works out well, for the overlapping, grazed, 100' or so diameter circles around burrows merge together so the entire colonies are free from tall plants that might conceal predators. (They also cut unpalatable plants from these circles.) Normally, regrowth of new vegetation within these circles remains in balance with the amount of food required. In these large, open towns, prairie dogs intermingle and, using their upright posture for better vantage, warn each other of impending danger with short, high-pitched, doglike "barks."

Before the livestock invasion, some of these prairie dog towns were truly enormous, covering thousands of square miles and including millions of individuals. One was estimated to be 100 miles wide and 250 miles long (25,000 square miles) with *400 million* residents. In fact, prairie dogs were so incredibly numerous that the human mind can scarcely comprehend the numbers. More than 600,000 square miles (an area over 3 times the size of California) were occupied by an estimated *5-10 billion* prairie dogs! In other words, there were more prairie dogs in the West 150 years ago than there are now humans on Earth.

From these numbers alone, one can imagine the importance of prairie dogs to the Western environment. The rodents were a key food for countless millions of predators, including coyotes, wolves, foxes, eagles, hawks, owls, badgers, bobcats, and snakes. Their billions of old burrows gave shelter to burrowing owls, rabbits, spiders, crickets, ground squirrels, toads, box turtles, snakes, lizards, and numerous others. Their daily activities and burrowing action (along with that of gophers, squirrels, badgers, kit foxes, and others later killed off by ranching) aerated the soil; took organic matter and topsoil to lower levels; brought substratum to the surface and scattered it, subjecting it to weathering; and, by opening up deep holes, helped weather the substratum and turn it into soil. (Studies show that prairie dogs and some other burrowing rodents bring to the surface as much as 5 tons of subsoil per acre per year.) Their buried vegetation, runways, galleries, and holes helped counteract the packing effect of buffalo and other large-hooved animals. Burrows also helped water infiltrate to lower levels and conserve moisture, thus augmenting water tables. Indeed, some naturalists believe millennia of infiltration through billions of prairie dog holes was a major contributor to the huge Ogallala Aquifer of the southern plains, the largest store of underground water on the continent. (This aquifer has diminished rapidly, mostly due to pumping for livestock production, and may be depleted in 30 years.) Prairie dog mounds were vital components of the soil-air interface. Their foraging and surface activity helped prepare seedbeds, spread seeds, and create a diversity of conditions, thereby increasing fire, biotic, and zoologic diversity and, thus, ecosystem stability. The fresh soil they brought to the surface provided a medium for the germination of forbs, also augmenting diversity. At least 137 vertebrates, including pronghorn, buffalo, most birds, reptiles, amphibians, ground squirrels, mice, cottontails, jackrabbits, and predators, as well as arachnids, insects, and more were all more abundant around prairie dog towns than elsewhere on the open range. The towns were also important buffalo wallow and dust bath areas.

All this ended with the livestock invasion. Ranchers claim that cattle *increased* prairie dog numbers in the late 1800s by grazing off the grass and thereby "helping out" prairie dog towns. This is absolutely contradicted by research, common sense, and descriptions by Native Americans, early settlers, and explorers. The truth is, cattle depleted the prairie dogs' food source (causing it to range farther to keep fed, often into the mouths of predators) trampled their burrows, and ravaged their ecosystems. Prairie dogs are quite able to keep their towns free of tall vegetation without the assistance of cattle, sheep, or any other herbivore, as they had done for countless millennia. Actually, livestock helped greatly *reduce* the West's prairie dog population by 80%, to an estimated 1 billion by the early 1900s.

Western ranchers have always hated prairie dogs. The "damned varmints" ate "their" grass, and their cattle and horses sometimes broke legs in prairie dog holes. Later, the "unsightly" prairie dog mounds and holes made driving ranch vehicles over the open range difficult. As with so many other indigenous animals, the prairie dog became a scapegoat for destructive ranching, and prairie dog killing became a way for stockmen to release hostility and to imagine they were improving ranching conditions. In their profit-oriented way, contemporary range professionals found that 250 prairie dogs eat as much as a 1000-pound cow, so to them 1 cow = 250 prairie dogs, or 250 dead prairie dogs = the profit from 1 cow. A report by Daniel W. Ursesk disproves this greed-induced logic, and concludes that "Controlling black-tailed prairie dogs on rangelands in western South Dakota did not result in a positive increase in forage production after 4 years" (Ursesk 1985).

Defying reason, ranchers killed prairie dogs on principle. To people who had built their lives on unbridled exploitation of their surroundings, any animal that didn't have some obviously useful purpose deserved to die.

Ranchers actually transported sick [plague-infested] *rodents in trucks, sometimes across hundreds of miles, with the intention of infecting local communities of prairie dogs and reducing their numbers, thus allowing cattle to find more grass.*
--**Plagues and Peoples** by William McNeill

So early ranchers killed prairie dogs -- always -- with the weapons at hand: guns, poisons, traps, dogs, and, as above, disease. They shot as quickly as they could reload, put out as much poison as they could afford to buy, trapped as fast as they could reset, rewarded their dogs for dead prairie dogs, and released as many disease-infested rodents as they could import. But killing these seemingly numberless varmints was time-consuming and sometimes costly. Therefore, as usual, stockmen turned to the taxpayer.

Thus began in the late 1800s the official program to eliminate the prairie dog. By the early 1900s, the Biological Survey was dispensing strychnine-soaked grains. According to ranchers, however, this wasn't killing the animals fast enough. They demanded increased action. Soon federal, state, and local government agents assaulted prairie dog ranges with massive amounts of various poisons. The more they killed, the stronger grew the stockmen's desire for profits. By the 1920s, urged on by the government agents who also stood to gain, the ranching establishment was pushing for total extermination of the prairie dog.

After World War II, the prairie dog "control" program became a lustful, massive campaign of genocide against these peaceful creatures. Compound 1080 was added to the arsenal. Poison was used on all prairie dogs wherever livestock grazed -- in other words, nearly everywhere. Aircraft flew over their vast towns, broadcasting tons of poisoned bait. Soon, all the great colonies were destroyed. Billions of gophers, squirrels, rabbits, mice, seed-eating birds, insects, and microbes died along with the prairie dogs, as did the predators and scavengers that ate their toxic bodies. Some of the poison washed into waterways; some adhered to vegetation and was eaten by livestock. And, interestingly, the lack of rodents caused many larger predators to prey on livestock.

According to **The Wonders of Prairie Dogs** by G. Earl Price, altogether during the campaign *more than 800,000 square miles* of the West were poisoned. For a time it looked as though the industry would celebrate extermination or even extinction of the prairie dog.

This photo from the early 1900s reflects 1641 dead prairie dogs taken from 320 acres in Arizona. They were killed the previous day with 80 quarts of poisoned rolled oats. Only a fraction of the prairie dogs poisoned is shown because most of them die in their burrows. For decades, such mass annihilation by stockmen was commonplace throughout prairie dog habitat. *(Unknown)*

But the slaughter slowed in the 1950s, mainly because there were few prairie dogs left to kill. Also, the public was beginning to complain. People visiting National Parks and the few other areas where the rodents were protected enjoyed the "cute little animals." Others were concerned about the secondary effects of the massive poisonings. Under pressure and with little left to kill, the government discontinued most of its "control" program.

Prairie dogs reached a low in the early 1960s. They were extirpated from most areas, and healthy prairie dog towns were reduced to a few scattered locations. Today, despite ranching establishment misinformation, they have recovered only slightly. Towns of dozens or hundreds are found in some areas, but most colonies are too small even to maintain long-term genetic viability. Overall population is perhaps 0.25% of the pre-ranching number, and the Utah prairie dog is listed as Threatened.

It is unlikely that the prairie dog will ever significantly recover so long as the ranching establishment controls the rural West. Many stockmen still poison or shoot them whenever they can, as they have been conditioned to do from childhood. Many of these people think it great sport to sit at the edge of a prairie dog town and pick them off one by one as they pop up from burrows -- like a shooting arcade. One rural community in southwest Colorado, Nucla/Naturita, has even begun a "World Prairie Dog Shoot" to eradicate the "pests." The Forest Service, ADC, state and county agencies still kill them. In 1987, for example, the Forest Service spread poison on nearly 6000 acres and in 3000 burrows to kill prairie dogs (USDA, FS 1988). ADC killed 124,000 in 1988, mostly with poison. Execution methods also include drowning, sterilization, and hole plugging.

The Simmons Allotment [Pawnee National Grasslands, CO] *Management Plan (1983) prescribed 80 acres as the maximum prairie dog town size. Each year we measure the size of our prairie dog towns. This year, we found that the town exceeded the 80 acre limit. The Forest Service is obligated to follow their agreement and discourage* [mostly kill] *prairie dogs when the town size has exceeded the maximum acre limit.*
--Grant Godbolt, District Ranger, Pawnee National Grasslands, Colorado

Of course, effects from the loss of this low-trophic-level mammal reverberated throughout Western grassland ecosystems. For example, the burrowing owl, which eats prairie dogs and nests in their burrows, plummeted to a small fraction of its original population and has not recovered. Other indirect repercussions have been enormous. As a random example, the disappearance of the prairie dog helped force coyotes and other predators into hills and mountains, where they then depleted wild turkey, quail, and grouse populations.

Over the years control methods using toxic chemicals on Federal, State and private lands have not caused the decline of a single species of wildlife -- endangered or otherwise!
--Vern Vivion, past President, National Wool Growers Association

They lie.
--Mike Roselle

Another once-common grassland resident, the black-footed ferret, was so dependent upon prairie dogs that it is now among the most endangered mammal species on Earth. This mink-sized predator fed almost exclusively on blacktail prairie dogs, which also provided the ferrets with ready-made burrows for shelter and raising young. In turn, the ferrets imparted predator benefits to blacktail prairie dogs. With this strong, albeit seemingly lopsided, interdependency, the 2 species' ranges matched almost exactly.

(Robert Waldmire)

As with the prairie dog, the black-footed ferret was devastated by livestock grazing in the late 1800s. When the huge prairie dog poisoning campaign hit in the early 1900s, the ferret's fate was sealed. Not only was its food source nearly eliminated but, because it also eats carrion, it seems certain many were killed by eating poisoned prairie dogs. When the killing began to ease off in the 1960s, prairie dog numbers rose in some areas, but black-footed ferrets continued to decline. As scientists soon discovered, black-footed ferrets require *large* prairie dog towns in order to find both enough food and enough other ferrets to maintain genetically healthy populations.

From 1974 until 1981, no wild groups of black-footed ferrets were seen anywhere in North America, and many thought it time to declare the

Burrowing owls, once very common residents throughout prairie dog range, have been reduced to only a tiny fraction of their aboriginal population largely by the annihilation of prairie dogs -- which were a major portion of their diet and provided burrows for nesting -- and by other effects of the eradication campaign, livestock grazing, and other harmful ranching influences. *(Bill Girden)*

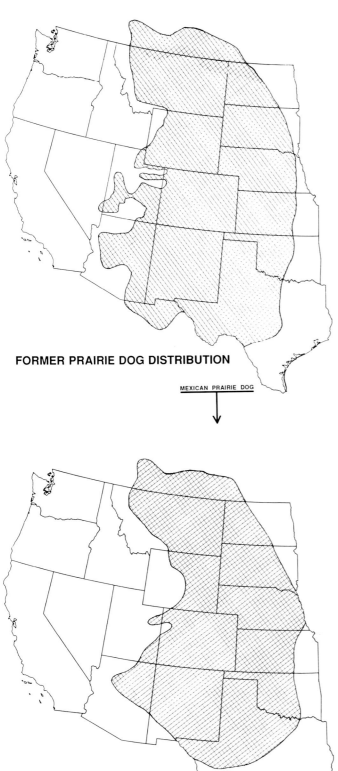

FORMER PRAIRIE DOG DISTRIBUTION

MEXICAN PRAIRIE DOG

The black-footed ferret was so dependent upon the blacktail prairie dog for food and shelter that their ranges matched almost exactly (the discrepency seen here in the western part of their ranges refects whitetail prairie dog habitat). When the prairie dog was wiped out by the ranching establishment, so was the ferret -- nearly to extinction.

**FORMER BLACK-FOOTED
FERRET DISTRIBUTION**

animal extinct. But in September of that year, near Meeteetse, Wyoming, a rancher's dog killed one that tried to eat from its food bowl. The rancher's wife took the lovely, furry, dead animal to a local taxidermist, who notified the government, who sent out scientists, who discovered a fair-sized colony of black-footed ferrets living among prairie dog towns nearby. Researchers studied and monitored the ferrets, but in 1985 the colony dwindled as plague decimated prairie dog towns and canine distemper -- possibly from ranchers' dogs -- killed some of the ferrets. By the end of 1985, an estimated 30 ferrets survived at Meeteetse. Following bitter fighting between government agencies, all remaining known wild ferrets were captured. They now await their fate in cages at the Sybille Canyon Wildlife Research Center in eastern Wyoming.

One has to wonder how many ferrets have been secretly dispatched by ranchers in recent years. A staunchly pro-ranching Wyoming state representative, Marlene Simons, in comparing the situation to wolf reintroduction, put it this way: "It's like black-footed ferrets. If you had a black-footed ferret in your back yard, you wouldn't want anyone to know about it, because then you couldn't get rid of it."

Tens of billions of prairie dogs have been killed in the ranching industry's massive secret war, but the massacre continues. Because the industry controls nearly all prairie dog habitat, prairie dog numbers remain minuscule, and the black-footed ferret faces extinction.

What might be missed are the endless miles of towns and the millions of wild dogs running, barking, wagging their tails, and stretching from horizon to horizon. That's what it was in the old days, but like those old days, the seemingly endless prairie dog towns are gone forever [are they?]*.*
--Last paragraph of **Wonders of Prairie Dogs** by G. Earl Price

Ranching competitors are under triple attack: (1) livestock ruin their habitat; (2) the ranching establishment kills off the survivors; and (3) ranching advocates are the most vehement and powerful opponents of reintroductions and recovery efforts.

The industry fights other lesser competitors, including moose and even mountain goats. A great many of its smaller competitors are more commonly known as "pests."

Pests

An illustration from a government ranching publication.

Webster defines "pest" as "a plant or animal that is harmful or injurious to man." A stock-man may consider a pest to be any small animal interfering with his ranching operation. A scientist may have a different idea, a naturalist another. There is much disagreement over the lines separating pests from other categories of animals, but this is largely a matter of semantics and perspective.

In this section, we will discuss those animals that the ranching establishment generally considers pests -- mostly the small mammals and insects that compete with livestock for herbage. Many of these so-called pests are simply competitors ranchers want to give a bad name so they may gain government assistance, or at least meet less resistance in their attempt to eradicate the animals. For example, a county agricultural agent is more likely to support a poisoning project to eliminate "a destructive infestation of pocket gophers" than "pocket gophers."

Other supposed pests are simply species at high points of their natural population cycles. Livestock interests, using the upswing to justify eradication, warn of the dire consequences of not "controlling the invading hordes." For example, if an "infestation" of Mormon crickets on a certain allotment isn't exterminated, we are told, it will permanently damage the environment. Yet, Mormon cricket population fluctuations are normal occurrences to which Western ecosystems have been well-adapted for millennia.

Other "pests" are more properly *pests*, but ranching is primarily responsible for their existence in the first place. As we have seen, overgrazing and range developments simplify biosystems and sometimes set up conditions favorable for population explosions of opportunistic animal species. Ironically, the more a profit-hungry rancher overgrazes a range, the more pests he creates to minimize those profits.

These ranching-induced pest explosions are the most destructive type, for the overgrazing and range developments that caused them also impair the natural systems that would otherwise limit their destructive impacts. For example, a livestock-caused increase in jackrabbit numbers would otherwise result in a corresponding increase in predators which would reduce jackrabbits before they were able to seriously intensify the impacts of livestock grazing.

Contrarily, an increase in jackrabbits under the full ranching scenario sets up a different set of circumstances. Because most predators have been eliminated, the jackrabbit population climbs far beyond normal limits. Jackrabbits eventually reach the point where they so overgraze the land that they and many other animals starve to death, soil erosion increases, etc. Or, population density may become so extreme that disease spreads and eventually reduces jackrabbit numbers far below their normal cyclical low point. Indeed, ranching-caused pest infestations have been linked to many of the plague epidemics over large areas of the West that annually claim myriad animals and several humans.

Though most pest infestations on Western public land are the *result* of overgrazing and range development (or acquisitive or delusional imaginations), ranchers blame the environment and make the taxpayer sponsor technological fixes, rather than reduce livestock numbers or range development. Thus have federal, state, and county governments become a pest eradication service for the ranching industry.

It wasn't always that way. In the late 1800s, ranchers themselves usually fought pests. They picked off rodents one by one with small caliber guns, poisoned and trapped as many as they could, taught their dogs to attack small animals on sight, and smashed with a shovel, rock, or bootheel those that weren't fast enough. These methods served ranchers for awhile, but the magnitude of the overgrazing and their voracity for profits eventually had them running to the government for large amounts of poison -- the most effective tool for killing pests.

The government first used toxic bait in 1885 in a campaign to kill grasshoppers. The poisoning campaign against insects and rodents gradually gained momentum, and by the 1930s was in full swing. In subsequent decades, science and technology provided new and more powerful toxins and methods of dissemination, enabling the ranching establishment to "treat" thousands of acres at a time.

Compound 1080, banned from public land for more than a decade, was reintroduced as a rodenticide in 1985 by EPA. A similar poison, Compound 1081 (sodium monofluoroacetamide) also joined the industry's arsenal of chlorinated hydrocarbons, organophosphates, strychnine, arsenic, and other rodenticides and insecticides.

That these toxins are environmentally hazardous should be obvious. After all, *they kill animals*! In fact, generally they kill even more non-target animals than do predicides. Malathion and other insecticides kill **most** insects -- especially carnivorous insects -- on contact, and some may bioaccumulate as they proceed through the food chain. Insecticide sprayed on a valley to kill grasshoppers, for instance, also destroys many or most other insects in that valley --

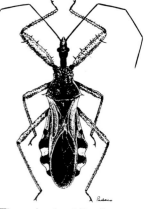

The spined soldier bug -- one of thousands of species of range insecticide victims.

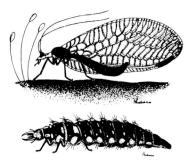

Lacewing, eggs, and larvae.

bees, bumblebees, beetles, butterflies, and lacewings included -- some of the animals that eat the poisoned animals, and sometimes aquatic life.

This was well-demonstrated to my family and me a few years ago by a rural neighbor. That year, he sprayed malathion on his large garden to kill grasshoppers and aphids. Within a few weeks, we began finding dead bodies of songbirds in the area, and that year we had fewer songbirds. (Incidentally, within a few weeks our neighbor's garden was once again suffering more insect damage than was our organic garden!)

Rodenticides are similar. They are placed, in the form of tainted grain, in rodent burrows, spread around "problem" areas, or broadcast from aircraft. Poison grain left to kill, say, kangaroo rats may also be eaten by squirrels, voles, mice, rabbits, insects, songbirds, doves, quail, javelina, and any other animal that eats grain. And these poisoned animals may in turn be eaten by coyotes, foxes, skunks, weasels, badgers, ringtails, ground squirrels, hawks, eagles, owls, jays, crows, ravens, various insects, and any other animal that eats carrion.

The ringtail of the southern half of the US West -- another indirect ranching victim. *(Helen Wilson)*

Massive poisoning projects can lead to violent biologic fluctuations. For example, in many areas during much of the year coyotes subsist mainly on small rodents. The large-scale extermination of rodents may eventually lead an area's coyotes to move elsewhere or die. If other conditions are favorable, the lack of coyotes in the area may then result in an even larger infestation of rodents than was poisoned in the first place -- which, even more ironically, may further lead to a temporary sharp increase in the number of coyotes. These coyotes are then hunted as livestock predators.

The eradication of much of an area's insects or rodents often means loss of a vital food source for many animals. For instance, the poison deaths of most of an area's insects may also mean the deaths of some of the area's birds, small mammals, fish, lizards, toads, and so on. Non-target species may be devastated *even if only the target species is poisoned* because the target species is reduced far below normal limits. If ants are eliminated from an area, so are ant lions. If pocket gophers are killed off, gopher snake populations fall.

● Rodents

Vast amounts of time and money have been spent on their control, often under the theory that the rodents were the cause rather the an effect of range damage. However, numerous studies have shown that the most effective means of control is a three-stand barbed-wire fence, which keeps out livestock.
--Raymond F. Dasmann, **Environmental Conservation** (Dasmann 1972)

Rodents are shunned as filthy, dangerous, and worthless -- essentially the opposite of what they really are. The ranching industry also justifies slaughtering rodents as a way to reduce the spread of disease, especially rabies. But according to the Humane Society, "A rodent has never been reported to be responsible for a case of human rabies anywhere in the world." Mounting evidence shows that rodent slaughtering activities actually foster the spread of many diseases (Grandy 1989).

Perhaps half of the 100 or so rodent species on Western rangeland are pursued as vermin by the ranching establishment. When their numbers reach "unacceptable" levels, rodents are poisoned *en masse* with various baits, or killed with whatever implements of death are available. Much of this butchery is done quietly on a local scale by ranchers and county and state agents, but collectively their impact is considerable.

Perhaps the rodent stockmen most love to hate is the **jackrabbit.** As much as the coyote it is their mortal enemy, and more so than the elk a loathsome competitor. "Popping" at jackrabbits with rifles and pistols is traditional and habitual to stockmen.

Three species of hare, or jackrabbit, are native to the West. The *antelope jackrabbit*, identified by its pale whitish sides and hips, inhabits mid-elevations of southern Arizona. The *whitetail jackrabbit* is found in the open, grassy or sagebrush plains of the northern 2/3 of the West. And the *blacktail jackrabbit*, the familiar "range" jackrabbit most persecuted by ranchers, lives on the open plains and deserts in all but the northern portion of the West. Jackrabbits have keen senses, run 45 mph, and jump 20 feet in a single bound. They eat grasses, forbs, and other succulent vegetation; range professionals figure 150 of them eat as much as one cow.

On many ranges jackrabbits are the most numerous and sometimes the *only* large animal. It is unquestionably true that livestock grazing (and predator control or other range development) can sometimes increase jackrabbit numbers, sometimes explosively. But many perceived infestations are attributable to normal population cycles (averaging 5 to 10 years) and the fact that on a barren landscape jackrabbits simply *appear* much more numerous, and eat more herbage, than any other wild animal. Historical accounts tell us that jackrabbits were abundant in the aboriginal West.

Jackrabbits are poisoned with "treated" grain, hay, and salt; shot; run over with vehicles; and killed by ranchers' dogs. When their numbers reach epidemic proportions, they may even be killed by the thousands in huge, organized roundups. Large numbers of people surround an area known to have rabbits, "close the ring" to a small circle, and then club the trapped animals to death in an orgy of brutality. In **Sacred Cows**, Denzel and Nancy Ferguson report that, "As recently as 1982, about 100,000 jackrabbits were slaughtered in such drives in southeastern Oregon" (Ferguson 1983).

Because in some areas up to 75% of coyotes' diet is jackrabbits, their slaughter forces coyotes to prey more on livestock. So the ranchers kill more coyotes, which later in turn allows jackrabbit numbers to rise.

Five species of **rabbit** inhabit the West: the *desert, eastern,* and *mountain cottontails,* and the *brush* and *pygmy rabbits.* The 3 cottontails upset stockmen, especially the desert cottontail, which lives in a variety of habitats throughout the southern and eastern portions of the West and eats many forbs and grasses. Given its dietary preferences, it competes especially with domestic sheep.

Cottontails are not so persecuted by ranchers as jackrabbits, but are nonetheless widely killed. They are much less likely to proliferate on overgrazed ranges. In fact, because cottontails require abundant ground-level vegetation for food and cover, overgrazing and range "improvements" have led to their decline over vast areas.

A rich variety of **ground squirrels** inhabit the West. All but 1 of 14 species eat significant amounts of green vegetation. So ranchmen kill them. Even the closely related rock squirrel, which eats very little greenery, is widely killed -- "guilt" by association, one must conclude.

Many ranchers shoot ground squirrels with .22 rifles or shotguns whenever possible, often just for sport or target practice. They and their government agents also kill the rodents with traps, strychnine-treated grain and other rodenticides, and poison gas. Much of the 1080 used as a rodenticide is used to kill ground squirrels, especially the California ground squirrel. Reportedly, about half a million pounds of strychnine-laced bait is used annually in the US -- mainly in the West -- and is responsible for the documented deaths of 5 California condors, 6 peregrine falcons, 15 golden eagles, and 31 bald eagles. Undoubtedly these documented cases represent only a small fraction of the actual kill.

Thirteen species of *Dipodomys,* the **kangaroo rat,** live in the West. These are nocturnal, mouse-like creatures with fur-lined cheek pouches, white side strips, long, fluffy-tipped tails, and well-developed kangaroo-like rear legs that enable them to hop 5 feet or more. They manufacture all the

water they need from starch in the seeds they eat (slightly augmented with the water from occasional greenery). Their arid to semi-arid habitat encompasses most of the West, especially the Southwest and California. Ranchers consider most species of kangaroo rats pests, and kill them or have them killed with surface-broadcast or air-dropped poisoned grain. Destroying these important tiny mammals has disrupted many ecosystems.

Kangaroo rat. *(Helen Wilson)*

Pocket mice are closely related to kangaroo rats, but are more mouse-like. Twenty species are known around the West, except in the Pacific Northwest. The species most common on ranched land, along with a number of other mice, are sometimes persecuted by the ranching establishment.

Pocket gophers, characterized by their fur-lined cheek pouches, tiny ears, digging claws, exposed double incisors, and short, hairless tails, live almost entirely underground. They are important as soil-forming agents, aid in water conservation and soil aeration, and provide prey to many predators. Because most species require ample, loose, cool, moist soil and succulent vegetation, overgrazing has had an adverse influence on pocket gophers in many areas. Pocket gophers dig burrows (that livestock could injure legs in) and eat roots, tubers, and some surface vegetation (that livestock could eat). Because of this, several of their 10 species are killed by ranchers and their government helpers with traps and poisons, often with strychnine-laced grain baits, and often on public land. The Forest Service alone reports "treating" 51,676 acres with pesticides in 1987 to kill pocket gophers (USDA, FS 1988).

Townsend mole. *(Helen Wilson)*

Voles, moles, marmots, and **woodrats** also are important components of Western ecosystems. Some species dig burrows, and many eat seeds or green vegetation. Therefore, many ranchers kill them.

●Grasshopper

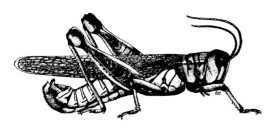

Hundreds of species of grasshopper are native to the US, each uniquely adapted to certain plant species and habitat. Studies by M.I. Dyer and U.G. Bokhari in 1976 show that Western plants evolved to benefit from grasshoppers and actually produce more biomass under their various impacts (USDA, APHIS 1986). Throughout the West, grasshoppers also are an important food source for countless wild animals, with some species subsisting mainly on these nutritious insects during parts of the year.

Grasshoppers exhibit irregular yet cyclical population fluctuations in response to the amount of ground cover, soil temperature, soil moisture, abundance of predators, and so forth. These fluctuations usually are limited, but if many conditions happen to coincide, an explosive increase in grasshoppers may occur, commonly involving a mixture of several different species. Livestock grazing and range development have greatly increased the incidence and severity of grasshopper population explosions by: exposing bare soil in which grasshoppers lay their eggs; causing surface soil temperatures to rise, thereby promoting egg development; simplifying ecosystems, thereby hampering natural limiting factors; increasing preferred forbs in some areas; and eliminating grasshopper predators.

Generally, the intensity of explosions is in direct proportion to the intensity of livestock grazing and/or range development.

On the other hand, by severely reducing plant biomass, eliminating native plants and changing plant composition, and by drying out and damaging the soil, ranching has in many areas reduced grasshopper populations far below natural, healthy levels. In other words, in the rural West ranching is the major factor causing both unnaturally extreme grasshopper population reductions *and* explosions.

When plant food in an area is inadequate, grasshoppers may migrate to adjacent areas, or some species may physiologically transform themselves into what are termed "locusts." Basically, locusts are grasshoppers that have developed the ability to fly long distances. Thus, when ranching causes a population explosion of grasshoppers -- and when this growing horde finds that livestock have already consumed the vegetation in their area -- they may mutate into locusts and fly off *en masse* in search of food. The food they find may be in a riparian area, a corn field, or your garden. But most likely it will be on other rangeland.

Grasshopper infestations caused untold damage to range resources last year and we certainly hope that APHIS will take vigorous action this year to bring these pests under control.
--National Cattlemen's Association, in a 1986 letter to APHIS

As early settlers transformed the natural Western landscape into livestock ranges and farms, their problems with grasshoppers increased proportionately. For example, one of the greatest grasshopper plagues in US history occurred in 1874 -- just when Western ranching and farming were getting in full swing. Increasing complaints by agricultural interests led Congress to establish the Entomological Commission in 1877, which eventually evolved into the USDA's Animal and Plant Health Inspection Service (APHIS).

Grasshopper problems continued through the years. An especially destructive period of infestations was the 1930s -- a decade when livestock pressure was at a peak. In 1937 Congress ordered USDA into the grasshopper war. After 1945 several deadly insecticides -- chlorinated hydrocarbons -- were added to the arsenal. In the 1960s these were largely supplanted by malathion, carbaryl (Sevin), and other allegedly nonpersistent insecticides; in the 1970s the organophosphate acephate came into general use.

"Just go ahead and spray over the house," rancher W.D. Wear Jr. said to state officials after learning that malathion applications to kill grasshoppers would begin the next day on his [mostly public land] ranch.

"We can't spray it over your trucks," replied William Gorman, assistant director of the eastern region for the state Commission of Agriculture and Horticulture, pointing to his nearby vehicles. "It will wreck the paint."
--5-13-86 *Phoenix Gazette*

Under a co-operative management agreement, APHIS and other federal, state, and local agencies now spray insecticide, mostly malathion, on an average of **2.64 million acres (0.4%) of Western rangeland annually**, a large percentage of it public land. Poison baits, usually bran, are also employed, though in far lesser amounts. Chemical industry and government agents roam the rural West, "identifying" areas "needing" "treatment" and "enlisting" ranchers to participate in the poison programs.

APHIS *et al.* may spray blocks of land having 10,000 or more contiguous acres when all ranchmen within the block consent to participate, and when grasshoppers occur at the average rate of 8 or more per square yard, though most spraying begins when hopper numbers reach 15-30 per square yard. At high population points, eight (or even 20) per square yard is not naturally an excessive rate, but it is generally considered the point at which grasshoppers begin to significantly compete with livestock. Since "only" an average of 2.64 million acres are sprayed each year under these co-op agreements -- and, according to a Winrock International (a chemical company) spokesperson, an estimated average of *10 million acres* (1.5%) of Western rangeland are "infested" annually with grasshoppers above the 8-per-square-yard limit -- the grazing industry constantly pressures government for more insecticide. Not to be outdone, APHIS claims that the 2.64 million acres poisoned annually is only *11%* of the Western rangeland that needs it. In other words, if it could APHIS would poison *4.4%* of Western rangeland for grasshoppers annually! (USDA, APHIS 1986 and USDA, USDI 1979) Additionally, the Forest Service reported spraying 363,000 pounds of insecticide on 608,000 acres to kill grasshoppers in 1986, and various other government agencies and ranchers add to the toxicant dissemination.

Acreage sprayed under the APHIS co-op program varies extremely from year to year, according to the intensity of infestations. In 1983, APHIS reported *no* spraying for grasshoppers. Only 2 years later, it dowsed *more than 13 million acres* with insecticide. In both 1986 and 1987, it sprayed millions of acres, largely in Idaho, Wyoming, and Montana, mostly public land; 1990 is expected to be another "bad" year in much of the West. Despite the spraying, there has been no overall downward trend in infestations.

All chemical insecticides are extremely non-specific, killing not only the intended insects but huge numbers of other insects, other invertebrates, and sometimes, depending on the circumstances, vertebrates. Even APHIS's ridiculously biased 1986 Environmental Impact Statement, *Rangeland Grasshopper Cooperative Management Program*, acknowledges

A ladybird beetle (ladybug) and eggs.

that the agency's 3 favorite insecticides -- malathion, carbaryl, and acephate -- "adversely affect" (that is *kill*) substantial numbers of bees, a variety of beetles, leafhoppers, moths, wasps, moth and butterfly larvae, ants, flies, caddisflies, mayflies, stoneflies, mosquitos, midges, ladybugs, "certain beneficial insect parasites and predators," and arachnids (USDA, APHIS 1986). Poison deaths of birds, fish, and other vertebrates are documented.

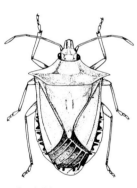

A stinkbug.

Indirectly harmed or killed are animals dependent upon insects for food such as songbirds, fish, and coyotes, and plants such as those dependent upon insect pollinators for propagation. For example, a reduction in the bee population may mean a reduction in flowering plants dependent upon bees for pollination. Further, though hundreds of species of bees inhabit the West, many plant species can be pollinated only by 1 or a few species of bees; some Threatened or Endangered flowers may be pollinated by a species of bee almost as rare as the flower itself, and their range may be quite limited, especially after a century of ranching. A malathion spraying covering tens of thousands of acres may consequently kill off not only the rare bees but dependent rare flowering plants as well.

Adding futility to insult, much evidence indicates that spraying huge blocks of land with insecticides sometimes creates conditions that later cause extreme infestations of certain spider mites, caterpillars, aphids, and, again, grasshoppers! No wonder it's called an "insecticide treadmill."

The aforementioned 1986 EIS also states that acephate has a half-life of 5 to 10 days in soil and 50 days in water, that carbaryl continues to kill for weeks after application, and that malathion (the fastest-killing and widest-spectrum poison of the 3) takes an average of a few days or more to stop killing. Additionally, these chemicals may combine with other artificial or naturally occurring chemicals to produce compounds of even greater toxicity. Few studies have been conducted on such synergistic effects. There is also evidence of a carcinogenic danger to humans. (USDA, APHIS 1986)

Most studies of these poisons' effects on wildlife cited in APHIS's EIS exhibit an almost laughable pro-insecticide bias. Many species, including almost all plants and most reptiles and amphibians, aren't even studied. The Environmental Protection Agency and numerous concerned groups and individuals have repeatedly contested the government's grasshopper spraying program on many issues, including its blatant disregard for Endangered species.

Where ranching is concerned, however, environmental protection and common sense rarely prevail. APHIS and other bureaucracies involved spout impressive-sounding professional jargon, ignore everyone who doesn't agree, and arrogantly continue the massive poisoning.

Nosema is a commercially available protozoan pathogen that infects the fat tissues of grasshoppers. Infection spreads throughout the grasshopper, disrupting circulation, excretion, and reproduction, leading to disfigurement and/or death.
--The IPM Practitioner (Sept. 1985)

There are alternatives to chemical insecticides. The *Nosema locustae* microbe described above is being tested by USDA, BLM, and other government and private entities with generally fair, if erratic, results. But the ranching establishment prefers its poisons, especially malathion, and mostly gives *Nosema* lip service. And though touted by environmentalists as the "safe, organic" method of killing grasshoppers, *Nosema* is only so in comparison to insecticides. It entails expenditure of time, money, and materials and, if it works, it drastically and artificially reduces grasshopper numbers, perhaps negatively affecting an ecosystem in many ways like insecticides. And how would it feel to die over a period of days from a disrupted circulatory system, clogged intestines, and "disfigurement"? Does it make sense to pretend grasshoppers can't feel when we see them writhing in agony? A typical 10,000-acre grasshopper eradication with *Nosema* kills about **4 billion** grasshoppers in this painful manner -- so a couple of ranchers *might* be able to graze 10 extra cattle for a year or two (and keep the range degraded, thus promoting continued grasshopper infestations!).

USDA vilifies the grasshopper as livestock's most significant insect competitor, and APHIS implies that more than $80 million in herbage is "lost" to this winged demon yearly (USDA, APHIS 1986). Its profit-minded calculators figure that 301,395 grasshoppers eat as much herbage as a cow. Thus, by inference we are supposed to believe that killing 301,395 hoppers will make room for 1 more cow on the range. APHIS uses these figures and this mentality to justify its "control" program, but there is little evidence that the program is economically or environmentally warranted;

there is much evidence to the contrary. The solution to the grasshopper menace is to remove livestock from the public's land. There would then be little "need" for the destructive farce called grasshopper control.

> *Grasshoppers on the public's range should be viewed as a protein source* [as they are in parts of Africa] *rather than an expensive inconvenience to our exploitation of the range by exotic, inappropriate livestock. If we consider the grasshoppers as "winged bison" we will have a better perspective of the consequences of our extermination actions.*
> --Randy Morris, "Chicken of the Desert Enterprises," Mountain Home, Idaho, in a letter to APHIS (Morris 1986)

Mormon crickets, the famous insects that plagued early Mormon settlers beginning in 1848, are actually wingless, long-horned grasshoppers native to semi-arid intermountain rangelands and lowlands. They have natural population cycles similar to other hoppers. The small, leaf-eating creatures stand accused by the ranching establishment of causing "extensive damage" to the Western range, especially in Utah, Colorado, Nevada, Oregon, and Washington. APHIS even claims that "Mormon crickets have been estimated to remove *44%* of the forage available to cattle and *48.6%* of the forage available to sheep" (USDA, APHIS 1986). It's enough to make one wonder how the West got along so well without APHIS & Co. around to protect it from itself. To prevent Mormon crickets from eating range forage and irrigated alfalfa during the 1990 growing season the various agencies sprayed insecticide on more than 700,000 acres in northern Nevada alone.

● Other insects

Even the tiny **ant** cannot escape the wrath of the ranching establishment. Ants are numerous and important participants in ecosystems on nearly all Western rangeland. Making contributions similar to those of rodents, they are a vital food source, soil- and mulch-forming agent, water infiltrator, diversity-enhancer and, of course, worthy in their own right.

Several species of *harvester ants* occur in the West, with the western harvester the most widespread. Something like prairie dogs, harvester ants build large mounds and clear the surrounding area of all vegetation for a radius of up to 10 feet. They forage on plants, especially seeds. Harvester nests can be 8 feet deep, with 60 chambers. An active nest may exist for 15 to 20 years and contain more than 10,000 worker ants.

Depending on environment, there may be from a few to 30 or more harvester mounds per acre. Also depending on circumstances, livestock grazing and range development may increase or decrease the number of mounds per acre. For example, a range seeding may drive away and kill ant predators and provide ants such an abundance of seeds and tender sprouts that they are able to thrive at rates of more than 40 mounds per acre. Overgrazing may favor large numbers of mounds in areas where dense vegetation has been thinned to the point that it no longer prohibits ants from establishing new colonies. In contrast, where ranching eliminates too much of their food source, it may reduce harvester ants (as it does most ant species).

With 25 mounds per acre, harvester ants may remove vegetation from 10% of the land. At this point (or before) ranchers and government agents may use chlordane or other poison against all harvester ants in an area; they attempt to kill the queen to kill the colony. However, some ranchers poison harvester (and other) ant mounds indiscriminately.

Harvester ant discs on severely degraded Idaho range. *(BLM)*

A harvester ant disc on remote, ungrazed range in northeast Utah. Note the lush vegetation.

Several small sucking insects are called **black grass bugs**. They thrive in and have infested millions of acres of crested wheatgrass and other exotic grass monocultures, though they are uncommon on healthy native vegetation. These insects are sometimes "controlled" with pesticides, by burning, or by intensive livestock grazing.

Many kinds of **grubs, moth and butterfly caterpillars, beetles, leafhoppers, stinkbugs, aphids, stem borers, thrips, mites,** and practically any **other small creatures** that eat or damage plants may be poisoned or burned when the animals are thought to be diminishing herbage and thus reducing livestock production. Vegetation harboring insect eggs and tiny pests may be burned or allowed to be grazed to nubs by live-

An aphid.

stock. Again, the perceived "infestations" may simply be the high points of natural cycles, the results of ranching activities or some other human factor, or coincidental alignments of natural circumstances.

The solution to all these pest problems is incredibly simple: **stop ranching.**

As with small mammals, most problems from insects on rangeland have been caused by human activities such as overgrazing or extensive land clearing and revegetation with monocultures that reduce habitat diversity.

--from the ranching text, **Range Management**, by Jerry L. Holechek *et al.* (Holechek 1989)

●Parasites

The pest category may also include livestock parasites. These myriad host-dependent little animals include **mites, lice, ticks, blood-sucking gnats and flies,** and **various parasitic larvae and worms.** Under natural conditions, parasites don't often affect their host so seriously as to kill it; to do

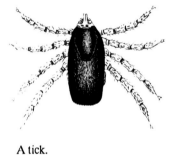

A tick.

so would be suicide. Sedentary concentrations of livestock, however -- especially those under stress by overgrazing and other ranching practices -- often create unnatural situations in which parasites so lack limiting factors that without intensive veterinary intervention they may reach epidemic proportions.

Perhaps the most celebrated campaign against a livestock parasite is APHIS's **Screwworm** Eradication Program. This exotic fly's larvae once killed thousands of cattle throughout the South and Southwest. Over decades, spending tens of millions of tax dollars, APHIS eventually eliminated the fly from the US by releasing tens of billions of sterile male flies in infested areas.

Farm [ranch] *property owners are exempt from registration and licensing requirements for pesticide application equipment, as is otherwise required under the Environmental Pesticide Control Act.*

--Wyoming Statute 35-7-363(a)(i)

For most livestock parasites, pesticides are the killing agent. They are applied to cattle and sheep with liquid or powder sprays, dipping vats, portable spray-dip machines, pour-on and spot-on treatments, backrubbers, and dusts. The poisons usually are applied by ranchers, often in a careless manner (as stockmen generally have little knowledge of proper application), and ranchers often use too much of the toxin (to "make sure" all parasites are killed), or gamble with dangerous substitute pesticides. Thus, cases of environmental harm, livestock and human poisoning are not infrequent. Even if used properly, these are dangerous toxins.

One example is famphur, a compound commonly sold under the name Warbex and used to kill lice. Some bird species (e.g., cattle egret) peck parasites from the backs of cattle, ingesting the poison. They may die, or may be eaten by eagles and other raptors which may also then die. According

to *High Country News*, 2 bald eagles in Lassen County, California, were found dead with signs of famphur poisoning. Even 4 months after application, the chemical can kill. One great horned owl died after eating a red-tailed hawk that had eaten a magpie contaminated with treated cattle hair. Evidence indicates that famphur has caused a decline of black-billed magpies throughout the West.

Studies have shown that other drugs used internally to kill parasites in cattle have killed earthworms, dung beetles, and other small creatures that come into contact with cattle feces. Without the aid of these animals, soil structure and fertility suffers and cowpies decompose much more slowly.

Additionally, some parasites (horn flies for example) are gradually becoming resistant to insecticides. As they do, stockmen use increasingly greater amounts of insecticide, or questionable substitute poisons.

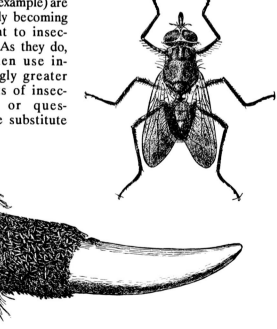

A horn fly (top), and horn flies on a cow horn.

USDA calls **mosquitos** a "scourge of livestock." The tiny winged Draculas may spread stock diseases or feast on livestock in such numbers that weight loss or even death occurs. Stock producers may seek "control" by spreading oil on larval waters or spraying toxins.

No-goods

The fourth category of ranching establishment animal enemy -- the one with the most members -- is the "no-good" group. Its basis stems directly from the Old West mentality that "The only good _____ is a dead _____!" This attitude remains prevalent among public lands ranchers.

So, **most rodent species** are shot, poisoned, trapped, run over, or killed by ranchers' dogs because "they're worthless varmints." **Scorpions, Gila monsters, centipedes, millipedes, black widows, tarantulas, ants, bees, bumblebees,** and **wasps** die because "they might hurt someone." **Bats, beaver, snakes, opossums, various rodents,** and **many others** die because "they carry disease." **Carp** and **suckers** are shot or caught, killed, and thrown away because "they're trash fish." **Worms, slugs, snails, spiders, beetles, crickets, cockroaches,** and **many other small creatures** are mindlessly squashed because "they're no good!"

Others are killed merely because they resemble offending animals. Thus, many ranchers kill not only livestock-predatory birds, but **all large predatory birds.** They kill not only plant and seed-eating squirrels, but **all squirrels.** They kill not only rattlesnakes and coral snakes, but **all kinds of snakes.**

A ranchman bashed in the head of this harmless gopher snake.

Birds are gluttonous and filthy.
--M.E. Ensminger, **The Stockman's Handbook** (Ensminger 1983)

Birds of many species are perceived as winged pests that spread disease and eat forage seeds. Stockmen shoot, poison, trap, or allow their cats to kill **magpies, crows, ravens, jays, mockingbirds, blackbirds, starlings, sparrows, swallows, pigeons, doves,** and **vultures** on both public and private land.

Skin of a porcupine killed by a local Forest Service permittee.

Wild animals (other than predators) that might physically harm livestock in some manner are another group of no-goods (or perhaps pests). For example, I know of a rancher who extirpated all **beaver** from a stream because one of his bulls got a leg stuck in a beaver dam and died. A professional range study even suggested eliminating beaver because they raise creek levels, thereby blocking the travel of ranchers and livestock!! Many ranchers shoot **porcupines,** ostensibly to reduce the chance of livestock being injured and infected by quills.

(Steve Johnson)

Rattlesnakes, feared as they are, are nonetheless beneficial to Western ecosystems. Millions of these fascinating reptiles of a dozen species inhabit the West. Yet only a few humans die from all snakebites (including bites from copperheads and cottonmouths) in the US annually, and most of these people have been harassing the snakes or are very young, sick, or old. Cattle and sheep -- omnipresent, clumsy, and liable to blunder almost anywhere -- are bitten comparatively often, occasionally dying from the poison or related complications. Stockmen also blame rattlesnakes for spooking their horses and for jeopardizing their own safety.

To eliminate rattlesnakes from the range, stockmen in the late 1800s began annual "rattlesnake roundups" in which local citizenry were enlisted in competitions to see who could bring in the most rattlers, dead or alive. In New Mexico, Texas, and Oklahoma today, ranchers still help organize rattlesnake roundups in which thousands of snakes are captured, mistreated, often tortured, and then killed. To drive snakes from their shelters and capture them, participants spray gasoline into thousands of underground holes and crevices, in the process killing many other animals, contaminating the soil, precluding denning and hibernating use by other animals, and polluting groundwater.

From fear, superstition, and general hostility toward Nature, ranchers probably more than any other group kill rattlesnakes. Judging from personal experience, I have to conclude that most stockmen try to kill every rattlesnake they see (and any snake resembling a rattlesnake), with guns, vehicles, shovels, rocks, and whatever they can lay hands on. More than 100 years of persecution, in combination with overgrazing and other ranching impacts, has devastated some rattlesnake species, extirpating them from many areas.

The coatimundi of the US Southwest: persecuted by stockmen, harmed by livestock grazing.

Other animal enemies are those that dig open burrows large enough for a cow, sheep, or horse to break a leg in. **Prairie dogs, ground squirrels, pocket gophers,** and **others** have already been mentioned. **Badgers** survive today at only small fractions of original numbers, yet they are still shot, poisoned, and trapped because they dig burrows. It is interesting that millions of buffalo shared the West with billions of prairie dogs, badgers, ground squirrels and other rodents, but ranchmen cannot tolerate even small numbers of these animals.

Wildlife that may prey on ranchers' poultry, rabbits, or other small domestic animals may likewise be considered no-goods. So, stockmen kill **raccoons, skunks, weasels, foxes,** and even **ringtails** and **coatimundis. Numerous other wild animals** are killed because they eat livestock feed stores or salt; some because they damage range "improvements."

Consider the impact simply from public lands ranchers' dogs and cats: Because these 30,000 stock raisers are allowed to graze livestock on public land throughout the West, their homes and businesses are -- far more than any other group -- located in close physical proximity to Western

public land. Most of these ranchers own dogs and cats, often packs of dogs and many cats. Most of the dogs are trained to kill wild animals, and the cats are allowed to.

These domestic predators (along with ranchers' abandoned dogs and cats) spend much time on public land, where they attack millions of wild animals annually, disturb wildlife, and spread disease.

Got a problem with squirrels? Poison the sons a bitches! Rattlesnakes in your area? Throw a stick of dynamite in their den! Bothered by magpies? Blast the fuckers with buckshot! Don't like lizards? Stomp 'em with a boot heel! More than literary dramatics, this is rangeland reality throughout the rural ranching West.

They're troublesome, dangerous, obnoxious, dirty, slimy, mean, stupid, ugly -- any conceivable reason will do. Each day for more than 100 years countless "no-goods" have been killed. Because these activities are remote and dispersed, their overall impact goes unrecognized. The ranching establishment would have us believe that this behavior is limited to a tiny minority of rancher "old timers," but it just ain't so.

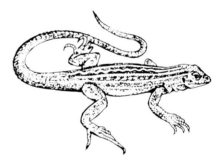

In conclusion, 30,000 stockmen are spread evenly across Western public lands, and the vast majority of them kill predators, competitors, pests, and no-goods with guns, traps, poisons, dogs, trucks, boots, and whatever means available. By now, you may wonder if there are *any* wild animals that stockmen don't consider enemies, or treat like enemies. Reportedly there are: aardvarks and penguins.

Livestock Management

If a fragile and delicate environment will support cattle, or even looks like it will support cattle, custom dictates that it be promptly and fully stocked and not a blade of grass "wasted."
--Denzel and Nancy Ferguson, **Sacred Cows** (Ferguson 1983)

Another facet of range exploitation may be termed "livestock management." Basically, this refers to **(1) what kind, (2) how many, (3) where, (4) when,** and **(5) in what manner** livestock are grazed. Livestock management for each public lands ranching operation is based on diverse environmental, economic, social, and political variables. (For more detail on livestock management, consult Calef 1960, Ensminger 1968, Hickey 1977, or Holechek 1989)

● **(1) What kind** of livestock are grazed ostensibly is determined by the agencies, though the permittee usually has more decision-making power in this regard. The livestock breed is almost exclusively the rancher's choice. In practice, both the kind and breed are largely traditional.

Range characteristics such as vegetative cover, topography, water, poisonous plants, diseases, predators, insect pests, and wildlife competitors are strong influencing factors. Cattle prefer level to gently rolling ranges, whereas sheep and goats are better adapted to steeper topography. Sheep and goats can better exploit brushy and "weedy" vegetation, but are far more prone than cattle to predation, and to a larger variety of predators. Sheep also require less water than cows, and are better able to obtain water from the plants they eat; sheep can even get all the water they need from eating snow. Consequently, the woolly animals are grazed in large areas of the West that are impractical for cattle.

Breeds grazed are determined similarly. For example, Brahman cattle -- big, strong, and drought-resistant -- often are raised in hot, dry areas with numerous predators. Other popular range cattle breeds include the ubiquitous, white-faced, spotted hereford (Gary Larson, where are you?), black angus, charolais, shorthorn, and Texas longhorn. Popular range sheep breeds include Suffolks, Columbia, and Targee. And the overwhelming range goat favorite is the angora.

To maximize allotment productivity, some ranchers graze a combination of livestock types and/or breeds having differing dietary preferences and range characteristics. Correspondingly, this also tends to maximize biotic and general environmental degradation.

However, according to M.E. Ensminger in **The Stockman's Handbook,** "Actually, economic factors -- often unrelated to range characteristics -- probably have the greatest influence on the selection and popularity of kinds of livestock" (Ensminger 1983). The unwise choice of livestock has caused much unnecessary environmental damage; still, more importantly, **no** kind of domestic livestock is suited to the Western range.

● **(2) How many** livestock a rancher is allowed to graze on an allotment is called the "stocking rate" and ostensibly is based on the allotment's "carrying capacity," or maximum number of livestock the allotment can support on a long-term basis without causing significant environmental damage. Stocking rate likewise refers to the density of livestock on the range, which is a function of how many livestock are grazed, where they are grazed, and for how long. The Forest Service defines carrying capacity as "the maximum stocking rate possible without inflicting damage to the vegetation or related resources" (O'Toole 1988).

Officially, the stocking rate for each allotment is set by the land management agency based on the amount of available herbage, range condition and potential, allotment characteristics, conflict with other land uses, and other pertinent factors. In practice, stocking rates are set more by tradition, permittee influence, "grazing advisory boards" composed of local ranchers, and actual use (which often differs greatly from permitted use) than by the agencies. If carrying capacity is defined to mean the number of animals beyond which significant environmental damage occurs, nearly every allotment in the West is stocked far beyond its carrying capacity; the average allotment is probably stocked several times higher than its so-called "carrying capacity." But carrying capacity is an abstract, arbitrary, malleable term that on the Western range has nearly always been interpreted to benefit stockmen. For example, damage from livestock cannot be "significant" -- thus carrying capacity cannot be exceeded -- so long as ranching advocates dictate the meaning of the word "significant." ("Hell, it ain't hurtin' the land none," "Our assessment detected no potential significant environmental impact," etc.) Further, in setting carrying capacities most range personnel neglect that many ranchers habitually stock allotments with more animals than are allowed by permits.

Of course it is a foregone conclusion that every allotment must be stocked with *at least* as many livestock as it will "support." As Ensminger puts it, "Too light stocking wastes forage . . . ."

The *methods* of determining stocking rates are likewise faulty. For example, herbage estimates used to determine carrying capacity are based more on total allotment herbage than on how much of that herbage will actually be available to livestock. An allotment producing a total of 1500 herbage AUMs may be allotted 100 head of cattle -- the number of animals that would eat 1200 AUMs in a year -- even if 500 of the AUMs are in areas too steep, remote, or far from water for cattle to use. So, the 100 animals have only 1000 available AUMs and further overgraze their accessible range. On all allotments some parts will be more heavily used than others, but this isn't adequately compensated for by many range professionals in their determinations of carrying capacity.

Similarly, range managers often fail to consider that, rather than consumed, much of an allotment's available herbage will be trampled and otherwise destroyed by livestock; this places an even greater strain on the range.

Nor do they consider that a stocking rate based on observations at certain times may not apply throughout the grazing season or from one year to the next. For example, livestock allowed to forage an area's abundant spring grass might cause minimal damage if withheld until mid-spring, but may thoroughly ravage the area in early spring when mucky soil is easily damaged by trampling and when young plants don't yet contain sufficient sugars and protein to rejuvenate leaves and stems lost to grazing. In another area, grass seeds may have already dropped when livestock graze in early September one year, but may still be developing -- and thus be destroyed -- when livestock graze in early September the next year. In yet another, high points in natural rodent population cycles may combine with the usual overstocking to devastate range vegetation at 10-12 year intervals, causing long-term decline.

Similarly, in setting stocking rates range professionals neglect the many extreme natural events that periodically and substantially reduce the carrying capacity of allotments. Studies at the Forest Service's Santa Rita Experimental Station in Arizona and elsewhere document that forage production sometimes fluctuates wildly from year to year in response to extremes of precipitation, temperature, storms, fire, and other influences. On much of the Western range, drought may reduce available forage to as little as 50% of the annual average. (Holechek 1989) Droughts there are so frequent and variable in their intensity that stocking the range on the basis of the average, industry-determined "carrying capacity" results in overstocking *almost half the time*, even by industry standards.

Stocking rates traditionally have been raised (legally or illegally) to take advantage of periods of high precipitation and increased herbage production, and then kept high as long as possible. Consequently, when drought or other "natural disaster" makes its periodic appearance, livestock numbers are even more out of proportion to what the ranges can support. The result is disastrous overgrazing, as occurred in Idaho in 1987 and throughout much of the West in 1990. For example, according to *High Country News* (1-21-90), in southeast Utah "cattle have eaten the dried annuals and are ripping perennial bushes out by the roots or chewing them down to stumps." Area resident Bill Hedden says the overgrazed range will "look like a parking lot or nuclear holocaust by the time they're done with it this winter," and there is nothing on the range now but "stumps of bushes, cow turds, and dirt."

Range professional Jared Smith wrote nearly a century ago:

The maximum number of cattle that can safely be carried . . .
is the number that the land will support during a poor season.
Whenever this rule is ignored there is bound to be loss.

To minimize harm to livestock, environmental damage, and taxpayer-sponsored "disaster" relief expenditures, prudent range managers should figure carrying capacities and set stocking rates for the *least* productive years, because by the time a drought or other periodic "natural disaster" occurs an ecosystem is likely already seriously overgrazed. Nature does not operate on fickle ranching schedules.

"Utilization" is the inverse of carrying capacity, being the percentage of herbage livestock remove from an allotment during a grazing period, whereas carrying capacity refers to the livestock that that food will support. The percent of utilization allowed ostensibly is determined by the land managing agencies based on most of the same factors used to determine stocking rate. Most public grazing permits allow livestock to consume 40%-70% of the above-ground biomass of forage plants. In fact, talk in professional range circles reveals that for most Western ranges 40%-70% depletion of herbage cover is widely perceived as "moderate" utilization.

Under natural conditions, wild ungulates generally did not remove nearly this percentage of vegetation. For example, on Africa's Serengeti Plain the world's greatest concentration of wild large herbivores consumes an average of only 20% of range herbage production annually (Ehrlich 1986). In other words, relatively speaking, our public land managers allow livestock to remove at least 2 to 3 times as much foliage from public rangeland as native herbivores do from Africa's Serengeti. (And, once again, large herds are not natural to most of the West.)

However, on-the-ground inspection of grazing allotments reveals that livestock typically consume an even greater percentage, often 80% or more of the herbage biomass. Agency personnel typically excuse this by saying that, though large areas may have 80% utilization, the allotment *as a whole* has lost "only" the permitted percentage. They explain that the allotment includes some areas inaccessible to or little used by livestock. Their explanation unfortunately does not lessen the damage to the heavily utilized bulk of the allotment.

BLM and some other land managing agencies use these tiny exclosures to help determine how much forage is taken by livestock. According to BLM range personnel with whom I spoke, this Utah cattle range has been "lightly grazed."

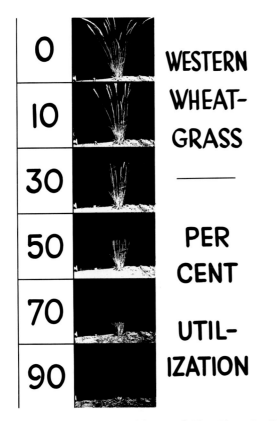

0	
10	
30	WESTERN WHEAT-GRASS
50	PER CENT
70	UTIL-IZATION
90	

--from *Estimating Range Use with Grazed-Class Photo Studies,* The University of Arizona, Cooperative Extension Service, and Agricultural Experiment Station.

Utilization estimates are also faulty in that they are based overwhelmingly on preferred, common livestock forage species -- often exotics -- and not on *all* native species. Thus, an estimate of 50% utilization may mean that 50% of preferred grass, 95% of a rare, leafy herb, and 5% of a thistle's above-ground biomass have been removed from an area. As discussed, livestock, cattle especially, generally consume a greater variety of plant species than do wild herbivores.

Additionally, utilization is based on the *current* productivity of the range, not on what it would be if left ungrazed, or what it was 150 years ago. This is another way in which the industry keeps our public land in a *dynamic state of degradation*; by reducing overall environmental health in small increments, and by basing each current assessment on conditions a little more degraded than those preceding.

Finally, utilization estimates are strongly influenced by the same economic, social, and political forces that determine stocking rates. I have more than once been told by agency range personnel that obvious 50% + utilization was actually 30% or less.

● **(3) When** livestock are grazed, or the season of use, is chiefly a function of range characteristics during each time period as they relate to economic and political considerations. The wide diversity of climate, topography, vegetative types, and human factors in the West means that ranchers practice a great variety of seasonal use patterns. But most public lands grazing falls within 5 categories: (1) *summer*; (2) *winter*; (3) *spring-fall*; (4) *spring-fall-winter*; and (5) *all-year*. Most cattle are turned out onto the range at or near the beginning of the

To the casual observer, this fenceline contrast may seem insignificant. However, cattle have stripped off roughly **90%** of the ground cover on the left side of the fence; the right side has been grazed only by deer, rabbits, mice, and other wildlife.

spring growing season and brought in in the fall or when herbage is exhausted.

Most high mountain areas of the West are grazed only in *summer* because cold and snow make grazing otherwise impossible. Often livestock are moved to lower mountain elevations or high plains to spend *spring and fall*. Throughout much of the temperate West animals are moved in *winter* to the warmer lowlands, where they subsist on range forage, pasture, hay, and/or other feed. In much of the cooler West where mountain pasture is unavailable, livestock are left on public ranges through *spring-summer-fall* and brought onto private land for supplemental feeding during winter. Finally, livestock are allowed to graze *365 days a year* on much public land in warmer portions of the Southwest and California where, sparse as it may be, forage and browse are available year-long; this amounts to about 1/5 of BLM and FS rangeland.

As mentioned, the average duration of use on public land is about 4 months per year. This is chiefly because during the rest of the year public land is simply uninhabitable or deficient in livestock feed. Even so, considering the fragility of most public land, most grazing seasons are far too long. Further, many ranchers try to maximize their use of "cheap grazing" on public land by bringing livestock onto allotments before and leaving them after the use dates on their permits.

For those desert lands so denuded that year-round grazing is no longer feasible, the BLM has developed "ephemeral" regulations that allow cattle and/or sheep to be trucked into these areas when rare wet winters result in a brief "desert bloom." . . . Often cattle and sheep are released into areas where rain has not arrived, or before the plants have even had a chance to sprout. Even where grazing begins at the peak of the season, livestock are often kept there long after the plants have been consumed, forcing further damage to the perennial plant species that have managed to survive over a century of such grazing.

--Steve Johnson, "Grazing Impacts on Southwestern Desert Lands"

● **(4) Where** livestock graze, or their distribution on an allotment, is determined by the kind and type of livestock grazed and the allotment's unique characteristics and environmental conditions in relation to range management and developments. Livestock, cattle especially, have a strong tendency to utilize the more level, grassy bottoms and ridgetops and concentrate around water and shade. To distribute them more evenly over allotments, ranchers build fences and water developments, salt strategically, ride the range, kill off livestock predators and pests that cause animals to congregate and seek protection, and employ a wide variety of grazing systems. Unfortunately, they distribute ranching degradations along with their livestock.

Worldwide, *herding* is the traditional means of forcing livestock to evenly utilize and maximize use of forage and browse. On the Western range sheep often are herded, or at least closely watched, rather than left completely untended for long periods, as is the case with the vast majority of cattle. Some sheep are herded with dogs. Some are now fitted with electric devices that automatically emit shocks to animals that stray too close to a sensing wire surrounding the herd; they eventually learn to stay away from the wire.

In general, however, herding has become rare in the US West, due mostly to high labor costs and the fact that so few modern Americans are willing to sleep on the ground (unfortunately), eat canned beans, and follow/drive a bunch of hoofed dullards around for months at a time.

● **(5) In what manner** livestock are grazed depends chiefly on the grazing system used. A "grazing system" is a particular scheme used for grazing livestock on the range. The type of grazing system used determines herbage intake and production; livestock distribution over the range; susceptibility to predators, disease, and parasites; and so forth. Generally, it depends on economic considerations particular to each ranch.

Each allotment management plan contains details of a grazing system supposedly designed for that individual allotment. In practice, the permitted system often is modified by the permittee as he sees fit, or through forces beyond his control. For example, a flood may destroy a fence and allow cattle to graze a portion of an allotment not scheduled to be grazed until the next growing season. Ranchers may be officially permitted to alter planned grazing strategies in response to declared emergencies. For example, during the 1990 "drought disaster" declared in Arizona, ranchers were allowed to abandon management plans and drive cattle into areas with more herbage and water.

There is no best grazing system. Certain kinds of grazing are generally preferable under certain circumstances. But countless studies demonstrate that for best results a grazing system must be designed to suit each particular range situation. This involves additional government and private time, work, and money -- additional time, work, and money the rancher often does not want to provide.

The environmental impact from grazing systems likewise varies with each range situation. Still, in most cases the differences in overall environmental impact from the various grazing systems are relatively insignificant. The stocking rate per total area grazed is nearly always a vastly more important factor.

Moreover, livestock grazing by any system is almost never more environmentally benign than non-grazing, regardless of circumstances. Over the years, nearly every conceivable grazing system, and combination of systems, has been tested. Consequently, there is no new "undiscovered" grazing system that will revolutionize public land ranching and make it economically practical or environmentally benign.

The basic [ranching] *strategy, regardless of grazing system, has been and seemingly continues to be to maintain the maximum number of livestock possible. . . . Stocking rate is and always will be the major factor affecting the degradation of rangeland resources. No grazing system can counteract the negative impacts of overstocking on a long range basis . . . .*

--Range professionals Pieper and Heitschmidt, in a 1988 paper

Though no 2 grazing systems are exactly alike, nearly every public lands rancher in the West uses (consciously or not) 1 or some combination of the following 4 basic grazing systems:

(a) *Continuous grazing.* Much of public land is grazed more or less continuously. This does not mean animals are necessarily grazed all year but throughout the period or periods when grazing is possible -- when adequate herbage is available and other conditions are conducive. On Forest Service and some other federal and state lands, supplemental feed occasionally is given to stretch animals' time on public range. (BLM officially allows only concentrated protein/mineral supplements, but much unauthorized feeding of other supplements does occur.) For the balance of the year, livestock usually are moved to private land to eat forage, pasturage, or stored feed. Or they are moved directly from public land to feedlots or slaughterhouses.

Most ranchers prefer continuous grazing to other systems because it generally entails less expense for fences, livestock handling, and planning and monitoring, and it maximizes herbage utilization in grazed areas. There is a persistent myth, spread mostly by proponents of rotation grazing, that continuous grazing necessarily begets worse overgrazing than other livestock grazing systems. Studies show that generally this is not true except in localized areas, such as riparian areas, where livestock are allowed to concentrate for long periods.

(b) *Rotation grazing.* In this system, an allotment is divided into several or many different pastures. A heavy concentration of livestock is placed on one pasture for a short period (usually a few days to a few weeks), while the others remain ungrazed. When the herbage in the first pasture is depleted, the animals are moved on to the next, and then to the next, until eventually returned to the first pasture when it has (ostensibly) once again regrown enough herbage to withstand another period of grazing. Thus, the mass of livestock is alternately moved at intervals from one pasture to another throughout a growing season. Depending on a host of variables, each pasture may be grazed 1 or more times per year.

Rotation grazing, largely in the form of range consultant Allan Savory's so-called "Holistic Resource Management," has experienced a surge of popularity in recent years, for political as well as economic reasons (see Chapter XII).

(c) *Rotation-deferred grazing*. This method divides an allotment into several grazing units. At least 1 unit remains ungrazed each year until after the seed crop has matured. The next year a second pasture is deferred while grazing on the first is delayed as long as possible to allow seedlings to become established. And so on. In this way, eventually each of the units is in theory rested and allowed to reseed.

(d) *Rest-rotation grazing*. Similar to rotation-deferred, rest-rotation grazing is a system in which one area of an allotment goes ungrazed for 2 or more growing seasons while all livestock are crammed onto the remainder of the allotment. Another area is then rested in the same manner while the herd is crowded onto the remainder of the allotment. And so on, rotating rest periods between areas. Supposedly, each area is rested long enough that livestock-palatable plants have a chance to recover. Concurrently, each area is grazed heavily enough that animals are forced to eat "undesirable" plants and "utilize" unpopular sites.

Though perhaps not evident in this photo, rotation grazing has stripped off more than 80% of the right pasture's above-ground biomass.

Maybe, when all else fails, the BLM will play a shell game, shuttling cattle from one pasture to another to create the illusion of better management while failing to face up to the fact that there are simply too many cattle on the allotment.
--Joseph M. Feller, "The Western Wing of Kafka's Castle" (Feller 1990)

Various rotation grazing systems (and combinations thereof) presently are in vogue with the government and many ranchers. They shuffle livestock back and forth between pastures in an attempt to take advantage of vegetation at different stages of growth. While touted as simulations of natural grazing, none of these systems reflects the behaviors of native herbivores. And, regardless of how they are shuffled about, livestock remain imported, inbred, hybrid, domesticated animals, under human control and living grossly artificial lives. While advertised as "progressive, scientific" range management, livestock kept on the move have not been shown to be significantly less destructive than those kept more sedentary (Holechek 1989). Also, many stockmen shun rotation grazing, complaining that the constantly moving stock burn up too many calories.

Use of rotation grazing systems is intended to not only placate those concerned about continued overgrazing, but to *increase* the number of livestock on public land. Critics call it "systematic overgrazing."

Another reason for the popularity of rotation systems is that during declared emergencies -- which are surprisingly frequent -- ranchers may graze their livestock on the normally ungrazed portions of allotments. For example, in 1990 Cochise County in southeast Arizona was declared a drought disaster area by the Governor. Permittees using rotation systems were allowed to move their cattle onto portions of allotments that otherwise were not scheduled to be grazed until some future date. Simply put, future overgrazing was almost guaranteed in order to provide livestock emergency herbage. When I asked the area BLM range specialist what would happen when the already-grazed portions could

Having clearcut the right pasture to bare dirt, sheep are driven to the pasture on the left to repeat the process. Central California BLM.

no longer support the previously planned grazing, he responded that "the cattle would either starve to death or have to be moved to private lands for feed." When I asked why livestock were being given priority over wildlife, he replied that livestock needed that forage. And why weren't ranchers required to move livestock to their private land during drought disasters? Same answer.

To implement rotation grazing, governments' long-range plans call for the construction of tens of thousands of miles of new barbed wire fences to divide our public land into ever smaller "pastures" for ever more intensive grazing management. Likewise planned are thousands of new stock watering tanks, roads, cattle guards . . . .

Agency people like all this because it increases their bureaucratic power and justifies their existence. Ranchers like it because they may be able to squeeze more cattle onto the same number of acres and have government pay most of the extra cost. And it looks good to the public because parts of the range are given "rests" from grazing and it seems as if something is being done about overgrazing.

Unfortunately, once again, the public and the land lose and ranching wins. Administration becomes more complex, difficult, and expensive, while the probability of permit violations and range abuse increases. Rancher and bureaucratic power spreads, while other public lands uses are limited and degraded. We the public pay for most of these extra so-called "improvements," while our land is grazed that much more heavily when it is grazed. Wildlife must somehow adapt its needs to the intensive on-off grazing cycles. Large animals increasingly are killed and restricted in movement by more and more fences. Livestock and their attendant problems are spread to areas previously grazed lightly, if at all. Ranching development is spreading like a cancer over our public land.

Routine ranching activities -- done tens of thousands of times each day -- disturb Western ecosystems.

Livestock management activities also include: rounding up and dispersing; collecting strays; separating sexes, age groups, and breeding stock; culling the old, sick, and infirm; branding, dehorning, castrating, and treating stock for disease and parasites; shearing sheep; and simply monitoring livestock. Disturbances from ranchers in vehicles, on horseback, on foot, or even in ultra-lights, airplanes, or helicopters during these and other management activities cause environmental damage and help fragment habitat. For example, the Forest Service notes in *Run Wild -- Wildlife/Habitat Relationships*, "Disturbances caused by cattle round-ups cause bucks to flee their home range to adjacent pastures."

A rancher in a noisy pickup truck upsets the wild animals in a remote canyon. An afternoon of branding calves leaves a small grassy flat in poor condition. A mounted cowboy, in scrambling to collect a stray calf, tramples a steep hillslope, killing vegetation and displacing soil. A herd of cattle driven across a valley during a roundup leaves a wide trail of trampled vegetation, terrified wildlife, and pulverized, exposed soil. (For example, the main detriment to the small Utah cactus, *Pediocactus winkerli*, when it was first listed as federally Endangered, was trampling from cattle being driven through its habitat from one grazing area to another.) Livestock loading, unloading, and servicing create especially degraded conditions, if not sacrifice areas.

All these activities harm the environment in many of the ways discussed in this book. Wild animals are forced from their nests and driven from their home ranges; separated from their young, group, or herd; hindered in mating; interrupted in feeding and watering; forced into the open where they are more vulnerable to predators; driven from shelter into harsh weather or hot sun; made to run away and expend valuable energy; robbed of sleep or rest; psychologically disturbed; and so on. The cumulative impact of 30,000 ranchers performing routine livestock management activities on public land is considerable.

Sheep in Bighorn National Forest, Wyoming, being driven to lower elevation pasture. *(George Robbins Photo, Jackson, WY.)*

I know of areas here where I live that abound with wild animals, large and small, until the sheep arrive. After a thousand sheep and the men and dogs move into an area . . . many wild animals, and most all of the larger ones, must go elsewhere, out of fear or lack of food . . . .
--Lynn Donnelly, Marble, Colorado, letter to the editor of *Colorado Outdoors*

Herding cattle across an Idaho BLM range: In some people, such scenes evoke a rustic nostalgia, but the environmental damage is very real.

Ranching developments such as roads, fences, and salt enable livestock to occupy and degrade all of the BLM sage country seen in this photo taken near Big Piney, Wyoming. *(George Robbins Photo, Jackson, WY)*

Thou shalt inherit the Holy Earth as a faithful steward, conserving its resources and productivity from generation to generation. Thou shalt safeguard thy fields from erosion, thy living waters from drying up, thy forests from desolation, and protect thy hills from overgrazing by thy herds, that thy descendents may have abundance forever. If any shall fail in this stewardship of the land thy fruitful fields shall become stony ground and wasting gullies, and thy descendants shall decrease and live in poverty and perish off the face of the earth.
--W.C. Lowdermilk, **Conquest of the Land Through 7,000 Years** (Lowdermilk 1975)

Understanding Range Development

This lengthy chapter has detailed the numerous ways the ranching establishment manipulates public land for its purposes and how this in turn affects the natural environment. Indeed, range development probably causes as much overall environmental damage as livestock grazing itself. So, why don't we recognize its impact on the Western landscape?

To begin with, many Americans' worldview is not unlike that of ranchers and range managers. They perceive the natural environment as a "resource base" to be manipulated for human goals. So, on those few occasions when they consider range development at all, most people support it if there is any alleged benefit.

Moreover, the average American understands the environmental effects of range development no more than those of livestock grazing, and for many of the same reasons. Most of it takes place out on the range, on the rarely visited half of the West. Similar to overgrazing, the impacts from many of these developments and activities are widely dispersed, subtle, insidious, and cumulative. Those that *are* recognized generally are accepted as rustic parts of the Old West -- the nostalgic barbed wire fences, the stoic windmills, the rugged dirt roads, the exciting roundups, the macho ropings and brandings, and, of course, the pastoral cattle and sheep -- all the stuff of romantic cowboy legends. And, even on a range where there is no discernable ranching impact whatsoever (a rare place indeed), there usually is a profound unseen influence nonetheless. Predator and competitor eradication efforts may have eliminated some native animals; the presence of ranchers and their stock may interefere with normal wildlife behavior; various ranching activities may have introduced harmful exotic vegetation; and so on.

Most of the public has likewise been duped into thinking that range developments -- fences, tanks, roads, vegetation removals, seedings, prescribed burns, predator "control," and so on -- are primarily to benefit wildlife, soil, water, and the public. They have no idea that: 30,000 public lands ranchers are spread evenly across 41% of the West; each is doing whatever he can to develop "his" average 12,000-acre grazing allotment for livestock; and thus each is doing significant environmental damage. Assisting them are about 700 Forest Service ranger and BLM resource area district offices, a dozen other federal agencies, and scores of state agencies, hundreds of county ranching-related programs, and countless private entities. In terms of distribution and diversity of impacts, ranching surpasses any other Western land use; in cumulate environmental damage, it far outweighs any other public land use. As with livestock grazing, ranching developments are nickle-and-diming the West to death.

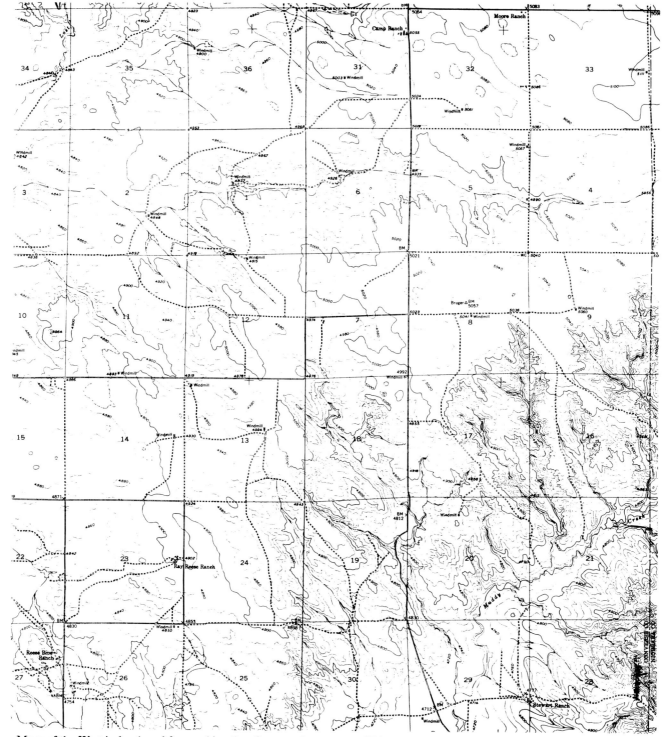

More of the West is developed for ranching than for any other purpose. This section of a USGS topo map reflects a 30-square-mile area of typical Wyoming range: scattered ranch headquarters, ranching roads accessing every square mile, numerous windmills and stock tanks. Even so, most ranching developments are not shown.

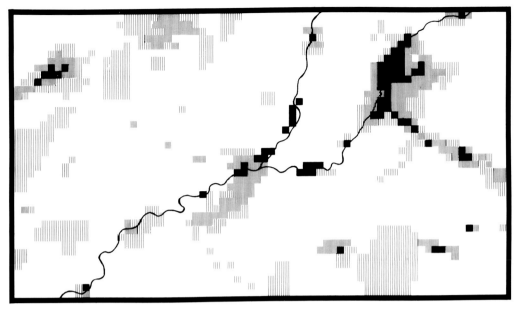

COMBINED NON-RANCHING HUMAN IMPACT -- AVERAGE WESTERN COUNTY, USA
TOTAL ENVIRONMENTAL IMPACT -- 1,000 POINTS

AVERAGE WESTERN COUNTY, USA

DEGREE OF ENVIRONMENTAL IMPACT

These maps portray stylized versions of hypothetical environmental damage in a fairly average rural Western County, the map above from non-ranching activities, the one below from ranching. Though non-ranching impacts stand out much more starkly and overall damage may *seem* worse, damage from ranching is actually twice as great.

| 10 miles |

Light Impact (0 points) — (Light or no ranching; tourist and visitor impacts: light hunting, heavy gathering; light ORV use; most acid rain; etc.)

Medium Impact (1 point) — (Medium ranching; select logging; heavy woodcutting; medium roading; medium ORV use; overhunting; utility lines; etc.

Heavy Impact (2 points) — (Heavy ranching; clearcutting; light development heavy roading; heavy ORV use; most farming; serious toxic spills; etc.

Extreme Impact (3 points) — (Cities and towns; most development; strip mines; dams and reservoirs; use of nuclear weapons; etc.)

RANCHING IMPACT -- AVERAGE WESTERN COUNTY, USA:
TOTAL ENVIRONMENTAL IMPACT -- 2,000 POINTS

The cattle ranch at left may be likened to a deadly parasite, slowly sucking life from tens of thousands of acres around it.

What we call "news" consists of crises -- sharply focused occurrences that are easy to report. Chronic, time-extended happenings don't have much chance when competing for time or space in the evening broadcast or morning newspaper.
--Dr. Garrett Hardin, "Sheer Numbers," *E* magazine (Nov/Dec 1990)

Compounding the lack of understanding, like overgrazing most range development is less an event than a process -- *a dynamic state of degradation*. We notice the obvious, destructive events, but not the subtle, ongoing impairment of the land. For example, it's not the past massacre of tens of billions of prairie dogs that is now most significant, but that killing thousands of prairie dogs every year (coupled with continued overgrazing) persistently keeps the animal from recovering. It's not so much that half a million miles of ranching roads were made on public land as that these roads are continually used and maintained and that each year more are built. As expressed by CNN news anchor Bernard Shaw, "there's often no daily development -- or, in news jargon, a peg -- to justify spending time on a story that will remain just as timely tomorrow, next week, or next year."

Unfortunately, many of us have a limited understanding of Nature. For example, we suffer from "park mentality" -- the belief that the ideal natural landscape resembles a well-manicured city park, with widely scattered trees devoid of lower branches, with a few, trim bushes, no organic ground litter, and short grass throughout. By claiming to be trying to create a similar landscape, range developers garner public support. But, like developed ranges, city parks are artificial, simplified, non-functional environments, maintained only through intensive management and the continued infusion of resources. We fail to realize that a wild, scruffy, teeming, untamed natural landscape is far more healthy, productive, diverse, and self-sustaining than any green, pretty city park.

With a lack of understanding or interest in the Western environment -- rangeland in particular -- the public defers judgement on range matters to "the range experts," who have thus essentially had free reign to develop public land for ranching.

In practice, stockmen, government range personnel, and private range professionals -- not the the public -- decide how most of our public land is managed. *(Paul Hirt)*

Basically, range development is the manipulation of livestock and the land for ranching purposes. From the combined environmental impact described thus far in this book, it almost could be said that *range development is the attempt to minimize all living things but livestock and their food plants.* With enough labor, materials, tax money, and environmental manipulation, nearly any place can be forced to produce livestock.

Range development, however, is more than simply a means of producing livestock. It is the physical manifestation of a millennia-old stock-man worldview which presumes that "mankind" is endowed by a god with dictatorial power over the Earth (see the end of Chapter XI). Thus, range development encompasses not only physical efforts to increase livestock profits but also deeply ingrained feelings and perspectives. Regardless of how destructive, wasteful, or even ineffectual range development might be, it will continue to be widely practiced by ranchmen so long as they remain in power.

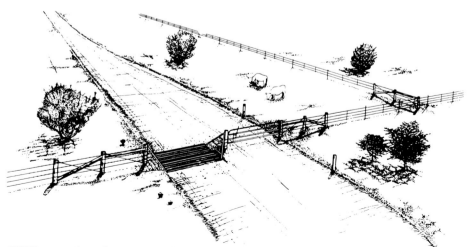

BLM conception of a proper, park-like range. *(BLM)*

Management is our business.
--BLM

Our government land managers generally share the aforementioned worldview, though they manifest it somewhat differently. Their self-declared primary function is *management*, and they aim to *manage*. The more the land is used, the more management is needed from the bureaucracies and the more influence they accumulate. Thus, administrators become nervous when land they "administer" is not being used, even for something as impractical as ranching.

So they manage under the doctrine of "multiple use" and regard public acres as so many slices of pie to be divided among "the users." Since ranching is the traditional and priority use on most public land -- and the only "significant" use on probably half of public land -- the agencies are terrified at the thought of ranching's abolishment. Without it, their basis for control over most land and much of their reason for existence would vanish. This helps explain why they so heavily and blindly support ranching regardless of the consequences.

Conversely, the more the land is developed, the more use it receives and the more administrative power the agencies acquire. The agencies therefore promote range development whenever and wherever possible -- causing the exploitation of tens of millions of acres that otherwise would experience little manipulation.

I'd begin by reducing the number of cattle on public lands. Not that range managers would go along with it, of course. In their eyes, and in the eyes of the livestock associations they work for, cutting down on the number of cattle is the worst possible solution -- an impossible solution. So they propose all kinds of gimmicks. More cross-fencing. More wells and ponds so that more land can be exploited. These proposals are basically a maneuver by the Forest Service and the BLM to appease their critics without offending their real bosses in the beef industry.
--Edward Abbey "Even the Bad Guys Wear White Hats" (Abbey 1986)

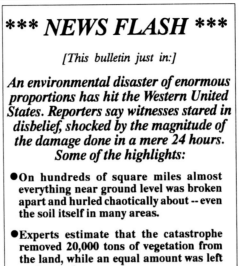

*** *NEWS FLASH* ***

[This bulletin just in:]

An environmental disaster of enormous proportions has hit the Western United States. Reporters say witnesses stared in disbelief, shocked by the magnitude of the damage done in a mere 24 hours.
Some of the highlights:

● **On hundreds of square miles almost everything near ground level was broken apart and hurled chaotically about -- even the soil itself in many areas.**

● **Experts estimate that the catastrophe removed 20,000 tons of vegetation from the land, while an equal amount was left broken and scattered.**

● **Witnesses said that wild animals died by the thousands and survivors desperately sought what scant food and cover remained. They stated that thousands more "seem to have been killed intentionally."**

● **An estimated 1 million tons of topsoil were displaced, washed, or blown away during the cataclysm, fouling waterways throughout the West. Additionally, a 5-square-mile area was so thoroughly ravaged that one spectator observed, "It looks like someone bulldozed it!"**

● **Hundreds of millions of gallons of surface water were lost, and some springs and streams vanished entirely. An estimated 1000 tons of harmful excretory wastes were discharged into remaining water sources, causing 20-30 persons to become ill.**

● **Authorities are predicting that monetary damages in lost resources for human use will total in the millions of dollars; other impacts have not yet been calculated.**

● **Unbelievably, federal disaster experts state that disasters of equal magnitude are expected to occur *each and every day for the next 120 years*, as they have for the past 120 years.**

*** *NEWS FLASH* ***

Now, in the late 20th century, ranchers/range managers fall into 2 seemingly divergent, though actually very similar, philosophical molds. The "old-timers" are still prone to beat the range into submission, like they've done for decades, like they'd break a wild horse. They see the land as theirs by right of manifest destiny, tradition, and the innate superiority of ranching. They believe Nature was created specifically for human use, that the world is a collection of resources, and that their challenge is to bring it under control for their benefit. They live in a self-absorbed, anthropocentric world where all entities within their realm are subject to their control or influence.

The "new-timers" deduce that if brute force won't work, they will outwit Nature (and the public). Through scientific knowledge and technological power, they *manipulate* the range into submission, like a test-tube experiment. They see control of the land as theirs by right of innate human superiority, intelligence, and technological capability. They believe Nature should serve those who have learned to manipulate it. Indeed, they don't believe there is such a thing as natural, but that the world is a huge, complex piece of clay, and they the sculptors. They see the planet as "Spaceship Earth*," and their ultimate challenge as learning how to operate it to produce and extract the desired resources.

*RELATED TRIVIA NOTE: Ferdinand Marcos left the book **Operating Manual for Spaceship Earth** halfway read on his nightstand when he fled the Philippines.

The new-timers are, of course, gradually replacing the old-timers. They peddle the new-and-improved, scientific, ecologically based range development, said to be the answer to all our ranching problems. Science and technology, they tell us, is the secret to benign exploitation. Scientific discoveries will enable us to apply advanced technological solutions to range problems and restore the West -- even beyond its aboriginal productivity!

In reality, these supposedly revolutionary new scientific discoveries are long-known ecological principles that the ranching establishment recently has discovered and learned to utilize to more fully exploit the range and the public.

The more edge effect a particular area has, the higher the wildlife population, because most wildlife species require several types of vegetation to meet their needs.
--**Range Management** (Holechek 1989)

Thus, for example, government agencies -- to the bewilderment of many conservationists -- nowadays often justify their range development practices by "managing for maximum diversity." Agency range professionals claim that when they manipulate the vegetation cover, the edges of the disturbed areas support animals from both of the adjoining habitats, as well as animals that need both kinds of habitat, and other animals that specialize on edges. Supposedly, these transition zones provide for greater overall numbers and diversity of wildlife than if the vegetation was not manipulated. This is known as "edge effect," and according to its promoters it simulates Nature's mosaic effect. Pretending that more edges mean more diversity -- and fully aware that "managing for maximum diversity" means greater support from conservationists, as well as, usually, more forage for livestock -- the agencies manage for maximum edge effect.

Some [brush control] projects in the past were carried out with little regard for wildlife, but now most are designed to produce a mosaic of vegetation types, thereby increasing grass production but leaving strips or islands of brush for wildlife cover.
--from *Progressive Agriculture* by the College of Agriculture, University of Arizona

The agencies argue that managing for maximum intensity and variety of disturbance produces maximum edge effect and therefore maximum diversity of habitat and wildlife. So they cavalierly herbicide strips through brushland, chain wide swaths through pinyon/juniper, prescribe burn segments of rangeland, promote logging and firewood cutting on mesas and ridges, plant seedings in bizarre designs, allow intensive goat and sheep herding in selected areas, and so on -- all under the wide, protective umbrella of "managing for maximum diversity." Of course, all this gives the bureaucracies the appearance of doing something useful.

Conservationists and others have been fooled and confused about diversity. Nature already "manages" ecosystems for optimal mosaic and edge benefit. Additional mosaics and edges increasingly detract from overall ecosystem health.

Moreover, the impacts of machines, herbicides, unnatural fires, exotic plants, livestock, and humans are vastly dissimilar to Nature's forces. The kinds of species that benefit most from these artificial intrusions are plant and animal "weeds." While indigenous species may be reduced or extirpated, these exotic and increaser species may thrive in human-altered landscapes, sometimes causing, at least temporarily, an overall increase in diversity in the disturbed areas. This type of management, with its countless, inherent unforeseen variables, often produces not even weeds but bare dirt, soil erosion, water siltation, wildlife declines, and so forth.

Furthermore, unlike most natural disturbances, artificial disturbances often adversely affect the interior of adjacent unaltered habitats. For example, the microclimates created by numerous artificially disturbed areas often reach well into nearby undisturbed areas and, in combination, may cause significant harmful changes in wind, humidity, temperature, etc. Likewise, predators, disease, parasites, and pathogens introduced from these artificial edges may harm interior wildlife. Edge effect management may or may not increase species diversity along edges, but nearly always it causes species declines to interiors.

Also, with intensive management for edge effect, native plants in undisturbed areas tend to disappear under an onslaught of exotics (often seeded intentionally) from the numerous edges. This reduces species diversity on a broader scale since the same weedy species tend to occur over and over.

Large blocks of habitat support more species than comparable smaller blocks totaling the same size. Many plant and animal species need large blocks of undisturbed land, and management for too much edge effect fragments their habitat. Studies in Brazil show that rainforest fragmented into 2 1/2-acre blocks is all edge, and even 250-acre blocks are 25% edge. Fragmentation is a main dynamic behind deterioration of habitat (see **Conservation Biology**, edited by Michael E. Soule, for a discussion of habitat fragmentation and edge effect).

All range developments, especially ranching roads, firebreaks, fences, seedings, vegetation eradications, prescribed burns, livestock

An artificial mosaic on northern Arizona BLM range. Marble Canyon is in the background.

management activities, sacrifice areas, heavy grazing, and livestock, increase habitat fragmentation. Most range developments require road building, which not only further damages and fragments habitat, but brings in more people. Further, once an area has been artificially altered, it must continue to be periodically redeveloped essentially forever to maintain its artificial state, for it will always strive to return to a natural state. Finally, the increased livestock grazing following these unnatural alterations often is the greatest detriment of all.

Human management does not create healthy ecosystems. Only natural disturbances, the products of Earth's evolution over millennia, can create natural abundance and diversity with an appropriate mix and interaction of species. Reed Noss, a landscape ecologist, expresses this concept well:

The ecological mosaic created by natural disturbance is a far cry from the checkerboard of isolated habitats created by modern humans. The natural mosaic is interconnected; the artificial patchwork is fragmented. . . . What we want is a full complement of native species in natural patterns of abundance. (Noss 1986)

As development continues to encroach on the natural world, naturalists and conservationists are continually called upon to answer the question, But what good is it [a given species]? . . . . Ecologist Marston Bates has suggested that the best response the naturalist can give to the question is to ask, What good are you?
--from **The Nature of Birds** by Adrian Forsyth

The only truly useless species is one that has become extinct.
--G. Jon Roush, "The Disintegrating Web," *The Nature Conservancy Magazine* (Nov/Dec 1989)

When a hurricane, tornado, avalanche, fire, clearcut, concentration of cattle, or other major disturbance changes a landscape, a dramatic shift in available nutrients may occur to certain favored species. In the case of a tornado, trees and brush may be uprooted, torn to pieces, and distributed about the landscape as organic litter, resulting in an increase in sunlight and soil nutrients to forb and grass species, eventually providing more food for, say, rabbits. In other words, the nutrients in the destroyed vegetation are redistributed to surviving and future plants and, in turn, to their dependent animal species. These species may then experience dramatic, albeit temporary, population increases.

Range managers have learned that by manipulating certain influences they may redistribute ecosystem nutrients, including sunlight, to favor selected species, usually forage grasses and livestock. This is a basis of modern range management and one of the secrets of how range managers can sometimes seem to magically produce certain plants and animals. Their tools include vegetation eradication, prescribed burns, intensive livestock herding, and so forth.

Consider a common scenario: a northeastern New Mexico valley is covered mostly with shrubs, the spaces between them showing exotic grasses and bare dirt. The local permittee pressures BLM to disc 800 acres. The shrubs are reduced to organic litter and, along with the existing litter layer and grass, are incorporated into the topsoil. Suddenly, soil nutrients, humus, microbes, and aeration

increase. Now, **if** sufficient moisture follows and temperatures and other variables happen to align, the exotic grass seeds in the churned up soil sprout and thrive, yielding a net increase in grass. The rancher is happy (at least for awhile), and BLM toots its horn.

Fortunately, Nature is not so easily enslaved. These variables rarely align to produce a best-case scenario. Rain may not come; the grasses may not have seeded well the preceding spring; pests may thrive in the simplified community and eat most of the seeds or seedlings; or storms may wash away the temporarily unprotected soil.

Perhaps more important, what increases do occur are usually *short-lived*. Often within a few years, as nutrients redistribute to recovering members of the ecosystem, they gradually move to lower levels than before implementation of the range development. A natural climax community -- or what passes for one while being overgrazed -- begins to reestablish itself.

On the same 800 acres before discing, organic material from the shrubs and grasses was released slowly and relatively evenly over time, providing the soil a continuous nutrient supply. When discing released the entire biomass of the 800 acres into the soil at once, humus dramatically increased. But over the next few years, this humus decomposed and new growth could not replenish it as had the original vegetation, especially while being grazed by livestock. Consequently, the humus eventually fell below original levels, grasses declined, and shrubs once again achieved dominance -- *with a net loss in ecosystem biomass and diversity*.

But, ranchers do not want this to happen. They want grass. So, they keep killing, burning, seeding, and herding, hoping and gambling they can maintain forage artificially, *while their livestock relentlessly counteract their efforts*.

This redistribution of rangeland nutrients for short-term increases in productivity is similar to what is happening all over the planet. Oil and mining companies "unlock" non-renewable resources and call it "progress." Timber interests cut aboriginal forests that will never recover their natural abundance and diversity. Farmers large and small take from the earth more than they return. And fishing outfits take maximum hauls from a finite ocean. Ranching makes Western range just as much a non-renewable resource.

I wanted to create a place where living things could thrive, when all the while I was killing the life that was there.
--from *Star Trek, the Next Generation* TV series

Under the influence of ranching, Western range productivity has been declining steadily for more than a century. Thus, to maintain traditional livestock levels the industry has been forced to "restore the range." This is *not* true range restoration, but attempted *forage* restoration -- another form of range development. In fact, most of the alleged "restoration" techniques are identical to the range developments discussed in this book. Under this banner of "restoring the range," the industry is developing the West for ranching even beyond previous levels of exploitation.

This is analogous to building taller smokestacks to reduce air pollution. True restoration would be a temporary effort -- to return "management power" to Nature so that future restoration would be unnecessary. True restoration would break the endless snowballing cycle of restoration-over-grazing-restoration-overgrazing.... True restoration would entail not only restoration techniques, but elimination of the ultimate cause of deterioration -- ranching. Range "improvements" treat the symptoms, not the cause.

Further obscuring their motives, the range controllers claim that their "restoration" efforts are vital to many rangelands because environmental damage has progressed beyond the point of natural regeneration. Not only this, because humans have irreversibly changed the land, they must henceforth take *permanent* control over natural processes.

Well, slow down! This theory has far-reaching implications. Are we to believe that after 5 billion years of natural existence the Earth suddenly cannot survive without eternal human supervision and maintenance? If this is the direction in which we are headed, won't the Earth ultimately be turned into a huge, complex human experiment? What kind of future would it be if humans determine every aspect of Earthly existence? What person has the knowledge or wisdom to direct the lives of trillions of diverse beings, their infinite number of interrelationships, and incredibly complex ecosystem dynamics? As writer/ecologist George Wuerthner writes, "Even our most complex inventions, such as spaceships and computers, are, by comparison to natural systems and processes, incredibly simple." And as ecologist Frank Egler points out, "Nature is not only more complex than we think, but more complex than we can ever think." Ecologist Jamie Sayen expands upon Egler's statement in "Taking Steps Toward a Restoration Ethic":

> ...systems reconstructed by humans are always biologically impoverished relative to similar natural systems, and are always more susceptible to invasion by exotics.
>
> Efforts to recreate or replicate damaged ecosystems can never succeed. Even if we knew all the parts (down to the site specific soil microbes and mycorrhizal fungi), we wouldn't begin to understand the web of relations. Furthermore, an undisturbed system today is quite different from what it was 100 or 1,000 years ago. It may have the same appearance, but changes caused by climate, disturbance, succession, adaptation and evolution change it in ways no historian, archaeologist, or ecologist can ever fully know. (Sayen 1989)

In other words, we cannot restore the Earth. Human interference with natural processes can only detract. We can only put back available missing pieces, stand back, and let Nature heal.

I firmly think that the vast bulk of degraded Western rangeland is capable of natural restoration if protected from further damage and given enough time. Most areas will heal surprisingly well, as has been demonstrated by the hundreds of sites around the West where ranching has been terminated. Harold Dregne of Texas Tech University reports in the UN's *Desertification Control Bulletin* (#15, 1987), "Enclosure studies around the world have demonstrated the potential for recovery of overgrazed and drought-affected pastoral lands, even during droughts." Unfortunately, humans are impatient, especially when clamoring for more livestock, and some areas may take decades or even centuries to heal.

Some range professionals cite cases where decades of protection from ranching have resulted in "no significant improvement" in range condition. This is misleading. First,

they conveniently ignore the vast majority of sites that show much improvement. Second, in most of the cases they cite there *has* been improvement, just not enough to seem "significant" to people who consider little more than livestock production. Often improvement is belittled to promote the impression that ranching is benign. Third, as explained, the size of the protected areas is generally inadequate. Finally, other detracting human influences often are overlooked.

Range professionals also cite instances where restoration projects seem to have improved range conditions. To be sure, there are cases where restoration management has been worth the tax money, effort, and resources expended -- some check dam projects, reintroductions of native grasses, and prescribed burns, for example. But the true successes are few and far between. Most restoration efforts fail to produce the calculated results, or expend more than is justified by the results; nearly all are followed by more of the intensive ranching that necessitated restoration in the first place. Failures go unpublicized, and the "successes" are generally misinterpreted by vested interests.

Artificial restoration should be used only as a last resort, especially when removing the cause of degradation is by itself not enough to reverse deterioration and prevent significant long-term damage. For example, rather than prescribing burns to restore a range, why not let natural fires burn? (Range manager's answer: unplanned fires do not fit into grazing schedules.) To quote Jamie Sayen again:

> Instead of attempting to control evolution or create ecosystems, we should work to restore the possibility of the evolutionary dance. We must rely upon the resiliency of Mother Earth, not on our species' cleverness." (Sayen 1989)

Many professionals use range studies to promote range development. Out of thousands of existing studies they carefully select a handful that "prove" what they want to prove -- that a preferred type of grazing system or range management improves range conditions, or minimizes decline. Or, they simply conduct their own relevant studies. The integrity of many of the studies is in doubt, but perhaps more importantly, most of the alleged "improvements" could not be made without infusions of outside labor, capital, and materials.

Nonetheless, they trumpet their "successes" as proof that there really are ways to raise livestock on the Western range without ruining it. Many of these ranching advocates claim to have discovered the magic scientific formula which if implemented on a large scale might save Western ranching.

These pros are often convincing, but their claims have little basis in reality. You cannot pick a few results from thousands of studies and claim them indicative of ranching in general. Likewise, because a certain method produced an apparent improvement under a unique situation does not mean that method will do the same elsewhere on the Western range.

Nearly every conceivable kind and combination of grazing and range development has been explored over the years. Yet the West remains in poor condition.

A thing is right when it tends to preserve the integrity, stability, and beauty of the biotic community. It is wrong when it tends otherwise.
--Aldo Leopold

An artist's depiction of unranched range in Douglas County, Nevada. *(Jan Rogers)*

Range development is an attempt to circumvent natural processes and subvert Nature for human purposes. One illusion held in range professional circles is that the more ecological knowledge you gather, the more control you can exert over the land and the more it will conform to your goals.

Consider the infamous Dust Bowl disaster of the 1930s. The farmers' attempt to force the shortgrass prairie to produce crops was ultimately as destructive and futile as the ranchers' attempt to force public land to produce livestock. In fact, though we rarely read of it in history books, overgrazing was not far behind farming as a cause of the Dust Bowl, and ruinous overgrazing continued throughout the ravaged 80,000-square-mile area of Kansas, Colorado, New Mexico, Oklahoma, and Texas even after thousands of farmers gave up farming and left. Vegetation cover on grazed Dust Bowl lands was reduced by at least 50%, frequently by 90%-98%, and the government provided emergency relief to ship thousands of starving cattle east to the tallgrass prairie. (Malin 1956, Vankat 1979) Scientists indicate an increasing likelihood of new farm-belt dust bowls, but large areas of overgrazed Western range have resembled dust bowls for decades.

This photo shows the edge of a range revegetation project, Gallatin National Forest, Montana. Increasingly intensive range manipulation puts humans in the improper position of dictating the nature of Nature *(USFS)*

The land has already been developed by Nature to its full potential.
--Ian Sinclair, **Live and Let Live**

We humans have come to think that we can do a better job of managing the land than the land itself can. Despite what we think, only Nature "manages" the environment appropriately; people can only *manipulate* it. Consider, for example, that studies show a single acre of grassland supports about 4 million invertebrates large enough to be seen with the unaided eye. Also on this acre may be hundreds of vertebrates, billions of microscopic organisms, and millions of plants of scores of species. Add to this the complex relations of sunlight, soil, water, mineral cycles, weather, and more. Though constantly evolving and dynamically changing in infinite ways, this assemblage exists together for millennia, to the overall benefit of nearly all participants. How can we better manage this acre, regardless of our intentions or how hard we try?

Nature already has provided the most abundant, diverse ecosystem possible for each unique set of climatic, geographic, geologic, and hydrologic conditions. It is the ultimate expert, having been working not for mere hundreds, but for *billions* of years. Scientists estimate that Nature has created more than *4 billion* different species since life began.

Even the simplest ecosystem is so incredibly complex that no person could begin to understand it, much less manage it appropriately. As the trillions of cells in our bodies function as one, similarly do the infinite components of natural systems. In our ignorance and conceit, we think we can function as the "brain" to manipulate the Earth, not realizing that the brain is actually the composite whole.

Yet, on occasion wildlife will be *less* abundant and diverse on rangeland in its natural state than if intensively manipulated by humans. In this case, the "correct" biosystem is still the natural one, for its very existence shows that in the long run it is the most appropriate biosystem for that environment and within the context of the greater Earth. And even if we were able to increase an ecosystem's overall biologic "productivity," how are we to know that long-term productivity and certain species will not be harmed by our interference? More is not necessarily better.

It seems that one of man's strongest desires has been to achieve stability: a steady-state system, devoid of the tumultuous ups and downs so characteristic of natural ecosystems. This means dampening the effects of flooding, drought, and fire, phenomena to which most of the flora and fauna are adapted.
--Steven P. Christman, Ph.D. (Christman 1988)

Moreover, the natural *combination* of ecosystem components is vitally important. The almost infinite number of unique *interrelationships* among and between individuals, species, non-sentient beings, cycles, and systems is what maintains healthy ecosystems. These dynamics have evolved over millions of years and cannot be artificially improved.

Consider the plants composing any Western ecosystem. It may seem that each species is trying to dominate all others. But if this were true, after millions of years of competition between thousands of plant species one species would likely have outcompeted the others in its area and taken over vast territories. Yet after countless millennia of supposed "ruthless competition" nearly every natural area in the West supports remarkably diverse plant communities -- dozens or even hundreds of different kinds of plants living together in complex intermixtures and mosaics. Each specie's welfare is ultimately best served as an integral component of the community. Each provides certain benefits to the whole, as the whole provides for each species -- something like the cooperation between the individual cells of a living being. In turn, each subdivision of an ecosystem -- plant, animal, soil, water, fire, air, mineral, chemical, or whatever -- interacts in ways that benefit the whole ecosystem as well as itself, and each ecosystem functions similarly within the context of the whole Earth, as does the Earth in the context of the solar system, and so on. Humans have lost the reality that we were/are/must be an integral and natural part of all this.

When human interference changes an ecosystem -- and ranching is most insidious in this respect -- these vital interrelationships break down, to the detriment of the individual, the species, the cycle, the system, the ecosystem, and the Earth. Snowballing damage results from the breakdown of naturally occurring interrelationships. In other words, harming the component parts of the environment damages a much greater portion of the whole than the sum of these immediately affected parts.

Further, the ranching establishment presents range development as a wholly positive effort to improve the range, but ignores that the outside materials and the human energy expended could have remained unused or put to better use. Take an average 1000-acre BLM African lovegrass seeding. Is it simply a noble attempt to restore overgrazed range? If the grass takes well, is it necessarily a success? What about the 1000 gallons of diesel, gasoline, and oil used by the bulldozer, tractors, and pick-up trucks -- petroleum that had to be mined, piped, stored, shipped, processed, stored, trucked, stored, and pumped again? What about the machinery's manufacture and maintenance? What about the lovegrass seeds, which had to be harvested, processed, shipped, stored, packaged, and transported? What about the 1000 hours of labor expended directly on the project by range personnel and ranchers? What about agency planning, paper work, computer time, phone calls, and office supplies? What about related developments (fences, roads, firebreaks, etc.), follow-up visits, and seeding maintenance? What about the fact that the area will have to be reseeded every 15 to 25 years? Couldn't all these resources have remained unexploited, or at least have been used for something more worthwhile than preparing the range for further overgrazing?

"Streamside Protection, Deschutes NF, Oregon," according to the Forest Service. The fence has fallen apart. *(USFS)*

Range "improvements" under the continued influence of ranching are innately non-permanent and must be constantly monitored, maintained, replaced, or renewed. As such, and because of their huge financial costs (Chapter VII) and environmental harm, they could more appropriately be called range "burdens."

Nevertheless, we are not given the option of simply removing livestock from our public land. We are forced to keep throwing tax dollars into range development to counteract ranching's inherent destructiveness.

At best, range development is a double-edged sword. While allowing stockmen to partially mitigate the impacts of ranching, it treats the symptoms, not the cause of the destruction. Like an overworked ulcer patient being advised to take antacids instead of changing jobs, it only prolongs the day of reckoning and allows the tumor to continue growing. While allowing stockmen to maintain or increase livestock production, it does so only by creating dependency on ever-larger and more complex management schemes. Like a narcotic addict needing more, ever MORE, getting more only leads to *needing* more.

As with long-vanished civilizations that plundered their resources and destroyed themselves, we are living on borrowed time. For them, it took many centuries of cumulative degradation before they perished. Modern science and technology has given us the ability to manipulate and exploit the environment as never before. For us, it may take only decades. The ranching establishment is "playing god " with 306 million public acres, and the results are proving catastrophic.

As I travel through the United States, I see much evidence of good stewardship in the form of vigorous, high-quality range forage for livestock and high quality habitat for wildlife.
--Joseph L. Schuster, Range Science Department, Texas A & M University (USDA, USDI, CEQ 1979)

If one considers the full ecological impact of livestock grazing, not just the narrowly defined parameters used by range managers, it is difficult to justify or defend livestock grazing for any reason on public lands.
--George Wuerthner, "Success on the Range"

Decades of overgrazing on the fragile, arid ranges has damaged riparian areas, forced out wildlife, threatened endangered species, ruined fisheries and turned large areas of viable range into wasteland. "Grazing on our public lands," says Democratic Representative Mike Synar of Oklahoma, "is producing an ecological and fiscal disaster."
--Michael Satchell, "Last Roundup on the Range?," *US News & World Report* (11-26-90) (Satchell 1990a)

Range Development Photos

A BLM chaining to rip out shrubs. *(BLM)*

A pipe-filled cattle tank on Nevada BLM land. The wooden box on the left prevents cattle from damaging the float valve. *(BLM)*

Propane-driven water pump, stock tank, and sacrifice area. *(BLM)*

A stock tank sacrifice area in the Coronado National Forest, Arizona. *(Paul Hirt)*

A windmill, metal tanks, corral, pens, ramp, and deteriorated range. BLM, Tembler Range, California.

Water developments and salting allow livestock to survive where they otherwise would not. Note the sacrifice area, cattle trails, degraded range, and fenceline contrast.

Sage ecosystems are destroyed by the hundreds or thousands of acres and seeded with livestock forage grasses. *(Nevada BLM)*

The dashed lines delineate road-side fences. Away from the rights-of-way, nearly all plants but exotic grasses have been excluded or precluded by ranchers and their cattle. A common Western scene.

An obliterated riparian zone runs through the center of the scene. A salt block sacrifice area is at the upper left-center; a ravaged spring area at center right; ranching roads; fences; cattle trails; and heavy grazing throughout. Note the roadside fenceline contrast.

Cattle production in central California.

The remains of a rattlesnake, killed by a stockman and left hanging on a fence post. BLM land.

A New Mexico BLM cattle tank sacrifice area littered with cow pies.

A BLM corral and water development. To supply the water pump, the electric line runs for more than a mile across public land.

Dozens of species of healthy, full-sized plants on the ungrazed roadside are reduced to stubbles of only a few species by cattle and their owners on the surrounding ranchland.

Corral, sacrifice area, cattle trails, and depleted range.

A cleared fenceline becomes a cattle trail.

Ranching at 9400' elevation in the Dixie National Forest, southern Utah.

A large Forest Service stock water dam and pond. Note the excavations on the hill, the roads, and the overgrazing. *(USFS)*

Deforested, overgrazed tablelands in the Gila National Forest, New Mexico.

A BLM corral sacrifice area. There are tens of thousands of such corrals and sacrifice areas on our public lands.

Bulldozing brush for ranching on BLM land. *(BLM)*

A stock tank graveyard.

This juniper deforestation for cattle has begun to regrow with juniper. Note the cleared fenceline.

From a capped spring, a pipeline runs for 7000' along this ridge to a cattle trough. *(Idaho BLM)*

A corral, pens, stock scale, and loading ramp on state land.

A large stock tank under construction on Montana NF. *(USFS)*

Montana stock water development under construction. *(USFS)*

Bulldozing a BLM stock tank. *(BLM)*

A portable stock ramp and pen, Manti-LaSal NF, Utah.

Here, corrals tie directly into cliffs. Heavy grazing throughout.

A very large stock tank on BLM range seeded with exotic forage grasses. *(BLM)*

A 10,000-gallon holding tank, well, well house, pipelines, special utility line, fences, sign, and rancher's trailer. *(BLM)*

Firebreak, ranching road, fence, deforestation, and overgrazing.

Discing is a hopeless attempt to farm the Western range. *(BLM)*

Grading a firebreak along a freeway to prevent forage fires.

Many ranching roads become eroded drainages.

A fence set in bedrock in the Sierra foothills, central California. Fence builders killed most of the cryptogams on the right.

A large stock tank on BLM range in Coconino County, Arizona. Note the size of the van at center-right.

A trailer for hauling horses and cattle. Intensive activity on wet soil here has damaged the soil and created a sacrifice area.

Notice the roadside fenceline contrast here, but also understand that most of the scenic landscape in the background is damaged. The gated culvert doubles as a stock underpass.

Hundreds of thousands of sacrifice areas are virtual moonscapes. Note that a pipe exclosure protects the storage tank from cattle damage.

Another cattle tank sacrifice area. A solar heater helps prevent ice capping so cattle may exploit the range in winter. (Some tanks are propane-heated.)

Corrals, pens, chutes, and ramps on BLM land.

A 2-mile-long pipeline feeds this cattle water trough. *(BLM)*

Fencelines cleared through thick brush harm the land both directly and by providing increased access to cattle and humans.

A culvert and the fill of a ranching road on right; new and obsolete fences on left.

A new cattle tank being constructed in the Coconino National Forest in central Arizona. This tank is sponsored by taxpayers, as are by far most stock tanks on public land.

A water pipeline for cattle being installed on BLM land.

A water pipeline leads over this hill to a stock tank on public land beyond. Note the roadside fenceline contrast in foreground.

Range developments allow ranchers to more fully exploit public land.

A portion of a soil erosion control project on BLM cattle range in central New Mexico. Such projects are not linked to ranching by BLM.

Long after it was herbicided to recreate grassland lost to livestock grazing, this once heavily vegetated portion of Avra Valley, Arizona, remains a wasteland. Tens of millions of acres of Western range have been herbicided to increase or maintain livestock grazing levels. *(Terrance Moore.)*

A tank sacrifice area. The windmill is supplemented by an electric pump. Note the roadside fence, fenceline contrast, firebreak, cattle trail, and ravaged range.

A galvanized iron water tank for cattle in the Black Hills National Forest, western South Dakota.

An auxillary public lands ranching operation concentrates livestock and human damage on this canyon bottom. Most of the riparian area here has been destroyed.

Tens of thousands of miles of destructive firebreaks "protect" ranchland often so denuded by livestock that it cannot carry fire. As always, note the fenceline contrast. California BLM.

Cattle create numerous parallel trails as they move through a saddle to and from an artificial water source and forage areas. Again, note the roadside fenceline.

Ranching damage surrounds a half-acre exclosure at high elevation in a Utah National Forest.

A stock tank, roadside fence and contrast, and depleted range. Note the lack of lower branches on the trees.

Deforestation for cattle in Kaibab National Forest in northern Arizona. Both sides of the fence are badly overgrazed.

CHAPTER V
LIVESTOCK SUFFER, TOO

I gave three distinct grounds for believing that nonhuman animals feel pain: behavior, the nature of their nervous system, and the evolutionary usefulness of pain.
--Peter Singer, **Animal Liberation**

A new health food store recently opened here in Tucson. The largest "natural" foods store in town, its immaculate shelves are well-stocked with everything from non-factory- farmed eggs to "Save the Whale" soap.

The meat/poultry/fish section of this "ranch market" is a big customer draw and features as its main attraction "the finest range-fed beef available -- 100% Rocky Mountain Pure." A colorful handout on the meat counter details how these beef cattle "graze on unfertilized mountain pastures, drink from snow-melt streams, breathe crystal clear mountain air, and are raised in a completely natural environment." On the cover, beautiful and rugged Colorado mountains sweep majestically into a deep blue sky. The foreground is filled by a large meadow scattered with cattle. The meadow is badly trampled and overgrazed.

Apparently many customers think so, for they buy this higher-priced range-fed beef not only because they believe it is "a clean, healthy alternative" but because "the cows don't suffer." If they only knew.

Most of us are comfortable with the familiar pastoral scenes where seemingly contented cows graze in the grassy countryside. Few of us consider that most of our images derive from memories of small, carefully fenced, well-watered private pastures. Even there most of the animals actually lead short and uncomfortable lives, but livestock on the open Western range generally have it much worse.

In cattle on range the first symptom is partial or complete blindness. This is followed by, or accompanied with, inability to use the tongue or swallow. The disease is termed "paralyzed tongue." Because of blindness, animals may wander aimlessly until exhausted, or stand and push against a solid object in their path for hours. Because of inability to swallow, animals may stand in water, unable to drink or they may try unsuccessfully to crop forage. Animals become thin and weak and die if treatment is not undertaken.
--Description of tansy mustard poisoning from "Poisonous Range Plants of New Mexico," New Mexico State University Cooperative Extension Service

Cattle commonly are turned out onto the open range in spring or summer, basically to fend for themselves, and then rounded up after the growing season. In some areas they are left on the range year-round. Generally sheep are more closely watched, often herded, although shepherds usually must each watch over hundreds or even thousands of sheep.

It is ironic that because most Western range is overgrazed and/or otherwise degraded, range livestock must cope with most of

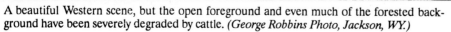
A beautiful Western scene, but the open foreground and even much of the forested background have been severely degraded by cattle. *(George Robbins Photo, Jackson, WY.)*

Granted, the meat from these animals usually is superior to that produced exclusively on crowded pastures and feedlots (and this particular ranch is widely considered the most organic large operation in the West). But do these cows really lead a life of pleasure in Rocky Mountain Paradise?

the same problems that wild animals do. But because these domesticated animals are unnaturally manipulated and have had much of their original instinct, intelligence, and agility bred out of them, they often are unable to do so. They frequently die or suffer due to starvation; thirst; exposure;

physical injuries; infections from foxtails, stickers, and thorns; poisonous plants; snake bites; lightning; fires (sheep especially); predators; disease and parasites -- problems most of which are much less common to the generally healthier and more closely supervised livestock on small private pastures.

For example, as I write this now in Tucson thousands of cattle on nearby overgrazed rangeland are dying of thirst and starvation, many with their mouths filled with spines from the cactus they ate. Cattle dying from thirst or starvation on the Western range is common, especially during prolonged dry spells and harsh winters when deep snow covers forage for long periods. Further, mostly because palatable plants on Western ranges have been depleted and toxic plants spread, annual range livestock mortality from poisonous plants averages 2%-5% (Holechek 1989); each year tens of thousands of range cattle and sheep suffer torturous poisoning deaths. Some cattle become addicted to locoweed and consequently die from starvation or thirst as they give up food and water in favor of the narcotic contained in the plant. Likewise, many range stock succumb to deficiencies or excesses of minerals. Others die from exposure during blizzards, extreme cold, or heat. Some become entangled in fences or loose barbed wire which strangles, maims, or holds them until they die from thirst, starvation, or exposure. Others die from drowning, quicksand, or falls.

This cow -- like 2%-5% of all range livestock annually -- ate too much toxic vegetation.

In fact, range livestock mortality from causes other than predation averages roughly 10% annually. An additional 2% of losses are blamed on predators; thus **roughly 12% of stock animals on the open range die from "natural" causes each year** (sheep losses are higher than cattle losses). Probably a larger percentage suffer from these hazards without dying.

(Jan Rogers)

This cow may have succumbed to disease or toxics from a nearby mineral spring.

Additionally, many range livestock are shot by hunters who mistake them for "game" animals, who don't like them competing with "game," or who simply want to shoot something big. Usually the animals are only wounded and amble off to suffer and perhaps die later. Others are shot or poisoned by people who don't want livestock on public land and by angry landowners who have suffered livestock damage. Also, hundreds, perhaps thousands, are poached annually. And thanks largely to "open range" laws that allow livestock to roam practically anywhere, thousands of cattle and sheep are injured or killed annually by vehicles on Western roadways.

This calf starved on a barren, overgrazed range. *(Steve Johnson)*

Bleeding at four points on its body, a big bull calf bucks to its feet and plunges headlong into a nervous wall of cattle at the far end of the corral. What [the rancher] had just done to that bull is enough to make any man cringe.
--1-22-82 *Wall Street Journal* (Ferguson 1983)

In addition to the above-mentioned hardships, ranchmen themselves subject range livestock to numerous brutalities, many of which originated with barbarous Spanish stockmen centuries ago. Animals are branded with hot irons, dehorned, castrated, and mutilated in the ears, cheeks, and neck for identification. They may be shocked, pushed, prodded, punched, roped, rounded up, dragged, kicked, whipped, and beaten. They are trucked great distances without adequate food, water, shelter, or rest, causing animals discomfort, injury, and death. (Trucking livestock to and from public grazing areas is increasingly common.) They may be injected, fed, dipped, sprayed, and otherwise treated with various insecticides, fungicides, fumigants, antibiotics, minerals, chemicals, and fertility drugs. Some suffer reproductive failure, birth deformity, bodily impairment, illness, and death from herbicides and pesticides sprayed on rangeland.

And, a fall from a cliff onto these boulders proved fatal to this cow.

These stockmen are violently jabbing, beating, and kicking the cattle in this trailer -- ordinary behavior on the Western range.

Range cattle usually mate when their owners allow them to and with whom their owners provide, not as they would naturally. Occasionally, beef cattle are artificially inseminated. Difficult or slow births may be assisted with clamps, hooks, pry bars, ropes, and even blocks and tackle. Though many ranchers have become proficient with these tools, most lack the knowledge or desire to minimize trauma to the animals, who frequently die from complications.

Young calves are vaccinated against disease present in their grazing areas. Still, many contact disease or suffer protein and other deficiencies while nursing from their ill or emaciated mothers. Calves are usually weaned by separation from their mothers at 6 to 8 months of age, rather than the 10-12 months Nature intended.

When large animals are dehorned there may be excessive bleeding. If this occurs, you may pick up the main artery on the underside of the cut with forceps and pull it until it breaks. The broken artery goes back into the softer tissues and usually bleeding stops.
--from *Beef Cattle Husbandry Study Course*, USDA

Most cattle are dehorned at an early age to prevent future damage to valuable beeves, hides, and cowboys, and because dehorned cattle are considered easier to handle (they cannot defend themselves as well). Younger calves are roped and held down; larger animals are restrained in dehorning chutes, pinch gates, squeeze pens, and cattle stocks, or thrown against and tied to any large, sturdy object. Usually horns are simply sawed or clipped off, though they may be burned off with hot irons or gouged out with patented dehorning spoons and tubes. All these methods are extremely painful. Sometimes caustic chemicals are applied to the horn area of young calves to prevent horn growth. When rain follows, or when the job is improperly done, the chemical gets into and burns the calves' eyes, sometimes blinding them.

Dehorning is such a shock to a body that often the animal will lose weight and not regain it until a week or two later. Cracked and slivered skull bones and lacerated blood vessels are not uncommon. Some animals even die from excessive bleeding, infection, or resultant parasites or introduced disease.

Most young male cattle are castrated, thereafter becoming "steers." The main reason this is done is that castrated cattle are more lethargic, therefore easier to handle and apt to gain more weight. Also, castration precludes unplanned breeding, prevents animals from developing well-proportioned, less profitable bodies, and is alleged to produce more tender, flavorful meat. Almost all castration is done by ranchers themselves, usually with knives. The scrotum is slit lengthwise or the lower portion cut away entirely, the testicles pulled out and cut or yanked off. (Men: Do you think this would hurt??) After these procedures, the animals often cry, lie down, and kick for an hour or more. Pain killers are not used. Other methods of castration include clamping off the testicles with a rubber ring called an "elastrator" or severely crushing the cords and blood vessels above the testicles with special pincers, after which the testicles eventually waste away for want of circulation. Or, the whole appendage may simply be severed with a pocket knife. As with dehorning, castration sometimes results in

excessive bleeding or infection and, in rare cases, death. Some cattlemen spay heifers, and most spaying is done by ranchers themselves, not veterinarians. The details of and complications arising from these operations are best left to the imagination.

Owners of livestock may treat animals belonging to them without being subject to penalties for practising veterinary medicine without proper licensing and permitting.
--Wyoming Statute 33-30-203(a)(i) and (v). (This law is similar to most in other Western states.)

Sheep commonly are "docked," that is, their tails are cut off, largely so droppings won't cling to their wool and draw flies. Docking is accomplished with knives, red-hot irons, chisels, crushing utensils (crushing rather than cutting reduces blood loss), pincers, and special constrictors which cut off the blood supply, whereafter the tail gradually atrophies and falls off.

Older sheep may also be subjected to "tooth-grinding," an operation some sheepmen think extends the productive life of sheep by improving their ability to crop short grass (sheep's teeth grow throughout their lives). Studies show this to be a false assumption; normal grazing prevents teeth from growing too long. In tooth grinding, a sheep is tied and gagged and its teeth reduced with pliers or some other tool. This may cause damage to gums or sensitive tooth pulp cavities, and thus extreme pain to the animal. (Clifton 1990)

To those who know the Western range, sheep shearers are notoriously brutal, but even the most well-intentioned shearers cause the animals much suffering. *(Dick Randall)*

In Western lore, sheep shearing is portrayed as a harmless, rustic activity. On the real range, accounts abound of mistreatment and cruelty by sheep shearers. Wool sheep are sheared each spring after lambing. If sheared too early in the season, they may succumb to exposure or associated disease. Because shearers often are hurried or careless, sheep sometimes are kicked and punched to subdue them, and they may have portions of their bodies cut or torn by shearing utensils.

Branding calves. *(Unknown)*

Ranchers take pride in their brands, for to them it is much more than a sign of ownership; it is a symbol of service -- a pledge of integrity of the man behind it and a mark of courage, character, and wisdom.
--from **Beef Cattle Science** by M.E. Ensminger (Ensminger 1968)

On the Western range, ownership, age, and breeding information are affixed on individual animals by means of branding, tagging, and bodily disfigurement. The most common method of establishing animal ownership is with brands. Each livestock operation has its own brand, which is registered with the state, similar to a copyright. No one else may legally use that brand. Usually the brand is burned permanently into the flesh of the animal's hip or thigh with a hot iron -- the celebrated *branding iron*. (This was also a favorite method of World War II Nazi torturers.) Many Western states *require* hot iron branding. Less commonly, the mark of ownership (and owner's courage, wisdom, etc.) is burned into the animal's flesh with caustic branding fluids. Some ranchers also brand cattle on their jaws or other body parts to indicate year of birth or other information.

Among other symbols of identification used on range livestock are earmarks. Ears are slit open with knives, or notches cut out with ear notchers. The types and number of disfigurements, location on ear, which ear, etc. indicate certain management information. Metal or plastic markers are also common, though less popular than mutilation. Clamped onto ears, they may rub or scratch the skin and cause infections or openings for parasite introduction. Quite often they fall or rub off and animals must be retagged; the colorful plastic numbers are a common sight lying in the dust on the open range.

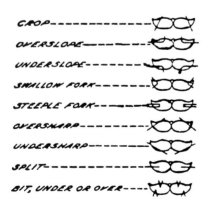

CROP
OVERSLOPE
UNDERSLOPE
SWALLOW FORK
STEEPLE FORK
OVERSHARP
UNDERSHARP
SPLIT
BIT, UNDER OR OVER

Nine common ear marks (mutilations) of cattle, from a stockman's handbook.

Other methods of identification: "Buds" are formed by slitting an animal's nose. "Dewlaps" are created by cutting a long flap from the loose skin of an animal's neck, so that the strip of skin hangs down as an identifying pendent. "Wattles" are made similarly by cutting a strip of skin down off the jaw bone.

The pendulous flaps on this cow's neck are "dewlaps."

The object of meat animal production is to deliver a salable animal at the packing house.
--Wesley Calef, **Private Grazing and Public Lands** (Calef 1960)

On top of all this, the vast majority of public lands cattle operations are geared to produce yearling heifers and steers ("feeder cattle") to send to commercial feedlots for fattening -- "building" as they say in the business -- before slaughter. So, **almost all public range cattle end up in feedlots**, along with most US cattle. Here they spend their last 100-120 days crammed together by the thousands (as many as 100,000), standing in their own excrement, with little or no shelter from the elements. They are fed a "hot" diet, high in concentrates and grains, scientifically designed to fatten them as quickly and cheaply as possible, supplemented with such delights as processed sawdust, feathers, newspaper, "plastic hay," sewage, tallow and grease, poultry litter, cement dust, cardboard scraps, and even their own excrement, all disguised with artificial flavors and aromas. They receive synthetic and natural hormones to make them grow fast -- as much as 3 pounds per day. From their terrible diet, crowding, unnatural living conditions, and mistreatment, animals commonly experience physical ailments and disease, for which they are given feed heavily laced with antibiotics. (For more on feedlots, see Mason 1980 or Fox 1986.)

Shipping fever is caused from multiple infection due to the interaction of viruses and bacteria, accentuated by environmental conditions creating physical tension or stress. Change in weather and feed, overcrowding, hard driving, lack of rest, and improper shelter all help usher in the disease.
--M.E. Ensminger, **The Stockman's Handbook** (Ensminger 1983)

A cattle feedlot. *(SCS,USDA)*

Whether from feedlot or directly from the range, in the US nearly all of the few million cattle grazed on public land at some time each year eventually end up at brutal commercial slaughterhouses, along with nearly all of the remaining roughly 35 million cattle produced exclusively on private land. They arrive tired, hungry, and dehydrated, often suffering from injuries and exposure from roundup, trucking, and mistreatment along the way; roughly 2 in 100 die in transit. (Globally, hundreds of thousands of sheep and cattle die during shipboard transport each year, and millions die during ground transport.)

The survivors are herded (or dragged behind a pickup truck, in the case of "cripples") into a noisy slaughtering building, where they witness others being killed and butchered before them. The slaughterhouse is filled with the screams of terrified animals; the brutal thump of the pneumatic hammer; the whir, whack, rip, and crunch of bodies being processed. The sticky air reeks of death. The cattle stand in line, awaiting the final insult. In the end, about 40% by weight of an average 800 pound cow becomes what we prefer to call "beef." [Apparently, life for the workers in these establishments is not much better; turnover rate and rate of injury are the highest for any profession in the US (Robbins 1987).]

A $1 hormone pellet transplant behind the ear means the animal [cow] *will consume approximately four fewer bushels of corn (a $20 savings) and reach market weight 18 days sooner (15% faster than if untreated).*
--**Beef** magazine

Feedlots and slaughterhouses make life on the range seem better, but do not be deceived; all are cruel components of the same industry. Also consider that nearly all steers and heifers (by far most cattle) spending time on public land live less than 2 years before slaughter, while breeding females are culled at around 8 to 10 years of age and breeding bulls at not much older. *Their ancient ancestors lived full lives as members of complex social herds for 20 to 25 years in the wild.*

Most ancestors from which contemporary cattle and sheep were developed established their particular species several million years ago. A wild ancestor of Eurasian cattle, the aurochs, was driven to extinction by hunting and habitat degradation in the late Middle Ages. Forebears of today's cattle are thought to have been domesticated some 9000 years ago in the Middle East. Ancestors of today's domestic sheep are the mouflon of Europe and urial of Asia; their domestication and herding began about 7000 years ago.

Since that time cattle and sheep have been extensively crossbred and inbred, and have lived unnatural lives of forced work and premature death. Today they little resemble in either appearance or behavior their ancient ancestors. In recent times hybridization has created decreasingly natural animals. Toxic chemicals common in today's livestock industry have also taken their toll on the animals' body and behavior. Today's cow and sheep, bred to be slow and to gain weight quickly, represent an ongoing experiment to maximize productiveness and minimize cost.

The rancher wants as many big, fat, docile, procreating animals as possible. Studies show that confined sheep and cattle expend about 30% less energy than free-ranging livestock (Holechek 1989). So even on the open range livestock are encouraged to minimize expended energy and weight loss. They are moved only when absolutely necessary, always slowly. Various injections and additives, castration, age and sex separation, fences, lack of predators, human mistreatment, and generally unnatural living situations all have created spiritless animals.

Further, many ranchers, feedlot operators especially, feed or inject their livestock with harmful tranquilizers, sex hormones, and steroids to induce them to gain more weight. Livestock "growth stimulators" include "Steer-oid," "Ralgro," and "Compudose."

"Improved" breeding techniques and genetic manipulation are other juicy carrots in front of ranchers' noses. Already the modern cow more resembles a huge, fat slug than a wild bovine. One is reminded of the futuristic Woody Allen comedy, *Sleeper*, with its 200-pound carrots and 10'-tall chickens. On the other hand, in northern Mexico, cross-breeding and genetic engineering have produced a profitable 3-foot-tall, 300-pound "minicow." According to the 2-28-88 *Denver Post*, "Ten minicows can graze on less than 3 acres of land [in this portion of northern Mexico], the area one normal cow requires."

Cross-breeding and genetic manipulation are cruel to the animals being tested, and often lead to gross deformities and birth defects. While some "preferred" characteristics may be passed to following generations, so too are new flaws that may go unnoticed or are ignored by the experimenters.

Advanced biotechnology now offers cloning, gene splicing, sex determination, and more as Woody Allen-sized carrots in front of the ranching establishment's nose.

As one example of the lengths to which the industry will go to make a buck, Donald Johnson, a biologist from Colorado State University, is (with tax money) experimenting with drugs called ionophores, growth enhancers similar to antibiotics. He knew that about 6% of what cattle eat is "wasted" in methane burps, and so theorized that if he could find a way to reduce bovine burping he could increase the efficiency of cattle growth. Says Johnson:

> Ionophores change the way cows ferment feed in the rumen by inhibiting certain kinds of microbes. In general, the ionophores worked well. We got the same growth with 6% to 7% less feed, and methane loss was decreased by 4% to 25%.

> On April 3, the US Patent and Trademark Office announced its intention to pursue a new interpretation of patent law which would allow patents to be granted on genetically-altered animals, with the exception of human beings.
> --The Animals' Agenda (Jul/Aug 1987)

Most of this chapter has focused on cattle, and indeed range cattle have fared somewhat worse than range sheep. Nonetheless, sheep experience most of the same open range and inflicted adversities described above, as do goats, horses, and other animals used for ranch stock. Various federal, state, and local laws and ordinances ostensibly protect the welfare of riding horses, dogs, cats, birds, and other pet and wild animals; however, due to the livestock industry's enormous power, few of these legalities apply to commercial "stock."

For example, if your neighbor repeatedly beats her horse, the horse could be impounded and the woman taken to court for animal abuse. However, if a rancher repeatedly beats his horse, even to death, the laws probably won't apply. If a troubled youngster tortures cats with a soldering iron, he breaks the law. Yet, thousands of public lands ranchers burn the flesh of millions of cattle and sheep each year with red hot irons, with the blessing of these same governments (as mentioned, many state laws even *require* hot iron branding). If a rural resident withholds food from his caged pet geese for weeks at a time, he may be subject to county legal proceedings. But if a rancher puts a hundred cattle onto an overgrazed range and half of them starve to death, then the government gives him emergency assistance.

In fact, because livestock deaths are considered a business loss entitling the owner to a tax break, some ranchers *intentionally* starve animals to death. For example, multimillionaire public lands rancher John Jay Casey deliberately starved to death many hundreds of his cattle for tax write-offs and habitually mistreated his animals. Over the years he was charged with hundreds of counts of animal cruelty. Yet he has been criminally charged only 4 times, resulting in 3 misdemeanor convictions and fines of a few thousand dollars. (Bowman 1987)

Try this experiment: Next time you see animal abuse, report it to the relevant city or county authorities. They will advise you of the animal protection law that applies to the situation and may even investigate. Then, find the worst case of range cattle or sheep abuse you can. Report it to the same authorities. They will at first be surprised and confused, and eventually will refer you to your state livestock board. Call the state livestock board and you will talk with a secretary who is similarly befuddled and knows little about livestock abuse legislation. If you are "lucky," you will to talk to one of the livestock board members, most of whom are ranchers. He (they're always men) will treat your concern for a lowly stock animal with controlled bemusement, or hostility, then more or less tell you that animal protection laws generally don't apply to livestock.

A few do, but since the state livestock boards administer livestock statutes, complaining does little good. Direct mistreatment and indirect abuse of livestock is omnipresent on the Western range, yet attempts to prevent it nearly always go nowhere.

> *Cows have got to be
> the most blantless creatures on earth.
> I mean, we eat them.
> We drink them.
> We wear them.
> They don't bite.
> Hell, they don't even shit on the sidewalk.*
>
> --from the movie *Endangered Species*

Ranchers treat their "stock" animals like meat-production units, like raw materials to be transformed into packaged goods, like "living factories," as one range professional put it. They have always considered cattle and sheep as growing, moving *products*, not feeling beings with lives of their own.

Unfortunately, ranchers are partly correct. Thanks to the industry's manipulative efforts, the modern cow and sheep, through no fault of their own, have lost many of their animal qualities. No longer are they physiologically or psychologically prepared for life. For example, the cow is one of the few animals on Earth that stands and sits in its own excrement, even on the open range, or evacuates its bowels in its own water. Cows and sheep make comparatively easy prey, and sheep especially are pathetically helpless against many predators. Cattle drift great distances during inclement weather and have a poor sense of territory. Unlike buffalo and other wild herd animals, cattle drift *with*, rather than against, prevailing storm winds, so they tend to move along with storms. They seldom paw snow off the ground in search of winter forage as do elk, deer, pronghorn, and horses. Their closest Western relatives, buffalo, thrust their heads into the snow and sweep their heads side to side, exposing large patches of forage, while cattle starve to death. Compared to wildlife, livestock also are ill-prepared for harsh winters because they have thin hides, store less fat for the winter, and their metabolic rate doesn't slow down nearly as much. When encountering a fence, a cow may walk back and forth until exhausted. When caught in a wildfire, it may stand in one place and roast to death, rather than flee or find protective cover; sheep frequently burn to death in fires, sometimes in great numbers. Cattle are bulkier, slower, less agile, and more obtuse than any large American ungulate. Unattended cattle on the open range usually die within a few years in most areas, while domestic sheep usually don't survive in the wild more than a few months without human assistance.

While domestication, intensive management, and manipulative breeding have created ever bulkier and more efficient livestock "eating machines," so have they created ever more awkward and lifeless animals.

Cows and sheep have devastated the West, but they are not to blame. They are only pawns in a deadly game of maximum profits. And, yes, they are animals and should be treated with respect. Yet, they are less truly *alive* than wildlife and should not have priority over wildlife in natural areas, on public land especially.

I sit on the downed tree and watch the black steers slip on the creek bottom. They are all bred beef: beef heart, beef hide, beef hocks. They're a human product like rayon. They're like a field of shoes. They have cast-iron shanks and tongues like foam insoles. You can't see through to their brains as you can with other animals; they have beef fat behind their eyes, beef stew.
--Annie Dillard, **Pilgrim at Tinker Creek** (Dillard 1974)

In conclusion, closing down feedlots and intensive pasture farms to instead raise livestock "out on the Western range" in a "natural" manner is nothing more than a wild pipe dream. As detailed above, open range ranching is very cruel to live stock. And, head-for-livestock-head, it is much more environmentally destructive.

Moreover, such a shift would be *impossible* -- an important consideration. It takes the public lands half of the West to produce only 3% of this country's beef, so it would take roughly *6 billion acres -- an area larger than North America* -- of comparable range to produce the beef produced by feedlots and intensive pasture farms. How can we squeeze 30 million cattle onto range that is now terribly overgrazed with the equivalent of only 1 or 2 million? Or, would it be better to cut down all forest in the Eastern US for pasture and increase US beef production by about 1/3? Now, reconsider that nearly 2/3 of the land area of the US is already used to produce livestock, and nearly all of this land that is grazable is already being grazed far beyond its carrying capacity. Obviously, open range livestock grazing is *not* a preferable, viable, or even compassionate alternative to factory farming or intensive pasture ranching.

If cattle and sheep must be produced in this country, they should be raised on farms in moist climates. They should be grazed very lightly on open, organic pastures, protected from predators, and when necessary brought into barns at night. They should remain physically, genetically, and (as much as possible) behaviorally unaltered. They should be treated well throughout their short lives and slaughtered locally in a compassionate manner. This is more how farmers in the East raised livestock for centuries, and, as long as meat animals are to be raised in this country, it is still the best way. To do so, we would, of course, have to drastically reduce livestock numbers.

Steve Allender of the National Cattlemen's Association . . . showed a list of strategies to the audience. First on the list was, "Don't educate the public." He said trying to argue the cattle industry's position too vigorously might raise the public's awareness . . . . The second strategy, Allender said, is "Deal with your strengths," that is work with the good public opinion [image] that farmers and ranchers have and try to reinforce it. The third strategy listed was . . . not to debate the extremists because it attracts attention which is currently focused on research laboratory animals, not cattle and sheep on the open range.
--11-21-90 *Laramie Daily Boomerang*, Laramie, Wyoming

Chapter VI
GLOBAL PERSPECTIVE

Cattle are the scourge of the Earth.
--Richard Rice, The Wilderness Society

The American West is world famous for cows and cow-men, perhaps more so than any other region on Earth. However, livestock production in less celebrated forms has a profound influence across the globe. To put Western ranching in perspective, to learn how it is interrelated with world livestock production, let's take a quick (and necessarily simplified) global livestock tour, starting with our overgrazed neighbor to the south:

Mexico is an incredible topographic labyrinth and includes everything from scorching deserts to pine-clad highlands to steamy jungles. The country shelters more than half of all migrating bird species in North America. It harbors the Earth's greatest array of reptile species and ranks second only to Indonesia in mammal species.

Cattle in the state of Sonora, Mexico. The new fence in the foreground is part of an intensified ranching development effort that includes devegetating and seeding millions of acres of lush aboriginal Sonoran desert and grassland.

A nearby area of Sonora not yet developed for ranching.

Unfortunately, Mexico is also one of the most degraded and threatened regions on Earth. With 90 million humans and 40 million cattle in only 1/5 the area of the US, it is overpopulated throughout. More than half of the country in nearly every landscape is grazed by livestock, and most of this land is plagued with overgrazing and ranching abuse. Many areas have been stripped of vegetative groundcover to bare dirt, and officials list accelerated soil erosion as one of Mexico's worst problems.

More than 60% of Mexico's original rainforest has been destroyed, largely to create cattle pastures, while overgrazing and brush and tree removal by ranchers keep it from growing back. Millions of acres of temperate and semi-arid tree and brush cover have likewise been eradicated. Predators such as jaguar, mountain lion, Mexican wolf, and bears have been eliminated from the vast bulk of their range, along with most other wildlife. To hint at the extent of ranching's environmental impact: Stockmen in Mexico and other tropical countries search out and kill millions of vampire bats in their roosts because the bats feed on cattle.

Due to human overpopulation, widespread poverty, and intensive competition for land, private land in Mexico has little protection from ranching. Due to these factors and general, institutionalized political corruption, Mexico's public land is likewise degraded. Additionally, more of Mexico's grain is fed to livestock than is eaten by people.

The [Mexican] jungle is burning, the great trees are being destroyed and the land is enveloped in a sinister darkness. No-one cares, people only seem to be thinking about the cattle.
--Gertrude Duby Blom, "The Jungle Is Burning," *Advance* magazine

To the east, in the **Caribbean Islands**, 1/4 to 1/2 of the land base of most islands has been deforested and converted to cattle pasture, with similarly tragic results. On **Espaniola**, where in 1493 Columbus introduced cattle, sheep, pigs, goats, and horses, only 9% of the forest that once covered nearly all of the island remains; much of the island continues to be overgrazed by cattle and goats. Cattle density in **Cuba** is among the highest on Earth, and much of the land is cattle pasture.

Throughout Central America, cattle grazing produces fewer benefits per unit of land deforested than any other form of land use. In Costa Rica, for example, the livestock cattle industry produces only $42 per square kilometer in export revenues, while the banana industry produces $6,036 on the same amount of land.
--Rainforest Action Network

The 7 nations comprising **Central America** cover only a tiny portion of the planet's surface, yet rank high in numbers of plant and animal species. **Costa Rican** cloud forest may support more species per unit of area than any place on Earth. A century ago, most of Central America was blanketed with luxuriant tropical rainforest, while the remainder was covered with drier tropical forest and mountain vegetation.

Today, fully half of Central America is cattle pasture, and about 2/3 of the region's arable land is dedicated to cattle production. Since 1960, over 40% of Central America's rainforest has been cut and converted to cow fields. Soil erosion and flooding are rampant.

As in most areas of the world where domestic livestock are grazed, Central American ranching is monopolized by a small number of powerful, wealthy ranching families. Also as in much of the world, these dominant land barons are a main cause of the region's long-standing social and political injustice. Contrary to popular opinion, they export only about 1/4 of Central America's beef, largely to the USA, where most of it ends up as fast-food hamburgers, lunch meat, hot dogs, and other processed meat. Most is eaten by Central America's urban elite.

In 1975 a United States reconnaissance satellite's heat sensor detected a sudden and intense warming of the Earth in the Amazon basin usually associated with an imminent volcanic eruption. A special alert mission was dispatched. And what did they find? A German multinational corporation burning down one million acres of tropical forest for a cattle ranch.
--Frances Moore Lappe, Food First (Lappe 1979)

Moving into **South America** we find an ongoing livestock catastrophe that dwarfs Central America's in total area. The **Amazon Basin** contains by far the Earth's largest contiguous rainforest. In what has been called "the biggest holocaust in the history of life," roughly 1/3 of the Amazon Basin's original rainforest has already been destroyed -- beginning when Europeans arrived in the 1500s, but occurring mostly in the past 2 decades. Satellite photos show about 31,000 square miles -- an area the size of Maine -- of Brazilian rainforest being cleared annually. **An estimated more than 70% of Amazon deforestation is for cattle ranching,** though ranching is sometimes used as a cover for other types of exploitation. Currently, there are more than 50,000 separate livestock operations in Amazonia.

Typically, prospective ranchers chainsaw, bulldoze, or chain all trees in large blocks of forest, allow the slash to dry, and then burn it. (Satellites have detected as many as 7000 fires burning in the Amazon in one day.) Soon thereafter, grass, forbs, shrubs, and small trees colonize the burned areas and the cattle are brought in. According to the Rainforest Action Network:

Unfortunately (or perhaps fortunately), these "instant cow pastures" don't last more than a few years. The nutrient-poor topsoil is soon depleted, and the land degrades from lush jungle to scraggly desert. Then the cattlemen move on to the next forest.

Recent evidence indicates that these ravaged areas are somewhat more resilient than at first thought. However, they are rarely allowed to recover, and are usually grazed until no longer able to support cattle, commonly a decade or two. When finally abandoned, they are beyond the point of recovering to anywhere near their original condition.

As part of an intensive national development program begun in the early 1970s, the Brazilian government (like the US) spent billions of tax dollars to encourage cattle production in the Amazon, offering free or cheap land, little or no taxes, and other assistance. According to a *Nature* TV documentary, "Rainforest ranchers stay in business only because of government subsidies." As with US public lands, Amazon destruction has little justification; only 3%-4% of Brazilian beef is produced there.

And as with "Indians" in the USA's Old West, thousands of indigenous Amazonians are being displaced by ranching and killed by introduced disease and alcohol. Many native resisters have been murdered outright by wealthy rancher "god-fathers" and their hired "pistoleros," as was recently Chico Mendez, the highly respected rainforest defender. Those local inhabitants who depend on sustainable forest products, such as rubber and Brazil nuts, likewise are victims of this relentless ranching onslaught (Amazonian Manifest Destiny?).

The planet's most species-diverse bioregion is quickly being devastated. At the present rate of deforestation, the Amazon rainforest will be all but gone within several decades.

I am a **rancher,** *and I will live like a* **rancher,** *even if the ecologist doesn't agree. . . . We* **ranchers** *are the biggest ecologists!*
--Darly Alves, powerful Amazonian stockman whose son recently admitted to having hired a professional killer to murder Chico Mendez, TV series The Reporters, 11-18-89

Even though a world-wide outcry today could conceivably save much of the Amazon, livestock production has already extensively damaged most of the remaining 2/3 of South America. Most of **eastern** and **southern Brazil, Uruguay,** and **Argentina** -- an area larger than the Amazon -- is heavily overgrazed and damaged by ranching developments. Here are more than 150 million cattle, perhaps 80 million sheep, and the world's most extensive intensive ranching area. This is where "gauchos" are the celebrated equivalent of US Western cow-boys. Most native animals, including the strange, humpless camels that grazed the plains when the Portuguese and Spanish arrived with their livestock 400 years ago, are gone, and surviving vegetation bears little resemblance to aboriginal grassland, semi-grassland, or other vegetation types. On the Argentine *Pampa*, for example, less than 1/4 of the remaining vegetation is native.

To increase forage, stockmen also have destroyed much of the region's original deciduous to semi-deciduous forest and scrub. Brazil's southern and eastern states, which encompasses more than half of the country, have lost more than 95% of their original Atlantic tropical forest cover, more to ranching than any other factor. Corn is the region's major crop, but roughly 1/3 of the corn is fed to livestock, along with major portions of its wheat, soybeans, and other crops.

In the northern portion of the continent, about half of both **Colombia** and **Venezuela** -- mostly the vast *llanos*, or plains -- are now dedicated primarily to 35 million cattle. Much tree and brush cover likewise has been cleared here to promote forage, and for cropland -- about 1 million acres per year in Colombia alone, where 25% of all land is said to have "serious" soil erosion problems. Predators and competing herbivores have been eliminated, along with most native wildlife.

Sheep, alpaca, goat, and cattle grazing is prevalent throughout most of the 6000-mile-long **Andes Mountains**, from the Caribbean shore to Tierra del Fuego. The UN identifies this region as one of the world's most threatened by pastoralism. The arid to semi-arid high plains and valleys, and some of the drier lowlands, are especially vulnerable to livestock damage, and much has been divested of nearly all plantlife. Native Andean camels -- llamas, vicunas, and guanacos -- once roamed the grassy high plateaus by the tens of millions, but livestock grazing has so ruined their habitat and sheep and goat ranchers and herders slaughtered so many of them as competitors that, despite recent recoveries, the llama and guanaco remain at only small fractions of their aboriginal numbers; the vicuna was listed as Endangered in 1969 before making its modest recovery under special protection. (All 3 are now semi-domesticated in most areas.) As with the California condor, two of the biggest threats to the Andean condor -- of which only about 1500 remain -- are livestock grazing and shooting and poisoning by stock raisers, who are likewise the main killers of other large predators and smaller competitors in most of the Andes.

Portions of the drier lowlands and west coast are also overgrazed, as is about half of **Bolivia**, from mountaintops down to rainforest. The US Embassy in Bolivia reports forest cover being removed at roughly 3/4 million acres per year, largely for livestock, and that overgrazing is changing river flows, stripping topsoil, and desertifying the land: "On the *Altiplano* [high plains], grazing animals remove virtually all plantlife."

Off southern Argentina in the Atlantic, Great Britain's **Falkland Islands** are little more than an overgrazed 6000-square-mile sheep ranch.

Out in the vast Pacific, many oceanic islands once covered with lush vegetation have been devegetated by or for goats, sheep, cattle, and/or feral pigs and goats. For example, **Easter Island** (famous for its huge, mysterious monoliths), now desertlike throughout, is thought to have once been mostly tree covered. Whether the forests were originally cut more for wood or to promote livestock grazing is uncertain, but livestock subsequently prevented them from growing back by eating saplings. **St. Helena**, in the South Atlantic, met a similar fate. In the South Pacific, more than half of 300-mile-long **New Caledonia** and about 1/3 of the 7000-square-mile **Fiji Islands** have been cleared and turned into pasture.

Small islands are particularly susceptible to livestock damage because they usually contain relatively simple ecosystems with fewer natural limiting factors (large predators, diseases, etc.) and lack adjacent terrestrial ecosystems to buffer impacts, allow wildlife to escape to, reintroduce extirpated species, etc. Ranching and feral livestock have upset the ecological balance on hundreds of small islands around the world. For example, goats introduced to Baja California's **San Benito Islands** and California's **San Clemente Island** multiplied without restraint and quickly transformed these botanical wonderlands into wastelands.

Back in the South Pacific, we move on to **New Zealand**, world-renowned for its sheep. With about 100,000 square miles, 80 million sheep, and 8 million cattle, New Zealand has the world's highest livestock density -- equivalent to about 1200 sheep per square mile. Much of the island nation is steep, rugged, densely forested, or otherwise unproductive for livestock, so density in areas actually grazed approaches 2000 sheep per square mile!

Were New Zealand not well-watered and lushly vegetated, it could not support even a fraction of these animals. However, environmental damage here can only be described as extreme. About half of the country now resembles an immense golf course covered chiefly with exotic vegetation. Forests that once blanketed most of the islands have been reduced to 5% of their original coverage. In large portions of the North Island "slips" -- or huge sections of topsoil -- are sliding off the overgrazed hills. In the worst areas, former subtropical and temperate forest is now virtual desert. Most of New Zealand's unique animal life is gone, and some species are extinct or in danger of extinction, due largely to livestock grazing and ranching practices. On this biologically isolated island realm -- where bats are the only native mammals -- the impact of nearly 100 million large, hooved quadrupeds is understandably profound.

New Zealand's big neighbor to the northwest, **Australia**, is grazed by twice as many sheep -- 160 million, or a population 8 times greater than the continent's human population. By far most of these are raised in the interior eastern third, while some are grazed on the far western grasslands and Mediterranean scrub. The island continent is also home to some 30 million cattle, most being raised along the relatively moist eastern coast. However, most of the remainder of Australia is also grazed by cattle and sheep; generally, livestock density decreases toward the arid, barren heart of the continent. Altogether more than 2 million of Australia's 3 million square miles are grazed. Ranching is impossible on most of the remainder because large portions of the interior are too dry and barren (partly as a result of past overgrazing), and some of the northern tropical forest is too dense.

Of all land uses ranching easily causes Australia's greatest environmental damage. The huge land mass drifted away to form "the island continent" more than 100 million years ago, before the evolution of large ungulates on the contiguous continents, so Australia never felt a hard hoof until 200 years ago when Europeans arrived with their cattle and sheep. In other words, the Australian environment did not evolve to include *any* hooved animals, much less domestic livestock.

Overgrazing has reduced or extirpated native vegetation throughout much of the continent and replaced it with more than 800 species of exotic "weeds," and bare dirt. About 3300 native plants are now considered rare or endangered, and more than 100 are extinct largely as a result. Cryptogamic crusts have disappeared in many areas. Soil erosion has increased tremendously; consequently, huge dust storms sometimes roll out of the overgrazed interior and over coastal cities. Natural water sources are greatly diminished, and soil salinity continues to rise. Cattle dung produces billions of troublesome bush flies. Sheep and cattle have eaten and trampled many small mammals and others out of food and shelter. So far, 18 of Australia's mammals are extinct and 40 are endangered, due more to ranching than any other factor.

Extreme overgrazing, especially by sheep, promotes massive grasshopper "invasions" and incredible population explosions of feral European hares. The exotic hare is now the most populous mammal in Australia, eating approximately 1/12 as much as the nation's livestock. Also helping to lay waste to the continent are many feral ungulates, spread largely by ranching -- an estimated 300,000 horses, 1.5 million burros, 570,000 cattle, 7 million pigs, 150,000 water buffalo, and 35,000 camels.

In their attempt to maximize production, Australian stockmen have degraded the land perhaps as much as their livestock. Ranching "improvements," including roads, are the most visible and harmful developments throughout most of the Australian outback. Millions of acres of brush, eucalyptus and other trees around the continent have been cut, chained, bulldozed, burned, herbicided, etc. for livestock; largely for this reason, less than half of Australia's aboriginal tree cover remains. Millions of acres of forestland in the north currently are being cleared for cattle and water buffalo. Denudation of woody vegetation, along with slaughter by ranchers and a drastic reduction of grass from overgrazing, has caused many of the smaller of the 62 species of Australian kangaroos to become endangered or extinct. Each year an estimated 3 million large kangaroos (and many other herbivores) are killed legally, plus an equal number illegally, mostly by or for ranchers to reduce grazing competition. Wallabies and pademelons once roamed the grasslands of Australia; today, due to overgrazing and attrition from ranchers, few survive but on offshore islands. Australia's primary large predator, the coyote-like dingo, is considered vermin and killed by the thousands annually. Ranchers slaughter millions of competing feral hares, but to help kill off the rodents they introduced European red foxes, stoats, and domestic cats, which now number in the millions and kill off burrowing marsupials and other natives as well.

The Australian ranching establishment is strikingly similar to that of the US West. The government leases grazing to a handful of powerful, wealthy stockmen, who essentially control about half of Australia with ranches of tens or hundreds of thousands of acres each. They pay only token grazing fees and are heavily subsidized by numerous direct and obscure means. Yet, they commonly represent themselves to the public as poor, dusty, downtrodden stockfolks; Crocodiel Dundees; or John Waynes.

As in the USA's Old West and now in Brazil's Amazon, the native peoples, here the Aborigines, are being forced from their homeland and into poverty, disease, and alcoholism, while their land -- their source of food, water, and other necessities -- is ravaged by overgrazing and range development. According to a recent *National Geographic* article, "Whites came in and killed any game they wanted, but when an Aborigine speared a sheep or calf he was an outlaw."

Australia is said to hold the world's record for environmental destruction relative to the size of human population -- 11 acres of land significantly damaged per human inhabitant. Livestock production is by far the main factor giving it this dubious distinction.

Moving north, to the equatorial west Pacific region, we find as yet relatively little livestock production, except sheep pasture on **Sumatra** and cattle pasture on **Java**, a large island with one of the world's highest concentrations of humans. Partly as a result, soil erosion, siltation, and flooding are serious on these 2 islands. However, the **Indonesian region** is the wettest large area on the planet, and though logging is increasing dramatically in some areas, most of the region is still covered with dense rainforest, on **Borneo** and **New Guinea** in particular. Unfortunately, to reduce population pressure on some islands, the Indonesian government is encouraging expanded settlement, including clearing of rainforest for livestock. An estimated 1 million acres of the island country are deforested annually.

The Philippines a few centuries ago was covered with one of the most prolific rainforests on Earth. Today, little rainforest remains and more than 1/3 the area of The Philippines is cattle pasture. Remaining rainforest is falling faster than almost anywhere else in the tropics, mostly for timber, but as elsewhere around the globe livestock and their owners prevent reforestation in many areas.

Japan also has several million cattle. Much of the land in its southern islands is dedicated to pasture.

Commercial livestock production on mainland **Southeast Asia** is limited mostly to **Thailand** and **Burma**, where much of the fertile lowland is used to produce about 20 million cattle. Still, livestock raising is spreading in the region where forests are cut, and the animals eat and trample young trees and prevent reforestation. Forest covered 80% of Thailand only 40 years ago; today, the 20% remaining is quickly being destroyed. When forested areas cleared for farming lose productivity, often they are converted to livestock production rather than being allowed to reforest. Also, over 2 million acres of former Thai forest now grow cassava, a fruit exported to feed European cattle. Water buffalo are raised as work animals throughout much of Southeast Asia, but they do much less harm than commercial livestock production.

There are nearly 1.5 million square kilometres of desert in China [16% of the nation] *including the Gobi Desert.... It is estimated that 1000 square kilometres are lost to desertification in China each year and that 85 per cent of the desert area of the country was caused in the first place by overgrazing, deforestation and excessive cultivation.*
--from *China Reconstructs* (Vol. 36[2], Feb 1987)

China ranks second both in world sheep and goat production. More than 120 million of the wooly animals graze nearly every portion of the US-sized country, while tens of millions of goats browse and graze generally the more rugged portions. The heaviest concentrations of both are in the north-central region and northern Manchuria, where accelerated soil erosion is nearly universal, plant cover is severely depleted, and nearly all large native animals are gone. The Chinese government recently implemented a massive grass and tree planting program to stem desertification in the north, but most of the grass dies and only about 10% of the trees reach maturity; livestock often eat the new grasses and tree saplings. Chinese scientist Zhu Zhenda reports in *Beijing Review* that "unless urgent measures are taken" desertification in China will consume an additional 200,000 square miles -- more than twice the size of Taiwan -- by the year 2000.

Most of west China is dry, and 2/3 of the region is utilized by nomadic sheep and goat herders; damage here is considerable. In the southwest, before the invasion of Mao's People's Liberation Army in 1950, Tibet had one of the most successful systems of environmental protection of any peopled region on Earth; Tibetan Buddhism extoled compassion for all life and forbade killing animals. The new regime, however, established collective farms and widespread intensive livestock grazing. Predators and competing animals, even moles and marmots, were slaughtered. Livestock numbers have risen 10-fold in many areas, and where large numbers of antelope, gazelles, musk deer, wild sheep and asses, wolves, foxes, leopards, and bear once roamed, huge herds of domestic sheep and yaks now graze. Recent expeditions through the region report denuded ranges, serious soil erosion, and virtually no wildlife. According to the UN, the Himalayan region is one of the most endangered ecosystems on Earth, largely from livestock production.

East China, where nearly a billion humans live, is mostly highly developed farmland. Nearly all of the nation's 60 million cattle are grazed on pasture and cropland there; altogether, about 1/3 of eastern China is grazed. However, pigs are China's primary meat animal (although most Chinese eat little meat), and more than 300 million are raised -- 40% of the world total and 5 times more than any other country. Relative to the amount of meat produced, Chinese pig production is much more efficient and less environmentally harmful than is cattle, sheep, and goat production.

North of China is **Mongolia**, an Alaska-sized, sparsely populated, semi-independent Soviet territory. Nomadic herding here is nearly omnipresent, and most of this cold, dry, barren land (original home of the tumbleweed) has been extensively damaged by livestock grazing. Recent research on the steppes of Inner Mongolia reveal a desertification rate among the highest on Earth.

Nearly half of the immense **Soviet Union** is cold northern forest, so livestock grazing in this nation is confined mostly to the southern and western regions -- still an area larger than the US. Here are broken woodlands, vast grassy steppes, extensive marshes, expansive deserts, 125 million cattle, and 160 million sheep. Globally, the USSR ranks first in number of sheep and second behind only India in number of cattle. About half of the mid-section and nearly all of the southern portion of the country are ranched or farmed for livestock, with a heavy environmental impact. For example, the saiga, a strange goat-like animal with short, straight horns and a large, thick snout, roamed mid-Asia by the tens of millions before being driven nearly to extinction by livestock production and overhunting. Now propagated as a stock animal, the semi-domesticated saiga population is about 1 million.

Large portions of central Asian USSR have been turned dry and barren by decades of overgrazing. Massive grass- and tree-planting restoration efforts here try to stem the tide. However, the cattle population increase in the USSR and **eastern Europe** in the second half of this century has been the highest of any region on Earth, as more and more grain is fed to livestock instead of people, more land is devoted to grazing, and rangeland is more heavily developed and stocked.

Scattered across the northern Soviet Union, semi-nomadic herders raise semi-domesticated reindeer across nearly 4000 linear miles of Arctic tundra and boreal forest. Modern breeding and handling practices and overstocking cause overgrazing in many areas, while related predator kills, developments, and human encroachment also damage these fragile Arctic to sub-Arctic ecosystems.

An Indian with a decorated sacred cow. *(BLM)*

India probably is the most overgrazed large country. With nearly 200 million cattle (15% of the world total), 50 million sheep, 17% of the world's goats, and other livestock competing with more than 800 million humans in an area only a little larger than the contiguous 11 western US states, the situation is critical. Though most of the Indian subcontinent is well-watered with monsoon rains and is naturally one of the most productive regions on Earth for humans and wildlife, livestock have rendered much of the country desertlike -- what is termed a "wet desert." Even the Great Thar Desert in northwest India does not have a truly arid climate, but has been turned into barren waste mostly by livestock.

Livestock are nearly everywhere in India, and Hindu "sacred cows" wander freely, multiplying unchecked, eating and trampling the already overburdened environment. Throughout most of India, native wildlife has disappeared; soil erosion is severe; water tables are dropping; streams are being converted from year-long to seasonal flow; rivers flow with sediment; silt clogs reservoirs and irrigation canals; and flooding is increasing. Overgrazing and deforestation in the Himalayan watershed cause landslides, fill reservoirs with silt, lower water tables, and flood the Ganges Plain. Where once elephant, rhino, buffalo, gaur, lion, tiger, leopard, 8 species of deer and antelope, and many primates roamed in great numbers, extinction, near-extinction, and scarcity are now the rule. For example, cattle and domestic buffalo are currently destroying the last tiny remnant of habitat of the endangered Asiatic lion. In southern India, cattle compete with and spread diseases to the last significant herds of wild Indian elephants, which also are killed as competitors by stock owners.

Little of India's original forest remains and what does is "intensely" overgrazed, according to government officials. Of the remaining 185 million acres of original forest (22%

of the country), 75 million lack tree cover and 25 million have only shrubs. Worse, satellite data show a loss of more than 3 million acres of Indian forest annually. Stock owners often fell whole trees to provide fodder to their hungry animals; saplings are eaten as soon as they sprout. Consequently, as do people in much of Asia, Africa, and Latin America, many Indians burn dry livestock dung for fuel -- at the further expense of the soil. But even dung is becoming scarce. In some areas people follow cattle around and compete for the plops as soon as they leave the animals' bodies; the winners dry their bounty in the sun.

Throughout most of India, cattle eat most edible plant material within reach. In some areas there is nothing left to eat, and their bloated bodies are seen being eaten by vultures or floating in the rivers, augmenting the manure, sediment, chemical, and sewage pollution. During droughts, they die by the hundreds of thousands. While people lie in the dust starving, children climb high into remaining trees to pull off leaves and twigs so cattle will not starve. In recent years, local governments have established fodder relief camps for starving cattle, much as they have food relief camps for starving people. India has extreme overpopulations of both humans and livestock; the populations of both have doubled since 1950.

The Great Thar Desert turns truly arid in neighboring **Pakistan**, where the huge southern Indus River Valley region receives only 4"-8" of precipitation annually. Scientific evidence indicates that several thousand years ago this region was covered with jungle -- even away from waterways -- and that livestock production has not only denuded vegetation but helped aridify the climate.

Moving west from Pakistan through the **Middle East** to **Turkey**, we find a rugged assortment of arid to semi-arid terrain, much of it mountainous. Nomadic herders (generally in the east) and livestock farmers (generally in the west) raise about 150 million sheep and uncounted millions of goats here on short grass, brush, small trees, and pasture. Turkey holds about a third of these animals, along with about 15 million cattle. From centuries of intensive pastoralism, most of the region is badly deteriorated.

Much of the "Holy Lands" of **Syria, Iraq, Lebanon, Israel, Jordan**, and the **Sinai Peninsula** once supported abundant grass and other vegetation, as well as wild animals. Millennia of overgrazing transformed most of the region into scenes of desolation. In *Conquest of the Land through 7,000 Years*, W.C. Lowdermilk relates how historic goat and sheep grazing "unleashed the forces of erosion" that "devastated" many areas. He describes how the forests that once covered much of Lebanon -- including the fabled "Cedars of Lebanon" -- were destroyed for building materials and, because livestock ate all small trees, never reestablished themselves, *except as 4 tiny groves protected by stone fences* from "the rapacious goats that graze down every accessible living plant on these mountains." (Lowdermilk 1975)

Large portions of the huge **Arabian Peninsula** are too dry, sandy, and barren for livestock, but evidence indicates that millennia of pastoralism is a contributor to this condition. Desertification appears to have progressed here for at least several centuries, but recently it has accelerated. Today, nomadic herders run domestic camels (a relatively less destructive trampler, though a more wide-spectrum eater), sheep, goats, and some cattle wherever they still can

-- on most of the subcontinent, especially the relatively moist southern highlands.

The Middle East generally has been overgrazed perhaps longer than any region on Earth; thus, desertification there has progressed to the point that little original soil, water, or wildlife remains. Contemporary grazing on about 3/4 of the region keeps it in a highly degraded condition.

We cross the Red Sea into **Africa**. Half of the world's livestock-dependent people live here, along with 15% of both the world's sheep and cattle and nearly 1/3 of all goats -- animals renowned for their ability to eat almost any plant (some kinds of goats can even *climb trees* to reach browse).

Africa's 183 million cattle, 197 million sheep, and 163 million goats are supported almost entirely by grazing and browsing. Most of the huge continent is used by livestock. Non-livestock Africa consists mostly of desolate portions of the Sahara, Namib, and Kalahari Deserts; what remains of the dense, central African tropical rainforest; the tsetse fly portions; scattered farming areas; and the few (partially) protected wildlife preserves. The image of Africa as a gigantic, unfenced wildlife landscape is wholly false. In fact, much more land is dedicated to livestock, and by far most wildlife is gone.

However, the infamous tsetse fly continues to spread deadly sleeping sickness to cattle, though not to wildlife. Large portions of central and southern Africa support some of the world's largest surviving wildlife populations in a comparatively healthy environment, mostly because humans have been unable to eradicate the tsetse fly to make way for cattle (or, in many areas, to *reinstate* cattle). For more than a decade, the United Nations' Food and Agricultural Organization (FAO) has waged a multi-billion dollar pesticide campaign to eliminate the tsetse fly over 70% of its African habitat -- about 10 million square kilometers, an area larger than the United States. The FAO's stated reason for the "war" on the tsetse is to open up potential ranchland (largely cut-over forest and woodland) so that *120 million* cattle may be raised there. These cattle would eat small trees and prevent regrowth of forest and woodland, increase soil erosion, compete with wildlife, transmit disease, etc.; the incoming ranchers would build fences and roads, kill predators, cut more trees, and so on. Thankfully, even though 200,000 tons of deadly active ingredient in insecticide has rained down on the tsetse areas, FAO has thus far been ineffective in most areas. Unfortunately, the FAO program is scheduled to continue another 30 years or more, and now the European Economic Community is pushing a plan to eradicate the fly and develop the tsetse area for ranching. (As for the tsetse's alleged deadly threat to humans, only 5 deaths have been recorded in 25 years.) [To protest FAO's war on the tsetse, write: FAO, United Nations, Via delle Terme di Caracalla, 00100, Rome, Italy.]

More surely than the bark of a gun, the lowing of cattle and bleating of goats sound trouble for wildlife. . . . Many in the wildlife community mourn the loss of the insect that, for its role in keeping out livestock and settlement, has been called "the best game warden in Africa." While I rode with one hunter, he rolled down his window and carefully shooed out a fly with the admonition, "Go and breed, you little bugger."
--Douglas B. Lee, "Okavango Delta," *National Geographic* (Dec 1990)

Aside from the tsetse areas, ranching and nomadic herding are common south of Africa's central rainforest, large areas of which have been cleared for livestock. Recent studies show mounting range deterioration throughout southern Africa. In the **Kalahari region**, cattle and range developments have ruined much of the grassland and semi-grassland, leading to the deaths of millions of antelope and other wild animals. In the late 1970s in the Kalahari, drought-stricken migrating wildebeests piled up against new cattle fences; 200,000 out of 230,000 migrants died of thirst because they couldn't reach water. Ranching and herding have also ravaged the land of, plundered the livelihood of, and made virtual slaves of thousands of Bushmen -- the tribespeople who had gathered and hunted here for more than 10,000 years. Many now live in shanties and tend cattle for their stockmen bosses.

A 1984 United Nations report states, "The degradation of rangelands caused by overgrazing is doubtless the most serious environmental problem facing **Botswana**." The nation's cattle outnumber people 2 to 1, and are a traditional measure of wealth. Much of the land is stripped bare, and during droughts starving goats climb atop cars to reach withered leaves and onto roofs to eat thatch. Having killed the tsetse with herbicides, ranchers are invading Botswana's last remaining wetlands. Thousands of miles of fences built to exclude wildebeests, zebra, antelope, water buffalo, elephants, and other wild animals thought to carry livestock diseases kill tens of thousands of these wild animals yearly; for example, more than 50,000 wildebeests died in 1983 alone. Like many others, the Botswanan government is dedicated to serving big-time ranchers, and many high government officials are themselves cattle barons.

Sheep ranching is intensive in **South Africa** and northwest in neighboring **Namibia**, though not elsewhere in southern Africa. Forty million of the fleecy beasts overgraze millions of acres of the scraggly brush and surviving grass there. In southeast Africa the populous Zulu tribe has evolved to regard cattle as indicative of wealth and status -- to the great harm of the environment.

Several hundred miles off Africa's southeast coast lies the island country of **Madagascar**, home to some of Earth's most unusual and varied wildlife. About 200,000 plant and animal species are native there, more than half of them endemic. When humans and their livestock first arrived in this 227,000-square-mile paradise only 1500 years ago, 4/5 was mantled with luxuriant tropical forest and lush savanna. Today, 60% of the forest has been cut or burned, largely to increase forage for cattle and goats, and, along with most of the former savanna, lies barren due to relentless overgrazing. *Thousands* of plant and animal species are already extinct, and grazing pressure continues to mount. The World Wildlife Federation identifies Madagascar as one of the world's 3 leading areas experiencing decline in biodiversity due to human influence.

Back on the mainland, moving north through eastern Africa, we find that large portions of the south have relatively few livestock, thanks to the tsetse fly and other deterrents. From central Tanzania northward through Ethiopia, however, cattle, sheep, and goat damage is moderate to severe. Portions of the coastal lowlands are overgrazed, and some of the dominant nomadic herders here *kill* anyone venturing onto their grazing territories. The 100,000-square-mile **Afar Triangle**, just west of where the Red Sea meets the Gulf of Aden, contains some of the lowest, hottest, driest, and most desolate land on Earth; yet, even here herders allow their goats, sheep, and camels to take what scant vegetation and fresh water still exits.

In the livestock-ravaged highlands, human starvation is periodic, as recently demonstrated once again in **Ethiopia**. Livestock plague the region's arable lands and make them more susceptible to drought and other natural vagaries in climate, frequently even eating crops. Bare dirt is spreading as stock raisers topple trees for fodder and livestock eat saplings and groundcover. The Masai, one of the region's large, nomadic herding tribes, has over the centuries become so over-specialized and dependent upon livestock that they sometimes allow their animals every last available leaf and drop of water in an area rather than risk losing their source of milk, blood (they drink it), and meat. Masai populations have tripled over the past 30 years; their livestock numbers have also soared and grazing pressure mounts.

The Ethiopian highlands were once among the most biologically diverse non-tropical forestlands on Earth; now they are among the most damaged. The rate of deforestation here is one of the highest anywhere, and only 3% of Ethiopia's original forest remains. Herders currently are driving livestock into the few remaining rugged areas not yet overgrazed. Recent reports from Ethiopia's northern mountains tell of the forest understory in previously ungrazed areas being stripped of every edible leaf and twig.

In northern **Kenya**, Lake Turkana (formerly Lake Rudolf), one of Africa's largest lakes, has shrunk dramatically in recent years. Many people think overgrazing of the vast Turkana Basin is the main cause. In southern Kenya, deforestation of mid-altitude brushland and upland forest to improve livestock pasture is occurring "at an alarming rate," according to the UN.

Not far south, in northern **Tanzania**, lies Africa's largest caldera, a 12-mile diameter, steep-walled crater named Ngorongoro. Mostly livestock-free since 1974, and protected from encroaching ranching, farming, and poaching, the grass-, shrub-, and tree-filled Ngorongoro is now one of the planet's greatest game preserves.

The vast belt of steppe and grassland from the Ethiopian highlands 3500 miles west to the Atlantic, from the Sahara 1000 miles south to the rainforest -- sometimes termed **the Sahel** -- is also a land of cattle, sheep, goats, and famine. Here, periodically, many thousands die from starvation; the emaciated people often are pictured lying in the dust beside their skeletal cattle -- *the cattle that symbolize their wealth and prestige!* As throughout much of the world, social inequities are largely to blame for the famines; however, contemporary livestock production is a major cause of these inequities, as well as an inefficient and destructive food production system. The Worldwatch Institute, a Washington, DC-based environmental think tank, states that "virtually all the rangeland [in this region] is "at least moderately degraded." According to ecologist Paul Ehrlich, "In the Sahel, the territory just south of the Sahara, and in Africa in general, cattle are playing a major role in this desertification" (Ehrlich 1986). The Sahel livestock population *quadrupled* between World War II and 1968, and remains many times higher than the land can accommodate.

Livestock grazing throughout the vast bulk of this region has turned thousands of square miles into wasteland, and continues to do so at an ever-accelerating rate. For example, **Mauritania** recorded only 43 sandstorms between 1960 and 1970, but 10 times this number in the following decade, with a record 240 sandstorms in 1983 alone. Officials here and throughout drier Africa report a main cause of devegetation and land degradation is herders breaking branches from the already small tree population to feed livestock, and cutting woody vegetation to build livestock enclosures. In **The Sudan**, about 30% of which has been seriously desertified during the past 50 years, thousands of square miles of forest are burned annually to increase livestock forage. And Lake Chad, the largest natural lake in northern Africa and one of the largest closed river basins in the world, has shrunk to merely 20% of its size only a few decades ago, mostly due to livestock-caused desertification and livestock production practices.

According to various sources, the **Sahara Desert** (or rather, desert-like condition) is expanding southward at a fluctuating, rough average of 2-6 miles per year, with livestock production the principal cause.

There were those who even claimed that the huge Sahara Desert was a man-made product caused by shepherds burning the jungle, and by the subsequent overgrazing of ever larger herds of goats and sheep. Modern research has proved this to be so.

--Thor Heyerdahl, **Fatu-Hiva**

Recent research has demonstrated that the Sahara was covered with trees as recently as 6,000 B.C., and that it was turned into a desert by nomadic tribes that burned the trees to provide grazing areas for their herds.

--Jacques Cousteau, **The Ocean World**

Only 6000 years ago the Sahara Desert was largely covered with trees, brush, and grass, and has since become arid. Much evidence also indicates that, as is the case in many of the world's drylands, livestock grazing was a significant contributor to this aridification. Contemporary livestock herding over more than 2/3 of the USA-sized, sandy, barren wasteland we now call the Sahara Desert continues to deplete what scant soil, vegetation, and water sources remain. Stock raising is carried on wherever possible with little regard for sustained yield or environmental consequences. However, livestock ownership here is less a matter of survival than tradition, honor, and glory.

The region all along the northern coast of Africa and south for many miles into the interiors of **Tunisia**, **Algeria**, and **Morocco** was 2000 years ago extensively utilized to provide livestock and crops to the Roman Empire. Much of it was covered with forests. Today, the climate has not changed much, but the area is largely desolate. W.C. Lowdermilk writes:

Over a large part of the ancient granary of Rome we found the soil washed off to bedrock and the hills seriously gullied as a result of overgrazing. . . . With the coming of the grazing culture, brought in by invading nomads from Arabia, erosion was unleashed by overgrazing of the hills. We can see here on the landscape how the soil mantle was washed off the upper slopes to bedrock. Accelerated runoff from the bared rock cut

gullies into the upper edge of the soil mantle, working it downhill as if a great rug were being pulled off the hills. In this manner has the country been seriously damaged, and the capacity to support a population much reduced. (Lowdermilk 1975)

Today, the region is still tremendously overgrazed by millions of cattle and tens of millions of sheep and goats. The United Nations reports that "Rangelands have been overgrazed with three head of cattle where only one could thrive . . . . Two-thirds of the land area of Tunisia is being eaten away by desertification." The Sahara is expanding north as well as south.

Far to the east, in **Egypt**'s richly fertile, intensely overpopulated Nile River Delta, much potential cropland is used instead for the less efficient production of 5 million cattle.

Overall, Africa rivals any continent in the extent of livestock production damage. Overgrazing, forest clearing, and other livestock production activities are major factors in the decline of most African endangered wildlife, including the gorilla. Between 1850 and 1980 Africa lost 60% of its forest cover, perhaps mostly to promote livestock. African stock raisers have killed millions of large herbivores as competitors, and because they think that wildlife spreads livestock diseases. Historically, disease epidemics *introduced by cattle* have repeatedly decimated Africa's wildlife, causing severe ecological disruptions. Livestock protection rivals, and in many areas exceeds, sport hunting and poaching as the main cause of predator mortality, with similarly profound environmental consequences. Stock raisers encouraging new growth burn many millions of acres unnaturally each year. Overgrazing has caused gigantic dust storms and accelerated hydraulic erosion, displacing much of the soil over vast areas. Africa's infamous locust invasions, caused mostly by overgrazing, worsen the devastation. (The US and USSR military are currently collaborating on laser technology to fight Africa's locusts.) Livestock production has displaced many native tribal cultures, and is, along with human overpopulation and unjust food distribution, the major anthropogenic cause of relentless famine in Africa. The continent's cattle, sheep, and goat population *doubled between 1950 and 1987*, and continues to increase at a high overall rate, despite sporadic and massive livestock die-offs.

Across the Mediterranean, about half the area of the **European subcontinent**, excluding the Soviet Union and Scandinavia, is used to produce livestock. Other than India, this region has the heaviest concentration of cattle on Earth. It also has some of the worst sheep grazing.

Mediterranean scrub and woodland has been particularly hard hit. Centuries of overgrazing by sheep and goats, and later cattle, as well as environmental manipulation by their owners, left *most* of this area eroded and impoverished. **Greece**'s ragged, scrubby condition may seem charming to us now, but its more fertile, verdant aboriginal character would have been more so. Much of **Yugoslavia**'s forest was destroyed in ancient times for and by goats, sheep, and cattle. Sheep and cattle turned whole regions of **Spain** -- once lush Mediterranean shrub/woodland and steppe -- desertlike, while stockmen cut and burned millions of acres of forest for their animals. (The Spanish were the greatest historic influence on ranching in the Western US.) The drier portion of southern **France** is being similarly desertified, and most of **Italy** has been devastated.

Very little of the Mediterranean region resembles its original character or environmental productivity, though paleontological studies show that today's climate is almost identical to the climate of ancient times. Georg Borgstrom, a widely respected authority on world food problems, has ranked the destruction of Mediterranean vegetation by goats and other livestock as 1 of the 3 worst ecological blunders in world history. (The other 2 were the Dust Bowl of the 1930s US, in which livestock were a major factor, and the deforestation of China's uplands around 3000 B.C., yet another instance where livestock have subsequently been the most potent human influence keeping the area in a degraded condition.)

Cattle and sheep in the **Pyrenees** compete with remaining wildlife and spread disease, while their owners kill the now-rare predators. Most of the grassy meadows in the **Alps**, once productive for wildlife, are denuded by livestock.

Nearly half of **central Europe**'s well-watered flatlands and hills is farmed for livestock or grazed as pasture, most of it heavily. The grass may be greener here than in drier southern Europe, but this does not represent benign land use; stocking rates are much higher; native vegetation has been displaced, wildlife habitat ruined, and soil erosion intensified.

In the soggy **British Isles** -- where more than half of the land has been converted to livestock pasture -- intensive, long-term sheep and cattle grazing has stripped the land of native vegetation, laid bare and damaged the soil, and even created sand dunes in some areas. Herders from the European mainland invaded the British Isles beginning about 6000 years ago, cut most of the forest that covered the land, and exterminated all bears and wolves. Livestock kept forests from growing back by eating and trampling saplings. Recent reports are that intensive sheep grazing, clearing of livestock fields, and tree planting have diminished the heather on English moors by 25% in 20 years. (The British were the second most powerful historical influence on ranching in the Western US.) **Ireland** is "the Emerald Isle," but by far most of it is livestock pasture; competition for forage there is so intense that some stockmen force their herds of cattle to swim a mile or more out to small coastal islands to graze. Thousands of tons of Irish *seaweed* is harvested and fed to livestock.

Even southern **Scandinavia** is home to about 10 million cattle and several million sheep, while much of northern Scandinavia is used for commercial reindeer. And according to an article in *National Geographic* (February 1987), sheep herders long ago stripped off virtually all of the forest that once covered much of **Iceland**, while subsequent overgrazing prevented it from growing back: "When the trees disappeared, so too did most of the well-drained soil, carried off by the incessant wind." About 20% of Iceland is grazed by sheep now, the remainder being barren, steep, covered with lava or ice, or excessively damaged by past grazing. Nearly all of **Greenland** is too barren, boggy, or ice-bound to be grazable, though some sheep are raised along its southern coasts.

Most of **Canada** is likewise ungrazable, being enveloped with cold, herbage-scarce conifer forest or Arctic tundra. However, about 200,000 square miles (an area 4 times larger than New York) of the Great Plains of central Canada, most of south-central British Columbia, and portions of southeast Canada are grazed, mostly by 11 million cattle. Most of this land is overgrazed, in the west much of it with a welfare public lands ranching system similar to that of the US. As in the US, Canadian ranchers are foremost among those exploiting the wild and opposing protection for wolves, grizzly bears, and large herbivores in ranching areas. For example, the Canadian Cattlemen's Association recently presented a position paper to the Canadian Ministry of Agriculture recommending that the entire population of the world's largest free-roaming buffalo herd be exterminated from Alberta's Wood Buffalo National Park, a UNESCO World Heritage Site, because some of the buffalo are infected with brucellosis and tuberculosis. (The buffalo have carried these diseases since contacting them from cattle in the 1920s, before their forebears were shipped in from overgrazed areas to the south at the insistence of cattlemen who wanted to make way for more cows.)

And so we return to the **USA**. In **Alaska**, other than Eskimo reindeer herding in the northern and western coastal lowlands, livestock production is thus far limited to cattle on Kodiak Island, some of the Aleutian Islands, and around Anchorage; a few thousand sheep are grazed, mostly near settled areas. However, range professional D.C.Tomlin estimates that 10-13 million acres of grassland in Alaska have "potential" for cattle, sheep, and horses. Tomlin thinks that, rather than being inherently impractical for producing livestock, these areas are simply not yet socially structured to maintain a ranching establishment.

Not so 4000 miles south. Firmly entrenched, big-time ranchmen graze cattle on more than 1/3 of the area of the **Hawaiian Islands**. Tropical and sub-tropical paradise has been converted to cattle ranches and cropland. Feral goats and pigs also do extensive damage.

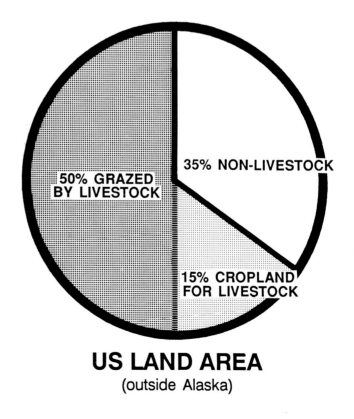

US LAND AREA
(outside Alaska)

According to the US Forest Service:

About 1/2 of the total land area of the continental United States is used for grazing livestock [by far mostly for cattle]. This area amounts to about 1 billion acres. (USDA, FS 1983)

Food production experts report that, in addition, more than 2/3 of the 444 million acres of cropland in the **48 states** (15% of the contiguous US) are planted with livestock feed (56% for beef cattle). Roughly 80%-90% of all grain grown in the US is used to feed meat animals, mostly cattle, and about 40% of all US farm produce, including grain, is fed to livestock. To feed a typical American requires about 2 acres of cropland (more than 1/3 of which is used to grow food for beef cattle) and 4.4 acres of grazing land (nearly all of which is used for beef cattle). And, according to Worldwatch Institute, about 50% of all water used in the US goes to produce livestock or livestock feed, mostly for cattle, and a much greater percent of *consumptive* -- generally non-recyclable -- US water use is by the livestock industry.)

Therefore, **65% of the US outside Alaska is somehow employed in the production of livestock!** Most of this land is significantly impacted. While most American rangeland may look good compared to North Africa, the Middle East, or India, remember that *the US has been overgrazed and overcultivated for only a century, not millennia,* as has been the case in most of the "Old World." The vast bulk of the remainder not currently used for livestock is incapable of producing livestock, or is intensively used for other purposes. Some of this land suffers indirectly from livestock production, or from lingering influences of past livestock production.

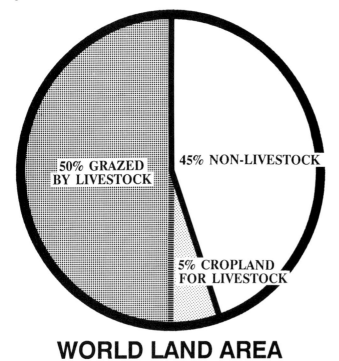

WORLD LAND AREA

Altogether, about 50% of the Earth's land surface is grazed by domestic livestock -- (23% as "rangeland") -- while an additional 5% is farmed for livestock. Again, nearly all of the remainder is unsuitable for producing livestock, or is developed for other purposes. FAO estimates that *70% of the Earth's land surface is potentially grazable.*

The cows which dot this jungle-turned-to-pasture appear like white specks from above, and they begin to seem like cancer cells eating away at Mother Earth.
--Daniel Dancer, environmental photo-journalist

●**Tropical rainforests** are in many ways Earth's most important ecotype. They are the oldest continuous ecosystems, most having remained more or less in their present form for tens of millions of years. Experts estimate that although they cover only 2% of the Earth's surface, tropical rainforests are home to at least half of the 10-20 million animal species (most are insects) and perhaps 120,000 of the more than 280,000 plant species on the planet (including those in the oceans). Some recent estimates are that as much as 4/5 of the animal species and 1/2 of the plant species on Earth may depend on tropical rainforest habitat. Additionally, as many as 30,000 plant species and millions of animal species are thought to be as yet "undiscovered," most of them in rainforests. Tropical rainforests are crucial to the Earth's atmospheric balance, play a key role in moderating its climate, contain more than half this planet's live wood and unfrozen fresh water, and are the source of numerous food and medicinal plants. According to *US News and World Report*, in terms of ecological and human impact, loss of the Earth's rainforests would be tantamount to losing 80% of the world's vegetation.

Only a few centuries ago rainforest covered about 14%, or 8.2 million square miles, of the Earth's terrestrial surface. Axe, chainsaw, bulldozer, fire, hoof and mouth have reduced this to about 6%, or 3.5 million square miles. The United Nations FAO estimates that more than 41 million acres of world rainforest, by far mostly in the tropics, were completely and permanently cleared in 1990, up from 25 million in 1980. Additionally, more than 50 million acres are thought to be grossly disrupted annually. This would indicate that *more than 1.5% of the biome is being destroyed and 2% heavily degraded annually* (at constant 1990 rates). Satellite data indicate that in 1987, 20 million acres of rainforest were cleared in the Brazilian Amazon alone. The National Academy of Sciences estimates annual deforestation at *50 million acres* -- an area the size of England, Wales, and Scotland combined. Either estimate equals more than one acre per second. At this rate, the vast bulk of the Earth's remaining tropical rainforest will be gone within a single human life-span.

Contrary to popular images, the man with a chainsaw is as likely to be cutting for pasture as for wood. Livestock production is a leading cause of world rainforest denudation. However, because rainforests store most of their nutrients in the vegetation -- rather than in the soil, as do most terrestrial ecosystems -- cleared rainforest makes moderate to poor livestock pasture. When rainforest slash is burned, nutrients are lost as heat and smoke or rendered inaccessible to regrowth, as rainforests generally are not adapted to fire. Much of the regrowth that does occur is eaten or trampled by livestock. The thin soil, never before directly exposed to sun, wind, raindrops, or hooves, becomes drier than ever before, and is therefore damaged and easily eroded. Sediments damage waterways. Deforested land gradually loses productivity and stocking rates drop accordingly. Livestock grazing is the last commercial use

(Rainforest Action Network)

rainforest soils can support, so even in areas where the forest initially is cleared for some other purpose, livestock production often prevents restoration. Conversion of rainforest to pasture has been identified as the most destructive of all possible uses while, overall, livestock production is a (possibly *the*) major factor preventing world rainforest regeneration.

Burning rainforest for pasture also contributes to the buildup of CO_2 in the atmosphere, accelerating global warming by way of the "greenhouse effect." Some scientists think that about 25% of human-caused greenhouse gases come from burning rainforest.

Experts estimate that every quarter-pound of beef costs about 55 square feet of rainforest and thousands of individuals of hundreds of species. They say that during the past 600 million years the Earth's rate of species extinction was roughly 1 per year. Now they estimate the rate at *more than 3 per day* -- perhaps as high as 1 per hour -- scores of times higher than during the great ice age extinctions and during the demise of the dinosaurs. This is estimated to be the highest extinction rate in Earth's 4-billion-year history of life, roughly 1000 times higher than normal background extinction. At the present rate of acceleration, species extinction will reach *several hundred per day* in the early years of the next century. Scientists project that in the next 30 years more than 1 million species will become extinct and that *only a few human generations down the line the Earth may contain less than half as many plant and animal species as it once did!*

The planet's mantle of trees has already declined by a third relative to preagricultural times, and much of that remaining is damaged or deteriorating. Historically, the demand for grazing land is a major cause of worldwide clearing of forest of most types. Currently, livestock production, fuelwood gathering, lumbering, and clearing for crops are denuding a conservatively estimated 40 million acres of the Earth's forestland each year.

● Worldwide, grasses of more than 10,000 species once covered more than 1/4 of the land. They supported the world's greatest masses of large animals. Of the major ecotypes, **grassland** produces the deepest, most fertile topsoil and has the most resistance to soil erosion. Livestock production has damaged the Earth's grassland more than has any other land use, and has transformed roughly half of it to desertlike condition. Lester Brown of the Worldwatch Institute reports that "Widespread grassland degradation [from livestock grazing] can now be seen on every continent."

●Deserts and desertlike conditions have expanded proportionately, not only into former grassland but into shrubland, brushland, and even into former forest. In preagricultural times, only about 1/5 of the planet's land surface was desertlike. Mostafa K. Tolba, Executive Director of the United Nations Environment Programme (UNEP), summarizes the results of scientific studies by the UN:

> Based on climatic data, more than a third of the earth's surface is desert or.semi-desert . . . . Based on vegetation and soil criteria, however, it was found that 43 percent of the earth's land surface was desert. The difference . . . was man-made desert.

In 1977, experts attending the United Nations Conference on Desertification in Nairobi agreed that the greatest cause of world desertification in modern times has been livestock grazing (as did the US Council on Environmental Quality in 1981). They reported that grazing was desertifying most arid, semi-arid, and sub-humid land where farming was not occurring. Seven years later UNEP compiled, from questionnaires sent to 91 countries, the most complete data on world desertification ever assembled. According to the resultant 1984 assessment, more than 11 billion acres, or 35% of the Earth's land surface, are threatened by new or continued desertification. UNEP estimated that more than 3/4 of this land -- the vast majority of it grazed rangeland -- had already been at least moderately degraded. About 15 million acres (the size of West Virginia) of semi-arid or subhumid land annually are reduced to unreclaimable desert-like condition, while another 52 million arid acres annually are reduced to minimal cover or to sweeping sands -- more due to livestock grazing than any other influence. The world's "deserts" are expected to expand about 20% in the next 20 years.

Thus, livestock grazing is both the greatest cause of world desertification *and* the greatest detriment to the Earth's deserts.

The Worldwatch Institute estimates that each year 24 billion tons of topsoil over and above natural erosion are displaced from the Earth's surface due to human activities. Livestock grazing and livestock crop production cause accelerated soil loss over more of the globe than any other land use.

From woodland to grassland to desert, throughout most of the inhabited globe, livestock production is a primary cause of environmental deterioration *and sustained degradation* -- that is, prevention of recovery. Many ancient civilizations -- in southern Europe, North Africa, Arabia, the Indus Valley, India, central Asia and elsewhere -- declined under its impact, and the vast majority of countries have serious livestock problems now.

According to *New Scientist* (5-6-89), world cattle population has **doubled** in the past 40 years, and now stands at **1.3 billion**. In other words, the rate of cattle population expansion is even higher than that for humans! In total biomass, cattle now outweigh humans about 2 to 1. The United

Nations reports that the world's domestic sheep population increased 9% between 1974 and 1982 -- 3 times faster than the cattle population for those years -- while other sources indicate a continuing high rate of increase. Today, there are also about 1.3 billion domestic sheep, and (though they eat only about 1/5 as much as cattle) pound for pound, they are in some ways more destructive grazers/browsers. Countless millions of goats, pigs, buffalo, camels, alpacas, and other domestic stock add to the impact, while millions of feral goats, pigs, and other escaped or introduced livestock have ravaged environments in many areas. Projections for cattle, sheep, and goat populations indicate that high increase rates probably will continue to the year 2000 and beyond.

These dramatic livestock population increases reflect not only human population increases but modernized and expanded range development, including predator slaughter, roading, water development, fencing, vegetation manipulation, changes in grazing systems, and much more. As discussed, these and traditional, related human activities and methods of management often cause as much environmental damage as do the animals themselves. Much of this livestock increase also reflects increased feedlot and cropland livestock production; however, reports indicate increases in rangeland grazing pressure in most grazed regions.

The soil loss and degradation, water depletion and pollution, flood and sediment damage, desertification, deforestation, wildlife destruction, cropland loss and damage, energy and other resource waste, social and political inequities, and unjust resource utilization inherent to livestock production are all major contributors to hardship, poverty, and global conflict.

Now, all this would *seem* much less a tragedy if livestock production supplied great amounts of food for people. Livestock grazing and farming stand roughly together as the planet's leading causes of environmental decline (aside from human overpopulation and a more abstract but also fundamental cause, our withdrawal from Nature -- the 2 main problems underlying the rise of agriculture and livestock domestication). However, while about 10% (3.7 billion acres) of the Earth's terrestrial surface is cropland, *nearly half of this land is used to grow food for livestock.* Moreover, **non-livestock farming produces several times more in total food value for humans than all livestock production,** cropland and rangeland. (Half of the world's fish catch is also fed to livestock.)

According to Worldwatch Institute, altogether roughly 1/3 of the plant food grown on Earth that could be eaten by people is instead fed to livestock. According to world food and agriculture expert Frances Moore Lappe, the figure is 40%-50%. This food -- grain, legumes, fruit, vegetables, nuts, and seeds (even animal products) -- loses approximately 80%-90% of its food value to humans when cycled through livestock rather than being eaten directly by people. In other words, *we are being consumed by the livestock we think are sustaining us.*

In **State of the World: 1989**, Worldwatch Institute identifies 4 principal causes of global land degradation: (1) overgrazing; (2) overcultivation of croplands; (3) waterlogging and salinization of irrigated lands; and (4) deforestation. Let's more clearly identify these causes: (1) *Overgrazing*/ranching may be the greatest single cause of environmental degradation. (2) As stated above, roughly half of the world's *cropland* is used for livestock. (3) A large portion of the world's *irrigated land* (irrigated land comprises 15% of all cropland) is irrigated to produce food for livestock, and much of this land is damaged by trampling livestock. (Irrigation accounts for 3/4 of global human water use, and more than half of the world's irrigated lands are already significantly damaged.) (4) Again, livestock production is a major cause of world *deforestation* and, perhaps more importantly, *prevention of reforestation*.

Thus, (aside from human overpopulation) livestock production is not only the planet's greatest environmental degrader, but, relative to what it provides humans, it is by far humanity's most environmentally destructive pursuit. Most of the Earth's arable and grazable land is already heavily used and is declining in productivity. Attempts to increase livestock production on existing and newly opened land are intensifying the environmental crisis and exacerbating global famine and social conflict.

Exaggeration? Fabrication? Not at all. The role of livestock production in world problems is **universally underplayed** due to many factors explained in this book.

> *Animal agriculture is the single most environmentally destructive industry in the world.*
> --Physicians Committee for Responsible Medicine

Chapter VII
WELFARE RANCHING

Although cattle grazing in the West has polluted more water, eroded more topsoil, killed more fish, displaced more wildlife, and destroyed more vegetation than any other land use, the American public pays ranchers to do it.
--Ted Williams, "He's Going to Have an Accident" (Williams 1991)

The environmental consequences discussed in the first part of this book by themselves more than justify ending public lands ranching. But, adding insult to injury, we the people are forced to subsidize this plunder. That's right; piles of our tax and private dollars allow the ranching establishment to overgraze our land and develop it for ranching. By exploiting America's fondness for cow meat and cow boys, fostering a healthy public image, exercising its overwhelming political might, and simply maintaining the status quo for more than a century, stockmen have stuck us with the bill -- without our consent or even our knowledge.

As has been detailed, ranchers, government and private entities have been working together for decades to convert our public land into profitable livestock ranches. Despite millions of range developments, they have not been successful; public land remains inherently "a lousy place to raise livestock." Federal studies show that even though the average grazing allotment size per rancher is about 12,000 acres, only about 5% of permittees have herds large enough -- about 500 head of cattle -- to provide sole support for a family (Luoma 1986). However, perhaps most of these large operators are businesses, not families; most of those that are families are wealthy independent of their public ranching operations; and both businesses and families derive most of their livestock feed from *private* land.

They perpetuate a land abuse system -- often called *welfare ranching* -- that eats up billions of tax and private dollars. In fact, in terms of net production public lands ranching is among the most heavily subsidized businesses in America. All levels of government give liberally, from federal to state to county, and even some cities, as do many private entities, willingly or not. Most stockmen themselves admit that most public lands ranching operations would collapse without this artificial support structure. What does this say for an industry whose members boast of self-sufficiency and resourcefulness? According to Steve Johnson, as Southwest Representative for Defenders of Wildlife, "The popular conception of the rancher as a rugged individualist is strikingly at odds with reality." Tom France of the National Wildlife Federation maintains that "Grazing is as close to a pork-barrel issue as the West gets."

Payments to the agriculture industry are called subsidies. In the urban sector, subsidies are called welfare.
--Harvey Duncan, Hanna, Wyoming

Cattle ranching on the public lands of the American West is the most sacred form of public welfare in the United States.
--Edward Abbey

Welfare ranching has become a way of life for the 22,000 Western BLM and Forest Service permittees, as well as most of the 8000 or so stockmen on other Western federal, state, and county lands. This tiny minority -- whose public ranching domain encompasses 41% of the West -- lives well off the liberal generosity of the rest of us 250 million Americans. Partly for this reason, partly because only the wealthy can afford to buy public lands ranches, users of public grazing land are the nation's largest and wealthiest livestock operators. For example, despite the fact that merely 3% of this country's cattle feed comes from public land, an incredible 90% of all US cattlemen owning 1000 or more cattle hold public grazing permits. (Ferguson 1983)

At the same time, a large percentage of those who graze public land run their operations at a subsistence level or as a secondary business, that is, as a tax write-off or source of extra income that will never fold with endless subsidization. Like other public ranchers, these "ranchers" pay minuscule grazing fees, almost no property taxes on their private land, and are kept in "business" with openhanded government and private technical, material, and financial assistance. They include numerous and powerful politicos, businessmen, and corporations such as Union Oil, Getty Oil, Texaco, Phelps Dodge, and Anheiser-Busch, along with investment partnerships, feedlot operators, agribusiness companies, railroads, land speculators, foreign investors, doctors, lawyers, actors, and whoever else has half a million bucks or so to slap down on a public lands ranch.

Also included are more than a few underworld figures. They find ranches perfect "front" businesses -- comfortable and isolated strongholds where they may engage in criminal activity unhampered or, if necessary, "lie low" until things "cool off on the outside." A case in point is a large Forest Service ranching operation down the road from where my family and I lived in southwest New Mexico; it was known to locals as a hideout for the Mafia, including in the past the underworld dignitary Al Capone.

With an indomitable line-up like this, is it any wonder welfare ranching continues unchecked?

They lease the land for less than market value; the mortgage value of the right-to-lease is a lucrative source of capital; and for some of them, the entire operation is a tax write-off. They complain that they have a "bad deal" because of agency meddling and neglect. On the other hand, they make large campaign contributions to assure they get to keep their bad deal.
--Jim Fish, Director, New Mexico BLM Wilderness Coalition

The government and private sectors subsidize public graziers in innumerable ways. Much is given openly in the form of ranching-assistance efforts. These most direct subsidies include low grazing fees, range developments, and ranching administration, and total roughly $100 million annually. In an article by columnist Jack Anderson, Oklahoma Representative Mike Synar states that if Congress decided to grant these subsidies to all US livestock producers, based on the fact that federal lands ranchers represent less than 2% of US livestock producers, the subsidy (not including low grazing fees) would cost taxpayers more than $2 billion annually. Including low grazing fees, the figure would surpass $7 billion.

However, a vastly greater amount is subsidized *indirectly*, in multitudinous ways often having little apparent connection to ranching. Consequently, it is impossible to compile precise subsidy information on public lands ranching; no government agency nor private entity I am aware of compiles such records. For example, through hundreds of federal/state/county/private funded Agricultural Extension Service offices, public lands ranchers receive millions of dollars worth of assistance annually; because accounting does not distinguish between beneficiaries, no one has any idea how many millions. Extension Service agents I spoke with would not venture even a rough guess. Other indirect subsidies include range "restoration" projects, university range programs, range experimental stations, research and testing programs, federal wool incentive payments, livestock disease and parasite control, and much, much more.

Of the money the public unknowingly spends on public lands ranching each year, how much is intentionally hidden and how much simply reflects tradition/status quo must necessarily remain a matter of debate and subjective analysis. For instance, state fish and game departments commonly design "wildlife enhancement" projects that benefit livestock interests as much, if not more. Exactly what percent is actually designed for ranching is anyone's guess.

In any event, 20 years of observation have left no doubt in my mind that government agencies habitually mislead the public about ranching subsidies. Facts and figures are juggled and misinterpreted; assessments are distorted; hidden costs and ill-defined projects are buried in obscure government reports; range developments, activities, and their effects are not made public or are misrepresented.

More than for any other public land user, subsidization for ranching comes in disguise, concealed under labels such as "riparian enhancement," "soil conservation," "range research," "fire prevention," "type conversion," "wildlife water development," "cooperative management," "aesthetic enhancement," "open range," "access improvement," "watershed seeding," and dozens of others. These shrewd euphemisms are used to draw more dollars into the ranching trough without public or legislative interference. Known as "institutionalized ripoff," it has become even more prevalent in recent years as multiple use mandates force the agencies to increasingly conceal subsidies from scrutiny.

This subsidization system is protected by an unwritten policy that absolves the ranching establishment from accountability for its influences. Thus, for example, when one of Oregon's finest trout streams, the Donner and Blitzen River, was virtually destroyed by overgrazing, BLM expressed concern but said it could do nothing until "wildlife funds" were appropriated to fence cattle out (Ferguson 1983).

This covert policy operates at even the most basic level. A Forest Service district ranger picks up a dozen salt blocks at the local feed store "as a favor" for an influential rancher. A BLM range specialist helps Rancher Jones round up stock under guise of "checking out the range conditions." A state range manager can get a stockman friend "a good deal on a cattle guard for your new fence . . . maybe even get it for nothing if we play our cards right." Government employees spend time chasing cattle and sheep out of unauthorized areas, closing gates, and mending broken or cut fences, rather than insisting that the ranchers responsible do so.

These little stories are day-to-day reality on the Western range; I've seen them all and more. There are, of course, many conscientious agency employees. Still, much covert, mutual back-scratching is prevalent between government officials and stockmen. Both realize that they have a good thing going at the public's expense, so why jeopardize it by letting the public find out?

In sum, government "range" (ranching) expenditure statistics are only the tip of the public lands ranching fiscal iceberg. Total tax and private expenditures are not only many times higher, but cannot be accurately measured. Nevertheless, we can study available information, read between the lines, scrape off some of the crap, and try to get a better look. The remainder of this chapter makes that attempt.

Those who receive special benefits and services from the federal government should be the ones to bear the costs of these services, not the general taxpayers.
--President Ronald Reagan, "hobby" rancher

Grazing Fees

"That's right, cousin," the ringtail answered. "The ranchers around here rent this land from the US Government for almost nothing. And most of them treat it as if it's not worth a dime! They put too many cows on the land, trying to raise as much beef to sell as they possibly can. You can't blame them, I guess, if the Government lets them get away with it."
--Gerry Bishop "Adventures of Ranger Rick," *Ranger Rick* (March 1985)

The low price of grazing fees on public lands is probably the longest-running scandal in the West.
--J.J. Casserly, "Financial Farce of US Grazing Fees," 4-4-85 *Arizona Republic*

A *grazing fee* is a periodic assessment charged ranchers for the privilege of grazing livestock on public land. Over the years federal, state, county, and city governments have used a great variety of parameters in determining the price to be charged. Because BLM, FS, and most other government agency grazing fees -- even at their highest level -- have rarely exceeded 1/3 of fair market value, they are the most conspicuous form of welfare to public lands ranchers.

During the initial decades of Western ranching, stockmen paid nothing to graze their animals unrestricted on public land. Conversely, unlike today they received few government subsidies, other than political, legislative, and judicial favoritism.

Subsidies increased gradually in the late 1800s, and when the Forest Service was established in 1905 it felt justified in unimposing a 5-cent-per-AUM grazing fee on the newly designated FS grazing permittees. (Different FS areas had different base values; 5 cents was the average fee charged.) The new fee, which went into effect in 1906, was defined by the Forest Service as "reasonable," though it didn't even cover administrative costs; $0.05/AUM was equivalent to about $0.80/AUM in today's dollar, or only a small fraction of what the herbage would have been worth on the private market.

Nevertheless, many ranchers labeled the new fee "outrageous." Through their political power structure they pressured Forest Service Director Gifford Pinchot and President Teddy Roosevelt to revoke the grazing fee. When the two wouldn't budge, the ranching-enamored Congress retaliated by drafting a bill to withdraw presidential authority to create National Forests in several Western states. Roosevelt quickly designated 16 million acres of new National Forests in those states, and then signed the bill into law. The industry raged against the Forest Service and filed a lawsuit, though to no avail.

FS grazing fees remained extremely low, fluctuating between $0.03 and $0.15/AUM until 1940. The Forest Service had apparently learned its lesson, for when in 1920 the House Committee on Agriculture tried to increase fees up to 300% (from the existing $0.13/AUM average), the agency opposed the attempt.

On the other hand, several government agencies, some of the public, and many private stockmen complained that Forest Service permittees were being unfairly subsidized with low grazing fees. Subsequently, a comprehensive study, the Rachford Appraisal, was conducted from 1920-24 to "provide a basis for fair and justifiable fees." Per the Rachford report, grazing fees were, beginning in 1924, to be annually appraised relative to livestock prices. Stockmen again objected and deferred the new fees for 4 years. In 1928 the new fee system was finally implemented, but it did not significantly raise the grazing fee. In fact, the fee was actually decreased dramatically, to $0.07-$0.09/AUM, in the early 1930s due, ostensibly, to the Great Depression.

If we charge no fee it would amount to a government subsidy, and a government subsidy is always subject to scrutiny, criticism, and investigation. You stockmen set some fair fee . . . we will want fees for our own protection.
--F.R. Carpenter, first Director of the Division of Grazing

In 1934 powerful cattle ranchers pushed through the Taylor Grazing Act and created the Division of Grazing, which became the Grazing Service in 1939 and, combined with the General Land Office, the Bureau of Land Management in 1946. During its first year of operation the Division of Grazing charged no grazing fee. Thereafter, until 1946, it charged the same $0.05/AUM fee as did the early Forest Service, ostensibly based on administrative costs.

For 2 main reasons early FS and BLM grazing fees were set only at token levels. First, as mentioned earlier, public lands ranchers were the major formulators of both of these agencies, and subsequently they exerted much control over their operation. Second, low fees made it much more likely that disgruntled ranchers would cooperate with the new federal grazing programs.

Of course, as with the Forest Service fee, the $0.05/AUM BLM fee never covered even the cost of range administration. So during the mid-1940s a coalition of agency, political, and private interests made the first serious attempt to raise the Grazing Service fee. It was promptly crushed by the ranching colossus. In fact, the Grazing Service was punished for its involvement; its budget was slashed by 50%, its range staff was reduced from 250 to less than 50 and, in 1946, it was eliminated altogether and replaced with the Bureau of Land Management. Consequently, the new BLM was so short on funds its first year that grazing "advisory" boards allotted range "improvement" funds to help pay range salaries (Foss 1960).

However, pressure to raise the BLM grazing fee continued, and in 1947 a fee study and recommendation, the Nicolson Plan, was formulated. Under its authority, the fee finally was raised -- to $0.08/AUM, where it stayed until 1950. This fee likewise failed to recover administrative costs, and in 1951 and 1955 BLM officials convinced permittees that other nominal increases were needed to partially compensate for increased administrative costs and inflation. After all, how could ranching subsidies be implemented without funding?

The Western ranching interests did not want to pay fees representing the true value of the forage, and they were particularly desirous not to have any principle established under which grazing fees would ever be related to the value of forage.
--Wesley Calef, **Private Grazing and Public Lands** (Calef 1960)

But even these increases scarcely kept pace with inflation, and everyone knew that federal grazing fees were still embarrassingly low. In 1954 BLM's "cost of administration" concept was abandoned and the method for determining the grazing fee was changed to reflect the going price of beef and mutton at Western markets. Consequently, the 1955 BLM fee was raised to a whopping $0.15/AUM. Since then BLM has gradually increased the fee in response to market trends, inflation, and pressure from US budget officials. Forest Service fees since 1928 rose similarly. In 1980 BLM and FS grazing fees peaked at $2.36/AUM and $2.41/AUM respectively -- still less than 1/3 fair market value -- after which the 2 agencies began charging the same fee.

Meanwhile, Congress passed the Federal Land Policy and Management Act (FLPMA) of 1976. FLPMA established a policy to "receive fair market value of the use of the public lands and their resources unless otherwise provided for by statute." Two years later, Congress enacted on a temporary 7-year basis the possible statutory exemption mentioned in FLPMA. This statute, the Public Rangelands Improvement Act (PRIA), contained a formula for setting grazing fees. PRIA provided that during the 7-year experimental period the Departments of Agriculture and Interior were to evaluate the fee and other options, then recommend fees for 1986 and beyond. (Com. on Govt. Oper. 1986) The resulting study, *Grazing Fee Review and Evaluation* (which cost the Departments $4 million to conduct) showed clearly that the fees charged for grazing federal land were far below those charged for private land (USDA, FS and USDI, BLM 1986).

THE PRIA GRAZING FEE FORMULA

(from *Grazing Fee Review and Evaluation* -- USDA, FS and USDI, BLM 1986)

BASIS OF FORMULA:

The PRIA formula consists of a base value of $1.23 per AUM that is updated annually through a series of indexes that measure changes in the private grazing land lease rates, the price of beef cattle, and the costs of livestock production. The base period for the indexes is 1964 to 1968. The PRIA formula is:

$$\text{Calculated fee (CF)} = \$1.23 \times \frac{FVI + BCPI - PPI}{100}$$

Where:

CF = The Calculated Fee to be charged, which Congress defined as fair market value, which is the estimated economic value of livestock grazing to the user, and where annual increases or decreases in the fee are limited to a plus or minus 25% of the previous year's fee.

$1.23 = The base value established in 1966 through the Western Livestock Industry Survey (WLIS).

FVI = The Forage Value Index, an index of annually surveyed private land lease rates, 1964-1968 = 100.

BCPI = The Beef Cattle Price Index, an index of USDA annually reported prices of beef cattle over 500 pounds, 1964-1968 = 100.

PPI = The PRIA Prices Paid Index, indexed prices that producers of livestock pay for selected production items, 1964-1968 = 100.

Subsequently, since 1978 the annual federal grazing fee has been calculated according to the PRIA formula, which multiplied the number of AUMs a rancher uses by a predetermined rate based on changes in private grazing land base rates, beef cattle prices, and livestock production costs. These estimated production costs are based on numerous factors, such as prices of ranching supplies, fuel, rentals, repairs, new equipment, utilities, insurance, etc. They are set at arbitrarily high levels, rather than on what ranchers actually pay. Livestock losses to predators, poison plants, drought, and so on are treated essentially as deductions, and ranchers commonly inflate these estimates. The PRIA formula itself is likewise loaded, arbitrary, hypothetical, and confusing, with its base rates, price indexes, weighted averages, alternative bases, and so on. PRIA was created by the public lands ranching establishment to assure low grazing fees.

In short, the revenue collected from ranchers for public allotment grazing is computed by multiplying the total number of AUMs used times the PRIA grazing fee formula: AUMs X PRIA formula = grazing fee. This means that a stockman, corporation, or cattle or sheep company is charged a grazing fee based on "ability to pay" and not as a competitive, commercial enterprise using public land. This sliding grazing fee formula is similar to the ability-to-pay fee formulas used in many government welfare programs. Thus, when beef prices fell and production costs rose in the mid-1980s, the federal grazing fee was reduced to $1.35-$1.40/AUM for 5 years straight.

When the PRIA formula expired in 1985, Congress did not renew it. Instead, in February of that year, in a slick move that infuriated many reform advocates, rancher Ronald Reagan rode to the rescue and (while vacationing at his California ranch) promulgated an executive order directing the Secretaries of Agriculture and Interior (at their advisal) to permanently adopt the PRIA fee formula -- contrary to initial proposals by the White House Office of Management and Budget to increase the fee. Both Secretaries promptly did so, with a new provision that established a floor of $1.35/AUM. Consequently, the federal grazing fee remained $1.35/AUM through 1987. BLM spokesperson Joe Zilincar stated that without the minimum, the grazing fee would have dropped below $1.00/AUM.

The agencies accepted their marching orders despite their own 1986 report, *Grazing Fee Review and Evaluation*, which appraised the average market value of federal lands grazing at $6.65/AUM in 1983 (USDA, FS and USDI, BLM 1986). President Reagan's executive order conflicts with the spirit of FLPMA to "receive fair market value of the use of public lands and their resources" (Com. on Govt. Oper. 1986).

In 1987 a group of Congresspersons led by Oklahoma Representative Mike Synar (a private land cattle rancher) introduced legislation that would have raised the grazing fee from the then-current $1.35/AUM to $9.00/AUM, and that would have appropriated 25% of fee revenue to help restore degraded riparian areas. The ranching political establishment reduced this proposal by half in committee and then killed it when it reached the Senate floor.

In 1988, several factors -- Synar's bill, public pressure, revelations about public lands ranching's economic and environmental impacts, and increasing inflation of beef

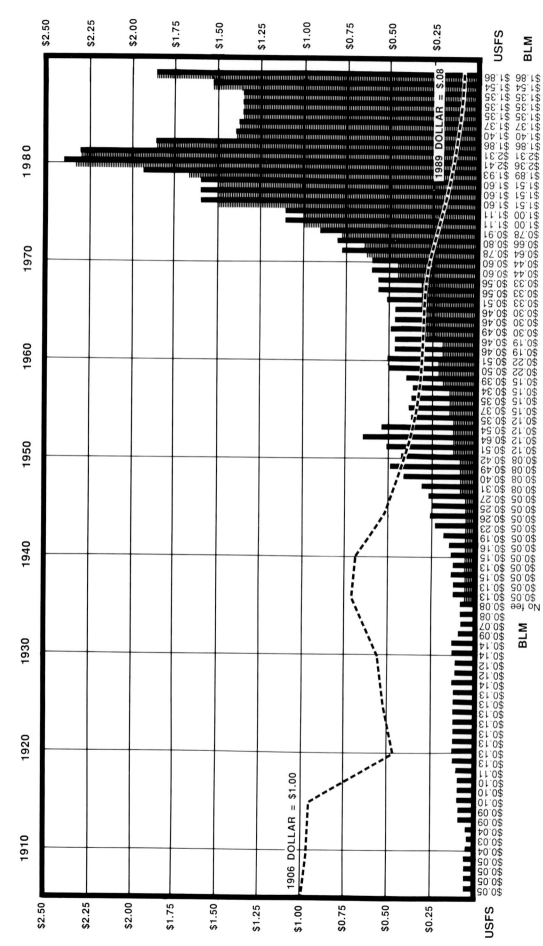

FEDERAL GRAZING FEES AND THE DECLINING DOLLAR: 1906-1989

(Sources: USDA, USFS, USDI, BLM 1986 and the Dow Jones Irwin Business and Investment Almanac)

prices -- combined to raise the grazing fee by 14%, to $1.54/AUM.

Also in 1988, the Natural Resources Defense Council and 8 other conservation organizations sued the federal government (*NRDC v. Hodel*) in an attempt to force it to raise the grazing fee to fair market value. The ranching industry again flexed its mighty muscles. One of its chief legal collaborators, Mountain States Legal Foundation, intervened in the case and the court ruled that the grazing fee did not violate any relevant statutes and, instead, that it fell under the broad authority of the Secretaries of the Interior and Agriculture.

In 1989, under the same influences described above, the federal grazing fee was raised 17% to $1.86/AUM. Much of the media, playing up the "poor, noble rancher," portrayed these 2 small increases as "drastic." Because the fee had always been extremely low, that is how it seemed to some people. In fact, however, the fee could have been raised 400% and still not have reached fair market value! According to the California Wilderness Coalition, real estate appraisers conservatively calculate that the increase to $1.86/AUM brought the fee up to only 20%-29% of the market value of federal grazing privileges.

Moreover, USDA in 1989 predicted that the federal grazing fee is likely to remain at this low level for many years. In 1990 its projection got a good start when the grazing fee was *reduced* 5 cents to $1.81/AUM, ostensibly in response to increasing production costs. However, beef prices currently are near an all-time high; when they drop the grazing fee probably will decrease even further. In other words, the huge gap between the federal fee and private fees will probably continue to widen.

Even if grazing fees are raised in the future, Reagan's executive order limits the increases to a maximum of 25% per year. At that rate, if the fee was raised from 1990's $1.81/AUM at the maximum each year -- an almost impossible scenario -- it would take *nearly 8 years* just to reach the average herbage fee paid for private rangeland. This assumes an inflation rate of zero, rather than the common 5%-10%, and the unlikely possibility that the cost of leasing private grazing will not rise.

After recent rule changes, National Forests in the East are divided into 6 grazing sub-regions, where grazing fees charged range from $0.84/AUM to $4.36/AUM in 1990. The new rules gradually phase out fixed fees and phase in competitive bidding; a "grandfather clause" allows ranchers to continue paying fixed fees until grazing permits change "ownership." So far, roughly 1/5 of the 1000 or so Eastern National Forest permittees are on the competitive fee system, though they pay on the average only slightly more than those on the fixed fee system.

Another bid to raise the grazing fee occurred in 1989, when Georgia Representative George Darden introduced legislation that would have rewritten the fee formula. And the latest attempt was once again organized by Representative Synar -- an amendment tacked onto a 1990 federal appropriations bill that would have raised the fee gradually to $8.70/AUM, or approximately fair market value. Both proposals occurred in the midst of a fiscal crisis in which Congress was desperate to trim fat from the federal budget, yet both were as usual promptly squashed by the ranching establishment's political behemoth. Synar vowed he would "be back again and again until we stop cattle rancher welfare once and for all . . . ."

The federal government allows ranchers to "lease" a land expanse nine times the entire state of New York for less than the rental cost of a single office building in downtown Manhattan.
--Robin Hur, "Six Inches from Starvation" (Hur 1985)

We're pleased with the current [grazing fee] system. We have never said we want to pay less than the value of the product. We want to pay what's fair.
--Ronald Michieli, Director of Natural Resources, National Cattlemen's Association

The history of the federal grazing fee "controversy" has been extremely one-sided. Ranchers must be said to have won each and every year, for they have never paid even 1/3 fair market value, and have averaged 1/5 to 1/10 what the range was worth. By far most proposals to increase the fee have been defeated, while those nominal increases that have been allowed scarcely keep up with inflation. Fees have been reduced in response to drought, wars, and depression, and there have been at least 4 moratoriums on scheduled increases, all for various reasons. Every decade since federal grazing fees were instituted stockmen have lamented to Congress about inflation, economic downturns, rising production costs, wartime hardships, livestock surpluses, low livestock prices, predation, drought and blizzard, rustlers, poor range conditions, and any other crisis that ostensibly justified continued minuscule grazing fees. Indeed, records show that nearly every fee raise proposal in history has met a flurry of these complaints. From the tenacity of these overwhelming problems, one might get the idea that public land is not a good place to raise livestock.

Ranchers, since 1934, pay fees for their use of public lands. Since 1966, these have been set at fair market value as determined through national studies.
--BLM

In most instances, the costs between private leases and public leases are comparable.
--Peter Decker, public lands rancher, former director of Colorado Agricultural Department

They lie.
--Mike Roselle, progressive activist

The BLM and FS grazing fee was **$1.81 per AUM** in 1990, while various other government agencies charge fees ranging roughly from $1/AUM to $15/AUM, with the vast majority of these AUMs going for under $3. (On federal ranges, calves graze for *free* until 6 months of age, and up until a year of age if they enter public land before 6 months of age, with the rancher paying only for the mother, even though calves eat forage and a lactating mother eats more [USDI, BLM 1978].)

In contrast, grazing fees on the Army's McGregor Range in southern New Mexico and the Navy's Boardman Bombing Range in northeast Oregon are determined by competitive bidding and approach fair market value. Ranchers there gladly pay an average of about $7-$8/AUM, even though precipitation at both of these installations averages less than 10" annually. Surrounding federal grazing, of course, goes for only $1.81/AUM. Buffalo National Wildlife Refuge in Texas charges $13/AUM -- perhaps the highest federal grazing fee in the country -- and has no lack of takers. (Matteson 1989)

In 1984 BLM and FS defined "fair market value" as "The amount that livestock owners would probably pay for the grazing use if it were offered for rent or lease in the open market" (Tittman 1984). According to the federal government's own *Grazing Fee Review and Evaluation*, the fair market value of the grazing privilege on federal lands was $6.65/AUM in 1983, or nearly 5 times higher than the $1.40/AUM federal grazing fee that year (USDA, FS and USDI, BLM 1986). The report also revealed that rates charged for private AUMs averaged about $7 during the early 1980s. In **Sacred Cows**, Denzel and Nancy Ferguson place the private lease rate at $8.83/AUM in 1983 (Ferguson 1983), while University of Colorado researchers Kerry Gee and Albert Madsen reported that government statisticians estimated -- in *Agricultural Prices*, USDA, Statistical Reporting Service, Washington, DC, Dec 30, 1983 -- that the 11 Western state average private grazing lease rate was $10.32/AUM that year (Gee 1986). Rates continued to rise in the 1980s, along with inflation. According to most estimators, private lease rates currently average roughly $8-$12/AUM; *$10.00/AUM is probably close to average fair market value in the West.*

Thus, today we find the BLM and Forest Service still selling ranching privileges for roughly **1/5** as much as do owners of private rangeland. Consequently, grazing fees represent only a small percentage of public ranchers' operating costs. Stockmen pay $21.72 to feed a cow on public lands herbage for a year (12 AUMs). If you have ever fed a cow, horse, pig, chickens, dog, or even a cat for a year, you'll appreciate this bargain. According to the Committee for Idaho's High Desert, "1 AUM provides a total weight gain of 28 to 90 pounds per cow. At 50 cents per pound wholesale each AUM produces $14 to $45 ($168-$540/year) for the rancher."

Just as the federal government collects fees for camping in public land campgrounds, the BLM and USFS collect grazing fees from ranchers whose cattle and sheep harvest public land forage.
--Mosley, *et al.*, *Seven Popular Myths About Livestock Grazing on Public Lands* (Note: The average cost for a night's camping in a federal campground would buy a public lands rancher about *4 months* of public forage for his cow.)

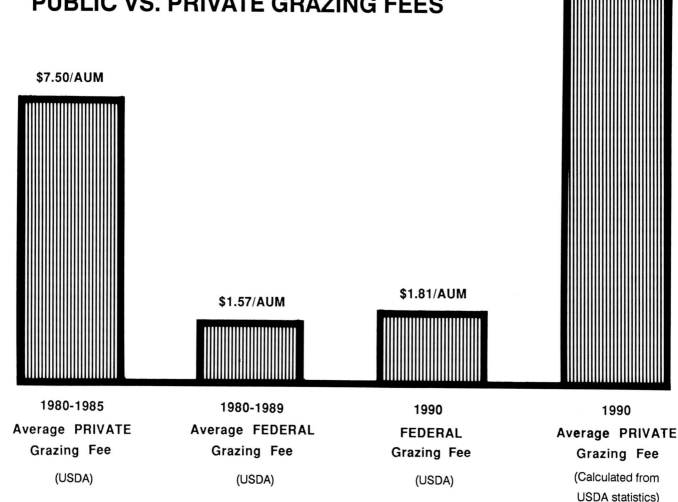

PUBLIC VS. PRIVATE GRAZING FEES

$10.00/AUM

$7.50/AUM

$1.57/AUM

$1.81/AUM

1980-1985
Average PRIVATE
Grazing Fee
(USDA)

1980-1989
Average FEDERAL
Grazing Fee
(USDA)

1990
FEDERAL
Grazing Fee
(USDA)

1990
Average PRIVATE
Grazing Fee
(Calculated from
USDA statistics)

Commercial river runners are especially distressed at the low fees charged ranchers for their grazing cattle because they, the river runners, have to pay $1.90 per person per day, which works out to around $57 per month. There is no environmental impact from these people (they pack out all their trash) yet each of them is charged 42 times more than a head of cattle that does impact the environment.

--Helene Klien, Ft. Lauderdale, Florida

The privileged few who use our rangeland for livestock are practically *given* the forage and browse! As reported in the Committee on Government Operations' 1986 *Federal Grazing Program*, "The difference in the appraised market value and actual grazing fees paid under PRIA average $75 million per year in Government revenue foregone" (Com. on Govt. Oper. 1986). If we divide this $75 million evenly among the 22,000 Western BLM and FS permittees, we find each being subsidized $3409 per year by low grazing fees alone. This aligns with a 1980 study (when grazing fees were about 10% higher) showing each permittee being subsidized approximately $3500 annually by low fees.

In fairness to taxpayers and to competitive stockmen on private land, as long as public lands ranching is allowed, herbage should be offered at the going market rate, or be sold by competitive bidding, as are leases for timber, mineral and oil, etc. Better yet would be open bidding (see Chapter XII).

In every case where the federal government puts up AUM's for bid, they bring in 4 or 5 times more than the standard fee. I'm talking about exactly the same kinds of range, the only difference being that one fee was set by Congress and the other by the free market. ... If it did cost so much more to graze public land, then the boys wouldn't bid those forage prices so high. But even if it did cost more to graze public land, my reaction as a cattleman is, "so what!" If it's too expensive, then don't graze it. Go somewhere else or get out of business. In any event, don't ask me as a competitor in the market place to subsidize your operation.

--from a letter by Lonnie Williamson of the Wildlife Management Institute to the President of the Nevada Cattleman's Association

Public lands graziers argue that the tiny fees are "fair" or even "excessive" because federal rangeland is less productive than private and the costs of maintaining fences, herding livestock, transportation, and so on therefore are higher. With brilliant reverse psychology, John Ross, Executive Vice-president of the California Cattlemen's Association says that, "Ranchers will always tell you the fees are too high, but basically the formula is a fair formula" (Hartshorn 1988). Some professional industry lackeys even recommend doing away with grazing fees altogether, as in the good ol' days. For example, a grazing fee study by John Fowler, professor of agricultural economics at New Mexico State University, concludes that grazing fees on some New Mexico state rangelands should be eliminated because ranchers can't afford them (McClellan 1985).

Few would argue against the claim that public land is generally less conducive to practical ranching than is private land. But it is ridiculous to suggest that additional production costs are 5 times as high, as many ranchers claim, or

even twice as high. Indeed, an extensive study of grazing fees by the federal government in 1986 found that production costs for cattle and sheep on public land were only slightly higher than on private -- $3.28/AUM compared to $2.75/AUM for cattle and $4.53/AUM compared to $3.89/AUM for sheep (USDA, FS and USDI, BLM 1986). That's **16%** and **14%** higher -- **not 500%** -- as claimed by welfare ranchers. The study calculated that, based on comparisons with private land grazing fees, in 1986 the market value for grazing a cow on public lands was $6.40 to $9.50 per month (O'Neill 1990).

At any rate, whatever expenses a public lands rancher incurs above and beyond the price of the herbage should have nothing to do with how much is charged for the herbage. Basing the grazing fee the government charges on ranchers' expenses is like a tire dealer basing the price of tires on the kinds of roads customers drive on.

Perhaps BLM PR man Joe Zilincar can set us straight. He says the grazing fee system was not set up to "return dollar for dollar. It's based on the cost of production." Since he claims that "producer" costs are far higher on public land than on private, we might ask him why public land is grazed at all. According to Zilincar, it is because "there is more public land than private land." (They don't call him "Bogus Logic Joe" for nothing.) Arizona Senator Dennis DeConcini, defending his powerful ranching constituency, expands upon Joe's twisted rationality:

Many ranchers are forced to graze Federal lands because of the lack of private lands in the West. Additionally, the conditions of rangelands in the arid regions of the Southwest are very different from the private grazing regions of the East and Midwest. For these reasons, a larger land area is necessary to sustain the needs of livestock. ... I support the current [grazing fee] formula, because ranching families need to be protected.

The contention that public lands grazing fees should be kept artificially low to compensate for the higher costs of grazing public lands is a self-defeating argument. However much more it may cost to graze public land than private is just that much more reason why it makes no economic sense to graze public land in the first place. It is not logical to subsidize an unneeded business that is inherently unprofitable. The unspoken contention is that ranchers should to be kept in business artificially because they are somehow more worthy than other people of being subsidized.

Public lands ranchers certainly maintain a vast competitive advantage over their private counterparts. In fact, simply by virtue of their geographic proximity to and use of public rangeland, they enjoy numerous subsidies unavailable to the other 97% of the nation's livestock producers -- who must buy land or lease ranchland at fair market value, pay taxes, finance many or most ranching developments, and so on. Therefore, it would be in the best interest of private stockmen to demand an end to public ranching.

Though some are doing so, by far most private lands stockman remain locked into a traditional system of "cowboy camaraderie" -- self-perpetuating mutual support and machismo that require approval of *all* ranching, regardless of what form it takes. Further, long-time public ranching expert Steve Johnson thinks that the livestock industry uses the public lands rancher as a "hood ornament" -- an insignificant, though prominent, publicly appealing cowboy/western figurehead.

They may not fully understand, but private lands ranchers thus hurt themselves in 2 important ways. First, they support their unfair competition. Second, and perhaps more important in the long run, they align themselves with a comparatively wasteful industry which probably will only continue to lose public support until it finally collapses. By association, the public may begin to perceive private lands ranching as little different than public (which, in environmental terms, it is). Because Western ranching has always ridden high on a platform of public sympathy, erosion of public support could well mean decline for Western private land ranching as well (no great loss to the Western economy or to the American meat supply).

F. Dale Robertson, Chief   Nov. 6, 1987
U.S. Forest Service
U.S. Dept. of Agriculture
P.O. Box 96090
Washington, DC 20090

Dear Sir,

As a full-time cattleman with a lifetime of experience in this highly competitive and economically treacherous business, I am disturbed by your agency's refusal to extract full market value from leasees now grazing cattle on the public lands of the West. A decade or so ago I thought the unfair taxpayer subsidies to the West's welfare ranchers were going to be phased out, and that fair market value on leases and permits would become actual policy _and_ practice.

I am currently paying $9/AUM for leased grass here in south-central Oklahoma. In the past 15 years I have paid as little as $7/AUM and as high as $10/AUM. My 78 year old father can only remember a few times when grass was worth less than $2/AUM -- in the past 60 years! The $1.35 - $1.50 you are charging is offensive to every cattleman I know who is aware of this practice.

Now I'm finding out that you want to abandon the fair market value policy without ever giving it a real try. This year my 500 head of cattle on leased grass will cost $54,000 for grass alone. At the standard Forest Service rate of $1.35/AUM I would be paying $8,100, or $45,900 less than fair market. Where's my subsidy money? -- I want to know where to apply. I'd like to know why you're giving up on fair market rates on public lands permits.

Sincerely,

David Sheegog
3SJ Land & Cattle Co.
Pauls Valley, OK

Not even bothering to go through the trouble of grazing livestock to fleece the taxpayer anymore, many permittees have taken to *subleasing* the herbage on "their" allotments. The permittee leases his base property, yet retains owner-ship of the ranch. The lessee, who then controls the base property, is treated by BLM like a permittee. The new permittee pays the federal grazing fee for the public land and pays the ranch owner *an undisclosed amount* for the lease itself.

Subleasing, per se, is not allowed on Forest Service land; however, FS officials say that they detect an average of 1 or 2 subleasing cases a year on each of the West's 98 National Forests (undoubtedly many more are not detected). Additionally, much illegal subleasing occurs on BLM land, and subleasing payments are concealed by confusing arrangements that defy the attempts of outsiders, including BLM, to uncover and prove. (Stein 1989) The US General Accounting Office concurs: "Unless reported by the permittee, livestock lease arrangements are difficult to identify" (USGAO 1986a).

In 1984 appraisers for both the BLM and Forest Service uncovered more than 2000 secret subleasing deals providing the original holder of the grazing permit "the opportunity to profit at the expense of the Treasury" (Com. on Govt. Oper. 1986). A recent study by Colorado State University researchers found more than 900 cattle permittees were subleasing "their" BLM allotments. Considering there are only about 19,000 BLM permittees altogether, 900 (almost 5% of the total) seems to indicate a serious problem. And one further wonders how many subleasers were not revealed.

These 900 were subleasing at an average rate of $7.76/AUM -- more than 5 times the then-current $1.35/AUM grazing fee charged by the federal government. Most of the difference went into ranchers' pockets. For example, according to the 5-11-87 *Reno Gazette-Journal*, multimillionaire Willard Garvey collected $120,000 rent in 1986 from a Humboldt County, Nevada rancher, while the government received only $14,587 in grazing fees for that public land. A 5-23-89 *Los Angeles Times* article states, "In one extreme case, a rancher along the Idaho-Oregon border reportedly paid more than $26 an AUM -- almost 20 times the government rate -- to graze cattle on a parcel that was 97% public land" (Stein 1989). This arrangement lasted 3 years, costing the rancher $18,000 annually, while the original permittee paid the government $891 annually.

BLM has "investigated" many cases of subleasing, though apparently with little intent of doing much about them. In 1984 Congress enacted legislation to recapture some of this lost government income, and instructed BLM to begin taking steps to do so. But BLM, by utilizing loopholes in its regulations, had by 1986 managed to collect only $8000 on 2 allotments accounting for the difference between $1.35/AUM and the fees actually charged, even though it had identified 633 "illegal subleases." This $8000 doesn't even cover the administrative cost to recover the funds. Failure to collect the difference on these 633 subleases alone represents a loss of government revenue of probably over $1 million. (Com. on Govt. Oper. 1986)

In the 1986 Congressional report by the Congressional Committee on Government Operations, *Federal Grazing Program: All Is Not Well on the Range*, the following conclusions were reached:

This insignificant amount [$8000 recaptured by BLM] is due to a narrow and questionable interpretation of the statute, delays in administrative proceedings, inadequate recordkeeping, and a "hands off" attitude toward permittees who benefit *financially from these arrangements. As a result, Congress' efforts to collect for the public fair market value in, at least, those instances in which market forces yield payment of a fee greater than that paid into the Treasury have met with failure.* (Com. on Govt. Oper. 1986)

Responding to the outrageous situation, an Inspector General's report stated: "One solution to the problem of subleasing, in our opinion, is an increase in the grazing fees to market value, which would eliminate most of the potential for subleasing grazing privileges at a profit."

The beneficiaries of this federal largesse [federal grazing sub-leasing] include the family of the head of the BLM, Robert Burford, as well as the multimillionaire businessman Willard W. Garvey, who heads a national tax protest group and opposes most other kinds of federal subsidies that don't pay off for him directly.
--9-30-87 *Sacramento Bee*

The federal grazing fee also creates many associated administrative problems. Generally, grazing fee bills are prepared and mailed out in advance, and permittees are supposed to pay their grazing fee charge *before* letting their livestock onto allotments. If bills are paid late, it is technically defined as "trespass" -- unauthorized grazing subject to penalty. However, the Inspector General's office in a 1984-85 investigation of BLM offices in Idaho, Montana, Nevada, New Mexico, and Oregon estimated that roughly 60% of all grazing fee payments involved some form of delinquency. The IG reported that BLM does not vigorously follow up on delinquent bills and is failing to collect trespass charges when permittees fail to pay their fees in advance. IG found that 105 of 180 bills for 1985 grazing fees they investigated were not paid until *after* livestock had been placed on the allotment -- and **no** trespass notices were issued. Further, only 5 delinquent bills were issued. The IG conservatively estimated potential trespass fees in the 105 cases they investigated would total anywhere from $58,000 to $173,000. (Com. on Govt. Oper. 1986)

A number of other associated administrative expenses caused by permittees are not recaptured by either BLM or FS. These include duplicate billing charges where the permittee was at fault, allotment use changes where the agencies do work supposed to be done by the permittee, and inadequate service charges for replacement billing.

Who controls the land, controls wealth.
--Calvin Black, infamous San Juan County, Utah, Commissioner

It's a right. Grazing permits are bought and sold. They're recognized by the IRS. They're taxed. No one else can graze my [public] land or sell my permit but me. It's mine.
--Bob Piva, Sawtooth National Forest, Idaho, permittee (Jones 1991a)

When base properties are sold, grazing permits are waived to the government, which nearly always reissues them to the purchasers. (Occasionally permits are reissued to purchasers of allotment livestock.) In effect, it is nearly impossible to obtain a grazing permit without buying a base property. This means that because grazing fees are ridiculously low as compared to the true market value of the

herbage they represent, government AUMs are sold as if they were part of private property when a ranchman sells his base property. Combined with the value represented by other subsidies, this is generally known as *permit value*. In their 1984 appraisal report on the fair market value of public grazing lands, the BLM and Forest Service state that "permit value can be defined as a leasehold value that accrues to the holder of the lease when contract rent is less than economic rent or fair market rent value" (Tittman 1984).

Thus, a cost averaging from $400 to $1500 for each cow authorized on a federal grazing permit, or an average of about $80 per AUM, is added to the price of the deeded property when sold (Ferguson 1983). Quite often the value of the public grazing allotment permit actually *exceeds* the value of the deeded property, house and improvements. An increase in the grazing fee or a decrease in livestock numbers would immediately lower ranch value, so of course public lands ranchers and their banks oppose such reasonable moves.

~~~~~~~~~~~~~~~~~~~~~~~~~~~~~~~~~~~~~

~~~~~~~~~~~~~~~~~~~~~~~~~~~~~~~~~~~~~

A typical ad for a Western public lands ranching base property, from a Utah newspaper.

I recently received a call from a realtor (a millionaire public lands rancher) who specialized in public lands ranches. A friend in Kansas had asked me to keep my eye out for a base property with a BLM and/or FS permit, for he wanted to buy it, *not* run livestock on the allotment for 5 years, and then challenge the government in court when the agency tried to force him to graze the allotment or tried to take the permit away and reissue it to someone else. Answering my query, the realtor told me of 4 public lands ranches for sale in southeast Arizona.

All had permits allowing the grazing of between 50 and 100 cattle on allotments yearlong, and all had extremely inflated asking prices because of it. One was merely 56 acres of deeded property not worth more than $100,000, but with 14,720 acres on a Forest Service grazing permit the asking price was $383,000. Another was only a 20 acre ranch with no house or substantial improvements thereon, yet the owner felt comfortable asking $254,000. According to the realtor, the land could not possibly have been worth more than $5000/acre, yet the owner could reasonably ask $12,700/acre simply because of the attached BLM and state land grazing permits! These examples are typical of public lands ranches around the West.

Say that Rancher Bob owns 10,000 acres. His neighbor, Rancher Bill, owns only 1,000 acres but controls a grazing permit for 100,000 acres of public land. Yet, because of the permit value, Bill might sell his property on the open market for as much as, or even more than, Bob.
Jon R. Luoma, "Discouraging Words" (Luoma 1986)

Public lands ranchers even take out loans using permits as collateral. A 1979 survey of appraisers and loan officers in New Mexico showed that they considered Forest Service permits to be worth $944 to $1163 per animal unit and BLM permits $667 to $888 per animal unit (Ferguson 1983). Some ranchmen have taken federal agencies to court over proposed livestock reductions, contending that the government is taking "their" property (Synar 1986). Here in southern Arizona, after a man inherited a public lands ranching operation from a deceased parent, IRS taxed him on the value of the grazing permit as well as the ranch. Indeed, grazing permits are handed down through the generations like priceless family heirlooms. Obviously, both the government and private sectors consider public lands grazing permits of great value.

If low grazing fees and other forms of government assistance were not really welfare subsidies, then the grazing privilege would carry little or no market value. It would amount to little more than a permit to run a business utilizing public land, not a guarantee of permanent government assistance. As it is, when someone acquires a public lands grazing permit with a purchased deeded property, he is not so much buying the privilege of grazing publicly owned land as use of the many subsidies that go with it.

In theory, all permit values combined should represent roughly the amount the public ranching industry is subsidized over and above the private. Just for fun, let's assume that the value of each BLM and FS ranching operation is $500,000 (probably fairly accurate). With 22,000 permittees, the combined value would be $11 billion. Assuming that the average permit value was only 1/3 the value of the base property, we still find the subsidy value represented by Western grazing permits to be $3.66 billion. Because private ranching is also subsidized, however, this would represent how much *more* is spent on public ranching than on private

-- not the total subsidy value. And, of course, this does not take into consideration other net losses to the government and public: degradation of natural resources, decreased use of public land, expenses incurred due to unfair open range laws, and so forth -- all of which could also be regarded as indirect subsidies.

The grazing fee system has other detrimental effects. Because they pay so little to use public range, many ranchers figure they might as well milk it for all it's worth. So they relentlessly pressure the agencies to maintain traditional, very high stocking rates. Because fee receipts per each animal grazed are so low, generally the agencies feel the need to maintain high numbers of livestock just to bring in whatever meager ranching income they can. However, even if livestock numbers were reduced drastically, expenditures on the government's ranching infrastructure would decrease little because most management is based on the mere presence of livestock, not their actual numbers.

Similarly, no matter how poorly ranchers run their operations, the sliding grazing fee is geared to keep them in business. Ranchers may therefore run shoddy, inefficient operations, overgraze and otherwise abuse the land, and then rely on cheap grazing to compensate. Thus, some say low grazing fees traditionally favor range abuse and further subsidization.

Throughout the history of the Taylor Act administration, only a small part of the total grazing receipts has gone ultimately into the federal treasury. . . . Half of all receipts were to be turned over to the states in which they were collected, with the state legislatures being required to expend the monies in the counties collected. I found it a startling exemplification of the political power of the range stockmen to discover that these funds were invariably turned over to the grazing district advisory boards to be expended for range improvements . . . ."
--Wesley Calef, **Private Grazing and Public Lands** (Calef 1960)

(Greg Pentkowski)

By authority of the Taylor Grazing Act, BLM today manages approximately 90% of its grazing land under that law's Section 3 (permits) and 10% under Section 15 (leases). Grazing fee receipts from Section 3 lands are disbursed as follows: Only 37.5% ($4.5 million in 1987) goes to the US Treasury. Some 12.5% goes back "in lieu of taxes" to the states from whence it came. Most of this small amount ($1.5 million in 1987) is used for state and county development, some of which benefits stockmen. Through the Range Betterment [sic] Fund, the remaining 50% ($5.9 million in 1987) *goes back to the grazing districts from whence it came, to be allocated by grazing "advisory" boards for ranching developments.* So tightly are these range "betterment" funds controlled by the "advisory" boards that they are commonly termed "advisory board funds." The BLM and Forest Service, in their *Appraisal Report Estimating the Fair Market Value of Public Rangelands in the Western United States Administered by the USDA-Forest Service and USDI-Bureau of Land Management*, state that:

> The advisory boards derive their funds from the portion of the grazing fees that are returned to the state and local county for range improvements. These funds are spent in a manner similar to improvement funds appropriated to the agencies. (Tittman 1984)

The US Treasury receives *nothing* from Section 15 BLM grazing fee receipts. Half ($1.5 million in 1987) goes to the Range Betterment Fund, from which it is disbursed for range developments in the grazing districts it came from. The other 50% goes back to the states from whence it came; again, some of this benefits lessees. (USDA, FS and USDI, BLM 1986; USDI, BLM 1988)

The Forest Service's grazing fee receipts are disbursed similarly to BLM's. Half ($4 million in 1987) goes into the Range Betterment Fund, to be returned to the National Forests for ranching development. Another 25% ($2 million in 1987) goes to back to the states for disbursement to the counties of origin for roads and schools, some of which benefit permittees. The remaining 25% ($2.0 million in 1987) goes to the US Treasury. (USDA, FS 1988)

In other words, BLM and FS permittees actually pay more than half of their federal grazing fees right back to themselves for ranching development. This means that the *actual* 1990 grazing fee, rather than $1.81/AUM, is less than $0.90/AUM, or **less than 1/10 fair market value**. This works out to about 3 cents per day per cow -- roughly what it costs to feed a hamster.

Less than 1/3 (31%) of federal grazing fee receipts end up in the federal Treasury. In 1987 all BLM and FS grazing fees combined yielded only $21 million and netted the US Treasury only **$6.5 million**. Yet, in their blind dedication to their ranching cohorts, the agencies contradict their own statistics. Verbatim from BLM's 1987 report, *Public Lands Statistics*: "Receipts from Section 3 grazing use at $1.35 per AUM returned $11,892,137 to the U.S. Treasury during the fiscal year 1987" (USDI, BLM 1988). And, verbatim from the Forest Service's 1987 report, *Report of the Forest Service: Fiscal Year 1987*: "The range program was funded at $31.4 million [including range "betterment" funds] in 1987, and returned $8.1 million to the Treasury from grazing fees" (USDA, FS 1988). The agencies tell us that they collected about $20 million from grazing fees for the US Treasury in 1987, when actually the Treasury netted only 6.5 million.

FEDERAL GRAZING FEE DISBURSEMENTS:1987

(Source: USDA, FS and USDI, BLM 1986; USDI, BLM1988a; and USDA, FS 1988)

50%
($5.9 million)

Range Betterment Fund for range development on BLM districts where fees collected

37.5%
($4.5 million)

US Treasury

12.5%
($1.5 million)
States, in lieu of taxes

BLM -- Section 3 lands
Total -- $11.9 million

50%
($1.5 million)

Range Betterment Fund for range development on BLM districts where fees collected

50%
($1.5 million)

States where fees collected

BLM -- Section 15 lands
Total -- $2.9 million

50%
($4.0 million)

Range Betterment Fund for range development on National Forests and USFS Regions where fees collected

25%
($2.0 million)

US Treasury

25%
($2.0 million)

Counties where fees collected

Forest Service
Total -- $8.1 million

Public lands ranchers' $6.5 million contribution represents about 1/180,000 of the federal government's annual income (US Dept. of Com. 1986). If derived from anyone but ranchers, this amount would command scarcely any notice by a Congress almost overwhelmed by a multitude of enormous fiscal concerns.

Moreover, while the federal government netted this $6.5 million in 1987, it reported spending about 10 times that amount directly on ranching programs that year, with the BLM and Forest Service spending about $34 million and $31.5 million respectively. Less than $10 million of this $65 million was grazing fee money returned through the Range "Betterment" Fund, resulting in a net loss of roughly **$50 million** to the US Treasury. (USDA, FS 1988 and USDI, BLM 1988)

Bear in mind that government figures reflect only money spent directly on ranching programs as defined by the US government, and do not include the many obscure and secret costs (detailed in the next section). Even if stockmen were to pay grazing fees several times fair market value, revenues would not begin to cover expenditures.

BLM and FS themselves report spending an average of $4.50/AUM directly on ranching programs, leaving a deficit of about $2.54/AUM on ranching programs alone ($2.54 x 20 million 1987 BLM and FS AUMs = $50.8 million lost). Furthermore, between 1979 and 1983, BLM received only 11.1 cents for every dollar it spent directly on reported ranching programs, while the Forest Service received only 21 cents on the dollar. A federal study has shown that the government spends about $10 on range "improvements" for each $1 it collects in grazing fees. This compares to an average ratio of $1 spent for every $3 collected from timber, firewood, recreation, power, land lease, rights-of-way, and other commercial public lands users (of course this study does not reflect many of the indirect costs of grazing, timber, or other programs).

The Forest Service reported that the total revenues collected from all commercial National Forest users in 1986 was $1.72 billion. In comparison, gross receipts from grazing fees amounted to only $8.1 million, or 0.47% of the total receipts collected. (USDA, FS 1988) BLM reported receiving about $220 million from all commercial users in 1987, while its grazing receipts amounted to only $14.3 million, or about 6%, of the total. Thus, of the agencies' combined revenues of nearly $2 billion, only $22.4 million -- or about 1% -- came from ranching receipts. If money returned to ranchers through the Range Betterment Fund is included, the figures are $11.2 million and 0.5%.

Further, since 1983 federal oil, gas, and mineral revenue has been received by the Department of the Interior's Mineral Management Service (MMS), rather than the agencies that administer the land. In 1987 MMS collected $621 million in total on-shore mineral royalties in the 11 Western states, nearly all of it from BLM and FS land. (USDI, MMS 1988) So, annual receipts from Western federal land users actually total more than $2.5 billion, of which ranching's net contribution is about 4/10 of 1%. In other words, though the ranching industry utilizes and degrades more public land than all other commercial users combined, it paid about 230 times less than other commercial users combined to do so.

Furthermore, even the *annual worth* of public lands livestock grazing is less than what we taxpayers spend on it. The forage and browse consumed by livestock on BLM and FS land produce an estimated total livestock market value of only **$390 million** annually (Ferguson 1983), and all Western federal, state, county, and city grazing lands combined produce perhaps **$500 million** worth of livestock annually. This $500 million is about half what taxpayers spend on public lands ranching each year.

Compare this $500 million figure to the 1987 value of all US cattle, including dairy cows, which is $41.3 *billion*. Americans spend more each year on strawberries ($504 million), birdseed ($517 million), and jogging shoes ($572 million). In 1990, outdoor recreationists spent about $80 billion, or roughly 160 times more than the value of public lands livestock. They would spend much more if not for environmental degradation and user competition from public lands ranching. (US Dept. of Com. 1986)

> *In his book* Livestock Pillage, *Edwin G. Dimick compares the economic values derived from the 6 major "multiple uses" of public land identified by the federal government -- water, timber, minerals, wildlife, outdoor recreation, and livestock. From statistics compiled from federal publications, Dimick summarizes that of the 6, livestock is not only the least valuable and least cost-effective, but by far the biggest detractor from the other multiple uses.*

Abusive grazing practices on federal land are acquiesced to by the Forest Service and Bureau of Land Management because of the political clout of certain western ranching interests that have grown fat on gigantic government subsidies. The needs of huge numbers of hunters, fishermen, campers, farmers, municipalities, and nature lovers for well-watered ecosystems have been subordinated to the greed of a few who are creating deserts for short-term profits.

--Paul Ehrlich, **The Machinery of Nature** (Ehrlich 1986)

Regardless of the economic loss, the whole fee controversy obscures the main problem -- public lands ranching. If the grazing fee was raised to fair market value, or even $100/AUM (assuming any rancher would pay this), by far most of its environmental, political, social, and even economic problems would remain.

(For a more complete discussion of grazing fees, see Calef 1960, Foss 1960, Voigt 1976, Com. on Govt. Oper. 1986, or USDA, FS and USDI, BLM 1986)

Squandering Our Taxes

Dear Brandholder,

"Stand on your own two feet" independence. That's a brand you and I wear with pride. It's a trait you and I share as Idahoans . . . as Americans . . . and especially as cattlemen.
--Public lands rancher Vern France, for the Idaho Cattle Association

The cowboy is a symbol of rugged individualism, of Western independence. No handouts, no special favors, just man and his determination against the elements. How odd, then, that ranching is the most government-subsidized industry in Wyoming.
--Scott Farris, Lander, Wyoming

The BLM and Forest Service annually spend about 50 million federal tax dollars directly on ranching in excess of grazing fee returns -- an average annual subsidy of at least $2273 for each of the agencies' 22,000 Western grazing permittees. Let's look closer at where our money goes.

BLM and FS provide *at least* matching funds for nearly all range developments, and the great majority are financed mostly or wholly by the agencies, often augmented by other federal, state, and/or county agencies. The federal government's 1986 report, *Grazing Fee Review and Evaluation*, states that from 1978 to 1984 permittees contributed an average of only $0.16 per AUM (BLM) and $0.30 per AUM (FS), compared to an average federal subsidy of $3.00 and $6.00 per AUM, respectively (USDA, FS and USDI, BLM 1986). In other words, the taxpayer forks over roughly 20 times more for ranchers' range "improvements" than ranchers do; stockmen pay only 5% of the cost of ranching developments on public land. Moreover, this neglects that many ostensibly non-ranching developments are designed to benefit ranching, and that many stockmen habitually inflate their development expenditure figures.

> *For example, in 1977, the total private range improvements constructed on all BLM rangelands in 11 western states included 9 miles of pipeline, 17 springs, 1 water catchment basin, 1 well, 24 cattle guards, and 14 miles of fencing.*
> --Denzel & Nancy Ferguson, **Sacred Cows** (Ferguson 1983)

Furthermore, when range developments are made under BLM "improvement permits," permittees are allowed to retain ownership in proportion to their original investment. In practice, often some portion of the "improvement" value a rancher assumes ownership of actually is contributed by the agencies. When a rancher sells a grazing permit with a base property, these values are transferred to the new owner. (Tittman 1987)

Because BLM does not account for range development expenditures by project, it is difficult to determine just where and how BLM range funds are spent. Likewise, BLM does not have an accurate inventory of range developments on BLM land, so no one really knows what is out there. It is also reported that BLM often spends range development funds on projects that are not allowable under guidelines set down by their parent funding sources. (Com. on Govt Oper. 1986)

BLM is required to prepare cost benefit analyses for range projects. Yet more than 1/3 of the project files examined by the Inspector General's office in 5 locations in 1985 did not contain cost benefit analyses. Further, BLM often spends money on range projects that are not supported by required cost benefit analyses. (Com. on Govt. Oper. 1986) For example, according to the Committee for Idaho's High Desert, "It costs from $11.70 to $43.50 for the BLM to spray grasshoppers to prevent them from eating $1.35 (1 AUM) of forage." BLM's response? None -- it has no valid economic justification for grasshopper spraying.

BLM and FS both "improve" the range essentially whenever, wherever, and however they see fit, assuming they have the funding. Following is a general rundown of range "improvement" costs.

Forest Service employees installing a fence. *(USFS)*

Those ever-present barbed wire fences that criss-cross our public land and line our roads cost roughly $2000 to $4000 a mile to build, and an average of perhaps $10 to $20 annually per mile to maintain (depending on terrain and economic variables). Taxpayers bear most of the cost. Large sections of fence damaged or destroyed by "natural disasters" (fire, flood, earthquake, landslide, etc.) usually are repaired or replaced using tax money. I read of one case where a fire started by a permittee on his private land burned onto adjacent Forest Service land and destroyed a portion of fence and cattleguard braces. A Forest Service range conservationist called the next day offering new wooden posts.

Taxpayers provide thousands of human "walk-overs" on public land.

On the Pacific Coast in Los Padres National Forest, California.

BLM and FS construct several thousand miles of fence yearly. Each year other federal agencies, states, counties, and cities erect thousands of additional miles for ranching purposes, or to keep livestock out of developed and agricultural areas, watersheds, parks, recreation areas, seedings and tree plantings, natural areas, riparian zones, etc.

A 400' well, electric pump with concrete foundation, solar panels on a concrete base, and 5000-gallon holding tank on a special gravel bed. Note the fencing to prevent cattle from damaging equipment. Water is piped to a nearby stock water trough. Costs include never-ending monitoring, maintenance, repair, and replacement. *(BLM)*

A BLM cattle watering development on a remote east-central Nevada range.

A tax-funded, 12'-high holding tank for cattle. *(BLM)*

The several hundred thousand stock ponds and other stock watering systems that dot our public land vary greatly in price, according to the size and complexity of the projects. Their cost ranges from a few hundred dollars to $100,000 or more; most fall into the $2000 to $10,000 range. Several thousand new water developments are built by BLM and FS each year. Maintenance costs are high.

Believe it or not, livestockmen in Oregon successfully sued the BLM during the '70's when a water development failed and cattle were lost. Like suing Santa Claus, huh?
--Edwin G. Dimick, **Livestock Pillage of Our Western Public Lands** (Dimick 1990)

Range vegetation manipulation projects also vary greatly in cost. The 2 agencies annually spend several million dollars to "treat" hundreds of thousands of public acres with machinery, herbicides, prescribed burns, and grass seedings. The initial cost to seed crested wheatgrass, for example, averages around $40 per acre. After an allotment is seeded by

BLM's 267,193-acre Vale Seeding Project in eastern Oregon cost about $307,692 per permittee affected. *(BLM)*

the government and the permittee is able to produce more welfare cattle, he still pays the same $1.81/AUM grazing fee. The Southern Utah Wilderness Alliance recently prepared a cost-benefit analysis of BLM's draft EIS for its proposed vegetation management program; it revealed that federal expenditures would be $320 for every $1 returned.

The Forest Service's $30.5 million 1986 range program included: construction of more than 3860 structural improvements, such as fences, water developments, and pipelines; treatment of 12,000 head of cattle for ticks and lice; placement of 315 poisoned bait stations to kill ants; spraying of 23,000 acres with herbicides and 600,000 acres with pesticides; and "forage improvement," such as burning, seeding, and mechanical treatment, on about 100,000 acres. Planning, monitoring, inventory, and administrative costs for implementing these range developments are included in range program budgets, along with general administrative costs. Other range-related expenses include, according to the Forest Service, "salaries and benefits, travel, transportation of things, supplies, materials, and equipment, and other contractual services." BLM's fiscal information on all this is very sketchy.

Approximately 90% of the mass of an iceberg floats below the surface of the water. The ranching subsidies outlined so far collectively comprise what is termed agency "range programs." Now we begin the arduous task of plucking out and revealing the indirect, unseen, and covert subsidization of public lands ranching -- a combined tax burden that represents the submerged ice.

The only [recent] *improvements* [on my allotment] *have been two* accidental *fires, one water tank* for wildlife, *the seeding of the Billy Mountain burn* for erosion control, *and over 10 miles of drift fence which I have built with materials* furnished by county range funds and the BLM. [emphasis added]
--Philip Krouse, Oregon public lands rancher, in a complaint to the Forest Service over the lack of range "improvements"

A cattle-depleted crested wheatgrass seeding on BLM land near Walti Hot Spring, Lander County, Nevada. Though stockmen are the only significant beneficiaries, American taxpayers spend millions of dollars on such seedings. This one is marked "Keystone Seeding."

As detailed in Chapters III and IV, many BLM and FS projects not identified with ranching are designed as much, if not more, for ranching than for their alleged purposes; and, *most* agency programs are geared to benefit ranching in some manner. Indeed, the agencies spend far more on ranching development indirectly through these ostensibly non-ranching efforts than through the ranching programs themselves -- usually to the detriment of the parent program. The statistics below are taken from the most recent BLM and Forest Service annual reports (USDI, BLM 1988 and USDA, FS 1988) and from BLM's *Budget Justifications, Fiscal Year 1989* (USDI, BLM 1988a). Because few figures on ranching expenditures exist, conclusions, while hard to refute, are necessarily conjectural.

The Forest Service spent nearly half a billion dollars on its Timber program in 1987, while BLM spent $7.1 million on its Forest Management program. Among the timber-related activities intentionally designed to promote ranching are brush disposal, fuelwood cutting, and timber thinning. As mentioned, some logging projects are also covertly designed to create more grazing land, or at least land that is more grazable. Additionally, forest management in grazing areas must allow for (and is sometimes complicated by) fences, gates, grazing plans, rancher access, and livestock themselves. Reforestation and soil erosion control tree plantings, usually of pine or fir, frequently are damaged or destroyed by livestock that eat and trample the small trees and damage structural improvements.

While only a relatively small proportion of the Forest Service's Timber budget is attributable to ranching, it nonetheless probably totals several million dollars. BLM's forest program is much more geared

A stock tank on public land.

toward ranching -- including, for example, woodland "removal of shrub stands by mechanical chaining to improve range conditions . . . ." A knowledgeable inside source informed me that roughly 1/3, or more than $2 million, of the BLM's annual forest management budget is ascribable to ranching.

Instead of ridding the Trout Creek Mountains of livestock [to improve trout habitat], the Vale [BLM] District spent considerable sums of public funds in an attempt to improve fish habitat. Thousands of willow seedlings were planted, 49 small trash collector dams were constructed to improve pool habitat, and several miles of fence were built to keep livestock out of some riparian areas.

[Due mostly to livestock:] By 1980 nearly all the willows were gone. Flooding destroyed 60% of the trash catcher dams and siltation reduced the habitat effectiveness of the remainder.
--George Wuerthner, "A Case of Poor Public Range Policy" (Wuerthner 1990a)

In the Trout Creek Mountains, the BLM plans to spend $400,000 over the next several years [the early 1990s] installing fences, pipelines, reservoirs, and other improvements on 500,000 acres to protect fish and fragile desert streams from cows. The agency takes in about $87,000 in grazing fees annually from the ranchers who lease the four grazing allotments.
Kathie Durbin, "Storm Brews Over Livestock Grazing" (Durbin 1991)

This area of Prescott National Forest, Arizona, was replanted with ponderosa pine saplings in 1972. The half-acre at right was fenced from cattle. *(Rod Mondt)*

Ranching's fiscal impact on federal mineral, oil, and gas programs is obscure, but a definite relation does exist. For example, mining operations are often fenced to exclude livestock. Ranching roads are rerouted. Conflicts arise over access to or use of water sources, and the government must play referee. When mineral, oil, and gas activities impact ranching or vice versa (and because ranching is nearly omnipresent, they usually do), management plans and administration must be altered. The BLM's 1987 minerals management budget was nearly $80 million, while the Forest Service's was $27 million.

"AND JUST THINK, LITTLE FISHY, THIS WAY YOU AND THE COW CAN BOTH LIVE IN THE STREAM !/ "

(Ginny Rosenberg)

Spruce Grove, Mendocino National Forest, California. *(Rex Kowz)*

"This fence was constructed by the Forest Service to control [exclude] livestock grazing and to protect important wildlife habitat." *(Don Morris)*

As detailed elsewhere, federal wildlife programs are largely at the mercy of the ranching industry. In 1987 the Forest Service spent $42.6 million on its Wildlife and Fish Habitat Management program. Funds were used to "treat" 124,138 acres with prescribed burning, herbicides, mechanical devices, and seedings; to plant trees and bushes; to develop water sources; to fence livestock from riparian areas; to build instream structures; and so on. Most of these projects benefited ranching, while many were necessitated by ranching. Likewise, BLM spent about $17 million in 1987 on its Wildlife Habitat Management program for "58 fence modifications, 611 instream structures, 124 new water facilities, 40,995 acres of prescribed burns, 242 water facility improvements, 148 miles of fences [mainly to exclude livestock], 16 spawning bed stabilization projects, 81 streambank stabilization projects, 314 acres of chainings, 2773 acres of seedings," and other developments.

For example, several years ago cottonwood along the Gila River Box in Arizona was not regenerating due to livestock grazing. In response BLM planted and fenced individual cottonwood saplings and installed drip irrigation. The project was funded through the district's *wildlife* budget. (Wuerthner 1989) Recently it was destroyed by marauding cattle.

The BLM's wildlife program is much more heavily geared to ranching than is the Forest Service wildlife program. It is safe to assume that at least $15 million annually of combined BLM and Forest Service wildlife expenditures are necessitated by, or designed to benefit, ranching.

A fenced cottonwood in the Gila River Box, Arizona. *(George Wuerthner)*

Under stockmen's relentless pressure to eliminate livestock competitors, BLM has spent *well over $100 million* in federal taxes on its Wild Horse and Burro program since the late 1970s. While thousands of horses and burros already languish in federal corrals awaiting adoption, BLM reported that it appropriated $14,735,000 in 1988 to capture, hold, and make available for adoption an additional 8500 animals. In 1980 BLM reported that it "expended an average of $100,000 per year to fund" research projects at 6 Western colleges and universities to explore methods to reduce free-roaming horse populations and their competition with livestock. The Forest Service says it captured and made available for adoption 156 horses and burros in 1987, though it doesn't state in its fiscal report how much it spent doing so. In sum, about $12-$15 million annually is spent by the agencies to remove free-roaming horses from public land, mostly to placate the ranching establishment.

BLM's Wild Horse Distribution Center in Burns, Oregon. *(BLM)*

These [BLM instream restoration structures] *remain functional within the ungrazed Lower Big Creek study site because they have been relatively undamaged by livestock. Outside the exclosure, however, where heavy grazing continues, most of the structures have been destroyed by livestock trampling and subsequent streambank erosion.*
--William Platts and Rodger Nelson, "Characteristics of Riparian Plant Communities and Streambanks with Respect to Grazing in Northeastern Utah" (Platts 1989)

A structure designed to stabilize bank erosion on central New Mexico BLM cattle range.

This "Watershed Restoration Project" is basically a livestock grazing enhancement project. Coronado National Forest, Arizona. The roadside has been devegetated.

The 1987 FS fiscal report shows that its Soil and Water Management program spent about $34 million (some of these funds are appropriated from timber sales). As an "example of a watershed improvement project," the report includes a photo of a newly bladed dirt tank in a meadow. The caption reads, "Benefits provided for improved wildlife habitat and increased forage production" -- but the tank will be used by far mostly by cattle, and it is located in an area already endowed with water sufficient for wildlife but insufficient for cattle.

BLM spent $17.3 million in 1987 on its equivalent program, Resource Conservation and Development. Included were "brush control, seeding, soil stabilization, water detentions and diversions, dikes, pipelines, reservoirs, spring developments, water catchments, wells, cattleguards, and fencing," much of it necessitated by destructive ranching. Much of this activity was unquestionably *designed* to benefit ranching, yet it is all listed under a non-ranching category.

The gully erosion is caused mostly by a livestock-degraded watershed and the direct impact of cattle on the drainage itself.

A BLM attempt to reduce range soil erosion -- a foot high post-and-wire-mesh fence.

An erosion control structure on cattlized BLM range in central New Mexico. Most of these types of developments are located in remote areas, so few Americans ever see them.

This cutbank stabilization structure on BLM range in Socorro County, New Mexico, probably cost several hundred thousand dollars. Note the size of the human figures at top-center.

Ranching is the only permanent, general consumptive activity allowed in designated Wilderness Areas. Roughly half of Western Wildernesses are grazed by livestock, and ranching detracts from their management, environmental health, and public use more than any other land use. BLM spent over $7 million on Wilderness Management in 1988, probably at least $1 million of this to build ranching-related developments, mitigate ranching impacts, minimize conflicts due to ranching, and accommodate Wilderness planning to ranchers' demands. The Forest Service administers 70 times more Western Wilderness than does BLM, and spent $10.3 million in 1987 on its management.

Forest Service benches upended and damaged by cattle.

On their 1987 Recreation programs, the Forest Service and BLM spent approximately $100 million and $15 million respectively (excluding Wilderness funding). Ranching heavily influences these programs. For example, hundreds of Western campgrounds have been fenced to exclude cattle. Those that are not are often trampled and denuded by invading cattle, and helpless campers are left with dust, flies, and cowpies. Livestock damage tent sites, tables and benches, barbecue grates, water lines, drainage ditches, fences, walkways, signs, docks, backpacking shelters, ramadas, buildings, and other recreational developments. Livestock diminish and pollute drinking water sources, necessitating water developments, filtration, and chlorination. To protect natural areas, as well as archaeological and historical sites, hundreds of fences have been erected, while areas left unprotected often have been damaged. Much of the West's 200,000 or so miles of foot trails is trampled, eroded, and covered with livestock excrement. Recreation planning and management must be geared to accommodate ranching; hunting and fishing are adversely affected. And so on. It is probable that public lands ranching forces the Forest Service and BLM to spend at least an extra several million dollars annually on their Recreation programs.

We are in the process of developing a plan to conduct a two stage controlled burn on a 2560 acre area of ponderosa pine and chaparral on the Walnut Creek Allotment. . . . In addition, we intend to construct a 3 wire pasture division fence . . . to better implement the Summer Flex pasture rotation system on the allotment.

--Emilio S. Lujan, District Ranger, Prescott National Forest, Arizona

Fire fighting and prevention, while costly to the public, is often lucrative to the livestock grazier. If not for ranching much of it would be unnecessary, especially on rangelands where there is usually little considered "of value" other than forage and fences to protect. Funding for FS fire fighting and protection in 1987 was $284 million. Most of this amount was, of course, attributable to the protection of structural developments and saleable timber, but ranching also figures prominently. BLM's 1987 Firefighting and Rehabilitation budget was $83 million. Two-thirds of the fires fought with this money were on rangeland; nearly all of the remaining third was on grazed forest, and only 1% was on "commercial forest."

How many fires could be allowed to burn naturally instead of being suppressed to protect forage, range "improvements," 30,000 public lands ranch headquarters, and livestock? How many destructive fires are indirectly or directly the result of public lands ranching: cheatgrass, "weed," and brush "invasions"; artificial forage monocultures; range activities that start accidental fires; range arson; and range fire suppression that allows fuel to build up to dangerously high levels? (For example, ranching-spread cheatgrass is credited with extending Idaho's fire season by 2 months [ONDA 1990].) How much of the brush disposal, herbiciding, controlled burning, and forest thinning done in the name of fire prevention is actually done to benefit public lands ranching? No one knows for sure, but it is clear that without public lands ranching fire prevention costs could easily be reduced by millions of dollars per year.

In 1990 there were more than 375,000 miles of maintained dirt roads in National Forests (Foreman 1991). Federal appropriations of $63 million were used in 1987 to perform road maintenance on FS roads. If we assume only 10% of these costs were attributable to ranching, it adds up to $6.3 million -- approximating the $8.1 million taken in from FS grazing fees that year. Forest Service road construction funding that year was $233 million. An overwhelming percentage of these new roads were logging roads; yet if merely 1% were ranching roads their cost would amount to $2.3 million.

Far more miles of road traverse BLM land, where there is probably several times as much driveable land. Many BLM staffers have admitted to me that by far more of the roads on BLM land are for ranching than for any other purpose. Most are built and maintained by counties and states. Some are engineered by BLM and contracted out for construction and maintenance. The contractees are sometimes the same permittees using them for ranching -- the local rancher with a Cat and blade -- so in effect these people are paid by the government to build and maintain their own range developments.

According to a phone interview with BLM engineering staff in Washington, DC, the actual amount spent on road maintenance is buried in the BLM's budget for buildings, recreation, facilities, and transportation. But they indicated that roughly $3-4 million annually has been spent in recent years on BLM road maintenance. Funding for road construction has been much less, and available only sporadically in recent years; permittees are encouraged to build BLM roads themselves! However, an Arizona BLM official stated that $300,000 was procured for road construction in that state in 1988.

Though roads are a major form of ranching development on public land, neither the Forest Service nor BLM link road construction and maintenance to range programs. And many are constructed and maintained by these and other agencies with taxpayers' money under pretenses. These include "old logging roads" (that happen to still be maintained and that services ranching areas), "fire fighting access roads," "wildlife maintenance roads," "forest management roads," "administrative roads," and (the all-time favorite) "general public access roads" (which were often never requested by the general public, are rarely used by the general public, and just happen to lead to a range development or livestock foraging area).

Large cattle guards such as this cost tens of thousands of tax dollars each.

The next time you bounce over one of those tens of thousands of cattle guards in rural areas, picture $3000 to $25,000 tax dollars floating off to that big ranch in the sky. Our collective generosity also provides those tens of thousands of "CATTLE GUARD," "CATTLE XING," "WATCH FOR LIVESTOCK," "CLOSE THE GATE!," and allotment boundary signs. BLM alone reports spending well over $1 million each year installing and maintaining signs.

The Forest Service spent $15 million in 1987 maintaining its 11,200 buildings and related support facilities, and $25.7 million constructing new facilities. Most of this activity was

in the West; perhaps a few million dollars of it would not have been necessary without public lands ranching. The BLM spent about $5 million in 1987 on building construction and maintenance; chalk up another million to ranching.

A partial cost of buildings and their maintenance is another obscure cost of public lands ranching. Utah BLM Henry Mountain Resource Area headquarters.

FS and BLM expended roughly $10 million on law enforcement in 1987. Because the 22,000 ranchers spread evenly across Western federal land exert such powerful control and so heavily impact this land, special agents and law enforcement rangers from these agencies (and state police and county sheriffs) spend much time settling conflicts between ranchers and other public lands users. Disputes over trespass, access, and use are especially numerous, and threats and assaults by stockmen and their hired help are common. Officials also must investigate and process those accused of harming livestock, interfering with ranching operations, and tampering with range developments. Further, the extensive webwork of ranching roads has introduced much of the illegal activity, such as the looting of archaeological sites, that occurs on public land. In sum, public lands ranching probably adds more than a million dollars annually to BLM and Forest Service law enforcement programs.

The Forest Service produced 94 publications pertaining to range and grazing in 1986, and dozens more indirectly relating to ranching. Along with dozens produced by BLM, this amounts to hundreds of thousands of dollars expended annually.

BLM's Planning and Data Management program spent $24.6 million in 1987, and will spend twice as much in 1989. The purpose of the program is to "improve resource management decisions" and to develop an effective data management system. This involves problem identification and analysis, conflict resolution, coordination with other agencies, public relations, and modernization of data processing. Because much of this relates directly to ranching, we may assume that at least several million dollars of this program would be unnecessary without public lands ranching.

The Forest Service spent $27 million, and the BLM $12 million, on survey-related activities in 1987, a small portion of it due to ranching allotments. BLM and National Forest land management plans, Environmental Impact Statements, appeals processes, etc. are also sponsored by the federal government. Ranching is involved in much of this, to the tune of millions of dollars.

The Forest Service received roughly $150 million from government sources in 1987 for research. Ranching-related research included watershed management and rehabilitation; wildlife, fish, and range; and fire and atmospheric sciences. The multi-million dollar Rocky Mountain Forest and Range Experiment Station in Ft. Collins, Colorado, is one of 8 regional experiment stations. Drop a few million more into the public ranching trough.

Aside from range programs and possibly roads, perhaps the single biggest expenditure category for federal ranching is general administration, for which in 1987 FS and BLM spent $263 million and $87 million respectively. That year the Forest Service listed 27,400 full-time, 2901 part time permanent, and 15,783 temporary employees, while the BLM employed 6814 full-time personnel.

The agencies' range programs include salaries for their hundreds of full-time range specialists. But thousands more employees in other programs and general administration spend part of their time on ranching-related matters, trying to accommodate their specialties to the exorbitant demands and destructive impacts of the livestock industry. These include everyone from road maintenance crews to wildlife biologists to recreation staff to upper level bureaucrats. (Even the President of the United States and his staff must meet with public ranching representatives, study and sign appropriation bills, and consider livestock industry needs when dealing with matters pertaining to Western federal lands.) Non-range personnel -- BLM resource area managers and FS district rangers, particularly -- spend countless hours each year listening to ranchers' complaints; writing reports; conducting "educational" tours for the public; attending range-related meetings, hearings, and such; assessing base properties, applications, permits, and fee matters; and communicating with politicians on range affairs. Much time, effort, and money also is expended attending meetings of, and pandering to, grazing "advisory" boards. Agency clerks prepare and check grazing permits, changes in permit conditions, bills, sales of base properties, and all sorts of ranching arrangements. Little of this is linked to ranching fiscally.

Obscure general administrative costs also include utilities; office supplies and activities; procurement and contracting; purchase and maintenance of vehicles, equipment, and supplies; landscaping; and much more. The BLM and Forest Service also maintain state and regional offices, respectively, and both have headquarters in Washington, DC, where regulations and policies affecting ranching administration are established.

In conclusion, from the above we may conjecture that very roughly **$200-$250 million**, total, is spent annually by the BLM and Forest Service directly and indirectly on public lands ranching -- *not* $65 million or so as claimed by these agencies. This corresponds closely to the common "educated guess" that roughly 1/4 of the BLM budget and 1/15-1/20 of the Forest Service budget are dedicated to ranching. (Logging-related expenses eat up well over half of the Forest Service's annual budget.) In 1987 the Forest Service was funded at $2.2 billion and the BLM at $659 million. These amounts multiplied by 1/20 and 1/4, respectively, would equal about $100 million and $165 million, or $265 million total.

I retired from the position of Central Region Habitat Biologist, Oregon Dept. of Fish & Wildlife in 1982. For the last 27 years of the 29 in that position I have planned, programed, administrated and physically worked on cooperative habitat projects of various kinds on and with the Ochoco Forest. Through my Regional Habitat program I have spent thousands in public funds, more than I'd like to admit, on these cooperative projects through the years. Projects, few if any of which would have been needed were it not for livestock grazing. Projects such as erosion seedings, fire rehab seedings, prescribed burns, vegetation control, water developments, tree and shrub plantings and miles of fencing; all projects considering for continuance of livestock grazing or habitat conditions resulting from it.
--Harold H. Winegar, in letter to Ochoco National Forest Supervisor, 12-18-86 (Winegar 1986)

BLM and Forest Service expenditure on public lands ranching is enormous, but even this pales compared to taxes spent by other federal, state, county, and city entities.

Predator control is built in to the federal budgets, institutionalized within the bureaucracy, and regarded not as a subsidy, but as a right of the livestock industry.
--Bernard Shanks, **This Land Is Your Land** (Shanks 1984)

The US Department of Agriculture's Division of Animal Damage Control (ADC), under APHIS, employs more than 700 field workers and scores of other personnel. Operating in conjunction with state agencies, counties, and private ranchers, it slaughters "injurious" animals, disseminates information, and conducts research. ADC states, "The protection of livestock is the primary operational program of Animal Damage Control." Much of this activity occurs on public land.

According to Steve Johnson, Southwestern Representative for Defenders of Wildlife, ADC spends about $21 million annually in 14 Western states. Arizona, for example, receives the smallest share of funds -- roughly $550,000 annually. Of this amount US taxpayers contribute about 80%, while the state and counties provide nearly all the remainder. Arizona ADC spent about half a million dollars in 1985, mostly to protect livestock, while confirmed losses of sheep, cattle, and poultry to predators totaled less than $60,000. While ADC was killing coyotes and other predators that year, ADC's 1985 *Annual Report* revealed that about $474,000 worth of crop damage was caused by jackrabbits -- a favorite prey of coyotes. (Johnson 1987a)

Other examples illustrate ADC's mentality: Livestock losses to mountain lions in New Mexico were estimated at $30,000 in 1983, yet government agents spent $90,000 to kill the cats. As mentioned, near Browning, Montana, the federal government recently spent $41,000 to have agents shoot from helicopters and remove 6 wolves -- 1 of the only 2 known packs to have recolonized the 48 states in half a century. Their crime? Eating a reported $3147 worth of livestock, for which the owner was compensated $2239 by Defenders of Wildlife (Wuerthner 1987). A more recent ADC killing of only one wolf in northwest Montana cost $40,000. It costs the public more than $200 per animal for agents to shoot coyotes from airplanes and helicopters (Woolsey 1985). In 1988 ADC in California spent $3.2

million to kill 32,368 mammals -- almost $100 for each dead critter -- for allegedly causing $1.4 million in livestock, poultry, and crop losses (Satchell 1990). In Wyoming in 1989, where 4634 stock animals were reported killed by predation at a loss to ranchers of $340,000, ADC spent $1.35 million to kill 7472 predators (Reitman 1990). Montana ADC spent $1.25 million in 1989 to kill predators, though predators there reportedly killed only $235,567 worth of livestock that year (Milstein 1991). During the first year of James Watt's administration ADC spent more money killing predators than the federal government spent protecting all Endangered species (Shanks 1984). In response to increasing opposition to ADC, the General Accounting Office currently is investigating the agency in preparation for a critical analysis of the ADC program.

If taxpayers are asked to pay for predator control -- especially on public lands -- I feel ranchers should have to pay predator supporters like myself some compensation for the loss of each animal destroyed. Ranchers are depriving me and other public lands users the pleasure and experience gained from having predators like wolves around.

--Howie Wolke, outfitter, environmental activist (Wuerthner 1987)

Filling Reagan's cowboy boots, President Bush recently requested a 14% increase for ADC in 1990. According to *US News and World Report* (2-5-90), ADC's 1990 budget will be $29.4 million ($19 million for states west of the Mississippi), plus roughly $15 million in state funds; more than 60% of the total is directed toward protecting livestock. ADC's recently completed long-term management plan EIS cost an additional $1.7 million. Many states and some counties contribute to the annual kill with their own tax-sponsored predator "control" programs. And, state game & fish departments capture and relocate predators suspected of killing livestock, or sponsor hunts to kill them.

In recent years the US Fish & Wildlife Service, USDA's Animal Research Service, other government agencies, and land grant universities have implemented hundreds of projects testing methods of killing and deterring predators and of assessing predator damage. A major portion of all this serves public lands ranchers.

USDA's Animal and Plant Health Inspection Service (APHIS) conducts research on, and eradication programs against, ranching "pests" and livestock parasites and diseases. Along with state, local, and private contributors, it spends many millions of dollars each year to benefit public lands ranching. For example, APHIS currently is spending money experimenting with methods of eradicating several range plant "invaders."

The kangaroo rat: persecuted by APHIS as a livestock competitor. *(Steve Johnson)*

The total cost of the program [grasshopper spraying on 175,000 acres in southeast Arizona, half of it public land] *is expected to come to approximately $600,000, with the state paying $325,000, the federal government $265,000 and the ranchers the balance* [$10,000, or 1.66%].
--5-13-86 *Phoenix Gazette*

In 1985 APHIS spent $35 million to kill grasshoppers in the West, mostly on public ranges. It cost us more than $2 per acre for this "service." Current prices are roughly $3- $4 per acre. Commonly APHIS sprays insecticide on grasshoppers when they number about 15 per square yard, or about 68,000 per acre. At this point, grasshoppers on 1 acre eat about 23% as much as a cow, and poisoning grasshoppers on about 4.4 acres (a cost of roughly $15.40) would prevent them from consuming as much herbage as a cow eats (currently, ostensibly $1.81 per month). Thus, if a spraying eliminated all grasshoppers for an average 4-month public lands grazing season, it would cost $15.40 to prevent grasshoppers from eating $7.24 worth of herbage. And, as mentioned, spraying does not reduce future infestations; evidence indicates that the opposite is true.

To protect livestock, APHIS has spent over $200 million since 1958 to eradicate the screwworm fly and keep it away from US borders. As mentioned, the screwworm fly is exotic; there would have been little problem with the insect in the US had it not been introduced and spread by livestock.

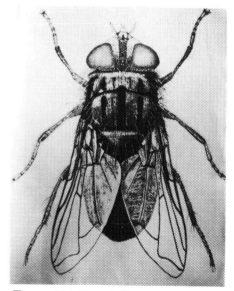

The multi-million dollar screwworm fly. *(USDA)*

The primary responsibility of the US Animal Health Association is to establish uniform methods and rules for the control of livestock brucellosis. USDA's Veterinary Services is responsible for the control and eradication of many other livestock diseases, as well for preventing foreign livestock disease from entering the US. Stockmen can receive financial assistance to eradicate some diseases, and owners of livestock destroyed due to certain diseases are eligible for indemnity payments from the federal and state governments. Under federal law, the Secretary of Agriculture may declare a national emergency to stop any communicable disease that threatens livestock. The US Public Health Service, concerned with the prevention and treatment of disease in humans, must also concern itself with disease and parasites transmittable to humans from commercial livestock.

ADC and government departments of health and game & fish inoculate and treat wild animals for disease, or kill them. We are told that these efforts are to protect wildlife and the public, yet often they are actually designed as much or more to protect *livestock*. This is true even of the antirabies campaigns. Livestock are quite susceptible to rabies. Sometimes all possible disease-carrying wild animals in an area are destroyed, whether they are carriers or not. And sometimes livestock spread disease to wild animals in the first place.

The US Department of Agriculture's Soil Conservation Service (SCS), whose chief is rancher William Scalding, employs 300 classified range consultants, 150 consultants with range degrees in other classified jobs, and 160 others who are range-trained. SCS spends tens of millions of dollars annually on programs relating to livestock production, and an average of **$30 million** per year on programs directly related to range management. (USDA, SCS 1979) The agency assists ranchers technically and materially with brush management, fencing, stock ponds, range "treatment" and seeding, and other ranching developments. For example, SCS currently is developing a new irrigation system for ranchers on Mill Creek, near Livingston, Montana; the 29 local ranchers will pay $1 million and taxpayers $2.5 million for the project (Wuerthner 1989).

SCS had a budget of $687 million in 1988 (OMB 1989). Its programs indirectly benefitting or partially necessitated by public lands ranching include erosion and flood control, watershed restoration, soil surveys, forage plant research, resource inventories, publications, technical advice, "natural disaster" assistance, and general administration. Mostly due to ranching, 10% of all US soil erosion occurs on Western public land. So, we may safely assume that SCS spends at least several million dollars annually due to public lands ranching.

Under the Food and Agricultural Act of 1962, SCS also administers Resource Conservation and Development (RC&D) areas, whose purpose is "Speeding up resource development and environmental protection [the 2 *complement* each other??] in multicounty areas . . . ." Most of the West is divided into RC&D districts, and their offices assist ranchers with planning and implementation of ranching development and cost-sharing for range "improvements." SCS funds most of this, but states and counties also contribute.

USDA's Agricultural Stabilization and Conservation Service (ASCS) was established to protect and promote domestic agriculture, including the grazing industry. Through a complex system it administers low-interest loans, production adjustments/price supports, emergency agricultural activities, cost-sharing (including costs for range development), and whatever responsibilities Congress assigns. USDA maintains an ASCS office in each county, directed by a committee of local ranchers and farmers. Federal outlays through ASCS average $12-$15 billion and the agency itself spends about $1-$2 billion annually, though the amount spent on public lands ranching is anyone's guess (OMB 1989).

The Commodity Credit Corporation (CCC) is a government-owned entity for which ASCS provides operating personnel. CCC provides ranchers and farmers fiscal management support. Through CCC, other federal agencies and the private sector, and through legal exemptions, Western ranchers take out tens of millions of dollars in low-interest loans annually. The millions of dollars of interest foregone raises the rest of America's interest rates correspondingly.

USDA's Farmers Home Administration (FmHA) provides ranchers ownership, "improvement," construction, and repair loans, as well as loans to restore ranching-damaged land. Other special FmHA assistance includes loan deferrals and refinancing, as well as emergency loans. In 1987 grazing associations owed $56.7 billion for low-interest loans; individual ranchers owed billions more (USDA 1987). "Repayment is scheduled according to the borrowers ability to pay . . . ."

The federal Farm Credit Administration (FCA) is responsible for the regulation and examination of those entities comprising the cooperative Farm Credit System -- the federal land banks that loan money to ranchers and farmers.

Other federal, state, and county agencies help ranchers with exportation, taxes, insurance, credit, cooperatives, electrical and telephone service -- all ultimately at public expense.

The National Wool Act of 1954 declares it the policy of Congress to encourage the domestic production of wool and mohair. Thus, through "incentive payments," sheep and goat ranchers are heavily subsidized. When wool prices are low, incentive payments are commensurately high. Annual incentive payments to public lands ranchers average in the *tens of millions of dollars*; $2.5 billion has been handed out since 1955 (Reitman 1990). Funds for incentive payments are derived from wool tariffs, which are assessed against imported wool. (Tariff funds, however, don't cover all associated costs to administer the program.) Wool tariffs raise the price of wool to the American consumer and, since US wool is poorly prepared and generally inferior to its foreign counterpart, lowers the quality of wool on the American market. To further support the sheep industry, the US has negotiated agreements with foreign nations to limit the amount of wool and synthetic fabrics they export to this country. (National Audubon Society 1973)

Our governments have paid out *billions* of dollars in "disaster relief" funds to public lands ranchers over the years in response to flood, fire, blizzard, drought, pests, disease, and other "natural disasters." Assistance also includes emergency hay, water, fencing, pesticides, inoculations, seedings, sandbags, water projects, loans of heavy equipment, livestock transportation, and practically anything ranchers request -- this, even though the "disasters" were often the results of overgrazing and/or improvident ranching development. In 1988, for example, some 380 million pounds of feed were purchased by ranchers for "drought-sticken" livestock under the ASCS emergency feed program at a cost to taxpayers of about $140 million (Atwood 1990). In August 1989, President Bush signed a $900 million appropriation for disaster relief to "flood and drought-stricken" farmers and ranchers.

Further, investigation has shown that disaster funding is often based on inflated AUMs. For example, I was recently informed by a Washington rancher that public lands ranchers there were being paid drought relief funding based on a loss of forage per acre much greater than the land was capable of producing.

COUNTY DECLARED EMERGENCY AREA

DECLARATION ALLOWS LIVESTOCK PRODUCERS TO APPLY FOR HELP

Mojave County was declared an emergency feed area Friday by the U.S. Department of Agriculture's (USDA's) Agricultural Stabilization and Conservation Service (ASCS). According to Steve Drye, ASCS's county executive director, county livestock producers who are forced to "supplement feed" their cattle can apply for assistance through the ASCS office.

The program is available to all agricultural producers who earn at least 10 percent of their gross annual income from livestock production, Drye said. . . . "People must file an application with us. Then they can purchase any feed they need and submit the invoice back to the ASCS for reimbursement," the executive director said.

--7-17-89 *Mojave Miner*, Kingman, Arizona

(Governor Rose Mofford subsequently declared 5 other counties -- about half of the state -- drought disaster areas, making ranchers there eligable for the special funding.)

Flooding caused by public lands ranching results in untold damages. Federal, state, county, and city governments have spent **many billions** of tax dollars over the years to repair and realign roads, rebuild and enlarge bridges, install culverts, channelize drainages, riprap banks, haul fill, remove debris, repair structures, revegetate, and build flood control dams -- when what was really needed was a reduction in livestock numbers and range development.

The Beef Board spent its $85 million budget largely on promotion.
--Report of the Secretary of Agriculture: 1987

A host of public relations firms and livestock industry lobbyists work together to secure tax monies to fund research on livestock production and to promote the consumption of livestock products. Essentially a public relations firm, USDA's Agricultural Marketing Service spends millions of tax dollars annually promoting the livestock industry, including public lands ranching. The federal Beef Research and Information Act of 1976 established "a program of research, information, and promotion for beef cattle and beef products."

Inspectors for USDA's Food Safety and Inspection Service (FSIS) examined 121 million head of livestock for disease and toxins in 1987. FSIS also enforces consumer safety regulations pertaining to livestock products, disseminates literature on the safe handling of meats, and enforces proper labeling. USDA's Office of Transportation promotes more efficient transportation of agricultural products, including livestock. USDA's Packers and Stockyards Administration enforces regulations pertaining to auctions, stockyards, packing houses, and other facets of buying and selling livestock. The US Department of Health and Human Service's Food and Drug Administration is charged with, among other things, protecting the livestock industry from illegal competition and testing the industry's drugs and pesticides.

USDA's Agricultural Research Service spends millions of our dollars "cooperating with local ranchers."

USDA's Agricultural Research Service (ARS) and Cooperative State Research Service use biologic knowledge (and $908 million in 1988) to search for ways to make farming and ranching more profitable. For example, ARS conducts ranching studies on its 50,000-acre United States Livestock Experimental Station near Miles City, Montana; the 194,000-acre Jornada Experimental Range near Las Cruces, New Mexico; and the large US Sheep Experimental Station in Idaho. USDA's Economic Research Service and National Agricultural Statistics Service use economic knowledge (and $109 million in 1988) to search for ways to make farming and ranching more profitable. And USDA's multi-million dollar National Agricultural Library in Beltsville, Maryland, is well-stocked with ranching literature. (OMB 1989)

Numerous other government research establishments serve ranchers. USDA operates an agricultural Research Center, with headquarters also in Beltsville, Maryland, and other laboratories and offices throughout the country. The Denver Wildlife Research Center spends tax dollars on research to find a better anti-predator sheep collar. The Science and Education Foundation employs range conservationists to search for less destructive, more profitable ways to graze livestock. The National Science Foundation and National Academy of Sciences both expend time and money promoting ranching. Even the Veterans Administration gives priority assistance to stockmen!

The Soil Conservation Service states that no less than **110** government entities in some manner serve farmers and ranchers. (Public lands ranchers silently ride the farmers'

coattails in some of these.) Ranching-related expenditures are buried in these agencies' budgets, and it would take many thousands of dollars and the Freedom of Information Act to ferret them out. (I haven't the money or ferrets but encourage others to do so).

This large, earthen flood control dam probably would not have been built if not for livestock grazing in the watershed. Southern New Mexico BLM.

Flood damages in southern Arizona in October 1983 alone were estimated at half a billion dollars. Range soil scientist Bob Dixon states, "The October 1983 flooding in Tucson was caused by the overgrazed watersheds of the Rillito and Santa Cruz Rivers." *(Bob Dixon)*

Flooding caused by public lands ranching necessitates thousands of riprap projects and more and larger bridges.

Flood damage from a heavily grazed watershed.

A stabilization project along the Rio Grande River, New Mexico.

In the Department of the Interior, aside from BLM, the Fish and Wildlife Service, National Park Service, Bureau of Outdoor Recreation, Geological Survey, and Bureau of Reclamation all are in some way involved with public lands ranching. For example, the US Geological Survey operates research stations that conduct livestock grazing studies on public land. Because public lands ranching so heavily affects US wildlife, FWS must add millions more to its half-billion-dollar annual budget than would otherwise be necessary. Likewise, public lands ranching's impact on Western waterways has added millions to the Bureau of Reclamation's annual billion-dollar budget. National Park Service reports reveal that millions of dollars more are spent annually on, and because of, legal and trespass ranching than are netted through grazing fees. And the National Park Service and numerous other government agencies have spent millions of dollars simply on land surveys to locate legal boundaries for ranching purposes, often in an attempt to mitigate grazing trespass.

The US General Accounting Office (GAO) is the investigative arm of Congress. In promoting fiscal responsibility in government, GAO scrutinizes agencies that administer public lands ranching. For example, it conducted 11 studies of BLM and its ranching program from 1986-89 -- a few million more tax dollars obscurely expended.

Those busy beavers, the US Army Corps of Engineers, whose total annual budget is over $3 billion, spend millions of dollars extra each year because public lands ranching has increased flooding, lowered river levels, and silted reservoirs and harbors. Thousands of Western dams, even including large ones such as Glen Canyon on the Colorado and Navajo on the San Juan, were designed in whole or part to reduce flooding and siltation from upstream overgrazed ranges.

Large-scale Western water projects, sponsored mostly by the Army Corps, Bureau of Reclamation, and other federal and state agencies with hundreds of millions of tax dollars annually, also benefit public lands ranchers, though usually on their private lands rather than then public lands allotments. Cornell economist David Fields and his associate Robin Hur report that direct and indirect water subsidies to the livestock industry in California alone total $26 *billion* annually. The Bureau of Reclamation sells private and public lands ranchers irrigation water for as little as a quarter-cent per ton, though costs to provide it may be more than 100 times that. (Hur 1985a) On the average, the government subsidizes irrigation at $54 per acre per year (Wuerthner 1989). Bureau of Reclamation statistics indicate that taxpayers paid $534 million to deliver water to Western irrigators (mostly stockmen) in 1988 (Wuerthner 1990b). According to Fields and Hur:

> Reports from the General Accounting Office, the Rand Corporation, and the Water Resources Council show that *every dollar spent by state governments in irrigation subsidies actually costs taxpayers over seven dollars in lost wages, higher living costs, and reduced business income... most of the water goes to produce livestock, either directly or indirectly. Thus, current water use practices now threaten to undermine the economies of every state in the region.*" (Robbins 1987)

Onward.... The US Government Printing Office prints, binds, and distributes scores of publications promoting public lands ranching. US and state court systems have spent millions of dollars contesting public lands ranchers on numerous and various issues. (More than $2 million was spent over 18 years on court battles with the aforementioned rampant grazing permit and regulation violator John Jay Casey alone.)

The Environmental Protection Agency (EPA) researches and monitors environmental threats and enforces environmental legislation. EPA spends hundreds of thousands of dollars (unfortunately not more) annually monitoring and combating various impacts of public lands ranching. EPA funded, for example, a slick 1990 publication titled *Livestock Grazing on Western Riparian Areas* (Chaney 1990). Similarly, the Council on Environmental Quality (CEQ) helps "to formulate and recommend national policies to promote the improvement of the quality of the environment" by assessing the impacts of public lands ranching.

Congress also appropriates special monies for, or because of, public lands ranching. For example, Congress recently ordered a $200,000 study performed by independent biologists to assess the feasibility of reintroducing wolves to Yellowstone National Park. The reintroduction plan detailed in the resulting report, *Wolves for Yellowstone*, is being adamantly fought by public lands ranchers. Wildlife advocate George Wuerthner maintains that not only should wolves and other animals extirpated by the ranching industry be reintroduced, but that the industry responsible for their extirpation should foot the bill.

> *... the incentive payments, the tariffs on foreign wool and mutton, the subsidized killing of competing wildlife, the experimental breeding stations that are located all over the United States and that cost the taxpayer several million a year (most industries research their own products, but the sheep industry doesn't) -- if all these subsidies were ended and the industry had to operate as a real free enterprise, it would collapse overnight.*
> --Comment on sheep industry by Dick Randall, former federal predator "control" agent

Western states and counties spend huge sums of tax money on public lands ranching. For example, Wyoming appropriated $22.5 million in state funds directly to agriculture in 1980-81, along with about $10 million in agriculture-related funds. Probably $5 million or more of this went to public lands ranching.

Each Western state has a State Department of Agriculture which renders various services to the public lands rancher. State livestock departments work to minimize livestock disease and enforce regulations pertaining to buying and selling livestock. And every Western state funds a state livestock board, which has broad administrative and advisory responsibilities pertaining to livestock matters within the state. For example, the Wyoming Livestock Board was established "for the purposes of supervising and protecting the livestock interests of Wyoming from theft and disease and to recommend legislation fostering the livestock industry." Today, it spends more than $2 million annually.

All Western states and some counties maintain pest, disease, and parasite eradication programs for the ranching industry. State veterinarians and livestock sanitary commissions also administer to its needs. Owners of diseased stock ordered killed by state veterinarians are usually compensated by the state for the value of the animals lost plus related expenses. Montana has spent about $30 million just trying to rid its cattle of brucellosis.

State associations of conservation districts coordinate and focus efforts on ranching. Some Western state statutes authorize the creation of livestock districts which are given various regulatory powers. Some states have special legislation designed to assist ranchers in the marketplace. Some have special non-profit commissions, committees, and councils to promote ranching. Some have special water, irrigation, and watershed improvement districts and boards designed to promote stockmen's interests.

Various state agencies fund and/or help secure low-interest loans for ranching programs.

State forestry departments often include range development as part of their forestry programs, as do other state land managing agencies.

Public lands ranching has proven costly to Western state game & fish departments, most of which cater heavily to hunting and fishing interests -- their main sources of funding. They spend millions of dollars to manage and reintroduce species diminished or extirpated by ranching. Under pressure from ranchers, they vaccinate wildlife to prevent the spread of livestock disease -- disease that is often spread by their stock. State game & fish departments also run fish hatcheries. When streams are degraded by livestock and "trash" fish "invade," state game & fish biologists "treat" with rotenone and replant with hatchery trout. The fish hatcheries themselves experience reduced water flow, siltation, and pollution from upstream ranching. These costs are absorbed with "wildlife" funds. Thus, millions more dollars quietly drop into the ranching trough.

Though permittees are already compensated for predator losses by lower grazing fees, tax write-offs, and more, in some states ranchers are further compensated by fish & game departments. In Wyoming, for example, if a mountain lion kills a calf the Game & Fish Department is responsible for paying the rancher the value of the calf. Each year the Wyoming Game and Fish Department also compensates ranchers about $750,000 for deer and antelope hunted on their private lands, and some $250,000 for wildlife damage to private forage or crops. Colorado spends more than $1 million annually on its compensation program, handing out about $180,000 a year for "game depredation," $34,000 of this just for livestock killed or injured by mountain lions. Many of the payees are public lands ranchers. Idaho ranchers recently procured $500,000 from the state legislature for depredation payments. Idaho and other states even dispatch state fish & game employees to shoot elk and other competitors that get into private pastures and haystacks.

A "study committee" is pushing for a similar compensation program in Arizona. According to Richard Stephensen, Legislative Liaison for the Arizona Game & Fish Department, "The study committee consists of two cattlemen, one wool grower, the head of the state lands commission (who has already voiced his support for the program), two legislators who are both cattlemen, and two members of the Arizona Game and Fish Commission, one of whom is a cattleman." Stephensen says ranchers have calculated that someone owes them $325,000 a year just for the livestock *salt* they claim wild animals use, including that used on public land!

State fish & game departments even supply ranchers with special fences and large wooden panels to keep elk, deer, and pronghorn out of their haystacks, and construction materials to keep them out of their barns. Some states reimburse permittees for damages done (or claimed) to fences and other range "improvements" by wildlife. Professional claims adjusters have found large percentages of these claims to be fraudulent. For example, ranchers have filed claims for wildlife damages to decades-old fence posts already rotted off at the ground, and based them on the value of newer fences.

Public lands ranchers are subsidized in other obscure ways at hunters' and anglers' expense. For example, the Federal Aid to Wildlife Restoration Act requires a manufacturers' tax on hunting equipment throughout the country. The collected tax monies are apportioned to the states. The Western states spend part of the money covertly on ranching and on mitigating its destructive influence on wildlife. For instance, hunting and fishing license fee dollars in Colorado were used to chain pinyon-juniper to increase livestock forage and help keep deer and elk at higher elevations (read "off private ranchlands") during winter.

The Arizona Game & Fish Department publishes 2 handbooks which, by its own admission, are largely designed to teach ranchers how to kill coyotes and mountain lions (Woolsey 1985, Shaw 1985).

Despite the conflicts caused by the inherent incompatibility of ranching and wildlife, most state fish & wildlife personnel remain heavily pro-ranching. Like the rest of us, they are enamored of ranching and cowboy mythology.

All Western states maintain vegetation eradication and reseeding programs for stockmen's benefit, as do many counties, often in the form of weed and pest control districts, etc. Montana taxpayers alone spend over $5 million annually to kill "weeds" usually caused by overgrazing. In Texas, literally hundreds of millions of tax and private dollars have gone into killing dense mesquite, also caused mostly by livestock. In every Western state but Colorado, Arizona, and New Mexico, authorities may legally enter any private land to eradicate "weedy" vegetation -- and then charge the landowner (Bingham 1990).

Hundreds of Western state-sponsored fire stations fight range fires, most partly or chiefly for the benefit of stockmen.

Fire protection on state land (most of which is open rangeland) usually is provided by cooperative agreements between state land departments, BLM, FS, and/or individual counties. State, county, and even city and community fire departments are frequently called in to battle large fires on federal rangeland. According to **Statistical Abstract of the US: 1987**, Western states spend roughly $100 million per year on fire protection (US Dept. of Com. 1986).

To facilitate movement of livestock across highways, aqueducts, large pipelines, etc., special livestock underpasses, overpasses, and crossings are designed and constructed by county, state, and federal agencies. Three highway underpasses are shown above; thousands run under roadways throughout the West, and cost the public *tens of millions* of dollars. Some double as drainages; in these cases livestock concentrations exacerbate roadway erosion. Most are fenced, so as to funnel livestock through, and gated; many have corrals built on; and all become yet another type of sacrifice area. Look for them.

BLM says ranchers cannot drive stock trucks on the plateau under current road conditions. Thus, cattle must be trailed up the road some dozen miles. This, according to the BLM, means the bulls arrive with tired, sore feet, and that they can't perform their primary function. Therefore, the roads must be improved.
--Randy Morris, Chairman, Committee for Idaho's High Desert

Western county road building and maintenance budgets range from $1 million (sparsely populated Carbon County, Wyoming) to $15 million (Pima County, Arizona) to $30 million (San Bernardino County, California -- the nation's largest county). There are 3041 counties in the US, with a combined road budget of roughly $8 billion, for an average US county road budget of about $2.6 million. There are 407 counties in the West. (US Dept. of Com. 1986) If we multiply the $2.6 million figure by 407, we get a combined Western county road budget of slightly over $1 billion. However, even though county road density is generally higher in the East, Western counties average nearly 3 times the size of those in the East; further, Western road expenses are higher, so we may estimate the combined annual Western county road budget at roughly $2 billion.

What part of this $2 billion is spent on public lands ranching roads no one can say because accountants make no such distinctions. Nevertheless, consider that: (1) 41% of the West is grazed government land; (2) more roads -- more than half a million miles -- serve ranching than anything else (3) many roads traversing other public and private land provide ranching access to public land (most logging roads are not county-maintained and should therefore not be factored); and (4) many Western states and counties have special programs specifically designed to improve rural roads for ranching. It seems reasonable then to assume that perhaps **$200 million** annually of this $2 billion road budget is spent on public lands ranching.

Most livestock and cattle guard warning signs are sponsored by counties and states -- an annual million-dollar-plus expenditure.

The 11 Western state governments spend roughly $7 billion annually on road building and maintenance. Only a small percentage of state roads function primarily as public lands ranching roads, but tens of thousands of miles of state highways stretch across public grazing land. Most are fenced to exclude livestock and have numerous related developments such as cattle guards, livestock underpasses, and signs. Thus do Western state highway departments also spend millions of dollars annually on public lands ranching.

The US government spends billions on federal highways and freeways in the West, tens of thousands of miles of which cross public ranching land. Likewise, millions of federal dollars annually are spent on ranching-related develop-ments. For example, some of the cut-and-fill portions of roadways on hillsides must be constructed wider than they otherwise would be to allow for livestock and rancher access, fencing, and cattleguards -- a significant cumulative expenditure. Just one freeway livestock underpass may cost hundreds of thousands of dollars. Some public ranches even have their own freeway offramps.

This gravel ranching road on BLM land in New Mexico is elevated, drained with ditches and culverts, reflector-marked, signed, and fenced on one side -- all at public expense.

Blading a ranching road on BLM land.

Roadside, BLM range, New Mexico. Waste concrete has been dumped along a culvert (itself quite large to accommodate runoff from damaged watersheds) to help prevent road erosion.

County workers installing a barbed wire fence to keep cattle off the roadway in Prescott National Forest, Arizona. Roadside fences alone cost millions of dollars annually.

Government maintains this paved road chiefly for use by just 1 public lands rancher.

A *double* cattle guard, apparently to make *doubly* sure no cattle get misplaced. Cattle guards in public roads soak the public for millions of dollars.

Research by Dr. Denzel Ferguson shows that when a cow pie hits hot asphalt, "the cow pie dries, curls up at the edges, and pulls up huge hunks of pavement with it." The process appears responsible for many of the potholes on roads around the rural West, where cattle often wander freely across paved roadways. *(Denzel Ferguson)*

Cooperative Extension Service (CES) offices are found in the courthouse of almost every county in the West. They are staffed with county agricultural agents (or farm advisors), who are assisted by specialists in various fields. CES offers a variety of services, mostly for agriculture, including referral, consultation, technical assistance, testing, training, and information in the form of publications, videotapes, news announcements, and workshops. In many rural counties, ranchers are CES's main constituents. The Western states and many agricultural colleges also maintain CES offices. Funding for CES is a confused mosaic of federal, state, county, and university monies, in the West totaling tens of millions of dollars annually. USDA's Extension Service, the federal participant in the CES program, was budgeted at $358 million in 1988 (OMB 1989).

Many high schools have vocational agriculture departments that train future public lands ranchers. These are financed through county property taxes and other government funds.

Future Farmers of America (FFA) is the youth agricultural program of the state boards of education. Almost every Western high school agriculture program has an FFA chapter, and there are college offices, state district offices, and a national office. FFA's total annual budget is in the millions, though only a small percentage of this comes from government sources. Similarly, the 4-H is a youth agricultural program of the Colleges of Agriculture at every land grant college in the country, implemented in every Western county by agricultural college faculty and/or the county CES. The 4-H organization, funded through land grant colleges, CES, SCS, and other public and private sources, spends millions of dollars training future farmers and ranchers, some of them for public lands ranching.

Every Western state university has a college of agriculture, each with a range department. They educate future ranchers, conduct range studies, provide technical assistance, produce literature, sponsor range seminars, etc. Some unknown and disproportionate amount of the federal government's annual $800 million in grants for agricultural research and development benefits public lands ranching.

Scoring these grants is big business to the range staff at many of these (and other) schools.

The College of Agriculture at the University of Arizona in Tucson is typical as Western state agricultural colleges go. It has a total annual budget of nearly $50 million, 80%- 90% of which comes from federal, state, and county governments. The College of Agriculture consists of 25 or so divisions, one of which is the School of Natural Resources, which administers the Range Department -- the department most devoted to public lands ranching. Many of the other divisions also are significantly involved with public lands ranching, especially Animal Sciences, Soil and Water Science, the Cooperative Extension Service, and the Range Experimental Station. Because public ranching is so politically significant and encompasses so large an area, it receives a disproportionately large amount of attention at Western agricultural colleges. Separate accounting is not kept, but we may surmise that of the roughly $40-$45 million in government monies spent by this college of agriculture yearly, at least $1 million goes to public lands ranching.

Thus, the tax money lost to public lands ranching at 11 Western state agricultural colleges is probably at least $11 million annually. This would not include indirect costs, such as general administration and buildings. Nor does it include agricultural programs at scores of other Western colleges and universities. There are other hidden subsidies. For example, at the request of the Agricultural Commissioner of Los Angeles, the Department of *Psychology* at California State College, San Bernardino, conducted predator aversion experiments in the Mojave Desert to placate complaining sheep ranchers (Defenders of Wildlife 1982). Arizona State University currently is conducting a study on how elk and cattle affect each other -- a study co-funded by the government, wildlife groups, and the ranchers who hope to gather evidence to use against the state's elk population.

Scattered here and there on Western public land are ranching experimental ranges, areas, and stations. Some are tens of thousands of acres in size (for example, Santa Rita Experimental Range south of Tucson, Arizona, encompasses some 50,000 acres). Usually they are permanently financed with federal, state, and/or county monies, often involving agricultural colleges. For example, the state agricultural experimental station in Wyoming was funded with $4,874,380 in state taxes in 1980-81. Methods of grazing, fencing, vegetation manipulation, seeding, fertilizing, predator "control," etc. are tested for the ranching industry.

Summers and her husband, Charles, own 20 acres nearly surrounded by the Marley property. The couple paid $873 in property taxes last year on their parcel. In contrast, Marley and his daughter own about 380 times more land but paid only $660 in taxes on it last year. Why the disparity? The Marley land is classified by the county assessor as grazing ranchland. Had it been classified as rural vacant land, like the Summerses' parcel, Marley and his daughter would be assessed with a property tax bill of about $744,000 a year, county officials said.

--8-14-88 *Arizona Republic*

Taxes and private grants support dozens of range-related research stations conducting hundreds of projects.

State and county laws give ranchers huge property tax breaks on private holdings, base properties and improvements. Commonly a public lands rancher will pay $40 or $50 a year on his 80-acre property, home and improvements (paying no taxes, of course, on "his" public lands grazing allotment), whereas a non-rancher owning the same private property would pay $2000 or more. A rancher owning and grazing thousands of rural acres might pay a few hundred dollars property tax, while a non-rancher would pay *hundreds of thousands* on the same land. For example, the average assessed value for Wyoming's 23 million acres of private grazing land was $3.71/acre in 1980, while farm land was assessed at almost $100/acre and non-agricultural land at many times more than that.

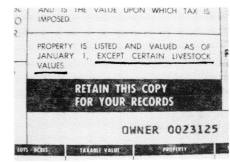

Because it ran cattle, the corporate owner of a 321,000-acre ranch (recently purchased by The Nature Conservancy) encompassing nearly the entire Animas Mountain range in southwest New Mexico paid only $8000 in property taxes. A non-rancher would have paid many, many times this amount on the appraised $16.5 million property. (2-7-88 *Albuquerque Journal*)

Why the difference? Ostensibly, according to most ancient state and county tax laws, it is because ranching is a costly business that provides food to consumers, or something like that. Yet, other costly businesses that provide much more necessary goods and services are not subsidized with dirt-cheap property taxes.

You know these people [land speculators] *are in the process of submitting development plans, but they throw out a few cows and shift the tax burden to everyone else.*
--Pima County, Arizona, attorney

Similarly, "rent-a-cow" schemes are gaining popularity with land speculators around the West. Though their intent to eventually sell or develop the land is obvious, they simply rent or buy a few cows to give the appearance of a livestock operation. Their land then qualifies as grazing land, rather than rural vacant land, and they pay practically nothing for property taxes.

The *Arizona Republic*, in a 1984 article, notes that a land investment firm, Nationwide Resources Corporation, paid $4.5 million for undeveloped real estate in Pima County, Arizona. In 1987 the firm reduced its property tax from $92,000 to $150 simply by renting a few cows and qualifying for the county ranchland property tax exemption! In a 1985 lawsuit by the firm, the county court took away the county assessor's authority to determine whether the use of livestock is a ploy to keep property taxes low. In another case, according to the Pima County Assessor, the owner of 640 acres worth over $3 million paid less than $100 in property taxes in 1985 because of a few cattle on the land. Without the cows the owner would have been charged about $53,000.

This taxpayer ripoff is common throughout the West. **Western county governments are being bilked of hundreds of millions of property tax dollars annually because of ranchland exemption laws.** The public, as usual, makes up the foregone revenue.

As a result of these unfair laws, few owners of undeveloped acreage can afford *not* to graze their vacant property. In other words, *livestock grazing is practically mandated on all private rural lands of appreciable size*. Accordingly, only ranchers, land speculators, and the wealthy (often one and the same) can afford to own medium to large rural parcels. Since these larger properties and ranchlands are the only real estate available in many rural locales, this prevents many non-ranchers (including people who would protect the land) from owning property and living in rural areas -- another important way ranchers maintain rural dominance. (Additionally, aside from tax reasons, most large rural land owners feel strong pressure to lease their land for grazing -- "to promote a helpful and co-operative local public image," as one told me.)

These tax scams have disastrous results on the land, and the livestock. As speculators take advantage of unjust property tax exemptions, previously ungrazed land is stocked with cattle. As county assessors and government attorneys (both at government expense) threaten and battle with rent-a-cow land speculators to force them to pay rightfully due taxes, speculators expand livestock operations to make them appear valid under existing tax exemption laws -- if need be even to the point of carrying out full-blown livestock operations. To them it is worth the cost to avoid paying taxes. Livestock may suffer due to ill-conceived operations and/or because the land is not suitable for livestock grazing. For example, on private land north of Tucson cattle currently are eating cholla cactus to survive because the land owners want to qualify for a property tax break.

If capital gains taxes on land had to be paid at the time of sale, destructive ranchland exemptions could be eliminated. Wealthy ranchers and speculators will not allow this reform, however.

In a similar scam, special agricultural exemptions allow ranchers or alleged "ranchers" to develop property as ranchland that otherwise would be protected by various city, county, and state legalities. The crafty rancher may use these exemptions to develop private property (or in some cases even a grazing allotment) to enhance its financial potential for ranching and/or for other alleged purposes. Thus, Texas billionaire H. Ross Perot, by claiming to be developing land for goat grazing, may legally clear trees from 200 acres (in preparation for building hotels and condos); if he had not claimed the ranching exemption, he would have had to submit to the city of Austin for approval (and possible denial, as the land is vital habitat of the Endangered golden-checked warbler) of the clearing.

> *It will be another 9 years before this place [private ranch] comes back to me and after that time I am going to make sure that another damn cow never walks on this land.*
> --Mary Sayrs, Moro, Oregon, personal correspondence

Western counties spend more than $1 billion annually on natural resource, parks, and recreation programs. Some of this cost is necessary because their resources have been degraded by ranching.

Some city properties, parks, and structural improvements have likewise been damaged. Hundreds of Western communities have spent millions of dollars fencing livestock away from domestic water sources, importing water, or pumping groundwater to counterbalance that lost to livestock grazing.

Postal service, police and fire protection, ambulance service, health services, school busing, and more all are substantially more expensive for the taxpayer to provide to remote, widely dispersed public lands ranchers than to perhaps any other group in the West. If the public rancher had to pay taxes on these services proportional to how much is spent on him, other taxpayers would save millions of dollars annually.

In late 1983 a workshop was held in Tucson, largely in response to demands by influential Arizona stockmen. They wanted something done about growing vandalism and "ecotage" of their ranching developments. A committee was formed, and, under the auspices of the Commission on the Arizona Environment, a program was implemented. Using tax-based monies and private, tax-deductable contributions from the same stockmen and other wealthy, commercial interests, the Commission created pro-ranching literature, signs, advertisements, commercials, and a toll-free, 24-hour-staffed 1-800-VANDALS informant hotline. A similar hotline was recently established at the request of Nevadan graziers -- 1-800-SABOTAGE.

Fight Vandalism
In Our Out-of-Doors

CALL 1-800-VANDALS

A typical small town rodeo grounds -- one of hundreds around the West partially sponsored by taxes. Willard, New Mexico.

The taxpayer sponsors public lands ranching in scores of other obscure ways:

● Land buyouts and swaps between government agencies and public lands ranchers commonly favor ranchers over the public.

● State and county fairs receive government funds to finance projects that benefit public lands ranchers.

● The Sonoran overgrazing/temperature study mentioned earlier was financed by the National Aeronautics and Space Administration (NASA) for $1 million.

● In Wyoming, gas tax rebates to ranchers and farmers totaled $2,503,810 in 1980-81.

● Taxpayers sponsor ranching-related conferences, hosted by cities and government agencies.

● The Arizona State Legislature recently authorized a special Range Research Task Force to evaluate range management practices and assist state ranchers. A special investigative unit administered by the Arizona State Livestock Board and a special law enforcement task force composed of members of various government agencies was assigned to pursue and arrest cattle rustlers. (Criminal police have developed a special method of identifying fingerprints on cow horns.)

● Julie Rechtin, an employee at Lava Beds National Monument in northeast California, writes that in 1987 Modoc National Forest came out with its long-range forest plan. The plan considered small cuts in livestock numbers in some of the most heavily grazed areas of the forest. Worried, the Modoc Cattlemen's Association obtained $2500 *from the Modoc County Supervisor's office* as part of $5000 to hire Resource Concepts, a Carson City consultant firm, to review the plan and help formulate opposition strategy.

● Similarly in New Mexico, the Luna County Commission recently voted to spend $20,000 in taxes over the next 10 years to pay a Wyoming legal firm to help county public land users (mostly ranchers) privatize management and developments on public land, as well as the land itself. As part of the "Arizona-New Mexico Coalition of Counties," a growing number of Southwest counties -- 11 at latest count -- have done likewise. Little-known arrangements such as these are common around the rural West.

● Also similarly, a large percentage of rural Western community chambers of commerce actively promote public lands ranching. They sponsor conferences, publish and distribute promotional literature, disseminate policy statements, present awards, woo the media, and generally do whatever they can to help local stockmen. Most chambers are funded primarily by community and/or county taxes.

● Western ranchers often are exempt from: planning and zoning restrictions, building regulations, sight requirements, health regulations, animal control laws, wetlands protection laws, minimum wage laws, alien labor laws, child labor laws, OSHA requirements, provisions of the Worker's Compensation Act, Unemployment Compensations Act requirements, wage reporting requirements, motor vehicle compensatory fees, most fuels tax, ad valorem taxation on livestock, taxation on stock as personal property, sales and use taxes on livestock and some ranching supplies (including feed), numerous credit laws, public lands closures and use restrictions, county special use permits, and almost anything else that would threaten them financially.

> *Probably no other group in the West receives as much special treatment as do ranchers, in so many obscure ways. In Western states, stockmen are exempt from: numerous vehicular legal requirements, including safety equipment, title, registration, and licensing (even for public roadways); fire and building codes; electrical licensing requirements; normal road width restrictions for stock driveways; licensing requirements for fairs and exhibitions for agricultural purposes; merchant licensing requirements for selling agricultural products; and much more. In trailing livestock, ranchers can legally drive their herds down the middle of roadways, even through small communities. Aside from highway department employees and law enforcement officers, ranchers are the only people permanently authorized to pull onto freeway rights-of-way and enter gates (many of which are installed specifically for their use). Only stockmen are allowed to regularly occupy single locations on BLM or FS land for more than 2 weeks at a time. And so on. Ranchers are even exempt from military draft in time of war!*

We may safely conclude that without public lands ranching, each year taxpayers would save *at least $1 billion** -- roughly twice the annual livestock value of public lands ranching! In sum, public lands ranching is a massive government give-away to a tiny, pampered minority. It makes no economic nor food production sense.

*Note: Soon after completing this chapter, I was informed by a prominent US Geological Survey research ecologist that a well-documented study by a staffer at US Forest Service regional headquarters in Albuquerque likewise found that roughly $1 billion in taxes is spent on public lands ranching annually. The forester's superiors, I was told, forbid release of the document.

As far as the term "welfare ranching" goes, there is no such thing. Ranchers do not receive any subsidies or aid of any kind from any government agency.
--Arizona public lands "rancher's wife" Beth Hawkes, 2-3-90 *Arizona Daily Star*

They lie.
--Mike Roselle, progressive activist

BANK ROBBERY? HELL... THIS IS GREAT
TRADITION OF THE OLD WEST!!!

(T.O. Hellenbach)

Other Losses

The closer look in the previous section reveals that the various levels of government spend not merely a few million dollars but at least **$1 billion** each year due to public lands ranching -- a subsidy of about $400 per cow year. This is a considerable public burden, yet *private* expenditures on, or because of, public lands ranching probably exceed $1 billion annually. And even this dollar loss seems to pale compared to the other burdens the public is knowingly or unknowingly forced to endure, including an incalculable loss in the quality of life and natural surroundings. What follows is a loosely organized discussion of these impacts.

Perhaps the best place to start is with ranching itself. Harold Dregne, Professor of Soil Science at Texas Tech University, roughly estimates the value of potential forage lost due to past and present overgrazing to be approximately $200 million per year (Chaney 1990). This suggests that if today's grazing industry was dropped into the pre-livestock West (minus the native competitors) it would produce $200 million/year more in today's dollars than it currently does. This assumes, of course, that this level of grazing can somehow be maintained indefinitely; there is no real evidence that anything approaching this level can be achieved without overgrazing or maintained without mass subsidization. The whole proposition is, in the end, self-defeating. Generally,

the more grazing, the less production per unit area of range; the less grazing, the more production per unit area of range.

Growing an ear of corn takes about 26 gallons of water; a pound of beef requires close to 25,000 gallons of water.
--Earth Island Journal (Spring 1991)

As detailed earlier, ranching has significantly decreased water production throughout most of the West by damaging watersheds, riparian areas, and water courses. Also, livestock and livestock feed producers account for 70% of all water consumed in the West, mostly for irrigation (Hur 1985a). In most rural Western counties, stockmen utilize more water than all other users combined.

These factors leave less water for municipal, recreational, industrial, and navigational uses and make remaining water more difficult and expensive for other users to procure. As an extreme example, to "save water" some Phoenix restaurants require customers to ask for a glass of drinking water; meanwhile nearby stockmen pour millions of gallons on pastures! Farmers, rural communities, and cities -- usually downstream from public lands ranching -- must take water from what surface flow remains, pump it from the ground, or import it from without. Because ranching has so heavily depleted streamflow, farmers along many Western waterways must build holding dams or pump groundwater, thereby often doubling or tripling irrigation costs.

Most of the water diverted from streams in the West is used to grow hay and crops for livestock, and most Western water development is government-subsidized. *(George Wuerthner)*

Rather than direct their efforts toward banning livestock from watersheds, waterless victims commonly squabble amongst themselves and build more water developments. Under the dominant ranching reality, simply removing livestock is rarely considered a viable option.

A growing number of individuals and organizations contribute labor and money to watershed improvement projects on both public and private lands.
--Livestock Grazing on Western Riparian Areas (Chaney 1990)

Without public lands ranching, *billions* of dollars worth of watershed protection and restoration projects, dams, weirs, reservoirs, dikes, levees, canals, wells, pumping stations, pipelines, and other water developments would be unnecessary. Many of these are privately funded developments on private land.

For example, many rural residents have been forced to drill wells because ranching has fouled or dried up creeks and springs. Likewise, because ranching has lowered water tables, many more wells must be drilled especially deep to reach good water. Professional well-drilling currently costs about $15-$20 per foot; water tables in many areas have fallen a score or more feet due to ranching. As hundreds of thousands of rural residents have had to drill wells in affected areas, this loss alone probably totals tens of millions of dollars.

By damaging watersheds and reducing streamflow, public lands ranching has significantly reduced hydroelectric power potential and has increased production expenses. Increasingly numerous and expensive smaller projects have been built to meet power demand.

More than 80% of electricity production in the Northwest is hydroelectric. Economists calculate that the region loses 17 billion kilowatt hours -- more than 10% -- of its electricity per year to irrigation use by stockmen. (Hur 1985a) Probably an even greater yet inestimable amount is never realized because overgrazing has reduced streamflow in the first place.

Economist Robin Hur further estimates that if the livestock industry as a whole had to pay all expenses for the water it uses, common hamburger meat would cost $35 per pound (Hur 1985a). This cost is borne indirectly by the taxpayer, the consumer, and the environment.

By depleting Western community water supplies, public lands ranching raises production and storage costs -- and therefore water prices -- to consumers. Most communities drawing drinking water from surface waters fence their watersheds or water sources to keep livestock out. Consumers absorb this extra cost as well. In unfenced watersheds, ranching lowers water quality with chemical, mineral, biological, and sediment pollution. Once again, taxpayers and consumers absorb the extra cost for water treatment, not to mention having to drink the lesser-quality water. Even household plumbing systems can be affected by buildup from increased mineralization.

As the public has shelled out billions of tax dollars for flood damage caused by public lands ranching, so has it spent billions of private dollars. Overgrazing and range developments cause untold devastation to downstream landowners, residents, and businesspeople, including destruction of buildings, improvements, vehicles, gardens, and farms; cutting, gullying, and eroding the land; polluting wells; and killing farm animals and pets. In 1963 annual flood damages due to excessive runoff from BLM land alone were estimated at more than $14 million (Sprague 1974); current damage costs probably are several times higher. Over the years thousands of people have been left homeless, and scores have lost their lives.

By far most Western water comes from public land, and ranching is the major reason for increased flooding from these lands. On any given year damages from floodwaters racing off Western public land total in the tens or hundreds of millions of dollars. Though probably most flood damages are a consequence of unwise development in floodplains and drainages, much damage would not occur without ranching damaging the land and increasing the incidence, size, and ferocity of floods.

Since the 1800s, floodwaters have consumed hundreds of thousands of acres of bottomland -- the most fertile, productive farmland in the West. Since most is private, this represents a loss of hundreds of millions of dollars in real estate values. However, the loss is far greater if cumulative, long-term loss in productivity to humans and Nature is considered.

Fill excavated from this hill is used to replace bottomland washed away by increased flooding. The entire scene exhibits serious overgrazing.

Fifty years ago these oil field pipes in California were underground. Severe downcutting, caused mostly by an overgrazed watershed, has left them useless.

Sediment produced from overgrazed watersheds can drastically reduce the capacity and economic life of irrigation, water supply, flood control, and hydroelectric reservoirs.
--Livestock Grazing on Western Riparian Areas (Chaney 1990)

Damage caused by sediment deposits in the United States is estimated at $500 million annually (Ferguson 1983). Considering that (1) much of this sediment damage occurs in the West, where there are countless reservoirs, irrigation projects, and other developments, (2) public range in the West accounts for about 10% of total US sediment load (USDA, SCS 1980), and (3) ranching is the major cause of soil erosion on public rangeland, we can safely conclude that public lands ranching is responsible for at least $10 million in sediment damages annually.

Roughly 75% of ranching-eroded sediments eventually pour into Western waterways, lakes, and reservoirs, thus reducing their useful lifetimes and harming agriculture, hydroelectric production, fisheries, and water-based recreation. For example, the Arizona Department of Environmental Quality reports that ranching-caused sedimentation in the Salt River watershed "will gradually eliminate much of the current reservoir capacity which provides a dependable water supply to the Phoenix metropolitan area." Sediments in floodwaters likewise bury culverts, drainage ditches, ponds, roads, crops, and anything else in the way.

Sediments from Western public land are carried into harbors and bays as far away as the Mississippi River delta.

Irrigation canals are a common recipient of this increased sedimentation, in addition to suffering trampling by cattle. Loss of bottomland leaves these canals without a medium in which to flow. Expanding cutbanks leave them breached and useless. Lowered waterway beds and decreased streamflows often mean inadequate elevation differences and water momentum for gravity flow irrigation, necessitating pumping or importation. To counter all this, Western water users spend millions of dollars on rerouting, dredging, bank stabilization, check dams, flumes, culverts, floodgates, pipelines, cut and fill, channelization, and fences to keep livestock out.

This cow became trapped in a sediment-filled canal and died. Curiously, it contributed to its own demise by helping overgraze the range and unleash the deadly sediments. *(Howard Wilshire)*

It is conservatively estimated that human activities cause the loss of 500 million tons of topsoil from public land each year, most of it due to ranching (Akers 1983). If we assume an annual topsoil loss caused by public lands ranching of only 200 million tons, and calculate the value of topsoil at only 50 cents per ton, this alone adds up to $100 million annually -- about 5 times what the BLM and Forest Service grossed from grazing fees in 1987. If multiplied by more than a hundred years of ranching, it totals $10 billion.

But can you put a price on soil? Without it most terrestrial life ceases, streamflows diminish . . . its loss is incalculable.

A common Western scene: The irrigation canal in the foreground has been extensively damaged by cattle. The open flat in the background is part of the millions of acres of Western riparian bottomland that have been converted to sterile livestock pasture. Rio Grande Valley, central New Mexico.

An unknown experiment with various conifers has no chance of success without protective fencing. Note the prolific roadside vegetation.

overgrazed Idaho rangelands and served as a breeding ground for the beet leafhopper. It being a drought year, the leafhoppers abandoned the parched, overgrazed ranges and moved onto nearby sugar beet farms. Ninety percent of the sugar beet crop in 6 counties was destroyed, forcing the closure of 2 sugar factories and putting 500 people out of work. In 1938-39 Mormon crickets infested 20 million acres of overgrazed Great Basin range and destroyed an estimated 75% of the grain and vegetable crops in the immediate area. Though seldom this extensive, these types of damages from ranching-caused pest infestations are regular occurrences in the West and Midwest.

Plant "invaders" spread across overgrazed Western ranges and infest private fields and pastures, choking out crops and pasturage. They overrun orchards, yards, gardens, and real estate. They harm farm animals, pets, and people. Scientists believe the overgrazing-induced invader yellow star thistle poisons hundreds of Western horses each year and harms thousands of others.

Even public lands ranching's impact on the honey bee (of which 1 species is native to the West) represents a significant economic loss. Over the years, Western beekeepers have failed to realize tens of millions of dollars of income due to the continual overgrazing that reduces wild flowers in most areas and due to range developments, especially insecticide spraying. As a result of APHIS grasshopper spraying, much of it on public land, Idaho beekeepers in 1985 lost 20%-30% of the state's commercial bees, worth more than $1.7 million (Morris 1986, USDA, APHIS 1986). An equally significant negative influence is caused by the decline in pollinating insects on Western farms, orchards, and gardens.

As mentioned previously, ranching has depleted many indigenous Western plants once important as sources of materials for basketry, clothing, ornamental products, and medicine. As well it has diminished hundreds of plant foods, such as grain amaranth; acorns; watercress; miner's lettuce; ground beans; Indian ricegrass and potatoes; wild plums, celery, turnips, and cucumbers. (Some 2500 of the roughly 14,000 plant species in the 11 Western states may be edible [Dimick 1990].) It has reduced plant and seed sources for experimental, agricultural, reclamation, and landscaping purposes. Depleted herbage has also left riding and pack stock less to eat.

Ranching has reduced the amount of firewood available on most of the Western range. Though livestock grazing has caused an increase in brush and trees in some areas, most of this is scraggly growth and thus inferior as firewood. Trees and large bushes have been depleted by: overgrazing and overbrowsing (which lowers water tables, erodes soil, stunts woody plants, kills young plants, etc.); livestock physically breaking apart bushes and breaking off and trampling lower branches of trees; firewood cutting by ranchers; wood-consuming range "improvements" such as fences and corrals; and range developments such as forest thinning, brush eradication and seeding.

Because of these influences, ranching has also caused a drastic reduction of shade in many areas, especially along waterways -- and most so in areas with the least shade in the first place. Anyone who does much hiking in the open West knows the value of this loss.

When ranges are overgrazed and jackrabbit populations explode, jackrabbits sometimes abandon the livestock wastelands and invade nearby croplands *en masse*. Similarly, hungry grasshoppers, often in the form of winged locusts, and other ranching-induced pests sometimes invade ungrazed range, residential property, gardens, and farms. For example, in 1934 exotic weeds covered millions of acres of

(Anonymous)

Livestock-overgrazed ranges induce hungry wildlife to raid private haystacks (above), domestic vegetation (below), farms, and orchards. *(George Robbins Photo, Jackson, WY)*

If the sportsman want anything to shoot at they had better cooperate with the ranchers and get rid of the cyote and the Fox. [sic]
--Emmett Douglas, Bozeman, Montana public lands rancher

Hunters and fishers, especially, have been hurt by ranching. Though they have much latent power to change public lands policy, "sportsmen" are ironically among the least likely to complain about ranching. Much of this stems from social conditioning; our society fancies hunters and anglers as part of the Old West, right in there with ranchers and cowboys. The livestock industry promotes this mostly imaginary camaraderie to gain the support of sportsmen, and then uses them to help eliminate livestock predators, competitors, and pests.

American hunters and fishers spent about $40 billion in 1990. A recent Montana Department of Fish & Wildlife study shows that hunters and anglers spend $226 million yearly in Montana alone. According to USDA, the 1987 value of hunting provided on National Forests is estimated at $420 million, with the value of fishing at $223 million (USDA, FS 1988). BLM hunting and fishing is worth roughly 1/3 as much. According to professional appraisers, the value paid for hunting privileges alone in many areas exceeds the sale price of livestock. Each year, sportsmen spend more than 50 million days hunting and fishing on Western public land.

Cattle and domestic sheep are getting all the gravy, while deer, pronghorns, bighorns, and other wildlife are left to lick the bowl. . . . It is amazing to me that the American people, including the bulk of this nation's livestock industry, allows relatively few grazing permittees to defile public property and destroy fish and wildlife to such a degree.
--Lonnie Williamson, editor, *Outdoor Life* (Williamson 1983)

Meanwhile, the West has lost more than 90% of big "game" and most small "game" animals since the 1800s, more to ranching than to anything else. The "success" of deer recovery efforts has barely kept the Western hunter appeased. Still, hunters kill an estimated 250 million animals in the US each year. In the West a significant portion of these hunters are ranchers, many of whom surreptitiously seek to eliminate animal enemies. In short, ranching is the hunter's greatest competition.

Many private hunting organizations spend time and money mitigating ranching's impact on "game." For example, in recent years the non-profit Rocky Mountain Elk Foundation spent about $200,000 restoring ranching-degraded elk habitat in Central Arizona. While wildlife groups argue among themselves, ranchers control and abuse what matters most -- *the habitat.*

(George Wuerthner)

Likewise, ranching is the greatest detractor from fishing in most of the West. At least 20 species of "game" fish inhabit Western waters, and all of them are significantly harmed by ranching. The American Fishery Society in 1983 estimated that the cost of fishery resources lost and opportunities foregone on Forest Service land as a direct result of overgrazing was $112 million annually. This is 10 times more than was taken in from Forest Service grazing fees that year. Without fish hatchery programs and the construction of numerous reservoirs for fishing, Western fishers would be most unhappy. However, in general contrast to hunters, many sport fishers have become strong opponents of public lands ranching after recognizing its devastating effect on trout.

Regardless of one's opinion on hunting or fishing, their diminishment by public lands ranching represents not only a loss of government and private revenue but, to many, a loss of outdoor experience and supplementary food.

It is the first consideration in my own decision of where I will hunt elk and I'm convinced the avoidance of grazed areas is the most important element in the success of these hunts.
--Steve Gallizioli, Arizona Game & Fish Department, *Arizona Wildlife News*

While about 25 million Americans hunt and 60 million fish (and both numbers are dwindling), according to *US News and World Report* (2-5-90), *135 million engage in some form of non-consumptive wildlife use such as birding or Nature study. Loss of wildlife affects them as surely as it does the consumptive users, as what they derive from the experience is no less important.

Cattle have a tendency to congregate in level, moist, fertile areas with lush vegeta-

(George Wuerthner)

tion -- along creeks and rivers, around ponds and lakes, on hill and ridgetops, in meadows and grassy flats. Ranchers also prefer to graze their sheep and goats there. Thus, the most beautiful, productive, and desirable areas for people (and wildlife) are also the most heavily abused by ranching.

M.E. Ensminger writes in **Beef Cattle Science**, "Indeed, cattle and sheep are pleasing to tourists, who come to view the 'Old West.'" Are we that hopelessly indoctrinated!? It is hard to imagine why anyone would want to spend a vacation viewing a barren, fenced landscape pocked with sacrifice areas and scattered with dull-witted, bellowing cows. But for those so inclined, there are more than enough cattle and sheep to view on private rangeland (25% of the West). In fact, this is where 91.5% of all Western livestock will be found (Com. on Govt. Oper. 1986).

"How can this be multiple use?" I asked him, "when no one in his right mind can be in the same area without being eaten alive!?"
--Bill Howard, "The Multiple Abuse of Our Public Lands"

Cattle defecate about 15 times per day, and the average pie is about the size of a dinner plate. Who hasn't stepped in one? Each meadow muffin can produce as many as 1500 flies. Flies are an obvious problem in areas with large livestock populations and to humans sometimes become nearly intolerable -- biting flies and gnats especially.

At least I always thought there was a definite correlation. But then one warm spring day our local grazing permittee set me straight. He assured me that the swarms of flies and gnats that for weeks had made life miserable for our family did not come from the surrounding thousands of putrid piles dropped by his cattle. "No, this is a common misconception," he explained. "In reality, flies are born right up out of the dirt." Perhaps he was right; there was a lot of bare dirt around.

Cows moo. They also bleat, bellow, bawl, grunt, and snort. Only the victim kept awake for hours night after night can appreciate how incessantly loud and grotesque they can be. Some cattle and sheep wear bells, which also clang loudly or tinkle throughout the night. Public lands visitors and nearby residents are commonly subjected to these obnoxious noises. However, vehicular and related noise from ranching roads is perhaps the greatest source of noise pollution on most public land. And nearby ranching base properties provide public lands visitors the pleasures of barking dogs, gun shots, heavy equipment, machinery, water pumps, generators, and other exotic sounds (all of these emanate from public land as well). Only stockmen can regularly create such a ruckus and not be cited for violating noise ordinances.

Smell is perhaps our most primitive sensation. Nature's myriad scents are as much a part of the wild as the sun and wind. The pungent fragrance of broken sage heightens awareness; sweet aroma from pine bark baking in the sun is immensely pleasurable; perfumed whiffs from unknown flowers are exciting. However, probably the most common smell in the West comes from cow shit. Its strong, musty odor drowns out and perverts natural scents. Cows are comparatively filthy animals; often you can smell them before you see or hear them.

Beauty springs from environmental health and integrity.

While ranching has increased unpleasant, unnatural noise pollution, it has also decreased Nature's music. A walk on the ungrazed right side of this fence reveals the wonderful sounds of life -- grass and leaves rustling in the breeze, crickets chirping, flying insects buzzing about, birds singing. Crossing over to the grazed side is eerie -- like stepping into a sound void.

Many visitors to public land come to enjoy its "visual resources." One of the most immediate, though immeasurable, results of overgrazing and range development is just plain ugliness. Trampled vegetation, bare dirt, muddied streambanks, dirty water, cowpies, fences, road scars, and sacrifice areas are more unsightly to most people than is undamaged landscape. Ranching's debasement of "watchable wildlife," such as large mammals and many birds; scenic vegetation such as cottonwoods, perennial flowering plants, saguaros, and tall grasses; verdant, flowing waterways; and unspoiled, undeveloped landscapes, has deprived millions of people of pleasures that should be theirs by right of birth.

While cattle may assault your senses, they may also assault your body directly. Many people have been attacked, some injured, and several killed by raging bulls and deranged cows on public land. For example, many years ago on BLM prairie in eastern New Mexico, in a small car on a very muddy ranching road, my family and I were chased for a mile by a huge demented bull; we spun through the muck barely fast enough to outrun it. Cattle may become deranged from illness, injury, stress, infection, or from eating narcotic or poisonous plants. Watch your children and pets.

Even hikers are feeling the pinch. "If you get one of those spiny seedheads in your legs and sit on it," rues Don Joley, a pest management specialist with California's Department of Food and Agriculture, "you know it in a hurry. It's miserable -- you can get pus building up and the spine can stay in there for a month -- and it smarts."
--Comment on the ranching invader yellow star thistle (Bashin 1990)

Ranching has spread tumbleweeds, goat heads, burrs, thistles, foxtail, catclaw, cactus, and other thorny or stickery plants across tens of millions of acres of public land. A few areas are now so thick with cactus and catclaw that they are virtually inaccessible to humans without protective gear (in some ways this may be a blessing, however). Have you ever come back from a hike to find your socks riddled with foxtails, or from a picnic to find them covering your shirt or blanket? An awn in your dog's eye? Clothing torn on catclaw? Spines in your shins? Stickers in your feet? Goatheads in your shoes?

[Note: I stand accused of "grasping at straws" here and on several other ranching impacts in this chapter. I disagree! Why shouldn't we expect to be able to throw down a blanket or go barefoot or enjoy a day without flies?! Remember, these impacts cause loss, inconvenience, discomfort, or bodily harm to millions of people on millions of acres.]

Loose strands of barbed wire catch and damage vehicles.

Barbed wire fences also degrade peoples' enjoyment of public land in many ways. They impede movement, necessitate the opening and closing of gates, and force the rerouting of many trails and roads, making them longer and thus spreading their destructive impacts.

Each July, Olson [an Oregon Fish & Wildlife Service employee] *makes a four-day loop through his district to count and classify sage grouse. Olson is always glad to take at least one other person along -- that way the passenger can get out of the truck to open and close the 52 cattle gates on his route.*
--Oregon Wildlife, 1990

Closing a rancher's gate: a hassle played out a million times a day on public lands around the West. BLM land, Vale District, Oregon. *(George Wuerthner)*

Fences are dangerous. How many people, while climbing over a fence or walking innocently along, have been cut by barbed wire? The number hurt on public land over the years must run literally in to the millions. Many people on horses, bicycles, and motorized vehicles have been seriously injured, and some killed, when they inadvertently collided with fences and gates. Fences are especially dangerous at night, when the strands are poorly seen. (Let me show you my stomach scars.) And who *hasn't* torn clothing on barbed wire?

Government publications warn about river running injuries and damages to watercraft due to fences across public waterways. A friend narrowly escaped serious injury and had his raft gashed. Most river runners have tales of barbed wire to tell. In **Run, River, Run**, Ann Zwinger writes of fences across rivers:

At low water level they may be far enough above the water not to be dangerous, but at high water they can be lethal. . . . Accepted procedure is to hold the paddle up vertically in front of your face, letting the wire slide up the shaft as your head goes under.

Fences across waterways hinder and sometimes injure river runners and damage their watercraft, while overgrazing and withdrawal for pasture irrigation lowers river levels.

Not measurable on the material plane, but important nonetheless, fences destroy the open-space feeling of the land. They are a ubiquitous eyesore.

DON'T FENCE ME IN
by Cole Porter, 1944

Oh, give me land, lots of land under starry skies above.
Don't fence me in.
Let me ride through the wide open country I love.
Don't fence me in.

Let me be by myself in the evening breeze,
Listen to the murmer of the cottonwood trees.
Send me off forever, but I ask you please,
Don't fence me in.

Just turn me loose, let me straddle my own saddle
underneath the western skies.
On my cayuse [Indian pony], let me wonder over yonder
till I see the mountains rise.

I want to ride to the ridge where the West commences,
Gaze at the moon till I lose my senses.
Can't look at hobbles and I can't stand fences,
Don't fence me in.

Hikers attempt to negotiate barbed wire on public land.

These [recreational] values have been substantially impaired by defendants' failure to exclude or restrict grazing. In addition, although BLM-administered lands are "public use" lands, the construction of fences on or around them often discourages and even precludes access to these lands, and, along with water developments and unsightly treatments of vegetation growing on these lands, considerably diminish aesthetic enjoyment.
--from a 1973 lawsuit by the Natural Resources Defense Council

My wife and I encountered at least three BLM "improved" camping spots that day, and each was so cluttered with fresh cow manure that we could only move on. It reminded me of a parallel situation in Nevada where livestockmen attempting to discourage use of public facilities, removed the tops of inlet water pipes into drinking troughs so that if a traveler stopped for a drink of water from the uncontaminated spout he instead would have to drink from the trough with the livestock.
--Edwin G. Dimick, **Livestock Pillage of Our Public Lands**

. . . [An Uncompahgre NF, CO volunteer] says a day rarely passes that he doesn't receive a complaint from campers who have to chase cattle from their campgrounds or spend restless nights amid cows mooing for their calves.
--Lisa Jones, "Overgrazing: Feds Move to End It" (Jones 1991a)

Livestock hooves pock-mark millions of acres of meadows, bottomlands, and flatlands across the West, sometimes making travel difficult. Many places are so covered with hoof holes and cow pies that you can't even find a decent spot to lay a sleeping bag. Mosquitoes breed in the rancid, water-filled holes and thrive on the blood of the numerous cattle, and later attack human visitors.

Ranching's degradation of the Western water system has affected a lot more than fishing and farming. No longer can we travel across public land simply drinking from natural water sources. Now we must shorten our trips, lug around water containers, go thirsty, or get sick. Medical bills due to livestock-polluted water alone are high.

Many public swimming areas are fouled and monopolized by ranchers and their livestock. Many others no longer exist. Hot springs have been either dried up or destroyed by overgrazing-caused floods. There is a wonderful hot spring on the San Francisco River in New Mexico's Gila National Forest. Located in a peaceful, beautiful, deep canyon, it is popular with locals and travelers. However, for many years visitors there were met not by the music of canyon wrens and a musty river bank aroma but by the clamor and stench of a gas-powered pump. Water was lifted through a pipe up the canyon wall to cattle on the mesa 500' above. The pump has since been damaged, then removed completely, but similar situations abound in the rural West.

Hike up a desolate desert canyon, gain the rim -- and be greeted by a bawling cow utterly impaled on a yucca. Backpack into a wilderness area and locate a rockface to climb. Struggle to the top and find the glorious amaranthine view you anticipated defiled by the presence of bell-tinkling, bleating, malodorous sheep. That is public lands degradation.
--David L. McWilliams, Rock Springs, Colorado, 3-2-88 *Casper Star-Tribune*

Millions of people enjoy hiking, camping, backpacking, and other "outdoor sports." But most important for many is simply *being* in Nature, *being* natural, *being* free. Nature provides humans infinite lessons on many facets of existence, such as form, function, meaning, time, substance, structure, relations, sense, self, and awareness. These lessons reflect "Nature's wisdom" -- billions of years of natural creation and existence. Moreover, Nature provides a context for life, the proper medium in which to interact with the planet.

When natural systems are altered the underlying principles are perverted, obscured, and rendered invalid. When Nature is no longer natural, the beauty, magic, purpose, and very essence of experience is diminished. Every unnatural environmental influence diminishes Nature's wisdom.

Once we encountered two enthusiastic young Germans traveling through the Southwest in a battered microbus. They were staying in those miserable, expensive KOAs. We got out a map and explained in halting Anglo-German about the wonderful public lands -- Volkslande. "All these cows we see, they are Volkskuhe (people's cows)?" they asked. No, we said, those are private cows and private fences. They were perplexed. "But how can there be private cows on public land?"
--Dennis Brownridge, Mayer, Arizona, personal correspondence

Visitors to Forest Service and BLM land in the US accounted for about 250 million visitor days in 1987, mostly in the West (USDA, FS 1988). Together with other public lands impacted by ranching, the figure would be at least 300 million. Although experience is poorly measured with dollars, if we place an arbitrary value of only $20 per day on each visitor day, we get a total visitor value of $6 billion. Even if only 1 of 100 of these visitors had the quality of their experience degraded by $5 by public lands ranching, it would amount to $15 million.

I remember hiking once on the Concord side of the mountain, when I discovered in a slightly burned area one of the rarest species on the mountain -- the Mt. Diablo Globe Lily, one of seven species of plant life found here but nowhere else on earth. When I returned later in the week, I was shocked to find my discovery, not eaten, but buried beneath a disgusting pile of cow flop.
--Sharon Seidenstein, Berkeley, California

Ranching inherently detracts from Nature, often in ways we do not appreciate or understand. For example, ranching has eliminated more wild flowers from the Western landscape than has any other land use (observe that colorful roadside wild flower displays often end exactly at the right-of-way fence). It desecrates countless fragile, unique, rare, and interesting natural phenomenon. Spider webs, pine cones, mushrooms, ant mounds, ground nests, weather-sculptured pieces of wood, graceful ripples in the sand, wild animal tracks, fragile mineral formations . . . all are ravaged indiscriminately.

Fragile and beautiful natural entities are precluded or destroyed by ranching. This sage skeleton could never have survived intact on a livestock range. Deer step gingerly around it, whereas cattle would have trampled it into scattered debris.

(George Wuerthner)

The biological and ecological values of prairie dogs are to some degree measurable or quantifiable. The social and esthetic values defy such measurement. How does one evaluate the experience of a family who spends an unforgettable hour at Wind Caves National Park watching and delighting at the antics of prairie dogs . . . .
--Robert Badaracco, in a conservation publication

How much is a prairie dog worth? An elk? A trout? A vole? A flower? A hot spring? A mushroom? A hollow log? A grassy creek bank? A delicate mineral formation? These things and the experiences humans derive from them are poorly measured with money. Nor can we measure the infinite suffering inflicted on wildlife during the past century, or the worth of billions of wild lives that simply never were.

However, the purpose of this chapter *is*, in part, to place a monetary value on "resources" degraded or lost due to ranching. The impacts detailed above and below show it to be *more than a billion dollars annually*.

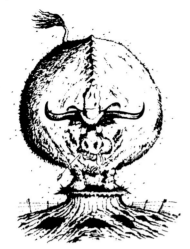

(Roger Candee)

Livestock operators pollute the public lands as freely as if they owned them. And the real owners -- the public -- are expected to accept the contamination of their outdoor sanctuaries by filth, flies, foul water, and fences.
--George Wuerthner, "The Price Is Wrong" (Wuerthner 1990b)

A cattle-trampled aboriginal campsite on BLM land in northeast Arizona.

I've put in a lot of pipe and never had to put up with all this archaeological crap!
--Sawtooth NF permittee Kyle Adams, in defense of his installation of an unauthorized water line on National Forest land (Williams 1991)

After the ranching establishment helped fuel the conquest and subjugation of Native American cultures, it even desecrated the sanctity of their memory. Most of the West has been grazed for a century, and each year millions of clumsy hooves have stomped and scraped the land's surface billions of times. Further, the areas where aboriginal peoples lived and spent most of their time -- level lands and along waterways -- are most heavily affected.

Through trampling, increased soil erosion, and flooding, artifacts such as pottery and chards; arrowheads, spear points, scrapers, knives, and other stone tools; and mortars and pestles have been displaced and broken. Thousands of historic and prehistoric village ruins, camping and hunting sites, and burial grounds have been ravaged. A travesty to the spirit of this continent's aboriginal peoples, it also has frustrated modern archaeologists.

Even prehistoric cave dwellings are not sacred to the sacred cow. I have hiked to many, only

The decline of needle-and-thread grass in much of the West is an unmeasurable aesthetic loss. *(Helen Wilson)*

to have cattle awkwardly stumble out at my approach. Cows like to siesta in the cave coolness on hot afternoons. The insides of many caves are a scrambled confusion of stinking cowpies and overwhelming dust, any artifacts long since pulverized.

Not as widespread as cows' hooves, but more thoroughly destructive to aboriginal remains, has been range development. Chaining, bulldozing, plowing, and other techniques used in vegetation manipulation, along with other range development, have ruined many sites and certain canyons, mesas, and other places held sacred by Native Americans. In cases where sites were known beforehand, the ranching establishment often proceeded with open callousness. More often, sites are discovered *after* being demolished.

Similarly, livestock and range development have damaged numerous historical sites of the Spanish and American cultures. Old Spanish settlement and encampment sites in New Mexico were damaged by chaining operations. Old Western cemeteries not well-fenced have had gravesites trampled. Cattle wander through Western ghost towns, trampling relics and damaging structures.

Special railroad underpasses for ranching roads and livestock movement cost railroads millions of dollars altogether. This one is *not* a drainage. Note the roadside fenceline contrast.

Railroad corporations owning or operating a line within the state are required to construct, maintain and repair sufficient fence connected with suitable cattle guards at all public road crossings to prevent livestock from entering railways. In addition, railroad corporations are liable to owners of livestock for damage or loss resulting from collision with trains and are required to post notice of the killing or injury.
--Wyoming Statutes 37-9-304 through 37-9-308

Public lands ranching necessitates thousands of special, gated railroad crossings for ranching roads.

Roughly 15,000 miles of railroad tracks stretch across the West, with perhaps a third of these miles on public land. Unlike last century, when "cattle catchers" on engines knocked cows out of the way, barbed wire (usually) now keeps cattle off the tracks. Special crossings are constructed for ranchers and their livestock at each of the thousands of places where ranching roads intersect railroad tracks. As with roads, railroads also have special underpasses for livestock. Again, the consumer ultimately foots the bill.

Structural developments on public and private ranges, such as in this oil field, must be protected with sturdy enclosures or risk damage from cattle. This cost alone totals millions of dollars, and is generally passed on to the consumer and taxpayer.

The dark patches in the foreground are crude oil from a pipeline damaged by trampling cattle and cattle-caused erosion.

When oil and gas drilling, mining, tourist development, powerline construction, organizational gatherings, movie making, and other activities on public land disturb ranching operations, users are required to compensate ranchers for the value of their ranching losses. This can include lost herbage, depleted water sources, damaged range developments, greater access costs, scared cattle, and just about anything else a rancher can dream up. Values commonly are inflated, and at times the scam is essentially subleasing. In New Mexico this type of compensation averages $28,000 per ranchman affected.

The [Henry Lake] foundation raised money from its members to permanently exclude livestock from the riparian area along a half-mile reach of stream. Foundation members took time off from jobs and vacations to build the fence to the rancher's specifications. The foundation paid the rancher a modest fee to cover the cost of maintaining the fence.
--from Livestock Grazing on Western Riparian Areas (Chaney 1990)

Many private organizations cater to the needs and demands of public lands ranchers, often under the misguided impression that they are doing something patriotic and worthwhile for America and its dusty, downtrodden cowboy. These include veterinary associations, advocacy groups, and scientific research groups.

Hundreds of environmental, conservation, sportsmen, recreation, and other groups have over the decades spent millions of dollars and hours studying land management plans, writing letters, making phone calls, implementing lawsuits, and so forth to mitigate the influences of public lands ranching. For example, in 1986 a range professor at Oregon State University founded the Oregon Watershed Improvement Coalition with the purpose of mediating disputes between ranchers and others and discussing range "improvement" ideas. The Nature Conservancy and other private groups spend millions of dollars acquiring or protecting ranching-damaged land in attempting to restore Endangered species, riparian areas, watersheds, etc.

In California's San Bernardino Mountains the Sierra Club, Deep Creek Flyfishermen, and others expended much effort and money building range developments to mitigate ranching's impact on waterways, hot springs, trails, and archaeological sites. The Izaak Walton League's Public Lands Restoration Task Force organizes outings where volunteers help restore overgrazed riparian areas by building instream structures, revegetating denuded areas, and repairing protective fences. Trout Unlimited, Oregon Watershed Improvement Foundation, Henry's Fork Foundation, Henry's Lake Foundation, and Chinook Northwest are a few of the many organizations that spend time and money on fencing and restoration projects for overgrazed waterways. BLM, FS, and other government agencies sponsor numerous volunteer outings to build and maintain fences; remove obsolete fences; revegetate denuded and damaged areas; eradicate "weeds" and brush; build erosion control structures; repair trails and facilities damaged by livestock; restore wildlife; study, monitor, build facilities for, and take care of ex-free-ranging horses and burros; protect archaeological sites -- *ad infinitum* (see USDI, BLM 1987, for example). Boy Scouts, Girl Scouts, Camp Fire, YMCA, YWCA, DeMolay, church, and other private groups conduct similar activities. And, hundreds of times a day around the West, individuals and small groups chase cattle and sheep out of "protected" areas, mend ranching fences, and assist public lands ranchers in diverse ways. The total value of all this volunteer effort and financial expense is in the millions of dollars annually. But, again, rarely do people confront, or even recognize, the ultimate cause.

Here, several men and women spend their weekend dismantling and removing an obsolete fence from Saguaro National Monument near Tucson, Arizona, so the barbed wire and posts will not harm wildlife and humans.

Any public utility may furnish free service to "caretakers" of livestock, poultry and other domestic animals.
--Wyoming statute 37-3-105

Through special legislation and consideration, stockmen often pay lower utility rates and less for construction and hookup of new utilities than do common people. And, electrical rates are lower for irrigators (mostly stock growers) than for the general consumer. The public, through higher taxes and utility rates, absorbs much of the extra cost for construction and maintenance of the huge utility network that services the 30,000 public lands ranches spread across the rural West.

Tens of thousands of miles of special phone and other utility lines and service roads benefit public lands ranches.

Similarly, many other commercial enterprises experience smaller profit ratios, or losses, in servicing public lands ranchers. For example, the rancher who lives an hour down a remote dirt road pays the same amount for delivered propane as the mechanic on the edge of town. The lower profit ratio in doing business with ranchers is compensated for by higher prices to other customers. We may term this privately based subsidization.

Workers must dismantle and rebuild fences to work on utility lines, which increases consumer cost.

(Unknown)

For the New Mexico Cattle Growers Association to act as plaintiff in the case in which the state Supreme Court ruled against phone-rate breaks for the elderly on assistance is the height of hypocrisy. Even if the rate-breaks would have cost members of the association a few cents each month on each month's phone bill, that pales in comparison to the subsidies that New Mexico ranchers -- especially those on public lands -- receive.
--B. Donald Schwartzenegger, letter to the editor, 9-20-87 *Albuquerque Journal*

Ranching spreads dangerous chemicals and biocides over thousands or millions of acres of public land each year. Some are known or suspected mutagens, carcinogens, or embryotoxins. Especially heavy concentrations of toxins may occur where livestock are treated for parasites and disease, herbicides and pesticides are handled, and ranchers spill or dump used oil, diesel fuel and various chemical mixtures. Any of the above may be hazardous to public lands visitors, or to downstream or nearby residents.

For example, the persistent, wide-spectrum Dow Chemical herbicide Tordon, a defoliant used in the Vietnam War, is also used to kill leafy spurge, an Asian perennial that may cause scours in cattle and "infests" (largely due to overgrazing) roughly 1.5 million acres of range in the north-central US. Residents in areas sprayed with Tordon have complained that it kills their gardens and trees; tests show the chemical exists in their water supplies too. While the government claims Tordon is harmless to humans, a resident near one sprayed area in Wyoming quipped, "When your plants die after being watered with the same water you drink, you think about it." (Hampton 1990)

Ranching traps and poisons kill and maim hundreds or perhaps thousands of pet dogs and cats each year. Traps also catch scores of people each year, injuring some. Bear and mountain lion traps are huge and can do serious damage to a human leg. One story is of an elderly woman who got caught in a bear trap and may have died had she not finally been able to pull the chain from the ground. Larry Sunderland, a Scottsdale, Arizona, resident, was hiking along a wooded road in the Coconino National Forest when his dog stepped into a scented, buried, steel-jaw trap. In trying to free the dog, Sunderland caught his own hand in the trap, causing profuse bleeding. After his visit to a hospital emergency room, the Arizona Game & Fish Department charged Sunderland with disturbing a trap -- a misdemeanor crime. Sunderland was so outraged he filed suit against AZ G&F, but lost. (Baylor 1989) Similarly, a California man seriously injured his hand while trying to free his horse from a leg-hold trap. When he threatened legal action against the trapper, he was instead cited by the California Department of Fish & Game for interfering with a trapline.

Each year ranchers shoot hundreds of pet and feral dogs that they find chasing livestock. Legally they may even shoot those only "in the vicinity" of livestock. They claim the dogs might run a little fat -- and therefore weight and profit -- off their cattle and sheep. Some even have it figured out mathematically: X yards running = Y ounces weight loss = Z dollars lost.

As I was walking on Forest Service land near my home in central Arizona several years ago, I noticed drag marks in the dirt leading to what appeared to be a crude grave.

Thinking I must have happened across some human murder victim, I gently scraped back a few inches of the loose soil to find fur -- a neighbor's beloved pet dog, with a bullet hole in its side. Later they told me they were aware that the local public lands rancher was the killer. Indeed, they said he had killed 2 of their other dogs. Laws in most Western states allow a rancher to kill any dog or other animal he claims killed, injured, bothered, or even *might* bother his livestock.

A sign posted on public range.

Many other unjust, antiquated laws created by and for stockmen a century ago still stand in every Western state. For example, cattle rustling is a third-degree felony in Utah, punishable by up to 5 years in prison and a $5000 fine. Rustling is likewise a third-degree felony in Arizona, with a minimum 3.75-year and maximum 25-year prison sentence. Western authorities manage rustling cases with utmost seriousness, like bank robberies. In Texas, cutting a livestock fence is a third-degree felony and can result in up to 10 years behind bars.

!!! NEWS FLASH !!!

April 23, 1989
Gila County, Arizona

A manhunt by deputies from the Gila and Yavapai County Sheriff's Departments and an Arizona State Department of Public Safety helicopter has resulted in the arrests of 3 bowhunters for the murder of a cow. [The cow was scheduled to die in a slaughterhouse in December.] The search began with the report of the shooting death of a cow in the Fossil Creek area of Gila County. The suspects were apprehended after an extensive all-day search in the rugged, mountainous area. Shooting another man's cow is a Class 5 felony in the state, with a minimum prison sentence of 1-6 years.

(Source: *Verde Independent*, Cottonwood, AZ)

So far as consistent with the purposes and provisions of this subchapter, grazing privileges recognized and acknowledged shall be adequately safeguarded, but the creation of a grazing district or the issuance of a permit pursuant to the provisions of this subchapter shall not create any right, title, interest, or estate in or to the lands [emphasis added].
--[Taylor Grazing Act] 43 U.S.C. 315b, amended by 43 U.S.C. 1701 (1982)

Imagine this: a Western scene, cowboys on horseback herdin' them doggies into a corral. The moos of the cows, the yips of the cowboys, a vast, rugged landscape as backdrop. An appropriately rustic, gravelly male voice says slowly, resolutely, "I work this land. [pause] I share it with others . . . ." A short lecture follows on people throwing trash around and not respectin' range improvements, thus the land. These vandals are hurtin' every public lands user, he says, ending with: "Help ensure continued access to all Arizona's outdoors." To prove the point, the video climaxes with a gate being locked, with what is presumably our public land behind it.

This "public service announcement" is being run by TV stations around Arizona these days. The message is clear: Ranchers work and respect the land. Respecting the land means respecting ranchers' "improvements," and if some people continue to damage range developments the public will be locked out of public lands. Unbelievably, the public accepts such drivel without a second thought as an *environmental* message. That the ad is a lie as much as a threat is, unfortunately, beyond most people. It demonstrates to what lengths stockmen will go to maintain their power. The ad is financed by the Arizona Game & Fish Department and the Arizona Cattlemen's Association, for which it doubles as a tax write-off.

On national TV Clint Eastwood, as hardassed as ever, says there's people out there damaging our public lands, particularly range developments thereon, and as far as he's concerned "these clowns can either clean up their act or get out of town." Make my day.

Take Pride In America Campaign Coordinated by the Department of the Interior

Out on the range, the machismo gets worse. For example, a Central Arizona permittee is known to shoot over the heads of visitors who dare "trespass" on "his" public lands allotment. Some stockmen make threats, post "no trespassing" signs, gate and lock roads, and even build illegal fences on "their" public land to prevent access. There are many cases of a road legally accessing public lands running past a rancher's house, with the rancher doing his best to intimidate the public from using that access -- often with many unwieldy gates, blockades, vicious dogs, menacing signs, and various frightening displays. Thousands of public lands visitors are harassed and threatened by ranchers. Some encounters end in violence.

In its pamphlet, "Backcountry Ethics," the Forest Service tells backcountry visitors:

--**DON'T** leave trash.

--**DON'T** disturb soil.

--**DON'T** disturb groundcover.

--**DON'T** girdle trees and brush.

--**DON'T** cut trees, limbs, and brush.

--**DON'T** use firewood or make fires.

--**DON'T** camp within 300 feet of water.

--**DON'T** pick flowers or disturb vegetation.

--**DON'T** clear away vegetation for your tent.

--**DON'T** put foreign substances in waterways.

--**DON'T** disturb historic and prehistoric sites.

--**DON'T** travel between trails or across meadows.

--**DON'T** camp in meadows; "you'll trample the grass."

--**DON'T** defecate on the soil surface or near waterways.

--**DON'T** let pack stock damage vegetation, soil, or water.

Meanwhile . . . stockmen and their stock do all these things and more -- with many times the impact of all other human visitors combined throughout most of the backcountry West.

I'm tired of cattle grazing all around us May-Sept. every year, always the threat of a trampled garden, etc. Why should we have to fence in our 25 acres to seal out range cattle?
--Meggie Blume, Eureka, Montana

. . . my property (as well as the National Forest) is constantly being desecrated by cattle from the surrounding forest. . . . My fencing, orchard, springs, and garden have all experienced destruction at the teeth and hooves of beef cattle.
--David Field, Covelo, California

The snow is melting fast in our canyon here in the south side of Palomar Mountain in Southern California, revealing the true extent of the damage caused by 7 days of uninvited cattle grazing. Broken water stand-pipes, hours of repair time in the dark while it's raining, hours spent trying to run the cattle out of our canyon, and more hours spent repairing fences are the result of this latest trashing by our neighbor's cattle.

We get no apology, no help from the owner of the cows, just grunts and sour looks; no offer of paying for our time or materials . . . .
--Bruce Druliner, Palomar Ranch, Santa Ysabel, California

As my neighbor found out when cattle destroyed the garden he had worked all summer, it is the landowner's responsibility to fence out unwanted animals.
--Roger Owens, Heber, Arizona

The above quotations are from among scores of similar letters I have received. "Open range" laws allow a rancher's livestock to range freely almost anywhere except on another rancher's land or allotment. Essentially, they absolve stockmen from legal responsibility for problems caused by their livestock or range management activities. They also allow ranchers to graze and profit from land they do not own or lease.

Open range laws were enacted during the early settlement of most Western states -- except in much of California, where a high farming and urban population partially overpowered stockmen and caused some big-time ranchers to move elsewhere. These blatantly unfair laws have caused hardship and expense to hundreds of thousands of innocent people over the years.

While public lands ranchers argue for the sanctity of their own private land, they rarely extend this respect to other rural property. Open range laws require private landowners who do not want livestock on their land to fence ranchers' livestock *out*, rather than ranchers to fence their livestock in. To meet state minimum legal requirements, fences must be constructed with 4 or 5 strands of barbed wire on deeply planted, close-set posts, with sturdy support posts at regular intervals. (If a cow is injured trying to squeeze through your illegal fence, you may be liable for damages to the cow!) Requirements vary slightly between states.

If not entirely enclosed with a strictly legal fence with closed, securely fastened gates, your land is legally available for grazing to the opportunistic ranchman. In fact, *most* unfenced and *much* legally fenced rural private property in the rangeland West is grazed *intentionally* by ranchers (this largely discounting land already grazed by the owner or under contract to be grazed). Maintaining a legal fence is no guarantee that your land will not be plundered. Cattle commonly break through legal fences and come through open gates. Many ranchers cut fences and leave gates open to gain access to larger private properties. And I just received a letter from a couple that owns 20 acres adjacent to Washington's Okanogan National Forest who fenced their land a few years ago, only to have the local rancher file a lawsuit to gain easement across their property for the purpose of moving cattle between allotments.

It seemed to me by the end of the fall that the cows must have been half-starved. The meadow had been reduced to a dry rubble by that time, yet the cows continued to chomp the seedless stalks. They ate the compost I foolishly set out to bury. They even ate the jar of Queen Anne's Lace flowers I left sitting by my cabin door.
--Cecelia Ostrow, musician, *Touching the Earth*

LANDOWNERS OF GRAND COUNTY

You have rights too!

A suit is being filed against the BLM and the U. S. Forest Service, alleging that they have been negligent and irresponsible in their management practices of public lands adjacent to private property. In their lack of sensitivity to the needs and problems of private land owners in the county, they have knowingly assisted in the infliction of personal and private property damages.

LANDOWNERS

If you have received damage to your property or person due to the policy of grazing cattle next to your private property, please notify: The Coalition for Responsible Management of Our Public Lands, Box 50, Moab, Utah 84532. We are currently gathering data as to the kind and degree of property damage involved. Describe the damages by breaking them down into three groups:

1. Estimated actual property damage, such as, broken pipe, crop damage, water pollution, building damage, etc. This should include cost of repair or replacement. Include your labor at $10.00 per hour, plus all material expenses.

2. Estimated cost for fencing out livestock being grazed adjacent to your property. Include labor and materials as well as annual maintenance expenses.

3. Personal psychological stress. The continuing destruction of one's homestead can be a very depressing problem in one's life. The court's are often very sympathetic to this type of personal injury.

All claims can be extended back to the 1943 grazing ordinance. This suit may take years to complete, and may go through many courts and appeals. But, should the C.R.M. win this battle, all of your legitimate damage losses will be reimbursed.

PAID POLITICAL ANNOUNCEMENT

A notification in a Grand County, Utah, newspaper.

"They came through the barbed wire fence and just destroyed my garden about two weeks ago," said Kathy Sheldon, 29. "They ate all the corn, they ate my tomatos and they ripped up the drip irrigation system." . . . *"The cows tear down my fence and eat my plants," McGee said. "They eat my garden. They eat my bushes. They eat my trees. And they're not a bit afraid of you."* . . . *"I have a 6-year-old daughter and my main concern is for her safety," said the 31-year-old man. "I have a barbed wire fence around my yard, but they keep tearing it apart to get in to eat the grass."*

--8-2-87 *Arizona Daily Star*

Thus do rural landowners and residents very often experience close-up the sight, sound, and smell of cattle. They encounter cow pats on their yards, sidewalks, and patios. They endure eaten and trampled gardens, fruit trees, landscape vegetation, and lawns. They suffer damage to driveways, drainages, vehicles, homes, porches, sheds, well houses, lawn furniture, walls, fences, pipes, planters, pools, swing sets, and anything else damaged by a gouge, shove, or stomp from an awkward, half-ton animal.

Without a protective fence, this central Utah garden would be plundered by cattle from the adjacent Fishlake National Forest grazing allotment. Note the cattle-depleted range in the foreground, which is part of the private property. Many stockmen consider private land near or adjacent to "their" allotment to be essentially part of the allotment.

Public lands cattle also plunder farms, orchards, and nurseries; when rangelands are overgrazed and barren, that juicy greenery is irresistible to hungry cattle. They ravage hay supplies and grain stockpiles. They break pipes. They knock down fences, allowing farm animals to escape. They damage tourist facilities and degrade the experience of customers. They invade any unfenced businesses near public lands. They create hazards on and damage private drives and roads, even airplane runways.

I have visited several small Western communities where cattle wander freely throughout -- yards, streets, parking lots, sidewalks, vacant lots, parks, school grounds. These towns are stripped of most vegetation, littered with cowpies, and experience much physical damage.

Free-ranging cattle also raid private Nature preserves, such as the Arizona Nature Conservancy's Hassayampa River Preserve. Many preserves list legal cattle trespass as their #1 problem.

Who says the "Wild West" is dead?

The monetary loss that public lands ranching causes rural folks is unarguably in the millions of dollars annually. Decreased Western property values (from eroded bottomland, degraded vegetation, depleted water, the presence of livestock, etc.) incurred from legal or trespassing livestock total in the billions.

Lonnie Williams, a forester who owns 640 acres on the mountain, says he's tired of cattle eating his young trees. "I give the cattle credit for destroying 75% of the seedlings I've planted over the past seven or eight years," Williams says. "That's $5,000 in growing stock." . . . . [The cattle are] a big problem because I have to fence them out," says Loyal Fleener, whose wheat farm is adjacent to open range east of Deary.
--June 1986 Moscow, Idaho, *Tribune*

While living in the Gila National Forest in the late 1970s, we and most residents experienced numerous problems from the local permittee's cattle, which moved freely between National Forest and private property. Like us, some owners fenced their land, but the cattle invariably broke through. Talking to the rancher and Forest Service proved useless.

We circulated a petition listing 9 major complaints, requesting that the Forest Service ban cattle from the immediate area. Of the area's residents, 54 out of 69 signed the petition (some of those who didn't were the permittee's relatives). When presented the petition, the forest supervisor seemed bewildered by this unprecedented open rebellion against ranching, but he did nothing.

One resident, Mike Lusby, is recovering from multiple broken bones he suffered when his motorcycle struck a cow on the highway on June 17. Attorneys representing the cow's owner have notified Lusby that he is expected to pay for the animal, which was killed in the accident.
--8-2-87 *Arizona Daily Star.*

Imagine the impact from a 1000-pound cow to a car traveling 55 mph. Envision the bloody scene when a pickup tops a hill and plows into a flock of sheep. (Stockmen frequently drive herds and flocks down the middle of roadways.) Cattle wandering across roadways at night are especially dangerous, particularly black angus, which can be nearly impossible to see soon enough to miss. Cattle commonly plunge suddenly onto roadways; often they actually plow into vehicles rather than being hit. In many cases accidents occur when drivers swerve to miss livestock or cowpies at night. Stumbling cattle also kick rocks, branches, brush, and other hazardous debris onto roadways.

Each year thousands of motorists are involved in cattle-related vehicular mishaps. Hundreds of vehicles are damaged or destroyed, dozens of people are injured, and in most years some people are killed. A study showed that on a 25-mile stretch of State Highway 85 in Arizona's Organ Pipe National Monument alone there were 141 cow-car accidents in the late 1960s (Schultz 1971).

Open range laws also absolve ranchers from responsibility for their livestock on roadways (and as mentioned, on railways). These laws were unfair a century ago, but with today's high-speed, widespread vehicular travel they are a main cause of carnage on Western roadways.

If while driving you happen to hit a cow, **you** are required by law to pay the owner for damages to the cow. If the animal dies, you pay the claimed value of the cow on the open market. You may even be forced to pay for a partial value of its projected, unrealized offspring if it was a productive animal. Surprisingly often it turns out to be one of the rancher's most valuable animals. You may be required to pay to repair the fence if you crashed into it. All these prices commonly are inflated. Thus, when involved in a vehicular mishap with livestock the rule is: "Keep going!"

All this holds true even if a deranged bull plows unseen from the roadside into the side of your vehicle, or even if there are passenger deaths. In one well-known case, a woman with her baby was driving along a country road at night, hit a cow, and ran off the road into some water. The baby died immediately, but the injured woman was trapped in the vehicle and died a slow, suffering death. But the cow died too. The cow's owner sued the dead woman's husband for the price of the cow, and won.

Generally ranchers push the government to fence roadways; they rarely do so themselves. Nonetheless, tens of thousands of miles of roads crossing public land remain unfenced. Ranchers like this because livestock may graze the relatively verdant, well-watered roadsides, but dislike it because their animals may be hit by vehicles. But even where roads are fenced, ranchers often cannot resist allowing their animals onto the lushly vegetated rights-of-way.

A stockman has allowed these sheep onto this well vegetated highway right-of-way.

And even with the best of fencing, gates will be left open, fences will be cut, some cattle will break through, and floods, fires, and other natural disturbances will allow livestock onto roadways. Thus, even if all open range laws were overthrown, many vehicular mishaps with livestock would still occur.

Damage from a collision with a public lands cow. *(Julie Rechtin)*

Cattle guards also cause many vehicular accidents. A few years ago a local woman was killed while riding a bicycle down a steep hill; she hit a cattleguard and her front wheel crumpled. Particularly rough cattle guards can cause damage to a vehicle's frame, body, suspension, tires, and human occupants, even without an actual wreck. Paved-over cattle guards, cattle guard support/fence posts, and closed gates also have caused many mishaps and casualties. Add to all this the inconvenience and danger from thousands of slow-moving stock trucks rambling along rural roadways.

Your car is wrecked. You are hurt. The cow is dead. You sue the cow's owner. You lose and have to pay for everything, including the cow. It does not matter that the cow's owner was drunk on champagne and fell asleep watching Lawrence Welk before closing the gate to the corral.
--Rick Braun, Oregon Natural Desert Association (ONDA 1990)

US 163 between Valley of the Gods and Bluff, Utah. *(Eliot Kalman)*

Stop the Bull*@☆!
End Open Range

In conclusion, the effects on Western motorists alone are a fair argument for ending public lands ranching. Combined with the scores of other detrimental impacts and loss of more than 2 billion tax and private dollars described in this chapter (and this is by no means a complete list), we have an overwhelming economic case for ending public lands ranching. Adding these to the environmental, social, and political ramifications detailed elsewhere in this book, it seems unthinkable that any informed person could support public lands ranching. If not for social conditioning, we might realize that the lovable cowboy and his peaceful cows are a national disaster.

If ranchers were assessed the real cost of doing business in the West, particularly on public lands, the Western livestock industry would be unable to compete with livestock producers in more benign climatic regions. If the many external costs and liabilities associated with public lands livestock grazing were fully considered, livestock would be removed from all public rangelands and these lands would be managed instead for their recreational, wildlife, and biological values.
--George Wuerthner, "Counting the Real Costs of Public Lands Grazing" (Wuerthner 1989)

TOTAL PUBLIC & PRIVATE COSTS

$2 BILLION (VERY ROUGH)

TOTAL PUBLIC COSTS

$1 BILLION (VERY ROUGH)

**BLM &
FOREST SERVICE
ECONOMIC$**
(1987. Sources: Various
government publications.)

VALUE OF ALL LIVESTOCK

$390 MILLION

BLM & FOREST SERVICE
DIRECT & INDIRECT COSTS $225 MILLION
(ROUGH)

BLM & FOREST SERVICE
DIRECT COSTS $65 MILLION

GROSS RETURNS
NET RETURNS

$21 MILLION
$6.5 MILLION

ANNUAL EXPENDITURES   ANNUAL RETURNS

Chapter VIII
SOCIAL/CULTURAL ISSUES

... the greatest power of ranchers is not in the West; it's in our minds.
--Candace Crane, "In the Shadow of Livestock" (Crane 1989)

Ranching has discolored the West's social and cultural fabrics. More than a century of powerful rancher influence, rancher/cowboy mythology, ranching management structure, and ranching itself has had an overwhelming impact on people living in ranching areas -- *most of the rural West* -- and, indirectly, on those in urban areas as well. Because ranching has been institutionalized for so long, few people are aware of the extent to which it affects them. Because public ranchlands comprise 41% of the West, and because public lands ranchers tend to be the West's most influential stockmen, the influence of public lands ranching is especially significant.

Nonetheless, the issue's necessarily vague and subjective nature makes it difficult to write about, and nearly impossible to document. This will therefore be a short chapter relative to the importance of the subject matter. While Chapter I examined the establishment of this social hierarchy, this chapter will consider its development, present situation, and repercussions.

Ranching is the basis of a social system that is in many ways deleterious. That we unquestioningly tolerate these malevolent influences -- frequently even becoming unwitting apologists for them -- testifies to the extent to which our culture embraces the myth of The Cowboy.

As a representative of an occupational group, [the cowboy] has received perhaps more attention than any other worker in the world ....
--William W. Savage, The Cowboy Hero (Savage 1979)

At the onset, I must admit to bias -- a *pro-ranching* bias. Like everyone else in this country, I was reared on cowboy/rancher mythology. I dreamed of being a cowboy when I grew up, for cowboys embodied everything real men should be. Hamburgers were my sustenance, and steak the ultimate food. Grass was wasted if not eaten by a cow, and all ranchers were doing their damndest to feed a hungry world. To me, munching cattle were as much a part of the Western landscape as the endless barbed wire fences and the birds in the sky. In other words, I was an American kid. Like every American, my reality is saturated with cowboy romanticism.

The "cow country" furnished in time a wealth of material for the writer of fiction as well as themes for the artist and poet. Stories, pictures, and songs of the range region were produced in great abundance, and given wide circulation, serving to advertise the cattle business and in many cases to give an entirely false conception of the industry and the region in which it was carried on.
--from **The Range Cattle Industry** by Edward Dale (Dale 1960)

If we believe absurdities, we shall commit atrocities.
--Voltaire

Nearly the antithesis of his fictional counterpart, the real-life, historic average American cowboy was a sad spectacle. He was a scraggly, dirty man with tattered, ill-fitting clothes and an unmistakable smell. His poor sanitary habits, inadequate diet, alcoholic tendencies, and excessive time in the saddle made him weak and sickly. According to Old West authority Joseph McCoy, he was "the picture of malnutrition." He was rootless, shifty, self-serving, and prone to violent behavior, likely a social outcast, often criminal. When not doing mundane ranching chores, he spent his time drinking and smoking, playing cards, and generally doing little one could call exciting, heroic, or even romantic (here again, there are notable exceptions).

One hundred years ago America was no more impressed by a cowboy than by a railroad employee or shopkeeper. One hundred years ago, America considered cowboying just another profession, a decidedly uninspiring one at that.

Put simply, the cowboy became a hero because he was marketed as one ... public acceptance of the cowboy increased because entrepreneurs severed his connection with history by making him into what he never was. And he never was interesting.
--William W. Savage, Jr., **The Cowboy Hero** (Savage 1979)

While ranching gained prominence in the West, American society was growing and modernizing rapidly. In developing and defining its national character -- a character influenced largely by westward expansion -- the United States needed a standard model of excellence, a paragon to exemplify its highest-held values, a distinctively American stereotype to embody and represent America, to itself and to the world. In short, America needed a national hero.

In 1884 "Buffalo Bill" Cody, one of the West's great buffalo killers, presented William Levi Taylor, a.k.a. "Buck" Taylor, to the public as a featured attraction in his famous Wild West Show. Cody had already exploited virtually every Western stereotype, and was looking for something different to attract Eastern audiences. He tried a cowboy -- namely Taylor, who had formerly worked on Cody's ranch in Nebraska.

Because cowboys generally were held in such low esteem, Cody would have no easy task selling Taylor to the American public. But Cody was a talented promoter, well-known for his aggressiveness and willingness to take risks. He presented Taylor's past as a mosaic of hard work, privation, and hardship, laced with danger and adventure. Cody said that the tall, handsome cowboy possessed many remarkable qualities, among them great dexterity, strength, and endurance. All this garnered public interest, but to assuage peoples' negative image of cowboys, Cody also endowed Taylor with honesty, integrity, geniality, humility, sensitivity, and other goodly qualities. By inference, the public was intentionally led to believe that all this was somehow attributable to the Western cowboy lifestyle. Thus was America's cowboy image redefined. With traveling Wild West Shows, carefully staged photographs, books and magazines, Buck Taylor quickly became America's first cowboy hero.

Others followed. As you know, *hundreds* followed. Each came to symbolize certain qualities America wanted to see in itself. The cowboy, as the least European and allegedly most "American" of all American heros, came to represent the essence of America to itself. A new, quintessentially American figure was born -- a nebulous, malleable, composite self-image. The collective American psyche imbued this self-image with whatever qualities it needed to project upon itself. Thus, as never before in a single representative, the cowboy persona came to embody all that was assumed to be great and good about America. In short, cowboyism became America's most popular self-delusion.

Yet the mythic cowboy is shaped out of image, not out of substance. His wonderful adaptability is evidenced by his ability to represent many things to many people, to symbolize whatever our needs require . . . because his image is a very pliable kind of cultural clay.
--from **Cowboy -- The Enduring Myth of the Wild West** by Russel Martin

Many became proficient at exploiting the cowboy image for a buck. "Buck" Taylor himself became an actor, and all subsequent "cowboy" heros have been actors. Even the self-proclaimed sage of the sagebrush, Will Rogers, wasn't really a cowboy but became popular by pretending to be. In fact, extremely few cowboy heros were ever actual cowboys. Most Americans can name many cowboy heros who were *actors*, but not one who was actually a cowboy!

As cowboy mythology developed and expanded solidly upon its own self-delusions, it came to include not only cowboys, but ranchers (especially) and ranches, horses, cows, beef, and anything perceived as "Western." Ever since the birth of Buffalo Bill's cowboy hero a century ago, we Americans have enshrined anything having to do with cowboys or ranching -- *for in doing so we enshrine ourselves and our dreams!* We are all the product of a society that has blind dedication to anything it perceives as "Western," which unfortunately happens to include public lands ranching.

By the 1950's there were few Americans alive who had seen the Old West. It had become a legend -- the Great American Myth. . . . The Saga of the West continues to shape the dreams of a great many Americans.
--from the TV documentary *The West of the Imagination*

Regardless of how many times it is said that the cowboy era was a fraud and a myth, there remains that intangible something that lives on in the hearts of a lot of people.
--Cecil Garland, politician, rancher

Much has been written over the years about our Great Western Fantasy, particularly "the Cowboy Phenomenon." The vast majority of this literature is nothing more than an extension of the fantasy itself. Rather than helping us understand the fantasy, it perpetuates and becomes part of the fantasy to sell itself to the American public.

A few books and articles have done well in explaining the phenomenon. (One of the best is **The Cowboy Hero** by William W. Savage Jr.) They give a variety of reasons for our collective dedication to Western mythology: The myth has simply been passed down through the years; it is an outlet for our collective fantasies; in our modern, humanmade world, we keep the myth to maintain a feeling of closeness to the natural world; we are unable to reject it because we all develop a strong feeling of nostalgia for it as children; in a repressed society, we need the myth to vent our aggressions; the people who benefit from it promote it; and so on. These are all well-grounded explanations. Even so, they have done little to change society's overall perceptions. Even in the late 20th century, few of us understand why or how much we are influenced by The Great Western Fantasy. Because we are so accustomed to it, we cannot see what it really is or how much it affects us.

Today being a "cowboy" is more of an attitude than an occupation.
--Singer Bobby Bare

Begin with something as seemingly simple as a cowboy hat. Just another kind of headwear? Like a road worker's hard hat or gardener's straw hat? No way! As we all know, the cowboy hat *is* different. The man who puts on a cowboy hat suddenly becomes bigger, in more ways than one. In putting on this hat, he identifies himself as part of a select group. He takes on the attributes for which the cowboy hero is famous -- toughness, virility, self-confidence, independence, freedom, unlimited possibility. He expects and usually attracts more attention and respect from those around him.

He's all hat and no cattle.
--*Conservative Digest* editor Scott Stanley on 1988 Democratic Vice Presidential candidate Lloyd Bensten

The cowboy hat is a symbol. You've probably noticed that cowboy hats are worn on cloudy days, indoors, in stores, to the cinema, at the dining table, and even (at least in movies and TV commercials) to bed. Those wearing these hats are proclaiming, to themselves and to the world: "I am special. I am a cowboy (or like a cowboy) and all the wonderful things a cowboy is!"

Parents adorn their little boys with oversized cowboy hats because the contrast between the harmless child and *ultimate man* represented by the hat is perceived as cute. Many short men wear cowboy hats to increase their stature in the eyes of society. Some women wear cowboy hats because many men imagine them more sexually alluring that way. Urban cowboys wear them, sometimes as phallic symbols, proclaiming their virility.

Cowboys are the last real men in the world.
--From the movie "The Misfits"

In some bars a man can get into a fight simply by wearing a cowboy hat and "not being man enough" to wear one. As a popular bumpersticker reads, "If you ain't a cowboy, you ain't shit!" Don't agree? Well now, them's fightin' words! So we are told.

The cowboy hat is a cowboy hat!

Despite the continuing downtrend in cigarette sales in the US, Marlboro in 1990 had its best-selling year ever -- largely because its massive ad campaign features the immensely popular Marlboro Man cowboy-fantasy super-hero.

Cowboys are wiser, stronger, faster, better fighters, better drinkers, better lovers, more real, more courageous, and more exciting than other people. In American culture, so pervasive is this inflated cowboy image and self-image that a psycho-scientist might term it a case of "massive, institutionalized delusions of grandeur."

Take a walk down any American street -- or drive your Bronco, Brahma, Mustang, Lariat, Ranger, Rodeo, or Ranchero. The Marlboro Man's ultramasculine presence radiates. Billboards proclaim that you too can possess the attributes of a cowboy by smoking this brand of cigarette or drinking that brand of beer. Bars and restaurants are The Ranchers' Club, Cattle Company, Brandin' Iron, Golden Spur, Rodeo, Corral, Roundup, Water Hole, Bum Steer, Ragin' Bull . . . . Clothing stores promote "Western" clothing that is claimed to make you more of a man or woman. (Now in fashion with wealthy Easterners -- for $65 a pair -- are "Montana Broke" jeans -- used clothes certified to have been worn by a Montana cowboy.) Steak houses and fast food joints advertise their "Western"-style foods -- 1001 different items to choose from, but all made with *100% real beef*, all the best in the West! Grocery stores carry ranch dressing, cowboy-cooked canned beans, and ranch-style potato chips. Doctor, lawyer, and insurance company waiting rooms hang with humorous and rustic paintings and photos portraying likeable cowpokes, rangeland roundups, and nostalgic pastoral scenes. Even banks get into the game, dressing up their employees in cowboy costumes now and then to play up the small town, just-plain-folks angle and to add a little "excitement" to their stuffy atmospheres.

When the last [Marlboro Man] *television commercial ran in September, 1970, the narrator could state with some certainty, "Today, the West is everywhere." Indeed it was, for by then the Marlboro landscape conformed perfectly to the convolutions of the viewer's brain, with all that such conformity implied.*
--William W. Savage, Jr., **The Cowboy Hero** (Savage 1979)

If you want to understand what drives a society, study its commercialism. American advertising is dictated by our likes and dislikes, but conversely our likes and dislikes are dictated by advertising. With a deep-rooted, pervasive, and nostalgic cultural phenomenon like the Great Western Fantasy, commercialism and society's dominant paradigm mutually reinforce each other, creating a self-sustaining circle of delusion. Every day of our lives we are bombarded with images and ideas that, by intention or not, reinforce our support of ranching.

But the greatest thrill about it [starring in the movie "Back to the Future, Part III"] *was being a cowboy!*
--Actor Michael J. Fox

Turn on a television; it's no different. Fun-lovin' cowboys tear around the Western landscape in Ford Broncos, swilling Coors and Coca Cola. Used car salesmen in cowboy hats and boots try to sell you with their folksy honesty. Rugged, handsome ranchers splash on a certain kind of aftershave and take their pick from hordes of gorgeous, lusty women. Down-home-at-the-ranch realtors want to sell you a taste of "the good life" on your very own Western-style country ranchette. Hard-working, blizzard-bound ranchers in northern Montana recommend Alka Seltzer Plus for the sniffles. Comical cowboys push Pace Picante hot sauce -- an' they'll string ya up if ya don't like it! And rustle up some Fri-tos, paaarrt-ner! On the other hand, deadly serious, impeccably straight-shootin' cowboys reveal the "straight facts" about AIDS. Singin' cowboys sell Swanson TV dinners. Miller Lite super cowboys hog-tie 50-ton trucks. Cartoon cowboys peddle sugar-filled cereals to young buckaroos. Talking cowboy toilets hype "the toughest toilet bowl cleaner alive." Talking hamburgers urge you to buy them. The cows themselves talk, relaxing in lounge chairs and promoting their master's product as "pampered beef."

A study of 1000 nationally broadcast TV commercials found that fully **20%** featured or included cowboys and/or Western ranching in some form -- an amazing statistic considering that *less than 1/2000th* of the US population is Western cowboys and ranchers!

Cowboy-glorifying prime-time TV series like "Paradise" and "Young Guns" garner huge audiences, as did "Gunsmoke" and "Rawhide" in the past. Others feature fearless cowboy cops who clean up the bad guys single-handedly. Or cosmic cowboys who battle it out (and always win) with space monsters. Or small-time ranchers who work their fingers to the bone in pitiful tear-jerkers. Cowboy cartoons for the kids. And, of course, the standard cowboy-hero TV western movie -- at least 1 per day!; more than 4000 of them have been made by Hollywood in the past 75 years (Zaslowsky 1989). If you can't get enough cowboy stuff on regular TV, consider subscribing to the newly created Cowboy Channel on cable TV.

Last night I was watching a television. A movie ended, and suddenly a stereotypical "Western" scene filled the screen -- a quintessential saguaro-studded ranching landscape. Then, dramatically, a mounted cowboy entered the scene slowly, deliberately, from stage left. With infinite self-assurance, he rode into and usurped the scene. The camera joined him and panned with him slowly across the landscape. Clip-clop, clip-clop, clip-clop.

Then . . . music. Melodic guitar. A rich female voice, strained with emotion: "Don't . . . you . . . know . . . *pride* . . . comes . . . ea-sy . . . ." The lyrics rolled on, the music gradually building, swelling with pride, and, finally, after a minute, virtually exploding with patriotism.

Along the way, various more-common folks were shown doing more-common things. Then, the grand finale: mounted *cowboys* this time and . . . "We're Channel Eleven -- comin' in *prrooouuud* . . . and clear."

This is the stuff we were raised on, paaarrt-ners. Think about it.

Likewise, the radio waves carry cowboy commercialism and a steady stream of country and western tunes pitying or exalting fictional cowboys and ranchers in a hundred different ways. Interestingly, only an infinitesimally small fraction of "cowboy" singers ever were actual cowboys. In Tucson, even the rock-'n'-roll station is called "The Radio Ranch"; it broadcasts the new rock hit "I'm a Cowboy" (not to be confused with the Steve Miller classic, "I'm a Space Cowboy"). Dimestore novels and Western romances glamorize the Western ranching lifestyle and the people who live it. Children's books portray ranchers and cowboys as mythical heros, role models and paragons.

The proud symbol of a small-town high school.

Magazine and newspaper ads picture robust cowboys utilizing various commercial products, and their articles detail what a pitifully hard time financially strapped ranchers are having making it on the open range these days. Half-time shows at sports events feature beefy cowboys on large white horses, adrip with gold and silver, along with baton-twirling cowgirls. Hundreds of schools throughout the West proudly display the cowboy (and even the rustler) as their school emblem. And be assured, every parade must have its glittering equestrian cowboys -- symbols of all that is great and good. Last month I even attended a cowboy *opera*.

Contemporary religion likewise instills within the cultural psyche a belief in livestock production, with its flocks, sheep, shepherds, mangers, and other pastoral symbolism. Much of this is rooted in the Bible, which was written when nomadic livestock herding was in full-swing in the Middle East more than 2000 years ago. (Interestingly, icons of Jesus, crosses, and cowboys hang together over the mantles of countless homes in the rural West.)

Even our language predisposes us to accept ranching's omnipotence. For example, we call any open piece of rural land with grass or browse "grazing land" -- as if being grazed by livestock was its main intrinsic quality. We accept "range" to mean land for grazing livestock, though such land without livestock is still range. Without realizing it, we accept the blanket contention that the correct and ultimate use for all

ranchable land (about 80% of the West) is ranching. Likewise, anyone living on acreage in the rural West is said to live on a "ranch," though Webster defines "ranch" as "a large farm for raising livestock, as beef cattle, sheep, or horses." Most rural Western residents living on "ranches" don't live on ranches, though they like to pretend that they do. Friends in New Mexico resolved this dilemma by naming their 20-acre spread the "No Cattle Cattle Company."

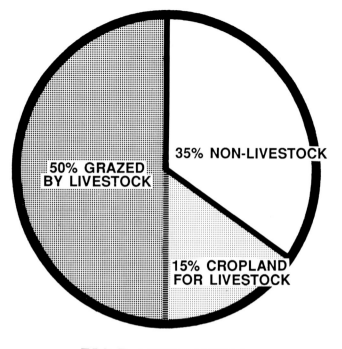

US LAND AREA
(outside Alaska)

Our society's reverence for cowboys and ranchers also extends to the product of their endeavors -- the *cow*. The bald eagle may be this country's official animal, but a good look around reveals that our real national animal is the cow. The cow is by far the most common large animal in this country. It accounts for many times more total biomass than any other animal species and outweighs America's human population more than 2 to 1. As mentioned earlier, in the US outside Alaska half of the water used, about 2/3 of the cropland (40% of plant food production), and 65% of all land is used to produce livestock, mostly cattle. Look again; the United States is a cow factory!

Beef is the backbone of the American diet and always has been.
--John Morgan, former president of Riverside Meat Packers (died in 1982 from colon cancer)

Further, cow meat (beef) is our national food. In some societies it is rice or fish or potatoes; many people around the world have never even eaten cow. But our society is so cow-oriented that few of us stop to think about it. In restaurants, we naturally expect most of the items on the menu to contain cow meat. At fast food joints, we order cow burgers, cow tacos, or cow sandwiches; what else is there? At the dinner table, the plate seems naked without some form of meat -- most often cow -- in the place of honor. Cow is the most common meat in almost any grocery store, taking up at least half of the space at most meat/fish counters. Why?

Steak has magical properties.
--1989 radio ad by Beef Board

And then, even beyond beef, there is . . . *steak!* -- a food worshipped almost religiously by our culture. Steak is the ultimate culinary item, the most desirable of all foods. When we want to impress our friends, when price is no object, when we want the very best, we buy the choicest part of the cow -- steak. Movie stars throw them on grills for TV cameras. Young men order them for their lovers to show how much they care. The affluent order them with pomposity in fancy restaurants. The poor only dream about them. Steak is a luxury item, a status symbol. Steak symbolizes the best of the best. Holy cow!

Ah yes, dairy!

The word conjures up pleasant, wholesome images of peacefully grazing milk cows and rosy-cheeked children. From childhood we are taught that (like meat) cow milk is the basis of 1 of the "4 basic food groups," and that it should be ingested in some form at every meal. This, despite the fact that humans are the only animals on Earth besides cows that drink milk from cows, that cow milk is difficult for all humans to digest, and that 20% of Caucasians and up to 90% of black and Asian people lack the lactose enzyme necessary to digest cow milk, causing cramps, bloating, and diarrhea upon drinking it.

Dairy promoters tell us that milk from cows is "the perfect food" for humans. This, despite the fact that cow milk has *no* fiber and is for many reasons the perfect food only for baby cows; physiologically, the most perfect food for adult humans is fruit. For years they drilled us with "Every body needs milk!" -- until the courts maintained that no human body needs cow milk, and in fact many are allergic to it. Then it was "Milk has something for every body," "Milk is a natural," "Milk does a body good," . . .

For decades our diet has been dictated by the Great Calcium Scare; without cow milk's calcium our teeth might fall out and our bones collapse. In truth most non-animal foods contain abundant calcium; it would be virtually impossible *not* to get enough calcium from a normal plant food diet. Heavy consumption of cow milk (normal for Americans) actually blocks the body's intake of calcium, contributing to this country's rising epidemic of osteoperosis. Without cow milk's "quality" protein, they imply, we will become frail and sickly. Yet, sufficient quality protein is easily obtained from a normal plant-centered diet, and Americans' excessive intake of protein is actually the *cause* of many of their health problems. The dairy industry tells us: "Whole milk is only 3.5% fat." However, by far most of milk's weight is water, and the amount of calories as fat in whole milk is 50%.

Today, professional advertisers tell us to "Get on a health kick!" with cow milk, while our extreme consumption of dairy products has been linked to numerous health problems. Yogurt a health food? What a joke!

(Diamond 1985, Robbins, 1987)

For generations, dairy has been synonymous with "pure," beef with "strong." And cattle have ranged over the soul of America, a symbol of wide-open spaces, broncbuster spirit and the bucolic life on the family farm.
--Molly O'Neill, "Cows in Trouble" (O'Neill 1990)

Finally, not only is the cowboy our national hero, the cow our national animal, cow meat our national food, but cow milk is, debatably, our national drink. A survey by Growers Journal of California in September 1982 explains: "Dairy products have the highest incidence of consumption of any major food category. Only 6% of Americans say they don't consume milk in some form." (Many of these people are *allergic* to it.) Americans consume more cow milk products per capita, and as a percentage of diet, than do people in any other region on Earth (Espenshade 1988). According to the *Los Angeles Times*, the US cow milk industry is directly subsidized with almost *3 billion* tax dollars annually (Diamond 1985).

As infants, most of us were suckled on milk from a large bovine ungulate, not from our human mothers! As children, we drank cow milk at meals. As adults, we pour cow milk on cereals and eat it as cheese, ice cream, yogurt, and dozens of other "dairy" products.

[The rodeo bull] doesn't buck because he is a wild and furious beast, but because an excruciatingly painful strap has been cinched, tightly, in the areas of his genitals and intestines. Sometimes a nail, tack, piece of barbed wire, or other sharp metal object has been placed under the strap, to further infuriate him. And just before the animal is let out of the chute, an electric prod known in the trade as the "hot shot," is applied to his rectum . . . .
--John Robbins, **Diet for a New America** (Robbins 1987)

Like other Western cities and hundreds of small Western towns, the city of Tucson (population 600,000) honors the mythical Cowboy with an annual "Rodeo Day." All city schools are closed so children can join 150,000 other worshipers at the Rodeo Day Parade, which kicks off the 4-day Tucson Rodeo. The pageantry includes hundreds of

cowboy-costumed cow people strutting on horses, cowboy-costumed marching bands, cowboy-costumed famous people and government officials riding in convertibles, all moving slowly along a large horseshoe-shaped route through downtown Tucson. (Interestingly, there are no actual range cows in the parade.) Until a few years ago this ranching extravaganza was sponsored largely by city taxpayers, but now the city "only" provides the grandstands,

special transportation and city busing, 175 police officers, fire engines, ambulances, free parking (the only day of the year), sanitation, and so forth.

A wealthy entrepreneur established the Tucson Rodeo as a tourist attraction in 1925. No other holiday exalts a small segment of American society, and no other holiday but Christmas and the Fourth of July comes close in fanfare and hoopla. Only Labor Day honors another American worker (*all workers combined*), and it is hardly a celebration. In the West there is no celebrated Construction Workers Day or Bank Employees Day or Textile Workers Day or Bartenders Day or Miners Day or Teachers Day or even Farmers Day, or any day so special for any other group of people.

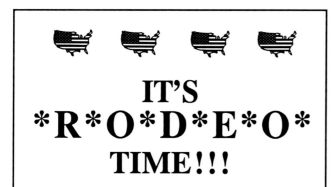

IT'S
*R*O*D*E*O*
TIME!!!

The original rodeo was a periodic gathering of local cow workers and owners. Its purpose was threefold:

First, it brought an area's stockmen together on a regular basis, giving them a sense of solidarity and a chance to better organize their scattered power bases, as well as buy and trade stock. This was important to an industry so widely dispersed geographically.

Second, it gave working cow people a competitive incentive to practice and perfect their ranching skills.

Third, the rodeo's crowd gave the cow boys a feeling of fun and excitement -- important in an occupation most of them considered lonely and boring.

To a lesser extent, the contemporary rodeo still serves these functions, but its main purposes have become: (1) make money, (2) bolster cowboy's self-image, (3) romanticize and promote the livestock grazing industry.

Many modern rodeo performers have never been livestock raisers, and much of modern rodeo has little practical application to ranching.

Today's rodeo is a carefully produced, self-glorifying exhibition. It is heavily advertised as a festive affair -- *an exciting event!* -- a place where "ordinary" [non-cowboy] folks can get a [fantacized] taste of the excitement of the cow raiser's [supposed] way of life.

Ya-hoo buckaroos!!!

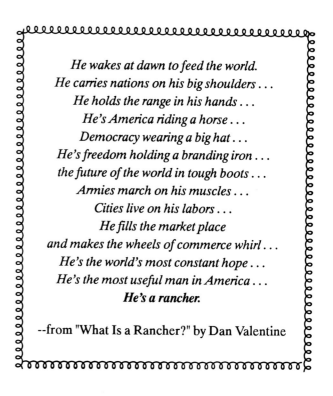

He wakes at dawn to feed the world.
He carries nations on his big shoulders . . .
He holds the range in his hands . . .
He's America riding a horse . . .
Democracy wearing a big hat . . .
He's freedom holding a branding iron . . .
the future of the world in tough boots . . .
Armies march on his muscles . . .
Cities live on his labors . . .
He fills the market place
and makes the wheels of commerce whirl . . .
He's the world's most constant hope . . .
He's the most useful man in America . . .
He's a rancher.

--from "What Is a Rancher?" by Dan Valentine

Cowboys are darned sure different.
--Rodeo cowboy, Wrangler Jeans radio ad, 1990

So who, really, is this mythical hero, the contemporary cowboy/rancher? The Hero is presented to the world as a plain-spoken, straight-shootin' man of brutal honesty -- a man so impeccably righteous he need never resort to falsehoods. Yet to those familiar with him, the rancher commonly is known to stretch the truth as tightly as the barbed wire of his fences. The Hero is publicized as extremely self-assured, capable, tough, fearless, quick-witted, and in every way a "real man" -- definitely someone to be reckoned with. The common rancher enjoys the special favor and protection afforded by his fictional counterpart, yet possesses these attributes no more than the mechanic or factory worker. The Hero is advertised as a hunk of masculinity, the ultimate in virility, a rangeland Romeo. But this fable has its roots in romantic days of olde when livestock tenders spent so much time on the range that their sexual imaginings (and inclinations) sometimes ran wild. The Hero is declared to be a very exciting and even mysterious individual. Yet, for all the hype the rancher remains just an ordinary fellow. The Hero is portrayed as a rugged outdoorsman, sweat-stained and calloused from years of strenuous work. Yet the average rancher labors no harder than the average American worker, relying on a variety of modern conveniences to do the bulk of the work; indeed, on the average he probably spends less time outdoors (and less time actually *working*) than the average construction worker. The Hero is described as living an admirably simple and down-to-earth existence -- a life of few material possessions or even desires to own them. Yet, the vast majority of ranchers are no closer to being "natural" than are their cows, and their material possessions would fill the average suburban home and 2-car garage several times over. Sure, some old, leathered cowfolks are interesting and likable characters. But so are many leathered old folks from many other trades, and most ranchers are not leathered.

The Rancher Hero, then, is a paragon, though his living counterpart is quite human. The Hero is everything virtuous and wonderful a hero should be. The Western rancher is . . . what he is.

The cowboy, shaded by a ten-gallon hat, his bowed legs hidden behind leather "chaps," his feet shod with sharp-heeled, quilted boots, is the premier American figure of romance. Herding, breeding, salting, protecting -- such are the homely occupations of the most popular figure in all fiction.
--Ross Calvin, **Sky Determines** (Calvin 1975)

This discussion only scratches the surface, but by looking at our culture from this different perspective, it becomes evident that we all are inundated every day of our lives with pro-ranching ideas and images. We are relentlessly indoctrinated, usually in ways we do not consciously recognize, to support the ranching establishment. Our society treats ranchers as superior and habitually supports them in whatever they do.

But America must have its myths. . . . Thus glorification of the cowboy is necessary. And everything that has been done to the cowboy has been done, consciously or unconsciously, to make him usable as a myth.
--William W. Savage, Jr., **Cowboy Life** (Savage 1979)

Perhaps we need heroes, real heroes. Perhaps not. Maybe we need our Western mythology or something like it. Perhaps not. But surely we don't need public lands ranching to preserve our Western legacy. As much as 86% of Western ranching would survive without it. Hell, by far most of our Western legacy would survive without *any* ranching! Indeed, the most sensible way to preserve the most worthwhile symbols of our Western legacy -- honesty, rugged independence, self-sufficiency, and resourcefulness -- would be to eliminate the wasteful and destructive public lands ranching system.

The most powerful, reactionary, and destructive little group in the Western states are still the public-lands ranchers; and they survive by hiding behind the cheap mythology of the "Cowboy": literally, a boy who looks after cows . . . .
--Edward Abbey

My heros have always been cowboys . . . .
--Waylon Jennings

In the United States, of course, we have traditionally honored the cowboy. . . . Our tiny planet deserves a new mythic hero.
--Jay D. Hair, Executive Vice-President, National Wildlife Federation

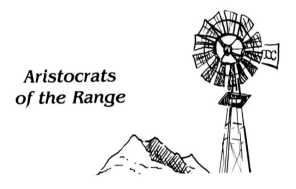

Aristocrats of the Range

Men in the cattle business were often picturesque and resourceful. Political and economic power gave them great self-confidence, spirit, and command. Being held in high regard by others caused them to become assertive, even arrogant. Early on, all this heady power began to be expressed as a distinct class consciousness.
--Denzel & Nancy Ferguson, **Sacred Cows** (Ferguson 1983)

The 26 Bar, once owned by actor John Wayne, Steeple L, H Bar V, Bar Flying V, Y Cross, C J and L A are just a few of the old-time brands that represent names like Brown, Udall, Sipes, and Butler.
--from a rural newspaper article

When you mess with ranching, you're fuckin' with people's identity.
--Anonymous rural resident

How many of us haven't at some time fantasized being the celebrated big-time rancher? Imagine:

Early one pleasant, sunny morning, you mount your fine steed and ride off into the nearby rugged hills, leaving your sprawling ranch headquarters far behind. You survey the vast Western landscape, a commanding view. Far below, small groups of cattle graze peacefully on grassy bottoms along a creek. Your eyes follow the creek downstream to where it joins a river and take in the pleasant, dollar-bill green of your large alfalfa field, awaiting harvest. In 4 directions your barbed wire fences and dirt roads melt into the horizon, well-defined symbols of a working ranch. Your allotment extends for miles all around. Though federal land, this is *your* domain -- your land more than anyone's -- and you feel security and stability in this. You ride proud. You *feel* important.

You relish your role. As a large ranch owner, you are respected, admired, envied, and, yes, feared by the local townspeople and other rural folks. They are well-aware of your eminence. They all want to know you and help you when they can. Even strangers, recognizing your clothing, manner, and bearing, cannot help but realize your significance. You command power and prestige. As an officer in half a dozen committees and associations, you are an influential political and social figure. You are a landowner, a personage, an establishment.

Ah, to be a cattle baron!

The ranchers are the landed gentry of the West, our self-proclaimed nobility, and they expect to be treated as such.
--Dave Foreman, "My Heros Have Always Been Cowboys" (Foreman 1986)

Historically, wealthy stockmen have tended to be loud-mouthed, boastful, and arrogant.
--Bernard DeVoto, **The Easy Chair** (DeVoto 1955)

Visiting a rural Western community you may spot the typical public lands ranchman -- the beefy, seemingly self-assured fellow, always in full ranching garb, swaggering down Main Street. He talks like he looks -- that stereotypical slow, deliberate, self-important, resonant bass, that wealthy stock-man drawl common to John Wayne, Rex Allen, Hoss Cartwright, and so many wealthy graziers.

Over at Hank's Coffee Shop as usual, you'll find a group of cowboy hats clustered around a table, caffeine-fired talk comparing ranching operations, envious customers at nearby tables venturing occasional suggestions. Next door at Bill's Barber Shop, patrons hang on Rancher Johnson's every word as he relates how he finally cornered an elusive

mountain lion. Down at the Mustang Tavern, the hats are lined up on bar stools and the bull centers around the new girl in town and the upcoming local rodeo. Up on the hill at the Lutheran Church (the only place *without* cowboy hats), the minister is praying for drought relief for "those of us fallen upon hard times." Out on the edge of town, the owner of Grant's Feed is helping Rancher Maddock load his pickup with rolls of barbed wire, fence posts, salt blocks, and hay.

Due to cowboy mythology and much else discussed in this book, public lands ranchers enjoy what may be termed "institutionalized social supremacy." They are among the most affluent and influential people in the rural West. Their relatives and private stockmen also lend support, and many influential non-ranchers find it advantageous to associate with and administer to these graziers.

Public lands ranchers cultivate relationships designed to heighten their social, economic, and political standing. Friendships with influential government land managers, politicians, businesspeople, community leaders, and other local VIPs ensure that stockmen's interests will be protected, and vice versa -- calculated, reciprocal back-scratching. For instance, would County Supervisor Hays recommend against predator "control" funding for the area including Rancher Jim's allotment? Jim's an old hunting buddy, and he's been losing calves to coyotes. Besides, Jim knows a lot of voters and pulls many strings.

Recently, the editor of a newsletter in a small New Mexico town had the audacity to run an article questioning the wisdom of public lands ranching. His biggest advertiser pulled out.

In most rural areas, public lands ranchers are like celebrities. The local populace adores the image of the Bonanza-like Western spread, the prominent ranching family, the noble-yet-sociable ranch owner. They envy all that supercilious prestige and power. They want part of it to rub off on them. They want to know ranchers, and they want other people to know that they know ranchers.

Conversely, stockmen cultivate a sociable image calculated to maintain public support. For most, this is easy because they are long-established locally and respected personages merely by being what they are. They strike up friendships with nearly anyone they so desire. They become community, church, and business leaders, are appointed and elected to boards, commissions, and committees by no other qualification than that they are large ranchers.

After attending Rancher Brad's annual beef bar-be-cue for 15 years, how could we complain about his cattle messing up Thompson Creek? After talking with him regularly at Kathy's Cafe, who would force him to pay for the damage his cattle did to their garden? After swilling beers with him at the Brandin' Iron, who would protest Brad getting drought relief funding for "his" over-stocked BLM allotment? We smile all the while. After all, *he is a rancher.*

People are socially, physically, and psychologically afraid to refute cowboyism. Whether they realize it or not, all rural folks are under unyielding pressure to support the ranching establishment.

Local BLM officials are quite probably strongly affected by adverse social pressures on themselves and their families. Most BLM offices are located in small western towns whose culture and livelihood are largely oriented to the range livestock industry. Public opinion is entirely that of ranching interests. Consequently, a district ranger who strongly antagonizes the local livestock interest will soon find himself and his family largely isolated from the social life of the community. Few managers or staff members experience this social disapproval, because they rarely antagonize the rancher community.
--Wesley Calef, **Private Grazing and Public Lands** (Calef 1960)

Government land managers are especially vulnerable to pressure from stockmen. They work with them often. They have the same friends. They eat at the same restaurants, drink in the same bars, go to the same churches, and attend the same community functions. Their wives are members of the same social clubs, and their kids go to the same schools. Most agency employees are unwilling to go against the grain; indeed, many envy and emulate the ranchers whose operations they are supposed to regulate.

In "Discouraging Words," Jon R. Luoma reports that social pressure from the ranching community has intimidated BLM personnel into backing down on needed grazing reforms. One BLM manager who tried to correct ranching problems "was reportedly forced to move to another district after his children were threatened and even beaten up in school." Bill Meiners, a retired BLM range specialist and now an outspoken critic of federal range policy, was in 1985 warned that his house would be bombed (Luoma 1986), as have been several other ranching reformers. Other tactics include petitions, harassing phone calls, legal persecution, repercussions by the business community, and vandalism.

The livestock industry's finesse at maintaining the status quo is legendary....
--Elizabeth Royte, "Showdown in Cattle Country" (Royte 1990)

One of our neighbors in rural central Arizona for 8 years was a transplanted upstate New York small-time politician and construction company owner. "Red" was a short, skinny, sickly man who to heighten his image always wore a cowboy hat and boots. He owned a 4-acre "ranch," the standard late-model, heavy-duty cowboy pickup, and even a couple of horses that left their small compound every few months when Red wanted to impress someone that he was a real cowboy. He completed his character with a deliberate, bow-legged walk, slow drawl, and jus'-a'good-ol'-boy grin. To make a long story short, Red was corrupt, bigoted, unhappy, lazy, and alcoholic (and never was a cowboy), yet despite all this "Ol' Red" maintained his cowboy image, and thus social acceptance and a surprising political following.

Several years ago, Geraldo Rivera was in town doing a story on farm [farm and ranch] foreclosures. In the course of his research, Rivera became involved in a physical altercation at the Rancher's Bar.... "Nobody even punched the guy," a hefty fellow told me. "It's just... see, he was poking into affairs that was none of his business, and he got his head runned through a wall."

--from "The Big Open" by Tim Cahill (Cahill 1987)

In most rural areas no other group exerts such influence on the local populace as do public lands ranchers. Rural residents are from birth conditioned to embrace the dominant cultural patterns, with ranchers generally at the top of the social pyramid. The situation is not unlike Medieval Europe, with large ranchers as the land-controlling aristocracy; government land managers, politicians, and private supporters as their loyal subjects; and the local citizenry as the unwitting common people.

Newcomers to the rural West soon discover that to "get along" they must conform to prevailing social expectations -- or pressures will be brought to bear. Those who challenge the ranching establishment quickly find themselves on the social shit-list. Suddenly, folks are less friendly to them. People gossip about them. They aren't invited to town meetings. Their kids are hassled at school. Even their scoops down at the ice cream shop get smaller. The local community quietly shuns them as unpatriotic troublemakers.

As a warning to stop our ranching-reform efforts, a local stockman shot our dog, skinned it, and dumped it near our house.

Ostracization increases. Nonconformists begin to feel lonely, outcast, troubled. Gradually, relentlessly, their will to resist is broken down. They find it easier to go with the flow, the status quo. Why make enemies? Why beat one's head against a wall? It may take years, but sooner or later they submit to the ranching imperative.

Those few who continue to contest "the way things are" face ridicule, harassment, threats, and physical assault. Historically, ranchers were well-known for using violence to get their way. To a lesser degree they still are. For example, soon after we circulated the stop-grazing petition mentioned in the previous chapter, local ranchers began packing holstered pistols as a show of force. Our dog was killed, skinned, and dumped along the road near our house. Vague threats hit the rumor circuit.

In response to their ranching-reform position, Denzel and Nancy Ferguson were physically ejected by 5 cowmen from a public dance in a small Oregon town and told they would be killed if they didn't leave the county (see Ferguson 1983). For his efforts, a friend in a small town in southeast Arizona was likewise threatened and permanently banned from local dances. We've all heard stories of knuckle-busting stockmen beating up alleged troublemakers in cowboy bars -- even murders. Some of it is true.

As a favorite bumpersticker reads, "Cowboy Country -- Love It or Leave It Alone!". More to the point -- support the ranching establishment or get the hell out!

(George Wuerthner)

Ranching's influence on the rural West's social/cultural fabric is, of course, not all negative. Its omnipresence provides certain threads of stability and tradition to a region often characterized by boom-and-bust. Scant threads do not a tight weave make, however, and in more ways ranching rots the fabric.

In Wyoming, "The Cowboy State," transplanted Californian writer Gretel Ehrlich, now reborn a rancher, champions the ranching cause like no other, making cowboy glorification an art form. To her, the ranching lifestyle is the ultimate in realism. Bobbi Birleffi, a native Wyoming filmmaker, offers this sensitive reaction to one of Ehrlich's cassette tapes:

Admitting newcomers who won't accept the official ranchers' version of things would amount to admitting that there is something wrong with Wyoming, something wrong with the way we treat each other and the land. That admission is inconceivable. So we continue to avenge ourselves on this terrible place and anyone who suggests otherwise.

People will tell you with pride that Wyoming is hard on women and horses. How plain do you need it said?

The Western ranching establishment is indeed hard on women and horses -- and anyone or anything that doesn't "fit in." Due to prejudice largely spearheaded by ranchers, many people find that they cannot live comfortably in rural Western communities. Thus, through upbringing and cultural tradition, stockmen banish opposition.

(Dave Foreman)

Western ranching (including government and private range programs), on public land especially, is dominated by male WASPs. Aside from Hispanic sheep herders in their north-central and a few smaller New Mexico enclaves, and several hundred scattered Basque sheep herders, non-WASP public lands ranchers are rare. In most areas a black man at a stockmen's association meeting would be like a parrot on the Arctic tundra. Stockmen argue that minorities are not well-represented in the ranching community because they don't have a ranching history. They weren't allowed to develop one, and for good reason they didn't want to. Put plainly, the Western ranching community generally rejects ethnic minorities and stains the social fabric of the rural West with its influence.

It likewise disfavors anyone who doesn't *believe* in ranching. For example, rural folks who propose removing cattle from sensitive natural areas are branded radical en*varmint*lists. Those who propose revoking Rodeo Day as an official town holiday are openly scorned as unpatriotic. Those who denounce branding as cruel become laughingstock under the dominant ranching mentality.

And it disdains those who would subvert the dominant paradigm. This includes everyone who doesn't measure up to the cowboy standard. For example, in small Western towns, few homosexuals dare come out of the closet, even those who are cowboys. Racial and religious minorities, atheists, social and political reformers, nonconformists, anarchists, hippies, greenies, pagans, back-to-the-landers, feminists, and an overwhelming diversity of other peoples are made to feel most unwelcome.

In a movie, book, or magazine, when a cowboy rides into town we all expect there's a'gonna be trouble, yes siree, and we'd be sadly disappointed if there wasn't. In our culture no figure so personifies the

glorification of violence. Perhaps ranching's most harmful social/cultural impact is its perpetuation of machismo and all it entails -- might is right, man over Nature and woman, egocentrism, an attitude that eating huge amounts of beef is patriotic and manly, brutality towards animals, and a generally wasteful, over-exploitive attitude.

"Big Cowboy Western knows just about everything," said Billy. --from a children's book. (*Greg Pentkowski*)

In the rural West, the macho cowboy is the ultimate in rugged masculinity, the yardstick by which all other men are measured. This is of course a ridiculous myth, even by macho standards. For example, who is tougher -- the cowboy sitting on a horse trotting across the range or the backpacker hauling 70 pounds for miles across rugged mountainsides? We all know the cowboy is, even if he spends half of his time sitting in a pickup or Cessna.

I could be anything. I mean, I could be a jet pilot, or a policeman, or the President of the United States. I could even be a cowboy.
--Chris Elliott, TV sitcom "Get a Life"

The cowboy/rancher is every male American child's role model, particularly in the rural West. When a boy puts a cowboy hat on his head and straps on his toy 6-shooter, he tastes the excitement of being in command -- *just like a real cowboy!* He fantasizes. By simply pointing his gun, he can make anyone do anything, or make them dead. If the Injuns or other bad guys get too thick, he can always gang up with his cowboy buddies and wipe them out. He can make any animal dead by pulling a trigger. He can make his horse do whatever he wants by spurring it hard enough. He controls a vast ranching territory as far as he can imagine, and whoever trespasses is in trouble. He knows what's right and makes everyone else do what's right. If they don't, they better watch out!

Around the world, the term "cowboy" has for good reason come to be used as a synonym for aggressive imperialism, particularly as practiced by the United States, but also by the Soviet Union, Great Britain, Japan, and other super-powers. Appropriately, US Secretary of State Jim Baker is a Wyoming rancher from a public lands ranching family, and Defense Secretary Dick Cheney also is a ranching-enamored resident of "The Cowboy State."

Fathers encourage their sons to grow into men based on the cowboy paragon. For example, older boys receive BB and pellet guns, then graduate to .22 caliber rifles. Emulating cowboys, they shoot bottles, cans, trees, cacti, birds, lizards, frogs, rabbits, and whatever moves or doesn't. When adults, they buy fancy pistols and rifles and become akin to real cowboys. The childhood desire to play cowboy is one of the principal inducements for American men to buy guns, worship them, and to use them indiscriminately.

Thousands of rural boys are taught to hate predators, competitors, pests, and no-goods -- *most* wild animals. They learn to mistreat domestic animals, that animals don't have feelings, and that they are here only for our use. They learn to exploit their surroundings however they see fit, that Nature has no real purpose beyond serving "mankind." They learn that ranching is inherently superior to other land uses, that ranching takes priority, and that ranchers are somehow better than common people.

They learn disrespect toward women, that females have their place. Little girls quickly learn their place. Consequently, there are 2 kinds of "ladies" in cowboyland. The "good woman" is the dedicated housewife who stands by her man, regardless of his possible indiscretions. She raises the kids, keeps house, has dinner ready on time, and has herself ready on time. She is a good advisor, but knows when to keep her mouth shut. The man "man"ages the family like he does the ranch.

The "bad girl" is the woman who has forsaken her conventional place in the established order. She cannot seem to learn proper dedication to a man. She may find her place on the bar stool.

Few ranchers are women, and most who are, are ranchers' widows or daughters. Most wives of stockmen describe themselves as "rancher's wife," and that indeed seems to be their main function. Aside from providing their husbands morale assistance and domestic servitude, most are members of the Cow Belles. Each Western county has a branch of the Cow Belles that meets regularly to plan projects that promote ranching and the beef industry. Activities include fund raisers; input at public hearings; displays at state and county fairs; presentations at schools; and production of "educational" material such as beef posters, brochures, slide shows, and recipes for distribution from local stores. Each county Cow Belle group is a branch of a state organization, which is a component of the National Organization of Cattle Women. Social pressure is heavy to become a member and act like a member, as a "rancher's wife" should.

Women were put on earth to reproduce, and are close to animals. Women's liberation is on an equal to gay liberation -- they are both ridiculous.
--Wyoming steer wrestler, *Animals' Agenda* (March 1990)

Many individual ranchers, of course, do not ascribe to the social/cultural circumstances described herein. To this day, however, causative influences do perhaps remain most common among Western stockmen, particularly public lands ranchers, who are on the whole the most reactionary and powerful faction of the Western ranching subculture. Because stockmen exert far more social/cultural power over the rural West than any comparable group, they are both the spearhead and a main driving force behind these influences.

In sum, though the ranching establishment is a traditional, stable Western institution, overall it has highly negative consequences for rural Western society. It creates a constant undercurrent of fear, even in those who support ranching. It demands acquiescence from all non-ranching factions and creates disunity among those factions. It largely controls the social structure, and tolerates little deviation. It promotes the cowboy paragon and consequent social injustice.

Perhaps our biggest obstacle to ending public lands ranching is social/cultural -- our unconditional worship and support for The Cowboy.

Chapter IX
POLITICS

Cattlemen like politics.
--A back-country Westerner

It is horrifying that we have to fight our own government to save the environment.
--Ansel Adams

Despite the evidence, many people find it impossible to believe that the same Uncle Sam who brought us Smokey the Bear, Woodsy Owl, and The Litterbug would allow America's public land to be desecrated by an elite handful of businessmen. Yet, there has always been an attitude of dedication and even subservience to the livestock industry throughout relevant segments of government. Indeed, much Western government was created by and remains composed of stockmen. Special treatment for ranchers has been institutionalized for so long that people either fail to recognize it or take it for granted.

"I didn't understand that, whatever the law says, we're not really committed as an agency [BLM] to multiple use -- we're committed to livestock grazing. Real enforcement is almost against our nature. It's not really a conscious decision -- it just comes historically out of our role as buddies to the ranchers. It's a very entrenched cultural imperative. My state director dressed like a cowboy, talked like a cowboy, thought like a cowboy, even chewed like a cowboy. He'd come through a system that had prepared him to make decisions based on the desires of the cowboys. How can we expect anything more?"
--BLM staffer, in "Discouraging Words" by Jon R. Luoma (Luoma 1986)

The government land managing agencies function as public relations fronts and apologists, concealing or rationalizing that which might harm the ranching industry. They juggle figures, sweep problems under the rug, and shrewdly promote industry causes. Excessive demands denied other commercial users often are granted freely to stockmen. Underlying it all is the knowledge that the American public will support nearly any measure that helps cowboys or increases beef production.

"Drought-stricken pasture," claims the Forest Service. *(USFS)*

You have to remember what the BLM is. It's a bunch of cattlemen running the public land.
--Jim Clapp, rancher, former BLM employee, founder of the Wild Horse Sanctuary in Shingletown, California (Atwood)

BLM, with more than 1/4 of its total operation geared to ranching, is often referred to as the "Bureau of Livestock Management" (sometimes the "Bureau of Livestock and Mining"). For the Forest Service logging comes first, with ranching an undisputed second. In the West, BLM has 11 state, 49 district, and 140 resource area (local) offices; every resource area is heavily grazed by livestock (BLM publications). The Forest Service has 6 regional, 98 National Forest, and 420 ranger district offices in the 11 Western states. Nearly every ranger district in every Western National Forest is managed for ranching. (USDA, FS 1988)

Symbolically, cattle graze landscape vegetation at a Forest Service Ranger District office; the cow on the left appears to be looking in a window. *(Jim Brown)*

The General Accounting Office reported in 1989 that the BLM "has often placed the needs of commercial interests ... ahead of other users as well as the long-term health of the resources."
--Brad Knickerbocker, "Cattle, Mining Strain Fragile Lands" (Knickerbocker 1990)

According to Bernard Shanks in **This Land Is Your Land**, nearly 85% of BLM line managers hold degrees in range management, forestry, or agriculture. Almost all were educated in Western universities, especially land-grant colleges that collaborate closely with the livestock industry. Fewer than 2% hold degrees in wildlife management, recreation, or other broad natural resource disciplines. (Shanks 1984) Most Forest Service personnel are aligned with the timber industry, yet a surprising number have ranching backgrounds, especially in the interior West. (Reportedly, one FS range manager combines interests -- sometimes tending his cattle on "his" grazing allotment as he patrols the FS ranger district on government time.)

Higher-ups at local agency offices are especially dedicated to ranching. In personal correspondence, an anonymous BLM biologist writes with unusual candor:

Managers are mostly clones of one another who got to the top by sucking butts and not upsetting any ranchers along the way. Their main concern is staying out of trouble and making the highest grade before retirement. Somewhere along the line most of them lost any land ethic they may have had.

Let me introduce myself. I am Don Case and I am Range Staff officer for USDA Forest Service in Sierra Vista. ... I have directly and indirectly been in the livestock industry most of my life and I feel a real need to help the industry when and wherever I can.

Recently, the livestock industry has had some bad publicity in the news media. Some of the reporting is true but most is fabricated and slanted to the view of the reporter. However, the person who reads this material can be persuaded that livestock grazing is a detriment to the land and total ecology. I do not think the industry is prepared to meet this kind of attack.
--Don Chase, Sierra Vista District Range Staff, Coronado National Forest, Arizona, in a 5-7-87 letter to the Cochise-Graham County Cattle Growers

It is understandable that government range managers have little desire to interfere with ranching operations. They know that their clout and share of funding depends largely on the number of AUMs and area of land grazed. The relevant government agencies have nearly as much motive to protect the status quo as do stockmen. Most have fed from the grazing industry trough, via the taxpayer, for decades. Indeed, these bureaucracies are integral parts of the ranching establishment.

November 7, 1986, at 11:30 A.M. has been established for the next permittee/Forest Service meeting. This particular meeting will be held at "The Little Outfit," Larry Robbins' ranch. It will be a pot-luck lunch as well, so bring a dish or two; a main dish and a salad or desert [sic]. Don't forget eating utensils. The Forest Service will provide drinks.
--from a typical notice for a Forest Service/permittee meeting

B.L.M.

One group of employees, usually the range management staff, could be seen, coffee cup in hand, emulating ranchers. The signs included rodeo belt buckles, western shirts complete with a can of Copenhagen in the pocket, well-worn cowboy boots, and twangy western accents. The caricature was startling, and the similarity to the rancher impressive. However, one difference was in attitude; in the presence of an influential rancher, the BLM cowboy was deferential. The rancher was aloof and superior.
--Bernard Shanks, **This Land Is Your Land** (Shanks 1984)

To better understand, consider the typical BLM office. The building is located along the main highway in this modest rural community, where both public lands ranchers and BLM employees live out their lives together. Walk through the front door and look around. In the entry, pick from shelves of handouts explaining BLM's mission and responsibilities, promoting the virtues of ranching, warning against damaging range "improvements," giving pointers on range management, and offering various ranching assistance. On the walls, see framed BLM credos, photos of rangelands, branding irons and lassos, perhaps an elk or deer head. Wall maps detail management plans and outline grazing allotments. The hat rack in the hallway is covered mostly with cowboy hats, and most of the employees' feet with cowboy boots.

Fifteen employees occupy the building. Two specialize in range management. Eight more are involved with ranching as "management specialists": specialists in fire; wild horse and burro; soil, air, and water; recreation and visual resources; wildlife habitat; multiple-use; and wilderness. The wilderness specialist is engaged with a ranchman, who is upset because BLM won't honor his request for a new fence in the nearby Wilderness Area. One of the range managers is on the phone with another rancher, trying to straighten out the matter of his grazing fee payment being 2 months late. The soil specialist is at his desk, diligently trying to incorporate traditional grazing levels into his recommendations for the resource area management plan. Everyone in the building has learned to consider ranching interests in whatever they do. To them continued grazing at or near traditional levels is as unquestioned as the sun rising each morning.

This hypothetical BLM resource area is typical. It encompasses more than 2 million acres, 90% of which is grazed. From each of its 150 permittees it takes in an average of about $800 in grazing fees annually, or a total of $114,280 per year -- the average for a BLM resource area. This isn't even enough to pay the 2 range specialists salaries ($60,000) and the ranching portions of 8 other employees' salaries ($60,000). (USDI, BLM 1988 and 1988a) Without ranching, funding would drop and some staff might be reduced to part time.

Range conservationists administer the grazing program on the Public Lands, in conjunction with wildlife biologists, soil scientists, hydrologists, environmental specialists, and other staff to insure that grazing use is in harmony with other resources and uses on the Public Lands.
--BLM, *Managing the Public Lands* (USDI, BLM 1987)

And there are federal agencies in place to oversee all of the public lands operations -- those agencies allow no overgrazing.
--Patty McDonald, Executive Director, Public Lands Council

Today most people think the federal lands are protected by government agencies. This is not the case. The agencies charged with protecting the public trust have a partnership with private developers. The essence of public-land management is to provide an economic subsidy to a handful of people and corporations. The public that owns the land is shortchanged.
--Bernard Shanks, **This Land Is Your Land** (Shanks 1984)

Range management is based on politics, and the ranching industry's political influence reaches down onto every grazing allotment.
--Ed Marston, Editor, *High Country News*

Under various laws and official mandates, government agencies are charged with administering proper ranching management, safeguarding the environment, and protecting the public's interests relative to public lands. That they have failed miserably should already be obvious. Nevertheless, it behooves us here to look closer. (For other studies of public ranching politics and administration, consult DeVoto 1955, Calef 1960, Foss 1960, Voigt 1976, Ferguson 1983, or Shanks 1984.)

Take BLM's 1.7-million-acre Jarbridge Resource Area in southwest Idaho, for example. It is a landscape of vast plains and awesome canyons containing outstanding existing and potential wildlife habitat. Yet, BLM's proposed resource management plan allocates 20 times more forage for cattle than wildlife. To achieve the livestock allocation, BLM now contends the plan must be amended to double livestock fences to 306 miles, triple livestock watering pipelines to 444 miles, and quadruple the number of livestock water developments. Livestock grazing would be increased 73% by altering vegetation on 300,000 acres of the Jarbridge

Plateau. Already, according to BLM itself, 42% of the resource area is in poor condition, and 29% is in exotic grass seedings which must be artificially maintained with tax money, essentially forever. Only 86 permittees ranch these 1.7 million acres (about 20,000 acres apiece).

In 1986, based on a negative staff report and overwhelming public opposition from many sectors, a BLM district manager in Idaho Falls denied the request of a few ranchers and farmers to build an "agricultural transport" road, the "Elgin-Hamer Road," through the winter range of Idaho's largest elk herd. (An existing road was less than a mile longer.) A local rancher/land baron even threatened to build fences to block the elk's migration if the road wasn't built. Finally, incensed, the ranchers went to see Interior Secretary Donald Hodel -- one of their political champions. The manager was promptly removed, and the road was built.

The Elgin-Hamer agreement required the road be closed during winter to protect elk. According to the Wildlife Management Institute, however, in January 1989 an employee of the Idaho Fish & Game Department flew over the area and saw the snowed-in road had been plowed and 1000 sheep were being trailed through, accompanied by a tractor and other vehicles. The offender turned out to be Jeff Siddoway, president of the Idaho Woolgrowers Association, maker of the aforementioned threat. He was later fined $50.

According to Norma Ames, assistant chief of game management for the New Mexico Department of Game & Fish:

In 1973 Game & Fish proposed to extend its jurisdiction to all wildlife, not just game species. But the legislature said no because of the fear of livestock people that we would protect the coyote.

In Arizona's Prescott National Forest, 1,248,110 acres of 1,250,613 acres (99.8%) are managed for ranching, and 78% is considered to provide "full capacity" grazing. Grazing fee receipts average about $376,000 annually, while the Forest spends several times this amount on ranching. The Forest's recent long-range management plan calls for continued grazing near traditional levels, even though the Forest's subsequent EIS stated that "The major cause of soil erosion and poor watershed conditions on the Prescott National Forest is overgrazing." The EIS also asserted that 99% of the Forest's riparian acres are in less than fair condition due to overgrazing; 46% of the Forest's range is in unsatisfactory condition; current permitted grazing use is 26,000 AUMs above the capacity of the range; planned grazing will cause lower water quality to "some riparian areas because of sedimentation and bacterial contamination from livestock grazing"; ranching will conflict with some recreational uses; and more. In other words, by the Forest Service's own admission the Prescott NF ranching plan will not comply with numerous legal mandates.

It is my decision to adopt the alternative which provides for rapid growing season rotation of cattle, moderate investment of project dollars, and a total stocking of 250 cattle yearlong [highest number of cattle of 6 alternatives]. ... Alternative 1 [no cattle] was not selected because it eliminates livestock use on areas that are suitable for grazing [ostensibly the entire allotment!].
--From Prescott National Forest Supervisor Coy G.

Jemmett's Notification of Decision, Walnut Creek Allotment Management Plan

With every other major commercial use of public land, the decision whether or not to permit the use is made on an individual, site-specific basis. Mining, woodcutting, utility corridors, developments, commercial recreation, and even logging are all permitted only in specified areas. Not so with ranching. From its inception, it has been given "highest use" blanket approval essentially everywhere with significant livestock forage or browse -- *about 3/4 of public land*. Our government accepts ranching unquestionably as a given, a constant, a kind of bedrock, a ubiquitous land management base upon which all else is contingent. And now our government declares that traditional use mandates future use. In other words, agencies never had a solid economic or environmental basis for their ranching programs in the first place -- only tradition and continued political imperative.

"Satisfactory" is used by the Forest Service to mean the land is producing [livestock forage, mostly] *at or above 40% of its biological potential.*
--(USDA, USDI 1979)

Roadside fenceline, Utah BLM.

Since their creation, the agencies have consistently strived to deceive the public and Congress that range conditions and trends are far better than they actually are. In so doing, they have 2 major objectives: (1) to show that they are doing a good job, thus promoting their bureaucracies, and (2) to protect their permittees, thus their bureaucracies.

The vast bulk of range the agencies describe as being in "satisfactory" condition is producing plant biomass at *less than 50% (some of it at less than 20%)* of its pre-livestock rate. For example, by industry standards an allotment rated in 100% "excellent" condition may still be only 50% as productive as it was aboriginally.

Further, range assessments don't adequately consider wildlife, species composition, water and soil, organic litter, and many other factors. Range condition as defined by the actions of government agencies is *not* assessed environmental quality; it is little more than a measure of herbage productivity for livestock. Maitland Sharpe, Director of Environmental Affairs for the Izaak Walton League put it like this:

> *In talking about the condition of the range, the author likened the range surveys to the body counts of the Vietnam War. . . . Many wildlife professionals seem persuaded that range surveys have, in practice, focused narrowly on forage species, that preferred livestock forage species have typically been selected as key species while critical browse species have not been so considered, and that critical escape, nesting, birthing, or rearing cover has not been considered at all. . . . As a result, range condition surveys tend to be largely assessments of grass.*
> (USDA, USDI 1979)

Even the US Soil Conservation Service -- a comparatively open-minded agency with an avowed "ecological approach" -- considers range with only 51%-75% climax species to be in "good" condition, with 76%-100% regarded as "excellent." "Poor" is 0%-25%, and "fair" 26%-50% (USDA, SCS 1976). We might reasonably ask what is "fair" about an ecosystem stripped of 1/2 to 3/4 of its natural vegetation. If a loss of half of rangeland productivity since aboriginal times was factored, range with 1/8 of its original climax vegetation could be classified "fair"! Moreover, even range professionals who profess to use the "ecological" method bias their range assessments to promote ranching (as explained in Holechek's **Range Management**). The agencies further deceive with the cruel hoax that modern science and technology can be increasingly applied to progressively improve the Western range indefinitely.

> *I spent a summer doing a vegetation survey (as a volunteer) a few years back. My job was to find out what the dominant vegetation types and conditions were. The BLM administers grazing permits without even knowing what is out there; it's like running a store without knowing what items you sell; and then only one volunteer could be sent to survey some 200,000 acres!!*
> --Todd Hoitsma, Yosemite, California, personal correspondence

All public grazing allotments are administered under management plans that ostensibly address environmental and land use concerns. However, most of these plans are basically just paper. While the agencies point to the plans as evidence of good stewardship, on-the-ground management usually bears minimal resemblance. The agencies are authorized to alter or amend these plans for any number of reasons, but ranchers routinely appeal and overturn unwanted proposed changes, calling in their political buddies to apply pressure if need be. Agency personnel are often branded "communists" for their attempts at reform.

But even with the best of intentions, no federal, state, or county agency has personnel sufficient to properly monitor and administer ranching on the acreage under its jurisdiction. In 1985, FS had 561 range conservationists and technicians (with cutbacks there are fewer now) overseeing 9000 grazing allotments covering 103 million acres -- an average of 16 allotments and 184,000 acres each (Joyce 1989). BLM range personnel watch over an average of 392,000 acres apiece (Jones 1991). A survey revealed that few of these people spend more time on the range than in the office anyway (Joyce 1989). A federal range manager may visit an allotment only once or twice a year, and in his lifetime he may never even see much of the land under his supervision. The Nevada state BLM office, for example, says that only about 1/3 of its allotments are inventoried in a given year. State land department field inspectors, responsible for monitoring an average of more than a million acres each, may not visit individual state grazing allotments for years. Many counties and cities do no monitoring to assess environmental impacts and impose no ranching restrictions whatsoever. Just pay the fee, thank you.

Indeed, most land managing agencies so lack monitoring personnel that they must obtain much or most of their information on allotment conditions *from permittees themselves*. Under these circumstances, how can the government possibly protect the land, even if it wanted to?

Moreover, the unit productivity of public land is so low that it would take more money to hire adequate personnel and maintain agency infrastructure to administer ranching than could be recouped in grazing fees or, in many areas, even net livestock value to the public. In other words, financing sufficient monitoring and administration of public lands ranching would preclude public lands ranching economically. Even at current (under)staffing rates, grazing fee receipts barely cover range managers' salaries.

> *Given the number of* [federal land] *technicians, the size of the districts under their administration, the number of duties they are obliged to perform, the equipment at their disposal, and the prevailing views of range managers concerning the intensity of inspection that is feasible, it is easy to understand why most range inspection is superficial, haphazard, and inadequate.*
> --Wesley Calef, **Private Grazing and Public Lands** (Calef 1960

Accurate scientific data for assessing range conditions and trends are likewise inadequate. Too few pertinent studies are conducted in too few locations; methods and implementation are questionable; and reports fail to consider numerous variables. Base data for determining range trends are lacking because so few useful, objective studies were conducted in the past. Ungrazed study plots are few, far too small, and affected by many unnatural influences. Thus, permitted grazing levels and ranching practices are based largely on guesswork, personal bias and, perhaps most of all, tradition. Even range wildlife professional Frederic H. Wagner, a long-time supporter of public lands ranching, seems to agree:

> *Since scientific measures of the structure of western ecosystems before the rise of livestock numbers do not exist, we will probably never understand fully the nature and magnitude of changes which have taken place. Even today, our efforts at measuring western vegetation are so inadequate that we will not have an accurate picture of changes in the next 50 to 100 years unless our present efforts are greatly increased.* (Wagner 1978)

Inter-agency and long-term range assessments are questionable partly because BLM, FS, and SCS all use different indicators to measure range health, and their evaluating techniques keep changing. Utah State University range professor Neil West says BLM has changed its evaluation methods at least 5 times in the past 50 years (Williams 1990). Ranching interests currently have a strong lobbying effort underway, and are forcing the agencies to begin using the terms "potential natural community," "late-serial," "mid-serial," and "early-serial" to describe range conditions. However, this amounts to a change in wording only, as indicated by public lands rancher Duane Slaathaug: "There seems to be a need to change the terminology so we are not using terms like 'unsatisfactory.'"

The agencies' determination of range condition in relation to carrying capacity is also inadequate and questionable. The number of livestock permitted usually is determined by visually examining the allotment, measuring and weighing sample herbage, and comparing the results against a standardized formula. The assessment allegedly reflects the allotment's current biotic state compared to its current biotic potential; the range condition, and thus the level of grazing permitted, is determined accordingly. As mentioned, the assessment does not reflect true biotic potential and is in many ways subject to error and the bias of agency personnel. Further, no method of determining carrying capacity used by government agencies adequately compensates for the many potential unforeseen variables, such as weather extremes, fire, market fluctuations, trespass, and poor livestock management. Perhaps most important, the mere use of the term "carrying capacity" denotes a presumption that any livestock grazing should occur there in the first place.

> *From time to time* [BLM range managers] *looked in and around some shrubs and identified a few of the grasses, then looked for five seconds at the area within a few yards to see whether they identified other similar grasses. From time to time they made remarks such as: "This range is in really fine shape"; "Man, there's a lot of good feed around here; there's plenty of feed"; "This range is in much better shape than when I was here ten years ago," and similar remarks.*
> --Wesley Calef, **Private Grazing and Public Lands** (Calef 1960)

The agencies' determination of herbage utilization is similarly flawed. Their several methods fall into 2 basic categories: visual estimates and estimates based on measuring devices. The most common is the visual survey, in which the range manager visually inspects an allotment and surmises how much herbage has been taken. Obviously, this method is highly subjective. Results are determined by the observer's memory, knowledge, skill, mood, and bias. In making an estimate, agency personnel often yield to the persistent underlying pressure to err on the side of the permittee. Measuring tools include tiny exclosures, thrown hoops, transects, and spot checking. These generally are more accurate than visual inspection, but once again results depend greatly on human and environmental variables.

Agencies often use tiny wire exclosures such as these to determine livestock herbage utilization on allotments. Ranchers may move them during grazing seasons to make it appear as if less herbage has been taken, and they are worthless as indicators of long-term environmental changes because they are so small and are relocated from year to year. BLM land, Cane County, Utah.

Each federal grazing permit contains a "preference" for a certain number of livestock, representing the maximum number of animals the permittee may put on the allotment. However, the preference is almost always set far higher (commonly 10%-30% higher) than even what the agencies consider carrying capacity, and the actual number of animals allowed is set informally each year or season. Thus, the exact number of livestock allowed to graze an allotment varies from year to year. According to BLM specialist Joseph M. Feller:

> The unrealistically high preference acts as a blank check, allowing the BLM and the permittee to agree informally each year or each season on the number of cattle that will graze the allotment.
>
> Since the actual number [allowed] is always less than the preference, the BLM can always claim that it is "reducing" the number of cattle on the allotment in order to protect the environment. The rancher can take his choice of either complaining about the oppressive "reduction" or boasting about his magnanimity in taking a voluntary "reduction" for nature's sake. (Feller 1990)

> ... The single-most difficult step to take in restoring abused ranges to a high level of productivity is the first and most essential act: reduce livestock numbers.

Harold Dregne, **Desertification of Arid Lands**

> To the observer, it appears that the ranchers administer the range about to suit themselves, at least so far as stocking rates are concerned. It is also my distinct impression that the district technicians think the range not just overgrazed, but so seriously overgrazed that, in view of the minor adjustments in stocking they are able to make, the situation is practically hopeless.

--Wesley Calef, **Private Grazing and Public Lands** (Calef 1960)

Under their contrived assumption that ranching is "mandated" to continue nearly everywhere it traditionally occurred, the agencies have ignored legislation, government directives, and even their own regulations to reduce livestock numbers to protect environmental quality and public interest, promoting instead taxpayer-sponsored range "improvements" to keep livestock numbers artificially high. Determined that reduced grazing is an absolute last resort, the agencies habitually promote range development to maintain traditional grazing levels, thus protecting their bureaucracies.

According to Phillip O. Foss in **Politics and Grass**:

> The stockmen naturally wish to encourage range improvement, but at the same time they apparently desire minimum regulation of grazing and a low grazing fee. These objectives place the stockman in a somewhat ambivalent position: if increased appropriations are obtained for range improvement, it is likely that closer supervision of grazing will also result. Increased appropriations are also likely to produce demands for increased grazing fees. (Foss 1960)

With the agencies' cooperation, stockmen minimize this conflict to their benefit by: obtaining subsidies under the guise of various alleged non-ranching programs; securing earmarked funds returned to states from grazing fees; formulating "cooperative arrangements" between agencies and permittees; and maintaining the sympathy of agencies and the public. As evidence of the above, the modest 15% cut in agency range staff made during the Reagan and Bush years has met with general approval from permittees (Cascade H.E.C. 1989). (In contrast, BLM wildlife and fisheries staff during those years were cut 34% and 54%, respectively.) According to former BLM biologist Richard Kroger, "The top range officials in Washington lobbied to reduce the agency's budget so that the land could not be monitored."

> The grazing industry is the most vocal and negative I've dealt with.

--Jim Baca, former New Mexico Commissioner of Public Lands, personal correspondence

Regardless of outward appearances, distressingly common across the ranching West is bureaucrat/rancher foul play -- string pulling, mutual back-scratching, deceit, taxpayer abuse, special treatment -- especially at local levels where affairs between ranchers and government employees rarely are exposed to public view. Public officials manipulate figures to cater to local livestock graziers, who are often powerful political, business, church, and social figures in their communities. Violations of permit conditions, regulations, and laws are shielded from scrutiny, as are questionable special arrangements.

For example, I know of a few surreptitious cases where ranchers are living in their own homes, complete with outbuildings and other improvements, *on National Forest land* with Forest Service approval. The justification given by a district ranger for one of these squatters was "He's an old rancher who's been there a long time." Another rancher was allowed to build a house on National Forest land because, a ranger said, if the house was situated on his own land on the other side of a large arroyo his kids couldn't make it to the school bus stop on the few days a year the arroyo floods. Indeed, because historic boundaries were vague and early ranchers often built houses and improvements wherever they wanted to anyway, today's public lands ranchers commonly have homes, outbuildings, and irrigated pastures on public land. For example, according to the California Desert Protection League, in BLM's East Mojave National Scenic Area a public lands ranching headquarters is illegally on BLM land, yet the rancher is allowed to continue business-as-usual. Such problems are usually cleared up by purchase, lease, or trade (or official disregard); non-ranchers rarely are given such special consideration.

Even today some ranchers purposely locate illegal improvements on public land. On BLM land in Utah I have seen ranchers growing alfalfa, with water developments to irrigate the crops. In Nevada I saw an unauthorized pipeline. On many public lands I have seen unauthorized ranching roads. A federal investigation in the late 1960s revealed at least 16,000 miles of unauthorized fence had been strung on Western BLM lands.

Many welfare ranchers sell publicly owned resources from "their" allotments. In Arizona, I have seen them selling sandstone slabs and fill dirt. Many supplement their incomes by illegally cutting and selling firewood. Some sell Native American artifacts. Some peddle live cacti, herbs, and shrubs as ornamentals. (Several Arizona ranchers recently were arrested for theft and sale of publicly owned cacti, including 12' saguaros worth thousands of dollars.)

Other permittees use public lands as settings for commercial ventures such as sightseeing tours, hay rides, campouts, archaeological outings, and guided hunts. These profit-making activities often cause environmental damage, and usually permits and fees are legally required. But many stockmen feel that public ranchland is theirs to do with as they please. Several years ago a southern Arizona public lands rancher advertised an overnight outing in the nearby National Forest. The event would consist of horses, covered wagons, a large camp, and however many people bought tickets. When, at the complaint of a local resident, the permittee was informed by FS district staff that a permit was required for such commercial activity (although FS assured him it had no intention of stopping the outing), he "was surprised" and stated that he had been "organizing rides in these mountains for 7 years."

No person shall by force, threats, intimidation, or by any fencing or inclosing ... prevent or obstruct ... any person from peaceably entering upon ... any tract of public land ... or shall prevent or obstruct free passage or transit over or through public lands.
--Federal Unlawful Inclosures Act

Some ranchmen charge access fees or hunting fees for public land to which they control access. For instance, 20 years ago Wyoming public lands sheep rancher Norman Palm and other ranchers banded together to form Elk Mountain Safari, Inc. They charged hunters $250 per year to gain access to public lands behind a locked gate on Palm's private land. Promotional literature listed "800,000 Acres of BLM, State and Private Leases" as "resources of Elk Mountain Safari, Inc." A federal district judge recently ruled the blocked access illegal.

Norman Palm is not unusual; many public lands ranchers control access to public land by locking gates crossing their private land, thereby monopolizing the public land behind them. Some even lock gates on "their" public land allotments -- gates that legally should remain unlocked at all times.

Ostensibly to protect the environment, areas of public land sometimes are closed to the public -- *but not to ranching.* Coconino NF, Arizona.

Several years ago a welfare rancher in our local area enlarged one of "his" stock tanks on "his" Arizona State grazing allotment by turning it into a sand and gravel pit. His buddies lived in campers by the excavation site for months, which is illegal. They operated a loader and drove dump trucks in and out from a busy highway only a hundred yards from and in plain view of the entire operation. The rancher came and went as work progressed.

Finally, when the pit had expanded to about 3 acres, I called the State Land Department. I was told that there were only 3 field inspectors for 9 million acres of state land and that the state could not take any action until someone officially notified the county sheriff. I did, and when the sheriff arrived at the excavation site a day later, the lawbreakers and their possessions had all mysteriously and suspiciously vanished. According to the State Land Department, such occurrences are common.

An example of subsidy abuse involves former Secretary of the Department of the Interior, William Clark. In April 1984 the environmental journal *Not Man Apart* reported that the Compound 1080 was being applied illegally on the Secretary's large California ranch by the California Department of Game & Fish to kill ground squirrels and coyotes, apparently with Clark's knowledge. Government safety procedures were being ignored, and the health of the area ecosystem was being compromised.

This spring, while floating the Rio Grande River, which forms the western border of Big Bend National Park, I counted 136 trespassing animals [cattle] *along the riparian zone.*
--George Wuerthner, "Counting the Real Costs of Public Lands Grazing" (Wuerthner 1989)

Cattle on Arizona State land broke through this fence into Buenos Aires National Wildlife Refuge, leaving the vicinity of the break inside the Refuge in as poor shape as the state land in the foreground. *(Steve Johnson)*

Six mounted rangers began the trek Monday to the Humphries Wildlife area in the Chama Valley [New Mexico] in pursuit of owners of 2,000 sheep who are occupying the land in defiance of a state agency, a spokesman said Monday. "The sheep owners cut a fence along the southwestern corner of the Humphries wildlife area and we just followed the grazing path left by the sheep," Game and Fish spokesman Jerry Maracchini said in an interview. . . . Game & Fish "won't make any arrests immediately, but will issue warnings to the lawbreakers," Maracchini said.
--8-22-89 Albuquerque Journal

Common knowledge throughout the rural West is that overstocking trespass -- running more livestock on an allotment than authorized -- is as common as not. The agencies customarily deny this, citing "official statistics" (paper livestock). However, for years I have seen overstocking and heard of it from so many rural residents, agency personnel, and even ranchers that it seems the grazier who doesn't overstock is an oddball. Reliable reports tell of ranchers stocking 2 or even 3 times as many cattle as called for on permits. Since agencies are understaffed and range personnel cannot easily count cows on 12,000 rugged acres, getting caught and penalized for overstocking is unlikely. "Understocking," or grazing fewer livestock than authorized on a permit, also occurs, though ranchers have little incentive to do this, for generally they (are supposed to) prepay for an agreed number of AUMs, regardless of how many their animals actually consume.

Another type of trespass occurs when a permittee turns livestock onto an allotment before opening date, after closing date, or during the wrong season. Many permittees do this routinely to maximize use of free public herbage, or simply because they are sloppy managers. For example, a millionaire rancher near Tucson has an agreement with Pima County to graze livestock on the Cienega Creek Natural Preserve for 4 months each spring, yet he has consistently grazed some of his animals there before and after the dates stipulated in the grazing agreement.

Yet another type of trespass occurs when a rancher turns stock onto a portion of an allotment not scheduled to be grazed at that time. He may do this because his animals have consumed too much herbage on the permitted portion, he has trespassed too many animals, a windmill in the permitted area breaks down, the trespassed area is more convenient to him, or for any of a number of other reasons.

Two other kinds of trespass involve grazing livestock on public land without a permit. One occurs when a rancher runs livestock on government land off-limits to grazing. Commonly, a permittee will allow or drive his livestock onto unauthorized BLM or National Forest land, or onto a little-visited portion of a nature reserve, recreation area, National Park or Monument, National Wildlife Refuge, state or county park -- where forage often is so abundant that the rancher cannot bear to let it "go to waste." The second type occurs when a permittee grazes stock on the allotment of another permittee. This generally is the type of trespass the government notices, for forage is "stolen" from the allotment's assigned permittee, who then raises hell with the relevant government agency.

Grazing permits stipulate the routes ranchers may use to move their stock to and from permitted grazing areas. These conditions are widely violated -- another form of livestock trespass. A traditional favorite trick of many stockmen is "trailing" their animals at a snail's pace across public land, moving them from one public or private grazing area to another, grazing them heavily as they go. Generally, permittees are not charged for trailing.

Finally, a last type of trespass occurs when a private land rancher runs livestock on public land. For example, according to Arcata, California's *Eco-News* (August 1989), cattle from adjacent private land have been intruding onto BLM's Kings Range National Conservation Area, south of Eureka on the remote northern California coast, threatening Endangered species and degrading riparian areas. BLM has done little to prevent the unauthorized grazing. As another example, an unidentified source reports that officials of Shasta-Trinity National Forest, California have for years allowed private cattle on Forest land there without permit.

Now add 40 percent to the government's AUM numbers, and you will have a fairly accurate range-use figure that takes the Standard Annual Trespass (SAT) into consideration. . . . When you consider that BLM typically permits three to four times the use the range can support on a sustained-yield basis,

you will realize that adding 40 percent to this use increases the overuse to five to six times sustainability. . . . It is happening on a grand, West-wide scale. It is "traditional" and entrenched.
--Bill Davis, "Our Living Desert Is Becoming a New Sahara" (Davis 1990)

Trespass of all kinds is commonplace. Some is accidental, as when livestock come through open gates or breaks in fences, or when a few cattle are left behind when a herd is moved to another grazing area or roundup. But much -- perhaps most -- is deliberate. Most trespass goes undetected and unreported; even if reported it is nearly impossible to prove that a stockman intentionally left a gate open, made a break in a fence, or left cattle behind. Regulations require fences to be wholly intact *before* livestock are moved onto an allotment, but ranchers also often intentionally allow fences to deteriorate so their animals may trespass.

When a trespass is reported, the offending rancher can declare it "nonwillful" and thus be subject to the minimum penalty -- an assessment to pay approximately fair market value for the forage -- by claiming that someone else left the gate open, or that the trespassing animals are not his, or that his hired hand was confused as to where the allotment boundary line was located, or that his animals were in trespass only a very short while when they were first observed and he was just about to round them up and move them back onto the authorized area at that time. Documenting even nonwillful trespass on lands of mixed or checkerboarded ownership, such as is common throughout large portions of the West, is nearly impossible because usually there are no identifiable property boundaries and it is difficult to establish precise periods of trespass.

Punishment for even the most serious "willful" violations commonly is only temporary impoundment of the rancher's trespassing livestock and/or an order to pay up to double the value of the stolen forage and/or cost of the impoundment. If the violator is an especially troublesome, long-term repeat offender, he may be subject to impoundment expenses and fined about 3 times fair market value. But according to the *Federal Register*, "for violations to be considered 'repeated' it must also be determined that the violations are 'willful'" (USDI, BLM 1978)." This usually is difficult, if not impossible, to prove.

As trespass charges rarely are significant, a rancher may not object to paying an assessment. If he does object, he may cause the agency grief by initiating a lengthy appeal process that may take years to resolve. Or, he may bring political or social pressures down upon the head of the official who dared implicate him in trespass transgression, thus bullying the official into reducing or dismissing the penalty.

However, when a trespass is reported agency officials often do *nothing* and patiently wait for the trespasser to remove his livestock of his own accord. The offender may be sent a warning letter or politely asked to remove his stock, and if it is done promptly the matter is forgotten. If the offense is particularly blatant or protracted, or if the permittee has a record of trespass, he may be issued a sterner warning. And if some more official notice is taken of the trespass, common practice is to make a deal with the ranchman before any official action is taken, so as to avoid burdening the stockman or making him hostile toward the agency.

Files obtained through the Freedom of Information Act show that most penalties levied by BLM are at the lower, nonwillful rate. One agency insider contends that the extent of violations is almost always reduced (McMillan 1990).

The agencies are supposed to count livestock to prevent trespass. However, they usually don't, and when they do they rarely do so unannounced, so ranchers have advance warning to adjust numbers or hide animals accordingly. Thus, when officials of Sawtooth National Forest, Idaho, responding to reports of overstocking, held an unannounced head count during an allotment roundup in October 1989, the event was recounted by ranchers in local papers as "Gestapo tactics" by "Forest Service bullies." (The FS officials were in the company of 2 lawmen in response to reports of physical threats against them.) The ranchers are demanding a government investigation. (Marston 1990)

Trespass is so difficult to detect, hard to prove, and tough to punish that ranchers feel they have nothing to lose, and much to gain, by trespassing. Wesley Calef, in **Private Grazing and Public Lands**:

Since no one insists that they [trespass charges] are punitive, they seem to me to be a positive incitement to trespass; a rancher might conclude that it was worthwhile to gamble on getting some free forage by trespass, since the worst that could happen to him would be to pay approximately the same price for the feed that he would otherwise have to pay some private landowner. (Calef 1960)

The 1986 Congressional report, *Federal Grazing Problem: All Is Not Well on the Range*, summarizes the trespass problem:

BLM does not have an effective trespass monitoring program to detect and prevent grazing trespass, is not diligent in pursuing and resolving the trespass cases that are reported, and is not recovering all costs associated with trespass cases. Available data also raises serious questions about the effectiveness of the Forest Service program. (Com. on Govt. Oper. 1986)

The trespass situation is exacerbated by the fact that on many allotments the agencies issue annual or seasonal grazing licenses, even while the standard 10-year permits are in effect. The conditions of these special licenses commonly are set by agency range personnel and permittees who meet informally once or twice a year. They may authorize different stocking rates, use areas, grazing periods, etc. than specified on the 10-year permits. Thus, for example, livestock numbers may be increased to take advantage of wet years and reduced in drier years. However, this lack of long-term commitment to environmental safeguards, combined with year-by-year pressure from stockmen, tends to encourage range abuse rather than protection.

Early stockmen made sure that trespass and all other grazing permit violations carried **no** criminal charges, no matter how intentional or how much damage occurs to the environment or personal property. When cornered with evidence of permit violations so conspicuous it cannot be ignored, the agencies typically plead their innocence and good intent by citing "legal requirements," "bureaucratic directives," "Congressional mandate," and other obscure references to the ranching imperative. We would like to do something but our hands are tied, they may further insist; though in fact federal and state laws give them authority to impound and sell livestock, revoke permits, levy fines, dictate ranching activities, and change permit conditions in response to permit violations. This last opportunity is sometimes utilized -- they change the conditions of the permit, *ex post facto*, to "eliminate" the permit violation!

Even where the agencies admit extreme abuse, they are loath to take action. According to an unknown writer:

> In the winter of 1987-88, the floor of Arch Canyon [Utah] looked like a war zone. The vegetation had been cropped off to the roots and the soil pulverized. There was just one clue to tip off the visitor that the damage had not been caused by a bomb: there was cow manure everywhere. Even the BLM recognized the damage. An inspection report described the grazing as "severe," and, in response to an inquiry from this author, the area manager acknowledged that the canyon had been "overutilized" by cattle.
>
> But... the BLM has stated its intention to renew the grazing permit for Arch Canyon for another ten years without any public input or environmental analysis.

What is necessary to cause a rancher's permit to be cancelled is indeed something to contemplate. One of the few stockmen in public lands ranching history to be barred from public land is the infamous John Jay Casey, an arrogant 73-year-old cattle baron said to possess 30,000 head and a net worth of nearly $100 million. For 30 years Casey contemptuously violated permit stipulations and grazing regulations hundreds of times on "his" allotments in 3 states. In Montana, the Forest Service revoked his grazing privileges only after his cattle repeatedly devastated thousands of acres of range and riparian area. BLM's Susanville, California, District logged 83 trespass actions against Casey before cancelling his permits in 1979. BLM officials in northern Nevada cited him *123* times before finally yanking his permits! Even now he intentionally trespasses cattle from his adjacent private lands. In several court cases, Casey has defended himself, saying he is no worse than many other cattlemen. According to a *Sacramento Bee* article, Casey "prefers that people think of him as just another dimeless buckaroo." (Bowman 1987)

The agencies do in some instances show backbone. In perhaps its most aggressive action yet, in southern Utah, BLM recently shot and killed a group of 17 cattle because the owner had repeatedly allowed them to trespass and overgraze an area of public land closed to livestock.

A 1984-85 internal audit by the Interior Department's Inspector General revealed rampant trespass. One BLM file showed a permittee had trespassed 3 years in a row, resulting in "heavy to severe" range damage. In another, BLM personnel actually watched a grazier truck "over 100 livestock" onto a parcel where the animals clearly did not belong. Both cases were dismissed "without penalty in order to maintain a good working relationship" with the ranchers. (Baker 1986)

One retired Nevada range conservationist estimates that illegal foraging exceeds authorized AUMs by up to a third (McMillan 1990). A spot check of aerial photos by the Inspector General during the 1984-85 audit revealed 4 times as many instances of apparent trespass as BLM acknowledged. In 1987, of the thousands of unauthorized use violations committed by permittees on BLM land that year, only 323 were officially recognized. Fines levied to recoup the value of stolen forage and other expenses averaged only $287 per offender, or a total of about $93,000 -- far less than

what BLM spent dealing with trespass that year. (USDI, BLM 1988) (The Inspector General estimates $1009 in administrative costs just to arrange a typical BLM lease.) However, BLM has no plans to increase fines. Meanwhile, the Forest Service acted on only 72 cases of unauthorized grazing use in 1987; half of these were for horses (USDA, FS 1988). A 1990 GAO report reaffirms that BLM trespass is rampant, that "Permittees and lessees operate essentially under an honor system with little threat of compliance of checks," and that many ranchers operate virtually unchecked (Jones 1991).

> Rather, in a perverse twist of logic, the BLM insists that to fail to renew a grazing permit, or to authorize a reduced number of livestock on an allotment, would be a major action that should not be taken without the most rigorous -- and virtually unattainable -- level of scientific certainty about the precise impacts of grazing on the environment.
>
> Combine this heavy burden of proof with the BLM's insistence that most of the range monitoring data collected in the past are flawed, throw in the BLM's self-induced lack of funds with which to collect more data -- throughout the Reagan administration the BLM successfully sought to reduce its own range management budget -- and you've got a perfect recipe to insure the cows never come home.
>
> --Joseph M. Feller, "The Western Wing of Kafka's Castle" (Feller 1990)

> The Chief, Forest Service, is authorized to revoke or suspend term grazing permits in whole or in part on all National Forest System lands and on other lands under Forest Service control:
>
> (a) For failure to comply with any of the provisions and requirements in the grazing permit; any of the regulations of the Secretary of Agriculture on which the permit is based; or, the instructions of Forest officers issued thereunder; and,
>
> (b) For knowingly and willfully making a false statement or representation in the permittee's grazing application, and amendments thereto.
>
> --Section 231.6, Regulations Governing Livestock Grazing on National Forest ...

> The authorized officer may suspend the grazing use authorized under a grazing permit or grazing lease ...
>
> --Subpart 4170.1-1, [BLM] Grazing Administration and Trespass Regulations (USDI, BLM 1978)

The Natural Resources Defense Council has explained BLM's authority over allotments:

> The Federal Range Code provides, inter alia, . . . that the district manager of each grazing district shall determine for the district and each component unit therein the proper numbers and types of livestock, the proper seasons of use and the maximum period of use during a year ... (NRDC 1973)

The same is true the Forest Service. In other words, permit conditions, area rules, regulations, and range management programs and procedures -- and therefore subsidies -- are all supposed to be determined by the agencies. Yet, in practice they are dictated more by "grazing advisory boards" than by the public employees we hire to do that job.

The Taylor Grazing Act of 1934 provided for the establishment of BLM, area, state, and national grazing "advisory" boards. Similar Forest Service livestock "advisory" boards were established in 1950 by Section 18 of the

Granger-Thye Act. About 840 are recognized and in operation. Other state and federal stockmen boards influence grazing policy for other ranched public lands.

[Public lands rancher] *Rep. William A. (Rory) Cross has been elected to a Bureau of Land Management advisory board less than five months after his sensational trial for allegedly threatening a BLM employee with a loaded gun. A second rancher who is fighting the federal agency in court also was elected to a two-year term on the BLM's grazing advisory committee. He is Norman Palm of Elk Mountain.*
--9-4-86 *Star-Tribune*, Casper, Wyoming

Members of area "advisory" boards are elected by permittees periodically by secret ballot. All permittees in each district are allowed to vote, though statistics show that only a small percentage do. Generally, the wealthiest and most influential stockmen in each area are elected, and by law nearly all board members must be ranchers. The very low turnover rate of board members exacerbates the incredible entrenchment of these bureaucracies. "Advisory" boards are not just legally recognized by the federal government; their members are actually sworn in as federal employees and serve 3-year terms! They meet regularly, with agency personnel often in attendance.

Under the Taylor Grazing Act, "advisory" boards are given the power to "make recommendations" on "any matter which they desire . . . or on which their advice may be requested." Their expressed purpose is to serve in an "advisory" capacity in allocating grazing privileges and supervising details of administration. In practice, boards exert a dominant influence in most federal ranching matters, from removal or transferral of uncooperative agency personnel, to funnelling wildlife funds into ranching development, to expanding grazing areas. No part of federal ranching administration is barred from their influence.

Through the Range so-called "Betterment" Fund, "advisory" boards dictate how grazing fee funds returned to the states for range development will be spent. These funds -- about half of all grazing fee receipts -- are spoken of as "advisory board money." Agency district managers act as foremen to oversee distribution and use of the funds.

"Advisory" boards also hold significant legislative power. The Taylor Grazing Act and its amendments give grazing boards "recommendary" capacity concerning federal grazing rules and regulations. In practice, "bills" are drawn up by board members, or are submitted by the legislature, and then acted upon by the boards in a legislative manner. For example, according to Gordon Griswold, president of the National Advisory Board Council (NABC) from 1940-1949:

The revised Code [Federal Range Code, which interprets the Taylor Grazing Act for application on the range] *was written in its entirety by livestock men at the first* [NABC] *meeting in Denver. The Grazing Service even asked if we would rather they weren't there.* (Foss 1960)

Federal range manuals derived from this code and many other rules, regulations, and directives established by the boards over the years still govern management of public lands ranching.

Various levels of federal administration may legally overrule "advisory" board "recommendations," but such action is almost unheard of. Few dare challenge the "advice" of "the

experts." Although called "advisory," these boards in practice decide how federal grazing lands are to be administered and range "improvement" funds expended.

In **Politics and Grass** Phillip O. Foss suggests that this system "may be a formalization and legal representation of the upper strata of a rural caste system." In a random study of a grazing "advisory" board in Oregon:

The board, when asked its advice, did not feel that it was giving advice, but that it was making a decision. It was essentially correct in this belief, because the range manager had overruled the board's "decision" only once during eight years as district range manager.

Later, Foss writes:

Do these conclusions indicate that the advisory board system is "home rule on the range?" Or do they suggest the presence of a rural caste system which decentralized administration has strengthened and crystalized? (Foss 1960)

The great majority of grazing "advisory" board members are also members (usually officers) of powerful livestock associations. In fact, the boards and livestock associations are so closely interrelated, and the views expressed by each are so similar, that one could be said to represent the other. They frequently work in league with each other and the agencies, and in many cases the associations have nearly as much "recommendary" influence as the boards. Board meetings commonly are scheduled to coincide with those of livestock associations, and the two sometimes join together with or against the agencies to fight proposed grazing fee increases, livestock reductions, etc.

Livestock association leaders are especially influential in county and state politics and in the US Congress. Many associations are great bureaucracies in their own right. The Washington, DC-based National Cattleman's Association, for example, with 300,000 members, is heavily involved in government affairs, public relations, management, education, and marketing. The Public Lands Council, also based in Washington, DC (only 3 blocks from the White House), is a potent public lands ranching lobbying establishment.

The National Cattlemen's Association, Public Lands Council, American Farm Bureau Federation, Association of National Grasslands, National Wool Growers Association, Society for Range Management, National Inholders Association, People for the West, Multiple Use Land Alliance, National Live Stock Producers Association, Western Livestock Producers Alliance, Western States Meat Association, Agriculture Council of America, American Meat Institute, American Sheep Producers Council, American Sheep Industry Association, National Council of Farmer Cooperatives, National Farmers Union, National Live Stock and Meat Board, livestock "advisory" boards, state and local stock associations, coalitions, lobbyists, lawyers, pressure groups, grievance committees, the Cow Belles, public relations programs, advertising campaigns, press conferences, publications and promotions -- all these and more are sustained by the highly organized livestock industry. Funding comes in the form of dues, fees, grants, donations, and overtly or covertly trickles down through various government programs. The Western ranching establishment is capable of exerting political leverage or coming up with large sums of money to meet nearly any threat to its power or profit. Tanja Keogh, in *U.S. Predator Control -- a Legacy of Destruction*, offers a typical example:

Our experience in attempting to ban leghold traps in Nevada County [California] shows the strength of these "good old boys." When hearings on this issue were scheduled, our local Agricultural Commissioner's office and area Farm Bureau Federation, consisting of a handful of area ranchers, were able to mobilize the entire California Farm Bureau Federation, Cattlemen's and Woolgrower's Associations, their many well-paid lobbyists and attorneys, the entire staff from the ADC office in Sacramento, professors from large agricultural colleges, other Ag and "sportsmen's" groups, and ranchers from every surrounding county. (Keogh 1988)

Nevada ranchers have filed a lawsuit challenging a Forest Service management plan that attempts to rehabilitate lands damaged by overgrazing in the Humboldt and Toiyabe National Forest. The Nev. Cattlemen's Assoc., a group called Nevadans for a Practical Wilderness Policy and six individual ranchers say the agency unjustly blames livestock for deterioration of streambeds, wildlife habitat, soil and watersheds on public land.
--High Country News (5-6-89)

The judicial system also is heavily influenced by the ranching establishment. Not a few judges are stockmen, have ranching ties, or are smitten by the concept of the noble, heroic cowboy. For example, US Supreme Court Justice Sandra Day O'Connor's family (politicians themselves) owns the Lazy B Cattle Company, which controls ranching on 133,000 BLM acres -- the largest BLM grazing permit in Arizona.

Stockmen have, individually and through their livestock associations and legal representatives, further solidified their power over the years with thousands of administrative appeals and numerous protracted lawsuits and threatened lawsuits designed to privatize public lands ranching, and also to contest grazing fee increases, stock reductions, responsible management, and environmental legislation. Likewise, stockmen and their political consorts have repeatedly attacked and stalled investigations, hearings, and studies by the agencies and Congress. All of this has had

a decided psychological impact on agency personnel, intimidating and demoralizing them, often causing them to abandon responsible administration. Time and time again the ranching establishment has thwarted needed reforms.

We have allotments that need an 80 percent reduction in cattle. But we're told to ease up on the ranchers, since they're also facing a drought.
--Jim Mower, range and wildlife staff officer, Wasatch-Cache National Forest, Utah (Zaslowsky 1989)

An October 1987 BLM management study of agency fishery and wildlife biologists indicated that more than half of those responding felt they were not working at full potential. The reason most often cited was lack of management support, usually due to ranching industry pressure. They said this was evidenced by (1) failure to treat wildlife recommendations as equal to commodity interest recommendations, (2) biologist positions not seen as necessary, and (3) lack of implementation of wildlife policy, regulations, and laws. Over half of those who had left BLM said they would return if management improved, legal and regulatory policies were more consistently applied, and the multiple use principle was taken more seriously. (Culhane 1981)

The following excerpt is from the US General Accounting Office's 1988 BLM riparian restoration project report:

The livestock industry's political power and ability to influence decisions has been documented in general studies. For example, the 1987 Audubon Wildlife Report stated that the livestock industry intimidates BLM into transferring, demoting, or firing field staff who take actions that upset local interests. The study also states that the industry applies pressure to have decisions by BLM field staff overturned at upper agency levels. It concluded that such tactics not only result in the policy changes sought by the industry, but can also cause BLM personnel to be wary about making tough land management decisions. Although most of the district staff said they thought this situation had been slowly improving over the last several years, we found this attitude to exist at many of the 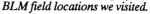 *BLM field locations we visited.*

In one district, the staff told us that the district essentially is directed by headquarters and the state office to make no decisions opposed by permittees. Further, BLM is not managing the permittees; rather, permittees are managing BLM. They gave many examples to document this situation. For instance, an area manager confronted a rancher he found cutting trees without authorization in a riparian area on BLM land and demanded the rancher halt the cutting. Soon after, the area manager was told by his district manager that word of the incident had gotten back to him as a result of the rancher's political connections. The area manager was told to apologize to the permittee and deliver the wood to his ranch.

In another instance, an area manager documented numerous instances of riparian area trespass and fence-cutting by a permittee. The area manager said that when he asked the district manager to act on the matter, the district manager stated that "he would not be a martyr to riparian [sic]." Area managers and other field staff in the district told us that it is common knowledge in BLM that management had taken adverse action against staff for trying to implement formal policy.

A biologist responsible for riparian programs in a field office told us that although BLM should be able to expect compliance on riparian management issues, the opposite is often the case. . . . He stated that BLM management has not taken action on this and many other compliance problems because they fear the political power wielded by certain permittees. . . . His concerns are based on his personal knowledge of many examples of field staff who tried to implement riparian programs against the wishes of local permittees and are harassed or transferred by management as a result. (USGAO 1988)

The basic motivating factor of any BLM official is to minimize stress in their lives. And in general, they minimize stress by not offending the cattle rancher.

--Joe Feller, BLM expert (Wheeler 1990)

At a recent meeting, a Bureau of Land Management employee made a remark that I accepted at face value when it was said; but the more I thought about it, the more absurd it became.

His comment was that he could take no strong stand on abusive public grazing practices because he had to have credibility with the permittees.

"Had to have credibility with the permittees"!

--Bryan Pridgeon, Burley, Idaho, in a letter to a local newspaper

Over the years the political power of ranchers and their lenders has often resulted in the transfer, early retirement, or dismissal of many federal employees who tried to reduce cattle numbers for the protection of the land . . . it is a rare employee who will seek grazing reductions today.

--Steve Johnson, SW Rep., Defenders of Wildlife

"I guess I didn't understand how things were supposed to work. I would 'trespass' a rancher [cite him], and right away my state director would be on the phone asking if I couldn't just take it easy on these guys.

"It finally gets to the point where you have three options, and I've seen this all over the BLM. You look for another job. Or you stick to your guns, and eventually BLM management will find another job for you -- that's what happened to me. Or you acquiesce and learn to live with it."

--A BLM range specialist in "Discouraging Words" by Jon R. Luoma (Luoma 1986)

There's an old saying in the Forest Service that if you cross a stockman, you can expect to be shipped to Siberia tomorrow.

--Jim Prunty, retired Forest Service official (Egan 1990)

From scores of conversations, telephone interviews, and letters, I have found that many agency employees believe that public lands ranching is "an economically and ecologically dubious proposition," as one Fish & Wildlife Service biologist put it. Dozens of BLM, FS, state, and other agency professionals have confided to me that public lands ranching ravages the land, that the grazing fee and other subsidies are grossly unfair, that ranchers have excessive political and social clout. But they add quickly, "Don't quote me on that," or "This is strictly off the record." As reported in a *Los Angeles Times* article, "All but a few of the dozens of BLM employees interviewed by *The Times* spoke candidly only with the assurance that their names would not be used (Stein 1989)."

An unnamed Wyoming BLM fisheries biologist writes in personal correspondence:

After 7 1/2 years with the BLM, I see the only solution to the degradation caused by grazing is total livestock removal from our public lands. Many in the BLM, at least 15%, feel the same way but only a few are willing to sign a petition saying so. Fear of reprisal is too great for most of us.

Steve Yates writes in "Windspirit of the West":

Even on national wildlife refuges and other public lands, ranchers fight reductions in grazing allotments with fervor and political clout; federal land managers find that it is flirting with professional suicide to even suggest grazing-allotment reductions, let alone actually push for them. (Yates 1988)

In 1981 Bob Buffington, director of the Idaho BLM state office and a 26-year veteran of the agency, was replaced, demoted, and eventually ushered out of BLM altogether for speaking out against overgrazing (Stein 1989). In Nevada's Toiyabe National Forest, identified by the Forest Service as the nation's most overgrazed National Forest, plans to reduce stocking rates that often exceed 80% utilization to a more "moderate" maximum 55%-65% utilization in riparian areas have met hostile opposition and a lawsuit from ranchers. The district manager and range conservationist for the Toiyabe were transferred to other Forests shortly after the controversy began. (Forest Watch 1989)

In Idaho's Sawtooth National Forest, rampant permit violations and devastating overgrazing induced Twin Falls District Ranger Don Oman to initiate moderate reforms, including the first enforcement action against cattlemen in the history of the Sawtooth -- a modest 10% stocking reduction on an allotment for 1990. Permittees and their political and agency cronies pressured Forest superiors to force Oman to accept a transfer; his refusal created a raging battle and perhaps more publicity than any confrontation yet. Some Twin Falls District permittees have threatened Oman with harm or death, and one of the largest, Winslow Whitely, even stated in the *New York Times*:

Either Oman is gone or he's going to have an accident. Myself and every other one of the permit holders would cut his throat if we could get him alone.

Asked if he was making a specific threat on the life of the district ranger, Whitely replied,

Yes, it's intentional. If they don't move him out of this district, we will. (Egan 1990)

Oman, himself raised on a Montana ranch, says that he has "been contacted by a number of people" in the Forest Service who are facing similar situations. (Williams 1991, Marston 1991)

In southwest New Mexico's Gila National Forest, ranchmen recently prevailed upon the Catron County Commission to make certain grazing cuts a violation of civil rights. Forest Service officials can be fined $10,000 and jailed for up to 10 years if they order a grazing reduction that is judged as being not related to permit violations, damage to resources, or drought-caused resource loss. (Jones 1991a)

Ranchers have always intimidated "uncooperative" agency personnel with warnings of political, economic, and social reprisal, browbeating, harassment, pounding on desks, threatening violence and, at times, physical assault. Some claim that this type of behavior is slowly decreasing. Perhaps, as expressed by *High Country News* editor Ed Marston, "the livestock industry no longer automatically gets its way." Still, oft-heard in the rural West is "These ranchers around here pretty much get what they want." Dennis Curtis of BLM's Arizona Strip District in St. George, Utah, said it plainly: "We can't tell ranchers what to do with their own allotment."

> *BLM land management policy is the product of 52 years of agency history. During the first 40 years of the BLM's history, the livestock industry was effectively the agency's sole constituency, exerting virtually unchecked influence on BLM grazing policy. . . . Over the past dozen years, the legal context for BLM range management has changed.* [emphasis added]
> --Anadromous Fish Law Memo, Lewis & Clark School of Law (Blum 1986)

In 1978, at the urging of the ranching establishment, the so-called "Public Rangelands Improvement Act" (PRIA) was passed. In addition to setting aside hundreds of millions of dollars for future ranching development, PRIA in Section 8 specified an "experimental" "cooperative management agreement" (CMA) program that essentially would transfer many BLM and FS land management responsibilities to grazing permittees, initially setting up "experimental stewardship programs." The little-known law required that the BLM and Forest Service draw up grazing allotment plans in "consultation, cooperation, and coordination" with stockmen. In other words, the law allowed the fox to guard the hen house.

In 1985, a federal district court (*Natural Resources Defense Council v. Hodel*) ruled the cooperative management program illegal and held that Congress had ordered BLM -- not private stockmen -- to administer ranching on public domain, "apparently because after years of rancher dominance of range decisions, it found substantial evidence of rangeland deterioration." Despite the ruling, BLM management basically remains controlled by permittees, while the Forest Service in its 1986 annual report stated, "Emphasis on permittees assuming more responsibility for livestock grazing management activities will be continued, which includes the maintenance and implementation of allotment management plans."

In reports on experimental stewardship, federal agencies have done their best to conceal mismanagement and environmental damage. For example, in its 1985 "Experimental Stewardship Program, Report to Congress," BLM and FS almost pompously proclaim tremendous improvements in range condition for each of 16 experimental stewardship program areas detailed in the booklet. In the grand finale -- an 18 page rundown of each individual program -- not a discouraging word is heard, nor is there any mention of the millions of tax dollars used to implement these programs.

Yet, buried near the middle of the booklet are facts hard to ignore: Only 6 (all ranchers) of 53 respondents to a public review draft on the program stated they thought range conditions on the stewardship areas had improved since the program's inception, and by a margin of 31% to 11% respondents didn't think the stewardship program was successful. Most of the remaining respondents clearly opposed the stewardship program, though the agencies' booklet tried to make it seem as if they didn't. (USDI, BLM and USDA, US 1985)

One of the strongest indications of the trend toward increased permittee control surfaced in May 1987 when BLM published a proposed rulemaking document in the *Federal Register*. The amendments were designed to prohibit livestock reductions and guarantee ranching priority over all other legally recognized multiple uses. They called for elimination of the current legal requirement (currently on the books, anyway) that livestock use must not exceed an area's carrying capacity. Further, by requiring that ranching-enhancing range developments be tried first, they relegated reduction of livestock numbers to protect other resources to a last resort action.

The proposed rules likewise deleted legal requirements that allotment management plans allocate forage among wildlife, watersheds, and other non-consumptive uses as well as livestock. They gave BLM discretion not to modify grazing permits, even if permits are in violation of land use plans. The proposed amendments resurrected the "cooperative management agreement" program, called for BLM give to up its authority to cancel grazing permits of ranchers who consistently violate federal or state environmental laws, and proposed that the penalty for grazing trespass be reduced even further. All this from BLM, not stockmen!

Numerous concerned groups and individuals protested, and the proposed rule changes have been shelved for the time being. But this was the third time these types of amendments had been proposed by BLM in 5 years.

What next? How about stockmen owning exclusive rights to water sources on public land -- even to the exclusion of wildlife? In 1981 BLM reversed its longstanding policy of filing for water rights on public rangeland, instead allowing grazing permittees (and nobody else) to file for and obtain water rights on public land in their own names. Before this, since 1926 development of public water sources by private individuals was allowed only through special use permit or cooperative agreement with BLM, which in effect permitted BLM to control the use of water. (Com. on Govt. Oper. 1986)

Former Secretary of the Interior James Watt changed all this by supporting measures which eventually were issued as an official BLM policy directive in 1981 by BLM Director Burford. The changes allowed permittees to become co-holders of water rights on public land, even when the water supply had been developed with federal funds. Two years later Burford went further and announced an updated policy allowing permittees exclusive rights to some water sources. As stated in *Federal Grazing Program: All Is Not Well on the Range*:

> *Where once it was presumed no one could monopolize the water, now BLM officials can decide on a case by case basis whether it is all right for a private individual to be given water*

rights on public land which were previously reserved for public use. The BLM is now assisting private individuals in filing for such water rights. (Com. on Govt. Oper. 1986)

A House Appropriations committee investigative staff report noted that this policy allows "permittees to have exclusive rights to this water in perpetuity, even if they were to sell off their base property and give up their grazing permit."

Western state laws already prohibited any person except a local rancher from staying or camping within a specified distance (generally 500' to 1/4 mile) of a water source for livestock.

This is not just a fight over cows and sheep. It's a fight over who controls public land.
--Rose Strickland, "Taking the Bull by the Horns" (Strickland 1990)

Basically, ranchers and agency personnel -- not the public -- decide how our public lands are managed and developed -- for ranching. *(Paul Hirt)*

The Endangered Species Act is the villain behind all this [predator reintroduction]. *We were asleep at the switch when it was passed. We saw nothing wrong with saving the whooping crane. But the list now is ridiculous. Who cares about a piping plover or a snail darter?*
--Joe Helle, Environmental Director, National Sheep Growers Association

Legislation intended to promote public lands ranching is worded, or *interpreted*, so as to seem to "mandate" universal intensive livestock grazing. Concurrently, laws enacted to protect the public and environment generally are so vaguely worded as to be malleable in the hands of the biased land management agencies whose job it is to interpret and enforce them. Utilizing this legislation to bring about even small changes in ranching administration is extremely difficult.

For hypothetical example, how could one *prove* under the Clean Water Act that grazing by 17 cattle in the upper reaches of an east-central California creek made 4 downstream hikers who drank from it sick? The Clean Water Act requires every federal agency with jurisdiction over any property or facility to comply with all substantive and procedural federal, state, and local water pollution laws regarding control and abatement. In other words, BLM and FS are supposed to follow all water pollution laws at all levels of government, including the Safe Drinking Water Act. The Clean Water Act defines pollution as "the man-made or man-induced alteration of the chemical, physical, biological, and radiological integrity of water." Livestock have obviously altered the chemical, physical, and biological integrity of surface waters throughout the West; even many federal studies acknowledge this. Yet the law is sufficiently vague so that the government is not held accountable.

Amendments to the Clean Water Act established in 1987 (Section 319) address "nonpoint" pollution (widespread pollution from multiple sources) and provided requirements and authorized resources for states to deal with the problem. Though ranching often is cited as the main source on nonpoint pollution on public land, little substantive reduction in ranching-caused water pollution has been accomplished through the Clean Water Act.

The Granger-Thye Act of 1950 gave the Secretary of Agriculture authority to issue grazing permits for up to 10 years. It also emphasized that "That nothing herein shall be construed as limiting or restricting any right, title, or interest of the United States in any land or resources." In other words, ranchers are not allowed to privatize grazing permits or public resources. Yet, for all practical purposes, they have been doing just that.

The Independent Agencies Appropriation Act of 1952 calls for federal land user fees to be "self-sustaining, uniform, and fair and equitable to the public and user." Yet numerous government reports show that the federal grazing fee is far below fair market value, that BLM and Forest Service range programs are nowhere near self-sustaining, that other users pay far more than do ranchers for the privilege of using public lands relative to the "resources" they use and the product or service they offer, and that ranching significantly detracts from other commercial and non-commercial uses of public lands.

Similarly, the federal government's "Bureau of Budget Circular A-25" of 1959 calls for users to pay "fair market value" for commercial use of federal land.

I had long suspected that "multiple" use was a semantics for making cattlemen, sheepmen, lumbermen, and miners the main beneficiaries. After they gutted and ruined the forests, then the rest of us could use them -- to find campsites among stumps, to look for fish in waters heavy with silt from erosion, to search for game on ridges pounded to dust by sheep.
--Supreme Court Justice William O. Douglas

We used to basically "rubber-stamp" our grazing permits. Now we take a closer look. And the more we learn about grazing impacts, the harder it seems to be to manage our rangelands to protect all the various resources out there.
--Inyo National Forest, California, employee (*Inner Voice* 1991)

True multiple use in the West occurred 200 and more years ago.
--Anonymous

The Multiple Use and Sustained Yield Act of 1960 directs federal agencies to manage federal lands for the multiple purposes of outdoor recreation and wilderness, wildlife and fish habitat, range, timber, land and water, and human and community development, rather than for a single use. The government expounds a lot on multiple-use -- big, fine words -- but only hollow rhetoric when government action (or lack thereof) gives priority to dominant-use ranching throughout most of the public lands West.

Two court decisions, *LaRue v. Udall (US Court of Appeals for the District of Columbia Circuit, 1963)* and *United States v. Fuller (US Supreme Court, 1973)*, established that a federal grazing permit does not create a "vested interest," and that the government may, for adequate reason, revoke a grazing permit without compensation to the permittee. Subsequently, however, the agencies have found adequate reason to revoke permits in only a handful of the most *extreme* cases.

The Wilderness Act of 1964 provided for the establishment and protection of Wilderness Areas. Federal agencies acknowledge that many Wilderness Areas are suffering from ranching damage, yet most ranching there continues at or near traditional levels.

According to the Forest Service, the National Historic Preservation Act of 1966 directs federal agencies "to identify and protect significant cultural resource properties" from "land-disturbing activities." Nothing has disturbed public land so much as ranching, yet to my knowledge the impact on cultural resources from millions of trampling livestock has never been legally questioned, while that from range development has been only rarely, and then with disillusioning results.

Section 101(b) of the National Environmental Policy Act (NEPA) of 1969 requires the federal government "to use all practical means" to "fulfill the responsibilities of each generation as trustees of the environment for succeeding generations," to "attain the widest range of uses of the environment without degradation," and to "preserve important . . . natural aspects of our national heritage." Big, fine words again, yet, according to range advocate Stuart Croghan, "The only effect the NEPA process had on the BLM and Forest Service is that now it costs the taxpayer 10 times as much for the same land abuse."

Federal agencies can write all the Environmental Impact Statements in the world. But cows will jump over the moon before they kick them off our public lands.
--Bill Marlett, Oregon Natural Desert Association

The Council on Environmental Quality, created pursuant to NEPA, has been issued guidelines on the preparation of Environmental Impact Statements (EISs). They require that impact statements be prepared even where federal actions are "localized in impact . . . if there is potential that the environment may be significantly affected." From this language, nearly every federal grazing allotment should be subject to an impact statement.

However, BLM refused to prepare grazing EISs until a 1974 lawsuit (*Natural Resources Defense Council v. Morton*) determined that BLM's ranching program is a "major federal action significantly affecting the quality of the human environment" and therefore subject to NEPA requirements. It ordered BLM to prepare EISs assessing "the specific environmental effects" of "particular permits or groups of permits" issued in each BLM district, including "the detailed analysis of local geographic conditions necessary for the decision-maker to determine what course of action is appropriate under the circumstances." As ordered, BLM has been producing grazing EISs, but these have been consistently superficial and designed to protect ranching interests. Apparently the federal government does not consider ranching impact "significant" regardless of the damage.

The renewal [of the Endangered Species Act in 1988] *also ends a four-year struggle with several senators, including several from the West, who have attempted to block the act. The Western senators wanted the act to include provisions for hunting threatened species that wander onto* [private] *ranchlands* [25% of the West].
--*High Country News*

The Endangered Species Act (ESA) of 1973 is a conservation milestone. It directs federal agencies to ensure that their actions do not jeopardize Threatened and Endangered species, and requires that they help bring about their recovery. As detailed earlier, many Threatened and Endangered species continue to decline under ranching impacts. Yet ranching on most federal land continues, mostly unchallenged and at or near traditional levels. The ranching establishment currently is lobbying strongly to weaken or overturn the Endangered Species Act.

In **Livestock Pillage of Our Western Public Lands**, Edwin G. Dimick relates that, in response to the Endangered Species Act, the Eastern Oregon BLM in the late 1970s hired a botanist to go through the motions of determining which area species were in danger and why. The resulting report was never released to the public; Dimick suggests that it may have revealed ranching-incriminating evidence. (Dimick 1990)

The Forest and Rangeland Renewable Resources Planning Act of 1974 requires the Secretary of Agriculture to develop, implement, and revise land and resource management plans for the National Forests to provide for multiple use and sustained yield. Yet, ranching pressures continue to deplete resources faster than they regenerate, and other public lands uses continue to be impaired.

The National Forest Management Act (NFMA) of 1976 restated the Multiple Use Act's mandates and specifically provided that federal land use plans prepared under NFMA must "include coordination of outdoor recreation, timber, watershed, wildlife and fish, and wilderness." The Act additionally requires the "identification of the suitability of lands for resource management" -- not blanket use wherever a use is possible, as is the case with federal lands ranching. "Suitability" is defined as "the appropriateness of applying certain resource management practices to a particular area of land, as determined by an analysis of the economic and environmental consequences and the alternative uses foregone." The federal government itself has established that much of federal lands ranching is inappropriate, i.e., economically unjustified, environmentally destructive, and/or that it conflicts significantly with other uses. NFMA regulations contain numerous other provisions which if followed verbatim would greatly curtail National Forest ranching. Yet, Uncle Sam refuses to adhere to his own mandates when it comes to cowboys. (PNFF 1987)

Before 1976 federal land management was governed by a hodgepodge of some 3000 land laws, often outdated and sometimes contradictory. The Federal Land Policy and Management Act of 1976 (FLPMA) largely overrode earlier laws and mandated responsible stewardship. It ordered federal agencies to develop land use plans "in a manner that will protect the quality of scientific, scenic, historical, ecological, environmental, air and atmospheric, water resource, and archaeological values . . . [and] that will provide food and habitat for fish and wildlife and domestic animals." The act also mandated "multiple use and sustained yield" and insisted that the nation receive fair market value for lands and resources.

Yet, FLPMA amounts to little more than an admission that the public range continues in poor condition, and that heavy subsidization must continue in order to maintain conventional levels of ranching. FLPMA has done little to improve the range. For example, overwhelming scientific evidence indicates that overgrazing continues to cause widespread and accelerated soil erosion and riparian degradation on BLM land. The US General Accounting Office, the investigative arm of Congress, conducted 11 studies of the BLM from 1986-89 and in early 1989 summarized their findings in testimony before Congress:

> For substantive progress to be made, we believe there will have to be a fundamental change in the approach of the agency responsible for day to day management of the public lands. For this to occur, BLM will have to abandon its historical identification with the interests of livestock permittees and other commercial interests. In its stead, BLM and Interior management will have to demonstrate the institutional will to effectively implement the principles of multiple-use and sustained-yield as mandated by FLPMA. Business-as-usual simply will not do if the Congress' expectations as set forth in FLPMA are to be realized.

> When I worked as a botanist for the BLM in the 1980s, one of my assignments was to inventory BLM lands for areas with outstanding biological, geological, and archaeological attributes and make recommendations to protect these sites as ACECs. After I submitted my first recommendation, I was called into my supervisor's office . . . I had to redraw my boundaries to exclude all areas that were being grazed or could potentially be grazed, or risk rejection of the entire area.
> --George Wuerthner, "How the West Was Eaten" (Wuerthner 1991)

As a result of *NRDC v. Morton*, Congress ordered BLM to prepare environmental impact statements for the land under its administration. By most accounts, BLM has failed miserably. Subsequently, FLPMA required the Secretary of the Interior to "develop and revise land use plans for all public lands based on multiple use sustained yield principles, giving priority to designation and protection of areas of critical environmental concern (ACEC)." According to a review by the Natural Resources Defense Council (NRDC), within 12 years only 2% of 332 million acres in Alaska and 12 Western states had been designated ACECs. NRDC states:

> We found that the "ACEC" program has not resulted in enhanced protection for these important areas," and, moreover, that BLM has avoided designating ACEC's in areas impacted by livestock grazing. . . . It appears to us that [BLM] has not designated sites threatened by livestock in order to avoid upsetting its powerful grazing constituency.

FLPMA also reiterated the agencies' own existing regulations requiring public participation in land management decisions. FLPMA required public input in "all decisions that may have significant impact on federal lands." Again, ranching has more impact on federal lands than any other use, yet typically the agencies trivialize its influence,

interpret these mandates as to preclude public participation, proceed without requesting public input, infinitely delay acting upon public input until interested parties give up (a favorite trick), or simply disregard what opposing public input they receive (thank you for your letter; we'll add it to our files, etc.).

The Soil and Water Resources Conservation Act of 1977 "provides for the conservation, protection, and enhancement of the Nation's soil, water, and related resources for sustained use" (USDI, BLM 1988). Public lands ranching has obviously depleted "the nation's soil, water, and related resources" (USDA, SCS 1981 and others). As usual, legalities are ignored as the agencies cater to stockmen.

The Public Rangelands Improvement Act (PRIA) of 1978 declared that the goal of range management "shall be to improve the range conditions of the rangelands . . . ." Yet, according to specialists, "The PRIA defined 'range improvement' so broadly as to be virtually meaningless."

PRIA established "multiple use councils," ostensibly to ensure diverse input from all public lands users. But, according to Jon R. Luoma in "Discouraging Words," a 1984 study by the NRDC showed

> that the environmentalist representative in the Salmon, Idaho, district was a drive-in theater owner nominated by the local Farm Bureau. In the Boise district, the "environmentalist" was a woman who had opposed establishment of a BLM protection zone for portions of the Snake River Canyon for one of the greatest concentrations of raptors in the world. In Lakeview, Oregon, the "public at large" representative was a rancher and chairman of the county Republican party. On seven of the fifty councils, ranchers were the wildlife representatives. On ten of them, ranchers were the "elected officials." On nine, ranchers represented the "public at large." On seven they represented environmental interests, on two nonrenewable-resource interests, and on another two, transportation interests. (Luoma 1986)

Stipulations in BLM grazing rules and regulations prohibit graziers from "violating any Federal or State laws or regulations concerning conservation or protection of natural and cultural resources or the environment including, but not limited to, those relating to air and water quality, protection of fish and wildlife, plants, and the use of chemical toxicants" (USDI, BLM 1978). Stockmen violate such laws not only frequently but blatantly, yet BLM and other agencies seldom take enforcement action.

Even the Taylor Grazing Act of 1934 directs the Secretary of the Interior "to preserve the land and its resources from destruction or unnecessary injury . . ." (USDI, BLM 1976) In recent major actions Congress mandated that environmental values be protected, even if BLM must sacrifice "the greatest economic return or the greatest [livestock] unit output." In 1978 Congress directed BLM to see that "multiple use" prevailed. To what end?

In 1984 Congress directed BLM to collect subleasing profits and return them to the US Treasury. Thirteen months later, the agency responded by issuing new regulations defining "subleasing" so narrowly that hardly any money has been captured. (Com. on Govt. Oper. 1986)

In 1985 Congressman Jim Weaver introduced a House bill that would have ordered BLM and FS to protect and restore ranched land under their supervision, as well as to implement a modified market value fee system and abolish grazing "advisory" boards. It was quickly quashed.

If the intent of the various environmental and public land laws was rigorously enforced, 75% of public lands ranching would be shut down.
--Rose Stickland, vice chair, Sierra Club Public Lands Committee

In recent decades, Congress has passed more than 40 laws protecting environmental quality. Many of these and scores of other laws, regulations, directives, ordinances, and court decisions (see Glustrom 1991) are intended to guarantee public participation in land use planning, fair market value for sale or lease of public resources, true multiple use, sustained yield, and environmental health. The government has at its fingertips overwhelming evidence of ranching's harmful impacts. Yet in practice, with powerful stockmen and the pro-ranching agency, judicial, and political systems deciding how they should be interpreted, enforced, or ignored, there has been little progress in any of these areas with regards to ranching.

(Julie Rechtin)

Historic users of public lands have long considered the land their own. Although they have never been successful in having title or rights to the land recognized by the federal government, ranchers have enjoyed considerable success in having federal policy tailored to meet their needs and to protect their access.
--from **Federal Lands** by Sally K. Fairfax and Carolyn E. Yale

Federal ownership or control of land is a form of communism.
--Wyoming Representative Frank Barrett, leader of grazing industry public land grab attempt in 1946

From the beginning, stockmen have been successful in resisting the agencies' modest attempts to enforce regulations and reduce livestock numbers. However, in the 1970s conservation groups won a number of court cases and Congressional battles which, *at least in theory*, would have forced the agencies to crack down on abuses.

The "Sagebrush Rebellion" was the industry's counterattack -- a bold attempt to break the agencies once and for all. It began in 1979 when the stockmen- and miner-dominated Nevada state legislature seized 49 million acres of BLM land (70% of the state) and passed an act claiming state ownership. Other western states with powerful public-lands-exploiting establishments soon followed suit -- Utah, Arizona, New Mexico, and Wyoming passed similar acts within a year. Western newspapers and television took up the cry of this "new," "revolutionary" force. In late 1979 Utah's Senator Orrin Hatch introduced a bill that would have transferred title of 200 million acres of BLM and Forest Service land west of the 100th meridian to 13 western states -- and through cheap sale eventually mostly to *ranchers'* ownership.

In early 1980 rancher Ronald Reagan declared, "I am one who supports the Sagebrush Rebellion. Count me in as a rebel." After becoming President he brought many of the Sagebrush Rebels to Washington and allowed them to set up a command post inside the Interior Department. The ringleader of the group was Joseph Coors, the Colorado millionaire beer king and rabid anti-environmentalist. Shortly thereafter, so many of Coors' followers were appointed to administration positions that they became known as Reagan's "Colorado Mafia." The infamous James Watt was named Interior Secretary when Reagan's first choice, wealthy Wyoming Governor Clifford Hansen, withdrew after learning he would have to divest himself of BLM grazing permits. Appointed to head EPA was extreme anti-government-regulation advocate and lawyer Anne Gorsuch. And made BLM Director was none other than a leader of the Sagebrush Rebellion's fight to destroy the BLM, Robert "Hereford" Burford. (Gorsuch and Burford were close, so close they later married.)

In the past, if a BLM director wanted to let the grazing interests tell him how to make decisions, he had to bother with a telephone call. Burford doesn't have to do that. He just has to ask himself.
--Johanna Wald, senior attorney, Natural Resources Defense Council

Burford is widely considered the most anti-conservation Director ever to head BLM. One of unbelievably many millionaire BLM ranchers, well-known as a trespasser of livestock, he held grazing permits to 32,000 BLM acres when nominated Director. Unlike Clifford Hansen, through complicated and sleazy legal acrobatics Burford "rearranged" his involvement in public lands ranching to avoid conflict of interest charges. The Ethics Office didn't buy it, however, and wrote, "The arrangements contemplated [by Burford] appear to leave him in retention of interests." Burford cited a special loophole in the ethics law, and the next day Interior Secretary James Watt (a ranching zealot and close personal friend), granted him a waiver. (Miller 1983)

While Director, Burford maintained direct ownership of 25% of title to 9600 acres, including the base property for BLM grazing permits, while transferring the permits to his sons. Burford explained, "The legal vehicle of two partnerships is being used to allow me to retain interest in the deeded land as an investment for future retirement." Burford signed a statement declaring "I hereby recuse myself while serving as Director of the Bureau of Land Management from making any decisions which directly affect grazing permits which I now own." Subsequent evidence strongly suggests that Burford did indeed make many decisions that benefited him regarding his sons' grazing leases and his ownership of property. (Miller 1983)

Meanwhile, "Burford's" largest parcel of public land, the Little Salt Creek Allotment near Grand Junction, Colorado, was and still is overrun with scraggly brush and cheatgrass, heavily eroded, and nearly devoid of native grass, as it has been for decades. An old livestock exclosure on the allotment contains thriving stands of lush perennial grasses. Attempts by a new BLM recruit and a few others at the local BLM office to improve the condition of the Little Salt Creek and other allotments in the area by reducing grazing pressure ended when political strings were pulled.

With Watt, Gorsuch, Burford, and their brethren at the helm, 20 years of environmental progress (relatively speaking) in the United States quickly came to a halt. As stated in "What *Really* Happened at EPA" in July 1983 *Reader's Digest*, "When Watt, Burford, and Gorsuch arrived in Washington, they knew precisely what the President wanted them to do: deregulate the environment." (Miller 1983)

And that they did. First, they staffed top levels of their agencies with ranching industry and other big business lawyers, lobbyists, public relations professionals, and such -- the very same people who had been fighting so hard against the environmental protections they were now supposed to enforce. Second, they used Reagan's budget-cutting programs as an excuse to further deregulate. Burford, in order to give fellow ranchers more power over public lands, used budget cuts to reduce the number of employees in BLM's Range Management Division and to prevent effective enforcement of grazing regulations. The effort was largely successful. In fact, James Watt was so pleased with Burford's crippling of the BLM that he proclaimed victory for the Sagebrush Rebels and stated he had become "a rebel without a cause."

Back to Hatch's bill: Though the Sagebrush Rebellion was promoted by many powerful stockmen and politicians from "the ranching states," the "rebellion" never had the widespread support claimed by its supporters. Even Arizona Governor Bruce Babbitt -- whose family holds grazing permits to much public land in the state -- called it "a land grab in thin disguise." Senator Hatch's bill, and

similar others, never reached the floor in Congress. However, the power play accomplished stockmen's main goal -- not taking outright ownership of federal lands so much as knocking down the already submissive BLM and Forest Service even further, thus enabling the industry to reap the benefits of ownership without the responsibilities. The process is delicately explained in the range textbook **Range Management**:

> *Provided that grazing privileges are maintained and grazing fees are kept reasonable it is advantageous to most ranchers for these lands to remain in federal ownership. Taxes, costs of maintaining physical structures (fences, corrals, water developments, roads), and interest in land purchase money would make grazing uneconomical for most ranchers if they were forced to buy federal grazing lands.* (Holechek 1989)

Even so, some 1 million acres of federally owned Western land *have* passed into state hands since the Sagebrush Rebellion put the pressure on.

A book was written during the Sagebrush Rebellion period expressly for the purpose of urging that BLM and FS rangelands be transferred to stockmen. **Locking Up the Range** was sponsored by Pacific Institute, a flowery-sounding, "independent, tax-exempt, research and educational" front for ranchers and other public land exploiters. The book "documents" that the federal government has "locked up" as public land hundreds of millions of acres of Western range that rightfully belong to stockmen.

The Sagebrush Rebellion is only the latest in a long string of public-land-grab attempts by the ranching establishment designed to periodically "put the agencies in their place," if not actually take the land (thus putting the agencies *out of business!*). The first came soon after gentleman rancher Teddy Roosevelt created federal forest reserves in 1891. Stockmen wanted control of the reserve lands "returned" to the states (where it never was), and thus eventually to them.

Another rebellion came during the 1920s when Western ranchers and their Congressmen, bolstered by support from President Hoover, once again tried to convince the Congress and public that the states -- thus, ultimately *ranchers* -- could better manage 200 million acres of public land than the federal government. This campaign fell apart over disagreements about methods of land transfer. Stockmen also didn't want to pay a suggested $1 per acre minimum to buy the land. (Shanks 1984)

In the mid-1940s Congressional bills introduced by Nevada Senator Pat McCarren, Wyoming Representative Frank Barrett, and Wyoming Senator E.V. Robertson (the latter a wealthy public lands rancher) would have transferred title to the vast bulk of Western federal land, including large portions of National Parks and Monuments -- *as well as rights to timber, oil, minerals, hydroelectric power and other resources thereon* -- to public lands graziers, either directly through cheap sale or indirectly via the states. The American National Livestock Association and National Woolgrowers Association formally agreed that this Texas-plus-California-sized public acreage should be offered for sale at 10 cents per acre, with ranchers having first right of purchase to the lands they held permits to graze (nearly all of it). Under increasing public protest, the schemes did not result in changes in land ownership, but they did eliminate any naive ideas the Forest Service and Grazing Service might have had about responsible management. (DeVoto

1955) Another uprising in the 1950s punished the agencies for their attempts at more responsible administration and forced them to toe the line.

Likewise, the recent Sagebrush Rebellion was successful in that the Forest Service soon backed off from many of its ranching reforms and the Bureau of Livestock Management became even more subservient. Following the "rebellion," the $2.36/AUM grazing fee dropped each year for 4 years in a row, eventually hitting $1.35/AUM, where it stayed for the next 3 years. Jay Wilson, executive vice-president of the California Wool Growers Association, sums it up succinctly, saying BLM responded to the Sagebrush Rebellion in a "positive" manner (Hartshorn 1988). Wildlife advocate Dan Dagget concurs: "They think the Sagebrush Rebellion is over and they won. No one's going to tell them what to do on their ranch [allotment]."

DK Ranch -- the private land -- is actually 3 miles down the road, which runs through National Forest the entire way and provides access to a hundred other residents.

As long as our civilization is essentially one of property, of fences, of exclusiveness, it will be mocked by delusions.
--Ralph Waldo Emerson

For more than a century, federal political establishments have remained consistently and heavily supportive of public lands ranching. The Reagan administration admittedly was more biased than most, but the Bush administration thus far has proven little different. Symbolically, on his first visit to China President Bush gave the Chinese Prime Minister a pair of cowboy boots embossed with US and Chinese flags. More recently, on his highly publicized visit to Washington, newly elected Russian President Boris Yeltsin was compelled to don for the media a large, white cowboy hat. Senate Minority Leader Bob Dole explained the gift to Yeltsin: "It's for big people and . . . for great leaders."

I asked him [BLM Director Cy Jamison] when the overgrazing on public lands will stop. He said there was no overgrazing on public lands -- at least on paper. Every allotment is within its carrying capacity.
--Sports Editor Pete Cowgill, 3-30-90 *Arizona Daily Star*

To replace rancher Bob Burford as BLM Director, George Bush appointed Cy Jamison, a country boy from the "little cowboy town" of Ryegate, Montana, a former BLM employee, and for 10 months liaison to the White House for James Watt. At the time of his appointment Jamison was an aide to ultra right-wing Republican Montana Representative Ron Marlenee (who now sits on the Interior National Parks and Public Lands Subcommittee). Both are staunch defenders of public lands ranching. Jamison is "a good choice" says Patty McDonald, Public Lands Director for the National Cattleman's Association. "We have worked with Cy on a lot of things." 'Nuff said.

Bush's nominee to oversee the Forest Service and Soil Conservation Service as Assistant Secretary of Agriculture was James Cason, ranching advocate and former Watt deputy. However, Congress rejected Cason's appointment due to mounting public opposition. The continuing Chief of the Forest Service, F. Dale Robertson, recently showed his true colors when before a conference of ranching interests he told the assembled that together they should adopt a strategy of ignoring those calling for reform of public lands ranching and expand their efforts to "increase the producers' [ranchers'] credibility." More recently, President Bush nominated Indiana hog farmer James Moseley to fill the post.

The new US Fish & Wildlife Service Director, John Turner -- a former state senator who owns a ranch in Jackson Hole, Wyoming -- is said to be a concerned wildlife advocate, though it remains to be seen if he will lower livestock from the top of the rangeland totem pole any more than his predecessors did. So far Turner seems to be doing his best to sweep ranching problems under the carpet. Bush's choice for Park Service Director was James Ridenour, a friend of Vice President Dan Quayle and whom many conservationists castigate as another James Watt. A 4-30-89 *Los Angeles Times* article states that "Although his 'mind is open,' Ridenour expressed sensitivity to the concerns of ranchers." Also appointed by Bush were Manual Lujan as Interior Secretary and Constance Harriman as Assistant Secretary for Fish, Wildlife, & Parks. Both are ranching advocates and were vocal supporters of James Watt while he was Interior Secretary.

Given public indifference, a built-in place in government infrastructure, and more or less permanent control of relevant federal, state, and local political systems, the ranching industry bureaucracy undoubtedly is one of the most impervious and enduring of any.

Phillip O. Foss, in **Politics and Grass**, summarizes his findings on stockmen's political influence:

As compared with the total population, western stockmen are few in number, but in range states they rank high in wealth, prestige, and influence. Not only are they influential in state politics but they also carry considerable weight in Congress, especially the Senate. There are few groups of comparable size, if any, which are as politically powerful as are the western stockmen. (Foss 1960)

In her book, **God's Dog**, wild horse expert Hope Ryden describes ranchers as, "unquestionably the best-organized political force in the West. Considering that they represent a rather small fraction of the total Western population, it is surprising to what extent they control state capitols, run state conventions, and send representatives to Washington."

Indeed, federal grazing permittees represent about 0.037% (or 1 out of 2727) of the population in the West and 0.0088% (or 1 out of 11,363) of all American citizens (Com. on Govt. Oper. 1986, US Dept. of Com. 1986). Writer/ecologist George Wuerthner considers Arizona:

> The state has only 3,792 livestock producers, and of these only 1,323 graze livestock on federal lands. Yet these 1,323 exercise more control over the federal lands in Arizona than do Arizona's other 3.3 million residents. (Wuerthner 1989)

High Country News publisher Bob Marston (who supports the concept of public lands ranching) states, "In practice, a rancher's political influence is roughly one hundred times greater than that of a non-rancher in the West." A conservative estimate.

The 1981 book by Paul J. Culhane, **Public Lands Politics**, though obviously intended to be a resource for commercial exploiters of public lands, indicates the extent to which ranchers influence rural politics. In 1973 Culhane conducted research in random BLM and FS administrative units in 3 geographic regions of the West. The research involved interviews with local agency officials and key interest group leaders, questionnaires sent to group leaders, and the collection of documents. From the results, Culhane extrapolates:

> The largest single category of groups was the rancher-grazing associations, with over one-quarter of all participants. When BLM advisory board members, all of whom are ranchers, are included, the importance of the livestock industry in the three regions is evident.

In fact, Culhane's statistics showed that the livestock industry had almost 2 1/2 times as many participants as any other interest group involved in local level public lands management politics (though they comprised only a small fraction of public land users). Culhane summarizes:

> Stockmen constitute the largest single category of participants in local public lands politics. They have ties to professional community [sic] (including agency professionals) through SRM [Society for Range Management]. Many local government officials in the three regions, including a number of town mayors and most county commissioners, were stockmen; almost all the irrigation groups, and many of the conservation and RC&D [Resource Conservation and Development] districts, were led by or primarily served stockmen. Finally, stockmen were the primary constituency or customer group for all the local government officials, local businessmen, and realtors in the sample, irrespective of formal affiliations with the livestock industry. (Culhane 1981)

An article in *Oregon Ike* (a publication of the Izaak Walton League) states:

> The number of stock allowed has been determined more often by the political influence of the rancher or corporation; the strength or laxity of the officials in charge; the influence of the local advisory board; its importance to the county tax structure; and the influence of the local banker.

According to Phillip Foss:

> The principal decision-makers of the federal grazing activity include the advisory board members, leaders of stockmen's associations, a small number of congressmen, and some members of the federal grazing bureaucracy. (Foss 1960)

Ronald Reagan described the late Secretary [of Commerce, Malcolm Baldrige, who died in a rodeo accident in July 1987] *as direct and unpretentious. He told of how Baldrige had ordered his staff to interrupt him for only two types of phone calls. "I was one," the President said, "and any cowboy who rang up was the other."*
--*Time* magazine

Stockmen, their "advisory" boards and associations meet regularly at ranches, with agency staff, private range pros, and/or politicians (who are often ranchers themselves) in attendance. Thick slabs of beef and calculated cowboy camaraderie assure public lands ranchers of preferential treatment. *(BLM)*

With 17 western states holding 34 seats in the Senate, there will always be enough votes to guarantee that the livestock industry's interests are not overlooked.
--Sava Malachowski, "Bloody Shame" (Malachowski 1987)

I don't think, in the final analysis, Congress has the guts to raise the [grazing] fees or radically restructure the [federal lands ranching] system.
--Gerald Hillier, Manager, California Desert District, BLM

The Western ranching establishment profoundly affects the US Congress. Many senators and representatives obtain most of their information on federal range policy from "advisory" boards, stockmen's associations, and stockmen themselves. These are no mere lobbyists; many Congresspersons consider them *the* experts and their recommendations to be imperatives. Combined with the many professional lobbyists they hire, they exert overwhelming influence.

Many Congressmen themselves are involved in public lands ranching. For example, powerful former Senator Paul Laxalt -- one of Ronald Reagan's closest friends, his 1980 campaign manager, and former Republican National Chairman -- is a northern Nevada public lands sheep rancher. Representative Joe Skeen, a southern New Mexico public lands sheep rancher, sits on the all-important House Appropriations Committee. Senate minority whip Alan Simpson is a Wyoming public lands rancher from an influential ranching family. The families of Representatives Robert Smith of Oregon, Larry Craig of Idaho, and Jim Kolbe of Arizona hold public lands grazing permits. Many others are mentioned in this book.

Most federal legislators, those in the East especially, admire the fabled, heroic Western rancher and thus provide fertile ground for ranching industry misinformation and misrepresentation. For example, livestock associations often fly in (allegedly) poverty-stricken-but-courageous-and-patriotic-to-the-end, small-time ranchers to Washington and parade them before Congressional sessions and committee meetings, especially during appropriations time. Already ranching-enamored and under pressure, politicians are moved, and subsidy approval usually is forthcoming.

Moreover, as political scientists have noted, the Congressional committee system -- *not the general Congress* -- is this country's actual decisionmaking body. Committees may be further specialized into subcommittees, which are in essence specialized mini-legislatures. Most actual legislative process occurs at these levels. Because of the specialized nature of subcommittees, few other than the lawmakers involved in the issue at hand participate in them. This is especially so with public lands ranching -- a seemingly obscure "Western" issue in which few Eastern Representatives or Senators have much knowledge or interest. They defer participation to those they perceive as "experts" -- in this case those close to the livestock industry in the West. According to the 5-23-89 *Los Angeles Times*, "This leaves BLM in the domain of lawmakers elected in rural western constituencies where cattlemen and miners usually are among the wealthiest, most influential, and politically active citizens" (Stein 1989).

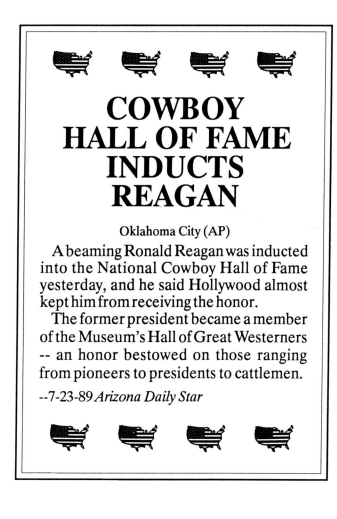

COWBOY HALL OF FAME INDUCTS REAGAN

Oklahoma City (AP)

A beaming Ronald Reagan was inducted into the National Cowboy Hall of Fame yesterday, and he said Hollywood almost kept him from receiving the honor.

The former president became a member of the Museum's Hall of Great Westerners -- an honor bestowed on those ranging from pioneers to presidents to cattlemen.

--7-23-89 *Arizona Daily Star*

In other words, the *actual* Congress that formulates legislation and dictates administration of federal ranching is composed of small groups of Congressmen from the Western "range states." Most have strong ranching ties. Many are "owned" by the grazing industry and can always be counted on to vote in its favor, or are themselves public lands ranchers. Add to this continuing contributions by livestock interests to political campaigns and political action committees. Even some US presidents were ranchers or owned ranches, including Reagan, LBJ, and Teddy Roosevelt. Is it any wonder our federal government does not tamper with the status quo?

The New Mexico Senate March 13 easily confirmed former New Mexico Cattle Growers president Bob Jones to the state Game and Fish Commission. . . . With ranchers packing the Senate gallery, the Senate Rules Committee voted 7-1 after a four-hour March 12 hearing to recommend that Jones be confirmed. The full Senate concurred the next day, voting 30-3 without debate.
--High Country News (3-30-87)

The ranching industry's power at the state, county, and local levels is even more overwhelming. Many governors have been ranchers or came from ranching families, recently including: New Mexico's Bruce King and Gary Corruthers; Arizona's Bruce Babbitt; Wyoming's Edgar Herschler, Stan Hathoway, and Clifford Hansen; Colorado's Roy Romer; Montana's Ted Schwinden; Idaho's Cecil Andrus and John Evans, and California's hobby rancher Ronald Reagan. The ranching establishment likewise includes a great many (far too many to begin to list here individually) state legislators, state board and commission members, county supervisors, county board members, game & fish officials (*most* Western game & fish commissioners have ranching backgrounds), sheriffs, judges, small town mayors, and other state, county, and local officials.

(Unknown)

The influence of this political octopus is so extensive throughout every relevant sector of government that some say the industry has its own "special private government." According to Phillip Foss, "The special private government attaches itself to most of the trappings and authority of the general public government and very likely the public assumes that it is in fact an integral part of the general public government" (Foss 1960).

Because of all this, rural areas of the West are said to be "overrepresented" (proportionately) in state legislatures and the US Senate. If elected and appointed in proportion to their small numbers, ranchers would comprise less than 1% of Western local, county, state, and federal politicians representing rural areas, while public lands ranchers would comprise 1 among hundreds of these officials. Only 3% of Wyoming's residents are employed in all agriculture, yet they -- mostly ranchers -- make up 30% of the state's legislators. (Duncan 1987) About 1% of Montana's 1 million residents are ranchers, yet stockmen compose approximately 1/3 of politicians in the state.

Though no study I am aware of has documented figures, it seems likely that 1/5 to 1/3 of all politicians in or representing the rural West are ranchers, with probably most being public lands ranchers. Rural Westerners in most areas *expect* many, or even most, of their political representatives to be ranchers. It isn't unusual to have one's county supervisor, state representative and governor, Congressional representative, and Senator all be stockmen. And most non-rancher politicians are from ranching families or are associated with influential ranchers.

Probably only the real estate business rivals politics as a stronghold of ranching interests. Again, is it any wonder that public lands ranching continues unhampered?

Welfare ranchers learned an important political lesson long ago. They learned that a loud mouth overrides any amount of scientific evidence in the eyes of a politician.
--Stuart Croghan, public lands advocate

Public lands ranching has long been a political octopus, its tentacles reaching into every policy-making body that might control exploitation of the land -- state governments, Congress, and federal agencies.
--Jon R, Luoma, "Discouraging Words" (Luoma 1986)

(1) Ranchers and their private supporters, (2) land managing agencies, (3) "advisory" boards, (4) stockmen's associations, and (5) politicians and political structures -- each of these by themselves is a powerful public ranching bureaucracy. The close collaboration between all 5 forms a seemingly invincible combination greater than the sum of its component parts. It is difficult to comprehend the subtle-yet-immense political power exerted by the ranching establishment over the rural West. Thus, the effort to end public lands ranching is also a struggle for political justice.

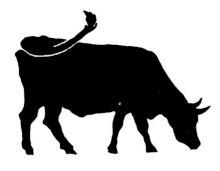

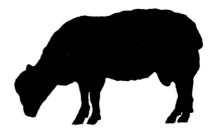

Publications and Public Relations

Put simply, it is not financially, politically, or socially advantageous to produce literature confronting the ranching imperative. And few people are inclined or able to spend months or years of their life on a major work almost guaranteed to make enemies and produce little or no income. The same holds true for audio, video, and other forms of communication. Consequently, most of what we see, read, and hear is heavily biased to favor public lands ranching. That's what sells, pays, and garners social esteem.

Various federal, state, and county agencies put out an incredible number and variety of livestock-oriented leaflets, folders, papers, pamphlets, periodicals, bulletins, brochures, booklets, and books. Nearly all of these publications are available to stockmen "free of charge" -- that is, courtesy of the taxpayer.

Their authors understand the unwritten rules and guidelines designed to protect the ranching industry and the agencies' self-serving involvement in it. Most of this literature is loaded with hollow rhetoric, misrepresentation, and outright falsehoods, along with plentiful breast-beating bullshit.

When the word "overgrazing" is found at all in government publications, it is almost always in the *past* tense. "Multiple use" is used nearly as a synonym for livestock ranching. The words "livestock" or "range management" in a sentence are commonly accompanied by words like "benefit wildlife" or "protect watersheds." Public lands ranching is a "developing science" with glorious potential. By semi-official decree, the word "desertification" is no longer used by the federal government in relation to the Western range. Public lands ranchers are now "producers" -- a word with only positive connotations. Ranching developments have been called "range improvements" for decades, and now the agencies have even taken to calling them "range accomplishments." And so forth. (Send for USDA's *Livestock Grazing Successes on Public Range -- USDA 1989* in bibliography.)

Government ranching-related publications.

Be ye not deceived.
--Holy Bible

Visit any large Western university library and you will find aisles lined with hundreds of publications, government and private, geared toward ranching. The periodicals room contains a dozen different livestock journals, magazines, and newsletters. And, of course, you can pick from *thousands* of fictional and "non-fiction" Westerns -- romanticized tales of cowboys and ranchers in the Old and New West. The authors of this literature are well paid and appreciated for their work.

At this same library you will find many publications on public land use, environment, science, politics, special interests, and even ranching that discuss uncomplimentary aspects of Western ranching, some suggesting modest reforms. Only a small handful do so in detail, and only 3 sizable writings encompass public lands ranching as a whole (see bibliography).

United States
Department of
Agriculture

Forest Service,
Pacific Southwest
Region

Los Padres
National Forest

1989-90 Accomplishment Report

Los Padres National Forest

The stockmen seem to hope that by improved public relations methods they may be able to secure additional appropriations for range improvement without losing their present autonomy in the grazing districts and without raising their grazing fees.
--Phillip O. Foss, **Politics and Grass** (Foss 1960)

These 2 photos are taken from the Forest Service pamphlet *Livestock Grazing Successes on Public Range*. The top photo portrays a barren and degraded riparian area; the bottom photo shows the same scene 10 years later as mostly greenery. We are told that this was accomplished through improved grazing management "with no reduction in livestock numbers." A close look at the top photo, however, reveals *patches of snow* at upper left (indicating that the photo was taken in winter, when vegetation would be barren of foliage), and that much of the woody vegetation had recently been cut as well. This propaganda piece is found in every BLM and Forest Service office in the West. The Public Lands Council helped produce the handout, but contributed only a token $500 to its cost. *(USFS)*

Produced in partnership by:

The Forest Service, Bureau of Land Management, and Public Lands Council

Photos and graphics in government publications portray what the ranching establishment wants us to see -- luxuriant, grass-filled meadows grazed by fat, healthy cattle and sheep, before and after shots of the most successful range restoration projects, the best grass seedings at their height of productivity, wild animals drinking from stock tanks,

ranchers and range managers smiling and shaking hands, and romantic scenes of cattle round-ups and windmills silhouetted against sunsets. These are not selected randomly, but are carefully chosen or created to showcase ranching and its government bureaucracies in the best possible light. In these times of increasingly professional, more effective manipulation of public opinion, the agencies consciously avoid portraying embarrassing situations. For instance, in a recent conversation with BLM's Public Affairs office in Washington, DC, in response to a request for photos of BLM overgrazing an official told me, "We used to get a lot of overgrazing photos [from state and local BLM offices] in the 50s and 60s, but no one sends us the overgrazing photos anymore."

The cover of a BLM pamphlet depicts a domestic sheep posed in noble fashion on a mountain top, *a la* bighorn.

While some government productions (such as the "Operation Respect" pamphlet portrayed on the following page) are comically amateur, most read more like professionally produced insurance company promotion pamphlets or travel agency brochures. Like Pepsi Cola, Merrill-Lynch, and IT&T, government agencies have become public relations specialists. They know what drives the American public, what it wants, what it fears, how to influence opinion and minimize opposition. For instance, 27 Montana Forest Service staffers recently completed 2-week marketing courses at Montana State University because, according to one, "our credibility with the public is suspect."

Shortly after these Brahman cattle were released onto this very lightly grazed, well-grassed Texas range, SCS took publicity photos. *(SCS, USDA)*

I would have liked here to examine the contents of various publications, but space does not allow. Suffice it to say that it behooves the prudent reader to read between the lines.

The ranching industry itself also keeps the public and the politicians snowed with a plethora of TV spots, radio commercials, billboard messages, and print ads (as if these media aren't already saturated with cowboy worship). For the 20th anniversary of Earth Day, the National Cattlemen's Association and Beef Promotion and Research Board ran a full-page ad in *The New York Times* proclaiming in large, bold letters **EVERY DAY IS EARTH DAY FOR AMERICAN CATTLEMEN** and claiming all sorts of related environmental benefits to the Western range.

NEW MEXICO

The New Mexico Cow-Belles and their ranching families, the Bureau of Land Management, USDA Forest Service, New Mexico Department of Game & Fish, and the New Mexico State Land Office join together to ask you to be our good neighbor.

The industry sponsors promotional presentations and exhibits at public schools, as well as at civic and private functions. It endears the public to ranching with productions at fairs, parades, holiday celebrations, and other special events. To further increase its palatability, the industry has begun placing women in high-profile, public relations positions. It holds press conferences in which these women stand before the cameras with baby lambs in their arms, asking for more predator "control."

A recent TV news broadcast included a story on how last summer's high rainfall had finally relieved hard-pressed local ranchers from relentless drought. A couple of particularly scruffily dressed cowboys were shown driving some cows out onto the open range, while the reporter explained the tough times they'd been having for so long before the rains. You couldn't help but pity these poor, hard-working fellows and wish them the . . . but hey . . . what's that name again? I know him; he's no destitute, dusty cowpoke, but an extravagant, multi-millionaire grazier -- powerful, arrogant, a trespasser of livestock and builder of unauthorized ranching developments on public land. The public will eat it up!

How many newscasts misrepresenting wealthy public lands ranchers as dusty, downtrodden cowpokes have I seen recently? Or staged photos of little boys with oversized cowboy hats on horseback alongside their rancher daddies in newspapers and magazines? Or TV commercials with 3-year-old cow-babies swinging lassos?

And as if all this weren't enough, every time someone dares use their First Amendment rights to express their opposition to public lands ranching, the industry immediately sounds the alarm and activates its highly organized defamation and misinformation network. The unfortunate individual is soon cowering under a barrage of disparaging letters, telegrams, and phone calls from rancher good guys and their loyal supporters throughout the West.

EVERY DAY IS EARTH DAY FOR AMERICAN CATTLEMEN

The American cattleman is still hard at work out there. We're out West, down South, up North, back East and in the Midwestern heartland. Sometimes we wear a 10-gallon hat with a suit and tie . . . ride a pickup truck instead of a horse. We've even traded our dusty ledger books for computers. But some things haven't changed — we still do business on a handshake. And we still work hard to care for the land that is our livelihood and our future.

Cattlemen own or manage more land in this country than any other industry. We raise our cattle primarily on the hundreds of millions of acres of U.S. land unsuitable for crop production. But that land produces renewable resources like grass and forage. We use those resources, as well as feedgrains and harvested roughage not edible by humans, to produce a healthful, nutritious food for humankind. We are stewards of the miraculous cycle of *sun* to *grass* to *cattle* to *human food*.

We take our responsibility for natural resources seriously. We invest millions

of our own dollars every year to maintain and improve the land and water we use. It's an investment in food for the 21st century . . . and an investment in future generations of cattlemen.

In the process of raising cattle, we also help Mother Nature. Cattle grazing helps strengthen and replenish vegetation — it's a lot like mowing your lawn.

Wildlife also benefits from our care of natural resources. Cattle grazing keeps plant life fresh and succulent, providing a healthy habitat for the many species of wildlife which share our lands. And when nature isn't kind — when there are blizzards, windstorms, fire or drought — we help minimize nature's damage.

Cattlemen are partners with the land — we live and work close to the Earth every day. We're proud to celebrate the 20th Anniversary of Earth Day, April 22 — because **every day** is Earth Day for American Cattlemen.

National Cattlemen's Association
The Beef Promotion and Research Board

The beef quality grade "USDA Good" was renamed "USDA Select" to present a more positive image for this grade of beef . . . . The decision to change the name was made in response to a petition from the Public Voice for Food and Health Policy, supported by other consumer and health organizations, as well as the National Cattlemen's Association and the American Meat Institute.
--Report of the Secretary of Agriculture, 1987

Other Public Ranchlands

Although comprising 85% of all grazed government land (excluding Indian reservations), BLM and Forest Service holdings are just 2 of the many kinds of public ranchlands in the US. Various other agencies administer government land for stockmen's benefit.

We thought you'd like to see this

Bureau of Land Management

PUBLIC LANDS ☆USA☆

(Bob Dixon)

U. S. DEPARTMENT OF THE INTERIOR
Bureau of Land Management
Washington D.C. 20240

**An ad we might see . . .
If there was truth in advertising.**

● Wilderness

As an apologist for the ranching community, I believed that we environmentalists only had to explain "wilderness" to ranchers. Then we could unite to combat the common threat from mining, dam construction and summer-home subdividers. But I was absolutely wrong.
--Randy Morris, Committee for Idaho's High Desert

Wilderness Areas are administered by 4 parent federal land managing agencies -- Forest Service, BLM, National Park Service, and US Fish & Wildlife Service -- under authority of the Wilderness Act of 1964 and FLPMA of 1976. Thus far, about 28 million acres, less than 4% of the 11 Western states, has been officially designated Wilderness. In the lower 48, about 32 million acres, or under 2%, is Wilderness. (USDI, GS 1987, US Dept. of Com. 1986) For every acre of Wilderness in the Lower 48 at least 2 other acres are under asphalt or concrete (Shanks 1984). Still, approximately 10% of the contiguous 48 states remains "wild," as defined by Section 2(c) of the 1964 Wilderness Act (Foreman 1989).

Unfortunately, this remaining relatively wild land is falling quickly to exploitation, including ranching. According to Howie Wolke in **The Big Outside**, wilderness on US public land is disappearing at the rate of at least 2 million acres per year. Outside Alaska, few places in the US are more than 10 miles from a *constructed* road, and no place is more than 21 miles. (Foreman 1989)

The National Wilderness Preservation System is this country's remaining wildest country -- a last refuge for wildlife and human interaction with Nature (see Driver 1985 for a thorough discussion of Wilderness significance). Yet, essentially it amounts to little more than a collection of the areas least desirable for human occupation and exploitation -- inaccessible areas, rocks and ice, steep mountainsides, rugged canyonlands and badlands, barren deserts, and swamps. Conversely, the most productive, level, accessible lands were taken as private property, mostly by ranchers and farmers, and are now the most abused. In short, public lands are the leftovers and Wilderness is the leftovers of the leftovers.

Cattlemen from Cochise and Graham counties have persuaded Rep. Morris K. Udall, D-Ariz. ["the environmental congressman"], to back down on his proposal to add 55,000 acres to the Galiuro wilderness northwest of Willcox. . . . Udall called the proposal "unwise" and added, "I recognize the importance of the cattle industry in Southern Arizona and I will not suggest passing a bill which would put obstacles in the way of a healthy cattle industry."
--*Tucson* magazine (9-1-77)

The Wilderness Act of 1964 was written and legitimatized largely under supervision of the ranching industry; opposition from powerful stockmen might otherwise have killed it. To gain the industry's support, wilderness advocates had to settle on the following language in the enabling legislation:

Section 4(d)(4)(2) . . . the grazing of livestock where established prior to the effective date of this Act, shall be permitted to continue subject to such reasonable regulations as are deemed necessary by the Secretary of Agriculture.

Subsequently, regulations generally have not been considered "reasonable" if they conflict with ranching interests.

In other words, ranching has continued basically unhampered in most areas even after designated Wilderness. In fact, roughly half of Western Wildernesses are ranched; most of the remainder are essentially unranchable. And, as with nearly all public lands, trespass grazing in Wildernesses is rampant; especially since their remoteness makes detection unlikely.

The Wilderness Act also contains language allowing predator "control," even from helicopters, and the construction and maintenance of water developments, fencing, and all other range developments deemed necessary for the continuance of ranching at traditional levels. Regulations allow ranchers to maintain and in some cases construct ranching developments with heavy equipment, leaving many roads cherry-stemmed into Wildernesses. The Act also mandates continued possession of base properties; therefore many Wildernesses contain private ranchlands in, or cherry-stemmed into, their boundaries, and access to them -- with pickups, bulldozers, and whatever -- is assured. (Some ranchers have profited handsomely by selling excess adjacent private lands at inflated prices for addition to Wilderness Areas.)

The main effect the Wilderness Act had on ranching was in prohibiting the use of motorized equipment within Wilderness, except as above and for "emergency purposes." Supplying feed to starving livestock, pumping water to thirsty animals, and rescuing endangered animals have been interpreted as emergencies, and some ranchers are known to drive into Wildernesses despite the law. However, the ban on motorized vehicles has had minimal impact on most ranching operations in these areas because most Wilderness is inaccessible to vehicles in the first place. Even so, many permittees vehemently oppose Wilderness ostensibly because ranching is not practical without the use of motorized vehicles.

... in some circumstances, the presence of livestock may even add to the wilderness experience.
--M. Rupert Cutler, Assistant Secretary of Agriculture for Conservation, Research, and Education (USDA, USDI, CEQ 1979)

Each Spring I pack up my gear and, with my burro, head for the trails.... The map's [of Marble Mountain Wilderness, California] *legend showed that pasturing my animal while visiting these sensitive meadows "might cause permanent damage," so we carried feed. But upon arriving I found the meadows and surrounding forest permeated with cow dung. Every water source for miles was contaminated by the cows, which defecate and urinate as they wallow in the water through the heat of the day.*
There were but few wildflowers in this area -- mostly poisonous species -- yet wildflowers were abundant and luxurious on the ungrazed ridge I found....
--Bill Lewinson, Hyampom, California, in a letter to a local newspaper

I have recently returned from a backpacking trip to the Carson-Iceberg "Wilderness" Area, along the Pacific Crest Trail, south of Ebbetts Pass.... crawling with cattle.... wherever I went... there they were.... This is no Wilderness, but a Ranch.
--David Loeb, San Francisco, California, in a letter to the Toiyabe National Forest Supervisor

I have recently returned from an extended wilderness trip to southern Utah ... incredible amount of overgrazing ....
During my two months of exploring Utah I did not find any canyon or Wilderness Area where cattle were not or had not been present.
--Michael Areson, Santa Cruz, California, in a letter to Utah federal agencies

Aside from commercial guide services, ranching is the only permitted permanent commercial general use of designated Wilderness Areas. In most of the areas where it occurs, ranching has degraded Wilderness and the Wilderness experience far more than any other factor -- in many areas more than all other human influences combined.

For instance, in the alpine Big Blue Wilderness of southwest Colorado, thousands of sheep graze through the summer, even above 13,000' elevation. The shepherds camp there for months at a time, as only stockmen are allowed to do. You can hear them shooting at

Cattle overgrazing an aspen-fir forest in Gros Ventre Wilderness, Wyoming. According to writer/ecologist George Wuerthner, in Wilderness "Livestock grazing causes far more environmental damage than all human recreation use combined." *(George Wuerthner)*

coyotes and other "varmints" most nights, their shots booming out like cannons through the crisp, clear, high-mountain air. Irate hikers and backpackers have renamed the area "The Big Blue Barnyard."

Sheep grazing alpine meadows in Absaroka-Beartooth Wilderness, Wyoming. *(George Wuerthner)*

In much of America's first Wilderness Area, the Gila in southwest New Mexico, cattle grazing is so severe that the groundcover has been reduced to bare dirt. We lived in this area for a few years, only half a mile from the Wilderness boundary. In extensive foot travel in the immediate area, I found little difference in ranching impact between the designated Wilderness and the adjacent National Forest. During one walk, I discovered miles of new fence. A wide swath of trees and brush had been cleared, scores of trees had been cut for fence material, others were girdled with barbed wire, and waste materials were scattered about.

In northern Utah's Mount Naomi Wilderness, helicopters skim along the tree tops as gunners blast away at coyotes, as they have done legally for 15 years. In Arizona's rugged Superstition Wilderness east of Phoenix, cattle ravage what few riparian areas remain. In Northern California's Trinity Alps and Marble Mountain Wildernesses Areas, summer herds of cattle turn verdant glacial meadows into closely cropped, trampled quagmires. In most of Southern California's dozen scattered coastal range Wildernesses, ranching degrades what is left of California condor wild habitat. In many northern Rocky Mountain Wilderness Areas, sheep and cattle

Rutted cattle trails, Trinity Alps Wilderness, California. *(Bill Lewinson)*

ranching harms high mountain meadows, competes with native wildlife, and destroys predators, including the wolf and grizzly. With unintentional ambiguity, Jerry Holechek relates in **Range Management**:

> Because of esthetics and its fragility, large tracts of alpine tundra have been turned into wilderness areas. Presently, this area is grazed primarily by sheep that are herded. (Holechek 1989)

> . . . that particular allotment is called the Bull Springs Allotment [in central Arizona's Mazatzal Wilderness]. A total of 160 cattle graze yearlong on approximately 32,000 acres. . . . We will in developing our management plan address these [riparian destruction] issues and try to solve them within the guidelines that Congress has set for us concerning development of ranges found within Wilderness Areas. Hopefully we will solve some of these problems associated with cattle on this allotment without having to build too many new fences which in turn can be offensive to some wilderness users.
> --Stephen L. Gunzel, District Ranger, Tonto National Forest, personal correspondence

Ranching industry pressure usually is an important consideration in creating Wilderness Areas. Rather than protecting whole ecosystems, many Wilderness boundaries simply include "worthless" areas and exclude the more productive ranching areas. If not for opposition from permittees, the 90,000-acre Paria Canyon-Vermillion Cliffs BLM Wilderness Area on the central Utah-Arizona border could easily have contained the 100,000-acre Paria Plateau instead of only the rugged canyons and cliffs surrounding it. NPS's Craters of the Moon Wilderness Area in central Idaho might have encompassed large portions of the surrounding Snake River Plain, which is largely undeveloped and has no commercial use other than ranching. The boundaries of Arizona's Coconino National Forest's Wet Beaver, West Clear Creek, and Fossil Springs Wilderness Areas conform almost perfectly to the rims of deep, steep-walled canyons so as not to include any upland grazing areas; and, as with many Wildernesses, their boundary lines were carefully drawn to exclude heavily grazed riparian bottomlands. A million-acre Wilderness could probably be established in southwest Wyoming's Red Desert and southwest Idaho/southeast Oregon/northern Nevada's Owyhee country, among many other ranching areas. Dave Foreman writes in **The Big Outside** that "Vast areas of the Great Basin and Southwest could be designated Wilderness were it not for the livestock industry" (Foreman 1989).

> With support from non-ranchers, the BLM has recommended several Wilderness Areas for the Owyhee; but bowing to pressure from local ranchers, almost all proposed areas include only the bottoms and sides of the major river canyons cutting through the plateau, leaving the flatlands out of BLM recommendations.
> --George Wuerthner, "The Owyhee Mountains, Range Abuse and its Ecological Effects" (Wuerthner 1986)

Wilderness Study Areas (WSAs) are large undeveloped areas of public land being considered for Wilderness. If found suitable, they are added to the National Wilderness Preservation System; if not, they are released to "multiple use" -- chiefly commercial exploitation. Their suitability is determined by the federal agencies after study of their natural characteristics and input from the public and commercial interests. In practice, Congress passes Wilderness legislation based largely on agency recommendations.

The hundreds of WSAs in the West encompass many millions of acres. Most are ranched, many heavily, and industry resistance has prevented and will prevent many from being designated Wilderness. *Tens of millions* of additional acres did not qualify for WSA status because ranching development spoiled their wild character.

Some ranchers intentionally blade roads into WSAs so they won't qualify for Wilderness. In southern Utah's Capitol Reef National Park, BLM is building new range developments with motorized vehicles in an area recommended for Wilderness. Charlie Watson, director of the National Public Lands Task Force, reports on ranching degradation in the glaciated, high-mountain Blue Lake WSA in northwest Nevada:

> *Startling photographic evidence was brought back this summer, by an expedition headed by Prof. Ross Smith (Univ. of Nevada/Reno), showing that (1) Blue Lakes basin had myriad new "cow trails" over fragile slopes, (2) that Outlaw and Hollywood Meadows had been "trashed" by overgrazing cows, and (3) that vital Leonard Creek Lake's entire shoreline had been reduced to a mud wallow.*

> *What about environmental extremists who want to steal your grazing land out from under you and lock it up as wilderness . . . or a national park . . . or riparian area?*
> --from Idaho Cattle Association promotion letter

On the whole, ranchers have been the most vehement, persistent, and (along with the timber industry) powerful opponents of Western Wilderness. For instance, 6 Nevada permittees currently are suing the Forest Service, saying that plans for the Toiyabe and Humboldt National Forests call for too much Wilderness. The Idaho Cattle Association has a "formal policy of opposing all additional Wilderness," and fights bitterly any attempt to protect Idaho public lands as Wilderness. In October 1984, the Western states Farm Bureaus, Cattlemens Associations, and the National Wool Growers Associations met in Salt Lake City. Here are excerpts from a statement on Wilderness adopted by the delegates:

- Any wilderness legislation adopted by Congress should include . . . language that specifically authorizes timely use of motorized-mechanized equipment in wilderness areas to allow graziers and the management agency to care for livestock, range improvements, fences and to control predators.

- Exclude wild and scenic rivers.

- Provide for increased grazing allocations whenever range conditions allow such increases.

- Provide control of noxious weeds, insects and diseases where they pose a threat to adjacent lands.

- In a good-faith effort, we will continue to work vigorously to modify these restrictions, and to minimize additional wilderness areas . . . .

> *The selection of wilderness is a necessary part of proper range use, but the selection must be made by reasonable, practical criteria, not by blind emotion, like a child running through a toy store with his father's credit card.*
> --Jeanne W. Edwards, Nevada public lands rancher [Note: At the time of Edwards' quote -- 1988 -- *less than 0.1%* of Nevada was designated Wilderness.]

> *I don't think there is integrity to wilderness without addressing livestock grazing. It's antithetical to what wilderness is.*
> --Andy Kerr, Conservation Director, Oregon Natural Resources Council (Durbin 1991a)

Public lands ranchers often complain bitterly of how "the government is locking up all the land in Wilderness Areas." They grumble about Wilderness restrictions, some declaring with facetious machismo, "We'll end up having to put diapers on our cows." Many currently are clamoring for more vehicular access, new range developments, even stocking increases in Wilderness.

Meanwhile, this group grazes 73% of all publicly owned land (41% of the West) and is subsidized with 2 billion tax and private dollars annually, continues ranching much of the 4% of the West now called Wilderness, degrades this land more than anyone, and is one of the main reasons America is forced to protect natural areas as Wilderness in the first place.

Range expert Randy Morris writes, ". . . what sort of wilderness do you have when the dominant ungulate of the ecosystem is the range cow?" A Wilderness Area with ranching is **not** a true wilderness.

> *A coalition of seven Oregon environmental groups has unveiled a proposal to designate 6 million acres in Eastern Oregon managed by the Bureau of Land Management as wilderness, national parks, preserves, monuments, and wildlife refuges. . . . The main sticking point in the* [proposed Oregon High Desert Protection Act] *appears to be its suggestion that livestock grazing be phased out over a 10-year period on all federal lands designated as wilderness, preserves, national wildlife refuges, or wild and scenic river corridors.*
> --Kathie Durbin, "High Desert Wilderness Plan Offered" (Durbin 1991a)

Stockmen have also more than any other group blocked potential scenic and natural areas, state parks, Wild and Scenic Rivers, National Parks and Monuments, and other protective designation. And since (to maximize use of forage and browse) the West's thousands of base properties are strategically dispersed throughout the West, stockmen, by arguing for the "sanctity" of private property, have had great leverage to extinguish plans for protected areas. Similarly, as legal owners of 25% of the West, stockmen are the strongest voice against public acquisition of private land for environmental protection. And, if not for historic dubious acquisition by stockmen, many private lands in the West would now be public.

If public lands ranching was terminated and all ranching roads were closed, probably an additional **1/3 or more** of Western public land (more than 100 million of over 300 million acres) could qualify for Wilderness designation. For example, roughly half of Nevada is public land significantly impacted only by ranching and, if not for ranchers' stranglehold, most of this could be designated Wilderness.

If private ranching in the West was ended, another 150 million or so acres, including many of the West's best riparian areas, could eventually be restored. In all, ending ranching could probably free about **1/3 of the West** to become designated or de facto wilderness! Doing so would reduce US beef production by only about 10%, and only minimally affect other human use in that area.

Cessation of grazing on private land outside the 11 Western states could free an additional *200 million* or so acres. Eastern pasture could then grow back into forest or grassland wildlife habitat; parts of it could be used for more efficient food production. Additionally, if all US livestock feed production were replaced by plant food production for humans, *more than 40% of US cropland* -- roughly 170 million acres -- could be restored to environmental health, with no reduction in US food supply. In other words, about 370 million acres of the most fertile land in the US could be released from food production -- *with no loss of food or jobs*. That is, the same number of workers could grow an equivalent amount of food on vastly less land. (Robbins 1987 and US Dept. of Com. 1986)

Approximately half of the former tallgrass prairie of the Midwest could be turned into immense Wildernesses or National Parks and restocked with native wildlife. Large portions of California's Central Valley could be returned (eventually) to its native vegetation, elk, pronghorn, fish, reptiles, insects, waterfowl, badgers, foxes, and grizzlies. Half of Utah's irrigated riparian bottomland could grow cottonwoods, willows, grasses, flowers, and other wildlife, rather than alfalfa, clover, and livestock grains.

In all, replacing livestock food production (including cropland used to grow livestock feed) with plant food production for humans conceivably could free about 620 million acres, or **33% of the US outside Alaska**, for other use, or non-use, or Wilderness, again, with no reduction in US food supply. Not a likely scenario, admittedly, but *the potential is there, and the means are available*.

Throughout the West, public lands ranchers are the most vocal and militant lobby against environmental protection and wilderness designation.
--Dave Foreman, leading Wilderness expert, co-author of **The Big Outside** (Foreman 1989)

● National Grassland

When many years ago I first heard those words, they brought to mind vast open spaces where buffalo roamed free amid tall grasses blowing in the Midwestern breeze. I fantasized wildflowers in abundance, huge prairie dog towns, few roads and fewer fences. I envisioned National Grasslands as the grassland version of National Parks.

When I first visited a National Grassland, I couldn't figure out where it was. Where the map indicated National Grassland seemed no different than the rest of the over-grazed prairie we had been driving through. They are National Grasslands in name only, for they closely resemble the overgrazed, overmanaged, intensively fenced and developed private land around them. A more appropriate name would be Special Federal Ranchlands.

National Grasslands are administered by the US Forest Service, and are largely Dust Bowl lands "rescued" by USDA and added to the USFS System in 1954. Nineteen NG's cover 3.8 million acres, mostly on the Great Plains; well over a million acres are in the 11 Western states. Most National Grasslands are a confused patchwork of federal, private, and state lands, making administration and enforcement of permit conditions and grazing regulations difficult.

Moreover, administration, permit issuance, and recordkeeping on National Grasslands are all formulated by grazing associations; they sign "agreements" with the Forest Service, which has "oversight" responsibilities. In essence, National Grassland permittees are even more self-regulating than BLM and FS permittees, though no less heavily subsidized.

National Grasslands never had an established grazing fee; each grazing association pays a different fee. In 1987, 1479 NG permittees paid from $0.46-$2.74/AUM. Through the Conservation Practices outlined by Title III of the Bankhead-Jones Farm Tenant Act of 1937, National Grasslands permittees are allowed to deduct the claimed value of their contributions to range developments and even administration from their grazing fees. (Tittman 1984) The situation invites corruption, taxpayer ripoff, and land abuse.

The grasslands are rich and varied ecosystems. But when all the average tourists see is miles of grazed land with miles of cows and cowpies, they think -- how boring! . . . . We get sick and tired of driving all over the National Grasslands and the thing we see most of is cows and cowpies!
--Mr. & Mrs. C.J. Bishop, Littleton, Colorado, in a letter to the Forest Service

• National Wildlife Refuge

Cattle grazing in Red Rock Lakes National Wildlife Refuge, Montana. *(George Wuerthner)*

National Wildlife Refuges (NWRs), administered by the US Fish & Wildlife Service (FWS), are the only federal lands in the US where wildlife has officially been given higher priority than recreational and commercial activities. Federal law states that no recreational or commercial use shall be permitted on these lands unless the Secretary of the Interior determines that these activities are compatible with the primary purposes for which Refuges are established. Though most are basically waterfowl refuges (commonly known as "duck factories"), NWRs are nonetheless the most important system of wildlife reserves in the US.

Still, 156 of the 368 NWRs in the 17 Western states and the Pacific Islands allow commercial livestock grazing and/or haying (Mollison 1989). A report from a comprehensive study conducted by Cornell graduate student Beverly I. Strassmann reveals that in 1986 about 1400 permittees grazed cattle on 2,432,300 acres and harvested hay (sometimes using irrigation) on almost 30,000 acres, mostly in the West (see Strassmann 1983 and 1983a). About 70% of this acreage was in 3 states -- Montana, Nevada, and Oregon. Additionally, during drought years FWS sometimes opens ungrazed Refuges or portions of Refuges to "emergency haying" for livestock.

Though ranched lands represent only a small portion of the 88 million acres in the National Wildlife Refuge System, *they comprise 77% of all Refuge land that can be used for ranching.* The remaining ranchable land is protected by constraints of laws like the Endangered Species Act or by economics. Strassmann reports that total AUMs grazed in 1980 were 374,849, or 41% more than reported by FWS. (Strassmann 1983)

As you may have guessed, many Refuges have ranching problems. At Sheldon NWR in Nevada, a portion being grazed produced 72% fewer pronghorn fawns than when cattle were excluded. At Bosque del Apache NWR, New Mexico, crane populations nearly tripled after cattle were removed from most of the Refuge. At Red Rock Lake NWR in Montana, the leading cause of moose calf mortality is entanglement on livestock fences.

Predator "control" occurs, often covertly, on some Refuges. More than 800 coyotes have been killed, ostensibly to benefit wildlife, in the past few years at Malheur NWR in Oregon; the Refuge plans to continue predator "control" for at least another 5 years. Hunting and trapping, often by or for the ranching industry, is encouraged on 256 out of 435 NWRs in the US. On some Refuges, native hay meadows are flood-irrigated to increase livestock forage, often flooding nests and nesting areas. Hay mowing machinery kills many birds and other wildlife; the animals often crouch and remain motionless when the mower approaches. Haying also decreases the long-term productivity of Refuges by repeatedly removing organic biomass. Ranching activities spread alfalfa and other exotic plant species which compete with native vegetation and harm native animals. Livestock diseases and parasites are transmitted to Refuge wildlife. Other documented ranching detriments to NWRs are too numerous to mention here, but many are detailed elsewhere in this book. Even though probably most Refuge managers are ranching advocates, a recent GAO report states that more than 60% of the managers of Refuges grazed by livestock consider ranching a major problem.

Refuge scam: Ranchers farm crops, most of which go to livestock. Riparian bottomland is transformed into crop monocultures that benefit only a few (mostly hunting) species. Stockmen pay little or nothing. Here at Bosque del Apache NWR in central New Mexico, 1400 acres are farmed by local ranchers.

Almost any excuse is used to expand or continue livestock grazing. For example, on my refuge, my range con would like to allow cows to graze wet meadows down to stubble to provide goose browse -- even though we have only a dozen geese on the whole refuge. Never mind that an ungrazed meadow is far more valuable to most of the refuge's wildlife.
--Rock Lakes NWR manager Barry Reiswig (Wuerthner 1991)

Strassmann's report documents extensive environmental damage, including overgrazing of riparian habitats, wildlife mortality due to collisions with fences, and mowing of migratory bird habitat during breeding season. It states that a few wildlife species may benefit from grazing management, but most do not. Those that do "could be served equally well or better by prescribed burning." The report concludes that livestock grazing and haying, as currently implemented "does more harm than good," and notes that "This conclusion is strengthened when one considers that for the majority of wildlife species there are no data indicating that even controlled grazing can be beneficial, while numerous studies report that grazing adversely affects these species."

Grazing at Fish Springs NWR, Utah, eliminates cover for ducks and other nesting waterfowl. *(George Wuerthner)*

Refuge grazing fees are figured on a Refuge-by-Refuge basis. FWS doesn't keep track of all figures, but Strassmann found they averaged about $4.44/AUM in 1980 -- roughly half of fair market value at the time. She also found that Refuges chose permittees overwhelmingly by tradition, lottery, or negotiated sale rather than truly competitive bid.

According to the results of a questionnaire sent out by Strassmann, National Wildlife Refuge managers reported spending $919,740 to administer cattle grazing and haying in FY 1980. According to FWS, Refuge grazing (@$4.44/AUM) and haying permits in 1980 brought the federal government $973,431. So, superficially it appears FWS broke even on its ranching program. But this is not the case. Nineteen percent of Refuge managers refused to answer the survey question on expenditures. The costs of degraded wildlife habitat and restoration efforts were not counted, nor were related general administrative costs. And, as always, numerous other significant indirect and obscure costs were not included in reported figures. For example, ranching roads on NWRs are not financed by ranching funds; FWS spends thousands of dollars annually to feed elk on Wildlife Refuges so they won't compete with livestock in nearby areas; and NWRs must pay to fence out livestock from adjacent public lands. It is safe to assume that National Wildlife Refuges lose well over $1 million annually to public lands ranching.

Refuge managers have wide discretion for issuing permits, setting permit conditions, and managing ranching activities. However, stockmen's inordinate influence over the

management of many NWRs is apparent. For example, Hart Mountain National Antelope Refuge in southeast Oregon allots 7 times more herbage to cattle than to pronghorn. At many Refuges, livestock matters consume more than a third of Refuge funds and staff time. Sheldon NWR in Northeast Nevada and several others spend *most* funding and staff time on ranching. In order to protect their jobs, managers and staff understandably tend to portray their ranching programs in a favorable light. Strassmann's report sums it up well, stating that "refuge programs primarily accommodate the economic needs of permittees rather than the ecological needs of wildlife."

Nearly all of the refuge funding goes toward managing cattle owned by eight permittees. What little is spent on wildlife is mostly damage control. It's not making things better for wildlife, unless you call mitigating livestock making things better. While I have people to build and maintain fences, stock ponds, water pipelines, and other developments for the permittees and a range conservationist to oversee the grazing program, I don't even have one biologist on my staff -- and this is supposed to be a wildlife refuge!
--Barry Reiswig (Wuerthner 1991)

There has been a general trend toward reducing livestock numbers and use on NWRs in recent years, largely as a result of lawsuits and Congressional actions. Nevertheless, FWS plans future livestock *increases*. For example, a 1983 memorandum from FWS Director Robert Jantzen stated that "Refuges with potential for increasing grazing activity should immediately initiate plans for increasing grazing in accordance with guidelines outlined in the Refuge Manual." Ranchers and managers at many NWRs, including Malheur, one of the largest ranched NWRs, are pressuring for more livestock.

Ranching is not only the greatest detriment to Western National Wildlife Refuges but also the foremost hindrance to the creation of new NWRs. For example, the Animas Mountains in extreme southwest New Mexico are a "biological melting pot" of even greater potential, where wolves, jaguars, thick-billed parrots, and much more could re-establish, and where 22 Endangered species currently live. A private 321,000 acre ranch encompasses most of the mountain range and adjacent valleys. During the late 1980s plans by FWS to purchase 200,000 acres of the Gray Ranch and establish the Animas National Wildlife Refuge met hostile opposition from nearly all local ranchers, even though, according to FWS, *livestock grazing would continue unhampered as a "wildlife management tool."* Said one, "The federal government has no business owning land." Scoffed another, "You don't hire cowboys. You hire left-over hippies." And, according to Denny Gentry of the New Mexico Cattle Growers Association, "We're opposed to any purchase of private land by a government entity unless an equal amount is put back into private [ranchers'] ownership." (2-7-88 *The New Mexican*) Answering the ranchers' wishes, Secretary of the Interior Manuel Lujan, Jr., a former New Mexico congressman, and then-New Mexico Governor Garrey Carruthers, a public lands rancher, helped block State Senator Jeff Bingaman's proposal to appropriate funds to buy the ranch. (Current Governor Bruce King is likewise a wealthy public lands rancher opposed to the proposed Refuge.)

In January 1990 The Nature Conservancy closed a deal to buy the entire 321,000 acre ranch for $18 million in what is thought to be the largest private land acquisition in "conservation" history. The Nature Conservancy's idea was to eventually transfer title to most of it to FWS for the Wildlife Refuge. However, to try to gain area ranchers' approval for the Refuge, both The Nature Conservancy and FWS have pledged to lease the vast bulk of the "refuge" for livestock grazing and said that they have no plans to reintroduce

wolves. Indeed, there is speculation that pressure from local ranchers will force a livestock *increase* on the land, and that the ranchers will never allow it to become a National Wildlife Refuge. Currently 15,000 head of cattle roam the ranch, and -- despite reports that it is in "excellent" condition -- much of the ranch is in fair or poor condition after a century of overgrazing. (Wolf 1990) Late word has it that a group of surrounding ranchers have threatened to chain off all roads leading into "the ranch."

● National Park Service

Grazing on park land is permitted where authorized by law or permitted for a term of years as a condition of land acquisition.

Grazing and raising of livestock is also permitted in historic zones where desirable to perpetuate and interpret the historic scene.
--National Park Service Guideline NPS-53, Special Park Uses

America's National Parks are world famous for their beauty and grandeur. Since the late 1800s Congress has been setting aside these lands as the most unique and impressive examples of untrammeled Nature in this country. Today they comprise the most extraordinary system of natural preserves on Earth.

Naturally most Americans think their National Parks and Monuments are protected from commercial exploitation. And generally they are, outside of certain heavily visited locations where concessionaires are permitted to operate

stores, gas stations, lodges, and other services deemed necessary for tourists. However, ranching is once again the glaring exception. A little history:

As with FS, BLM, state, and other public lands, most lands in the West chosen for the National Park Service (NPS) system were open to ranching before such designation. More so than any other group, the stockmen holding permits to graze these lands and owning strategic inholdings influenced their ultimate fate.

In some cases, the federal government was able with generous offers to buy out grazing permits, base properties, and/or private ranchlands or make special deals with stockmen to establish ranching-free Parks. Many ranchers increased their wealth and power as a result; some left the livestock business, others expanded their ranching operations elsewhere.

In many instances, however, stockmen (supported by their political representatives) refused to relinquish "their" grazing permits to proposed Park lands, even though usually most of their forage and browse needs were met by other lands. They used their substantial influence to force the government into special agreements that allowed them to continue ranching the new Park lands, either in perpetuity or for a period of years. Consequently, some Parks (Sequoia, for example) have over the years paid off ranchers and phased out ranching, while others (Great Basin, for example) plan to continue ranching indefinitely. Currently, a bill to expand Craters of the Moon National Monument in southern Idaho and turn it into a National Park contains language mandating continued livestock grazing at near-traditional levels. A proposal by the Hell's Canyon Preservation Council to turn Hell's Canyon National Recreation Area into a National Park is shackled with wording designed to continue ranching indefinitely. New Mexico's newly designated El Mapais National Monument also plans to continue ranching.

Cattle in El Mapais National Monument, northwest New Mexico. *(Dale Turner)*

Some stockmen owning base properties and/or other ranchland within proposed Park boundaries required that as a condition of acquiring these private lands the government allow them to continue traditional ranching in the new Parks. Others refused to yield their private lands, and as a consequence some Parks, such as Zion and Black Canyon of the Gunnison, still contain private ranches within their borders.

Some ranchers even convinced the government to allow them to maintain ranching operations in new Parks under guise of "preserving the historic Old West" for the benefit of tourists; Pipe Springs NM in northern Arizona is a disgraceful example. These and some other NPS units actively promote ranching. However, ranching in many Parks proceeds only under the ardent objections of Park supervisors and staff.

In the 11 Western states the National Park Service currently administers 23 National Parks, 47 National Monuments, 11 National Recreation Areas, and 17 National Memorials, Historic Sites, Historic Parks, Battlefield Parks, Seashores, and such. These 98 NPS units cover about 17 million acres, or 2.3%, of the West. Somewhat less than 3 million acres of this land is open to commercial ranching, including 7 National Parks, 7 National Monuments, 5 National Recreation Areas, and 7 National Memorials, etc. Many NPS units outside the West also allow ranching -- even Haleakala National Park in Hawaii.

Sawtooth National Recreation Area, central Idaho.

Livestock production on NPS lands, which is by far mostly cattle ranching, is administered by the National Park Service or, in several cases, adjacent federal land management agencies. Ranching impact generally is less severe than for any other public or private ranchland category in the West. However, some NPS units have serious problems and in most units historic ranching damage lingers (Yosemite, Canyonlands, and Petrified Forest, for example). Some NPS and even some non-NPS ranchers are granted permission to trail livestock across NPS lands.

A down gate and deteriorating fence on the south boundary of Grand Canyon National Park, Arizona.

Most NPS stockmen pay the same micro-fee charged other federal permittees under the PRIA formula. As with BLM and FS permittees, the government sponsors nearly all of their range developments and guarantees construction and maintenance of any range "improvements" deemed necessary for continued ranching. NPS reports indicate that NPS spends *millions* of tax dollars each year on or because of ranching -- at least several times what it takes in from grazing fees. Many of these reports complain of fiscal waste on ranching management, personnel tied up with ranching matters, overgrazing and structural damages to Parks, as well as cattle in campgrounds, visitor centers, picnic, recreation, and other tourist areas.

> *... there is no authorized cattle grazing in the park ... There are inholdings of private land and many acres of private and public land along Zion's boundaries where grazing is permitted. Maintaining fence along the boundary is a large task. Although we have a very good fence crew, it needs to be bigger to completely exclude cattle. We also badly need additional managers to patrol for cattle trespass and other violations.*
> --Harold L. Grafe, Superintendent, Zion National Park, Utah, in a 8-18-89 letter

Rivaling and perhaps surpassing permitted ranching as a problem on National Park Service lands is trespass grazing. The Parks' relatively lush vegetation is a magnet for hungry livestock, which commonly break through fences or come through open gates, perhaps with a little help from their owners. Ranchlands border nearly all Parks in the West, and the thousands of miles of protective fences in often rugged terrain are difficult and expensive for NPS to maintain. Thus, the job descriptions of many NPS employees, even in "ungrazed" Parks, include patrolling for trespassing livestock; closing gates; chasing cattle, sheep, and horses out of tourist areas and off Park land; rounding up, moving, and caring for trespass animals; repairing developments and mitigating environmental impacts; dealing with permittees; and building and mending fences.

Most Western Parks report problems from trespass livestock. A 1986 project statement by Kings Canyon National Park in California, for example, states that impacts from trespassing cattle include "trampling of wetlands, conversion of grass to feces, formation of cattle trails, extra erosion, fecal deposition in streams, and destruction of sedges ...." The statement requests "$300,000 for the first year and $20,000/yr thereafter for increased patrol and fence maintenance." A similar Organ Pipe Cactus National Monument (Arizona) statement requests $195,000 for fencing, patrol and other management due to "serious" trespass problems "which could multiply manifold" if protective measures are not taken. At world-famous Grand Canyon National Park, officials state that trespass grazing has caused changes in soil, native wildlife, and vegetation; they likewise request more protective fencing. In northwest California's Redwood National Park, 117 cattle and horses were reported to have trespassed 1170 acres in 1984 (the latest figures available); recently $22,000 was expended there to modify 4 miles of the boundary fence because elk were dying on it.

Roughly *half* of all Western National Parks are trespassed more or less regularly by livestock from adjacent public and private lands, or from NPS allotments themselves. The

Rocky Mountain Region of NPS reports in its *Summary of Livestock Grazing for 1987* that livestock trespassed 11 of its 14 grazed units and ate 8% as much herbage as permitted animals. However, as with other federal lands, officially recorded amounts probably represent only a small fraction of actual trespass. I have several times witnessed trespassing cattle or sheep which were undiscovered, ignored, or chased out of Parks without official recognition.

Wyoming's U.S. Senator Clifford Hansen held, in the Tetons, the largest grazing permit in all the Park Service -- for 569 cattle. The permit had originated as trespass grazing in clear violation of federal law years before. The record was clear -- the Park Service would have to enforce its own laws and regulations and cancel Hansen's permit and others like it. . . . The chief ranger was a tall, experienced man who carefully read my memorandum before he called me into his office. He clapped a fatherly hand on my shoulder and looked both concerned and sympathetic. "Young man," he said, "I don't care what you find in those records; as long as Cliff Hansen sits on the Senate Interior Committee, we ain't going to fuck with his cows."
--Bernard Shanks, **This Land Is Your Land** (Shanks 1984)

Let's examine the ranching situation on several NPS units:

In Wyoming's Grand Teton National Park, 24,000 acres are grazed by 1600 cattle owned by 8 permittees. Most of this is in the beautiful, grassy, and profitable Snake River Valley; political string pulling secured continued ranching here. Park visitors are encouraged to view the overgrazing cattle, fences and other range developments as part of the natural scenery.

Southern Utah's Zion National Park is world famous as a land of spectacular, steep-walled canyons and colorful rock formations. Though none of the Park is legally grazed, Zion hosts a private cattle ranch within its boundaries and provides it with guaranteed access. One adjacent permittee drives herds of cattle through a portion of the Park each spring. Reports show that in 1987 200 trespassing cattle grazed 1200 AUMs on 5400 Park acres, upsetting fragile riparian corridors and desert ecology. Herds of sheep also trespass Zion's verdant high country, but little of this is officially recognized or challenged. Other than visitor use and related development, ranching is Zion's most serious threat.

Throughout the grazing season, we assisted permittees with livestock management on the Park as often as possible. This fostered good working relations with the permittees.
--*Resource Management Plan Updates, 1989, Great Basin National Park*

The recently created, largely overgrazed Great Basin National Park in east-central Nevada would have encompassed hundreds of thousands of acres of basin and range if it were meant to truly represent the basin and range province. Under pressure from stockmen the proposed Park's size was reduced until all that remained was 77,100 acres -- *all in the steep mountains*, which are of course the least livestock-productive rangeland. Thus, Great Basin National Park contains no basin! Language in the Park bill -- without which the bill probably would not have been passed

-- allows grazing to continue at more or less pre-existing levels indefinitely. A Park brochure assures tourists that "cattle grazing [is] an integral part of the Great Basin scene." It fails to say that visitors will see hundreds of cattle en route to the Park and will hardly wish to see more, especially in the campgrounds, where they now graze. On the sides of the Park's 13,000' Wheeler Peak, you may (as I have) find cattle above 10,000'.

Big Bend National Park in southwest Texas is a designated World Biosphere Reserve. Historic ranching there was so destructive that even now, several decades after ranching was banned, much of the Park bears little resemblance to pre-livestock times. And though most of the Park is making a gradual recovery, trespassing livestock, mainly from Mexico, so heavily degrade the Rio Grande canyon that in many areas riparian systems are trashed and cottonwood regeneration is virtually non-existent. (Wuerthner 1989)

Cattle-caused gully erosion, Big Bend NP. *(George Wuerthner)*

Even Channel Islands National Park off the Southern California coast has livestock problems. Ranching there is scheduled to be phased out over the next decade; however, officials report that, largely from past and present overgrazing, all the islands have high rates of soil erosion. Other problems include vegetation destruction, disturbance of archaeological sites and loss of artifacts, trail damage, and sloughing of sea cliffs.

Cattle in Capitol Reef National Park, Utah. *(George Wuerthner)*

Until a few years ago, 1800 to 2500 cattle grazed more than 145,000 acres between October and May in southern Utah's fantastic Capitol Reef National Park. A century of grazing had stripped off native vegetation, caused serious soil erosion, dried up springs and creeks, severely harmed the few remaining riparian areas, destroyed most of the cryptogamic layer, and helped extirpate bighorn sheep and other wildlife. Cattle and numerous ranching developments disturbed Park visitors and degraded the fragile desert scenery.

When the Park was created from Capitol Reef National Monument and surrounding public lands in 1971, the 30-some existing permittees agreed to phase out grazing by 1982. However, that year Utah Senator Jake Garn and other ranching-advocate politicians introduced legislation to extend grazing in the Park for the lifetimes of the permittees and their heirs. Congress compromised by extending grazing until 1994. The Park Supervisor recently attempted to buy-out the permits, but the politicos pushed through a provision extending grazing for permittees who don't want to sell; it will extend ranching for their lifetimes and even for those of sons and daughters living in 1971. Today, negotiations and generous pay-offs have induced most stockmen to sell "their" permits, but several permittees still ranch the Park. (Zuni Reincarnation 1986 and Sierra Club publications)

Ranching in northwest Colorado's 200,000-acre Dinosaur National Monument has also been reduced in recent years, from about 120,000 acres on 22 allotments to about 80,000 acres on 11 allotments. A phase-out program similar to Capitol Reef's allows permittee family members to retain grazing privileges for their lifetimes, or to cash them in. And like Capitol Reef -- though ranching in the Monument is waning -- its legacy will remain for decades or centuries: grasslands converted to sage and bare dirt, devastated wildlife (bighorns, for example, were extirpated mostly due to ranching by the early 1950s), depleted soil and waters, ravaged riparian areas, increased flooding (which damages the Monument's dinosaur fossil beds), and many road cuts and sacrifice areas.

Black Canyon of the Gunnison National Monument in west-central Colorado encompasses a 20-mile portion of the rugged Gunnison River gorge and some rangeland above it. Several permittees run nearly 1000 cattle on about 7000 acres (the remainder is inaccessible or dominated by cliffs). The owner of one ranch inholding has threatened to bulldoze an access road, clear brush, build stock ponds and ranch structures, harvest Christmas trees, and generally create as big an eyesore as possible unless the Park Service makes a lucrative offer for a scenic easement on his 600 acres and allows him to retain actual title. Another Monument rancher recently was paid a generous $2.1 million for his 4200-acre ranch inholding and given grazing privileges within the monument for 20 years.

Glen Canyon National Recreation Area spreads across 1.25 million acres in southeast Utah. Its infamous Glen Canyon Dam entombs some of the most wonderful river canyons on Earth under the dead waters of "Lake" Powell. Nearly 1 million fragile, arid to semi-arid NRA acres are included in 38 grazing allotments that supported only 554 cattle in 1987/88 (about 1800 acres per animal). Most of the remaining 1/4 million acres is under water. Several government agencies presently are conducting tax-sponsored studies for a management plan for long-term livestock grazing on Glen Canyon NRA.

The 1.5-million-acre Lake Mead National Recreation Area of southernmost Nevada, northwest Arizona, and southwest Utah is host to the largest National Park Service ranching operation of all -- about 1.1 million acres. Aside from the Colorado River and "Lake" Mead itself, the entire NRA is low-elevation, hot, arid, and sparsely vegetated. An Eastern livestock producer might think of turning cattle out on this burning desert as a cruel joke. But the joke is once again on the public and its land, as well as the livestock. BLM resource area offices in Nevada, Arizona, and Utah provide ranching administration and assistance on the NRA for 20 permittees and their cattle. The huge bovines trample and erode the fragile desert soil, crush the cryptogams, and consume the scant greenery. They congregate around the area's few water sources and along the "Lake" Mead and Colorado River shorelines, where they invade campgrounds and foul beaches. *We* pay to fence them out of the locations popular with tourists and a few of the most environmentally sensitive areas. Aside from the usual seasonal grazing, in much of Lake Mead NRA stockmen are allowed to bring in their cattle whenever wet weather produces a "surplus" of forage or browse -- what is termed "ephemeral grazing." Hundreds of miles of ranching roads degrade the area and provide for vastly increased human impact.

This gate has 2 locks -- one for the Park Service and one for the rancher. Three allotments cover most of the 5000-acre Coronado National Memorial in southeast Arizona. Staff complain of overgrazing, fiscal waste, and cattle disturbing picnic areas, the visitor center, trails, residences, and a maintenance yard.

A water development and corral for cattle in Coronado National Monument.

Point Reyes National Seashore north of San Francisco is largely a livestock operation. Eighteen permittees graze beef cattle, dairy cows, and sheep on about 25,000 acres, and cultivate an additional 2000 acres for oats and rye -- together, roughly 40% of the Seashore. This includes the most sensitive portion of the Seashore, with 23 rare plant species and 4 animal species targeted for protection (due partly to ranching impacts). Ranching roads, fences, outbuildings, and resident ranch headquarters mar recreational use, and harm and preclude wildlife. Overgrazing strips native vegetation, spreads "pest" species such as thistle and poison hemlock, and increases flooding. Herbicides, pesticides, and livestock wastes pollute fresh and salt water. These influences, and increased soil erosion calculated at 110,000 tons annually, threaten the health of the Drakes and Limantour Estuaries, the last 2 estuaries on the California coast in a semi-natural state. NPS currently is throwing hundreds of thousands of tax dollars at the problem, rather than simply halting livestock operations.

Several miles south, just across the bridge from San Francisco, commercial cattle and horses graze more than 2000 acres of Golden Gate NRA.

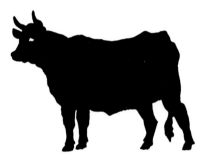

Through the years ranchmen have been foremost among those working to prevent establishment of new National Parks. In some cases they halted them altogether, and often they were able to limit their size. At present, in California's Mojave Desert a half-dozen permittees are fighting tooth-and-nail to prevent the transformation of BLM's East Mojave Scenic Area into Mojave National Park. The ranchers graze only about 3000 cattle on the arid 1.6 million acre expanse -- *roughly 1 cow per square mile* -- but their opposition is a formidable barrier to Park designation. On the 210 million acres in the Midwest that were once tallgrass prairie, there are no National Parks or Monuments, and less than 3% of original grassland remains (though in degraded condition). Ranchers there have thus far beat back serious attempts to establish a Tallgrass Prairie National Park, first in Kansas and then in Oklahoma.

And of course, many potential Parks will never be realized because stockmen own outright about 1/4 of the rural West, including many locations that might otherwise have become Parks.

Nearly every NPS unit where ranching has been banned shows significant recovery: Grand Canyon, Petrified Forest, Rocky Mountain, Yellowstone, Yosemite, Sequoia/Kings Canyon, Canyonlands, Arches, Bryce, Natural Bridges, Wupatki, Devils Tower, and many more. In 1978-79 livestock were removed from Organ Pipe National Monument in southwest Arizona. Previously most of the expansive 500-square-mile Monument was desolate due to decades of ranching abuse. Today, even this arid desert is relatively verdant. (Schultz 1971 and Warren 1987)

Where grazing is permitted and its continuation is not in the best interest of public use or maintenance of the park ecosystem, it will be eliminated . . . .
--National Park Service Guideline NPS-53, Special Park Uses

Wupatki National Monument in northern Arizona is beginning to recover from a century of ranching.

Recovery from ranching in Arches National Park, Utah. *(George Wuerthner)*

• Military and other federal

The United States Army, Navy, Air Force, Marines, Coast Guard, Corps of Engineers, Bureau of Reclamation, Department of Energy, Agricultural Research Service, Department of Transportation, and other federal entities also lease lands for livestock ranching -- roughly 2-3 million acres altogether. On the whole ranching administration on these lands is conducted more responsibly than on most government lands, and ranching's impact here generally is less harmful.

Grazing fees charged for most of these federal lands are determined largely by competitive bid and average roughly $4-$10/AUM -- usually about 1/3 to 3/4 fair market value in the local area. But bidding here rarely is truly competitive; as with all public ranchlands, traditional permittees enjoy many covert favors and special arrangements that help them retain control. Newcomers are discouraged and thwarted in various ways.

The US Army's expansive Fort Hunter-Liggett is nestled in the beautiful hills and valleys just inland from the central California coast. Prime annual grassland/oak woodland, about 110,000 of its 165,000 acres are open to ranching from November through June. Competitive bidding for 4 leases is administered by the US Army Corps of Engineers, while on-the-ground administration is conducted by the Army, which employs a full-time range conservationist. Competitive bids recently have averaged about $6-$7/AUM, but in the past reached as high as $18/AUM. A sergeant at Hunter-Liggett refers to the lessees as "a few big shots" who "control all grazing."

Three other nearby central California coast military reservations also lease ranching via similar competitive bid and administration. About 10,000 acres at the Army's Fort Ord are open to sheep ranching, as are portions of Vandenberg Air Force Base. Cattle ranching is supervised by the Corps of Engineers on 20,000 acres of Camp Roberts, a former Army base now leased to the state for National Guard use. And, 2 sheep ranchers graze 31,000 acres of California's south coast Marine Corps Camp Pendleton, while cattlemen ranch the adjacent Fallbrook Naval Weapons Station and even the Seal Beach NWS in the midst of Orange County's metropolitan expanse.

Under BLM administration and grazing fees, one permittee ranches 35,000 acres of Nellis Air Force Base in southern Nevada, in addition to "his" 300,000 BLM acres. Ranching on the US Department of Energy's Hanford Reservation in Washington is administered by the Washington Department of Natural Resources. In 1988, about 50,000 acres here were divided between 4 lessees, while the remaining 300,000 acres were used as a buffer zone for DOE's radioactive activities. Lessees pay $4.65/AUM -- less than half fair market value. A few miles west, the US Army administers 6 ranching leases on 194,000 acres of the 264,000-acre Yakima Firing Range. Competitive bid fees for cattle and sheep grazing there average $5.62/AUM.

Perhaps the most widely publicized example of superior public lands ranching administration is the US Army's 271,000-acre McGregor Range in southern New Mexico. Grazing fees on the Range's 15 grazing units are determined by competitive bid and average about $7/AUM, while the fee on adjacent BLM land was, of course, only $1.81/AUM in 1990. Additionally, BLM, which administers ranching on the McGregor Range, annually sets minimum bids which ostensibly finance all administrative costs (the falseness of this claim is detailed elsewhere). Further, the Army controls access and assumes no responsibility for safety or damages, while BLM allows no subleasing, maintains "only" wells and pipelines, retains ownership of all permanent structural "improvements," requires prompt and full bid payments, monitors cattle movement on and off the range, and enforces (relatively speaking) strict penalties for violations. Interestingly, even with the "high" fee and all these restrictions, there is no lack of prospective graziers. Range condition on the McGregor Range, though not excellent, is much better than on comparable surrounding land. (Johnson 1987)

• State

Nothing in history suggests that the states are adequate to protect their own resources, or even want to, or suggests that cattlemen and sheepmen are capable of regulating themselves even for their own benefit, still less the public's.
--Bernard DeVoto, **The Easy Chair** (DeVoto 1955)

As Western states were added to the United States in the 1800s, they were granted land, primarily as compensation for loss of sovereignty to the federal government (to placate the states and minimize their opposition to federal annexation). Texas, essentially an independent nation before statehood, had much greater leverage and was able to transfer almost all of its land from federal to state and eventually to private ownership. Thus, today 98% of Texas is privately owned, mostly by ranchers, and almost universally overgrazed.

Originally, land grants to the Western states constituted about 5% of their area; the states received the 16th and 36th sections of each township, except Utah and New Mexico which each received 4 sections. Nevada, which received the smallest grant area, got just under 3 million acres, or an area about the size of Connecticut, while New Mexico received the largest, a 10-million-acre portion (twice the size of Massachusetts). As the years passed, ownership patterns changed. Some states sold holdings for revenue. Some bought or traded land for various reasons. Today, some states own more than originally and some less; all except Nevada retain about 2 million acres or more.

Most state land was established for the purpose of supporting education, including state colleges, while smaller land grants were provided for state institutions, internal improvements, and other purposes. Typically, Western states passed laws around the turn of the century requiring state lands to be used to return the highest possible revenue to state school systems. Subsequently, they have developed a wide variety of revenue-gainers and administrative procedures. State lands are leased for logging, mining, farming, rights-of-way, billboards, movie-making, recreation, and many other commercial purposes -- and, of course, most of all for ranching. All imaginable forms of natural resources are sold from state land. And each year thousands of acres of Western state land are sold outright, usually to the highest bidder.

In their economic self-interest, the Western states have interpreted their school trust laws as strict mandates to -- above all else -- generate **maximum profit** from state lands. Consequently, states have shown little inclination to protect land under their administration from reckless exploitation, and state lands generally are the most abused of all government lands in the West. Had the Sagebrush Rebellion been successful in its avowed goal of transferring federal lands to the states, it would have made the longstanding ranching disaster on these lands even worse.

State land leased for grazing purposes (nearly all) carries no stipulations concerning the number of livestock to be grazed, season of use, or length of grazing period. These matters are entirely within the discretion of the lessee.

--Wesley Calef, **Private Grazing and Public Lands** (Calef 1960)

In telephone interviews with officials of various Western state agencies (*a hellish ordeal!!!*), the great majority of the 60 or so contacted -- even range managers -- told me they had no idea how much of their land was ranched, how many AUMs were consumed, what grazing fee was charged, how much tax was spent, or even how much land was under their jurisdiction! For example, of the 60 only *1* (in California) could tell me how much land was owned by the state. Some officials were reluctant to share what little information they had; others were openly hostile (Washington and Colorado particularly). This is understandable when you consider that many state officials are ranchers or tied to the ranching industry. Yet, despite all the ignorance and resistance, I was able to compile the following:

The 11 Western states presently own approximately 46 million acres -- roughly 6% of the West. About 36 million acres, or nearly 80%, is used for livestock ranching.

STATE-OWNED LANDS RANCHING
(1989 telephone interviews and USDA 1989)

STATE	TOTAL ACRES (Millions, approx.)	GRAZED ACRES* (Millions, approx.)	$/AUM (1988) (State land departments only)	FEE DETERMINATION
ARIZONA	9.7	8.8	$1.19	FORMULA
CALIFORNIA	1.9	0.1	$1.35	SAME AS FEDERAL
COLORADO	3.3	3.0	$4.00	BOARD SET
IDAHO	2.6	2.1	$3.27	BIDS AND BOARD SET
MONTANA	5.6	4.1	$2.59	FORMULA
NEVADA	0.3	0.1	$4.00 (Rougherage, various agencies)	VARIES
NEW MEXICO	9.5	8.9	$2.59 (Average)	FORMULA
OREGON	1.8	0.7	$2.50	BOARD SET
UTAH	3.8	3.4	$1.54	SAME AS FEDERAL
WASHINGTON	3.7	1.2	$4.20	VARIES
WYOMING	3.8	3.6	$1.65	FORMULA
TOTAL	46.0	36.0	$2.26 (weighted average)	————

* Includes state departments of land, wildlife, parks & recreation, and other large state land administrators, but not state departments of highways, forestry, and corrections, state universities, and other state entities administering smaller areas, totaling perhaps 2 to 3 million acres.

State land departments administer more than 90% of all state land and state lands ranching. In 1988 they charged a weighted average fee of $2.26/AUM -- about 30% higher than the federal fee, but less than 1/4 fair market value. As with federal fees, state land department fees are consistently low and generally vary little from year to year.

State departments of wildlife, parks & recreation, and occasionally others also administer significant amounts of Western state land. These agencies usually charge $6 to $12 per AUM, sometimes more, as one official told me "making one wonder why state land departments and the federal government are not doing the same." Lesser amounts of state land -- totaling perhaps 2-3 million acres -- are administered by state departments of forestry, highways, agriculture, corrections, state military, state universities, and other state entities. Some of these lands are leased for ranching, usually for most of fair market value.

The figures I was able to obtain indicate that in 1988 the 11 Western states sold approximately 7 million AUMs on 36 million acres for roughly $15 million. This represents roughly 1/3 of the AUM use and fee return of Western federal land.

Interestingly, though states have a supposed mandate to maximize income from state land, raising grazing fees to near fair market value seems out of the question due to ranchers' clout. So the states partially compensate by allowing extremely heavy stocking under the assumption that more livestock = more fee revenue. Nevertheless, because state ranching produces such a tiny percentage of livestock, yields so little revenue compared to total expenditures, and degrades the environment and competes with other land uses, terminating state lands ranching would greatly benefit the economies of Western states.

State lands ranching is unbelievably diverse and confused. Ownership patterns often are a mosaic or checkerboard. Each state has its own regulations and administration procedures, and numerous state agencies sell ranching under an array of long and short-term leases and permits, rental agreements, and other legal arrangements, mostly stipulated lease agreements. Regulations and lease conditions are scarce and enforcement is lax or nonexistent. For example, in Arizona restrictions are few and the state "monitors" ranching mainly *by mailing lessees questionnaires.*

Though state land administrators often pretend otherwise, state grazing leases are renewed virtually automatically. Wesley Calef notes in **Private Grazing and Public Lands** that "Only unusual circumstances will cause a state land administrative agency to refuse a lease renewal requested by the lessee (and the lessee almost invariably does want it renewed)" (Calef 1960).

Consequently, ranchers utilize state land -- even more than federal -- like private property, likewise without having to purchase property or pay property taxes. According to Chuck Griffith, Northern Rocky Mountains state regional executive for the National Wildlife Federation:

> *Since these school lands were first established, the average grazing permittee has considered them "his," not unlike the attitude of the federal grazing permit holders. Such grazing leases are treated by banks and other lending agencies as tangible, privately owned assets.*

One Washington private lands rancher told me he was amazed to hear a neighbor say that their ranch was "handed down" through the family for generations. He knew that "their ranch" consisted almost entirely of a few thousand acres of Washington State land.

Technically, most state lands are off-limits to people without commercial permits or special permission. But in practice state land generally is administered as public domain in New Mexico, Arizona, Oregon, Washington, Idaho, Utah, and Nevada. However, stockmen exercise **de facto** control over much of this land with warning signs, fences, locked gates, threats, and physical assaults.

The other Western states more actively prohibit public access, though widespread enforcement is impractical due to the huge areas involved and to insufficient personnel. Some states give ranchmen the power to control access to the state land they ranch. For example, Montana's state land department traditionally has allowed grazing lease holders to control access; much of the state land there is posted and the public is literally locked out. Recent legislation in Colorado gives lessees complete access control. The Utah state wildlife agency attempted unsuccessfully to draft a similar bill in 1987. In Wyoming the state education department director has recently reinterpreted the law to prevent ranchers from denying access to hunters and anglers, though they may deny it to backpackers, rockhounds, and other "recreationists." In most states where public use is permitted, if you wish to obtain a permit to use state land for camping or some other purpose, the state land department will first "check with" the local ranching lessee.

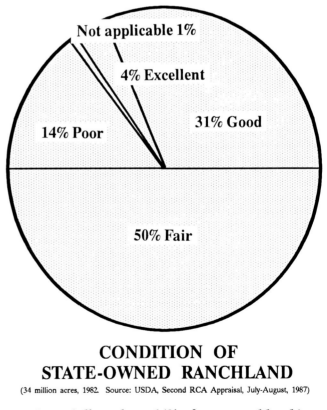

CONDITION OF
STATE-OWNED RANCHLAND

(34 million acres, 1982. Source: USDA, Second RCA Appraisal, July-August, 1987)

(Essentially, at least 64% of state ranchland is functioning at less than half of its potential.)

Various state parks, state-operated regional parks, and state land trusts are ranched, often as a condition of their establishment. Many of these lands are purchased and set aside for the expressed purpose of preserving their natural character for the enjoyment and use of the people. Others are acquired with the intent of protecting Threatened or Endangered species, outstanding scenery, or some other natural attribute. Livestock grazing detracts from their original purpose, sometimes resulting in heated conflicts between graziers, other users, and administrators. Here are excerpts from a letter by John O'Donnell, one of the directors of California's East Bay Regional Park District:

The East Bay Regional Park District is comprised of 65,000 acres of land . . . . We intend to buy 20,000 more . . . 55% of our acreage is leased to cattle ranchers. . . . . When I drive one of my constituents along our property line and ask them if they've ever been on the land, their answer is always the same; they look at the barbed wire and the herd of cattle and say no, that's private land. . . . I would rather see Tule elk or pronghorn on the land. . . . The Park District even has it's own Rangeland Manager, but we do not have a wildlife manager.

State ranchland in west-central New Mexico. By far most vegetation ends at fence.

In Arizona, less than 1000 ranchers graze livestock on 8.8 of the state's 9.7 million acres -- 12% of the state. They produce less than 1/1000 of US livestock. The Arizona State Land Department brings in an average of about $1 million per year from these lessees, yet the various governments spend many times this amount on or because of state lands ranching. (In contrast, the state lottery nets $120 million/yr.) The current 1990 fee is "way up" from years past -- to $1.40/AUM, or less than 1/5 what private herbage goes for in the state. Grazing fee income accounts for roughly 1% of state land revenue. According to Extension Service Range Specialist Don Floyd, stocking rates on state land are the highest of any public lands category in Arizona -- about 9 cattle per square mile. Overstocking and trespassing are customary. Accordingly, most Arizona state land is tremendously overgrazed.

In Oregon, only 43 lessees graze 536,000 acres -- more than 75% of Oregon's state ranchland -- and altogether less than 200 lessees graze 700,000 acres. At $2.50/AUM, they contribute only a few hundred thousand dollars a year to state school funding, while expending far more state funds under various programs.

Washington's less than 200 lessees control most of the state's 1.2 million acres of ranchland. At $4.50/AUM, its grazing fee is the highest of any Western state. Yet, in 1988 from all lessees Washington collected only $582,120 -- about 0.3% of the state's total $193 million state trust land revenue. At least $2-$3 million of its $32 million state lands budget is expended on ranching, for fire management, insect and disease control, riparian restoration, roads, maintenance and supplies, range personnel, general administration, and more. (WA St. Dept. of Nat. Res. 1988 and 1989)

In Montana, 4.1 of 5.6 million acres of state land are leased to ranchers for $2.59/AUM. Like most state land, most of Montana's ranchland has suffered greatly from overgrazing and range development. Additionally, the state has tentative plans to sell large portions of its land to wealthy ranchers. In response, the Montana Coalition for Appropriate Management of State Land sued the Montana State Land Department for mismanagement, failure to actively implement the existing multiple use law, and to discourage sale of state land.

New Mexico's state land is among the most devastated anywhere, mostly by ranching. Stockmen there run livestock on more state land than in any other state -- 8.9 of 9.5 million acres, or 12% of the state. Their average $2.59/AUM grazing fee provides only about 2% of the Land Office's annual revenue. In 1985, in a bold move to increase state school revenue, State Lands Commissioner Jim Baca attempted to raise the fee to near fair market value. His plan was promptly crushed by the ranching establishment; a Santa Fe district judge threw out the proposed fees, saying in effect that grazing fees should be based on how much ranchers say they are able to pay, not on what the ranching is actually worth.

Most of the Great Plains states conduct ranching on state lands, causing similar environmental and economic problems. For example, on a large state-land ranch in Texas, 22 lawyers, owners of the base property, are known to have each received about $50,000 in subsidies in 1987.

Even Hawaii, about 1/3 of which has been cleared of tropical and sub-tropical forest and is now pasture, leases livestock grazing on state land. Ranching there is dominated by big-time stockmen. Ranchers on the Big Island currently are battling state biologists and environmentalists over the fate of the nearly extinct 'alala, or Hawaiian crow. Experts agree that the 'alala's only hope for survival is for state biologists to capture the few remaining wild birds and add them to the 10 already in a captive breeding program. The state had planned to do just that, but backed out when the owners of the McCandless Ranch, who hold a grazing lease for the state land where the birds live, refused to allow researchers or biologists into the area. Some speculate that the owners don't want scientists on the ranch because they might find other Endangered species, a situation which might result in the government curtailing ranching operations. Experts say that destruction of food sources and habitat by livestock grazing and forest cutting for ranching, timber, and development have decimated the 'alala.

The 36 million acres of ranched Western state land are of great environmental importance and potential. Yet as a whole they are the most severely overgrazed public lands, monopolized by a small number of powerful stockmen who don't produce enough livestock to begin to justify ranching them. To my knowledge, there has not been one serious, comprehensive study of the utilization and administration of state lands with regards to ranching. In sum, the secretive, often-corrupt state lands ranching industry is an even bigger rip-off than the federal.

State land behind this sign is treated essentially as private property.

● County

Western counties also own millions of acres as public parks, nature reserves, flood control and watershed protection areas, and so on. Many of these lands, larger parcels especially, are ranched under a wide variety of arrangements, often as a result of contract stipulations when the land was sold by ranchers to counties. Grazing fees generally are substantially higher than for federal land, though still well below fair market value. Ranching damage here is also extensive, though usually not so bad as on state lands. Land use conflicts are common.

● City

Many Western cities own surprisingly large amounts of undeveloped land in outlying areas, some of which are leased for livestock grazing. Ranching here usually is loosely regulated; consequently, these lands are often badly abused. Some cities also own large parcels of land far removed from their geographic locations, often for the purpose of procuring or protecting watersheds. The City of Los Angeles, for example, owns hundreds of thousands of overgrazed acres hundreds of miles north in the Owens Valley for water purposes (ironically, it could create more water by ending ranching there). The City of Scottsdale, Arizona, owns a large ranch in Mojave County, more than 100 miles away. Happily, the Scottsdale City Council recently voted to end sheep grazing on the ranch to prevent the possible transmission of life-threatening diseases to bighorn sheep in the area.

● Other

And some quasi-governmental bodies administer ranchlands -- various commissions, directorates, land trustees, and other semi-official entities. Ranching arrangements on these lands vary greatly.

● Indian Reservation

Indian reservations, supervised by the Interior Department's Bureau of Indian Affairs as "federal trust" lands, are not public land except to Native Americans. They encompass roughly 55 million acres in the US, 44 million in the West. About 40 million acres are grazed by livestock, perhaps 35 million in the 11 Western states -- nearly all that can be.

One-fourth of reservation livestock are owned by non-Native Americans under joint agreement between the Bureau of Indian Affairs and Native Americans. Most of the remainder of reservation grazing is controlled by a relatively small number of influential Native Americans, similar to the US public lands ranching establishment. Of course, many poor Native Americans do own a few cattle, sheep, goats, and/or horses for meat, milk, wool, transportation, and/or "tradition," but the commonly held notion that profits from reservation livestock are shared equitably among all is false, and most land damage is caused by commercial animals.

Goats eat nearly anything; they have stripped the foreground bare and the lower branches from the bushes. Navajo Reservation, AZ, between Tuo-noz-poz and Tus-naz-eye. *(Katie Lee)*

The Bureau of Indian Affairs is notoriously corrupt, as are many tribal councils and chairmen (former Navajo Chairmen Peter McDonald, for example, who was recently convicted and jailed on conspiracy and fraud charges, including those related to the purchase of a 491,432-acre ranch). Consequently, on most reservations influential stockmen maintain much power and receive special favors and obscure subsidization.

About 10 per cent of the Papagos [Indians, Arizona] own 90 per cent of the cattle. These local sheiks and politicos call the shots and maintain the status quo. Even drought is to their benefit, since it tends to weed out some of the smaller operators.
--Arizona Daily Star

According to the photographer, this winter range exhibits "drastic abuse" from livestock. Wind River Indian Reservation, Wyoming. *(George Robbins photo, Jackson, WY.)*

Fort Apache Indian Reservation, Arizona.

Sheep and goat grazing on the Navajo Indian Reservation, Arizona.

Ranching impact on most Indian reservations is severe, and has virtually ruined the environmental health of many. For instance, in **Desertification in the United States** David Sheridan identifies the 15-million-acre Navajo Reservation in northeast Arizona as one of the 3 areas of severe desertification in North America -- a "badly eroded land base with little of its natural grasses and low shrubs intact and vigorous" (Sheridan 1981). The Navajo are perhaps the most live-stock-dependent tribe in North America. Also among the most degraded reservations are the Hopi, Apache, Papago, and Hualapai in Arizona (all almost entirely grazed, which along with the Navajo encompass 1/4 of the state), Fort Hall in Idaho, Crow in Montana, and Yakima in Oregon. Combinations of cattle, sheep, goats, and horses on some reservations, such as the Navajo, are especially destructive. Much reservation land formerly serving many uses and providing natural resources is now practically worthless for anything but grazing livestock, if even that.

Though ranching has ravaged their reservations perhaps as thoroughly as all their other land uses combined, few Native Americans would consider abandoning their supposed "traditional means of livelihood." Those with longer memories recall that Spanish and Euro-American conquerors introduced them to cattle and sheep to help pacify ("civilize") them and settle them onto reservations. They understand that their ancestors gradually lost their natural relationship with the Earth as their domestic animals gutted the land that once provided them with physical and spiritual fulfillment.

● Private

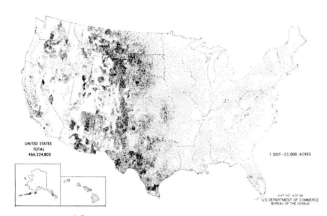

FIG. 1.2. PRIVATELY OWNED PASTURE OTHER THAN CROPLAND AND WOODLAND.

The widespread overgrazing of private lands in Texas, and throughout the West, is as disturbing to me as the overgrazing of public lands.
--David D. Diamond, M.S. in botany, Ph.D in Range Science, Austin, Texas

Finally, while 41% of the West is public ranchland, an additional 25% is private ranchland. (Including Indian reservations, 70% of the West is commercially ranched.) Nearly 40% of the West is privately owned, and 62%, or about 184 of 295 million acres, of this land is used for grazing livestock. Most of the remaining 38% is used for private residences and businesses in cities and towns; therefore, private land is even more dedicated to ranching than is public.

Indeed, it is truly amazing how much of our private property we Americans devote to 4-legged grazers. Visit a typical rural Western settlement. Most people who own several to several hundred acres have fenced the boundaries and turned them into barren pastures with cattle, sheep, goats, and equines. Non-grazed land is restricted to fenced homes and yards, businesses, and vacant lots. Out on the open private range, almost the only ungrazed land is that which *cannot* be grazed.

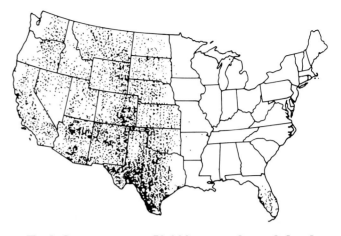

Each dot represents 50,000 acres of non-federal ranchland in fair or poor condition: 1982.
(Source: *National Resources Inventory*, SCS, USDA)

Not having even the scant protection provided by government supervision, many private lands are wrecked by ranching. An SCS appraisal of the 1982 National Resources Inventory data indicates that 71% of non-federal ranchland in the West is being "inadequately managed," mostly as pertaining to livestock numbers and duration of grazing (Atwood 1990). Conversely, lack of government influence allows some ranchers to practice lighter stocking and more benign ranching management. On the whole, however, private ranchlands are probably in worse condition than are public lands; percentage-wise, more private range is accessible to livestock, is more highly developed for ranching, and has been ranched longer. The 1975 BLM survey report concluded that about 68% of private rangeland was in fair or poor condition (Ferguson 1983). This seems to indicate that the ranching industry is managing the land it gained ownership of as poorly as the public land it is permitted to

Private range in California.

ranch. SCS (under)estimates about the same percentage of private rangeland in "unsatisfactory" condition as does BLM (under)estimate for its rangeland. In 1987 SCS reported the condition of private range in the contiguous US as 4% excellent, 31% good, 47% fair, and 17% poor, with range conditions stable on 69% of this land, improving on 16% and declining on 15% (Willard 1990). In other words, nearly 2/3 of private range -- more than 270 million acres -- is functioning at less than half its potential, and about as much of private range is declining as improving.

In *Livestock Grazing and the Livestock Industry*, Frederic H. Wagner estimates that cattle numbers in the West are now at an all-time high, that forage demand for western livestock today is at an alltime high, and notes that "it seems possible that they [private rangelands] are experiencing some of the heaviest pressures they have received in the history of the West" (Wagner 1978). Even so, in the 1989 USFS publication, *An Analysis of the Range Forage Situation in the United States: 1989-2040*, Linda A. Joyce concludes, ". . . the supply of forage from private lands in 2040 is projected to increase by 52% over the 1985 levels" (Joyce 1989).

Because, aside from farmland, private ranchland generally is the most productive land in the rural West, it often *appears* (even to range professionals) to be in better condition than it actually is, especially compared to the relatively rugged, dry, barren, public rangeland. The more productive private ranchland should support more wildlife than public ranchland does, and in some cases, such as pronghorn in Wyoming, it does. Yet, throughout most of the West more wildlife survives on public land where it is afforded a higher degree of protection from ranching and attrition from ranchers and others.

Private ranchland. As always, note the fenceline contrast.

California's private ranchland is the worst. Even SCS, which generally is protective of ranching, says that *46%* of the state's non-federal rangeland is in *poor* condition -- producing (primarily for livestock) at **0%-25%** of its present potential; Idaho is second with 29% (USDA, SCS 1981). This is largely a reflection of California's overall longer history of ranching; early Spanish settlers began overgrazing its lush grasses in the 1600s. Additionally, although California rangeland receives less summer precipitation than any other state's, ranchers nevertheless often graze it through summer. According to a major interagency study of California's San Joaquin Valley, of the 4 million acres of grazing land there, 3.2 million, or 80%, "have problems."

Perhaps most of the 30,000 or so Western public lands ranching privately owned base properties are located in or near riparian areas, most of which consequently have been severely degraded.

Demarcating his private ranching domain, a Utah stockman has spray-painted "THIS IS PRIVATE PROPERTY NO TRESSPASSING [sic]" on a rock face directly over an Anasazi pictograph. *(Kelly Cranston)*

Worth special mention here are the Western "railroad lands." To speed colonization of the West, the federal government very early on encouraged construction and westward extension of railroads by means of large land grants. These grants initially totalled more than 94 million acres, consisting of alternate sections extending in a checkerboard pattern 10 to 40 miles on each side of the right-of-way.

Because checkerboarded railroad sections alternate with sections of BLM, FS, state, and/or other private lands, stockmen usually exercise de facto control of ranching on these lands as well. In this way stockmen have been able to block up huge tracts of public and private land. Many ranchers consider and manage these parcels, especially state and BLM lands, as their own. Because these lands usually are unsurveyed and unmarked, administration is difficult and the public and government generally defer control to stockmen.

Over the years most railroad lands were purchased by stockmen. Today, less than 20 million acres are still held by the railroads, and most of these are leased to stockmen. Railroad lease agreements generally don't restrict the number of livestock, period of use, etc., so these lands are among the most overgrazed in the West. Due to past and present ranching abuse, some are so wasted that they are considered virtually worthless even by ranchers.

CHAPTER X
BENEFITS OF PUBLIC LANDS RANCHING

By now, some skeptical readers may be thinking, "Yeah, maybe most of this book is true. But what about the *other* side? What about public lands ranching's contributions?" In the interest of presenting a more complete picture of the issue, therefore, this chapter is dedicated to public lands ranching benefits.

Public lands ranching:

- Produces 3% of US beef.

- Keeps some people wealthy.

- Keeps some people powerful.

- Helps maintain some people's accustomed lifestyle.

- Helps keep bureaucrats busy.

- Allows us to feel like we are doing something useful with otherwise "useless" public land.

- Requires endless miles of barbed wire fences, which occasionally catch ORVers.

- Provides humans roaded access to every nook and cranny of public land and opens the West to widespread exploitation.

- Reduces groundcover, allowing hikers easier travel and the ability to spot venomous snakes more easily.

- Gives hunters *something* to shoot at (cows).

- Helps -- ever so slightly -- to preserve "our Western legacy."

- Promotes excessive beef consumption, and thus helps reduce human overpopulation.

- Provides material for Gary Larson cartoons.

- Maintains remote base properties that serve as excellent sites for criminal hideouts and narcotics laboratories.

- Provides an excellent example of how tyrannical, wasteful, and destructive a special interest can be without public awareness or opposition.

Bumpersticker seen in New Mexico:

> **TO PROTECT ALL HIS CREATIONS
> GOD CREATED RANCHERS**

We have all encountered much misinformation and many romantic renderings of ranching, but how much real evidence do we have to justify public lands ranching?

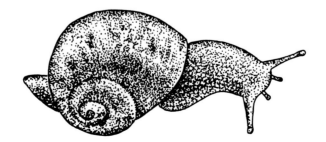

Chapter XI
JUSTIFICATIONS/MYTHS

(Nola Burger)

In ranching's early years, brute force ruled the range. Stockmen took what they had the power to take and felt little need to justify their actions or presence on public land. In the early 1900s, as more people came West and population grew, public land increasingly was used for purposes other than ranching. Accordingly, ranchmen were increasingly hard-pressed to excuse their dominance and destructive practices.

At first it was mostly a matter of defending "their" land from competitors. Ranchers simply claimed to have the "right" to control public land because they were there first (conveniently overlooking the Native American people and wildlife they helped eliminate). Over time, as multiple use gained acceptance, this claim became less tenable. So, through the years stockmen necessarily have developed increasingly complex and diverse stratagems for justifying a business that is inherently unjustifiable.

Much of this rationale has been passed down through the years in the same way as Western legends and tall tales. Ranching custom and the unwritten, self-perpetuating code of cowboy comraderie compel stockmen to promote these fictions. As with the Easter Bunny and Santa Claus, by mutual agreement what is known to be untrue is treated as reality. Ranchers largely can't be blamed for promoting these fables; they were raised on them and see them as not only part of their ranching legacy but as a necessary protection against what they perceive as an increasingly hostile society.

Other justifications have been deliberately fabricated in recent years as part of the industry's modern promotion strategy. Some are specifically designed to appeal to popular virtues such as patriotism, teamwork, thriftiness, and fair play. Others are scare tactics. Many of these arguments can be very convincing to the uninformed. Each has at least a grain of truth, as does any fabrication. Ranching advocates offer them brazenly, hoping that impressiveness of presentation will obscure content, thinking that our

Today, 100 years after the cattle and sheep drives and range wars that figured so prominently in the settling of the West, livestock grazing continues as a valid, authorized use on public range. Livestock grazing produces food and fiber, along with many other environmental, economic, and social benefits.
--Livestock Grazing Successes on Public Range (USDA 1989)

We have provided the most abundant, economical, and safest food supply in the world, while practicing conservation methods that ensured that the environment is protected.
--National Cattle Growers Association news release, spring 1990

The secret to lying is to always tell big lies, never small ones.
--Joseph Goebbels, Nazi Propaganda Minister

society's ignorance, indifference, and cowboy religion will protect their myths. The ranching establishment has learned the fine art of public relations.

Over the years most of these justifications have become highly standardized. They fall into a score of basic approaches.

● What problem?

I've worked 6 years as a Forest Service botanist, mostly on the Inyo [California] NF, and am livid at what I've seen, experienced, and confronted in habitat devastation, rancher rhetoric & clout, and FS apathy toward the mere acknowledgment of even a problem existing.
--Jim Andre, Bayside, California, personal correspondence

Believing denial the best defense, many in the ranching establishment simply refuse to acknowledge that there is or ever was a problem. They feign surprise at the very suggestion:

What!? -- peaceful, grazing cows and sheep harm the land? Ridiculous! Some armchair environmentalist must have thought that one up. You don't believe that crap do you?

Thus, if you do you are led to feel like a gullible, desk-bound fool. This works on many people who know little about ranching or who strongly embrace cowboy mythology.

The agencies, as public affairs agents, commonly disregard or trivialize ranching impacts. As a small but common example, this morning I read a publication entitled "Proposed Coconino National Forest Plan." In it the Forest Service describes the 12 "issues of concern" for this central Arizona National Forest. Curiously, ranching is not among them. There is only an incidental reference to some live-stock-caused damage to riparian areas *in the past*. Though undeniably ranching stands with logging as this Forest's most harmful influence, apparently the public should not even consider it a problem, much less a major issue. Ranching advocates insist that there is no positive *proof* that ranching harms the land. To them, of course, no evidence constitutes proof.

● Well, ranching's not so bad compared to . . . .

When denial didn't work, ranchers blamed the problems on wild horses, weather, hunters, off-road vehicles, vandals, or -- most recently -- elk.
--Rose Strickland "Taking the Bull by the Horns" (Strickland 1990)

***The flyer portrays a rugged Western landscape in silhouette. To the right, outlined in white, a city sprawls across the flatlands. A road extends from the city to the left, toward what remains of the wild. On the far left, up on a bluff, a lone, mounted cowboy surveys the encroaching distant city. A river, etched in orange lines, symbolically separates the cowboy from modern society.

The flyer was distributed by the Tucson Public Library to advertise audio tapes labeled "The Wilderness Still

Lingers." The message is clear: Cowboys are an integral part of the wilderness, valiantly-but-futilely trying to protect their home and the West from the relentless onslaught of modern civilization -- a sadly unalterable destiny. The scene evokes melancholy, and sympathy for wilderness and cowboy.

But there is more. Barely visible in the river gorge, a bridge crosses the river. Will the cowboy cross that bridge into the modern age? Hell no! This is a one-way bridge, representing civilization's inevitable advancement against defenseless cowboy/wilderness. Further, parts of the cowboy and horse are outlined in pink; no other part of the flyer is that color except the text used to describe the wilderness audio cassettes. In other words, the cowboy is our link to the wilderness.

Ironically, the writers featured on these cassettes include strong supporters of ranching reform, even Edward Abbey, a leading critic of public lands ranching. Also ironic is that this irrevocable symbol of the wilderness -- the cowboy/rancher -- has not only done more than anyone to ruin the wild West, but has also done more to prevent remaining Western natural areas from being protected.

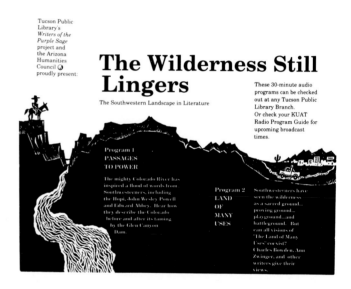

Tucson Public Library's *Writers of the Purple Sage* project and the Arizona Humanities Council proudly present:

The Wilderness Still Lingers

The Southwestern Landscape in Literature

These 30-minute audio programs can be checked out at any Tucson Public Library Branch. Or check your KUAT Radio Program Guide for upcoming broadcast times.

Program 1
PASSAGES TO POWER

The mighty Colorado River has inspired a flood of words from Southwesterners, including the Hopi, John Wesley Powell and Edward Abbey. Hear how they describe the Colorado before and after its taming by the Glen Canyon Dam.

Program 2
LAND OF MANY USES

Southwesterners have seen the wilderness as a sacred ground... proving ground... playground...and battleground. But can all visions of "The Land of Many Uses" coexist? Charles Bowden, Ann Zwinger, and other writers give their views.

***The video portrays an elderly Navajo woman on horseback driving sheep across a vast, barren Navajo landscape. In the distance, like an immense, evil citadel, stands the coal-fired Four Corners Power Plant, one of the largest and dirtiest electric-generating facilities in the US.

The message is clear. Here is a traditional way of life being symbolically, if not physically, assaulted by the juggernaut of industrial civilization. Furthermore, science and technology, impersonal and uncaring, can be extremely destructive, whereas the rustic family activity -- livestock grazing -- is relatively harmless. The two are ironically side by side.

It **is** ironic -- because the woman's sheep, along with other livestock on the reservation, have done more damage to Navajoland than all the reservation's power plants and coal strip mines combined. It is also ironic because now that Navajo land is severely degraded by overgrazing it isn't much use for anything but continued overgrazing.

***The front page photo of the conservation journal *High Country News* is half-filled by "Brutus," a 26-story-high strip-mining shovel turned tourist attraction near West Mineral, Kansas. Like a small toy in comparison, a black angus cow runs before the gigantic iron monster.

Symbolism run amok! Here is a poor, defenseless cow, and by inference its poor, defenseless rancher owner, and by inference the poor, defenseless ranching subculture, under attack from the ruthless, unstoppable modern monster of exploitation.

Ironically again, stockmen and their cows have done more to ruin the West than a thousand of these gigantic strip-mining machines. But to write this is blasphemy!!! Regardless of reality, our American Cowboy remains the personification of the Western landscape.

The point is, images similar to those above, though delusions, pervade our society. Grazing livestock, folksy cowboys, rustic windmills, etc. often are (even by environmentalists) contrasted against contemporary culture to represent benign simplicity, naturalness, innocence, contentment, truth, pride, and other virtues. Because of its outward predominance in Western history, ranching recalls the past -- bygone times, the good ol' days, when things were as things should be. Ironically once again, we have seen that ranching is not the antithesis but the vanguard and compatriot of the exploitive, growth-oriented modern worldview.

Usually the first thing a country does in the course of economic development is introduce a lot of livestock. Our data are showing that this is not a very smart move.
--Cornell University nutritional biochemist T.C. Campbell

Backpackers leave body wastes and campfire ashes in the wilderness areas; ecologists pollute the biosphere and other areas they study; bird watchers disturb the habitat of the birds they watch; campers leave residues and trample vegetation, so do hunters and anglers; herds and flocks of livestock trample and defecate on grass and water just as they did in Biblical times. So, too, do all wild herbivores, and even fish must defecate.
--T.C. Byerly, Staff Consultant, Winrock International (suppliers of range "improvement" equipment) (USDA, USDI, CEQ 1979)

Some say the best defense is a good offense. As Western ranching has come under increasing resistance in recent years, ranching proponents have begun a concerted effort to promote the idea that ranching isn't really a problem when compared to other uses. Using diversionary tactics to deflect opposition, many have taken to condemning the "real destroyers of public lands" -- strip-miners, irresponsible hunters, off-road vehicle users, backpackers, vandals,

and those fiendish litterbugs. (Curiously, stockmen almost universally support logging, which is the second most overall destructive use of Western public lands. Less trees mean more grass.)

By focusing attention on other public lands abusers, ranchmen take the heat off themselves. By displaying opposition to other destructive uses, they portray themselves as environmentally concerned, thus suggesting that they certainly would not harm the land.

New Mexico public lands rancher Sid Goodloe declares in *Harper's Magazine*, "let's talk about the real problem on our public lands -- the damage being done to them by off-road vehicles." South Dakota rancher Linda Hasselstrom sums up her argument in a letter to *High Country News*: "If we ban cattle grazing, let's be consistent and ban all use of public lands that will damage the land or wildlife . . . [and] ban skiers from mountains where any living wild animal has been observed." Maybe we should also ban public lands birders, those unchaste ruffians who gleefully trample delicate purple asters and terrorize great blue herons.

This all-or-nothing, black-or-white approach is used often by stockmen and their apologists. It is an old debating trick -- using shades of grey to justify or trivialize extremes. No distinction is made in *degree* of abuse, which would allow us to *prioritize* mitigation of the abuses. The point consistently side-stepped is that public lands ranching is **the** most destructive, **least** justifiable of all public lands uses.

It's a felony to deface a Forest Service sign, but perfectly OK for cows to destroy an entire watershed!
--Denzel and Nancy Ferguson (ONDA 1990)

Personal experience has led me to write that cattle alone have done thousands of times more to degrade our natural surroundings than all the tourists, fishermen, picnickers, hikers, backpackers, birders, and naturalists combined. Philip Fradkin claims in "The Eating of the West" that "The impact of countless hooves and mouths over the years has done more to alter the type of vegetation and landforms of the West than all of the water projects, strip mines, power plants, freeways, and subdivision developments combined." On the other hand, Colorado public lands rancher Art Johnson claims in a letter to *High Country News* that "When you look at the massive and permanent damage done by mining, oil development, major road building, deforestation, hydro projects, ski resorts, etc., the damage done by present grazing practices on public lands is minor." While most people naturally tend to think that the truth must lie somewhere between these extremes, careful consideration of the obscure nature of ranching and its overall impact leads me to believe that Philip Fradkin and I are *understating* the case.

Ranching promoters maintain that we must treat all uses equally. If we ban ranching, then let's ban 'em all, including hunting and skiing, hiking and birding. They know, of course, that few of these other uses ever will be banned.

There is another important ulterior motive behind this twisted logic -- *eliminating competition*. As discussed previously, ranching negatively affects many other uses of public land. Inversely, these other uses sometimes conflict with ranching.

For example, many stockmen dislike ORV enthusiasts because they kill grass, scare cattle, leave gates open, and vandalize range developments. Ranchers may sound like the environmentalists they claim to be when ranting and raving against the evils of ORV use, but their primary motive is eliminating competition.

They ignore the fact that the removal of the vegetation cover by livestock and the extensive network of Western ranching access roads is a major cause of the ORV problem, and that most ranchers are themselves off-road vehicle users. With massive pickup trucks, 3- and 4-wheelers, and dirt bikes, stockmen patrol allotments in all kinds of weather, on road and off, causing far more damage than other ORVers in most of the West. Thus, any argument against ORV use is an argument against ranching.

Ranchers sometimes discourage mining on public land because it reduces grazing and scares cattle. However, where mining development results in improved access, an influx of money to the local economy, or other perceived ranching benefits, they tolerate or encourage it. (As mentioned, by law stockmen are more than compensated financially for reduced grazing and other inconveniences caused by mining operations on allotments.)

bad, are likely to oppose ranching -- and most ranchers simply don't like "those hippie types." So they denounce hikers and backpackers as "the true despoilers of the West," "outsiders" who trample the land, pollute the water, litter, leave gates open, and scare cows. They "use the resources and don't even pay a fee to do so!"

Sure, there are rainforest destruction, wholesale slaughter of dolphins by the tuna industry, wanton harvesting of animals for their pelts by the fur industry, toxic and hazardous waste and a whole panoply of other crimes that we have committed against the planet. But recognition of these facts does not excuse the rape of the West that has been perpetrated by ranchers and their cattle.
--David A. Huet, in a letter to the *Tucson Weekly* (9-26-90)

These days, public display of environmental concern is a necessary part of any commercial land-use strategy. Stockmen, set in their ways and used to getting what they want, were slow to learn this. Mostly since the "ecology movement" of the 1970s they have come to realize that feigning environmental concern, as distasteful as it might be, helps garner support and minimize competition.

(Roger Candee)

Stockmen have mixed feelings about hunters. On one hand, they encourage and support hunting to eliminate their animal enemies. On the other, stockmen push for stronger controls over hunters because hunters sometimes scare livestock, cut locks and fences, leave gates open, and shoot holes in water tanks. Some hunters, discouraged by the lack of game on Western ranges, have taken to hunting cattle. But most ranchers themselves are "hunters," or at least have no qualms about knocking off predators, competitors, pests, and no-goods.

Stockmen especially disdain hikers and backpackers, accusing them of numerous sins. Their hostile feelings seem based mainly on socio-political factors. People who appreciate rather than exploit public land make ranchers look

All this is not to say that some ranchers are not truly concerned. As with any group, some are working to reverse environmental degradation, both on and off their allotments. Unfortunately, because any kind of ranching is inherently detrimental, even these ranchers continue to damage the range with both livestock and development. Their hard work and good intentions create an unfortunate situation where the support they garner perpetuates the innately harmful, wasteful welfare ranching they practice.

● *Ranching may once have been destructive, but not now that it's scientific.*

The record is clear. The ranges are improving and most of the rangelands are best used for grazing . . . there's no reason to argue for not grazing.
--Thadis Box, Utah State University range professional

Our grandfathers and great grandfathers overgrazed, but that's all over now.
--An Arizona public lands rancher, in a local newspaper

Assistant Secretary of the Interior David O'Neal told members of the New Mexico Cattle Growers' Association to fight critics by producing "data proving our rangelands are getting better."
--*The Animals' Agenda* (March 1991)

Nearly every ranching publication contains some reference to the "uncontrolled" livestock devastation of long ago. Each then openly or by inference goes on to claim that range conditions are much better now than in those wild, unrestricted days.

This often is the second line of defense when initial attempts to make ranching seem harmless fails. It goes something like this: "Uncontrolled" grazing ravaged the range a century ago. Since range condition was terrible then, it must be better now. Since it is better now, range conditions are improving. Since range conditions are improving and we have ever-expanding science and technology for "controlled" grazing, range condition will continue to improve indefinitely, eventually even surpassing aboriginal condition.

This is faulty logic, but the basic assumptions behind it may be even more faulty. Past grazing was "uncontrolled" insofar as it was not administered by the government and livestock were mostly unfenced. However, then as now the *mass* of domestic animals were the major factor behind the devastation, not the lack of administration and fences. Indeed, in some ways the large, nomadic herds on the open range then caused less environmental damage per head than livestock do now. The claim that "controlled" grazing is necessarily more benign is as much a myth as the promise that control of the atom would bring us "a world of peace" and "life of effortless plenty."

Are range conditions really better now? Things may *seem* better than a hundred years ago when much of the West was stripped as bare as a billiard table (though much is still that bare). However, as mentioned, even government studies show that roughly 50% of Western range productivity has been lost to cumulate livestock impact. In a report to the President's Council on Environmental Quality, Frederic H. Wagner and 2 other range experts "concluded that 3/4 of the western ranges were producing at less than half their potential at the time [1968]" (Wagner 1978). A 1984 Senate report estimated that 76% of BLM range was in either fair or poor condition, unable to produce more than half its estimated aboriginal potential (Williams 1990). A 1980 SCS estimate was that more than half of Western rangeland was producing at less than 40% potential and that more than 85% was producing at less than 60% potential (Chaney 1990). Several other reports indicating little or no change have already been mentioned. In other words, the land is actually producing much less forage now, though individual forage plants in grazed areas may on the average be larger than, say, in the 1880s or 1930s because they are not always cropped to the ground.

If we define range condition as the overall, long-term health and integrity of the rangeland environment, today's conditions probably are significantly worse than a century ago. A century ago, livestock were simply turned out and allowed to reproduce in greater and greater numbers until the land could no longer support them. Although this caused many kinds of immediate environmental harm, other kinds of damage and more serious long-term damage would not become apparent for decades.

In the late 1800s livestock stripped the herbaceous cover, then starved if they were not removed from the range. Even so, *the distribution, composition, and density of native vegetation all were still basically intact.* Native species covered most of their aboriginal range; vegetation was composed mostly of natives; and individual plants were relatively closely spaced, though eaten to nubs. Over subsequent decades native species have declined drastically as increasers, invaders, and bare dirt spread relentlessly. Distribution, composition, and density have progressively declined as long-term impacts compounded.

CONDITION OF BLM-MANAGED PUBLIC RANCHLAND

Source	Condition class (percent)				
	Excellent	Good	Fair	Poor	Unknown
NRDC/NWF @ (1985)	1.9	27.1	42	29	0
BLM range managers (GAO 1988)	6	23	31	12	28
Official BLM report (1987)	3	30	39	19	9

@Natural Resources Defense Council and National Wildlife Federation. Based on an analysis of the grazing environmental impact statements done by BLM between May 1978 and June 1985, covering about 118 million of the 165 million acres of public ranchland administered by BLM.

Range Conditions, Then and Now

The BLM range now, according to the BLM. *(BLM)*

Dropped out range conservationists have told me that they have seen drastic reductions in forage in the last 10 years, and expect the trend to continue.
--Anonymous New Mexico State Land Department official

Each passing year more soil erodes from the Western range. There is less soil now than ever before because excessive soil erosion continues while the creation of new soil cannot nearly keep pace. The greatly reduced topsoil supply and the loss of tens of thousands of acres of bottomland have caused a chain reaction of destructive environmental changes, including substantial loss in biological health and productivity.

Likewise, continual overgrazing has contributed to a progressive diminishment in streamflows and water tables, and thus in dependent wildlife. Evidence indicates that overall water pollution due to livestock also has grown steadily worse.

Ranching continues to harm wildlife. Granted, there have been reintroductions and increases of some species' populations in recent decades. However, much of this recovery has required massive human intervention, and little of it can be credited to ranching. Each year we expend more resources to maintain or increase numbers of some "game" animals, often to counterbalance ranching's malevolent influences. This creates the *illusion* of recovery. Meanwhile, ranching causes many of the less popular native species to continue their inexorable declines, some toward extirpation or extinction. The overall wildlife picture is not better than in the past.

Additionally, a century ago, though much of the West was ravaged by livestock, large areas remained ungrazed because they were inaccessible or too far from water. For example, until the early 1900s many of the natural forest meadows had never been grazed by livestock because they were too remote or were surrounded by impenetrable brush or trees. Aboriginal, densely vegetated forests had not yet been thinned by timbering. Large portions of arid to semi-arid range were too far from water for livestock to utilize.

In recent decades, more ranching access roads, modernized livestock and supply transport (including helicopters), livestock access developments, and artificial water sources

have allowed livestock to spread to almost every nook and cranny of our public range. This important factor is underappreciated by most range analysts. Though some public land has been built on or otherwise withdrawn from livestock use (only 4% in the US since 1958 [Joyce 1989]), rangeland overall is being more thoroughly grazed, and previously ungrazed land has been turned into grazing land.

Range developments a century ago were simple and rare. Today, science and technology have provided the means to mitigate some of the more serious range management detriments (though always at the expense of other natural components and other ecosystems). This has enabled the ranching establishment to damage the land more thoroughly in more ways than early ranchers would have imagined possible. Each year there are more and more fences, roads, stock watering devices, salt blocks, seedings, and other destructive range developments.

Federal records show livestock range herbage consumption on public lands down somewhat from earlier times, *but roughly stable since the 1950s.* Even accounting for today's larger cattle, agency exaggeration, and other factors, there probably has been an overall, small reduction in livestock biomass since historic peak periods. We are told that this represents a "sincere attempt to control overgrazing." More correctly it means *the long-term productivity of the Western range continues to decline -- even with the aid of billions of dollars in range "improvements."* Thus, some experts believe relative livestock *pressure* on the Western range is now at an all-time high. (In the West as a whole, the cattle population is at an all-time high.)

The highest historic peaks in livestock numbers give us the false impression that lower levels represent responsible use. Yet, even disregarding these highest peaks, livestock pressure on public land has consistently remained extremely high from the 1870s until present; **even the lowest points represent a severely harmful influence.**

BLM's own 1984 report -- which has been criticized as slanted to portray BLM range improvement -- stated that, while 5% of BLM range was rated excellent, 31% good, 42% in fair, and 18% in poor or very poor condition, 18% was improving, 68% was stable, and 14% was declining (USDI, BLM 1984). It is safe to assume that if BLM says nearly as much of its land is deteriorating as improving, probably more is deteriorating than improving. After the General Accounting Office conducted 11 studies of BLM in 3 years, it reported to Congress in 1989:

We found that almost 60% of the grazing allotments for which BLM range managers had current status information were in less than satisfactory condition. Further, only about one-fourth of the allotments whose status was known were improving while the remainder were either stable or declining. Despite this generally unsatisfactory condition, range managers told us that a significant portion of grazing allotments continued to be overstocked. Moreover, on 75% of the allotments threatened with overgrazing, BLM had not scheduled any action to reduce authorized grazing levels. [emphasis added]

(Mentioned earlier was a 1987 SCS report estimating as much US private range deteriorating as improving.)

The mouth of Cave Creek Canyon, Chiricahua Mountains, southeast Arizona. A 1908 photo (top) shows a range well covered with native grasses eaten close to the ground by cattle, widely scattered with shrubs. The same scene in 1956 (below) is dominated by bare, rocky ground and thorny brush. *(Unknown)*

A freeway right-of-way west of Laramie, Wyoming. The resident photographer adds, "This is common all over Wyoming and getting worse." *(Harvey Duncan)*

Range condition as defined by the ranching establishment is an arbitrary, biased, misleading term, based mainly on perceived present potential of the land to produce herbage for livestock, rather than on environmental health and integrity. Furthermore, how much environmental good is allegedly "productive" range in allegedly "good" condition when herbage is cropped to stubble for most or all of the year?

In sum, today's public range is in a **dynamic state of degradation.** Most evidence indicates that the greatest rate of overt rangeland damage probably occurred during the initial livestock invasion of the late 1800s and during a few peak use periods in the first half of this century. But these high rates of degradation in large part simply reflect that the most susceptible environmental components succumbed first. Compared to these peaks, the overall *rate* of environmental damage has in some ways declined. However, in some ways it has not. *Progressive* deterioration continues and *cumulative* degeneration intensifies. Thus, overall ranching *pressure* is probably near an all-time high. Ranching **is** as bad as it used to be, if not worse.

● *Ranchers aren't responsible for harming public land because it is the government's responsibility to protect this land.*

Last night, I once again heard a public lands rancher stand up in front of a crowd and make this claim. It deserves no response.

● *Ranchers lead simple, earthy lives, so they have developed a special closeness to and respect for Nature.*

The Fantasy.

Ranchers are rugged outdoorsmen, right? They make a living out there on the range, close to the land. From working on the land for so long they have developed a thorough knowledge of, and strong feeling for, the environment. They are poor, hard-working people who lead simple, natural lives. So the story goes.

Back in the real world, we find that most ranchers are not rugged, adventurous outdoorsmen, but are instead rather ordinary businessmen. Generally they attend to their livestock and ranching chores in fancy pickup trucks (sometimes ultra- lights, airplanes, or helicopters), do their work with the most modern equipment available, and rarely spend a night outdoors. They see the environment more as obstacle than companion. Through the years I have been shocked to discover just how little most stockmen understand or appreciate the land they ranch.

The common perception that ranchers lead a simple existence, a natural life close to the Earth, is but for few exceptions not true. In the first place, most Western stockmen are well-situated and accustomed to a comfortable lifestyle. Moreover, the very nature of public lands livestock grazing necessitates large, complex, and expensive ranching operations. And because Western land, public land especially, is so poor for raising livestock, profit-to-expense ratio is usually very low. A livestock operation netting $100,000 per year may spend several times that amount for not only ranching labor, supplies, repairs, utilities, transport, etc., but to maintain the accustomed lifestyle in a remote location. If public and private subsidies are factored, the "business" becomes so unprofitable as to be laughable. A visit to a public lands ranch is a lesson on waste:

Simpson and "his wife" own an 80-acre base property. Around the headquarters compound rests an assortment of heavy equipment -- tractor, bulldozer, backhoe. Pieces of machinery lie in various states of repair and disrepair. Against a shed wall stand drums of kerosene, creosote, asphalt emulsion, diesel fuel, gasoline, motor oil, and hydraulic fluid. Behind the shed, we find a grease pit and a small trench for used oil.

The large barn is stocked with straw, hay, salt blocks, and bags of cattle, horse, dog, and chicken feed, cement, and fertilizer. A few seldom-ridden horses stand in their stalls; a horse corral is adjacent. The horses are handy for certain chores (and for fun and visitors), but the vast bulk of ranch work utilizes motorized vehicles -- including the pickups, stock truck, jeep, and ATV parked over with the family car, horse trailer, heavy equipment trailer, utility trailer, live-in trailer (for extended stays on the range), and several junk vehicles near the ranch house. Simpson's single-prop Cherokee awaits him at the end of a nearby quarter-mile-long dirt runway.

The compound also contains cattle corrals, holding pens, chutes, ramps, a stock tank and scale. Sheds and outbuildings bulge with tools and supplies, most seldom but eventually used. Here we find auto and truck parts, vehicle repair tools, windmill components, water pumps, chainsaws, generators, equestrian gear, branding implements, sheet metal, sheet and rolled plastic, tarps, torches, sprayers, mowers, power post hole diggers, chains and ropes, come-alongs, hydraulic jacks, drills and presses, wire stretchers, welding equipment, carpentry tools, table saws, an air compressor, electrical equipment, veterinary supplies, firearm supplies, varmint and insect poisons, weed killers, *ad infinitum*. Under the overhangs of some of the buildings are a cement mixer, wheelbarrows, piles of fence posts and stays, old gates, rolls of mesh and barbed wire, pipe (CPVC, ABS, and galvanized iron), lumber, roofing materials, concrete blocks, ladders, propane tanks, stove pipes, screens, rebar,

angle iron, hoses, haying machinery, farm implements, old tires, animal traps, and so on. Tacked and nailed on the wall of one old shed are deer heads, rattlesnake skins, and coyote carcasses. The hound pens and chicken coops occupy most of the shady space under a lone ponderosa pine.

Six miles of dirt road snake from ranch headquarters down the valley to the well-maintained gravel road leading to town. The dirt road is usually impassable several days a year, but the county does a good job of keeping it open. Along the dirt road, mail is delivered daily to 3 widely spaced mailboxes, all owned by public lands ranchers who own the best bottomland along the valley and control permits for ranching on surrounding public land. The other 2 ranchers have children, who are picked up and dropped off by school buses each weekday.

Back at Simpson Ranch, electrical wires from the main house and various buildings meet at a central utility pole; from there a line of power poles marches to the horizon. Telephone wires, installed 15 years ago through a special discount to ranchers, also run along these poles. The large propane storage tank that serves the main ranch and guest houses is filled every few months by a delivery truck that makes the 17-mile journey from town. Although propane is the main house's principal heat source, the ranch family burns a few cords of wood in the fireplace and wood heater each winter to save money; after all, the wood is free from public land. The ranch house isn't exactly "Little House on the Prairie"; it is large, comfortable, and equipped with the latest conveniences. A satellite dish picks up TV waves. An extra bedroom serves as the ranch office.

The Simpson's domestic water comes from a fenced spring half a mile up a nearby canyon, capped off and run down the canyon through a 2" galvanized iron pipe into a 10,000-gallon holding tank above the house. Water for cattle (when at headquarters) and horses comes from a small reservoir. Late each spring, after the threat of flooding has mostly passed, Simpson uses a bulldozer to scrape a diversion dam across the valley's seasonal creek, diverting the flow through a ditch into the reservoir. The reservoir also helps irrigate a 12-acre pasture, which occupies the most fertile bottomland along the creek below the house. During periods when the reservoir is full, Simpson allows it to overflow and run back down into its natural course (or what passes for "natural" after being channelized and rip-rapped). Though the creek no longer flows for extended periods, when it does, water is diverted directly to pasture and stock via irrigation ditches.

For years Simpson has dumped garbage, brush, trash, scrap material, and assorted junk into an arroyo a couple hundred yards behind the house. Like many ranchers, he feels a curious security in this time-honored accumulation.

Due to intensive activity by vehicles, machinery, horses, cattle, and people, the compound area for a radius of hundreds of feet is stark, bare earth. Most days this is a source of dust, but it becomes a cursed muddy quagmire after a rain. Nevertheless, the ranch family is glad for the barren zone around their living area as it helps keep the bugs and varmints at bay.

Simpson has tried to raise a few fruit trees near the house, fencing them from the horses and loose cattle with 5 tight strands of barbed wire on close-set posts. The attempt has been moderately successful, with most of the stunted trees' upper branches still intact. A lawn and ornamental bushes survive within a chain link fence adjoining the house.

From the compound, dirt roads radiate in every direction, following the creek up and downstream, accessing every part of the valley bottomland, cutting up steep hillsides, winding along ridgetops and canyon bottoms. The stockman can drive from the ranch house almost anywhere. On his ATV, he can zip down to the diversion dam to check the water flow, or down the valley to irrigate the pasture. In his jeep, he can 4-wheel it up to the springhead to check the water intake or drive the 7 rugged miles along ridgetops to check cattle on the high mesa on the far side of the 12,300-acre allotment. In one of his heavy-duty pickups, it takes only an hour to reach a fence post cutting area 35 miles away, or half an hour to go to town to pick up supplies.

During the 18 years Simpson has "owned" the allotment, the Forest Service and other agencies have provided the following: 7 dirt and 3 metal stock tanks; a concrete dam; a pipeline; 2 windmills; 3 brush and 5 pinyon/juniper removals totaling 1450 acres; 2 noxious weed control projects for 470 acres; 3 seedings and reseedings for 870 acres; poison spray twice for grasshoppers on 900 acres; poison grain for gophers and ground squirrels; coyote and mountain lion eradication; disease inoculation for hundreds of cattle; 16 miles of new fence and 8 1/2 miles of replacement fence; 4 cattle guards; 3 gates; 8 miles of dirt roads; and 6 "Watch for Livestock" and "Cattle Guard" signs. Nobody keeps track, but the cost of all these "improvements" totals about $200,000. Simpson has contributed some of his own range developments, generally the cheaper ones.

Other assistance comes in various forms from the feds, the state, the county, range pros, the ag department at the university. Most he is glad to receive, though sometimes he feels that others are trying to run his ranch and his life.

Part of a public lands ranching headquarters -- houses, barns, sheds, trucks, heavy equipment, etc. Note that the riparian bottom has been virtually destroyed. Central Utah.

Except perhaps for the airplane, Simpson's hypothetical ranching operation is typical of public lands ranches. Ranchers may live far from town, but this in no way means they live simply, much less naturally. While most of us will continue to envy the popularized down-home Western lifestyle, we should realize that this dream has little to do with the reality of public lands ranching. A small percentage of

stockmen, especially in the wilder areas of the West, may live this way, but the celebrated Western lifestyle generally is better exemplified by small-time miners and homesteading hippies than by ranchers. Regardless, we should not condone a group's harmful activities because we envy or sympathize with their lifestyle.

As a whole the stock ranching business in its goals and management is much like other businesses. The rancher wants the greatest net financial return with the least expense and effort. He figures herbage amounts, livestock weights, and ranching expenses on his pocket calculator. He records receipts and expenditures and market trends on computer spreadsheets.

The stockman is not out there to commune with Nature, but to make money and maintain the status quo. If through the years he happens to gain an appreciation for the natural world he and his livestock denigrate, it is incidental to his primary purposes. As a society, one of our biggest misconceptions is that knowledge of or physical proximity to Nature necessarily begets respect for Nature. Ignoring obvious signs to the contrary, we are further willing to believe that an appreciation for Nature necessarily overrides the desire for profits and power enough to beget benign use.

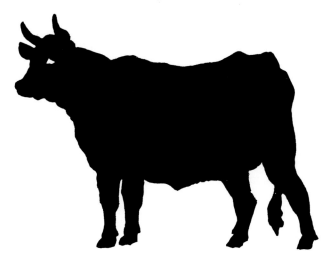

"Our goal is to produce the greatest weight gain in our cattle with the least financial expense possible."
--4-"H" youth

● *Ranchers are the true conservationists. Their livelihood depends on a healthy range, so they wouldn't damage the environment.*

We are the original ecologists. We're the ones who originally came West, took it on ourselves to produce something from nothing. We are dependent on the ecology.
--Jim Connelley, president, Nevada Cattlemen's Association, 1-2-90 *Tucson Citizen*

Such arguments often are impressive, especially to city dwellers. The first half of this book reveals that they have no basis in reality.

Some public lands ranchers have joined conservation organizations in recent years, often taking positions of power to which they are accustomed -- a main reason most large conservation organizations refuse to challenge the ranching establishment. While some seem truly concerned for environmental welfare, most seem more concerned with other things. That is, they have come to understand that co-opting the very groups that might otherwise oppose their exploitation of public land is good public relations and good politics. For example, a contribution from the X-9 Ranch will reasonably assure that the local Sierra Club will not interfere with the X-9's public ranching operation, especially when the X-9 owner is a Sierra Club board member. A few hundred dollars and a membership fee is a small price for a wealthy stockman to pay to protect an operation worth a million. Additionally, the environmental image he gains from his association with the Sierra Club minimizes opposition from other conservation groups, politicians, and the public.

Beyond images, public lands ranchers generally oppose activities that would threaten their income levels and social/political standing and support those that would strengthen them; environmental impact is incidental. In the 2-million-acre "Arizona Strip" north of the Grand Canyon, where devastating overgrazing has continued for a century, ranchers are encouraging new uranium mines, including one within 15 miles of the Grand Canyon itself. Though ranching is the only land use to speak of over most of the area, and since (aside from the uranium miners) stockmen comprise by far the strongest political force in the area, stockmen welcome uranium mining there for the improved road network it provides and as "a boost to the local economy."

Southern Utah's Burr Trail, a 66-mile stretch of dirt road between the small town of Boulder and "Lake" Powell, has long been considered one of the most scenic roads in North America. Winding through a million-acre expanse of relatively undeveloped red rock desert that includes Wilderness and Wilderness Study Areas, a National Park, and archaeological sites, the Burr Trail is a popular mountain bike trail. Yet, some area businesspeople are pushing to have it developed to boost tourism and fatten their wallets. With $2 million in Utah taxes, they plan to have Burr Trail widened, re-routed, and paved, infringing on wildlife and wilderness, increasing vehicular traffic by an estimated 2000%, and degrading the road's scenic qualities. Local public lands ranchers support the plan because it would improve their access, and, again, "boost the local economy."

In contrast, public lands ranchers are now in league with thousands of people in protest of a proposal by the US Air Force to withdraw 1.5 million mostly BLM acres in southwest Idaho for a bombing range. If implemented, the proposal might reduce grazing for some of the area's 60 or so permittees, though they would be financially compensated. Two hundred people testified at a recent hearing on the proposal; several were ranchers, who received most of the media attention simply because they are ranchers.

Similarly, ranchers in southwest Montana's Big Hole Valley presently are joined with conservationists in calling for Wilderness designation for much of the National Forest surrounding the 100-mile-long valley. The Forest Service plans to allow clearcutting on large areas of the thick forest on the steep hillsides north and west of the valley. All 17 Big Hole Valley ranchers oppose the proposed logging and have reluctantly accepted Wilderness designation as the only feasible way to stop it, even though past and present ranching keeps most of the valley bare of trees and is the valley's greatest environmental detriment. While their alleged "collective regard for the land" has impressed some conservationists, the ranchers' primary concern is that clearcutting will increase watershed runoff and hurt their ranching operations (if logged, the steep slopes would provide a minimal amount of pasture anyway).

As in most river valleys in the rural West, the Big Hole ranchers own most of the private land and dominate the valley, especially in the lower elevations. Any intrusion into their area is a potential threat to their ranching operations and to their local power structure.

The Big Hole issue demonstrates the enormous power of the ranching establishment. A coalition of conservation organizations with thousands of members could battle against the proposed clearcutting with only a low probability of success. But throw in 17 local ranchers and suddenly you have "one of the most influential conservation groups in southwestern Montana," as reported in the conservation newsletter *LightHawk*. A handful of local stockmen equals an army of ordinary Jane and John Does.

Thus, public lands ranchers sometimes support environmental protection -- usually ostentatiously -- by proclaiming their positions to the press, as if their involvement suddenly gives the issue real significance. How many times have you heard these exact words?: "As a _____ (fill in state) public lands rancher with a deep, abiding respect for the land, _____ (fill in complaint or demand)." Their modernized public relations strategy has given public lands ranchers a more palatable conservation image, but they will never be and *cannot* be true conservationists, much less environmentalists, for public lands ranching by its very nature is environmentally unsound.

In other words, it is easy to be a "conservationist" when proposing to conserve something besides the land you ranch. You can call yourself an ecologist because you have learned ecology in your attempt to manipulate ecosystems for ranching. And anyone can send in $35 for a Sierra Club membership and claim to be an environmentalist.

Stockmen's destructive legacy speaks for itself. They stand without equal as enemies of conservation.

They came into the West, they killed off the native wildlife, they've stripped the West of vegetation and continue to declare war on the few remaining predators. And now they have the nerve to call themselves environmentalists.
--Jim Fish, Public Lands Action Network, 4-28-90 *Albuquerque Tribune*

All of the ranchers' arguments are specious. They claim to love the land. Well, I have known people who beat their spouses black and blue all the while claiming they love them dearly.
--David A. Huet, letter to the editor, *Tucson Weekly* (9-26-90)

Sure, some (not most) ranchers and cowboys spend much time on land and some have learned a lot about the land. Some even have a personal relationship with the land. But even for

most of these people the relationship seems to be more like that of a rapist who appreciates the firmness and smell and taste and beauty of his victim's body.
--Anonymous

The rancher (with a few honorable exceptions) is a man who strings barbed wire all over the range; drills wells and bulldozes stock ponds; drives off elk and antelope and bighorn sheep; poisons coyotes and prairie dogs; shoots eagles, bears, and cougars on sight; supplants the native grasses with tumbleweed, snakeweed, povertyweed, cowshit, anthills, mud, dust, and flies. And then leans back and grins at the TV cameras and talks about how much he loves the American West.
--Edward Abbey "Even the Bad Guys Wear White Hats" (Abbey 1986)

● *Grazing is a useful tool for managing public lands.*

. . . livestock grazing is accepted as a legal, legitimate, and desired tool for improvement or maintenance of public rangelands.
--David Jolly, Chief, SW Region, USFS

The fact is, many public agencies and other cow apologists resort to absurd fantasy attempting to justify the nonsensical tradition of grazing public lands. The current strategy is to contend that cows are good for everything -- water, fish, wildlife, vegetation, soils, etc. It seems only a matter of time before we hear that a cow in your back seat will result in better gas mileage!
--Denzel and Nancy Ferguson (ONDA 1990)

The theory that livestock can be a "useful tool" for managing public lands was concocted in the 1960s and 1970s in response to mounting environmental concern and subsequent pressure for ranching reform. Industry "scientists" and "range experts" were marched in with bogus studies to publicize the idea that livestock can be used for environmental *manipulation*. Reality was turned on its head, and suddenly livestock became a potential benefit rather than actual detriment. The campaign has been moderately successful in dissipating anti-ranching energy, and in many cases is even being used to justify intensified ranching.

Today, though the useful tool argument is increasingly used, the ranching establishment has yet to demonstrate real success in using livestock to improve environmental quality. Indeed, results have been erratic, accomplished only with the aid of expensive range developments, and beneficial to only a few ecosystem components -- at the expense of many more ecosystem components. Ranching in any form has shown an almost unequivocally overall negative impact on Western rangeland.

Most studies were superficial and ignored the complex inter-relationships between large herbivores and other plant and animal life. Other studies were plain silly. Out of this phony research the argument emerged that cattle were a wildlife management "tool" that could benefit many wildlife species. Before long, both stock raisers and academicians portrayed the cow as the finest friend of the western rangelands. Such a

conclusion was ridiculous, but the ranchers had "scientific" evidence to rationalize their livestock grazing.
--Bernard Shanks, **This Land Is Your Land** (Shanks 1984)

● *Ranchers provide range developments and stewardship essential to a healthy environment.*

Throughout the first half of this book we have seen that the opposite is true.

● *Ranchers provide a necessary public service on public lands.*

According to George Bell, who runs a large public lands ranching operation in southern Arizona:
If there were no [public lands] ranchers, all this [public] land would have to be taken care of by the Forest Service and BLM. We help people who get lost on the land; we deal with fires; all kinds of things.

This represents another justification that looks good only on the surface. First of all, Nature does not need to be "taken care of." Rather, it mostly needs to be left alone. Such administration, when required, is the legal responsibility of the agencies, not stockmen. And sure, ranchers may occasionally give directions to lost motorists or report wildfires. But their detriments far outweigh such insignificant contributions. As detailed, they also intimidate public lands visitors, start fires, necessitate the opening and closing of gates, cause livestock to wander onto roadways, detract from recreational use, and so on.

● *Without the use of public lands as calving grounds, the Western livestock industry would collapse.*

The falseness of this claim is explained in Chapter II.

● *Without livestock grazing the public forage resource would be wasted.*

At the onset of this line of reasoning we usually are presented the shopworn argument, "Grass that isn't eaten by livestock is wasted." Consider the words of Ronald A. Michieli, Executive Director of the Public Lands Council:
These animals [public lands livestock] are solar factories. They take a renewable resource which would otherwise be wasted and turn it into edible food and other products which man desires and needs.

This may have gone undisputed 50 or 100 years ago, but many people have come to appreciate that something isn't wasted or worthless if it isn't turned into greenbacks or hamburger.

Colorado public lands rancher's wife Marj Perry asserts, "It [public ranching] is an ideal way of converting grass to protein." So, what is ideal about spending $2 billion in tax and private monies annually to have our public land degraded by a politically and socially dominant minority to produce 3% of our livestock -- especially when the average American already consumes twice the amount of protein recommended by nutritionists?

FORAGE WOULD HAVE LITTLE VALUE SAVE FOR LIVESTOCK.

A photo from an SCS ranching publication. Note the caption. *(SCS)*

● *If you don't graze the land, how else are you going to use it?*

Why do we think that all usable land must somehow be used by humans? Why would we consider this a mandate to put livestock on the land? Yet, this is the automatic response from many Americans to the idea of removing livestock from public lands. More than anything, cultural conditioning creates this reality.

The ranching establishment gives more professional, yet no more substantial, explanations.For example, Steve Williams, Range Manager for the Arizona State Land Department, writes, "The rural areas vary in nature and character, but really aren't suited for anything but grazing." He should tell that to a fisher, camper, or nature photographer. He should tell that to a desert tortoise, bobcat, frog, butterfly, bunchgrass plant, hillside, or stream.

● *"Grazing is a traditional, legitimate use of public lands."*

--Robert M. Williamson, Director of Range Management, BLM

Public lands graziers claim they have the "right" to ranch our public lands, saying "We've been running cattle here since before you were born, son!" or "My great, great grandfather homesteaded this place in 1879." By this line of reasoning, we might say that pirates have the right to plunder ships at sea because they have been doing so for centuries, or that a king has the right to the throne because his ancestors conquered the kingdom a hundred years ago. As ecologist George Wuerthner notes:

> *The only defense for the continuation of public lands grazing is that it is a traditional use of public lands. . . . Dumping raw sewage into our rivers was traditional also.* (Wuerthner 1989)

Similarly, we are told that ranching should continue wherever stockmen have "established grazing rights." This almost sounds reasonable -- until you stop to consider that ranching has traditionally occurred almost every place that it now occurs, which is to say almost everywhere there is enough vegetation to keep a cow or sheep alive, which is to say 73% of Western public land, which is to say 41% of the West.

And what of the 40,000-year-old tradition of the Native Americans that ranchers killed or displaced, or the ancient traditions of the Western ecosystems they devastated?

--We all must make a living.

--We all use natural resources.

--We all impact the environment, or have someone else do it for us.

The ranching establishment often uses these calculated truisms as arguments to rationalize public lands ranching -- the well-worn tactic of justifying black or white by expounding upon shades of grey. It shifts the blame and belittles the destruction.

Yes (though there are obviously far too many people on the planet), everyone should have an equal opportunity to have a place to live and earn a living. However, when just one person or family monopolizes and degrades thousands, or even tens or hundreds of thousands, of publicly owned acres, under heavy subsidization, to provide their income and produce a relatively tiny amount of food for society, it is time to draw the line.

> *I don't think it's a fair statement to make that public grazing is a major destructor of land. Use of that kind is historic. . . . A lot of the permittees have been out there a long time -- three or four generations in some cases.*
>
> --Joe ["Bogus Logic"] Zilincar, public relations spokesman for BLM's national office

● *Public lands grazing must be saved to preserve our ranching legacy.*

> *In one place, the city council set aside an ecological reserve -- with cattle! Their reasoning was that the cattle are part of San Diego's history, so they stay.*
>
> --Dave Sage, Solano Beach, California, personal correspondence

> *Sympathizers to the ranchers claim that a "valuable cultural resource" would be lost if the ranchers and their livestock were removed* [from Mt. Diablo State Park, California]. *Even if the ranchers are defeated, a "demonstration ranch" with about 200 head of cattle would remain, "to reflect this county's history . . . ."*
>
> --Sharon Seidenstein, Berkeley, California, personal correspondence

> *The sight of cattle or sheep and cowboys or sheepherders on a well-managed range is an attractive part of western lore for our mainly urban population.*
>
> --from *Progressive Agriculture* by the College of Agriculture, University of Arizona (College of Agriculture 1981)

Texas historian Walter Prescott Webb once said that "Westerners have developed a talent for taking something small and blowing it up to giant size." The ranching establishment often claims that ranching must be preserved because it is vital to our Western legacy. Further twisting reality, it alleges that, as one rancher put it, "many people view pastures as natural scenery."

What is really being said here? Are cows and fences part of Nature? Why must public lands ranching's 18% contribution to Western livestock production be preserved to save our Western legacy? As well say we had to save the Rambler to save the American automobile industry. Moreover, why hasn't the government preserved (that is heavily subsidized) the thousands of Western shoemakers or weavers or glassblowers or Native Americans or grizzly bears or riparian areas to save our Western legacy?

What is really being assumed is that ranchers and ranching are somehow more important than anybody or anything else. In real terms, stockmen simply maintain a more powerful public image and carry more clout.

For decades, the ranching establishment has been imprinting in the American psyche the message that the ranchman is "the keeper of the Western flame," that "the living legend of the cowboy" (public lands rancher) must be preserved or the last vestige of the Old West will die. They warn us that if the public lands rancher "fades into history" (gets booted off public land), the Great Western Epic will end and our cherished Western Romance will be lost forever.

Yet, most ranching in the West is on private land and will continue with or without public lands ranching. Moreover, little of the romantic Old West we hold most dear is based on actual livestock ranching; by far most would survive even if *all* ranching was ended. Further, rather than a bunch of rustic, sweat-stained cowpokes, *most* public lands ranchers are well-situated and influential. They comprise a powerful, highly organized, heavily financed, hard-nosed business -- not a romantic legacy.

By and large stockmen's involvement in our Western legacy has been bloodstained, destructive, and wasteful. Why we should preserve such a legacy, except perhaps in books and movies, is a question we should ask.

Don't get me wrong; I love the legends of the Old West. . . .
But the days of longhorns, trail drives, rustlers and gunfighters are long gone. What little remains of the West's wilderness -- as opposed to the Wild West -- needs to be conserved.

It's become too precious to sacrifice to a sappy nostalgia for the frontier, to a business that cannot survive except for massive government subsidies.
Besides, cattle ranching has done irreparable damage to the West. . . .
The hard truth is that we don't need the West's cattle ranches anymore. They're as much a historical oddity as the steam locomotive and whalebone corset.
--Richard Lessner, "Dancing With Wolves: Ranchers Should Lose This War" (Lessner 1991)

● *No serious, knowledgeable person would propose ending public land ranching.*

Interestingly, this claim is made more often by conservationists than by stockmen. A person who opposes ranching is a person whose social acceptance and self-image are on the chopping block. A person who embraces America's cowboy imperative and promotes only modest reforms designed to perpetuate ranching need not fear ostracization and gnawing inner guilt. Thus most conservationists distance themselves from "the radical fringe" and breathe easy.

Most ranchers know better. They of all people understand why the concerned, well-informed person is the *most* likely to call for an end to public lands ranching.

● *If livestock are banned from public lands, the Western livestock industry and rural Western economies will collapse.*

It's time to set the record straight. Livestock grazing on public (and private) lands helped settle the west and build our nation, and today continues to play a major role in many local economies. Agriculture is the nation's largest industry, and the cattle industry is the largest segment of American agriculture.
--Patty McDonald, Executive Director, Public Lands Council

One of welfare graziers' favorite tricks is lumping public lands ranching together with the entire livestock industry, and agriculture in general, to increase its apparent importance. Another example of this is a statement by Pamela Neal, Executive Vice President of the Arizona Cattle Growers Association, in an *Arizona Daily Star* article on public lands ranching: "Cattle is the largest commodity in the state's agricultural group." Nowhere in the lengthy article does she acknowledge just *how much* public lands ranching contributes to the state's agricultural industry. The obviously sympathetic author of the article further states, "Hinging on the outcome of this battle [over increasing grazing fees to fair market value] could be the death of the state's $1 billion cattle industry and *a piece of Arizona tradition* [italics added]." These kinds of claims are as common as they are misleading. (*Seven Popular MYTHS About Livestock Grazing on Public Lands* takes this to the extreme; see Mosly 1990.) As Bernard DeVoto writes in **The Easy Chair**, "they are telling the truth, but not enough of it." Unfortunately, many uninformed Americans are eager to believe whatever a cowboy tells them.

Back in the real world, we find that Arizona's *gross* total income from cattle is less than half this $1 billion figure and that beef cattle represent only about 1/3 of the state's overall agricultural production. Only 32% of Arizona's livestock are produced by federal land -- more than any state but Nevada at 38%, which is 70% BLM and 10% FS land, almost entirely grazed. Further, though about 45% of non-Indian reservation Arizona is grazed federal land, altogether there are only about 1000 federal lands ranchers in the state -- 0.025% of the population, or 1 out of 4000 residents.

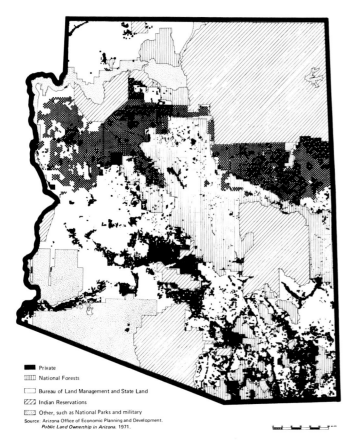

- ■ Private
- ⊞ National Forests
- ▢ Bureau of Land Management and State Land
- ▨ Indian Reservations
- ▦ Other, such as National Parks and military

Source: Arizona Office of Economic Planning and Development.
Public Land Ownership in Arizona, 1971.

LAND OWNERSHIP IN ARIZONA
(Dark gray areas represent private checkerboarded with public.)

All publicly owned lands in the 11 Western states combined produce only **18%** of the West's livestock -- hardly essential to the survival of the Western livestock industry. Only **17%** of Western stock producers use public land at all (Com. on Govt. Oper. 1986), and most of these ranchers don't depend on public ranching to stay in business.

They [wildlife groups] have had their goddamn boot heel in our [stockmen's] neck now for the last 10 years and they do not let up, and I don't think you'll have an economic base in Wyoming that can support the schools or cities or hospitals. But I don't think they give a shit.
--Lee Coffman, President, Wyoming Wool Growers Association, *High Country News* (11-23-87)

If the livestock producer were to be forced off the public range, it would be impossible to maintain a viable livestock industry.
--Hubbard S. Russel, Jr., Chairman, Private Lands and Water Usage Committee, National Cattlemen's Association

Many small cities and towns in the West would be destroyed economically if all grazing were taken off the public land.
--[illegible signature], Deputy Director, Acting, BLM, "stock" response, 1988

To take cattle off public lands, as some preservationists suggest, would cripple the state's [New Mexico's] economy as well as the economy of the entire West.
--Public lands rancher James M. Jackson, *Natural Resources Journal* (Summer 1989)

These statements represent an even more preposterous fairy tale -- that if livestock are banned from public land the economies of the rural West will be ruined and the people living there will become destitute. One Colorado welfare rancher even suggested that it would be "a form of genocide." Here in Arizona -- one of many so-called "cattle states" -- a recent study claims that if public lands ranching were ended the state economy would lose most of $302 million contributed by Arizona ranchers (1-25-89 *Arizona Republic*). The study was commissioned and funded by the Arizona Cattle Growers Association (ACGA), headed by an agribusiness professional at an agricultural college, and presented to the public by a public relations firm hired by ACGA. It was conducted using results of surveys mailed out to 601 selected ranchers, with only 180 ranchers responding. Each dollar spent was counted "three times to indicate the way income is spent locally." Results were based on extremely inflated dollar figures, and dollars spent included everything from ranchers spending money at movie theaters to BLM range managers buying food and gas while making trips to grazing allotments. *Economic minuses due to ranching were not reflected*, nor were the results of a recent Arizona State University College of Business study showing that all agriculture, including ranching, feedlots, and crop production, accounts for just 7% of the gross economic product in Arizona's 13 *rural* counties. Nor was any indication given that ranchers would still spend a comparable amount of money locally whether they ran livestock on public land or not. Such bogus studies are common, and typify ranching industry misinformation (indeed, the Forest Service and BLM are currently using the above and other slanted studies to promote ranching).

The fact is, even though *most* of the area of *most* Western counties is ranched, very few counties earn more than 5% of their gross income from ranching, *even including private lands ranching*. In studies of 20 local Western ranching areas, Steve Johnson, Southwest Representative for Defenders of Wildlife, found not one having more than 3% of its economy based on ranching. Indeed, if other factors are considered, livestock grazing actually *detracts* from many, if not most, local economies -- even the well-known "cattle countries" and "cow counties."

Mojave County in northwest Arizona, for example, encompasses some 13,000 square miles, and more than 80%

of it is grazed by cattle. Yet this overwhelmingly rural county derives only 0.8% of its total income from ranching and all other agriculture. Ranching is the county's greatest environmental detriment, and an overall economic detriment.

Grant County in southwest New Mexico derives less than 5% of its gross income from livestock grazing, even though 90% of its 3000 square miles is grazed. Ranching there has caused drastic reductions in game and fish, the elimination of many natural water sources, erosion of topsoil and loss of hundreds of acres of valuable bottomland, extensive public and private property damage, decreased recreational income, extensive flood damage to small communities and the county seat, and more. Despite bold proclamations by Grant County stockmen and their agency collaborators, ranching certainly causes a net loss to that county's economy.

Northeast Nevada's 8500-square-mile White Pine County is likewise typical. It boasts being one of Nevada's "Cow Counties" and is in fact composed of 76.6% BLM land, nearly all of which is grazed. The stockmen who rule over most of White Pine County assert that the county's economy would collapse without ranching. Yet White Pine County derives only 4% of its gross income from all ranching, public and private. Again, ranching's detrimental influences may actually cause a net loss of income to the county.

Eastern Montana is the region of the West perhaps most dependent on livestock grazing. But even here most counties derive only small income percentages from ranching -- tiny percentages from public lands ranching (90% of Montana livestock are on private land). In Wyoming, the alleged "Cowboy State," where only about 2000 public lands permittees graze about half of the land, less than 5% of the state's income is derived from public lands ranching. (Various government sources)

ing operations. Therefore, even if their contributions outweighed their detriments, the benefits could hardly be significant.

As for employment, few industries come close to ranching in the paucity of jobs created compared to taxes and resources consumed. Alan Durning notes in **State of the World: 1990** that "ranching is the least labor-intensive agricultural activity in the country." A review by the Congressional Research Service shows that only 3.6% of the commercial employment based on the 7 National Forests in the Greater Yellowstone ecosystem is attributable to livestock

A Peruvian sheep herder on Idaho BLM land. *(George Wuerthner)*

operations (Wuerthner 1991). In other words, public lands ranchers hire few employees. Many of their hired hands are transients or illegal aliens, are part-time and/or temporary and poorly paid. More and higher paying jobs could be created by ending public lands ranching.

Without public lands ranching, net incomes would probably *increase* for most rural economies. For example, in Idaho hunters and fishers pay 15 times more for hunting and fishing licenses than all ranchers on BLM and FS ranchland in the state (1/4 of the state) pay in federal grazing fees. Without degradation of game animal habitat and attrition from ranchers, game animals populations in Idaho would soar.

Because public lands ranches cover an average of more than 12,000 acres each, local rural economies are usually affected by only several to a score or so public lands ranch-

(Greg Pentkowski)

The agencies allege that public lands ranching is "important locally." Likewise, one could say, so is poodle grooming "important locally." The agencies say they need to prop up public lands ranching to "stabilize the local economies of the rural West." What kind of double talk is this when the industry must have *permanent*, massive government financial and technical assistance to survive?

So much for the myth of ranching as the "backbone" of rural Western economies.

One BLM employee who has been studying the impact of public lands ranching on the West said she was able to find no significant economic impact. "And there was no real social impact. I decided there was only a mythical impact. Everybody's in love with the myth of the American cowboy."
--Jon R. Luoma, "Discouraging Words" (Luoma 1986)

● *Together, we can work to create a better future for rangeland management . . .*

Changing public values and demands bring complexity and focus attention on the need for cooperation among all users of rangelands. Successful partnerships between permittees, State, and Federal managers form a strong base on which to build a positive future for the public range.
--*Livestock Grazing Successes on Public Range*, "Produced in partnership by: The Forest Service, Bureau of Land Management, and Public Lands Council" (USDA 1989)

This one is designed to appeal to our faith in science and technology, if not our optimism, patriotism, and teamwork. By planning for a co-operative future, the ranching establishment lays the foundation for future public lands ranching. In recent years, this has become a public relations approach.

Ranching, we are told, is a "developing science," and it is merely a matter of time before scientific breakthroughs allow us to solve its problems. Livestock grazing will become an exciting new tool of progressive rangeland management! With American spirit and ingenuity, we will not only halt environmental deterioration, but eventually double -- hell, *triple* -- livestock production!!!

This contrived optimism is no substitute for reality. We have yet to see much improvement in the overall condition of the public range, even with billions of tax and private dollars poured into management, developments, and restoration. Enthusiasm, glittering promises, and intensified rangeland manipulation are not substitutes.

Though many people already propose ending public lands ranching -- and many more would if made aware of the situation -- our government refuses to even acknowledge the possibility. Not one BLM resource area, Forest Service ranger district, or state land department division has made a *significant* permanent overall reduction in ranching, much less ordered a complete cessation.

Yet countering this interest [in environmental responsibility] has been the widespread growth of a feeling that science and technology will resolve any real emergency and bring us to a condition of effortless plenty.
--Paul B. Sears in **Deserts on the March** (Sears 1967)

● *We're all in this together, good neighbor, good buddy. (A.k.a., honey is sweeter than cow shit.)*

This one's similar to the above, with an added emotional twist. When ranchers turn on the folksy charm, who can resist? No one can garner sympathy like a dusty ol' cowpoke. When, hat in hand, a Western-garbed permittee in his slow drawl says he knows "there's room for improvement" but how hard he's "been a'tryin' to do a better job" than his overgrazin' grandpappy did, could you cancel the poor, sincere fellow's permit and turn him out onto the cold streets? When he asks you if you'll join with him and work to improve the range, are you going to tell him no? Hell no! You would seem a heartless scoundrel -- as he well knows! I have seen even confirmed stop-public-lands-ranching advocates melt under the influence. You cannot resist. At this point all you can do is meekly suggest modest reforms, or more likely point your finger at the government and demand more range "improvements."

What a song and dance! In truth, the vast majority of these po', hardworkin' ranch folk are not really poor at all, and do not work any harder than the rest of us.

They do not relent, however: We must work together, they plead. It's not us and them; no. Join us, they say -- *join us!*

What does this *really* mean? Mostly it means do not resist your ranching neighbors. Help them preserve the status quo. With your time, energy, and tax dollars, help them mitigate their destructive ranching impacts and restore your overgrazed ranges -- *so they may raise more cattle and sheep!*

● *If you don't keep us in business, we'll be forced to sell out to the developers.*

If we are forced from the public lands, we have two alternatives. First, we can manage our lands for domestic livestock only [no change], or, secondly, we can sell to the "developers." None of us want this, so please don't force us into it.
--J.W. Swan, First Vice-President, Idaho Cattlemen's Association (USDA, USDI, CEQ 1979)

Rather than a grain, this argument contains a small pebble of truth. The thinly veiled threat -- *blackmail* -- has for years been used effectively to quell opposition.

Many stockmen imply that if they were to cease ranching, public lands would be opened up to developers. Although they know full well that public land is rarely bought, sold, or commercially built upon, they fool some uninformed people.

Perhaps most public lands ranchers are not so bold as to imply this outlandish threat, but many do maintain that if they are "driven out of business" (is receiving welfare a "business"?) by enforced restrictions, higher expenses, decreased subsidies, and/or reduced grazing, they will then sell their private lands, including base properties, to developers who will turn the rural West into a squalor of condominiums and subdivisions. This ominous warning is false in several ways.

First, (as detailed above and below) the argument applies mainly to private, not public, lands ranching (though with alternatives available it need not apply to private ranching either). And by supporting public lands ranching we put more pressure on private ranchers to sell out because we give their more heavily subsidized competitors an even more unfair advantage.

Next, few public lands ranchers would be inclined to sell their base properties and get out of welfare ranching even if not making a profit on the public lands ranching portions of their operations. As mentioned, government reports reveal that public land provides an average of only about 1/3 of permittees' total livestock needs (and, yes, calves can be born and raised just as well, or better, on private land). As we also have seen, many permittees are not serious stock raisers but ranch instead for extra income, tax write-offs, "front" business, family tradition, status, hobby, etc.

Next, if they did sell out, why would public lands ranchers -- people who claim "a deep, abiding respect" for their land -- sell it to developers rather than to more responsible owners? As highly desirable as most ranch properties are, there would be no lack of environmentally concerned buyers, many who would pay a good price and take better care of the land than ranchers have.

Next, many public lands ranchers already have sold off their "excess" land (privately owned land in excess of minimum base properties required for public lands grazing permits) -- and not because they were "driven out of business." Consider how many Western ranching operations are named "_____ Land and Cattle Company." Most public lands ranchers either do not need all their private land to maintain ranching operations, do not need public lands grazing to maintain operations, use public lands ranching as a tax write-off or source of extra income, or are more or less independently wealthy. So, for most public lands ranchers, excess land is not necessary anyway. Cutting off their subsidies and artificial props would not induce them to sell off their excess land, much less their base properties.

Because ranching properties are among the most well-watered, fertile, and strategically located lands in the West, generally they command high prices. The private lands associated with public lands ranching are especially coveted since they are bordered or surrounded by public land and protected from nearby development, and often are located in spectacular natural settings. Many public lands ranchers realized their land's substantial financial potential long ago and sold off all land not essential to their ranching operations. Others have sold off bits and pieces over the years for various reasons. Sale of excess property is one of the main reasons that such a high percentage of public lands ranchers are so rich and powerful; many have become millionaires. Far from being the end result of hard times for public lands ranchers, sale of excess land has given them even greater economic, social, and political clout.

Unfortunately, much of this excess land *has* been sold to developers for housing developments, vacation cabins,

resorts, campgrounds, hunting camps, and so on (ironically, often resulting in conflicts over the grazing practices of the rancher who sold the land in the first place). However, a similar amount of excess land would have been sold regardless of the public lands ranching situation.

On the other hand, much of this land has ended up with better caretakers, environmentally speaking, than stockmen. Through purchase, trade, or special arrangement, cities, counties, states, and the federal government acquire it to protect watersheds, to halt flooding and soil erosion, for recreational purposes, and so on. Other land is protected as publicly owned nature preserves, reserves, refuges, parks, etc. Still other is acquired by private conservation organizations such as The Nature Conservancy, Defenders of Wildlife, and the Wilderness Society, or by hunting and fishing groups, or by conservation-minded individuals. For various objectives, ranching usually has been curtailed or eliminated on these lands, with dramatic success in most cases.

Next, even if every public lands rancher in the West was suddenly "driven out of business" and forced to sell his permit, nearly all base properties eventually would be sold to other ranchers because base properties are necessary for public lands ranching operations, no matter who picks up the permit. Government agencies essentially mandate continued grazing on nearly every allotment; if one person doesn't graze it, another will. With endless subsidization, technical and working assistance, essentially permanent grazing tenure, prestige, and power all institutionalized as part of the grazing permit, there is no lack of ranchers wanting permits, even if a former permittee was not making it and decided to sell. Base properties and permits nearly always are sold together. Each new permittee needs a base property, which nearly always will turn out to be the existing base property. Ranchers want to headquarter their operations on suitable base properties, close to their grazing allotments. And because taxes on large properties for non-graziers are astronomical, few besides ranchers can afford or are inclined to buy them. Base properties remain nearly invariable in number and location. With our government bending over backward to keep stockmen in business, it would take a major shift in public lands policy to change this situation.

Lastly, even if public ranching were banned, undoubtedly most former permittees would retain base properties as the private ranches, vacation get-aways, and rural residences they are, while some would turn them into dude ranches, hunting camps, wilderness guide bases, and other business ventures. Why would they sell out these established, comfortable country estates simply because their livestock no longer obtained some portion of their diet from public land? As above, few permittees would have to or be inclined to. Of those comparatively few base properties that were sold, a similar percentage would end up under the protection of the conservation-minded entities mentioned above.

To protect base properties once public ranching was ended, there are many reasonable and feasible possibilities. These include special programs to assist former permittees with management, stringent zoning ordinances, redirection of welfare ranching subsidies, and restrictions on who former permittees could sell to. Probably the best solution is for the government to buy out all base properties and return them to public ownership. This approach has proven successful with many National Parks and other public reserves.

But, ranching advocates warn, what about the fate of public lands themselves once livestock are removed? Wouldn't such removal create a "void" that could be filled only by some other kind of exploitation? Won't the government want to put the land to use? Won't the big strip mining companies, clearcut loggers, road builders, ORVers, and other environmental rapists come marching in?

The answer is a resounding "NO!" *These exploiters are already doing this* almost every place they can, and with the government's blessing. In fact, it is largely the huge network of ranching roads that allowed the exploiters access to nearly every nook and cranny of the West in the first place. The ranching industry conquered most of the Wild West and has been instrumental in its overdevelopment. Removing livestock from public land would simply mean no livestock or new range developments on the public's land -- *less*, not more, exploitation.

Ranchers decree that we must choose one or the other -- ranching or another form of exploitation. This is analogous to being given the option between having your mother raped or beaten up. But now we actually have both.

Aside from all of this, most development is due to overpopulation and rampant consumerism, rather than to the availability of land for building. Millions of acres of rural Western ranchland are available for sale and development right now, but only a small percentage of this land is actually being developed (other than for ranching). By far most rural Western real estate bought and sold is bought and sold among ranchers, who continue to own outright roughly 25% of the West. Availability of even more ranchland for sale will not cause substantially more development.

Unhappily, development of the rural West is a reality and probably will continue, with or without livestock. The choice is not between development and ranching, but between development *with* ranching and development *without* ranching. We only compound the destruction by supporting public lands ranching.

> **RANCHING DOES NOT PROTECT THE WEST. RANCHING EXPLOITS AND PROMOTES EXPLOITATION OF THE WEST.**

● *Without public lands ranching people would go hungry and the price of a hamburger would skyrocket.*

If you succeed [end public lands ranching], *I hope you get the joy of paying $15 a pound for a tough bull, like they do in China, which, by the way is where I wish people like you were.*

--Bonnie Udall, Arizona public lands rancher's widow, personal correspondence

Suggesting that we start growing all beef on private lands, the average public [sic] *would probably be paying $25.00 for a hamburger.*
--"A cattleman," Palm Springs, California, personal correspondence

I think people should realize that when they recommend a reduction [in livestock numbers on public lands], *they are not reducing domestic livestock grazing, but they are reducing food supply for the world.*
--J.W. Swan, First Vice-President, Idaho Cattlemen's Association (USDA, USDI, CEQ 1979)

They [cowmen] *realize that cattle on public lands contribute nearly 50 percent of the beef cattle in the U.S. food chain.*
--Mary Monzingo, ZR Hereford Ranch, Benson, Arizona, letter to editor, 3-10-88 *Arizona Daily Star*

Federally owned rangelands provide about 10% of the feed requirements of livestock in the United States.
--from **Range Management: Principles and Practices**, a textbook on contemporary range management (Holechek 1989)

. . . 18% of the [sic] *U.S. beef is raised on public lands.*
--Society for Range Management

Therefore, the grass forage of public grasslands needs to be continued [sic] *for ruminant (primarily cattle and sheep) production to prevent worldwide famine.*
--Robert E. Miller, D.V.M., Johnstown, Colorado, in a letter to *Colorado Outdoors*

Most of the people who make these (dare I say *ridiculous*?) claims know that only 3% of this country's beef comes from all public lands. But they also realize that we are a gullible, cowboy-crazed society.

In truth, the amount of food produced by public lands ranching is insignificant to US food supply. More plant food could probably have been grown on private Western bottomland washed away by ranching-caused flooding than is now produced by public lands ranching. Far more cattle are raised on the 2 million private pasture acres in Vermont than on the 55 million public acres in Nevada (USDA 1987).

As for "feeding a hungry world" (where some 20 million people die of malnutrition each year), the minuscule amount of public lands-grazed meat exported to other nations does *nothing* to feed the hungry. Little if any of it winds up in the hands of those suffering from hunger or malnutrition. Poor people cannot afford expensive luxury items like imported beef. Most of it ends up in well-stocked refrigerators in wealthier nations such as Canada, Great Britain, and Japan. Moreover, the US accounts for only 2% of world beef exports, while importing almost 9 times this much. (The US produces only 9% of world beef, and far less than 1% of world sheep.) (Espenshade 1988)

Terminating public lands ranching would likewise have little effect on the price or availability of meat in the American supermarket. According to Brigham Young

University economist Ardon Pope, Mormon bishop and son of a ranching family, we could kick every cow off public land and at most the cost of beef might temporarily rise 2%. The nation's beef supply would be diminished almost imperceptibly. Rest assured -- McDonald's would not have to change its price list, and hamburgers would keep rolling off the grills by the billions.

Agriculture Department figures show that Americans now consume an average of about 100 pounds of beef per year (and 1.6 pounds of lamb and mutton) (USDA 1987). Just how much are we willing to pay for the 3 pounds of this provided by public lands ranching? Wild game animals and game birds already provide a larger amount, while non-commercial fishing provides even more. If livestock were removed, public land would provide much more wild fare. We could all just as well eat plant food instead of cow meat in a few meals each year.

Clearly, if one believes the claim of Nevada cattlemen that they are feeding the country and the world, then one would also believe that the President of the Nevada Cattlemen's Association can urinate in San Francisco Bay and raise the water level in Hong King Harbor.
--Don Molde, "The Western Livestock Industry -- Last Bastion of Free Enterprise or Heavily Subsidized Environmental Disaster?" (Molde 1984)

WE FEED COWS FIELDS OF GRAIN, BUT LEAVE HUMAN STOMACHS EMPTY.

(Ginny Rosenberg)

● *If we don't maintain public lands ranching, more tropical rainforest will be cut down to make up for the lost beef.*

Some well-meaning individuals -- often impelled by ranching industry misinformation -- boldly make this warning, thinking they are doing the world a favor. Invariably they fail to understand the destructiveness of public lands ranching, how little of this country's beef comes from public land, or the dynamics of beef imports and exports. Public lands ranchers have been using these misinformed people to promote their destructive business. Statistics belie their claim.

In historic times more than half of the world's tropical rainforest has been cleared, and roughly half of this area currently is used to graze livestock. Probably less than 10% of the world's total rainforest-area beef is exported and less than 5% of the world's exported beef comes from rainforest areas (Espenshade 1988). The US accounts for about 20% of the world's beef imports (Espenshade 1988); about 5% of the US beef supply is imported (US Dept. of Com. 1986); and roughly 10% of US beef imports are from rainforest areas (USDA 1987). Finally, again, only 3% of US beef comes from public land.

Since official statistics are lacking, from all this I have roughly estimated that about 0.5%, or 1/200, of all US beef is rainforest beef, and that the US uses about 2% of the world's tropical rainforest beef. Thus, indirectly the US uses roughly 1%, or 1/100, of the world's tropical rainforest area to produce beef. (Of course US beef import impact is greater on some rainforest areas than on others.)

Now, theoretically, if pubic lands ranching was banned the US could make up for this lost beef by importing 6 times as much rainforest beef -- in which case the US would use about 1/17 of the world's rainforest area to produce beef. In this scenario, we could "save" 1/17 of the world's tropical rainforests by saving public lands ranching.

In reality, this is a nearly impossible, worst-case scenario, and is based on faulty logic. If public lands beef was "lost" -- if there was a demand for that missing 3% -- why would we suddenly "make it up" with only rainforest beef? If increased beef imports were somehow necessary, why wouldn't 90% of it be imported from *non-rainforest* sources, as it currently is? Under this scenario, we could save 1/170 of the world's rainforests by saving public lands ranching.

But why couldn't we slightly increase grain belt, pasture, and/or feedlot beef production? Why couldn't the 3% loss be absorbed by the continuing reduction in US beef consumption? Why couldn't people eat a tiny bit more grain? Moreover, those cattlemen clearing the rainforest for ranching unfortunately have no lack of customers for their product and will continue to clear rainforest regardless of a 3% fluctuation in US demand for beef.

More importantly, the argument for supporting public lands ranching over rainforest ranching for environmental reasons is self-contradictory. Because it takes many times more land area per cow, Western public lands ranching is, *beef pound for beef pound*, easily as environmentally destructive as tropical rainforest-area ranching.

Livestock production is a primary cause of world tropical rainforest destruction, but the continuation or elimination of US public lands ranching is such an infinitesimally small factor in that destruction that it is hardly worth the paper to write about it. The American ranching establishment's incessant campaign to get people to eat more beef probably has resulted in the destruction of more rainforest than has been "spared" through public lands ranching's beef "contribution."

If we can't meet the demand for beef within the United States, will the third world countries such as Brazil, be encouraged to speed up the deforestation of their rain forests to increase livestock production? The consequences of taking cows off public lands may be of greater detrimental significance to the environment of the nation and the planet then [sic] it appears.
--Public lands rancher James M. Jackson, *Natural Resources Journal* (Summer 1989)

In the United States, challenges to publicly subsidized grazing have not yet brought changes in policy, even though environmental damage rivals that of the Amazon rain forest.
--Sharon Bloyd-Peshkin, "Grazing Our Way to Disaster" (Bloyd-Peshkin 1991)

● *Meat is a natural food and essential to human health, so livestock grazing is essential.*

If we kick ranchers off the public lands, what are people going to eat? People need meat.
--Colorado public lands rancher

The presumption that heavy meat eating is natural and necessary to humans is one of the greatest fallacies of modern times, one the ranching establishment is only too happy to take advantage of. Now, hold on! Before you throw this book down in disgust, read this section through:

What we eat is a very personal matter. People are easily offended when you question what they put into their bodies. Personally, I find it offensive to be told that eating large amounts of beef is natural and healthy, that I should be doing it or supporting it. However, though I have been almost wholly plant-eating for more than 20 years, animal-eating does not bother me. I see nothing wrong with a hawk catching a rabbit and crushing its skull, then ripping its guts out and eating them. I watch with fascination. I've no problem with hungry people eating animals (hopefully not Endangered species); I occasionally do so myself. This is simply part of the wonderful instinct to survive. It is only natural to eat what is available when the body needs sustenance.

Nevertheless, both scientific study and common-sense observation reveal *Homo sapiens* as a slightly omnivorous plant-eater, not an omnivore. Our teeth, jaws, tongue, saliva, salivary glands, stomach, digestive juices, intestines, liver, urine, skin pores, and more are all those of a plant-eating animal. According to Harvey Diamond in **Fit for Life**, "There is not one anatomical faculty the human being has that would indicate that it is equipped for tearing, ripping, and rending flesh for consumption (Diamond 1985)." Look at your hands. They are perfectly evolved for picking fruits, berries, nuts, vegetables, and the like, not for ripping through tough hide into flesh, as are omnivores' claws. We

scarcely have what are inaccurately termed "canine" teeth, which all large truly omnivorous mammals have -- and even vegan (one who eats plant foods almost exclusively) gorillas have, for defense. With our extreme slowness, delicate skin, fragile bodies, and complete lack of natural weapons, we are not equipped to pursue, battle, and kill most wild animals for food (without the aid of technology, including primitive weapons -- a relatively recent development, as reflected by our very minimal subsequent physiological evolvement toward omnivorism).

Well then, how about our psyche, our instinct? Don't we naturally crave meat? Naturally, no; socially and culturally, yes. How many of us, when hungry, upon seeing a rabbit have the overwhelming urge to jump on it and sink our teeth into its neck, bite into its underside and eat the heart, liver, other guts, and, lastly, the meat, then lap up the spilled blood, as would a truly omnivorous large mammal? Maybe if we were starving; otherwise we wouldn't eat it unless it was properly "prepared." We always cook our meat, usually smother it with sauces and spices, and commonly disguise it within other foods. (Some practices of some native peoples are a partial exception, but these were also relatively recent developments, anthropologically speaking.) In contrast, nearly all plant foods may be eaten natural and unadulterated. How many of us would pluck a ripe, juicy pear from a tree and eagerly sink our teeth into it?

The meat, dairy and egg industries tell us: Animal products constitute 2 of the "Basic 4" food groups. The meat, dairy and egg industries don't tell us: There were originally 12 official basic food groups, before these industries applied enormous political pressure on behalf of their products.
--John Robbins, **Diet for a New America** (Robbins 1987)

Despite overwhelming evidence to the contrary, modern society clings blindly to its mandated assumption that we are omnivores. To preserve the myth, the livestock industry, US government, and food service industry spend *hundreds of millions* of dollars annually on advertising. (In comparison, the combined annual budget of the 7 major environmental organizations in the US is only $125 million.) Consequently, today we believe eating excessive amounts of cow meat is not only natural and healthy, but even patriotic and exciting.

The National Livestock and Meat Board makes it a point to "reach the children of the land at an early age," and "prepare them for a lifetime of meat-eating."
--John Robbins, **Diet for a New America** (Robbins 1987)

Mary Ryan of the California Beef Council, outlined the work of the council promoting beef with advertising campaigns on television and magazines through the coming months. She said the council is now targeting unique areas including Hispanics, Asians, health care experts and fitness enthusiasts, food editors and the youth market.
--3-30-89 *Santa Maria* [CA] *Times*

The Beef Industry Council has the rights to the popular Gary Larson's cow cartoons from "The Far Side" collections. These cartoons are featured in special ads aimed to reach foodservice operators.
--*Beef* magazine, January 1987

Though US beef consumption fell from a high point of 127 pounds per capita in 1976 to 108 pounds per capita in 1986 (USDA 1987) (or from 81 pounds in 1974 to 64 pounds in 1989, when different criteria for what constitutes "beef consumption" are used), the livestock industry is mounting a multi-million dollar advertising campaign to convince people to eat more of it: "Beef -- Real Food for Real People." The campaign, launched by the Cattlemen's Board and Beef Industry Council in January 1987, spent $29 million in the first 28 weeks alone for TV spots, print ads, and radio commercials. In 1991 the campaign continues in full swing.

On TV the ultra-masculine and brutally sincere James Garner advises us to eat more beef -- *real* food -- if we want to be real people and says you can't really trust those who don't. Sexy Cybill Shepard glamorizes the meat -- "People have a primal, instinctive craving for hamburgers -- something hot and juicy," and recalls the Madison Avenue adage that you "sell the sizzle, not the steak." Shepard likewise states that she doesn't trust anyone who doesn't eat beef. She was later quoted as saying she hardly ever ate the

stuff herself, while Garner checked into a hospital for quintuple coronary artery bypass surgery. Then came model Kim Alexis -- who later admitted that she rarely ate beef. And then Jeff Juliano, the man who played the part of the original Ronald McDonald, was revealed to be vegetarian.

The cow meat pushers were further embarrassed when it was discovered that the handsome, blond cowboy holding an American flag pictured on their promotion posters in supermarkets across America was taken directly from a Hitler Youth poster from World War II Germany. The Nazi youth was given a hat and chaps, his shirt color changed, the swastika on his tie transformed into a longhorn, and his swastika flag substituted with the stars and stripes.

In recent years America's long-time "King of Meats" has been taking a beating. For reasons not understood by cattlemen, beef suddenly has become the whipping boy for food faddists, diet book authors -- and even some scientists and nutritionists.
--from a promotional pamphlet by the National Cattlemen's Association

While vested interests proclaim cow meat to be "nutrition you can sink your teeth into," scientific studies consistently show that it causes untold death and suffering. Documented by Pulitzer Prize nominee John Robbins in **Diet for a New America**, daily consumption of animal products (mainly beef in the US):

● **increases the risk of heart disease -- the most common cause of death in the US -- by more than 300%**

● **causes high rates of colon cancer -- the most common life-threatening cancer in the US**

● **increases the risk of breast cancer by nearly 400%**

● **increases the rate of fatal prostate cancer 3.6 times**

● **roughly doubles the risk of osteoporosis (weak bones and teeth; 20 million Americans have this disease)**

A New Mexico public lands ranch. As always, note the fenceline contrast.

- **significantly contributes to the incidence of strokes; pancreatic, stomach, endometrial, cervical, ovarian, and even lung cancer; sterility; multiple sclerosis; salmonellosis (a bacterial disease, with over 4 million known cases a year in the US); trichinosis (worms, mostly from pork); kidney stones; kidney disease; peptic ulcers; hiatial hernias; gallstones; diverticulosis; irritable colon syndrome; hypoglycemia and diabetes; hypertension; asthma; arthritis; hemorrhoids; constipation; and obesity**

- **increases the amount of pesticides in mothers' milk 35 times**

- **is the source of 55% of pesticide residues in the US diet (DDT, malathion, parathion, aldrin, kepone, dieldrin, chlordane, heptachlor, endrin, mirex, PCBs, PBBs, toxaphene, lindane, etc.). (USDA tests less than 1 of 250,000 slaughtered animals for toxics, and for only 10% of chemicals known to be present in the US meat supply.)**

Robbins writes, "Thousands of impeccably conducted modern research studies now reveal traditional assumptions regarding our need for meats, dairy products and eggs have been in error (Robbins 1987)."

Each year 1.5 million Americans are crippled or killed prematurely by heart failure, stroke, cancer, and other "killer" diseases that have been linked conclusively with the consumption of animal products . . . . Yet, the USDA actually encourages the consumption of animal products by promoting the "four basic food groups," which suggests that one-half of our dietary calories should come from meat and dairy products.
--Alex Hershaft, president, Farm Animal Reform Movement

Cow meat averages 25%-36% fat (much of it saturated fat) compared to 3%-4% for wild animals; 70%-80% of saturated fat eaten by Americans comes from animal products. Beef's cholesterol content is very high; virtually all of the cholesterol eaten by Americans comes from animal products. Beef

has virtually no fiber. It is difficult for humans to digest properly, which hampers extraction of its nutrients. It putrefies in our intestines -- which are long and designed for plant eating -- producing various toxins not produced by decaying plant matter, taking an average of 4 days to make the digestive journey rather than a day and a half as for plant foods. Cow meat is devoid of carbohydrates, the most readily usable source of energy, contains very little calcium, and has only fair vitamin content. It contains harmful added nitrates and hormones. (Partly because of this, thousands of young American boys and girls, some of them barely out of diapers, have grown large breasts, sprouted pubic hair, etc.) The residues from pesticides, hormones, growth stimulants, insecticides, tranquilizers, radioactive isotopes, herbicides, antibiotics, appetite stimulants, and larvicides found in beef batter our immune systems, damage our gene pool, and cause birth defects, sterility, and neurological disorders. Beef usually is processed, adulterated in various ways, and, by the time it reaches the supermarket shelf, partially decomposed. (Generally animal matter decomposes into harmful substances much more quickly than does plant material.)

Does this sound like a natural food for humans? If we were omnivores would a diet containing even 25% meat create these health problems? Are our bodies trying to tell us something?

Despite mass production and endless subsidization, cow also even costs more than most foods of comparable nutritional value -- and far more than the retail price indicates if public and private subsidization are included.

At your next cookout amaze your hosts and throw that T-bone to the dog. Better yet, eat the dog.
--Ecologist B. Don Schwarzennegger

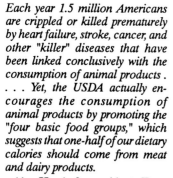

(Roger Candee)

But how can the human body get enough protein without animal foods?! Ghastly images of protein-starved, Third World stick figures haunt our memories. It has been said, only partly in jest, that only our fear of death itself rivals our fear of protein deficiency.

Well, how does the vegan gorilla get protein? How did we vegan hominids get it for 12 million years? The amount of calories as protein in human milk is 5%; nutritionists consider this is the optimum amount of calories as protein for humans. Many plant foods compare with (and some exceed) meat in protein content, and most contain sufficient protein. Rice has 5%, wheat 15%, and broccoli 45%. Even carrots have 10% of calories as protein. With a plant food diet, even containing **no** animal products, it is virtually impossible *not* to get enough protein in one's diet!

Also according to nutritionists, the average American's 106-gram daily protein intake is already almost twice the US government's average recommended daily allowance (RDA) of 54 grams. RDAs have a built-in safety margin of almost twice the actual need, which means the average American gets *between 3 and 4 times* more protein than the body wants. (Diamond 1985) According to a USDA survey, even the average American vegetarian consumes 150% as much protein as the RDA, or *between 2 and 3 times* more than the optimum amount for good health.

According to **The Times Atlas of the World**, people in the US and Canada eat *more* animal protein and *less* plant protein than any other region on Earth. These 2 countries derive well over 2/3 of their protein from animal foods, while the rest of the world derives well over 2/3 of its protein from plant foods. In other words, rather than being the basis of good health, America's extremely high-meat, high-protein diet is a major reason it has the world's highest rates of heart disease, digestive tract problems, and various cancers. No, the world's starving masses are not dying simply from protein deficiency, but from deficiencies in calories and carbohydrates and minerals and vitamins and fiber and every other nutritional component.

This isn't to say that people in the world's poorer regions wouldn't eat more meat if they could. Like the "great" wealthy cultures they strive to emulate, Third World cultures have come to measure "progress" by the amount of meat they can afford. Meat is a status symbol, to both the individual and the society. We believe the more meat in the pot, the better off we are.

But don't we need "complete" protein to build strong, healthy bodies? Yes. Haven't we been taught for decades that "complete" protein can be obtained only from animal products? Yes, but merely thinking something for a long time doesn't make it true.

Amino acids are the building blocks of protein. Our bodies manufacture perhaps 16 of the 25 (so far known to science) amino acids needed to make protein. But nine of them, called essential amino acids, must come directly from food. The human body digests food protein, splits it into its component amino acids, and from these constructs the protein it needs. We easily obtain the 9 amino acids needed to manufacture complete protein from a plant food diet, as we have for millions of years. The current assumption that humans require "complete" protein available only from the bodies of animals is based mostly on research on lab rats in the 1940s. (Akers 1983)

To be turned into usable protein in our bodies, these 9 amino acids need not be ingested in the so-called "proper combination," a "complete protein" combination found only as animal protein or a complicated combination of plant foods, as popularized in Frances Moore Lappe's vegetarian best-seller, **Diet for a Small Planet**. Both meat and some plant foods contain all 9 amino acids. Moreover, the human body *stores* amino acids in the blood -- in an "amino acid pool" -- and doles them out in the proper amounts when needed. As long as all 9 are replenished regularly, from whatever sources, they will be readily available for the manufacture of protein. Any natural, varied plant food diet easily provides all 9. And in an emergency the body can extract amino acids from cells and redistribute them where needed. Lappe now maintains that she was mistaken: protein combining is unnecessary, a notion with which a growing number of experts agree. Further, many amino acids in meat are destroyed when meat is cooked, as it nearly always is by humans (and for good reason should be).

In **A Vegetarian Sourcebook**, Keith Akers writes: "It is almost impossible to avoid getting enough protein on almost any calorically adequate diet" (Akers 1983). Nathan Pritikin, considered by many the foremost expert on nutrition in recent years, similarly observed:

Vegetarians always ask about getting enough protein. But I don't know any nutrition expert that can plan a diet of natural foods resulting in a protein deficiency, so long as you're not deficient in calories. You need only six percent of total calories in protein . . . and it's practically impossible to get below nine percent in ordinary diets.

Then what about the mysterious, magic vitamin B12? Won't we perish without it? Isn't it found naturally only in animal foods, and isn't this proof positive that we humans are naturally omnivorous?

Even most vegans believe this one. (Then again, for more than a century much of the world considered chocolate a potent aphrodisiac.) Vegan gorillas need B12 too. Where do they get theirs? And cows? In the healthy individual, the stomach secretes a substance called "intrinsic factor," which makes available to the body the B12 created by the bacterial flora in the large intestine (similar to the way our bodies manufacture vitamins B1 and B6). For many years it was blindly presumed that the human body did not independently produce B12 in this manner or, that if it did, this B12 could not be utilized (inexplicably, making humans the only vegan animal on Earth that produced B12 but could not utilize body-produced B12). Recent studies by Dr. Keiichi Morishita and others indicate that the human body does indeed manufacture B12, and that it is absorbed and utilized. This body-produced B12 is the same as that produced in the bodies of other vegan animals, and, as it has been for millions of years, is wholly adequate for our needs. Vitamin B12 is also found in many plant foods, though in minute amounts.

An extremely rare disease called pernicious anemia results from B12 deficiency. According to John Robbins, however:

. . . the only instances of pernicious anemia known in the medical literature have resulted from an extremely rare metabolic dysfunction which causes an inability to metabolize the vitamin. There are no cases on record of pernicious anemia resulting from a pure vegetarian diet. (Robbins 1987)

The Times Atlas of the World shows that although the US and Canada rank third highest out of 8 world regions in the number of calories consumed by humans daily, these 2 heavy meat eating countries expend many times more energy in the form of non-renewable resources to produce a meat food calorie (even a range-grazed meat food calorie) than the rest of the world does to produce a plant food calorie. In fact, a detailed 1978 study by the US Departments of Interior and Commerce ("Raw Materials in the United States Economy, 1900-1977, Technical Paper 47") revealed that the production of meat, dairy products, and eggs accounts for about 1/3 of all raw materials used for any purpose in the United States! If we ate plant foods instead, only about 1/50 of our raw materials consumed would be for food production. (Robbins 1990)

Similarly, economists Robin Hur and David Fields estimate that if the US switched from a meat- to plant-centered diet, "A typical household of three could expect to save $4,000 a year in the short run. . . . Savings on health care alone could be expected to reach $100 billion within five years." (Robbins 1990)

America's extremely high meat intake *does* reflect our great wealth. But rather than contributing to our being "well-fed," it detracts greatly from our overall food potential, as well as wasting money and resources and causing tremendous environmental harm.

Food	Food calories produced per calorie of fossil fuel energy input
Corn (Mexico)	83.33
Sorghum (The Sudan)	38.46
Rice (The Philippines)	9.50
Wheat (India)	9.06
Oats (US)	2.47
Potatoes (US)	2.18
Corn (US)	1.80
Wheat (US)	1.71
Soybeans (US)	1.45
Rice (US)	1.25
Beef (rangeland, US)	*.28*
Eggs (US)	.25
Lamb (rangeland, US)	*.16*
Milk (US)	.14
Broilers (US)	.07
Catfish (US)	.04
Beef (feedlot*, US)	*.03*

* Remember, nearly all public lands cattle eventually go to feedlots.

(Source: Akers 1983)

(Greg Pentkowski)

Likewise, Keith Akers reports that studies show no correlation between vegan diet and B12 deficiency, or any other serious health problem (Akers 1983).

From within or without, the healthy human body requires only about 0.1 microgram (*one ten millionth of a gram*) of B12 daily. Most commercial vitamin B12 supplements supply **10,000** times or more this amount per dose. The body conserves B12 and can store enough of it to last 5 years or longer. In other words, theoretically, if a strict vegan consumed 1 vitamin B12 tablet, B12 from that tablet could be stored and used by the body for *years*. Additionally, when B12 passes from the body in bile salts, it can be reabsorbed through the intestinal wall (and perhaps elsewhere) and recycled, so that very little of it actually leaves the body. Animal foods do contain vastly greater amounts of vitamin B12 than do plant foods, but this is of no importance since our bodies independently manufacture and store what we need.

In fact, meat consumption *hampers* the body's production of intrinsic factor and thus the absorption of B12. So, heavy meat eaters, especially those who drink alcohol to excess (and, for biochemical/physiological and even psychological reasons, the two often occur together), are actually more likely to develop the dreaded B12 shortage than vegans. Not that some vegans don't develop vitamin B12 deficiency, and many other nutritional problems. Just that, like so many in our modern society, their deficiencies are not caused by a vegan diet, but by an overall *lousy* diet.

But isn't animal flesh the iron-rich food; don't we need it to get enough of this essential mineral? Then why is iron-deficiency anemia the most common nutrient deficiency in the US -- a nation of meat gluttons? Other factors are involved, but once again, a meat-centered diet may block the body's absorption and use of iron.

Thiamin, niacin, B6, vitamin C, phosphorus, fiber, calcium, fat, calories? Whatever nutritional component in question will be supplied more properly by a vegan than meat-centered diet.

Well then, isn't it true that, unlike wimpy plant foods, meat gives one strength and endurance? To build a hard, meaty body, doesn't it make sense to eat a lot of meat? (Many advertisers even subtly imply that it will make a man's penis grow larger and firmer -- and stay hard longer during sex.) Doesn't the fuel from plant food just "burn off" quickly, whereas that from meat is (as advertised) potent, long-lasting energy? *Isn't meat a power food?*

How many millions of misguided, macho muscle men, believing these myths, make meat their main course at every meal? Because beefy, brawny types are the most likely to believe it in the first place, the myth may seem to be true. But don't they wonder how the buffalo can produce a half-ton of hard muscle from blades of grass? Or how the grass-eating horse can run for hours at high speed? Or how the gorilla, perhaps the strongest large animal for its size on Earth, can build its amazing physique from leaves, stalks, fruit, and other plant foods almost exclusively? Or how many of the world's top athletes can be vegetarian?

Sure, you can become big and bulky with a fatty, hormone-infested, meat-centered diet, especially if you pump iron 3 times a week. And as a placebo meat can do amazing things. But it is no more of a power- and body-building source than plant foods containing equivalent nutrients. (Indeed, much evidence suggests the opposite.) Nutrients, from whatever source, are nutrients. Health, strength, and endurance (and sexual proficiency) come not from gobbling down meat, but from natural eating and natural living.

All this leads into one of the most sensitive subjects -- the psychology of traditional, heavy meat eating. It would take more pages to begin to explore this issue than we can afford here, but because it is so important to understanding why we support the ranching industry, I will consider it briefly.

First and foremost, *culture more than anything dictates individual reality*. When a certain behavior has for centuries been an integrated component of the cultural whole, it is extremely difficult for the individual to realize the extent to which that culture has evolved to reinforce belief in that custom in each individual psyche. Cultural beliefs tend to be self-perpetuating entities over which the human participants have little objective control.

For example, up until early this century American women were supposed to wear dresses, never pants. Of course, there was no significant physical reason why women could not have worn pants (or that men could not have worn dresses, for that matter), but the prevailing reality was "Women wear dresses." To men and women alike, it was almost beyond belief that women would want to wear pants. A woman who did was likely to be scorned as homosexual or crazy. Conversely, because of this mandated reality via social pressure, few other than homosexual and crazy women could conceive of wearing or would want to wear pants, *thereby reinforcing the common cultural reality*.

Today, we think ourselves an advanced, enlightened culture. Yet to be considered more attractive our women remove their natural body hair and cover their faces with colored substances; to gain acceptance our men tie slender pieces of cloth around their necks; our doctors slap newborns and put them in plastic boxes (then cut the foreskin off the males' penises!); our priests drop magic water on babies' heads to ward off the Devil; and most of our people think that our political unit, the USA, is inherently -- and even spiritually -- superior to all others on Earth. Most of our people consider these behaviors and beliefs not cultural manifestations but "reality" itself. The point is, we were born into this predetermined "reality" with little ability or desire to objectively comprehend it, much less formulate an alternative and live it out within the context of the prevailing culture.

So it is with omnivorism. Our cultural reality dictates that "Humans are omnivores." This preordained reality never was based on facts, but on its own continuance over the centuries. We were raised to accept, not to question, those beliefs.

Each member of society tends to embrace his or her traditional, assigned role in the cultural whole. Therefore, the popular vegetarian stereotype -- pale and skinny, impotent, timid, a little queer, a "bleeding heart" who is "afraid to kill an animal" -- often is quite accurate. These individuals in turn reaffirm society's prevailing conviction that vegetarianism does indeed diminish health and that it is practiced by "inferior" persons.

Hence, the beef industry's new slogan: "*Real* food for *real* people." It wasn't designed to *convince* people that beef is more real than plant foods or that beef-eaters are more real than plant-eaters, but to *preserve* our culture's long-standing myth. Though only 3% of US citizens thus far have adopted a plant food diet, this vegetarian trend already represents the loss of billions of dollars to the livestock industry. The slogan is a clever, though desperate, attempt to stave off growing awareness that meat actually is *not* a very real food for humans after all.

Despite centuries of ignorance, mythology, and prejudice, despite unceasing commercial persuasion, and despite the stigma of the stereotypical wimpy vegetarian, the movement toward a more natural plant-centered diet continues to grow. Realizing that their culture lost touch with what is natural long ago, more people are trying to reestablish it in their own lives. They try to minimize society's many pressures to feel inferior or somehow less real for not eating large amounts of meat, and they find they don't need meat at all to be healthy, strong, and real.

The world's longest-lived peoples are the Vilcabambas of Ecuador's Andes, the Abkhasians near the USSR's Black Sea, and the Hunzas of Northern Pakistan's Himalayas. Researchers report that all 3 are totally vegetarian or close to it. "But what about the Eskimos?" every good skeptic must ask. They seem(ed) to thrive on nothing but fish, seal, walrus, and whale (though not beef). By necessity, the indigenous peoples of extremely cold climes are the most meat-oriented on Earth, though they do eat some plant foods. Extreme cold does seem to make the human body much more amenable to a fatty, meat-centered diet. After thousands of years, these peoples have even begun to show physiological changes toward carnivorism. Still, even they remain overwhelmingly vegan in body. It is speculated that being the world's greatest consumers of animal flesh is a major reason the Eskimos, Laplanders, Greenlanders, and Russian Kurgi have the world's lowest average life expectancies, often only about 30 years (Robbins 1987).

[Note: Much of the following discussion on early human diet (and of the rise of pastoralism in the following section) may also be speculative -- though no more so than prevailing theories. Substantial and mounting evidence suggests that it is correct. For many reasons, traditional scientific study has provided us a very misleading picture of certain aspects of early humans.]

The Eskimos are the extreme. Relatively few ancestral human groups (or even existing primitive tribes) derived more than a minor portion of their food from animal sources. Contrary to our popular image, the great majority were not hunters or hunter-gatherers but *gatherers or gatherer-hunters*, subsisting primarily on fruits, berries, leafy greens, vegetables, herbs, nuts, tubers, grains, seeds, honey, and such. As related by Riane Eisler in her important work, **The Chalice and the Blade**, scientific evidence suggests that, "meat eating formed only a minuscule part of the diet of ancestral primates, hominids, and early humans." Dr. Oliver Alabaster, director of the Institute for Disease Prevention at George Washington University, concurs:

Fruits, nuts, cereal, and vegetation were the basis of the human diet over the millennia. Our modern diet is really an anathema to our whole historical evolution.

During earlier hominid history, we were even less likely to eat animals, as reported by the eminent anthropologist Dr. Alan Walker in his studies of fossilized teeth:

No exceptions have been found. Every tooth examined from the hominids of the 12 million-year period leading up to Homo erectus *appeared to be that of a fruit eater.*

When relatively recently hominids overpopulated their natural habitat in the well-vegetated tropics* and many were forced out into colder and dryer regions where hominid plant foods were less abundant, they were forced to kill animals for food, clothing, and shelter. During subsequent ice ages, they came to rely even more heavily upon animals for survival. When local game animals were depleted, they invaded new lands or began domesticating and raising livestock. Thus did those who would shape recent human history become habituated to heavy meat eating.

* Those hominids remaining in the tropics eventually also depleted their habitat and for other reasons came to rely more heavily on animal foods, but this is another story. Native Americans, also habituated to excessive meat consumption, are descended from heavy meat eating peoples who had lived in the cold regions of Asia for millennia and gradually worked their way across the Bearing Strait perhaps 40,000 years ago.

Leaving its natural habitat in the tropics was perhaps the most hazardous step ever taken by the human-like animal. To survive, *Homo erectus* has from that point on been forced to adopt unnatural and harmful ways of living, and to greatly alter its surroundings to provide for its needs as an inherently tropical, plant-eating animal.

Our popular vision of our "lowly" human ancestors -- cowering in caves; cold, hungry, filthy, and disease-ridden; clothed with ill-fitting animal skins; venturing out into the cruel world only to hunt game or club each other over the head; surviving on greasy mastodon parts -- is probably the antithesis of most early humans.

All this has broad implications as to the alleged "naturalness" of many traits we traditionally have been conditioned to believe inherent-

ly human, including omnivorism, hunting...clothing, housing...warfare, science, technology, and the whole shebang. But this is another book....

In recent millennia, as these powerful, war-like pastoral tribes and the dominating cultures and colonial empires from which they grew spread their influence around the globe, meat eating became symbolic of status, wealth, and power. Lack of meat came to be seen as a sign of poverty, weakness, and general inferiority.

We are primates, and primates are all vegetarians with only rare meat consumption by certain species. All the protein, minerals, and vitamins the human body needs are easily obtained from plant sources. The taste for meats and other fatty foods is like a substance abuse to which we are addicted early in life.
--Dr. Neal Barnard, President, 30,000-member Physicians Committee for Responsible Medicine

With this history, heavy meat eating in contemporary times has become a psychological need for most of the Earth's people. *As we have drawn further away from the natural world, what we eat has become increasingly arbitrary -- based on social and cultural considerations, not instinct and bodily function.* William J. Mayo, founder of the Mayo Clinic, in an address to the American College of Surgeons states, "Meat-eating has increased 400% in the last 100 years." (America's beef consumption has likewise grown along with its cowboy obsession, and now, according to the editors of Consumer Reports, "The United States, with less than one-twentieth of the planet's people, consumes one-fourth of the planet's beef.") In our modern, competitive world, meat eating has become so strongly associated with accepted values that it is a rare individual who dares step outside cultural norms and even suggest that we are not omnivores.

Still, more and more people continue to shed their culturally installed preconceptions in favor of common sense, as scientific evidence that humans are naturally vegan continues to accumulate. As mentioned, literally thousands of studies already suggest as much, but now findings from the most comprehensive study of the issue yet conducted strongly reinforce the concept. In 1983 Cornell University researchers, aided by Chinese scientists, began a continuing study of the dietary habits of thousands of Chinese and comparing them to those of Americans. Among their recently released findings:

● Chinese get more than enough protein; Chinese consume 1/3 less protein than Americans, but only 7% of their protein comes from animal sources compared to 70% for Americans.

● Consumption of animal protein itself significantly raises the incidence of heart disease and cancer.

● Fat intake should account for 10%-15% of caloric intake, rather than the 30% or more commonly ingested by meat-centered Americans (interestingly, the average American's body is 15%-30% fat, compared to the optimum 10%-15%).

● *Chinese consume 20% more calories than Americans, but Americans are 25% fatter* (no, the Chinese are not starving, as for 50 years we have been indoctrinated to believe).

- Cholesterol counts for Chinese ranged from 88 to 165 milligrams per 100 milliliters of blood, compared to 155 to 274 milligrams for Americans.
- The average Chinese adult with her/his heavily vegetarian diet consumes twice as much iron as does the average American.
- Chinese get plenty of calcium and have lower rates of osteoporosis than American animal product eaters.
- Chinese ingest 3 times more dietary fiber than Americans, nearly twice as many vegetables, 4 times as much grain, 1/11 as much sugar, 1/5 as much fats and oils, 1/4 as much meat, and 1/88 as much cow milk product.

The director of the study, Cornell University nutritional biochemist T. Colin Campbell, maintains that only in the last few thousand years have meat and animal products become prevalent in the human diet: "That's not nearly enough time to evolve new mechanisms to give us protection from those kinds of foods. . . . Animal foods, in general, are not really helpful and we need to get away from eating them." Campbell is writing a book on the reasons why recent humans have begun eating so much meat, and the preliminary findings of the study were recently published as a 900-page monograph. (*Arizona Daily Star* 1990) After studying the diets and health histories of 88,751 female nurses, Dr. Walter Willet of the Brigham and Woman's Hospital in Boston concluded, "The optimum amount of red meat you eat should be zero."

Baboons, raccoons, opossums, chickens, and peccaries are omnivorous. Orang-utans, chimpanzees, gibbons, gorillas, (our 4 closest relatives) and humans are all vegan or nearly so.

We humans are "omnivorous" in that we can extract some nutrients from most things organic, be they oranges, animal parts, or grass clippings. Similarly, wolves are "omnivorous" in that they can extract nutrients from oranges, animal parts, or grass clippings. Nevertheless, neither humans nor wolves are true omnivores. Throughout prehistory, we have eaten animals in time of need and lightly supplemented our normal diet with animals, especially those easily caught such as insects, shellfish, and certain reptiles and amphibians. Eating meat occasionally is natural to humans, but eating large amounts routinely is not. To me, what is natural is what is best (though often this "rule" must be compromised in an increasingly unnatural world).

Unfortunately, people generally perceive and do what their culture dictates, despite any evidence to the contrary. Our modern circumstance decrees that we are omnivores, and our thoughts and actions are compelled by this imperial edict. We become frightened and reactionary when our very reality develops cracks. So now, throw this book down in disgust if you must.

To conclude, it is untrue that eating animal flesh is essential to human health. For example, my 2 sons, 13 and 15, have eaten meat only several times in their lives and are in excellent health. Likewise, it is untrue that a diet containing more than a small percentage of meat is natural to the human animal. Livestock grazing is thus not justified on the basis of nutritional need.

Tell me, do you ever wonder where that wonderful prime rib and succulent T-bone steak came from? . . . As you sit at your tidy table some evening in the future and feast on a patty of vegetable protein and sea weed, you can contemplate on whatever happened to that good old beef steak! Long live the rancher and his cows!
--Nancy E. Brown, letter to the editor, 1-30-90 *Red Rock News*, Sedona, Arizona

(SCS, USDA)

- ## God put the land here for ranching.

Regardless of one's convictions as to how we all got here, the fact remains that man and cattle are a part of the scheme of things, just as are other mammals, reptiles, birds, and all the rest.
--Public lands rancher's widow Peggy Monzingo, in a letter to a local newspaper

Mary Vass, another long-time public lands rancher (or, "rancher's wife," as she prefers) in Wyoming, once told me:

I believe grass was put here by the Good Lord for us to raise livestock. If you don't graze this public lands grass, what are you going to do with it?

When I answered, "Not much; I'd leave it mostly for wild animals and the rest of Nature," she responded, "Now, what are you going to *do* with all those wild animals?"

Mrs. Vass's words represent much more than she might imagine. Her conviction is shared by today's public lands ranchers in particular and the Western ranching community in general. It is echoed by the men who "conquered" the West and continue to exploit it for short-term personal gain, men who consider the land little more than a collection of resources put here by "God" for competitive human use (which even if true would still not justify such short-sighted exploitation). It is seen in Western Manifest Destiny -- the subjugation of Native Americans; the bloody range wars;

social, economic, and political ascendancy; and the relentless war against "the wilderness." And it is reflected by our modern culture more than we might imagine or care to acknowledge.

Mrs. Vass, in her seemingly unassuming way, reflects a belief system, an ideology that sees humanity above and apart from Nature and evolution as a divinely preordained, linear progression toward ever-increasing human dominance. The roots of her words go far into prehistory. Indeed, the taproot from which Mrs. Vass's worldview grew likely had its seed in the rise of aggressive, warlike pastoral tribes in the "Old World" thousands of years ago.

From their beginnings perhaps 12 million years ago, most hominids lived in unitary coexistence with Nature. As *Homo sapiens* evolved, its unique intelligence made it a very successful species, and it thus eventually overpopulated its natural habitat in the tropics ("overpopulated" meaning exceeding natural limits). Other species would have been confined by various environmental factors, but humans pushed into less favorable habitats and survived by using fire, making clothing, and building increasingly more efficient shelters -- by (temporarily) outwitting Nature. Most settled into the more benign, productive portions of their new world, where eventually they developed civilizations based on farming -- a human invention that began roughly 10,000 years ago to produce food in overpopulated habitat and areas where humans were not native.

But continuing overpopulation there and in the tropics caused other peoples to be cast into the less productive hinterlands, where even greater changes in their cultures took place. There, struggling merely to survive, they gradually came to view Nature as an enemy -- to be thwarted or conquered -- rather than as the benevolent companion it generally had always been. Because plant foods were much less abundant, these peoples necessarily changed from a plant- to animal-centered diet and developed weapons and skills needed to hunt large prey. Because hunting gained immense importance and men -- generally faster and stronger than women and not encumbered by bearing and nursing infants -- became the hunters, the cooperative social systems these peoples had in the tropics gradually evolved into authoritarian patriarchies. The most aggressive and successful males became dominant chieftains. Woman were cast into a subordinate role, along with children, animals, and Nature in general (see Carolyn Merchant's **The Death of Nature**).

To stay with the roaming and migratory animals they came to depend on, these peoples necessarily developed highly nomadic lifestyles. As they became more efficient hunters, they often depleted local food animals and had to move into new areas to find enough to eat. When these new territories were already occupied by other hunting bands, conflict erupted. The bands with the best hunting weapons and skills usually won.

With this new, aggressive competition developing, communication broke down, leading hunting groups to increasingly distrust one another. Accordingly, trade also broke down, leading them to rely increasingly on pillage rather than exchange to replenish their diminishing resources. As time went on, these bands learned that in order to survive they needed to improve their fighting skills as much or more than their hunting skills. They modified their hunting

weapons for use against humans. Gradually, they evolved from nomadic hunting bands into savage, pirate-like warrior-tribes.

Some eventually perceived greater efficiency and dependability in domesticating and grazing wild sheep, goats, and cattle, and became nomadic and semi-nomadic herders. This rise of animal husbandry gave them a feeling of control over their environment, further alienating them from Nature and worsening their aggressive tendencies. The larger, more dependable food supplies provided by pastoralism gave them an even greater ability to wage war against their neighbors. The ability to derive sustenance from wild game or livestock anywhere the animals could forage or browse provided them mobility and prolonged access to nearly any area they desired. Subsequent domestication of the horse gave them even greater mobility and power to overcome their enemies.

When they overgrazed their land, the warlike pastoralists drove their livestock into neighboring territories and battled for dominance. They killed their competitors, took "their" women into slavery, looted and destroyed property, and added the stock to their herds. Appropriating the losers' resources, the victors increased their power exponentially. Meanwhile, hunting declined almost completely before the onslaught and overgrazing of the powerful pastoralists. Now a man was judged by the number of livestock he possessed, as he still is today in many parts of the world, including the American West. Indeed, archaeologist Marija Gimbutas' description of one of these pastoral warrior-cultures bears striking resemblance to the male-dominated ranching subculture of today's rural West:

> The Kurgan system was composed of patrilineal, socially stratified, herding units which lived in small villages or seasonal settlements while grazing their animals over vast areas.

Gimbutas relates that the Kurgan "exalted virile, heroic warrior gods" [macho, gun-toting cowboy heros] and "glorified the lethal power of the sharp blade" [6-shooter]. This phallic symbolism and the power structures it enforces have been passed down through subsequent dominator societies and live on today in rural Western America.

Meanwhile, as these pastoral warrior-tribes expanded their domains they began to encroach upon the settled, generally more peaceful agrarian civilizations. In **The Chalice and the Blade**, Riane Eisler describes this early threat:

> At first it was like the proverbial biblical cloud "no bigger than a man's hand" -- the activities of seemingly insignificant nomadic bands roaming the less desirable fringe areas of our globe seeking grass for their herds. Over the millennia they were apparently out there in the harsh, unwanted, colder, sparser territories on the edges of the earth . . . . (Eisler 1987)

However, as their growing lust for power led to ever-greater conquests, their influence on these agrarian cultures became profound. The most ruthless and violent were the most efficient conquerors, amassing great wealth and power. Among these were the well-known "barbaric hordes" that swept out of the steppes and deserts and across Eurasia beginning around 7000 years ago. The most powerful began directly attacking the bountiful agrarian civilizations. Eisler describes "increasingly massive incursions of the extremely mobile, warlike, hierarchic, and male-dominated pastoralist peoples" (Eisler 1987). W.C. Lowdermilk, in *Conquest of the Land though 7,000 Years*, repeatedly describes the conflict between pastoral peoples and agrarian peoples:

> *Invasions of nomads out of the grasslands and desert . . . . From time to time they have swept down into the plain to bring devastation and destruction upon the farming and city peoples of the plains. Such was the beginning of the Cain and Abel struggle between the shepherd and the farmer.* (Lowdermilk 1975)

To make a long story short, eventually even the most peaceable of the agrarian cultures were either conquered or forced to adopt war-oriented postures to defend themselves. (See, for example, Andrew Schmookler's **Parable of the Tribes**.) The influence of aggressive pastoral hordes thus wholly redirected prevailing human culture. A new system, based on the power to dominate rather than cooperate, emerged and was spread through Europe, most of Asia, eventually North America and all other areas colonized by Europeans and Euro-Americans. (The Roman Empire, for example, was largely an outgrowth of this new system, and a main reason Rome invaded northern Europe was because it had seriously depleted the Mediterranean region with overgrazing livestock and deforestation for livestock.) The new dominant paradigm placed one religion over all others, man over woman, the powerful over the weak, the upper class over the lower classes, people over animals, and humanity over Nature. This worldview has been passed down through many empires, kingdoms, and nation-states, and is still with us. In modern America, it is perhaps best represented by the religious intolerance, machismo, environmental plunder, entrenched social and economic hierarchies, and domineering political power of the Western ranching establishment. Only in recent decades have we begun to question this predominant worldview.

[A footnote: Humans' new-found ability to use animals for food allowed them access to virtually every portion of the planet's land (and even water) surface. This allowed *Homo sapiens* to occupy -- and denigrate -- non-human habitat throughout most of the world -- habitat not suited to and easily damaged by the exotic, overwhelming human species.]

Thus was our "fall from grace" precipitated not by Eve or serpents or evil demons but by warlike pastoralists who had earlier been the first humans cast out of their comfortable natural habitat into a seemingly cruel and alien world. So we see that herdsmen and their animals, through necessity borne of circumstances, became the first great despoilers of the "Garden of Eden" -- the bountiful natural world that had existed basically unspoiled since its beginnings billions of years ago. And thus did powerful stockmen introduce to the world the first great social/cultural system based on human domination rather than cooperation between humans and the planet -- a system that influences our reality to this day. Thus, public lands ranching is not, of course, divinely preordained, but determined by relatively recent world cultural evolution.

[Note: All this is not to suggest that pastoralists are "the root of all evil." They were, through a chain of circumstances beyond their control, cast into the role of leading humanity away from itself and into this different reality.]

> *. . . the existing image of the lone cowboy hero in popular culture runs counter to the deep sociality that has always been intrinsic to human nature. The myth fosters privatism and deludes us into the "wishdream" of being totally independent*

one day like the cowboy hero.
--Douglas C. Bowman, **Beyond the Modern Mind**

The word *Devil* came into the Jewish religion from the time when the Hebrews were captives of Babylon, and thence into Christianity. According to Zoroaster, devas or devils "are the originators of all that is bad . . . and are constantly thinking of causing the destruction of the fields and trees." This connotation has its origin in the fact that their former fellow tribesmen, the Indians, were running their cattle, sheep and goats over their fields, destroying them. . . .

Zoroaster's followers fenced their fields off from this destruction which created further fighting with the "deva worshippers." The Persian word *pairi-daeza*, meaning a "beautiful garden fenced in," was taken over in the Old Testament as the word *paradise*, and thence spread over the whole civilized world.
--Doloras LaChapelle, Earth Wisdom

SYMBOLISM

Ritual
Ceremony
Custom
Culture

All begin as natural expressions
All, even the most primitive
Quickly become traps
Inferior substitutes for Nature

Humanized symbolism replaces
Naturalism
Never restoring, never attaining parity with
What it supplanted, what it buried

Wedging us ever further from ourselves
From the Earth

--LJ, somewhere between Nature and Culture

● *Give us po', hard-workin' folks a break, won't ya; don't destroy our cherished way of life.*

"You can't avoid one conclusion," says a BLM staffer. "The permittees are one of the most pampered groups in the country. We protect their life-style and insure that they get to graze their animals at minimum cost. We assure that they have no competition. We look the other way when they trespass or sublease for profit. We give them low-interest loans and a disproportionate voice in the management of the resource they profit from. What other business gets pampered that way? And they're really just businessmen -- businessmen with special clothes and a special hat and a special twang in their voices, and we listen to them and just give them whatever they want."
--from "Discouraging Words" by Jon R. Luoma (Luoma 1986)

OBSEQUIOUS LAMENT OF THE
PUBLIC LANDS RANCHER

(Greg Pentkowski)

If all the rationalization and hard-sell doesn't work, as a last resort the plead-for-sympathy approach usually does. It comes in many different forms, all designed to evoke our pity for the poor ol' dusty cowpoke. Thus, for example, when a few years ago the New Mexico State Land Department had the audacity to attempt to raise the state land grazing fee closer to fair market value, the NM Cattle Growers and NM Farm and Livestock Bureau labeled it a "shameful attack on a financially-strapped minority. . . Because of the ranchers' economic conditions, we just can't stand it. . . . We have an environment very conducive to disaster" (McClellan 1985). Well hand me the goddamned Kleenex!

The American public has long had immense sympathy for anyone in the ranching business. That most public lands ranchers are materially secure and socially and politically powerful is unknown to most Americans, but seems to have little bearing on our feelings anyway. And, in these days of striving to save the family farm, it is especially easy to commiserate with public lands stockmen who claim to be in that poverty-stricken boat. In reality, the public lands rancher bears little resemblance to the traditional, small-time farmer.

"*This thing* [soil erosion] *has been going on for centuries; it was going on before there was a cow in Wyoming . . . . Why blame it on the poor shepherd and little old cowboy that's trying to make a living here on these hills?*"
--Wyoming Senator Frank Barrett in 1946, from **The Easy Chair** by Bernard DeVoto (DeVoto adds: "There are places in Wyoming where the poor shepherd and little old cowboy have accelerated erosion several hundred thousand percent.") (DeVoto 1955)

Undoubtedly some public lands ranchers *are* struggling financially, even with plentiful government and private assistance. (As detailed, roughly 2 billion tax and private dollars annually are lost to public lands ranching -- an average of $66,666 for each public lands permittee; compare this with the average amount a family of four receives on welfare each year -- $6,492.) A few permittees are selling out of the ranching business altogether. But this simply means that their ranching operations have not been providing enough profit to make staying in the ranching business worth the effort. This is to be expected occasionally for, as we have seen, public land is a lousy place to raise cattle. As Tom Bonar, an Arizona permittee using 200,000 public acres, complains, "How's a guy supposed to make a living?"

Well, most of us are struggling to make it. But does the locksmith expect the government to supply work materials and guarantee permanent employment? Does the construction worker insist that the government grant special utility rates and waive taxes on home and property? Does the grocer demand that the government sell her/him agricultural products at 1/5 fair market value? Of the many commercial groups in this country, public lands ranchers expect more and a greater variety of assistance than perhaps any other.

Why is it a tragedy when a ranch fails, but no big deal when my shoe store goes under?
--Small businessman at a 1985 Wyoming Republican Party issues conference

Jim Chilton, another Arizona public lands grazier, grumbles, "I'm a native Arizonan, and I've worked hard all my life. When someone calls me a welfare recipient, I just boil." On an emotional level, this may seem admirable. But think about it; does hard work alone mean someone is not on welfare, or that the work being done is worthwhile?

When a business is heavily subsidized, it is a form of welfare, whether the recipient works hard or not. Furthermore, work is not a virtue when the results are destructive. "Work" is simply directed effort. It may be beneficial, harmless, or destructive. Many ranchers are hard working; many are not, as is the case with most professions. Supporting welfare ranching because some stockmen work hard makes no sense, nor is it fair to the other workers of this country. Indeed, one of ranching's greatest appeals is that (though it does take much money) it requires as much or little effort as the stock raiser wants to spend; "just throw some cows out there and you're in business," as they say. (Personal observation suggests that very many public lands ranchers spend as much time in coffee shops as on the range.)

The author demonstrates that you cannot believe everything as presented. *(Lynne Bohi)*

Although they love to dress up like Gabby Hayes, ranchers are businessmen, and like all businessmen they want to minimize overhead and maximize profits.
--Richard Lessner, "Dances With Wolves: Ranchers Should Lose This War" (Lessner 1991)

Despite reality, the ranching establishment keeps arousing our sympathies and romanticism: "We're just plain common-folk, tryin' hard against all odds to make an honest living," they declare. Not only that, they are (take your pick): "providing red meat for a growing America (or world)"; "working people"; "the forgotten folks at the bottom of the economic pyramid"; "the salt of the earth"; "promoting the pioneer spirit"; "preserving our Western legacy"; and so on. With such syrupy schmaltz, who could refuse these poor downtrodden their dirt-cheap grazing fees, subsidized range developments, and profuse special treatment? Few commercial enterprises stoop to such heights of calculated self-pity and pretentious false modesty in an attempt to maintain government and public support. And they'll lay it on

thicker and heavier as needed, even going so far as to question the patriotism and morality of those who would deny them.

The ranchers making these claims are usually the same ones who can afford to take jets or drive their fancy, $15,000 pickups from across the West to attend a 3-day stockmen's convention for $60 a night at some posh hotel -- so they can stand up and make their pitiful claims! Sometimes, however, a stockmen's association will fly in a truly destitute, dusty public lands cowpoke to tell his tear-jerking tail of woe and misery for the media or Congress. What a show!!

Various interests want all livestock removed; other interests want the resources developed to permit livestock to safely use the resources. Whether the public lands are to continue to provide opportunity for those seeking to make a living or to provide enjoyment for those who have already secured their means of livelihood is an often raised question. [Drive a semi between these lines!] (USDA, USDI, CEQ 1979)
--Idaho Governor and public lands rancher John V. Evans, 1979

The underappreciated but irrefutable fact is that most of the 30,000 or so Western public lands ranchers (1.9% of US ranchers) live quite comfortably. About 20% are described by the US government as "large" operators -- those permitted to lease more than 5000 AUMs (the equivalent of roughly 400 cattle). By far most of these ranchers would be considered wealthy by the average American. GAO identifies 11% of all BLM permittees as corporations, while an additional 8% are described as "partnerships" and another 5% as "other" than individuals (USGAO 1986). Forest Service and other government agency figures are similar. Most of these entities hold substantial wealth, and in recent years this group includes a growing number of powerful Japanese investors. Idaho, 70% publicly owned, has a higher percentage of millionaires than any other state, largely because wealthy ranchers so thoroughly dominate its public and private lands (Ferguson 1983).

This not-unusual public lands ranching headquarters in central California includes structural developments worth more than $1 million.

THE COMPLEET
CONTEMPORARY CATTLEPERSON *

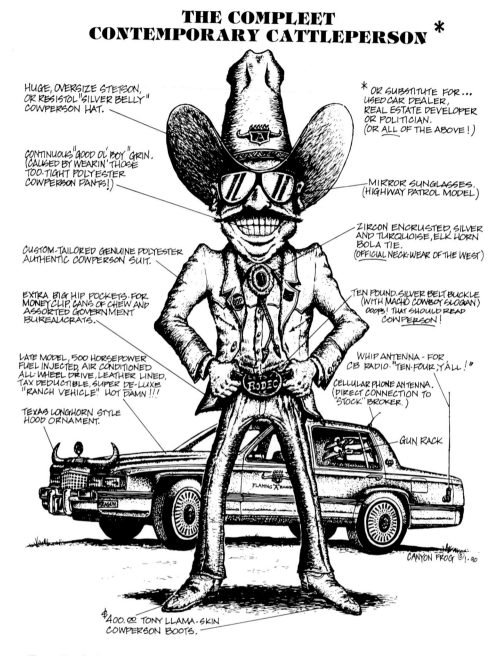

HUGE, OVERSIZE STETSON,
OR RESISTOL "SILVER BELLY"
COWPERSON HAT.

CONTINUOUS "GOOD OL' BOY" GRIN.
(CAUSED BY WEARIN' THOSE
TOO-TIGHT POLYESTER
COWPERSON PANTS!)

CUSTOM-TAILORED GENUINE POLYESTER
AUTHENTIC COWPERSON SUIT.

EXTRA BIG HIP POCKETS. FOR
MONEY CLIP, CANS OF CHEW AND
ASSORTED GOVERNMENT
BUREAUCRATS.

LATE MODEL, 500 HORSEPOWER
FUEL INJECTED, AIR CONDITIONED
ALL-WHEEL DRIVE, LEATHER LINED,
TAX DEDUCTIBLE, SUPER DE-LUXE
"RANCH VEHICLE". HOT DAMN!!!

TEXAS LONGHORN STYLE
HOOD ORNAMENT.

$400.00 TONY LLAMA-SKIN
COWPERSON BOOTS.

* OR SUBSTITUTE FOR ...
USED CAR DEALER,
REAL ESTATE DEVELOPER
OR POLITICIAN.
(OR ALL OF THE ABOVE!)

MIRROR SUNGLASSES.
(HIGHWAY PATROL MODEL)

ZIRCON ENCRUSTED, SILVER
AND TURQUOISE, ELK HORN
BOLA TIE.
(OFFICIAL NECK-WEAR OF THE WEST)

TEN POUND, SILVER BELT BUCKLE
(WITH MACHO COWBOY SLOGAN)
OOPS! THAT SHOULD READ
COWPERSON!

WHIP ANTENNA - FOR
CB RADIO. "TEN-FOUR, Y'ALL!"

CELLULAR PHONE ANTENNA.
(DIRECT CONNECTION TO
"STOCK" BROKER.)

GUN RACK

CANYON FROG © 1-90

(Roger Candee)

Of the remaining (roughly 2/3) described as "medium" to "small" individual operators, many are land speculators, politicians, wealthy businessmen, doctors, lawyers, actors, country and western singers . . . even rock stars! For most of these people, ranching is not a profession, but a tax write-off, source of extra income, weekend hobby, vacation get-away, or a way to impress people (we're spending the weekend . . . *at our ranch*). Romance, recreation, and achievement of desired social status or political power are the primary motives for many operators. Still other public ranching operations are pursued simply to maintain family tradition.

This leaves probably less than 50% "medium" to "small" ranchers. A large percentage of even these stockmen are financially endowed. As mentioned, most public lands ranchers derive only a minor portion of their net income from public lands ranching. Many own other businesses, such as retail stores, automobile dealerships, insurance outlets, and financial institutions, or hold regular jobs or political offices in town, and cowboy only on weekends. A great many of these ranchers have become independently wealthy through inheritance and/or by selling off their "excess" private land.

Of the remaining 20%-30% (?) -- the medium to small-time "working ranchers" -- the majority are well-off, to say the least. These stockmen maintain essentially permanent ranching tenure (and subsidies) on public land and usually own or hold substantial equity in their homes and improvements, base properties, livestock, vehicles, machinery, and other tangible and intangible assets. In many cases wives work as waitresses, retail clerks, beauticians, etc. and bring home other income.

Of the remaining less than 10% (?) (perhaps less than 3000) who are not well-situated, few are truly poor. Regardless, with many practical alternatives available (see next chapter), even the poorest have no good excuse to keep their livestock on the public's land.

Everyone wants the family farm to survive, and nostalgia looms especially large in the West, where cowboys have always held the greatest fascination for Americans. Working a spread that runs from here to the horizon comports with the classic American image of freedom and rugged individualism.
--Dyan Zaslowsky, "A Public Beef" (Zaslowsky 1989)

If we calculate the average public grazier's income based solely on public lands ranching (as most permittees purposefully do), we get a distorted picture. If 22,000 federal lands ranchers are divided into the $390 million in annual livestock value derived from grazing BLM and FS land, we find that each permittee sells his public lands livestock for only $17,727 annually. Even disregarding ranching expenses (which could easily dwarf this figure), this amount hardly exceeds the poverty level for most families. Perhaps they really are as poor as they claim?

No. Their livestock graze public land an average of only about 4 months each year. For the remaining 8 months, their animals subsist on private land. A year is 3 times longer than 4 months, and 3 X $17,727 = $53,181 per year. Additionally, some of most BLM and FS permittees' livestock spend *no* time on BLM or FS land or on other publicly owned land, so we may safely surmise that the average federal permittee grosses far more than $53,181 annually from livestock sales. Moreover, as mentioned, most public lands ranchers have a second or even third or fourth source of income. These include other jobs, political office or influence, direct and indirect ranching subsidies, "special arrangements" with government agencies, hunting and access fees, interest, dividends, royalties, commissions, rentals, and sale of public resources. Some ranchers, for example, have amassed considerable wealth from fees paid by energy companies to drill for oil and gas on the ranchers' land. Many have become independently wealthy through inheritance and/ or sale of "excess" real estate. Thus, claims by most permittees of poverty based on low income from public lands grazing are grossly deceptive.

This isn't a matter of survival, or generally even of lifestyle, but of profit and power. On the whole, public lands ranchers have a much higher net income and far greater total assets than the average American; a remarkably large percentage are millionaires. They hold immense influence and prestige. What reason is there for pity? The American public has been taken for a century-long ride by these sympathy miners.

The rancher's self-image as the last hard-working, most independent member of American society grew with the popular western movies. Western stockraisers, as Bernard DeVoto explained, believed in their own mythology. No finer welfare system was ever developed. It combined aristocratic arrogance toward a public agency with high social status and financial rewards.
--Bernard Shanks, **This Land Is Your Land** (Shanks 1984)

These welfare ranchers are experts at telling tales of woe. . . . Everyone is crying about the poor rancher that will lose his job. Has any welfare rancher ever stepped forward to help you keep your job? . . . No one worried about the poor crutch-makers who lost their jobs when Jonas Salk invented the polio vaccine, and no one is going to miss the welfare rancher.
--Stuart Croghan, LaGrande, Oregon

And so we find that the ranching establishment's justifications for ranching have little basis in reality. The next chapter will explore the most commonly proposed alternatives to traditional public lands ranching, concluding with a description of one of the most workable and responsible long-term solutions.

Chapter XII
ALTERNATIVES

Notwithstanding the semi-facetious BENEFITS OF PUBLIC LANDS RANCHING, some readers may still think this book dwells on the negative and offers no solutions. I would counter that it dwells on public lands ranching -- an overwhelming negative -- the elimination of which **is** the solution. Allowing the subsequent environmental, economic, social, and political improvement is one of the most *positive* things we could do for the West.

And yet, while many people recognize that ranching is a negative influence overall, few in our cowboy-oriented society realize the extent of its influence and fewer still can conceptualize banning it from public land. Instead, they offer alternatives.

Reform

If you talk about making people quit ranching, you put up an instant red flag. They'll throw your head up against the wall up here in eastern Montana. If, on the other hand, you say we want to help you ranch in a different way, to manage the land better and make a profit without government subsidies, then maybe they'll listen.
--Charles Jonkel, Institute of the Rockies

But total eviction of the cattle and sheep would not be much of a victory. The real victory will be reform of public land ranching so it becomes an asset to the West rather than its present liability.
--Ed Marston, publisher, *High Country News* (3-12-90)

Reform is fine -- except when that to be reformed is inherently impractical. Given enough hidden subsidization, special assistance, and publicized misinformation, banana plantations in Minnesota could be made to seem feasible.

Public lands ranching has been undergoing reformation since the early 1900s; little has changed, though. This book has mentioned dozens of legislative acts and amendments, policy directives, and judicial rulings designed to reform ranching. They have had varying effects on the agencies, yet all of them combined have not much changed public lands ranching. For example, though NRDC's 1973 lawsuit forced BLM to go through the motions of preparing EISs for 212 grazing areas on 150 million acres, the EISs have, according to NRDC, resulted in little discernible benefit to the land.

Still, even most conservationists remain deluded that the solution is to study ecology and reform ranching accordingly. Does understanding Minnesotan ecology and how bananas grow make growing bananas in Minnesota practical? Wouldn't a more reasonable approach be to decide not *how* but **if** public land should be used for ranching?

Carrizo Plain is a 50-mile-long valley nestled between coastal mountain ranges in south-central California. A visitor in 1886 described it: "In the spring, native bunch grasses, reaching as tall as the side of a horse, grew thick on the undulating land, turning to naturally cured hay in the summer. Wild horses, elk, deer, and antelope were abundant on the plain." A subsequent century of ranching has left it remarkably barren and devoid of wildlife. In 1988 The Nature Conservancy, in cooperation with BLM and the California Department of Fish & Game, purchased 8 contiguous ranches on the plain -- 85,000 acres altogether -- that eventually will be sold to the agencies as the core of a 180,000-acre reserve. To help restore several Endangered species, the Conservancy has implemented "a much stricter grazing management regime." However, though limited progress has been made, in a late 1990 visit to the "reserve" I saw overwhelming overgrazing and precious little recovery (even taking into account the current drought). An interview with cowboy-like managers of the "reserve" indicated that ranching will continue. It seems certain that (without intensive, expensive range restoration) significant recovery will not occur until ranching is terminated.

receive fair market value for its herbage, the fee would have to be raised 10-fold, to about $20/AUM. Moreover, the federal grazing fee is simply the price the government charges for grazing livestock (like a feed store selling hay); it does not compensate the roughly $1 billion a year in additional tax subsidies. To cover this cost, with half of fees going to the Range "Betterment" Fund, permittees would have to pay approximately $80/AUM, or more than 40 times the current rate. To recompense the additional non-tax-related values already outlined, they might have to pay $200/AUM or more. Fat chance, especially when permittees already complain about $1.81/AUM!

If the federal government was somehow forced to reform ranching administration to fully protect the environment and public interest, what would happen? It would quintuple the grazing fee; terminate the Range "Betterment" Fund; eliminate subsidies; close ranching roads and dismantle fences; end predator and pest programs; ban livestock from all environmentally sensitive areas; drastically cut remaining livestock numbers; strictly enforce all grazing regulations; disallow monopolization; eliminate "advisory" boards, unfair laws, and special political consideration . . . in other words, it would essentially shut down the vast bulk of public lands ranching. What little remained wouldn't begin to justify the infrastructure needed to keep it going! Ranching reform is a contradiction in terms -- a pipe dream.

After all these years of effort, we still face the same set of problems: seriously abused public lands with devastated streamside areas, ravaged fisheries and wildlife habitat, chronic soil erosion, weed invasions, sick watersheds, and degraded trails and campsites. . . . My husband says range reform is like cold fusion.
--Rose Strickland, Sierra Club Grazing Subcommittee Chair (Strickland 1990)

Raised Grazing Fees

Perhaps the most commonly suggested alternative is raising grazing fees to make them comparable to the cost of leasing private ranching. Through this simple act the public would finally receive a fair price for the herbage it collectively owns. Or would it?

As mentioned, about 1/2 of federal grazing fee receipts are returned to the Range "Betterment" Fund for ranching development. Thus, for the American public to actually

Many environmentalists believe higher fees would reduce grazing pressure because generally public lands ranchers stock heavily to take advantage of cheap herbage. The herbage-to-animal profit ratio makes this practical, even if the high level of grazing lowers average animal weight or if some animals starve. Higher grazing fees supposedly would remove this motivation. However, a good look at leased private ranchland suggests that this is largely wishful thinking.

According to Johanna Wald, public lands attorney for the Natural Resources Defense Council, "By being set so low, the fees are denying the agencies the ability to do their job better, if not right" (Zaslowsky 1989). While undoubtedly this idea has merit, the fact remains that the grazing fee system is set up to promote ranching more than stewardship; the more money it returns through fees, the more ranching justifies and expands itself. The system was designed to be self-perpetuating.

Some people presume (or hope, in many cases) that higher fees would be the straw that broke the camel's back -- that public lands ranching would then collapse like a house of cards. However, many borderline ranchers might overstock allotments or increase trespass to recoup this extra expense, perhaps out of spite, to judge from the warnings of some. Higher fees would eliminate some inefficient, uneconomic, submarginal, and speculative operators (some of the most irresponsible), but other ranchers are always waiting to procure those leases. Moreover, since fees are only a small portion of operating costs, even a large increase would be unlikely to shut down an operation not already on the brink. Most operators, especially large ones, could easily pay market value. Higher fees probably would tend to force smaller operators out of business, allowing larger ones to buy them out and expand. (It seems likely, however, that raising the grazing fee to fair market value would result in less than 5000 of the West's 30,000 or so public lands ranchers selling their grazing permits -- and very few of these would be impelled by actual poverty.)

Supporters of the traditional micro-fees have terrified the hamburger-addicted public by claiming that beef prices would skyrocket if ranchers were forced pay what herbage is worth. For example, Arizona Congressional Representative Jim Kolbe (from an influential public lands ranching family) responded to Oklahoma Representative Mike Synar's 1988 bill to raise the federal grazing fee by saying, "I doubt opponents would be willing to pay three to four times the price of beef at their local supermarkets." Kolbe . . . well . . . misrepresents the truth.

Suppose federal permittees were forced to pay fair market value of roughly $10/AUM, and suppose they compensated by raising the selling price of their cattle 5-fold, and suppose feedlots and meat companies bought their animals at this ridiculous price and incorporated this beef into the national supply. Since all federal land beef is only 2% of the national supply, if the rest was priced at $1 per pound and public land beef was $5 per pound, the overall increase in beef prices would be to $1.08 per pound, not the $3-$4 claimed by Kolbe.

According to long-time range reform advocate Randy Morris and others higher grazing fees would mean more money available for not only ranching administration but ranching development -- that is, for expanded environmental degradation. They would probably further entrench the ranching establishment and give stockmen even more social/political clout. Additionally, by paying more for fees (and higher taxes as well), the industry would convey an improved image (which in a sense would be deserved). However, this better image could lend validity to an inherently impractical land use, giving the public the misimpression that everything's fine now.

Raising grazing fees *may* be an improvement. But it is no solution.

Several reformers have suggested basing grazing fees on permittees' environmental impact. A rancher who badly overgrazed an allotment would pay a very high fee; one who did minimal damage would pay a minimal fee. This may sound good in theory. However, if it worked in practice the rancher causing minimal damage and paying a minimal fee would graze a minimal number of livestock. In other words, most public lands ranching would be terminated anyway. More likely, as they currently do, the agencies would simply misinterpret range conditions to cater to stockmen, and widespread overgrazing and trespass would continue. Covert subsidization, political abuse, and all the rest would remain largely unchanged. This too is no solution.

Competitive or Open Bid Leases

Another alternative is leasing ranching by competitive bid, as on some Department of Defense, Indian reservation, state, and other public and private land. Timber; oil, gas, and minerals; and other public resources are leased by competitive bid, so why not livestock herbage?

Under this scenario, public land would be offered for ranching lease to the highest *qualified* bidder (preferably with a reasonable floor fee, perhaps to cover administrative costs). Lease rates would then approximate those on private land -- fair market value. Leases could be issued for a period of 5 or 10 years. Because ranchers would no longer have lifetime guarantees of ranching privileges, they would be less likely to treat public land as their own, the government would procure more administrative power, and other users would gain proportionately more influence. Thus, selling the idea to stockmen would require a miracle.

Wyoming Game & Fish takes competitive bids for its land and receives $5-$8/AUM. California sells ranching permits for some of its land to the highest bidders. Oklahoma put grazing leases up for bid and quadrupled grazing income. The Army's Boardman Bombing Range in northeast Oregon averages $7-$8 on its competitive bids.

In competitive bidding areas, grazing fees average much higher than for land with set fees. However, they still average only about 1/2 to 2/3 of fair market value. If competitive bidding were used for all BLM, FS, state, and other public land now on set fees, fees on those lands would probably average even lower due to relative political influence and somewhat higher ranching expenses.

While competitive bidding probably would be an improvement over set fees, the new system would have many of the same drawbacks as the old, as well as some others. For example, it assumes an open marketplace -- nearly the antithesis of the ranching situation in most of the rural West. As now happens with most competitive bid ranchland, entrenched ranchers would acquire most of the leases. And the necessarily wide geographic distribution of Western ranches makes it difficult for distant ranchers to bid high. This, plus "special arrangements," tradition, and social and political influence, favor the status quo. The competitive bid system could thus encourage grazing monopolies as large, established operators collaborated, combined, and expanded exponentially, as was the case in ranching's early days.

As for improving range conditions, competitive bidding would fail unless a significant portion of the increased revenue went toward administrative changes, monitoring and enforcement. Though competitive fee-leased land generally is in better condition than fixed-fee land, the difference is due almost entirely to tighter regulations, lower permitted stocking rates, and stricter enforcement by agencies quite differently oriented than BLM, FS, and most state land departments. Finally, as usual, even if competitive bids reached fair market value, they would not begin to end subsidization, political abuse, and all the rest.

When someone wants to cut timber on your [public] forests he has to enter a sealed bid against all others who want to bid and can make the required guarantees. Not the cowboy and the shepherd, types who are always bellyaching about bureaucratic tyranny.
--Bernard DeVoto, **The Easy Chair** (DeVoto 1955)

The proud, independent rancher as the paragon of the free enterprise system? Forget it, he's a welfare bum. I heard one good ol' boy state at a grazing fee hearing last year, "Open bidding would destroy the very concept of free enterprise."
--Dave Foreman, "My Heros Have Always Been Cowboys" (Foreman 1986)

While competitive bidding between stock raisers would seem appropriate to this country's capitalist system, *open* bidding would seem even more so, especially under the multiple-use concept. Conservation, hunting, fishing, outfitting, hiking, backpacking, and other interests would then have the opportunity to use public land now degraded by ranching for other purposes. If they would pay as much as ranchers for the use (or non-use) of this land, cause less environmental damage and taxpayer waste, and provide services for a greater number and wider range of people, then why shouldn't our government administer such a system? Why shouldn't our government favor a true *multiple* use, *free* enterprise system?

Perhaps an open bid system would be preferable to fixed fees or closed bid between stockmen, but it too has serious drawbacks. Because much Western range is of little economic interest to other users, and because most graziers could pay much higher fees, ranching-as-usual probably would continue on most Western public land. Range condition on these allotments would not improve much, if at all. Also, those stockmen who won the bidding might feel an even greater possessiveness over public land and expect greater control over it, further entrenching dominant-use ranching.

Those groups and individuals with the most money and profit potential -- ranchers in most of the West -- probably would monopolize most of the land. Abuse might increase and multiple use suffer. Perhaps more than traditionally, the less affluent, less powerful, and less exploitative public interests would be stuck at the bottom of the totem pole. Further, those who leased public land purely to protect and restore the environment would be caught in a ransom-type situation. In essence, they would be paying the government large sums of money to do what it should have done all along -- protect the land. Also, improved allotment conditions would force higher competing bids from stockmen when leases came up for bid. Thus, conservationists would be punished for their good stewardship. Conversely, the more a rancher degraded an allotment, the lower subsequent competing bids from other users would tend to be.

There is another, more practical, consideration with an open bid system: what would become of those millions of range developments? Would the government allow fences to be torn down, roads closed, and stock tanks to wash away on non-grazed allotments when future ranching is always a possibility? How could environmental restoration proceed with them? But why waste millions of dollars to maintain them if no longer needed?

While open bidding seems the best of the alternatives mentioned so far, even it is a poor solution.

Game Ranching

Wildlife worth preserving should be wild.
--Raymond F. Dasmann, **Environmental Conservation** (Dasmann 1972)

The concept of game ranching is appealing to many -- it seems a perfect compromise between conservationist and rancher. In this alternative, we simply replace domestic ungulates with wild ones. The rancher continues ranching, and -- presto! -- the range is restored.

Game ranching on large private ranches has recently gained popularity because continued range deterioration, competition from intensive livestock production, reduced beef and mutton consumption, and growing public opposition to environmental degradation make livestock ranching decreasingly attractive. Rather than sell out, a small percentage of private ranchers are turning to game ranching. They manage private land for selected wildlife, receive permission from state game & fish departments to set extended hunting seasons and bag limits, and charge hunting fees, sometimes producing several times as much income as they did from livestock.

However, public lands ranchers generally do not advocate game ranching because (1) wildlife on public land (ostensibly) is public property and (2) most base/private properties are not large enough to support significant game populations. So, though game ranching on public land -- even if it required *more* subsidization -- generally is preferable to livestock ranching, its widespread use would require a major and unlikely shift in land use policy.

In many parts of the West, a cow has a lot less economic value than an elk.
--Bruce Babbitt while Arizona Governor, whose family runs one of the largest public land ranching operations in the state

Game ranching has one overriding purpose -- to make money -- and 2 basic orientations -- hunting and meat production. Thus far, nearly all Western game ranches are geared more toward hunting. For example, Wyoming Republican legislator Jim Hageman charges $100 per person to hunt deer on his eastern Wyoming ranch. Brad Eade of the Laguna Ranch near Coalinga, California, says, "We've cut down on cattle by 50% and increased our hunting tremendously." His ranch's hunting program now earns twice as much as his cattle did. Utah's largest game ranch is the Deseret Ranch 110 miles northeast of Salt Lake City. The mountainous 200,000 acres were used primarily for livestock until 1977, when a trophy game emphasis was adopted. Now, the state of Utah allocates a certain number of hunting licenses to the ranch each year, and customers pay from $100 for a non-guided deer hunt to $2000 for a catered 2-week elk hunt. Wildlife business at the ranch employs 3 persons full-time and earns about $250,000 annually.

In recent years, scores of ranchers, particularly in California, Wyoming, Colorado, and Utah, have reduced livestock to increase commercial "game" on portions of their private rangeland. However, they still represent only a tiny fraction of Western ranchers, and, moreover, little public land has experienced similar changes in management.

Exotic game ranching also is increasingly popular on private land, especially in Texas, where some 200 ranches use exotic species as a major source of income or to augment livestock operations. Many hunters gladly pay a high price to bag a gazelle or gemsbok.

However, buffalo, deer, elk, moose, pronghorn, and bighorn are eminently better suited to Western game ranching than are exotics or livestock. Compared to livestock, they require less water, fencing, herding and handling, treatment for parasites and disease, predator protection, and other management and range development. Wild meat, hides, and body parts generally are more valuable than those of livestock. Natives also cause relatively less environmental damage. Elk, for example, eat only 1/3 to 1/2 as much as cattle, produce about 40% more (and much leaner) meat per unit of herbage eaten, command twice the price, and do much less land damage per pound produced. Exotics compete with natives and spread disease and parasites. On some public lands, Big Bend National Park and Gunnison National Monument for example, feral exotics wander in from nearby game ranches and upset natural processes.

From the data gathered so far, it appears that, near Nairobi, the annual yield of lean meat from game ranches could be at least twice the poundage per acre as is taken from the best cattle ranch in the area.
--Paul Ehrlich, **The Machinery of Nature** (Ehrlich 1986)

Game ranching for meat production generally requires more financial investment and intensive management than for hunting. Even so, studies by wildlife biologists indicate that more meat could be produced on a sustained yield basis on Western public land through increased wildlife production (with livestock removed) than is currently produced with livestock.

Paul Ehrlich reports in **The Machinery of Nature** that since 1978 on their 20,000-acre ranch near Nairobi, Kenya, David and Carol Hopcraft have been raising mostly game animals, along with some cattle. Studies there have shown that in the past few years range condition has been improving even though animal biomass has increased some 35%. Harvesting antelopes and other wild animals is more efficient and humane than it is with cattle; cullers simply drive out on the range and shoot as many animals as needed. (Ehrlich 1986)

In the Western US, buffalo ranching is increasing, with the shaggy beasts at least partially replacing cattle on dozens of ranches. Being smarter, larger, stronger, faster, and more agile than cattle, buffalo can better survive harsh winters and protect themselves from predators. They have a more efficient digestive system and can graze "lower quality" vegetation. During grazing, they disperse more and are less selective than cattle. On the other hand, they hate and often walk right through fences, are hard to handle, and present a whole new set of instincts and behaviors for ranchers to deal with.

Due to clever advertising and health concerns, Americans are acquiring a taste for buffalo meat ("buf"?) -- higher in protein, lower in cholesterol, and, many say, more flavorful than beef. Buf is commanding high prices. Still, in the US only 10,000 buffalo are slaughtered and processed annually, compared to 60,000 beef cattle *daily*.

Ranchers have additional financial incentives for raising buffalo. Where livestock ranches double as dude ranches, resorts, hunting camps, and such, buffalo can be a novel tourist attraction. Some raise buffalo as big game animals, charging hundreds of dollars for the opportunity to ride out and shoot one. Often, the body is then sold or kept by the rancher, who may thus double his profit on the animal. Salable buffalo by-products are of superior quality and value to those of cattle, and include heads, skulls, tails, robes, leather goods, and jewelry made from bones and horns.

Pound for pound, ranch buffalo are less environmentally destructive than livestock. Nevertheless, buffalo *ranching* invariably is more destructive than is no ranching at all. Overgrazing and ranching overdevelopment was evident on most of the buffalo ranches I have visited, whereas range condition appeared good to excellent at Custer State Park (South Dakota), and Wind Cave, Badlands, and Yellowstone National Parks, where buffalo are semi-wild. And even buffalo ranching entails branding, roundups, fencing, road building, construction of water developments, predator slaughter, brush removal, and other management and development.

Research continues on buffalo genetics, crossbreeding, and inbreeding, as range professionals try to engineer the perfect "cattelo" and "beefalo." As buffalo popularity grows, ranching management intensifies and buffalo are raised more and more like cows, with increasingly similar results. Like cattle and sheep, ranch buffalo are slowly being turned into passive domestic creatures of the ranching establishment.

Is public land game ranching a workable alternative? Controversy already flares over game ranching on private land, with many people contending that no one should own free-roaming wildlife, especially animals that spend much of their time on public land. If ranchers removed livestock from public land and allowed wildlife to recover -- wildlife that would have been there naturally if not for ranching -- would it give them the right to profit from these animals? Should the public be charged by ranchers to hunt on its own land? Shouldn't wildlife on public land be public property, or no one's "property"?

If public land game ranching is to benefit the public and its land, it will have to be less like ranching and more like non-intensive wildlife management. In 1986 Bob Scott, a native of the "cowboy town" of Hamilton, Montana, unveiled his proposal for a large-scale "game range" in east-central Montana. Scott envisions transforming 15,000 square miles (about 10% of the state) of fenced, overgrazed livestock country into a huge game range/Nature reserve called "the Big Open." Domestics and fences would be removed, native game animals restocked, and the whole area allowed to restore itself to something more like the bountiful country Lewis and Clark reported in 1805 as teeming with wildlife. Presently, 363,000 sheep and cattle graze the "seriously degraded" area. Forty percent is public land.

Scott estimates that the Big Open would support 75,000 buffalo, 150,000 deer, 40,000 elk, 40,000 pronghorn, and 15,000 bighorn sheep, as well as much higher numbers of many other animals, and would be of greatly improved environmental quality. Perhaps $39 million annually would be generated from hunting fees alone, and household income for the area's 3000 residents would rise from (the reported) $15,000 to $28,000 a year. Writes Scott in personal correspondence, "We are telling them that converting to wildlife is **a higher economic return**, and we have the facts and market studies to prove it." Even the Soil Conservation Service seems to agree, as a recent report indicated that it would be cheaper to buy out all the ranchers and wheat farmers in eastern Montana than to continue government subsidies. The Big Open is one of the most workable large-scale game range proposals to date.

Yet, thus far it has gained little acceptance from the local populace. Though Scott tours the region giving talks and slide shows, trying to drum up support, few take him seriously. To the "good ol' boys" who dominate the region, the idea of someone telling them what to do hasn't set too well. Also, they are afraid to risk their traditional, subsidized way of life, and they worry about droughts, predators, and disease problems from wild animals. Some think the Big Open might be a plot by the government to take away their land. Scott has been scoffed, laughed, and yelled at. In one town, locals broke the windows out of his friend's car, thinking it was his. (Cahill 1987)

As usual, stockmen reign supreme. Their pressure, Scott says, keeps silent those who might otherwise support the idea. The loudest opponents prevail at public forums. Agencies won't study the idea without ranchers' approval.

On the Great Plains stretching from Texas to Montana, Frank and Deborah Popper have identified 139,000 square miles as being too unproductive to provide viable subsistence for local ranchers and farmers. They suggest that through a consortium of private and government owners this land be remanaged as the world's largest game preserve -- the Buffalo Commons. The cost? "Billions," according to Frank Popper, "but less than the current subsidy programs." Like Bob Scott, the Poppers have been denounced and threatened; they were furnished bodyguards for a public address in Nebraska. (Sidey 1990)

Thus, despite the eminent workability of the Big Open, Buffalo Commons, and proposals like it (see Popper 1988, for examples), the dreams will almost certainly be crushed under cowboy bootheels.

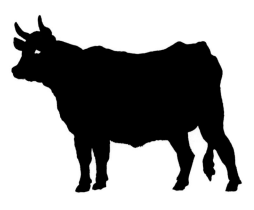

Savory's Salvation

Man's a clever little animal.
--Allan Savory

In recent decades, resistance to public lands ranching has grown steadily (though it is still not strong). The "ecology movement" of the 1960s and 1970s inspired open opposition to the industry's more flagrant abuses. There were calls for increasingly radical reform, with a growing minority demanding cessation of public lands ranching altogether.

The Imperial Graziers, fearing widespread rebellion and already experiencing decreasing profits, were mightily worried. They tried denial, rationalization, justification. They warned of economic disaster and the demise of The Hamburger. They forebode the end of Western Saga. They pled for sympathy. They pulled and pulled at their political strings. Some even threatened injury or death to anyone challenging the Royal Western Crown.

All this helped, but not enough. Even many of the Royal Ranchers' loyal government servants were clamoring for fewer Sacred Cows. Throughout the Grazing Kingdom, the graziers' 100 year reign seemed imperiled. Impending doom . . . desperation . . . and then . . . from far, far away, a Wise Man suddenly appeared.

The Wise Man gathered the despairing stockmen about Him, saying, "I am The Savoryor. Follow Me. Through Me ye shall find everlasting profit and power." The assembled were understandably skeptical, but worried nonetheless. "Fear not!" continued He, "Nay, the evil is not too many Sacred Cows, but too few. Verily, the West must have more livestock or fall to ruin!"

The congregation could scarce believe its ears.

But The Savoryor did not falter. "I am the Son of the God of Science. Gather together your scattered flocks into vast, moving herds; therein lies salvation."

Thereupon The Savoryor's words become Gospel and His followers devout. The Good Word spread far and wide across the Grazing Kingdom, and many hopeless graziers became Savorites.

Grazing Guru Allan Savory. *(Steve Johnson)*

Pay no attention to that man behind the curtain.
--from The Wizard of Oz

Allan Savory was born in 1935 in Rhodesia (now Zimbabwe), where his father was a big-time dam builder. With a background in sugar farming, biology, the military, and politics, Allan went into cattle/game ranching on his own land in 1964, and later bought an additional cattle ranch in southern Rhodesia. Published studies by Professor J.P.H. Acocks convinced Savory that short-duration grazing was a superior ranching approach and, with a partner, he established a counseling service to promote the idea. Subsequent failure of his cattle ranch, ostensibly from prolonged drought, and persecution resulting from his struggle to wrest power from Rhodesian leader Ian Smith induced Savory to come to the US in 1978, according to his present wife, "with little more than the clothes he was wearing and a few personal mementos" (and ownership of 7000 acres of his cattle/game ranch).

Savory knew that Western ranchers were seeking a panacea, so he set up another range consultant business, in Albuquerque, New Mexico and, for more than $100 per hour, taught ranchers how to use the short-duration grazing system he learned and redefined in Africa. In those early years, he popularized his teachings as "The Savory Grazing Method" or "SGM." Since a public land ranch's value and a stockman's borrowing power and clout are largely based on the number of animals grazed, Savory's claims such as "you can double the conventional or SCS [Soil Conservation Service] stocking rate" guaranteed him no lack of clients.

However, though SGM spread quickly through the ranching community, Savory soon realized that to gain the support necessary to implement his ideas on public land, he would also have to appeal to (as listed in one of his brochures) "environmentalists, university professors, private consultants, economists, government extension officers, bankers, businessmen, Native Americans, wildlifers, and foresters." So, he expanded SGM in scope and gave it the all-encompassing label "Holistic Resource Management," or "HRM."

In the 1980s, Savory skillfully and heavily marketed HRM as a progressive, scientific land management approach, to be used by nearly anyone to achieve nearly any land management objective -- even, somehow, mutually exclusive goals

simultaneously. He established an HRM Center in Albuquerque, where he taught HRM for $1000-$2000 per 1- or 2-week course. Center memberships went for $35/year and lifetime charter memberships for $10,000 (charter members receive a plaque). With the IRS in pursuit, Savory applied for and received non-profit status for his Center. With his growing gaggle of dedicated followers, Savory installed HRM branches around the West and flew about in his private plane conducting high-priced seminars and workshops at strategic locations. (Most were held at posh hotels and resorts, the "poor little ol' public lands ranchers" arriving via their late-model, heavy-duty pickups or private aircraft.) Savory's curious "holistic" approach to ranching garnered much publicity, including TV spots and articles in numerous publications. He started a quarterly newsletter entitled *The Savory Letter*, advertised widely, and distributed massive amounts of slick promotional literature.

What exactly *is* HRM? Savory calls it "a method of managing resources, involving planning and monitoring and replanning until desired goals are achieved." More fully, HRM is Allan Savory's malleable, theoretical concept of land management designed to lure and seduce every special interest group. With it, ecological interrelationships are carefully analyzed and manipulated; the results are then monitored and the management practices refined until the desired effect is achieved (or until the test fails).

If you think this sounds like a lot of mumbo-jumbo, you are right. Holistic Resource Management is a nebulous term and purposefully so; a malleable non-entity cannot be refuted and remains the property of its creator. What HRM really amounts to is studying ecosystems to more effectively and profitably manipulate them -- with Allan Savory as paid interpreter and advisor.

Of course there is nothing new in this "holistic, ecologic, scientific" approach. "Progressive scientists" (as Savory calls himself) have for decades been compounding their ecological knowledge to more effectively manipulate the environment. Many brilliant scientists are doing this now for big land-raping corporations and the military. Nearly every "scientific discovery" claimed by Savory has been known elsewhere for years. The approach is not new; the only things new are Savory's ecological interpretations and derivative plans to promote ranching.

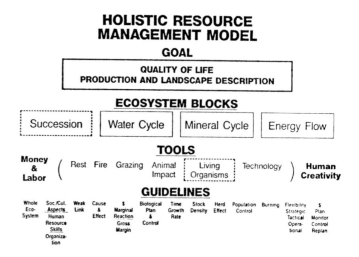

Range rest and reducing stocking numbers are the worst possible forms of range management.
--Allan Savory

As an aid to interpretation and manipulation of the environment, Savory created the "HRM Model." While the model may seem based on ecological principles, in practice (as with all aspects of HRM) it is used chiefly to promote Savory's ideas. The model lists 6 "tools" for resource management: (1) rest; (2) fire; (3) grazing; (4) animal impact; (5) living organisms; and (6) technology. I personally heard Savory say he advised the use of *fire* only once in his career (on a Navajo range when large numbers of cattle couldn't be brought in quickly enough). He repeatedly stresses that *rest* (non-grazing) is in the long run more destructive than is any level of overgrazing; that livestock are nearly always a more efficient management tool than other *living organisms* (e.g., wildlife); and that in by far most cases *technology* is a less useful tool than livestock. In fact, despite his claim that "the idea that I want to put cattle on the land is ridiculous, even childish," Savory's almost invariable solution to any land management problem (and, more accurately, the *goal* itself in the vast majority of cases) has been *grazing* and *animal impact*, i.e., *high-intensity, short-duration livestock* (almost always cattle) *grazing*, along with associated technological developments, mostly more fences, roads, salting, and water developments.

Savory's goal, dogma, and ultimate reality is **INTENSIVE SHORT-DURATION LIVESTOCK GRAZING**. It is HRM's basis, its overwhelming distinguishing feature, and essentially what keeps Savory in business. Nearly all HRM components -- that is, all of Savory's teachings and theories -- are in some way designed to advance intensive short-duration livestock grazing, and thus HRM -- creating a self-perpetuating entity.

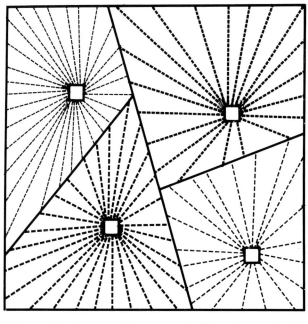

The future for public lands?

HRM students are taught how to implement intensive short-duration grazing on the land. (This includes public land managers; taxpayers have shelled out several hundred thousand dollars to teach them HRM.) Intensive SDG typically involves a wagon-wheel arrangement of fences, with water and livestock handling facilities at the center of the grazing area, or "cell," as Savory calls it. He recommends at least 12 and as many as 40 pastures, or "paddocks," per cell. Each paddock receives a week or less of extremely intensive livestock use, followed by a long period of non-use, and each paddock is grazed several times per growing season. (Compare this with native herds, which rarely grazed an area thoroughly more than once a year, usually once in several or more years.)

Coming under increasing fire for his plan to divide the West into literally millions of tiny, wedge-shaped fenced pastures, Savory recently began *espousing* (more than actually teaching) intensive herding as a way to minimize fencing. A huge number of tightly packed animals is herded slowly across an allotment until all areas are grazed; then the process is repeated, and so on.

Both methods allegedly "simulate" native ungulate herds, distributing grazing impacts more evenly over allotments, forcing animals to eat less palatable plants, trampling seeds and dead vegetation into the soil and creating seedbeds, allowing more sunlight for new growth, reducing soil compaction and erosion, increasing water percolation, benefiting wildlife, doubling livestock production, and perhaps even curing warts. All this sounds great in theory, but let's examine these claims.

Intensive livestock management, due to its very nature, cannot come close to simulating the behavior of wild animals. Native herds moved freely and randomly, not within political boundaries restricted by fences or where people drove or allowed them. They were composed of animals of varying ages which over years, generations, and millennia formed an array of social orders and interactions. Contrarily, most livestock are removed from the range before 2 years of age; composition and arrangement by sex, leadership ability, and other characteristics are corrupted; and human management impairs social interaction. Less-fit members of wild herds were culled occasionally by predators that kept herds cohesive and healthy, whereas a large percentage of the *most* fit livestock are removed annually by cowboys. Moreover, huge herds of ungulates were not native to most of the West, and domestic livestock cannot fill the ecological niche of vanished wildlife.

Savory counters that it will never be possible to bring wildlife back to anywhere near original range and numbers, so the most effective and available tool for managing the West is cattle. This pessimistic and self-serving attitude neglects that cattle ranching is the main reason wildlife cannot recover.

Savory may be right in claiming that HRM distributes grazing impacts more evenly over allotments. In fact, this probably is the main reason many ranchers experience a moderate increase in livestock production with HRM. According to Holechek *et al.* in **Range Management**:

Much of the increase in stocking rate claimed possible under short-duration grazing results from better livestock distribution (Dahl 1986). Confining a large number of animals to a small area for a short period improves uniformity of use and

forces the use of areas and plants not used previously.
(Holechek 1987)

Consequently, HRM may spread grazing *damage* more evenly over allotments and negatively affect a greater number and variety of wildlife.

While claims of doubling stocking rates with HRM are greatly exaggerated, many ranchers report moderate increases. Aside from more uniform grazing, much of this is probably due to the initial release of forage nutrients caused by intensive trampling; there are indications, however, of long-term decline. Some increase may be due to more efficient management, while much is due to more intensive management, including higher expenditures for planning, monitoring, fencing, herding, etc. Many claims of HRM increases are made during especially productive forage years (often when HRM publicity photos are taken). Others are made by imaginative ranchers deluding themselves that their last hope (HRM) is working or that their capital investment on HRM hasn't been wasted. Then, too, failed HRM operations are unlikely to be publicized, except when failures may be overtly blamed on non-adherence to HRM tenets.

One of Savory's key theories is that herds of large ungulates are the critical factor in maintaining Western range ecosystems. He explains that most of the West is prone to prolonged periods of adverse conditions for plant growth. These "brittle" (generally arid to semi-arid) environments lack the moisture necessary to decay and recycle dead plant (mostly grass) material, so livestock (preferably cattle, as sheep are not large enough) must physically knock it down and trample it into the soil.

Savory's theory is unsound in several ways. First, plants native to "brittle" environments are eminently adapted to them, so to them conditions are not "adverse." Second, it is untrue that dead plant material in these areas cannot decompose; it sometimes does so biologically near ground level during wet weather, causing standing material to eventually fall over. Depending on circumstances, dead plant material may also decompose chemically. Wind, rain, hail, and animals break it apart and knock it over. Nest-building and burrowing creatures work it into the soil. Termites, ants, and other microfauna decompose it. Many plant parts naturally detach from parent plants and fall to the ground. And, over much of the West, snowpack helps incorporate standing organic matter into the soil. Third, after its onset, heavy grazing of any kind leaves little organic matter to trample into the soil.

An ungrazed grass plant in southern Idaho. Last year's growth was matted down by snow, creating a mulch that protects and enriches the soil, preserves soil moisture, and so forth. HRM students are taught that old growth is "decadent" and that standing dead organic matter cannot be properly recycled without the help of livestock. *(George Wuerthner)*

Finally, like tree snags in forests, standing dead range plant material is itself an important, natural environmental component. Regardless, Savory claims like most ranchers that old-growth range plants are "useless" and "decadent." According to Savory, because dead material in "brittle" environments cannot decompose, it must be "tramped down" by livestock or it will grow so high and thick that it blocks sunlight from growth points and eventually kills itself. What is left is a perpetually sterile landscape filled mostly with tall, thick, sunlight-impenetrable dead grass.

Really? Even in the driest, coldest desert (where Savory says it takes longest for dead plant material to decay) can you imagine such a scene? In all my travels, I have never seen it. Some of that thick blanket of organic matter must eventually burn, decompose, or be knocked down naturally, allowing some new growth to occur (and with such abundance of organic material near ground level any cleared area would be highly favorable to new growth). Moreover,

Termites remove and help decompose dead plant material. Semi-arid range.

these "brittle" environments are exactly where plant growth is scarcest and sunlight most plentiful, leaving another of Savory's theories working against itself. It is hardly conceivable that any sun-drenched, "brittle" environment could support enough vegetation to crowd itself out and die out completely. The limiting factor in these areas is *water*, not sunlight.

Savory declares that HRM-style grazing improves water infiltration, decreases runoff, and reduces sediment load. Ample research shows that, generally, the exact opposite is true in the West (see Holechek 1989 for many examples). Short-duration grazing's intense hoof pressure compacts the under soil, thereby reducing water infiltration and increasing both runoff and sediment load. The soil's exposed, churned-up top layer can be devastated if a heavy rain or high wind follows soon thereafter. While grazing areas receive relatively long "rests" between HRM use, the time periods are not nearly long enough to allow full recovery. Evidence also indicates that HRM-style grazing generally is no less destructive to riparian areas and waterways than conventional grazing systems (see, for example, Marlow 1989).

Water is usually less available to wildlife under Savory's system than under conventional grazing systems because HRM water sources and developments generally are located at the center of grazing "cells," where livestock and human activity, environmental detriments, and fencing are most concentrated. Further, Savory claims that "all organisms are adapted to man" and that in the future it will be necessary to "semi-domesticate" wildlife to fit into HRM management schemes. He says that large wild animals will "follow closely behind as the [livestock] herd moves along" -- enjoying the many benefits of a freshly ravaged landscape, one must conclude.

Allan Savory's recipe for environmental salvation.

The 4 photos at right demonstrate the general growth pattern of many Western grass species. As an individual grass plant (top) spreads outward, the center portion dies (2nd from top). As the ring continues to expand, it fragments and creates new plants (3rd from top). These new plants spread and fragment and so forth in a dynamic natural balance that maintains a healthy grass cover (bottom).

HRM recruits also learn that:

- Seeds of native grasses are permanently in the soil, and one should never worry that any level of overgrazing will eliminate them.
- "It is the spacing and number of plants that matter, not their size and health."
- Native Western grasses (including bunchgrasses) are adapted to being cropped and trampled repeatedly each year.
- Cryptogams are a prime indicator of a deteriorating environment. (To underscore his postulation, commonly Savory scuffs apart the cryptogamic layer while walking on rangeland.)
- Soil capping is always bad.
- It is always beneficial to disturb the soil in some way -- *any way* -- especially with herds of livestock.
- Overgrazing is caused by animals grazing an area too long, and has nothing to do with their numbers. [For example, a herd of 100,000 cattle will not overgraze if left on a paddock for only 30 seconds.]
- The worst overgrazing is better than no grazing.

These claims, and similar others too numerous to list here, are refuted elsewhere.

Ungrazed Sevilleta National Wildlife Refuge, New Mexico -- a "deteriorating" range, according to Allan Savory.

To prove HRM grazing superior to non-grazing, Savory commonly cites from his special list of "deteriorating" non-grazed lands. (Curiously, these lands are always deteriorat-**ing**, never deteriorat-**ed**; Savory recently conceded that full "degradation could take between 4000 and 5000 years.") These include Chaco Canyon National Monument (his favorite) and Sevilleta National Wildlife Refuge (see quote and photo above) in New Mexico, the "pathetic" Natural Bridges National Monument and Canyonlands National Park in Utah, Petrified Forest National Park in northeast Arizona, and the Audubon Research Ranch in southern Arizona. These areas and other non-grazed lands throughout the West, Savory insists, are "overrested" from livestock grazing. To reverse deterioration and "get a handle on" management of these lands, HRM-style ranching is the best approach.

Over the last 4 years, I have conducted my dissertation research on yucca/yucca moth mutualism on the 228,000-acre Sevilleta Wildlife Refuge near Socorro, NM [see photo at top right]. The land has not been grazed for about 15 years and is beginning its recovery to grassland status. I have spent the last few months recording (to the best of my ability) the beauty of that land on slide film. Indeed, I am overwhelmed by it.
--Ollar Fuller, PhD in Biology, founder of Albuquerque Greens, personal correspondence

I have visited most of the places on Savory's special list and, rather than deterioration, I have seen remarkable recovery and relatively abundant wildlife. Most of the managers of these places seem to agree. For example, pertaining to the Audubon Research Ranch, where 20 livestock-free years has increased the proportion of groundcover from 20% to 80% and increased wildlife tremendously, Director Dr. Mark Stromberg says he believes Savory does not understand that heavy exploitation is not necessarily a part of all environments (Johnson 1987). Canyonlands National Park staff cite evidence of impressive recovery since the Park was formed -- and cattle were banned -- in the 1960s.

HRMers worst nightmare -- the dreaded dead center.

Grassland and wildlife waterhole in "overrested" Petrified Forest National Park, northeast Arizona.

Rest [from livestock] *is not doing nothing. It is doing something.*
--HRM advocate public lands rancher Wilbur Wood (Accordingly, humans must have been "doing something" for 5 billion years before they even existed.)

Savory likewise often cites a list of "success" ranches that demonstrate HRM's superiority to conventional ranching; it includes the Spurlock, Flying "M", and Date Creek in Arizona, the Davenport in New Mexico, and the Milton in central Montana. He infrequently identifies failures, except to say that they have not worked because managers are not adhering to his advice closely enough. Nonetheless, HRM failures, like the Dodson Allotment in Arizona's Apache-Sitgreaves National Forest, are common. In August, 1986, Supervisor Nick McDonough examined the allotment and found that there "was not enough grass left to carry the cows through the winter, or any reserve left for wildlife or plant vigor.... If our HRM operation doesn't do better, we won't start another."

As another example, I recently received a call from Oracle, a small community north of Tucson. The excited caller said that Savory-style heavy concentrations of cattle on an adjacent Forest Service allotment "are overflowing onto people's private property," damaging a riparian area, and polluting a water source used by a camp and local residents. Area landowners are banding together to force the Forest Service to take action.

Savory concurrently points at the worst conventional overgrazing to make HRM look better by comparison. This may impress the conservation community, but he often thereby contradicts himself, for conventional and HRM grazing share most of the same detriments. Indeed, numerous scientific studies indicate that generally HRM works best in moist climates, while in dry regions (most of the West) it may on the average be even more destructive than conventional grazing (Holechek 1987).

HRM-style ranching has been established longest in Savory's native Zimbabwe. In 1982 the World Bank/International Finance Corporation examined 7 ranches there where it had been practiced for periods ranging from 7 to 14 years. The Corporation found, "virtually no different effects attributable to grazing systems," and stated that most

of the small changes that did occur were due to "short-term changes in rainfall pattern." (Johnson 1987)

In a recent Rangelands article -- "Southern Africa's Experience with Intensive Short Duration Grazing" -- Certified Range Consultant Jon Skovlin states:

Having returned from 3 years of consulting in sub-Sahara Africa, I am amazed by the interest in and wide acceptance of intensive short duration grazing as popularized by Mr. C.A.R. Savory and his Holistic Resource Management (HRM).

Skovlin cites numerous studies refuting claims for HRM-style grazing, and provides this summary:

Claims for range improvement in southern Africa through Intensive Short Duration Grazing at double conventional stocking rates are not founded in fact. To the contrary, evidence in literature from Zimbabwe and elsewhere indicates it is impossible to have both heavy stocking and improvement in range conditions.... In Southern Africa, where SGM had its beginnings, many ranchers are disillusioned and most rangeland specialists contend there are too many shortcomings to recommend it as prescribed. (Skovlin 1987)

To date I have not seen one ranch where HRM is supposed to be practiced, in what would be considered a "brittle environment," the type of environment where his [Savory's] controversial grazing methods are supposed to be most effective, where I was convinced HRM had done the job it is supposed to do.
--Steve Gallizioli, former Arizona Game & Fish wildlife biologist, now a leading HRM advocate, personal correspondence

"Savory"-style herd grazing. *(Paul Hirt)*

... The excess of dead cover smothered the dominant grass itself, resulting in replacement by weeds.... Where hooved animals grazed, however, they removed excess leafage, and by trampling broke loose dead stalks preparing the way for new growth of grass ... trampling promoted the natural reseeding process.

This quote comes not from Savory's HRM text, but from an agriculturally-oriented book entitled **The Grasslands of North America** by James C. Malin, written in 1947. Malin was describing the findings of Russian scientist A.N. Formosov in a 1928 report on the Russian steppe.

A heavy concentration of animals is placed on a given area for a few weeks, after which all the stock are moved on to another area and are finally returned to the first field when the growth is sufficient to withstand another period of grazing.

This one comes from **Beef Cattle Science**, a textbook first published in 1951. It states that this grazing system is best suited to humid regions.

Intensive, short-duration, pasture rotation grazing has been around for centuries. "Savory's" system was used by English stockmen 300 years ago, and his HRM model is based largely on a French dairy system used a century ago. Likewise, intensive herding has been practiced by many cultures around the world for millennia. These peoples travel all year with their herds, seeking whatever forage and browse still survives. Chapter VI examined the devastating results of such pastoralism. The herding Savory advocates also was common in the Western US in the late 1800s and early 1900s. Thousands of shepherds drove massive herds of sheep and cattle, keeping them constantly on the move; in many areas we see their scars still.

For a century, a small minority of range professionals in Eurasia, Africa, New Zealand, and North America have been advocating high-intensity, short-duration livestock grazing. Savory simply modified the approach and popularized it in the West.

There is no such thing as natural. . . . Everything that exists is natural.
--Allan Savory, 1986

Philosophically, HRM also leaves much to ponder. Allan Savory is foremost among the new school of land managers who share the perspective that we must meddle more with Nature to create a "productive" world. He frequently contends that humans have so altered the environment that it can no longer independently function properly. Therefore, he explains, we must intercede and increasingly intensively "manage ecosystems" or they will "deteriorate." Furthermore, in most cases "grazing" and "animal impact" from livestock are the preferred ecosystem management tools. Apache-Sitgreaves NF Supervisor Nick McDonough (who helped initiate HRM on the Apache-Sitgreaves) echoes Savory's theory of progressive human intervention in saying "We believe man is capable of managing forests better than nature can manage forests."

In Savory's world, there is "no such thing as a climax community." There are only "stages of succession," and "through skillful redirection of natural forces" (recall that he says there is "no such thing as natural") we should manipulate the environment (usually with cattle) to produce the "highest stage of succession" possible. This may sound halfway credible if you don't stop to consider that "skillfully redirected" "natural forces" are no longer natural. Under this reality rangelands, as well as deserts, brushlands, dense forests, swamps, and other "unproductive" areas, are redesigned to conform to human goals.

In other words, God is given human form. Sorry Earth; after 5 billion years of natural evolution we humans will take the helm from here (see Walter T. Anderson's **To Govern Evolution**).

HRM promotes the dangerous philosophy that humans are capable of, and should be, managing a planet. It does not recognize the integrity of the natural environment, its right to free existence, or humans' place in it. Instead, it places control of the natural world in the hands of HRM land managers who perceive the Earth as nothing more than a complexity of interrelationships which, if understood well enough, may be manipulated for human purposes. According to Savory, "There are only relationships, and it is only through the study and manipulation of these relationships that we can understand and manage our complex ecosystems."

This strikes me as not only pretentious and anthropocentric, but unrealistic and even immoral (if there is such a thing). HRM, as taught, asserts that *Homo sapiens* should assume the role of benevolent dictator over the Earth's environment, apparently with Allah Savory as chief luminary. Who among us has the knowledge to understand Nature's infinite interrelationships, or the wisdom to direct them? Who will hold the power to decide what form our surroundings will take? Power corrupts. Who controls the rural West now? And, the potential for unforeseen environmental harm grows roughly in proportion to our ability to manipulate the environment.

We, as human participants, have been an integral but small part of this planet's biosystem for perhaps a million years. We have fought to overcome Nature for only tens of thousands, and have overpowered it with brute force for only 200 or so. But we have never assumed the role of *ultimate controller*. HRM can only be seen as another step toward an Orwellion-type world where every action and function, human and non-human, is under the surveillance and unyielding control of whoever is in power.

Like the chickadee and the chipmunk, it [the Gila Monster] *has its place in its own environment, and attempts to remove it from the face of the earth place man in the uncomfortable position of deciding which animals besides himself are desirable inhabitants of the globe.*
--Peter Matthiessen, **Wildlife in America** (Matthiessen 1959)

Self-serving philosophy and promises of higher stocking rates and environmental salvation do not fully explain Savory's appeal. It lies more in the realm of psychology. Intentionally or not, Savory uses many effective indoctrination techniques to attract, convert, and endear people to his HRM religion.

First, like a candyman with a rainbow of flavors, he offers something to everyone, overlooking no one who might further his cause. Ranchers (at least 90% of his paying students) are promised profits and public favor, agency staff a way to justify bureaucracy and please permittees, conservationists an improved environment, hunters and fishers more wildlife, cities more water, the public expanded multiple use, and so on. Savory ballyhoos HRM as the means to any end -- snake oil supreme. Key, influential non-ranchers, including some agency range staff, SCS and state officials, university range professionals, politicians, and (especially) prominent anti-ranching advocates, are offered free attendance at HRM training sessions.

After getting their attention, Savory gains their trust. He portrays his cause as noble, selfless, and wholly scientific, asking those who *really care* to join him. In their first HRM class, ranchers are assuaged of possible guilt for overgrazing, range abuse, and ranch failure. Savory explains that they are blameless victims of a hopelessly antiquated ranching establishment. Fortunately, however, there is one bright ray of hope -- HRM.

Next, Savory *shocks* his students, shatters and rearranges their reality. He aggressively denounces the conventional livestock industry (his competition) for its many failures and refutes many beliefs held by ranchers and conservationists alike. Fertile seeds of doubt are sown.

Conventional reality is then systematically replaced with HRM reality. With decisive self-assurance, Savory unleashes a barrage of ideas, facts and figures, theories, revelations, visions. The students' heads reel as their former beliefs are dismantled, and as they try to assimilate all this new and unexpected input. They generally are very impressed, even dazzled, by Savory's apparent knowledge and wisdom. Many begin to see him as a scientific genius, and HRM as a breakthrough in enlightened, progressive thinking.

All along, Savory demands total, undivided attention to his every word. (At an HRM workshop, I was harshly reprimanded for taking notes while he spoke.) Ideas expressed that threaten HRM reality (there are few) are promptly dismantled and dispatched. Or, they may be absorbed as part of HRM if they don't threaten its overall infrastructure. Advance in detail is permitted; fundamental novelty is barred. Thus, HRM is a repository for co-opted data, reinforcing and building upon itself.

At the same time, Savory welcomes opposition. Indeed, he *thrives* on it, especially from traditional ranchers and anti-ranching advocates in the media. He well understands a main principal of martial arts -- use your adversary's energy to your benefit. Thus, arguments made against HRM focus more attention on it; energy used against it brings more energy to it. With his consummate power of reason, Savory turns each counterpoint against its perpetrator and negates even the most well-grounded argument. In each, he finds some fragment, magnifies it, and uses the comparison to justify his position. In the end, because HRM is a malleable, nebulous concept, it cannot be refuted -- it instead absorbs that which confronts it.

Those who still do not accept Savory's interpretation of reality -- no matter how well-informed -- are told they are simply ill-informed. They are pressured to believe that they will surely come to embrace HRM (see the light) when they learn more about it. Thus, so as not to seem ignorant or unenlightened (especially in front of their peers), they are drawn into the HRM mindset.

Indeed, peer pressure is used to keep devotees headed down the straight and narrow. Those not yet fully submitting to HRM are treated like junior partners. Those who begin to doubt are shown the error of their ways. Devotees are privy to various "HRM secrets." They come to feel like part of a select group involved in a vital cause. Self-identity and acceptance by the cult become dependent on one's level of commitment to HRM. Phony prophets and gurus often use the same approach.

Savory commonly uses black-and-white reasoning to support his claims; his followers, because they so badly need to believe, fill in the appropriate shades of gray. For example, students are sometimes taken on field trips to ranches where they are instructed to compare grazed, ungrazed, and HRM-grazed plots. Many cannot help but choose the lushly vegetated ungrazed plots as being in better condition. When this happens, Savory may take a couple of thoughtful puffs from his scholarly tobacco pipe. He might walk over to the ungrazed plot, yank out a handful of dead blades from old-growth grass and declare it "decadent." At this point, the errant student will realign his chain of thought to conform to Savory's world, despite the overwhelming evidence at his feet.

Those who continue to doubt HRM are castigated as stubborn or ignorant. In his newsletter, Savory has described HRM critics as "closed-minded," "cynics who fiddle while Rome burns," "standing in the way of science," and so forth. Involvement with non-believers continues only so long as they are seen as possible converts or as furthering his cause in some way. For example, in 1986 Savory invited me (a known stop-public-lands-ranching advocate) to attend a 2-day HRM seminar and a 5-day workshop free as his guest. During the workshop, Allan treated me like a visiting dignitary, even offering to let me stay for 2 weeks with him in his comfortable Albuquerque home while attending classes at the HRM Center ($2000 + value). Due to limited time and interest, I declined his offer, but we continued corresponding via letters. The romance didn't last long, however; as soon as he realized I was not to be counted among his flock, he ended communication. The last letter I received was from Jody Butterfield-Savory, his wife and editor of *The Savory Letter*, indicating Allan no longer wanted to "waste time" responding to my letters: "Please consider these matters closed. We expect no reply."

The Society for Range Management is the most prestigious range organization in the US. Its monthly publication, *Journal of Range Management*, is an endless series of scientific studies exploring range manipulation, with an overwhelming emphasis on livestock production. Savory understood that converting the Society to HRM would be one of the keys to his success, and for years he made that attempt. But the Society for Range Management was not to be regenerated, and it continued on its errant path, unenlightened by Savory's shining star. As Savory saw it, the Society was a staid, reactionary organization, incapable of perceiving HRM as a superior approach to range management. In 1986 Savory canceled his Society membership "because of the repeated attacks made on me personally and on behalf of the society."

Indeed, due mostly to his questionable scientific interpretations, Savory has garnered only moderate support and much opposition from the range science community. Word has it that the nation's largest stock growers organization, the National Cattlemen's Association, recently has also indicated a basic rejection of Savory's HRM.

Allan Savory, the man, is also greatly appealing. His rustic garb, utter self-assurance, and erect, almost militaristic bearing make him an arresting figure. With a complex and creative mind, Savory is knowledgeable (within his realm), interesting, and witty. His meticulous speech features a charming British colonial accent. He is even handsome, and quite popular with the cowgirls.

All this combines for charisma. Like most gurus, Savory is tremendously persuasive without seeming to try to be, and like most gurus he is most attractive to the naive, uninformed, and desperate. Most people cannot help but like him and, despite evidence to the contrary, find themselves *wanting* to believe him.

The real -- and tragic -- truth is that the resources of our lands have been, are being, and will continue to be abused by livestock grazing until the search for panaceas -- like the one Allan Savory espouses -- is abandoned, and meaningful changes in existing management are made.
--Johanna Wald, Senior Attorney, Natural Resources Defense Council

Savory claims that halting desertification is his main goal. Even assuming that this is so, good intent and impressive presentation are not enough. After 2 decades in Africa and a decade in the West, HRM has done little to halt desertification. To the contrary, it may be spreading it by distributing livestock and associated developments more widely over the range, and by prolonging ranching in areas where it otherwise might have been reduced or terminated.

Savory claims scientific objectivity, but maintains a nearly fanatic, single-minded devotion to cattle. He insists "there is no such thing as natural," then strives to "simulate natural processes." He professes trying to "skillfully redirect" Nature, then tries to *control* it. His declaration that humans (with him as overseer) know best how to manage Nature seems almost Napoleanic.

Holistic Resource Management is Holeistic Resource Management; it appears whole, but, like a colander, close inspection shows it to be full of holes. The truly *holistic* approach is to re-establish as many missing ecosystem components as possible, allow ecosystems to function as naturally as possible, then -- with minimum impact and in a sustainable fashion -- *cull* needed resources. Few would deny that in this overpopulated, overexploited world we are sometimes forced to compensate with some degree of protective and extractive management. However, rather than ever-increasingly "managing resources," we should try to reduce human population, minimize interference with natural processes, and move toward living more naturally.

Depending on how it is used, and on many other human and environmental variables, HRM-style ranching may in some cases be preferable to conventional ranching. However, it is in no way superior to non-ranching, except in terms of livestock production.

Why would we want to give the public rangelands over to the public?
--Public lands rancher Kirk Hanna, Colorado HRM member

Land management should not be a contest, wherein the person or group accumulating the most political power and/or ecological data gets to manipulate ecosystems. Allan Savory is a range consultant, and more than 90% of his customers are ranchers wanting ranching profits and influence. While the growing movement to end public lands ranching, if successful, would guarantee tremendous environmental improvement, Savory is co-opting this movement to promote his HRM.

Your kindly editor recalls reading a "balanced" environmental article in which a cattle rancher "philosophically" decided that the grizzly bear was "obsolete as a life form" and had "had its day" and would probably have to be eliminated even in Yellowstone. It apparently did not occur to the journalist (and certainly not to cattlemen) that perhaps the cattleman's operation was "obsolete as an economic lifestyle" and had "had its day" as a viable business.
--P.J. Ryan, Editor of *Thunderbear*

Logo used by the Arizona branch of Holistic Resource Management.

The Stockmen's Solution

Holistic Resource Management notwithstanding, ranchers have other plans for our public land. In 1983 the Public Lands Council, the powerful association of public lands graziers mentioned earlier, listed its set of alternatives in *The Western Livestock Industry and the Public Lands*. The following quotes from that publication are generally representative of the public ranching establishment:

● *... public lands must be managed on the local level by persons very close to the land.* [They want self-regulation on public land.]

● *... we believe, first, that private ownership and operation of the nation's land resources are in the national interest....* [They want all BLM and Forest Service land and "national grasslands **serving no real purpose**" (emphasis added) transferred to local and state levels, eventually to be sold "at reasonable low cost," or transferred "free" to ranchers.]

● *There are many sound and logical reasons why the continued and even expanded use of federal range by domestic livestock are in the national interest.* [They want currently ungrazed National Parks and Monuments, Wildlife Refuges, Recreation Areas, Wildernesses, and more opened up to ranching.]

● *... new law is needed that will provide the producers with long-term, assured, preferential tenure....* [They want more or less permanent grazing permits.]

● *In the event the permittee is deprived of further use of an improvement by the act of the government ... the appraised value ... should be due and payable to him.* [If the government should deny a permittee use of a range development he helped finance -- no matter how little he contributed -- the government must pay the permittee full cash value for that development.]

● *... we believe that the production of adequate food and fiber and the maintenance of the economic stability of the dependent local communities is of even greater importance* [than other public land uses]. [They want ranching given highest priority under the "multiple-use" concept.]

● *We therefore recommend ... new grazing fee structure and formula* [based on a government and industry collaborated grazing fee study]. [They want a new grazing fee formula that results in an *even lower* grazing fee.]

● *The generally adverse actions of the field personnel are resulting in more appeals* [lengthy complaint.] [They want agency range personnel divested of regulatory powers.]

● *Accordingly, we recommend that title to all waters arising on or flowing over federal lands, be transferred to the states....* [They want possession of all waters on or flowing across federal land -- most Western water -- transferred to the states so they may obtain exclusive rights to it.]

They don't want much, do they? They resemble terribly spoiled, bad-tempered (century-old) children, having always gotten their way, yet relentlessly demanding more and more.

In January 1989, the industry gathered for a special conference to consider how to combat growing opposition to public lands ranching. A subsequent report appeared in the Wildlife Management Institute's *Outdoor News Bulletin* (2-10-89):

Apparently over-indulging in loco weed, some attendees at the National Conference on Federal Lands held in Las Vegas, Nevada last month drafted federal legislation that would turn public lands over to livestock graziers.... Among the authors are the Public Lands Council and the Woolgrowers.

Among other things, the draft would designate "grazing areas" on 307 million acres of Bureau of Land Management and national forest land. Those areas would be dedicated to the "commodity benefit of the American people," specifically the grazing of domestic livestock. It would recognize a "possessitory interest" of grazing permittees in public lands. It would designate "grazing enterprise zones" and would transfer those lands to the permittee free, where it is determined that more than 50% of the "split estate values" (i.e., water rights, stock tanks, cattle guards, fences, etc.) are in private ownership. It would prohibit the federal government from acquiring western water rights from the states, and would prohibit Uncle Sam from cancelling grazing permits. It would declare livestock grazing the "dominant use" among all uses of federal rangeland. It would allow graziers to prohibit wilderness designations, wildlife habitat improvements and about anything else they so choose. And it would repeal all other statutes that conflict with it.

A Committee for Idaho's High Desert official titled the proposal "Sagebrush Rebellion III -- The Permittees Have a Wet Dream." Apparently the bill is serious, however, for the 5-23-89 *Los Angeles Times* reports that ranchers "have been looking around Washington for a member of Congress to sponsor the particularly aggressive piece of legislation." According to the *Times*, the proposed bill, called the National Rangeland Grazing System Act of 1989, would also

make it a felony punishable by 10 years in prison and a $10,000 fine for BLM workers to "present the private grazing permittee in a false light as a poor or incompetent grazer" by falsifying range conditions. (Stein 1989)

More recently, something called the American Freedom Coalition has been formed to help push the bill through.

Even more recently, Wyoming Representative Hansen has introduced a similar bill -- H.R. 473 -- to the 102nd Congress. This one would amend the Federal Land Policy and Management Act of 1976 so that "Whoever intentionally obstructs the operation of, or harasses any activity permitted under, a grazing permit or lease issued under this Act shall be imprisoned for not more than 5 years, fined in accordance with Title 18, United States Code, or both." This punishment might apply to a Forest Service ranger trying to reduce a stocking level, a hiker interfering with a coyote trap, or a camper throwing rocks at invading cattle.

The stockmen's solution, then, is a bad joke.

The general public has been misinformed that public land is strictly owned by the federal government, and that public land and wildlife should go together... we [permittees] have public lands that have an easement on them that comes before the general public and the right to run wildlife on them.
--Catron County Cattle Growers Association, in recent letter to the New Mexico State Game Commission

Cattlemen do not own the public range now; it belongs to you and me.... But they always acted as if they owned the public range and act so now; they convinced themselves that it belonged to them and they now believe it does; and they are trying to take title to it.
--Bernard De Voto (DeVoto 1955)

If something cannot be manufactured or built or grown without causing irreparable ecological damage, can't we strive to create something to take its place, or simply decide to do without it?

--Brian Tokar, **The Green Alternative**

Thorough examination of the alternatives makes clear that the best long-term solution is the simplest -- **end public lands ranching.** Anything less would be environmentally, economically, socially, and politically irresponsible.

Some environmentalists maintain that ending public lands ranching would punish the concerned permittee along with the reckless. However, while good intentions are nice, even the most conscientious permittee causes significant environmental damage, absorbs public subsidies, etc. Again, *any* kind of ranching is significantly more harmful overall than non-ranching.

The end of public lands ranching could be accomplished in many different ways, none as difficult as might be imagined. We could, as early stockmen did to gain control of the West, drive competitors off at gunpoint, kill the resisters, take their possessions, and burn their houses. That's how The Duke woulda done it!

> *. . . It is my decision to implement ALT A. This alternative will:*
> *1. Cancel the existing Term Grazing Permit and close the allotment to grazing . . .*
> --"Decision of Notice and Finding of No Significant Impact: Crown King Allotment [Prescott National Forest, Arizona] Management Plan," John W. Holt, District Ranger, Bradshaw Ranger District [Note: The permittee has appealed the decision.]

ENOUGH IS ENOUGH!

The Last Roundup

. . . the only way to attract the public's attention to the grazing abuses taking place now is to propose eliminating all livestock from our public ranges.

--90-year-old Earl Sandvig, raised on Montana ranch, former cowboy, Forest Service range specialist for 30 years, long-time "responsible management" advocate

We could tell ranchers to get their livestock off our land (as has been done on a handful of Western allotments). Stockmen could then continue raising their livestock on private land, or get into another business. A public lands grazing permit should have no inherent value, so no reimbursement would be necessary. This plan is good, but has 2 drawbacks -- (1) due to America's love affair with the cowboy, few people would support it, and (2) ranchers would retain ownership of environmentally critical base properties.

Perhaps a more acceptable approach is simply to calculate each permittee's annual AUM value and pay him or his widow that amount (adjusted for inflation) each year for the rest of his life to *not* ranch public land. If the annual rate was based on the grazing fee averaged over the past 10 years ($1.45/AUM), this would cost the federal government about $26 million annually -- a small fraction of what it now spends on the industry.

Or, we could figure the capital value of each permittee's AUMs and buy them outright. When ranchers sell federal grazing permits with land to each other, they commonly get from $25-$50/AUM. Even if we accept $50 as the average AUM value, we could buy all 18 million BLM and FS AUMs for about $900 million -- roughly the amount of taxes spent on public lands ranching in only 1 year. This plan is appealing because it would conclude the whole affair quickly.

Or, we could figure each welfare rancher's annual income from public ranching averaged over, say, a 10-year period and give him or his widow a yearly check for that amount for life (adjusted for inflation). This might amount to about $500 million annually -- approximately the net value of public lands livestock. This plan is even more unfair to the taxpayer, though still far preferable to the present situation.

Or, as one anonymous BLM staffer put it:

This nation went into a whole-herd dairy buy-out program to reduce the subsidies being paid to the dairy industry because of abuses and poor policy. Why couldn't we do the same thing to curb abuses of our public lands?

We could simply purchase their livestock and retire their permits and leases.

An economist could figure out the relative advantages and disadvantages of these various methods. We could even let welfare ranchers pick their own kind of subsidy; whatever they chose would be infinitely better than continuing welfare ranching.

These last 4 alternatives are all simple and eminently workable. They do, however, share one significant drawback -- they leave base properties in control of stockmen. Because most owners would continue ranching even without public lands allotments, base properties would continue to be heavily abused. There is also danger of some ranchers ("the original conservationists") selling to developers *out of spite*, as some have blatantly threatened to do if public lands ranching is terminated.

All 30,000 or so public lands ranch headquarters are the foci of huge sacrifice areas.

Aside from ecological considerations, continued ranching of base properties is a monopolization of potential farmland -- level, fertile, well-watered bottomlands, usually located in good growing climates. Rather than barren pastures producing further unneeded livestock, they could instead grow vegetables, fruits, nuts, and grains for local communities -- and reduce transportation and storage costs, lower food prices, and provide fresher, more healthful produce. Though generally they would have to work harder, many ex-public lands ranchers could turn to farming, and probably make more money directly from their operations. To this end the government could offer financial incentives by redirecting funds formerly expended on public lands ranching.

Former ranchers could also turn their former base properties into dude ranches, bed-and-breakfast operations, hunting and fishing camps, or centers for environmental study, Nature appreciation, horseback riding, historical tours, and pack and float trips. Ex-ranchers could rent out cabins or provide meals and services to public land travelers. All these enterprises would be enhanced by improved environmental quality. Already they provide a major source of income for many ranchers.

Governments could minimize development and other abuse of former base properties by strictly enforcing environmental laws, as well as zoning, building, and health regulations. And, as explained earlier, many former base properties would probably be purchased by more environmentally conscious owners.

Again, however, it would be much better for the 22,000 (or 30,000, including all public lands) Western base properties (and other environmentally critical private ranchlands) to be returned to public ownership. Remember, too, that many, if not most, base properties originally were transferred to private ownership through various degrees of fraud. Leaving them in private hands is inviting continued environmental disaster.

Several methods of public acquisition could be employed. Perhaps the simplest but least effective would be a program of voluntary sale. An ex-public lands rancher wishing to sell a former base property would be encouraged to sell to the government, which would then place it with the most appropriate land managing agency. Incentives could include offers of more than fair market value, waivers of related taxes and fees, and lucrative trades for environmentally less important government holdings.

Or, an ex-rancher wishing to sell could be required to sell to the government. In the meantime, periodic payments could be made to compensate him for stipulations permitting no sale, development, or abuse of the land. A modified version of this scenario would allow an ex-ranchman to retain ownership until death, at which time ownership would revert to the government and money reflecting the value of the land would be disbursed to the deceased's heirs.

However, the best solution ***** THE PREFERRED ALTERNATIVE ***** is simply to buy out all ranches, range developments, and AUMs, lock, "stock," and barrel, and be done with it!

Make no mistake; in the short run this would be expensive. At $500,000 apiece (probably close to average value), the 22,000 Western BLM and Forest Service base properties would cost about $11 billion. If the roughly $1 billion in federal, state, and county taxes currently spent each year on public lands ranching was carefully redirected to purchase former base properties, this amount could be raised in 11 years. Or it might be borrowed against this annual revenue. Many additional funding possibilities exist. The Land and Water Conservation Fund, set up in 1965 with revenue from offshore oil drilling, provides up to $900 million annually for federal land acquisitions. According to the House Water and Power Resources Subcommittee staff, between $260 million and $376 million in taxes is spent annually to supply federally subsidized water for irrigation of surplus crops (a large percentage of which are for livestock). As mentioned, ranchers receive millions annually in subsidies for irrigation for livestock purposes. These wasted subsidies, and many others, could instead fund land purchases. The US plans to spend $303 billion (directly) on "defense" in 1990, but only $14 billion to protect the environment -- a ratio of 22 to 1. If Congress would forego a few unneeded Stealth bombers or nuclear missiles, or reduce Star Wars, the full $11 billion could be redirected easily. Redirection of federal Department of Defense cutbacks could easily provide this amount. Private funding also could be raised, with tax write-offs as added incentives. Conservation, animal rights, recreational, hunting and fishing, scientific, educational, and other groups and individuals could raise millions of dollars. The point is, the money **can** be raised if there is the demand. Even if a special tax had to be levied to raise the $11 billion, it would cost only $44 per US citizen -- a small price to pay for perhaps the greatest environmental restoration program in world history.

If full funding was not immediately forthcoming, a program of systematic acquisition could be implemented. The most environmentally important properties would be priority acquisitions, while environmental safeguards were applied to the remainder.

As for the ex-public lands rancher, he (though loath to admit it) has over the years become financially and psychologically dependent on government aid, like many other welfare recipients. Some of the poorer welfare ranchers are "trapped" in their "profession," just as some other welfare recipients come to depend permanently on government assistance as their means of survival.

A phase-out could be implemented gradually so as not to cause undue hardship and allow ex-welfare ranchers time to readjust to the free enterprise system. Livestock reductions could be made in stages over 5 or 10 years, with compensatory payments made at each stage, perhaps also providing time to raise funds for purchasing base properties.

Using the annual $50 million or so (beyond grazing fee receipts) previously expended as BLM and FS range funding, former welfare ranchers might be temporarily employed to help rehabilitate the public land they damaged; who would (should) know better the problems they caused? This positive work would provide them excellent karmic therapy. They could help round up feral cattle; reintroduce extirpated species; dismantle and recycle fences, corrals, stock tanks and other range detriments; close and revegetate ranching roads; restore riparian and sacrifice areas; manually remove exotics; and so on. Ranch structures could be disassembled and recycled, or turned into visitor and management centers. As restoration proceeded,

former welfare ranchers could gradually be placed in other professions, some created by improved local environmental and economic conditions.

Other federal, state, county, and city welfare ranchers likewise could be placed in this rehabilitation program, as could many private lands (semi-welfare) ranchers. More than half of the West would then be freed from ranching. The tiny drop in the US beef supply could be compensated in perhaps 5 to 10 years by the continued reduction in beef consumption; or additional cattle be raised in the East, where pastures are 20 to 30 times more livestock-productive than Western rangeland.

Further, even if all 30,000 ex-public lands ranchers had to find new occupations (in reality, only a small percentage would) or go on "welfare" (direct government financial aid), their number would be insignificant on the national scale. For example, during the past 20 years **more than 300,000** US railroad workers had to find different jobs (US Dept. of Com. 1987), and their financial plight was far more serious than that of generally well-endowed public lands graziers. Did we shed buckets of tears for the ex-railroad workers? Did we keep them in the railroad business at any cost? And what about the many parts of the country currently experiencing a labor shortage?

All I want to do is get their cows off our property. Let those cowboys and ranchers find some harder way to make a living, like the rest of us have to do. There's no good reason why we should subsidize them forever. They've had a free ride. It's time for them to support themselves.
--Edward Abbey (Abbey 1986)

One of the main obstacles to wise management and protection of Western public land is the confusing land ownership pattern. Western history's great variety of government land disposal programs and agency acquisitions has produced a complicated array of land owners and administrators. Moreover, it has created a complex intermixture of land uses that often conflict with one another. Much of the West exhibits such a hopeless hodge-podge of owners, administrators, and uses that effective management and environmental protection are essentially impossible.

The National Park Service and US Fish & Wildlife Service have minimized this problem by acquiring large, solid blocks of land, as has the US military by default (though, still, few if any of these areas are large enough to preserve whole ecosystems intact, and most if not all are abused). Much Forest Service land likewise is relatively cohesive, though large sections in some areas are checkerboarded, and almost all National Forests are plagued with small inholdings -- mostly ranches in the best riparian areas or scattered patented mining claims. Most BLM, state, and county land is intermixed in a checkerboarded or chaotic jumble of properties with a diversity of government administrators and private owners.

Therefore, the various governments should strive to eliminate haphazard and checkerboarded ownership patterns. To repeat, first and foremost the public should eliminate ranching on its land and buy all base properties, most of which are inholdings or adjacent to public land. This is a crucial step toward wise and effective public land administration and toward protecting whole ecosystems intact. Furthermore, the public should buy other inholdings and adjacent private land and trade fragmented public land for adjoining private land to block up and consolidate public land.

Perhaps more importantly, the BLM, Forest Service, Fish & Wildlife Service, and several other federal land management agencies could be eliminated and replaced with an entirely new, simpler, and more effective land managing entity. This would eliminate much confusion, red tape, duplication of effort, agency squabbling, and bureaucratic imperialism. This new entity could be called the **DEPARTMENT OF PUBLIC LAND (DPL)**. States, counties, cities, and private entities could also place land into DPL administration, and foreign nations would be encouraged to create similar programs. To prevent the centralization and abuse of power, local governments could maintain general administrative control, with basic environmental protection laws applying and mandated integrated public participation.

The DPL concept is based on minimum land management and maximum protection of environmental quality, with encouragement of responsible human use. Indeed, this land would be open to all -- never for a fee -- as the most **PUBLIC** of all land.

Therefore, only non-commercial, low-impact uses would be permitted. Ranching, logging, commercial woodcutting, mining, buildings, roads, dams, utilities, and all other commercial uses and significant new developments would be banned. So would off-road vehicular travel and other medium- to high-impact activities, including those whose *cumulative* impact was significant. Hunting, fishing, plant food and material gathering, woodcutting, rockhounding, and other non-commercial consumptive uses would be responsibly regulated where necessary, and a fee equal to the market value of the resource taken charged. Campgrounds and recreational areas would be simple, with a minimum of development. Sensitive areas would be off-limits until recovery. Natural fire would be reintroduced and other natural processes would be allowed to proceed unimpeded. After prolonged, devastating abuse, public land finally would be allowed to begin natural restoration.

Artificial restoration of damaged public land would also be a major initial function of the Department of Public Land. In the early years, most of the roughly 50,000 former agency personnel could use their acquired skills to remove feral cattle, dismantle fences and other range "improvements," disassemble and recycle structural developments, close and revegetate roads, restore mined and logged-over areas, remove exotic plants and animals, reintroduce natives, and so on. Others would monitor the results. Gradually, as the most urgent tasks were completed and ecosystems began to heal, perhaps 30,000 of the 50,000-member staff would be transferred to other jobs in the public and private sector (some of which would be created by improved environmental quality), leaving a semi-permanent staff of only about 20,000. (Statistics derived from US government publications.)

Because DPL would make so much of our current federal land management bureaucracy and subsidization obsolete, and because the recovering land would be more productive for other uses, the federal, state, and local taxpayers ultimately would save billions of dollars (not to mention roughly equivalent private savings). Though the agencies that would become DPL now spend over $4 billion annually, they take in only about $3 billion from commercial users each year, causing a $1 billion annual deficit to the US Treasury (derived from US government statistics). The consolidated, simplified DPL would spend only about $1 billion annually, meaning the federal government would break even immediately. However, non-commercial, consumptive use revenue would increase along with environmental health and reduced competition, and, with other revenue generated from a recovering environment (money not spent by government on flood control, water acquisition, etc.), could be funnelled to DPL, making it revenue-producing.

With the billions of federal dollars saved through the years, the public could purchase and protect additional land under DPL. The system could eventually encompass half or more of the area of the US, including large portions of the East. Commercial exploitation would then be restricted almost exclusively to private land. Since only 3% of this country's livestock and (according to various sources) only 13%-20% of its wood products (72% of US forest is private) come from public land, this production lost would be minor, as would the compensatory additional strain on private land (all environmental laws should likewise apply to private land). As a large percentage of energy and minerals is derived from public lands, reduced production of energy and mineral "resources" would present a greater challenge, but could be compensated through conservation, increased recycling, increased efficiency, and reduced human population. (In fact, DPL could have a beneficial "reverse effect" on our political/economic system, slowing population growth.)

The Department of Public Land idea is based on a faith that Nature manages itself best -- *as it has for 5 billion years* -- but with a belief that Nature and humans are inseparable. DPL's ultimate function would be to ensure that public land remained natural, with natural human use.

This system of environmental protection (or something like it) could help carry the world through these times of anthropogenic crisis. It could provide a setting for humans and Nature to *coexist*, where we could rediscover our connection to the natural world and where Nature could proceed unhampered, neither off limits to the public nor vulnerable to destructive exploitation. It could help prepare the way for a future human existence based on oneness -- not conflict -- with the Earth. In short, the idea could evolve into a return to a healthy, natural world.

Cattle growers feel bashed these days, but the truth is that we have indulged them beyond belief. In what other business could a few people hold much of the continent hostage to a destructive industry with a trivial output? If any other tenants did to our property what cattle growers have done, they'd be booted out in a flash.

All the same, our nostalgia for the Old West makes us long for a happy medium. Isn't there a way to permit grazing at some non-destructive level?

A century of grim experience argues that there isn't. The only sound approach to grazing would be a rest and rotation system that would allow such low numbers of cattle that it would be hard to tell it from an outright ban.

. . . Arguing about how many cattle should be allowed on our public lands is like arguing about how many termites we

should permit in our houses. Ranchers should be given enough time to conquer their addiction to using our public lands. After that, the cattle should go.
--Donald M. Peters, Phoenix, Arizona, Guest Column, 5-30-90 *The Arizona Republic* (Peters 1990)

Livestock grazing abuse has and is scarring most of the public lands in the west that I have seen . . . Livestock grazing should be eliminated from all public lands in the United States.
--Edwin G. Dimick, 28 year veteran of FS, SCS, and BLM, **Livestock Pillage of Our Western Public Lands** (Dimick 1990)

Chapter XIII
A FUTURE FOR PUBLIC LANDS RANCHING?

In as little as 20 years, some people say, public lands ranching will be looked at as a living history exhibit, not a viable economic activity. Maybe that is what it is today, and maybe it's time we treated it as such.

--Dan Dagget, "Arizona Ranchers Are Ripping Off Wildlife" (Dagget 1990)

Today many people say there is no future in public lands ranching. They see the industry as a bloated relic from the Old West that soon will collapse under its own weight and go the way of whalebone corsets and the steam locomotive. To some, this is wishful thinking; to others, it is the sad fate of a heroic epoch.

As if to reinforce these predictions, many stockmen themselves maintain that even without opposition the industry won't last another 20 years. They complain that they are being driven out of business by the rising cost of ranching supplies, low beef prices (actually now near their *highest* level ever), excessive grazing fees, government interference, "goddamned en*varmint*lists," taxes, predators, bad weather, high fuel prices, rustlers, vandalism, foreign competition, and more.

These are, of course, the same grievances bemoaned for decades. Most of this self-pity is the same old ploy to maintain subsidies and public sympathy, and to defuse opposition. (Why work to end public lands ranching if it is dying anyway?)

While it is true that some operators have gone out of business in recent years, their former allotments certainly have not gone ungrazed. Indeed, federal statistics show a steady, annual 1%-2% of BLM and Forest Service grazing allotments vacant. (A large percentage of these are high elevation sheep allotments.) Would this be so if public lands ranching were on the verge of collapse? Discounting mounting opposition, several factors indicate that public lands ranching is far from coming to an end.

On my own leased forest lands, vegetation and soils are far from healthy. When my late husband and I purchased our ranch, the land was sick from overgrazing and USFS mismanagement. To heal the land, we chose to drastically reduce the livestock grazed on forest ranges. The USFS responded by threatening to terminate our permit unless we fully stocked our grazing allotment.

--Carolyn Lietzman, Carrizozo, New Mexico, *High Country News* (12-7-87)

First, the federal government has always claimed a "legal mandate" to maximize ranching on public grazing allotments. It uses the "multiple use" concept to reinforce this alleged universal mandate. According to the Forest Service, if a stockman for some reason decides not to graze an allotment for more than 3 years in a row (or if a non-rancher acquires a permit with the purchase of a base property), and even if he pays all the grazing fees but does not use a blade of grass, "The permit will be taken away and given to someone who *will* graze it." All permit holders *must* stock the range with at least the minimum number of livestock called for on their permits. State governments are even more insistent; county and city tax structures also virtually mandate ranching on large undeveloped acreage.

The U.S. cattle industry is beginning to turn back to raising cattle on range and forage because fattening and finishing cattle primarily on grains is becoming too costly. Thus, to cut production costs, this ecologically unsound industry is going to intensify its impacts on the natural environment.

--Dr. Michael W. Fox, **Agricide** (Fox 1986)

Second, massive ranching subsidization is institutionalized. Historically, government and private aid has always propped up public lands ranching in proportion to the level of assistance required, making its collapse virtually impossible regardless of its feasibility or malevolent influence.

Third, for more than a century stockmen have dominated the economic, social, and political power structures of the rural West. A rancher's clout traditionally has been based mostly on the land he controls. Thus, public lands ranching is incredibly entrenched in these Western power structures, and is perpetuated by them.

This is not to say that there has been no change in recent decades; obviously there has. Forest Service Range Management Director Robert Williamson has even declared,

The political clout that the livestock industry used to have is not there anymore. They think it's still there and they've tried to use it. But it doesn't work anymore.

Williamson probably intended his statement to diffuse opposition. The tiny grazing fees, "advisory" boards, political influence, unfair laws, agency acquiescence, overgrazed range, and more show clearly that stockmen still do carry overwhelming clout. But his statement does reflect change. How far this change is allowed to go remains to be seen.

Fourth, an important Catch-22 preventing significant change is this: Any improvement in range condition resulting from reduced grazing is used by the ranching establishment to justify increased grazing. As soon as the range starts to recover, it is once again stocked up with livestock, thus maintaining that dynamic state of degradation (or each series of grazing years contributing to a cumulate, long-term

A Forest Service depiction of proper, future range management. *(USFS)*

environmental decline). An area must warrant special administrative protection, or reach Sahara-like conditions, to finally go ungrazed. Even then it usually will again be grazed as soon as it is declared recovered.

For example, Nevada's Toiyabe National Forest (at 4 million acres second in size only to Alaska's Tongass) has been called the nation's most overgrazed national forest, even by Forest Service officials. Plans for modest grazing reductions over the next decade are overshadowed by long-term plans to *increase* livestock numbers once the Forest is judged to be restored.

Similarly, public lands ranching reforms will always be transitory so long as the industry's overall infrastructure remains intact. Dr. Denzel Ferguson, co-author of **Sacred Cows**, writes:

> . . . *We fought a huge battle at Malheur National Wildlife Refuge, and they reduced grazing to acceptable levels. As soon as we relaxed the pressure, the ranchers moved in and made new demands. Today, I am told that the situation is worse than ever! . . . . Local land managers live out in these communities and have no protection against pressures to increase grazing. Given these circumstances, as long as grazing is permitted, it will tend to be maximal, abusive, and not in the public interest. . . . It is surely an all or none phenomenon. In any event, until the entire conservation community is willing to demand complete removal of livestock from public lands, I see absolutely no solution to the problem.*

On 17 and 18 January 1989, a coalition of public lands ranching advocacy organizations held the first-ever conference devoted solely to exploring ways to squelch growing opposition. In a letter advertising the event to its members, the National Inholders' Association claimed:

> *The environmentalists have declared war on our range rights. We're within a few years of being driven off our grazing permit lands.*

Yet, though the threat of being "driven off" "their" public land was a central theme at the conference, few ranchers considered such eviction a serious possibility. Their focus at the conference was how best to combat ranching reductions and restrictions. The scare was designed to generate a stronger defense and garner public sympathy.

On March 16, 1990, a second major conference was held. This one took place at the Denver headquarters of the Society for Range Management (SRM), and included representatives from SRM, the Public Lands Council, ranching interests, and the government land management agencies

themselves. All attendees identified opposition to public lands ranching as the enemy and pledged to work together using various methods, including an expanded and intensified "public education" program. More conferences are planned.

Interestingly, while the ranching establishment whimpers about its imminent demise, it has big plans for our public land. Indeed, it has consistently maintained the long-range goal of *greatly increasing* livestock production there. For example, in 1974 the USDA Inter-Agency Work Group on Range Production estimated that red meat production on US rangeland could eventually be *tripled*. In 1979 Forest Service Deputy Chief Thomas C. Nelson projected:

> *In summary, when we look to the '80's and beyond, we see a future for rangeland characterized by:*
> *--A demand for range grazing that increases half again by the year 2000, and doubles by the year 2030.*
> *--An equilibrium of demand and cost on all* [public] *grazed areas of about 300 million animal unit months* [nearly twice current AUM's]. (Klemmedson 1979)

Also in 1979, Assistant Interior Secretary Guy Martin voiced his projection for BLM at a rangeland symposium: "Target: Double the current annual [public land] forage production to 11.2 million tons per year." Max Lieurance, BLM Division of Rangeland Management Chief, made this claim:

> *Vegetation production on the public rangelands managed by the Bureau of Land Management can be at least doubled. Without doubt, similar or even greater opportunities also exist on State and privately owned rangelands.*

Echoing BLM for the private sector at the same symposium, Thadis W. Box, Dean of the Utah State University College of Natural Resources, declared, "I believe that outputs of certain products, such as forage and red meat, can easily be doubled" (USDA, USDI, CEQ 1979).

In 1980, USDA was addressing all ranching factions when, in a major rangeland report entitled *An Assessment of the Forest and Range Land Situation in the United States*, it announced that:

> *The ultimate biological potential production from the range has been estimated at 566 million AUM's, more than 2 1/2 times the 1976 supply level of 213 million AUM's. This could be achieved by applying intensive management levels on all of the more than 1 billion acres of range* [in the US].

USDA further projected that the demand for Western range grazing would increase by more than 1/3 by the year

2030 and that with escalated government range development and other efforts, the Western range has the potential to double AUM production. USDA cautioned that due to practical restraints increased production in drier areas may be slower, but that "in humid areas where current yields per acre reach 3 AUM's, and under intensive management, yields of 6 AUM's per acre are expected by 2030." (USDA, FS 1980)

By 1988 the Forest Service had toned down previous projections a bit, claiming it was going to meet a 41% projected increase in US demand for range grazing by the year 2030 with a 5%-15% increase in National Forest System AUM production by that year (USDA, FS 1988). The BLM, US Fish & Wildlife Service, and some other federal agencies recently have made similar claims, while the wild declarations by money-hungry Western state land departments continue to explore the limits of fantasy.

It is believed that public grazing lands have the potential for a threefold increase in forage production under proper management.
--George D. Lea in **Grasslands of the United States**

To meet demand projections, most recent government land management plans call for long-range increases in livestock numbers. Curiously, some of these plans also call for initial minimal stocking reductions "to allow the land to recover full productivity" -- in other words, to foster these increases. Often the reductions are designed more to placate opposition; stocking levels rise as opposition dissipates. Some are last-resort attempts to restore critically abused areas, the hidden motivation being to restore livestock productivity.

Livestock have been banned from some of the most environmentally sensitive public lands. But most of these are small areas, and even here long-range plans usually call for future resumption of grazing after a specified period or when the land is deemed recovered. For example, BLM recently acquired 48,000 acres along a 40-mile riparian stretch in southeast Arizona, creating the San Pedro National Riparian Conservation Area -- the first of its kind in the US. Livestock were removed to allow recovery, but if after 15 years conditions have improved significantly (which they already have, according to BLM studies), the "moratorium" on grazing may be lifted. (The San Pedro NRCA Area bill was nearly killed by Wyoming Representative Malcomb Wallop, a front man for Western stockmen who feared the NRCA would set a precedent for government to take "public" waters from ranchers.)

The Nature Conservancy recently acquired grazing privileges to more than 50,000 acres of National Forest and BLM land with the purchase of the 4400 acre Muleshoe Ranch in southeast Arizona. To help restore the overgrazed range and damaged riparian areas, the Conservancy terminated all livestock grazing on the private land and convinced the Forest Service to retire permits and the BLM to agree to a 5-year grazing moratorium. With no ranching, the Muleshoe Preserve has made "a dramatic comeback." But local stockmen are pressuring and BLM is considering opening up some areas for ranching, and even the Forest Service may consider resumption if condition continues to improve.

MANTI-LASAL NATIONAL FOREST

United States Department of Agriculture   Forest Service

The cover of the Manti-La Sal National Forest, Utah, Management Plan.

A look at public land management plans would not lead you to think that public ranching is on the verge of extinction. For example, the recent Kaibab National Forest (north of the Grand Canyon) 50-year plan mandates continued ranching-as-usual, even though the Forest's own assessment shows more than half the Forest producing forage at less than half its natural potential. The plan says 24,645 acres of pinyon-juniper can be "cost-effectively treated" (chained) to increase grazing. Consider also the Mendocino National Forest (northwest California) plan, as reported by conservationist Don Morris:

Although the Forest Service admits that over 342,000 acres of the current 542,000 acres of grazing allotments are "unsuitable for range use" [due mostly to density of woody vegetation], they propose a "modest" 20% increase in grazing primarily due to new "transitory range" as a result of logging activities -- the proposed 40 acre hopscotch clearcuts will be bovine feedlots.

The Inyo National Forest (central-eastern California) plan is likewise typical, as reported by a local conservationist:

The Forest Service intends to increase grazing by livestock in the already severely overgrazed mountain meadows and sagebrush flats of the Inyo. Their justification, they admit, is pressure by the local livestock industry as well as "an expected increase in demand for red meat because of the increasing population of Southern California." Under PRF [preferred alternative], grazing of cattle, sheep, and wild horses would increase from 41,400 AUMs to 45,300 AUMs on 140,000 acres of "poor to fair" quality range.

Colorado ecologist David Lucas describes a BLM Resource Area Plan:

We stumbled onto the BLM's Henry Mountain [Resource Area] Grazing EIS, covering Capitol Reef [National Park] and the land east, over to and including the Henry Mountains. . . . The BLM Preferred Alternative would increase stock AUMs from 33,298 to 54,043 and game from 5,204 to 12,298 -- fancy figuring! This sleight of hand range management was to result from the treatment (herbicide spraying, chaining, etc.) of 24,300 acres, and building 119 reservoirs, 37 miles of pipeline, 38 troughs, and 17 miles of fence.

As mentioned, according to a report by the Committee for Idaho's High Desert, all 6 BLM resource areas in southern Idaho have recently released proposed management plans, all of which schedule increases in projected forage allocations to livestock, ranging from 13% to 66%.

The BLM acknowledges that overgrazing is the leading cause of the deterioration of its rangelands, but on 25% of the overgrazed allotments studied by the General Accounting Office, the BLM, bowing to rancher opposition and political pressure, has not recommended livestock reductions [not that they have on the remaining 75%].
--Bruce Hamilton, "Unfinished Business," *Sierra* (Sep/Oct 1989)

And so it goes on public land throughout the West. But ranchers have yet another ace up the sleeve. Usurping the agencies, they increasingly depict themselves as *managers* of public land, as well as livestock growers, and ranching as an integral and crucial component of public land management. This trend is reflected in the agencies' recent cooperative management efforts and self-imposed reductions in funding for ranching supervision, as well as stockmen's expanded efforts to extend their influence within public land user groups heretofore of little concern.

Public lands ranching is not dying; it is not being phased out; it is not being significantly reduced . . . in the long run it is to be *significantly increased*. The increase will be accomplished primarily with intensified vegetation manipulation, livestock developments, and uniform overgrazing, and by opening up new grazing land with expanded logging and brush clearing.

In The Shining Future, through ever-expanding science and technology, America's new-and-improved, modern, progressive range management will blossom. Contemplate excerpts from the contemporary range text **Range Management**:

During the night, the ranch computer automatically assembles several data bases to obtain current information on availability and prices of fuel, fencing, pump leathers, and vaccines; weather forecasts; and livestock markets. . . . Sensors in ear tags and implanted devices in the livestock are scanned for health, nutritional status, and estrus. . . . Rumen-regulating drugs and genetic engineering to produce more useful rumen microflora will provide increased potential for metabolizing range forage into useful nutrients. . . . The alteration of living cells plus advances in microculture, cell fusion, regeneration of plants from single cells, and embryo recovery and transfer will create new . . . . . (Holechek 1989)

Most public lands ranching is remote, unknown, and uncontested, such as this sheep and cattle grazing Wyoming's Bighorn National Forest.

The future productivity of livestock could be increased by the development and implementation of 150 current and potential technologies. These technologies span the entire spectrum of animal production from modifying and controlling the animal's environment to pest and disease control to manipulating and changing the animal's physiology.
--Linda A. Joyce, *An Analysis of the Range Forage Situation in the United States: 1989-2040* (for USFS) (Joyce 1989)

Most public lands ranches already use modern vehicles, equipment, and livestock technology, and many are to some degree computerized. The trend is toward more intensive planning, monitoring, and management, with increasing manipulation of the environment. For example, a recent development is the "Grazing Land Simulator," a digital computer that monitors rangeland management (financed by the Co-operative State Research Service, Co-operative Extension Service, BLM, FS, SCS, Bureau of Indian Affairs, and the National Cattleman's Association). Computerized symbols -- little cows, sheep, tanks, fences, roads, creeks, brush, trees, grass, and such -- appear on the screen, awaiting your command. Yes, now you can plan ecosystem management from the comfort of your own home! Or purchase the portable suitcase model for range use.

A tag with the code would be implanted in the sheep's hide. Monitoring systems that use satellites to track the location of a tagged sheep to within 15 feet soon will be available . . . . If a sheep wearing a transmitter were killed by a predator, a signal from the transmitter would help in quickly locating the dead sheep and possibly finding the predator . . . .
--1-22-90 *Arizona Republic* (Webster 1990)

Yes, the worst may be yet to come. For example, many ranching advocates are already calling for cloud seeding to "augment" natural precipitation (thus stealing it from other areas and perverting atmospheric dynamics). Advanced machinery will transform "worthless" natural landscapes into productive pastures. Formerly "useless" range vegetation will be harvested with special machinery and treated to make it palatable to livestock. Bio-engineering will "improve" livestock, while bio-manipulation will "improve" the range. Livestock of many kinds will be shuttled about the West in futuristic transport vehicles to take fullest advantage of the land. (Already, some Hawaiian stockmen shuttle their cattle between isolated grazing areas *with helicopters*.) Sophisticated mobile and stationary range sensors will monitor humans, vehicles, livestock, and the environment. Orbiting satellites will pinpoint available forage and browse.

A multi-video system that provides immediately useful narrow-band black and white imagery within the visible to near-infrared light (0.40- to 1.10um waveband) region of the electromagnetic spectrum was evaluated as a remote sensing tool to assess several rangeland ground conditions . . .
--J.H. Everitt and P.R. Nixon, "Video Imagery: A New Remote Sensing Tool for Range Management"

In sum, there is little reason to think that public lands ranching is waning. Degradation of the range will grow with the scientific and technological ability to manipulate the range. In the future, stockmen will continue to dominate the rural West. Ranching will remain the highest priority on most Western range under the pretense of multiple use. Profits will continue to be mined from an increasingly degraded environment, even if it takes twice as many range "improvements" or acres per cow or sheep. Ever more complex and costly range management systems will continue to artificially counteract ranching's inherent destructiveness and up production statistics -- to make it seem that range condition is improving. Taxpayers will continue to foot the bill. . . .

. . . . unless we do something about it. The next chapter explores the possibilities.

The next great environmental issue is going to be grazing and the desertification of public land.
--Larry Tuttle, Director, The Wilderness Society, Oregon office

(Roger Candee)

IF PUBLIC LANDS RANCHING WAS ENDED . . .

--Only about 30,000
of 1.6 million (2% of) US
livestock producers would be affected.

--The American public
would save billions of dollars.

--The rural West
would largely be freed from public
lands ranchers' social and political injustice.

--The American West
would experience one of the
Earth's greatest environmental restorations.

Chapter XIV
GET INVOLVED

Conservation Pledge

"I give my pledge as an American to save and faithfully to defend from waste the natural resources of my country — its soil and minerals, its forests, waters and wildlife."

Time was solutions to many of our problems were a bit simpler. A Winchester, a hard fist, or hard work went a long way when it came to protecting your own [public lands ranching operation]. Today, things aren't that simple.
--from Idaho Cattle Association promotion literature

If the public wants to assert ownership of its land, it will have to take it away from ranchers. That won't be easy. Nobody wants to take on John Wayne . . . . But that's the way the game is played. That's how the West must be won -- again.
--David Brown, author, wildlife biologist, former Chief of Game, Arizona Game & Fish Department

Stockmen have more power over the rural West and its people than any other group. The elite 30,000 public lands ranchers -- so used to getting their way for so long -- cannot be expected to release their century-long stranglehold on the public and its land voluntarily. And we cannot expect our ranching-oriented government to force them to.

Limited reforms have been made by small contingents of ranching victims, conservationists, animal rightists, hunters and fishers, as well as tax, political, and social reform advocates. However, fundamental and lasting changes require

increased public awareness and involvement, and, ultimately, much more widespread re-establishment with Nature. These are the main goals of this book.

Unfortunately, we have a long way to go. The American public suffers from unawareness, apathy, sheep-like behavior, a near-fanatic cowboy/Western obsession, and an increasing withdrawal from Nature. This, combined with worsening environmental conditions, affirms that we must begin making major changes soon.

Prerequisite, of course, is enough concern to spark a willingness to make those changes. The explosive movements for civil, women's, gay, and animal rights, and anti-war, anti-nuclear, health, and selected environmental issues in recent decades indicates that some of the American public **is** concerned and willing to get involved once it recognizes a need for change.

I've been amazed at how little attention public lands ranching gets, especially from environmentalists. Overgrazing may be America's least-known big environmental problem.
--Denis Jones, Hoboken, New Jersey

Therein lies the main hindrance. Many times I have been asked, "What's a BLM, anyway?" A surprising number of Americans don't realize that public lands even exist; still more don't understand what they are, where they are, or how they are abused. Easterners especially are amazed to learn that cattle and sheep graze public land, and that livestock developments are built there. Others think that cattle and sheep are indigenous Western animals. And, while probably most people are vaguely aware of public lands ranching, only a tiny percentage even begin to understand its repercussions. The average American probably knows more about Dolly Parton's hairdo than about the major land abuse of the West!

The situation is understandable, however. While the 11 Western states cover about 40% of the contiguous US, only 20% of Americans live there. In other words, Easterners comprise 80% of public land owners. If so inclined, they could easily overpower the Western ranching establishment and end public lands ranching. But Easterners remain even less informed -- thus uninvolved -- than Westerners on this issue. And, almost wholly separated from the reality of the Western range, Easterners are even more likely than Westerners to idealize ranching.

In the West, more than 4/5 of the people live in urban areas, insulated and isolated from happenings "out there" on the rural 99%. For most, contact with rural areas is limited to vacations to popular (usually ungrazed) tourist areas, highway driving, and travel stops in small towns. Moreover, Americans spend an average of more than 90% of their time indoors, and little of that remaining 10% meaningfully connected with Nature. Our prevailing culture provides us with little impetus to concern ourselves with the natural environment.

Anyone who goes beyond the city limits of almost any Western town can see for himself that the land is overgrazed.
--Edward Abbey (Abbey 1986)

You don't need a weatherman to know which way the wind blows.
--Bob Dylan

The best education is direct experience. Only in this way can one sufficiently understand ranching's environmental, economic, social, and political impact on the West -- something only partially communicated in a book. So, *get out there on the range!* Travel any direction from nearly any Western settlement and usually you will soon be "in the heart of ranching country."

Visit many locales and diverse terrain -- not just the popular parks and recreation areas, which usually are kept ungrazed to protect the land or for public relations purposes. These tourist areas cover less than 5% of Western public land but receive over 95% of the visitation. They are packed with people, while the remaining lands see only an occasional hiker or hunter and, of course, the local rancher. BLM land encompasses much more of the West than does Forest Service land, yet it receives less than 1/20 as many visitors. There is also state, FWS, Bureau of Reclamation, Department of Defense, Indian, county, municipal, and private range, the vast bulk of it open to the public or by request, most of it infrequently visited. Time on this land may be freer, more interesting, and more enjoyable than a closely supervised session of gawking at spectacular panoramas amidst throngs of tourists. And this is where you will begin to see what ranching has done to 70% of the West.

[Ranching critics are] *arm chair, desk bound, self ordained experts . . .* [who] *see a few cow chips and determine the* [sic] *livestock is devastating the range.*
--Hubert Lauzon, Arizona public lands rancher

Travel slowly through the rural West; you can't learn much from a vehicle at 60 mph. Use back roads, dirt roads, rough roads, no roads. Stop often; stop anywhere. Chances are better than 50-50 that you will stop on some kind of public land; chances are more than 7 out of 10 that you will be on ranchland. Chances are that you will have to climb over a barbed wire fence. . . .

Now that you are on the land, in the open air, close to the Earth, relax! Take time . . . . Shed the human-made world. Allow yourself to become part of your surroundings. In time, your mental, emotional, spiritual, and physical senses re-emerge, realign, and reunite into a new, heightened, and expanded awareness.

Use this awareness to experience and learn about this place. What is here, in this ecosystem? What entities, processes, cycles, systems? Why? How do they function? What is not here? Why? What should be here? Why isn't it? Try to imagine what the area might have been like 200 years ago. By now, you should be starting to see some of the ways in which ranching has influenced this place.

Consider the vegetation -- species, health, density, composition, distribution, the way it changes from place to place. Can you find wild animals or their signs? How has the area's soil been affected? Churned up? Compacted? Excessive erosion? How much bare dirt? Cutbanks? Cryptogams? How much organic litter? What is it composed of? Is it intact? Running water? Should there be? If there is, is it polluted? Cattle? Note their brands, hoof prints, bleating and bawling, fly-covered splats.

Notice the dirt ranching roads and where they lead. What effect are they having on the area? What do recent tire tracks indicate? Are there signs of off-road vehicle use? Observe stock tanks and how they are constructed. How much could that one have cost? What kind of machinery was used to build it, with what impact? Are there signs of woodcutting, excavation, arson, trapping? With your eyes, follow fences across the landscape. What purposes do they serve? How many gates? Where are they located? What access do they provide? Girdled trees? Note the variations in vegetation from ranching practices, especially fenceline contrasts (however, usually much damage occurs even where a contrast is not obvious or even evident). What have ranchers and range managers done to cause these changes? Try to spot sacrifice areas and discern why they have become degraded.

When you feel you know the area, leave and find a nearby, comparable *unranched* area -- perhaps a National Park or Monument, or a natural or scenic area. Walk out away from the roads, developments, and tourists and immerse yourself in the surroundings. Then compare notes. In most cases, the contrast will be impressive, if not remarkable.

Look at the land with new eyes. With experience, you will begin to see ranching's impact nearly everywhere, even in forms not mentioned in this book. Areas that previously seemed unspoiled will reveal surprising degradation. This may be a rude awakening but no problem ever disappeared by looking the other way.

What does "Free Our Public Lands!, stop destructive welfare ranching, end public lands livestock grazing" actually mean? How is welfare ranching so destructive? I don't understand. How could cows eating grass be so bad?
--J. Siciliano, Stamford, Connecticut, personal correspondence

Although direct experience is best, there are other ways to learn about public lands ranching. Libraries and book stores carry hundreds of publications that touch upon the subject. Some contain useful information. As mentioned, however, the vast majority are of, by, and for the ranching establishment, and separating information from misinformation and irrelevance may not be easy.

You can write government agencies and request pertinent information. In return you may receive stacks of promo handouts and pro-ranching form letters -- if anything. In conducting research for this book, I sent requests to 14 federal and state agencies involved in public lands ranching. Each letter was individually typed and specifically requested any available information on the agency's involvement with public lands ranching, including breakdowns on funding, responsibilities, and organizational structure. Each was politely and succinctly worded, requesting billing if there was a charge. Of the 14 agencies contacted, only 8 even bothered to respond; only 5 of those provided useful information, while none of them provided nearly the material requested. Follow-up letters yielded little more. Dozens of other requests over the years have produced similar results.

To get pertinent information from government agencies, you must: (1) possess infinite patience and persistence; (2) break into their files late at night; or (3) invoke the Freedom of Information and Privacy Act. In the last case you are required to submit a letter to the relevant agency requesting specified information under authority of the Act, allow weeks or months for research, and pay all related costs, often amounting to hundreds or thousands of dollars. (Public interest groups sometimes can obtain a waiver on costs. For more information on Freedom of Information requests, visit a library or contact the ACLU or other legal aid organization.)

You can phone agency officials, but this is even more like pulling teeth. I have rarely reached an intended official with less than a couple of long-distance calls. You can leave messages, but they usually don't return your calls. Most of those you do reach act more like stockmen than public servants.

Bureaucracy... they "forget" that you requested this information or that. Or they may forget that you were interested in this decision or that. Or they seem to ignore you. Or they seem intent on wearing you down. Or they seem to want to make you feel like you don't know what you are talking about. Or they try to intimidate you either overtly or covertly. Or they may try to coopt you. Or they may ridicule you or your efforts.
--Leslie Glustrom, *Participating in Livestock Grazing Decisions on the National Forests* (Glustrom 1991)

You can visit these people in their offices. They may be polite, bewildered, or hostile, but few will speak openly of what is really going on. To discourage you, they may pretend that you are the only oddball ever to question them about public lands ranching, or act like you are wasting valuable government time. They may perform a standard song-and-dance about ranching mandates, sustained yield, multiple use, responsible management, and how the range is now "better than ever." Most agency officials (whether they realize it or not) are professional PR men who defend the ranching imperative; that is largely how they made the grade. I can say without hesitation that many of them will intentionally mislead you if they get the chance.

You can talk with independent range consultants and range professionals at agricultural colleges, but they likewise are integral components of the ranching establishment. These "experts" juggle statistics and use convincing, rehearsed arguments. They may know 147 different grasses, but everything they know is structured to promote ranching. It's their job.

You can request relevant information from stockmen's associations. This usually results in more public relations brochures and form letters, or nothing. For instance, my request (under an assumed name) to the National Cattlemen's Association for information on their organization and its official policy on public lands ranching was answered 2 months later with this:

The information you have requested is for the most part available to members, and since NCA is a membership organization owned by members, I cannot provide you with the information you requested.

You can talk with ranchers themselves, but by virtue of their upbringing, conditioning, peer pressure, and vested interest, most are incapable of realistic dialogue. They may provide some interesting stories, but little reliable information. Tall tales and self-serving interpretations of reality are traditional within the ranching community. Also customary between ranchmen is an unwritten compact to never openly criticize another's ranching practices, even if abuse is severe and they hate each other's guts (sometimes making for humorous situations). They portray an image of folksy cowboy comraderie to the outside world, even if there is none. This blanket reciprocal support is an established means ranchers employ to help reaffirm their self-worth, protect the industry's favorable public image, and maintain cohesion of the power establishment.

The more perceptive modern stockman will want to maintain healthy public relations. He may invite you to his ranch for lunch and a tour. You'll meet the wife, eat barbecued hamburgers, and hear all about the many hardships of running a public lands ranch. You'll be shuttled about the allotment in his 4-wheel drive, visit the most impressive spots, take in the most successful range developments, and be dazzled by his range savvy all the while. To convince you of his sincerity and environmental commitment, you may be privy to a special range problem he's been having and his special efforts to solve it.

Unfortunately, we cowboy-crazed Americans, urban dwellers especially, are primed to believe nearly anything a rancher tells us. How are we to know differently? And, when a living legend speaks, you listen.

Consider this typical encounter. John and Jane Average-Middle-Class-American Jones have their annual 2-week summer vacations coming up. They want to do something really different this year, so they load the kids into the RV, leave the city behind, and head out for the beautiful badlands of southern Utah.

Their fourth day out, feeling adventurous, on a whim they turn off the main highway, bump over the cattle guard onto a small dirt road, and follow its twisting course along an arroyo and over a hill to a small creek. There being several large shade trees here, the Joneses decide to have a picnic. They pile out with their stuff, walk up the creek a few yards, and suddenly, there, wrapping barbed wire around an old cottonwood, is . . . *a cowboy!*

The Joneses have never seen an in-the-flesh cowboy at work before, and are nervous but excited.

Little Jimmy calls out, "Hey, are you a *real* cowboy!?"

A suitably rustic voice replies, "That's right, son. Been workin' this ranch 25 years."

Upon hearing this, Dad begins to worry. "I . . . I'm sorry. We didn't know where this road went. Is this private property?"

The rancher, wanting to sound sociable but maintain his authority, answers coolly, "Well, no not really -- BLM grazing land. Where're you folks from?"

Seizing this opportunity, Dad introduces himself, though rather self-consciously in his citified, pressed Levi lookalikes and jogging shoes. The two settle into a conversation,

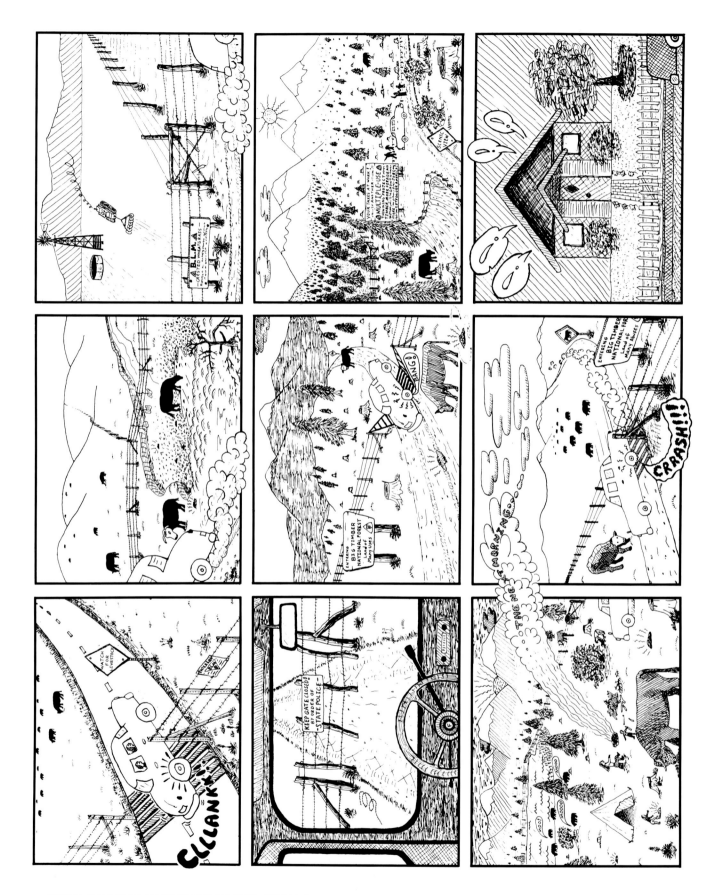

THE JONES FAMILY SETS OUT ONE DAY TO EXPERIENCE THE WILD WEST.

the rancher doing most of the talking, responding to John's queries about ranch life, while the family listens intently.

The stockman talks about the fence he's building, how it'll help keep better track of the cattle and how it needs to be stretched tight across this creek between these 2 trees so's it won't wash away in the next flood. He talks of what a hard time ranchers are having making a living these days, and of the many things working against them -- high prices; floods and droughts; the feds and their regulations; outsiders coming in and throwing trash around and leaving gates open and just not respecting the land and his livelihood; and predators, especially the coyotes that've killed 85 of his calves in the last few years.

"People just don't understand those damned coyotes," he declares. "If you don't keep them down, they'll just keep multiplying like rabbits and eat every animal around, *including all the wildlife!*" The cowboy tilts his hat up, fixes Dad with a serious look, and states dramatically, "Ever seen coyotes kill a calf?" Before Dad can answer, he continues, "Well, it ain't a pretty sight. In a big pack they come right up behind a running calf and just start bitin' off chunks of its tail. Just playing, not really wanting to kill the animal -- yet. They tire of that after awhile and start tearing into the rear legs, crippling the animal so's it can't walk or hardly move. Then they get the blood lust and just start ripping into the calf's belly and asshole -- while the calf just lays there struggling and bawling the whole time! No sir, it ain't a pretty sight!"

The rancher pulls his hat down at an angle across his eyes, indicating that the conversation is closing, and resolutely proclaims, "I've killed hundreds of coyotes, and they're still thick! These city people wantin' to tell us what to do and save every single damned predator just don't know what goes on out here. Well, what're they gonna eat when they close down the livestock producers, anyway -- *soy-ya burgers?!*"

John Jones, now feeling more citified, naive, and self-conscious than ever, ponders all this as he awkwardly shakes the cowboy's hand and allows him to return to his obviously important work. As John walks away, he's thinking, "Gosh, I've just talked with a *real* cowboy, a rugged outdoorsman who lives way out here and works this land and knows what he's talking about."

The average American understands little about actual ranching, to the great benefit of the industry. A compelling yet intimidating aura of mystery shrouds the celebrated stockman. We tend to fear and magnify what we don't understand. Thus, the Western rancher, already an exalted hero, becomes an almost overwhelming authority figure.

More reliable sources of public lands ranching information are scientific, conservation, and environmental organizations. They have already done the dirty work and are less biased by a profit/power motive. Many have been to some extent involved in the issue for decades and are happy to share their knowledge.

Some of the best sources are common folks who live near or spend much time on public land but are not so bound by ranching ties. Talk with rural residents, hunters, fishers, campers, hikers, backpackers, and naturalists.

People come out to look at the situation and they fall in love with these cowboys. It's the myth of the American West. The cowboys come off as the paragon of great American values. Now we're saying that they're destroying public lands.
--Tom France, National Wildlife Federation (Royte 1990)

The level of outrage on the part of the American people is not high enough. This is due to massive ignorance of the problem. This situation has not been helped much by various elements of the environmental community who have bent over backwards in placating the cowboys out of some half-assed romantic notion that cowboys represent a free lifestyle that is the cultural equivalent of wilderness.
--Public ranching critic

The cowboy and Mickey Mouse are the two greatest American heros.
--Dr. William H. Goetzman, TV documentary *The West of the Imagination*

Learning the issue is crucial, but only one of several major hurdles. We also need to overcome -- or at least redirect -- our national obsession with the sacred cow and sacred cowboy. One conservationist writes,

We must begin goring the sacred cow, treating the myth of the cowboy with the contempt it deserves. Shake the bastards' confidence that they are universally envied and adored.

In short, we must dismember the Marlboro Man.

*The West is the lovliest and most enduring
of our myths,
the only one
that has been universally accepted.*

--Bernard DeVoto

But dismembering the Marlboro Man won't be easy. As discussed, cowboyism permeates our culture. Questioning this institutionalized reality is like denouncing Christmas. Who would declare our mythological Western Hero not only mortal, but also the West's greatest despoiler? Fear of rejection keeps us from seeing clearly, making rational decisions, and acting appropriately.

There is, moreover, a small but monied "cowboy establishment" that deals in the preservation of the cowboy myth, linking it with the nebulous concept of western heritage, and arguing, in effect, that the cowboy is the last sentinel on the parapet of Americanism. Any research that results in information to the contrary is immediately suspect.
--William W. Savage, Jr., **The Cowboy Hero** (Savage 1979)

We need to separate fantasy from reality. For example, from early childhood we are conditioned to equate ranching with the great outdoors, with Nature. Few of us pull out of this mind-set long enough to realize that more than any other influence ranching has made the West *unnatural*. While we are shocked at the obvious destruction wrought by a bulldozing developer, we welcome the rancher, his livestock and developments (even *his* bulldozer!) as natural

parts of the Western scene, even if they do far more overall damage. While we imagine it the antipode, ranching is actually an integral component of Western development, its vanguard and promoter.

WE CAN KEEP THE ROMANTIC FANTASY AND GET RID OF THE COWS.

(Greg Pentkowski)

Likewise, we unthinkingly ordain the ranchman our exemplary rural inhabitant, even though ranchers comprise only a tiny fraction of the rural populace. We adoringly declare him the folksiest of folks, even though other rural groups live generally more earthy lives. We idealize ranching as the epitome of simple, natural living, even though, as we have seen, it is based on a highly complex, consumptive, exploitive infrastructure. Actually, many city apartment dwellers live simpler, more natural lives.

Yet, what 8 to 5, city-bound reader can resist romantic prose like this from the January 1989 **National Geographic**:

Somewhere else, I suppose, people are traffic jamming to offices and factories.

Not Steve Madsen. He's over by the Idaho-Nevada line, working alone on a ranch that runs for 37 miles across the headwaters of the Bruneau River. Most of the day he'll rassle with a horse named Blutcher. This sorrel is big and ornery enough to carry you straight up any canyonside, but you sure don't want to hammer horseshoes on the son of a gun by yourself....

One purpose of the cowboy myth is to vicariously fulfill our longings for everything missing from our routinized, bureaucratized, civilized lives. Ranching romanticism has for a century held immense appeal to Americans. But today the lure to escape to the popularized ranching lifestyle has become almost irresistible. Commercial interests now wage fierce competition to sell the American public their brand of Western fantasy. Their agents prowl the backcountry West, searching out the folksiest or toughest or most colorful cowhands, who are then set up, filmed, and offered to the public as representative of ranching in general. Other (most) promotions are fabricated with professional models, such as the Marlboro Man.

One popular TV commercial urges its audience to "live the legend!" *Imagine yourself in his cowboy boots!* As modern America grows, so does the ranching lure. Ironically, though each year the illusions, exaggerations, and deceptions grow more outlandish, the yearning to believe them grows stronger.

What we're really talking about here is the big lonesome heart of the West. Our culture has carried on such an epic romance here that the rest of the world tends to see all Americans as part cowboys. Maybe we are.
--Douglas H. Chadwick, "Sagebrush Country: America's Outback"

Rustic images promote public support for public lands ranching. But look at the land.

Why, really, is ranching so romantically appealing? Do Americans dream of stringing barbed wire, burning calves with hot irons, and driving about the landscape dumping salt blocks from pickups? No. What they really yearn for is a satisfying life in the wide open Western spaces. They want escape, relaxation, simplicity, contentment, security, independence, excitement, opportunity, wealth, status, power, and all the myriad nebulous things ranching rightly or wrongly represents -- not ranching.

Yet the public lands rancher, through association, uses their Western romanticism to make a clean sweep of their sympathies. The reality of ranching is minimized, the fantasy maximized. In a Western movie, when a couple of cowboys pull a bawling calf from quicksand, the event is a great humanitarian deed. On the real range, you can bet those two cowboys are a hell of a lot more concerned about the animal's dollar potential than the animal itself. Indeed, the things they do to animals would turn many people's stomachs.

To the American public, ranching represents the best of the West. Yet most people if they more fully understood ranching would find it offensive or repulsive.

Romanticism/nostalgia is one of the strongest human emotions. Nevertheless, if we realize that our sentimentality toward public lands ranching is *misdirected* as a result of lifelong, massive doses of cowboy romance, we may begin to overcome or redirect it. We don't have to embrace anything and everything "Western." Public lands ranching is a hard-nosed business, not a sentimental journey.

Under the symbol of the West, most of the West suffers.

Thanks to a barrage of "Western" motion pictures and TV dramas that were presented during their formative years, George and Martha Middle America sincerely believe they will never ever have a backyard hamburger barbecue if the Marlboro Man is not permitted to keep a'ridin' on public range. . . . The fact that the vast bulk of America's livestock is raised back East without a lot of yelling, hollering, horseback riding, and wearing of picturesque costumes is somewhat disappointing from a romantic point of view, but it is a fact that may lead to a more rational discussion of public land use.
--P.J. Ryan, editor of *Thunderbear*

And there are still more obstacles to overcome. Upon those who would challenge public lands ranching, various psychological pressures are brought to bear.

For example, as concerned persons become aware of the problem, many of them call for vast livestock reductions. But when confronted with a sob story of hard-workin', financially strapped cowpokes, they become guilt-ridden and back down. A vague but overpowering cowboy sentimentality wells up inside them, and suddenly potential activists are suggesting timid reforms or tax-sponsored range "improvements," rather than the needed stock reductions or removals. Meanwhile, these same ranchers chide "bleeding heart environmentalists" for trying to save Endangered species.

Want to avoid confrontation?
--Sit on a fence.
Wanna play it safe?
--Sit on a fence.
Don't care what happens?
--Keep sittin' on that barbed-wire fence.

The voice of moderation and compromise
While the Earth goes to hell

--Anonymous

As I reflect upon this situation, I see that values based upon an unpopular ethic are a luxury many people cannot afford to conceptualize, let alone embrace.
--Donald J. Barnes in *A Matter of Change* from **In Defense of Animals**

Stop-ranching advocates are castigated as closed-minded and selfish. Yet, all components of the ranching establishment are geared toward perpetuating ranching and their involvement in it. Detached, scientific objectivity is a myth used to quell opposition. Activists convinced to withdraw to extrinsic non-involvement are nullified as agents of change.

If you object to public lands ranching, you will likewise be scorned a fault-finder, a detractor -- someone with a negative attitude who only works *against* something. If you were a "constructive" person, they insist, you would be working to "improve" the grazing industry, not "tear it down." Being in the position of attacking the status quo puts you at a distinct disadvantage. In a recent local newspaper editorial, letters to the editor disputing public lands ranching were termed "a blast at ranchers and the rural West," while those from ranchers were portrayed as constructive comments by working folks trying to protect their livelihood and our Western saga.

If, understandably, you display emotion -- anger, sadness, etc. -- at ranching's environmental plunder, tax ripoff, social or political oppression, you are unlikely to be taken seriously. Meanwhile, public lands ranchers are *expected* to show anger, sadness, etc. because they are "personally involved" in protecting "their" interests.

What is right has always been called radical by those with a stake in things that are wrong.
--George McGovern, 1972

You allegedly promote a wild fantasy by an elite special interest group. You are a radical, escapist, malcontent, troublemaker, cow or cowboy hater. Your self-worth and validity are stripped away by a society that does not respect you or take you seriously unless you embrace its cowboy reality.

Pressures you never knew existed, pressures you cannot consciously comprehend, gradually dampen your spirit and erode your will to resist. As did a couple of "thought criminals" in George Orwell's **1984**, you may come to understand the overwhelming influence cultural reality has over each of us. Or you may never realize why your emotions seem at odds with what you think.

> ***Culture is the creator of our reality,***
> ***and a steamroller over nonconformity.***

Thus, people who feel comfortable tackling other issues often cannot stand the stress associated with the ranching issue -- perhaps most of all, the *self-imposed* pressure to support and promote ranching that compels each of us deep inside. This, combined with a lack of understanding of the issue, keep most potential stop-ranching activists from getting involved. According to Colorado activist Eric Holle,

Environmentalists can usually get folks riled about clearcutting, strip mining, dolphin slaughters, or toxic dumps. The more radical groups put their bodies in front of bulldozers, whalers' harpoons, or shipments of nuclear waste, and some even dangle 80 feet up in redwoods to save the last old growth forests. Yet even the most daring of the Earth-savers seem reluctant to take on the single greatest threat to our Western public lands: the cow.

Indeed, if even a fraction as many people had worked as long and hard on public lands ranching as most of these other issues, it would probably have been ended long ago.

It is one thing to pull on your Tony Lamas in the morning; it is another to feel a cowboy boot crash into your face.
--Tom Wolf, "'Wyoming' Is Dead -- Long Live 'Wyoming'" (Wolf 1988)

People's hesitancy to get involved is understandable, though, in light of other possible consequences. The ranching industry radically differs from all others in organization and distribution of power. Though comparatively not numerous, public lands ranches are so widely and strategically dispersed and effectively located throughout nearly all of the rural West that the arrangement would do any army general proud. They accommodate an extensive network of powerful -- *and well-armed* -- individuals and groups, capable of exerting not only economic, social, and political pressure, but physical force against whoever threatens the status quo.

Stockmen are used to getting their way -- so much so that they feel persecuted if they don't. They see violence as a legitimate, traditional means of defending their business interests and "their" territory from "outsiders." Meanwhile, the worshipping public supports violence as a rustic -- even admirable -- part of cowboy character. After all, John Wayne and the cowboy good guys were always justified in using force; weren't they always in the right?

Ranchers have used property damage, threats, harassment, and bodily harm to suppress opposition. Fortunately, however, when it comes to physical assault contemporary ranchers seem to be more vocalization than action. They talk tough to intimidate opposition and build self-confidence, especially when grouped together at meetings or in cowboy bars. But they rarely follow through with their threats, relying instead on their traditional macho image to keep people in line. While stockmen are famous for using force to get their way, few are the fearless rangeland gladiators they pretend to be. Like most bullies, they usually back down when confronted alone by those they seek to terrorize. Of the score of hate letters I have received in the past few years, most and by far the most hostile were from public lands "ranchers' wives" (as they almost invariably describe themselves).

This is not, however, to belittle the potential for violence. A gun or a can of gasoline and a match can make anyone a serious threat. In my years of involvement, I have heard (mostly second-hand) many threats against me personally. However, I have yet to be physically assaulted (other than having lug nuts on my vehicle loosened twice -- nearly causing high-speed wheel losses involving me, my two children, and friends -- and having a placard jerked from my hands at an otherwise peaceful demonstration). *Livestock Market Digest* Executive Editor Lee Pitts states that "there is a group of cowboys on public lands in the West who would like to string Jacobs up." I take that threat seriously -- but not too seriously. Those who take reasonable precautions should have little to fear. And as involvement in this effort grows, threats to individuals will decrease.

Fear remains prevalent, however. Over the years, scores of potential activists have confided to me that they would like to become openly involved, but are afraid due to ranchers' penchant for physical violence.

The widely dispersed nature of public lands ranching and its impacts likewise makes it extremely difficult to pin down and combat. Whereas activists usually can see definite progress (or definite lack of it) on most other issues, their efforts to reform or eliminate public lands ranching instead seem to disappear into some kind of black hole. Changes occur in small, often imperceptible increments and cannot be gauged by common standards of measurement. There is little central focus to hold one's attention and involvement, little evident progress or reward for one's efforts. In these contemporary times of instant gratification and jaded sensibilities, this may be discouraging, frustrating, or infuriating. It is easy to throw up your hands and quit, as many stop-public-ranching activists eventually do.

On the other hand, public graziers have a veritable catalogue of justifications for maintaining their power establishment. Any of these, and numerous other clever diversions, can be and often are employed to make sure potential opponents don't see the forest for the trees. With this issue, as perhaps no other, it is easy to lose oneself in trivialities. Keep the perspective. Don't let the vested interests obscure your vision with irrelevant obstacles.

The ranching establishment has yet another overwhelming but subtle means of maintaining the status quo -- assimilation. We are offered participation in grazing allotment and land management plans, a chance to speak at public hearings, memberships on boards and committees, invitations to meetings and conferences, visits to public lands ranches . . . . While all of these are potentially worthwhile pursuits, they are as well integral components of, and calculated to perpetuate, the status quo. They solicit minor modifications but reject and neglect any possibility of fundamental change. They cause one to become lost in a maze of trivialities and to lose commitment to the overall problem. And they are all based on the presumption that ranching should and will continue indefinitely at or near traditional levels.

In being allowed participation in this system, we come to believe that we can make a difference; when in fact the inherent structure of the system prohibits us from making any real difference. Through personal involvement in this system we come to feel part of it and in the long run to protect and promote it, regardless of original intent. By being integrated into and absorbed by the very system we need to change we are co-opted and neutralized as agents of real change.

If you are like me, you may strongly disagree with much of what someone does, or with what the group s/he represents does, but still like that person as an individual. Most of our imagined enemies become friends if we spend enough time with them.

For this reason, some perceptive public lands ranchers and their advocacy groups deliberately foster relationships between ranchers and those who oppose or might oppose public lands ranching. It is an ancient strategy -- a form of cooption. When an activist or potential activist becomes emotionally involved with a permittee, that person is much less likely to *feel* like opposing her new-found friend's ranching operation, or public lands ranching in general. Few of us are willing to invite rejection by a friend, especially when that friend warns that our potential actions would cause them hardship.

An example of this situation is the "6-6 Club" in Arizona. Six representatives each from the conservation and public lands ranching communities meet regularly in a social setting, allegedly to foster communication and cooperation between the two. This all sounds nice, but what has actually happened is that the stockmen maintain -- as always -- that their livestock operations shall never be significantly reduced, while some of the conservationists have been neutralized as agents of real change. Through cooptive socialization, the former activists are becoming decreasingly effective, and they now function primarily to *promote* their new comrades' public lands ranching operations by proposing various ineffectual mitigation techniques and disparaging stop-ranching advocates. These 6-6 members now enjoy the widespread social and political approval they never had with an "anti-cowboy" image.

Many stockmen do not, of course, purposefully misuse their relationships with those who might oppose public lands ranching, but generally friendships between stockmen and activists strongly favor the status quo. Most times when a rancher suddenly wants to be your friend, he has more than friendship in mind.

This is merely to discourage deceitful relationships and cooption and to encourage honest friendships and effective activism.

Natural existence has an elegant beauty, amazingly interactive diversity, and profound intelligence that beckons us home.

"This flower you want to save," asked the rancher testily, "is it good for anything?"

"We don't know yet. But if you see a bolt on the ground, do you throw it away?"

"Course not. I might need it some day."

"We feel the same way," said the botanist, "about the prairie carnation."

--from "Quietly Conserving Nature," *National Geographic* (Dec 1988)

Finally, while most Americans enjoy the great outdoors, few show much real connection to their surroundings. For most, Nature is merely a setting for "outdoor sports." Like most ranchers, they think of the environment as a collection of "natural resources" put here for human use or pleasure. Even the botanist quoted above seems compelled to justify the prairie carnation's existence with a claim of potential human use.

We must abandon these anthropocentric notions. Without a fundamental change in our relationship with Nature, there is little hope for long-term environmental health, or our own survival. We need to *reconnect* with the Earth, or we will ultimately ruin it (unless, of course, we destroy ourselves first -- a fair possibility). In the long run, this planet can only sustain itself -- including us -- if we allow it to return to a more natural existence by returning ourselves to a more natural existence.

Fortunately, this is entirely possible. Despite our seemingly irreconcilable split from Nature, each of us retains deep within the instinct to live naturally (though generally it fades more each year). Regardless of the artificial reality we create, we remain of, by, and for this planet. Ultimately, we may save the Earth only by *rejoining* it.

Meanwhile, we must act to neutralize the most serious environmental threats. Ranching, as the most harmful and least justifiable use of Western public land, needs our immediate attention.

Recreationist; hunter, fisher, or animal rightist; sightseer, picnicker, hiker, equestrian, biker, camper, or backpacker; vegetarian or meat-eater; environmentalist, conservationist, or affected consumptive user; naturalist, scientist, or archaeologist; social justice or political reform advocate; back-to-the-lander; watershed user, farmer, or private lands rancher; rural motorist or resident; taxpayer; Nature-ist; concerned Earth-dweller -- all have good reason to get involved. And, while such diverse interests can't always work together, in this case they may work for the same goal.

Having read this book, you know why public lands ranching must be stopped. The following section offers ideas on what you can do to help stop it. Choose something that interests you and suits you, then *do it*. Whatever you do, *keep involved* in some way. Good intentions are fine, but *action* is what matters most.

*** *Note: Please make copies of any or all of the following pages and distribute. (The Public Lands Ripoff page would go well on the reverse side of the petition.) Pages are standard 8 1/2" X 11" for easy copying.*

The single most significant issue we face, that of massive overgrazing of our public lands, is virtually being ignored. . . .

After years of fruitlessly trying to convince the national groups to help us, and months of personal soul searching, I have resigned my position as Northwest Director of the National Wildlife Federation. There is no doubt in my mind that if we are to end the senseless destruction of our public lands, we will have to do the job ourselves. . . .

*Since leaving the NWF, I have joined with other activists to set up a west-wide, grass-roots organization whose main function is to, quite simply, end public-lands welfare ranching. We are **not** interested in charging higher fees for the destruction of our public lands. We are **not** interested in expanding or maintaining grazing under the so-called "better management" scenario. The plain truth is, you **can not** manage livestock on fragile, arid public lands. We are no longer willing to spend days, months, or even years touring our ravaged lands with BLM employees and the cattle industry, listening to one excuse after another about why nothing can be done . . . .*

Please join with us.

--Bruce Apple, Executive Director, Rest the West

(Brush Wolf)

*** WHAT YOU CAN DO TO HELP ***
*** WHAT YOU CAN DO TO HELP ***

(Please copy and distribute this and the following pages.)

(Brush Wolf)

Protecting something as wide as this planet is still an abstraction for many. Yet I see the day in our lifetime that reverence for the natural systems -- the oceans, the rain forests, the soil, the grasslands, and all other living things -- will be so strong that no narrow ideology based upon politics or economics will overcome it.
--California Governor Jerry Brown

For more than a century the ranching industry has chomped, stomped, fenced, roaded, bladed, burned, churned, chained, poisoned, and generally trashed the West -- more so than any other land user. Yet, the Imperial Graziers -- using about 300 million acres of our public land and about 2 billion tax and private dollars annually -- relentlessly continue their business-as-usual. Reform is useless. One hundred years is long enough! If you think it is time to break their social and political grip over the rural West, if you want to save billions of dollars, if you want to restore public land to more natural health, then take action to stop public lands ranching.

● **Be informed.** Through the various means discussed in this book and other sources, learn about public lands and public lands ranching.

● **Communicate with others what you have learned.** Spread the real story of welfare ranching; arouse the sleeping masses.

● **Submit written comments or speak at public hearings on Bureau of Land Management, Forest Service, and other public land use plans.** Though "the planning process" largely is a game designed to promote traditional commercial interests, your input may help.

Two guides for public participation in ranching decisions in land use planning are available. One is for the Forest Service:

> *Participating in Livestock Grazing Decisions on the National Forests: A Citizen's Handbook*, 1025 Clubhouse Dr., Prescott, AZ 86303.

Another is for the BLM:

> *How Not To Be Cowed: An Owners' Manual for the Public Lands*, Southern Utah Wilderness Alliance, 436 Alameda, Salt Lake City, UT 84111.

Both are very worthwhile publications. Send a few dollars or whatever you can afford to cover costs.

BLM according to BLM.

● **Adopt an allotment.** BLM regulations and Forest Service policy provide for public participation in allotment management. Write the relevant local BLM or Forest Service office explaining how you are affected by ranching (it degrades your hiking, fishing, birding, swimming, aesthetic enjoyment, and/or whatever) in a certain area and request that you be designated an *affected interest* with respect to the grazing allotment(s) in that area. Once you are so designated, the agencies should consult with you whenever they formulate or amend an allotment management plan(s) or adjust livestock numbers on the allotment(s) in that area. Insist that they do. (See Feller 1990 in bibliography for details.)

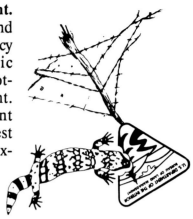

● **Write, phone, or visit elected representatives and others with power to make changes.** Ask them to do whatever necessary to stop public lands ranching. (Particularly, ask your political representatives to introduce legislation to ban it.) Take your stand and do not compromise.

Many politicians and other powers-that-be are as uninformed on this issue as the average citizen. Explain or demonstrate the ranching problem for them; provide statistics and visual aids if possible. Ask them what they plan to do about the problem, and then follow up later. Pursue the issue until they cannot ignore it.

They will have a hard time ignoring it if they see what you are talking about with their own eyes. Getting "VIPs" out on the range to experience ranching effects firsthand could be invaluable.

Letters generally carry more clout than phone calls, telegrams, and such, and are one of the best means of influencing policy decisions. They are most effective when expressed in your own words, handwritten or individually typed. Be brief, sensible, and to the point; tell them what you think and how you feel. Ask them exactly where they stand on the issue, and if they don't give you a decent answer, hound them until they do. Don't be intimidated by their aloofness or self-importance; they are *supposed* to represent you.

Make contact today, especially with:

- The President: 1600 Pennsylvania Ave., NW, Washington, DC 20500, (202) 456-1414

- US Senators: Senator ____, United States Senate, Washington, DC 20510, (202) 224-2115

- US Representatives: Representative ____, United States House of Representatives, Washington, DC 20515, (202) 225-7000

- The Secretary of the Interior: Secretary, US Dept. of the Interior, 18th & "C" Sts., NW, Washington, DC 20240, (202) 343-7351

- The Director of the Bureau of Land Management: Director, BLM, Dept. of the Interior, Washington, DC 20240, (202) 343-3801

- The Secretary of the Department of Agriculture: Secretary, US Dept. of Agriculture, 14th St. & Jefferson Dr., SW, Washington, DC 20250, (202) 447-3631

- The Chief of the United States Forest Service: Chief, US Forest Service, USDA, P.O. Box 2417, Washington, DC 20013, (202) 447-6661

- The Director of the United States Fish & Wildlife Service: Director, US Fish & Wildlife Service, Interior Bldg., 18th & C Sts., NW, Washington, DC 20240, (202) 343-4717

- The Director of the Environmental Protection Agency: Director, US Environmental Protection Agency, 401 "M" St., SW, Washington, DC 20460, (202) 382-2090

- Other Important Targets: State governors, senators, and representatives; state land departments and other agencies; county commissioners; public land user organizations; and any other entities with the clout to change land use policy.

- **Contribute time, energy, and money to organizations that work to reduce or eliminate public lands ranching.** (A partial list follows this section.) But don't just join and then expect the group to do the work for you; *your individual action* makes the difference! Most of these organizations need a good push to give them the courage to more effectively confront the ranching establishment.

- **Try to draw other groups into the stop-public-ranching effort.** Many diverse organizations don't yet realize that it is in their best interest to oppose public lands ranching. Inform them. Form coalitions.

- **Drive a wedge between private lands ranchers and their unfair competition -- public lands ranchers.** Communicate with private lands livestock organizations and individuals, enlightening them and asking them to withdraw their support for welfare ranchers.

> *Don't take yourself too seriously; recognize that your adversaries are not necessarily driven by evil; demonstrate a sense of humor; and don't try to con anybody.*
> --Brant Calkin, long-time environmental advocate

- **Dismember the Marlboro Man.** Promote the novel concept that cowboys and ranchers are mere mortals after all and do not warrant extra-special treatment.

- **Eat *less* beef.** This need not entail vegetarianism. Eating cow from nearly any source is relatively wasteful and destructive. Reducing our collective consumption of cow by 3% would make up the difference for what is produced on all public land. Any reduction in cow consumption will help the land, our health, and our economic well-being.

● **Boycott public-lands-raised meat.** Though usually it is very difficult to trace where a dead cow (or sheep) spent its life by the time it reaches a fast-food counter or supermarket shelf, it is possible in some cases. (If in doubt, don't buy.) Tell people why you choose to lessen beef consumption or boycott beef. (To support the national beef boycott, write: Fergusons, Star Route, Bates, OR 97817.)

● **Refuse to ranch.** Buy or rent a ranch and stop ranching. Obtain a public grazing permit and refuse to graze.

● **Organize locally.** Seek like-minded others in your area. Plan a protest, conference, endangered species fair, press release, or other action to educate people about the issue.

● **Canvass door to door.** Carry information and petitions; garner support; raise money.

Stop-public-lands-ranching petitions.

● **Organize a fund raiser.** A concert, video showing, bake sale, raffle, or whatever will raise money and draw attention to the issue.

A shopper eating lunch reads a free handout on public lands ranching she picked up in the store.

● **Use the power of the press.** Design and distribute stop-ranching bumperstickers, petitions, flyers, and such. (Ideas and source materials can be obtained from some of the organizations listed in the next section.) Make copies of worthwhile articles on public lands ranching and spread them around. *Make copies of these pages as a handout and spread them!*

Bulk printing can be surprisingly inexpensive. A 1-page fact sheet can be printed in bulk for less than a penny per sheet. *Free Our Public Lands!*, a 48-page, newspaper-sized tabloid I self-published in 1986, cost only 15 cents per copy to print 100,000 copies. Bumperstickers can be produced for less than 10 cents apiece.

Compile, borrow, or rent lists of concerned individuals and do bulk mailings. Mail literature to influential organizations, politicians, and others.

Printed matter can also be passed out on street corners, at parks and malls, and left on vehicles in parking lots. Information tables can be set up at fairs, outside stores, on campuses, etc. To reach public land users more effectively, hand out literature at public campgrounds, recreation areas, popular tourist spots, hunting or hiking club meetings, and the like. Go directly to the agencies and distribute materials to employees in BLM, Forest Service, state land, and other government offices. For true adventure, pass out your stop-ranching material at livestock association meetings.

IDEAS FOR STICKERS, POSTERS, ETC.

*BEEF: BAD FOR THE ENVIRONMENT, ECONOMY, HEALTH
*BOYCOTT PUBLIC LANDS BEEF
*COWS OFF PUBLIC LANDS
*DON'T WASTE PUBLIC LAND WITH CATTLE
*END OPEN RANGE
*END PUBLIC LANDS RANCHING
*GET LIVESTOCK OFF PUBLIC LANDS
*GET RANCHERS OFF PUBLIC LANDS
*LIVESTOCK DON'T BELONG ON PUBLIC LANDS
*LIVESTOCK GRAZING KILLS FISH & WILDLIFE
*NO MORE WELFARE COWBOYS
*NO MORE WELFARE RANCHING

*PROTECT OUR ENVIRONMENT: STOP PUBLIC LANDS RANCHING
*PUBLIC LANDS DON'T BELONG TO RANCHERS
*PUBLIC LANDS GRAZING = WELFARE RANCHING
*PUBLIC LANDS RANCHING RIPOFF
*PUBLIC WILDLIFE, NOT PRIVATE LIVESTOCK
*RANCHING RUINS PUBLIC LAND
*RANCHING RUINS SOIL, WATER, WILDLIFE
*RECLAIM PUBLIC LANDS: STOP WELFARE RANCHING
*STOP PUBLIC LANDS RANCHING
*STOP WELFARE RANCHING
*WASTE OF THE WEST: RANCHING
*WELFARE RANCHING = PUBLIC LANDS RIPOFF

● **Use the media.** Write letters to the editors of newspapers and periodicals. This is an easy way for anyone to express an opinion and expose the issue. Submit articles, photos, and graphics. Or, once you learn the issue, go on a radio or TV talk show. Urge the media to publicize the issue; provide them informative material; visit their offices and talk with them face to face. Anticipate, however, that they will glorify cowboyism at every opportunity -- and at your expense.

Or produce your own stop-ranching message and run it in the various media. Conversely, complain about and discredit misleading or inaccurate pro-ranching media disseminations.

● **Develop a stop-ranching educational program.** Present it to a school, church, special interest group, conservation or environmental organization, civic group, or the general public. Give a talk, concert, video or slide show, photo or other visual exhibit, or whatever. All these can be produced even by amateurs, and some organizations offer financial and technical help. Photo and various audio/visual exhibits can be displayed at fairs, museums, banks, and other public places.

● **Organize a stop-public-lands-ranching demonstration.** Many have already taken place around the West. They have been effective in reaching the public, and with increasing numbers of demonstrations (and therefore, increasing public awareness) the government is beginning to get a message it cannot ignore.

Demonstrations are a form of expression and communication. They can be as small and simple as a couple of people with signs walking up and down a sidewalk or as large and complex as you want to make them. Convey your message to as many people (and as many *influential* people) as possible, with the minimum expense and effort necessary to do so. Contact television, radio, and newspapers in advance, and make your demonstration offer something memorable to their viewers, listeners, and readers.

(Lynne Bohi)

Because public lands ranching occurs in every part of every Western state, possible locations for demonstrations are practically limitless. Any BLM, Forest Service, or state land office is good, as are many offices of federal or state fish and game departments, pro-welfare-ranching politicians, ADC, APHIS, SCS, ASCS, and county and state agricultural extensions are possibilities, as are colleges of range science, agriculture, and natural resources and livestock boards, agricultural committees, and stockmen's associations. Highly visible events, such as hearings, conferences, and conventions, are among the best targets for demonstrations. Other possibilities include parades, rodeos, and county fairs. Best of all, but perhaps most difficult to attract media to, is public land itself; stage an event or outing.

Romantic cowboy images parade below as protestors illegally hang a stop-public-lands-ranching banner high above. *(Mike Stabler)*

● **Consider planning a "non-violent direct action."** Civil disobedience or CD, is a symbolic, yet sometimes functional, illegal action. Protesters in these actions prepare for arrest, hoping that, whether they are arrested or not, more attention will be drawn to the issue. The plan might be to refuse cops' orders to disperse, physically block a roadway, occupy a government office, drive a cow off public land and into a nearby BLM office, or any of an infinite number of graphic possibilities.

Non-violent direct actions generally should be planned well in advance with the help of experienced protesters. Participants need to be honest, committed, and creative, and should understand what chances they are taking and be willing to accept the consequences. Direct actions involve an element of risk, but the results can be well worth it.

● **Consider legal action.** When (mis)management agencies are not protecting the land and politicians hardly listen, legal action is one possible alternative. Over the years, various public lands ranching-related lawsuits have been filed, though mostly with limited success. However, many legal avenues, some with great potential, have yet to be explored.

In fact, if existing environmental, pollution, land use, public welfare, and other laws were strictly enforced, public ranching operations would be shut down throughout nearly all of the West. National Environmental Policy Act; Clean Water Act; Endangered Species Act; Federal Land Policy and Management Act; Public Rangelands Improvement Act; agency failures to enforce grazing regulations; BLM and Forest Service policy directives requiring resource protection, true multiple use, and sustained yield; public participation in agency land management planning; legislation requiring fair market value for sale or lease of publicly owned resources; antiquated state open range laws; deficit state lands grazing -- all these and much more afford opportunities for legal action.

Public lands ranching is rife with indefensible practices. The public is beginning to reject the ranching imperative, and the courts eventually will have to uphold legal mandates. With a little time, effort, and money, important legal precedents could be set.

(Helen Wilson)

In Memory of the Slain Jaguar of the Chiricahuas

● **Take The Bull by the horns.** A growing number of people are disillusioned with a ranching-bound government that refuses to protect the public and its land. Their years of efforts and appeals to reform public lands ranching have yielded little substantive change, and our governments apparently do not intend to *ever* significantly curtail ranching (in fact, quite the opposite). A diversity of interests are tired of trying in vain to change the situation through culturally sanctioned means. They question a system that promotes the waste of the West, and that considers the implements of that destruction sacred.

Some of these people have begun sabotaging -- *monkeywrenching* -- the machinery and developments that enable the ranching establishment to ravage public land. They cut fences; leave gates open; drive cattle onto neighboring allotments; decommission destructive ranching machinery; damage pumps, windmills, and stock tanks; dismantle and burn corrals, pens, and ramps; close ranching roads; leave stop-ranching messages on livestock road signs; dispose of salt blocks; remove traps and poisons; and generally do what they can to thwart the industry's ability to continue business-as-usual.

To pursue this kind of environmental defense is a personal decision. Each individual who chooses to act, whether working in a small group or alone, should fully understand and feel comfortable with what s/he is doing. All participants should keep in mind that what they are doing *is* highly illegal, and that the consequences of arrest could

be substantial. Monkeywrenching is a form of *non-violent* direct action; that is, it should never endanger the physical safety of anyone. The job should be done as simply, safely, and effectively as possible.

[The author neither advocates nor disadvocates the above, but recommends the book **Ecodefense** (Foreman 1986) for those interested in such activity.]

● **Visit public land often.** Take the time to know it. While there watch for signs of overgrazing or overstocking, as well as permit violations, unauthorized developments, obsolete roads and fences, and other destructive range situations. If you see anything of the sort, report it to the appropriate government agency personnel (and perhaps the media). Whatever they say, demand that corrective action be taken, then follow up to see that they have done it.

● **Other possibilities for effective action are as unlimited as your imagination.** Here are 3 novel examples: (1) In Arizona one man is currently organizing a united year-long fast. Participants in the fast may commit themselves to abstaining from solid food for 1 week at a time as a symbolic protest against public lands ranching. (2) Activists in Colorado dumped 200 pounds of cow pies in front of a Forest Service district ranger office to protest destructive ranching in the nearby National Forest. (3) Many people have suggested as a symbolic protest mailing public land cow pies to the directors of government land managing agencies and selected politicians.

> *The concerned individual carefully considers many options. S/he chooses those that feel right, are fun and most effective. The important thing is to get involved and stay involved in some way, however small.*

CONTACTS

The following entities work to eliminate or reform public lands ranching; the first 6 advocate more or less total cessation, while the remainder thus far recommend various degrees of reform:

- **Free Our Public Lands!**, Lynn Jacobs (contact), P.O. Box 5784, Tucson, Arizona 85703, (602) 578-3173. Contact for information, literature, stickers, referral, and other help. Correspondence, questions, suggestions, support: all are welcome.

- **Public Lands Action Network**, P.O. Box 5631, Santa Fe, New Mexico 87502, (505) 984-1428. Publishes *PLAN* newsletter quarterly (dedicated solely to the public lands ranching issue).

- **Earth First!**, P.O. Box 5176, Missoula, MT 59806, (406) 728-8114. *(EF! Journal* office; EF! has no head-quarters.) Publishes *Earth First! Journal* 8 times yearly. Loans a stop-public-lands-ranching slide-show.

- *Wild Earth*, P.O.Box 492, Canton, NY 13617, (315)379-9940. Quarterly journal focusing on wilderness, wildlife, habitat, and biodiversity.

- **Ranching Task Force**, Linda Wells (contact), P.O. Box 41652, Tucson, AZ 85717, (602) 327-9973. Contact for information, literature, stop-public-lands-ranching slide-show, T-shirts, etc.

- **Rest the West**, Bruce Apple (contact), P.O. Box 68345, Portland, OR 97268, (503) 645-6293, 653-9781.

- **Natural Resources Defense Council**, 71 Stevenson St., #1825, San Francisco, CA 94105, (415) 777-0220. National NRDC publishes *Newsline* newsletter 6 times yearly and *The Amicus Journal* 4 times yearly; both available from 122 East 42nd Street, New York, NY 10168, (212) 949-0049.

- **Defenders of Wildlife**, 1244 19th St., NW, Washington, DC 20036, (202) 659-9510. Publishes *Activist Network News* newsletter bimonthly and *Defenders* magazine bimonthly.

- **National Audubon Society**, 950 Third Ave., New York, NY 10022, (212) 832-3200. Publishes *Audubon Activist* newsletter and *Audubon* magazine, both bimonthly.

- **Sierra Club Public Lands Committee**, P.O. Box 8409, Reno, NV 89507, (702) 747-4237. Publishes *Public Lands* quarterly, available from Sierra Club Public Lands Committee, C/O J. Hopkins, 3316 Cutter Place, Davis, CA 95616.

- **Sierra Club**, 730 Polk St., San Francisco, CA 94109, (415) 776-2211. Publishes *Sierra* magazine bimonthly.

- *The Animals' Agenda*, P.O. Box 6809, Syracuse, NY 13217 (subscriptions); P.O.Box 5234, Westport, CT 06881, (203) 226-8826 (other). Bimonthly animal rights magazine that takes public lands ranching seriously.

- *High Country News*, P.O. Box 1090, Paonia, CO 81428, (303) 527-4898. Biweekly journal focusing on Western land use issues; much on ranching.

- **Earth Island Institute**, 300 Broadway, Suite 28, San Francisco, California 94133, (415) 788-3666. Publishes *Earth Island Journal* quarterly.

- **The Wilderness Society**, 900 17th St., NW, #400, Washington, DC 20006, (202)842-3400. Publishes *Wilderness* magazine quarterly.

- **Environmental Defense Fund**, 257 Park Ave. South, New York, NY 10010, (212) 686-4191.

- **National Wildlife Federation**, 1412 Sixteenth Street, NW, Washington, DC 20036, (202) 637-3700. Publishes *National Wildlife* magazine bimonthly.

- **Wildlife Management Institute**, Suite 725, 1101 14th Street, NW, Washington, DC 20005, (202) 371-1808. Publishes *Outdoor News Bulletin* biweekly.

- **Association of Forest Service Employees for Environmental Ethics**, P.O. Box 11615, Eugene, OR 97440. (503) 484-2692. Publishes *Inner Voice* newsletter quarterly.

- **The Nature Conservancy**, 1815 N. Lynn St., Arlington, VA 22209, (703) 841-5300. Publishes *Nature Conservancy* magazine bimonthly; for political reasons usually does not publicly advocate cessation of ranching, but its actions often speak that language.

- *Wildlife Damage Review*, P.O.Box 2541, Tucson, AZ 85702. (602) 882-4218.A quarterly newsletter: "Our goal is the elimination of the Animal Damage Control program as it currently operates."

PUBLIC LANDS RANCHING ROUNDUP

According to government and private sources, livestock ranching on our Western public land:

- Utilizes roughly 75% of Western federal, state, and local publicly owned land -- **41% of the West.**

- Has destroyed more **native vegetation** than any other land use.

- Has destroyed more **wildlife and wildlife habitat** than any other land use.

- Has caused more **soil erosion and soil damage** than any other land use.

- Has destroyed more **riparian area** than any other land use.

- Has destroyed, depleted, and polluted more natural **water sources** than any other land use.

- Has caused more ruinous **flooding** than any other land use.

- Has caused more invasions of **animal pests and non-native vegetation** than any other land use.

- Has eliminated more beneficial **natural fire** than any other land use.

- Has been the cause of more developments on public land and **environmental damage from developments** thereon than any other land use.

- Produces only **3% of US beef.**

- Includes roughly 30,000 permittees -- only 16% of Western stockmen and only **2% of US stockmen.**

- Costs federal permittees only $1.81/AUM* in 1990 (a high year) -- about **1/5 fair market value**, causing an average annual loss of about $50 million to the US Treasury.

- Causes a total net federal, state, and local **tax loss of roughly $1 billion annually**, if all impacts from public lands ranching are considered.

- Causes a total net **private economic loss of roughly $1 billion annually.**

- Causes **untold hardship** to rural residents, motorists, and visitors.

- Produces an estimated **$550 million in livestock annually** -- far less than what taxpayers spend on the industry.

- Rarely contributes more than 5% gross to rural economies and probably **detracts from most local economies** if lost recreation opportunities, depleted natural resources, wasted local tax monies, damages to private property, etc. are considered.

- **Detracts more from other uses of public land** than any other land use.

- Has caused **more political and social problems** associated with Western public land than any other land use.

*AUM: Animal Unit Month or roughly the food required by a cow for 1 month

PETITION

We consider commercial livestock production on public/government land to be economically, socially, politically, and environmentally destructive and unjustifiable. We ask the President, Congress, Bureau of Land Management, Forest Service, states, counties, and other relevant government entities to take all measures necessary to eliminate all commercial livestock production on all public/government land.

Signature_____ Name(printed)_____

Address_____

Signature_____ Name(printed)_____

Address_____

Signature_____ Name(printed)_____

Address_____

Signature_____ Name(printed)_____

Address_____

Signature_____ Name(printed)_____

Address_____

Signature_____ Name(printed)_____

Address_____

Signature_____ Name(printed)_____

Address_____

Signature_____ Name(printed)_____

Address_____

Signature_____ Name(printed)_____

Address_____

Signature_____ Name(printed)_____

Address_____

*Please make copies and send to: your Senator, Representative, or other chosen relevant government entity.

PUBLIC LANDS RANCHING
* STATISTICS *
for the
ELEVEN WESTERN STATES
(Arizona, California, Colorado, Idaho, Montana, Nevada, New Mexico, Oregon, Utah, Washington, Wyoming)

RANCHING AND LAND OWNERSHIP

(Figures are based on 1986-87 USDA, USDI, and other federal publications. Figures are approximate and vary little yearly.)

• % of West administered by BLM (177 million acres)	24%
• % of BLM-administered Western land used for ranching (163 million acres)	92%
• **% of West ranched on BLM land (163 million acres)**	**22%**
• % of West administered by Forest Service (141 million acres)	19%
• % of Western Forest Service System land used for ranching (97 million acres)	69%
• **% of West ranched on Forest Service System land (97 million acres)**	**13%**
• % of West administered by BLM and Forest Service (318 million acres)	42%
• % of Western BLM and Forest Service System land ranched (260 million acres)	82%
• **% of West ranched on BLM and Forest Service land (260 million acres)**	**35%**
• % of West ranched on other federal land (5 million acres)	1%
• % of West federal land (360 million acres)	48%
• % of Western federal land ranched (265 million acres)	74%
• % of West ranched on state land (36 million acres)	5%
• % of West ranched on county, city, and miscellaneous government land (5 million acres)	1%
• **% of West publicly owned (418 million acres)**	**56%**
• **% of Western publicly owned land ranched (306 million acres)**	**73%**
• **% of West ranched on publicly owned land (306 million acres)**	**41%**
• % of West ranched on Indian reservation land (35 million acres)	5%
• % of West privately owned (295 million acres)	39%
• % of West not-ranched private land (106 million acres)*	14%
• **% of West ranched on private land (184 million acres)**	**25%**
• **% of West ranched (525 million acres)**	**70%**
• % of ranched West public land (306 million acres)	58%
• **Total land area of 11 Western states**	**750 million acres**

* Includes urban land, 12 million acres of livestock pasture, and 66 million acres of cropland, much of which is planted with livestock feed.

PUBLIC LANDS RANCHING
* STATISTICS *
for the
ELEVEN WESTERN STATES
(Arizona, California, Colorado, Idaho, Montana, Nevada, New Mexico, Oregon, Utah, Washington, Wyoming)

GRAZING PERMITTEES

(Figures are based on 1986-87 USDA and USDI publications. Figures vary little yearly.)

• Number of cattle and sheep permittees authorized to graze Western BLM land	19,146
• Number of cattle and sheep leasees authorized to graze Eastern BLM land	578
• Total BLM graziers	19,724
• Number of Western Forest Service System permittees (all livestock)	11,952
• Number of Eastern Forest Service System permittees (all livestock)	2044
• Total Forest Service System graziers	13,996
• **# of permittees, Western BLM & FS System land** (adjusted for overlapping use)	**approx 22,000**
• **#of permittees, all BLM and Forest Service System land** (adjusted for overlapping use)	**approx 24,000**
• **#of permittees, all Western publicly owned land** (adjusted for overlapping use)	**roughly 30,000**
• Number of cattlemen in US	approx 1.60 million
• Number of cattlemen in West	approx 0.18 million
• % of US cattlemen in West	approx 11%
• **% of US cattlemen in East**	**approx 89%**
• % of Western cattlemen ranching Western BLM & Forest Service System land	approx 12%
• % of Western cattlemen ranching Western public land	approx 16%
• % of US cattlemen ranching Western BLM and Forest Service System land	approx 1.4%
• % of US cattlemen ranching all BLM and Forest Service System land	approx 1.5%
• **% of US cattlemen ranching Western publicly owned land**	**approx 1.9%**
• % of US population represented by Western public land permittees (1 of 8333 US citizens)	approx 0.012%
• % of Western population represented by Western public land permittees (1 of 2000 Western residents)	approx 0.05%
• Average size of BLM and Forest Service System allotment	8500 acres
• **Average size of BLM & FS land used per Western permittee** (includes overlap)	**11,818 acres**

PUBLIC LANDS RANCHING
* STATISTICS *
for the
ELEVEN WESTERN STATES
(Arizona, California, Colorado, Idaho, Montana, Nevada, New Mexico, Oregon, Utah, Washington, Wyoming)

LIVESTOCK PRODUCTION (cattle and sheep)

(Figures based on 1986-87 USDA and USDI publications. Figures are approximate and vary little yearly.)

- **% of US livestock feed* supplied by Western BLM and Forest Service System land**   **2%**
- % of US livestock feed supplied by other Western public land   1%
- % of US livestock feed supplied by Eastern public land   less than 0.25%
- **% of US livestock feed supplied by all publicly owned land**   **3%**

- **% of US livestock feed supplied by private land in West (including Indian reservations) 18%**
- % of US livestock feed supplied by private land in East   79%
- **% of US livestock feed supplied by private land**   **97%**

- **% of US livestock feed supplied by West**   **21%**

- % of US rangeland livestock herbage** supplied by Western BLM & FS land   9%
- % of Western rangeland livestock herbage supplied by Western BLM & FS land   17%
- % of Western rangeland livestock herbage supplied by all Western public land   27%

- **% of Western livestock feed supplied by Western BLM and Forest Service System land 11%**
- **% of Western livestock feed supplied by all Western publicly owned land**   **18%**

- % of US sheep feed supplied by West   47%
- % of US sheep feed supplied by public land   15%
- % of US cattle feed supplied by public land   3%
- % of combined US sheep and cattle production represented by sheep (by weight)   2%

- % of US livestock production supplied by rangeland and pasture herbage   roughly 50%
- % of US livestock production supplied by livestock crops   roughly 50%

* Livestock feed refers to livestock food of any kind.

** Herbage refers to forage and browse.

PUBLIC LANDS RANCHING
* STATISTICS *
for the
ELEVEN WESTERN STATES
(Arizona, California, Colorado, Idaho, Montana, Nevada, New Mexico, Oregon, Utah, Washington, Wyoming)

LIVESTOCK PRODUCTION (Continued)

(1987 figures)

- Herbage used by cattle on Western BLM land — 9.6 million AUMs*
- Herbage used by sheep and goats on Western BLM land — 1.5 million AUMs
- Total — 11.1 million AUMs

- Herbage used by cattle on Western Forest Service System land — 6.2 million AUMs
- Herbage used by sheep and goats on Western Forest Service System land — 0.9 million AUMs
- Total — 7.1 million AUMs

- **Herbage used by cattle and sheep on Western BLM & FS land** — **18.2 million AUMs**
  (equivalent to 1.5 million cattle yearlong)
- Herbage used by cattle on Western publicly owned land — 27 million AUMs
- Herbage used by sheep on Western publicly owned land — 3 million AUMs
- **Herbage used by cattle and sheep on Western public land** — **roughly 30 million AUMs**
  (equivalent to 2.5 million cattle yearlong)

- **Cattle & sheep production, Western private land (incl. Indian)** — **roughly 170 million AUMs**
  (equivalent to 14 million cattle yearlong)

- **Cattle and sheep production in US** — **roughly 1000 million AUMs**
  (equivalent to 83 million cattle yearlong)

* An AUM (Animal Unit Month) is the amount of forage and/or browse (and/or other feed) required to feed a cow and her calf, a horse, or five sheep or goats for a month -- an average of about 900 pounds of herbage.

STOP THE
PUBLIC LANDS RIPOFF

PUBLIC LANDS RANCHING
* STATISTICS *
for the
ELEVEN WESTERN STATES
(Arizona, California, Colorado, Idaho, Montana, Nevada, New Mexico, Oregon, Utah, Washington, Wyoming)

ECONOMICS

(Figures based on 1986-88 USDA, USDI, and other government publications. Figures vary little yearly.)

- **1990 federal grazing fee** — **$1.81/AUM**
- 1990 average private land grazing fee (calculated from USDA figures) — approx $10.00/AUM
- 1980-85 average private land grazing fee (USDA survey) — $7.50/AUM
- 1980-89 average federal grazing fee — $1.57/AUM

- **% of fair market value represented by 1990 federal grazing fee** — **19%**
- % of federal grazing fee revenue returned to public ranching industry — more than 50%
- % of federal grazing fee revenue to US Treasury and parent states — less than 50%
- **Extracted 1990 federal grazing fee** — **$0.90/AUM**
- **% of fair market value represented by extracted 1989 federal grazing fee** — **9%**

- 1987 BLM and Forest Service grazing fee revenue — $21.0 million
- 1987 BLM and Forest Service grazing fee revenue net to US Treasury — $6.5 million
- 1987 BLM and Forest Service direct expenditures on public lands ranching — $65.0 million
- **Net loss to US Treasury in 1987** — **roughly $50 million**

- Annual BLM & FS direct and indirect expenditures, public ranching — roughly $160 million
- Annual tax loss to public lands ranching — very roughly $1 billion
- Annual private economic loss to public lands ranching — very roughly $1 billion
- **Total annual economic loss to public lands ranching** — **very roughly $2 billion**

- **Annual value of Western BLM & Forest Service livestock production** — **roughly $390 million**
- **Annual value of Western public lands livestock production** — **roughly $550 million**
- **Annual value of US livestock production** — **roughly $21 billion**

STOP
WELFARE
RANCHING!

QUOTATIONS

Quotation confesses inferiority.
--Ralph Waldo Emerson

The wisdom of the wise, and the experience of ages, may be preserved by quotations.
--Isaac D'Israeli

O sovereign Lord! since it has pleased thee to endue man with power and pre-eminence here on earth,
And establish his dominion over all creatures,
May we look up to thee,
That our understanding may be so illuminated with wisdom,
And our hearts warmed and animated with due sense of charity,
That we may be enabled to do thy will,
And perform our duty towards those submitted to our service and protection,
And be merciful to them,
Even as we hope for mercy.
Thus may we be worthy of the dignity and superiority of the high and distinguished station in which thou hast placed us here on earth.
--William Bartram, **The Travels of William Bartram**, 1773

Except as you, sons of the Earth, honor your birthright and cherish it well by human endeavor, you shall be cut down and perish in darkness . . . . Look you well, therefore, to yourselves in your posterity. Keep all close to the Earth, your feet upon the Earth, and your hands employed in the fruitfulness thereof.
--Babylonian prophet

The earth is very good in and of itself. It has abided by the celestial law, consequently we should not despise it, nor desire to leave it, but rather . . . strive to obey the same laws that the earth abides . . . .
--Brigham Young

And I brought you into a plentiful country to eat the fruit thereof and the goodness thereof; but when ye entered, ye defiled my land and made mine heritage an abomination.
--**The Bible**

He who spits on the Earth spits on himself.
--Old Native American saying

If we harm nature, we harm ourselves.
--Raymond Dasmann, **Environmental Conservation**

As man proceeds towards his announced conquest of Nature, he has written a depressing record of destruction, directed not only against the Earth he inhabits, but against the life that shares it with him.
--Rachel Carson

Increasingly, the world around us looks as if we hated it.
--Alan Watts

We abuse land because we regard it as a commodity belonging to us. When we see the land as a community to which we belong, we may begin to use it with love and respect.
--Aldo Leopold

Our approach to Nature is to beat it into submission. We would stand a better chance of survival if we accommodated ourselves to this planet and viewed it appreciatively, instead of skeptically and dictatorially.
--E.B. White

The Earth is sacred. You cannot improve it. If you try to change it, you will ruin it. If you try to hold it, you will lose it.
--Lao Tsu

"This Earth, this world. For a warrior there can be no greater Love. Only if one loves this Earth with unbending passion can one release one's sadness," Don Juan said.

"A warrior is always joyful because his love is unalterable and his beloved, the Earth, embraces him and bestows upon him inconceivable gifts.

"The sadness belongs only to those who hate the very being that gives shelter to their beings." Don Juan again caressed the ground with tenderness. "This lovely being, which is alive to its last recesses and understands every feeling, soothed me -- it cured me of my pains; and finally, when I had fully understood my love for it, it taught me . . . freedom."
--Carlos Castaneda, **Tales of Power**

Biological diversity and integrity of organic evolution are where I take my stand.
--Gary Snyder, Earth poet

When the animals come to us, asking for help, will we know what they are saying? When the plants speak to us, in their delicate beautiful language, will we be able to answer them? When the planet herself sings to us in our dreams, will we be able to wake ourselves, and act?

--Gary Lawless, Earth poet\activist

Wilderness is an anchor to windward. Knowing it is there, we can also know that we are still a rich nation, tending to our resources as we should -- not a people in despair searching every last nook and cranny of our land for a board of lumber, a barrel of oil, or a blade of grass . . . .

--Late Senator Clinton P. Anderson

We are living in very strange times and they are likely to get a lot stranger before we bottom out.

--Hunter S. Thompson

Why disassociate ourselves from a single atom beneath our feet? What is the purpose of presuming for dignity's sake alone that human life is dearer than other forms of life in the Cosmic Whole? Can we not exalt all life without losing our own prestige? Are we not a constituent of the whole?

--Calvin Rutstrum

Humankind is a strand in Nature's infinite web
A single, short strand
Shining in the sun
Glowing with the web
Spun together with all other forms of being
With such delicate and effectual precision
That when plucked upon
The web trembles

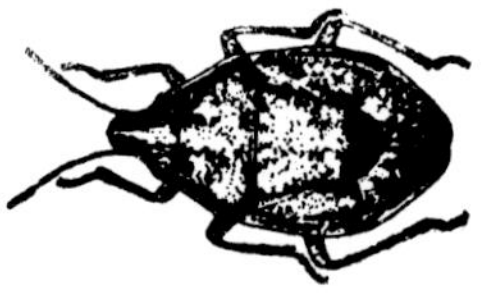

--LJ

This we know. The earth does not belong to man; man belongs to the earth. This we know. All things are connected like the blood which unites one family. Whatever befalls the earth befalls the sons and daughters of earth. Man did not weave the web of life; he is merely a strand in it. Whatever he does to the web, he does to himself.

--Chief Sealth, 1854

Nature's object in making animals and plants might possibly be first of all the happiness of each one of them, not the creation of all for the happiness of one. Why ought man to value himself as more than an infinitely small composing unit of the one great unit of creation? . . . . The universe would be incomplete without man; but it would also be incomplete without the smallest transmicroscopic creature that dwells beyond our conceitful eyes and knowledge.

--John Muir

The real wealth of the world is the living richness of the biosphere itself.
--Douglas C. Bowman, **Beyond the Modern Mind**

It's doing so well on its own
Won't you leave it alone?
--Cecelia Ostrow, musician

Can't the bastards leave anything alone?
--Edward Abbey

Let Nature take her own way; she understands her own affairs better than we.
--from the documentary *Amazon, Land of the Flooded Forest*

Whatever befalls in accordance with Nature should be accounted good.
--Cicero

Nature never did betray the heart that loved her.
--William Blake

Earth gives life and seeks the one
who walks gently upon it.
--Hopi Legend

Restore   the   Earth
Rejoin   the   Earth

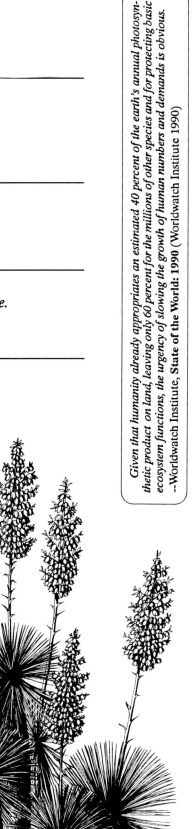

Given that humanity already appropriates an estimated 40 percent of the earth's annual photosynthetic product on land, leaving only 60 percent for the millions of other species and for protecting basic ecosystem functions, the urgency of slowing the growth of human numbers and demands is obvious.
--Worldwatch Institute, **State of the World: 1990** (Worldwatch Institute 1990)

PRINCIPAL LITERATURE CONSULTED
(partial list)
• Indicates Priority Reading

• **A**bbey, Edward. 1986. "Even the Bad Guys Wear White Hats: Cowboys, Ranchers, and Ruin of the West." *Harper's*. Jan: 51-55. (True grit, nitty-gritty -- an emotional portrayal of the ranching industry and its desecration of the West.)

Abdel-Magid, Ahmed H., M.J. Trlica, and Richard H. Hart. 1987. "Soil and Vegetation Responses to Simulated Trampling." *Journal of Range Management*. Jul: 303-306.

Advisory Committee on Predator Control. 1972. *Predator Control -- 1971*. Institute for Environmental Quality, University of Michigan, Ann Arbor, MI. 207 pages.

Ahlstrom, Mark E. 1985. **The Coyote.** Crestwood House, Box 3427, Mankato, MN 56002. 47 pages. (A good one for children; does a wonderful job of describing both the coyote and the ranching industry.)

Akers, Keith. 1983. **A Vegetarian Sourcebook: The Nutrition, Ecology, and Ethics of a Natural Foods Diet.** Vegetarian Press, Arlington, VA. 229 pages. (Some conclusions dubious, but this book contains much vital information on how our diet affects us and the world around us.)

Alderfer, R.B. and R.R. Robinson. 1947. "Runoff from Pastures in Relation to Grazing Intensity and Soil Compaction." *Jour. Amer. Soc. Agronomy*. 29: 948-958.

Anderson, D.C., K.T. Harper, and R.C. Holmgren. 1982. "Recovery of Cryptogamic Soil Crusts from Grazing on Utah Winter Ranges." *Journal of Range Management*. 35: 355-359.

Anderson, J.E. and K.E. Holte. 1981. "Vegetation Development over Twenty-five Years Without Grazing on Sagebrush Rangeland in Southeastern Idaho." *Journal of Range Management*. 34: 25-29.

Arizona Daily Star. 1990. "Humans Are Natural Vegetarians, Cornell Dietary Research Suggests." May 9: A14. (A major study adds to the mounting evidence that humans are naturally basically vegan.)

• Atwood, Charles Lee. 1990. *Restoring the Ravaged Range*. In **Audubon Wildlife Report: 1989/1990.** National Audubon Society. Pages 331-364. (A good overview, with reasonable, more-than-empty-rhetoric solutions.)

Baer, James L. 1985. "Arroyo Formation, Juab County, Utah, 1983." *Rangelands*. Dec: 245-247. (A good description of arroyo cutting.)

Bahre, Conrad J. and David E. Bradberry. 1978. "Vegetative Change Along the Arizona-Sonora Boundary." *Annals of the Association of American Geographers*. June: 150-161.

Bagwell, Steve. 1990. "Gridlock at Busterback." *High Country News*, P.O. Box 1090, Paonia, CO 81428. Mar 12: 22. (Water diversion for ranching harms anadromous fish.)

Baker, James. 1986. "An Internal Audit Indicts the BLM's Grazing Practices." *High Country News*. Mar 3: 12.

Bashin, Bryan Jay. 1990. "Superweed." *San Francisco Examiner*. Aug 19: *This World* supplement, pages 10-11. (An excellent report on the grazing invader star thistle.)

Baylor, Bryd. 1989. "Jaws: It's Inhumane, It's Cruel, and It's Legal." *City Magazine*, Tucson, AZ. Pages 46-49.

Becker, Philip S. 1988. *Diet and Ecology: The Environmental Ramifications of Agricultural Production of Animal-Derived Foods*. PAWS, P.O. Box 52262, Philadelphia, PA 19115. 57 pages. (This study of US livestock production's environmental effects is packed with amazing facts and figures.)

Behnke, R.J. 1976. *Biology and Management of Threatened and Endangered Western Trouts*. USDA Forest Service General Technical Report RM-28, Rocky Mountain Forest and Range Experiment Station, Fort Collins, CO. 45 pages.

Behnke, R.J. and R.F. Raleigh. 1978. "Grazing and the Riparian Zone: Impact and Management Perspectives." In *Strategies for Protection and Management of Floodplain Wetlands and other Riparian Ecosystems*, USFS Symposium, Dec 11-13. Pages 263-267.

Belnap, Jayne. 1990. "Microphytic Crusts: 'Topsoil of the Desert.'" *Permaculture Drylands Journal*. Spring: 4-5, 14.

Berry, Kristen H. 1978. "Livestock Grazing and the Desert Tortoise." *Transactions of the North American Wildlife and Natural Resources Conference*. 43: 505-519.

Bingham, Sam. 1990. "Barbarians Within Agriculture's Gates." *High Country News*. Mar 12: 17-18. ("Weed" eradication.)

• Bishop, Gerry. 1985. "Adventures of Ranger Rick." *Ranger Rick*, 8925 Leesburg Pike, Vienna, VA 22180. Mar: 10-14. (Another great one for kids! Rick and his friends visit the Western range and experience livestock grazing effects firsthand. After his story ran, Bishop was admonished for his honesty by his superiors in the National Wildlife Federation, who had been admonished by the ranching establishment.)

Bishop, Richard A. and C. Roger Hungerford. 1965. "Seasonal Food Selection of Arizona Mearn's Quail." *Journal of Wildlife Management*. 29: 813-819.

Bloyd-Peshkin, Sharon. 1991. "Grazing Our Way to Disaster." *Utne Reader*. Jan/Feb: 15-16.

• Blumm, Michael, Editor. 1986. "Livestock Grazing in Riparian Zones: Ensuring Fishery Protection in Federal Rangeland Management." *Anadromous Fish Law Memo*. Lewis and Clark Law School, 10015 S.W. Terwilliger Blvd., Portland, OR 97219. Oct: 19 pages. (Clearly and convincingly states the case for removing livestock from Western riparian areas; a good description of the effects of livestock grazing on riparian zones and waterways.)

Blydenstein, J., *et. al.* 1957. "Effect of Domestic Livestock Exclusion on Vegetation in the Sonoran Desert." *Ecology*. 38: 522-526.

Bock, C.E. 1984. "*Responses of Birds, Rodents, and Vegetation to*

Livestock Exclosure in a Semidesert Grassland Site." Journal of Range Management. 37(3): 239-242.

Bohn, Carolyn. 1989. "Management of Winter Soil Temperatures to Control Streambank Erosion." In *Practical Approaches to Riparian Resource Management: An Educational Workshop*, USDI, BLM. US Govt. Printing Office, Washington, DC 20402. Pages 69-71.

Bowman, Chris. 1987. "Cattle King Rides Roughshod over the Range." *Sacramento Bee.* Jan 29.

Box, Thadis W. and John C. Malechek. 1987. "Grazing on the American Rangelands." 9 pages. (Two leading ranching promoters provide a prime example of professional, distortion-ridden propaganda; former BLM Director Burford used this paper as a handout to those questioning BLM ranching.)

Brady, W.W., et. al. 1990. "Response of a Semidesert Grassland to 16 Years of Rest from Grazing." *Journal of Range Management.* 42(4): 284-288.

Branson, F.A. 1956. "Quantitative Effects of Clipping Treatments on Five Range Grasses." *Journal of Range Management.* 9: 86-88.

Branson, F.A. 1985. *Vegetation Changes on Western Rangelands.* Society for Range Management, 2760 W. Fifth Ave., Denver, CO 80204. 76 pages. (Branson writes like an apologist for the grazing industry, but provides useful info.)

Braun, Clait E. 1971. "Habitat Requirements of Colorado White-tailed Ptarmigan." *Proceedings of the Western Association of Game & Fish Commissioners.* 51: 284-292.

Braun, C.E., et. al. 1978. "Management of National Wildlife Refuges in the United States: Its Impact on Birds." *Wilson Bulletin.* 90: 309-321.

Briggs, H.E. 1934. "The Development and Decline of Open Ranching in the Northwest." *Mississippi Valley Historical Review.* 20: 521-536.

Broly, William. 1980. "The Sagebrush Rebels." *New West Magazine.* Nov 3.

Brower, Monty. 1988. "Lawman Len Sims, Alone on the Range, Hunts the Killers of Nevada's Wild Mustangs." *People.* [Date unknown]: 63-65.

Brown, David E. and David H. Ellis. 1977. "Status Summary and Recovery Plan for the Masked Bobwhite." US Dept. of Interior, Fish & Wildlife Service, Office of Endangered Species, Region 2, Albuquerque, NM. 18 pages.

Brown, David E. 1978. "Grazing, Grassland Cover and Gamebirds." *Transactions of the 43rd North American Wildlife Conference.* Pages 477-485.

● Brown, David E. 1984. **The Wolf in the Southwest: The Making of an Endangered Species.** The University of Arizona Press, 1230 Park, Suite 102, Tucson, AZ 85719. 195 pages. (Chronicles the relentless, bloody extermination of the Southwest's premier livestock predator; gently yet effectively worded.)

● Brown, David E. 1985. **The Grizzly in the Southwest.** University of Oklahoma Press, Norman, OK. 274 pages. (An account of the demise of the West's most magnificent animal, mostly at the hands of the ranching industry.)

Brown, David E. 1988. [Title unknown; on Endangered species.] *Wilderness.* Winter: 42-52.

Bryan, K. 1925. "Date of Channel Trenching (Arroyo Cutting) in the Arid Southwest." *Science.* 62: 338-344.

Buffington, L.C. and C.H. Herbel. 1965. "Vegetational Changes on a Semi-desert Grassland Range from 1858-1963." *Ecological Monographs.* 35: 139-164.

Bury, R. Bruce and Stephan D. Busack. 1974. "Some Effects of Off-road Vehicles and Sheep Grazing on Lizard Populations in the Mojave Desert." *Biological Conservation.* 6: 179-183.

Busby, F.E. and G.F. Gifford. 1981. "Effects of Livestock Grazing on Infiltration and Erosion Rates Measured on Chained and Un-chained Pinyon-juniper Sites in Southeastern Utah." *Journal of Range Management.* 34: 400-405.

Buttery, R.F. and P.W. Shields. 1975. "Range Management Practices and Bird Habitat Values." *Proceedings of the Symposium on Management of Forest and Range Habitats for Nongame Birds.* Tucson, AZ, May 6-9, 1975.

Buys, Christian J. 1975. "Predator Control and Ranchers' Attitudes." *Environment and Behavior.* March.

Cain, Stanley A., et. al. 1971. *Predator Control -- 1971. Report to the Council on Environmental Quality and the Department of the Interior by the Advisory Committee on Predator Control.* University of Michigan Press, Ann Arbor, MI.

● Calef, Wesley. 1960. **Private Grazing and Public Lands.** The University of Chicago Press, Chicago, IL. 292 pages. (An informative, professional, well-written -- though ranching-biased -- account of public lands ranching in relation to government administration, with special emphasis on the intermountain West.)

Call, M. and C. Maser. 1985. "Wildlife Habitats in Managed Rangelands -- The Great Basin of Southeastern Oregon -- Sage Grouse." BLM, Portland, OR.

Calvin, Ross. 1975. **Sky Determines: An Interpretation of the Southwest.** The University of New Mexico Press, Albuquerque, NM. 391 pages. (Romanticized, but relevant nonetheless.)

Carlton, Jasper and Keith Hammer. 1990. *Killing Roads: A Citizens' Primer on the Effects & Removal of Roads.* Supplement to May 1 *Earth First! Journal*, P.O. Box 5176, Missoula, MT 59806. 8 pages. (An excellent discussion on the impacts of roads and what we can do to reduce them.)

Carothers, S.W. 1977. "Importance, Preservation, and Management of Riparian Habitats: an Overview." In *Importance, Preservation, and Management of Riparian Habitat: A Symposium*, R.R. Johnson and D.A. Jones (eds.). *USDA Forest Service General Technical Report RM-43.*

Carr, Ann. 1986. "Holistic Resource Management." *Earth First! Journal.* Sep 23: 23.

Cascade Holistic Economic Consultants. 1989. "Change on the Range." *Forest Watch.* Sep: 21-25.

Chaney, Ed, Wayne Elmore, and William S. Platts. 1990. "Livestock Grazing on Western Riparian Areas." Northwest Resource Information Center, Inc., Eagle, ID. 45 pages. (Produced for EPA; another full size/color publication on ranching's impacts on riparian areas, in case studies.)

Chapman, H.H. 1948. "Modern Overgrazing of Livestock as the Direct Cause of Ruin of Southwest Agriculture." *Journal of Forestry.* 46 (12): 929.

Chapman, W.B., Jr. 1973. **Natural Ecosystems.** Macmillan Publishing Co., Inc., 866 Third Avenue, New York, NY 10022. 248 pages.

Chapman, W.R. 1919. *Production of Goats on Far Western Ranges: USDA Bulletin No. 749*. 35 pages.

Cheatham, Norden H., W. James Barry, and Leslie Hood. 1977. *Research Natural Areas and Related Programs in California*. In **Terrestrial Vegetation of California** by M.G. Barbour and Jack Major. John Wiley & Sons, 605 Third Ave. New York, NY 10016. Pages 75-108.

Christensen, Jon. 1990. "Sagebrush Rebels Try to Call the Shots in Nevada." *High Country News*. Jul 2: 1, 10-11.

Christman, Steven P. 1988. "Timber Management Is Not Wildlife Management." *Earth First! Journal*. Sep 22: 20-21, 25. (Excellent discussion of fire ecology and land management in general.)

Cleland, Robert Glass. 1941. **The Cattle on a Thousand Hills: 1850-1880**. Henry E. Huntington Library and Art Gallery. (Early California's Spanish livestock industry.)

Clifton, Catherine. 1989. "Effects of Vegetation and Land Use on Channel Morphology." In *Practical Approaches to Riparian Resource Management: An Educational Workshop*. USDI, BLM. US Govt. Printing Office. 121-129.

Clifton, Merritt. 1990. "The Myth of the Good Shepherd." *Animals' Agenda*. May: 24-28, 57.

College of Agriculture, University of Arizona. 1981. *Progressive Agriculture in Arizona: Special Issue: Arizona Rangelands*. College of Agriculture, University of Arizona, Tucson, AZ. 34 pages. (The epitome of absurdly subjective, intentionally misleading journalism -- a good example of public lands ranching promotion efforts.)

● Committee for the World Atlas of Agriculture, Editor. 1969-1976. **World Atlas of Agriculture**. Istituto Geografico de Agostini, Novara, Italy. 4 volumes. (This amazing collection of incredibly detailed maps portrays agricultural land use throughout the globe.)

● Committee on Government Operations. 1986. *Federal Grazing Program: All Is Not Well on the Range*. US Govt. Printing Office. 74 pages. (Well-written, informative, and right on the mark; an excellent treatment of welfare ranching.)

Conner, Patrick K. 1986. "Hooved Vandals." *The San Francisco Chronicle-Examiner*. Oct 26: 17-18.

Cook, W.C. and L.A. Stoddart. 1963. "The Effect of Intensity and Season of Use on the Vigor of Desert Range Plants." *Journal of Range Management*. 16: 315-317.

Cook, W.C. and R.D. Child. 1971. "Recovery of Desert Plants in Various States of Vigor." *Journal of Range Management*. 24(5): 339-343.

Cope, O.B., Editor. 1979. "Proceedings of the Forum -- Grazing and Riparian/Stream Ecosystems." *Trout Unlimited*, Denver, Colorado. 94 pages. (Much useful info on livestock effects in riparian areas.)

Costello, D.F. and G.T. Turner. 1941. "Vegetation Changes Following Exclusion of Livestock from Grazed Ranges." *Journal of Forestry*. 39: 310-315.

Cottam, W.P. and R.R. Evans. 1945. "A Comparative Study of the Vegetation of Grazed and Ungrazed Canyons of the Wasatch Range, Utah." *Ecology*. 26: 171-181.

Cotton, J.S. 1905. Range *Management in the State of Washington: USDA, Bureau of Plant Industry Bulletin No. 75*. 26 pages.

Cotton, J.S. 1907. *The Improvement of Mountain Meadows: USDA, Bureau of Plant Industry Bulletin No. 117*. 29 pages.

Council for Agricultural Science and Technology. 1974. "Livestock Grazing on Federal Lands in the 11 Western States." *Journal of Range Management*. 27: 174-181.

● Council on Environmental Quality and the Department of State. 1981. **The Global 2000 Report to the President: Entering the Twenty-First Century**. Blue Angel, Inc., 1738 Allied St., Charlottesville, VA. 22901. 960 pages. (This monumental work includes much information on livestock production's devastating impact on the planet; when the Reagan administration took office it squelched distribution of the report and unofficially banned the word "desertification" from future federal publications.)

Crane, Candace. 1989. "In the Shadow of Livestock." *Animals*. Sep/Oct: 18-23. (Good overview of public lands ranching.)

Crested Valley Wildlife Management Authority. 1974. "Habitat Requirements for Ground-nesting Waterfowl and Effect of Grazing and other Cover Removal Activities on Nesting." CVWMA, Box 640, Creston, British Columbia, Canada.

Crosby, Alfred W. 1988. **Ecological Imperialism: The Biological Expansion of Europe, 900-1900**. Cambridge University Press. 368 pages.

Croxen, Fred W. 1926. *History of Grazing on the Tonto*. Fred W. Croxen, Senior Forest Ranger, Tonto National Forest, AZ. 11 pages.

Culhane, Paul J. **Public Lands Politics**. 1981. The Johns Hopkins University Press, Baltimore, MD 21218. 398 pages. (Studies "interest group influence on the Forest Service and the Bureau of Land Management.")

Daddy, F.M., J. Trlica, and C.D. Bonham. 1988. "Vegetation and Soil Water Differences among Big Sagebrush Communities with Different Grazing Histories." *The Southwestern Naturalist*. 33(4): 413-424.

Dadkhah, M. and R.W. Gifford. 1980. "Influence of Vegetation, Rock Cover, and Trampling on Infiltration Rates and Sediment Production." *Water Resources Bulletin*. 16(6): 979-986.

Dagget, Dan. 1988. "*El Tigre* Doesn't Live Here Anymore." *Earth First! Journal*. May 1: 1, 8-9. (The jaguar and the grazing industry's campaign against it.)

Dagget, Dan. 1990. "Arizona Ranchers Are Ripping Off Wildlife." *High Country News*. Mar 26: 16.

Dahne, Julius. 1990. "BLM May Spray More Rangeland with Deadly Insecticide." *High Country News*. Dec 17: 3.

Dale, Edward. 1960. **The Range Cattle Industry**. University of Oklahoma Press, Norman, OK. 207 pages.

● Dasmann, Raymond F. 1972. **Environmental Conservation**. John Wiley & Sons, New York, NY. 473 pages. (One of the best books on general ecology and human influence; good discussion on ranching.)

Daubenmire, R.F. 1940. "Plant Succession Due to Overgrazing in the *Agropyron* Bunchgrass Prairie of Southeastern Washington." *Ecology*. 21: 55-64.

Daubenmire, R.F. and W.E. Colwell. 1942. "Some Edaphic Changes Due to Overgrazing in the *Agropyron-Poa* Prairie of Southeastern Washington." *Ecology*. 23: 32-40.

Davis, Bill. 1990. "Our Living Desert Is Becoming a New Sahara." *High Country News*. Aug 27: 12.

Debano, Leonard F. and Larry J. Schmidt. 1989. "Interrelationship Between Watershed Condition and Health of Riparian Areas in the Southwestern United States." In *Practical Approaches to Riparian Resource Management: An Educational Workshop*," USDI, BLM. 45-51. (A good discussion of watershed dynamics.)

Defenders of Wildlife. 1982. *1080: The Case Against Poisoning Our Wildlife*. Defenders of Wildlife, 1244 Nineteenth St., NW, Washington, DC 20036. 20 pages.

DeLamater, Rick and Wendy Hodgson. 1986. "Agave Arizonica: An Endangered Species, a Hybrid, or Does It Matter? Presented on Nov 7, 1986 at the California Native Plant Society Meeting, Rare & Endangered Plants: A California Conference on Their Conservation & Management." 6 pages.

• DeVoto, Bernard. 1955. **The Easy Chair**. The Riverside Press, Cambridge, MA. 356 pages. (One of the few writers who had the courage to reveal the sleazy politics of public lands ranching; over 100 pages on the issue, still highly relevant.)

• Diamond, Harvey and Marilyn. 1985. **Fit for Life**. Warner Books, Inc., 666 Fifth Avenue, New York, NY 10103. 241 pages. (Swallow your machismo or machisma, control your knee-jerk reaction against "wimpy, faddish health food nuts," and read as the Diamonds soundly debunk the great meat/milk myth.)

Dillard, Annie. 1975. **Pilgrim at Tinker Creek**. Bantam Books, Inc., 666 Fifth Avenue, New York, NY 10019. 279 pages. (Contains only 1 paragraph on cows, but it's a good one and this outstanding book awakens and reawakens awareness of this mystical living Earth.)

• Dimick, Edwin G. 1990. **Livestock Pillage of Our Western Public Lands**. Edwin G. Dimick, P.O. Box 265, Caldwell, ID 83606. 293 pages. (Dimick, backed by 50 years experience on the Western range, explains the environmental and economic pillage he has seen and calls for an end to public lands ranching; 1 of only 3 books on the subject.)

Disney Films. 1960s. *The Legend of Lobo*. Walt Disney Films. (Not literature, of course, but a great film for young and old alike; portrays predator "control" efforts from a wolf's perspective.)

Dixon, R.M., J.R. Simanton, and L.J. Lane. 1978. "Simple Time-power Functions for Rainwater Infiltration and Runoff." *Proc. 22nd Annual Meeting of the AZ-NV Academy of Science, Am. Water Res. Assoc., 8-79-89. Flagstaff, AZ, April 14-15, 1978*.

Dogmeat, Arthur. 1986. "Sheep Kill Grizzlies." *Earth First! Journal*. Sep 23: 5.

Downer, Craig. 1985. "In Defense of America's Wild Horses." *Earth First! Journal*. Nov 1: 22-23.

Driver, B.L., Roderick Nash, and Glen Haas. 1987. "Wilderness Benefits: A State-of-Knowledge Review." Pages 294-319 in *Proceedings of the National Wilderness Conference, Fort Collins, CO, July 23-26, 1985*. Intermountain Research Station, Ogden, UT 84401. (An excellent discussion of the benefits derived from Wilderness.)

Duce, J.T. 1918. "The Effect of Cattle on the Erosion of Canyon Bottoms." *Science*. 67: 450-452.

Duncan, Harvey. 1987. "Statement of Harvey Duncan of the Wyoming Wildlife Federation Before the House Interior Subcommittee on National Parks and Public Lands Regarding Livestock Grazing Fees on BLM and USFS Lands, Sept 21." 4 pages.

Durbin, Kathie. 1991. "Storm Brews Over Livestock Grazing." *The Oregonian*, Portland, OR. Feb 17: A22-A23. (Good coverage of the overall issue.)

Durbin, Kathie. 1991a. "High Desert Wilderness Plan Offered." *The Oregonian*. Apr 29: B1, B4.

Egan, Timothy. 1990. "Ranchers vs. Rangers Over Land Use." *New York Times*. Aug 19. Section 1, page 20.

Ehrlich, Paul R. 1986. **The Machinery of Nature**. Simon & Schuster, New York, NY 10020. 320 pages. (The well-known overpopulation expert presents a fascinating discussion on various aspects of ecology; portions pertain to ranching.)

Eisler, Riane. 1987. **The Chalice & the Blade**. Harper & Row, Publishers, 10 East 53rd Street, New York, NY 10022. 261 pages. (Reassesses humans' relationship with each other and their surroundings. Abstract, redundant, overcompensatory against men, and thoroughly anthropocentric; nonetheless a revolutionarily important work!)

Elmore, Wayne and Robert L. Beschta. 1987. "Riparian Areas: Perceptions in Management." *Rangelands*. Dec: 260-265.

• Ensminger, M.E. 1968. **Beef Cattle Science**. The Interstate Printers and Publishers, Inc., Danville, IL. 1020 pages. (A complete description of the business of cattle from the cattleman's perspective.)

Ensminger, M.E. 1983. **The Stockman's Handbook**: 6th Edition. The Interstate Printers and Publishers, Inc., Danville, IL. 1192 pages.

Espenshade, Edward B., Jr., Editor. 1988. **Goode's World Atlas, 17th Edition**. Rand McNally & Company. 367 pages. (Good livestock statistics and maps.)

Executive Office of the President of the United States, Office of Management and Budget. 1989. **Budget of the United States Government**. US Govt. Printing Office. 650 pages.

Fairfax, Sally K. and Carolyn E. Yale. 1987. **Federal Lands: A Guide to Planning, Management, and State Revenues**. Island Press, Suite 300, 1718 Connecticut Ave., NW, Washington, DC 20009. 252 pages.

• Feller, Joseph M. 1990. "The Western Wing of Kafka's Castle." *High Country News*. Mar 12: 9-11. (A law professor, trying to protect a portion of southeast Utah from further overgrazing, immerses himself in the BLM grazing allotment management "public participation" process, giving the reader an excellent look into the inner workings of BLM.)

• Ferguson, Denzel and Nancy. 1983. **Sacred Cows at the Public Trough**. Maverick Publications, Drawer 5007, Bend, OR 97708. 250 pages. (The most thorough account of the effects of public lands ranching yet compiled -- must reading!)

• Ferguson, Denzel and Nancy. 1984. "Sacred Cows at the Public Trough." *Earth First! Journal*. Aug 1: 14-15. (More useful info on public lands ranching than on any other 2 pages.)

Fish, Jim. 1987. "Triple Dipping the Public Till." *The Rio Grande Sierran*, Rio Grande Sierra Club, Albuquerque, NM. Page 5. (The son of a rancher reflects on public lands ranching.)

● Foreman, Dave. 1986. "My Heros Have Always Been Cowboys." *Earth First! Journal*. Feb 2: 18. (A brief but compelling rundown on why we should end public lands ranching; includes alternatives.)

Foreman, Dave. 1991. **Confessions of an Eco-warrior**. Crown Publishing, New York, NY. 350 pages. (Contains a fine chapter on public lands ranching.)

Foreman, Dave and Bill Haywood. 1987. **Ecodefense: A Field Guide to Monkeywrenching -- Second Edition**. Ned Ludd Books, P.O. Box 5141, Tucson, Arizona 85703. 311 pages. (A how-to guide on physically and non-violently thwarting environmental exploitation; includes a section on ranching.)

Foreman, Dave and Howie Wolke. 1989. **The Big Outside**. Ned Ludd Books, Tucson, AZ. 470 pages. (A comprehensive inventory of all of America's large remaining roadless areas, with discussions on wilderness history, ecology, destruction, and threats.)

Foreyt, W.J. and D.A. Jessup. 1982. "Fatal Pneumonia of Bighorn Sheep Following Association with Domestic Sheep." *Journal of Wildlife Disease*. 18: 163-168.

Forsling, C.L. 1927. "Grazing Control Is Needed for Proper Watershed Protection." In **USDA Yearbook, 1927**. Pages 350-351.

Forsling, C.L. 1931. "A Study of the Influence of Herbaceous Plant Cover on Surface Runoff and Soil Erosion in Relation to Grazing on the Wasatch Plateau in Utah." *USDA Technical Bulletin #220*.

● Foss, Phillip O. 1960. **Politics and Grass: The Administration of Grazing on the Public Domain**. University of Washington Press, Seattle, WA. 236 pages. (Within the cultural limits of 1960, Foss chronicles the stockmen-dominated political development and administration of public ranching.)

Fox, Michael W. 1986. **Agricide, The Hidden Crisis That Affects Us All**. Schocken Books, 62 Cooper Square, New York, NY 10003. 194 pages. (Chock full of useful info.)

● Fradkin, P.L. 1979. "The Eating of the West." *Audubon*. 81: 94-121. (A good introduction to the ranching problem.)

Frischknecht, Neil C. and Maurice H. Baker. 1972. "Voles can Improve Sagebrush Rangelands." *Journal of Range Management*. 25: 466-468.

Gallizioli, Steve. 1976. "Livestock Vs. Wildlife." *Forty-first North American Wildlife and Natural Resources Conference*. Washington, DC., Mar 1976.

Gallizioli, Steve. 1977. "Overgrazing: More Deadly than Any Hunter." *Outdoor Arizona*. [Date unknown]: 24-31.

Gallizioli, Steve. 1977a. "Overgrazing on Desert Bighorn Ranges." *Transactions of the Desert Bighorn Council*. Pages 21-22.

Gardner, J.L. 1950. "Effects of Thirty Years of Protection from Grazing in Desert Grassland." *Ecology*. 31: 44-50.

Gary, H.L., S.R. Johnson, and S.L. Ponce. 1983. "Cattle Grazing Impact on Surface Water Quality in a Colorado Front Range Stream." *Journal of Soil and Water Conservation*. 38: 124-128.

Gee, C. Kerry and Albert G. Madsen. 1986. *The Cost of Subleasing Federal Grazing Privileges, Project Report*. Colorado State University. 8 pages.

Gifford, G.L. and R.H. Hawkings. 1978. "Hydrologic Impact of Grazing on Infiltration: A Critical Review." *Water Resources Research*. 14: 305-313.

● Gleason, Henry A. and Arthur Cronquist. 1964. **The Natural Geography of Plants**. Columbia University Press. 420 pages. (A great book with wonderful pictures; will really help you understand plants.)

● Glustrom, Leslie. 1991. *Participating in Livestock Grazing Decisions on the National Forests*. 1025 Clubhouse Dr., Prescott, AZ 86303. 87 pages. (Effective public involvement in FS livestock grazing decisions, with useful appendixes, including FS regulations.]

Goodson, N.J. 1982. "Effects of Domestic Sheep Grazing on Bighorn Sheep Populations: A Review." In *Biannual Symposium and Goat Council*. 3: 287-313.

Goodwin, John G., Jr. and C. Roger Hungerford. 1977. "Habitat Use by Native Gambel's and Scaled Quail and Released Masked Bobwhite Quail in Southern Arizona." *USDA Forest Service Research Paper RM-197*, Rocky Mountain Forest and Range Experiment Station, Fort Collins, CO. 8 pages.

Gorsuch, David M. 1934. "Life History of the Gambel Quail in Arizona." *University of Arizona Bulletin 5(4), Biological Science Bulletin No. 2*. 89 pages.

Grandy, John W. 1989. "Comments of the Humane Society of the United States before the Colorado Division of Wildlife on a Proposal to Restrict the Use of Cruel Devices in Trapping Wild Animals, Thursday, July 13, 1989." 8 pages.

Green, Douglas M. and J. Boone Kauffman. 1989. "Nutrient Cycling at the Land-water Interface: the Importance of the Riparian Zone." In *Practical Approaches to Riparian Resource Management: An Educational Workshop*. USDI, BLM. US Govt. Printing Office. 61-68.

Griffiths, D. 1910. *A Protected Stock Range in Arizona: USDA, Bureau of Plant Industry Bulletin No. 177*. 28 pages.

Gunderson, D.R. 1968. "Floodplain Use Related to Stream Morphology and Fish Populations." *Journal of Wildlife Management*. 32: 507-514.

Hampton, Bruce. 1990. "Herbicide Causes Plants to Die *En Masse* in a Wyoming Drainage." *High Country News*. Jul 30: 5.

Handwerg, K. 1980. *Grazing Fees and Fair Market Value*. Cascade Holistic Economic Consultants, Eugene, OR. 20 pages.

Hansen, R.M. and L.D. Reid. 1975. "Diet Overlap of Deer, Elk, and Cattle in Southern Colorado." *Journal of Range Management*. 28: 43-47.

Hanson, H.C., L.D. Love, and M.S. Morris. 1931. *Effect of Different Systems of Grazing by Cattle upon Western Wheatgrass Type of Range: Colorado Agricultural Experimental Station Bulletin No. 377*. 82 pages.

● Hardin, Garrett. 1968. "The Tragedy of the Commons." *Science*. 162: 1243-1248. (Some conclusions are dubious, but this is a good philosophical essay on problems inherent to common ownership of land, focused on public lands ranching. Considered a classic.)

Hartshorn, J.K. 1988. "Truce or Consequences." *California Farmer*. May 7: 29-32.

Hastings, James Rodney and Raymond M. Turner. 1965. **The Changing Mile**. The University of Arizona Press, Tucson, AZ. 317 pages. (Comparative photos showing vegetation changes over the decades, but none from before the livestock invasion. The text often contradicts itself and its conclusions are sometimes dubious, but it still contains useful info.)

Haws, Austin B., *et. al.* 1982. *Rangeland Insects of the Western United States*. Utah Agricultural Experiment Station. 64 pages.

Heady, Harold F., *et. al.* 1974. "Livestock Grazing on Federal Lands in the 11 Western States." *Journal of Range Management*. 27(3): 174-181.

Herbel, C.H. 1955. "Range Conservation and Season-long Grazing." *Journal of Range Management*. 8: 204-205.

Hickey, Wayne C., Jr. 1977. *A Discussion of Grazing Management Systems and Some Pertinent Literature (Abstracts and Excerpts) 1895-1966*. USDA, FS. 323 pages. (Drawn from 115 papers on grazing management selected to promote grazing systems over continuous grazing.)

Hitchcock, A.S. 1935. **Manual of the Grasses of the United States**. US Govt. Printing Office. 1039 pages. (Probably the best book on US grasses.)

Holechek, Jerry L., Rex D. Pieper, and Carlton H. Herbel. 1989. **Range Management: Principles and Practices**. Prentice Hall, Englewood Cliffs, NJ 07632. 501 pages. (The contemporary textbook on managing the land for meat animal production. The authors spend half of the book defining the problems inherent to livestock grazing and the other half futilely trying to mitigate those problems.)

Honeycutt, Patricia S. 1987. "Public Lands Grazing or How to Create Desert While Paying Your VISA Bill." *Forest Watch*. Jan: 8-12. (Briefly explores welfare ranching.)

Hood, R.E. and J.M. Inglis. 1974. "Behavioral Responses of Whitetailed Deer to Intensive Ranching Operations." *Journal of Wildlife Management*. 38: 488-498.

Howard, Richard P. and Michael L. Wolfe. 1976. "Range Management Practices and Ferruginous Hawks." *Journal of Range Management*. 29(1): 33-37

Hull, A.C. and M.K. Hull. 1974. "Presettlement Vegetation of Cache Valley, Utah and Idaho." *Journal of Range Management*. 27: 27-29.

Humphrey, Robert R. 1962. **Range Ecology**. The Ronald Press Company, New York, NY. 234 pages.

Humphrey, Robert R. 1967. **The Desert Grassland**. The University of Arizona Press, Tucson, AZ. 74 pages.

Humphrey, Robert R. 1987. **90 Years and 535 Miles: Vegetation Changes Along the Mexican Border**. University of New Mexico Press, Albuquerque, NM. 448 pages. (Compares photos taken in 1892-1893 -- a period of extreme drought, *after* many years of extreme overgrazing -- at boundary monuments in 205 locations along the US-Mexican border with recent photos of the same locations.)

• Hur, Robin. 1985. "Six Inches from Starvation: How & Why America's Topsoil Is Disappearing." *Vegetarian Times*. P.O. Box 570, Oak Park, IL 60303. Mar: 45-48. (An informative and eye-opening synopsis of US soil erosion.)

Hur, Robin and David Fields. 1985a. "America's Appetite for Meat Is Ruining Our Water." *Vegetarian Times*. Jan: 16-18.

Hyde, Dayton O. 1986. **Don Coyote**. Arbor House Publishing Company, New York, NY. 245 pages. (The owner of a 6000-acre private ranch in Oregon, overcoming social pressures from local ranchers, befriends a coyote, which eventually teaches him the value of predators and Nature intact. Hyde is the ultimate "benevolent land steward.")

Inner Voice. 1991. Association of Forest Service Employees for Environmental Ethics, P.O. Box 11615, Eugene, OR 97440. Summer: 1-10. (This issue of *Inner Voice* -- a publication normally overwhelmingly concerned with logging issues -- focuses on Forest Service ranching.)

• Jacobs, Lynn. 1986. *Free Our Public Lands!* P.O. Box 5784, Tucson, AZ 85703. 48 pages. (An overview of the environmental, economic, social, and political effects of public lands ranching -- a tabloid with many photos and graphics.)

Jacobs, Lynn. 1988. "Amazing Graze." *Desertification Control Bulletin*. United Nations Environment Programme, Nairobi, Kenya. Nov 17: 13-17. (A summary of public lands ranching.)

Jarchow, James L. 1987. *Report on Investigation of Desert Tortoise Mortality on the Beaver Dam Slope, Arizona and Utah*. Neglected Fauna International, 2720 West San Juan Terrace, Tucson, AZ 85713. 20 pages.

Jawson, M.D., *et. al.* 1982. "The Effect of Cattle Grazing on Indicator Bacteria in Runoff from a Pacific Northwest Watershed." *Journal of Environmental Quality*. 11: 621-627.

Jeffries, D.L. and J.M. Klopatek. 1987. "Effects of Grazing on the Vegetation of the Blackbrush Association." *Journal of Range Management*. 40: 390-392.

Jessup, David A. 1985. "Diseases of Domestic Livestock Which Threaten Bighorn Sheep Populations." *Desert Bighorn Council 1985 Transactions*. Pages 29-33.

Johnson, Aubrey Stephen. 1978. "Pronghorns, Fences, and Ranch Mortgages." *Defenders*. [Date unknown]: 8-11.

Johnson, Aubrey Stephen. 1978. "Ranching: High Cost of an American Myth." *Defenders*. [Date unknown]: 324-327.

Johnson, Aubrey Stephen. 1985. "Desperation Leads Ranchers to Ghost Dance with the 'Guru of Grass' -- Allan Savory." *Forest Watch*. Jan: 13-19.

Johnson, Aubrey Stephen. 1985a. "Just Whose Home Is the Range?". *Defenders*. Jul/Aug: 14-17.

Johnson, Aubrey Stephen. 1987. "Testimony of Aubrey Stephen Johnson, SW Rep., Defenders of Wildlife, before the Subcommittee on National Parks and Public Lands Committee on Interior and Insular Affairs, US House of Reps. on Grazing Fee Legislation, Sep 22, 1987." 5 pages.

Johnson, Aubrey Stephen. 1987a. "If It's a Wild and Free Animal, then Kill It!" *High Country News*. Oct 15: 13-14.

Jones, K.B. 1981. "Effects of Grazing on Lizard Abundance and Diversity in Western Arizona." *The Southwestern Naturalist.* 26: 107-115.

Jones, Lisa. 1991. "Federal Study Finds Few Illegal Grazers Fined by BLM." *High Country News.* Feb 25: 6.

Jones, Lisa. 1991a. "Overgrazing: Feds Move to End It." *High Country News.* Apr 8: 1, 10-12. (A report on several current public lands ranching political battles, with an oddly inappropriate title and conclusion, however.)

Joyce, Linda A. 1989. *An Analysis of the Range Forage Situation in the United States: 1989-2040. General Technical Report RM-180.* Rocky Mountain Forest and Range Experiment Station, Fort Collins, CO. USDA, FS. (Ten-year assessment mandated by the Forest and Rangeland Renewable Resources Planning Act of 1974; a mostly redundant and unredeeming document that promotes the party line.)

Kay, Charles. 1986. "Streambed Basics." *Montana Magazine.* Jul/Aug: 72-73.

Kay, Charles. 1988. "Leave It to the Beavers." *Montana Magazine.* May/Jun: 15-16.

Keller, C.R. and K.P. Burnham. 1982. "Riparian Fencing, Grazing, and Trout Habitat Preference on Summit Creek, Idaho." *North American Journal of Fisheries Management.* 2: 53-59.

Kellogg, W.W. and S.H. Schneider. 1977. "Climate, Desertification, and Human Activities." In *Desertification: Environmental Degradation in and around Arid Lands,* ed. M.H. Glantz. Westview Press, Boulder, CO.

Keogh, Tanja. 1988. U.S. Predator Control -- a Legacy of Destruction. *Earth First! Journal.* Mar 20: 18-19. (Excellent).

Kessler, W.B. and R.P. Bosch. 1982. "Sharp-tailed Grouse and Range Management Practices in Western Rangelands." Pages 133-146 in J.M. Peek and P.D. Dalke (eds.), *Wildlife-livestock Relationships Symposium: Proceedings 10.* University of Idaho Forest, Wildlife, and Range Experiment Station, Moscow, ID.

Kirsch, L.M. 1969. "Waterfowl Production in Relation to Grazing." *Journal of Wildlife Management.* 33: 821-828.

Klemmedson, J.D. 1956. "Interrelations of Vegetation, Soils, and Range Conditions Induced by Grazing." *Journal of Range Management.* 33: 134-138.

Klemmedson, James O. and Paul E. Parker. 1979. *Public Rangelands and Federal Policy -- Choices and Consequences.* The Society of American Foresters. 31 pages.

Knickerbocker, Brad. 1990. "Cattle, Mining Strain Fragile Lands." *The Christian Science Monitor.* May 23: 7.

Knoll, G. and H.H. Hopkins. 1959. "The Effects of Grazing and Trampling upon Certain Soil Properties." *Transactions of the Kansas Academy of Sciences.* 62: 221-231.

Knopf, F.L. and R.W. Cannon. 1982. "Structural Resilience of a Willow Riparian Community to Changes in Grazing Practices." Pages 198-207 in J.M Peek and P.D. Dalke, Editors, *Wildlife-livestock Relations Symposium: Proceedings 10,* University of Idaho, Forestry, Wildlife, and Range Experiment Station, Moscow.

Koford, Carl B. 1953. **The California Condor.** National Audubon Society, 950 Third Ave., New York, NY 10022. 154 pages.

Kratz, Andrew & James Kagan. 1986. "Grasslands Amid the Forests." *The Nature Conservancy News.* Jun/Jul: 10-13.

Lacey, J.R. and W. Van Poollen. 1981. "Comparison of Herbage Production on Moderately Grazed and Ungrazed Western Ranges." *Journal of Range Management.* 34: 210-212.

Lappe, Frances Moore. 1986. **World Hunger: 12 Myths.** Grove Press, New York, NY. 208 pages.

Lappe, Frances Moore and Joseph Collins. 1979. **Food First: Beyond the Myth of Scarcity.** Ballantine Books, New York, NY. 619 pages. (Tends to trivialize human overpopulation, yet contains much useful information.)

Larson, F. and W. Whitman. 1942. "A Comparison of Used and Unused Grassland and Mesas in the Badlands of South Dakota." *Ecology.* 23: 438-445.

Laycock, W.A. 1967. "How Heavy Grazing and Protection Affect Sagebrush-Grass Ranges." *Journal of Range Management.* 20: 206-213.

Laycock, W.A. 1969. *Exclosures and Natural Areas on Rangelands in Utah (Research Paper INT-62).* USDA, Intermountain Forest and Range Experiment Station, Ogden, UT. 44 pages.

Laycock, W.A. and P.W. Conrad. 1967a. "Effect of Grazing on Soil Compaction as Measured by Bulk Density on a High Elevation Cattle Range." *Journal of Range Management.* 20: 136-140.

Leopold, Aldo. 1924. "Grass, Brush, Timber, and Fire in Southern Arizona." *Journal of Forestry.* 22(6): 1-10.

Leopold, A. S. 1951. "Ecosystem Deterioration Under Multiple Use." Presented to the Wild Trout Management Symposium, Yellowstone National Park, Sep 26, 1974. 5 pages.

Leopold, Luna B. 1985 [assumed]. "Vegetation of Southwestern Watersheds in the Nineteenth Century." *The Geographical Review.* [Date unknown]: 294-316.

Lesperance, A.L., P.T. Tueller, and V.R. Bohman. 1970. "Competitive Use of the Range Forage Resource." *Journal of Animal Science.* 30: 115-122.

Lessner, Richard. 1991. "Dancing With Wolves: Ranchers Should Lose This War." *The Arizona Republic.* Apr 1: A12. (An aggressive, barely concealed call for an end to public lands ranching -- by a deputy editor of Arizona's largest newspaper.)

● Leydet, Francois. 1977. **The Coyote,** Defiant Songdog of the West. University of Oklahoma Press, Norman, OK. 221 pages. (This enthralling book looks closely at the ranching industry's predator control efforts.)

Loft, Eric R., *et. al.* 1987. "Influence of Cattle Stocking Rate on the Structural Profile of Deer Hiding Cover." *Journal of Wildlife Management.* 51 (3): 655-664.

Lorz, H. 1974. "Ecology and Management of Brown Trout in Little Deschutes River, Oregon." Department of Fish & Wildlife, Portland, OR.

Lowdermilk, W.C. 1975. *Conquest of the Land through 7,000 Years.* US Govt. Printing Office. 30 pages. (In 1938 Dr. Lowdermilk was commissioned by the US government to study the historic causes of disastrous soil erosion around the globe.)

• Luoma, Jon R. 1986. "Discouraging Words." *Audubon*. Sep: 87-104. (A well-researched article; page for page one of the best summaries of public lands ranching.)

Lusby, G.C. 1970. "Hydrologic and Biotic Effects of Grazing Vs. Non-grazing near Grand Junction, Colorado." *Journal of Range Management*. 23: 256-260.

Mack, Richard N. 1981. *Invasion of Bromus Techtorum* [cheatgrass] *into Western North America: An Ecological Chronicle*. Elsevier Scientific Publishing Company. 22 pages.

Mack, Richard N. 1984. "Invaders at Home on the Range." *Natural History*. Feb: 40-47. (Discusses plant invaders.)

Mackie, Richard J. 1970. "Range Ecology and Relations of Mule Deer, Elk, and Cattle in the Missouri River Breaks, Montana." *Wildlife Monographs*. 20: 79.

Mackie, Richard J. 1978. "Impacts of Livestock Grazing on Wild Ungulates." *Transactions of the North American Wildlife and Natural Resources Conference*. 43: 462-476.

Maidenburg, H.J. 1973. "The Livestock Population Explosion." *New York Times*. [Date unknown]: Page 1, Finance section.

Malachowski, Sava. 1988. "Bloody Shame." *Penthouse*. Oct: 106-112. (Good article on predator slaughter.)

Malin, James C. 1956. **The Grassland of North America**. Edwards Brothers, Inc., Ann Arbor, MI. 469 pages. (Discard the farming portions and abundant misinformation and you have an interesting study of grasslands and grassland ecology.)

Marcuson, P. 1977. "The Effect of Cattle Grazing on Brown Trout in Rock Creek." Montana Fish & Game Department, Helena.

Marlow, Clayton B. *et. al.* 1989. "Response of a Southwest Montana Riparian System to Four Grazing Management Alternatives." In *Practical Approaches to Riparian Resource Management: An Educational Workshop*. USDI, BLM. US Govt. Printing Office. 111-116.

Marquiss, R. and R. Lang. 1959. "Vegetational Composition and Ground Cover of Two Natural Relict Areas in the Red Desert of Wyoming." *Journal of Range Management*. 12: 104-109.

Marston, Ed. 1990. "Ranchers' Hold on Agency Revealed" (and accompanying article). *High Country News*. May 7: 6-10.

Marston, Ed. 1991. "Rocks and Hard Places." *Wilderness*. March: 38-45.

Marten, Robert. 1991. "The Technology of Torture." *Earth First! Journal*. May 1: 37. (A right-on expose of trappers and trapping.)

Mason, Jim and Peter Singer. 1980. **Animal Factories**. Crown Publishers, New York, NY. (An excellent look at factory farming, including the feedlots where nearly all public lands cattle end up.)

Matteson, Mollie. 1989. "National Wildlife Refuges of the West: A Primer." *Earth First! Journal*. Sep. 22: 35.

Matthews, Jim. 1987. "Hunting 'Til the Cows Come Home." *Fins and Feathers*. [Date unknown]: 52-55.

Matthiessen, Peter. 1959. **Wildlife in America**. The Viking Press, New York, NY. 304 pages.

McClellan, Doug. 1985. "Ranchers Decry 'Shameful' Fees." *The El Paso Times*, El Paso, TX. Jun 8.

• McCoy, J.J. 1974. **Wild Enemies**. Hawthorne Books, Inc., New York, NY. 210 pages. (Good overview of Western predators and the ranching industry's war against them.)

McGinty, W.A., F.S. Smeins, and L.B. Merrill. 1979. "Influence of Soil, Vegetation, and Grazing Management on Infiltration Rate and Sediment Production of Edwards Plateau Rangeland." *Journal of Range Management*. 32: 33-37.

McLean, A. and E.W. Tisdale. 1972. "Recovery Rate of Depleted Range Sites under Protection from Grazing." *Journal of Range Management*. 25: 178-184.

McLuhan, T.C. 1971. **Touch the Earth: A Self-Portrait of Indian Existence**. E.P. Dutton & Co., New York, NY. (A wonderful collection of quotes from people who felt their natural connection with the Earth.)

McMahan, C.A. and C.W. Ramsey. 1965. "Response of Deer and Livestock to Controlled Grazing in Central Texas." *Journal of Range Management*. 18: 1-7.

McMillan, Doug. 1990. "Grass-roots Rustling." *High Country News*. Jul 2: 11.

McMillan, Ian. 1968. **Man and the California Condor**. E.P. Dutton & Co., New York, NY. 191 pages.

McNamee, Thomas. 1985. **The Grizzly Bear**. Alfred A. Knopf, Inc., New York, NY. 308 pages. (Insufficient discussion of the ranching problem, but a good study of the grizzly.)

McNulty, Faith. 1970. **Must They Die?: The Strange Case of the Prairie Dog and the Black-footed Ferret**. Doubleday & Company, Inc., Garden City, NY.

Meehan, William R. and William S. Platts. 1978. "Livestock Grazing and the Aquatic Environment." *Journal of Soil and Water Conservation*. 33: 274-278.

Mentzer, L.W. 1950. "Studies on Plant Succession in True Prairie." *Ecological Monographs*. 21: 255-267.

Merchant, Carolyn. 1979. **The Death of Nature**. Harper & Row, New York, NY. 348 pages.

Miller, James Nathan. 1983. "What *Really* Happened at EPA." *Reader's Digest*. Jul: 59-64. (Intriguing look at the sordid politics of Reagan's "environmental" staff.)

Milstein, Michael. 1991. "A Federal Killing Machine Rolls On." *High Country News*. Jan 28: 1, 12-14. (Excellent report on ADC.)

Mohler, J.R. 1923. **Diseases of Cattle: a Special Report by the USDA**. US Govt. Printing Office. 563 pages.

Molde, Don. 1984. "The Western Livestock Industry -- Last Bastion of Free Enterprise or Heavily Subsidized Environmental Disaster?" *American Forum*. Feb: 10-11.

Morgan, James K. 1971. "Ecology of the Morgan Creek and East Fork of the Salmon River Bighorn Sheep Herds and Management of Bighorn Sheep in Idaho." M.S. Thesis, Utah State University. 156 pages.

Morris, Randall E. 1985. *An Analysis of Wildlife and Wildlife Forage Allocations by the BLM on Six Ranges of Public Land in South Idaho*. Committee for Idaho's High Desert, P.O. Box 2863, Boise, ID 83701. 9 pages.

Morris, Randall E. 1986. "Chicken of the Desert." *Earth First! Journal*. Jun 21: 19. (This hilarious satire introduces a viable alternative to the USDA's grasshopper [winged bison] extermination program: replace beef production with grasshopper harvesting and thereby greatly increase food yield.)

Mosley, Jeffrey C. *et. al.* 1990. *Seven Popular MYTHS About Livestock Grazing on Public Lands.* University of Idaho, Idaho Forest, Wildlife, and Range Station. (Indicating that the ranching establishment is indeed getting worried, 3 professional range prostitutes at 2 land grant colleges wrote this propaganda booklet specifically to quell growing opposition to public lands ranching; it has been widely discredited.)

● Muir, John. 1961. **The Mountains of California.** Doubleday & Company, Inc., Garden City, NY. 300 pages. (A superb book, with some parts pertinent to livestock grazing.)

Nabhan, Gary. 1986. **Gathering the Desert.** The University of Arizona Press, Tucson, AZ. 209 pages. (A fine work on native desert plants used by Native Americans.)

National Audubon Society. 1973. *Federal Subsidies to the Sheep and Goat Industry.* National Audubon Society, New York, NY. 11 pages.

● National Audubon Society. 1991. *The New Range Wars.* Turner Broadcasting System, Inc., Box 105366, Atlanta, GA 30348. 1-hour film. (The only feature-length documentary on public lands ranching. Ranching establishment pressure induced Ford Motor Company to pull its sponsorship for the program.)

National Wildlife Federation and the Natural Resources Defense Council. 1985. *Our Ailing Rangelands: Condition Report -- 1985.* National Wildlife Federation, 1412 Sixteenth St., NW, Washington, DC 20036, NRDC. 40 pages.

National Wildlife Federation and the Natural Resources Defense Council. 1989. *Our Ailing Rangelands, Still Ailing: Condition Report -- 1989.* NWF, NRDC. 40 pages.

● Natural Resources Defense Council *et. al.* 1973. *Civil Action No. 1983-73 in the United States District Court for the District of Columbia: Complaint for Declaratory Judgement and Injunctive Relief.* Natural Resources Defense Council, 90 New Montgomery, Suite 620, San Francisco, CA 94105. 23 pages. (The key lawsuit filed by NRDC and others that forced BLM to at least go through the motions of preparing EISs for BLM lands.)

Neumann, A.L. and Roscoe R. Snapp. 1969. **Beef Cattle.** John Wiley & Sons, New York, NY. 768 pages.

Noss, Reed. 1986. "Do We Really Want Diversity?" *Earth First! Journal.* Jun 21: 20. (The 1-page length of this article belies the importance of its message: "managing for diversity" is not necessarily managing for environmental health.)

Nowakowski, Nancy A. *et. al.* 1982. *Run Wild: Wildlife/Habitat Relationships.* For the US Forest Service, SW Region. US Govt. Printing Office. 10 pages.

Ogden Standard-Examiner. 1984. "BLM Sued Over Grazing Policies." Jun 3: 6D.

Olson, Jack. 1971. "The Poisoning of the West." *Sports Illustrated.* Mar: 8, 15, and 22.

O'Mary, C.C. and Irwin A. Dyer. 1972. **Commercial Beef Cattle Production.** Lea & Febinger, Philadelphia, PA. 393 pages.

O'Neill, Molly. 1990. "Cows in Trouble: An Icon of the Good Life Ends Up On a Crowded Planet's Hit List." *The New York Times.* May 6: Section 4, pages 1, 4.

Oppenheimer, H.L. 1971. **Cowboy Arithmetic.** Interstate Printers and Publishers, Danville, IL. 246 pages.

● Oregon Natural Desert Association. 1990. *Desert Ramblings.* Nov-Dec: 1-6. (This special issue of *Desert Ramblings* features several fine short articles on public lands ranching and a boycott of same.)

Orodho, A.B., M.J. Trlica, and C.D. Bonham. 1990. "Long-term Heavy Grazing Effects on Soil and Vegetation in the Four Corners Region." *The Southwestern Naturalist.* 35(1): 9-14.

Orr, H.K. 1975. "Recovery from Soil Compaction on Bluegrass Range in the Black Hills." *Transactions of the American Society of Agricultural Engineers.* 18: 1076-1081

O'Toole, K. Ross. 1976. **The Rape of the Great Plains: Northwest America, Cattle and Coal.** Little Brown, Boston, MA.

O'Toole, Randal. 1988. **Reforming the Forest Service.** Island Press, Washington, DC. 254 pages. (Far too little on ranching, but a strong critique of the FS timber program.)

Overmire, Thomas C. 1964. "The Effects of Grazing upon the Habitat Utilization of the Dickcissel (*Spiza americana*) and Bell's Vireo (*Vireo bellii*) in North Central Oklahoma." *Dissertation Abstracts.* 25: 1425.

Pacelle, Wayne. 1988. "Wyoming's Predator Defender: An Interview with Dick Randall." *The Animals' Agenda*, P.O. Box 5234, Westport, CT 06881. Jan/Feb: 4-8. (A former predator control agent, Dick knows what he's talking about.)

Packer, P.E. 1953. "Effects of Trampling Disturbance on Watershed Condition, Runoff, and Erosion." *Journal of Forestry.* 51: 28-31.

● Palmer, Katey. 1988. "Return of the Natives." *Earth First! Journal.* Dec 21: 26. (A succinct, scientific explanation of why livestock don't belong on Western bunchgrass rangelands.)

Patterson, Robert L. 1952. **The Sage Grouse in Wyoming.** Sage Books, Denver, CO. 341 pages.

Peacock, Doug, Editor. 1988. *Independent Grizzly Bear Report.* Earth First! Journal. 16 pages.

Pearce, Fred. 1989. "Methane: the Hidden Greenhouse Gas." *New Scientist.* May 6: 37-41.

Peden, D.G., et al. 1974. "The Trophic Ecology of *Bison bison* L. on Shortgrass Plains." *Journal of Applied Ecology.* 11: 489-495.

Peters, Donald M. 1990. "Give Me a Range Where Never Is Heard a Discouraging Herd." *The Arizona Republic.* May 30: A10. (This guest editorial by a Phoenix attorney is perhaps the best short piece on public lands ranching I've read.)

Pickford, G.D. 1960. "The Influence of Continued Heavy Grazing and of Promiscuous Burning of Spring-fall Ranges in Utah." *Ecology.* 13: 159-171.

Pieper, R.D. and R.K. Heitschmidt. 1988. "Is Short-duration Grazing the Answer?" *Journal of Soil and Water Conservation.* 43: 133-137.

Pimentel, David. 1976. "Land Degradation: Effects on Food and Energy Resources." *Science.* Vol. 194: 149.

Pimentel, David and Martha. 1979. **Food, Energy, and Society.** John Wiley & Sons, New York, NY. 165 pages.

Platts, William S. 1978. "Livestock Interactions with Fish and Aquatic Environments: Problems in Evaluation." *Transactions of North American Wildlife and Natural Resource Conference.* 43: 498-504.

Platts, William S. 1981. "Streamside Management to Protect Bank-channel Stability and Aquatic Life." Pages 245-255 in D.M. Baumgartner (ed.), *Interior West Watershed Management: Proceedings from a Symposium*. Cooperative Extension, Washington State University, Pullman, WA.

Platts, William S. 1989. "Compatibility of Livestock Grazing Fisheries." In *Practical Approaches to Riparian Resource Management: An Educational Workshop*. USDI, BLM. US Govt. Printing Office. 103-110.

Platts, William S. 1990. "Fish, Wildlife and Livestock: Protection of Riparian Areas." *Western Wildlands*. Summer: 16-19.

Platts, William S. and Rodger L. Nelson. 1989a. "Characteristics of Riparian Plant Communities and Streambanks with Respect to Grazing in Northeastern Utah." In *Practical Approaches to Riparian Resource Management: An Educational Workshop*. USDI, BLM. US Govt. Printing Office. 73-81.

• Pope, C. Arden III. 1987. "More Than Economics Influences Allocation of Rangeland Resources." Choices. 1030 15th St., NW, Suite 920, Washington, DC. 20005. Fourth Quarter: 24-25. (A fresh look at how romantic image affects the economics of public lands ranching -- from an associate professor at an agricultural college, Mormon bishop, and son of a ranching family!)

Popper, Deborah Epstein and Frank J. 1988. "The Fate of the Plains." *High Country News*. Sep 26: 15-19.

Potter, Albert Franklin. 1905. *Grazing Lands, Western United States* (map). USDA. (This vintage map is a real classic; it is big and with shading and crosshatching shows the basic kinds of livestock grazing that occurred on about 80% of the West at the turn of the century; it remains mostly applicable.)

Potter, L.D. and J.C. Kremetsky. 1967. "Plant Succession with Released Grazing on New Mexico Rangelands." *Journal of Range Management*. 20: 145-151.

Potvin, M.A. and A.T. Harrison. 1984. "Vegetation and Litter Changes of a Nebraska Sandhills Prairie Protected from Grazing." *Journal of Range Management*. Jan: 55-58.

Prescott National Forest Friends, *et al*. 1987. *Statement of Reasons in Support of the Appeal of The Land and Resource Management Plan and Environmental Impact Statement for The Prescott National Forest*. Pages 25-63. (An excellent challenge of the land use plan of Arizona's Prescott National Forest based on its failure to comply with numerous legal mandates; could apply to the range portions of nearly any FS or BLM plan.)

Public Lands Council. 1983. *The Western Livestock Industry and the Public Lands*. Public Lands Council, 220 Livestock Exchange Bldg., Denver, CO 20004. 14 pages. (In black and white, this powerful organization of public lands ranchers lists its plans for the takeover of our public lands and the theft of tax dollars. Not a joke!)

Rauzi, F. and F.M. Smith. 1973. "Infiltration Rates: Three Soils and Three Grazing Levels in Northeastern Colorado." *Journal of Range Management*. 26: 126-129.

Reed, M.J. and R.A. Peterson. 1961. *Vegetation, Soil, and Cattle Responses to Grazing on Northern Great Plains Range: USDA, Forest Service Technical Bulletin No. 1252*. 79 pages.

Reitman, Jude. 1990. "Our Incredible War on Wildlife." *E* magazine. May/Jun 1990. 36-41, 64.

Reynolds, T.D. 1979. "Response of Reptile Populations to Different Land Management Practices on the Idaho National Engineering Laboratory Site." *Great Basin Naturalist* 39: 255-262.

Reynolds, T.D. and C.H. Trost. 1980. "The Response of Native Vertebrate Populations to Crested Wheatgrass Planting and Grazing by Sheep." *Journal of Range Management*. 33: 122-125.

Rich, L.R. and H.G. Reynolds. 1963. "Grazing in Relation to Runoff and Erosion on Some Chaparral Watersheds in Central Arizona." *Journal of Range Management*. 6: 322-326.

Rickard, W.H. and C.E. Cushing. 1982. "Recovery of Streamside Woody Vegetation after Exclusion of Livestock Grazing." *Journal of Range Management*. 35: 360-361.

Rickard, W.H., W.D. Vresk, and J.F. Cline. 1975. "The Impact of Cattle Grazing on Three Perennial Grasses in South-central Washington." *Journal of Range Management*. 28: 108-112.

Robbins, Jim. 1987. "The Continuing Saga of the West's Wild Horse." *High Country News*. Mar 16: 8-12.

Robbins, Jim. 1991. "Are Cowboys Killing the West?" *USA Weekend*. Apr 19-21: 4-6. (Shallow, loaded, predictable -- the same standard struggling-cowboy-hero formula used so much by the popular media.)

• Robbins, John. 1987. **Diet for a New America**. Stillpoint Publishing, Box 640, Walpole, NH 03608. 390 pages. (A well-written, well-researched, very informative account of animal foods production and its consequences; highly recommended.)

Robbins, John. 1990. *Realities 1989*. EarthSave, P.O. Box 949, Felton, CA 95018-0949. 11 pages. (Documented vital facts on the animal foods industry excerpted from **Diet for a New America**.)

Robbins, John. 1989a. "The Ground Beneath Our Feet." The *Animals' Voice*, P.O. Box 1649, Martinez, CA 94553. Feb: 59-65. ("There is not a single aspect of the ecological crisis that would not be immediately and profoundly improved by [switching to a plant-centered diet]." For the Earth's sake, if not your body's, read what Robbins has to say.)

Roberts, Paul H. 1963. **Hoof Prints on Forest Ranges**. The Naylor Company, San Antonio, TX. 151 pages. (Roberts, a long-time FS official, though obviously infatuated with ranching trivia and romanticism, provides useful information on early ranching on public forests.)

Rosetta, Noel. 1985. "Herds, Herds on the Range." *Sierra*. Mar/Apr: 42-47. (Summarizes public lands ranching.)

Rowley, William D. 1985. **U.S. Forest Service Grazing and Rangelands: A History**. Texas A & M University, College Station, TX.

Royte, Elizabeth. 1990. "Showdown in Cattle Country." *The New York Times Magazine*. Dec 16: 60-70. (A fairly good summary of the issue.)

Rummell, R.S. 1951. "Some Effects of Livestock Grazing on Ponderosa Pine Forest and Range in Central Washington." *Ecology*. 32: 594-607.

Russo, John P. 1956. *The Desert Bighorn Sheep of Arizona: A Research and Management Study.* Arizona Game & Fish Department. 153 pages.

Sacramento Bee. 1987. "BLM's Cash Cows." *The Sacramento Bee.* Sep 30: Forum section, page 4.

● Sampson, A.W. and L.H. Weyl. 1918. *Range Preservation and Its Relation to Erosion Control on Western Grazing Lands: USDA Bulletin No. 675.* 35 pages. (Good discussion of soil-livestock dynamics.)

Sampson, R.N. 1981. **Farmland or Wasteland: A Time to Chose.** Rodale Press, Emmaus, PA.

Satchell, Michael and Joannie M. Schrof. 1990. "Uncle Sam's War on Wildlife." *US News & World Report.* Feb 5: 36-37.

Satchell, Michael. 1990a. "Last Roundup on the Range." *US News & World Report.* Nov 26: 30-32. (A good though brief article.)

Savage, William W., Jr., Editor. 1975. **Cowboy Life: Reconstructing an American Myth.** University of Oklahoma Press, Norman, OK. 208 pages. (Selections from 13 writers on Western history provide diverse interpretations of the original 1800s cow-boy and his life; with photos.)

● Savage, William W., Jr. 1979. **The Cowboy Hero.** The University of Oklahoma Press, Norman, OK. 179 pages. (Our brain cells are saturated with cowboy/rancher mythology. This fascinating and perceptive book helps us distinguish fantasy from reality -- highly recommended!)

Savory, Allan. 1988. **Holistic Resource Management.** Island Press, Washington, DC. 512 pages. ("The Grazing Guru" details his methods of ecosystem manipulation and defines his infrastructure for planetary management by humans.)

Sayen, Jamie. 1989. "Taking Steps Toward a Restoration Ethic." *Earth First! Journal.* May 1: 14-16. (In contrast to the above: We can't fix Nature . . . we can put back the pieces and allow Nature to heal herself." Many important, original ideas discussed.)

Schlesinger, William H. *et al.* 198?. "Biological Feedbacks in Global Desertification." *Science.* Mar 2: 1043-1048.

Schmidt, William E. 1989. "Nature Sows Life Where Man Brewed Death." *New York Times.* Mar 12: Section 1, pages 1, 15.

Schmutz, Ervin M., Charles C. Michaels, and Ira Judd. 1967. "Boysag Point -- A Relict Area of the North Rim of Grand Canyon in Arizona." *Journal of Range Management.* 20: 363-369.

Schultz, Robert L. *et al.* 1971. *Range Conditions on the Organ Pipe National Monument.* USDI, BLM. 24 pages.

● Sears, Paul B. 1967. **Deserts on the March.** University of Oklahoma Press, Norman, OK. 178 pages. (Outlines destructive land use in the US from an environmentally responsible perspective; generally good eco-philosophy, somewhat overbearing, even naively patriotic at times -- but written in 1935.)

Seton, Ernest Thompson. 1929. **Lives of Game Animals. Vol. 3, Part 1.** Doubleday, Doran, Garden City NY. 412 pages.

Shands, William E. and Robert G. Healy. 1972. **The Lands Nobody Wanted.** The Conservation Foundation, Washington, DC.

● Shanks, Bernard. 1984. **This Land Is Your Land.** Sierra Club Books, San Francisco, CA. 310 pages. (Chronicles public lands administration by land use, with a fine chapter on ranching.)

Sharp, A.L., *et al.* 1964. "Runoff as Affected by Intensity of Grazing Rangeland." *Journal of Soil and Water Conservation.* 19: 103-106.

Shaw, Harley G. 1985. *Mountain Lion Field Guide.* Research Branch, Arizona Game & Fish Commission, Phoenix, AZ. 43 pages. (Funded by Arizona hunters and anglers, produced by the Arizona Game & Fish Department, this is little more than a handbook, mainly for ranchers, on how to kill mountain lions.)

● Sheridan, David. 1981. **Desertification of the United States.** Council on Environmental Quality. 142 pages. (Portions document and discuss ranching as a cause of desertification in the West.)

Sidey, Hugh. 1990. "Where the Buffalo Roamed." *Time.* Sep 24: 53-56.

Sierra editors. 1990. "Thoroughly Cowed." *Sierra.* Sep-Oct: 37. (*Sierra*'s editors provide one of the most appropriate short appraisals of the stop-public-ranching effort.)

Singer, Peter. 1975. **Animal Liberation.** Random House, New York, NY. 301 pages.

Skovlin, J.M., P.J. Edgerton, and R.W. Harris. 1968. "The Influence of Cattle Management on Deer and Elk." *Transactions of the 33rd North American Wildlife Conference.* Pages 169-181.

● Skovlin, Jon. 1987. "Southern Africa's Experience with Intensive Short Duration Grazing." *Rangelands.* Aug: 162-166. (Certified Range Consultant Skovlin, after 3 years in Africa where Allan Savory claims great victories for HRM-style grazing, states that he is "amazed by the interest and wide acceptance of intensive short duration grazing as popularized by" Savory and HRM.)

Smith, Arthur D. 1961. "Competition for Forage by Game and Livestock." *Utah Farm and Home Science.* 22: 8-9, 23.

Smith, D.A. and E.M. Schmutz. 1975. "Vegetation Changes in Protected Versus Grazed Desert Grassland Ranges in Arizona." *Journal of Range Management.* 28: 453-458.

Smith, Jared G. 1895. "Conditions of the Prairie Region." In **USDA Yearbook of Agriculture**: 1895. Pages 309-324.

Smith, Jared G. 1899. *Grazing Problems in the Southwest and How to Meet Them: USDA, Division of Agrostology Bulletin No. 16.* 47 pages.

Smith, Richard J. 1977. "Conclusions." In *Proceedings of a Seminar on Improving Fish and Wildlife Benefits in Range Management.* Biological Services Program, FWS, Washington, DC (FWS OBS-77/1).

Smith, Richard J. 1978. **Condor Journal: The History, Mythology, and Reality of the California Condor.** Capra Press, Santa Barbara, CA. 135 pages.

Soule, Michael E., Editor. 1986. **Conservation Biology: The Science of Scarcity and Diversity.** Sinauer Associates, Inc., Sunderland, MA. 584 pages.

Sprague, Howard B., Editor. 1974. **Grasslands of the United States: Their Economic and Ecologic Importance.** The Iowa State University Press. 220 pages. (Not a book on grasslands, but on using grasslands for ranching.)

Stein, Mark A. and Louis Sahagun. 1989. "Ranchers Turn a Profit by Subletting U.S. Land." *Los Angeles Times*. May 23: Section 1, pages 26-27. (A good article on subleasing, fees, and politics.)

Stephenson, G.R. and Anne Veigel. 1987. "Recovery of Compacted Soil on Pastures Used for Winter Cattle Feeding." *Journal of Range Management*. Jan: 46-48.

Stoddart, Laurence A. 1945. *Range Land of America and Some Research on Its Management*. Utah State Agricultural College, Fourth Annual Faculty Research Lecture, Logan, UT. 32 pages.

Stone, Judith. 1989. "Bovine Madness." *Discover*. Feb: 38-42.

● Strassmann, Beverly I. 1983. "Grazing Programs on Federal Rangelands and Refuges: Consequences for Wildlife, Beef Production, and Fossil Fuel Use." MS Thesis. Cornell University, Ithaca, NY. 167 pages. (A good description of the impacts of ranching on National Wildlife Refuges.)

Strassmann, Beverly I. 1983a. "Effects of Cattle Grazing and Haying on Wildlife Conservation at National Wildlife Refuges in the United States." *Environmental Management*. Vol. 11, No. 1: 35-44.

● Strickland, Rose. 1990. "Taking the Bull by the Horns." *Sierra*. Sep-Oct: 46-48. (A long-time ranching reformist skillfully addresses the futility of ranching reform.)

Suk, T., *et al*. 1986. "Water Contamination with Giardia in Backcountry Areas." *Proceedings of the National Wilderness Conference, USDA, Ogden, UT*. 238-239.

Szaro, R.C., S.C. Belfit, and J.N. Rinne. 1985. "Impact of Grazing on a Riparian Garter Snake." Pages 359-363 in *Riparian Ecosystems and Their Management: Reconciling Conflicting Uses*. Proceedings of the Symposium. US Dept. Agric. For. Serv. Gen. Tech. Rep. RM-120, 523 pages. Rocky Mountain Forest and Range Experiment Station, Fort Collins, CO.

Taylor, D. 1986. "Effects of Cattle Grazing on Passerine Birds Nesting in Riparian Habitat." *Journal of Range Management*. 39(3).

● Thwaites, Reuben Gold. 1959. **Original Journals of the Lewis and Clark Expedition, 1804-1806, in Seven Volumes and an Atlas.** Antiquarian Press Ltd., New York, NY. 2704 pages total, plus a 52-part atlas. (One of the best descriptions of the Western landscape before it was ravaged by ranching and other human influences, as well as a glimpse into the unbelievably pernicious, exploitive, wasteful mentality of those who conquered the West.)

Tiedemann, A.R. *et al*. 1987. "Responses of Fecal Coliform in Streamwater to Four Grazing Strategies." *Journal of Range Management*. Jul: 322-329.

● Tittman, Paul B. (FS) and Clifton E. Brownell (BLM). 1984. *Appraisal Report Estimating Fair Market Rental Value of Grazing on Public Lands*. USDA, FS and USDI, BLM Washington, DC. 281 pages. (Mandated by PRIA; one look at this monstrous statistical nightmare should convince anyone of the absurdity of ranching public lands.)

Trueblood, T. 1980. "They're Fixing to Steal Your Land." *Field and Stream*. [Date unknown]: 40-41, 166-167. ("They" is mostly stockmen.)

Turkowski, Frank J. 1975. "Dietary Adaptability of the Desert Cottontail." *Journal of Wildlife Management*. 39: 748-756.

Turner, Dale S. 1989. "A National Wildlife Refuge System?" *Earth First! Journal*. Feb 2: 1, 5.

Turner, Raymond M., *et al*. 1980. *Arizona Range Reference Areas (General Technical Report RM-79)*. USDA, Rocky Mountain Forest and Range Experiment Station, Ft. Collins, CO. 34 pages, with map. (Gives descriptions and shows locations of most livestock exclosures in Arizona. Similar reports have been prepared for other Western states; yet, few exclosures have been studied for comparative purposes.)

United Nations Environment Program. Various issues. Various articles. *Desertification Control Bulletins*. UNEP, P.O. Box 30552, Nairobi, Kenya. (Good sources of information on world livestock production impacts.)

US Council on Environmental Quality. 1975. *Environmental Quality: 6th Annual Report of CEQ*. US Govt. Printing Office.

US Department of Agriculture. 1987. **Agricultural Statistics: 1987**. US Govt. Printing Office. 541 pages.

US Department of Agriculture. 1988. *Report of the Secretary of Agriculture: 1987*. USDA. 53 pages.

US Department of Agriculture, APHIS. 1986. *Rangeland Grasshopper Cooperative Management Program, Final Environmental Impact Statement as Supplemented -- 1986*. USDA, APHIS. About 300 pages.

US Department of Agriculture, APHIS. 1987. *Rangeland Grasshopper Cooperative Management Program, Final Environmental Impact Statement -- 1987*. USDA, APHIS, PPQ.

US Department of Agriculture, Forest Service. 1962. *Rotation Grazing Management*. USDA, Forest Service, Region 2. 11 pages.

US Department of Agriculture, Forest Service. 1970. *Regulations Governing Livestock Grazing on National Forest Service System Lands and Other Lands Under Forest Service Control*. US Govt. Printing Office. 26 pages.

US Department of Agriculture, Forest Service. 1980. **An Assessment of the Forest and Range Land Situation in the United States**. USDA, FS. 631 pages. (This is the assessment required by the Forest and Rangeland Renewable Resources Planning Act of 1974 as amended by the National Forest Management Act of 1976.)

US Department of Agriculture, Forest Service. 1983. **Beef Cattle Husbandry Study Course**. USDA, Forest Service, Southern Region. 254 pages.

US Department of Agriculture, Forest Service. 1988. *Report of the Forest Service, Fiscal Year 1987*. USDA, FS, Washington, DC. 188 pages.

US Department of Agriculture, Forest Service. 1987. "Finding of No Significant Impact: Grazing Fee Formula for Livestock Grazing, National Forests in the 16 Western States." USDA, FS. 23 pages. (The Forest Service's official, yet baseless, excuse for charging ranchers about 1/5 what livestock herbage is worth.)

US Department of Agriculture, Forest Service, Range Management. 1987. *Grazing Statistical Summary, FY 1988*. US Govt. Printing Office. 94 pages.

US Department of Agriculture, Forest Service, Southwestern Region. 1991. "Rangeland Ecosystem Management." 4 pages. (The Forest Service response to growing opposition: a stylish title, eco-rhetoric, policy distortion, contrived optimism, baseless and nebulous reform promises, and a list of strategies designed to "increase credibility" of public lands ranching.)

US Department of Agriculture, Forest Service, USDI, BLM, and Public Lands Council. 1989. *Livestock Grazing Successes on Public Range: USDA, FS Program Aid # 1439*. USDA, FS. 16 pages. (A fancy, full-color pamphlet; a literally unbelievable propaganda effort.)

US Department of Agriculture, SCS. 1976. **National Range Handbook**. SCS, USDA, P.O. Box 2890, Washington, DC 20013. 154 pages.

US Department of Agriculture, SCS. 1979. *Briefing Paper: SCS Range Program Funds*. SCS, USDA. 3 pages.

US Department of Agriculture, SCS. 1981. *America's Soil and Water: Condition and Trends*. USDA, SCS. 33 pages. (The basic facts on US soil and water conditions, as perceived by SCS.)

US Department of Agriculture, USDI, BLM. 1986. **Grazing Fee Review and Evaluation**. US Govt. Printing Office. 99 pages.

US Department of Agriculture, USDI, CEQ. 1979. *Rangeland Policies for the Future, Proceedings from a Symposium*. US Govt. Printing Office. 114 pages. (Printed statements of speakers -- mostly empty drivel designed to promote public lands ranching.)

• US Department of Agriculture and USDI Secretaries. 1986. **Grazing Fee Review and Evaluation, Final Report, 1979-1985**. USDA, FS and USDI, BLM, Washington, DC. 99 pages. (Loaded with useful charts, graphs, and fiscal info on public lands ranching.)

US Department of Commerce, Bureau of Census. 1986. **Statistical Abstract of the United States: 1987**. US Govt. Printing Office. 960 pages.

US Department of the Interior. 1990. *State of the Public Rangelands: 1990*. USDI, BLM. 12 pages. (Breast-beating.)

US Department of the Interior, BLM. 1951. "Rebuilding the Federal Range." USDI, BLM. Pages 8-11.

US Department of the Interior, BLM. 1976. *The Taylor Grazing Act of June 28, 1934: Information Bulletin No. 5 (with updates)*. US Govt. Printing Office. 8 pages.

US Department of the Interior, BLM. 1978. *Range Management and Technical Services: Grazing Administration and Trespass Regulations*. Federal Register, Vol. 43, No. 129. 20 pages.

US Department of the Interior, BLM. 1984. *50 Years of Public Land Management*. USDI, BLM. 28 pages.

US Department of the Interior, BLM. 1987. *Managing the Public Lands*. USDI, BLM. 56 pages. (Yet more breast-beating bullshit by the BLM.)

US Department of the Interior, BLM. 1988. **Public Land Statistics, 1987**. US Govt. Printing Office. 220 pages.

US Department of the Interior, BLM. 1988a. **United States Department of the Interior Budget Justifications, F.Y. 1989**. BLM, USDI. 413 pages.

US Department of the Interior, BLM and USDA, FS. 1980. *Third Report to Congress, June, 1980: Administration of the Wild Free-roaming Horse and Burro Act*. US Govt. Printing Office. 39 pages.

US Department of the Interior, BLM and USDA, FS. [1985? no date given]. *Experimental Stewardship Program: Report to Congress*. USDI, BLM. 67 pages. (A laughable propaganda effort designed to give ranchers more power on federal rangelands.)

US Department of the Interior, BLM *et al.* 1989. *Practical Approaches to Riparian Resource Management: An Educational Workshop*. US Govt. Printing Office. 193 pages. (Contains 53 scientific papers and abstracts on riparian dynamics and management, many relating to livestock grazing, some of which are quite informative.)

US Department of the Interior, FWS. 1976. *Final Environmental Impact Statement on the Operation of the National Wildlife Refuge System*. FWS, Washington, DC.

US Department of the Interior, FWS. 1981. *Kofa National Wildlife Refuge Final Environmental Impact Statement: Proposal to Eliminate Cattle and Wild Burros on Kofa National Wildlife Refuge*. FWS, Washington, DC.

US Department of the Interior, FWS. 1990. "Bighole Fence in the Pakoon Spring Allotment -- Biological Opinion." FWS, Phoenix, AZ. (Excellent documentation of ranching effects on the desert tortoise.)

US Department of the Interior, Minerals Management Service, Royalty Management Program. 1988. *Mineral Revenues: The 1987 Report on Receipts from Federal and Indian Leases*. USDI, MMS, RMP. 109 pages.

• US Department of the Interior, USGS. 1970. *Federal Lands* (map). USDI, USGS, Reston, VA 22092. (This color-coded US map portrays lands under the administration of various federal agencies.)

  • US Department of the Interior, USGS. 1985. *Potential Natural Vegetation* (map). USDI, USGS. (This highly detailed and beautiful, multi-colored map of the US shows 106 different potential natural vegetation types; includes thorough discussion on reverse.)

US Department of the Interior, USGS. 1987. *National Wilderness Preservation System* (map). USDI, USGS. (Shows all designated Wildernesses in the US, by agency; reverse side provides acreages.)

US Environmental Protection Agency and BLM. 1979. *Livestock Management and Water Quality Protection*. US Govt. Printing Office.

US General Accounting Office. 1986. *Rangeland Management: Profiles of Federal Grazing Program Permittees*. GAO, Washington, DC 20548. 23 pages. (Pie graphs portray BLM permittees.)

US General Accounting Office. 1986a. *Rangeland Management: Grazing Lease Arrangements of Bureau of Land Management Permittees*. GAO, Washington, DC. 17 pages.

• US General Accounting Office. 1988. *Public Rangelands: Some Riparian Areas Restored but Widespread Improvement Will Be Slow*. GAO, Washington, DC. 85 pages. (As all government publications, this one cannot envision the permanent removal of livestock, but presents an excellent case for just that. It also describes obstacles to better management caused by agencies and permittees.)

US General Accounting Office. 1988a. *Rangeland Management: More Emphasis Needed on Declining and Overstocked Grazing Allotments*. GAO, Washington, DC.

US Senate. 1936. "The Western Range." 74th Congress, 2nd Session: Senate Document 199. US Govt. Printing Office.

Uresk, Daniel W. 1985. "Effects of Controlling Black-tailed Prairie Dogs on Plant Production." *Journal of Range Management*. 38: 466-467.

Vale, T.R. 1975. "Presettlement Vegetation in the Sagebrush Grass Area of the Intermountain West." *Journal of Range Management*. 28: 32-36.

Vale, T.R. 1980 [assumed]. "The Sagebrush Landscape." Unknown periodical. Pages 31-37.

Vankat, John L. 1979. **The Natural Vegetation of North America**. John Wiley & Sons, New York, NY. 261 pages.

Vass, A.F. 1926. *Range and Ranch Studies in Wyoming: Wyoming Agricultural Experimental Station Bulletin No. 147*. 150 pages.

● Voigt, William, Jr. 1976. **Public Grazing Lands, Use and Misuse by Industry and Government**. Rutgers University Press. 359 pages. (An exhaustingly thorough look at the complex, sordid political history of public lands ranching. On the inside cover of my copy, Voigt notes, "The title should have been 'Rape of the Western Range.'")

● Wagner, Frederic H. 1978. *Livestock Grazing and the Livestock Grazing Industry*, pages 121-145, in **Wildlife in America**. Howard P. Brokaw, Editor. Council on Environmental Quality, Washington, DC. (Wagner provides, within the scope of his ranching-oriented vision, useful descriptions of ranching's effects on Western wildlife.)

Wagner, Frederic H. 1978a. "Western Rangelands: Troubled American Resource." *Transactions of the North American Wildlife and Natural Resources Conference*. 43: 453-461.

Wagstaff, Fred J. and C. Ardon Pope III. 1987. "Finding the Appropriate Forage Value for Analyzing the Feasibility of Public Range Improvements." USDA, FS, Intermountain Research Station, Ogden, UT. US Govt. Printing Office. 4 pages.

Wallace, L.L. 1987. "Effects of Clipping and Soil Compaction on Growth, Morphology, and Mycorrhizal Colonization of *Schizachyrum Scoparium*, a 4-carbon Pathway Bunchgrass." *Oecologia*. 72: 423-428.

Warren, A. and J.K. Maizels. 1977. "Ecological Change and Desertification." In *Desertification: Its Causes and Consequences*, Secretariat, UN Conference on Desertification, Nairobi, Kenya, 29 Aug to 9 Sep. Pergamon Press, Elmsford, NY.

Warren, Peter L. and L. Susan Anderson. 1987. *Vegetation Recovery Following Livestock Removal Near Quitobaquito Spring, Organ Pipe National Monument*. Cooperative National Park Resources Study Unit, University of Arizona, Tucson, AZ 85721. 40 pages. (Through photos, witness the amazing, magical transformation of a grazed wasteland into a healthy riparian area and desert.)

Washington State Department of Natural Resources. 1988. *Agricultural and Grazing Lands Program*. WA St. Dept. of Nat. Res., Public Affairs Office, Cherberg Bldg. QW-21, Olympia, WA 98504. 59 pages. (This report serves as a random example of the economic and environmental absurdity of Western state lands ranching.)

Washington State Department of Natural Resources. 1989. *Totem: Fiscal Year 1988 Annual Report*. 24 pages. (Includes state lands grazing.)

Weaver, J.E. and F.W. Albertson. 1940. "Deterioration of Midwestern Ranges." *Ecology*. 21: 216-236.

Weaver, J.L. 1987. "Underground Plant Development in Its Relation to Grazing." *Ecology*. 11: 543-547.

Webb, R.H. and S.S. Stielstra. 1979. "Sheep Grazing Effects on Mohave Desert Vegetation and Soils." *Environmental Management*. 3: 517-529.

Webster, Guy. 1990. "Bar Codes, Satellites in Sheepmen's Future, Conferees Told." *Arizona Republic*. Jan 22.

Weller, M.W., B.H. Wingfield, and J.P. Low. 1958. "Effects of Habitat Deterioration on Bird Populations in a Small Utah Marsh." *Condor*. 60: 220-226.

Welsh, G.W. 1971. "What's Happening to Our Sheep?" *Wildlife Digest*. Arizona Game & Fish Department. 8 pages.

Weltz, Mark and M. Karl Wood. 1986. "Short-duration Grazing in Central New Mexico: Effects on Sediment Production." *Journal of Soil and Water Conservation*. Jul-Aug: 262-266.

Wheeler, Ray. 1990. "One View of Joe Feller: He Doesn't Give Up." *High Country News*. Mar 12: 12. (Relating to public participation in BLM allotment management.)

White, R. 1989. "We're Going Wild." *Trout*. Summer: 39.

White, Richard. 1983. **The Roots of Dependency: Subsistence, Environment, and Social Change among the Choctaws, Pawnees, and Navojos**. University of Nebraska Press, Lincoln, NE. 433 pages. (Discusses the decline of Native American culture as caused by invading cultures; in attempting to defend "traditional" Native American stock raising, White makes several serious misassumptions.)

Wilderness Society. 1989. *How to Appeal Forest Service Decisions: A Citizen Handbook on the 1989 Appeals Regulations*. The Wilderness Society, 1400 Eye St., NW, Washington, DC 20005.

Willard, E. Earl. 1990. "Northwest Rangelands: Evolution of a Temperate Ecosystem." *Western Wildlands*. Summer: 2-6.

● Williams, Mark London. 1988. "Stockman." *Earth First! Journal*. Sep 22: 28. (A captivating short story of one rancher's personal struggle.)

Williams, Clayton. 1963. "Range Exclosures within the State of Wyoming." *Wyoming Range Management*. 170: 1-19.

Williams, Florence. 1990. "The West's Time Capsules." *High Country News*. Mar 12: 6-7. (An informative article on livestock grazing in general, including discussion on the West's relict ungrazed areas.)

Williams, Florence. 1990a. "Who's at Home on the Range?" *High Country News*. Mar 12: 8.

Williams, Ted. 1988. "Bringing Back the Beast of Lore." *Modern Maturity*. Jun-Jul: 44-51. (On recent wolf reintroduction efforts.)

● Williams, Ted. 1991. "He's Going to Have an Accident." *Audubon*. March/April: 30-39. (Valuable insight into ranching administration by the Forest Service.)

Williamson, Lonnie. 1983. "Raping the Rangelands." *Outdoor Life*. Dec: 11-13. (Good public ranching article from a hunter's perspective.)

● Winegar, Harold H. 1977. "Camp Creek Fencing -- Plant, Wildlife, Soil, and Water Response." *Rangeman's Journal*. Feb: 10-12. (Describes the amazing results of simply fencing livestock out of a 4-mile section of a small Oregon stream.)

Winegar, Harold H. 1982. "Streamflow Augmentation Through Riparian Recovery." Riparian Workshop, Desert Conference IV, Apr 3, 1982. 5 pages.

Winegar, Harold H. 1986. Letter to Supervisor, Ochoco National Forest, Oregon, Dec 18. 6 pages.

Wolf, Tom. 1985. "Grazing Fees: Making a Good Deal a Fair Deal." *Northern Lights*. Jul/Aug: 18-20.

Wolf, Tom. 1988. "'Wyoming' Is Dead -- Long Live 'Wyoming.'" *High Country News*. Sep 26: 14, 18. (This one grabs cowboy mythology by the scruff of the neck and kicks the bullshit out of it.)

Wolf, Tom. 1990. "The Gospel According to Pete Tatschl." *High Country News*. Mar 12: 25-27. (Livestock removal vs. Holistic Resource Management.)

Woolsey, Norman G. 1985. *Coyote Field Guide*. Research Branch, Arizona Game & Fish Commission, Phoenix, AZ. 43 pages. (Funded by Arizona hunters and anglers, produced by the Arizona Game & Fish Department, this is essentially a handbook for ranchers on how to know and kill coyotes.)

Worldwatch Institute. 1989. **State of the World: 1989**. W.W. Norton & Company, New York, NY. 300 pages. (Good source.)

Worldwatch Institute. 1990. **State of the World: 1990**. W.W. Norton & Company, New York, NY. 253 pages.

Wuerthner, George. 1986. "The Owyhee Mountains: Range Abuse and Its Ecological Effects." *Earth First! Journal*. Aug 1: 14-15.

Wuerthner, George. 1987. "Pulsated Equilibriums in Ecological Systems." *Earth First! Journal*. Feb 2: 26. (A good discussion of cyclical balance in natural systems.)

Wuerthner, George. 1988. "Ranchers and Refuges: 3 Case Studies." *Earth First! Journal*. Sep 22: 22-23, 35.

Wuerthner, George. 1988a. "Wolf Recovery Stopped Dead." *High Country News*. Nov 23: 10-14. (Recent wolf reintroduction situation in the northern Rockies and Yellowstone.)

● Wuerthner, George. 1989. "Counting the Real Costs of Public Lands Grazing." *Earth First! Journal*. Aug 1: 22-23. (This is an excellent overview of public lands ranching in the Western US.)

● Wuerthner, George. 1989a. "Public Lands Grazing: What Benefits at What Cost?." *Western Wildlands*. Fall: 24-29. (Scaled down and somewhat different version of the above.)

Wuerthner, George. 1990. "Bison and Brucellosis." *Earth First! Journal*. June 21: 10-11.

Wuerthner, George. 1990a. "A Case of Poor Public Range Policy." *Earth First! Journal*. June 21: 11.

● Wuerthner, George. 1990b. "The Price Is Wrong." *Sierra*. Sep-Oct: 38-43. (Another excellent treatise.)

● Wuerthner, George. 1991. "How the West Was Eaten." *Wilderness*. March: 28-36. (Yet another fine overview.)

Yates, Steve. 1988. "Windspirit of the West." *Audubon*. May: 42-47.

Yensen, D.L. 1981. "The 1900 Invasion of Alien Plants into Southern Idaho." *Great Basin Nat*. 41: 176-183.

Yoakum, Jim D. 1975. "Antelope and Livestock on Rangelands." *Journal of Animal Science*. 40: 985-992.

York, John C. and William A. Dick-Peddie. 1968. "Vegetation Changes in Southern New Mexico During the Past Hundred Years." Pages 157-166 in W.G. McGinnies and B.J. Goldman, Editors. *Arid Lands Perspective*. American Association of the Advancement of Science and the University of Arizona Press.

Young, Cheryl A. 1985. **The Wild Horse in Nevada**. Nevada State Museum, Carson City, NV 89710. 33 pages.

Young, James A., B. Abbott Sparks. 1985. **Cattle in the Cold Desert**. Utah State University Press, Logan, UT 84322-9515. 250 pages. (Like all range professionals afriad to be professionally ostracized for questioning the wisdom of public lands ranching, Young suffers from "ranching apologist syndrome." His book is, nonetheless, an informative look at ranching in the Great Basin.)

Young, Stanley P. and Hartley H.T. Jackson. 1978. *The Clever Coyote*. University of Nebraska Press, Lincoln, NE. 411 pages. (Though claimed to be unbiased, this book by two federal predator killers is a thoroughly warped, hateful, execrable presentation of anti-coyote mentality and activities; enlightening.)

Zaslowsky, Dyan and the Wilderness Society. 1983. **These American Lands -- Parks, Wilderness, and Public Lands**. Henry Holt and Company, Inc., 521 Fifth Avenue, New York, NY 10175. 336 pages.

● Zaslowsky, Dyan. 1989. "A Public Beef." *Harrowsmith*, The Creamery, Charlotte, VT 05445. Jan/Feb: 38-47. (Written with literary skill, this informative article is an excellent and generally accurate portrayal of public lands ranching.)

Zimmerman, G. Thomas and L.F. Neuenschwander. 1984. "Livestock Grazing Influences on Community Structure, Fire Intensity and Fire Frequency within the Douglas-fir/Ninebark Habitat Type." *Journal of Range Management*. Mar: 104-110. (See references therein for numerous fire/livestock studies.)

Zuni Reincarnation. 1986. "Cows Own Capitol Reef National Park." *Earth First! Journal*. Sep 23: 19.

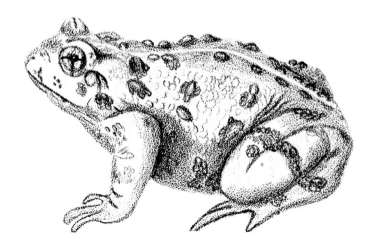

INDEX
(Includes sources of quotations)

(Helpful hint: Cross-referencing with the Table of Contents can help define the nature of a listing.)

PHOTO CREDITS

(Does not include government sources)

Babb, Geoff, 140
Bernshaw, Elliott, 153
Bohi, Lynne, 517, 562
Brown, Jim, 214, 439
Caprio, Tony, 144
Cockerill, Joanne, 226
Conner, Charles, 42
Cranston, Kelly, 7, 90, 94, 128, 485
Dancer, Daniel, 153
Dixon, Bob, 64, 83, 105, 248, 393, 465
Duncan, Harvey, 192, 493
Farm Animal Reform Movement, 70, 85
Ferguson, Denzel, 398
Fonseca, Julia, 215, 237
Foreman, Dave, 104, 437
Ginser, Richard, 35

Girden, Bill, 304
Hirt, Paul, 65, 92, 113, 132, 156, 193, 205, 278, 324, 331, 453, 531
Hood, Bonnie, 276
Johnson, Steve, 24, 48, 69, 74, 89, 96, 103, 116, 117, 118, 127, 133, 224, 265, 274, 283, 287, 292, 313, 348, 390, 446, 526
Kalman, Eliot, 420
Kowz, Rex, 384
Lee, Katie, 481
Lewinson, Bill, 109, 467
Mondt, Rod, 51, 384
Moore, Terrance, 341
Morris, Don, 385
Peacock, Doug, 115
Peterson, Nancy, 172, 225

Randall, Dick, 256, 258, 259, 260, 261, 277, 279, 280, 286, 287, 349
Rechtin, Julie, 419, 456
Robbins, George, 53, 111, 120, 130, 131, 207, 209, 215, 228, 293, 300, 320, 321, 346, 406, 482
Stabler, Mike, 563
Tebbel, Paul, 256, 283
Turner, Dale, 43, 472
Wilshire, Howard, 73, 78, 404
Wuerthner, George, 36, 46, 61, 63, 70, 86, 87, 88, 89, 90, 92, 93, 95, 99, 101, 114, 127, 140, 171, 172, 190, 194, 199, 213, 214, 250, 260, 265, 274, 280, 295, 385, 402, 406, 407, 408, 409, 436, 466, 467, 470, 471, 474, 476, 501, 528

ILLUSTRATION CREDITS

(Does not include government sources)

Burger, Nola, 487
Brush Wolf, 209, 267, 557, 558
Candee, Roger, 125, 166, 290, 412, 490, 508, 518, 545
Gila Trout, 51
Hellenbach, T.O., 402
Jacobs, Sky, 288

Leydet, Francois, 208, 254, 275
Lone Wolf Circles, 139, 258, 272
Millet, Peg, 279
Pentkowski, Greg, 34, 124, 132, 378, 437, 501, 510, 516, 552
Rainforest Action Network, 365
Rogers, Jan, 329, 347

Rosenberg, Ginny, 80, 110, 384, 505
Stiles, Jim, 156, 203, 257
Twachtman, Eric, 133
Waldmire, Robert, 304
Wilson, Helen, 15, 36, 44, 48, 66, 126, 138, 283, 302, 307, 308, 412, 563
Zaelit, John, 255, 256, 258